AMERICAN GOVERNMENT

TEACHER EDITION

FOURTH EDITION

bju press®

Greenville, South Carolina

Note: The fact that materials produced by other publishers may be referenced in this volume does not constitute an endorsement of the content or theological position of materials produced by such publishers. Any references and ancillary materials are listed as an aid to the student or the teacher and in an attempt to maintain the accepted academic standards of the publishing industry.

AMERICAN GOVERNMENT
Fourth Edition

Coordinating Writer
Joseph Jarrell, MS, MA

Contributing Writers
Kirsten Alexander, MEd
Lois Oldenburg, MS
John Seney, MA
Sarah Weaver, MEd, MA

Previous Edition Writers
Tim Keesee, EdD
Dennis Peterson, MS

Editor
Ben Sinnamon, MA, MLIS

Biblical Worldview
Brian Collins, PhD
Bryan Smith, PhD

Book and Cover Concept
Drew Fields

Book and Cover Design
Dan Van Leeuwen

Project Coordinator
Dan Berger

Page Layout
Sarah Centers

Permissions
Sharon Belknap
Sarah Gundlach
Elizabeth Walker

Illustration
Drew Fields
Jim Hargis
Del Thompson

Consultants
Linda Abrams, MA
Sonia Johnson, EdD
Gail Nicholas, MEd

Academic Oversight
Rachel Santopietro, MEd
Jeff Heath, EdD

Photo credits appear on pages 486–88.
Teacher Edition photo credit: xviii–1 © iStock.com/AndreyKrav

© 2020 BJU Press
Greenville, South Carolina 29609

First Edition © 1989 BJU Press
Second Edition © 2004 BJU Press
Third Edition © 2014 BJU Press

Printed in the United States of America
All rights reserved

ISBN 978-1-62856-544-7

15 14 13 12 11 10 9 8 7 6 5 4 3 2

CONTENTS

FEATURES OF THE BOOK iv

UNIT I: AMERICA'S FOUNDATIONS
Chapter 1: The Only Sure Foundation 2
Chapter 2: Forms of Government 14
Chapter 3: Christianity, the Church, and Government 40

UNIT II: THE CONSTITUTION
Chapter 4: Constitutional Beginnings 54
Chapter 5: The United States Constitution 80
Chapter 6: Federalism 124
Chapter 7: State and Local Government 140

UNIT III: THE LEGISLATIVE BRANCH
Chapter 8: The Structure of Congress 166
Chapter 9: The Powers of Congress 186
Special Section: A Trip to Washington, DC 206

UNIT IV: THE EXECUTIVE BRANCH
Chapter 10: The Road to the White House 222
Chapter 11: America's Highest Office 248
Chapter 12: The Federal Bureaucracy 274
Chapter 13: Foreign Policy 302

UNIT V: THE JUDICIAL BRANCH
Chapter 14: The Judiciary 332
Chapter 15: Civil Liberties, Civil Rights, and Civil Responsibilities 354

UNIT VI: PARTY POLITICS
Chapter 16: The Party System 376
Chapter 17: Campaigns and Elections 400
Chapter 18: Public Policy and Politics 420

APPENDICES
A. Party Control of Congress 446
B. Presidential Elections 450
C. Presidents of the United States 454
D. Justices of the US Supreme Court 456
E. How to Write to Public Officials 458
The American's Creed 459

GLOSSARY 460

INDEX 474

PHOTO CREDITS 486

AMERICAN GOVERNMENT, Fourth Edition, is a survey of United States government and is intended to give the high-school student a solid foundation of knowledge about how our government and political processes work.

The ultimate purpose of any Christian course of study is to produce students who are conformed to Christ's image and possess a Christian worldview. For the student who is developing his understanding of America's government, how it works, and his responsibilities to it, there may be no more valuable study.

Many students think the study of America's government will be boring or depressing. Some students believe that government is primarily about laws and taxes. Others believe that many people in our nation's leadership are self-serving and hungry for power; in some instances they are, sadly, correct on both counts. Others feel powerless to change the system, so they ignore the government until it directly affects them. However, your teaching of this course can transform your students' attitude toward America's government—and can equip them to take steps to improve our government.

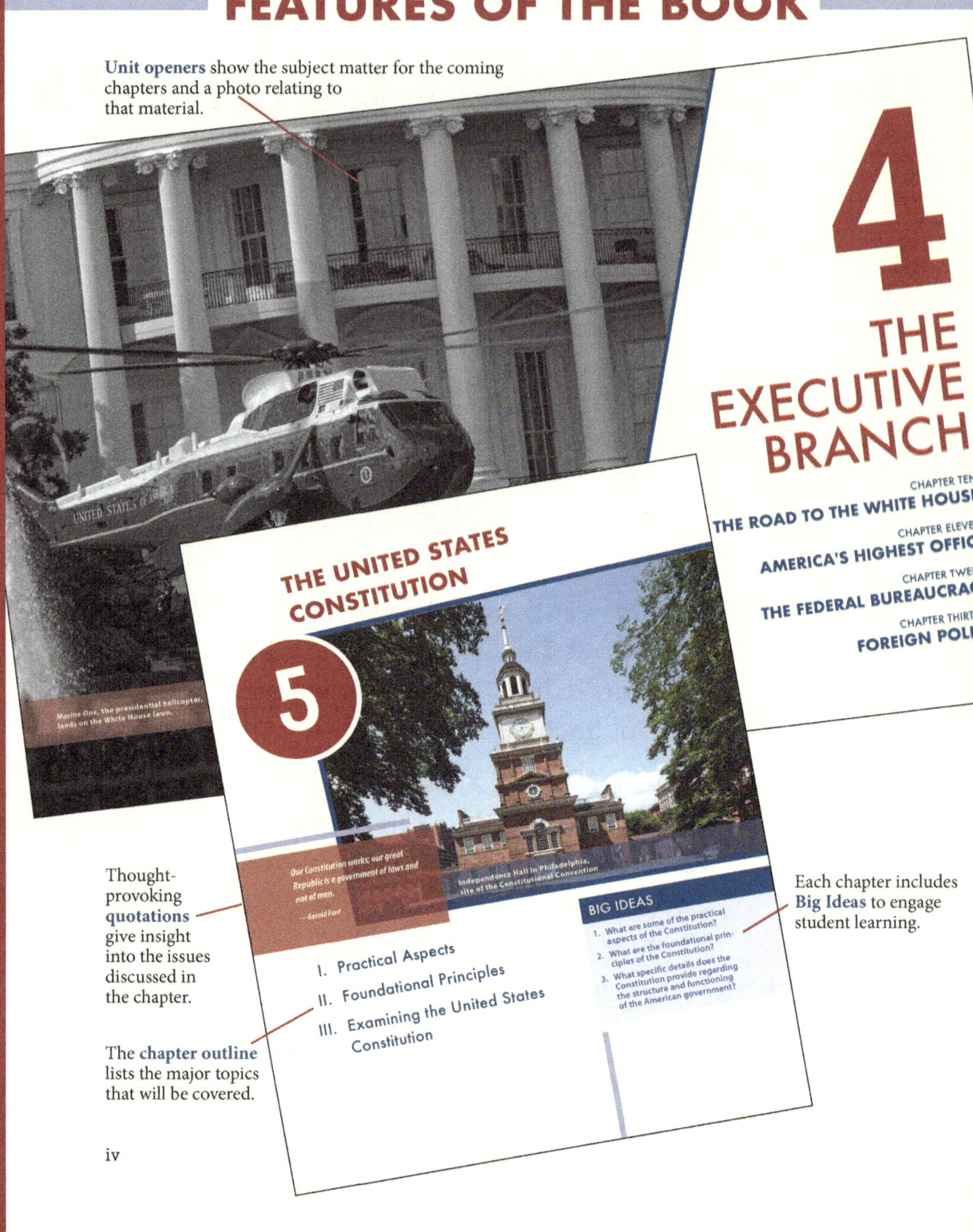

The Teacher Edition

The Teacher Edition of *AMERICAN GOVERNMENT*, Fourth Edition, has been designed to help you teach government more effectively. Many tools have been provided to allow you to incorporate more student participation and to promote the higher-order thinking skills that are essential for the high-school student.

As you prepare to teach each chapter, survey the suggested materials and activities as well as additional information in the Teacher Edition. Then select the items that best meet your students' needs.

It is recommended that you begin each lesson with a review of past material, asking for student feedback so that you can accurately determine whether the students are learning. The suggested activities are designed as a part of the educational experience and complement the student text. Suggested materials lists and adequate directions should make these activities easy to incorporate.

Scheduling

Each chapter has two to five sections. Some sections can be completed in a part of a day (and thus can be combined with other sections), while some will require a full day. Other sections will require additional time. Your students' abilities, your own interests, and the complexity of the material will help determine how you schedule lessons.

Lesson Plan Overview

A lesson plan overview for the course is provided in the front of this Teacher Edition. While American Government is a one-semester course in most schools, others offer it for a full year. See the suggestions at the end of the lesson plan overview if you are teaching a full-year government course.

Student Edition

The Student Edition contains the following features:

- Eighteen chapters divided into six units
- An outline structure and bold-faced headings and terms in each chapter
- Margin and feature boxes to supplement the material and encourage further study
- Scores of infographics
- Hundreds of photographs and several original political cartoons
- A Section Review after each section
- A fully developed Chapter Review after each chapter
- Appendices containing several tables of government data and a guide for writing to public officials

Current Issues and Events

It is highly recommended that a regular discussion of current events be an integral part of the entire government course. Such discussions provide fresh applications and illustrations of material in the student text and encourage the students in the civic virtue of following the news. Relating news stories to topics in the textbook will strengthen student awareness that government issues affect our daily lives.

Consider requiring students to maintain a notebook (electronically or in printed form) that includes news stories that are being discussed during the current semester. If an election is occurring, particular attention should be given to political campaigns and important issues being debated.

Side-Margin Notes

Chapter Goals

The first section in the side margin of each chapter contains the chapter goals. These are objectives that your students should be able to achieve while studying the chapter.

Section Objectives

Your students should achieve the section objectives, shown in the side margin at each new section, while studying that portion of the chapter. Both chapter goals and section objectives are suggestions that you may adapt as necessary.

Additional Information

Information in the side margins corresponds to material in the student text. It can be shared with the students as you desire and can be used to stimulate discussion.

Bottom-Margin Notes

Suggested Materials

The materials list in each chapter gives all the items needed for the activities suggested in the chapter. This will assist you in gathering what you will need for teaching.

Section Review Answers

At the end of each section are the answers to the Section Review questions. (Some questions, especially critical-thinking questions, will not have page numbers associated with their answers because the students will have to "think beyond the textbook.")

Chapter Review Answers

At the end of each chapter are the answers to the Chapter Review questions. (As is true of some Section Review questions, especially critical-thinking questions, there will not be a page number associated with some answers.)

Additional BJU Press Materials

The *American Government Student Activities* includes exercises that provide access to relevant primary sources, interpretation of historical events, and chapter reviews to prepare the students for chapter tests. Also available is an answer key for the *Activities* that includes the answers to all the activity questions and also indicates whether each activity is for reinforcement of information in the student text, enrichment, or review.

Premade *American Government* tests and an ExamView test bank are available. Each includes a variety of questions, including true or false, multiple choice, short answer, and essays.

Visit TeacherToolsOnline.com for additional resources.

Terms in bold type draw attention to important facts, ideas, people, or definitions.

Margin information boxes offer intriguing bits of information.

Charts, diagrams, infographics, and maps help the students visualize information, including statistical data.

Teaching Strategies

Suggested teaching strategies are provided throughout the bottom-margin notes. Some of these activities are labeled with icons to help you identify the type of activity without reading the entire description. Activities without icons are often suggested discussion topics or other teaching ideas.

Bible-study activities provide valuable discussion opportunities and enhance the students' decision-making skills. Visual displays, charts, maps, and video activities help visual learners. Special-speaker activities encourage personal involvement. Writing activities enhance communication skills, and group activities promote student cooperation and positive interaction.

Critical-thinking skills are developed throughout the suggested activities. The icons for these activities are as follows:

 Between the lines

 Bible Study

Bulletin Board

Charts and Graphs

Field Trip

Group Activity

 Homeschool Activity

Investigation

Listening

Maps

Music

Outside Reading

Special Speaker

Video

Website

Writing

Political cartoons convey information, often in a humorous manner.

Section reviews help the students remember what they have learned so far.

The **Chapter Review** asks students about terms and concepts to help them think critically, improve understanding, and prepare for assessments.

General Course Objectives

1. Analyze civic life, politics, and government. (Chapters 1–3)
2. Analyze the foundations of the American political system. (Chapters 1–4)
3. Assess the government's embodiment of the purposes, values, and principles of our democratic republic. (Chapters 5–14, 16–18)
4. Evaluate the relationship of the United States to other nations and to world affairs. (Chapters 13, 18)
5. Critique the role of citizens in our government and in society. (Chapters 1, 15; Appendix E)
6. Relate biblical worldview themes to the structures and functions of American government.

Homeschool Ideas

The flexibility inherent in the homeschool schedule allows parents and students to focus on specific topics. As much as possible, allow your student to pursue interesting topics. Taking field trips to historical sites that influenced colonial government (e.g., Independence Hall in Philadelphia or the House of Burgesses in Williamsburg, Virginia), attending a legislative session at the state or national level, watching court proceedings, or attending local governmental or political events can bring information in the student text to life.

The homeschooling parent can use most of the suggested activities. For convenience, some activities have a homeschool icon.

Mock Senate and Mock Trial

The back of the Teacher Edition contains the information needed to conduct a mock Senate and a mock trial. Additional details about both of these activities can be found at TeacherToolsOnline.com.

Explaining the Gospel

Because one of the greatest desires of Christian teachers is to see their students trust in Christ, we have placed a helpful outline in the back of the Teacher Edition entitled "Explaining the Gospel."

BIBLICAL WORLDVIEW THEMES FOR
AMERICAN GOVERNMENT

An American government course taught from a biblical worldview helps students understand the principal ideas related to government.

Many institutions (families, schools, businesses, etc.) have developed in order to fulfill the Creation Mandate. In a fallen world, institutions may act unjustly. Government is the institution intended by God to ensure justice within other institutions. However, in a fallen world, governments often seek to usurp the roles of other institutions. Christians should press for justice and righteousness in all institutions.

God made humans to form governments that serve certain purposes. **Ensuring justice** is one of the clear biblical purposes for government (Ps. 72:4; Prov. 29:4). Justice is conformity to the order that God built into creation. For example, because God created humans in His image, they have certain rights and responsibilities toward other humans that government should maintain.

Providing for national defense and public safety is a specific way that governments ensure justice. But Christians should evaluate whether specific military or law enforcement actions are truly just.

The law should **encourage moral behavior** (1 Pet. 2:14; Rom. 13:3). Laws set the moral tone for a nation (Prov. 14:34). Christians ought to advocate for moral laws while recognizing that only God's grace can change human hearts.

Governments should **address poverty** without creating dependency (cf. Ps. 72:12; Deut. 14:28–29; 15:12–16). Government policy should encourage work but provide a safety net for those in need.

Government also **provides order** for citizens by regulating activities such as transportation and commerce. This facilitates the carrying out of the Creation Mandate.

	Unit 1			Unit 2				Unit 3	
	c 1	c 2	c 3	c 4	c 5	c 6	c 7	c 8	c 9
Institutions	E (2)					Ev			
Purposes of Government				E		Ev	Ev (2)		Ev (2)
Justice	E, Ev			Ev					
Defense/Safety	E								
Promote Morality	E, Ev								
Framework for Poverty	E								
Provide Order	E								
Mixed Form of Government		E (2)			E				
Ideologies		E	E					E	
Church/State			E, F, A						
Responsibilities and Virtues	R, E, Ev, A	E, F	F						

Key: R = Recall; E = Explain; Ev = Evaluate; F = Formulate; A = Apply

Mixed Form of Government

A good system of government will mix rule by one, rule by a few, and rule by the many—all for the common good. Mixing these forms of government checks the power of sinful leaders.

Ideologies and Idolatry

Political ideologies, like socialism, populism, libertarianism, or nationalism, all propose ways to save society from the problems that afflict it. But they identify some part of God's good creation, rather than sin, as the problem. They then look to some theory, rather than to God, for salvation. Thus political ideologies can be a kind of idolatry that Christians must be able to discern.

Church and State

Throughout history Christians have struggled with how the church and state ought to relate. The best model recognizes that all of life is religious. Thus the church should maintain a biblical witness to and influence on the state. But the church and state are distinct institutions. Neither should seek to usurp the functions of the other institution.

Christian Responsibilities and Virtues

Christians have four obligations with regard to government: prayer, participation, submission, and witness. There are also four key political virtues: prudence, boldness, humility, and respect (Prov. 8:12, 15–16; Titus 3:1–2).

	Unit 4				Unit 5		Unit 6		
	c 10	c 11	c 12	c 13	c 14	c 15	c 16	c 17	c 18
Institutions			Ev				E		F
Purposes of Government			E (2)						
Justice					E, Ev	Ev, F			
Defense/Safety				Ev, F (2)					
Promote Morality	E, Ev	F		Ev					
Framework for Poverty									
Provide Order									
Mixed Form of Government									
Ideologies							Ev (2)		F, A
Church/State						Ev		Ev	A
Responsibilities and Virtues	E, Ev (2)	F				Ev	Ev	F	A

Key: R = Recall; E = Explain; Ev = Evaluate; F = Formulate; A = Apply

BUILDING ACADEMIC RIGOR WITH AMERICAN GOVERNMENT

1 — Desired Learning Outcomes

What do I want students to learn?

- Reading skills in informational texts
- Social studies literacy
- 21st century skills—collaboration, creativity, critical thinking, problem solving, technology literacy
- Considering political issues from alternative viewpoints, including a global perspective
- Biblical worldview development regarding governments and institutions, the purposes of government, mixed forms of government, ideologies, church and state, and Christian responsibilities to government

2 — Teaching and Learning Supports

How will I help students learn?

- Essential questions and bolded discipline-specific vocabulary
- Guided analysis of key American documents and other source materials
- Socratic dialogs
- Use of technology
- Collaborative activities and projects in researching, speaking, listening, and writing
- Class discussions
- Mock Senate, mock election, and mock trial activities
- Visual interpretation of political cartoons, graphs, and process diagrams
- Cross-curricular connections
- Current events in government and politics

3 — Evidence of Understanding

How do I know if students have learned?

- Completing frequent and varied preassessments and formative assessments
- Developing historical context and literacy in the study of primary and secondary source materials
- Analysis of political processes and their results
- Answering high-level questions
- Written and oral communication
- Formulating and applying Christian positions on the purposes of government and Christian responsibilities toward government

A PANORAMA OF ACADEMIC RIGOR

THE LEARNING ENVIRONMENT

Learning happens in a context. Physical and social environments create this context. For students to be stimulated and engaged and to perform at high levels, they need an environment that connects with and shapes their interests and values. Students need a flexible environment that adapts in order to remedy their deficits and capitalize on their proficiencies. They need an interactive environment that intrinsically motivates them by giving them structure, freedom, and choices in learning. They need a safe environment that invites questioning, risk taking, and honest discussion. Most importantly, students need positive relationships with mentors and peers and one-on-one time with caring, responsible instructors and parents. This kind of environment does not happen by accident; an educational climate like this must be crafted.

THE TEACHER'S ROLE

The teacher is the person who crafts this learning environment. The teacher creates a learning community with high educational expectations, ignites interest and passion to help students persevere in challenging educational tasks, and inspires them by providing models of learning. The teacher instructs, supports, critiques, and praises the efforts of growing learners, thereby laying a foundation for lifelong learning. On this foundation the teacher will help students transfer their knowledge, understanding, and skills to life while helping shape their worldview.

THE LEARNING EXPERIENCE

The textbook opens doors to the world of the learning experience. It captures student interest and significantly contributes to the educational environment. Educational and technological resources enable the teacher to develop knowledge, understanding, and skills in a scaffolded sequence to build a foundation that students can transfer to life. Teachers use educational tools to craft relevant, authentic learning experiences that develop curiosity, creativity, and problem-solving skills in a variety of contexts. These kinds of learning experiences allow students to take responsibility for their learning and discover the joy of serving God with their foundational knowledge and skills.

LESSON PLAN OVERVIEW

Lesson	Page Number	Student Activities	Content Objectives and Biblical Worldview
Chapter 1: The Only Sure Foundation			
1	2–5	1	**The Necessity of Government** Explain the origin of government as a God-ordained institution. Evaluate anarchy based on biblical teaching regarding human depravity.
2	5–9	2–3	**The Obligations of Government** Explain righteousness and justice. Explain government's primary biblical obligations. Evaluate governmental policies and actions regarding punishing unrighteousness and rewarding righteousness.
3	9–13	4–5	**The Obligations of the Governed** Assess the importance of praying for government officials. Analyze the ways that citizens may participate in government. Evaluate political issues in light of biblical commands about citizens' responsibility to submit to government. Identify ways to be a good testimony to government officials. Review
4			Test
Chapter 2: Forms of Government			
5	14–20	1	**Types of Government** Compare systems of government. Explain the relationships between the different levels of government. Contrast the parliamentary and presidential means of choosing an executive.
6	21–22		**American Government** Describe the United States' method of dividing the national government. Summarize the different responsibilities accorded to the national and state governments in the United States.
7	22–29	2–3	**A Brief History of Democracy** Trace the development of democratic principles. Identify the Founding Fathers' contributions to democratic government. Differentiate between *democracy* and *republic*.
8	29–34	4	**Characteristics of Democracy** Describe the strengths and potential weaknesses of majority rule. Explain the principles of equality and liberty. Analyze the roles of compromise and individual worth in a democratic system.
9	34–39	5	**Conditions for Democracy** Explain why opportunity and education are important in a democracy. Defend the idea that moral responsibility is necessary for the health and strength of a democracy. Review
10			Test
Chapter 3: Christianity, the Church, and Government			
11	40–43	1–2	**Christianity and Government in History** Survey Christian involvement in government during the Roman Empire, the Reformation, and in early America. Explain John Locke's view of religious toleration. Define *pluralism*.
12	44–51	3–4	**The Bible, the Church, and Pluralism** Defend a biblical view of the relationship between church and state against contrary viewpoints. Explain the role of ideologies and a Christian worldview in the formulation of political ideas. Determine a biblical view of Christian involvement in political issues. Propose ways a Christian may react to the problems created by pluralism. Review
13			Test
Chapter 4: Constitutional Beginnings			
14	54–65	1–2	**Colonial and Confederation Eras** Identify the factors that influenced American colonial governments. Analyze the processes by which the colonies sought to address their grievances with England. Assess the Articles of Confederation's weaknesses.

Lesson	Page Number	Student Activities	Content Objectives and Biblical Worldview
15	66–72	3	**Constitutional Convention** Outline the three major compromises reached at the Constitutional Convention. Analyze the role of political compromise in a free society.
16	73–79	4–5	**Ratification Controversy** Analyze the arguments presented by the Federalists and Anti-Federalists. Explain the significance of the ratification of the Constitution. **Review**
17			**Test**
Chapter 5: The United States Constitution			
18	80–87	1–2	**Practical Aspects** Explain the effect of the Founding Fathers' view of human nature on the writing of the Constitution. Evaluate different approaches to interpreting the Constitution. Identify the characteristics of the Constitution that make it adaptable to change. Describe the methods of amending the Constitution.
19	87–93	3–4	**Foundational Principles** Explain six basic principles contained in the Constitution. Relate foundational principles of American government to biblical principles.
20	94–123	5	**Examining the United States Constitution** Identify the three branches of government and explain their major functions. Explain the purpose and significance of the Bill of Rights. Evaluate the impact of constitutional amendments on the US government. **Review**
21			**Test**
Chapter 6: Federalism			
22	124–28		**The Partitions of Power** Define *federalism*. Differentiate between delegated powers, enumerated powers, implied powers, and reserved powers. Explain the interaction between state and federal governments.
23	129–31	1	**Developments in Federalism** Describe the system of dual federalism that once existed in the United States. Identify the significant events that increased the powers of the federal government. Evaluate different forms of federalism from a biblical worldview.
24	131–33	2	**Financing Federalism** Distinguish between the various forms of federal grants. Explain revenue sharing.
25	133–39	3–4	**The Challenges of Federalism** Identify the factors that maintain the distinctions between state and national governments. Describe problems that result from federal funding to state governments. **Review**
26			**Test**
Chapter 7: State and Local Government			
27	140–47	1	**State Governments** Explain the constitutional basis for states' powers. Delineate the responsibilities of state government. Outline the responsibilities of the different branches of state government. List the states' sources of revenue.
28	148–52	2–3	**Local Governments** Identify the various forms of county and municipal government. Explain the role of special districts in local government.
29	152–58		**State and Local Politics** Chart and explain typical political party organization on the state and local levels. Explain election and voting processes used in state and local politics.
30	159–63	4	**Interstate and Intergovernmental Relationships** Identify the types of interstate relationships. Describe the interaction of federal and state governments. **Review**
31			**Test**

Lesson	Page Number	Student Activities	Content Objectives and Biblical Worldview
Chapter 8: The Structure of Congress			
32	166–77	1	**Framework** Describe Congress's bicameral structure. Explain how the House and Senate officials lead their respective chambers. Evaluate controversial issues relating to members of Congress. Summarize the procedures regarding congressional sessions.
33	177–85	2–4	**Legislative Workings** Analyze the purposes and types of congressional committees. Explain the processes for passing bills in the United States Congress. Review
34			Test
Chapter 9: The Powers of Congress			
35	186–97	1–2	**Enumerated Powers** Delineate the powers specifically given to Congress in the Constitution. Relate the powers of Congress to the biblical purposes of government.
36	197–200		**Implied and Nonlegislative Powers** Explain the implied powers of Congress. Explain the nonlegislative powers of Congress. Relate the implied and nonlegislative powers of Congress to the biblical purposes of government.
37	201		**Denied Powers** Explain the powers the Constitution denies to Congress.
38	201–5	3–5	**Congressional Criticism** Cite various reasons Congress is criticized. Evaluate the criticisms Congress commonly receives. Review
39			Test
Chapter 10: The Road to the White House			
40	222–24	1	**Presidential Qualifications** Explain the constitutional requirements and desired qualities for the office of president. Outline common career paths for the presidency.
41	225–34	2	**Nomination** Describe the origins, purposes, forms, and course of presidential primaries. Summarize the preparations, participants, and procedures of national party conventions.
42	234–42	3–4	**Election** Evaluate some influences on campaign strategies. Analyze the role of debates in presidential campaigns. Explain the importance of Election Day. Evaluate the role of the Electoral College.
43	242–47	5	**Inauguration** Explain the significance of the orderly transitions that occur after American elections. Describe the presidential inauguration procedures. Review
44			Test
Chapter 11: America's Highest Office			
45	248–62	1–2	**Presidential Powers** Analyze six major areas of presidential responsibility. Describe constitutional restrictions placed on the president. Explain additional powers given to the president.
46	267–71	3–4	**Executive Organization** Outline the responsibilities of the vice president. Explain the origin and role of the Executive Office of the President (EOP). Describe the cabinet departments and other administrative agencies.
47	271–73	5–6	**Governing Wisely** Identify pitfalls of the presidency. Appraise the factors that influence assessment of presidents. Review
48			Test

Lesson	Page Number	Student Activities	Content Objectives and Biblical Worldview
Chapter 12: The Federal Bureaucracy			
49	274–79	1	**Bureaucratic Development** Explain the features and benefits of bureaucracy. Evaluate the factors that have contributed to the growth of bureaucracy in our government.
50	280–94	2–3	**Bureaucratic Structure** Describe the major departments within the executive branch. Outline how the federal bureaucracy functions.
51	294–301	4–5	**Bureaucratic Practices** Summarize why the federal bureaucracy has been called the fourth branch of government. Describe ways the bureaucracy is held accountable for its actions. Delineate the problems created by a powerful bureaucracy. Describe some distinctives and achievements of American bureaucracy. **Review**
52			**Test**
Chapter 13: Foreign Policy			
53	302–5	1	**Foreign Policy Goals** Describe the four basic goals of American foreign policy. Relate American foreign-policy goals to the biblical purposes of government.
54	306–10	2	**Foreign Policy Development** Describe the changes in America's foreign policy from 1790 to the present.
55	311–17		**Policymakers** Explain how the president helps shape foreign policy. Describe the work of agencies and departments within the executive branch that are involved in foreign policy. Explain how Congress impacts policymaking for foreign affairs. Analyze media influence on foreign policy.
56	317–23	3	**Policy Methods** Describe how diplomacy, treaties, and multinational organizations help achieve US foreign policy goals. Evaluate the use of foreign aid and sanctions. Analyze the role of military action and espionage in the implementation of foreign policy.
57	323–29	4	**Challenges Abroad** Identify challenges that face US national security. Determine a Christian response to national security challenges. **Review**
58			**Test**
Chapter 14: The Judiciary			
59	332–37	1	**Sources of American Law** Explain the scriptural foundation of American law. Explain the historical foundation of American law.
60	338–44		**Structure of the Courts** Explain judicial federalism. Describe district courts and circuit courts of appeals. Analyze the workings of the US Supreme Court.
61	344–49	2	**Selection of Judges** Explain the selection process for state and federal judges. Describe the factors that influence Senate confirmation of federal judges.
62	349–53	3–5	**Constitutional and Legal Change** Define *judicial review*. Evaluate the impact of Supreme Court decisions on the legal system. **Review**
63			**Test**
Chapter 15: Civil Liberties, Civil Rights, and Civil Responsibilities			
64	354–62	1–2	**Civil Liberties Guaranteed in the First Amendment** Distinguish between civil liberties and civil rights. Appraise civil liberties that are protected by the First Amendment.
65	362–67	3	**Other Constitutional Civil Liberties** Identify the constitutional guarantees regarding security rights. Examine the judicial procedures that are guaranteed in the Constitution. Explain whether the Constitution provides a right to privacy.

Lesson	Page Number	Student Activities	Content Objectives and Biblical Worldview
66	367–70		**Civil Rights** Define *substantive due process* and *procedural due process*. Describe the struggles African Americans faced in their effort to obtain civil rights. Describe voting rights and requirements.
67	371–73	4–5	**Civil Responsibilities** Explain the origins of liberties and rights. Describe the dangers of an overemphasis on liberties and rights. Explain the responsibilities citizens have to their government and present a biblical view of civil rights. **Review**
68			**Test**
Chapter 16: The Party System			
69	376–79	1	**Parties and Their Functions** Define *political party*. Explain the major functions of political parties.
70	379–88	2–3	**The Two-Party System** Explain why a two-party system developed in America. Analyze the characteristics of a two-party system. Summarize the historical development of parties. Identify party systems in other nations.
71	388–91	4	**Third Parties** Describe the types of third parties. Explain the importance of third parties.
72	391–94		**Party Organization** Explain the fragmented nature of political parties. Outline the components of the two major parties at the national level. Describe the organization of political parties at the state and local levels.
73	394–99	5	**Party Decline** Analyze the changes that have contributed to the decline of American political parties. Describe the role of independent voters in the political process. Explain the impact of media on political campaigns. Assess the impact of party decline on American politics. **Review**
74			**Test**
Chapter 17: Campaigns and Elections			
75	400–5	1	**Candidate Nomination** Describe the requirements for becoming a candidate. Discuss important steps a candidate should take after meeting the requirements for a position. Describe the various methods used to nominate candidates.
76	405–10	2	**The Campaign Trail** Explain the advantages of incumbency in campaigns. Describe how the coattail effect impacts elections. Analyze the media's influence on political campaigns.
77	410–15	3–4	**Elections and Voting** Explain what occurs on Election Day. Explain how voting requirements have changed. Describe the role that social, religious, economic, and other factors play in American elections. Identify the various methods of voting.
78	415–19	5	**Campaign Finance** Describe the laws that govern campaign funding. Analyze the campaign finance reforms that have been instituted. Assess the impact of campaign funding reform. **Review**
79			**Test**
Chapter 18: Public Policy and Politics			
80	420–22		**Government and the Public** Explain *public opinion* and *public policy*. Distinguish between liberalism and conservatism.
81	423–25	1	**Public Policy** Define *domestic policy* and *foreign policy*. Describe how public policy is developed and implemented.

Lesson	Page Number	Student Activities	Content Objectives and Biblical Worldview
82	425–30	2	**Public Opinion** Delineate the different sources of public opinion. Describe various means of measuring public opinion. Analyze dangers associated with public opinion.
83	430–35	3	**Interest Groups** Identify the purposes of interest groups. Distinguish between the various types of interest groups. Describe the activities of interest groups.
84	436–45	4–5	**Mass Media** Evaluate the major types of media that shape public opinion. Summarize the powers and the limitations of media. Evaluate how politicians use media. Describe the impact of media propaganda. **Review**
85			**Test**

Suggestions for a One-Year Government Course

Most schools offer American Government as a one-semester course; however, if your school schedules it for a full year, below are some suggested ways to use the additional days.

- Increase the amount of time you spend on most or all chapters.
- Spend additional time examining current events, particularly those relating to government issues. Perhaps spend one day a week discussing them or designate the first few minutes of class (two or three days each week) for such discussions.
- Increase the class time you allot for mock Senate (see p. 489) and mock trial (see p. 498) activities.
- Schedule additional field trips to places related to government (such as courts; local commission or council meetings; city, county, or state government offices; and polling places during an election year).
- Invite additional speakers to the class (see suggested speakers throughout the Teacher Edition's bottom-margin notes).

Sculptures of Presidents Washington, Jefferson,
Theodore Roosevelt, and Lincoln at Mount Rushmore

1

AMERICA'S FOUNDATIONS

CHAPTER ONE
THE ONLY SURE FOUNDATION

CHAPTER TWO
FORMS OF GOVERNMENT

CHAPTER THREE
CHRISTIANITY, THE CHURCH, AND GOVERNMENT

1. Determine why government is necessary.
2. Analyze government's obligations to its citizens.
3. Explain a citizen's obligations to the government.

Highlight

Emphasize that the overall goal of this course is for the students not only to learn the mechanics of American government but also to develop a Christian perspective. The students should be able to discern ungodly aspects of the government and propose godly remedies for those problems.

THE ONLY SURE FOUNDATION

1

He that ruleth over men must be just, ruling in the fear of God. And he shall be as the light of the morning, when the sun riseth.

2 Samuel 23:3–4

Chiseled into the stone behind the Speaker's rostrum in the chamber of the House of Representatives is the national motto: "In God We Trust."

I. The Necessity of Government

II. The Obligations of Government

III. The Obligations of the Governed

BIG IDEAS

1. Why is government necessary?
2. What are the government's obligations to its citizens?
3. What are a citizen's obligations to the government?

SUGGESTED MATERIALS

Section I
- Activity 1 from Chapter 1 of the *Student Activities*

Section II
- Activities 2–3 from Chapter 1 of the *Student Activities*

Section III
- Special speaker (see p. 9)
- Recorded segments of talk radio and televised news programs
- Comment feeds from websites
- Activities 4–5 from Chapter 1 of the *Student Activities*

Teacher Resources

Visit TeacherToolsOnline.com for resources to enhance the lessons.

King David's last words, shown at the opening of this chapter, describe the kind of ruler that brings blessings to his country (2 Sam. 23:3–4). Such a ruler must be just and must fear God. David describes this ruler in poetic language: he is like the rising of the sun on a cloudless morning or like grass that springs up after rain. David's ideal was not simply a guide to his successors in Israel, nor was it merely an anticipation of the perfect reign of Christ that will come at the end of time. David speaks generally of any leader.

The early Christians brought the gospel to Roman officials. They recognized that their rulers, like all other people, needed a Savior (1 Tim. 2:1–6). And since they knew that the Savior they preached is also the King of Kings, they were convinced that all human lords must acknowledge their greater Lord (1 Tim. 6:14–15; Rev. 1:5). Thus, the last words of David are not the outmoded advice of a long-dead king. Those words remain God's mandate for all rulers. If a government desires to be blessed by its Maker, it must be just. And a government can be truly just only by committing itself to rule in the fear of God.

Of course, "ruling in the fear of God" means different things to different people, but God has revealed His expectations in Scripture. They are the only sure foundation for this textbook, which analyzes human government generally and US government particularly. This opening chapter begins the task by examining what the Bible reveals about the reason for government, the duties of government, and believers' response to government.

I. The Necessity of Government

Simply stated, **government** is any system of public rule or authority. This definition is as broad as the vast array of types and levels of government that exists throughout the world. Literally thousands of governments are in operation, from simple county or town organizations to the complex machinery of national governments. Examining the various forms of government and the history of their operation can easily cause discouragement. Often, human government moves too slowly to correct certain injustices but at other times moves too swiftly to "correct" that which needs no correction. "If human government can do no better than it has," the skeptic in us all has wondered, "perhaps society would be better off without it." This view, however, fails to reckon with the Bible's teaching about the nature of God and His world and the problem of human depravity.

Guiding Questions

1. Why did God establish governments?
2. How do the concepts of human depravity and anarchy relate to each other?

US Capitol in Washington, DC

Section I Objectives

1. Explain the origin of government as a God-ordained institution.
2. Evaluate anarchy based on biblical teaching regarding human depravity.

Fear of God

Although "ruling in the fear of God" may mean different things in different aspects of government, the Bible does state which government actions a ruler should allow and disallow.

A ruler who fears God will not commit murder (Gen. 20:11); mistreat the disabled or the elderly (Lev. 19:14, 32); take advantage of the poor (Lev. 25:35–36); oppress his subjects (Lev. 25:17, 39–43); or otherwise abuse his position (Neh. 5:15). He will instead study the Bible (Deut. 17:18–19); love truth and hate covetousness (Exod. 18:21); and, in general, avoid sin (Prov. 16:12).

A ruler who fears the Lord acknowledges his place in subjection to God (Ps. 9:20) and brings glory to his nation.

Noah Webster on the Basis of Laws

"The moral principles and precepts contained in the Scriptures ought to form the basis of all our civil constitutions and laws. . . . All the miseries and evils which men suffer from—vice, crime, ambition, injustice, oppression, slavery and war—proceed from their despising or neglecting the precepts contained in the Bible."

The Necessity of Government

Some people think that government is necessary only because of the Fall. According to this view, once sin is removed, the human race will exist in a kind of holy anarchy. As James Madison wrote in *Federalist* No. 51, "If men were angels, no government would be necessary." Direct the students to use the following passages of Scripture to evaluate these ideas.

Genesis 1:27–28; 2:15, 18
God wants humans to rule over the world. Even when there were only two humans, God ordained an authority structure between them.

Romans 13:1
God ordained human government authority.

Matthew 19:28
In the New Creation, the disciples will sit on twelve thrones, judging the twelve tribes of Israel.

Luke 19:16–19
In the New Creation, some Christians will rule over cities.

Revelation 21:23–24; 22:1–2, 5
The Father and Christ will rule over the New Creation. Kings will continue to rule over nations in the New Creation, and all the redeemed will rule.

Activity 1: An Election Sermon by Abraham Williams, 1762

This activity is designed to help the students learn to examine and analyze original sources.

Thoughts about the Origin of Government

In modern times there have been various views about the origin of government. For example, in the sixteenth and seventeenth centuries many kings began to claim that they were head of both church and state by "divine right." Because their power came directly from God, they argued there was no power greater and should be no "checks" on them. That belief posed two major problems: (1) Scripture does not specify that an unlimited monarchy is the proper form of government (or, given the Bible's teaching about human depravity, that it would be a wise form to adopt) and (2) the Bible does not make rulers the head of the church.

Philosopher John Locke (1632–1704), who will be discussed more in coming chapters, criticized "divine right." He believed that Genesis 1:28 gave all humans equal rule over the earth; consequently, government could only exist by the "consent of the governed." If a government trampled people's rights instead of protecting them, he believed the people had a right to rebel. However, some of Locke's critics have noted that the Bible clearly states that governments are ordained by God (Rom. 13:1) and that rebelling against the government is forbidden.

Philosopher Edmund Burke (1729–1797), a longtime member of the British parliament, argued that a government gradually changes while it works to meet the needs of its citizens. While he believed that governments must respond to the needs of the people, he argued that rash actions and violent attempts to change the government could lead to barbarism and mob rule.

Origin of Government

The fundamental principles of government are woven into the fabric of the universe. God created a world in which government would exist. In fact, one of the most important themes in Scripture is the "government" of God—what we generally call God's "kingdom." God, because He is God and Creator, is King over the entire world. But when the Bible speaks about "the kingdom of God" it isn't always talking about God's direct rule over all things. It is often talking about God's rule through humans.

The human race is unique among God's creation because God made humans in His own image and gave them dominion over the whole earth (Gen. 1:26–27). The phrase "made in the **image of God**" means that God gave humans qualities that reflect His own character. These traits include reason, moral capacity, spirituality, sociability, and emotion. Such traits enable mankind to exercise good and wise dominion (or governing authority) over God's world as He commanded (Gen. 1:28). This first command of God to man is often called the **Creation Mandate**.

It is important to note that God made all humans in His image and gave them the high calling of managing His world. But, from the beginning, He intended that there would be an authority structure within humanity. God placed Adam in charge of maintaining the Garden of Eden, and He appointed Eve to be his helper (Gen. 2:15, 18). Clearly, God never intended every human to fulfill the Creation Mandate in the same capacity. Some are to be leaders in this endeavor, and some are to be helpers.

Some have argued that government emerged as the result of the rule of fathers over their extended families—and that this justified the hereditary and absolute rule of kings. Others have argued that government should have the consent of the governed because Genesis 1:26–28 gives all humans the right to rule over the world, but says nothing about some humans ruling over other humans. Notably, the Bible does not tell us how the first government or any government formed. It simply tells us that government is an institution created by God (1 Peter 2:13) and that the governing authorities that exist "are ordained by God" (Rom. 13:1).

Organization is necessary whenever there is a task or mission to be accomplished. If humans are to be effective and efficient in their responsibility of fulfilling the Creation Mandate, a system of authority or government is essential.

The Problem of Human Depravity

Government is necessary, not only because of the fundamental nature of the world, but also because of sin. God made humans in His own image, and therefore they were originally good (Gen. 1:26–27, 31). But when Adam and Eve chose to disobey God, the image of God in them—and in all their descendants—was severely marred. The result of this tainting of God's image is called **human depravity**. Saying that humans are depraved, however, does not

The Fall and Anarchy

Instruct the students to evaluate the absence of government by using the following biblical arguments:

Romans 13:1–7
Every human being is obligated to obey his government leaders because God created government to organize and rule over society. And in a fallen world, God has ordained government to punish evildoers.

1 Peter 2:13–17
Government has the obligation to punish evildoers and reward those who do right. Therefore, Christians should obey and honor their governmental officials.

Genesis 9:6
Because humans are made in the image of God, God demands that murderers be put to death by other humans. According to Romans 13 and other passages, government is the institution that has this obligation.

Deuteronomy 14:28–29
In a fallen world, poverty is an ever-present problem. In ancient Israel, the Israelites were to pay a 10 percent tax on their gross income every three years. This wealth was collected in the towns and distributed to the Levites, orphans, widows, and sojourners.

mean that all are horribly wicked. Rather, it means that every part of each human's being (mind, will, and emotions) has been twisted by his fall into sin.

One of the consequences of depravity is that the human race cannot thrive (or even survive) unless a system of public rule is in place to protect humans from wickedness. Recognizing the severity of human depravity, God long ago instituted the punishment that has traditionally served as the defining right of government: the death penalty (Gen. 9:6; Rom. 13:3–4). To right wrong deeds and to restrain evil intentions, government has the authority to punish, even, under certain circumstances, to take human life.

Those who sincerely believe that humanity would be better without government do not have a proper understanding of human depravity. Left unrestrained, the human race would destroy itself. **Anarchy**, or absence of government—the goal of some people's political philosophy—is always frightfully tragic and mercifully short-lived whenever it appears on the stage of history. In each generation, the human race learns the painful lesson that any government is essentially better than no government.

Human Government on the New Earth

Government will not pass away when Christ decisively ends sin. On the new earth, nations will continue to exist and have rulers (Rev. 21:24). One of the reasons Christ came to earth as a man was to fulfill the Creation Mandate that Adam and all his descendants failed to fulfill righteously (Heb. 2:5–9). The good government of the Son will last for eternity on the new earth, and humans will exercise leadership under His supreme rule (Rev. 22:3–5).

The seeds of government are found in the Creation Mandate, and government will persist throughout eternity. Sin, however, complicates attempts to achieve just governments in the present. It also causes Christians to think carefully about how governments should function.

Section Review

1–2. In the first paragraph of the chapter, two characteristics of an ideal ruler are mentioned. What are they?

3. Define *government*.

4–5. Explain the Creation Mandate. How does it relate to government?

6. Why does human depravity demand government?

✷ Why will government continue to exist for eternity even when people are no longer evil and in need of restraint?

II. The Obligations of Government

The Bible reveals not only why human government exists but also what it should do. A central obligation of government is to ensure justice (Deut. 1:10–18; 1 Kings 10:9; Ps. 72; Jer. 22:2–5). Related to this, governments are to provide for national defense and public safety (Rom. 13:4; Deut. 20:4) and to provide a framework for addressing poverty (Ps. 72:12–14). In addition, the laws that governments pass should promote moral behavior (1 Peter 2:14). Finally, government must provide order in a society.

Fall and Redemption

Genesis 9:6 and James 3:9 indicate that God's image in humans was not destroyed by the Fall. However, other passages emphasize that this image was marred by sin and that redemption is possible only through Christ's atoning work at Calvary (2 Cor. 5:17; Titus 3:5).

Section II Objectives

1. Explain righteousness and justice.

2. Explain government's primary biblical obligations.

3. Evaluate governmental policies and actions regarding punishing unrighteousness and rewarding righteousness.

Sources of Rights

Rights emerge from the moral order, or creational norms, that God has built into the world. For instance, because God made humans in His image, it is wrong to murder a human. Thus, humans have a right to life.

Other rights are conferred in various ways. For example, Americans have a right to a trial by jury in certain cases; this is a right provided by the Bill of Rights (in Amendments VI and VII). Similarly, a business contract may confer some rights.

Note about Section Reviews

Throughout this textbook, each section review will normally include one or two starred items. These are designed to help students apply and improve critical thinking skills.

Section Review Answers

1–2. The ideal ruler is just and fears God. (p. 3)

3. any system of public rule or authority (p. 3)

4–5. The Creation Mandate is God's first command to humans; it orders them to practice good and wise dominion over God's world. Government is part of this dominion. (p. 4)

6. The sinful tendencies of human depravity make government necessary to suppress evil. (p. 4–5)

✷ Government's purpose is not solely to restrain sin. Government is also needed to provide structure and leadership. The good government of God's Son will exist throughout eternity.

Competing Views of Justice

Often, political debates revolve around competing views of justice. Is relegating religion to the margins of society just? Those whose religions encourage activity in the public square say no. But those who argue that religion poisons everything say yes. Unfortunately, as Western societies become more pluralistic, political philosophers seek to address the justice question in a way that avoids making moral judgments. The utilitarian says that justice means ensuring the greatest good for the greatest number. But what about the rights of the minority? Libertarians often assert that justice means respecting each individual's freedom to choose his own good. But this neglects the fact that humans live in community. The choices of one individual affect those around him. What is just when people's rights and freedoms conflict? Justice cannot be discussed without reference to morality and religion.

For Christians, the Scriptures are the only infallible source of moral guidance. But in a pluralistic society some have argued that religious people should keep religious arguments out of public discussions since not everyone will accept scriptural teaching. However, instead of promoting tolerance, prohibiting the discussion of religious and moral viewpoints only heightens conflicts because supposedly neutral approaches always have underlying moral and religious viewpoints—and savvy citizens recognize them. It is best, therefore, for a pluralistic culture to allow people of all viewpoints to make their cases from their own moral perspectives.

Ensure Justice

What Is Justice?

To ensure **justice** means that governments should encourage people to do right and to respect one another's rights. It also means that governments should punish wrongdoers, such as those who violate the rights of others.

Justice also requires that laws be administered equally. However, *equality* does not mean "equality of outcomes"—it means equal treatment when laws are enforced. For example, what if someone earns a reward that others do not? Is it unjust for him to claim it? No. What if a company, in violation of a written contract, cut every employees' pay by fifty percent? Is that just? No. Though everyone would be treated equally, none would be treated justly because the law was disobeyed.

When considering justice, we should think in terms of rights. Injustice occurs when a person's rights are violated. Americans like to talk about rights. They have "certain unalienable rights" from the Creator that are listed in the Declaration of Independence. They have constitutional rights that are noted in the Bill of Rights. Americans also have civil rights—that is, the right to participate as citizens in their nation's political sphere. And some people argue for more rights beyond these. Unfortunately, some claim rights for themselves without respecting the rights of others. Thus, the number of rights people claim multiplies.

President Barack Obama presented the nation's highest military award, the Medal of Honor, to Marine Corporal Kyle Carpenter in June 2014 in recognition of his heroic actions in Afghanistan in 2010.

This confusion results, in part, from rejecting God. Justice can be rightly understood only in relation to God because justice and righteousness are determined by who God is. His character is the standard for right and wrong. Being made in God's image gives humans their true rights (and also their responsibilities toward one another).

Rewarding Righteousness

Just governments reward righteousness. In the New Testament, the apostle Peter tells his readers that God appoints government leaders to praise those who act rightly (1 Peter 2:14). In Proverbs, King Solomon repeatedly emphasizes the importance of fulfilling this obligation. In Proverbs 17, for example, he warns against wrong-

---

Ensuring Justice: The Central Obligation of Government

Ask the students what biblical teachings indicate that all humans have rights that need to be respected. Answers should include the teaching of the image of God in humans from Genesis 1:26–27. Students should also mention Genesis 9:6, which mandates capital punishment for murderers because of the image of God in humans. Also, James 3:9 teaches that the rights conveyed by bearing the image of God extend even to the way people talk about one another.

Ask the students what biblical teachings support the claim that ensuring justice is a central obligation of government. Direct them to passages such as Deuteronomy 1:10–18 (cf. Lev. 19:15); 1 Kings 10:9; Psalm 72; Jeremiah 22:2–5; Romans 13:1–7; and 1 Peter 2:13–17. The students should learn from these passages that ensuring justice is foremost among a ruler's responsibilities and that government officials will be judged on this basis.

What Is Justice? What Is Righteousness?

As cited in the Teacher Edition margin note above, some argue that religious people should keep religious arguments out of public discussion. List such topics as abortion, gambling, and embryonic stem cell research. Discuss that for the Christian these issues, and others, must always be framed with biblical teachings in mind. A helpful resource is *Biblical Worldview* by BJU Press (see pp. 273–77 and the accompanying notes in that Teacher Edition).

Discuss the relationship between justice (p. 6) and righteousness (p. 7). Use the explanations in the text as a starting point.

ing a person who has done good (v. 13). And he says that anyone who declares the wicked righteous and punishes the righteous is an "abomination to the Lord" (Prov. 17:15, 26). Governments can reward righteousness through the laws they enact. For instance, legislation that removes tax penalties for marriage rewards righteousness, as does legislation that protects people who act as Good Samaritans.

Despite the Bible's many admonitions about governments' obligation to reward the righteous, leaders have often punished the righteous. More eager to preserve their sinful ways than to be changed by such praiseworthy examples, some rulers seek to silence the testimonies of good people. When governments choose this course of action, they choose their own undoing. All governments are themselves ruled by a far greater King. This King sees the deeds of all humans, and as the ultimate Judge of all, He will do right (Gen. 18:25).

Punishing Unrighteousness

Government officials must also punish the unrighteous. God appointed government to execute His wrath on those who do evil (Rom. 13:3–4). Proverbs has much to say concerning the government's responsibility in this regard. (See especially Proverbs 20:26 and 24:24.) According to the Bible, the government can force individuals to restore victims' property (Prov. 6:30–31), can inflict physical punishment (Prov. 20:30), and can even take life (Gen. 9:6; Rom. 13:4).

But this does not mean that the government should punish every wrong action. Some sins are more appropriately dealt with by parents, schools, employers, or others. Some sins—such as lust, covetousness, and secret hatred—are beyond any government's ability to detect or punish. The government should exercise prudence in what it punishes. For instance, God opposes divorce, but He regulated it in Old Testament Israel because of the hardness of the people's hearts (Matt. 19:3–9). This also might have been the case with the regulation of polygamy in the Old Testament. Legislators need wisdom to know when evil behavior warrants a government response and what that response should be.

> ### Righteousness and Justice
>
> Righteousness and justice often seem like two different concepts. Righteousness may seem like a personal virtue, whereas the term *justice* brings to mind courts and lawmakers that operate in public settings. But in the language of the New Testament, both ideas are expressed with the same words, and the two concepts are not distinguished. (**Righteousness** is conformity to a standard—conformity to the character of God.) In this textbook, the government's responsibilities will be discussed using both the terms righteousness and justice.

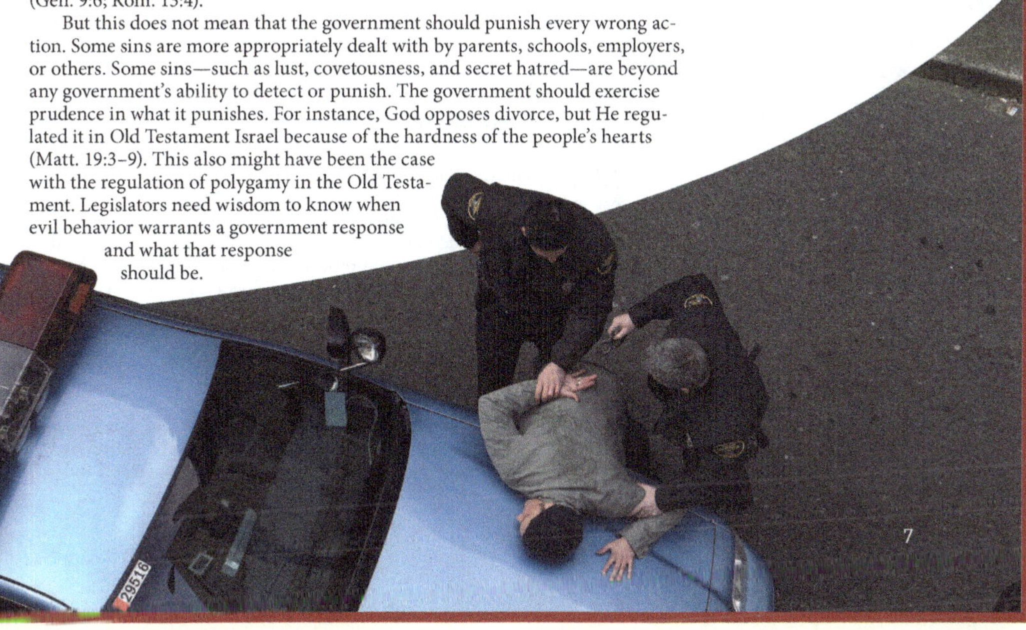

The Proliferation of Rights

The student text describes justice as respecting the rights that all people have as image bearers of God. However, in modern society the discussion of "rights" can produce some troubling results. For example, one danger is trying to expand rights to include such things as a certain standard of living or employer-provided abortifacients.

Furthermore, an emphasis on rights can lead to a selfish focus. Rights entail responsibilities; thus, the connection between rights and responsibilities is central to this discussion.

Evaluating Government Actions

Divide the class into small groups to discuss the topics of rewarding righteousness and punishing unrighteousness. Students should discuss these questions: What are examples of government being involved in such activities? What are instances in which the government is not involved but should be? How effective is government in rewarding and punishing? Encourage students to present their results to the class.

Activity 2: A Lesson from Literature

This activity is designed to develop application and analytical skills.

Activity 3: Psalm 72: God's Ideal for Government

Use this enrichment activity to hone Bible-study skills.

National Defense and Public Safety

Providing for the nation's defense and public safety are closely aligned with the government's obligation of ensuring justice. All are crucial aspects of the government providing for its citizens.

Moral Behavior

Many liberals believe that society should allow every individual to choose his or her own vision of life. However, conservatives have traditionally held that the law should encourage citizens to share morality. This is a biblical position. Peter says that the government should praise the good and punish the evil (1 Peter 2:14; cf. Rom. 13:3).

Provide National Defense and Public Safety

Governments also have the duty and authority to protect their citizens from foreign invasions. They should also prevent lawlessness within their borders.

A great host of injustices follow in the wake of a foreign invasion. Thus, historically, the threat of foreign danger is one of the primary reasons for government. As James Madison observed, "Security against foreign danger is one of the primitive objects of civil society." The Bible recognizes the legitimacy of this function of government but cautions rulers not to be hasty in going to war (Prov. 20:18; 24:6).

Governments support public safety by enforcing just laws. Policies should be in place that help deter sin against others. Because humans are made in God's image, they have a right to life. Murder violates this right, and therefore murder requires punishment to uphold justice (Gen. 9:6). Public safety includes more than just guarding against crime. Governments are called upon to respond to natural disasters and other emergencies; furthermore, they can support health services, especially during epidemics, and can fund medical research.

Address Poverty

Poverty is another major issue that governments must handle if they are to be just. David wrote that the ideal king would rescue the needy and help the poor when no one else assisted (Ps. 72:12). Work is the appropriate way to generate income (Prov. 10:4; 12:27; 22:29), and poverty programs that encourage people not to labor are unjust. Individuals who refuse to work should not receive money from those who do. The Mosaic Law modeled a government system in which the poor had their needs met while not deterring people from work (Ex. 22:25; Lev. 23:22; Deut. 14:28–29; 25:13–16).

Promote Moral Behavior

Governments also adopt laws that reflect and promote a moral code among citizens. The moral code established should reflect the character of God and honor the rights of humans. People sometimes argue that governments should not legislate morality, but in fact no law can exist in a moral vacuum. Laws always reflect some moral viewpoint, and they often influence the moral views of people in a nation. If a government is to praise good and punish evil (1 Peter 2:14), moral questions cannot be avoided. Nor should they be. As Solomon says, "Righteousness exalteth a nation, but sin is a reproach to any people" (Prov. 14:34).

Provide Order

Finally, governments bring order to society. Traffic laws determine what side of the road vehicles should travel and

Addressing Poverty

How to address poverty is a major point of debate in the American political system. Guide a discussion about how God addressed this problem in the nation of Israel.

According to Leviticus 23:22, what is one way that God ensured the poor could eat? *(The farmers were to leave food in their fields for the poor.)*

How does this regulation simultaneously uphold the principle that one ought to work to eat (2 Thess. 3:10) while also providing food for the poor? *(The poor still had labor gleaning the food left in the fields.)*

Poor people often have a cash-flow problem, and high-interest loans can make their long-term situation worse. How did Israel's law address this matter according to Exodus 22:25 and Leviticus 25:35–37? *(The poor were to receive interest-free loans.)*

If poor people could not pay their loans, they had to work until the loan was paid. How did the law that God gave to Israel ensure that these people did not immediately revert to destitution after paying their debts (Deut. 15:12–15)? *(The person for whom he worked is to generously provide him with parting gifts.)*

Was tax money ever used to provide for the poor (Deut. 14:28–29)? *(Yes, as mentioned at the bottom of the Teacher Edition p. 4, a ten percent tax was levied every three years for those in need.)*

Ancient Israel was an agricultural society, so these laws were never meant to be universally applied to all nations for all time. However, ask the class to brainstorm ways the principles found in God's law for Israel could help form contemporary policy about poverty.

what traffic patterns are the most efficient. In cases of natural disasters, governments often coordinate relief efforts. They keep official records such as birth certificates and marriage licenses. They are involved in developing zoning for land use, enforcing building codes, and maintaining public parks and libraries. Whether or not each of these precise functions needs to be administered by a government in every society, these are the kinds of ordering functions that governments have which enable a society to better carry out the Creation Mandate.

Section Review

1–5. What are five biblical obligations of government?

6. How do governments reward righteousness?

7–8. Should the government punish every wrong action? Why or why not?

9. Summarize how government should address poverty.

10–11. Should governments legislate morality? Explain.

★ In addition to the examples in the text, what are other ways governments provide order?

III. The Obligations of the Governed

We often forget that rights imply duties. For instance, though the Declaration of Independence states that we have the right to life, we must remember it also means we have the duty not to murder others. Thus, as we discuss government protecting our rights, we must consider the duties that Christians have toward government. What are those responsibilities?

Prayer

Christians have a duty to pray for their country and its leaders. This was also Israel's duty in exile in pagan Babylon. The Israelites were not allowed to be rebellious or even disgruntled. Instead, they were to promote the welfare of the city in which they were exiled. Prayer on the city's behalf was a primary way that they were to do this (Jer. 29:7).

In the New Testament, Paul makes prayer an explicit duty for believers when he urges them to pray

Students shown participating in the annual "See You at the Pole" event, at which thousands gather at their schools to pray

Officials as God's Ministers

Paul calls government officials "ministers" three times in Romans 13:4–6. He uses two words to do so. One word emphasizes that the minister is an agent of his master. Elsewhere in the Bible this word is used to describe Paul (Eph. 3:7; Col. 1:23) and Jesus (Rom. 15:8). The second word is used to describe angels (Heb. 1:7), Paul (Rom. 15:16), Epaphroditus (Phil. 2:25), and Jesus (as High Priest) (Heb. 8:1–2). This word denotes service and, in the case of government officials, public ministers under God.

Romans 13 indicates that Christians should not think of government as something apart from God's plan because "there is no power but of God." Government is an agent and servant of God to accomplish His will. To accomplish God's will, officials must understand right and wrong and therefore must fear God. Involvement in government is thus a legitimate and even necessary pursuit for Christians if they are going to do God's will on earth as it is done in heaven.

But officials who fail to follow God are still God's agents and servants because God uses their rebellion to accomplish His purposes, just as He used Balaam and Nebuchadnezzar.

Section Review Answers

1–5. to ensure justice, provide national defense and public safety, address poverty, promote moral behavior, and provide order (p. 5)

6. by passing and enforcing laws that encourage people to do right and that remove obstacles to doing good (p. 6–7)

7–8. No; some sins are internal, and some sins are more appropriately dealt with by other authorities, such as parents, schools, or employers. (p. 7)

9. Government should address poverty in a manner that doesn't reward people for not working. (p. 8)

10–11. Yes, because no law can exist in a moral vacuum. If a government is to praise good and punish evil, moral questions cannot be avoided. (p. 8)

★ Answers will vary.

  **Prayer for Government Officials**

Ask students to list reasons that praying for officials is important. Then direct them to work together to craft a prayer that includes the things that the Bible tells Christians to pray for regarding their government. Post the prayer and pray it together regularly.

The prayer should include requests for just, righteous, and self-controlled leaders who defend those deprived of justice, punish evildoers, and praise righteousness (Ps. 72:1–4; Rom. 13:1–7; 1 Pet. 2:13–17); leaders who fear God and consider that they will give an account to Him (Acts 24:25); the salvation of governmental leaders (1 Tim. 2:1–4); freedom for Christians to live godly lives without persecution (1 Tim. 2:1–4); and Christ's return to establish His kingdom on earth (Matt. 6:10).

Local Officials

Invite a local government official or police officer to speak about the importance of obeying laws and the consequences of not submitting to local authorities.

Paul's Political Environment

Some may say that the apostle Paul would not have commanded modern Christians to be subject to their authorities if he knew their government. However, Paul lived during the reign of the wicked emperor Nero.

Nero began ruling at sixteen under the supervision of his praetorian prefect, Burrus, and his tutor Seneca. During his early years, Nero governed well, despite his personal immorality. Nevertheless, he eventually killed his stepbrother, his wife, and his mother and ordered Seneca and his leading generals to commit suicide.

Perhaps Nero is best known for persecuting Christians after blaming them for the great fire that struck Rome in AD 64. Christians were crucified, sewn into animal skins to be torn apart by dogs, and burned as illumination for Nero's garden parties.

Paul's appeal to be tried by Caesar (Acts 25:11) was an appeal to Nero. Paul was probably martyred during Nero's persecution.

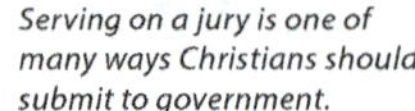

Believers should exercise their right to vote.

for all their authorities. At the very least, Christians should pray that the state will allow them to pursue godliness in peace and quiet. But Christians should pray for more than just that. Paul states that they should pray for government officials to be saved and to know the truth themselves (1 Tim. 2:1–4).

Participation

God wants Christians to be involved in government. The reason should not be hard to discern. If a government has believers involved in its operations, it is more capable of fulfilling its obligations well. Those who deny God and His law often have difficulty formulating a stable, accurate way to distinguish right from wrong. They may even treat good as evil and praise evil as good. Under unrighteous governments, God's people are often denied the liberty to obey God's commands.

In the United States, citizens enjoy the opportunity to participate freely in their government. This blessing is forbidden to millions living under dictatorial regimes. American citizens may participate in their government by voting, voicing their opinions, supporting a candidate, or even running for office themselves. Changing the government for the glory of God is far easier today than it was during the days of the Roman Empire. But such involvement demands that believers learn about government. Understanding the structure, the mechanics, and the operation of government is a necessary first step toward effective participation.

Submission

Whenever the New Testament discusses the issue of the Christian's relationship to civil government, it emphasizes the believer's obligation to obey and submit. In 1 Peter 2:13–17, Peter urges Christians to live in submission to their government to have a good testimony before critics of Christianity. Paul's reasoning in Romans 13 complements Peter's reasoning: a ruler is God's servant to execute His wrath on evildoers (vv. 4–5). God established government to bring order and justice to society. To do these tasks, government needs citizens who respect its authority by paying taxes, obeying speed limits, serving on juries, and performing other such duties. Even a corrupt government can fulfill much of God's will. Therefore, to disobey government is to violate one's conscience and rebel against God.

Since New Testament times, God's servants have often found themselves facing ungodliness in difficult situations. In some cases, the source of that ungodliness is the government. Paul faced ungodly government on two fronts—civil (Rome) and religious (the Sanhedrin). But even bold, blunt Paul remained respectful of those authorities. In fact, he was willing to stand trial and use their legal systems to his advantage. Just before Paul was to be whipped by Roman authorities, he appealed to them on the basis of his citizenship (Acts 22:25). He regarded his citizenship highly and politely reminded the authorities of civil laws relating to it. Later, when Paul stood before Felix, a Roman official who was known for his cruelty, he acted courteously and recognized Felix's many years of experience (Acts 24:10).

Serving on a jury is one of many ways Christians should submit to government.

Activity 4: Obligations of the Government and the Governed

Use this enrichment activity to examine Bible verses that deal with the responsibilities of government and those it governs.

Pressing for Justice

Develop projects that will provide an opportunity for students to participate in government. For example, ask the students to identify unjust governmental policies that they think should be changed. Be prepared to shape their understanding because some will likely be unable to identify local or state injustices without first investigating current events. Then lead the students in formulating steps that could be followed to effect changes.

Or suggest that the students participate in the campaign of an official who they believe will further biblical ends.

   ### Evaluating Political Discourse

Play segments of talk radio and televised news programs that include debates and discussions; also display select comment feeds from websites. Ask the students to evaluate these discourses with Scripture.

The following Scripture passages should shape the students' evaluation:

Titus 3:1–3
In the context of submission to governmental authority, Paul explains how Christians should conduct themselves toward everyone. Christians should not slander or otherwise verbally abuse anyone, especially a person in a role of authority. Christians should not be quarrelsome; they should always be gracious and considerate. Paul grounds his instruction in the fact that Christians were once no different from the sinners who ruled over them and lived around them. Christians are saved by grace, not by any merit of their own, so they should be gracious, not abusive, toward others.

Romans 13:1–7
Though Nero was emperor when Paul wrote

Yet Scripture's commands to submit to and obey government are always set in the context of God's authority structure: God maintains sovereignty over His creation, and the state is simply His instrument. If the government tries to force a Christian to violate a clear biblical command and the believer has exhausted every avenue of appeal, he must still obey the highest authority—God.

The Christian's response in such a situation is not so much a matter of disobedience as a principle of obeying the highest authority. When the hostile Jewish leadership in Jerusalem reminded the apostles that teaching in the name of Jesus was forbidden, the apostles declared, "We ought to obey God rather than men" (Acts 5:28–29). They then continued to obey the highest authority, preaching daily in the temple and in homes (Acts 5:42), just as Jesus commanded them in the Great Commission.

Even in such cases, however, the Christian's response is to be tempered with respect for government officials. The apostles continued to preach but did not organize a rebellion. Similarly, Daniel and his friends submitted to authority even when they disobeyed the king's command to eat meat and drink wine (Dan. 1). God's people must respect the government even if they must disobey it to obey God.

Witness

Because a Christian's first duty as a citizen is to pray for the salvation of his governmental leaders, evangelizing them should also be a priority. Paul demonstrated this passion for the souls of his rulers. On several different occasions, he pleaded with government officials to allow their lives to be changed by the gospel. Most memorable is his emotional appeal before Agrippa, a monarch who ruled the Jews (Acts 26:22, 27). Agrippa did not submit to the gospel that day, but many other people in government did convert to Christianity during Paul's life. In encouraging the saints at Philippi, Paul wrote to them that his imprisonment at Rome, though unpleasant, had advanced the spread of the gospel in the royal household (Phil. 1:13). At the end of that letter, Paul indicates that the gospel spread not only among those in the palace but also among many others, including those in "Caesar's household" (Phil. 4:22).

Christians also have a duty to testify to governments about their responsibility before God. When governments do wrong, Christians must confront them, calling for them to stop disobeying God and warning of God's judgment on that disobedience.

As we begin our study of American government, we explore a subject interwoven with the very fabric of American society, past and present. And we do so with the guiding lamp of Scripture to provide discernment. Christians must realize that their dual citizenship in heaven and on earth increases rather than diminishes their responsibilities. Because they have been enlightened by the truth of the gospel, Christians are responsible to declare to their rulers that the Christ who saves is also the Christ who is sovereign over earthly rulers (Rev. 1:5) and who therefore expects submission (Ps. 2:10–12). Through this declaration, God will be glorified, leaders will be blessed, and citizens can enjoy the blessing of good government.

Paying taxes is one of our responsibilities to our government.

The Highest Authority

The "highest-authority" principle, mentioned in the text, is easily clarified by an illustration from the military. Suppose a sergeant sent a private on an errand with strict orders to finish the job and return immediately. If the private's lieutenant were to stop him and issue a lawful order, the private would have to obey. Although the private may have failed to complete the orders of the sergeant, he did not disobey; he obeyed the higher authority. If his sergeant complained, the private could appeal directly to the lieutenant.

---

the book of Romans, Paul calls him God's servant and commands obedience to his decrees. Obviously, Christians must not obey commands that violate God's law (Acts 5:29); but otherwise they should generally obey government officials, viewing them as God's appointed servants.

1 Peter 2:13–17
Peter also lived under Nero's rule, and in this passage he tells Christians to honor the emperor. These verses demonstrate that Christians must honor the office of even wicked rulers. They should be careful to speak respectfully, even when they disagree with a ruler's policies and actions.

Acts 23:1–5
When Paul was confronted for reviling the high priest, he acknowledged his wrong by quoting Exodus 22:28, which says that people must not speak ill of their rulers.

James 3:9
In this verse, James warns Christians against using their tongues to curse others, who are also created in God's image.

Jesus and the Old Testament prophets did rebuke leaders with strong language (see Matt. 23:13–36; Amos 4:1). But there are two considerations to remember when harmonizing these instances with the verses listed above. First, these rebukes imply authority over the ones being rebuked. Jesus and the prophets had this authority. Second, when a Christian condemns an authority's practices or policies in strong language, he should be sure that Scripture stands behind the condemnation.

Christians must be forthright in defending truth and justice. But such candor should not conflict with the qualities of graciousness, consideration, and obedience.

Being a Testimony
Group the students and ask them to brainstorm ways that they can be a testimony to government officials. Instruct the groups to present their ideas.

Activity 5: Chapter Review
This review activity is designed to reinforce recognition of terms and other information.

True Patriotism

This embattled shore, portal of freedom, is forever hallowed by the ideals, the valor and the sacrifices of our fellow countrymen.

The limestone memorial on which these words are etched faces the graves of almost 9,400 World War II soldiers buried at the Normandy American Cemetery above Omaha Beach. Words like these stir strong feelings of patriotism in most American citizens.

Patriotism, defined simply, is love and devotion to one's country. However, it has also been defined as "the hatred of other countries disguised as the love of [one's] own" or as "the last refuge of a scoundrel." These negative definitions reflect the horrors committed in the name of patriotism. For instance, in Germany, the Nazis took patriotism to an extreme in which the government was not only honored but also worshiped. Unquestioning support for the state characterizes the corruption of patriotism.

Consequently, it is vital that Christians have a proper perspective of patriotism. True patriotism arises from a spirit of thankfulness for the blessings of good government. But good government does not rise spontaneously. It comes about through particular circumstances—often by the toils and the prayers of faithful citizens and ultimately by God's grace. As citizens reflect on individuals and events that helped shape their government, they must remember that God, not the state, should be the main object of their gratitude.

Patriotism also arises from love for neighbor. Christians should be devoted to their country because they should seek for the welfare of their neighbors (Jer. 29:7). Love for neighbor can include serving in the armed forces to defend one's country against enemies or serving in government to help enact wise laws that will benefit a community.

Love for neighbor includes more than the social and political welfare of one's country. The Christian recognizes that the spiritual welfare of his neighbors is also important. In fact, the social and political welfare of a nation is in many ways tied to its spiritual welfare. Therefore, a Christian knows that patriotism involves sharing the Word of God and being a Christlike example to a needy nation.

Sadly, America has drifted from a heritage that was deeply rooted in godly principles. But rather than simply lament this decline, Christian patriots must pray passionately for their nation and fervently desire to establish principles that honor God. While patriotism includes such actions as voting, singing the national anthem, saluting the flag, and honoring patriots past and present, it has an even deeper meaning for the Christian.

American cemetery in Normandy, France

Section Review

1. Discuss the first duty that a Christian has toward his government.
2. Why should a Christian fear to disobey his government?
3. How should a Christian determine whether to obey a specific command from his government?
★ Why does failure to confront rulers about wrongdoing violate the Great Commission?
★ One example of extreme patriotism is given in the text. Discuss it and list other examples.

Memorials

Ask students to research a local memorial or monument. Then take them to visit it. Discuss why it was built. Was it built immediately after the event that it commemorates or many years later? Did just a few local activists initiate its construction, or did it have wide community support? Does it have significance for the students, or would it be appreciated mainly by earlier generations?

Section Review Answers

1. Christians should pray for it and its leaders, and they should pray that government will permit Christians to pursue holiness in peace; they should also pray for the salvation of government officials. (p. 9–10)
2. because disobedience will cause him to violate his conscience and disobey God (p. 10)
3. He should not obey a law that forces him to disobey a clear biblical command. (p. 11)
★ If believers fail to confront rulers about rulers' obligations, then those believers fail to take the gospel to every segment of society.
★ Nazism in Germany was a twisted and extreme form of patriotism. Its unquestioning support of state was very dangerous. Other instances of extreme patriotism would include many Communist controlled governments and the government of Italy during the rule of Benito Mussolini.

CHAPTER REVIEW ANSWERS

Making Connections

1. David describes a ruler in poetic language. His words apply to any leader. He states that rulers must be just and must fear God. (p. 3)
2. Humans are unique among God's creation because God made humans in His own image and gave them dominion over the whole earth (Gen. 1:26–27). Humans have qualities that reflect His own character (such as reason, moral

CHAPTER REVIEW

People, Places, and Things to Remember

government
image of God
Creation Mandate
human depravity
anarchy
justice
righteousness
patriotism

Making Connections

1. Explain King David's last words and their significance.
2. Explain how humans are unique among God's creation.
3. Why is anarchy dangerous?
4. Outline a biblical approach to addressing poverty.
5–8. Summarize the four obligations, or duties, mentioned that Christians have to government.

Developing Civics Skills

1. If you were involved in government, how could you ensure that you ruled justly?
2. Should a legislator try to pass a law that punishes sin if he knows that the majority in Congress will vote against it and that the majority of the nation is opposed to it?

Thinking Critically

1. According to the Bible, what would an ideal government look like?
2. Since the Bible is the ultimate guide for human government, why do Americans not support a monarchy such as the kind Israel had?
3. What are the differences between equality before the law, equality of opportunity, and equality of outcomes? Why are some equalities unjust?

Living as a Christian Citizen

1. Increasingly, secularists often oppose Christian involvement in government on the grounds that Christian religion and morality should not be forced on the nation. Write an essay or an editorial arguing for the Christian's right to participate in American politics.
2. Outline some ways that you can be a testimony to government officials.

capacity, spirituality, sociability, and emotion). (p. 4)

3. Human society ultimately destroys itself when it is in a state of anarchy. Any government is essentially better than no government. (p. 4–5)
4. Poverty should be addressed in such a way that the poor have their needs met while not deterring them from work. (p. 8)
5–8. Christians have a duty to pray for government, participate in government, submit to government, and witness to government leaders. Christians should pray that the state will allow them to pursue godliness in peace and quiet and for the salvation of government officials. Participation in American government includes voting, voicing opinions, supporting a candidate, or even running for office. Christians should submit to government as long as they are not disobeying God in the process. Finally, Christians are responsible to declare to their rulers that Christ saves and is sovereign over earthly rulers. Evangelizing should be a priority. (p. 9–11)

Developing Civics Skills

1. by making decisions that match up with God's character as revealed in the Bible (p. 6)
2. The answer will vary depending on several factors, including the current importance of the issue, the desirability or viability of compromise, and the matter of whether the broader issue deserves debate to make the law's passage more likely.

Thinking Critically

1. God-honoring government arises only with the help of the Spirit and the advance of the gospel.
2. God had specific purposes for Israel that are not exactly applicable to us today. God clearly reveals the necessity of government but does not prescribe a certain form.
3. Equality before the law means that judgments are rendered according to the facts of a matter and not according to social standing, wealth, or other factors. It is rooted in the facts that all people are made in God's image and that God is not a respecter of persons. To deny a person equal opportunity before the law is unjust.

   Equality of opportunity is an ideal. Technically, it is impossible because people have various abilities and disabilities that affect their opportunities. Equality of outcome is seen as social justice by some people. Its proponents try to equalize wealth. In practice, however, attempting to ensure equality of outcome can lead to injustice. It often means depriving some people of things for which they have worked.

Living as a Christian Citizen

1. Answers may include some of the following. Professing Christians make up a large proportion of the American population and have a right to political participation and speech like everyone else. All laws originate from a particular point of view; why should the Christian view be ruled out? God made the world with certain norms; secular attempts to defy those norms will result in a broken society. Examples may be provided from contemporary society to show how immorality has resulted in a broken society. In other words, students can show that Christians are truly concerned for the welfare of their society.
2. Answers may include writing a gospel letter, sharing one's testimony in the course of meeting with an official, working on a campaign with a candidate both to promote a good candidacy and for opportunities to share the gospel.

1. Identify the differences between the various forms of government.
2. Examine the American system of government.
3. Outline a brief history of democracy.
4. Assess the characteristics of democracy.
5. Analyze the conditions necessary for democracy.

FORMS OF GOVERNMENT

2

British Parliament building in London

The best form of government is that which is most likely to prevent the greatest sum of evil.

—James Monroe

I. Types of Government

II. American Government

III. A Brief History of Democracy

IV. Characteristics of Democracy

V. Conditions for Democracy

BIG IDEAS

1. What are the differences between the various types of government?
2. How is the American system of government structured?
3. How has democracy developed and changed over time?
4. What are the characteristics of democracy?
5. What are the conditions necessary for democracy?

SUGGESTED MATERIALS

Section I
- Activity 1 from Chapter 2 of the *Student Activities*

Section II
- Special speakers (see p. 22)

Section III
- Activities 2–3 from Chapter 2 of the *Student Activities*

Section IV
- Questionnaire (see p. 31)
- Activity 4 from Chapter 2 of the *Student Activities*

Section V
- Special speaker (see p. 36)
- List of facts or copies of sample test for prospective naturalized citizens (see p. 37)
- Activity 5 from Chapter 2 of the *Student Activities*

Teacher Resources
Visit TeacherToolsOnline.com for resources to enhance the lessons.

Additional Reading
A good foundational resource for the teacher is *Government: An Ideal Concept* by Leonard Read. Though first written more than sixty years ago (later updated), it still provides excellent material.

The world contains a wide variety of governments. Some governments operate without the people's consent, others allow only limited popular involvement, and still others allow a great deal of popular involvement and acknowledge the people as the source of their power.

I. Types of Government

Great differences exist among the nations' governments. There are many varieties and combinations throughout the world. To clarify the differences, we examine in this section (1) various systems of government, (2) the relationship between the levels of a nation's governments, and (3) the methods some governments use to elect their executives.

Systems of Government

One major difference among systems of government is the level of citizen participation in the decision-making process.

Monarchy

Monarchy is a form of government in which a single person, such as a king or queen, is the leader. It is usually an inherited position and the person normally rules for life. It is one of the most common forms of government in history and flourished well into the nineteenth century, until an antimonarchical attitude began to gain wide acceptance. Many philosophers and theologians had long believed that the best form of government was a monarchy that included democratic and aristocratic checks on the **monarch**. Most monarchies today are **constitutional monarchies** in which the government is typically administered by a democratically elected parliament. The monarch is merely a ceremonial head of state.

Usually, a monarchy is a government in which supreme authority is invested in one who rules for life. Supreme authority does not mean sole authority. Historically, most monarchies functioned along with other governmental bodies, such as a senate, a diet, or a parliament. These aristocratic groups, sometimes elected, could serve as checks on monarchs' absolute authority.

Often, monarchies operate with hereditary succession. The heir apparent—usually the monarch's eldest son or, if there are no sons, eldest daughter—is called the crown prince or the crown princess. Once it becomes hereditary, a monarchy is called a **dynasty**, or a house. Occasionally, monarchs are elected. For instance, in the Holy Roman Empire, certain nobles chose the emperor. Monarchs in the past were often **absolute monarchs**—they had unlimited power.

Monarchy, the form of government that God chose for the nation of Israel, was rooted in the promises of the Abrahamic Covenant (Gen. 17:6). Even before Israel was a monarchy, God's people expected that God would one day provide a king for them (Gen. 36:31; 49:10). In the early years of Israel's

Guiding Questions

1. What are the similarities and differences between the various systems of government?

2. What relationships exist between the different levels of government?

3. How does the method of choosing a chief executive differ in the presidential and parliamentary systems?

---

1. Compare systems of government.

2. Explain the relationships between the different levels of government.

3. Contrast the parliamentary and presidential means of choosing an executive.

Monarchy, Democracy, and Aristocracy

As noted in the text, many philosophers and theologians have long thought that the best form of government combines elements of monarchy, democracy, and aristocracy.

Students may be unfamiliar with the textbook's usage of aristocracy and aristocratic. In this instance, the terms do not refer to those who are born into positions of privilege and wealth (as they sometimes mean), but rather to rule by the best and wisest citizens.

Divine Right of Kings

Advocates of the divine right of kings took something that the Bible did say (that the governments that exist have their authority from God) and said it meant something that the Bible did not assert (that any checks on the king's power were illegitimate). Notably, many theologians have historically favored mixed forms of government rather than the divine right of kings theory.

The Best Government

Refer to the side margin notes above and the feature box on page 17 entitled, "Mixed Forms of Government." You may need to explain that monarchy is "rule by one," aristocracy is "rule by a few," and "rule by many" is democracy.

Discuss the following: Did the United States experience rule by the best and wisest of its citizens in the founding era? Do the wisest and best rule today? What steps can be taken to ensure the best and wisest citizens occupy government offices?

Lord Acton

Lord John Emerich Edward Dalberg Acton (1834–1902) was perhaps the most significant Roman Catholic intellectual in Victorian England. He was educated in Munich, Germany, under the direction of Johann Joseph Ignaz von Döllinger, a notable church historian. Briefly a member of Parliament, Acton served as a confidant of Prime Minister William Gladstone. As a professor at Cambridge University (1895–1902), Acton emphasized that history is a rigorous, "scientific" discipline, and he made a special study of the nature of political freedom.

Anarchy in Iraq

When coalition forces toppled Iraq's dictatorial government in 2003, they soon witnessed the consequences of anarchy. After Saddam Hussein was driven from power, many Iraqis looted government buildings taking anything they could carry. Soon other Iraqis begged coalition troops to stop the theft and violence.

monarchy, constitutional and democratic elements existed in the government. The nation's elders played a role in choosing the king (2 Sam. 2:4; 5:1–4; cf. 2 Kings 11:17). The king, like his people, was bound by God's law (Deut. 17:18–20). Israel was also unique because God Himself decided who would be king (1 Sam. 9:16).

However, the Bible is also realistic about the problems that can arise with a monarchy. Saul became king because the Israelites demanded a king at the wrong time with wrong motives. They wanted to be like other nations, and they wanted a king to defeat their enemies (enemies that God would defeat if Israel remained faithful to Him). But God warned them what the inappropriate behavior of a monarch would be like: he would take the best of their produce, the best of their animals, and the best of their young men and women to work for him until the people cried to God for deliverance (1 Sam. 8:10–19). Such a king was just as much a judgment on Israel as was an enemy invader.

A monarchy can be a good system if the monarch's power is limited by the law and by checks and balances. If a limited monarchy falls into the hands of a wicked or gullible ruler, the people at least have some recourse against tyranny. But if an absolute monarch is wicked, the people have no way of correcting the situation except through prayer or revolution, and the latter option often conflicts with God's command to obey government officials.

Adolf Hitler, dictator of Germany (1933–45)

Absolute Monarchy or Dictatorship?

Usually there is little difference between these two forms of government. Absolute monarchs have unlimited power, and thus are dictators. However, though monarchy is hereditary, dictators may or may not pass power to another family member.

Dictatorship

The nineteenth and twentieth centuries saw a growing desire to replace monarchies with democratic forms of government. Although many monarchies disappeared or became increasingly limited in the twentieth century, that century also included a number of **dictatorships**. In a dictatorship the government acts without the people's consent or input. An elite ruling class—such as the military, the wealthy, or a powerful family—usually wields absolute power, often seeking to control every aspect of the people's lives (**totalitarianism**).

Dictatorial governments are typically autocratic or oligarchic. In an **autocracy**, one person rules with supreme authority. In an **oligarchy**, an elite group (e.g., a single political party, such as the Nazi, Fascist, or Communist Party) rules. Sometimes this elite group is self-appointed, dividing the governmental departments among its members.

Dictators usually rely on fear imposed by military or police power to gain and keep control within a country and to maintain respect in the world. For example, Saddam Hussein, who ruled Iraq from 1979 to 2003, maintained order and supported his regime through fear. His desire for power led Iraq into wars with Iran, Kuwait, and finally the United States and a coalition of other nations, culminating in a wrecked Iraqi economy; the loss of thousands of lives; the downfall of Hussein's regime; and eventually his capture, trial, and execution.

Good rulers can do much good, and limitations protect people against bad rulers. But absolute monarchies and dictatorships are destructive. As British intellectual Lord Acton wrote, because of human depravity, "power tends to corrupt, and absolute power corrupts absolutely." There is only one truly good absolute monarch—Jesus Christ. One day He will rule the world from Zion with absolute power (Ps. 2:6–9).

Comparing Governments

Group the students and assign a country to each group. Direct each group to research that nation's government. Assign nations that provide a representative sample of various government systems (i.e., one with a constitutional monarchy, one with an absolute monarchy, one with a dictator, one with anarchy). Encourage the groups to present their findings to the class.

Somalia in 2017 after a truck bomb explosion

Anarchy

We made reference to anarchy in Chapter 1. According to the *Oxford English Dictionary*, it is "a state of lawlessness due to the absence or inefficiency of the supreme power." To the anarchist, complete freedom (total lack of restraint) is ideal; therefore, any government, including a democratic government, is an unnecessary evil. Anarchy's underlying theory is that people do not need a superior force to ensure that they live together peacefully. In her book *The Political Theory of Anarchism*, April Carter states, "Society may create the kind of individuals who have strongly internalized values and can live cooperatively and freely without the threat of force." In contrast, Thomas Hobbes, a seventeenth-century philosopher, asserted that without government humans would continually fight and live "nasty, brutish, and short" lives.

Although the idea of people living together peacefully in complete freedom sounds great, the Bible teaches that such a utopia will never be realized because humans are inherently sinful (Jer. 17:9; Rom. 13:1–4; Eph. 2:3). As noted in Chapter 1, even in eternity, when the redeemed are sinless, government will exist in the form of a monarchy. In other words, even when sin is eradicated, anarchy is not acceptable. Anarchists' belief that government is evil attacks God's wisdom and goodness. No matter how good anarchy sounds, Christians must reject it because this theory contradicts Scripture.

History also demonstrates the impracticality of anarchy. For example, beginning in the 1990s war and strife destroyed much of the nation of Somalia—both politically and economically. With bitter fighting between tribal factions, the country had no functioning national government. Tribal factions controlled areas, and bands of heavily armed ruffians waged bloody conflicts. After twenty years of chaos, a new government was established in 2012. That government continues to struggle to bring stability to a country ravaged by decades of anarchy.

Popular Governments

A system in which the people participate is called a **popular government**. Popular governments exist when political power resides with the people, not with a monarch or an elite group. Two types of popular government exist: democracy and republic.

Democracy: The eighteenth-century philosopher Immanuel Kant developed a theory of ethics based on human dignity. In his theory every human has equal worth and rights that must be respected. Kant's ideas form the basis for modern liberal democracy.

Though not a perfect government, democracy is an example of participatory government. Unlike those living under repressive regimes, citizens of democracies have a voice in how they shall be ruled. The word *democracy* has come to mean many things, and the system is certainly not without its critics. Even democracy's strengths reveal some weaknesses. Liberty may be promoted at the expense of virtue, equality at the expense of proper respect for authorities, and individualism at the expense of the community; such problems reveal that the Bible's values and those of democracy do not always align. But, despite its

Mixed Forms of Government

Forms of government can be condensed to three types: rule by one, rule by a few, and rule by many. A number of writers have noted that mixing these forms of government can preserve the good parts of each while safeguarding against their bad tendencies. The structure of the United States government certainly reflects this concept. For instance, a single ruler can provide decisive leadership. But he can also become a dictator. So the United States has a single head (the president) who provides leadership while also having a legislative branch, rule by the few. The president and the lawmakers are elected by the many (the people), which allows the many to check the one and the few. Citizens make laws through their representatives, which allows the few to check the many.

Thomas Hobbes

Thomas Hobbes (1588–1679), an English philosopher, proposed that the driving force of humanity is self-preservation. Hobbes himself suffered from many fears, which led him to develop a political philosophy that emphasized the fear of death and the need for security. Hobbes supported the ideas that government should be based on social contract and that government should be absolute. (He preferred an absolute monarchy.) He rejected Christianity, fully embracing materialism. It is reported that at death Hobbes said, "I am about to take my last voyage, a great leap in the dark."

Kant and the Christian

Christians can agree with Kant that all people have equal worth and that people should respect one another's rights. But Christians also have some fundamental disagreements with him. Kant believed that each individual's reason, and that reason alone, creates moral obligations. But Kant believed that the state must not coerce anyone to follow a particular morality; rather, he said that the state should keep people from harming one another.

Unlike Kant, Christians believe that morality is founded in God's revelation—both natural and special revelation. And they must reject the idea that supporting biblical morality within a system of laws violates the rights of people who have different beliefs.

Current Events

Assign the students to search newspapers, magazines, and websites for examples of anarchy in foreign countries. For instance, nations sometimes experience anarchy when people are left with little or no government during a civil war or following the collapse of a dictatorship. Choose a day for the students to present the information that they find.

Kant and Republics

Kant believed that only republics can safeguard the rights of humans. Engage the students in a discussion about whether Kant's thesis is correct. They should note that while republics have certain features that tend to protect individual rights, no form of government is the solution to injustice. Republics and democracies can become tyrannical, and monarchies can be just and fair. When under the influence of Christian teaching, any of these systems can ensure justice. But it remains true that some political structures are more open to abuse than others. For this reason, Christian political thinkers over the centuries have preferred systems that give the people a voice and the power to check abuses and that enable the government to check the passions of the populace.

Japan's Legislature

Japan's National Diet, or Kokkai, has two chambers—the House of Councillors (San-giin) and the House of Representatives (Shūgiin). The House of Councillors consists of 242 seats, and the House of Representatives consists of more than 450 seats. Both chambers are elected by the people. The leader of the majority party (or the leader of the majority coalition) that wins the legislative elections becomes the prime minister of Japan.

Democracy Versus Republic

In *Federalist* No. 10, Madison contrasted a republic with a democracy.

> The two great points of difference between a democracy and a republic are: first, the delegation of the government, in the latter [republic], to a small number of citizens elected by the rest; secondly, the greater number of citizens, and greater sphere of country, over which the latter [republic] may be extended.

shortcomings, democracy under the rule of law remains the form of government in which liberty, equality, and individualism find their best blend.

Democracies are usually divided into two types: direct or indirect. **Direct democracy**, also called pure democracy, is a government in which the people *directly* affect the government's policies and actions through gatherings resembling those of the ancient city-state Athens or New England town meetings. Each citizen hears the proposals and arguments and then participates directly by voting. Today, direct democracy is rare because of geographic and population limitations.

In **indirect democracy**, also called representative democracy, the people elect individuals to operate the government on their behalf. The people then keep these representatives accountable by holding frequent elections. Modern examples of indirect democracy exist in Japan, Canada, France, and the United States.

Republic: The founders of the United States were from the outset attached to the idea of a republic. Article IV, Section 4, of the Constitution requires that the United States guarantee a republican form of government for each state of the Union.

The *Oxford English Dictionary* defines a **republic** as a "state in which power rests with the people or their representatives." America's government, then, can be called a "democratic republic" because it is republican in structure and democratic in principle. The people are sovereign, but they elect representatives to exercise the government's powers according to written laws. The term "constitutional republic" also accurately describes our government.

It is important to remember that not every country which states that it has a democratic or a republican government fulfills those claims. For example, the former Soviet Union, which was also known as the Union of Soviet Socialist Republics (USSR), is a historical example of a government that asserted principles of freedom and popular participation but did not practice those principles. Today the People's Republic of China and the Democratic People's Republic of Korea (North Korea) sound like popular governments, but they are actually two of the most repressive nations in the world.

"I pledge allegiance to the flag . . . and to the republic for which it stands."

Relationships Between Levels of Government

A second way to understand government is to examine the relationships between different levels of government. Are the different levels of government closely or loosely related? Various answers to this question can be found in the following systems: unitary, federal, and confederate governments.

Unitary Governments

In the **unitary system**, governmental power resides in the central government; but, unlike a dictatorship, this government receives all its power from the people. Once established, the central government creates local units to help administer government. Since these units exist by the central government's authority, they can theoretically be disbanded if the central government later considers them unnecessary. The unitary system is the most commonly used form of government and is found in Great Britain, France, Japan, and Israel.

Activity 1: Systems of Government

This activity reinforces material in the text and requires students to use outside resources.

Voter Turnout

Around election time, various media outlets often feature stories about voter turnout. The assumption behind most of these stories is that high voter turnout is good and low voter turnout is bad. Discuss aspects of this assumption that may be true (e.g., low turnout may indicate that people are apathetic or that they think the political process is broken, or perhaps they are relatively satisfied with the government). Also discuss aspects of this assumption that may be false (e.g.,

it may be better to have a few voters who understand the issues at stake than many voters who have little understanding of the candidates and their differences). Guide a discussion about what makes an informed voter.

Federal Governments

Federalism divides a nation's power between national and regional governments. (When different governments simultaneously assert authority over the people, the situation is also called federalism.) In one instance, the regional government, such as a state or province, might exert more influence. On another occasion, the national government might be more influential. A constitution rules the nation's various levels of government, delegating powers to each. The federal system guards against tyranny by separating the government's powers, but this separation also impedes the efficient working of the national government. Federalism works well in large countries consisting of people with differing goals and needs. The national government governs the nation as a whole, but regional governments meet specific groups' needs within defined geographic areas. The United States, Brazil, Germany, and India are modern examples of governments that divide power between national and regional governments.

Confederate Governments

In a **confederate government**, regional governments retain supremacy and delegate few tasks to the national government. The powers held by the national government are exercised only by the states' permission. The Articles of Confederation established a confederate government in early American history. Another example is the Confederate States of America, established in 1861. Also, the countries of the European Union (EU), more than two dozen in number, exemplify a modern confederacy. Each member country retains its individual sovereignty while loosely combining with other countries to promote integration in European economics and politics. For example, the EU issued a new currency called the euro for its members' use; however, each country could choose whether to participate. Exercising their sovereignty, the United Kingdom, Sweden, and Denmark chose not to use the new currency. (Much later, in 2016, the United Kingdom voted to withdraw from the EU).

Although many people use the term federal government to refer to the national government of the United States, this use is technically inaccurate. In the US system all state governments and the national government combined compose the federal government.

Electing the Chief Executive

The third means of categorizing governments is analyzing the relationship between the legislative (law-making) and executive (law-enforcing) branches. Is the executive branch an independent branch of the government, or is it an extension of the legislative branch? Is the national leader, or chief executive, elected by the people or by the legislature? These questions distinguish two categories concerning the legislative and executive branches.

Presidential System

In a **presidential system**, the people elect the head of the executive branch, independently of the legislative branch. This leader is normally called the president. This

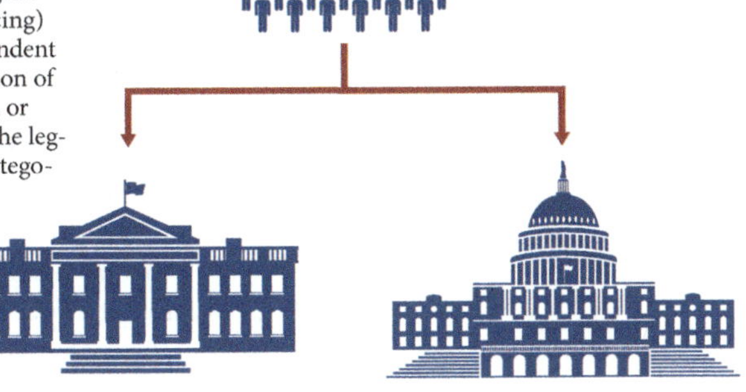

Presidential System

Origin of Parliament

Although Parliament's origins are debated, Simon de Montfort (ca. 1208–65) played a role in its creation. King Henry III was an autocratic ruler whose poor leadership, expensive military campaigns, and lavish living alienated his nobility. After Henry clashed with his barons, the barons forced him to sign the Provisions of Oxford (1258), which delegated some of his power to a council of fifteen, called Parliament. This power-sharing venture failed when Henry (with the pope's approval) abolished it and intensified his autocratic tendencies.

Simon de Montfort then led a rebellion of nobles and commoners against Henry in 1264. Initially, Montfort was successful, capturing both Henry and his son Edward. During his period of control, Montfort consulted the other nobles before making policy decisions, but his influence eventually dwindled. To compensate for his loss of power, Montfort expanded representation in Parliament by inviting towns to send representatives to that body.

After fifteen months, Montfort's coconspirator, the Earl of Gloucester, joined the king's party and helped Edward defeat and kill Montfort. Nevertheless, Montfort's expansion of Parliament was not forgotten; and in the future, the lesser nobility and townsmen were invited to attend sessions of Parliament.

House of Commons (lower house of British Parliament)

10 Downing Street,
residence of the British prime minister

Parliamentary System

practice is well-known to Americans but is in the minority worldwide. Benefits of this system include the president's accountability to the people and the executive branch's ability to operate independently of the legislative branch. But this system also has disadvantages, such as inefficiency. Differences in policy between the branches can create stalemates that slow or even stop the governing process.

In addition, dictatorships seem to rise more easily out of the presidential system, in which the power is strongly invested in one person.

Parliamentary System

The **parliamentary system**, in which the legislative and executive branches are inseparably linked, is more widely practiced worldwide than the presidential system. The parliamentary system differs from the presidential system in the method of selecting the national leader. The candidate whose party wins the most votes in a district becomes that district's representative in Parliament. The majority party (the party that has a majority of the members) in the Parliament then appoints the chief executive, the prime minister, who establishes a cabinet to run the affairs of the country. Although this system enables the executive and legislative branches to work together efficiently, it has dangers. Without independence, the executive branch is susceptible to domination by the legislative branch. Therefore, a strong legislature with competing parties is less likely to devolve into tyranny.

David Cameron (left) was British prime minister from 2010 to 2016. Theresa May (right) held that position from 2016 to 2019.

Section Review

1–3. What three broad categories are used to classify governments?

4. On what do dictatorships usually rely for power?

5–9. Identify five terms used in this section to describe the US government.

10. Who chooses the executive head in the parliamentary system?

★ How do a pure democracy and an indirect democracy differ?

★ Which do you think is better—a parliamentary system or a presidential system? Why?

Choosing Leaders

The charts on pages 19–20 show some differences between presidential and parliamentary systems. Instruct the students to examine the images and then ask questions to generate discussion. What does each visual indicate? In which system do the people have the greatest voice in choosing their leaders? What are advantages and disadvantages of each system? Do you think one produces a stronger leader than the other? How would you defend your answer?

Section Review Answers

1–3. systems of government, relationship between government levels, and methods of electing an executive (pp. 17–20)

4. Dictators rely on fear imposed by military or police power. (p. 16)

5–9. democratic republic, constitutional republic, indirect democracy, representative democracy, and republic (p. 18)

10. the majority party in Parliament (p. 20)

★ A pure democracy allows every citizen to directly participate, but in a republic the people elect representatives to run the government.

★ Students should incorporate the advantages and disadvantages noted in the text.

II. American Government

American government is divided into national and state levels. This section merely introduces those levels, while Chapter 7 examines the state and local levels to provide clearer insight into America's federal government system. Furthermore, the three branches of our government are summarized here, but Chapters 8–15 are in-depth studies of those branches.

National Government

The heart of American government is the Constitution. It limits the authority of the national government by assigning it specific **delegated powers** that allow the government to serve the country effectively.

The division of our national government into three branches—legislative, executive, and judicial—limits the government's power and protects the people's freedom. (These branches are explained in Articles I, II, and III of the Constitution.) Each branch exercises specific powers and contributes to the government's overall operation.

Legislative Branch

The legislative branch makes the nation's laws. Of the three branches, it has the closest ties to the people, who elect the representatives. The legislative branch is divided into two houses, collectively called **Congress**. The lower house is called the **House of Representatives**, and the upper house, the **Senate**.

Executive Branch

The executive branch enforces the nation's laws. The **president** is the chief executive officer and is therefore the head of the executive branch. The president—with the "advice and consent" of the Senate—chooses people to head the various government departments. These officials (known collectively as the cabinet), along with the vice president, the Executive Office of the President, and several agencies, help the president execute (enforce) laws passed by the legislative branch.

Judicial Branch

The judicial branch interprets the nation's laws. It judges whether the acts and laws of the other two branches are constitutional and decides how laws should be applied. The Constitution instituted the **Supreme Court**, the highest

---

Montesquieu

James Madison supported separation of powers between the legislative and executive branches of government. The ultimate source of his argument was *The Spirit of Laws* (1748), written by Charles-Louis de Secondat, Baron de Montesquieu (1689–1755), a French aristocrat. Wealthy enough to devote himself to intellectual pursuits, Montesquieu traveled around Europe (and in the highest political circles), investigating the nature of humans and their governments.

Montesquieu was no advocate of democracy or revolution, but he was a powerful critic of absolute monarchy. He believed that a legislature of educated aristocrats who had a genuine interest in serving the people could establish an honest and efficient government. His ideas were well received in his own day and became even more influential during the late eighteenth century. The framers of the American Constitution, for instance, were enthusiastic readers of *The Spirit of Laws*.

---

1. Describe the United States' method of dividing the national government.

2. Summarize the different responsibilities accorded to the national and state governments in the United States.

Bicameral Legislature

In *Federalist* No. 51, Madison argued for a bicameral legislature based on republican principles.

> In republican government, the legislative authority necessarily predominates. The remedy for this inconveniency is to divide the legislature into different branches; and to render them, by different modes of election and different principles of action, as little connected with each other as the nature of their common functions and their common dependence on the society will admit.

In other words, Madison believed that a bicameral legislature checks the legislative branch's tendency to be more powerful than the executive and judicial branches.

Montesquieu

He favored a mixed form of government because he feared that both unlimited monarchy and unchecked democracy would lead to tyranny. He thought that a nation should be ruled by its best and wisest men; however, he also recognized that the virtue such a form of government required would too often not be achieved. His advocacy of the separation of powers was a way to reckon with the reality that men with little integrity often gain positions of power.

Compromises

Remind the students that the distinction between the House of Representatives and the Senate is the result of the Great Compromise. Discuss the issues that played roles in the deliberations at the Constitutional Convention, especially the competing interests of small states and large ones. Discuss the benefits and the potential dangers of compromise and the need for biblical guidance when making such a decision.

Judge Selection

Guide a discussion using questions such as the following. What is the danger of selecting judges by election? Why is this a danger? What is the danger of allowing the executive or the legislature to appoint judges? What is the danger of appointing justices for life? What are the benefits? Would elected judges be more conservative or liberal in their rulings than appointed judges? Also discuss the dangers of electing someone based on his popularity. (*The most popular candidates are not always competent or godly.*) Help the students apply this lesson to their own friendships and to student government.

court of the land, to be the final judge for all questions concerning American laws. In addition, the national government created lower, or less important, courts to lighten the Supreme Court's caseload.

State Government

The second part of American federalism is state government. The American government consists of fifty sovereign states united for the common good of all. Each state retains all powers not delegated to the national government or prohibited to the states by the Constitution. Each state operates by its own constitution, which is guaranteed by the US Constitution to establish a republican form of government.

Within the state government, there are subdivisions that form the local government. These subdivisions—such as counties, townships, and municipalities (cities)—most directly affect the lives of people.

Section Review

1–3. List the three levels of American government.

4–6. List the three branches of the national government.

7. What powers are retained by the states?

8–10. What are three different subdivisions of local government?

★ Explain the responsibilities of each branch of the national government.

Guiding Questions

1. How did democratic principles develop?
2. What were the Founding Fathers' contributions to democratic government?
3. What is the difference between *democracy* and *republic*?

III. A Brief History of Democracy

Developments in Athens

The word *democracy*, often used to describe popular government, comes from two Greek words: *demos* (the people) and *kratos* (authority, or government). Therefore, **democracy** means "government by the people."

Greeks who lived in the city-state of Athens during the fifth and fourth centuries BC created the first society that was a "government by the people." But Athenian democracy excluded most of Athens's population, including females, slaves, and foreign residents. Furthermore, Athens was usually directed by a small group of aristocrats. Modern Americans would not consider the Athenian government truly democratic, but then neither would Athenians consider the American government democratic. In Athens, citizens were proud to exert their rule directly, not through elected representatives. They probably worked harder at governing themselves than any other group of people before or since. But Athenian democracy contained a serious weakness: the assembly's final say was often unchecked by established law. Another problem involved popular leaders called demagogues, who could manipulate the assembly with emotional speeches.

Developments in Rome

The Roman Republic also incorporated democratic principles and functioned remarkably well between the fifth and first centuries BC. Although aristocratic families supervised the Roman Republic, popular assemblies elected their leaders and ratified important governmental decisions. Magistrates called tribunes were

Greek and Roman Influence on the Lincoln Memorial

The influence of Greece and Rome extends beyond government. The Greek and Roman cultures made their marks in American symbolism and architecture as well. The Lincoln Memorial, for example, shows the influence of both cultures.

Henry Bacon, architect of the Lincoln Memorial, deliberately designed it to resemble the Greek Parthenon because he thought a memorial to Lincoln should take its design from a monument in democracy's birthplace. The Lincoln Memorial is 188 feet long, 118 feet wide, and 99 feet tall. It has a colonnade of thirty-six Doric columns representing the thirty-six states existing during Lincoln's presidency. Each column is 44 feet tall with a diameter of 7 feet 5 inches at the base. Bacon divided the memorial into three chambers that are also patterned after the Parthenon.

The statue of Lincoln is 19 feet tall and made of twenty-eight separate pieces of marble. Sculptor Daniel Chester French wanted to portray Lincoln as a powerful president during war, so he used Roman symbols for power and authority. For instance, he patterned Lincoln's chair after the Roman curule chair (in which Roman officials sat), which signified authority. Also, the arms of Lincoln's chair are decorated with fasces, bundles of rods that symbolized authority in ancient Rome.

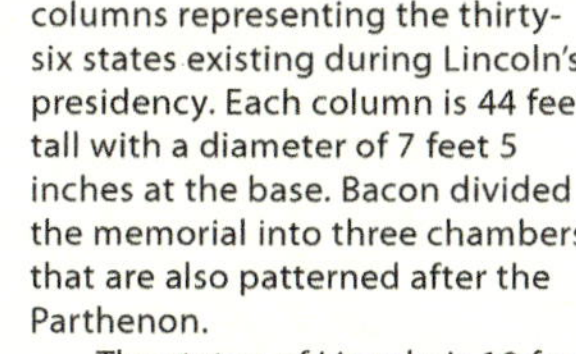

Parthenon (left) *and Lincoln Memorial* (right)

even charged to protect individuals' rights against abuses by the powerful. But once Rome conquered most of the lands bordering the Mediterranean, the republic degenerated into an empire governed by emperors and their armies. America's founders were very familiar with the popular governments in Greece and Rome. *The Federalist Papers* (Nos. 6, 9, 18, 38, 63, and 70 especially) abounds with lessons drawn from classical history.

Developments in England and the Colonies

Much more important for American democracy was the development of popular government in England. Being an island, England was somewhat isolated from the almost constant warfare on the European continent. It was also far from Rome, the seat of Catholicism. In their conflicts with other European states and the Roman Church, English kings, more than other monarchs, needed at least the appearance of popular approval. Though it at first had limited power, the English Parliament clearly dominated its kings by the eighteenth century.

Because England had such a great influence on the development of democracy in America, it is important to examine some of England's foundational documents. Foremost among them are the Magna Carta and the English Bill of Rights.

City-States

Venice, Milan, and Pisa are notable examples of historical city-state republics. Nevertheless, these small-scale republics were generally led by an oligarchy of nobles or merchants, and citizen participation was limited.

Activity 3: Thucydides: Pericles's Description of Democracy in Athens

This activity requires students to analyze original sources.

Importance of a Constitution

Discuss the specific dangers of a democracy that does not have a constitution. Would minorities be in danger of oppression if the majority were not checked by a constitution? (*Yes, history reveals that to be so.*) Remind the students of the need for constitutional protections of the rights of minorities. If the United States did not have a constitution, would the country be stable? The history of Athens exemplifies how unstable a democracy is without a constitution.

Development of Democracy

Assign a research paper. Instruct students to choose one of the following topics: ancient Athens, Rome, Florence, Pisa, Venice, Milan, Pericles, or Solon (or any other person or place significant to the development of democracy). Depending on the length of the paper, this project could serve as either a summary report or an examination of each topic's contribution to democracy today.

King John

In contrast with his brother Richard, who was nicknamed Lion-hearted, John was known as Lackland and Softsword. He was known as Lackland because, as the fourth son of Henry II, he did not have much land to inherit. He was called Softsword because of his propensity to make treaties. His distrust and abuse of the English nobility led to his humiliation at Runnymede.

The peace produced at Runnymede was doomed to fail for several reasons: (1) some of the barons were radicals who did not want peace; (2) Pope Innocent III opposed the Magna Carta; and (3) King John did not want to restrict his royal privileges.

King John of England constantly demanded money from his subjects, yet he always seemed short of cash. His foreign wars, construction projects, and mercenaries were expensive, and he willingly trampled the feudal rights of his barons to pay for his pastimes. But after the king's reputation was further diminished by his 1214 defeat in France, John's barons met at Runnymede and forced him to set his seal to a list of demands that became known as the **Magna Carta** (the Great Charter). The Magna Carta was primarily a document restoring the feudal rights of English barons, but it contained principles that caused it to later be heralded as a foundational document of constitutional government.

For instance, it established the "law of the land" as superior to the king's demands. It also provided the basis for **due process**, which requires certain legal procedures to be followed to protect the rights of the accused.

King John's consent to the Magna Carta lasted only two months. Pope Innocent III was only too happy to nullify the agreement after John appealed to him. The Magna Carta, though, continues to leave an enduring mark, especially through its constitutional descendants. Its principles laid the foundation for

Magna Carta AD 1215

John, by the grace of God King of England, Lord of Ireland, Duke of Normandy and Aquitaine, and Count of Anjou, to his archbishops, bishops, abbots, earls, barons, justices, foresters, sheriffs, stewards, servants, and to all his officials and loyal subjects, Greeting. . . .

(1) First, that we have granted to God, and by this present charter have confirmed for us and our heirs in perpetuity, that the English Church shall be free, and

shall have its rights undiminished, and its liberties unimpaired. That we wish this so to be observed, appears from the fact that of our own free will, before the outbreak of the present dispute between us and our barons, we granted and confirmed by charter the freedom of the Church's elections—a right reckoned to be of the greatest necessity and importance to it—and caused this to be confirmed by Pope Innocent III. This freedom we shall observe ourselves, and desire to be observed in good faith by our heirs in perpetuity.

To all free men of our kingdom we have also granted, for us and our heirs for ever, all the liberties written out below, to have and to keep for them and their heirs, of us and our heirs: . . .

(17) Ordinary lawsuits shall not follow the royal court around, but shall be held in a fixed place. . . .

(30) No sheriff, royal official, or other person shall take horses or carts for transport from any free man, without his consent. . . .

(38) In future no official shall place a man on trial upon his own unsupported statement, without producing credible witnesses to the truth of it.

(39) No free man shall be seized or imprisoned, or stripped of his rights or possessions, or outlawed or exiled, or deprived of his standing in any other way, nor will we proceed with force against him, or send others to do so, except by the lawful judgment of his equals or by the law of the land.

(40) To no one will we sell, to no one deny or delay right or justice. . . .

(45) We will appoint as justices, constables, sheriffs, or other officials, only men that know the law of the realm and are minded to keep it well. . . .

(63) It is accordingly our wish and command that the English Church shall be free, and that men in our kingdom shall have and keep all these liberties, rights, and concessions, well and peaceably in their fullness and entirety for them and their heirs, of us and our heirs, in all things and all places for ever.

Historical Perspective

Discuss the importance of leverage, as illustrated by the English barons' ability to gain concessions from King John. Often, people complain about taxes, laws, the behavior of government officials, or the humanistic bent of modern politics. Help your students realize that God has given them the opportunity to make their desires known in government affairs—a privilege enjoyed by few people in history. Help them understand that they have leverage with the government: the government needs their votes and their tax dollars. Their involvement can have just as dramatic an impact as the Magna Carta if they use the advantages God has allowed them to have.

freedoms that would eventually extend to all Englishmen. (The excerpts from the Magna Carta in this chapter represent the most important sections.)

The **English Bill of Rights** (1689) marked the beginning of a democratic government in England. After a civil war, a failed commonwealth, and a heavy-handed King James II, the English invited William and Mary to ascend to the English throne, but only after the couple agreed to the English Bill of Rights, which limited the monarchy's power and asserted the people's rights. William and Mary's rise to power under these limitations is known as the Glorious Revolution of 1688.

The English Bill of Rights was the most important development in constitutional government since the Magna Carta. It reflected much of the thinking of John Locke, who held that government—in this case, a monarchy—is responsible for protecting citizens' lives and property. According to this philosophy, if a ruler fails to meet his obligations, the people are justified in overthrowing him. During the next century, the English Bill of Rights, with its advocacy of limited government and personal liberty, would have an enormous impact on America's Declaration of Independence and Constitution.

The US Founders' Contributions

Although they were influenced by the democratic developments discussed in this chapter, America's founders made their own valuable contributions and innovations to democratic republican government.

Most modern Americans fail to appreciate the problems with which the founders grappled. Determining a successful balance between rule by a monarch and rule by a mob was daunting. The founders also struggled with new and difficult political questions.

The two major issues they confronted were (1) how to incorporate democratic ideas into the new American government and (2) how to make a democratic republic work in a vast territory.

Democratic Ideas

Many of America's early leaders feared direct democracy and the instability of a government in which a majority could become little more than a mob. They also distrusted the ability of the general public to govern themselves. Mobs could be fickle and prone to make snap decisions that could lead the nation into disaster; in addition, the masses might not have enough wealth and property to provide incentive for stable government. In short, the great fault of direct democracy was that it could potentially degenerate into tyranny.

America's Founding Fathers signing the Declaration of Independence

Despite the founders' misgivings about democracy, many of them were democratic in their thinking. They eloquently set forth such democratic ideals as liberty and equality in the Declaration of Independence:

> We hold these truths to be self-evident, that all men are created equal, that they are endowed by their Creator with certain unalienable rights, that among these are life, liberty and the pursuit of happiness.—That to secure these rights, governments are instituted among men, deriving their just powers from the consent of the governed.

Benjamin Franklin

Benjamin Franklin was perhaps the most democratic of the Founding Fathers, as was manifested in the constitution drafted for the state of Pennsylvania in 1776. (Franklin presided over the convention and helped write the document.) This constitution established a unicameral legislature—the Assembly—that had the authority to make Pennsylvania's laws, elect its president, dismiss state supreme court justices, and impeach magistrates. This all-powerful Assembly was elected annually, and representation was based on population and location. The state's president was elected yearly and had no veto power. Every man over age twenty-one who owned property, paid taxes, and swore allegiance to Pennsylvania was considered a citizen.

John Cotton on Democracy

New England Puritan John Cotton commented, "Democracy, I do not conceyve [believe] that ever God did ordeyne as a fitt government eyther for church or commonwealth. If the people be governors, who shall be governed?"

Thoughts about Democracy

Lead a class discussion regarding the following questions:

How are checks on monarchy similar to checks on majority rule?

(Just as an absolute monarch needs a check on his power so he will not abuse it, so the people, when they become rulers, need a check on their power so that they will not abuse it. Human nature is such that power without restraint will lead to abuses.)

How does a republican form of government seek to address the problems of a purely direct democracy?

(It seeks to ensure that virtuous people are placed in ruling positions. The people are given a role in governing, but there are limits on their authority. When the Constitution was first adopted, the people voted directly for the House of Representatives; the state legislatures appointed senators; the Electoral College selected the president; and the president appointed federal judges. Over time this system moved in a more democratic direction.)

Does a republican form of government solve the problems of direct democracy?

(It addresses some of them, but the students should realize that no form of government solves every problem. The basic problems of government find their root in human depravity. Some forms of government are more effective than others in managing sinful ambitions, but no form of government can solve the root problem of sin. Government is important but cannot be seen as a panacea to a nation's ills.)

William and Mary

King James II's replacement was his son-in-law William III, Prince of Orange and Stadholder of the Netherlands, and James II's oldest daughter, Mary. William and Mary agreed to abide by the English Bill of Rights.

Although William was unpopular with the nobility and was never accepted as an Englishman, he made several contributions to his adopted country. First, by prudently asserting royal prerogative, William preserved the stability and strength of the Crown. Second, he mediated a peace between feuding parties. Third, he promoted religious toleration; and fourth, he strengthened both the English and Dutch militaries.

English Bill of Rights AD 1689

Whereas the Lords Spiritual and Temporal and Commons assembled at Westminster, lawfully, fully and freely representing all the estates of the people of this realm, did . . . present unto their Majesties . . . a certain declaration in writing . . . in the words following, . . .

Whereas the late King James the Second . . . did endeavor to subvert and extirpate [destroy] the Protestant religion and the laws and liberties of this kingdom; . . .

[The king's actions] are utterly and directly contrary to the known laws and statutes and freedom of this realm; . . .

And thereupon the said Lords Spiritual and Temporal and Commons . . . being now assembled in a full and free representative of this nation, . . . do in the first place (as their ancestors in like case have usually done) for the vindicating and asserting their ancient rights and liberties declare:

1. That the pretended power of suspending the laws or the execution of laws by regal authority without consent of Parliament is illegal;
2. That the pretended power of dispensing with laws . . . as it hath been assumed . . . of late, is illegal;
3. That the commission for erecting the late Court of Commissioners for Ecclesiastical Causes, and all other commissions and courts of like nature, are illegal and pernicious;
4. That levying money for or to the use of the Crown [king] . . . without grant of Parliament . . . is illegal;
5. That it is the right of the subjects to petition the king. . . .
6. That the raising or keeping a standing army within the kingdom in time of peace, unless it be with consent of Parliament, is against law;
7. That the subjects which are Protestants may have arms for their defence suitable to their conditions and as allowed by law;
8. That election of members of Parliament ought to be free;
9. That the freedom of speech and debates or proceedings in Parliament ought not to be impeached or questioned in any court or place out of Parliament;
10. That excessive bail ought not to be required, nor excessive fines imposed, nor cruel and unusual punishments inflicted;
11. That jurors ought to be duly impanelled and returned, and jurors which pass upon men in trials for high treason ought to be freeholders;
12. That all grants and promises of fines and forfeitures of particular persons before conviction are illegal and void;
13. And that for redress of all grievances, and for the amending, strengthening and preserving of the laws, Parliaments ought to be held frequently.

William and his wife, Mary, became British monarchs in 1689.

The founders sought to preserve these ideals in a stable government while avoiding the pitfalls of the past. First, they recognized the source of these problems—humans' sinful nature. The mob-rule tendency of direct democracy is the result of humans' inclination to do wrong when unrestrained. To protect indi-

✝ The Monarchy

Shortly after he retired from the presidency, Thomas Jefferson wrote to a friend about the European monarchs he knew or knew about from his time in Europe. He thought that by intermarrying and by spending their time in idleness and sensuality they had all become fools.

However, is monarchy inherently wrong? Explore with your students the Bible's teaching on monarchy by contrasting Christ's monarchical rule in the Millennium with Samuel's warning to Israel about what a king would do (1 Sam. 8; Rev. 19:11–16). Mention that human depravity is what perverts monarchy. Even King David, who was "after [God's] heart," had personal failures. But David's reign points to a better reign under the perfect King, the Lord Jesus.

vidual liberty and equality from the power of an unruly majority, the founders set constitutional limits.

The Constitution limits both the government and the governed. The government is limited by its division into three branches: the legislative, the executive, and the judicial. Also, each branch is checked by the other branches so that no department takes more than its share of power. And the government is limited in its power over its citizens by the **Bill of Rights**, the first ten amendments to the Constitution.

The Constitution limits the power of the governed by restricting their influence on the national level. Reflecting the founders' belief that the general public should not have too much direct control over government, the Constitution makes the House of Representatives the only body elected directly by the people. Other top officials, including the president, are elected indirectly by the people. Senators were initially elected by their respective state legislatures rather than by the voters because senators were intended to be representatives of their respective states. The president is elected indirectly through the **Electoral College**. Under Article II, Section 1, of the Constitution, each state has a number of electors equal to that state's representation in Congress. (For example, if a state has eleven representatives in the House of Representatives and two senators, it has a total of thirteen electoral votes.)

Governing a Large Area

Until the late 1700s, neither a republic nor a direct democracy had ever been successful over a large geographic area. Eighteenth-century Enlightenment thinkers, such as Rousseau and Voltaire, noted that direct democracy was practiced only on a very small scale. Similarly, republics survived only in small settings. It was also widely believed that successful self-government required a population of similar self-interests. Participatory government, therefore, seemed unlikely to succeed in a country as diverse and large as the United States. The founders, however, had other ideas about how to unite thirteen states into a national republic while preserving democratic ideals.

They established self-government by representation. This republican practice was not new, but the United States was the first to establish it on a large, national scale based on state population.

Representation provides a degree of self-government by allowing citizens to choose their own leaders. It also solves the problems of time and space that come with direct democracy on a large scale. What would happen if all US citizens had to leave their jobs and families to vote on laws in Washington, DC? Factories would shut down, crops would go untended, and society (as well as the traffic in and around the capital) would generally come to a standstill. Representative government avoids such problems.

The system of federalism forged at the Constitutional Convention permitted democratic practices of

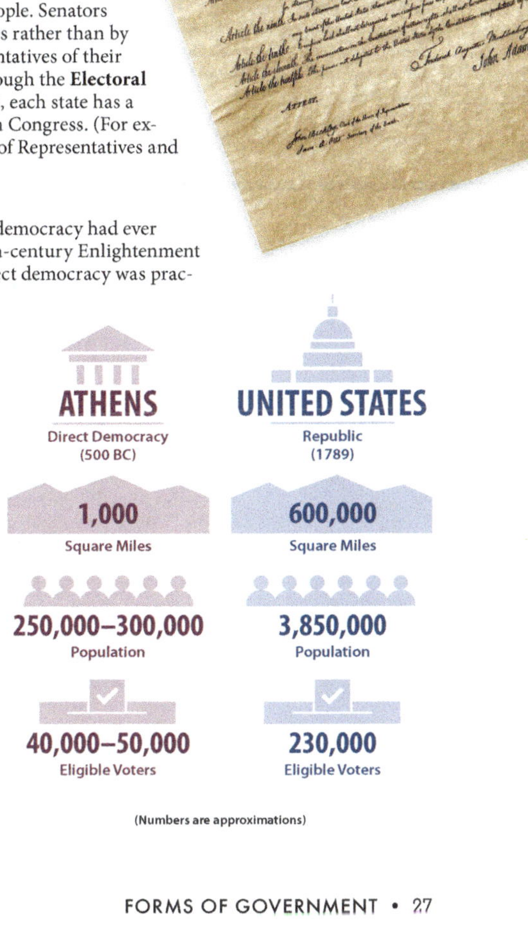

Enlightenment

Our founders were greatly influenced by Enlightenment thinking, which stressed the individual over the state. John Locke wrote,

> To understand political power aright, and derive it from its original, we must consider what estate all men are naturally in, and that is, a state of perfect freedom to order their actions, and dispose of their possessions and persons as they think fit, within the bounds of the law of Nature, without asking leave or depending upon the will of any other man.

The social contract theory of Hobbes, Locke, and Rousseau held that humans, who are essentially free, give up some liberty to ensure order in and the protection of society. These philosophers believed, however, that government must remain limited so that people can live freely within the bounds of law.

Enlightenment and the Bible

Discuss with students whether the social contract theory of the Enlightenment is biblical. (More information about this will be presented in Chapters 3 and 4.) Guide the discussion so that students understand that though the social contract theory is not discussed in the Bible, it recognizes that people are not unattached individuals who are always able to make choices about their relationships with others. For example, we are born into a family, with all the associations and responsibilities that entails. Likewise, people are born into a particular nation. Mention that citizens will not usually have the opportunity to institute a social contract. However, they are still required to submit to the authorities that God has allowed to be established.

Divisiveness

Divisiveness, disagreement, and differences of opinions are not just problems in government; they also plague churches. For example, the apostle Paul rebuked the Corinthians when they broke into factions (1 Cor. 1:10– 3:23). Perhaps your students have witnessed churches suffering division over minor issues. Of course, there are biblical reasons for separation, such as the presence of false teachers or unrepented sin. However, factions that develop over minor things, like personality conflicts, violate Christ's command in John 13:34–35.

Democracy by Internet?

Could the internet make representative government unnecessary by circumventing the problems inherent in a geographically large area? The increased use and accessibility of the internet make direct involvement in the government possible. One potential benefit is that all citizens could participate in discussions and vote from their homes or cities, avoiding travel and lodging costs. The internet could make direct democracy possible on a never-before-seen scale. Of course, the issues of computer illiteracy, computer security and reliability, and limited time to adequately discuss and understand political issues are just a few of the difficulties that would have to be addressed when considering direct democracy by internet.

However, even if direct democracy via the internet *could* occur, *should* it be implemented? As noted in this chapter, there are many problems with such a government. Would voters have the expertise required for decision making? Would individuals place more importance on what is best for the nation than on their own personal, and sometimes selfish, considerations? Would the majority listen to the concerns of the minority? Would voters make wise, thoughtful choices rather than rash decisions?

local government and protected democratic principles of liberty and equality—all under the umbrella of a republican national government.

Democracy or Republic?

Was the United States founded as a democracy or as a republic? Part of the difficulty in answering that question lies in the way the founders used the terms.

To James Madison, *democracy* meant a direct democracy and *republic*, a representative democracy. Thomas Jefferson, however, defined *republic* as "a government by its citizens in mass, acting directly and personally, according to rules established by the majority." That definition seems to equate a republic with a direct democracy. John Adams offered yet another definition of *republic*: "an empire of laws, and not of men."

So what did the founders mean when they wrote in the Constitution that the "United States shall guarantee to every state in this Union a republican form of government" (Article IV, Section 4)? The answer seems to lie in what they avoided. The founders distrusted pure democracy because it had so often degenerated into tyranny, and they also feared a tyranny of the majority. Thus they established a republican form of government to circumvent the danger of mob rule.

The difference between a democracy and a republic, then, was that the founders restrained mob rule by writing a constitution and by removing government operations from the majority's direct control. The founders' attempt to avoid oppression by the majority meant that America's initial government was not a democracy but a representative republic ruled by a constitution and based on democratic principles.

The Constitution's framers instituted representative self-government that bridged distances and shared power with citizens on the local level. However, constitutional provisions and unfolding events over the next two centuries would increase the democratization of the republic.

Milestones in Democracy

The third section of this chapter briefly describes some of the landmarks in the history of democracy. Assign students to create displays for the classroom to highlight and explain these (Athens, Rome, the Magna Carta, the English Bill of Rights, the Declaration of Independence, and the Constitution). Alternatively, students could prepare a slide presentation describing each.

Section Review

1. Where did the first significant example of pure democracy occur?
2–3. What two major questions confronted the framers of the US Constitution?
4. What human characteristic did the nation's founders recognize would make direct democracy a poor choice for our government?
5. What features did the founders include in the Constitution to ensure that the majority would not tyrannize the minority?
★ Reread the feature box entitled "English Bill of Rights." Which three of the thirteen items do you think are most important? Justify your answer.
★ Is the United States a democracy or a republic? Explain your answer.

IV. Characteristics of Democracy

The word *democracy* is widely used in today's world. As mentioned earlier, even Communist leaders in China and North Korea refer to their countries as democratic, but any Chinese or North Korean citizen bold enough to criticize those countries' governments is subject to severe punishment.

Communist countries refer to themselves as *economic* democracies because their citizens supposedly enjoy economic equality, at least by those countries' definition of *equality*. However, democracy has been understood since the days of Pericles, the famous Athenian ruler, as a *political*, not an economic, system. Of course, every democracy has its own distinctive features given the particular influences in the country where it develops. Democracy in the United States differs from democracy in Canada, which differs from democracy in Japan. Yet all these governments are political systems that share certain characteristics, making them democracies in the traditional sense.

Majority Rule

E. B. White, a well-known American author, said that "democracy is the recurrent suspicion that more than half of the people are right more than half of the time." This somewhat humorous definition underscores an important characteristic of democracy: the principle of **majority rule**—that is, a majority of the electorate makes decisions that bind the entire electorate. Democratic republics contain two kinds of majorities: a popular majority and a representative majority. A **popular majority** comprises the majority of all citizens, or at least the majority of all voters who participate in their government through free elections. A **representative majority** is a majority of elected officials, such as members of Congress. There may, in fact, be a great gulf between the will of the popular majority and that of the representative majority. For example, a February 2011 Rasmussen poll found that 65 percent

Guiding Questions

1. What are the strengths and potential weaknesses of majority rule?
2. What are the definitions of *equality* and *liberty*?
3. What is the role of compromise and individual worth in a democratic system?

Kim Jong-un became the dictator of North Korea in 2011.

"Complaints are everywhere heard from our most considerate and virtuous citizens, equally the friends of public and private faith, and of public and personal liberty, that our governments are too unstable, that the public good is disregarded in the conflicts of rival parties, and that measures are too often decided, not according to the rules of justice and the rights of the minor party, but by the superior force of an interested and overbearing majority."

—James Madison,
Federalist No. 10

Section Review Answers

1. Athens, Greece (p. 22)
2–3. how to incorporate democratic ideas into the new government and how to make a democratic republic work in a vast territory (p. 25)
4. humans' sinful nature (p. 26)
5. The founders divided the government into three branches and included the Bill of Rights in the Constitution. (p. 27)
★ Students will likely emphasize items 1, 4, 6, 8, 9, 10, and 13.
★ The United States is both a democracy and a republic. We call it a democracy because the people hold ultimate power. We call it a republic because it is not monarchical, and it is ruled by law.

Which Is Better?

Is majority-plurality representation better for a nation than proportional representation? Rather than trying to answer that question, it is probably more helpful to note that each system has its own distinct advantages and disadvantages.

Electing a Representative Majority

Democratic societies use several methods to select representation. Each has its advantages and disadvantages. Two common systems are majority-plurality representation and proportional representation.

Majority-Plurality Representation

This electoral system, also called the first-past-the-post system (FPTP) because it is often likened to a horserace, awards the position to the candidate who wins the highest percentage of votes—even if he lacks the majority. For example, if Candidate A wins 42 percent of the votes; Candidate B, 36 percent; and Candidate C, 12 percent, then Candidate A wins the seat although he did not obtain the majority of the votes. FPTP is often criticized because it does not fairly represent the people's will. For example, in a vote to fill ten seats in the legislature, Party A wins 59 percent of the votes, and Party B wins 41 percent. In this system, it is possible for Party A to win 100 percent of the legislative seats if Party A wins the most votes in each district. This leaves Party B (and its voters) with no representation in the legislature, though it received 41 percent of the vote.

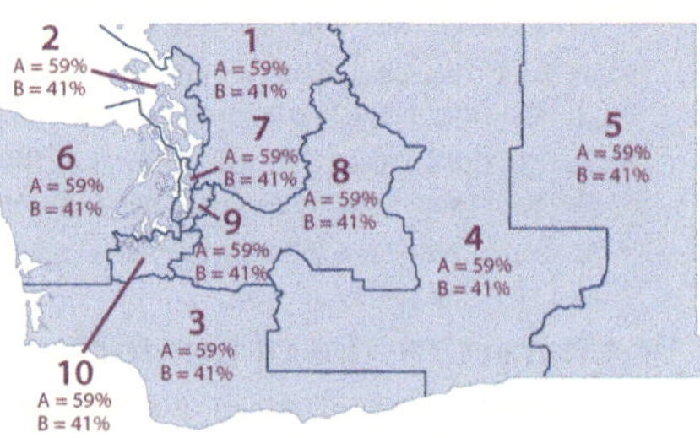

Proportional Representation

In this system, the number of seats won by a party equals the percentage of voters who supported that party. For example, in a legislature of one hundred seats, a party that received 59 percent of the votes would earn fifty-nine seats. This procedure works well in countries with multiple parties because even small parties can receive seats. Furthermore, the legislature more accurately reflects the views of all segments of society.

Majority-Plurality Representation	
Advantages	
Usually condenses the voters' choices to fewer contenders, simplifying the voting process	
Handicaps third parties, thus providing a more efficient and stable government	
Disadvantages	
Enables a party to gain a higher percentage of seats in the legislature than the percentage of votes it received	
Limits minority-party voters' opportunities to influence the government	

Proportional Representation	
Advantages	
Gives minority parties a greater voice in the legislature	
Represents the citizens' will more accurately	
Disadvantages	
Promotes multiple parties, thus leading to less efficient and less stable government	
Provides a potentially confusing list of slightly differing candidates for citizens to choose from	

of those surveyed favored prayer in public schools, yet a prayer amendment has consistently failed to receive the necessary support in Congress.

The representative majority is, therefore, not necessarily representative. Because representatives might not know what the popular will is on every given issue, they must make decisions based on the best available information. Furthermore, representatives must sometimes make decisions they feel are in the nation's best interest even if a popular majority does not agree. Yet if a representative consistently thwarts the will of his constituents, voters can register their com-

Is the Majority Always Right?

Fisher Ames (1758–1808) was one of America's lesser-known Founding Fathers. Born in Dedham, Massachusetts, he was a graduate of Harvard and a gifted orator who served in the Massachusetts legislature and in Congress. Show the following quotation to your students.

> They say, while a faction is a minority, it will remain harmless by being outvoted; and if it should become a majority, all its acts, however profligate or violent, are then legitimate. For, with the democrats, the people is a sovereign who can do no wrong, even when he respects and spares no existing right, and whose voice, however obtained or however counterfeited, bears all the sanctity and all the force of a living divinity.

Discuss with students the consequences of believing that the majority is always right. Help students refute this belief biblically. (See Exod. 23:2.)

Going Against Public Opinion

Instruct students to write essays exploring situations in which it might be a good thing for representatives to oppose public opinion. Help the students by directing their thinking to moral issues about which the populace and representatives might disagree (e.g., abortion, homosexuality, or responses to terrorism).

plaints at the ballot box, and that representative might be unemployed after the next election.

The principle of majority rule has been criticized as potentially repressive to the minority's rights and opinions. One question understandably rises concerning majority rule: why should 51 percent of the people be able to impose their will on 49 percent of the people? Several observations help answer this question.

First, majority rule is a better approach to governance than is unanimity (total agreement before action can be taken). Unanimity creates a great problem because, with this condition, even one negative vote can stop a proposal regardless of how widely it is supported. Unanimity, in effect, makes a "majority" of one. This was one of the chief flaws of the United States government under the Articles of Confederation (1776–89). Amending the articles required the unanimous consent of the states, which meant that one state could obstruct the wishes of all the rest.

Second, the majority is not a fixed, well-defined group. A citizen could vote with the majority on one issue and find himself in the minority when voting on the next. In a **pluralistic society** (one in which there are many diverse religious, ethnic, and political groups) differing opinions and ideas coexist. Thus the views held by a majority of citizens are often varied and, sometimes, unpredictable.

Third, in a successful democracy, majority rule must account for minority rights. The rule of law must limit the majority's power so that, to cite an extreme example, the majority cannot enslave the minority as the Nazis enslaved the Jews during the Second World War.

In the United States, the minority's rights are protected by the Constitution. But both the minority and the majority must respect the law. If a group loses at the polls or if its representatives fail to translate their interests into laws, it must not try to change the government by unlawful means.

Presidential inaugurations are an example of times when personal opinions must be set aside and the majority and minority must respect both the laws and each other. In 2000, Al Gore and George W. Bush competed for the Oval Office. The vote tally was extremely close and the election was highly controversial. Bush was not declared president until December because of contested ballot counts in Florida; but in January 2001 he took the oath of office. Standing near his predecessor, Bill Clinton (of the opposing party), Bush recited the oath; with the concluding petition "So help me God," all the power of the presidency was transferred to him. Likewise, the January 2017 inauguration of Donald Trump was a contentious event. There were protests before, during, and after Inauguration Day and some were violent. Supporters of Trump's opponent, Hillary Clinton, noted that her popular vote total exceeded his by more than three million (though Trump won the vote in the Electoral College). Nevertheless, with Hillary Clinton present at the ceremony, the transition of power occurred as scheduled. Americans generally take for granted the ease with which new presidents take office. In many countries, bitter and very bloody power struggles between factions surround leadership changes.

Donald Trump (left) *and Hillary Clinton* (right) *in one of their 2016 presidential debates*

Minority Rights

Discuss the importance of balancing majority rule with minority rights. Emphasize that *minority* does not refer simply to ethnicity. In elections the supporters of a losing candidate find themselves in the minority, and Bible-believing Christians plainly constitute a minority in society.

 How Often Are Students in the Minority?

To demonstrate that no one is always in the majority, develop a questionnaire and ask students complete it. The questionnaire should cover various political, social, biblical, and personal topics, such as the death penalty, imprisonment, taxation, welfare, Social Security, minimum wage, favorite sports teams, and favorite activities. The students can answer the questionnaire anonymously and then their collected answers can be compared to local and national surveys in addition to their class peers.

Incorrect Views about Equality

Equality is often misunderstood. Humans are equal because all are made in the image of God; however, equality does not mean hierarchies should not exist. For example, within the family, the husband and father holds a special role (Eph. 5:22–24; 6:1–4), and children are to honor and obey their parents (Prov. 1:8). Furthermore, the young are instructed to honor the elderly (Lev. 19:32), and church members are to value the teaching of their pastor (Eph. 4:11–12; Heb. 13:17).

The Changing Concept of Liberty

Liberty has always been an American ideal. But Americans' understanding of what liberty is has changed over time.

In the following passage, David Hall describes the Puritan view of liberty.

> No one of [the Puritan] mindset expects a referendum to decide whether God got it right. . . .
>
> Similarly, the "liberties" enumerated in the Massachusetts "Body of Liberties" (1641) were, for the most part, protections against unauthorized and unjust actions of the civil state, not doorways to personal freedom.

David D. Hall, *A Reforming People: Puritanism and the Transformation of Public Life in New England* (New York: Alfred A. Knopf, 2011), xvi.

Finally, the majority principle must be accompanied by other principles. Democracy does not consist only of majority rule—that would more nearly define *mobocracy*. There must also be present both the principle of individual equality under the law and the freedom of political action by which the minority may legitimately confront and even become the majority. Most importantly, democracies need shared moral principles. Democracies without morality can become as tyrannical as any dictatorship.

Equality

The second democratic principle is equality. When Thomas Jefferson wrote that "all men are created equal" in the Declaration of Independence, he was not referring to absolute equality. All people differ from one another in various physical, social, financial, educational, and cultural ways, as well as in ability, personality, and background. Rather, the democratic principle of **equality** means *political* equality, or legal equality, its chief characteristics being equality of justice and equality of the franchise (vote).

Equality under the law was what the framers of the Declaration of Independence and the Constitution envisioned. Every citizen, regardless of station in life, would enjoy constitutional guarantees of liberty. Jefferson defined this chief characteristic of political equality in his first inaugural address.

> It is proper you should understand what I deem the essential principles of our Government[:] . . . equal and exact justice to all men, of whatever state or persuasion, religious or political; . . . freedom of religion; freedom of the press, and freedom of person under the protection of the habeas corpus.

In fact, justice cannot exist apart from equality. The law must be blind to a person's name, income, race, and social status and must provide each citizen with equal protection and enforcement of the law.

Voting has also become an important aspect of political equality. Although the matter was not as important to the framers of the Constitution as were guarantees of justice, the framers' pioneering effort provided an essential foundation for the franchise. America's founders forged a democratic republic in a world of nations usually headed by royalty and structured by birth and rank. Equality was a driving force for these men; it broke barriers of social caste and gave Americans a standing before kings and princes that did not require so much as a curtsy. Yet political equality in voting was a *growing* reality in America. Restrictions of race, sex, and income were gradually lifted, so that today all American adults enjoy equality of the ballot.

"We hold these truths to be self-evident, that all men are created equal."
—Declaration of Independence

Equality of opportunity is also important to democracy. Equal opportunity ensures that no one is restricted based on sex, religion, or ethnicity from educational, occupational, or political opportunities. As mentioned in Chapter 1, this equality does not mean "equality of outcomes"—it means equal treatment when laws are enforced.

Liberty

Liberty is a key term in our political vocabulary and a fundamental characteristic of our democratic system. Liberty entails personal and political freedom. Personal liberties such as freedom of conscience, freedom of association, and freedom of expression involve not only the right to worship openly but also the

---

Created Equal

Nathaniel Ames, the eighteenth-century writer, said that "all Men are by Nature equal, but differ greatly in the sequel." As a class, compile a list on the board of the many ways in which people are not equal. Emphasize the founders' idea of political equality. Equality involves fairness—a level playing field for all.

Discuss also why people have varying opinions about what constitutes equality. This would be a good time to review the differences between equality before the law, equality of opportunity, and equality of outcomes. Ask students to explain the difference between these three concepts.

Activity 4: Walter Williams: Democracy and Majority Rule

This enrichment activity helps the students understand the dangers of majority rule. It provides clear examples and statistics regarding this issue.

opportunity for political associations and the expression of opinions. Political liberty involves the right to vote, campaign, and hold elective office. In short, it is the freedom to influence the government through any legitimate means available.

Both liberty and equality are closely linked in America's democratic system. But current trends distort the meaning of liberty. Liberty apart from Christian morality often becomes a license to do evil. For example, sensuality and even pornography are defended today in the name of freedom of expression.

Necessity of Compromise

The fourth democratic principle is the necessity of compromise. In a popular government, compromise is permissible—even necessary—because there are as many opinions as there are voters. Without compromise, opposing opinions could hamper or even stop a democracy's legislative processes. Compromising on methods and nonmoral issues allows each opinion to further important objectives without causing gridlock in legislation. For a democracy to operate smoothly, differing factions must be willing to compromise on nonessentials.

As beneficial as compromises are, however, believers should never compromise on the truth. While seeking to find a balance that best represents the majority's wishes, a Christian statesman cannot overlook God's thoughts on issues like murder, abortion, homosexuality, and poverty relief—even if popular opinion demands otherwise. The Christian must obey God rather than compromise to accommodate humans' desires (Acts 5:29).

Christians in government need the virtue of prudence, the wisdom necessary to know how to best achieve a good goal, to discern what can be compromised and what cannot. Compromising on God's laws is not an option, but Christians should not hesitate to compromise on issues that do not contradict God's Word. That type of compromise allows democracies to function and represent the majority's wishes.

Individual Worth

The fifth principle of democratic government is the fundamental worth of every individual. Each individual must be recognized and respected as a distinct being loved by God (John 3:16) and created in His image (Gen. 1:27; 9:6). If not, the result will be that a majority or an elite will oppress those they deem less worthy or of lesser value.

Individual worth does not entitle one to ignore or reject the majority's will. The majority is not a faceless mob but a group

Compromise

Edmund Burke, an eighteenth-century British member of Parliament who argued in behalf of the American colonies, wrote, "All government, indeed every human benefit and enjoyment, every virtue and every prudent act, is founded on compromise and barter." While compromise concerning amoral issues might bring peace and prosperity to a country, government leaders must guard against a policy of appeasement. Winston Churchill wrote (referring to the events leading to World War II), "An appeaser is one who feeds a crocodile, hoping it will eat him last."

Fragile Freedom

Emphasize that a free society is rare and often fragile. Each generation must assume responsibility for freedom's continuance.

Prudence in Compromising

To teach the students about the role of prudence in the legislative process, choose a current issue or series of issues and ask the students to determine what the ultimate goal of each issue should be. Instruct them to define the obstacles that impede reaching each goal. The students should also identify the kinds of compromises that would violate important values or prevent them from reaching the future goals.

Distinctive Features of Democracy

Assign students the task of devising a graphic organizer showing the characteristics of democracy. It should include the items mentioned in this section (majority rule, equality, liberty, necessity of compromise, and individual worth). Invite students to place the organizer on the classroom board or screen and explain each component.

of individuals united in a common goal. Individual worth does, however, protect the minority of individuals from majority coercion. In a democracy, individual worth protects the minority from oppression but does not allow them to do whatever they please.

Section Review

1. What is the difference between a popular majority and a representative majority?
2–5. Give four observations concerning majority rule in America that show why that principle has been effective.
6–7. In what two ways are all American citizens equal?
★ What is the difference between personal and political liberty?

V. Conditions for Democracy

Democracy has had varying degrees of success throughout the world. Many of the new democracies formed since World War II struggled against enormous obstacles in their bid for political liberty. A number of these nations were carved from Europe's colonial holdings and had little experience in self-government. Consequently, some soon faced civil war, Communist plottings, or dictatorship. What conditions, then, contribute to the success of a democratic system?

Opportunity

A democratic system must provide a person the opportunity to improve himself economically, expand himself educationally, and involve himself politically. Such opportunity boosts prosperity, provides channels for productive energy, and prevents social unrest.

Economic opportunity provides a sense of hope and enhances prosperity. That prosperity, in turn, results in a larger middle class. If a country lacks a middle class and has great extremes of economic conditions (i.e., a small wealthy class and a large poor class), democracy will struggle. Political division may result.

To what extent should the government try to reduce economic inequities by ensuring citizens' basic welfare? Who is responsible to care for the destitute, the poor, and the unemployed—the government or Christians?

From a biblical perspective, it is clear that individuals should help the poor and disadvantaged. James notes that Christians' relationship with God involves helping the needy (James 1:27). Families bear a responsibility to help family members (1 Tim. 5:16). Churches also have a responsibility to care for members, such as widows (1 Tim. 5:3–16).

Yet the famous American theologian, Jonathan Edwards, cautioned against relying entirely on "voluntary charity." Other Christian leaders have observed that when God framed the government of Israel, the laws He established included a safety net that provided for people in need while stifling neither individual charity nor the incentive to work (Exod. 22:25; Lev. 23:22; Deut. 24:12–15).

Welfare programs in the United States help many needy individuals. However, some programs have structural flaws that violate important biblical and democratic principles. For example, some encourage continued dependence on the government. Some are expensive and saddle future generations of Americans with burdensome debt. One way in which Christians can demonstrate love to their neighbors is to assist in the development of welfare reforms that retain a basic safety net while also providing incentives, training, and means for each individual to have productive employment.

Haiti's Struggle

Haiti's struggle for democracy has been both heroic and tragic. Today Haiti has an annual per capita income of approximately $730, which makes Haiti one of the world's poorest nations. Three decades of corrupt and cruel leadership under the Duvalier family and their ruthless secret police made the change to a democratic government difficult.

After the overthrow of Jean-Claude "Baby Doc" Duvalier in 1986, the first free elections in a generation resulted in significant violence. Military leaders, determined to control the elections, were responsible for much of the bloodshed. Candidates for president were assassinated, and voters were gunned down at polling places. About five hundred Haitians were killed in election-related violence.

Although Haitians have had a number of democratic elections since 1990, violence and political upheaval still plague the nation, causing suspicion regarding whether democratic principles have been established. Natural disasters (numerous hurricanes and earthquakes) have further strained the ability of even good leaders to provide a stable government in Haiti.

Struggling for Democracy

Haiti is just one example of a nation that has faced many difficulties in its attempt to establish a democratic government.

Assign students to research the leading obstacles (corrupt, and sometimes ruthless, politicians; abuse of power by military leaders; prevalence of poverty; and occurrence of many natural disasters). You may require students to briefly address all these issues or ask them to concentrate on just one problem.

Question students about their findings. Which item has posed the greatest difficulty for Haiti? How could problems have been handled differently? What can be done today to assist the nation in establishing a stable democracy? How important are opportunity, education, and moral responsibility to the formation and maintenance of democracy?

Comparing Governments

Periodically in this textbook, a feature box will be presented that compares the United States to another country. The emphasis in each box will be on government. We begin these comparisons by looking at the world's second most populated nation, India.

For Richer or for Poorer: Democracy in the United States and India

Democracy in America is assumed. Widespread land ownership and the English political tradition have produced a climate of respect for economic and political liberty, which is guaranteed by representative government. With a desire to protect property and with a high literacy rate, Americans are willing and able to secure their democracy from threats. Compared with most of the world's population, America's citizens are wealthier and better educated; therefore, democracy in America should, and does, work well.

But what about democracy in a relatively poor nation with about one billion people? Prospects for democracy are not as good in such a case. Nonetheless, India has maintained its democracy. India is divided by language, religion (mostly Hinduism and Islam), ethnicity, and caste. With an economy eroded by dramatic population growth, much of India remains poor. In addition, religious and ethnic violence and border wars with Pakistan and China have threatened its stability.

But surprisingly, India's democracy endures. The British left a strong civil service in India, which provides basic services and unites Indians from various backgrounds. The Congress Party, which has usually dominated since 1947, enjoys wide acceptance because it was the party of the independence movement. And although the family of Nehru (the first Indian prime minister) has been important, no one charismatic leader has dominated as in some other developing nations.

Also, opposition to the Congress Party was severely divided, and that ensured Congress Party power even when the party garnered less than a majority in elections. Furthermore, the Indian military has been loyal to the democratic system.

Only once was democracy challenged. In 1975, Prime Minister Indira Gandhi declared emergency rule, limiting the press and the activities of opposition groups. Fortunately, these conditions lasted only twenty-one months, and elections were held in 1977. Increasingly, India has become a two-party nation. The Congress Party has lost some national elections, and lower-caste Indians are playing a more important role.

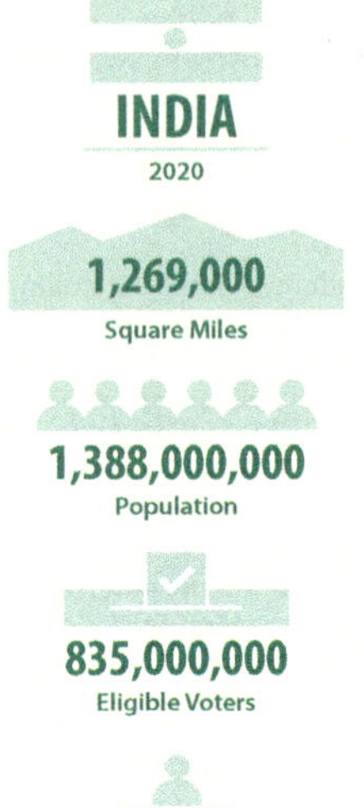

(Numbers are approximations)

Educated Society

An educated society is also an important element of a successful democratic system. Of course, citizens must be literate to read news articles and cast intelligent votes, but they must also be educated for **civic thinking**. Civic thinking involves an understanding of the political ideas and institutions that shape America's government, an appreciation for America's heritage, and an ability to evaluate current issues and national direction.

Although education is important, it does not guarantee the success of democracy. There was certainly no system for universal education in 1787, yet

Comparing and Contrasting

Discuss the major differences between India and the United States shown in the feature box above. Perhaps assign students to research additional points of comparison.

What obstacles have hindered the development of democracy in India? What has aided the nation in its efforts? What happened in 1975? By contrast, what advantages has the US enjoyed that have made it easier to establish a democratic government than in most countries?

Christian Professor

Invite a Christian professor (perhaps one of your former professors) to speak to your students concerning the importance of education for Christians. Although education is important for economic and political reasons, ask the speaker to focus on learning as a means of becoming a mature Christian for the glory of Jesus Christ.

the founders' efforts survived. Neither is education a remedy for all problems. Before World War II, Germany was one of the best-educated countries in Europe, yet that did not prevent its fledgling democracy from being crushed by Nazism under Adolf Hitler.

Today, despite our widespread systems of public and private education, many citizens remain ignorant of America's heritage and political ideals. That does not provide an encouraging picture of the future of our participatory government. For example, in 2011, the US Department of Education released test results from the National Assessment of Educational Progress (NAEP). The scores for American students were lower for history than any other subject, including reading, math, and science. In 2015, additional NAEP test results were equally discouraging. Of the more than eleven thousand eighth graders who were tested in United States history, only 1 percent scored "advanced," while 17 percent scored "proficient." The remaining 82 percent tested at the "basic" or "below basic" levels. Similar results were posted for the more than nine thousand eighth graders who took the civics test. While only 2 percent scored "advanced" and 22 percent scored "proficient," the remaining 76 percent performed at the "basic" or "below basic" levels.

Diane Ravitch, a New York University research professor of education, expressed concern about some of the dismal test results. She said, "All of these students will be voters. . . . They will be making decisions in the voting booth

Importance of Education

As the quotes in the feature box below indicate, education is important for every society. But, education that is not grounded in moral values and with a biblical worldview can be devastating for a country.

Education: A Necessity in a Free Society

People have understood since centuries past that a free society could not exist without education. The following are quotations from well-known men concerning education's importance.

"A popular government, without popular information, or the means of acquiring it, is but a prologue to a farce or a tragedy; or, perhaps both. Knowledge will forever govern ignorance: and a people who mean to be their own governors, must arm themselves with the power which knowledge gives."
—James Madison

"If a nation expects to be ignorant and free, in a state of civilization, it expects what never was and never will be."
—Thomas Jefferson

"Education makes a people easy to lead, but difficult to drive; easy to govern but impossible to enslave."
—Henry Peter Brougham

"Education is a better safeguard of liberty than a standing army."
—Edward Everett

"Next in importance to freedom and justice is popular education, without which neither justice nor freedom can be permanently maintained."
—James A. Garfield

Additional Reading

Two good biographies dealing with education during our nation's formative years are *Noah Webster: The Life and Times of an American Patriot* by Harlow Giles Unger and *McGuffey and His Readers: Piety, Morality, and Education in Nineteenth-Century America* by John H. Westerhoff III.

Civic Knowledge

Test the students' civic knowledge. Quiz them on the names of current and recent political leaders, including your state's governor, US senators, and members of the US House of Representatives. Also ask questions about voting age, the definitions of simple government terms, and the source of quotations, such as "We the people." The exercise should precede a general class discussion and need not be graded. The results might challenge the students to learn more about their government and reveal specific weaknesses that you can later rectify.

For an alternative exercise, print copies of the sample test given to prospective naturalized citizens, and see whether your students can pass it.

Activity 5: Chapter Review

The review questions in this activity build students' recognition skills and enhance test preparation.

Public Opinion

In his book *Democracy in America*, Alexis de Tocqueville wrote,

> Whenever social conditions are equal, public opinion presses with enormous weight upon the minds of each individual; it surrounds, directs, and oppresses him; and this arises from the very constitution of society, much more than from its political laws. As men grow more alike, each man feels himself weaker in regard to all the rest; as he discerns nothing by which he is considerably raised above them, or distinguished from them, he mistrusts himself. . . . Not only does he mistrust his strength, but he even doubts of his right; and he is very near acknowledging that he is in the wrong, when the greater number of his countrymen assert that he is so.

that influence our lives. They should be well informed and capable of weighing the contending claims of candidates, especially when the candidates rest their arguments on historical precedent."

Moral Responsibility

Another necessary condition for the strength and survival of a democratic republic is moral responsibility. Moral responsibility strengthens democracy in a number of ways. First, moral responsibility among citizens implies submission to the rule of law. Apart from the rule of law, democracy would rapidly degenerate into tyranny or worse. For Christians, submission to the rule of law does not stem simply from concern for social order; it stems from a concern for obeying God, who commands obedience to human authority (1 Pet. 2:13–15).

Moral responsibility also provides a standard for judging the majority's actions. Alexis de Tocqueville observed that one of the greatest dangers in a democracy is the power of public opinion. Moral responsibility counteracts the force of public opinion by asking what is right rather than what is popular.

In this respect, moral responsibility also determines the limits of compromise. As noted earlier, Christians must not compromise on biblical principles, but what should they do in a democracy where political compromise is necessary? Christians must exercise the virtue of prudence (Prov. 8:12–16). For instance, a prudent Christian legislator may vote for a bill that limits abortions under certain conditions even though he would prefer to outlaw all abortions. (Of course, such a lawmaker should not vote for a law that would prevent the legal protection of unborn human life.)

"Unless there is some strong ground for opposition to majority opinion, it inevitably prevails. This is the really dangerous form of the tyranny of the majority, not the kind that actively persecutes minorities but the kind that breaks the inner will to resist because there is no qualified source of nonconforming principles and no sense of superior right."

—Allan Bloom,
The Closing of the American Mind

Morally responsible Christians should also demonstrate the virtues of boldness, humility, and respect. As some biblical positions become increasingly unpopular in American culture, Christians will need boldness to articulate those positions publicly. Such boldness should be coupled with humility (Matt. 5:5). When attacked, the Christian should not become angry or resentful nor respond with abusive speech, insults, or slander (Titus 3:1–3). Because the Christian is motivated by love for his neighbors, rather than quest for power or prestige, he should endure attacks to advance a position that he believes is for the common good. He should demonstrate the virtue of showing due respect to others.

Democracy is a word that has been widely used and misused. Yet its common use indicates its common appeal, even where democracy is only claimed but not practiced. Democracy in its best sense embodies the ideals of liberty and equality within a system that promises opportunity. It is a government of people under the law, providing the liberty that freedom-loving people desire and tyrants fear.

Section Review

1–3. What three main conditions are necessary for a successful democracy?

4. What dangers arise when people lack economic opportunity?

5. How does moral responsibility help moderate the majority's power?

★ Why is accurate civic thinking critical to a democratic system?

★ What does it mean for a Christian to be prudent when considering compromise?

Problems with Public Opinion

As noted in the margin above, Alexis de Tocqueville states that the power of public opinion is a great danger in a democracy. Show students the first sentence from the quotation. Ask students to name specific ways in which public opinion "surrounds, directs, and oppresses." Discuss some of their answers and ways to limit the dangers public opinion may produce.

Section Review Answers

1–3. opportunity, an educated society, and moral responsibility (pp. 34–38)

4. The poor people lose hope. If there is a small (or nonexistent) middle class, the contrast between the poor and the rich is glaring. Political division may result. (p. 35)

5. Moral responsibility implies submission to the rule of law and provides a standard for judging the actions of the majority. It asks what is right, rather than just what is popular. (p. 38)

★ The citizenry must be well-informed, well-prepared, and well-educated to think accurately. Education prepares citizens to make wise decisions in voting for the best candidates, to discern between good and bad legislation, and to react appropriately by praising the good and condemning the bad.

★ Students should include the definition of prudence (it is the wisdom necessary to know how best to achieve a good goal). Students might include the following example or a similar one. A prudent Christian legislator may vote for a bill that limits abortions under certain conditions even though he would prefer to vote to outlaw all abortions.

Making Connections

1. Reread the section entitled "Popular Governments" on pages 17–18. Briefly explain the basics of how popular government functions in the United States.

2–4. How do unitary, federal, and confederate governments differ?

5–6. Distinguish between how a nation's leader is chosen in a presidential system and a parliamentary system.

7–9. Summarize the three conditions necessary for a successful democracy.

Developing Civics Skills

1. What does the Declaration of Independence mean when it says that "all men are created equal"?

2. Why did America's founders choose the federal system of government?

Thinking Critically

1. Why would a direct democracy be impractical for the United States?

2. What conditions are necessary for democracy to spread and flourish in Third World countries?

Living as a Christian Citizen

1. In the last century many new nations were created, most notably in Africa from the 1960s onward. Imagine that a new nation with a largely Christian population has asked you to propose a governmental structure that accounts for Christian principles. Describe this form of government, and be sure to explain the biblical reasons for your structure. Also explain the weaknesses of pure monarchy or pure democracy.

2. Modern democracy attempts to avoid the issue of what is good for society by focusing on respecting perceived individual rights, including indulgence in pornography, drugs, and gambling. If you were a legislator, how would you explain to your colleagues that this approach to legislation is flawed?

People, Places, and Things to Remember

monarchy
monarch
constitutional monarchies
dynasty
absolute monarchs
dictatorships
totalitarianism
autocracy
oligarchy
anarchy
popular government
direct democracy
indirect democracy
republic
unitary system
federalism
confederate government
presidential system
parliamentary system
delegated powers
Congress
House of Representatives
Senate
president
Supreme Court
democracy
Magna Carta
due process
English Bill of Rights
Bill of Rights
Electoral College
majority rule
popular majority
representative majority
pluralistic society
equality
civic thinking

Developing Civics Skills

1. All citizens have political equality, which is equality of justice and equality of franchise (vote).

2. It limits the government's power and establishes checks and balances not only within each level of government but also within and among all the branches.

Thinking Critically

1. The United States is too populous and too geographically far-flung to make pure democracy practical.

2. Answers will vary. There must be economic opportunity that produces a substantial middle class, and the people must be educated in order to understand the benefits of democratic government. The people must also be morally responsible, or their abuse of power will destabilize their governments.

Living as a Christian Citizen

1. Students should develop mixed forms of government that account for the weaknesses of the various pure forms of government. The students may note that pure monarchy can easily become tyrannical and that pure democracy has nothing to check the sinful inclinations of the majority. Students may say that strong democratic emphases sometimes undermine biblically based authorities, such as parents and pastors.

2. Students may emphasize that all sinful activity harms more than the sinner himself. Laws cannot make people good, but they do often set the tone for what a society accepts. A society that neglects morality in the framing of its laws will soon degenerate.

CHAPTER REVIEW ANSWERS

Making Connections

1. The United States is an indirect democracy, or representative democracy. Citizens have a voice in the government as they choose representatives to operate the government. The leaders are elected for short terms and cannot remain in power unless the people reelect them. (pp. 17–18)

2–4. In the unitary system, governmental power resides in the central government, which receives all its power from the people. A federal government divides a nation's power between national and regional governments. In a confederate government, regional governments retain supremacy and delegate few tasks to the national government. (pp. 18–19)

5–6. In a presidential system, the people elect the head of the executive branch. In a parliamentary system, the candidate whose party wins the most votes in a district becomes a member of Parliament. The major party in Parliament then appoints the chief executive, the prime minister. (pp. 19–20)

7–9. Citizens in a successful democracy need economic opportunity and an educated society and must demonstrate moral responsibility. (pp. 34–38)

CHRISTIANITY, THE CHURCH, AND GOVERNMENT

3

Our Constitution was made only for a moral and religious people. It is wholly inadequate to the government of any other.

—John Adams, 1798

Pilgrims Going to Church by George Henry Boughton

I. Christianity and Government in History

II. The Bible, the Church, and Pluralism

BIG IDEAS

1. How would you describe the relationship that has existed between Christians and government?

2. What is the role of Christians within our pluralistic society?

SUGGESTED MATERIALS

Section I
- Activities 1–2 from Chapter 3 of the *Student Activities*

Section II
- Activities 3–4 from Chapter 3 of the *Student Activities*

Teacher Resources
Visit TeacherToolsOnline.com for resources to enhance the lessons.

Three hundred years after the birth of Christ, the Faith He founded spread from a persecuted minority to the ruling class in the Roman Empire. Christians who previously suffered for their faith now had the opportunity to influence those who sat on thrones.

Chapter 1 presents the Bible's teaching on the obligations of government and the governed. But not all governments follow God's standards. Believers must learn to thrive in societies that persecute or ignore them or that even institute a single state church, allowing no competition. Over the centuries, many have tried to resolve these issues; we can learn from their successful ideas as well as from their unsuccessful ones.

I. Christianity and Government in History

Jesus and Constantine

"If they have persecuted me, they will also persecute you," Jesus told His followers (John 15:20), and it did not take long for persecution to begin. Jesus' prediction was soon fulfilled by zealous Jews and Romans.

The New Testament records the spread of the gospel among the Romans, which led to the spiritual conversion of some government officials (Acts 13:12; Phil. 1:12–13). But these conversions did not end Christians' suffering. As time passed it became very difficult for a Christian to serve in the Roman government or military since politicians and soldiers often had to offer a sacrifice to Roman gods and worship the emperor, practices in which Christians refused to participate.

Persecution of Christians in the Roman Empire abruptly ended in AD 313 with the Edict of Milan issued by Emperor Constantine. Eusebius, a church historian, saw the triumph of the gospel in Constantine's acceptance of Christianity. The apostle Paul's instructions to pray for the conversion of kings so that Christians might live "quiet and peaceable" lives seemed to have borne fruit (1 Tim. 2:1–2). Yet Constantine's embrace of Christianity raised new questions for the church. Should Christian rulers conduct offensive war? How should they treat other religions? Does a Christian emperor have authority over the Christian church, or should he submit to church leaders? How can the government develop just laws?

Throughout the Middle Ages, churchmen and political rulers tried to answer these questions. Predictably, they often disagreed about which authority was supreme. Many believed that a shared morality should be a concern of government—and a shared morality, they thought, required a shared religion. Though limited toleration of Jews and Muslims existed in certain parts of Europe, many leaders viewed religious freedom as a destabilizing evil rather than as a God-given right.

The Reformation

The Reformation shattered the illusion of religious unity in Europe. For the first time in many centuries, the church (which was actually the Roman Catholic Church led by the pope) divided into many churches (Lutheran, Anglican, Anabaptist, and others). However, that dramatic shift did not stop many from believing that a stable society rests on the foundation of a shared religion. The Reformation merely allowed each ruler to choose the religion to be practiced in his state.

Christianity and Government

Guide the students in creating a timeline that marks the significant events described in Section I. They should state on the timeline why each event is important.

Alternatively, divide the class into teams of two or three, and direct each team to construct a timeline. Encourage the students to vote on the best timeline based on appearance as well as content. Display the winning timeline.

Activity 1: Mayflower Compact, 1620

This activity will help students understand an important primary source, the Mayflower Compact.

Natural Law

In John Locke's day many people believed that having a shared religion was necessary in order for a society to have a shared conception of public virtue. But Locke argued that natural law can provide the basis for such shared ideas, even among adherents of different religions.

Guide the students through the following scriptural evidence for natural law.

Romans 2:14–16
In this passage, Paul teaches that the Gentiles, who did not have the law of Moses, still sometimes did what the law required because the law was written on their hearts.

Romans 1:18–32
In their hearts, people know that idolatry, homosexuality, covetousness, envy, murder, deceit, pride, and other sins are wrong and deserve to be punished by death. (The word *death* in this passage refers to eternal punishment.)

1 Corinthians 5:1
People have a sense of morality. In this verse, Paul rebukes the Corinthians for tolerating behavior that even unbelievers find repulsive.

Genesis 12:10–20; 20; 26:6–11
There is a recognized standard of right and wrong that governs the behavior of unbelievers and enables them to critique even God's people.

John Locke on Toleration

John Locke's view of toleration rested on a particular view of the state and its purposes and of the church and its purposes. His *A Letter Concerning Toleration* explains his beliefs. Excerpts are contained in Activity 2 of the *Student Activities*.

Locke's basic premise was that the state exists only to protect "civil interests." So issues related to property, the physical well-being of citizens, and the cohesion of society fall within its domain. Locke believed that rulers do not have power over religious matters because God did not grant them such power. Rulers, he said, may exercise only "outward force," whereas genuine religion is a matter of the mind and heart.

Locke defined the term *church* as "a voluntary society of men, joining themselves together of their own accord in order to the public worshipping of God in such manner as they judge acceptable to Him, and effectual to the salvation of their souls." He concluded that since a church is "a voluntary society," it may prescribe laws only for those who voluntarily join it. In addition, he thought that since the church is concerned with worship and souls, it need not concern itself with matters of the state.

But this led to the very destabilization people feared. European Protestants and Catholics raised armies and fought many battles to determine whether Protestantism would survive or the Roman Catholic Church would regain its former dominance. In addition, fluctuations in English rulers' religious views caused political struggles in England.

John Locke

This is the world into which British philosopher **John Locke** (1632–1704) was born. As a young man, Locke accepted the mindset of the day that everyone must strictly follow the monarch's religion. Such submission, he thought, was the only way to keep the peace.

But in 1665 Locke was sent on a diplomatic mission to the German city of Cleves. There he beheld a rare sight: Protestants and Catholics living in harmony. The city, due to its unusual political circumstances, allowed its citizens to choose their own religion.

This experience transformed Locke's thinking. He saw that this toleration in Cleves removed the disputed matter of religion from the already sensitive area of politics—and therefore led to peace, no matter what faith each person followed. But how was the state to promote public morality if people could choose their own religion? Locke found the solution in what is termed **natural law**. This is the belief that all people have a conscience and recognize that certain moral truths exist in nature. These traits, he believed, were enough to hold a society together.

Early America

Englishmen began immigrating to North America shortly before John Locke's birth. In many cases these colonists were fleeing religious persecution. In America, they established local governments that guaranteed them the right to worship God as they saw fit. Those colonists believed that governments founded upon Christian principles would provide moral stability.

By 1787, when leaders of the world's newest nation drafted its constitution, John Locke's arguments for religious toleration were readily received. Influenced by Locke's writings and the encouragement of American religious leaders, the First Amendment to the Constitution begins, "Congress shall make no law re-

Mayflower Compact

The **Mayflower Compact**, signed in 1620 by forty-one men aboard the *Mayflower*, established a temporary government for the Pilgrims' pioneer community. This government was based on the idea of a covenant—that is, that God had a covenant, or agreement, with His people and that they in turn had a covenant with one another to pursue common goals. This principle of **social contract**, that people agree to submit to a government in exchange for the protection of their rights, became a key component of American political thought and practice.

The students should conclude from this survey that God wrote a natural law on the human heart that is unavoidable as people look at the creation around them.

But the existence of natural law does not necessarily confirm Locke's view that natural law can produce shared concepts regarding public virtue. Instruct the students to read the following verses and evaluate the purposes Scripture gives for natural law and natural revelation.

Acts 14:13–17
To testify of God's existence and His goodness toward sinners

Romans 2:14–15
To restrain sin

Romans 1:18–20; 2:14–16
To render people inexcusable when God judges them

Encourage the students to evaluate the limitations on natural law's role of providing common morality for a society.

Romans 2:14–15; 1 Corinthians 8:7, 12; 1 Timothy 4:2; Titus 1:15; Hebrews 9:14; 10:22
Romans 2 explains that people do not always act according to natural law. Furthermore, if the conscience is the way that God's law is made known to a person, then the state of that person's conscience must be taken into account. The conscience may be weak, defiled, or seared.

Romans 1:18
Paul affirms that unbelievers have access to the truth, but he also teaches that they suppress the truth. The natural knowledge of God they have serves only to condemn them.

1 Corinthians 5:1; 1 Peter 4:3–4
Unbelievers do have a sense of morality, but it is grossly distorted. Paul's point in 1 Corinthians 5 seems to be that if even unbelievers can see that a behavior is immoral, it must really be immoral. He is not making a positive comment on their overall ability to arrive at sound moral conclusions.

A Christian should be confident when making a public case on an issue of morality. However, he should also be aware that unbelievers will not always yield to his arguments. They may use all their intellectual abilities to suppress the truth they naturally know.

specting an establishment of religion, or prohibiting the free exercise thereof." Thus, the "establishment clause" and the "free exercise clause" are key concepts concerning religion and government in America.

The Rise of Pluralism

In the half-century between the War of 1812 and the Civil War, America experienced deep religious change. The Second Great Awakening brought millions of believers into the evangelical fold, especially after 1820. Evangelical Protestants became the largest subculture in America. As a result, most Americans shared a common outlook on morality and the authority of the Bible. Evangelical Protestants founded many centers of higher education and established various influential societies to deal with social ills, such as drunkenness, illiteracy, and poverty.

Locke seemed to be correct. A nation conceived in religious liberty was working. Despite denominational differences, the moral foundation of America looked secure.

But after the Civil War, a large influx of Roman Catholic, Jewish, and Eastern Orthodox immigrants diminished Protestant dominance. Liberal European Protestant theology (which denied many fundamentals of the Scripture) also infiltrated American seminaries and schools, undermining confidence in the Bible.

By the twentieth century, humanists and secularists were pushing for a broader interpretation of the establishment and free exercise clauses. They argued that this brief statement mandated strict separation between religion and government. This secular argument gained popularity in the public mind as the United States became more religiously diverse. In addition to various Christian denominations, Muslims, Hindus, Buddhists, agnostics, and atheists comprised an increasing percentage of the population.

Today **pluralism**, which can be defined as the coexistence of a diversity of ethnic, social, religious, and political backgrounds, is increasingly common in America. Various groups, with different views of right and wrong, all live in the same society. This new reality challenges Christians to consider carefully how believers should behave in relation to political matters.

—First Amendment

Timothy Dwight was president of Yale College during part of the Second Great Awakening.

Yale University was established in 1701 as a Christian institution of higher education.

Section Review

1. Why did it become difficult for Christians to serve in the Roman government and military?

2. Why did many medieval and early modern Christians believe that states needed a common religion?

3. Why did the Reformation result in religious wars in Europe?

4–5. What was John Locke's solution to Europe's religious conflict? What was his basis for shared morality?

6. What is natural law?

★ Locke's religious toleration approach worked when various forms of Christianity were the primary competing religious options. Would his approach work in a society with greater religious diversity?

★ Why was the Mayflower Compact significant?

Activity 2: John Locke's Views Regarding Religious Toleration

This activity examines some of Locke's ideas about the relationship between government and the church.

Section Review Answers

1. Roman military and government service often involved offering sacrifices to pagan gods and worshiping the emperor. (p. 41)

2. They believed that stable states need a shared morality and that shared morality is impossible to achieve without a shared religion. (p. 41)

3. The Reformation shattered the illusion of religious unity in Europe, but many people still valued a shared religion. In each nation the religion of the ruler became the religion of the nation. Religion thus became a highly contentious political matter. (pp. 41–42)

4–5. religious toleration; natural law (p. 42)

6. the belief that all people have a conscience and recognize that certain moral truths are built into nature (p. 42)

★ Answers should mention that differing religious worldviews lead to great disagreement about what is moral and immoral.

★ It established a temporary government for the Pilgrims' pioneer community. The principle of social contract, that the government is formed by the consent of the governed, is a key component of the document and is at the heart of American political thought and practice.

1. Defend a biblical view of the relationship between church and state against contrary viewpoints.
2. Explain the role of ideologies and a Christian worldview in the formulation of political ideas.
3. Determine a biblical view of Christian involvement in political issues.
4. Propose ways a Christian may react to the problems created by pluralism.

Guiding Questions

1. How would you defend a biblical view of the relationship between church and state against contrary viewpoints?
2. What is the role of ideologies and a Christian worldview in the formation of political ideas?
3. What is a biblical view of Christian involvement in political issues?
4. How might a Christian react to problems created by pluralism?

II. The Bible, the Church, and Pluralism

Pluralism poses a serious challenge to John Locke's theory. Can a society based only on natural law succeed? Locke faced limited religious pluralism: Catholics and Protestants. Though the theological differences between those two groups are significant, the groups still agree on many moral issues. However, the melting pot of America has resulted in a much broader form of religious pluralism, adding Hindus, Muslims, religious liberals, and others into the mix. In addition, a large dose of secularism began to influence society.

Secularism's basic thesis is that religion is a private matter that should stay out of public spaces. Most secularists say that Christianity is fine on Sunday (and Judaism is fine on Saturday), but religion should not dictate laws. They also believe that it should be excluded from science labs, corporate boardrooms, and public schools.

How, then, does society answer moral questions? Do women have the right to choose an abortion? Can scientists conduct research on embryos? Should homosexual marriage be accepted? Is pornography a legitimate form of free speech? Should divorce be allowed for any reason? Should the government tax the rich heavily to support the poor?

The various groups in American society—religious and nonreligious—answer these questions differently because each group has different values. Some groups, for example, value personal freedom so highly that they see limits on abortion as immoral. But Christians traditionally view abortion as murder because they believe that every person, from conception, bears the image of God. Those who value personal freedom enough to allow doctors to kill babies also tend to see homosexual marriage as a matter of individual freedom. Many Christians, however, view homosexuality as immoral behavior and believe that public approval of such behavior will encourage its spread and increase moral damage. Those who try to help liberate people from homosexual sin may be labeled bigots by those who contend that homosexual marriage is a civil right. American Christians live in a society with multiple definitions of *morality*. How should they handle this situation?

Church and State

First, let us examine the relationship of the church and the state, two institutions established by God.

Absolute Separation of Church and State

Some people promote absolute separation between church and state (with church being broadly defined as "any religious influence"). They conclude that courthouses should not display the Ten Commandments and that public school valedictorians should not quote Scripture in their commencement addresses. In addition, they insist that local governments should not open their sessions with prayer.

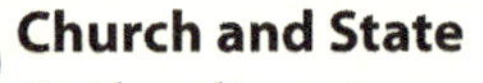

Church and State

Guide a discussion on the dangers of absolute separation of church and state. (After each discussion topic, a sample observation is given.)

(Someone's moral values will always prevail in a society. Christians should resist attempts to exclude their moral views.)

Guide a discussion of how the church and the state can relate in a positive way.

(The state, as a minister of God [Rom. 13:4], ought to protect religion. However, Scripture opposes coercion in matters of worship. Furthermore, the state has no competence in matters of doctrine, nor does it have biblical justification for interfering with the government of the church.)

Discuss the different challenges the church faces under different kinds of governments.

(In the first place, the Christian church does not require a specific form of national government in order to function in a way that pleases God. For instance, the church can maintain its witness even under hostile governments. But under persecution, Christians face the temptation to turn from Christ. Conversely, when the church has influence in a society, it may do great good publicly. But in that situation, it faces temptations to abuse its power or to rely on political schemes for its advancement. In no situation is the church free from temptations.)

This is the classic secularist view. Secularists assume that *separation of church and state* means "no religion in public life." They bring lawsuits against crosses on public monuments.

But the true power of secularism is more subtle. For example, instead of a politician using Scripture to justify opposition to same-sex marriage, secularism in society leads him to say, "I'm not here to impose my personal views on anyone; I'm just saying that marriage in every society has always been between a man and a woman." This may at first sound acceptable. But why should other societies' practices have any bearing on the way we do things? Are not all moral views in some sense personal?

Secularism views religious arguments on political matters as irrelevant. According to the secularists, if a person opposes abortion for religious reasons, his arguments should be ignored.

Sadly, like the politician mentioned above, some Christians have a secular perspective of politics. To them, the church is about worship and spirituality. Though they see how the Bible should shape personal life, they believe public life falls outside the church's jurisdiction. They do not believe Christianity should have a role in politics. Instead, they often adopt a particular political ideology to guide their thinking.

State over Church

Absolute separation of church and state is a relatively new idea. In the Byzantine Empire, the church and the state had a definite relationship: the state ruled over the church. The emperor saw himself as the defender of the church's orthodoxy. He had to believe what the church taught, but he served as its head. He could call church councils and participate in church matters. In medieval western Europe, rulers often exercised control over the church by appointing its leaders. This practice was known as lay investiture. The term is derived from the fact that such rulers were "laymen" or non-church officials. During this period, the lay investiture controversy led to one of the greatest struggles between church and state.

Some actions that Christians consider moral—such as believing that people should live according to their biological gender or teaching individuals how to become Christians—will seem immoral to many secularists. Consequently secular leaders may exert authority over Christians. For example, in some places laws dictate how a person may or may not address someone who identifies as transgender. Another example of the state's dominance over the church is the government of North Korea. In that officially atheistic nation, evangelizing is illegal because such work is deemed immoral.

There is no neutrality in moral issues. Every government makes decisions based on a particular view of morality. If a government chooses an unbiblical moral stance, conflict with the church will be inevitable. This may result in a situation like that which existed in the Byzantine Empire, where the state ruled over the church.

Church over State

Yet another view is that the church should have authority over the state. In the Middle Ages, the Roman Catholic Church declared its dominance over

Concordant of Worms

By the end of the first millennium AD, many wealthy men had left their estates to the Roman Church upon their deaths. Churchmen were appointed to oversee these estates; this created a potential conflict of interest. On one hand, these leaders were required to be loyal to their spiritual superior. On the other hand, they owed allegiance to their political superior (often a king). Gradually, a struggle, known as the lay investiture controversy, developed over which superior would invest the churchman with his political and spiritual responsibilities.

After many disagreements, the pope and the Holy Roman Emperor reached an agreement about handling the issue within the Holy Roman Empire. In the Concordant of Worms, a document signed in the city of Worms in 1122, these two leaders agreed to share power in the region.

Such a dispute provides a clear example of the struggle between the church and the state during the Middle Ages. But formal agreements did not always resolve the question of which power was superior.

Relations Between Church and State

Absolute Separation of Church and State

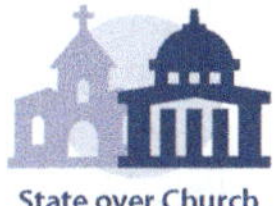

State over Church

Church over State

The Bible and Government

Even though the Bible is not a manual for government, it has had a profound influence on the development of government theory and practice. The kings of Israel were commanded to write their own copies of the Mosaic law (Deut. 17:18–20). From the Middle Ages until about the middle of the nineteenth century, legal theorists and government leaders often referred to the Bible to support their political views. For example, the controversial notion of a divine right of kings, which played an important role in European history, was derived from an interpretation of Scripture. However, that idea ignored the fact that the Bible leaves room for the people to play a role in government (2 Sam. 5:1–5) and permits limitations on the ruler's authority (2 Chron. 26:17–18).

Thomas Hobbes referred often to the Bible in his *De Cive*. John Locke used Scripture in his *Second Treatise of Government*. And both Robert Filmer's *Patriarcha* and Algernon Sidney's *Discourses Concerning Government* (written in response to Filmer's *Patriarcha*) proposed a political philosophy based on Scripture.

Activity 3: Jefferson and the "Wall of Separation"

This activity gives the students experience in comparing primary sources (in this case, correspondence between Jefferson and the Danbury Baptists) that are related to the principle of separation of church and state.

Compartmentalizing Christianity

The Puritans did not believe in compartmentalizing Christianity. For them, the Bible was a guide for all areas of life, including education and government. Discuss the ways that modern society and even professing Christians separate Christianity from many aspects of life. Discuss the dangers of such an attitude.

Useful Resource

In *How the Nations Rage: Rethinking Faith and Politics in a Divided Age*, author Jonathan Leeman notes that many people think that the government rules over the political realm while the church rules over the religious realm. They see these as two distinct areas of life. Those individuals rightly understand that the church and state are different institutions, but they are wrong to think that the political and the religious can be separated.

Leeman states that other people recognize that the religious and political parts of our lives are intertwined, so they want to merge church and state somehow so that the church rules the state or the state rules the church. But, he says, these people fail to recognize that God gave the church and the state distinct responsibilities.

Distinction and Influence in the Nineteenth Century

In his book *Church, State, and Original Intent*, Donald L. Drakeman states,

> Supreme Court Justice Joseph Story's *Commentaries on the Constitution* . . . proffered an opinion about how Americans during the founding era believed that Christianity should "receive encouragement from the State" that sounds quite different from Jefferson's "wall of separation."

Story's view was as follows:

> Probably at the time of the adoption of the Constitution, and of the [First] Amendment . . . the general if not the universal sentiment in America was, that Christianity ought to receive encouragement from the State so far as was not incompatible with the private rights of conscience and the freedom of religious worship. An attempt to level all religions, and to make it a matter of state policy to hold all in utter indifference, would have created universal disapprobation [disapproval], if not universal indignation.

Pope Innocent III

governments in western Europe. It allowed the state to perform political functions, with the understanding that the church held more power.

Exercise of this power was demonstrated during the reign of Pope Innocent III (r. 1198–1216). He excommunicated King John of England and declared that the king's feudal lords no longer owed allegiance to John. The feud between the two leaders continued until the king accepted the demands the pope had made. Innocent also forced Philip II, king of France, to set aside his third wife and take back his second wife (his first wife had died in childbirth). However, not all kings accepted the decrees of the Catholic Church. In 1303, when Pope Boniface VIII tried to exercise papal power, the French king removed him from power.

The church ought not to exercise power over the state because God has not given the church the responsibility to rule. God has given that responsibility to the state (Rom. 13:1). While the church should influence the state regarding moral matters, when churches have gained political power over the state the outcome has often been the corruption of the church rather than the improvement or purification of the state.

Distinction and Influence

Christians may find themselves in societies where one of the above views prevails, but, as we have seen, each is flawed, and none should be sought as a goal.

Almost all Christians today believe that the state and the church should be distinct in some way. There is a biblical basis for this position. Even in Israel the king and the high priest were not the same man. When King Saul and King Uzziah tried to change that, God was unhappy (1 Sam. 13; 2 Chron. 26). This truth is also implied in the New Testament era, when God's people are not closely identified with any specific state.

But the secular insistence on the absolute separation of church and state is not really about keeping institutions separate; it is about removing religious influence from public life. The Christian cannot accept this approach for two reasons. First, the Bible applies to all of life, not just to private, religious matters. Second, laws are based on moral positions. Every legislator's vote should promote a better life for citizens—but what qualifies as a "better life" remains a moral question. Whose definition will we use? It is dishonest for secularists to portray their morals as neutral and exclude others.

The Christian church, unlike the state, functions through the preaching of God's Word. Its role is not to formulate specific public policies. And it certainly does not promote its views through any kind of physical coercion. Rather, the church equips its members to demonstrate to the world, by word and deed, what is right and what is wrong—in short, what is a better life. And the church does its best to inform non-Christians about God's moral standards.

The ideal relationship between the church and the state would preserve the institutions' distinct functions while giving Christians a significant moral influence on the nation. The church would disciple people from all vocations, including judges, politicians, doctors, lawyers, and others influential in public life, teaching them to observe everything Jesus commanded. In this relationship the church's influence would be persuasive, not coercive.

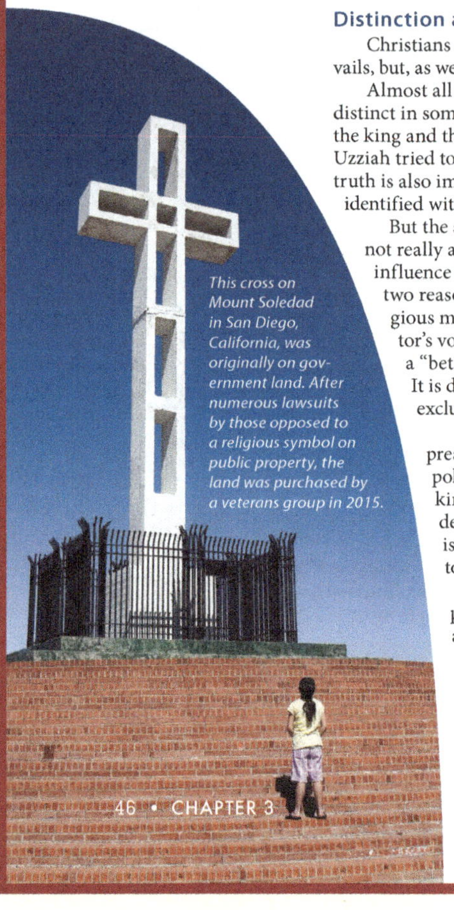

This cross on Mount Soledad in San Diego, California, was originally on government land. After numerous lawsuits by those opposed to a religious symbol on public property, the land was purchased by a veterans group in 2015.

Pluralism

Many current conflicts in American society find their root in different moral views. Relate the following situations to your students, and instruct them to evaluate the different moral viewpoints in each situation. Ask them how each moral conflict could be settled. (After each situation, a sample observation is given.)

In 1878 the Supreme Court ruled that Mormons would not be permitted to practice polygamy, partly because the practice undermines a healthy society. But the Mormons taught that plural marriage contributed to human salvation and that it gave the participants greater glory in heaven.

(There is a conflict between religious liberty and public morality in this case. In general, Christians support religious liberty in order to protect their own freedom to worship God. But this does not mean that any behavior can be tolerated as long as it bears a religious label. As John Locke noted, "No opinions contrary to human society, or to those moral rules which are necessary to the preservation of civil society, are to be tolerated by the magistrate." Making moral judgments is an inevitable part of governing, and Christians should insist on the superiority of Christian moral judgments.)

In 2001 President George W. Bush decided to limit funds for embryonic stem-cell research, saying, "I . . . believe human life is a sacred gift from our Creator. I worry about a culture that devalues life." In 2009 President Obama reversed President Bush's limitations. In his explanation, President Obama argued that "we [must] make scientific decisions based on facts, not ideology." He also said, "As a person of faith, I believe we are called to care for each other and work to ease human suffering."

(Both presidents made moral claims. But President Obama connected his moral claims only to the potential positive results of the research. According to Obama's speech, moral evaluation should be prohibited from influencing scientific decisions, and ideologies should be strongly distinguished from scientific facts. But this is itself an ideological posi-

Because our world is fallen, there is a danger that has proved very powerful in the United States. Citizens can develop a civil religion that is only superficially similar to true Christianity. Monuments and presidential speeches may quote the Bible, and legislators might gather for prayer during wartime—but the core elements of Christianity, the truths about human sin and our utter dependence on God, are disregarded.

Christians and Political Issues

Abortion is one of the most controversial issues in American politics. As a result, some lawmakers campaign on the position that they personally oppose abortion but do not wish to impose their religious beliefs on others. That may appear reasonable, but if the term *abortion* were replaced with terms for other violent acts, how would that sound? "He personally opposes rape and murder, but he does not want to impose his religious beliefs on others." "She does not like the idea of soldiers maiming civilians, but she views the issue as a matter of individual choice."

Society has a way of making some sins seem plausible and commonplace, sins that from God's

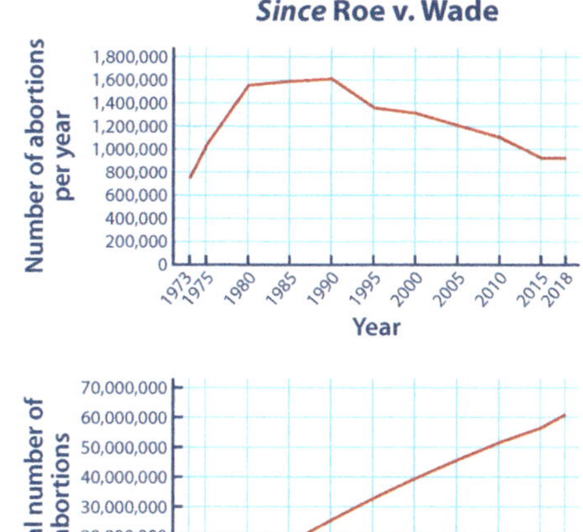

Political Ideologies

Ideologies are beliefs that guide an individual or group based on an underlying worldview. Dr. Nancy Love, a political scientist, says that ideologies tend to have three parts: an analysis of society, a vision for improvement, and a strategy for accomplishing goals. Thus, ideologies identify problems in society and then propose solutions.

But what makes something a **political ideology**? It focuses on solving societal problems with the application of political power; it goes beyond questions of government structure to examine all aspects of civilization. For example, communism claims that divisions of class and wealth are evil and identifies the solution as the elimination of private ownership. The right to own property would not exist in a pure (ideal) communist society. Libertarianism emphasizes individual freedom, though it often ignores the fact that granting some liberties to individuals (such as abortion) can violate the rights of others (such as the unborn's right to life).

Since ideologies result from worldviews, they often conflict with the Christian worldview. The Bible provides an analysis of human nature and existing society and offers a vision of a better future. Unfortunately, though many Christians see how the Bible should shape their personal lives, they do not see a role for Christianity in politics. Instead, they adopt another ideology from a competing worldview.

tion—one that reduces all truth to that which some scientists assert. Christians should challenge the assertion that scientific claims should be the defining ideology of our culture, and they should proclaim the negative consequences of following such an ideology.)

Several rulings in the last part of the twentieth century and the first part of the twenty-first century forbade public school science teachers to teach about origins from any other viewpoint than an evolutionary viewpoint.

(In this situation, there is a conflict between a naturalistic approach to origins and a theistic, or even specifically Christian, approach. A Christian teacher should present both positions while showing that the biblical record clearly supports the creationist position.)

After completing this exercise, the students should recognize the difficulty that faces a society composed of multiple religious viewpoints. Those viewpoints affect day-to-day policies, and competing religious groups often advocate different positions on those policies. Some wish to solve this problem by forcing all religious viewpoints out of the public square, but that is itself a religious position. It also violates the free exercise of religion.

Political Ideology and Worldview

Guide a discussion about these two topics. What is the relationship between the two? What are some examples of political ideologies that conflict with the Christian worldview? How should Christians handle such conflicts?

Misunderstanding Liberty

One of the difficulties in publicly discussing moral matters from a Christian perspective is many Americans' attachment to specific and unbiblical ideas about liberty. Misconceptions about liberty are common in American history. On the verge of the American War for Independence, Isaac Backus published a work called *An Appeal to the Public for Religious Liberty, Against the Oppressions of the Present Day*. In this work, he wrote, "The general notion of liberty, is for each one to act . . . as he pleases."

It is common for people to reject Christian moral positions as encroachments on their liberty. As Backus noted,

> It is supposed by multitudes, that in submitting to government we give up some part of our liberty, because they imagine that there is something in their nature incompatible with each other. But the word of truth plainly shews, that man first lost his freedom by breaking over the rules of government; and that those who now speak great swelling words about liberty, while they despise government, are themselves servants of corruption.

perspective are shocking and degrading. This tendency is evident by shifts in terminology. There has been a massive rise, for example, in cohabitation in America (unmarried couples living together). But if any politician were to publicly appeal to the Bible denouncing this, many voters would object. "You cannot force your religious views on other people!" "You cannot legislate morality!" "What people do in their bedrooms is none of your business!"

Natural Law

Christians disagree about how to respond to these charges. Some, following John Locke's reasoning, believe that Christians should not use the Bible to determine public policy. They insist that Christians and non-Christians both have the gift of reason.

On the issue of cohabitation, natural-law theorists argue that marriage brings commitment to relationships while cohabitation robs women and children of financial and familial security. And they appeal to a number of sociological studies to prove their point.

These arguments are valid because natural law does exist. The apostle Paul said that non-Christians who do not have God's law often "do by nature the things contained in the law" (Rom. 2:14). This is one reason why societies full of sinful people are not as bad as they could possibly be. Even people who have not read the Bible generally know that murder, theft, adultery, and deceit are bad—and that saving lives, giving to charities, remaining faithful to marriage vows, and being honest are good.

But, in Romans, Paul says that unregenerate people also suppress the truth of God's law. So, for instance, in modern America, abortion, software piracy, frequent divorce, or lies about coming late to work do not seem wrong to many individuals.

Natural-law arguments are not invalid; they simply do not go far enough. Natural-law theorists are also in danger of subtly confirming the thesis of secularism by eliminating religious reasoning.

Reasoning from natural law will not necessarily convince people any better than arguing from Scripture. The conscience is weak (1 Cor. 8:7, 12), defiled (1 Cor. 8:7; Titus 1:15), seared (1 Tim. 4:2), and impure (Heb. 9:14; 10:22). Thus, even the best Christian argument against sinful behavior may provoke anger rather than change.

Applying Scripture to Political Matters

Scripture applies to all of life, including the concerns of government, and should be applied appropriately. Mere reliance on natural law is not enough. For example, Scripture has much to say about divorce. The Mosaic code, the laws of the Old Testament, permitted it (Deut. 24:1–4); however, it also placed some restrictions on the practice. In the New Testament, Jesus teaches that God's intention from the very beginning was that a husband and a wife remain married for their entire lives. Moses gave permission for divorce only because of the hardness of people's hearts.

Both the Mosaic Law and Jesus' teaching remain relevant and instructive. Today no-fault divorce—divorce in which the

---

Old Testament Laws

Christians who appeal to the Bible on moral issues may receive a challenge like the following: "Sure, the Bible has some verses condemning homosexuality, but it also prohibits eating shellfish or wearing clothes with mixed fabrics!" Indeed, those restrictions are noted in the laws mentioned in the Old Testament.

How should Christians approach this argument? Paul clearly says that believers are under the New Covenant, not Old Testament laws (Rom. 7:4–6; 1 Cor. 9:21; 2 Cor. 3:3).

But God's expectations listed in Exodus through Deuteronomy have not entirely changed. Murder is still wrong because it still violates the image of God in man (Gen. 9:6). Adultery is still wrong because it still breaks God's original design of marriage between one man and one woman (Matt. 19:4–6). Homosexuality is still wrong because it is also contrary to God's original design (Matt. 19:4–5; Rom. 1:26–27). Though the symbols and ceremonies of those Old Testament laws do not apply today, God's moral expectations remain the same in every era.

✝ The Christian and Censorship

Some secularists object to censorship of obscene material on the grounds that censorship imposes a moral standard on people, who should be free to make their own choices.

Guide a discussion from a Christian perspective addressing censorship. (A sample observation is given below.)

(Sex is good within the context of marriage; a sexual relationship should be personal, rather than impersonal [Gen. 2:23–25]. Furthermore, a God-honoring sexual relationship provides the security of lifelong, exclusive commitment [Gen. 2:24; Matt. 19:4–6]. Grounding these truths is the fact that both males and females are bearers of God's image [Gen. 1:27]. Obscene, pornographic material degrades those portrayed [primarily women] by treating them as mere objects to be used for others' pleasure. Pornography also degrades the character of the person who willingly views it, and it also affects society's expectations and practices.)

In engaging moral issues, the Christian assumes that there are basic moral truths that unbelievers know, even if they seek to suppress them. Unbelievers have some conception of what is good, even though that view is distorted. The Christian's goal is to show that virtue cannot be achieved apart from Christian grounds. But this goal is difficult to reach because in a fallen world many are determined to suppress the truth that Christians seek to proclaim.

Current Events

Encourage the students to bring news articles containing examples of government leaders who have taken stands based on biblical principles. For example, students could focus on those who oppose abortion or the legalization of drugs or pornography.

Instruct the students to evaluate the arguments the leaders have made regarding these issues. They should identify the strongest arguments and look for ways to strengthen the weaker arguments.

spouse seeking a divorce does not have to prove any fault on the part of the other spouse—has become common. Christian legislators should examine this problem from a biblical perspective. Those lawmakers will recognize that today's society may necessitate some divorce legislation, as in Moses' day. However, they should encourage individuals to strive for God's ideal—marriage between a man and a woman for life. Legislators who address this issue should examine the negative social consequences of no-fault divorce and mount a case for the public benefit of divorce legislation that encourages lasting marriages. In doing so they demonstrate the importance of a biblical worldview. Such actions are crucial; no country can constantly live contrary to the laws of God and escape His wrath.

Addressing the Issue of Pluralism

Pluralism is a significant challenge Christians face in dealing with political matters. The political clashes that are shown on television screens every day can often be traced to different worldviews. Of course, not every political disagreement is this serious, and the various political parties agree on many things. But the most intense arguments about public issues become so heated because there are fundamental issues of truth at stake. They create what is called the **culture wars** ("a conflict between groups with different ideals, beliefs, and philosophies").

It is impossible to limit all moral questions to the private realm. Moral decisions always affect other people. For instance, most Americans would rightly recoil if employers were permitted to deny black Americans employment solely on the basis of ethnicity. That is morally wrong. Is it right, therefore, to force Christians to hire a pastor who openly affirms his homosexual desires and his homosexual relationships? Some people would say that this violates the church's right to its religious beliefs. Others believe that refusing to hire a homosexual to serve as a pastor is a form of discrimination. This conflict cannot be resolved without addressing worldview differences.

Go and Do

How can Christians gain influence in political matters despite pluralism? They must understand the political process—how the system works and how to accomplish things. Much of this textbook addresses this issue.

However, knowing the specifics of how the government functions is only part of the task. Christians should also seek to persuade unbelievers. Although unbelievers may attempt to suppress the truth, the Bible tells us that, deep down, they do know it (Rom. 1:20–32). Christians should develop arguments that encourage

Negative Social Consequences of Divorce

Increased dropout rates

Poverty

Depression/ Mental health problems

Rejection of faith

Abuse

Suicide or Early death

Increased likelihood of children of divorce divorcing

Substance abuse/ Addiction

These negative consequences are frequently associated with divorce though not necessarily caused by it.

What Is Liberty?

In his book, Isaac Backus defined *liberty* thus:

> The true liberty of man is, to know, obey and enjoy his Creator, and to do all the good unto, and enjoy all the happiness with and in his fellow-creatures that he is capable of; in order to which the law of love was written in his heart, which carries in [its] nature union and benevolence to [the supreme] Being in general, and to each being in particular.

Regarding the protection of this liberty, Backus concluded, "All nations have found it necessary to submit to some government in order to enjoy any liberty and security at all."

Consequences of Divorce

Negative social consequences that arise from actions (such as divorce) are a demonstration that people are living contrary to the way God designed His world to work. In public policy debates, Christians and non-believers often agree that the consequences of divorce are undesirable. Such discussions often provide Christians an opportunity to make clear the basic Christian beliefs that lead them to oppose divorce.

Note that the graphic on this page is not stating that the consequences listed are all caused by divorce; however, clearly divorce often leads to many harmful outcomes.

Divorce

Refer to the graphic above entitled "Negative Social Consequences of Divorce." Guide a discussion by asking questions. What lessons can be learned by looking at the list? What are additional consequences of divorce? What biblical principles should Christians voice in public policy debates about divorce?

The note in the Teacher Edition right margin ("Consequences of Divorce") will assist with the discussion.

Marriage

Guide a dialogue using the two pictures on this page as a starting point. After discussion questions below, a sample observation is given.

Is marriage about love rather than gender (as noted in one of the pictures)? (*Marriage involves many issues, both love and gender among them. The Scriptures give some very specific instructions regarding marriage being between a man and a woman.*)

Are there cases in which people love each other, but marriage is not proper? (*Yes. For example, marriage between brothers and sisters, parents and children, and a married person and another married person are not allowed in our society. Hence, it is both reasonable and acceptable that laws establish some requirements for marriage.*)

What is love? (*Biblical love is not merely a feeling of personal delight and desire for someone. Biblical love is a desire for the other person's good, and their good is ultimately found in God. To desire someone in a way that contradicts God's law is not truly to love them.*)

Tolerance

In addition to misconceptions about liberty, another problem Christians encounter when discussing moral matters is the prevalence of unbiblical ideas about tolerance.

Theologian D. A. Carson argues that the definition of *tolerance* is changing. Under the old definition, people could hold strong beliefs, grant others the same privilege, and debate about the merits of their ideas. But the new tolerance demands acquiescence to all views; it rejects dogmatism while being itself dogmatic.

This has profound effects on Christianity. As Carson noted in *The Intolerance of Tolerance*,

> The charge of intolerance has come to wield enormous power in much of Western culture. . . . It functions as a "defeater belief." A defeater belief is a belief that defeats other beliefs—i.e., if you hold a defeater belief to be true (whether it is true or not is irrelevant), you cannot possibly hold certain other beliefs to be true: the defeater belief rules certain other beliefs out of court and thus defeats them. . . .
>
> Put together several such defeater beliefs and make them widely popular, and you have created an implausibility structure: opposing beliefs are thought so implausible as to be scarcely worth listening to, let alone compelling or convincing. . . .
>
> [For this reason,] the new tolerance tends to avoid serious engagement over difficult moral issues, analyzing almost every issue on the one axis tolerant/intolerant, excluding all others from the pantheon of the virtuous who do not align with this axis.

people to confront the truth they are trying to avoid. This also means that Christians need to understand their opponents' perceptions. Christians must recognize those truths and use them to expose the error in their opponents' positions.

To challenge unbiblical thinking in public requires boldness. Christians who argue for biblical positions will often be labeled as bigoted and their positions as harmful. The Christian also has to remember his goal. He is not trying to merely win an argument, he is seeking to persuade. Much of today's political discourse—on talk radio, on television, and in online discussion—has degenerated into insulting and abusive comments. Christians, like their Lord, should have a different spirit. They should engage in political discussion with humility and respect. They should demonstrate that they are motivated by love for others, seeking their true good.

But Christians must not be naive. Some worldview clashes provoke people to violence. Christians must be willing to face persecution even though persecution in America is seldom physical. When Jesus defined persecution in the Beatitudes, He mentioned slander and other types of verbal abuse endured for the sake of His name. However, for many Christians around the world, persecution exceeds hurtful speech. The torture and execution of Christians in North Korea, China, and Pakistan foreshadow what could someday come to America. American Christians are sometimes tempted to trim their message to avoid ridicule and increase their public influence. But the kingdom of heaven is given to those who suffer persecution to advance the cause of Christ (Matt. 5:10).

Finally, and most importantly, Christians must see the gospel as the ultimate solution to the problems created by pluralism. Those seeking to change society first need the gospel for themselves. Transformed Christian families can show the love of Christ, neighbors can serve their community, and churches can minister to those that society neglects; these small good works often have profound effects. Yes, Christians should strive for moral laws that restrain sin and convict sinful hearts. However, no lasting change will take place without divine regeneration of individuals.

The relationship of church and state has led to some difficult questions over the centuries. And the current situation in the United States presents additional challenges. Righteousness exalts any nation, and Christians should work toward the ideal regardless of the society in which they live. The kingdom of Christ will endure when all other empires have crumbled to dust.

Section Review

1. What is the basic thesis of secularism?
2. Why do Christians traditionally view abortion as murder?
3–4. Cite two reasons why Christians cannot accept the removal of religious influence from public life.
5. Why is it impossible to say that moral questions should be limited to the private realm?
★ Why do secularists seek the absolute separation of church and state?
★ How should Christians seek to gain influence in political matters?

Activity 4: Chapter Review

This activity will reinforce terms and other information contained in the chapter.

Section Review Answers

1. Religion is a private matter that should stay out of public spaces. (p. 44)
2. They believe that every person, even the unborn, bears the image of God. (pp. 47–48)
3–4. First, the Bible applies to all of life, not just to private, religious matters. Second, legislation is based on a moral position. (pp. 48–49)
5. Moral decisions affect other people, not just an individual. (p. 49)
★ They seek to remove all religious influence from public life.
★ They should understand the political process. They should seek to persuade unbelievers and rely on the fact that right and wrong are written on the human heart. Christians should also try to understand opponents' positions to reveal the errors in their reasoning. Above all, Christians must rely on the gospel's power to transform lives.

CHAPTER REVIEW

People, Places, and Things to Remember

John Locke
natural law
Mayflower Compact
social contract
pluralism
political ideology
culture wars

Making Connections

1. Why was Locke's conception of religious toleration considered attractive and workable in the early United States?

2. Explain the natural-law approach to Christian involvement in public matters.

3–4. Should Christians expect persecution from unbelievers? Why or why not?

Developing Civics Skills

1. Many Christians have sought to overturn the legalization of abortion since 1973. What do you think are the most useful measures for reversing the legalization of abortion in today's political climate?

2. Is reduction of poverty a legitimate concern for government? Why or why not?

Thinking Critically

1. Should Christians seek to reduce the divorce rate through political means? Why or why not? How would they do so?

2. Politicians often create government programs to reduce the financial gulf between those they call "the rich" and "the poor." Should Christians support such programs? Why or why not?

Living as a Christian Citizen

1. Select a political discussion regarding a topic important to Christians (it may be online or recorded from television or radio). Assess how well the person reflects the virtues of boldness, humility, and respect while representing a position with which Christians would most align. Rewrite the dialogue to reflect these traits where there are shortcomings in the discussion.

2. Choose a topic on which Christians can take a biblical position (abortion, sexual morality, work/welfare, etc.) and formulate a brief argument that makes use of Scripture and which also seeks to persuade those who are not Christians.

CHRISTIANITY, THE CHURCH, AND GOVERNMENT • 51

Governments should enact legislation encouraging work. While a government will never be able to eliminate poverty, it can take action to limit it and assist those who need help.

Thinking Critically

1. Students might note that while divorce is a sin problem that will only be solved by the gospel, bad laws can exacerbate the situation and good laws can improve it. Efforts to reduce the divorce rate are a public-policy matter since divorce produces negative societal effects that have been documented and are widely recognized. There are various reform methods. States could rescind no-fault divorce laws. In nonviolent situations, waiting periods and reconciliation classes could be instituted to assist in preserving marriages.

2. Some students may support such programs. Others might mention that Christians should support the government penalizing businesses that take advantage of the poor (e.g., lenders that charge exorbitant rates). They might also endorse other legislation. Other students might say that the government should not be empowered to take from the rich to give to the poor because charity is the responsibility of individuals, churches, and private organizations.

Living as a Christian Citizen

1. Students should address the virtues mentioned in the assignment.

2. Students should create an argument that makes effective use of Scripture while also being persuasive to a broad audience.

CHAPTER REVIEW ANSWERS

Making Connections

1. Locke's view was attractive because the colonies had included people who were fleeing religious persecution. They had established local governments that guaranteed the right to worship God as they saw fit. (p. 42)

2. It believes that Christians should not use the Bible to determine public policy. They and non-Christians should rely on reason to make decisions. (p. 48)

3–4. Christians should expect persecution because Christ endured persecution and warned His followers to expect it. (pp. 49–50)

Developing Civics Skills

1. Students may say that incremental changes seem to be the most effective way to reduce the number of abortions. Several states require minors seeking abortions to have parental consent. Some states require a woman who wants an abortion to have an ultrasound, hear her baby's heartbeat, and undergo a waiting period between consultation and the actual abortion.

2. Answers will vary. Government should provide a framework for dealing with poverty. The Mosaic law required the government to provide a measure of relief to the poor, though this support was in conjunction with other groups.

The Declaration of Independence and the Constitution are among the documents on display at the National Archives in Washington, DC.

2

THE CONSTITUTION

CHAPTER FOUR
CONSTITUTIONAL BEGINNINGS

CHAPTER FIVE
THE UNITED STATES CONSTITUTION

CHAPTER SIX
FEDERALISM

CHAPTER SEVEN
STATE AND LOCAL GOVERNMENT

Chapter Goals

1. Identify the influences and crises that shaped America during the colonial and Confederation periods.
2. Assess the major decisions reached during the Constitutional Convention.
3. Describe the concerns and disagreements regarding the ratification of the Constitution.

CONSTITUTIONAL BEGINNINGS

4

The Constitution of the United States was not made merely for the generation that then existed, but for posterity—unlimited, undefined, endless, perpetual posterity.

—Henry Clay

Scene at the Signing of the Constitution of the United States by Howard C. Christy

I. Colonial and Confederation Eras

II. Constitutional Convention

III. Ratification Controversy

BIG IDEAS

1. What influences and crises shaped America during the colonial and Confederation periods?
2. What major decisions were reached during the Constitutional Convention?
3. What were the concerns and disagreements regarding the ratification of the Constitution?

SUGGESTED MATERIALS

Section I
- Pictures of events, individuals, and documents covered in this chapter
- US map
- Activities 1–2 from Chapter 4 of the *Student Activities*
- Special speaker (see p. 61)

Section II
- Handout template
- Activity 3 from Chapter 4 of the *Student Activities*

Section III
- *The Federalist Papers*

- Activities 4–5 from Chapter 4 of the *Student Activities*

Teacher Resources
Visit TeacherToolsOnline.com for resources to enhance the lessons.

The Constitution is a powerful, eloquent, yet immensely practical legal instrument. It was written because American leaders were forced to deal with difficult issues facing a new nation. The men who gathered in Philadelphia to draft the Constitution were an impressive group; they had distinguished themselves on the battlefields and in the statehouses of the youthful nation. Two future presidents, George Washington and James Madison, were among them, as were twenty-eight future congressmen. Thomas Jefferson, who was in France during the Constitutional Convention, praised these Constitution makers by calling them "an assembly of demi-gods [half-gods]." Although their work was elevated, these men were really mere humans. They argued among themselves, devised compromises, fretted over how history would remember them, and prayed for God's direction and blessing on their efforts.

This chapter examines the historical context of the Constitution—the document's authors, the national problems they struggled to solve, and the way their solutions produced a republic that has been a model of successful self-government for over two centuries.

I. Colonial and Confederation Eras

Political Influence and Innovation

America was largely an English export. The men and women who crossed the Atlantic to settle the American wilderness generally transported political, social, and religious patterns and values from the Old World, especially from England, to the New World. Anne Bradstreet was America's first poet. Her poems, first published in 1650 under the title *The Tenth Muse Lately Sprung Up in America*, provide interesting insight into the extent of English culture in early America. Bradstreet's flowers are English flowers; the birds, English birds; and the landscape, Lincolnshire, England.

During its early development, American colonial government was also an English export. The mother country mainly influenced three areas: local government, legislative government, and limited government. **Local governments** were organized quickly in the New World, providing order and leadership for isolated pioneer communities. The English influence on local government is still evident in American vocabulary, which includes terms such as *grand jury*, *sheriff*, *bailiff*, *township*, and *county*, all of which are rooted in English governance.

The **legislatures**, the lawmaking bodies, that were established in each of the colonies were influenced by the English Parliament. As early as 1619, for example, the Virginia colony organized the **House of Burgesses**—the first representative assembly in the New World. These colonial assemblies reinforced the principle of representation, encouraged political participation, and provided leadership training in the difficult art of self-government.

Limited government was already a centuries-old principle in England when the first colonists waded ashore

Virginia House of Burgesses at Colonial Williamsburg

Constitutional Beginnings

Construct a timeline based on the key events covered in the chapter. If possible, find pictures of events, individuals, and documents. Display this in the classroom.

Additional Resources

Check the following books for more information on the people and principles that influenced the War for Independence and the Constitution:

- *Lion of Liberty: Patrick Henry and the Call to a New Nation* by Harlow Giles Unger
- *American Sphinx: The Character of Thomas Jefferson* by Joseph J. Ellis
- *The Radicalism of the American Revolution* by Gordon S. Wood
- *The Great Rehearsal: The Story of the Making and Ratifying of the Constitution of the United States* by Carl Van Doren
- *Founding Brothers: The Revolutionary Generation* by Joseph J. Ellis

Then and Now

Compile a list of areas in which the United States has changed since 1787 (e.g., lifestyles, education, currency, transportation, politics, technology, and entertainment). Construct a "Then and Now" display for the classroom or the school hallway.

King George III

George III was not so much a conscious tyrant as a king of limited ability advised by inept counselors. He was noted for his devotion to his wife, Charlotte, (a rare quality among European royalty) as well as for his personal bravery. For example, he endured several assassination attempts with courageous composure. Yet as a political leader he was hopelessly out of his element, both with the American colonies and with Parliament.

In addition, King George suffered from photosensitivity, seizures, and mental problems. Between 1811 and 1820, he was periodically confined, sometimes in a straitjacket, to his rooms in Windsor Castle. Before he died in 1820, he became blind and insane. The cause of his illness is uncertain. Many believe his condition might have been a result of porphyria, a hereditary disease.

Power of Parliament

Initially, the focus of colonial criticism was the British Parliament, in which colonists had no representation. The Declaration and Resolves of the First Continental Congress asserted that it was unjust for Parliament to use taxation as a means of raising revenue in the colonies. Rather, the Congress said, Parliament could establish taxes only on imperial trade that was intended to enrich the entire empire. The Congress denied Parliament's right to levy internal taxes, such as the Stamp Act, because the colonies were not represented in Parliament. However, the British believed every member of Parliament represented everyone in the British Empire.

King George III

The Stamp Act required colonists to use special paper, bearing stamps like these, for almost all printed materials. Colonists resented the tax required to obtain the stamp.

in America. Since the writing of the Magna Carta in the thirteenth century, Englishmen believed that they had certain rights that the government could not take from them. Government was limited by laws that everyone, including the king, was bound to obey.

While the English influence on colonial government was understandably extensive, Americans also placed their own stamp on their politics. For example, the representative assemblies throughout the colonies exercised increasing authority over the royal governors. It is no accident that this power shift followed the 1688 Glorious Revolution (see Chapter 2), in which Parliament firmly established its authority over the king. In retrospect, this event contributed to American independence in ways no one could have foreseen. Bolstered by the unparalleled strength that Parliament now commanded, the colonial legislatures assumed the right to levy taxes; alter colonial constitutions; and, in some cases, appoint or approve royal officers.

Britain's attitude toward the aggressive American colonial governments was quite lenient, especially during the first half of the eighteenth century. The growth in colonial political power and experience was gradual and was nurtured by official British neglect and America's geographic remoteness. Three thousand miles of ocean did much to assist the progress of self-government in America. Britain's preoccupation with various wars also played a role. Within the colonies, poor roads, swollen rivers, and slow transportation meant that distances between people were greater and that government was less centralized than in the old country. However, the growing confidence of the colonial legislatures, born out of political gains, was soon to meet its most formidable challenge as the winds of change blew from the distant shores of England.

Tension and War in America

Years after the War for Independence, John Adams concluded that the war began not in 1775 on the battlefields of Lexington and Concord but rather in the 1760s. By then, several significant events were making America ripe for independence.

In 1760 Montreal, the last French stronghold in North America, surrendered to the British. The French and Indian War was nearing its end for the colonies. The French defeat removed a major obstacle from the path of American expansion. At the same time, the war left Britain with a huge debt; Parliament soon demanded that the colonies help shoulder the burden. Also in 1760, a twenty-two-year-old prince named George III ascended to the throne. The young king fully intended to act on his mother's advice to "be a king" by reasserting the political strength of the Crown, which had been on the decline for more than a century. His reckless efforts, however, combined with the incompetence of his advisors and parliamentary supporters, strained and eventually snapped the British hold on the American colonies.

Beginning with the Stamp Act in 1765, Parliament passed a series of taxes and trade restrictions on

Government Terms

Much of the language used in American government reflects influences from the English system of government. Ask students to research the etymology of the following terms and report on their findings.

bailiff	grand jury
bureaucracy	impeachment
cabinet	inauguration
census	mayor
congress	president
constitution	republic
county	senate
democracy	sheriff
federal	township
governor	veto

Providence in Geography

Using a US map, discuss how geography (physical dimensions, natural boundaries, natural resources, climate, etc.) affected the development of US government both in this formative period and throughout the nation's history. Discuss topics such as forms of government, methods of representation, campaigns, elections, economic interests, and foreign policy. Remind the students that God's providence affects not only humans' actions but also geographic boundaries. (See Acts 17:24–26.)

Boycotts

Boycotts are still used as tools of political persuasion. Instruct the students to collect news articles about recent or current boycotts. The articles could discuss subjects such as nations that are boycotting other nations, or interest groups (or individuals) that are boycotting particular businesses. In each case, assign students the following questions: Who is doing the boycotting? What group is the target of the boycott? What items are being boycotted? What goals does the boycotter have? Does the boycott seem successful?

the colonies that produced more resentment than revenue from America. That same year, the British government also imposed a peacetime army on the colonies and passed laws forcing the colonials to provide food and housing for the soldiers. Many colonists were outraged by these actions.

Over the next ten years, Britain continued to tighten its economic and military hold over the colonies. Having enjoyed years of self-government largely free of parliamentary interference, the colonies were alarmed that the taxes and troops were imposed without their consent. Tempers and violence flared on both sides. British customs officials were often tarred and feathered or burned in effigy by radical elements in society. British soldiers and colonists harassed each other. On March 5, 1770, the British opened fire on a group in Boston that was hurling snowballs and insults at the soldiers. When the smoke cleared, eleven citizens lay in the snow, five of them dead. The Boston Massacre, as many colonists called it, strengthened American protests and fueled the growing Patriot movement.

Organized colonial resistance, both military and political, came to a head—surprisingly enough—over tea. Britain's attempt to monopolize the tea trade was greeted with outrage and calls throughout the colonies for a **boycott** (an act of protest in which business is withheld or refused). Many homes and taverns banned the drink from their tables, and coffee became the favored brew of many Patriots. A week before Christmas in 1773, a group of Bostonians shouting, "Boston Harbor a teapot tonight!" effectively ended the governor's attempt to distribute three shiploads of English tea. When the colonists dumped the chests of tea overboard, royal officials were infuriated and demanded that the colonists be punished. Parliament adopted the Coercive Acts, which were called the Intolerable Acts in the colonies. These laws closed the Boston port until the cost of the destroyed tea was repaid; revoked the Massachusetts colonial charter; required that any British officials in Massachusetts who were accused of crimes would be tried in another colony or England; and required the housing and feeding of British soldiers in American homes.

The American colonists, however, resisted. Responding to calls from the Virginia and Massachusetts Assemblies, the **First Continental Congress (1774)** gathered in Philadelphia in September with representatives from every colony except Georgia. Numbered among this assembly were such leaders as Samuel and John Adams of Massachusetts and Patrick Henry and George Washington of Virginia. Although the British government did not authorize its meetings, the Congress met for two months. It issued a declaration of grievances to George III; and, more importantly, defined the colonists' political rights as Americans, not simply as British subjects. John Adams wrote at the time that "the foundation . . . of all free government, is a right in the people to participate in their legislative council" and added that Americans were "entitled to a free and exclusive power of legislation in their several provincial legislatures."

Boston Tea Party (December 1773)

Second Continental Congress

Spark in Boston

Before the Boston Massacre, tempers had been rising in Boston for several months over the presence of British soldiers and scattered acts of violence. One source of tension was a dispute involving British soldiers who were working as rope makers during their off-duty hours. Unemployed Bostonians, in particular, resented losing employment to the "lobster backs." Insults were hurled on both sides, and some soldiers vowed revenge. Though some citizens in the mob that gathered in front of the Customs House had clubs and swords, most were unarmed, not believing that the soldiers would actually shoot. The British officer in charge, Captain Thomas Preston, did not order his soldiers to fire into the crowd, but he did not immediately restrain them.

Engraving of the Boston Massacre

Paul Revere's engraving of this event was an effective piece of Patriot propaganda. In it, Revere renamed the Customs House "Butcher's Hall" and the British officer appears, inaccurately, to be ordering his soldiers to fire.

Captain Boycott

Colonists could not use the term *boycott* when protesting the English tea trade because the term did not yet exist. It was coined more than a hundred years later. In 1880, a notorious English land agent, Captain Charles Cunningham Boycott, raised the wrath of Irish tenant farmers by refusing to lower their rents. In response, the Irish Land League, led by nationalist Charles Parnell, called on everyone in the locality to refuse to deal with Boycott. The practice soon spread elsewhere under the name of its infamous target.

State Government

As the students study the formation of US government, direct their attention to their own state's history and the formation of its government. Group the students and assign each group a different aspect of the state's government. One could compile information about one or two major individuals who influenced the state's constitution. Others could explore the influence of particular economic, religious, political, and social issues. Another group could compile a timeline of important state, national, and international events. Another could compare the state's form of government with that of other states. Each group may designate a liaison to exchange useful information with other groups. Each group can present its findings in an oral and written manner.

Assign your homeschool student to research and write a report on your state's history and government, addressing the issues listed in the preceding group activity. The student could also expand the report to cover the history and government of your town or county (or parish or borough, if you live in Louisiana or Alaska, respectively).

Loyalists

Not all colonists supported independence from England. Some were loyal to the mother country for political, religious, and economic reasons. Many believed they were fairly represented by Parliament and that taxes to fund the colonies' defense were acceptable. Others thought Parliament had exceeded its bounds with various acts; however, they did not think that those actions justified war. Furthermore, some Loyalists (or Tories) feared that independence might lead to mob rule and tyranny. Christians, like other groups in the country, had varying opinions. Some were Patriots while others were Loyalists.

By the time the assembly reconvened as the **Second Continental Congress** during the late spring of the following year, shots had been fired in Lexington and Concord, Massachusetts. Soon, the desire for complete independence was gaining momentum. However, that view was certainly not unanimous. Many colonists remained loyal to Britain for political, religious, and economic reasons. Many of these **Loyalists**, or Tories, feared independence would lead to mob rule and tyranny.

American Independence—1776

Two major tasks lay before the Second Continental Congress: to deal with the military emergency around Boston and to discuss a formal declaration of independence. To address the military emergency, Congress dispatched George Washington to forge the ragtag volunteer militias around Boston into a Continental army. As for the **Declaration of Independence**, its basis was a June 1776 resolution proposed by Virginia delegate Richard Henry Lee: "These united colonies are, and of right ought to be, free and independent states." The task of creating the formal document was left to a committee of five appointed by Congress: Benjamin Franklin, John Adams, Robert Livingston, Roger Sherman, and **Thomas Jefferson**. The committee unanimously agreed that its youngest member, thirty-three-year-old Jefferson, would do the actual writing.

What Jefferson penned in elegant fashion was nothing new. Rather, he brought together established "self-evident" principles of government that he thought justified the colonies' break with England. Indeed, without such a clear statement the colonies would appear to be in lawless rebellion—something European governments would certainly not view favorably. The result was a document that reflected the **Age of Enlightenment**, the philosophical and intellectual movement in eighteenth-century Europe that emphasized reason and thought.

Consistent with the Enlightenment, the Declaration stressed the importance of natural laws that govern the universe—and, in this case, government. In the introduction, Jefferson presented four major laws, or truths:

1. All humans "are created equal."
2. All humans "are endowed by their Creator with certain unalienable rights," which include "life, liberty and the pursuit of happiness."
3. Governments are established "to secure these rights."
4. If governments become "destructive of these ends," they may rightfully be abolished and replaced.

The idea of natural law has a long history. The apostle Paul refers to it in Romans 2:14–16 (cf. Rom. 1:32), and Paul's readers, whether Roman, Greek, or Jewish, would have understood the concept. In the thirteenth century, philosopher and theologian Thomas Aquinas distinguished between divine law (law found in Scripture) and natural law (law discovered through conscience or observation of the world).

Franklin, Adams, and Jefferson were the primary members of the Declaration committee.

Activity 1: Declaration and Resolves

The first part of this activity centers on excerpts from the Declaration and Resolves sent to King George III. The second part requires each student to gather information about a particular signer. This activity enhances analytical skills and skills in using original sources.

The Fourth of July

Independence Day is obviously an important part of American culture. Instruct your students to research holidays that other countries celebrate to mark important political events in their history. Some suggested holidays are as follows:

Australia: Australia Day, January 26
Brazil: Independence Day, September 7
Canada: Canada Day, July 1
China: National Day, October 1
Cuba: National Revolution Day, July 26
Egypt: Revolution Day, July 23
France: Bastille Day, July 14
India: Republic Day, January 26
New Zealand: Waitangi Day, February 6
Norway: Constitution Day, May 17
Switzerland: National Day, August 1

According to Aquinas, divine law directs people toward their spiritual good, and natural law directs people toward their natural good; human laws are therefore to be based on natural law, not Scripture. Reformation leaders also believed in natural law, and they thought it explained why pagan nations would often enact just laws. But they tended to deny that a person or a nation can consistently understand natural law rightly apart from Scripture. As the Reformation gave way to the Enlightenment, however, natural law took center stage. Enlightenment philosophers emphasized natural law because it

John Locke's Views

As previously noted, one of the most significant philosophers of the Enlightenment was Englishman John Locke (1632–1704). His writings profoundly influenced America's Founding Fathers, including Thomas Jefferson. In *Second Treatise on Civil Government*, Locke explains a natural-law basis for government and justifies political revolution. Locke's Enlightenment views were similar to views of government developed by covenant theologians in the sixteenth and seventeenth centuries. They developed the idea that nations exist in the context of a covenant between God and each nation and a covenant between the people and their rulers. Locke focused more on a government contract between the latter. For the most part, this **social contract theory** seems to be a secularization of seventeenth-century Christian political thinking.

Comparing the ideas and wording of Locke's *Second Treatise* with Jefferson's Declaration gives some indication of Locke's influence on Jefferson.

John Locke and the Declaration

In his influential work *The Declaration of Independence: A Study in the History of Political Ideas* (1922), historian Carl Becker treats the Declaration as a purely secular expression of Enlightenment thinking. Becker based his thesis on his beliefs that Jefferson was heavily influenced by John Locke and that Locke's writings imply that nature is a better way to know God's will than the Bible.

Many writers disagree with Becker's view. They assert that, though Locke was an Enlightenment thinker, a close examination of his writings makes it clear that Locke is neither a deist nor a secularist. In *Starting with Locke* (2011), Greg Forster (a recognized Locke scholar and a conservative Christian) writes positively about Locke while recognizing Locke's theological deficiencies.

It is important to note that even Christians who admire Locke admit he was not entirely orthodox and that he wanted deists and others tolerated within Anglicanism. In this way, he contributed to the doctrinal decline of the Anglican church in the eighteenth century.

Declaration of Independence—1776 to Today

The Declaration of Independence truly embodies the "Spirit of '76." Largely the work of Thomas Jefferson, it opens with one of the most powerful and eloquent statements of personal liberty, proceeds to enumerate the "repeated injuries and usurpations" that George III committed against his American subjects, and concludes that separation from Britain is necessary. Serious men debated, wrote, and signed the Declaration—men who pledged to each other and to future generations their "lives, [their] fortunes, and [their] sacred honor." The spirit of liberty in the

Declaration became the rallying cry for Patriots and freedom.

The actual document has had a fascinating history all its own. During the early years of the Republic, the Declaration, though valued, was not viewed as a national treasure. The youthful country, lacking a sense of history and pressured by the demands of war and peace, gave little thought to the parchment. When the British burned Washington during the War of 1812, the document was taken away in a linen sack and stored overnight in a barn in northern Virginia.

Following the War of 1812, however, America's growing appreciation for its heritage brought the Declaration into the national spotlight—a position it has retained ever since. But, as historian Dumas Malone noted about the Declaration, "While immortal in spirit, it was by no means imperishable in form." Handling, temperature changes, and the fading

effects of light greatly harmed the old parchment. Even restoration attempts sometimes did damage. In 1940 a detached corner of the document was crudely repaired with tape that turned the color of molasses within a few years.

However, new technology has increased the Declaration's long-term survival chances. In 1952, shortly before being moved to the National Archives in Washington, the document was placed in a helium-filled case with sensors to monitor humidity and other atmospheric conditions. Nearly fifty years later the Declaration was moved again to an even more sophisticated case, as were the Constitution and the Bill of Rights. Perhaps the most interesting evidence of the value Americans place on their Declaration of Independence came after the Japanese attacked Pearl Harbor in 1941. The Declaration was transferred from Washington and stored with the gold in a vault at Fort Knox, Kentucky, for almost three years.

What Were They Reading?

Jefferson and his peers relied on many sources as they formed a new government. Group the students and instruct each to gather information about one of the following writers on whose work the Founding Fathers relied:

- John Locke
- Montesquieu
- William Blackstone
- Algernon Sidney

Each group should write a report that includes information on the writer's background, major writings, and major contributions to political theory.

Activity 2: John Locke's Views Regarding Government

This activity contains some excerpts from John Locke's *Two Treaties of Government*. In the document Locke defends the Glorious Revolution that occurred in England in 1688. Many of his ideas were later used in the writing of the Declaration of Independence. This activity provides another opportunity for students to analyze original sources.

Jefferson's Beliefs

Thomas Jefferson's deism is manifest in a project he undertook while he was president. Jefferson compiled for his own use a version of the New Testament that eliminated any references to Christ's miracles or His deity. (He later misplaced that "Bible" and compiled another one, which is now housed at the Smithsonian.) Jefferson denied the infallibility of Scripture, believing that the apostle Paul and the Gospel writers corrupted Jesus' teachings and were guilty of "giving their own misconceptions as [Jesus'] dicta [teachings], and expressing unintelligibly for others what they had not understood themselves."

Nevertheless, Jefferson was by no means unaffected by Christianity. He believed that Christ's teachings were "the most sublime and benevolent code of morals which has ever been offered to man." How tragic that a man as educated and gifted as Jefferson would praise Christian morals but, evidently, fail to embrace the salvation that Christ offers.

The Unanimous Declaration of the Thirteen United States of America

When in the course of human events, it becomes necessary for one people to dissolve the political bands which have connected them with another, and to assume among the powers of the earth, the separate and equal station to which the laws of nature and of nature's God entitle them, a decent respect to the opinions of mankind requires that they should declare the causes which impel them to the separation.

We hold these truths to be self-evident, that all men are created equal, that they are endowed by their Creator with certain unalienable rights, that among these are life, liberty and the pursuit of happiness. That to secure these rights, governments are instituted among men, deriving their just powers from the consent of the governed. That whenever any form of government becomes destructive of these ends, it is the right of the people to alter or to abolish it, and to institute new government, laying its foundation on such principles and organizing its powers in such form, as to them shall seem most likely to effect their safety and happiness. Prudence, indeed, will dictate that governments long established should not be changed for light and transient causes, and accordingly, all experience hath shewn, that mankind are more disposed to suffer, while evils are sufferable, than to right themselves by abolishing the forms to which they are accustomed. But when a long train of abuses and usurpations, pursuing invariably the same object, evinces a design to reduce them under absolute despotism, it is their right, it is their duty, to throw off such government, and to provide new guards for their future security. Such has been the patient sufferance of these colonies; and such is now the necessity which constrains them to alter their former systems of government. The history of the present king of Great Britain is a history of repeated injuries and usurpations, all having in direct object the establishment of an absolute tyranny over these states. To prove this, let facts be submitted to a candid world.

He has refused his assent to laws, the most wholesome and necessary for the public good.

He has forbidden his governors to pass laws of immediate and pressing importance, unless suspended in their operation till his assent should be obtained; and when so suspended, he has utterly neglected to attend to them.

He has refused to pass other laws for the accommodation of large districts of people, unless those people would relinquish the right of representation in the legislature, a right inestimable to them, and formidable to tyrants only.

He has called together legislative bodies at places unusual, uncomfortable, and distant from the depository of their public records, for the sole purpose of fatiguing them into compliance with his measures.

He has dissolved representative houses repeatedly, for opposing with manly firmness his invasions on the right of the people.

He has refused for a long time, after such dissolutions, to cause others to be elected whereby the legislative powers, incapable of annihilation, have returned to the people at large for their exercise; the state remaining in the meantime exposed to all the dangers of invasion from without, and convulsions within.

He has endeavored to prevent the population of these states; for that purpose obstructing the laws for naturalization of foreigners; refusing to pass others to encourage their migrations hither, and raising the conditions of new appropriations of lands.

He has obstructed the administration of justice, by refusing his assent to laws for establishing judiciary powers.

He has made judges dependent on his will alone, for the tenure of their offices, and the amount and payment of their salaries.

He has erected a multitude of new offices, and sent hither swarms of officers to harass our people, and eat out their substance.

He has kept among us, in times of peace, standing armies without the consent of our legislatures.

He has affected to render the military independent of and superior to the civil power.

He has combined with others to subject us to a jurisdiction foreign to our constitution, and unacknowledged by our laws; giving his assent to their acts of pretended legislation:

For quartering large bodies of armed troops among us:

For protecting them, by a mock trial, from punishment for any murders which they should commit on the inhabitants of these states:

For cutting off our trade with all parts of the world:

For imposing taxes on us without our consent:

For depriving us in many cases, of the benefits of trial by jury:

Historic Words

Select some of the opening lines of the Declaration for the students to memorize and then recite or write.

Grievances

The Declaration of Independence contains a list of grievances that the colonists directed toward King George III. Assign one grievance to each student. Since the Declaration often states the grievances in general terms, direct the students to research specific details about their assigned grievances. Their findings can be presented in one-page reports or in brief oral presentations.

Next, guide a discussion regarding whether the grievances met the standard established by John Locke. Remind the students that Locke said rebellion was acceptable when a government becomes tyrannical. (Adherence to that idea would mean that the biblical requirement to submit to government would not apply to citizens of that government).

Ask students the following: How can people legitimately declare a government is tyrannical? Would a single abuse of power lead to such a designation? The likely answer will be that repeated problems and repeated violations of freedom would be necessary.

Discuss the significance of the phrase "a long train of abuses and usurpations" mentioned in the Declaration of Independence.

For transporting us beyond seas to be tried for pretended offenses:

For abolishing the free system of English laws in a neighboring province, establishing therein an arbitrary government, and enlarging its boundaries so as to render it at once an example and fit instrument for introducing the same absolute rule into these colonies:

For taking away our charters, abolishing our most valuable laws, and altering fundamentally the forms of our governments:

For suspending our own legislatures, and declaring themselves invested with power to legislate for us in all cases whatsoever.

He has abdicated government here, by declaring us out of his protection, and waging war against us.

He has plundered our seas, ravaged our coasts, burnt our towns, and destroyed the lives of our people.

He is at this time transporting large armies of foreign mercenaries to complete the works of death, desolation, and tyranny, already begun with circumstances of cruelty and perfidy scarcely paralleled in the most barbarous ages, and totally unworthy the head of a civilized nation.

He has constrained our fellow citizens taken captive on the high seas to bear arms against their country, to become the executioners of their friends and brethren, or to fall themselves by their hands.

He has excited domestic insurrections amongst us, and has endeavoured to bring on the inhabitants of our frontiers, the merciless Indian savages, whose known rule of warfare, is an undistinguished destruction of all ages, sexes and conditions.

In every stage of these oppressions we have petitioned for redress in the most humble terms: our repeated petitions have been answered only by repeated injury. A prince whose character is thus marked by every act which may define a tyrant, is unfit to be the ruler of a free people.

Nor have we been wanting in attentions to our British brethren. We have warned them from time to time of attempts by their legislature to extend an unwarrantable jurisdiction over us. We have reminded them of the circumstances of our emigration and settlement here. We have appealed to their native justice and magnanimity, and we have conjured them by the ties of our common kindred to disavow these usurpations, which, would inevitably interrupt our connection and correspondence. They too have been deaf to the voice of justice and of consanguinity. We must, therefore, acquiesce in the necessity, which denounces our separation, and hold them, as we hold the rest of mankind, enemies in war, in peace friends.

We, therefore, the representatives of the united states of America, in general congress assembled, appealing to the Supreme Judge of the world for the rectitude of our intentions, do, in the name, and by authority of the good people of these colonies, solemnly publish and declare, that these united colonies are, and of right ought to be free and independent states; that they are absolved from all allegiance to the British Crown, and that all political connection between them and the state of Great Britain, is and ought to be totally dissolved; and that as free and independent states, they have full power to levy war, conclude peace, contract alliances, establish commerce, and to do all other acts and things which independent states may of right do. And for the support of this declaration, with a firm reliance on the protection of divine Providence, we mutually pledge to each other our lives, our fortunes, and our sacred honor.

The lap desk on which Jefferson wrote the Declaration

Thomas Jefferson Reads His Declaration

Invite "Thomas Jefferson" to present the Declaration before the class. Ask someone in your school, church, or community to read the Declaration in a way that emphasizes its language. Encourage the person to dress in period clothing; and if he is knowledgeable about Jefferson, ask him to field questions from the class.

The Signers' Religious Views

A list, such as the one on this page of the student text, can provide only a general picture of the signers' religious beliefs because some religious affiliations are denominational and others are not. It is possible, for example, for someone to attend an Episcopal church and be a deist (Jefferson is an example) or to be both a Congregationalist and a Unitarian. Probably half the Declaration's signers were deists or had deistic leanings.

Deism was on the rise in the eighteenth century and reached its peak during the revolutionary and early national periods. Yet even at its peak, it was limited primarily to some of the intellectuals that graduated from colleges that had grown theologically liberal. This explains why a mixture of orthodox and unorthodox men participated in the founding of our country. In the early nineteenth century, by God's grace, the nation moved in a decidedly evangelical direction.

Secularists sometimes use the deism of some of the founders to argue that Christianity should be excluded from political discussions. But the founders, even those influenced by deism, were not hostile toward religion's influence in public life. Many, though not orthodox Christians themselves, believed that Christianity had an important role in fostering morality in the nation.

provided a rationalistic way for people with different religious backgrounds to agree about morals and legislation.

The Declaration proceeded to list grievances against King George, stating that he had not only neglected the colonists' rights but also sought actively to destroy them. Their attempts at reconciliation had failed, and some colonists believed that fighting for independence was their only alternative against submitting to what they believed to be tyranny. The Declaration claimed for the colonies the political authority to conduct foreign affairs, which had previously been the role of Great Britain, as proof of their independence.

Jefferson drafted the Declaration and submitted it to the other committee members. Franklin and Adams made minor changes, and the committee submitted the document to Congress on June 28, 1776. On July 2, Congress approved the Declaration. Late in the afternoon of July 4, the final draft was ready. It would take several days, even weeks, for news to spread throughout all the colonies. Although the document had been approved, the official copy was not prepared and signed until August 2. As president of the Continental Congress, **John Hancock** signed first with a large, bold signature. He reportedly said, "There, King George will be able to read that without his spectacles."

As the War for Independence raged, two developments shaped America's emerging politics. First, the Second Continental Congress functioned as the national government. The various roles of government, such as controlling finance and foreign relations, were largely managed by committees. Second, by 1777 new state governments were formed that superseded colonial administrations. Since local representative government was viewed as a check against tyranny, the power of state legislatures was enhanced and executive power was weakened. Also, the states resisted yielding their taxing power to the Continental Congress. Having removed Parliament's interference in their local affairs, they were not eager to submit to another "outside" government, though they would cooperate when it was in their best interest to do so. These two factors—a weak legislative central government and strongly independent state governments—molded the nature of United States government during the formative years following the American victory in the War for Independence.

The Articles of Confederation

After independence was declared in 1776, the Second Continental Congress endeavored to establish a central government based on the consent of the newly formed state governments; the result was the **Articles of Confederation**. Supported by advocates of states' rights such as Patrick Henry and Thomas Jefferson, the articles proposed a central government with characteristics very similar to those of the provisional Second Continental Congress. At the same time, the articles bound the various states into a "firm league of friendship." By November

Faith of the Founding Fathers

Consider sharing the following reference materials with your class: Gregg L. Frazer's *The Religious Beliefs of America's Founders: Reason, Revelation, and Revolution*, Edwin S. Gaustad's *Faith of the Founders: Religion and the New Nation, 1776–1826*, and David L. Holmes's *The Faiths of the Founding Fathers*.

Neighboring States

Although the Bible says little about how states in a union should treat each other, it says much about the relationship of neighbors in general. Encourage your students to review the following verses and apply them to interstate relations.

Specifically consider the issues of resources, labor, law, aid, defense, and diplomacy.

- Psalm 101:5
- Proverbs 3:28–29
- Proverbs 11:12
- Proverbs 14:21
- Proverbs 16:29
- Proverbs 24:28
- Proverbs 25:9
- Proverbs 25:17–18
- Matthew 19:19
- Romans 15:2

1777, the Articles of Confederation were sent to the thirteen states for approval. This approval process, called **ratification**, required the unanimous consent of the states and was therefore difficult to complete. Eleven states ratified the articles quickly. New Jersey followed by 1779, but Maryland did not do so until 1781 because of a squabble with Virginia over western land claims. The ability of one state to impede the others under the Articles' provisions was a sure indication of problems to come.

The Articles provided broad powers to the states, as detailed in Article II.

> Each state retains its sovereignty, freedom, and independence, and every power, jurisdiction, and right, which is not by this Confederation expressly delegated to the United States, in Congress assembled.

The national government consisted of a **unicameral**, or one-house, legislature without a national executive or judiciary. Members of the Confederation Congress were chosen for one-year terms in a manner determined by each state legislature. States could send from two to seven representatives, but each state had only one vote in the national assembly regardless of the size of the state's population or delegation.

The crucial weakness of the Articles of Confederation was the national government's inability to enforce its policies. For example, Congress was authorized to build a navy and establish a banking system, but it could only *request* funds from the states; it could not levy taxes. Strapped for cash, the Confederation Congress once proposed a modest import duty, only to be thwarted by Rhode Island. During its existence, the Confederation government barely had enough funds for basic operating expenses.

Congress was also authorized to raise an army and declare war if necessary, yet the national government could only *request* the states' cooperation in such an effort. In fact, when the Barbary pirates seized American ships and crews in the Mediterranean, the Confederation Congress could not afford to pay the demanded ransom, much less raise a navy to crush the pirates.

The weakness and ineptitude of this Congress did not encourage men of action and vision to participate. For only three days during the period from October

Articles of Confederation		
Weakness	**Federalist Papers** debate	**Constitution solution**
Congress was unable to take action directly against individuals.	No. 15	Art. VI, clause 2
Congress lacked power to enforce federal law.	No. 21	Art. I, Sec. 8, clause 15; Article II
Congress lacked power to raise revenue through taxes.	No. 21	Art. I, Sec. 8, clause 1
Congress lacked power to regulate commerce.	No. 22	Art. I, Sec. 8, clause 3
Congress lacked power to raise military forces.	No. 22	Art. I, Sec. 8, clauses 12–13
Regardless of size, each state had one vote in Congress.	No. 22	Art. I, Sec. 2, clause 3
Unanimous agreement of states was needed to amend the articles.	No. 22	Article V
There was no provision for national courts.	No. 22	Art. III, Sec. 1
Congress consisted of only one house (unicameral).	No. 22	Art. I, Sec. 1
Articles were not ratified by the people (through conventions).	No. 22	Article VII
Congress lacked sole power to coin money.	No. 44	Art. I, Sec. 8, clause 5
Government lacked separation of powers.	No. 84	Art. I, Sec. 1; Art. II, Sec. 2; Art. III, Sec. 2

Northwest Ordinance

The government under the Articles of Confederation was by no means totally ineffective. For example, while the Constitutional Convention was meeting, the Confederation Congress enacted the Northwest Ordinance, which provided a system of government for western lands stretching north of the Ohio River to the Great Lakes and west to the Mississippi River. Each of the territories that the ordinance created (eventually there were five) was to be administered initially by a governor, a secretary, and three judges appointed by Congress. When the number of free adult males in a territory reached five thousand, the territory could elect a bicameral legislature and send a nonvoting member to Congress. When a territory had sixty thousand free inhabitants, it could apply for statehood on an equal footing with already-existing states. The Northwest Ordinance also provided western citizens with a bill of rights and forbade slavery. Historian Ray Allen Billington commented that the Northwest Ordinance of 1787 "did more to perpetuate the Union than any document save the Constitution."

What If?

Guide a discussion about what might have occurred if the Articles of Confederation had been retained. First, discuss whether the Union would have stayed together. What issues might have pulled it apart? How would the Confederation affect relations with other countries? Next, examine how our government would be different today if the Articles of Confederation were still in effect. What would be the major benefits or drawbacks of that situation?

1785 to May 1786 was there a quorum of states present to conduct business. Obviously, state legislatures had little regard for the Confederation Congress. Most were occupied with commercial disputes and petty jealousies with their neighboring states. George Washington expressed his fears for the nation in a letter to James Madison in 1786: "No morn ever dawned more favourably than ours did; and no day was ever more clouded than the present. Wisdom and good examples are necessary at this time to rescue the political machine from the impending storm."

Calls for Change

The deteriorating condition of the Confederation government was viewed with disappointment and alarm by those men who had worked so diligently to secure American independence. John Hancock wrote, "How to strengthen and improve this union, so as to render it more completely adequate, demands the immediate attention of these states. Our very existence as a free nation is suspended upon it." John Jay also voiced his concern about the weak Confederation: "I am uneasy and apprehensive; more so than during the war." George Washington shared Jay's fears: "We are fast verging to anarchy and confusion. . . . Thirteen sovereignties pulling against each other; and all tugging at the federal head; will soon bring ruin on the whole."

Two events focused the states' attention on the national government's woes and triggered changes that would result in a redefinition of national union. First, a commercial dispute between Virginia and Maryland over navigation rights on the Potomac River brought representatives from both states to Alexandria, Virginia, in 1785 to negotiate a settlement. The hospitable George Washington invited the men to meet at his home, **Mount Vernon**, just a few miles away. The meetings were friendly and quite productive, settling in just three days matters of navigation, fishing rights, and uniform currency. Hoping to apply the success of the Mount Vernon meetings on a national scale, where commercial disputes were nagging problems, the Virginia legislature called on all the states to send representatives to Annapolis, Maryland, in September 1786 to "recommend a federal plan for regulating commerce."

George Washington's home, Mount Vernon

Unanimous Consent

To demonstrate the difficulties of acquiring unanimous consent, as the Articles of Confederation required, ask the students to vote on a series of school or classroom issues. Allow each student one vote. If unanimous consent is not achieved, engage in debate and make compromises and concessions to try to achieve unanimous consent on a subsequent vote. (The students must have legitimate reasons for their votes. They should not vote against the majority just to cause a deadlock. However, they may initiate a stalemate regarding an issue about which they have little interest if that helps them gain an advantage on an issue about which they have strong beliefs.)

Too Weak? Too Strong?

The United States no longer suffers from a weak central government, such as that under the Articles of Confederation. In fact, some argue, the present federal government dominates state and local governments and may be too strong. Contrast these two situations, and discuss the problems of each.

The **Annapolis Convention** was poorly attended. Only five states sent representatives, amounting to only a dozen delegates, but the convention provided the setting for a momentous invitation. Alexander Hamilton drafted a proposal that his fellow delegates quickly accepted—namely, that the states send delegates to Philadelphia in May 1787 to "devise such further provisions as shall appear to them necessary to render the constitution of the Federal Government adequate to the exigencies [needs] of the Union." In the meantime, the call to convene received an added sense of urgency because of some disgruntled farmers in western Massachusetts.

Economic depression plagued the nation during the postwar period. It was fueled by wartime disruptions and by the Confederation Congress's inability to deal with interstate commerce disputes or to restrict the circulation of inflationary paper money. These hard times resulted in a popular uprising in Massachusetts in 1786 and 1787: Daniel Shays led a small army of debtor farmers to close county courthouses to prevent farm foreclosures and prison sentences for indebtedness. The Massachusetts state government, which had resisted the debtors' repeated calls for reform and assistance, dispatched a large force that easily routed the farmers.

Shays's Rebellion

Shays's Rebellion resulted in little bloodshed, and all its leaders, including Shays, were quickly pardoned. However, its real impact lay in the fear of anarchy generated throughout the state legislatures. This fear convinced many to support a revision of the Articles of Confederation. In fact, just one month after the battle between the farmers and the militia, the Confederation Congress gave its reluctant endorsement to the proposed meeting in Philadelphia.

As early as 1781, Alexander Hamilton understood that "the republic is sick and wants powerful remedies." The Confederation's symptoms of weakness only worsened as the pressures of governing revealed the Confederation's chronic defects. The "powerful remedies" Hamilton prescribed would be devised in Philadelphia throughout the long, hot summer of 1787.

Section Review

1–3. In what three major areas did England influence American colonial government?

4–5. What two events in 1760 brought about changes in British colonial rule that would eventually lead to American independence?

6. Beginning in 1773, what were some actions Americans took in an attempt to obtain relief from Britain's tightening control?

7–8. What two significant political factors during the War for Independence profoundly molded the nature of the United States government following the war?

9. What was the crucial weakness of the Articles of Confederation?

★ Is natural law apart from Scripture a sufficient basis for human law? Why or why not?

★ How did Shays's Rebellion impact America?

Shays's Rebellion

In a letter to James Madison on November 5, 1786, Washington expressed his thoughts about Shays's Rebellion.

What stronger evidence can be given of the want of energy in our governments than these disorders? If there exists not a power to check them, what security has a man for life, liberty or property? To you, I am sure I need not add aught on this subject, the consequences of a lax, or inefficient government, are too obvious to be dwelt on. Thirteen sovereignties pulling against each other, and all tugging at the federal head, will soon bring ruin on the whole; whereas a liberal, and energetic constitution, well guarded & closely watched, to prevent encroachments, might restore us to that degree of respectability & consequence, to which we had a fair claim, & the brightest prospect of attaining.

Review Answers

1–3. local government, legislative government, and limited government (p. 55)

4–5. Montreal surrendered to the British; George III ascended to the throne. (p. 56)

6. tea boycott began; Boston Tea Party occurred; First and Second Continental Congresses convened (pp. 57–58)

7–8. a weak legislative central government (the Second Continental Congress) and strongly independent state governments (p. 62)

9. the inability of the national government to enforce its policies (p. 63)

★ Though medieval Christians and Enlightenment philosophers would answer yes (for different reasons), Reformation leaders tended to disagree. They believed that both creation and the minds of unregenerate people are corrupted by the Fall (Rom. 8:5–6; Eph. 4:17–18). This corruption, their followers would say, skews people's perception of natural law. This is more evident today than at the time of our nation's founding because religious pluralism has increased. The various viewpoints in modern America result in many competing value systems.

★ Fear of anarchy spread throughout the states; many became convinced that the Articles of Confederation must be revised to handle the problems with governing.

1. Outline the three major compromises reached at the Constitutional Convention.
2. Analyze the role of political compromise in a free society.

Violated Instructions

Many of the state legislatures instructed their delegations to the Constitutional Convention to only amend or improve the Articles of Confederation but nothing more. In proposing, debating, and voting on a totally new governmental system, those delegates violated their instructions.

News Blackout

George Washington insisted on the news blackout "lest [the delegates'] transactions get into the newspapers and disturb the public repose."

1. What three major compromises were reached at the Constitutional Convention?
2. What is the role of political compromise in a free society?

George Washington (below); the Assembly Room in Independence Hall, where the Constitution was written (bottom)

II. Constitutional Convention

Toward a New Government

Rain fell steadily, offering a cool change from the oppressive heat that had settled on the city. The wet weather halted the sewer construction that was underway as rain filled the trenches and washed mud down the untidy streets. As the delegates entered the door of the State House (now known as Independence Hall) in their dripping cloaks and hats, they bore little resemblance to the "demi-gods" that Jefferson declared them to be. Yet as they gathered in the Assembly Room where eleven years earlier the Declaration of Independence had been signed, a sense of anticipation arose—they knew they were making history. Madison boasted that their work would "decide forever the fate of republican government."

On that rainy morning of May 25, **1787**, the **Constitutional Convention** began (it was originally called the Philadelphia Convention). Ahead of the delegates lay four months of difficult debates and tough questions. At first, the discussions moved rapidly. The first item of business was to choose a president of the convention. **George Washington**, whose very presence helped ensure the success of the delegates' work in the people's eyes, was elected unanimously to head the convention.

Next, two important procedural rules were adopted, the first being a rule of secrecy. No discussion of the con-

A Day in the Convention

Assign each student to research one of the days on which the Constitutional Convention was in session. The students can research the days using Madison's notes, Max Farrand's *Records of the Federal Convention of 1787*, and other resources readily available on the internet. Each student should present his findings in a one- or two-page paper that includes a paragraph summary of the day's events, background information concerning the major speakers of the day, and an explanation of any major constitutional issues that were addressed.

vention's activities was to take place outside the hall. This rule was designed to reduce speculation in the newspapers and protect the delegates from unnecessary public pressure. Although it is difficult to imagine such a rule working today over a four-month period without a single leak to the press, it worked in 1787. Fortunately, records of the convention's activities do exist. Several delegates kept notes, and the secretary of the convention, William Jackson, kept an official journal that recorded the delegates' resolutions and votes. The most-detailed notes, however, were made by the man whose political knowledge and immense influence earned him the title Father of the Constitution—**James Madison**. Like many other delegates, Madison chose not to publish his notes immediately. In fact, his notes were not published until 1840, more than fifty years after the convention and four years after his death.

> *"When you are in the minority, talk; when you are in the majority, vote."*
>
> —*Roger Sherman*

The second procedural rule that the convention adopted was to organize as a committee of the whole. This meant that the entire assembly could function as a committee, permitting informal discussions and flexibility in voting. This decision greatly facilitated the essential compromises that were to come.

After setting the ground rules, the delegates faced the question of whether the Articles of Confederation should be scrapped altogether or simply revised. On May 30, acting on a resolution by Gouverneur Morris of Pennsylvania, the delegates agreed overwhelmingly that "a national government ought to be established consisting of a Supreme Legislative, Judiciary, and Executive." Remarkably, just five days after the assembly convened, the most fundamental question was settled. A new national government—restructured and redefined—would provide the leadership to make the United States united, both in name and in fact.

Conflicts and Compromises

Not everything continued as smoothly as it had during the convention's opening sessions. Because the delegates represented various states and regional interests, difficult issues lay ahead of them; the delegates would need patience, wisdom, and flexibility to hold the convention together. Three major issues required compromise: representation, slavery, and commerce.

Representation

How the states were to be represented in the new government was surely the most difficult question for the delegates. The battle lines were drawn between the states with large populations (such as Virginia, Pennsylvania, and Massachusetts) and the states with smaller populations (such as New Jersey, Delaware, and Maryland).

James Madison gave a great deal of thought to the composition and structure of the new Congress. His thorough study

Chronology of the Constitutional Convention (1787)	
May 14–24	Preliminary meetings
May 25–28	Organization
May 29	Proposal of Randolph (Virginia) Plan and Pinckney Plan
June 15	The Paterson (New Jersey) Plan and revolt of the "small-state" delegations
June 15–30	Two weeks of debate over the two major plans
June 30	Compromise committee appointed
July 5	Report of the compromise committee proposing that there be proportional representation in the lower house and equal representation in the upper house and that all money bills should originate in the lower house
July 16	Compromise adopted
August 15–23	Debate on the powers of Congress (Art. I, Sec. 8 and 9)
August 24–25	Debate on the powers of the president
August 29	The "three-fifths" clause, the slave trade, and the commerce clause
September 12	Report of the Committee of Style and Arrangement
September 17	Signing of the Constitution and adjournment

James Madison

James Madison, the Father of the Constitution, was elected to the Continental Congress when he was twenty-nine. Madison was one of the most formidable political thinkers of his day and was well-read in the major works of the Enlightenment, especially those by Voltaire, Diderot, Montesquieu, and Locke. Madison's detailed diary of the convention is the most complete record available of the floor debate. In a comment about his remarkable journal, Madison recalled, "I was not absent a single day, nor more than a casual fraction of an hour in any day, so that I could not have lost a single speech unless a very short one."

Benjamin Franklin's Ride

In 1787, Benjamin Franklin was eighty-one years old and virtually immobilized with gout and gallstones. To avoid being jostled in a carriage, he rode in a glass-windowed sedan chair that was imported from Paris and carried by prisoners from Philadelphia's Walnut Street Jail.

Biographies of the Delegates

Instruct each student to research one of the delegates to the Constitutional Convention by investigating that delegate's background, occupation, religious life, and impact on the debates or the ratification process. Create a one-page template that the students can use to present their findings. Leave an area on the handout for each student to write a one- or two-paragraph summary about the delegate. Also include a square where each student can place a copy of the delegate's portrait. The students' completed biographical sketches can be compiled into a binder or PDF for reference.

The Virginia Plan vs. the New Jersey Plan		
	Virginia Plan	**New Jersey Plan**
Author	James Madison	Collaboration
Presenter	Edmund Randolph	William Paterson
Balance of power	Strong national powers	Strong state powers
Executive branch	• Consists of one executive • Chosen by legislative branch • Able to veto acts of Congress	• Consists of several men • Chosen by legislative branch • No veto power
Judicial branch	• One supreme court (possibly more), plus lower courts • Appointed by legislative branch • Able to veto acts of Congress	• One supreme court • Appointed by executive office • Appointed for life • No veto power
Legislative branch	• Bicameral congress • Able to override executive- and judicial-branch vetoes	• Unicameral congress • Limited powers to tax and to regulate trade
Representation in Congress (See illustration on page 70.)	• House of Representatives chosen by the people • Senate chosen by the House of Representatives from nominees submitted by state legislatures • Both chambers based on population or revenue	• Equal representation of states in Congress

and careful planning resulted in a proposal known as the **Virginia Plan**, which became the basis for much of the Constitution.

Madison's Virginia Plan, which was introduced to the convention by Edmund Randolph, advocated a **bicameral**, or two-house, congress. The number of representatives was to be based on state population or on the amount of revenue a state provided for the national government. Election to the House of Representatives would be by popular vote. This lower house would, in turn, elect members of the Senate, the upper house, from nominees submitted by the state legislatures.

In contrast to the Confederation Congress, the legislature under the Virginia Plan was given greatly expanded powers. For example, the new Congress would be able to enforce its laws over the states and elect both the chief executive and the judicial branch. These two branches, the executive and the judicial, could jointly veto congressional acts, although their veto could be overridden by a vote in both houses of Congress.

Since representation under the Virginia Plan was based on state population, the plan naturally favored the larger states. The smaller states quickly reacted to this proposal, setting forth what they called the **New Jersey Plan**. Presented by William Paterson of New Jersey, this plan advocated a unicameral congress, maintaining the one-state, one-vote principle of the Confederation. Congress, under the New Jersey Plan, would also elect a "federal executive" of more than one person. These members could be removed by a majority vote of the state governors.

The convention nearly reached a deadlock over the issue of how representation would be determined. John Dickinson, representing Delaware, conceded that "some of the members from the small States wish for two branches in the General Legislature, and are friends to a good National Government." "But," he added, "we would sooner submit to a foreign power, than submit to be deprived of an equality of suffrage, in both branches of the legislature, and thereby be

Prudent Compromise

The art of political compromise is still necessary today. Discuss some current legislation in Congress or in your state or local government. Often, an issue will be divided along party lines.

Choose a controversial issue, and clearly define the two or more positions regarding it. Ask the students what they think each side wants to achieve. Then ask whether there is a compromise solution. You might want to divide the class into several groups and ask each to suggest a solution. In each case, discuss whether the proposed compromise is acceptable from a Christian perspective. Emphasize to students the importance of prudence (the wisdom to know how to best achieve a goal and to discern what can be compromised and what cannot).

Follow the legislative process in Congress or in your state or local government to learn the final outcome for the controversial issue. Was a compromise successfully reached? Did both sides gain something while giving up something else? If so, was the compromise a good solution?

thrown under the domination of the large States." While the small states feared disenfranchisement through domination, the large states feared disenfranchisement through lack of representation, arguing that basic democratic principles favor proportional representation.

For weeks, long debates and short tempers, aggravated by the hot weather, threatened to break up the convention and, with it, hopes for a strong, stable government. Roger Sherman of Connecticut, influenced by Benjamin Franklin, offered the embroiled assembly a solution to its dead-end debating. Sherman was a Christian who had an unwavering testimony for Christ. John Adams referred to him as "that old Puritan, honest as an angel." Sherman put together a skillful compromise that salvaged both the convention and the Constitution. The

Roger Sherman: Uncompromising Compromiser

"He was a man of approved integrity; a cool, discerning Judge; a prudent, sagacious politician; a true, faithful, and firm patriot. He ever adorned the profession of Christianity which he made in youth; and, distinguished through life for public usefulness, died in the prospect of a blessed immortality."

These words from Roger Sherman's tomb testify of the personal and public faith of one of America's Founding Fathers. Sherman became a member of the First Continental Congress in 1774 at age fifty-three. During his years as a public servant, he placed his signature on the Articles of Association of 1774 (which proposed a boycott of British goods), the Declaration of Independence, the Articles of Confederation, and the Constitution—the only person to sign all four. He also served on the five-member committee responsible for drafting the Declaration of Independence. During the debate over constitutional representation, Sherman made his most notable contribution through the Connecticut Compromise.

A fellow representative once said, "If I am absent during the discussion of a subject, and consequently know not on which side

to vote, I always look at Roger Sherman, for I am sure if I vote with him I shall vote right." Among his peers, Sherman had a reputation for wisdom, honesty, and integrity. Thomas Jefferson labeled him "a man who never said a foolish thing in his life," and Nathaniel Macon said, "Roger Sherman had more common sense than any man I ever knew."

What made Sherman's "common sense" so uncommon was that it was rooted in his faith and public walk with God. From his youth, Sherman had professed Christ and made his faith foremost in whatever he endeavored to do. In his early years he was a shoemaker, a merchant, and a surveyor. His skills as an astronomer were great enough for him to supply calculations for a New York almanac. Besides serving in national government, he was mayor of New Haven and a distinguished lawyer. His career included a judicial appointment to the Connecticut Supreme Court. Sherman emphasized prayer and daily Bible reading to his fifteen children. A devoted son, he cared for his aged mother in his own home. He was also classified as a theologian by the likes of John Witherspoon, Jonathan Dickinson, and Jona-

than Edwards, with whom he corresponded. His church in New Haven, Connecticut, asked him to help revise its creed. Statements from that document show Sherman's firm belief in the biblical truth by which he lived: "I believe that God . . . did send his own son to become man, die in the room and stead of sinners, and thus to lay a foundation for the offer of pardon and salvation to all mankind, so as all may be saved who are willing to accept the gospel offer."

Few politicians, past or present, clearly exemplify such obedience to God's command for government leaders to be "minister[s] . . . for good" within society (Rom. 13:4).

Reaction to Franklin's Request for Prayer

Though Franklin's recommendation for prayer had support, several delegates opposed it because they feared public opinion. They said that they would receive harsh criticism for starting prayers after having had several weeks of sessions, leading the public to suspect that the convention was struggling. Others noted that the public would react worse if they rejected the proposal than if they were late in beginning a good thing. A final objection came in the reminder that the convention had no funds, not even enough to provide for a chaplain's services. The convention voted to adjourn rather than vote on Franklin's suggestion. When the delegates reconvened, they did not mention the matter again, and deliberations continued without public prayer.

Representation Solution?

Like William Paterson, David Brearley (another delegate from New Jersey) hotly opposed proportional representation in the national legislature. Perhaps in jest, he proposed that if the large states insisted on such a scheme, Congress should erase the existing boundaries and divide the country into thirteen equal parts.

Character Counts

Roger Sherman was distinguished by his reputation for honesty, integrity, and wisdom. Sherman's example is a logical starting point for a discussion regarding the qualities of a good politician. Instruct each student to list at least five qualities that a politician should possess, along with one or two passages of Scripture about those qualities. Conclude the activity by discussing the need for Christian politicians like Sherman, whose faith affected all areas of his life.

Heated Debate

Neither side immediately accepted Roger Sherman's compromise. Although Sherman first proposed it on June 30, it was initially rejected.

At one point, Gunning Bedford of Delaware made a particularly pointed attack on the delegates of the large states: "I do not, gentlemen, trust you." And he warned that, rather than face ruin from the Virginia Plan, the small states might look elsewhere for help—to "foreign powers who [would] take [them] by the hand." Such a remark was too strong even for like-minded delegates. Rufus King of Massachusetts hoped that it arose only from "passion" and noted that he would "never . . . court a foreign power" for relief.

Extensive debate continued regarding Sherman's proposal. On July 16, the Connecticut Compromise was approved.

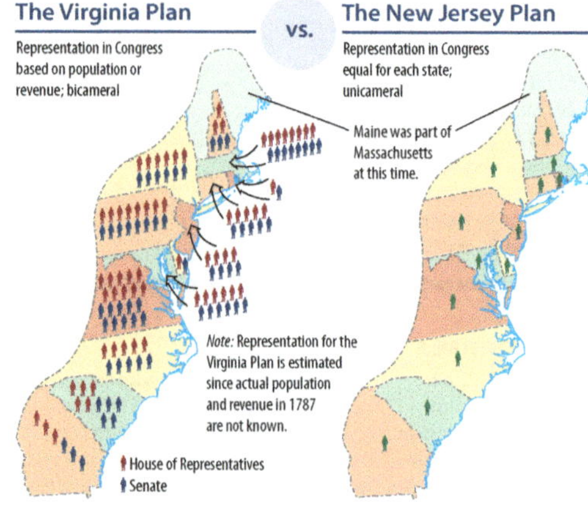

The Great Compromise

House of Representatives		Senate	
Virginia	New Jersey	Virginia	New Jersey
Based on population		Same number from each state	

Effect of Three-Fifths Compromise on the House of Representatives
3rd US Congress, 1793

	Free	Slaves*	Representatives not counting slaves	Representatives counting slaves
PA	430,636	3,737	13	13
MD	216,692	103,036	7	8
VA	454,983	292,627	14	19
SC	141,979	107,094	4	6

Based on the 1790 census and 1 representative per 33,000 people as established by the Apportionment Act of 1792; *(total number of slaves)

Connecticut Compromise, or **Great Compromise**, proposed the bicameral congress mentioned in the Virginia Plan. Representation in the House of Representatives would be based on state population. However, the Senate would have an equal number of representatives from each state, regardless of a state's population. Sherman's proposal is a classic example of political compromise: both sides got something, and both sides were denied something.

Slavery

Another divisive issue confronting the delegates of the Constitutional Convention was whether slaves should be counted in determining congressional representation for states. Almost one-third of the people in southern states were enslaved African Americans. Although slavery existed predominantly in the agricultural South, it was not confined to that region. (Pennsylvania, for example, had several thousand slaves at the time.) Delegates from southern states argued that slaves should be counted. Delegates from states that had few slaves opposed such action, partly because enslaved people could not vote. Consequently, the issue of how slaves should be counted caused heated debates among the delegates.

Finally, the delegates reached a numerical compromise known as the **Three-Fifths Compromise**. Under this unusual settlement, three-fifths of a state's slaves would count toward its representation in the House of Representatives, but a slave state would also have to pay taxes on the slaves at the same rate. This compromise did not resolve the issue of slavery but merely postponed it.

Commerce

The third critical issue was commerce. Part of the original motivation behind calling the Philadelphia Convention was the Confederation's inability to deal with interstate and international trade. While most delegates agreed that Congress needed a role in commerce, they disagreed over the extent of that role. The South was especially concerned that the new Congress might halt the slave trade and try to raise revenue through export duties that would hurt the Southern economy, which depended on the export of raw goods, such as cotton, timber, and indigo.

A compromise, however, settled the issue. The agreement gave Congress power over foreign and interstate commerce. In exchange, the legislative branch was forbidden to interfere with the slave trade for at least twenty years (until 1808) or to impose any export duties on the states.

How to Count Slaves

The issue of whether or not slaves should be counted in determining congressional representation for states was contentious at the Constitutional Convention.

Why was the matter significant? *Counting all slaves would greatly benefit states with a large number of slaves by dramatically increasing their representation in the House of Representatives. Conversely, not counting them would significantly weaken slave states' political influence.*

Why did opponents of slavery criticize the Compromise? *They argued that it further institutionalized slavery and made discussions about emancipation of slaves less likely. They also did not think that even a fraction of a population that had no voters should be counted for representative purposes.*

Two Great Leaders

Of the fifty-five delegates who participated in the Constitutional Convention, two left notable imprints on the final document. The governmental ideas of James Madison laid the foundation of much of the Constitution's content, and the writing style and literary eloquence were largely the work of Gouverneur Morris of Pennsylvania.

Gouverneur Morris was a brilliant attorney and writer who, in 1777 at the age of twenty-five, helped draft the New York State Constitution. He served in the Continental Congress, signed the Articles of Confederation, and then became the most outspoken delegate at the Constitutional Convention. He was a persuasive debater with a colorful personality. Years later, he represented Pennsylvania in the US Senate (1800–1803).

During the convention, the thirty-five-year-old Philadelphia lawyer used his wooden leg to pound the floor for emphasis during some of his many speeches.

James Madison of Virginia, who would later become the nation's fourth president, has often been called the Father of the Constitution. He was only thirty-six years old at the time of the convention, but he possessed a wealth of knowledge about governmental forms and constitutional law. He formulated major points for the new government and frequently offered his thoughts in convention debates. His ideas formed the Virginia Plan, although he did not take personal credit for it, and he spoke more times during the Philadelphia meetings than did any other delegate except Morris. He not only stayed active in the meetings' debates but also managed to take meticulous notes, preserving the best-detailed account of the event.

After the delegates reached agreement on most points of their governmental plan, they selected Madison, Morris, and three other men to be the Committee of Style and Arrangement. Morris took the lead.

Morris turned a mass of ideas into an organized document with clarity and style. As Madison later wrote, "The finish given to the style and arrangement of the Constitution fairly belongs to the pen of Mr. Morris. . . . A better choice could not have been made, as the performance of the task proved."

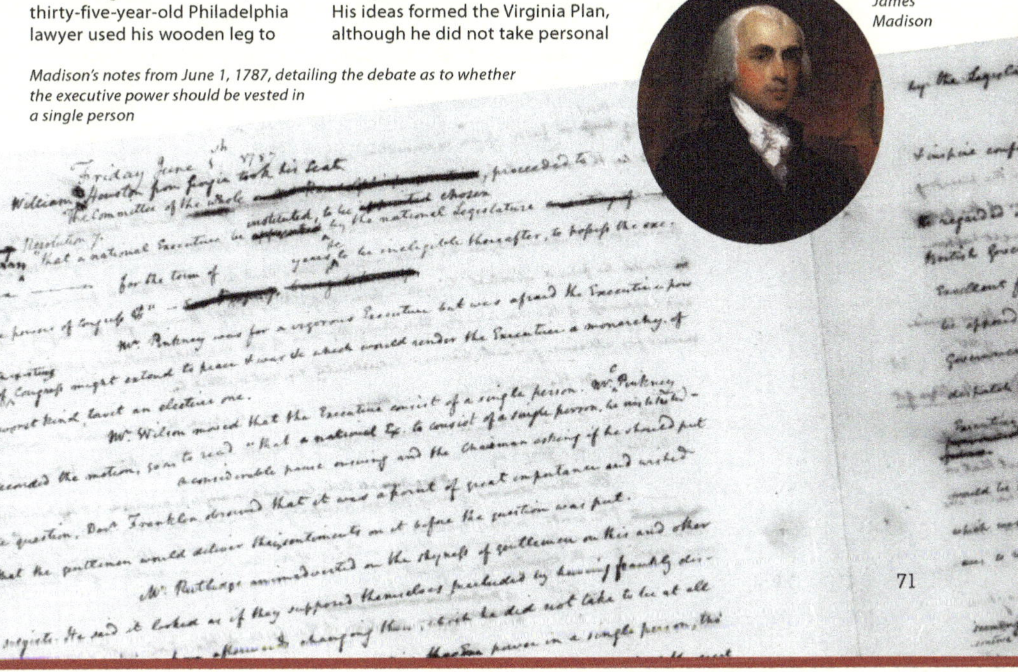

Gouverneur Morris

James Madison

Madison's notes from June 1, 1787, detailing the debate as to whether the executive power should be vested in a single person

71

Activity 3: The Constitution and Limited Government

This activity develops the students' analytical and evaluation skills.

An Economic Interpretation

In 1913, historian Charles A. Beard published his influential work *An Economic Interpretation of the Constitution of the United States*. Beard, a progressive, argued that the founders were motivated primarily by economic self-interest rather than by ideals or a desire to promote the greater good. By arguing that the Constitution was selfishly created, Beard hoped to advance the notion that the Constitution should be interpreted to meet society's changing economic and social needs. Supreme Court Justice Oliver Wendell Holmes Jr. was unhappy with what he called the "covert sneer" that ran through the work.

Beard classified the delegates into categories based on their source of wealth. Those who were most likely to gain from the Constitution, he argued, were those with personalty (personal property, such as stocks and bonds). Those who were least likely to gain held their wealth in the form of realty (land).

Subsequent historians, such as Forrest McDonald and Robert Brown, contended that Beard's categories were arbitrary and artificial. Brown also noted that any increase in the delegates' wealth after 1787 proved little about their interests before the convention. The delegates, like anyone else watching the ratification process, could anticipate financial opportunities.

Other Agreements

Besides the three major compromises, many other agreements helped fashion the language of the Constitution and shape our national government. For instance, a dispute over the election of the president was resolved through the creation of the Electoral College, which gave direct power to neither the people nor Congress but to intermediate electors. The issue of power over treaties was resolved by giving the president power to make them but then requiring the Senate to approve the treaties. It should be no surprise that the Constitution has been referred to as a "bundle of compromises."

Much of the Constitution, however, did not require compromise. Its authors readily agreed on broad, basic principles, such as limited government. The constitutional compromises primarily dealt more with procedure than with principle.

Compromise is an important part of our political process. Differences of opinion are only natural in a free society. Therefore, when legislators representing various regions and interests meet to make laws, compromise and flexibility are often necessary to get a majority to agree. The politically involved Christian must exercise wisdom when asked to compromise. He must ask himself whether the issue is moral. If it is a moral issue, he must ask whether it is something that should be legislated. He must also determine whether the political disagreement is over the goal or the means for reaching it.

Although the constitutional compromises created mixed emotions among the delegates and the states, they drew the states together into a working union despite sectional differences. On **September 17, 1787**, after four months of exhausting work, the delegates gathered to sign the official engrossed copy of the Constitution. It was not a perfect document, but, as Madison correctly observed, no human government is perfect; therefore, he noted, "that which is the least imperfect is . . . the best government."

Some delegates viewed the Constitution as considerably flawed and refused to sign it. Several prominent leaders, including George Mason of Virginia, objected that it lacked a bill of rights to safeguard individual liberty. In his notes from the convention, Madison recorded Mason's blunt statement that "he would sooner chop off his right hand than put it to the Constitution." Such opposition foreshadowed the difficult months ahead as the Constitution endured the scrutiny of the ratification process throughout the states.

Section Review

1–2. What two key procedural rules, established at the beginning of the Constitutional Convention, greatly facilitated the convention's progress?

3. Who is known as the Father of the Constitution?

4. What major agreement did the Constitutional Convention reach after only five days of meetings?

5. What questions should a Christian legislator ask himself when asked to compromise?

★ Identify the three major areas in which delegates to the Constitutional Convention had to compromise, and explain the reasoning behind those compromises.

★ Why do people in a free society need to make political compromises?

No Perfect Government

Use Madison's remarks in the next to last paragraph of this student page and the questions below as a springboard for discussion. What are some imperfections of our government?

What is the perfect government? When will a perfect government exist? *when Christ's kingdom is established on earth*

Section Review Answers

1–2. a rule of secrecy outside the convention hall; organization of the convention as a committee of the whole (pp. 66–67)

3. James Madison (p. 67)

4. The convention would establish a new national government—restructured and redefined. (p. 67)

5. Is the issue a moral one? Is it something that should be legislated? Is the disagreement over the goal or the means to reach it? (p. 72)

★ representation (Some wanted representation based on state population, but others wanted equal state representation, so the delegates compromised by establishing a bicameral legislature in which one house had equal representation by state and the other house had representation by population.)

slavery (Some wanted to count slaves toward representation, but others did not, so the delegates compromised by counting three-fifths of any state's slaves toward representation while taxing them at the same rate.)

commerce (The delegates disagreed about the role Congress should have in regulating trade. A compromise gave Congress power over foreign and interstate commerce. In exchange, the legislative branch was forbidden to impose any export duties on the states or to interfere with the slave trade for at least twenty years, until 1808.)

★ Compromise is an important part of the political process. Disagreements are common and addressing those issues is essential for governing to take place.

III. Ratification Controversy

The public speculation that had been brewing for weeks about the closed-door convention was quelled with the publication of the Constitution in Philadelphia's daily, the *Pennsylvania Packet*, just two days after the delegates adjourned. But the months ahead held perhaps the most difficult and crucial political struggle that the Republic has ever known—the fight for ratification. Madison summarized the issue thus:

> The question on which the proposed Constitution must turn is the simple one, whether the Union shall or shall not be continued. There is in my opinion no middle ground to be taken.

As the signers of the Constitution traveled home to sell the new government, nagging questions plagued their minds. Article VII required that the Constitution be approved by nine of the thirteen states. But the disapproval of one or more powerful states, such as Virginia or Massachusetts, would be enough to scuttle the Union because of the political and geographic divisions it would create.

Special ratification conventions were held in each state. The **Federalists**, as advocates of the Constitution were called, were pitted against the **Anti-Federalists**, who opposed the new plan of government. Their debates were fierce, their pens tireless, and their votes often close. No national organization directed either the pro- or antiratification forces, and the states often debated the Constitution's merits in light of petty local issues.

The Federalist Papers

The Anti-Federalist forces wasted no time in their attacks on the Constitution. Just one week after the text was first published, a New York newspaper began a series of Anti-Federalist articles written under the pseudonym Cato. Cato was in fact the governor of New York, George Clinton. Other articles denouncing the works of the Philadelphia Convention soon appeared. They used the aliases Brutus and Sydney.

Alexander Hamilton, returning from the convention, responded to the Anti-Federalist charges with newspaper articles of his own under the pen name Publius (Latin for "public man"). Hamilton enlisted the help of James Madison and John Jay in this war of words. From October 1787 through the following spring, the trio wrote eighty-five well-reasoned essays that were widely read not only in New York but also in other states where ratification lay in the balance.

Of the eighty-five essays, all signed "Publius," Hamilton wrote over half, and Madison wrote about one-third. Jay, who became seriously ill during the project, wrote five essays. A few were joint efforts by Hamilton and Madison. The essays were compiled and published in two volumes in May 1788 as **The Federalist Papers**. This work answered the Anti-Federalists' objections by carefully explaining and forcefully defending constitutional provisions of power and predicting dire consequences if the Constitution were rejected. Hamilton warned in *Federalist* No. 1 that the "fate of an empire" hung upon the question

Alexander Hamilton

James Madison

John Jay

Guiding Questions

1. On what matters did Federalists and Anti-Federalists disagree?
2. Why was the ratification of the Constitution such a significant event?

Section III Objectives

1. Analyze the arguments presented by the Federalists and Anti-Federalists.
2. Explain the significance of the ratification of the Constitution.

Public Debate and Pseudonyms

In the colonies and Great Britain, there was a long tradition of public debate through the writing of sophisticated essays. Benjamin Franklin, for example, once wrote a series of fourteen articles under the pen name Silence Dogood for the *New England Courant*; and he later started the Junto, or Leather Apron Club, in which members wrote essays on political and intellectual issues and debated them. Such essays often attempted to imitate the style of classical Roman writers, and their authors frequently used Roman pseudonyms.

Publius, the pen name of the Federalists, means "the people" or "the public man." The Anti-Federalist name Brutus referred to two famous Romans: the supposed founder of the Roman Republic in 509 BC, and a conspirator who helped assassinate Julius Caesar on the grounds that Caesar was suppressing political freedom in Rome. The name Cato referred to an earlier opponent of Caesar who became a martyr of the Roman Republic. The name Sydney, another Anti-Federalist pseudonym, referred to Algernon Sidney (1622–83), a Whig leader executed for treason based on questionable evidence during the reign of Charles II.

Powerful Ideas

The fight for ratification is a reminder that not all conflicts are settled on the battlefield. Federalists and Anti-Federalists fought a war of ideas. Although the maxim "The pen is mightier than the sword" might be a cliché, Alexander Hamilton and many other authors used the pen to great advantage during the ratification process. Discuss today's war of ideas with your students. Examine how ideas are spread in our culture. Also discuss ways that Christians can spread ideas contained in God's Word. You might suggest that the students follow the example of the participants in the ratification debate by writing the editor of your local paper about a current issue. Students might also post their opinions on a blog or forum online.

The Main Essays in *The Federalist*

The following Federalist essays are considered the best of *The Federalist Papers*: Nos. 1, 2, 6, 9, 10, 14–16, 23, 37, 39, 47–49, 51, 62–63, 70, 78, and 84–85.

The Finger of God

Some of the founders saw God's providential hand in the writing of the Constitution. Alexander Hamilton said that "without the finger of God, [the Constitution] never could have been suggested and agreed upon by such a diversity of interests." In *Federalist* No. 37, James Madison wrote, "It is impossible for the man of pious reflection not to perceive in [the creation of the Constitution] a finger of that Almighty hand which has been so frequently . . . extended to our relief in the critical stages of the revolution."

However, unlike the Declaration of Independence the Constitution makes no reference to God. That concerned many American Christians in the eighteenth century. In contrast, an analysis by Pew Research has found that today God or the divine is mentioned at least once in each of the fifty state constitutions. Overall, the terms appear two hundred times in those fifty documents.

The Federalist Papers Today

Although *The Federalist Papers* was written more than two hundred years ago, many of its topics are still current issues. Whether the topic is defense spending, term limits, tax policies, or presidential nominations, *The Federalist Papers* offers important insight into the people who helped establish the American government. But *The Federalist Papers* was not always accurate in its predictions. For instance, Alexander Hamilton stated that the Senate would rarely reject nominees to office chosen by the president. He did not foresee that the rise of political parties would make some nominations contentious. Still, *The Federalist Papers* often reveals how American government works and, even more importantly, the tradition or values upon which the Founding Fathers based their decisions.

Presidential pardons offer a good example of how government works. Every president has the opportunity to offer pardons—usually done at the end of his term of office. In *Federalist* No. 74, Hamilton explains why such a power was given to one man.

> The President. . . . is also to be authorized to grant "reprieves and pardons for offenses against the United States, except in cases of impeachment." . . . The criminal code of every country partakes so much of necessary severity, that without an easy access to exceptions in favor of unfortunate guilt, justice would wear a countenance too sanguinary [bloody] and cruel. As the sense of responsibility is always strongest, in proportion as it is undivided, it may be inferred that a single man would be most ready to attend to the force of those motives which might plead for a mitigation of the rigor of the law, and least apt to yield to considerations which were calculated to shelter a fit object of its vengeance. The reflection that the fate of a fellow-creature depended on his *sole fiat* would naturally inspire scrupulousness and caution.

Regarding pardons of treason, Hamilton continues,

> But the principal argument for reposing the power of pardoning in this case to the Chief Magistrate [the president] is this: in seasons of insurrection or rebellion, there are often critical moments, when a well-timed offer of pardon to the insurgents or rebels may restore the tranquillity of the commonwealth; and which, if suffered to pass unimproved, it may never be possible afterwards to recall. The dilatory [delay-causing] process of convening the legislature, or one of its branches, for the purpose of obtaining its sanction to the measure, would frequently be the occasion of letting slip the golden opportunity. The loss of a week, a day, an hour, may sometimes be fatal.

These justifications for presidential pardon—the opportunity to show mercy and provide necessary peace—help explain Gerald Ford's pardon of Richard Nixon in 1974. They also show how a president might abuse his power by using the presidential pardon for purposes that the Founding Fathers did not intend. Like the Constitution, *The Federalist Papers* is more than just a collection of historical documents. It continues to provide insight into today's issues through the wisdom of yesterday's leaders.

"[The Federalist Papers is] the single most authoritative source of insight into the original intentions of the Constitution's framers."

—Robert T. McKenzie, historian

of ratification and that the states could expect danger and dismemberment if the Anti-Federalists got their way.

Considering the circumstances under which *The Federalist Papers* was written, it is a remarkable work, a comprehensive commentary on republican government. In fact, Jefferson called it the "best commentary on the principles of government which ever was written."

A Closer Look

Encourage each student to examine one of the essays in *The Federalist Papers* or an essay by an Anti-Federalist. In a one-page report, each student should identify (1) who wrote the essay, (2) when it was written, (3) what main topics it addresses, and (4) the argument(s) that the author states. In addition, the students could research any examples used in the essays' arguments and comment on them. They should also note any political philosophers/writers quoted in the essays.

Potent Papers

Guide an examination of some current issues that are directly addressed in *The Federalist Papers*. Provide a copy of *The Federalist Papers*, and look at the following essays for these topics:

- Security and defense: Nos. 23–29
- State powers: Nos. 44–45
- Separation of powers: Nos. 47–49
- Taxation: Nos. 30–36
- Checks and balances: No. 51
- House of Representatives: Nos. 52–61
- Senate: Nos. 62–66
- President: Nos. 67–77
- Judiciary: Nos. 78–83

Battles in Virginia and New York

Delaware led the way by unanimously ratifying the Constitution on December 7, 1787. Within about two months five more states added their consent to the Constitution. However, the toughest fights lay ahead in Virginia and New York, where the Anti-Federalists were better led and organized. Although the required nine states ratified by June 1788, the stakes were quite high, since the consent of both these key states was crucial to the success of the new government. In a very practical sense, nine were not enough. If New York failed to ratify, New England would be separated from the rest of the nation; and if Virginia voted nay, that vote would sever the South.

In Virginia the Federalist forces were led by James Madison, while the Anti-Federalists had the fiery orator Patrick Henry as their spokesman. Henry was joined by two nonsigning Constitutional Convention delegates—Governor Edmund Randolph (who eventually changed his mind and voted with the Federalists) and George Mason. Richard Henry Lee, who had signed the Declaration of Independence, also opposed ratification. However, the Anti-Federalists' boast that they were the true heirs of 1776 rang rather hollow since George Washington and Thomas Jefferson (after some persuasion from Madison) supported the Constitution.

Motives of the Anti-Federalists varied. Some used the ratification issue to further their political ambitions. Others opposed the Constitution because they opposed the national government's power to tax. Others, including Patrick Henry, opposed it because it curbed state

Chronology of the Ratification of the Constitution	
Delaware	Ratified 30–0 (December 7, 1787)
Pennsylvania	Ratified 46–23 (December 12, 1787)
New Jersey	Ratified 38–0 (December 18, 1787)
Georgia	Ratified 26–0 (January 2, 1788)
Connecticut	Ratified 128–40 (January 9, 1788)
Massachusetts	Ratified 187–168 (February 6, 1788)
Maryland	Ratified 63–11 (April 28, 1788)
South Carolina	Ratified 149–73 (May 23, 1788)
New Hampshire	Ratified 57–47 (June 21, 1788)
Virginia	Ratified 89–79 (June 25, 1788)
New York	Ratified 30–27 (July 26, 1788)
North Carolina	Rejected 184–84 (August 4, 1788); finally ratified 194–77 (November 21, 1789)
Rhode Island	Ratified 34–32 (May 29, 1790)

Source: Adapted from *The Convention and the Constitution* by David G. Smith

Patrick Henry

Edmund Randolph

George Mason

Richard Henry Lee

Patrick Henry

Patrick Henry was a fearless defender of personal liberty. The Virginian is best remembered for his demand at St. John's Church in Richmond in March 1775. There he proclaimed, "Give me liberty, or give me death!"

Henry refused to attend the Constitutional Convention, saying that he "smelt a rat." After the Constitution was ratified, however, he supported it.

Activity 4: Patrick Henry, Anti-Federalist

This activity gives the students experience in analyzing original sources (in this case, excerpts from speeches by Patrick Henry).

George Mason said at the Richmond Convention, "Grant us amendments . . . and we will cheerfully . . . unite with those who advocate it [the Constitution]."

How Federalists and Anti-Federalists Differed

The Federalists and Anti-Federalists differed in their philosophies of government. The Federalists supported a strong central government while the Anti-Federalists focused on strong state governments. The following issues were among those debated during the ratification process, and they illustrate the differing viewpoints of the two sides. (The Federalists' viewpoints on these issues are taken from Essays 10 and 14 of *The Federalist Papers*, in which Madison defends the Constitution.)

1. The Proposed Constitution and Convention Legitimacy

Federalists: Believed they had the right to construct a new document because they were appointed to the Constitutional Convention by legitimate means.

Anti-Federalists: Thought that the convention should have amended the Articles of Confederation and that delegates exceeded their bounds when writing the Constitution.

2. The Fate of the Union and the States Under the Proposed Constitution

Federalists: Believed that the strength of the government outlined in the proposed Constitution would be sufficient to protect the people's liberties and general good. Believed that weakness would encourage the Union to split into separate confederacies.

Anti-Federalists: Opposed breaking up the Union but said that the proposed Constitution was not the answer. Thought that it would demote the states to administrative districts and take away the people's liberties and self-government rights.

3. The Lack of a Bill of Rights

Federalists: Thought that a bill of rights was unnecessary since the Constitution did not give the federal government power to interfere with or infringe on individual rights. (Some Federalists, such as John Adams and Thomas Jefferson, wanted to include a bill of rights.)

Anti-Federalists: Presented as the strongest argument against the proposed Constitution its lack of a bill of rights (because the Constitution had no provision to defend individual civil liberties).

4. Amending the Constitution

Federalists: Believed that the amending process under the Articles of Confederation was too difficult since all states had to agree on a single issue.

Anti-Federalists: Said that the proposed Constitution's amending process was too easy and that unanimous consent of all the states was a more appropriate method.

The ratification process was not limited to these issues. Other matters debated were the presidency, powers and representation of Congress, the judiciary, a permanent national capital, slavery, and religious tests for voting and holding office. These debates over the Constitution's ratification proved to be the most important in American history.

power. Henry, a strong advocate of states' rights at Virginia's ratification convention in Richmond, even challenged the wording of the Preamble: "Who authorized them to speak the language of, 'We, the People,' instead of 'We, the States'?" he asked. "States are the characteristics, and the soul of a confederation."

Henry and his colleagues feared that the consolidation of power in the hands of a strong national government would be a step toward tyranny. They and Anti-Federalists in other states were unhappy with the absence of a bill of rights protecting individual liberty. Federalists were not opposed to personal freedom, but many of them thought that a list of specified rights was unnecessary. Hamilton thought that a bill of rights would, in fact, be dangerous since specifying rights might more easily invite the government to assume power in *unspecified* areas.

On this point, however, the Virginia Federalists eventually compromised, agreeing to send recommendations for amendments in conjunction with ratification. Madison pledged that following ratification he would do everything possible to see that a bill of rights became law. That compromise and pledge swayed a few undecided delegates, and the Constitution was approved in Virginia by a vote of 89–79.

Ratification Debate

Stage a debate between "Federalists" and "Anti-Federalists" regarding various questions at issue during the struggle for ratification. The students should identify the arguments by key Federalists and Anti-Federalists.

As part of this debate, invite students to analyze which arguments better align with the biblical purposes of government identified in Chapter 1. They may conclude that on a given argument both sides fail to align or that both sides equally meet the biblical purposes of government. In some cases, they may argue that one side's view fulfills the purposes more than the other.

At the Same Time

In late April 1789 George Washington was inaugurated as the first president. Shortly afterward, the French Revolution began. Refer students to the Declaration of the Rights of Man and the Citizen. It was the defining French document of the early Revolution and was adopted in August 1789. Thomas Jefferson was in Paris as the US ambassador at the time and actually edited and helped craft this document.

Discuss the changes made to government in the United States with the ratification of the Constitution compared to those made in France during the French Revolution. Note the significant differences between the violence that became commonplace in France and the peaceful establishment of the new government in the United States.

Meanwhile, a similar battle raged in Poughkeepsie, New York. New York was the last major obstacle to constitutional government, and Governor Clinton and his Anti-Federalist forces held a commanding majority in the ratifying convention against the pro-Constitution delegates led by Hamilton. However, with the news of the Federalist victory in Virginia, the New York Anti-Federalists suffered a fatal setback. A number of Clinton's delegates, perhaps thinking of their own political futures, defected to the Constitution camp when they realized that the collapse of the Virginia Anti-Federalists made their own opposition a lost cause. By a slim margin, New York approved the Constitution on July 26, 1788, becoming the eleventh state to ratify.

The words of the Constitution now became the reality of working government. Elections for Congress were set, and a date fixed—March 4, 1789—for its members to meet in the temporary capital of New York City.

A Nation Arises

George Washington was unanimously chosen by the Electoral College to serve as the first president. He took the oath of office on April 30, 1789, from the balcony of Federal Hall on Wall Street in New York City. The great Virginian placed his hand on the Bible and promised to preserve, protect, and defend the Constitution, adding, "So help me God." He then kissed the Bible. The streets filled with the sound of cheering crowds, ringing bells, and booming cannon salutes. The experiment in liberty had begun.

The Constitution is not a perfect document, but it has demonstrated remarkable durability and adaptability for well over two centuries. It has also provided a model of successful self-government for other nations, confirming the observation

George Washington sworn in as the first president of the United States

Activity 5: Chapter Review

This activity contains chapter review questions that help reinforce the students' recognition skills and aid in test preparation.

Inauguration Bibles

George Washington was sworn in using a large leather-bound Masonic Bible. The same Bible was also used by Warren Harding, Dwight Eisenhower, and George H. W. Bush. George W. Bush intended to use it, but because of its fragility and inclement weather on Inauguration Day, he used a family Bible instead.

Several other presidents have used family Bibles, including Lyndon Johnson, Jimmy Carter, and Ronald Reagan. Occasionally, the Bible has been opened to a particular passage of Scripture. Woodrow Wilson used Psalm 119, and Calvin Coolidge used John 1. Ronald Reagan had his Bible opened to 2 Chronicles 7:14, a text about repentance and seeking God.

At least five presidents, including Barack Obama and Donald Trump, have used two Bibles during inaugural ceremonies. In 2009 and 2013, Obama used the Bible on which Abraham Lincoln took the oath for his first term in 1861. In 2013 he also used a second Bible, one that had been owned by slain civil rights leader Martin Luther King Jr. (When January 20 falls on a Sunday, as it did in 2013, presidents take the oath of office twice—in a private ceremony that day and again at a public ceremony the following day. During the private ceremony on Sunday, January 20, 2013, Obama used a Bible belonging to his wife's grandmother. The next day at the public ceremony, he used the Lincoln and King Bibles.)

In 2017, Donald Trump used a Bible that was a gift from his mother in 1955 (given shortly before his ninth birthday) and the Lincoln Bible that had been used in the previous two inaugurations.

of British prime minister William Gladstone that it was "the most wonderful work ever struck off at a given time by the brain and purpose of man."

Washington's inauguration was both an end and a beginning. It marked an end to the struggle to gain liberty and self-government that began in 1776, and it heralded a *national* beginning. Benjamin Franklin put it best in 1787, while observing the delegates signing the Constitution. Madison recorded that

> Doctor Franklin, looking towards the President's chair, at the back of which a rising sun happened to be painted, observed to a few members near him, that painters had found it difficult to distinguish in their art, a rising, from a setting, sun. I have, said he, often and often, in the course of the session, and the vicissitudes of my hopes and fears as to its issue, looked at that behind the President [of the Convention], without being able to tell whether it was rising or setting; but now at length, I have the happiness to know, that it is a rising, and not a setting sun.

Section Review

1–5. Who were the main leaders of the Anti-Federalists?

6–8. Who were the main leaders of the Federalists?

9–10. What were the two most crucial state conventions in the ratification of the Constitution?

11–12. What factors led to the final approval of the Constitution in the two most crucial states?

★ Explain the two major arguments Patrick Henry presented against adoption of the Constitution. Do you agree or disagree with those arguments? Defend your answer.

★ How significant was *The Federalist Papers*? Explain your answer.

The Rising Sun chair, mentioned by Benjamin Franklin, can be seen at Independence Hall in Philadelphia.

Section Review Answers

1–5. George Clinton, Patrick Henry, Edmund Randolph, George Mason, and Richard Henry Lee (p. 75)

6–8. Alexander Hamilton, James Madison, and John Jay (p. 73)

9–10. the conventions in Virginia and New York (p. 75)

11–12. A few undecided Virginia delegates were swayed by Madison's promise to do everything possible to obtain a bill of rights, and some New York Anti-Federalists switched sides after the Virginia Anti-Federalists failed to block ratification. (pp. 75–77)

★ It curbed state power and it lacked a bill of rights. Answers will vary regarding the second part of the question.

★ They were crucial to ratifying the Constitution. They not only addressed the objections of Anti-Federalists, they also provided a commentary on the principles of republican government. In addition, they helped persuade many people that the Constitution should be adopted.

Making Connections

1–3. Explain three major ways in which colonial governments were influenced by English government.

4–6. Explain three English actions that threatened colonial governments and angered many colonists.

7. On what fundamental issue did the delegates to the Constitutional Convention quickly agree?

8–9. Identify the states where the greatest threat to the ratification of the Constitution existed. What compromise was the deciding factor in the success of ratification?

Developing Civics Skills

1. Evaluate the efforts of the Second Continental Congress to create a central government.

2. Were the Articles of Confederation doomed to fail? Why or why not?

Thinking Critically

1. How did Jefferson justify the colonies' break with England in the Declaration? Do you agree with that justification? Defend your answer with scriptural reasons.

2. With which position—Federalist or Anti-Federalist—do you agree with? Defend your answer.

Living as a Christian Citizen

1. When the government does something that seems unjust, how should a Christian respond? Consider Jeremiah 22:13–17; Acts 16:37–39; 22:25–28; 1 Timothy 2:1–4; 1 Peter 2:13, 21–23; 3:13–17.

2. Propose some alternatives to the Three-Fifths Compromise and explain the strengths and weaknesses of each. Discuss the likelihood that the alternative would have received the approval of the Constitutional Convention or the states.

People, Places, and Things to Remember

local governments
legislatures
House of Burgesses
limited government
boycott
First Continental Congress (1774)
Second Continental Congress
Loyalists
Declaration of Independence
Thomas Jefferson
Age of Enlightenment
social contract theory
deism
John Hancock
Articles of Confederation
ratification
unicameral
Mount Vernon
Annapolis Convention
Shays's Rebellion
Constitutional Convention (1787)
George Washington
James Madison
Virginia Plan
bicameral
New Jersey Plan
Connecticut (Great) Compromise
Three-Fifths Compromise
September 17, 1787
Federalists
Anti-Federalists
The Federalist Papers

Thinking Critically

1. Jefferson based his argument on humans' unalienable rights established by natural laws. According to Jefferson, since the king had repeatedly violated those rights, the colonists were justified in seeking independence. Answers will vary for the second part of the question.

2. Students will provide varying answers, depending on which side they choose to defend.

Living as a Christian Citizen

1. Christians should speak against unjust governmental actions as the prophets did in the Old Testament (Jer. 22:13–17). Following the example of Paul, they should also use legal means to challenge unjust actions (Acts 16:37–39; 22:25–28). Christians should also pray for governmental officials to act justly (1 Timothy 2:1–4). However, Christians should be prepared to suffer injustice for righteousness' sake, knowing that God will eventually judge all rulers (1 Peter 2:13, 21–23; 3:13–17).

2. Answers may include: (1) Counting all persons, even slaves, as full persons for the purpose of representation. This alternative would increase the power of slave states by giving them greater representation in Congress. It would incentivize increasing the slave population of slave states. This alternative was unacceptable to the free states. (2) Counting only free persons for the purposes of representation. This approach would have had the benefit of neither rewarding slavery nor increasing the power of slave states. However, it was unacceptable to the slave states. (3) Representation could have been based on the number of eligible voters. This option also neither rewarded slavery with greater representation nor increased the power of slave states. However, it would have placed an incentive for the states to expand the number of eligible voters, which the founders (with their concern about the excesses of democracy) might have been hesitant to promote.

CHAPTER REVIEW ANSWERS

Making Connections

1–3. From the English, Americans adopted (a) English terminology and organization of local governments, (b) the idea of representative legislatures, and (c) the concept that laws protected individual rights and limited government. (pp. 55–56)

4–6. England passed a series of taxes and trade restrictions, imposed a peacetime army on the colonists, and required colonists to provide food and housing for the army. (pp. 56–57)

7. on the need for a restructured national government (p. 67)

8–9. New York and Virginia; Madison's promise to support a bill of rights (pp. 75–77)

Developing Civics Skills

1. Answers will vary. State governments feared a strong central government and resisted yielding their power, so the Congress under the Articles was weak. The Confederation's primary weakness was its inability to enforce its policies. (pp. 62–63)

2. Yes; among other reasons, the Confederation was unable to enforce its policies. (pp. 62–64)

1. Explain the practical aspects of the Constitution.

2. Outline the foundational principles of the Constitution.

3. Analyze the specific details the Constitution provides regarding the structure and functioning of the American government.

THE UNITED STATES CONSTITUTION

5

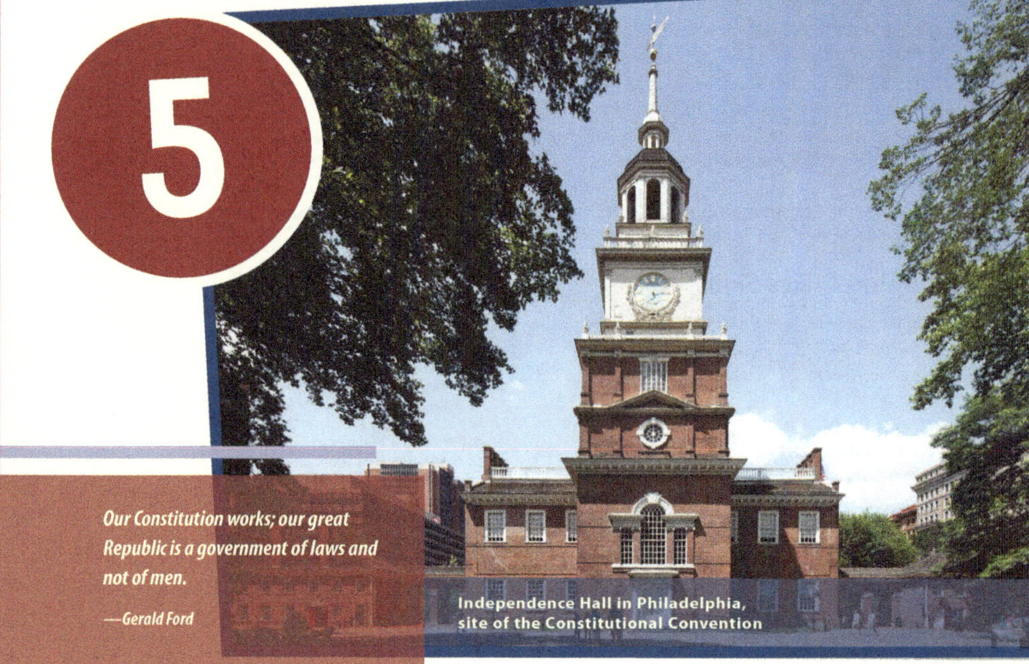

> Our Constitution works; our great Republic is a government of laws and not of men.
>
> —Gerald Ford

Independence Hall in Philadelphia, site of the Constitutional Convention

I. Practical Aspects

II. Foundational Principles

III. Examining the United States Constitution

BIG IDEAS

1. What are some of the practical aspects of the Constitution?

2. What are the foundational principles of the Constitution?

3. What specific details does the Constitution provide regarding the structure and functioning of the American government?

SUGGESTED MATERIALS

Section I
- Activities 1–2 from Chapter 5 of the *Student Activities*

Section II
- Activities 3–4 from Chapter 5 of the *Student Activities*

Section III
- Special speaker (see p. 95)
- List of patent numbers (see p. 99)
- Copy of your state's constitution
- Copies of Supreme Court opinions on treason cases
- Copy of a church constitution
- Maps of the United States

- Copy of Billy Sunday's sermon "Get on the Water Wagon"
- Activity 5 from Chapter 5 of the *Student Activities*

Teacher Resources
Visit TeacherToolsOnline.com for resources to enhance the lessons.

Dwarfed by the glass-and-steel towers of Philadelphia, the old State House still stands, stubbornly resisting the sprawl of the modern metropolis. Over two centuries have dramatically altered the skyline, and the building where the Constitution delegates argued—and eventually agreed—seems locked in the distant past. Those delegates have long ago passed from the scene, their debates have been silenced by time, and the pages of their writings have yellowed with age. Although a few of those delegates became household names, most of them have drifted into obscurity. The Constitution they forged more than two hundred years ago has outlived its creators. Our Constitution, now in its third century of governance, immortalizes principles that transcend its eighteenth-century setting.

Since its inception, the United States has grown from a rural seaboard country of four million to a large industrial superpower. Our Constitution has shown remarkable resilience during that time, shaping and being shaped by the nation's character.

Today our Constitution is the world's oldest in continuous use. But its effect has not been confined to America. The constitutions of most nations have been written or revised since 1970. (Only about a dozen were penned before World War II.) The US Constitution was a model for many of these new constitutions; in fact, the Constitution has been described as America's "most important export."

This chapter offers a closer look at the Constitution, beginning with its practical character and general principles and ending with the actual text of this remarkable cornerstone of our government.

I. Practical Aspects

The Constitution is not an outdated, dusty document; it is a practical tool for governing. The Constitution's success is due to the founders' understanding of human nature and the document's inherent adaptability.

Realistic View of Human Nature

The Constitution's framers wrote with a realistic view of human nature. They recognized humans' desire for freedom and their capacity to govern, but they also had a clear understanding of humans' tendency to sin.

The Constitution, however, is not a Christian document. In fact, God is not mentioned in the work. But the Constitution's framers lived in a society where Scripture was prevalent, and their thinking was often influenced by basic biblical principles. James Madison wrote in *Federalist* No. 51,

> What is government itself, but the greatest of all reflections on human nature? If men were angels, no government would be necessary. If angels were to govern men, neither external nor internal controls on government would be necessary. In framing a government

"The Declaration [of Independence] provided the philosophical basis for a government that exercises legitimate power by 'the consent of the governed.' . . . The Constitution delineated the structure of government and the rules for its operation, consistent with the creed of human liberty proclaimed in the Declaration."

—Edwin Meese III,
US Attorney General (1985–1988)

Fundamental Differences

Guide a discussion about how a different view of human nature might have affected the Constitution. Specifically look at the roles and powers of the executive, legislative, and judicial branches. How might these powers have been combined into a single authority?

Activity 1: Why Was the Constitution Written?

This activity provides experience in analyzing original sources.

Why Is Government Needed?

As noted above, in *Federalist* No. 51, James Madison commented, "If men were angels, no government would be necessary." Though that statement reflects a biblical view of fallen human nature, it is not based on a biblical view of why government exists. Refer to the note at the bottom of page 3 (Chapter 1) for further explanation.

Intentionally Broad

If the framers tried to provide every detail and answer every objection, their work would never have survived the convention. More importantly, a detailed document would have quickly become outdated.

Right to Privacy?

The so-called right to privacy that the Supreme Court noted in some of its rulings in the 1960s was cited in the 1973 *Roe v. Wade* case, which legalized abortion.

which is to be administered by men over men, the great difficulty lies in this: you must first enable the government to control the governed; and in the next place oblige it to control itself.

This distrust of human nature—the realization that people tend to misuse power and to be corrupted by power—was a major reason America's founders divided authority within the national government and included checks and balances to prevent the concentration and abuse of power.

The French Revolution demonstrates what happens when governments are planned around an idealistic, unbiblical view of humans. Radicals during that period hoped to banish Christianity from public life. Consequently, for a time, the nation was governed by the guillotine rather than by moral principles. In contrast, America's Constitution provides a stable, practical guide for governing because it was written by men who understood both their capacity to rule and their need for restraint.

Constitutional Interpretation

The founders understood that they were not prophets who could predict America's future problems or write a document to solve all future problems. Rather they wrote a brief and general charter. The original document is only about four thousand words long, and its twenty-seven amendments extend its length to only about seven thousand words. Unlike some state constitutions, which are over ten times longer, the Constitution is not overladen with detail. Instead, it provides a framework with minimal structure and guiding principles that has the flexibility to meet the demands of change.

Because the Constitution is a guide rather than a detailed manual on governing, it has been open to various interpretations over the years. As early as Washington's administration, people differed over how far such interpretations should go. Those who believe that closely following the text of the Constitution is important and that any interpretation should be kept to a minimum have traditionally been known as **strict constructionists**, while others prefer the term originalists. Those who take a broader and more flexible approach to constitutional interpretation have traditionally been known as **broad constructionists**. They are also called loose constructionists or living constitutionalists.

Constitutional interpretation has contributed to both the document's durability and the controversies surrounding the national charter. Some interpretation arises naturally from the text. For example, America's vast federal bureaucracy, which numbers more than two million civilian employees, is not mentioned in the Constitution; yet Article II, Section 3, states that the president "shall take care that the laws be faithfully executed." The bureaucracy has grown out of the president's responsibility to see that constitutional laws are implemented and programs administered.

Other interpretations are not so readily tied to the text. For example, in the last quarter of the twentieth century, federal courts have issued a number of rulings about a constitutional right of privacy. The founders certainly favored the right of privacy, by which they meant that a law-abiding citizen should be protected from unnecessary government intrusion into his life and home. However, in *Griswold v. Connecticut* (1965) the Supreme Court interpreted amendments such as the Third (which prohibits the forced quartering of soldiers) and the Fourth (which protects citizens from unlawful searches and seizures) to imply a broader constitutional right of privacy. The *Griswold* decision overturned a

The guillotine was used to execute thousands during the French Revolution (1789–1799).

Dilute or Expand

Examine the Supreme Court's interpretation of the Fourth Amendment in *Griswold v. Connecticut* (1965) to explain how a broad interpretation of the Constitution is achieved. In his dissenting opinion, Justice Hugo Black objected to the decision's inference that the Constitution contained a right to privacy. He critically noted,

> One of the most effective ways of diluting or expanding a constitutionally guaranteed right is to substitute for the crucial word or words of a constitutional guarantee another word or words, more or less flexible and more or less restricted in meaning. This fact is well illustrated by the use of the term "right of privacy" as a comprehensive substitute for the Fourth Amendment's guarantee against "unreasonable searches and seizures." "Privacy" is a broad, abstract and ambiguous concept which can easily be shrunken in meaning but which can also, on the other hand, easily be interpreted as a constitutional ban against many things other than searches and seizures.

Discuss the outcomes of adopting such a "broadening" philosophy.

How Should Government Officials Interpret the Constitution?

"[The Constitution] is to be interpreted, as all other solemn instruments are, by endeavoring to ascertain the true sense and meaning of all the terms; and we are neither to narrow them, nor to enlarge them, by straining them from their just and natural import, for the purpose of adding to, or diminishing its powers, or bending them to any favorite theory or dogma of party. It is the language of the people, to be judged of according to common sense, and not by mere theoretical reasoning. It is not an instrument for the mere private interpretation of any particular men."
—*Supreme Court Justice Joseph Story*

"The Constitution was not made to fit us like a straitjacket. In its elasticity lies its chief greatness."
—*Woodrow Wilson*

"Once judges depart from originalism, once they are no longer guided by the original meaning of the Constitution in resolving the cases that come before them, their very claim to the power of judicial review becomes open to question."
—*Keith E. Whittington, Professor of Politics, Princeton University*

"Ultimately, though, I have to side with [Supreme Court] Justice Breyer's view of the Constitution—that it is not a static but rather a living document, and must be read in the context of an ever-changing world.

How could it be otherwise? . . . Anyone looking to resolve our modern constitutional dispute through strict construction has one more problem: The Founders and ratifiers themselves disagreed profoundly, vehemently, on the meaning of their masterpiece. . . . It is unrealistic to believe that a judge, two hundred years later, can somehow discern the original intent of the Founders or ratifiers."
—*Barack Obama*

The US Supreme Court hears arguments regarding the interpretation of the Constitution in this courtroom.

Final Word

The question of who would have the final say in constitutional interpretation was not settled at the Constitutional Convention. Although available records indicate that some of the delegates leaned in favor of the Supreme Court, the issue was never fully debated since its controversial nature might have derailed the whole effort.

In *Federalist* No. 78, Alexander Hamilton was more direct. He said that judges should interpret the law and that the Constitution is the fundamental law of the land. He believed that in a conflict between a legislative enactment and the Constitution, the courts should prefer the Constitution to a statute.

Activity 2: Strict or Broad Constructionist?

This activity enriches the students' analytical and evaluation skills by having them interpret various judges' quotations about the Constitution.

Connecticut law forbidding the sale of contraceptives. It also set a precedent for the courts by which the right to privacy provides an umbrella for a variety of liberal social causes, such as abortion and homosexual rights.

Adapting the Constitution

More than a century ago, Charles Evans Hughes, governor of New York and later a Supreme Court justice, correctly observed, "We are under a Constitution, but the Constitution is what the judges say it is." Given the Constitution's flexibility and general character, interpretations and new applications are to be expected. However, as you will learn in Unit V, when judges depart from the original meaning of the Constitution, they may subject the country to an array of shifting opinions that vary widely based on the opinions of those who sit on the Supreme Court.

Congress also has a role in adapting the Constitution to the nation's needs. Article I, Section 8, clause 18, authorizes Congress "to make all laws which shall be necessary and proper for carrying into execution the foregoing powers, and all other powers vested by [the] Constitution in the government of the United States." The Constitution's framers added this **"necessary and proper clause,"** sometimes called the "elastic clause," to give Congress the authority to complete its tasks.

Congressional legislation often defines the extent of constitutional power. For example, the Constitution grants Congress the right to establish lower courts, which it has done by providing additional courts and judges as the nation and the

backlog of cases have grown. In short, Congress puts the Constitution into practice by writing laws, establishing programs, and appropriating funds to meet national demands within constitutional guidelines.

Presidential actions also apply, expand, and adapt the Constitution. Long-standing executive precedents may carry the weight of law although they are not specifically noted in the Constitution. For example, the founders established no limit on the number of terms a president can serve; however, Washington's self-imposed two-term limit set a precedent that lasted until Franklin

President Obama meeting with advisors in the Oval Office

Roosevelt sought and won third and fourth terms in 1940 and 1944. In response to Roosevelt's precedent-breaking terms, the Twenty-Second Amendment was passed, making the two-term tradition the law.

A president may also *assume* powers that are not specifically given and thus expand the Constitution's meaning and the power of his office. Before passage of the Twenty-Fifth Amendment in 1967, upon the president's death the vice president was authorized to assume the *responsibilities* of the presidency but not necessarily the office itself. When this succession issue was first raised in 1841 by the

Clause for Consideration

Discuss the benefits and inherent dangers of the necessary and proper clause. (*The clause empowers Congress to meet emergency demands, which change over time. But the clause is also potentially dangerous when it is treated as a blank check to expand federal power.*)

death of William Henry Harrison, John Tyler refused the title "Acting President" and assumed full control of the executive branch. Fewer than ten years later, Vice President Millard Fillmore took charge of the White House after the sudden death of President Zachary Taylor. Taylor's cabinet members went through the formality of offering their resignations to Fillmore, not expecting him to accept them, but they were wrong. Fillmore chose a new cabinet, demonstrating his firm grip on the presidential helm despite the absence of a specific constitutional grant of full power.

The Amendment Process

In addition to interpreting and applying the Constitution through the various branches of government, there is a more formal means of adapting the Constitution to meet changing needs—the amendment process.

The Constitution provides for its own amending in Article V. There are two major phases of the amendment process: proposal and ratification. **Amendment proposal** (the formal introduction of an amendment) may be made in two ways: either by a two-thirds vote in both houses of Congress or by a special national convention called at the request of two-thirds of the states. In practice, only the first method has been used; therefore, the proposal process is largely a federal responsibility.

Once an amendment is proposed, it must undergo the formal approval process called **ratification**—a state-level responsibility. Like the proposal process, ratification may also be effected by two means: either by the approval of three-fourths of the states' legislatures or by the approval of three-fourths of special state ratification conventions. The latter method is how the Constitution was originally approved. The choice of ratification method, though, is left up to Congress, and only the Twenty-First Amendment (which repealed Prohibition) has been ratified by state conventions.

The Process of Amending the Constitution

1. Proposal

290 + 67 or **34**

Representatives (⅔)   Senators (⅔)
(If all present and voting)

State legislatures (⅔) request a national convention

2. Ratification

38 or **38**

State legislatures (¾)

State conventions (¾)

Conventional Approach

No amendments have ever been proposed by a national convention because no national conventions have ever been called. Twenty–eight of the many state legislatures have called for a national convention to consider a balanced-budget amendment—only six states short of the required thirty-four.

As noted in the text, the amendment that repealed Prohibition (Amendment XXI) is the only amendment to be ratified by special state conventions.

When to Amend

Because amendments are so difficult to ratify, most interest groups seek other ways to bring about change, usually through legislation or court decisions. In two circumstances is a constitutional amendment desirable: (1) if a proposed law would otherwise be unconstitutional (e.g., a law to establish an income tax or to repeal Prohibition) or (2) if a proposed law addresses a matter of national importance that needs clarification (e.g., a law about presidential succession).

Current Amendments

Amendments are the one legitimate way that present-day Americans can reshape the Constitution. Conduct a search for constitutional amendments that have been considered by the current session of Congress. Discuss the purpose of the amendments, their merits, and their drawbacks. If possible, research the action taken in Congress.

State Amendments

As you discuss this section, assign the students to research the amendment process for your state's constitution. This may be a group or individual project.

Unratified Amendments

Here is the text of a few proposed but unratified amendments.

Anti-title Amendment (1810): "If any citizen of the United States shall accept, claim, receive, or retain any title of nobility or honour; or shall, without the consent of Congress, accept and retain any present, pension, office or emolument of any kind whatever, from any emperor, king, prince, or foreign power, such person shall cease to be a citizen of the United States, and shall be incapable of holding any office of trust or profit under them, or either of them."

Slavery Amendment (1861): "No amendment shall be made to the Constitution which will authorize or give to Congress the power to abolish or interfere, within any State, with the domestic institutions thereof, including that of persons held to labor or service by the laws of said State."

Equal Rights Amendment (1972):
"Section 1. Equality of rights under the law shall not be denied or abridged by the United States or by any State on account of sex.

"Section 2. The Congress shall have the power to enforce, by appropriate legislation, the provisions of this article.

"Section 3. This amendment shall take effect two years after the date of ratification."

Failed Amendments and Proposals

Only thirty-three amendments have ever been proposed for ratification—meaning that they received the necessary two-thirds vote in Congress. Of these, twenty-seven have actually been ratified. However, many more amendments have been submitted for consideration: more than eleven thousand have been offered during more than two centuries. These failed amendments come from all parts of America's political and social landscape and range from the absurd to the profound. On the more serious side, generally, are amendments that passed the proposal stage yet went unratified. These six are listed first, followed by a sampling of amendments that were simply submitted, but never received Congressional approval.

Proposed but Unratified

Article I of the Bill of Rights, 1789

Based representation in the House of Representatives on a system that called for 1 representative for every 30,000 citizens until the total number of representatives reached 100; for 1 representative for every 40,000 until the total number of representatives reached 200; and, finally, for 1 representative for every 50,000 people. Based on this final representative scale, there would be over 6,660 members of the House of Representatives today.

Ratified by eleven states

Anti-title Amendment, 1810

Forbade US citizens to accept any title of nobility from any king, prince, or foreign state. Citizens doing so would have their citizenship revoked and be incapable of holding any office of honor or profit under the United States.

Ratified by twelve states

Slavery Amendment, 1861

Forbade Congress to make any amendment to the Constitution that would give it power "to abolish or interfere" with state domestic institutions, specifically slavery.

Ratified by two states

Child Labor Amendment, 1924

Gave Congress power to "limit, regulate, and prohibit" child labor when workers were under the age of eighteen.

Ratified by twenty-eight states

Equal Rights Amendment, 1972

Provided equality under the law for men and women.

Ratified by thirty-five states (though five of these later revoked their ratification)

Voting Rights for Washington, DC, Amendment, 1978

Provided citizens of Washington, DC, with the same representation in Congress as the states.

Ratified by sixteen states

Submitted but Not Formally Proposed

1876: The Senate shall be abolished.

1878: An executive council of three shall replace the office of president.

1893: The nation shall hereafter be known as the United States of the Earth.

1893: The army and navy shall be abolished.

1894: God and Jesus Christ shall be recognized in the Constitution as the supreme authorities in human affairs.

1916: All acts of war shall be put to a national vote. All those affirming shall be registered as a volunteer for service in the United States Armed Forces.

1933: The wealth of any citizen may not exceed $1 million.

1948: Citizens shall have the right to segregate themselves from others.

1971: Citizens shall have the unalienable right to an environment free of pollution.

1989: Naturalized citizens who have been citizens eleven years shall be eligible for the office of president.

1990: The flag shall be protected by the Constitution from physical desecration.

1991: English shall be the official language of the United States.

1997: Citizens shall have the right to a home.

1999: Life is declared to begin at conception, and thus the Fifth and Fourteenth Amendments apply to the unborn.

2003: Children of illegal immigrants shall not be US citizens.

2008: Marriage shall be defined as a union of one man and one woman.

2009: US senators shall be limited to two terms for a total of twelve years, and US representatives shall be limited to three terms for a total of six years.

2015: The Sixteenth Amendment (which instituted the income tax) should be repealed.

2016: The Electoral College shall be abolished.

2018: A balanced budget should be adopted each year. (Basically, the expenditure in the federal budget should not exceed the amount of revenue collected.)

Failed Amendments and Proposals

Some items listed in the feature box above provide biblical issues for discussion.

Recognition of God and Jesus Christ as supreme authority (1894): While Christians need to maintain an institutional distinction between church and state, it is appropriate for governments to acknowledge the lordship of Christ (Rom. 13:1–7). At the time this amendment was introduced, cultural consensus around this matter was weakening. Of course, enforcement by a constitutional amendment would have been impossible.

ERA (1972): While Christians support legal equality for men and women, many Christians were concerned that this amendment would be used to reject biblical teaching about scriptural differences between men and women (cf. Eph. 5:22–33; 1 Tim. 2:8–15).

Life begins at conception (1999): This measure, to protect human beings from murder, received widespread support among Christians.

Marriage should be defined as a union of one man and one woman (2008): This reflected a biblical view of marriage (Matt. 19:4–6). It was proposed as the matter was becoming a controversial issue in the nation.

Generally, Congress sets a seven-year time limit in which an amendment must be ratified, or it expires. Amendments Twenty-One and Twenty-Two actually spell this out as one of their provisions. One notable exception is the Twenty-Seventh Amendment, which was proposed in 1789 as part of the original Bill of Rights but went unratified until 1992—over two hundred years later. During the ratification period, even if a state fails to approve an amendment once, the proposal can be submitted for approval again and again.

Of the twenty-seven amendments that have passed ratification, the first ten amendments, known as the **Bill of Rights**, were added in 1791 and were closely tied to the original ratification effort. Therefore, only seventeen amendments have been approved since the first session of Congress.

The small number of passed amendments reflects the Constitution's stability. Interest groups or regions of the country have not easily bent the Constitution to suit their particular desires. Generally, only amendments with broad appeal are ratified.

Amendments are difficult to ratify and are often unnecessary. Congress may pass laws to deal with most problems. However, the amendment process remains an important aspect of the Constitution's success. Amendments provide a means of permanently providing solutions that enjoy widespread popular support (e.g., the law that gave eighteen-year-olds the vote) or correcting major deficiencies in the operation of the national government (e.g., clarifying presidential succession).

Section Review

1. What is the difference between a strict constructionist and a broad constructionist?
2. Explain the "necessary and proper" clause.
3–4. What are the two major phases in the amendment process?
5. What are the various ways an amendment may pass through these phases?
★ How did a knowledge of human nature help the framers of the Constitution?
★ Read the feature box entitled "How Should We Interpret the Constitution?" After reading each quote, identify whether that quote supports a broad constructionist view or a strict constructionist one. Which of the two views do you support? Why?

II. Foundational Principles

While all of the Constitution's principles are not explicitly stated in its text, the basic ones are defined, embedded, or assumed within the document. These underlying principles of the Constitution were not invented in Philadelphia; the delegates gathered them from years of careful study of governments and political thinkers and from the painful lessons learned from the failed Confederation. All these basic principles deal in some way with the issue of government power—how to divide, balance, limit, and allot it. With these principles, the Constitution's framers forged a working balance that has provided America with liberty, order, and an enduring charter.

Recision

Once a state ratifies an amendment, its decision is usually considered final. However, some states have tried to revoke their ratification. In 1868, both New Jersey and Ohio rescinded their ratification of the Fourteenth Amendment. But a concurrent resolution by Congress declared their initial decisions to be final. Just before the Civil War, in secession resolutions, South Carolina and several other Southern states rescinded their ratification of the Constitution. And more recently, Tennessee, Kentucky, Idaho, South Dakota, and Nebraska rescinded their ratification of the Equal Rights Amendment (ERA). (Even with their ratification, the ERA fell short of the thirty-eight states needed for the amendment to pass.) The validity of recision has yet to be tested in the Supreme Court, but in 1978, the Senate voted 54 to 44 against recognizing state recision of ERA votes.

Section II Objectives

1. Explain six basic principles contained in the Constitution.
2. Relate foundational principles of American government to biblical principles.

Section Review Answers

1. A strict constructionist relies on a close adherence to the text of the Constitution, with a minimum of expanded interpretation; a broad constructionist takes a more flexible approach to interpreting the Constitution, reading into it things that the text does not explicitly say. (p. 82)
2. The "necessary and proper clause" gives Congress the authority to make laws that are necessary to complete its tasks. (p. 84)
3–4. Proposal and ratification (p. 85)
5. An amendment is proposed either by a two-thirds vote in both houses of Congress or by a special national convention called by two-thirds of the states. An amendment is ratified either by three-fourths of the states' legislatures or by three-fourths of special state ratification conventions. (p. 85)
★ Knowing humans' tendency to misuse and be corrupted by power, the framers divided authority within the national government and included checks and balances.
★ Woodrow Wilson and Barack Obama are broad constructionists. Joseph Story and Keith E. Whittington are strict constructionists. Answers will vary. Those that choose the strict constructionist's view may say that we should not stray from the founder's original intentions. Those that choose the broad constructionist's view may say that we should broadly interpret the Constitution in light of today's culture and society.

Limited Government

Limited government is a major theme in the Constitution, indeed, one of its foundations. It means that government does not have absolute power but rather is limited to those powers that the people have given it. The Constitution is designed to establish boundaries of power for the government and limits on liberty for the people. Because it is a *written* document, the bounds of authority are not subject to the rulers' whims. Written declarations of rights or demands were nothing new in 1787, but a written constitution that was distinct and superior to regular legislation was a novel idea.

The American colonists had lived under the unwritten British constitution. It was actually a collection of legislation, traditions, and even assumptions. However, these laws and customs were not superior to Parliament. Many colonists believed that this fact allowed Parliament to disregard American rights.

All this was a recent memory for the Philadelphia delegates. They charted a new course of action, establishing the Constitution, the laws Congress enacted, and treaties as the "supreme law of the land." This provided stability and safeguards for personal liberty. Thus, a central purpose of limiting government is to protect individual freedom. As stated in Article VI, the supremacy clause of the Constitution places not only the governed but also the rulers under the Constitution's authority. *No one* is above the law.

The founders understood that unchecked, concentrated power is another form of tyranny, so they built certain obstacles into the system that would hinder the expansion of government power without harming the government's ability to maintain a stable political system. These limitations involve the next two principles: the separation of powers and checks and balances.

> "It is agreed on all sides, that the powers properly belonging to one of the departments ought not to be directly and completely administered by either of the other departments. It is equally evident, that none of them ought to possess, directly or indirectly, an overruling influence over the others, in the administration of their respective powers. . . . After discriminating, therefore, in theory, the several classes of power, as they may in their nature be legislative, executive, or judiciary, the next and most difficult task is to provide some practical security for each, against the invasion of the others."
>
> —James Madison, *Federalist* No. 48

Separation of Powers

To prevent any group or individual from gaining too much control, the founders divided national power into three separate branches: the legislative branch (dealt with in Article I), the executive branch (Article II), and the judicial branch (Article III). This **separation of powers** is not just theoretical. All three branches are housed in different buildings in Washington, DC—Congress, at the Capitol; the president, at the White House; and the Supreme Court, at the Supreme Court Building.

Influenced by the writings of Aristotle and Montesquieu, the founders differed with the British parliamentary system and the Confederation government, which lumped executive functions with the legislative branch. Under the Constitution, in broad terms, Congress makes the laws, the president executes and enforces the laws, and the courts interpret them.

Although these branches are separate, they are not independent. Their responsibilities intersect in many areas, and some cooperation is necessary for the national government to function properly.

The Written Word

Assign groups of students to consider why it is important that the Constitution is a *written* document. Direct the students to consider how the written form enhances the value of the Constitution and how our nation would be different if the Constitution were merely a set of ideals passed orally through the generations. Ask them to think about other important documents that are in writing, such as contracts, wills, or family trees. Despite the obvious diversity of these things, they have been placed in writing for similar purposes—so that a record of information can be consulted in the future, especially when controversy occurs. The students might also consider specific instances in which their families have placed items in writing (e.g., family rules, chores lists, or reminder lists).

This section is ideal for discussing examples of how families use written documents. Discuss the preceding topics, emphasizing how writing things has helped (or could help) in your family situation.

What If?

Discuss the importance of checks and balances to the separation of powers. Instruct the students to imagine that no such separation exists in the Constitution and to suggest ways in which various branches could dominate the others.

Checks and Balances

Though separation of powers is often thought to be synonymous with **checks and balances**, there is an important difference. If there were only a division of power in the national government, one branch might expand its powers and dominate the other branches.

The principle of checks and balances, however, thwarts such an accumulation of power. For example, Congress can pass a bill; but the president can reject, or **veto**, the bill if he opposes it. However, his veto may in turn be overridden by a two-thirds vote in both houses of Congress. Another example involves the president's power to appoint federal judges and other top-level officials and his authority to make treaties. The Senate must approve the president's nominees and treaties, and the Supreme Court may nullify acts of both Congress and the president if a majority of justices interpret an act as unconstitutional.

One particularly high-profile example of checks and balances is Congress's power of **impeachment** (formally charging the president, federal judges, or other officials, with misconduct). For instance, in 2010, the House of Representatives impeached and the Senate convicted federal judge G. Thomas Porteous on four articles of impeachment, including accepting kickbacks and lying to the Senate and the FBI. Even within the impeachment process, however, accumulation of power is avoided because the Senate must either convict or acquit the defendant of all impeachments.

Checks and balances hinder the concentration of power and thus protect personal liberty. There is an obvious disadvantage, however: the system is sometimes inefficient. In fact, checks and balances can actually make it difficult for a branch to function properly. For example, in 1987, the Democrat-controlled Senate blocked Republican President Ronald Reagan's Supreme Court nomination. That nominee, Robert Bork, failed to receive the required Senate approval after months of debate and controversy. Similarly, the Republican-controlled Senate refused to consider a Supreme Court nomination made by President Barack Obama, a Democrat. After the death of Supreme Court Justice Antonin Scalia in February 2016, Republicans blocked the scheduling of hearings or a vote regarding Merrick Garland, the Obama nominee. Republicans successfully kept the seat

Impeaching Federal Judges

In 2010 G. Thomas Porteous became the fifteenth federal judge in US history to be impeached. He was only the eighth to be removed from office. Four others were acquitted by the Senate, and three resigned before the outcome of their trials.

Power Quiz

Instruct the students to spend a few minutes reviewing the "Separation of Powers" and "Checks and Balances" diagrams. Divide the students into three teams—executive, legislative, and judicial. Then, referring to the powers listed in the diagrams, ask a student on a team to identify the branch of government that performs a specific function. The student should not receive assistance from team members or consult the student text. A correct answer equals one point for the student's team. An incorrectly answered question should be asked to the next team. Add more questions to increase the length of the game or to ensure that each student is asked a question.

Checks and Balances

Group the students and direct each group to research the government structure of a nation, paying particular attention to any systems of checks and balances that exist in each country. Assign one or two students to research the country's constitution to distribute to the group's other members. Direct another student to create diagrams illustrating a country's branches of government and its checks and balances. Other students could compile information into a written presentation, and others could develop an oral presentation. (Consider assigning only countries with English as an official language because government documents and information in English will be easier to find.)

A Case for Judicial Review

Besides *Marbury v. Madison*, another important Supreme Court case that reinforced judicial review was *Martin v. Hunter's Lessee* (1816), a case involving state rather than federal legislation. Writing for the majority, Justice Joseph Story argued for uniformity within the US legal system.

> A motive of another kind, perfectly compatible with the most sincere respect for State tribunals, might induce the grant of appellate power over their decisions. That motive is the importance, and even necessity, of uniformity of decisions throughout the whole United States upon all subjects within the purview of the Constitution. Judges of equal learning and integrity in different States might differently interpret a statute, or a treaty of the United States, or even the Constitution itself; if there were no revising authority to control these jarring and discordant judgments and harmonize them into uniformity, the laws, the treaties, and the Constitution of the United States would be different in different States, and might perhaps never have precisely the same construction, obligation, or efficacy in any two States.

unoccupied until their presidential candidate, Donald Trump, was elected and inaugurated. President Trump's nominee, Neil Gorsuch, was approved in April 2017, more than a year after the vacancy occurred.

There are other instances of **gridlock**, a political stalemate or deadlock, that have resulted because of checks and balances. This has occurred, in part, when different political parties have controlled different branches of national government. For example, in the 1980s and 1990s, national government shutdowns occurred lasting short periods, culminating in December 1995 when a Republican-controlled Congress and President Bill Clinton, a Democrat, feuded about financial issues. Congress refused to pass the president's budget proposal, and the president blocked congressional bills by exercising his veto. The result was a twenty-one-day government shutdown that left some 280,000 government workers temporarily out of work. Each side tried to convince voters that the other side was to blame for the crisis. More recently, in 2013, disagreements between Democratic President Barack Obama and the Republicans in Congress resulted in a sixteen-day shutdown that affected 800,000 government workers. Two brief shutdowns occurred in February 2018 when President Donald Trump and Congress could not agree on spending measures. Such gridlock appears likely to continue.

The advantages of checks and balances outweigh the problems that sometimes develop. Some argue that the inefficiency of the process serves to further limit governmental power and protect personal liberty.

Judicial Review

Closely tied to the principle of checks and balances is the principle of **judicial review** (the judicial branch's power to review the constitutionality of laws passed by the legislative branch or of actions taken by the executive branch). Laws or actions that contradict the judicial interpretation of the Constitution can be struck down or overturned.

Although the principle of judicial review is assumed today, it is not clearly defined in the Constitution. In fact, Thomas Jefferson, an opponent of judicial review, argued, "Certainly there is not a word in the Constitution which has given that power to [the judiciary] more than to the Executive or Legislative branches."

However, another Founding Father, Alexander Hamilton, explained the basis of the principle in *Federalist* No. 78.

> The complete independence of the courts of justice is peculiarly essential in a limited Constitution. By a limited Constitution, I understand one which contains certain specified exceptions to the legislative authority; such, for instance, as that [Congress] shall pass no bills of attainder [a law that permits punishment without a trial], no *ex post facto* laws [legislation that makes laws retroactive], and the like. Limitations of this kind can be preserved in practice no other way than through the medium of courts of justice, whose duty it must be to declare all acts contrary to . . . the Constitution void.

The principle of judicial review was not asserted until 1803 when Chief Justice John Marshall used it in the landmark Supreme Court case ***Marbury v. Madison***. A more recent judicial-review case involved the Line Item Veto Act (1996), which allowed the president to veto specific parts of a bill rather than the whole thing. In 1998, the Supreme Court declared the act unconstitutional because it would have changed the constitutional process by which a bill becomes law.

Current Gridlock

Instruct students to find magazine, newspaper, or online articles detailing current examples of gridlock in our government. Take time to discuss any major situations and to examine the cause of each instance of gridlock—usually partisan politics.

On the Docket

Discuss any current cases in which the Supreme Court is deciding the constitutionality of an issue. Discuss how the Supreme Court might rule.

Government in the United States and South Africa

The US Constitution provides numerous ways for the three branches of the national government to prevent one another from becoming too powerful. Compromises among different interests are also reflected in the Constitution. The two divisions of Congress represent a balance between the interests of large states and those of small ones. The House is based on population (thereby favoring large states); and the Senate contains two representatives per state, thus small states have the same power in that chamber as large states. Furthermore, to determine population for purposes of representation and taxes, the Constitution stated that three-fifths of slaves would be counted; this was a compromise between slave states and nonslave states.

In this textbook, we often compare our government to the systems in other nations. It is noteworthy to contrast our Constitution, written in 1787, to the current constitution of the Republic of South Africa, adopted in 1997. By that year, white-minority rule and apartheid (official policy of racial segregation) had finally ended. Balancing different parts of the new government and various ethnic and political interests was a painstaking process that produced one of the most complex constitutions in the world.

South Africa contains a "rainbow" of ethnic groups and cultures: a black majority (the dominant African National Congress and the Zulus); a white minority (those of European ancestry); an Asian minority (Indians); and a Coloured minority (the South African term for those of mixed ancestry). Thus, the challenges of developing a system that fairly governed all segments of the population were great.

South Africa's constitution borrows from several sources: German, American, Swiss, British, Indian, and South African history. South Africa is divided into nine provinces, comparable to American states. Its parliament is divided into two bodies. The National Assembly has four hundred members—two hundred elected nationally and two hundred from the nine provinces. The National Council of Provinces consists of ninety members. Ten are chosen by each of the nine provincial legislatures.

Throughout the South African system are many similarities to the American system. For example, in neither is the president elected directly by voters. Whereas the Electoral College elects the US president, the National Assembly chooses the South African leader.

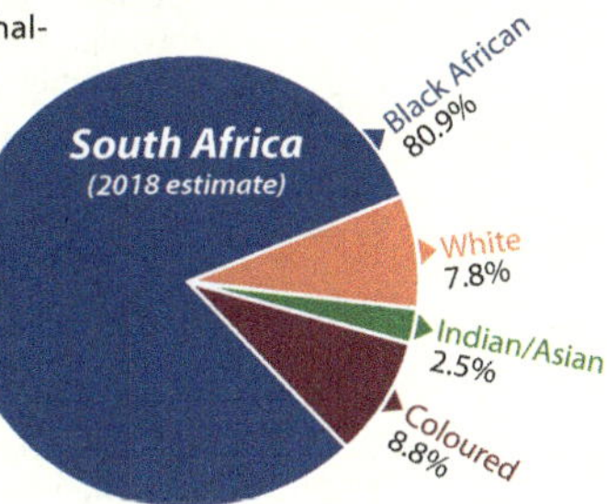

Federalism

Federalism is the division of power between national and state levels of government. The federal system was a unique contribution in its day; it developed from the political realities of the colonial and Confederation periods.

The thirteen separate colonies had grown along the eastern coast of America. Begun at different times, for different reasons, and with differing economies, climates, populations, and political systems, they nonetheless forged a loose-knit team to defeat the British and form a new government. At first, the central government was a confederation of thirteen fiercely independent state governments, an arrangement that soon began to fray at the seams.

The Constitution's framers represented these sovereign states, but most of the delegates also recognized the need for the strength and order of unity. From the need to balance state and national interests came federalism. This federal system not only divides power but, as Chapter 6 details, also accommodates differences in various regions by giving people a greater voice in their affairs on the state and local levels.

Comparing Governments

The feature box at left is another in the continuing series in the Student Edition that compares the United States government to one of another country. The first comparison dealt with India (p. 36).

Importance of Federalism

Federalism is not biblically mandated. However, it is a key component in our government that helps accomplish a biblical goal—limited government.

Federalism's Changes

Obviously, the current government is very different from that created by the Founding Fathers. Ask the students to imagine that those men could be transported from the past to the present. Encourage the students to speculate on what the Founding Fathers would think about the federal system as it exists today. What major changes might they note in American government?

We the People?

One of the loudest objections to Morris's Preamble phrasing came from the fiery orator Patrick Henry. Speaking at Virginia's ratification convention in June 1788, he asked,

> What right had they to say, "We, the People"? My political curiosity, exclusive of my anxious solicitude for the public welfare, leads me to ask, who authorized them to speak the language of, "We, the People," instead of, "We, the States"? States are the characteristics, and the soul of a confederation. If the States be not the agents of this compact, it must be one great consolidated National Government of the people of all the States.

In response, fellow Virginian Edmund Randolph replied,

> Why not? The government is for the people; and the misfortune was, that the people had no agency in the government before. . . . What harm is there in consulting the people, on the construction of a government by which they are to be bound? Is it unfair? Is it unjust? If the government is to be binding on the people, are not the people the proper persons to examine its merits or defects?

The Tenth Amendment contains the clearest definition of federalism:

> The powers not delegated to the United States by the Constitution, nor prohibited by it to the states, are reserved to the states respectively, or to the people.

Nevertheless, with the United States' rise to world power and the growing economic interdependence of its people, the constitutional power given to the states originally has waned. However federalism continues to be a crucial and innovative part of American government.

Popular Sovereignty

The Enlightenment emphasized the idea of **popular sovereignty**—that the people are the ultimate source of their government's authority. Though there is a biblical basis for involvement of people in government, popular sovereignty sometimes conflicts with scriptural commands to obey existing authority, which God established. Nevertheless, in the United States, God establishes rulers through the vote of the people. Consequently, America's rulers are accountable not only to God but also to the people.

Popular sovereignty, like other foundational principles, is not explicitly stated in the Constitution. Rather, it is a general theme. Many point to the Preamble's opening phrase—"We the people"—as evidence of the strength of the popular sovereignty theme. This emphasis, however, is a later one. The original draft of the Preamble listed each of the thirteen states.

> We the people of the states of New-Hampshire, Massachusetts, Rhode-Island and Providence Plantations, Connecticut, New-York, New-Jersey, Pennsylvania, Delaware, Maryland, Virginia, North-Carolina, South-Carolina, and Georgia, do ordain, declare and establish the following Constitution for the government of ourselves and our posterity.

When the members of the Committee of Style and Arrangement, headed by Gouverneur Morris, put the final touches on the Constitution's text, they foresaw the difficulties that could arise from listing all the states as consenting when some were hostile to the Constitution and ratification. An uphill battle for ratification loomed. Morris, a skilled editor, solved the problem with this revision.

> We the people of the United States, in order to form a more perfect union, establish justice, insure domestic tranquility, provide for the common defence, promote the general welfare, and secure the blessings of liberty to ourselves and our posterity, do ordain and establish this Constitution for the United States of America.

Therefore, when it was first penned, "We the people of the United States" was more a triumph of editorial eloquence than a major tenet of popular sovereignty.

The principle of popular sovereignty is most accurately expressed in the Constitution through representation and amendment provisions. Representation allows the people to have a voice in their government through their elected officials. The Constitution's framers, fearing the fickleness of public opinion, sought to limit the directness of the people's voice on the national level by providing direct election only for the House of Representatives. As democratic participation expanded over the years, however, this limitation came to be viewed as too restrictive. The result was the Seventeenth Amendment (1913), which provided for the direct election of senators as well. (Opponents of this amendment argue that the founders intended senators to represent the state governments rather than

Activity 3: Popular Sovereignty

This activity, which focuses on Alexis de Tocqueville's comments regarding popular sovereignty, enhances skills in using original sources.

Activity 4: Differing Viewpoints Regarding Judicial Review

This activity contrasts opinions of two Supreme Court justices—Antonin Scalia and Stephen Breyer—regarding how judges should make decisions on cases presented to them.

directly represent the people. They contend that the amendment left the states without a voice in the national government.)

The amendment process also demonstrates the workings of popular sovereignty. Amendments are another expression of the people's sovereignty because those that survive the difficult ratification process typically do so because of widespread popular support. Upon adoption, they supersede Congress's laws, the president's actions, and the courts' decisions. Chief Justice Marshall stated this point powerfully: "The people made the Constitution, and the people can unmake it. It is the creature of their will, and lives only by their will."

Self-government is no easy task. It does not occur by accident, and it is not a well-oiled, self-propelled machine. The people of each generation must grapple with their government—use its principles and adapt its process to make it work for their day. They must also carefully guard the privilege of self-government from those who would twist its power to their own advantage.

Conclusion

Whereas some constitutions are simply parchments full of empty promises, the US Constitution is a cornerstone for ordered liberty, true self-government, and personal liberties that have made America a "city set upon a hill" for millions around the world living under repressive regimes. Christians can be grateful for both the Constitution and the wisdom of its writers. The Founding Fathers created a system that deliberately mixed various forms of government. The president, a single leader, provides leadership. The Congress consists of a relatively small group, 535 members from a population over 335 million, who are charged with the responsibility of making the laws. Of course, the people of the country have the power to elect the president, indirectly through the Electoral College, and the members of the legislative branch.

While the American believer's chief source of authority is Scripture, he has an obligation to respect and obey the Constitution because it is the foundation of our legal system and our government. The Constitution and its first ten amendments have guaranteed Americans' liberties, such as freedom of worship, freedom of speech, freedom of the press, and freedom of association. However, these guarantees are empowered not by custom but by commitment—a commitment that each generation must make to defend the law and cherish their liberties.

Section Review

1–6. What six basic principles are the foundation of the Constitution?

7. What is the difference between separation of powers and checks and balances?

8–9. What is the obvious disadvantage of checks and balances? What benefits overshadow this disadvantage?

10–11. What is popular sovereignty? Where is this principle most accurately expressed in the Constitution?

★ Why did Hamilton believe that judicial review is necessary?

★ Was the Seventeenth Amendment a good change or a bad one? Defend your opinion.

Soviet Promises

The three constitutions of the former Soviet Union are prime examples of constitutions that made promises but fulfilled few of them. Under the threat of imprisonment and even death, only the most courageous tried to exercise their theoretical rights. Here are some excerpts from the 1936 Soviet Constitution.

Article CXXIV

In order to ensure to citizens freedom of conscience, the church in the USSR is separated from the state, and the school from the church. Freedom of religious worship and freedom of anti-religious propaganda is recognized for all citizens.

Article CXXV

In conformity with the interests of the working people, and in order to strengthen the socialist system, the citizens of the USSR are guaranteed by law:

(a) Freedom of speech;

(b) Freedom of the press;

(c) Freedom of assembly, including the holding of mass meetings;

(d) Freedom of street processions and demonstrations.

These civil rights are ensured by placing at the disposal of the working people and their organizations printing presses, stocks of paper, public buildings, the streets, communications facilities and other material requisites for the exercise of these rights.

Section Review Answers

1–6. limited government, separation of powers, checks and balances, judicial review, federalism, and popular sovereignty (pp. 87–93)

7. Separation of powers divides the national government into three distinct branches. "Checks and balances" refers to the power that each branch exerts over the others. (pp. 88–90)

8–9. Checks and balances make the government inefficient, but they limit government power and protect personal liberty. (pp. 89–90)

10–11. Popular sovereignty is the belief that the people are the ultimate source of their government's power. This principle is expressed in the Constitution through its plans for representation and the amendment process. (pp. 92–93)

★ Hamilton believed that judicial review is necessary to limit legislative authority.

★ Some will say the Seventeenth Amendment was a problem because it left the states without a voice in the national government. Others will say it was good because it demonstrated popular sovereignty at work.

Section III Objectives

1. Identify the three branches of government and explain their major functions.
2. Explain the purpose and significance of the Bill of Rights.
3. Evaluate the impact of constitutional amendments on the US government.

Justification for the Preamble

The Preamble of the Constitution not only outlined the purposes for the government but also helped justify the closer union between the states. Supreme Court Justice Joseph Story wrote in 1840 that the "more perfect union" mentioned in the Preamble promised to "diminish the causes of war, that scourge of the human race; . . . enable the national government to protect and secure the rights of the whole people; . . . diminish public expenditures; . . . insure respect abroad, and confidence at home; and . . . unite in one common bond the interests of agriculture, of commerce, and of manufactures."

III. Examining the United States Constitution

Guiding Questions

1. What are the three branches of American government and their major functions?
2. What is the purpose and impact of the Bill of Rights?
3. How have the constitutional amendments affected the US government?

Explanation

Preamble

The **Preamble** introduces the Constitution by explaining its nature and purpose. First, it states the source of the government's power: "We the people." Second, the Preamble establishes the purposes of government to
1. "form a more perfect union,"
2. "establish justice,"
3. "[e]nsure domestic tranquility,"
4. "provide for the common defence,"
5. "promote the general welfare," and
6. "secure the blessings of liberty to ourselves and our posterity."

Much of the Preamble's text comes from Article III of the Articles of Confederation, which states,

> The said States hereby severally enter into a firm league of friendship with each other, for their common defense, the security of their liberties, and their mutual and general welfare, binding themselves to assist each other, against all force offered to, or attacks made upon them, or any of them, on account of religion, sovereignty, trade, or any other pretense whatever.

Article I: The Legislative Branch
Section 1: Authority

Article I deals with the **legislative branch** of government, whose primary function is to make laws. This power belongs to Congress, which has two houses: an upper house called the Senate and a lower house called the House of Representatives. A two-house legislative system is called a **bicameral** system.

Section 2: The House of Representatives

(1) Members of the House serve two-year terms; all House seats are up for election at the same time. House members have always been elected directly by the people.

The United States Constitution

[*Note:* The numbers preceding each clause were added to separate individual clauses under each section; they were not in the original document. Capitalization and some spellings have been modernized. Sections in italic type are no longer in force or have been superseded by amendments or both.]

Preamble

We the people of the United States, in order to form a more perfect union, establish justice, insure domestic tranquility, provide for the common defence, promote the general welfare, and secure the blessings of liberty to ourselves and our posterity, do ordain and establish this Constitution for the United States of America.

Article I: The Legislative Branch
Section 1

All legislative powers herein granted shall be vested in a Congress of the United States, which shall consist of a Senate and House of Representatives.

Section 2

1. The House of Representatives shall be composed of members chosen every second year by the people of the several states, and the electors in each state shall have the qualifications requisite for electors of the most numerous branch of the state legislature.

Preamble

Invite students to memorize the Preamble to the Constitution. Test memorization by having the students recite or write the Preamble.

The Articles

By the end of their study of this chapter, students should be able to give a basic outline of the Constitution, using the article numbers as their outline. They should also know the contents of each amendment comprising the Bill of Rights.

2. No person shall be a representative who shall not have attained to the age of twenty-five years, and been seven years a citizen of the United States, and who shall not, when elected, be an inhabitant of that state in which he shall be chosen.

3. *Representatives and direct taxes shall be apportioned among the several states which may be included within this Union, according to their respective numbers, which shall be determined by adding to the whole number of free persons, including those bound to service for a term of years, and excluding Indians not taxed, three-fifths of all other persons.* The actual enumeration shall be made within three years after the first meeting of the Congress of the United States, and within every subsequent term of ten years, in such manner as they shall by law direct. The number of representatives shall not exceed one for every thirty thousand, but each state shall have at least one representative; *and until such enumeration shall be made, the state of New Hampshire shall be entitled to choose three, Massachusetts eight, Rhode-Island and Providence Plantations one, Connecticut five, New-York six, New Jersey four, Pennsylvania eight, Delaware one, Maryland six, Virginia ten, North Carolina five, South Carolina five, and Georgia three.*

4. When vacancies happen in the representation from any state, the executive authority thereof shall issue writs of election to fill such vacancies.

5. The House of Representatives shall choose their speaker and other officers; and shall have the sole power of impeachment.

Section 3

1. The Senate of the United States shall be composed of two senators from each state, *chosen by the legislature* thereof, for six years; and each senator shall have one vote.

2. Immediately after they shall be assembled in consequence of the first election, they shall be divided as equally as may be into three classes. The seats of the senators of the first class shall be vacated at the expiration of the second year, of the second class at the expiration of the

---

(2) To qualify for office in the House of Representatives, a person must
    a. be at least twenty-five years old,
    b. have been a citizen for at least seven years, and
    c. be a resident of the state he represents.

(3) The number of representatives each state may elect is determined by its population, according to the agreement of the Great Compromise. Also, any direct federal taxation of the states must be distributed according to population. Amendment XVI, however, makes the income tax an exception to this rule. Special arrangements were made by the Three-Fifths Compromise for counting slaves, indentured servants, and Indians in the population; but since the end of slavery and the beginning of Indian citizenship, these rules no longer apply. Today, House membership is set at 435. There are also 6 nonvoting members: one each from Washington, DC; Puerto Rico; Guam; American Samoa; the Northern Mariana Islands; and the Virgin Islands. A counting of the population, called a **census**, is taken every ten years to determine how many representatives each state may elect. After each census, the number of representatives each state is allotted (in the House of Representatives) is changed based on the new population statistics. This process is called reapportionment.

(4) Vacancies in the House of Representatives are filled by special elections called by the state governors.

(5) The leader of the House, called the Speaker of the House, is elected by the House members. The House has "the sole power of impeachment" (the power to file charges against a major federal official).

Section 3: The Senate

(1) Each state has two senators, according to the terms of the Great Compromise; each serves a six-year term. Senators were first elected by state legislatures to represent state governments in the national government. Since the passage of Amendment XVII in 1913, senators have been elected directly by the people.

(2) The Constitution makes arrangements for one-third of the senators to face election every two years. By this method, the Senate can act with continuity from one session of Congress to another because no more than one-third of the senators will be new to the body following an election. Experienced senators who did not stand for election at that time can help keep order through the transition.

The process for filling Senate vacancies was changed by Amendment XVII, which allows state governors to appoint replacements or call for special elections to select them.

House Vacancies

The Founding Fathers believed that House vacancies would be rare and would involve individual cases of death, disability, or disqualification. Therefore, the months needed to call and hold an election would not be a problem. But the terrorist attacks of September 11, 2001, suggested that the enemies of America might launch a massive attack on government leaders. (A plane that crashed in Pennsylvania was believed to be headed toward the White House or the Capitol.) Lawmakers have since discussed how to deal with a situation in which as much as two-thirds of Congress is killed or incapacitated. A constitutional amendment allowing emergency temporary appointments (to fill House vacancies) by state governments (as is true for senatorial vacancies) has been considered.

Census Taker

Invite someone who has served as a census worker to speak to the class about the experience. Ask him to share how he got the job, what he had to do on the job, and why he did those tasks for the job. He could also share anecdotes or distribute a sample census form to increase the students' interest and help them understand this topic.

County Statistics

Assign students to find census statistical data about different counties (or boroughs or parishes) in their state using the official census website. The students could use bar and pie graphs to illustrate some of their findings. They may search for statistics about topics such as age of the population, ethnic groups in the population, persons per square mile, income level, educational level, home ownership, and ancestry.

Explanation	The United States Constitution

(3) To serve as a US senator, a person must
  a. be at least thirty years old,
  b. have been a citizen for at least nine years, and
  c. be a resident of the state he represents.

(4) The leader (president) of the Senate is the vice president of the United States. He votes only in case of a tie. In case of a fifty-fifty split in party affiliation, the party of the vice president becomes the majority in the Senate.

(5) The Senate elects its own **president pro tempore**, who serves as leader of the Senate when the vice president is absent. (*Pro tempore* simply means "for the time being.") The president pro tempore is third in line in the presidential succession, following the vice president and the Speaker of the House.

(6) The Senate acts as a trial court for impeachment cases. Two-thirds of the senators must vote for conviction to remove an official from office. If the president is impeached, the chief justice of the Supreme Court, rather than the vice president, presides over the trial.

(7) If the House impeaches an official and the Senate tries and confirms the charges, Congress may punish the official only by removing him from office and barring him from holding any government offices in the future. Even so, the person can be tried in a regular civil or criminal court afterward and sentenced to further punishment if found guilty.

Section 4: Election and Assembly

(1) State legislatures have the right to administer congressional elections in their states, but they must follow any regulations established by Congress. For instance, national law requires that secret ballots be used in these elections. Congressional elections are held on the Tuesday following the first Monday in November in even-numbered years.

(2) Congress must meet at least once a year. Originally, it began its session on the first Monday in December. Now it first meets at noon on January 3 because the date was changed by Amendment XX.

---

fourth year, and of the third class at the expiration of the sixth year, so that one-third may be chosen every second year; *and if vacancies happen by resignation, or otherwise, during the recess of the legislature of any state, the executive thereof may make temporary appointments until the next meeting of the legislature, which shall then fill such vacancies.*

3. No person shall be a senator who shall not have attained to the age of thirty years, and been nine years a citizen of the United States, and who shall not, when elected, be an inhabitant of that state for which he shall be chosen.

4. The vice president of the United States shall be president of the Senate, but shall have no vote, unless they be equally divided.

5. The Senate shall choose their other officers, and also a president pro tempore, in the absence of the vice president, or when he shall exercise the office of president of the United States.

6. The Senate shall have the sole power to try all impeachments. When sitting for that purpose, they shall be on oath or affirmation. When the president of the United States is tried, the chief justice shall preside: and no person shall be convicted without the concurrence of two-thirds of the members present.

7. Judgment in cases of impeachment shall not extend further than to removal from office, and disqualification to hold and enjoy any office of honor, trust or profit under the United States: but the party convicted shall nevertheless be liable and subject to indictment, trial, judgment and punishment, according to law.

Section 4

1. The times, places and manner of holding elections for senators and representatives, shall be prescribed in each state by the legislature thereof; but the Congress may at any time by law make or alter such regulations, except as to the places of choosing senators.

2. The Congress shall assemble at least once in every year, and such meeting shall be on *the first Monday in December,* unless they shall by law appoint a different day.

Youngest and Oldest

Ask a volunteer to research the youngest and oldest members of the current US House and Senate.

Section 5

1. Each house shall be the judge of the elections, returns and qualifications of its own members, and a majority of each shall constitute a quorum to do business; but a smaller number may adjourn from day to day, and may be authorized to compel the attendance of absent members, in such manner, and under such penalties as each house may provide.
2. Each house may determine the rules of its proceedings, punish its members for disorderly behavior, and, with the concurrence of two-thirds, expel a member.
3. Each house shall keep a journal of its proceedings, and from time to time publish the same, excepting such parts as may in their judgment require secrecy; and the yeas and nays of the members of either house on any question shall, at the desire of one-fifth of those present, be entered on the journal.
4. Neither house, during the session of Congress, shall, without the consent of the other, adjourn for more than three days, nor to any other place than that in which the two houses shall be sitting.

Section 6

1. The senators and representatives shall receive a compensation for their services, to be ascertained by law, and paid out of the treasury of the United States. They shall in all cases, except treason, felony and breach of the peace, be privileged from arrest during their attendance at the session of their respective houses, and in going to and returning from the same; and for any speech or debate in either house, they shall not be questioned in any other place.
2. No senator or representative shall, during the time for which he was elected, be appointed to any civil office under the authority of the United States, which shall have been created, or the emoluments whereof shall have been increased during such time; and no person holding any office under the United States, shall be a member of either house during his continuance in office.

Section 5: Procedures

(1) Each house judges its own elections. A **quorum** is the minimum number needed to transact business. In Congress, a simple majority (just over half the members) constitutes a quorum. A **sergeant at arms** in each house is responsible to find absent members who are needed to constitute a quorum.

(2) The House and the Senate make their own rules for establishing committees, presenting bills, and establishing other needed procedures. A disorderly member can be expelled by a two-thirds vote of the body in which he is serving.

(3) Each house keeps a journal, or record, of what it does each day. Today this is called the **Congressional Record**. Some congressional proceedings may be kept secret, but a written record of any vote is kept if one-fifth of those present request it.

(4) Since the houses work together to pass legislation, one house cannot adjourn (go out of official session) for more than three days or move its meeting to another location without the other's permission.

Section 6: Benefits and Restrictions

(1) Senators and representatives are public employees who are paid salaries by the US Treasury. Both senators and representatives receive an annual salary of $174,000. (The Speaker of the House, the president pro tempore of the Senate, and the majority and minority leaders earn more.) They also receive allowances for travel, office expenses, and the **franking privilege** (the right to send official mail free of charge). In addition, they cannot be arrested going to or from the House or Senate (except for treason or other serious crimes), nor can they be arrested for what they say on the floor of the House or Senate. This precaution gives members of Congress the freedom to voice even unpopular ideas without fear of being arrested to prohibit their participation in Congress.

(2) To become a member of Congress, a person must resign any other federal offices he holds. Once elected, he cannot take any federal office created by his house of Congress until his term is ended, and he cannot take an office that Congress has increased the pay for during his term until his term is expired. This prevents members of Congress from giving themselves positions with increased salaries.

Expelled, Censured, or Reprimanded Congressmen

Only five members of the House of Representatives have ever been expelled from office. The first three expulsions came during the Civil War after those three members were charged with supporting the Confederacy. In 1980, Michael "Ozzie" Myers (D-PA) was expelled from the House after an FBI hidden-camera operation revealed that he had accepted a bribe. The most recent expulsion involved Jim Traficant (D-OH), who was expelled in 2002 following his conviction for bribery, racketeering, and tax evasion. Once he was expelled, he was sentenced to eight years in a federal prison.

In addition to expulsion, members of Congress can be censured or reprimanded (the least severe of the three). Twenty-three representatives have been censured, and ten have been reprimanded. The most recent censure involved Charles Rangel (D-NY). In 2010 he was censured for improperly soliciting funds and failure to pay income taxes. Recent reprimands include Joe Wilson (R-SC), who yelled, "You lie!" during a speech by President Obama to a 2009 joint session of Congress. In 2012 Laura Richardson (D-CA) was reprimanded for using her congressional staff during a reelection campaign.

Fifteen US senators have been expelled, the first being William Blount (D-R-TN) in 1797. The other fourteen were Democrats expelled during the first two years of the Civil War for supporting the Confederacy. Eighteen other senators had expulsion proceedings against them, but the Senate failed to get the two-thirds vote necessary to expel them or the member retired or resigned. Nine senators have been censured.

The *Congressional Record*

Locate the *Congressional Record* online, and identify activities that are currently occurring in the House and Senate.

Section 7: Lawmaking

(1) Bills dealing with taxation must start in the House, but the Senate may make changes to these bills. The Senate is not totally without power to initiate monetary legislation. Appropriations bills, which allocate funds, can be initiated by the Senate, as can revenue bills not dealing with taxation.

(2) For a bill to become law, it must be passed by both houses and signed by the president. This is part of the system of checks and balances. If the president opposes the bill, he may return it to the body where it started, stating his objections. This is a veto. Congress may override the president's veto with a two-thirds vote of both houses; then the bill becomes law. If the president neither signs nor vetoes a bill that comes to him, it becomes law in ten days as long as Congress remains in session. If he does not sign a bill and Congress adjourns within ten days, the bill is vetoed automatically. This is called a **pocket veto**.

(3) All acts requiring approval of both houses of Congress (except the decision to adjourn Congress) require the signature of the president, or Congress must override his veto by a two-thirds vote of both houses.

Section 8: The Enumerated Powers of Congress

(1) Congress has the power to tax. Congress can lay (impose amounts or a system) and collect taxes; duties (taxes on imports); and excises (internal taxes on the production, sale, consumption, or use of certain items, such as telephones).

(2) It has the power to borrow money. The government usually borrows money by selling bonds or certificates, which it pledges to repay later with interest.

Section 7

1. All bills for raising revenue shall originate in the House of Representatives; but the Senate may propose or concur with amendments as on other bills.
2. Every bill which shall have passed the House of Representatives and the Senate, shall, before it become a law, be presented to the president of the United States; if he approve he shall sign it, but if not he shall return it, with his objections to that house in which it shall have originated, who shall enter the objections at large on their journal, and proceed to reconsider it. If after such reconsideration two-thirds of that house shall agree to pass the bill, it shall be sent, together with the objections, to the other house, by which it shall likewise be reconsidered, and if approved by two-thirds of that house, it shall become a law. But in all such cases the votes of both houses shall be determined by yeas and nays, and the names of the persons voting for and against the bill shall be entered on the journal of each house respectively. If any bill shall not be returned by the president within ten days (Sundays excepted) after it shall have been presented to him, the same shall be a law, in like manner as if he had signed it, unless the Congress by their adjournment prevent its return, in which case it shall not be a law.
3. Every order, resolution, or vote to which the concurrence of the Senate and House of Representatives may be necessary (except on a question of adjournment) shall be presented to the president of the United States; and before the same shall take effect, shall be approved by him, or being disapproved by him, shall be repassed by two-thirds of the Senate and House of Representatives, according to the rules and limitations prescribed in the case of a bill.

Section 8

The Congress shall have power

1. To lay and collect taxes, duties, imposts and excises, to pay the debts and provide for the common defence and general welfare of the United States; but all duties, imposts and excises shall be uniform throughout the United States;
2. To borrow money on the credit of the United States;

Scripture and the Constitution

American Christians rightly respect the Constitution as the law of the land, but Christians must also recognize that no writing other than the Bible is without error. The Constitution probably would not have been adopted without the Three-Fifths Compromise, but the Constitution's implicit recognition of slavery was a wrong that needed to be corrected. As you discuss this chapter, ask the students whether there are any other parts of the Constitution that stand contrary to Scripture. Ask them to suggest amendments that would rectify the errors.

<table>
<tr><th></th><th></th></tr>
</table>

3. To regulate commerce with foreign nations, and among the several states, and with the Indian tribes;

4. To establish an uniform rule of naturalization, and uniform laws on the subject of bankruptcies throughout the United States;

5. To coin money, regulate the value thereof, and of foreign coin, and fix the standard of weights and measures;

6. To provide for the punishment of counterfeiting the securities and current coin of the United States;

7. To establish post offices and post roads;

8. To promote the progress of science and useful arts, by securing for limited times to authors and inventors the exclusive right to their respective writings and discoveries;

9. To constitute tribunals inferior to the Supreme Court;

10. To define and punish piracies and felonies committed on the high seas, and offences against the law of nations;

11. To declare war, grant letters of marque and reprisal, and make rules concerning captures on land and water;

A group of newly naturalized US citizens saying the Pledge of Allegiance

(3) It has the power to regulate trade with foreign nations, within the country, and with the Indians.

(4) It has the power to regulate naturalization and bankruptcy laws. **Naturalization** is the process by which a foreign-born person gains citizenship. Bankruptcy is the way a debtor is declared unable to pay his creditors.

(5) It has the power to control the currency system and the standard weights and measurements used in the country.

(6) It has the power to punish those who illegally interfere in the currency system. The term counterfeiting means "forging or copying something (money in particular) and using it illegally."

(7) It has the power to provide needed offices and roads for postal service. Post roads are roads used for delivering the mail. They became the basic routes of the US highway system. This clause was also used as the legal basis for the creation of the interstate highway system.

(8) It has the power to issue copyrights and patents. Copyrights are issued by the Library of Congress to protect authors' works (and their heirs' rights to those works) from infringement. Patents are granted by the Patent Office in the Department of Commerce, and they protect inventors from having their inventions or ideas taken by others for use or profit. The Patent Office also registers trademarks.

(9) It has the power to establish federal courts other than the Supreme Court. The federal court system is like a pyramid with the Supreme Court on top. Beneath the Court are thirteen circuit courts and the Court of Appeals for the Armed Forces. Next are the ninety-four district courts located throughout the states; courts with special jurisdiction (e.g., over taxes, trade, and veterans); and courts of review for specific military branches.

(10) It has the power to determine what acts committed at sea are crimes and to commit offenders operating in US waters or attacking US ships to federal courts for trial. Piracy is the act of robbing ships at sea. Other offenses against international law, such as terrorism and hijacking, are included under Congress's jurisdiction.

(11) It alone has the power to declare war. Although the president is commander in chief of the armed forces, Congress holds many powers that keep the president's military powers in check and ensure civilian control of the military. Nevertheless, presidents have been permitted to commit troops to limited military engagements. The 1973 War Powers Act somewhat curtailed presidential power in this area; however, smaller military engagements continue to occur without congressional authorization.

Letters of marque and reprisal, also discussed in this clause, were once used to permit private vessels to be

Indian Nations

At first, the American government treated Indian tribes both inside and outside the United States as independent nations. However, today Indian tribes are regarded as dependent nations with only limited independence under the Constitution.

Patent Office

Patents are issued by the US Patent and Trademark Office in three broad categories—utility, design, and plant patents.

Utility patents are the most common of the three. They include patents on inventions noted for their usefulness. A utility patent describes an invention and how it works. Examples of utility patents include patents on new types of machines, compounds, tools, chemicals, and software.

Design patents are given not for the usefulness of items but for their appearance. Even a well-known product, such as a bicycle, can be granted a design patent if it has a unique and innovative appearance.

Plant patents are patents for newly invented or discovered asexual plants.

Official Wars

In only five wars has Congress made an official declaration of war.

1. The War of 1812 (1812)
2. The Mexican War (1846)
3. The Spanish-American War (1898)
4. World War I (1917)
5. World War II (1941)

In other wars (the Korean War, the Vietnam War, the 1991 Gulf War, and the antiterrorist wars in Iraq and Afghanistan), Congress voted to authorize the president to use force for various purposes but did not call for an official declaration of war.

Searching for Patents

Visit the US Patent and Trademark Office online. Most patents registered after 1975 can easily be viewed there. After searching for some utility, design, and plant patents, make a list of their numbers to distribute to the class. Assign students, individually or in groups, to find patent information using these numbers.

The War Powers Act

The War Powers Act was passed in 1973 and stipulated that before and during the time the president introduces US armed forces into hostilities, he shall consult with Congress regularly. Within forty-eight hours of activating US troops, he must notify the leaders of Congress of

1. the circumstances that make the intervention necessary,

2. his constitutional and legislative authority for activating the troops,

3. the estimated scope and duration of the action, and

4. other information that Congress shall request.

The action must be ended within sixty days unless Congress approves of an extension or declares war during that time.

Hamilton on the Militia

In *Federalist* No. 29, Alexander Hamilton stated,

> [The militia] will not only lessen the call for military establishments, but if circumstances should at any time oblige the government to form an army of any magnitude that army can never be formidable to the liberties of the people while there is a large body of citizens, little if at all, inferior to them in discipline and the use of arms, who stand ready to defend their own rights and those of their fellow-citizens.

outfitted to fight in wartime and to capture enemies and their goods. Such permissions are no longer issued.

(12) It may create an army, but it cannot assign money to support the army more than two years ahead of time. Army appropriations (monies set aside for the armed forces) are limited to two years to prevent a takeover or other misuses of power by the military.

(13) It has the power to create a navy and vote for money to support it. America's first navy was actually created prior to the Constitution by the Continental Congress in 1775. However, it disbanded after the War for Independence. Congress, acting under clause 13, created a new navy in 1794 to protect US merchant ships in the Mediterranean.

(14) It has the power to make the rules for the armed services. Active-duty military personnel are bound by military law rather than civil law. This fact is reflected in the establishment of separate courts to deal with military cases. Military judges hear the cases, and prosecution and defense attorneys are provided by judge advocates—officers in each military branch under the Judge Advocate General (JAG)—who supply legal advice and services.

(15) It may call the state militias into service for the national government under certain conditions. The modern militia, known as the **National Guard**, is under dual control of state and federal governments. This change allows National Guard forces to support regular forces abroad; the conditions of this clause originally limited the National Guard to domestic situations only.

(16) It has the power to organize, arm, and discipline militias, but the states appoint officers and train these troops. When called into national service, the militia is under federal control as part of the armed forces. However, by its nature, the militia is also a check against the power of a standing army.

(17) It has the power to make laws for the District of Columbia and for all other federal properties, such as forts or bases. Today this power also applies to properties such as post offices, national historical sites, cemeteries, forests, parks, and fisheries.

(18) It has the power to do what it believes is "necessary and proper" to carry out any listed power. (This "necessary and proper clause" is sometimes also called the **elastic clause**.) To borrow money, for example, Congress can sell bonds and even create a bank. The Supreme Court can check this power by deciding whether the laws Congress passes by this authority are really necessary and proper.

12. To raise and support armies, but no appropriation of money to that use shall be for a longer term than two years;
13. To provide and maintain a navy;
14. To make rules for the government and regulation of the land and naval forces;
15. To provide for calling forth the militia to execute the laws of the Union, suppress insurrections and repel invasions;
16. To provide for organizing, arming, and disciplining, the militia, and for governing such part of them as may be employed in the service of the United States, reserving to the states respectively, the appointment of the officers, and the authority of training the militia according to the discipline prescribed by Congress;
17. To exercise exclusive legislation in all cases whatsoever, over such district (not exceeding ten miles square) as may, by cession of particular states, and the acceptance of Congress, become the seat of the government of the United States, and to exercise like authority over all places purchased by the consent of the legislature of the state in which the same shall be, for the erection of forts, magazines, arsenals, dockyards, and other needful buildings;—and
18. To make all laws which shall be necessary and proper for carrying into execution the foregoing powers, and all other powers vested by this Constitution in the government of the United States, or in any department or officer thereof.

Under Federal Authority

Guide the students as they list properties in your local area that are under federal jurisdiction based on Article I, Section 8, clause 17, of the Constitution.

<table>
<tr><th>The United States Constitution</th><th>Explanation</th></tr>
</table>

Section 9

1. *The migration or importation of such persons as any of the states now existing shall think proper to admit, shall not be prohibited by the Congress prior to the year one thousand eight hundred and eight, but a tax or duty may be imposed on such importation, not exceeding ten dollars for each person.*

2. The privilege of the writ of habeas corpus shall not be suspended, unless when in cases of rebellion or invasion the public safety may require it.

3. No bill of attainder or ex post facto law shall be passed.

4. No capitation, or other direct, tax shall be laid, *unless in proportion to the census or enumeration herein before directed to be taken.*

5. No tax or duty shall be laid on articles exported from any state.

6. No preference shall be given by any regulation of commerce or revenue to the ports of one state over those of another; nor shall vessels bound to, or from, one state, be obliged to enter, clear, or pay duties in another.

7. No money shall be drawn from the treasury, but in consequence of appropriations made by law; and a regular statement and account of the receipts and expenditures of all public money shall be published from time to time.

8. No title of nobility shall be granted by the United States: and no person holding any office of profit or trust under them, shall, without the consent of the Congress, accept of any present, emolument, office, or title, of any kind whatever, from any king, prince, or foreign state.

Section 9: Powers Forbidden to the Federal Government

(1) Congress could not interfere with the slave trade until 1808, and it could not tax slavery out of existence by levying heavy taxes on slaves. Congress did indeed abolish the importation of slaves on January 1, 1808, the earliest possible date. However, an illegal slave trade and the legal interstate trade continued to flourish.

(2) Congress may not take away a person's right to the writ of habeas corpus except in times of extreme danger. A **writ of habeas corpus** (Latin for "you should have the body") forces authorities who arrest a person to quickly bring him before a judge and charge him with a crime or else release him. Therefore, a person cannot be held prisoner unless a credible charge of a crime is made against him. People in dictatorships and other repressive regimes do not have this important right, so they may be held as prisoners indefinitely at the whim of government officials.

(3) Congress cannot pass a **bill of attainder**, which permits punishment without a trial, or an **ex post facto law**, which makes the law retroactive. Actions that were legal when they were committed cannot be prosecuted as illegal afterward.

(4) Congress cannot levy an unequal direct tax. For example, it cannot make Californians pay a special tax of one hundred dollars when people from Ohio have to pay only fifty dollars. But Amendment XVI made the income tax an exception. (People who make more money than others pay more income tax.)

(5) Congress cannot tax the states' exports. This means that neither goods exported to other nations nor goods exported to other states may be taxed.

(6) Congress cannot give preference to any port or state through its laws, and it cannot tax trade between the states, even if that trade is carried on by sea or another water passage.

(7) Money from the Treasury can be spent only if Congress approves, and a record of income and expenditures must be published. An **appropriation** is a specific amount of money set apart for a certain purpose. This clause gives Congress the "power of the purse." Today, the secretary of the treasury is in charge of the government's financial report.

(8) The United States cannot grant titles of nobility (duke, earl, baron, etc.), nor can its officeholders accept titles, presents, or emoluments (compensation) from foreign countries without Congress's permission.

Madison on Slavery

In *Federalist* No. 42, James Madison stated,

> It were doubtless to be wished, that the power of prohibiting the importation of slaves had not been postponed until the year 1808, or rather that it had been suffered to have immediate operation. But it is not difficult to account either for this restriction on the general government, or for the manner in which the whole clause is expressed. It ought to be considered as a great point gained in favor of humanity, that a period of twenty years may terminate forever, within these States, a traffic which has so long and so loudly upbraided the barbarism of modern policy; that within that period, it will receive a considerable discouragement from the federal government, and may be totally abolished, by a concurrence of the few States which continue the unnatural traffic, in the prohibitory example which has been given by so great a majority of the Union.

Habeas Corpus

By including the right of habeas corpus, the Founding Fathers drew on a political tradition that went as far back as the Magna Carta, which states,

> No free man shall be seized or imprisoned, or stripped of his rights or possessions, or outlawed or exiled, or deprived of his standing in any way, nor will we proceed with force against him, or send others to do so, except by the lawful judgment of his equals or by the law of the land.

Madison, the Constitution, and Slavery

Group the students and instruct each group to discuss one of the following questions regarding Madison, the Constitution, and slavery (use the excerpt from *Federalist* No. 42 in the margin note at top right to assist with this activity).

What was Madison's view toward the slave trade? Were there other ways of handling slave trade at the Constitutional Convention that would have still resulted in the completion of a document that could have been ratified? What elements in American political life made it difficult, if not impossible, to settle the slavery issue without having a civil war? As noted in the text, Congress later abolished the slave trade. What is the significance of the date on which that was done, and what are your thoughts about that legislation?

Financial Report

The secretary of the treasury's responsibility to provide a government financial report is outlined in US Code, Title 31, Section 331(c), which states,

> On the first day of each regular session of Congress, the Secretary shall submit to Congress a report for the prior fiscal year on the total amount of public receipts and public expenditures listing receipts, when practicable, by ports, districts, and States and the expenditures by each appropriation.

Hamilton on Titles

In *Federalist* No. 84, Alexander Hamilton commented on the Constitution's prohibition against granting titles of nobility.

> Nothing need be said to illustrate the importance of the prohibition of titles of nobility. This may truly be denominated the cornerstone of republican government; for so long as they are excluded, there can never be serious danger that the government will be any other than that of the people.

Section 10—Powers Denied to the States

(1–3) This section gives the national government exclusive power to enter into treaties, coin money, and control various other governmental functions. The section also ensures certain rights by adding some federal restrictions to the states, including prohibitions against passing bills of attainder and ex post facto laws and granting titles of nobility. Congress also has authority to approve or disapprove certain state actions, such as charging import taxes and keeping military ships in peacetime. However, states may respond to attacks if they are invaded. By limiting state powers, the Constitution strengthens the central government and produces a more united government.

Questions on Article I

1–6. What are the six purposes of government as outlined by the Constitution's Preamble?

7. What is the primary function of the legislative branch?

8–9. What are the respective roles of the House and Senate when a major federal official has committed a crime?

10. What is a veto?

11. How can Congress override a veto?

12–14. In Section 9 of Article I, Congress has limitations regarding three legal powers. Identify these (see clauses 2 and 3).

★ Which power of Congress do you think is the greatest? Why?

Section 10

1. No state shall enter into any treaty, alliance, or confederation; grant letters of marque and reprisal; coin money; emit bills of credit; make any thing but gold and silver coin a tender in payment of debts; pass any bill of attainder, ex post facto law, or law impairing the obligation of contracts, or grant any title of nobility.

2. No state shall, without the consent of the Congress, lay any imposts or duties on imports or exports, except what may be absolutely necessary for executing its inspection laws: and the net produce of all duties and imposts, laid by any state on imports or exports, shall be for the use of the treasury of the United States; and all such laws shall be subject to the revision and control of the Congress.

3. No state shall, without the consent of Congress, lay any duty of tonnage, keep troops, or ships of war in time of peace, enter into any agreement or compact with another state, or with a foreign power, or engage in war, unless actually invaded, or in such imminent danger as will not admit of delay.

Article I Answers

1–6. to form a more perfect union, to establish justice, to ensure domestic tranquility, to provide for the common defense, to promote the general welfare, and to secure the blessings of liberty to Americans and their children (p. 94)

7. to make laws (p. 94)

8–9. The House files charges (impeachment), and the Senate acts as a trial court. With a two-thirds agreement, the Senate can convict the offender and remove him from office. (p. 96)

10. the rejection of a bill by the president after it has passed through Congress (p. 98)

11. by gaining a two-thirds vote in support of the bill from both houses (p. 98)

12–14. Congress may not suspend writs of habeas corpus (except in times of extreme danger) or pass bills of attainder or ex post facto laws. (p. 101)

★ Answers will vary.

Article II: The Executive Branch
Section 1

1. The executive power shall be vested in a president of the United States of America. He shall hold his office during the term of four years, and, together with the vice president, chosen for the same term, be elected, as follows:
2. Each state shall appoint, in such manner as the legislature thereof may direct, a number of electors, equal to the whole number of senators and representatives to which the state may be entitled in the Congress: but no senator or representative, or person holding an office of trust or profit under the United States, shall be appointed an elector.
3. *The electors shall meet in their respective states, and vote by ballot for two persons, of whom one at least shall not be an inhabitant of the same state with themselves. And they shall make a list of all the persons voted for, and of the number of votes for each; which list they shall sign and certify, and transmit sealed to the seat of the government of the United States, directed to the president of the Senate. The president of the Senate shall, in the presence of the Senate and House of Representatives, open all the certificates, and the votes shall then be counted. The person having the greatest number of votes shall be the president, if such number be a majority of the whole number of electors appointed; and if there be more than one who have such majority, and have an equal number of votes, then the House of Representatives shall immediately choose by ballot one of them for president; and if no person have a majority, then from the five highest on the list the said house shall in like*

Article II: The Executive Branch
Article II deals with the **executive branch** of government, whose primary function is to carry out (enforce) the nation's laws.

Section 1: The Authority and Office of the President

(1) Both the president and vice president serve four-year terms. The four-year term strikes a balance by allowing enough time for the president to act with firmness and a level of independence in office, while hindering any officeholder from accumulating too much power.

(2) The **Electoral College**, composed of electors from each state, elects the president. Currently, the college is made up of 538 electors; this number equals the total number of senators (100) and representatives (435) each state has in Congress, plus 3 electors from the District of Columbia, which gained representation by the terms of Amendment XXIII. The electors who participate in this electoral process are usually prominent party members, and each usually pledges his vote to the candidate popularly elected by his state. However, there is no federal provision requiring the electors to vote this way; and, barring state regulations, they are free to vote as they choose.

(3) The Senate and House of Representatives oversee the counting of the electoral votes. If no candidate receives a majority of the votes, the House of Representatives chooses (with each state receiving one vote) the new president. Under such circumstances the Senate must choose a vice president. The House made the presidential choice in two elections—1800 and 1824. The Senate chose the vice president for the 1836 election. Other details of this procedure were replaced by Amendment XII in 1804 because of the difficulties that arose after the formation of political parties.

First Reading
The first draft of the Constitution, proposed on August 6, 1787, had a different version of Article II, Section 1.

The Executive Power of the United States shall be vested in a single person. His stile shall be, "The President of the United States of America;" and his title shall be, "His Excellency." He shall be elected by ballot by the Legislature. He shall hold his office during the term of seven years; but shall not be elected a second time.

Longer? Shorter?
Debate the pros and cons of the length of the president's term of office. Why might a shorter term be better? (*greater accountability to the people, greater check on power, and less time in office for an ineffective president*) What would be the disadvantages of a shorter term? (*more time spent campaigning, a more unstable executive branch, and little time to gain experience in the office*) Why might a longer term be better? (*more stability for the office, greater experience in office, and fewer ties to party politics*) What would be the disadvantages of a longer term? (*less accountability, more time for a bad president to do damage, and more time to "work the system"*)

Presidential Succession

In 1792 Congress passed legislation stating that in the event of removal, resignation, death, or inability of both the president and vice president, the president pro tempore of the Senate would become president. The Speaker of the House was then next in the line of succession.

In 1886, Congress altered the line of succession to replace the president pro tempore and the Speaker with the officers of the president's cabinet, and the secretary of state became first in line. The secretary of state followed the vice president in the line of succession from 1886 to 1947. In 1947, President Truman returned the removed officers to the line of succession; however, he switched their order.

(4) Congress determines the time for the president's election. Election Day is the first Tuesday after the first Monday in November, and the electors meet in mid-December at their respective state capitals to cast their votes.

(5) The president must
   a. be a natural-born citizen,
   b. be at least thirty-five years of age, and
   c. have been a resident of the United States for at least fourteen years.

(6) In 1947, Congress established the present line of succession:
   a. vice president, as stated in the Constitution;
   b. the Speaker of the House of Representatives;
   c. the president pro tempore of the Senate; and
   d. the members of the president's cabinet in order of the creation of their departments (secretary of state, secretary of the treasury, secretary of defense, attorney general, etc.).

Amendment XXV, however, made provision for the appointment of a new vice president when that office is vacant, so it is unlikely that succession would fall on anyone other than a vice president.

(7) The president's salary stays the same throughout his term. In 2001, it was increased from $200,000 to $400,000 per year.

(8) The president's oath of office is dictated by the Constitution. The word *affirm* is offered because some religions object to the use of the word *swear* (see Matt. 5:34–37). George Washington added "So help me God" to the end of the oath, and that addition has become tradition.

manner choose the president. But in choosing the president, the votes shall be taken by states, the representation from each state having one vote; a quorum for this purpose shall consist of a member or members from two-thirds of the states, and a majority of all the states shall be necessary to a choice. In every case, after the choice of the president, the person having the greatest number of votes of the electors shall be the vice president. But if there should remain two or more who have equal votes, the Senate shall choose from them by ballot the vice president.

4. The Congress may determine the time of choosing the electors, and the day on which they shall give their votes; which day shall be the same throughout the United States.

5. No person except a natural born citizen, *or a citizen of the United States, at the time of the adoption of this Constitution,* shall be eligible to the office of president; neither shall any person be eligible to that office who shall not have attained to the age of thirty-five years, and been fourteen years a resident within the United States.

6. *In case of the removal of the president from office, or of his death, resignation or inability to discharge the powers and duties of the said office, the same shall devolve on the vice president, and the Congress may by law provide for the case of removal, death, resignation or inability, both of the president and vice president, declaring what officer shall then act as president, and such officer shall act accordingly, until the disability be removed, or a president shall be elected.*

7. The president shall, at stated times, receive for his services, a compensation, which shall neither be increased nor diminished during the period for which he shall have been elected, and he shall not receive within that period any other emolument from the United States, or any of them.

8. Before he enter on the execution of his office, he shall take the following oath or affirmation:—"I do solemnly swear (or affirm) that I will faithfully execute the office of president of the United States, and will to the best of my ability, preserve, protect and defend the Constitution of the United States."

Qualifications for Office

Although the Constitution outlines qualifications for the office of president, some unstated factors are important as well. Ask the class to think of some of these tacit qualifications. Note the number of presidents who achieved a college-level education, held elected office before their election to the presidency, were married, and were members of a major party.

Some other unstated qualifications have changed along with society, such as being a male and a Protestant. Although no woman has yet become president, the idea of a woman president is much more acceptable now than in the past. John F. Kennedy broke the religious qualification barrier when he became the first Catholic president. You might also discuss moral qualifications. Scandals have thwarted some presidential candidates' hopes for office and threatened to unseat some who were elected.

God is clear in His Word about the qualities a leader should possess. Discuss Exodus 18:21; Deuteronomy 17:14–20; and 2 Samuel 23:2–4. Help the students see God's expectations for rulers in these passages.

Exodus 18:21

Leaders should have integrity. The public should have confidence that their leaders will not betray the trust placed in them. Leaders should also have ability. A candidate may identify himself as a Christian yet still be unqualified to hold an office.

Deuteronomy 17:14–20

This passage contains many particulars regarding Israel's kings that are not directly applicable today. Nonetheless, ideally, rulers should know God's law and fear God. They should fulfill their duties in submission to the law of the land and to God's law. This ideal is not always attainable, but it remains a worthy goal.

2 Samuel 23:2–4

This passage says that just rulers who fear God are a great blessing.

<table>
<tr><td>

The United States Constitution

</td><td>

Explanation

</td></tr>
</table>

Section 2

1. The president shall be commander in chief of the army and navy of the United States, and of the militia of the several states, when called into the actual service of the United States; he may require the opinion, in writing, of the principal officer in each of the executive departments, upon any subject relating to the duties of their respective offices, and he shall have power to grant reprieves and pardons for offences against the United States, except in cases of impeachment.

2. He shall have power, by and with the advice and consent of the Senate, to make treaties, provided two-thirds of the senators present concur; and he shall nominate, and by and with the advice and consent of the Senate, shall appoint ambassadors, other public ministers and consuls, judges of the Supreme Court, and all other officers of the United States, whose appointments are not herein otherwise provided for, and which shall be established by law: but the Congress may by law vest the appointment of such inferior officers, as they think proper, in the president alone, in the courts of law, or in the heads of departments.

3. The president shall have power to fill up all vacancies that may happen during the recess of the Senate, by granting commissions which shall expire at the end of their next session.

Section 3

He shall from time to time give to the Congress information of the state of the Union, and recommend to their consideration such measures as he shall judge necessary and expedient; he may, on extraordinary occasions, convene both houses, or either of them, and in case of disagreement between them, with respect to the time of adjournment, he may adjourn them to such time as he shall think proper; he shall receive ambassadors and other public ministers; he shall take care that the laws be faithfully executed, and shall commission all the officers of the United States.

Section 2: The Powers and Duties of the President

(1) Though Congress has some authority to check the president's military powers, his resources as commander in chief are many. Without a declaration of war, the president may approve secret operations, dispatch military patrols, and take other military actions. After Congress declares war, he has wide powers to direct military operations. It was a president who ordered the atomic bombs to be dropped on Japan in World War II, and it was a president who ordered American troops into the undeclared wars in Korea and Vietnam.

The phrase "in each of the executive departments" became the basis for the establishment of the president's cabinet. George Washington's cabinet included only four departments (state, treasury, war, and attorney general). Currently, there are fifteen departments, and several non-cabinet officials, such as the vice president, may be included in cabinet meetings.

Included among the president's powers is the power to grant **reprieves** (temporary postponement of punishment) and **pardons** (complete forgiveness of a crime and its consequent punishment). The president also has the power to offer amnesty, which is a general pardon to a group.

(2) This clause contains some of the checks and balances that Congress has over the president. The president or his diplomats may make treaties, but the Senate must approve them by a two-thirds majority. The president appoints ambassadors, ministers, consuls, judges, and other officials as allowed by the Constitution with approval of the Senate. Other positions are filled through the civil-service system used since 1883 to distribute government jobs according to merit, rather than as awards to friends (which occurred under the "spoils system," or patronage system).

(3) The president can fill vacancies in offices without Senate approval if the Senate is out of session. (These appointments are called recess appointments.) This clause was originally added to avoid long delays in government action when poor roads or weather kept senators from meeting. Today, presidents can avoid confirmation hearings this way, although they risk alienating the Senate or the public by overusing this power.

Section 3: The Duties of the President

a. The president gives Congress the required information in a written message or in a speech, called the State of the Union address, which is usually given near the end of January of each year.

b. The president can suggest that Congress pass certain legislation.

Presidential Impeachments

Only two presidents have been impeached—Andrew Johnson and Bill Clinton, and neither of them was convicted. Both of them remained in office following their acquittals.

In late 2019, the House began impeachment inquiry hearings regarding President Trump. The proceedings centered on whether Trump had acted inappropriately when he witheld funding for military assistance from Ukraine.

Although the House of Representatives held hearings that moved steadily toward the impeachment of Richard Nixon, he resigned before he could be impeached.

Governors

Assign students to research the office of governor in their state. In particular, ask them to compare the qualifications, election, powers, and duties of that office with those of the US president. Obtain a copy of your state's constitution, and make copies of pertinent sections.

News of Presidential Actions

Assign students to gather newspaper, magazine, and online articles about current presidential actions that correspond to various presidential duties.

c. He can convene (call into official session) both houses. This has been done rarely to deal with national emergencies, such as when President Wilson convened Congress to declare war on Germany in April 1917 and when President Franklin Roosevelt called a special session of Congress to deal with the Great Depression in March 1933.

d. If the House and Senate cannot agree on adjournment, the president can intervene.

e. He oversees diplomacy with ambassadors and public ministers. This is an important presidential power in the area of foreign affairs.

f. The president grants military officers their commissions.

Section 4: The Process of Impeachment

The president and other high officials can be impeached (have charges filed against them with the intention of removing them from office) for treason, bribery, other high crimes (felonies, such as murder and arson), and misdemeanors (lesser misdeeds). If the House of Representatives files such charges and the Senate convicts the accused of the charges, the official will be removed from office. If the Senate does not convict him, however, he may remain in office after impeachment.

Questions on Article II

1. What is the primary function of the executive branch?

2–4. What are the three qualifications for becoming president?

5. How long is the president's term of office?

6. What is the current line of presidential succession if the president is removed from office?

7. What powers does the president possess with which he can impact judicial decisions?

★ Which presidential power do you think holds the greatest potential for abuse? Why?

Section 4

The president, vice president and all civil officers of the United States, shall be removed from office on impeachment for, and conviction of, treason, bribery, or other high crimes and misdemeanors.

In 1998, Bill Clinton became the second president to be impeached. The first had been Andrew Johnson in 1868.

Article II Answers

1. to carry out (enforce) the nation's laws (p. 103)

2–4. must be a natural-born citizen, be at least thirty-five years old, and have been a US resident for at least fourteen years (p. 104)

5. four years (p. 103)

6. (a) vice president, (b) Speaker of the House of Representatives, (c) president pro tempore of the Senate, and (d) members of the cabinet in the order of the creation of their departments, beginning with the secretary of state (p. 104)

7. The president appoints certain judges. He may grant pardons and reprieves or offer amnesty. (p. 105)

★ Answers will vary.

Article III: The Judicial Branch

Section 1

The judicial power of the United States, shall be vested in one Supreme Court, and in such inferior courts as the Congress may from time to time ordain and establish. The judges, both of the Supreme and inferior courts, shall hold their offices during good behavior, and shall, at stated times, receive for their services, a compensation, which shall not be diminished during their continuance in office.

Section 2

1. The judicial power shall extend to all cases, in law and equity, arising under this Constitution, the laws of the United States, and treaties made, or which shall be made, under their authority;—to all cases affecting ambassadors, other public ministers and consuls;—to all cases of admiralty and maritime jurisdiction;—to controversies to which the United States shall be a party;—to controversies between two or more states;—*between a state and citizens of another state,*—between citizens of different states,—between citizens of the same state claiming lands under grants of different states, and *between a state, or the citizens thereof, and foreign states, citizens or subjects.*

2. In all cases affecting ambassadors, other public ministers and consuls, and those in which a state shall be party, the Supreme Court shall have original jurisdiction. In all the other cases before mentioned, the Supreme Court shall have appellate jurisdiction, both as to law and fact, with such exceptions, and under such regulations as the Congress shall make.

Article III: The Judicial Branch

Section 1: Authority

Traditionally, the function of the **judicial branch** has been to interpret the law. This function is not listed in the Constitution; it was established through court cases, especially the case of *Marbury v. Madison* (1803), which founded the principle of judicial review. This principle allows the Supreme Court to rule on the constitutionality of federal laws. That court, the only one specifically identified in the Constitution, is the nation's highest court; however, inferior, or lower, courts may be and have been created by Congress. They include circuit courts of appeals and federal district courts, as well as tax, claims, and military courts. Federal judges are appointed by the president with Senate approval, and they do not have specific terms of office. They may serve as long as they behave well; their service usually lasts for the remainder of their lives unless they retire, resign, or are impeached.

Section 2: Jurisdiction and Procedure

(1) This clause lists the cases that the federal courts must decide. No other courts can have jurisdiction in those cases. Amendment XI, however, returned the jurisdiction of cases between a state and citizens of another state (or another country) to the state courts.

(2) **Original jurisdiction** means that a case can start in the court in question and that the court has first opportunity to hear and decide the case. **Appellate jurisdiction** means that the case must first have been tried in a lower court before it can be appealed in a higher court.

Jurisdiction

Assign students to determine which US district court and which US circuit court of appeals serves your area. You could also assign other cities throughout the country. The following are examples of jurisdictions:

- Chicago, IL (district: Illinois Northern; circuit: Seventh)
- Manchester, NH (district: New Hampshire; circuit: First)
- Roanoke, VA (district: Virginia Western; circuit: Fourth)
- Sacramento, CA (district: California Eastern; circuit: Ninth)
- Honolulu, HI (district: Hawaii; circuit: Ninth)
- Midland, TX (district: Texas Western; circuit: Fifth)
- Casper, WY (district: Wyoming; circuit: Tenth)
- Camden, NJ (district: New Jersey; circuit: Third)

American Taliban

In 2002 John Walker Lindh, known as the American Taliban, avoided being charged with treason, partly because of the strict guidelines for conviction. Prosecutors knew it would be hard to provide two witnesses to prove that Lindh performed treasonous acts.

Espionage

Conviction of espionage often results in life imprisonment, although in one especially high-profile case it resulted in execution. In 1953 Julius and Ethel Rosenberg were found guilty of espionage, having provided the Soviet Union with American nuclear secrets. Both were executed by electric chair at Sing Sing Prison in New York State.

Jefferson on Juries

"With respect to the value of this institution [juries] I must make a general observation. We think in America that it is necessary to introduce the people into every department of government as far as they are capable of exercising it; and that this is the only way to ensure a long-continued and honest administration of its powers."

<table><tr><th>Explanation</th><th>The United States Constitution</th></tr></table>

Explanation

(3) A criminal trial is generally held in the same judicial district where a crime was committed, unless the defendant cannot get a fair trial there. The common method for trial is by jury.

Section 3: Treason

(1) **Treason** is defined specifically so that no one can be accused unjustly. It consists of going to war against the United States or giving aid and comfort to the enemies of the country. To be convicted of this crime, the accused must confess that he committed the crime or two eyewitnesses must testify to the fact in an open court.

(2) The punishment for treason is set by Congress and may extend only to the life of the accused himself, not to his family. Few people have actually been charged with treason. More often, they are charged with espionage, a lesser crime that is easier to prosecute.

Questions on Article III

1. What is the traditional function of the judicial branch?
2. What is the only court specifically identified in the Constitution?
3. What constitutional requirements of treason limit the abuse of accusations?
★ What do you think is the greatest weakness of the Supreme Court?

Article IV: Interstate Relations
Section 1: Full Faith and Credit
This section requires each state to respect the public records, laws, and court decisions of other states.

Section 2: Rights and Responsibilities
(1) If a citizen of a state passes through another state or moves there, he still keeps all his rights as an American citizen.

(2) A governor can request that a criminal who fled to another state be returned to the state where the crime was committed to stand trial. The process of returning the criminal is called **extradition**. However, the request for extradition may be denied by the governor of the state to which the criminal fled.

(3) Runaway slaves were to be returned to their owners on demand. This clause explains why the Underground Railroad existed in Northern states. To avoid extradition, some fugitive slaves escaped to Canada with the help of abolitionists through a series of safe houses and secret routes. Once outside the country they could

The United States Constitution

3. The trial of all crimes, except in cases of impeachment, shall be by jury; and such trial shall be held in the state where the said crimes shall have been committed; but when not committed within any state, the trial shall be at such place or places as the Congress may by law have directed.

Section 3
1. Treason against the United States, shall consist only in levying war against them, or in adhering to their enemies, giving them aid and comfort. No person shall be convicted of treason unless on the testimony of two witnesses to the same overt act, or on confession in open court.
2. The Congress shall have power to declare the punishment of treason, but no attainder of treason shall work corruption of blood, or forfeiture except during the life of the person attainted.

Article IV: Interstate Relations
Section 1
Full faith and credit shall be given in each state to the public acts, records, and judicial proceedings of every other state. And the Congress may by general laws prescribe the manner in which such acts, records and proceedings shall be proved, and the effect thereof.

Section 2
1. The citizens of each state shall be entitled to all privileges and immunities of citizens in the several states.
2. A person charged in any state with treason, felony, or other crime, who shall flee from justice, and be found in another state, shall on demand of the executive authority of the state from which he fled, be delivered up, to be removed to the state having jurisdiction of the crime.
3. *No person held to service or labor in one state, under the laws thereof, escaping into another, shall, in consequence of any law or regulation therein, be discharged from such service or labor, but shall be delivered up on claim of the party to whom such service or labor may be due.*

Treason Cases

The United States has only brought charges of treason approximately thirty times since the Constitution was ratified. If possible, find copies of the Supreme Court's opinions in the following three treason cases: *Cramer v. United States* (1945), *Haupt v. United States* (1947), and *Kawakita v. United States* (1952). Assign students to groups, one for each case. Each group should review its case and create a profile that includes the facts of the case, the Court's decision (with some explanation), and important historical precedents referred to in the decision. Students could also research famous treason cases such as those involving Aaron Burr, John Brown (treason against Virginia), and Tokyo Rose.

Article III Answers

1. to interpret the law (p. 107)
2. the Supreme Court (p. 107)
3. The definition of treason is limited to levying war against the United States or giving aid and comfort to its enemies. Conviction demands the testimony of two witnesses or a public confession in court. (p. 108)
★ Students may mention that a small group of judges has tremendous power. Others may say it does not have the authority or power to enforce its decisions.

What If?

Guide a discussion about what the United States might be like if the full faith and credit clause did not exist. Ask how many students have moved from one state to another. Discuss the changes such moves require (e.g., new addresses, drivers' licenses, auto tags, and voter-registration cards). Speculate about the amount of additional paperwork that would be required without such a clause. Also suggest the impact that the clause's absence would have on the criminal-justice system. How does this clause ultimately contribute to the goals established by the Preamble of the Constitution?

<table>
<tr><th>The United States Constitution</th><th>Explanation</th></tr>
</table>

Section 3

1. New states may be admitted by the Congress into this Union; but no new state shall be formed or erected within the jurisdiction of any other state; nor any state be formed by the junction of two or more states, or parts of states, without the consent of the legislatures of the states concerned as well as of the Congress.
2. The Congress shall have power to dispose of and make all needful rules and regulations respecting the territory or other property belonging to the United States; and nothing in this Constitution shall be so construed as to prejudice any claims of the United States, or of any particular state.

Section 4

The United States shall guarantee to every state in this Union a republican form of government, and shall protect each of them against invasion; and on application of the legislature, or of the executive (when the legislature cannot be convened), against domestic violence.

---

avoid being returned to their former owners. Southerners demanded a fugitive-slave law that would compel Northern states to return runaway slaves to their owners. In 1865, Amendment XIII abolished slavery and, with it, the purpose for this clause.

Section 3: Powers of Congress

(1) Congress admits new states to the Union, but if a state is formed out of another state or by the combination of "two or more states, or parts of states," the legislatures of the affected states must also approve.

(2) Congress is in charge of regulating US territories. Today, this applies to such areas as Puerto Rico, Guam, American Samoa, the Northern Mariana Islands, and the US Virgin Islands, but these possessions are usually given a large measure of self-government. For instance, Puerto Rico has many powers that the fifty states also enjoy, but it is exempt from certain federal tax measures and language laws. However, Puerto Rico and other territories lack voting representation in Congress.

Section 4: Requirements and Guarantees

When a state submits its constitution, that state must have a republican form of government. The federal government guarantees the survival of that republican government by protecting the states from invasion or by handling domestic violence when a state legislature or a state's governor requests help.

Questions on Article IV

1. What is each state required to respect?
2. What request does not have to be respected by other states?
3. What kind of government are new states required to have?

Fugitive Slave Laws

Article IV, Section 2, clause 3 states that runaway slaves were to be returned to their owners on demand. By 1850, the issue of returning such individuals had become a very contentious issue. That year, as a part of the Compromise of 1850, a stronger Fugitive Slave Act was passed. The law established a new, and controversial, process. Special federal commissioners now judged fugitive slave cases. They were paid ten dollars if they ruled for the slave owner and five dollars if they ruled against. Proponents asserted that the higher payment was justified on the grounds that ruling against an alleged fugitive required more paperwork. Opponents charged that the higher payment was effectively a bribe to influence the decision.

Those who opposed the new law also expressed other concerns. They feared that African Americans who were actually free persons would be seized on the pretext that they were runaway slaves. They objected to the fact that though owners could bring witnesses forward, the alleged runaways were prevented from testifying on their own behalf. Citizens who for conscience reasons opposed slavery were still required to participate in the return of runaway slaves. Opponents viewed this as unjust.

Article IV Answers

1. the public records, laws, and court decisions of other states (p. 108)
2. an extradition request (p. 108)
3. a republican government (p. 109)

Religious Tests

Some delegates, such as Oliver Ellsworth, argued that a religious test would discriminate against honorable people. After all, a person of integrity would not affirm a religious oath if he believed differently, but an unscrupulous person might consent even if he did not believe.

Others argued that requiring elected officials to affirm their belief in God or in the inspiration of the Scriptures, as many states did at the time the Constitution was adopted, was not wrong. They asserted that even if some men were dishonest, the expectation for a Christian government was maintained. Many of the states at the time that the Constitution was adopted tolerated all religions but expected their leaders to embrace basic Christian beliefs.

Article V: Amending the Constitution

Two-thirds of both houses of Congress may present proposed amendments, or two-thirds of the states may call for a convention to propose amendments to the Constitution. Ratification, or approval to put an amendment into effect, requires approval by three-fourths of the state legislatures or three-fourths of the states in their own conventions. When amendments are ratified, they become part of the Constitution, but no amendment may ever be made to take away equal representation in the Senate (without a state's consent).

The two clauses that were protected temporarily from amendment dealt indirectly with the importation and taxation of slaves. While this article protected the institution of slavery for twenty years, not all the Founding Fathers necessarily supported slavery. For example, James Madison hoped that the institution would die on its own in the allotted twenty years.

Questions on Article V

1–2. What groups have the power to propose amendments?

3. How much approval is needed to ratify an amendment?

4. What provision of the Constitution can never be changed without the consent of a state?

★ Why do you think the framers purposefully make it hard for amendments to be ratified?

Article VI: Constitutional and National Supremacy

(1) The new government under the Constitution would accept all debts and agreements made previously by the Confederation government. This clause assured foreign creditors that the new government would not erase debts made under the Articles of Confederation. A moral obligation to repay those debts remained.

(2) Known as the **supremacy clause**, this clause upholds the following as the supreme (highest) law of the nation:

    a. The US Constitution

    b. Laws of the national government

    c. Treaties

State and local laws must always abide by the limits placed by the Constitution and federal legislation.

(3) All national and state officers must affirm their support for the Constitution. However, holding specific religious beliefs is not a prerequisite for holding public office.

Article V: Amending the Constitution

The Congress, whenever two-thirds of both houses shall deem it necessary, shall propose amendments to this Constitution, or, on the application of the legislatures of two-thirds of the several states, shall call a convention for proposing amendments, which, in either case, shall be valid to all intents and purposes, as part of this Constitution, when ratified by the legislatures of three-fourths of the several states, or by conventions in three-fourths thereof, as the one or the other mode of ratification may be proposed by the Congress; provided that *no amendment which may be made prior to the year one thousand eight hundred and eight shall in any manner affect the first and fourth clauses in the ninth section of the first article; and that* no state, without its consent, shall be deprived of its equal suffrage in the Senate.

Article VI: Constitutional and National Supremacy

1. All debts contracted and engagements entered into, before the adoption of this Constitution, shall be as valid against the United States under this Constitution, as under the Confederation.

2. This Constitution, and the laws of the United States which shall be made in pursuance thereof; and all treaties made, or which shall be made, under the authority of the United States, shall be the supreme law of the land; and the judges in every state shall be bound thereby, any thing in the constitution or laws of any state to the contrary notwithstanding.

3. The senators and representatives before mentioned, and the members of the several state legislatures, and all executive and judicial officers, both of the United States and of the several states, shall be bound by oath or affirmation, to support this Constitution; but no religious test shall ever be required as a qualification to any office or public trust under the United States.

Article VII: Ratifying the Constitution

The ratification of the conventions of nine states, shall be sufficient for the establishment of

---

Article V Answers

1–2. both houses of Congress; a national convention (called at the request of two-thirds of the states) (p. 110)

3. three-fourths of the state legislatures or three-fourths of state conventions (p. 110)

4. States cannot be deprived of their equal number of representatives in the Senate. (p. 110)

★ to prevent the people (or the government) from making whimsical or dangerous changes to the Constitution

True Supremacy

Although the Constitution is the highest law in the land, Christians are bound to obey God rather than man when their mandates conflict (Acts 5:29). Discuss with students a scenario in which the First Amendment might be interpreted in ways to restrict Christian religious freedoms. Students should interact with the following Scripture texts:

- Matthew 5:10–12; 2 Timothy 3:12; 1 Peter 4:12
  Christians should not be surprised or dismayed at persecution.
- Acts 16:37–39; 22:25–29; 23:27; 25:8–12
  Christians may appeal to their rights as citizens.
- Acts 23:2–5; Romans 13:1–7; Titus 3:1–3; 1 Peter 2:13–25
  Christians should remain respectful even in their speech toward authorities. As was true of Christ, they may have to bear unjust suffering.

this Constitution between the states so ratifying the same....

Done in convention by the unanimous consent of the states present the seventeenth day of September in the year of our Lord one thousand seven hundred and eighty-seven and of the independence of the United States of America the twelfth. In witness whereof we have hereunto subscribed our names,

George Washington, president and deputy from Virginia

Delaware
George Read, Gunning Bedford Jr., John Dickinson, Richard Bassett, Jacob Broom

Maryland
James McHenry, Daniel of St. Thomas Jenifer, Daniel Carroll

Virginia
John Blair, James Madison Jr.

North Carolina
William Blount, Richard Dobbs Spaight, Hugh Williamson

South Carolina
John Rutledge, Charles Cotesworth Pinckney, Charles Pinckney, Pierce Butler

Georgia
William Few, Abraham Baldwin

New Hampshire
John Langdon, Nicholas Gilman

Massachusetts
Nathaniel Gorham, Rufus King

Connecticut
William Samuel Johnson, Roger Sherman

New York
Alexander Hamilton

New Jersey
William Livingston, David Brearley, William Paterson, Jonathan Dayton

Pennsylvania
Benjamin Franklin, Thomas Mifflin, Robert Morris, George Clymer, Thomas FitzSimons, Jared Ingersoll, James Wilson, Gouverneur Morris

Questions on Article VI

1. What provision did the Constitution make for debts contracted before its ratification?

2–3. What is the second clause of Article VI known as, and what does it state?

4. What can never be a qualification for seeking public office?

★ Does the third clause of Article VI prohibit citizens from taking a candidate's religion into account when deciding whom to support? Explain your answer.

Article VII: Ratifying the Constitution

Nine of the thirteen states had to ratify the Constitution to begin the operation of the new government.

No one from Rhode Island signed the Constitution because no delegates from the state were sent to the Constitutional Convention. However, Rhode Island did ratify the Constitution in 1790—and was the last of the original thirteen states to do so.

Questions on Article VII

1. How many states had to ratify the Constitution before it took effect?

2–3. Which of the original thirteen states did not have a representative sign the Constitution? Why?

Independent Rhode Island

Rhode Island's actions during this period may be attributed to its democratic localism and its tradition of autonomy. Rhode Islanders tended to resist all central governments, whether those governments sat in London or Philadelphia. In addition, Rhode Island relied on paper money, which was favored by its agricultural interests; this put it at odds with Article I, Section 10, of the Constitution.

A debtor revolt in the 1780s put the agrarian faction in control of Rhode Island's legislature, and that legislature not only refused to send delegates to the Constitutional Convention but also rejected eleven attempts by other factions to hold a ratifying convention. The legislature finally relented in 1790, eight months after George Washington became president (and after the city of Providence threatened to secede from the state). The vote on the Constitution favored ratification by the narrowest of margins (34–32), with some notable Anti-Federalists abstaining.

Despite strong Anti-Federalist sentiment, Rhode Island finally ratified the Constitution because of George Washington's prestige, the support of major Rhode Island newspapers, the passage of the Bill of Rights, and the proposed federal assumption of state debts.

Church Constitutions

Locate a copy of a church constitution for the students to examine. Direct attention to the amendment process, if there is one. Are there certain stipulations about the amendment process, like those found in Article V of the US Constitution? Note that some church constitutions have portions that are unamendable, usually because they refer to doctrinal matters. If these portions were changed, the biblical purpose of the church could be destroyed.

Article VI Answers

1. All prior debts were valid against the United States, as they were under the Confederation. (p. 110)

2–3. the supremacy clause; the US Constitution, the laws of the US government, and treaties are the supreme law of the land (p. 110)

4. a religious test (p. 110)

★ No; the government cannot impose a religious qualification, but citizens may take a candidate's religion into account when voting in elections.

Article VII Answers

1. nine (p. 111)

2–3. Rhode Island; it sent no delegates to the convention. (p. 111)

Wars of Religion

Desire for religious freedom in the United States was spurred by religious intolerance in Europe during earlier centuries. Insistence on one official faith contributed to many "wars of religion," both between and within nations. Even in England, Protestant Dissenters (e.g., the Pilgrims and the Puritans) faced religious discrimination that prevented their participation in the government.

The Second Amendment's Intent

In recent times, the Second Amendment has become more controversial. Violent crimes and accidents (especially ones involving small children) have led to more legislative interest in gun-control laws. Nevertheless, the original purpose of the amendment remains the same: to guarantee the right to keep and bear arms.

Christians thinking about this topic have two issues to consider. First, they must consider what the Constitution says. Second, they must consider how Scripture applies to what the Constitution says. Even if a Christian concludes that the Constitution permits armed resistance to tyranny, he must ask whether the Bible permits such resistance. At the time of the Revolutionary War, some American Christians reasoned that Calvin's law of the lesser magistrate gave them the right to armed resistance when they resisted under the auspices of elected officials. Many contemporary Christians do not believe that the law of the lesser magistrate is supported by Scripture. Calvin himself stressed obedience to magistrates, and Paul and Peter did so as well, even in the context of persecution (Rom. 13:1–7; 1 Pet. 2:13–17). If necessary, Christians must be willing to forgo their rights for Christ's sake (1 Cor. 9:18–19).

The Bill of Rights (Amendments I–X)

James Madison introduced twelve amendments on July 21, 1789. Of these, one failed the process and one went unratified for over two hundred years until 1992, when it became the Twenty-Seventh Amendment. The other ten were ratified in a little more than two years and are now known as the Bill of Rights. Although the Bill of Rights went into effect on December 15, 1791, the freedoms it listed already existed. However, the Bill of Rights protected them from federal government interference, ensuring their continuance. The Constitution and Bill of Rights secure the people's liberties. The ten amendments that compose the Bill of Rights illustrate the principles of limited government. At first, the limitations in the Bill of Rights applied just to the central government but not directly to the states. For example, state taxes were levied to support state churches until 1818 in Connecticut and until 1833 in Massachusetts. Supreme Court decisions have since bound the states to abide by most of the stipulations in the Bill of Rights.

Amendment I: Freedom of Expression

The First Amendment ensures five freedoms:
1. religion,
2. speech,
3. press,
4. assembly, and
5. petition.

Because this amendment guarantees freedom of religion, Congress cannot establish any church or denomination as a state-sponsored church. Recently, some judges have interpreted the First Amendment as meaning that religious expressions in public forums are prohibited and that religious motivations in forming public policy are forbidden. In some cases, the free exercise of religion has been limited to freedom of worship.

In addition, some Christian businesses that decline to participate in same-sex weddings or Christian adoption agencies that will not place children in same-sex households have been banned from continuing those practices. Other Christians have been unable to freely exercise their religion in the workplace. In these cases the free exercise of religion has been pitted against perceived civil rights violations.

Freedom of speech is important to our political system because it permits criticism of officials' actions. Freedom of speech is not, however, unlimited. **Slander** (defaming a person verbally) or **libel** (defaming a person in writing) are not included, and neither is any speech advocating the violent overthrow of the American government. According to the precedent set by the 1735 trial of John Peter Zenger (see Chapter 15), truth is the

Amendments to the Constitution
Amendment I: Freedom of Expression

Congress shall make no law respecting an establishment of religion, or prohibiting the free exercise thereof; or abridging the freedom of speech, or of the press; or the right of the people peaceably to assemble, and to petition the government for a redress of grievances.

Bill of Rights Checkup

After the students have read the section on the Bill of Rights, direct them to close their books. Use questions such as the following to quiz them on their knowledge:

- Which amendment guarantees the right to bear arms? (*the Second Amendment*)
- Which amendment prohibits excessive bail requirements? (*the Eighth Amendment*)
- Which amendment guarantees freedom of the press? (*the First Amendment*)
- Which amendment guarantees free exercise of religion? (*the First Amendment*)
- What two amendments deal with unstated rights? (*the Ninth and Tenth Amendments*)
- Which amendment gives the accused the right to a grand jury? (*the Fifth Amendment*)
- Which amendment gives a person the right to a speedy trial? (*the Sixth Amendment*)
- Which amendment prohibits forced quartering of troops in homes under most circumstances? (*the Third Amendment*)
- Which amendment prohibits the government from taking private property without compensation? (*the Fifth Amendment*)
- Which amendment prohibits unreasonable searches and seizures? (*the Fourth Amendment*)
- Which amendment allows a jury trial in cases involving more than twenty dollars in value? (*the Seventh Amendment*)

Guns and Crime

A frequently cited reason for gun control is the belief that gun control will reduce crime. Proponents of increased gun control argue that guns are too accessible. Opponents of gun control note that some countries that have strict gun bans continue to have high crime rates, as do many US states and cities with strict gun-control laws. Conversely, they argue that wherever citizens have greater freedom to own, carry, and use firearms, crime is lower. They cite the adage "When guns are outlawed, only outlaws have guns." Ask students which view they support and ask them to clearly state arguments supporting their beliefs.

Amendment II: The Right to Bear Arms

A well regulated militia, being necessary to the security of a free state, the right of the people to keep and bear arms, shall not be infringed.

Amendment III: No Quartering of Troops

No soldier shall, in time of peace be quartered in any house, without the consent of the owner, nor in time of war, but in a manner to be prescribed by law.

Amendment IV: No Unreasonable Searches and Seizures

The right of the people to be secure in their persons, houses, papers, and effects, against unreasonable searches and seizures, shall not be violated, and no warrants shall issue, but upon probable cause, supported by oath or affirmation, and particularly describing the place to be searched, and the persons or things to be seized.

Amendment V: Rights of the Accused

No person shall be held to answer for a capital, or otherwise infamous crime, unless on a presentment or indictment of a grand jury, except in cases arising in the land or naval forces, or in the militia, when in actual service in time of war or public danger; nor shall any person be subject for the same offence to be twice put in jeopardy of life or limb; nor shall be compelled in any criminal case to be a witness against himself, nor be deprived of life, liberty, or property, without due process of law; nor shall private property be taken for public use, without just compensation.

---

only valid defense against false accusations of libel or slander.

Without the right of assembly, there could be no clubs, political parties, churches, or political meetings except those approved by the government. Assemblies must be peaceable, however; violent mobs are not protected by this amendment.

Amendment II: The Right to Bear Arms

This amendment forbids Congress from infringing on citizens' right to keep weapons. This provision was necessary for two reasons: (1) to ensure that state militias would continue to exist and (2) to ensure that individuals had a right to own firearms.

Amendment III: No Involuntary Quartering of Troops

This amendment protects citizens by forbidding military intrusion into their homes. It reflects the colonists' resentment of Britain's efforts to force them to take soldiers into their homes.

Amendment IV: No Unreasonable Searches and Seizures

This amendment guarantees the privacy of homes from illegal searches. It does not keep authorities from conducting legal searches or seizures, but it does require them to get search warrants first and thereby protects citizens from indiscriminate intrusions.

Amendment V: Rights of the Accused

In a trial, a **grand jury**, composed of a panel of citizens, considers the prosecution's case against the accused. Its finding is used to determine whether there is enough evidence against the accused to warrant a jury trial to determine guilt or innocence.

This amendment ensures that no citizen can be forced to give evidence against himself. In addition, no person can be tried twice for the same crime if a legal judgment was reached in the first trial; and a person cannot be imprisoned, have his property taken away, or be sentenced to death without a fair and proper trial (**due process**). Private property can be taken by the government to use for public purposes (a process called **eminent domain**), but the owner(s) must receive compensation. For instance, the government can take land needed for the building of a highway, but it must pay a fair price for that land.

Search and Seizure

Details about search and seizure rules and procedures are found in Title 18, Section 2, Chapter 205, of the US Code. The code includes such specifics as when an officer may break a door or window.

> The officer may break open any outer or inner door or window of a house, or any part of a house, or anything therein, to execute a search warrant, if, after notice of his authority and purpose, he is refused admittance or when necessary to liberate himself or a person aiding him in the execution of the warrant.

Incorporation

The process by which state laws have become bound by the Bill of Rights is known as incorporation. This concept will be presented to the students in Chapter 15.

This nationalization of the Bill of Rights did not happen immediately, nor has all the Bill of Rights been incorporated. Divide the students into teams to find at least three Supreme Court cases in which the Court ruled that parts of the Bill of Rights had become applicable to the states through the due process clause of the Fourteenth Amendment. Some important cases are as follows:

Gitlow v. New York: First Amendment (1925)

De Jonge v. Oregon: First Amendment (1937)

Cantwell v. Connecticut: First Amendment (1940)

Everson v. Board of Education: First Amendment (1947)

Louisiana ex rel. Francis v. Resweber: Eighth Amendment (1947)

In re Oliver: Sixth Amendment (1948)

Wolf v. Colorado: Fourth Amendment (1949)

Mapp v. Ohio: Fourth Amendment (1961)

Gideon v. Wainwright: Sixth Amendment (1963)

Malloy v. Hogan: Fifth Amendment (1964)

Griswold v. Connecticut: Ninth Amendment (1965)

Duncan v. Louisiana: Sixth Amendment (1968)

Eminent Domain

Debate the pros and cons of eminent domain. Give examples of the abuse of this principle (e.g., some would say when the government takes private property to allow a developer to build a shopping center or resort).

<table>
<tr><td>

Explanation

Amendment VI: Rights of the Accused in Criminal Trials

Because some political trials in England were held in secret and lasted for years (while the accused remained in jail), the right to a speedy, public trial was important to the framers. An accused person has the right to see and face his accuser and his witnesses. The court calls a witness to appear by serving a **subpoena** (a document requiring a person to appear in court as a witness). Accused individuals have the right to have an attorney to defend them.

Amendment VII: Rights of Citizens in Civil Trials

An individual in any court case involving money or property valued over twenty dollars can demand a trial by jury. Juries are composed of randomly selected members of society who meet certain qualifications. Thomas Jefferson regarded juries as a further way to involve the public in government (popular sovereignty) and check government power.

Amendment VIII: No Cruel, Unusual, or Unjust Punishment

Bail (money paid to guarantee a court appearance, allowing the accused to be free while awaiting trial) may be required, but it must not be excessive. Unusual punishments included whipping, hanging by the heels, branding, and confining in stocks. This amendment outlawed such abuses. It is the courts' right to decide when bail and fines are excessive and when punishments are cruel or unusual.

Amendment IX: Unspecified Rights of the People

Before the adoption of the Bill of Rights, some Americans feared that by specifying certain rights, some would assume that unspecified rights did not exist. This amendment helped calm those concerns by stating that if the Constitution does not list a specific right, that right may nonetheless exist. For example, the right to move and settle somewhere or to choose an occupation are unlisted, yet Americans still have them. Amendment X also addresses this issue.

</td><td>

The United States Constitution

Amendment VI: Rights of the Accused in Criminal Trials

In all criminal prosecutions, the accused shall enjoy the right to a speedy and public trial, by an impartial jury of the state and district wherein the crime shall have been committed, which district shall have been previously ascertained by law, and to be informed of the nature and cause of the accusation; to be confronted with the witnesses against him; to have compulsory process for obtaining witnesses in his favor, and to have the assistance of counsel for his defence.

Amendment VII: Rights of Citizens in Civil Trials

In suits at common law, where the value in controversy shall exceed twenty dollars, the right of trial by jury shall be preserved, and no fact tried by a jury, shall be otherwise re-examined in any court of the United States, than according to the rules of the common law.

Amendment VIII: No Cruel, Unusual, or Unjust Punishment

Excessive bail shall not be required, nor excessive fines imposed, nor cruel and unusual punishments inflicted.

Protesters in front of the US Supreme Court denounce the death penalty as a violation of the Constitution.

Amendment IX: Unspecified Rights of the People

The enumeration in the Constitution, of certain rights, shall not be construed to deny or disparage others retained by the people.

</td></tr>
</table>

Death Penalty

After the students have read the examples of unusual punishments given in the explanation on this page, ask them to notice what is not included in that list (the death penalty). Also have them consider the wording of the Fifth Amendment, which states that no person can "be deprived of life, liberty, or property, without due process of law." (Consequently, according to the Constitution, one can be deprived of life if there is due process of law.) Discuss current public opinion about the death penalty. Also point out the lack of a death penalty in Europe and other parts of the world. Finally, ask them to look at relevant Scripture passages (Gen. 9:6; Exod. 21:12–14; Num. 35:30–31).

<table>
<tr><th>The United States Constitution</th><th>Explanation</th></tr>
</table>

Amendment X: Reserved Rights of the States or the People

The powers not delegated to the United States by the Constitution, nor prohibited by it to the states, are reserved to the states respectively, or to the people.

Amendment XI: Suing States

The judicial power of the United States shall not be construed to extend to any suit in law or equity, commenced or prosecuted against one of the United States by citizens of another state, or by citizens or subjects of any foreign state.

Amendment XII: Separate Ballots for President and Vice President

The electors shall meet in their respective states and vote by ballot for president and vice-president, one of whom, at least, shall not be an inhabitant of the same state with themselves; they shall name in their ballots the person voted for as president, and in distinct ballots the person voted for as vice-president, and they shall make distinct lists of all persons voted for as president, and of all persons voted for as vice-president, and of the number of votes for each, which lists they shall sign and certify, and transmit sealed to the seat of the government of the United States, directed to the president of the Senate;—the president of the Senate shall, in the presence of the Senate and House of Representatives, open all the certificates and the votes shall then be counted;—the person having the greatest number of votes for president, shall be the president, if such number be a majority of the whole number of electors appointed; and if no person have such majority, then from the persons having the highest numbers not exceeding three on the list of those voted for as president, the House of Representatives shall choose immediately, by ballot, the president. But in choosing the president, the votes shall be taken by states, the representation from each state having one vote; a quorum for this purpose shall consist of a member or members from two-thirds of the states, and a majority of all the states shall be necessary to a choice. *And if the House of Representatives shall not choose a president whenever the right of choice shall devolve upon them, before the fourth day of March next following, then the vice-president shall act as president, as in case of the death or other constitutional disability of the president.—The*

Amendment X: Reserved Rights of the States or the People

The states or the people possess any rights that the Constitution does not forbid them to have. The federal government cannot take such rights away from them. And not all the federal government's powers are expressly stated in the Constitution. Certain powers are implied by the very fact that a government must govern.

Amendments XI–XXVII

The following seventeen amendments have been passed since 1791. Some corrected problems or more fully explained subjects. Some are related to one another, such as those passed during Reconstruction, and they deal with problems or ideas from a given time period. Others deal with single issues.

Amendment XI: Suing States
(proposed March 4, 1794; ratified February 7, 1795)

Amendment XI states that a citizen of a state (or of a foreign country) may not sue another state in a federal court without that state's consent. Suits must be pursued in a state's own courts.

Amendment XII: Separate Ballots for President and Vice President
(proposed December 9, 1803; ratified June 15, 1804)

The provisions of this amendment replaced those outlined in Article II, Section 1, clause 2, which had created some awkward political situations. Instead of voting for two people, electors now vote separately for the president and vice president. Thus the possibility of a tie between the president and vice president, such as the one that occurred in 1800, is eliminated. The amendment also prevents the selection of a president and a vice president from opposing parties, which might make it difficult for them to work together for the nation's good. Later, Amendment XX changed Inauguration Day to January 20, so the date for the House to hold a special presidential vote was moved to an earlier date.

This amendment also provides resolution of deadlock in the Electoral College. The House breaks the deadlock in the case of the president, and the Senate does the same for the vice president. Because the vice president may have to act as president under certain circumstances, he must meet the same qualifications for office as those established for the president.

Amendment X

When Amendment X was originally proposed, two delegates suggested changing its wording to read "The powers not expressly delegated…" However, Madison and most of Congress rejected this change on the grounds that "it was impossible to confine a Government to the exercise of express powers; there must necessarily be admitted powers by implication, unless the constitution descended to recount every minutiae."

Awkward Situations

The awkward situations referred to in the student text involved the elections of 1796 and 1800. In the first, John Adams and Thomas Pinckney represented the Federalists for president and vice president against Thomas Jefferson and Aaron Burr, who represented the Democratic-Republicans. Political infighting among the Federalists caused Adams to receive the most electoral votes, followed by Jefferson rather than Pinckney. As a result, President Adams spent a contentious term with Vice President Jefferson, head of the opposing party.

In the 1800 election, it was nearly the same matchup—John Adams and Charles Cotesworth Pinckney (Thomas Pinckney's brother) for the Federalists and Thomas Jefferson and Aaron Burr for the Republicans. This time the Republicans won, but both Jefferson and Burr received the same number of electoral votes. The election was thrown to the House of Representatives to decide which of the two should be president. Finally, on the thirty-sixth ballot, Jefferson was chosen.

Two confusing consecutive elections were enough to demonstrate the need for a constitutional amendment.

Amendment X

Discuss how the vagueness of Amendment X (in contrast to the more specific wording of "not expressly delegated") allowed the national government to grow. Debate whether that growth was a necessary part of governing a growing nation or a needless appropriation of power by the federal government.

No Twelfth Amendment

Imagine a scenario in the most recent or upcoming presidential election in which the Twelfth Amendment does not exist. Ask the students to consider an actual situation in which the president and vice president were from separate parties. Ask the students whether their opinion of the amendment would change depending on who is elected to be president and vice president.

Amendment XIII, Section 2

Amendment XIII empowered Congress to establish necessary legislation to end slavery. However, there were limits to this power. For instance, in the case *Hodges v. United States* (1906), the Court found that Congress could not ensure equal access to public accommodations based on this amendment. In other words, racial discrimination was not ended by Amendment XIII. Additional laws had to be enacted to eliminate that problem.

Amendment XIV, Section 2

By the Three-Fifths Compromise of the Constitution (Article I, Section 2, clause 3), states counted three-fifths of their total slave population in determining representation in Congress. After the Thirteenth Amendment abolished slavery, all black Americans were included in that determination. However, blacks were often still denied voting rights; this meant that southern states received more representatives in Congress than they had before the Civil War while they continued to prevent most black Americans from voting in the elections of those representatives. Fearing that this change would give southern Democrats an advantage, northern Republicans added Section 2 of Amendment XIV, which lowered the representation of any state that prevented blacks from voting. Nevertheless, when southerners continued to keep black Americans from voting, northerners did not invoke this provision of the amendment.

Reconstruction Amendments (XIII–XV)

Amendments XIII–XV were all ratified just after the Civil War and deal with problems of that era.

Amendment XIII: Slavery Abolished
(proposed January 31, 1865; ratified December 6, 1865)

Although Lincoln's Emancipation Proclamation declared an end to slavery in the states that comprised the Confederate States of America (CSA), a constitutional amendment was needed for two main reasons. First, the president based his authority to free the slaves on the war powers granted to him as commander in chief in Article II, Section 2, of the Constitution. Thus the proclamation might have seemed to lose its validity after the war. Second, the Emancipation Proclamation abolished slavery only in the Southern states that seceded from the Union. Provision had to be made for the remainder of the nation.

Section 1—The amendment declares that "involuntary servitude," or forced labor, and slavery are illegal anywhere in the United States. One exception is that forced labor can be a part of the punishment of a person convicted of a crime.

Amendment XIV: Citizenship Defined
(proposed June 13, 1866; ratified July 9, 1868)

Section 1—By this amendment all people—white or black, slave or free—who were born in the United States or naturalized are both American citizens and citizens of the state in which they live. A state cannot deprive any person of life, liberty, or property without due process (a fair trial based on just laws and following proper procedures). This amendment extended the entire Bill of Rights to all citizens equally and decreed that all future laws should be the same for every citizen.

Section 2—This section prevented Southern states from counting black citizens for representation in Congress while preventing them from voting. The Fifteenth Amendment made this section unnecessary.

person having the greatest number of votes as vice-president, shall be the vice-president, if such number be a majority of the whole number of electors appointed, and if no person have a majority, then from the two highest numbers on the list, the Senate shall choose the vice-president; a quorum for the purpose shall consist of two-thirds of the whole number of senators, and a majority of the whole number shall be necessary to a choice. But no person constitutionally ineligible to the office of president shall be eligible to that of vice-president of the United States.

Amendment XIII: Slavery Abolished

Section 1. Neither slavery nor involuntary servitude, except as a punishment for crime whereof the party shall have been duly convicted, shall exist within the United States, or any place subject to their jurisdiction.

Section 2. Congress shall have power to enforce this article by appropriate legislation.

Amendment XIV: Citizenship Defined

Section 1. All persons born or naturalized in the United States, and subject to the jurisdiction thereof, are citizens of the United States and of the state wherein they reside. No state shall make or enforce any law which shall abridge the privileges or immunities of citizens of the United States; nor shall any state deprive any person of life, liberty, or property, without due process of law; nor deny to any person within its jurisdiction the equal protection of the laws.

Section 2. Representatives shall be apportioned among the several states according to their respective numbers, counting the whole number of persons in each state, excluding Indians not taxed. But when the right to vote at any election for the choice of electors for president and vice-president of the United States, representatives in Congress, the executive and judicial officers of a state, or the members of the legislature thereof, is denied to any of the male inhabitants of such state, being twenty-one years of age, and citizens of the United States, or in any way abridged, except for participation in rebellion, or other crime, the basis of representation therein shall be reduced in the proportion which the number of such male citizens shall bear to the whole number of male citizens twenty-one years of age in such state.

Amendment Maps

Provide the students with maps of the United States. Then assign each student one of the twenty-seven amendments. Instruct students to use different colors to indicate (a) which states were in the Union when the assigned amendment passed and (b) whether each state ratified or rejected the amendment. You might want to establish uniform color codes for ease of grading.

Reconstruction Amendments

As you cover the Fourteenth and Fifteenth Amendments (two of the Reconstruction Amendments), discuss with your students the civil-rights movement of the 1960s and current issues with racism. Help students understand that laws not only provide for justice but also set the expectations of society. For instance, outlawing racial discrimination sends the message that society will not tolerate racial discrimination.

However, when a nation legalizes or tolerates sins that it ought to outlaw, it sends a signal that such sins are acceptable. For instance, when the Supreme Court legalized same-sex marriage, it became normalized for the country.

Section 3. No person shall be a senator or representative in Congress, or elector of president and vice-president, or hold any office, civil or military, under the United States, or under any state, who, having previously taken an oath, as a member of Congress, or as an officer of the United States, or as a member of any state legislature, or as an executive or judicial officer of any state, to support the Constitution of the United States, shall have engaged in insurrection or rebellion against the same, or given aid or comfort to the enemies thereof. But Congress may by a vote of two-thirds of each house, remove such disability.

Section 4. The validity of the public debt of the United States, authorized by law, including debts incurred for payment of pensions and bounties for services in suppressing insurrection or rebellion, shall not be questioned. But neither the United States nor any state shall assume or pay any debt or obligation incurred in aid of insurrection or rebellion against the United States, or any claim for the loss or emancipation of any slave; but all such debts, obligations and claims shall be held illegal and void.

Section 5. The Congress shall have the power to enforce, by appropriate legislation, the provisions of this article.

Amendment XV: Black Voting Rights
Section 1. The right of citizens of the United States to vote shall not be denied or abridged by the United States or by any state on account of race, color, or previous condition of servitude—

Section 2. The Congress shall have the power to enforce this article by appropriate legislation.

Amendment XVI: Income Tax
The Congress shall have power to lay and collect taxes on incomes, from whatever source derived, without apportionment among the several states, and without regard to any census or enumeration.

Amendment XVII: Direct Election of Senators
The Senate of the United States shall be composed of two senators from each state, elected by the people thereof, for six years; and each senator shall have one vote. The electors in each state shall have the qualifications requisite for electors of the most numerous branch of the state legislatures.

Section 3—Former Confederates could be banned from public office. Four years after the amendment was ratified, the ban was lifted for almost all former Confederates, except certain government officials and military officers. In 1898, Congress lifted the ban entirely.

Section 4—Neither the federal government nor state governments were required to pay certain debts related to the Civil War and abolition of slavery.

Amendment XV: Black Voting Rights
(proposed February 26, 1869; ratified February 3, 1870)

Section 1—"Race, color, or previous condition of servitude" cannot prevent any citizen from voting. Unfortunately, some Southern states attempted to deprive African Americans of the right to vote by some of the tactics noted below.

1. **Literacy tests**—required voters to pass a literacy test in order to vote
2. **White primaries**—restricted party primaries and candidate selection to whites only
3. **Grandfather clauses**—allowed previous voters and their relatives to vote without facing a literacy test or other requirements (this allowed most white voters to avoid the new voting regulations)
4. **Gerrymandering**—drew district lines so that black voters had less influence

Progressive Amendments (XVI–XIX)
Amendments XVI–XIX are sometimes called the Progressive Amendments because they were passed during the Progressive Era (1890–1920).

Amendment XVI: Income Tax
(proposed July 2, 1909; ratified February 3, 1913)

Rather than using state population to set a tax base, Congress was given the power to tax individual incomes by standard rates according to the amount of each citizen's income.

Amendment XVII: Direct Election of Senators
(proposed May 13, 1912; ratified April 8, 1913)

By this amendment, the people, rather than the state legislatures, gained the right to elect their senators. Anyone qualified to vote in all state legislative elections is also qualified to vote in a US Senate election. Senate vacancies may be filled by special election or, if state law permits, the governor may appoint someone for the remainder of the term of office.

Income-Tax Attempt
Congress attempted to establish an income tax to help finance the Civil War. Initially, the income tax was declared constitutional, but a later case reversed that decision. The Sixteenth Amendment put the issue to rest by giving Congress the express power to levy the tax.

Senate Reform
Popular pressure for the Seventeenth Amendment came about for several reasons. First, legislative election of senators was tainted by corruption. In fact, between 1866 and 1906, nine cases of bribery were brought before the Senate. Second, election by legislatures too often led to deadlocks or long delays. As a result, some states went years without full representation in the Senate. Third, newspapers—especially those owned by publisher William Randolph Hearst—promoted the popular election of senators.

Critics of the amendment noted that it changed the founders' original intent. The Senate was intended to be the state governments' voice in the national government, just as the House was to be the people's voice in the national government. But this amendment gave the people another two votes per state.

Senate Debate
Lead the students in a debate regarding the value of the Seventeenth Amendment. Those supporting the amendment should discuss the need for senators to be accountable to the people in a democratic system of government. Those opposing the amendment should focus on the fickleness of public opinion and on how the Seventeenth Amendment has forced senatorial candidates to wage even more expensive campaigns than their counterparts in the House.

Amendment Report
Assign each student to write a one-page report about one of the constitutional amendments. You may either randomly assign the amendments or give the students their choice of topic. Each report should detail the historical background of an amendment, including the arguments for and against it and how it was ratified. Any major Supreme Court cases argued on the basis of the amendment should also be included, as well as any other information on the amendment's impact. Reports may also include images related to the topic. (If illustrations are included, the reports will be more than one page.)

Prohibition Initiative

The initiative for the Prohibition amendment was spearheaded by temperance organizations, such as the Woman's Christian Temperance Union and the Anti-Saloon League. Further support arose from patriotic impulses during World War I: distilling liquor consumed vast quantities of grain that might have been used as food, and beer was associated with Germans.

Tennessee's "War of the Roses"

By the summer of 1920, thirty-five states had ratified the Nineteenth Amendment. The approval of just one other state was needed. Amendment supporters in the Tennessee legislature wore yellow roses. Their opponents wore red ones.

When the suffragists counted the colored roses in the legislators' lapels, they were dismayed to find a tally of 49 red roses and 47 yellow roses. In the first roll-call vote, however, one legislator switched his position, and the vote was tied at 48–48. It remained tied during the second roll call.

Meanwhile, one legislator, Harry Burn, an opponent of womens' suffrage, received a telegram. The twenty-four-year-old read the message, put the telegram in his vest pocket, and returned his attention to the debate. When the voting resumed, Burn voted aye, pushing the tally to 49–47 in favor of ratification of the amendment. But not everyone was happy. Burn had to climb out a third-floor window of the capitol to escape an angry crowd.

Later, when someone commented that Burn voted aye although he had a red rose in his lapel, Burn replied, "Yes, but I had a telegram from Mother in my breast pocket!" Phoebe Ensminger Burn was somewhat responsible, therefore, for ratification of the Nineteenth Amendment.

<table>
<tr><td>

Amendment XVIII: Prohibition
(proposed December 18, 1917; ratified January 16, 1919)

In US history **Prohibition** refers to the nationwide ban on the manufacture, sale, or transportation of liquor. Congress passed the Volstead Act in 1919 to define "intoxicating liquors" and to enforce Amendment XVIII. This amendment was repealed by Amendment XXI in 1933.

Section 1—Congress focused on stopping the production and distribution of alcohol with a goal of affecting consumption.

Section 2—Initially, under the Volstead Act, the Internal Revenue Service assumed primary responsibility for enforcing the act. After eleven years the Department of Justice took charge. Enforcement proved to be very difficult given the sheer size of the nation and the number of people willing to disobey the law.

Section 3—This was the first amendment to have a ratification deadline attached. Several others since then have had similar provisions.

US agents destroying alcohol during Prohibition

Amendment XIX: Women's Suffrage
(proposed June 4, 1919; ratified August 18, 1920)

Section 1—By this amendment, women were given the right to vote. The right to vote is also called **suffrage**, or the **franchise**. A women's suffrage amendment had actually been introduced in Congress as early as 1878. Consistent pressure by women's suffrage groups, the increasing number of women in the work force, and female support for and service during World War I contributed to ratification. The final state needed for ratification, Tennessee, accepted the amendment by a narrow vote of 49–47.

</td><td>

When vacancies happen in the representation of any state in the Senate, the executive authority of such state shall issue writs of election to fill such vacancies: provided, that the legislature of any state may empower the executive thereof to make temporary appointments until the people fill the vacancies by election as the legislature may direct.

This amendment shall not be so construed as to affect the election or term of any senator chosen before it becomes valid as part of the Constitution.

Amendment XVIII: Prohibition

Section 1. *After one year from the ratification of this article the manufacture, sale, or transportation of intoxicating liquors within, the importation thereof into, or the exportation thereof from the United States and all territory subject to the jurisdiction thereof for beverage purposes is hereby prohibited.*

Section 2. *The Congress and the several states shall have concurrent power to enforce this article by appropriate legislation.*

Section 3. *This article shall be inoperative unless it shall have been ratified as an amendment to the Constitution by the legislatures of the several states, as provided in the Constitution, within seven years from the date of the submission hereof to the states by the Congress.*

Amendment XIX: Women's Suffrage

Section 1. *The right of citizens of the United States to vote shall not be denied or abridged by the United States or by any state on account of sex.*

Section 2. *Congress shall have power to enforce this article by appropriate legislation.*

</td></tr>
</table>

Billy Sunday

One of the most vocal advocates of Prohibition was Evangelist Billy Sunday. Obtain a copy of his most famous "booze sermon," entitled "Get on the Water Wagon," which he typically preached at least once in every campaign city. You might read parts of it aloud or ask someone from your school or church to deliver the sermon. Some audio clips of Sunday's messages are also available.

This topic provides an opportunity to discuss the pastor's role in discussing political topics. There are some topics that are clearly moral issues that a pastor needs to address if he is faithfully preaching God's Word. These include, but are not limited to, issues such as abortion, marriage, just and unjust wars, poverty, and creation and evolution. To avoid discussing these issues simply because they are politically charged would be wrong.

The church has a specific mandate revealed in Scripture that defines its mission. Most agree that the biblical mission of the church does not involve lobbying for or against particular candidates. The Bible does not provide the church with particular policy prescriptions even on the issues noted above, and a pastor would be overstepping his calling to tell the congregation that they ought to support such prescriptions. However, on occasion, there is legislation that is clearly momentous and clearly unbiblical, to which a pastor or church may feel biblically bound to address.

Amendment XX: Lame-Duck Amendment

Section 1. The terms of the president and the vice president shall end at noon on the 20th day of January, and the terms of senators and representatives at noon on the 3rd day of January, of the years in which such terms would have ended if this article had not been ratified; and the terms of their successors shall then begin.

Section 2. The Congress shall assemble at least once in every year, and such meeting shall begin at noon on the 3rd day of January, unless they shall by law appoint a different day.

Section 3. If, at the time fixed for the beginning of the term of the president, the president elect shall have died, the vice president elect shall become president. If a president shall not have been chosen before the time fixed for the beginning of his term, or if the president elect shall have failed to qualify, then the vice president elect shall act as president until a president shall have qualified; and the Congress may by law provide for the case wherein neither a president elect nor a vice president elect shall have qualified, declaring who shall then act as president, or the manner in which one who is to act shall be selected, and such person shall act accordingly until a president or vice president shall have qualified.

Section 4. The Congress may by law provide for the case of the death of any of the persons from whom the House of Representatives may choose a president whenever the right of choice shall have devolved upon them, and for the case of the death of any of the persons from whom the Senate may choose a vice president whenever the right of choice shall have devolved upon them.

Section 5. Sections 1 and 2 shall take effect on the 15th day of October following the ratification of this article.

Section 6. *This article shall be inoperative unless it shall have been ratified as an amendment to the Constitution by the legislatures of three-fourths of the several states within seven years from the date of its submission.*

Amendment XXI: Repeal of Prohibition

Section 1. The eighteenth article of amendment to the Constitution of the United States is hereby repealed.

Amendment XX: Lame-Duck Amendment
(proposed March 2, 1932; ratified January 23, 1933)

This amendment shortened the period in which a sitting president, senator, or representative can be a "**lame duck**" (an official who is still in office but has not been reelected). Lame-duck presidents have less political power; thus, presidents' administrations are usually least effective during their lame-duck periods. The amendment also addresses the issue of presidential succession in case of the president's death, incapacitation, or disqualification for office.

Section 1—The dates for starting terms changed from March 4 to January 20 for presidents and to January 3 for senators and representatives. Improvements in transportation and communication technology made a lengthy delay unnecessary: election results could easily be tabulated and reported, and elected officials could gather quickly to assume their offices.

Section 2—Congress must convene at least once a year. Following a November election, Congress shall convene the following year on January 3. Before this amendment, the new Congress was not required to convene until December of the year following the election; this resulted in an interim period of thirteen months. Today, the new Congress meets seventeen days before the president's inauguration. This ensures that the old Congress does not oversee his election if there is a deadlock in the Electoral College.

Section 3—If the president-elect dies before taking office, the vice president-elect takes his place. If a president-elect has not been determined by Inauguration Day, the vice president acts as president until a president is chosen. If both the president and vice president die or are disqualified for office, Congress is responsible for determining succession. Under this authority, Congress passed the Presidential Succession Act of 1947, which places the Speaker of the House, the Senate president pro tempore, and cabinet officials successively after the vice president.

Section 4—Congress must decide what to do if a candidate dies before the House or Senate decides an election (following a lack of a majority vote in the Electoral College).

Section 5—This amendment was ratified in 1933 and took effect on October 15 of that year. Consequently, the president already in office had his term shortened by approximately six weeks.

Amendment XXI: Repeal of Prohibition
(proposed February 20, 1933; ratified December 5, 1933)

The Democrats included the repeal of Prohibition as part of their platform in the 1932 election. This amendment was ratified shortly after Roosevelt took office.

"Bathtub Gin"

Some manufacturers of the ingredients of alcoholic drinks slyly placed a "warning" on their packaging; it stated that following certain steps would produce an alcoholic liquid that was illegal if produced, sold, or transported. This only encouraged people to follow those steps—and resulted in what became known as "bathtub gin."

Organized Crime

Much of the crime from 1919 to 1933 was linked to Prohibition. Organized crime saw Prohibition as a way to make money, much as drug dealers and drug cartels view drugs today. This led to "turf wars" as various crime groups sought to control the booze business in particular areas. People were killed, law-enforcement officials were bribed, and moral laxity increased.

Perhaps the most famous Prohibition enforcement agent was US Treasury agent Eliot Ness, who battled organized crime in the Chicago area with his team of agents known as the Untouchables. His prize catch was mobster Al Capone, who was arrested, convicted, and imprisoned, not for violating Prohibition, but for income-tax evasion.

Current Lame Ducks

Ask the students to think about current lame ducks, whether they are Senate or House members, the president, or those involved in state and local politics. Speculate how being a lame duck affects a politician's administration of his office.

Explanation	The United States Constitution

Section 1—This amendment repealed Prohibition as outlined in Amendment XVIII.

Section 2—However, states and territories were allowed to regulate the sale of alcohol within their borders.

Section 3—Unlike other amendments, Amendment XXI was ratified by state conventions rather than state legislatures. Lawyers for anti-Prohibition groups promoted this form of ratification because they feared that state legislatures were controlled by rural prohibitionist legislators.

Amendment XXII: Presidential Terms Limit
(proposed March 21, 1947; ratified February 27, 1951)

In 1940 and 1944, Franklin D. Roosevelt broke a tradition established by George Washington by running for a third and a fourth presidential term. Although World War II might have justified his actions, many people feared that the extra terms gave too much power to one man. After the war, this amendment was proposed to ensure that the two-term limit became law.

Section 1—Presidents can be elected for only two terms in their own right. If elevated from the vice-presidency during the second half of a previous president's term, a vice president who becomes president can serve a maximum of ten years. Harry Truman, who became president shortly after Roosevelt's death in office, was exempted from this provision, but he declined to run for a third term in 1952.

Amendment XXIII: Voting Rights for Washington, DC
(proposed June 16, 1960; ratified March 29, 1961)

By 1960, Washington, DC, had a population of over 750,000—more than that of several individual states. However, it still lacked voting rights in presidential elections until this amendment was passed.

Section 1—By this provision, residents of the District of Columbia can vote in presidential elections. The district has three electoral votes, and its electors follow the procedures outlined in Amendment XII.

Section 2. The transportation or importation into any state, territory, or possession of the United States for delivery or use therein of intoxicating liquors, in violation of the laws thereof, is hereby prohibited.

Section 3. *This article shall be inoperative unless it shall have been ratified as an amendment to the Constitution by conventions in the several states, as provided in the Constitution, within seven years from the date of the submission hereof to the states by the Congress.*

Amendment XXII: Presidential Terms Limit

Section 1. No person shall be elected to the office of the president more than twice, and no person who has held the office of president, or acted as president, for more than two years of a term to which some other person was elected president shall be elected to the office of the president more than once. *But this article shall not apply to any person holding the office of president when this article was proposed by Congress, and shall not prevent any person who may be holding the office of president, or acting as president, during the term within which this article becomes operative from holding the office of president or acting as president during the remainder of such term.*

Section 2. *This article shall be inoperative unless it shall have been ratified as an amendment to the Constitution by the legislatures of three-fourths of the several states within seven years from the date of its submission to the states by the Congress.*

Amendment XXIII: Voting Rights for Washington, DC

Section 1. The District constituting the seat of government of the United States shall appoint in such manner as the Congress may direct:

A number of electors of president and vice president equal to the whole number of senators and representatives in Congress to which the District would be entitled if it were a state, but in no event more than the least populous state; they shall be in addition to those appointed by the states, but they shall be considered, for the purposes of the election of president and vice president, to be electors appointed by a state; and they shall meet in the District and perform such duties as provided by the twelfth article of amendment.

Term Limits

Ask the students to discuss what might have occurred had George Washington not stepped down after two terms as president. Think about presidents, besides Franklin Roosevelt, who would have likely run for a third or fourth consecutive term if Washington had not set a precedent.

Section 2. The Congress shall have power to enforce this article by appropriate legislation.

Amendment XXIV: Poll Tax Abolished

Section 1. The right of citizens of the United States to vote in any primary or other election for president or vice president, for electors for president or vice president, or for senator or representative in Congress, shall not be denied or abridged by the United States or any state by reason of failure to pay poll tax or other tax.

Section 2. The Congress shall have power to enforce this article by appropriate legislation.

Amendment XXV: Presidential Succession and Disability

Section 1. In case of the removal of the president from office or of his death or resignation, the vice president shall become president.

Section 2. Whenever there is a vacancy in the office of the vice president, the president shall nominate a vice president who shall take office upon confirmation by a majority vote of both houses of Congress.

Section 3. Whenever the president transmits to the president pro tempore of the Senate and the Speaker of the House of Representatives his written declaration that he is unable to discharge the powers and duties of his office, and until he transmits to them a written declaration to the contrary, such powers and duties shall be discharged by the vice president as acting president.

Section 4. Whenever the vice president and a majority of either the principal officers of the executive departments or of such other body as Congress may by law provide, transmit to the president pro tempore of the Senate and the Speaker of the House of Representatives their written declaration that the president is unable to discharge the powers and duties of his office, the vice president shall immediately assume the powers and duties of the office as acting president.

Thereafter, when the president transmits to the president pro tempore of the Senate and the Speaker of the House of Representatives his written declaration that no inability exists, he shall resume the powers and duties of his office unless the vice president and a majority of either the principal officers of the executive department or of such other body as Congress may by law provide, transmit

Amendment XXIV: Poll Tax Abolished
(proposed August 27, 1962; ratified January 23, 1964)

Some states required citizens to pay a tax before they could vote (known as a **poll tax**). After the Civil War, several Southern states implemented this tax as a means of keeping some people, particularly poor African Americans, from voting. So called "grandfather clauses" (a stipulation that if your father or grandfather had voted before a certain year the tax would not apply to you) exempted many white voters from paying this tax.

Section 1—The payment of a poll tax to a state in any federal election was forbidden. Poll taxes were still allowed at the state election level until they were declared unconstitutional in the Supreme Court case *Harper v. Virginia Board of Elections* in 1966.

Amendment XXV: Presidential Succession and Disability
(proposed July 6, 1965; ratified February 10, 1967)

Amendment XXV clarified a number of issues about presidential succession: who would take power if something happened to the president. These issues were on Americans' minds following the assassination of President Kennedy in November 1963.

Section 1—The vice president becomes president if the president dies, resigns, or is removed from office. This clarified some ambiguity caused by Article II, which states that the "powers and duties" of the presidency "devolve on the vice president" in such cases but does not say whether the vice president actually becomes president.

Section 2—If the vice-presidency becomes vacant, the president can appoint a new vice president with the approval of both the House and the Senate.

Section 3—When the president cannot perform his duties, he can transfer them to the vice president.

Section 4—If an executive or congressional panel declares to Congress that the president cannot fulfill his duties, the vice president assumes them until the president declares himself capable. If there is disagreement between the president and the panel as to his competency, Congress resolves the issue with a two-thirds vote in both houses.

This provision solved the problem of an unforeseen and possibly long-term incapacitation of the president. Such occasions occurred with Presidents Garfield and Wilson and could have occurred with President Kennedy.

Amendment XXIII, Section 2

Authorized to enforce Amendment XXIII with legislation, Congress required that voters in Washington, DC, live there for one year and be at least twenty-one years old to vote. The age requirement was later lowered by the Twenty-Sixth Amendment.

Amendment XXV, Section 2

Amendment XXV was first used when Spiro Agnew resigned as vice president. President Nixon then nominated Gerald Ford to become vice president. Later, when Nixon resigned and Ford became president, Ford nominated Nelson Rockefeller to the vice-presidency. It was the first time that both a president and a vice president served without being elected to office by the people.

Amendment XXV, Section 3

See page 269 of this text for a description of three occasions when this part of the amendment was invoked (during the Reagan administration in 1985 and during the George W. Bush presidency in 2002 and 2007).

Incapacitations

After being shot, President Garfield lingered nearly three months before he died, creating a constitutional predicament. Woodrow Wilson suffered a stroke near the end of his presidency, leaving his wife, Edith, to nurse him and help manage White House business. When Amendment XXV was proposed, the assassination of President Kennedy was fresh in the minds of legislators. It was not difficult to imagine a situation in which the president could survive but be incapacitated indefinitely.

Activity 5: Chapter Review

The students may use this activity to review the chapter's terms and their definitions in preparation for the chapter test.

Voting-Age Reform

Whether to lower the voting age to eighteen was a recurring issue in American history, especially during wartime. It surfaced after the Civil War, as well as during World War II, the Korean War, and the Vietnam War. Advocates of the change argued that if a person is old enough to be drafted into military service and possibly give his life, he should be considered old enough to vote.

Even before the adoption of the Twenty–Sixth Amendment, four states (Georgia, Alaska, Kentucky, and Hawaii) had minimum voting ages below age twenty-one.

Explanation	The United States Constitution

Amendment XXVI: Vote for Eighteen-Year-Olds
(proposed March 23, 1971; ratified July 1, 1971)

Pressure for voting-age reform grew through the youth rebellion of the 1960s and the course of the Vietnam War—an unpopular war with many, and one in which eighteen- to twenty-year-olds bore the brunt. Amendment XXVI was ratified by the states in record time.

Section 1—The national voting age was lowered to eighteen for both federal and state elections.

Amendment XXVII: Congressional Pay Raises
(proposed September 25, 1789; ratified May 7, 1992)

This amendment states that any pay increases approved by Congress cannot take effect until after the next Congressional election. In contrast to Amendment XXVI, which was ratified in record time, Amendment XXVII took over two hundred years to be ratified. James Madison originally proposed it as part of the Bill of Rights, but only six states ratified it. Since no time limit was placed on the amendment's ratification, it remained active, though largely forgotten. Ohio added its ratification in 1873 to protest a congressional pay raise, but no other state ratified the amendment for over one hundred years.

Finally, the amendment resurfaced in the 1980s after members of Congress voted for pay raises for themselves. Enough states ratified the amendment by 1992 for it to become part of the Constitution. The amendment ensured that Congress would have greater accountability to the people. After adopting a pay raise, the public can express its approval or disapproval of members of Congress who supported a raise by deciding whether to vote for their reelection.

within four days to the president pro tempore of the Senate and the Speaker of the House of Representatives their written declaration that the president is unable to discharge the powers and duties of his office. Thereupon Congress shall decide the issue, assembling within forty-eight hours for that purpose if not in session. If the Congress, within twenty-one days after receipt of the latter written declaration, or, if Congress is not in session, within twenty-one days after Congress is required to assemble, determines by two-thirds vote of both houses that the president is unable to discharge the powers and duties of his office, the vice president shall continue to discharge the same as acting president; otherwise, the president shall resume the powers and duties of his office.

Amendment XXVI: Vote for Eighteen-Year-Olds

Section 1. The right of citizens of the United States, who are eighteen years of age or older, to vote shall not be denied or abridged by the United States or by any state on account of age.

Section 2. The Congress shall have power to enforce this article by appropriate legislation.

Amendment XXVII: Congressional Pay Raises

No law, varying the compensation for the services of the senators and representatives, shall take effect, until an election of representatives shall have intervened.

Questions on the Amendments

1. What are the first ten amendments usually called?
2–6. According to Amendment V, what are five rights of the accused?
7. What was the primary reason for separate ballots, for president and vice president, in the Electoral College?
8–11. In spite of the Fifteenth Amendment, four tactics were often used in some Southern states to prevent blacks from voting. Name these.
12–13. What are Amendments XVI–XIX also called? Why?
14. Who elected senators prior to Amendment XVII?
15. What is the only amendment that repealed another amendment?
★ Why did some fear that the Bill of Rights might endanger rights rather than protect them? How did the Bill of Rights address this concern?

Answers to Questions on the Amendments

1. the Bill of Rights (p. 112)
2–6. A grand jury must determine whether there is enough evidence to warrant a jury trial; no person can be tried twice for the same crime if a legal judgment was reached in the first trial; no person can be forced to give evidence against himself; and no person can be imprisoned, have his property confiscated, or be sentenced to death without a fair and proper trial; private property cannot be taken by the government unless fair compensation is given. (p. 113)
7. In 1800 the votes for president and vice president were tied. The change was to prevent this from occurring again. (p. 115)
8–11. grandfather clauses, white primaries, literacy tests, and gerrymandering (p. 117)
12–13. Progressive Amendments; because they were passed during the Progressive Era (p. 117)
14. the state legislatures (p. 117)
15. Amendment XXI (pp. 119–20)
★ They feared that unenumerated rights would not be considered rights. Amendments IX and X made it clear that this was not the case and that unlisted rights are reserved to the states and the people.

5 CHAPTER REVIEW

Making Connections

1–3. Briefly describe the primary function of each branch of government.

4–5. Explain the purpose and impact of the Bill of Rights.

6–12. Seven amendments changed voting procedures or voting rights. List and explain these.

Developing Civics Skills

1. Evaluate two laws that were recently passed and explain how they relate to the six principles that are the foundation of the Constitution.

2. Various interpretations of the First Amendment argue (a) that it demands an exclusion of religion from public matters, (b) that it prohibits establishing a state church and favoring one denomination over another, or (c) that it simply gives the states jurisdiction in matters of religion. Based on your knowledge of American history, which interpretation do you think best represents the intent of the Founding Fathers?

Thinking Critically

1. Why is the amendment process difficult?

2. Has the Tenth Amendment become obsolete? If so, what factors have rendered it obsolete? If not, how is it still effective?

Living as a Christian Citizen

1. Imagine that you are a delegate to the Constitutional Convention. Write an essay that explains the relationship that the new government should have with Christianity.

2. In Chapter 2 (see margin box on page 17) and in the conclusion of Section II in this chapter (see page 93) reference is made to the mixed form of government used in our country. Briefly defend the wisdom of creating such a system. Consider biblical principles in composing this defense.

People, Places, and Things to Remember

strict constructionists
broad constructionists
necessary and proper clause
amendment proposal
ratification
Bill of Rights
limited government
separation of powers
checks and balances
veto
impeachment
gridlock
judicial review
Marbury v. Madison
federalism
popular sovereignty
Preamble [to the Constitution]
legislative branch
bicameral
census
president pro tempore
quorum
sergeant at arms
Congressional Record
franking privilege
pocket veto
naturalization
National Guard
elastic clause
writ of habeas corpus
bill of attainder
ex post facto law
appropriation
executive branch
Electoral College
reprieves
pardons
judicial branch
original jurisdiction
appellate jurisdiction
treason
extradition
supremacy clause
slander
libel
grand jury
due process
eminent domain
subpoena
bail
literacy tests
white primaries
grandfather clauses
gerrymandering
Prohibition
suffrage
franchise
lame duck
poll tax

Amendment XXIV (Poll Tax Abolished) outlawed poll taxes as a requirement to vote. (p. 121)

Amendment XXVI (Vote for Eighteen-Year-Olds) lowered the voting age to eighteen for both federal and state elections. (p. 122)

(Note: Some students might mention that Amendment XIV says that states which deny the right to vote to voting-age citizens could have their representation in Congress reduced.)

Developing Civics Skills

1. Students should refer to some of the principles noted on page 94.

2. Those who argue for the first option must ignore a great deal of religious involvement in public life in the early days of the Republic. The second option is probably the best interpretation. For the third option, there is little evidence from the early national period that anyone thought that the federal government would infringe on the states in the matter of religion.

Thinking Critically

1. The framers wanted only the most well-considered and widely supported measures to pass.

2. Those who say yes might say that the obsolescence is due to the national government's steady rise in political and economic power at the states' expense. Those arguing for its relevancy might say that it is an important limit on the power of the federal government and an important protection of the rights of the states and the people.

Living as a Christian Citizen

1. Ideally, the students will acknowledge both God's supremacy over the nation and the Bible's importance as the moral basis for the nation's laws while recognizing that the government should not try to compel religious belief or practices.

2. Answers may include an acknowledgement that the Bible does not mandate any particular form of government, but its view of human nature means that it is wise to limit the power of every part of government. Thus, students may note that separation of powers, checks and balances, judicial review, and federalism help give the people a voice in government while also limiting their power and the power of those that govern.

CHAPTER REVIEW ANSWERS

Making Connections

1–3. The legislative branch makes the laws, the executive branch executes and enforces the nation's laws, and the judicial branch interprets the laws. (p. 88)

4–5. The Bill of Rights was designed to protect certain rights from the federal government's interference. It impacted government by carrying on the principles of limited government. (p. 112)

6–12. Amendment XII (Separate Ballots for President and Vice President) allowed electors in the Electoral College to vote for the positions of president and vice president separately. (p. 115)

Amendment XV (Black Voting Rights) gave black people the right to vote, though unfortunately attempts were made to limit this. (p. 117)

Amendment XVII (Direct Election of Senators) allowed the people rather than the state legislatures to elect senators. (pp. 117–18)

Amendment XIX (Women's Suffrage) gave women the right to vote. (p. 118)

Amendment XXIII (Voting Rights for Washington, DC) gave the residents of Washington, DC, the right to vote in presidential elections and gave them votes in the Electoral College. (p. 120)

1. Analyze the interaction of the two major divisions in American federalism.

2. Chart the development of American federalism.

3. Explain the financial aspects of federalism.

4. Evaluate the challenges of American federalism.

FEDERALISM

6

The states can best govern our home concerns and the general government our foreign ones.

—*Thomas Jefferson*

The national government provides highway funds that are essential to building roads in each state.

I. The Partitions of Power

II. Developments in Federalism

III. Financing Federalism

IV. The Challenges of Federalism

BIG IDEAS

1. How do the two major divisions within American federalism interact?

2. What are some of the major issues associated with the development of federalism?

3. How have federal grants been implemented to assist with financing federalism?

4. What challenges has federalism faced?

SUGGESTED MATERIALS

Section I
• Special speaker (see page 127)

Section II
• Activity 1 from Chapter 6 of the *Student Activities*

Section III
• Two "grants" of "$500,000" (see page 132)
• Activity 2 from Chapter 6 of the *Student Activities*

Section IV
• Activities 3–4 from Chapter 6 of the *Student Activities*

Teacher Resources

Visit TeacherToolsOnline.com for resources to enhance the lessons.

Federalism is a system in which governmental power is divided into two or more levels, usually a central government and component state governments. In the United States, government is divided between the national government in Washington, DC, and fifty state governments. Although they are distinct, the two levels of government often overlap in responsibilities. The Constitution gives to both the authority to govern.

This federal system is a basic constitutional principle and one of the outstanding achievements of the 1787 Philadelphia Convention. Federalism is based on the beliefs that limited government restrains tyranny and that one way to limit government is to divide power among several entities.

Inevitably, conflicts arise between the levels of government, even though both draw their power from the people. It is not easy to determine whether constitutional barriers can effectively restrict the central government from infringing on states' integrity while still allowing the central government to perform its legitimate duties. One of the causes of the Civil War was disagreement regarding the rights of states and the powers of the federal government. Much later, some presidents tried to reduce the national role in the federal system but were generally unsuccessful. For instance, both Richard Nixon and Ronald Reagan sought to develop a "new federalism" that would return power to the states and reduce the national government's involvement at the local and state levels.

Ideally, the national government is supposed to meet national needs, whereas state governments are to serve state needs. Distinguishing between the two is often a matter of debate. At its best, federalism is cooperative coexistence between those governments.

Jerry Brown served as governor of the most populous state, California, from 1975–83 and 2011–19.

I. The Partitions of Power

The Constitution outlines the division between national and state governments. It gives both levels specific powers, and both are denied certain powers through constitutional limitations.

National Power

The national government has **delegated powers** (powers given by the Constitution) that define the limits of its authority. Delegated power is not only a grant of authority but also a limitation because the power is ultimately bound "by the chains of the Constitution," as Jefferson stated. This delegated authority of the national government takes two forms—enumerated powers and implied powers.

Enumerated powers, sometimes called expressed powers, are specifically written into the Constitution. The Constitution gives the three branches of government particular powers, such as the congressional powers in Article I, Section 8, to collect taxes, regulate commerce, and declare war and the president's powers in Article II to appoint officials and negotiate treaties.

Implied powers are not stated in the Constitution but are *derived* from enumerated powers. Although they are not specifically mentioned in the Constitution, certain actions might be necessary or convenient in exercising enumerated powers. The national government's passage of laws requiring the institution of a

1. Define *federalism*.
2. Differentiate between delegated powers, enumerated powers, implied powers, and reserved powers.
3. Explain the interaction between state and federal governments.

US Presidential Power

In addition to the broad power of Congress, broad power has been given to the president, as specified in Article II, Sections 2–3, of the Constitution. However, the Constitution does not clearly define the scope of executive power; thus many presidents and many executive-branch agencies have expanded their powers.

Broad and Narrow Interpretations

Broad interpretations of the national government's enumerated (expressed) and implied powers and narrow interpretations of the states' reserved powers were partly responsible for the federal government increasing its powers.

Guiding Questions

1. What is *federalism*?
2. What is the difference between delegated powers, enumerated powers, implied powers, and reserved powers?
3. How do the state and federal governments interact?

Law and Personal Liberty

Read aloud Galatians 5:14. It states, "For all the law is fulfilled in one word, even in this; Thou shalt love thy neighbour as thyself." Guide a discussion about law and personal liberty. Laws are needed because humans do not fulfill the second-greatest commandment—love your neighbor as yourself. If everyone perfectly obeyed that law, there would be no need for laws against stealing, murder, or other crimes. In a sense, the myriad laws in the United States serve as a reminder of human depravity. Because people do not obey the second-greatest commandment, societies must have laws to regulate behavior. Consider the necessity of your school handbook. How many rules could be discarded if everyone perfectly lived out the second-greatest commandment?

Libertarians often wish to limit government interference not only in economic matters but also in moral areas. But the more wicked a society becomes, the less free it may be because people will demand more laws for protection from others' wickedness. A truly conservative approach, not to mention a biblical one, recognizes that laws that encourage a moral society are foundational for a truly free society.

Comparing Governments

The feature box at right is another in the continuing series in the Student Edition that compares the United States government to one in another country. The earlier comparisons dealt with India (p. 36) and South Africa (p. 91).

Federalism in Australia

A good example of federalism is the Australian government. In fact, the federal structure of Australia's government is based on that developed by America's Founding Fathers in 1787. Political power in Australia is distributed between a national government based in Canberra and the governments of Australia's six states.

At the national level, the legislative branch consists of a bicameral parliament. As in the United States, the two bodies of Australia's legislative branch are called the Senate and the House of Representatives. The Senate consists of 76 senators—12 from each of the six states and 2 from each of the two territories. The House of Representatives has 151 members and is based on the populations of the states.

Each state also has its own parliament and constitution. As in the United States, powers not enumerated in the national constitution or granted to the national government are reserved to the states. (Australia calls these powers residual powers.) However, the national government now dominates state governments, mostly because of its power of taxation. Australian states receive national grants, but (as is the case with US categorical grants) these grants have strings attached.

Federalism in the United States and Germany

As we continue the comparison of America's government with those of other nations, we should note that the governments of the United States and the Federal Republic of Germany have many similarities. Each is an example of federalism.

After Germany became a nation in 1871, the kaiser (emperor) granted regional governments some important powers. Following World War II, Germany was divided into democratic West Germany and Communist East Germany. Though Germans had hoped for a unified country, that was not accomplished until decades later.

West German voters did not directly elect the body that produced their constitution in the late 1940s. Elected leaders from West German regions chose the members of the constitutional assembly, which wrote the constitution, called the Basic Law, for the Federal Republic of Germany. Furthermore, the Basic Law was ratified by regional legislatures, not by a national referendum, or vote.

After Germany was finally reunited in 1990, the Basic Law provided for sixteen states (three are cities), or *Länder*, which are much like US states. Each German state has a legislature. The majority party in a German state legislature elects a chief, called a minister-president, just as voters in American states elect a governor.

The Bundesrat, Germany's upper house in Parliament, reflects the states' power in the federal government. Members of the Bundesrat are chosen by state legislatures. In the United States, the people of a state elect its US senators. Originally, before the Seventeenth Amendment, state legislatures selected senators somewhat as Germany now does.

The size of a German state's delegation depends on population, with larger states having more votes. But in the US Senate each state has two senators, regardless of population. In the Bundesrat, each representative must vote as the state government tells him, while US senators may vote as they wish.

The Bundestag, Germany's lower house, deviates from the federal system because it, not the people, elects the chancellor; in that sense Germany's political system resembles the British parliamentary system. Similarly, in the United States, elected officials in the Electoral College determine a presidential election. In theory, however, the American people are still involved because they choose the electors, who in turn vote for the president.

Members of the Bundestag are chosen through a complicated system that allows for two votes by the public—one by district and one by party. In the district vote, one member is elected from each district, just as one House member is elected from each congressional district in America. In the party vote, each voter selects the political party it prefers. Parties are then entitled to a percentage of the seats in the Bundestag roughly equal to their share of the vote nationwide.

The lower house of the German Parliament, the Bundestag, meets in the Reichstag building in Berlin (above).

minimum wage in all states was based on its power to regulate commerce "among the several states." Though some questioned the broad application of this power, congressmen supporting the minimum wage cited the **necessary and proper clause** (Article I, Section 8, clause 18), which states that Congress is permitted

> to make all laws which shall be necessary and proper for carrying into execution the foregoing powers, and all other powers vested by [the] Constitution in the government of the United States, or in any department or officer thereof.

Minimum-Wage Laws

Discuss the pros and cons of minimum-wage laws and the government's right to enforce them. Instruct students to consider the following points. When FDR signed the first federal minimum-wage law in 1938, he stated that it would improve the standard of living for many Americans. Minimum-wage proponents traditionally argue that full-time workers should not live in poverty. They also assert that government needs to act as a "check" on the greed of some businessmen who take advantage of their workers to produce higher profits. However, others argue that minimum-wage laws do more harm than good. Because of high hourly wages, employers are forced to raise prices or hire fewer workers. Higher product prices lead to higher costs of living and create a need for even higher wages. Also, if an employer chooses to hire fewer workers, entry-level positions become more scarce—a development that affects many younger workers.

Invite students to research alternatives to the minimum wage (i.e., ways to help workers without creating some of the claimed negative effects of minimum wage).

Poverty and Scripture

The Bible consistently speaks of poverty as an evil. In an ideal society, there would be no poverty (Deut. 15:4). Of course, this ideal is not yet achieved because of sin (Deut. 15:5, 11).

Because of poverty, the Mosaic code regulated how people harvested fields (Lev. 19:9–10) and how property was to be redeemed by a poor person (Lev. 25:25). The Mosaic code also provided a social safety net in the form of required lending to the poor and indentured servitude (Deut. 15:7–14). In addition, the Mosaic code regulated how often an employer must pay a poor employee (Deut. 24:15), and it warned employers not to oppress poor workers (Deut. 24:14).

Does government do enough to care for the poor? Ask students to state their opinions on that issue. Remind them to consider biblical teaching when reacting to the question.

Because that clause greatly enlarges the scope of national power and has at times been stretched to cover congressional acts, it is often also called the **elastic clause**.

State Power

According to the Tenth Amendment, the powers not delegated to the national government or denied to the states are reserved for the various states and their citizens. These **reserved powers** provide states with considerable freedom to exercise authority as they choose. States may, for example, establish systems of public education for their residents, implement state income taxes, enact laws regarding speed limits and seat-belt usage on their roads, and ban or permit liquor sales to eighteen-year-olds. Authority over those areas is not given to the national government or denied to the states; therefore, the states may exercise power in those areas. A state may even determine its own forms and rules of government, such as the extent of the governor's veto power or whether its legislative branch will consist of one or two houses. (Nebraska, for example, has a unicameral system, whereas the other forty-nine states have bicameral systems.)

When fifty separate governments make laws in many areas, the result is often substantial diversity. Certain businesses might decide to locate in a particular state because its laws are more favorable to their industry than are those of other states. Or the residents in a state might circumvent its laws by traveling to a neighboring state, where laws may be more relaxed, to obtain such things as firearms or marriage licenses. Sales tax provides a good example of how differing laws can produce friction between adjoining states. To reach states that have no sales tax (presently, those states are Alaska, Delaware, Montana, New Hampshire, and Oregon), residents of neighboring states frequently cross state borders to take advantage of savings; and, in so doing, they reduce their own states' revenue.

Although each state has much power over its own affairs, there are limits to its authority. The Constitution places specific restrictions on states, many of which are outlined in Article I, Section 10. For example, a state may *not* make treaties, declare war, or coin its own money. In addition, the supremacy clause and subsequent Supreme Court decisions, such as *McCulloch v. Maryland* (1819), prohibit states from taxing national institutions within their borders.

The Bill of Rights places restrictions on both state governments and the national government. The Tenth Amendment is far more than a simple sentence.

> The powers not delegated to the United States by the Constitution, nor prohibited by it to the states, are reserved to the states respectively, *or to the people.* (italics added)

"The powers not delegated to the United States by the Constitution, nor prohibited by it to the states, are reserved to the states respectively, or to the people."
—Tenth Amendment, US Constitution

"While the national government was to do a few very important functions well, the bulk of government powers by design remained at the state and local level, where it could have more discretion and responsibility."
—Matthew Spalding,
We Still Hold These Truths: Rediscovering Our Principles, Reclaiming Our Future

States set their own speed limits and seat-belt laws.

Some Key Events

Robert Donnelly, former chief justice of the Missouri Supreme Court, argued that three key events eroded state powers in relation to the national government:

1. The Seventeenth Amendment made senatorial elections more democratic but removed a bond that connected the national Senate to state governments.

2. *Cooper v. Aaron* (1958) reaffirmed the Supreme Court's position as chief interpreter of the Constitution. The decision declared that state governments are bound by the Court's decisions.

3. *Garcia v. San Antonio Metropolitan Transit Authority* (1985) held that Congress has the authority, based on the commerce clause of the Constitution, to require state and local governments to provide minimum wage and overtime pay to its employees.

Other factors that might have played a role in expanding federal power include the United States' rise to world power and global economic interdependence.

Whether the erosion of state power is good or bad continues to be the subject of debate. For example, in the case of *Cooper v. Aaron* (1958), noted above, the Supreme Court prevented the state of Arkansas from delaying desegregation of its schools. That decision was a victory for African Americans who had faced widespread discrimination and inequality at educational institutions. In other instances, the increased power of the national government has created greater controversy.

Christian Businessman

Invite a Christian businessman to discuss whether your state is "business friendly." Ask that person to discuss what this term means and how states can balance their need for tax money with their need for businesses to stimulate and fuel the economy.

Incorporation

The First Amendment was not originally applicable to the states. For instance, Massachusetts levied state taxes to support a state church until 1833. However, the Supreme Court's interpretation of Amendment XIV eventually expanded certain guarantees of the Bill of Rights to cover state actions as well, and the result was a further limitation of state power.

This federal limitation of state power prevents states from establishing state churches (for example, a Mormon majority cannot create a state church in Utah). During the period of Jim Crow laws in some states, this limitation also ensured the rights of black citizens.

Refer to the note at the bottom page 113 of the Teacher Edition and to pages 362 and 364 of the Student Edition for further discussion of incorporation.

No government within the federal system may deny a citizen such constitutional rights as freedom of worship and the right of due process. In addition, power not given to the national government or assumed by state governments is reserved for the people; that is, where no law prohibits a certain action, responsible citizens are free to act.

"When I took the oath of office, I pledged loyalty to only one special interest group: 'We the people.'"

—Ronald Reagan

Within each state is a variety of local governmental units, such as counties, cities, and townships. Unlike national and state governments, local governments are not mentioned in the Constitution. Traditionally, local units of government have served primarily to implement state laws. Because local authority is derived from state authority, city government may not ignore state government. Nevertheless, recent trends have enhanced the role of local government. The growth of suburbs and the complex expansion of government services have resulted in a more flexible relationship between the statehouse and the city halls and county commissions (or county councils) within its jurisdiction.

This interdependence of state and local governments reflects a similar interrelationship within the entire federal system. During the US government's history, however, various forces have blurred lines of distinction and strengthened the national role at the states' expense.

Constitutional and National Supremacy

Understanding the potential for conflict between state and national governments, the founders included Article VI, clause 2 (known as the **supremacy clause**), in the Constitution to establish the proper relationship between the two:

> This Constitution, and the laws of the United States which shall be made in pursuance thereof; and all treaties made, or which shall be made, under the authority of the United States, shall be the supreme law of the land; and the judges in every state shall be bound thereby, any thing in the constitution or laws of any state to the contrary notwithstanding.

Under the US federal system, the states have the constitutional right to pass their own legislation and judge their own cases, but their laws and judicial rulings cannot contradict the Constitution, national law, or Supreme Court rulings.

Section Review

1. Define *federalism*.
2. Explain why the necessary and proper clause is sometimes called the elastic clause.
3. Which constitutional amendment guarantees the reserved powers of the states and of the people?
4–5. Which two levels of government are mentioned in the Constitution?
6. Which level of government is not mentioned in the Constitution?
★ Evaluate the validity of the statement "There ought to be a law against that."
★ Federalism involves a division of powers between different levels of government. Why is it important for citizens to know which responsibilities are assigned to a particular level of government?

Supremacy Clause

Review the supremacy clause (Article VI, clause 2), discussed in this section. Although that clause can be abused, discuss what would happen if the supremacy clause were absent from the Constitution.

Section Review Answers

1. a system in which governmental power is divided into two or more levels, usually a central government and component state governments (p. 125)
2. because it enlarges the scope of national power and because it has been stretched to cover congressional actions (pp. 126–27)
3. the Tenth Amendment (p. 127)
4–5. state and national governments (pp. 125–28)
6. local governments (p. 128)
★ Students might say that the proper test of legislation is whether it encourages people to act justly and righteously or infringes on God-given rights and responsibilities.
★ Answers may include that citizens need to know to whom they must answer if laws are violated and whom they should contact if they want to change laws. Students may also mention that citizens should be able to recognize when a level of government overreaches its bounds or when it fails to meet its responsibilities.

II. Developments in Federalism

Conflicts

In the early years of the Republic, states played a much more important role in the lives of their citizens than did the national government. When travel across states could take days or weeks rather than hours, when there were no interstate highways and few bridges spanning swollen rivers, the country was, in a very real sense, much larger than at present. States were more isolated, more independent, and more important in the nation's social and political structure. In 1831 Alexis de Tocqueville observed that "in America the legislature of each state is supreme; nothing can impede its authority." Though an exaggeration, these comments make clear the importance of state governments.

The states' status as a potent political force did much to shape federalism. The states and the national government are two pillars supporting a federal structure. State political strength was bolstered by the relative weakness of the national government and by constitutional provisions, such as reserved powers and state legislatures' ability (before Amendment XVII) to select US senators. Powerful voices, including those of Thomas Jefferson and James Madison of Virginia and John C. Calhoun of South Carolina, defended decentralization of the government.

Of course, the national government did hold supreme power. Its role was well established, both by the Constitution and later by the rulings of the US Supreme Court. During the years that John Marshall served as that court's chief justice (1801–1835), the court decisions did much to expand the powers of the national government.

However, federalism was sometimes the source of disagreement. Clearly defining the roles of state governments and the national government was not always easy. For example, James Madison, the Father of the Constitution, vetoed Congress's public-works legislation with this message in 1817:

> I am not unaware of the great importance of roads and canals and the improved navigation of water courses, and that a power in the national legislature to provide for them might be exercised with signal advantage to the general prosperity. But seeing that such a power is not expressly given by the Constitution, and believing that it can not be deduced from any part of it without an inadmissible latitude of construction and a reliance on insufficient precedents; believing also that the permanent success of the Constitution depends on a definite partition of powers between the general and the state governments . . . I have no option but to [veto the bill].

During the early years of the nation and well into the twentieth century, **dual federalism** existed. Under this system, national and state governments were sovereign within their own spheres. Of course, clashes occurred regarding policies. Conflict arose in Congress; in the courts; and, during the Civil War, even on the battlefield. Nevertheless, dual federalism, or dual sovereignty, continued to dominate certain aspects of the political system. But eventually, new factors—economic, political, and social—gradually redefined the nature of federalism in America.

John Marshall

Federalism and Abortion

Should laws regarding abortion be instituted on the national level or the state level? Lead students in a discussion regarding this question.

Some conservatives argue that abortion should be settled state by state to protect federalism. Ask students to evaluate this position, and to provide a rationale for issues that should be decided on a state level and for those which should be decided on the national level.

Discuss with students that the federal structure of our national government takes into account differences between regions. However, remind them that moral laws, such as prohibiting the murder of the unborn, do not need to consider regional differences. Murder is always wrong everywhere. Nonetheless, students may note that the federal structure of the United States enables more conservative states to enact limitations on abortion.

Davy Crockett Regarding Federal Spending

David "Davy" Crockett served in Congress as a representative of Tennessee from 1827 to 1831 and from 1833 to 1835. While in the House, Crockett discussed a bill to appropriate funds for a naval officer's needy widow. Speaking to his colleagues, he said,

> I have as much respect for the memory of the deceased, and as much sympathy for the sufferings of the living . . . as any man in this House, but we must not permit our respect for the dead or our sympathy for a part of the living to lead us into an act of injustice. . . .

He then pledged he would give a week's pay to help the poor widow, and rather than give public funds for charity, he suggested that his fellow congressmen should likewise contribute. Though all the House seemed to favor the bill before Crockett's speech, after his opposition, the legislation was not passed.

The next day, Crockett commented to a friend,

> There are in that House many very wealthy men—men who think nothing of spending a week's pay, or a dozen of them, for a dinner or a wine party when they have something to accomplish by it. Some of those same men made beautiful speeches upon the great debt of gratitude which the country owed the deceased—a debt which could not be paid by money—and the insignificance and worthlessness of money, particularly so insignificant a sum as $10,000, when weighed against the honor of the nation. Yet not one of them responded to my

At one time, a three-layer cake (above) could have illustrated the relationship between America's local, state, and national governments. Modern federalism, however, is better illustrated by a marble cake (below) in which the three divisions are less distinct.

The Growth of Interdependence

In the first half of the 1800s, clashes between the governments of the slave states and the national government intensified. Those states protested attempts to outlaw slavery in new states and territories and asserted that the federal government was interfering with state sovereignty. With the end of the Civil War, the supremacy of the federal government was firmly established.

After the war, America continued to industrialize. Farmers left their farms and, with an influx of immigrants from Europe, flocked to cities, transforming the United States from an agricultural to an industrial nation. Railroads, with thousands of passengers, crossed state lines as if the borders did not exist. Instead of buying basic necessities from local general stores, Americans began to order unseen goods from strangers halfway across the country. The interdependence of producers and consumers who lived far from one another further reduced the importance of state lines and increased the need for national legal uniformity.

Governments at all levels also grew larger as increased productivity and a higher standard of living allowed more taxes to be taken with less detriment to taxpayers. When the United States emerged as a world power at the end of the nineteenth century, the federal government expanded its revenue base to maintain its international position. Passage of the Income Tax Amendment (**Sixteenth Amendment**) in 1913 eventually created a large source of federal money permitting increased spending and increased power to the national government.

During World War I, the federal government took control of the railroads and expanded its regulatory powers over major corporations and even entire industries. American perception of the federal government shifted greatly during the Great Depression, which began in 1929, when economic collapse exhausted state welfare funds, and the American public clamored for federal relief. In 1933 the newly inaugurated Franklin D. Roosevelt (FDR) began implementing a series of social and economic programs to address the poverty and unemployment of the Depression. These programs spanned the 1930s and were known collectively as the **New Deal**. Although the New Deal programs were often organized at the state level, there was no question as to which level of government was providing the funds. Thus, the New Deal vastly expanded the federal government's power.

New federal programs appeared during the 1950s and 1960s. Lyndon Johnson, who became president in 1963, introduced a number of initiatives aimed at eliminating poverty, supervising voting rights, and promoting greater national involvement in education and health care. The result of the **Great Society**, as these programs were called, was even further expansion of national government power and prominence.

During the 1980s, President Ronald Reagan spoke of a "new federalism" that would reduce national government involvement and spending at the state level, and he did curb federal regulation to a certain extent. President Richard Nixon had also discussed "new federalism" and similar changes soon after he took office in 1969. Nevertheless, the growth of the federal bureaucracy and the comparative decline in state power continued under both Nixon and Reagan, though at a lesser pace than during the New Deal and Great Society eras.

Federal Spending

Assign groups of students to consider the issue of the national government's use of money. Use the primary source material provided in the Teacher Edition margin notes entitled "Davy Crockett Regarding Federal Spending" (on this page) and "Federal Funding" (on the next page). You may wish to distribute copies of the information or project it on a screen.

Instruct students to evaluate the comments Davy Crockett and Franklin Pierce made. Do you agree with their viewpoints? Why or why not? If you were a government official would you have handled the situations differently? How do the instances noted relate to issues of federal spending today? After discussing the questions within their groups, students can present their views to the class.

Activity 1: Federalism's Development

The timeline chart in this activity requires the students to describe legislation and events and identify the impact of each.

FDR surrounded by some of the many New Deal programs he created

Section Review

1. How does the role of states today differ from their role in the early years of the American Republic?
2. What event firmly established the supremacy of the federal government?
3. What event in America's history significantly shifted Americans' perception of the federal government?
4–5. Which two presidents spoke about "new federalism"?

★ Describe the concept of dual federalism.

★ Briefly describe the New Deal and the Great Society and explain how they impacted federalism.

III. Financing Federalism

Federalism today is much more complicated than the simple model outlined in the Constitution. It has been transformed, partly because of the tremendous amount of federal resources available. Hundreds of programs have been created to assist the states with everything from education and social services to public transportation and law enforcement.

Federal **grants-in-aid** (the transfer of money from the federal government to state or local governments) represent a major portion of the federal budget as well as a key force in implementing national policies on the local level. Federal grants are not new, although in the nineteenth century they came primarily in the form of land grants. Cash grants did not become a significant form of state aid until the New Deal era (see Section II), and the grants remained relatively modest until the 1960s. Today, however, federal grants-in-aid amount to more than $700 billion

Guiding Questions

1. How are the various forms of federal grants different?
2. What is revenue sharing?

proposition. Money with them is nothing but trash when it is to come out of the people. But it is the one great thing for which most of them are striving, and many of them sacrifice honor, integrity, and justice to obtain it.

Federal Funding

In the mid-nineteenth century, President Franklin Pierce vetoed a bill to provide funds for the indigent insane. He stated,

[If] Congress is to make provision . . . the fountains of charity will be dried up at home, and the several states, instead of bestowing their own means on the social wants of their own people, may themselves . . . become humble suppliants for the bounty of the federal government, reversing their true relations to this Union.

New New Federalism

Ronald Reagan's "new federalism" was preceded by the new federalism announced by President Nixon in 1969. Nixon's program called for a shift to revenue-sharing grants that would give the states federal funds with fewer strings attached and would transfer more responsibilities to the state level. (See page 133 of the Student Edition.)

Section III Objectives

1. Distinguish between the various forms of federal grants.
2. Explain revenue sharing.

Section Review Answers

1. In the early years of the Republic, states played a more important role in the lives of citizens than did the national government. This was due to a number of factors—the relative weakness of the federal government, the reserved powers noted in the Constitution, and the state legislatures' ability to elect US senators. (pp. 129–30)

2. the end of the Civil War (p. 130)

3. the Great Depression (p. 130)

4–5. Richard Nixon and Ronald Reagan (p. 130)

★ Dual federalism is a system in which national and state governments exercise authority within their own spheres. It existed from the early years of the nation until well into the twentieth century.

★ The New Deal was a series of programs created by President Franklin D. Roosevelt to address the poverty and unemployment of the Depression. The Great Society was a number of initiatives from President Lyndon Johnson aimed at eliminating poverty, supervising voting rights, and promoting greater federal involvement in education and health care. Both of these programs expanded the national government's power and prominence.

Local Grants

Contact your mayor, a councilman, or other local leaders, and ask about some of the federal-aid grants that your community currently benefits from. Consider establishing a time to speak with one of these individuals by conference call or by video conference.

Direct your students to research other local programs that are federally funded, and discuss those programs' merits and weaknesses.

Overlapping Terms

The terms used to describe grants-in-aid—*categorical grants*, *block grants*, and *revenue sharing*—denote broad categories that sometimes overlap. For example, President Reagan proposed block grants that actually had more characteristics of revenue sharing. Not only do the terms sometimes overlap, but the projects that grants finance often overlap as well. For instance, at one time, as many as four different congressional committees controlled water and sewer grant programs.

annually. This money is distributed to state and local governments primarily through categorical grants and block grants. In addition, for more than a decade (1972 to 1986) federal funds were distributed through a process called revenue sharing.

Categorical Grants

Categorical grants are given to state and local governments for a specific purpose and, like all other federal monies, come with certain guidelines for their use. For example, a categorical grant given to Chicago for low-income daycare may not be used to refurbish city parks. Other restrictions may also accompany federal aid, such as minority-hiring quotas or environmental-protection guidelines. In addition, categorical grants generally require the recipient to provide matching funds for a project as well as an agency for managing the money.

Categorical grants may be either formula grants or project grants. **Formula grants**, as the name implies, are governed by demographic formulas in a given area. For example, unemployment figures may be used in composing a formula to determine the proportion of federal aid for a job-training program. By contrast, **project grants** allow the national government greater discretion in deciding how much aid will be given to a project.

Categorical grants are the most common—and the most controversial—form of federal aid. The controversy centers on "strings" attached to federal money. Through these accompanying regulations, the national government often becomes involved in areas of state authority, such as public education and urban policy; this involvement tends to erode the national and state distinctions of federalism.

The states are under no obligation to accept federal aid, but they usually actively lobby in Washington for additional funding. The millions, and sometimes billions, of dollars available to the states are often irresistible, despite the accompanying government stipulations. States often note that if they do not take the funding another state will do so.

The interstate highway system, begun while Dwight Eisenhower was president, was completed primarily through the use of grants from the federal government. Although the government did not force states to participate in building the roads, states received an offer that none refused. The national government established categorical grants with generous terms: for every dollar a state placed into the superhighway fund, the federal government would provide nine dollars. The interstate highway grants paid a substantially higher percentage of project cost than the typical federal program.

Block Grants

A second method of federal-aid distribution is the block grant. Begun in 1966, this grant is designed to streamline federal aid to states and localities. **Block grants** simplify state or city administration of federal funds because they provide more flexibility than the more closely monitored categorical grants. Block grants combine several categorical grants under a general umbrella, such

Federal Aid to State and Local Governments

Dollars (in billions) / Year

Grants with Strings Attached

Discuss the requirements that are often attached to federal funds, and discuss how those strings may force an institution or state to follow policies with which it disagrees in order to gain the money. An example that the students might understand is their home situation. Most students receive housing, clothing, food, and some spending money from their parents. As long as the students are in this position, they are required to follow their parents' rules. The same is true with federal funding.

Help the students see the benefits and dangers of federal funding. For example, when granting aid, the federal government might attach a requirement that prohibits discrimination against same-sex marriage. Adhering to this rule would violate a Christian's view of marriage as defined in Scripture. In such a case, a Christian would have to reject the funding.

Block versus Categorical

Divide the class into two "cities." Each city will choose a mayor; the other students will serve as council members. Give each city "$500,000" for urban renewal. One city will receive the money as a block grant, and the other will receive it as a categorical grant. The city receiving the block grant should determine how to spend its urban-renewal grant and devise a means to account for expenditures. The city receiving the categorical grant should be given directions about how the grant should be spent. For example, you could say that $125,000 must be used for new streetlights, $125,000 could be used for sidewalks, $150,000 could be used for road repairs, and $100,000 must be used to improve mass-transit services. Then, direct students to discuss some additional stipulations that the federal government might designate.

Compare how each city used its grants. Discuss the advantages and disadvantages of block and categorical grants.

as law enforcement or education, but involve fewer federal regulations and less red tape. For example, if Indianapolis wants to revitalize its inner city, it need not apply for a dozen categorical grants in areas such as housing, recreational facilities, and minority business loans; instead, the city may simply apply for a block grant for urban development.

Revenue Sharing

Federal aid has also been distributed through **revenue sharing**. As an official program, revenue sharing began in 1972 under Richard Nixon. It was eventually dismantled in 1986 as a part of the budget cuts enacted by the Reagan administration. Revenue sharing was not new; its practice can be traced as far back as the Jefferson and Jackson administrations.

In revenue sharing, the national government allocated some of its tax revenues to the states. Nixon's revenue sharing was an attempt to return policy control to the states and reduce federal intervention; it required no matching funds from recipients. Obviously, revenue sharing enjoyed great popularity with governors, state legislators, and mayors.

Nixon signing the message about his revenue-sharing plan that he proposed to Congress

The difference between early revenue sharing and that during the Nixon-to-Reagan period was that in the past, revenue was shared only when there was a surplus in the national Treasury. But during the 1970s and 1980s, federal revenue was shared when there was really none to share. The billions of dollars in shared revenue added to the rising tide of the federal debt.

Section Review

1. Provide a basic description of categorical grants.
2. What are block grants?
3. Explain revenue sharing.
★ Is it a good idea or a bad one for states to accept federal funds for public education? Support your answer.

IV. The Challenges of Federalism

Maintaining Federal Distinctions

As explained earlier, federalism is the division of political power between two or more governmental levels. This division is maintained through constitutional provisions and political pressures. But strong political pressures often threaten rather than maintain this division.

The Constitution actually has little to say about what the national government can or cannot do in its relationship with the states. One requirement placed on the national government is that it must honor the states' territorial rights (Article IV, Section 3). For example, Congress may not create a new state out of part of Alaska without the consent of the Alaskan legislature.

<table>
<tr><td colspan="2">**Guiding Questions**</td></tr>
</table>

1. What factors maintain the distinctions between state and national governments?
2. What problems result from federal funding to state governments?

Reagan's Reform Attempt

When President Reagan took office in 1981, a major proposal of his new federalism program was the consolidation of more than eighty categorical grants into six block grants. His intent was to reduce the federal bureaucracy's control and give more freedom of administration to the states in areas such as health services, energy and emergency assistance, and state education. Congress, however, refused to approve Reagan's proposal; instead, it formulated its own program of block grants and categorical grants that kept most federal controls in place.

Section IV Objectives

1. Identify the factors that maintain the distinctions between state and national governments.
2. Describe problems that result from federal funding to state governments.

Activity 2: Revenue Sharing

This activity provides students experience in studying and evaluating original sources (in this case, statements by Nixon and Reagan about revenue sharing).

Section Review Answers

1. Categorical grants are funds given to state and local governments for specified purposes if certain requirements are met. This kind of grant is the most common, and it is either administered according to a formula or targeted to certain projects in such a way that the federal government controls its use. (p. 132)

2. Block grants involve broader categories, fewer restrictions, and, hence, less federal control. (pp. 132–33)

3. Revenue sharing involved giving grants of money to state and local governments from tax revenues; it had fewer strings attached and was designed to reduce intervention by the federal government. In recent years, these types of grants existed from 1972 to 1986. (p. 133)

★ Students may say that state acceptance of federal education funds can pose some problems. For example, it can condition states to expect those funds as a continuing source of revenue; furthermore, the requirements that accompany the grants may be stringent. On the other hand, some students may say that the funding may enable states to accomplish educational goals that might be otherwise unachievable due to lack of money.

An early instance of the federal government attaching regulations to its grants to states was in the Morrill Act of 1862. If states used federal land grants to establish state land-grant colleges, the federal government required the states' institutions to teach certain subjects and make annual reports regarding their finances and programs.

In 1957, President Eisenhower sent troops to Little Rock, Arkansas, to restore order as the first African American students integrated an all-white school there.

Article IV, Section 4 states the national government must guarantee that each state has a republican form of government. It further says the national government is obligated to protect the states from foreign invasion and to intervene if necessary to suppress domestic violence in a state. For example, in 1967 and 1968 President Johnson ordered army units to help quell violent riots that erupted in Detroit, Chicago, Baltimore, and Washington, DC.

There are also important political forces that help preserve the national and state levels of federalism. First, in our republican system, national officeholders are elected from the state and local levels; that is, members of Congress who pass laws in the national legislature represent 435 districts and 50 states—states and districts to whom these officials must answer. This accountability helps maintain a degree of independence for states and localities that might otherwise be overwhelmed by national power. Second, political parties are organized on the state level and are somewhat independent of their national organizations. This independence strengthens the parties' control over their national representatives and enhances the political identity of the states and districts.

Maintaining this identity is no easy task. As earlier portions of this text have explained, the changes in American law, society, and economy during the nation's history have helped alter the balance of federalism in favor of the national government.

National controls are reflected in state and municipal budgets, which are planned with available federal grants in mind. Localities may boost their revenues by millions if they provide matching funds for projects that support particular national policies. This forces local planners to think "federally" as they devise a budget.

Giving and Taking

Federal aid involves both services and controls. Billions of dollars in grants permit states to provide a variety of assistance to their citizens that would not be otherwise possible. But, critics note that such aid means that sometimes objectionable and cumbersome national policies must be implemented by state and local officials.

The fact that such grants give greater involvement to the national government in state and local policymaking has certainly produced controversy. Matters that were previously areas of state and local prerogative are sometimes entangled in a web of federal regulations. For example, from 1974 to 1987, federal

Activity 3: A Brief History of American Federalism

This activity contains excerpts from an article entitled "American Federalism, Past Present, and Future." It provides a good review of many issues mentioned in this and previous chapters regarding federalism. It also gives students an opportunity to analyze the ideas presented.

highway funds were withheld from states that did not adopt a maximum speed limit of 55 miles per hour. The primary reason for the regulation was to save fuel. All areas, including those where motorists could travel fairly safely at 80 miles per hour (such as flat areas in western states where there are few curves), had little choice but to follow the federal government's limit. Though a state was not forced to adhere to the regulation, the loss of highway funds made it impractical to ignore. Likewise, in 1984 Congress passed legislation that reduced federal highway funds to any state that allowed individuals below age 21 to purchase alcohol. The legal drinking age had previously been a state or local issue; however, with the new penalties in place, eventually all states complied with the federal guidelines.

In recent decades public education, long governed by state and local officials, has also faced new federal mandates. In some cases compliance has been mandatory, while in others the loss of federal funding that would accompany noncompliance has meant that few school districts have been able to ignore them.

Growing National Debt

The national debt is the amount of money the federal government owes. By 2020, it exceeded $23 trillion. That amount is more than quadruple the amount owed just two decades earlier. Giving federal aid to the state and local government contributed to the rapid increase in this amount. In 1970 the total amount of federal grants stood at an annual $24 billion; a decade later the figure was over $90 billion per year. As noted earlier in this chapter, the aid to state and local governments now surpasses $700 billion annually.

Special-interest groups and financially strapped states and cities have lobbied hard to retain financial and political benefits gained from continued aid. States have become so accustomed to aid from the national government that reductions damage their budgets.

Deficit and Debt

What is a budget deficit? It is the amount by which expenditures exceed income. For example, if the United States has $3.9 trillion in revenue (income) for a year, but it spends $4.8 trillion, the budget deficit would be $900 billion.

What is national debt? It is the amount of money that the government owes. Each year in which there is a budget deficit, the US government borrows more money and the national debt increases. As noted in this chapter, the national debt exceeded $23 trillion by 2020.

A more thorough discussion of the national debt is presented in Chapter 9 (pp. 187–89, 201).

National Debt

Guide a discussion about the issues of the national debt and the federal government's annual budget deficit. Be sure the students understand the distinction between these two. Lay a foundation for a lengthier discussion regarding the national debt that you can initiate when examining Chapter 9.

State Favoritism

Favoring some states over others is nothing new in the federal grant system. After the New Deal programs were implemented, observers in 1940 found wide variations between the taxes paid by states and the aid they received. For instance, Delaware paid $172 per capita in taxes in 1940 but received only $22.24 per person in aid, while citizens of North Dakota paid $21 per capita in taxes and received $79 per person in aid.

Reasons for the disparity may include the following factors: During the Great Depression, North Dakota and other plains states were hit by a severe drought that devastated crops and destroyed livestock. Per capita income in North Dakota dropped to 47 percent of the national average, and thousands of North Dakotans emigrated to California. Also, North Dakota is a fairly large state with a comparatively small population, so relief that the state government provides is more difficult to manage than it is in tiny Delaware. In addition, political patronage might have been a major factor affecting states' gains or losses in the "game" of vying for federal dollars.

Competition Between States

Another problem facing federalism involves the relationships and competition between the states. Friction between the states is nothing new; the Constitution was written, at least in part, to reduce the disagreements between the states that existed under the Articles of Confederation. Today, federalism and changing demographics, or population trends, have produced problems of a different sort.

All states do not receive the same proportion of federal aid. Some states receive more federal funds than their residents pay in federal taxes, whereas other states receive less. Critics argue that states that pay more than they receive are, in effect, subsidizing programs in states that pay less than they receive. This inequity produces clamor and competition for federal tax dollars and arguments among governing officials.

A growing regionalism within the country has also brought discord. For example, the Sunbelt, consisting of states in the South and the Southwest, has become an economic rival of the Frostbelt, which consists of the Northeast and the upper Midwest. Many areas of the Frostbelt struggle with older industries (e.g., steel and auto manufacturing); decaying cities; and a declining population. The Sunbelt, by contrast, enjoys a growing population and newer industries. This shift has been partly economic. Many southern and southwestern states have lower taxes and offer financial incentives for companies that relocate there. Population shifts from the Frostbelt to the Sunbelt have also been politically advantageous for the southern and southwestern states. For example, after the 2010

Which States Rely Most on Federal Aid
Federal Aid as a Percentage of State General Revenue, Fiscal Year 2015

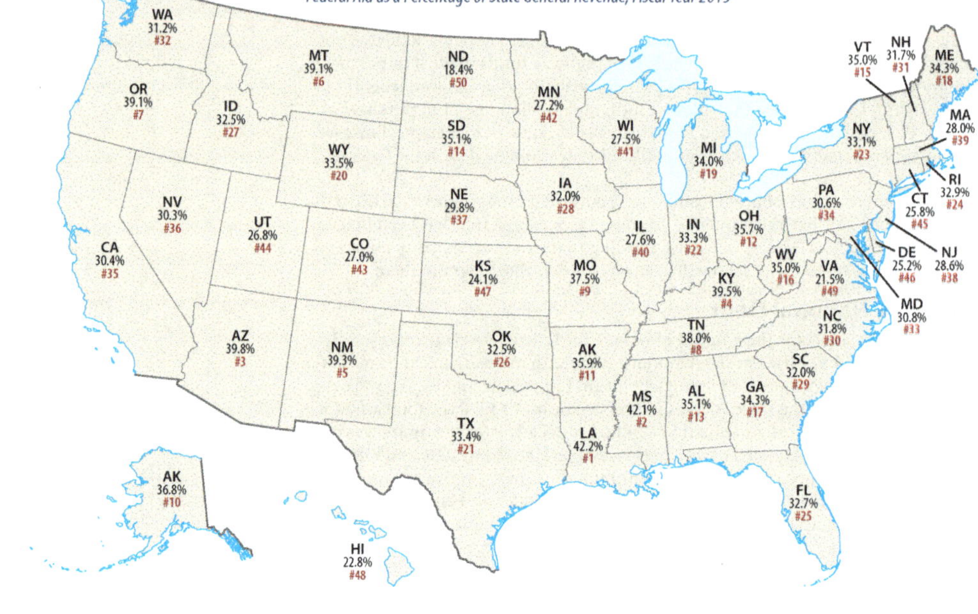

Federal Aid to States

Instruct students to carefully examine the map above. Which states rely most on federal aid? (*Louisiana, Mississippi, Arizona, Kentucky, and New Mexico*)

Which states rely least on federal aid? (*Delaware, Kansas, Hawaii, Virginia, and North Dakota*)

As noted in the text, some states receive more federal funds than their residents pay in federal taxes and other states receive less. Ask students whether they believe this is fair and instruct them to defend their answers.

Census, Sunbelt states gained more than ten new congressional seats—seats that the northern and midwestern states lost.

Sectional debate is increased by Congress's ability to favor one region over another through formula grants. Overall, the Sunbelt tends to edge out the Frostbelt in the struggle for federal funds, and many Sunbelt states get a better return on their federal tax dollars than do their northern rivals.

Federal funding is often tied to political control. In other words, the political party that controls the national government in a particular year often provides more funding to the areas that support its candidates. Though this has always been the case, it was particularly pronounced during the New Deal era. Federal grants, which were especially important during the economic crisis of the Great Depression, tended to pour into states that supported the political party of the New Deal's author, Democrat President Franklin Roosevelt. Conversely, other areas received less federal funding. As a result, voters who did not want to risk losing federal funds tended to continue voting for Democratic candidates. This trend continues today, and consequently, many voters support the political party that provides the most funding for their area.

Seats Lost or Gained by Reapportionment (based on the 2010 Census)

Lost

Two seats: New York and Ohio

One seat: Illinois, Iowa, Louisiana, Massachusetts, Michigan, Missouri, New Jersey, and Pennsylvania

Gained

Four seats: Texas

Two seats: Florida

One seat: Arizona, Georgia, Nevada, South Carolina, Utah, and Washington

Most of the money used to build the Gateway Arch in Saint Louis, Missouri, was provided from federal funds.

The Importance of the Census

Because representation in the US House is determined by the population within each state, completing the census is a very important process. Furthermore, because the number of electoral votes for each state is determined by the number of members the state has in the two houses of Congress, the census also has a direct effect on the election of the president.

Is the census count accurate? Some observers have asserted that there have been deliberate attempts to undercount or overcount the number of people in particular areas.

What questions should be included on the census form? In March 2018, the Commerce Department announced that the 2020 census would include a question about whether each US resident was a US citizen. The last time such a question was placed on all census forms was in 1950. The proposed question brought immediate controversy. While some praised the addition of the question, others denounced it. A legal battle ensued. In January 2019, a federal judge in New York ordered that the question regarding citizenship should not be placed on the census form. The Trump administration appealed the judge's ruling to the US Supreme Court. In June 2019, the Supreme Court ruled that the question could not be added to the census unless the government could provide "genuine justifications" for doing so. Instead of returning to court, the administration decided to not include the question in the census but rather to compile the data from other government agencies.

The census is addressed in several chapters of the Student Edition. Chapter 5 (p. 95) and Chapter 8 (pp. 168–70) give the greatest detail regarding this topic.

Census and Reapportionment

Use the margin box above as a springboard for discussing the relationship between the national census (which the Constitution mandates must occur every ten years) and the reapportionment of the US House of Representatives.

Ask students to research the impact of censuses over the past half century. What was the population of each state approximately fifty years ago? How many representatives did each state have in the US House at that time? What was the population of each state in the *last* census? How many representatives does each state have today? What trends are noticeable? Why do you think these trends have occurred?

Activity 4: Chapter Review

The questions in this activity cover the entire chapter and reinforce recognition skills that aid in test preparation.

Unforeseen Circumstances

The size and power of the federal government today would undoubtedly astound the Founding Fathers. They believed that any attempt to expand federal power would be met by considerable opposition from the states. In *Federalist* No. 46, Madison stated,

> Ambitious encroachments of the federal government, on the authority of the State governments, would not excite the opposition of a single State, or of a few States only. They would be signals of general alarm. Every government would espouse the common cause. A correspondence would be opened. Plans of resistance would be concerted. One spirit would animate and conduct the whole. The same combinations, in short, would result from an apprehension of the federal, as was produced by the dread of a foreign, yoke; and unless the projected innovations should be voluntarily renounced, the same appeal to a trial of force would be made in the one case as was made in the other. But what degree of madness could ever drive the federal government to such an extremity.

Of course, some contend that the Founding Fathers would likewise be amazed by much in modern society. Automobiles, aircraft, interstate highways, and stunning developments in technology would astonish the nation's early leaders. However, others argue that improvements in transportation, communication, and daily living are far different from changes in government structure.

Conclusion

Federalism has changed much since its principles were first outlined at the Constitutional Convention. Despite the many modifications, the federal system still provides enormous benefits and still serves our nation well.

One of the greatest advantages of federalism is the protection it provides against tyranny: it permits no single institution to hold *all* the reins of authority. James Madison, in *Federalist* No. 46, addressed those who criticized the Constitution. He noted:

> The federal and state governments are in fact but different agents and trustees of the people, constituted with different powers, and designed for different purposes. The adversaries of the Constitution seem to have lost sight of the people altogether in their reasonings on this subject. . . . These gentlemen must here be reminded of their error. They must be told that the ultimate authority . . . resides in the people alone.

Section Review

1–4. What four constitutional obligations does the national government have in relation to the states?

5–6. What two political forces help preserve the division between the state and national levels of government?

7. What is the basic point James Madison is making in the excerpt from *The Federalist Papers* at the conclusion of this chapter?

★ Why is it often difficult to reverse states' and districts' reliance on federal grants and to reduce federal budgets?

★ What are the primary advantages of federal grants? What are the disadvantages?

Section Review Answers

1–4. The national government must honor the states' territorial rights, must guarantee each state a republican form of government, must protect states from foreign invasion, and must intervene if a state needs help in suppressing domestic violence. (pp. 133–34)

5–6. Congressmen are responsible to the states and districts that elected them. Political parties are organized on the state level and are somewhat independent of their national organizations. (p. 134)

7. The power still lies in the hands of the people. The governments, both state and national, are agents of the people. (p. 138)

★ Each area that benefits from federal grants is usually very concerned about keeping the funding it receives and thus opposes cuts even if a reduction in federal spending is needed.

★ Advantages include the variety of types of assistance and assistance to citizens that would not otherwise be possible. Disadvantages include objectionable and cumbersome policies that must be implemented by state and local officials, greater involvement of the national government in state and local policymaking, increased national debt, and states that become dependent on the federal government's aid.

Making Connections

1. What clause in the Constitution has the federal government used to extend its power?
2. What constitutional amendment protects the reserved powers of the states and the people?
3–4. List and explain the two basic types of federal grants-in-aid used today.

Developing Civics Skills

1. Contrast a federalist system of government with a monarchy.
2. Research the national debt. What do you think are some of the problems it causes?

Thinking Critically

1. Why does a republican, federalist government structure require an honest and honorable population?
2. What Christian virtues are necessary in society to prevent a federalist government from becoming corrupt?

Living as a Christian Citizen

1. The American federalist system was created because of problems that arose under the Articles of Confederation. What problems have emerged under the current system? Outline a modified form of government, and explain how it resolves the stated problems.
2. In the United States, many of the most significant moral issues are decided by the courts rather than by legislatures. Is this good or bad for the country? Defend your thesis. If you think judicial determination of moral issues is bad, propose a change that would solve this problem.

People, Places, and Things to Remember

- federalism
- delegated powers
- enumerated powers
- implied powers
- necessary and proper clause
- elastic clause
- reserved powers
- supremacy clause
- dual federalism
- Sixteenth Amendment
- New Deal
- Great Society
- grants-in-aid
- categorical grants
- formula grants
- project grants
- block grants
- revenue sharing

tions; the interest on the debt costs hundreds of billions each year; and it is unwise to spend more money than you receive.

Thinking Critically

1. When the people play a large part in the governing process, they must have the morality necessary for good self-government.
2. Students may say that government officials must view themselves as God's agents and servants for the people. This means that they serve not for power or personal interests but for the common good. They may also mention that citizens must develop a concern for the common good instead of focusing on personal gain. Selflessness—or more broadly, love—is a necessary element in a federalist government.

Living as a Christian Citizen

1. Problems that might be listed include inefficiency, judicial activism, and increased power of special interests. Solutions should include an explanation of how the proposed changes will solve the problems and should note potential new problems that the changes might generate.
2. Students may say that an unelected judiciary that reshapes the nation's morality is not in the nation's best interest. Possible constitutional changes might include amendments that specify the limits of judicial review, modes of interpretation, or modes of recourse for clear judicial overreach.

CHAPTER REVIEW ANSWERS

Making Connections

1. the necessary and proper clause (the elastic clause) (pp. 126–27)
2. the Tenth Amendment (p. 127)
3–4. Categorical grants are given for a specific purpose and include certain guidelines for their use. Block grants combine several categorical grants under a general umbrella; they allow states to have more flexibility in administering funds. (pp. 131–33)

Developing Civics Skills

1. Federalism divides and distributes governmental powers between the national and state governments, whereas a monarchy, particularly an absolute one, centralizes all power in a single entity (the king or queen). Federalism provides a more flexible means of meeting regional needs because it allows leaders to be closer and more responsive to their people, whereas a monarch is usually far removed from the people whose needs he is supposed to serve. Federalism allows the people a degree of self-rule through their representatives at the various levels of government, whereas a monarchy vests all ruling power in one person's hands.
2. Some problems that students may note are that the debt will affect not only the present population but future genera-

STATE AND LOCAL GOVERNMENT

7

All politics is local.

—Thomas P. "Tip" O'Neill, Jr.
Speaker of the House (1977–87)

A city hall, such as this one in San Antonio, Texas, houses important offices for the local government.

I. State Governments

II. Local Governments

III. State and Local Politics

IV. Interstate and Intergovernmental Relationships

BIG IDEAS

1. How do state governments function and finance themselves?
2. What is the organizational structure of county and municipal governments?
3. How do political organization and the election processes work in state and local governments?
4. How do interstate and intergovernmental relationships work?

SUGGESTED MATERIALS

Section I
- Copy of your state's constitution
- Activity 1 from Chapter 7 of the *Student Activities*

Section II
- Special speakers (see pp. 150, 151)
- Activities 2–3 from Chapter 7 of the *Student Activities*

Section III
- Special speakers (see p. 154)

Section IV
- Activity 4 from Chapter 7 of the *Student Activities*

Teacher Resources
Visit TeacherToolsOnline.com for resources to enhance the lessons.

I. State Governments

State governments compose the second part of American federalism. The average citizen is most directly involved with state and local governments; therefore, they are the most integral parts of everyday government. In this respect, former Speaker of the House Tip O'Neill Jr. was correct when he said, "All politics is local." The national government could cease many of its operations for several days (which has occurred a few times when Congress could not agree on budget matters) without adversely affecting most people. The same cannot be said of state and local governments because those levels are where most people see and feel the day-to-day operations of government.

The American government consists of fifty states united for the common good of all the states. According to the **Tenth Amendment**, the states constitutionally retain all powers not delegated to the national government or prohibited to the states. States are limited not only by the powers delegated to the national government but also by their own constitutions. (Each state has its own constitution that must establish and ensure a *republican* form of government.) The fifty states that compose the United States of America exercise powers that are sometimes distinct from and at other times shared by the national government.

The Tenth Amendment protects the states from being dominated by the national government. The powers granted to the states by this amendment are extensive but necessary because state and local governments provide most of the services to the people. The Constitution gives the states the responsibility and power to—among other actions—police, educate, make land-use laws, and require licensing for professionals.

But the Constitution also limits states' powers in order to preserve the national government's powers. These limits are listed in Article I, Section 10, and in the Fourteenth, Fifteenth, Nineteenth, Twenty-Fourth, and Twenty-Sixth Amendments. (The cited amendments prohibit states from passing laws that would violate the privileges of US citizens.) Furthermore, Article I stipulates that states may not coin money or enter into any binding agreements with other states or nations. In addition, states may not raise or maintain armies or navies during peacetime, nor may they impose duties or levies on imports or exports.

To perform their responsibilities, states must have revenue, and they obtain it through various taxes and other sources. They must also have budgets by which they regulate their expenses. Some larger states have budgets that rival or surpass those of major nations. Unlike the US government, most state governments are required by their laws to have balanced budgets. Those states cannot legally run deficits. Some states borrow money to avoid deficits and eventually face a debt crisis. Other states use one-time grants to fund recurring expenses and experience crises during subsequent years when expenses continue but grants do not.

Tip O'Neill and President Reagan in 1985

Amendments Restricting State Power

Fourteenth: Every US citizen enjoys the rights and privileges of citizenship, and states cannot change that.

Fifteenth: Citizens cannot be denied their right to vote on the basis of "race [or] color."

Nineteenth: States cannot use gender to limit voting rights.

Twenty-Fourth: States cannot require that a poll tax be paid before a citizen can vote.

Twenty-Sixth: States are required to allow eighteen-year-old citizens to vote.

Section I Objectives

1. Explain the constitutional basis for states' powers.
2. Delineate the responsibilities of state government.
3. Outline the responsibilities of the different branches of state government.
4. List the states' sources of revenue.

Just a Reminder

There are two major caveats at the start of this chapter. First, the laws and political processes of the fifty states have similarities but many differences; thus, it is difficult to make broad, all-inclusive statements about how state and local governments operate.

Second, as is true in other chapters, the statements in the Student Edition and the Teacher Edition are correct at the time of publication. You will want to ensure, however, that they are still correct before teaching them.

Your State's Constitution

Obtain a copy of your state's constitution, and discuss its provisions with the students.

Your State's Blue Book

Most states periodically issue a "Blue Book." It provides a variety of interesting statistics and other information about a state's government, history, and county and municipal areas. If possible download a copy of your state's Blue Book to make your teaching of this chapter more relevant to the students.

The Broad Reach of "Public Safety"

Although crime prevention and law enforcement generally come to mind when one speaks of public safety, the term is much more far-reaching than it might seem at first.

Police responsibilities, for example, involve more than arresting bank robbers and distributing traffic tickets. They also include administering tests for drivers' licenses in many states, enforcing commercial transportation laws, educating schoolchildren in pedestrian and personal safety, conducting antidrug and anti-drunk-driving programs, and helping establish neighborhood watches. Other duties include issuing and conducting background checks for concealed-carry permits; enforcing parking codes; and collecting data about criminals and criminal activities in the state or local area and sharing it with other local, state, or national law-enforcement agencies.

Likewise, fire departments do more than extinguish flames. They conduct arson investigations; educate citizens about fire safety; inspect residences, businesses, churches, and factories to ensure adherence to the fire codes; and promote responsible use of fire and proper reactions to it.

Public safety also includes the work of health departments, which promote the health and well-being of people in the community, prevent and stem the spread of infectious diseases, and prepare and implement disaster plans for various scenarios.

Like the national government, state governments operate under a system of separation of powers. In that respect, states have the same branches as the national government: legislative, executive, and judicial.

Every state has three basic responsibilities:

1. Public safety: Education, enforcing law, ensuring public health and safety, and safeguarding morals are all state functions and responsibilities.
2. Commercial regulation: Each state government must ensure that business and industry within the state are conducted according to that state's laws.
3. Political subdivision oversight: State governments must keep counties, cities, towns, and special districts accountable in the performance of their duties regarding safety, taxation, and regulation.

Under these three broad categories are many specific tasks that each state performs, which include the following:

- approve the establishment and boundaries of new towns and provide funding as necessary
- build and maintain roads and highways, including the interstates, within the state
- charter corporations and issue business licenses
- conserve the state's natural resources and educate the public about them
- direct the education of students by overseeing state colleges and cooperating with local school boards
- ensure that laws, including those regarding marriage, family, divorce, child support, and alimony, are enforced
- maintain an employment service and mediate labor disputes
- oversee agriculture by disseminating agricultural information, operating pest-control programs, and promoting crop improvements and conservation
- oversee and fund welfare and the unemployment compensation programs
- oversee banking and insurance industries, performing actions such as granting charters, overseeing the work of auditors and examiners, and enforcing banking and insurance laws
- oversee healthcare practitioners and institutions throughout the state
- patrol state highways and enforce traffic laws, including those regulating commercial carriers (i.e., trucking and other means of commercial transportation within the state); assist local law enforcement as necessary; cooperate with national

An official from the Iowa Department of Natural Resources releasing trout into one of the state's lakes

What Do Law Enforcement Officials Do?

Remind the students about the many tasks law enforcement officials complete. Ask students to list additional items not mentioned in the Student Edition. Encourage them to share personal stories relating to family members who serve in such capacities. Stories could relate to personal sacrifices they have endured, catastrophes that have been averted because of their actions, ways in which members of the public have shown appreciation to officials, or perhaps occasions where law enforcement officials have endured insults.

Commercial Regulation

Ask the students to think of examples of how states regulate commerce within their borders. (Examples might include weight limits and size restrictions on trucks, standardization and inspection of gasoline pumps and scales, packaging requirements for various products, and health regulations in food-processing plants and eating establishments.)

agencies as necessary; and operate the state prison system

- prepare for and react to natural and wartime emergencies and cooperate with national law-enforcement officials for homeland security
- set and enforce health and safety standards for the manufacture and sale of raw and processed foods, inspect stores and restaurants, and ensure the standardization of weights and measures (e.g., commercial scales and gasoline pumps)
- set boundaries for election districts, especially during reapportionment, and legislate and oversee rules for elections
- set driving standards and issue drivers' licenses and license plates for private and commercial vehicles operated within the state
- perform other tasks designated by the legislature and approved by the governor

State Legislatures

Every state has a legislative branch that is responsible for passing that state's laws. State laws are different from national laws passed by Congress. In all but one state, the legislatures are **bicameral**; that is, the legislature has two separate houses—an upper chamber and a lower chamber. As mentioned in the last chapter, Nebraska's legislature is the lone exception: that legislature is **unicameral** (made up of only one house). That body is officially non-partisan; in other words, legislators do not have to declare affiliation with any political party.

The official names of the various legislatures differ from state to state. The most common name for the legislative branch is legislature, followed by General Assembly (nineteen states). Massachusetts and New Hampshire refer to it as the General Court, while North Dakota and Oregon call it the Legislative Assembly.

Similarly, the states call their lower house by various names, the most common being House of Representatives. A few call it the Assembly or the House of Delegates or the General Assembly. All states call their upper house the Senate. However, regardless of the names given to the houses, the distinction between upper and lower houses exists.

Generally, state legislatures possess all powers not specifically delegated to the executive or judicial branches (or both) in their respective states or prohibited by state or national constitutions. State legislatures have explicit powers to tax; maintain public schools; regulate business, industry, and commerce; and provide police protection. They also provide many more services considered necessary for the states' well-being. In addition, state legislatures can approve **gubernatorial** (i.e., the governor's) appointments, override gubernatorial vetoes, impeach state officials, and propose amendments to state constitutions.

The California Department of Forestry and Fire Protection uses aircraft to help stop wildfires.

Norris and Unicameralism

For years, a number of Nebraska lawmakers promoted the idea of a unicameral legislature, citing that it would be less expensive and more efficient than their bicameral body. In 1931 George W. Norris, US senator from Nebraska, visited Australia. He was impressed with the functioning of the unicameral legislature in the state of Queensland.

Upon returning to the United States, Norris tirelessly fought for a unicameral legislature for the state. Nebraska voters approved the concept in 1934.

Nebraska capitol in Lincoln

Unusual State Laws

Every state has some unique laws. Here are a few examples:

1. In Alabama a 1996 law declared that it was illegal to wrestle a bear. It was also illegal to, "for purposes of exploitation," surgically alter a bear (i.e., declaw it, remove its teeth, etc.). Apparently, it was legal to alter a bear if one did not intend to exploit the creature. This law was repealed in 2015.

2. In Flint, Michigan, it is illegal to wear sagging pants that reveal underwear or bare flesh. Though unusual, many applaud the law.

3. In New Jersey it is illegal to wear a bulletproof vest while attempting to commit murder. Violating this law could result in a punishment greater than that incurred by committing murder without a bulletproof vest.

4. In Wellington, Kansas, it is illegal to own more than four cats in a single household.

5. In Florida it is illegal to flash one's headlights to warn oncoming drivers of a speed trap ahead of them.

Laughable Legalities

Ask students to find and discuss examples of unusual laws in your state or local community. Many such laws were passed decades ago, and there were probably legitimate reasons for their passage at the time, but they have since become outdated.

Instruct the students to write to local officials (state representatives, county executives, or commissioners), urging them to repeal such measures.

Engage students in a discussion regarding obsolete laws and laws that they may consider to be unimportant or unfair. Are Christians still responsible to obey such laws? What should our attitude be toward such regulations?

State Executives

The chief officer of a state's executive branch is the **governor**, who is elected directly by the people of the state. The powers of the office vary from state to state, but the governor is responsible for administering the state government and enforcing state laws.

The governor can appoint and dismiss assistants in the executive branch, make budgets, and supervise the executive branch's staff. He is also the commander in chief of the state militia. The governor generally has power to veto bills from the legislature, call special sessions of the legislature, and even suggest legislation. Governors can check judicial power by pardoning and paroling convicted criminals, commuting (reducing) sentences, and issuing reprieves or stays of execution.

In addition to being the state's chief administrator and a major proposer (suggester) of legislation, the governor is the chief spokesman for the state and the head of his state political party. In the role of chief state spokesman, the governor receives official visitors, dedicates buildings or highways, and delivers speeches to various state or civic organizations. Increasingly, governors are the chief sales agents for their respective states, trying to entice business and industry to develop or expand operations in their states. This effort creates jobs, helps local and state economies, and, consequently, increases state and local revenues.

Nikki Haley was South Carolina's governor from 2011 to 2017.

While all governors have the power to veto a bill, forty-four states also give governors line-item veto power. (The exceptions are Indiana, Nevada, New Hampshire, North Carolina, Rhode Island, and Vermont.) This is the ability to eliminate one or more items from a bill without rejecting the entire measure. It is most commonly used on spending bills.

Governors in all states except two are elected for a four-year term. New Hampshire and Vermont elect their chief executive for just two years. Thirty-six states limit the number of terms the governor can serve (usually it is two terms).

In almost every state, the governor is assisted by a **lieutenant governor**, who functions somewhat like the vice president of the United States. He represents the state government at various functions and is often the presiding officer in the upper house of the legislature. In most states, he becomes the state's leader if the governor resigns, dies, is removed from office, or is unable to perform his duties. In some states, the lieutenant governor also serves on various boards, committees, task forces, or working groups. In general, however, the lieutenant governorship is a relatively weak, sometimes merely symbolic, position.

Gubernatorial Power	
Stronger Governors	**Weaker Governors**
Have line-item veto power	Have no line-item veto power
Appoint all cabinet members, who answer to the governor	Appoint no (or few) cabinet members or these members answer to the legislature
Have great influence over the budget process	Have little influence in the budget process

State Judiciary

The judicial branch of a state's government is responsible to interpret the law and oversee criminal cases. The highest state court is a **supreme court**; it is assisted by lower courts.

Unlike the judges for federal courts, who are appointed by the president, the selection method for state judges varies by state. Nearly all are chosen in one of

---

Office of the Governor

Instruct the students to research their state's office of governor and write a one-page report on whether the office is strong or weak. Also require them to research the governor's salary, length of term, and responsibilities as governor.

Report on Your State's Governor

Assign a group of students to research and present a report (oral or written) on the governor of your state. They should include the governor's background; political history; campaign strategies for winning the governorship; and views on important political, economic, and social issues in your state.

You may expand the report beyond the current governor and suggest that students research the youngest or oldest elected governor, the ratio of male to female governors, the ratio of "homegrown" governors to governors born out-of-state, the ratio of political party representation in the governorship, or other information.

three ways: popular election, appointment by the governor, or appointment by the legislature. More than half the states use the Missouri Plan for the selection of some judges. It combines the election and appointment methods.

Though there are variations of it, the Missouri Plan typically calls for a nonpartisan commission to review a list of potential judges. The members then provide the governor with the names of those they consider most qualified. Subsequently, the governor appoints one of the individuals from the list to a judicial vacancy. At the next election, usually a year or more later, the voters are asked to decide whether or not the judge should remain in office. If the people vote to not retain that judge, the election process begins again.

Which means of selecting state judges is best? That has been, and continues to be, a matter of debate. Some argue that judges should be directly accountable to the people, and thus should be elected. Others say the most qualified candidates might not be the most well-known ones or the best campaigners, and that appointment is better. Of course, there are obvious advantages and disadvantages of any method used.

State courts generally hear cases that involve anything outside the exclusive jurisdiction of federal courts. Specifically, most cases in state courts fall into the following categories:

1. Interpretation of state constitutions
2. Contract law, which deals with agreements between two or more people or entities and their respective obligations
3. Corporate and business organizations (establishing or dissolving and distributing the assets of corporations, partnerships, and limited liability corporations)
4. Election issues, including voting, voter registration, and legislative reapportionment
5. Family issues, including marriage, divorce, adoption, child support, and child custody
6. Municipal or zoning laws
7. Probate, which involves the validity of wills and the distribution of assets according to the desires of the deceased and the state's laws
8. Real property issues, which involve land and anything growing on, attached to, or built on it
9. Sale of goods
10. State criminal issues (Most crimes are of this nature.)
11. Personal-injury cases
12. Traffic issues involving state roadways and driving regulations

Generally, the states' supreme courts (called by various names) are located in the states' capital cities, but even those courts may occasionally hear oral arguments elsewhere if necessary.

The number of judges sitting on the states' supreme courts, the way they are selected, and the length, or term, of their service varies by state. In four states, the justices serve for life "during good behavior" (though two have a mandatory retirement age of 70). The other states' justices have terms ranging from a minimum of

Typical State Court System Organization

COURTS OF LAST RESORT
(variously named)
- Supreme Court (46 states)
- Court of Appeals (MD & NY)
- Supreme Judicial Court (MA)
- Supreme Court of Appeals (WV)

INTERMEDIATE APPELLATE COURTS
(in about half the states)

MAJOR TRIAL COURTS
(various combinations of these in the states)
- Chancery court
- Superior court
- Circuit court
- Other courts
- District court

COURTS OF LIMITED JURISDICTION
(various combinations of these in the states)
- Probate court
- Traffic court
- Justice court
- County court
- Magistrate court
- Municipal court
- Summary court
- Other courts
- Police court

State Supreme Court Trivia

How states select justices to serve on their supreme court
- Six states use partisan elections.
- Sixteen states use nonpartisan elections.
- Ten states' governors appoint justices with the legislature's consent.
- Two states' legislatures elect justices.
- Sixteen states use the Missouri Plan.

Number of justices on the states' supreme courts
- Five states have nine justices.
- Twenty-nine states have seven justices.
- Sixteen states have five justices.

Length of term for justices
- In only four states do justices serve for life.
- Fifteen states have terms of six years.
- Eleven states have terms of eight years.
- Thirteen states have terms of ten years.
- Five states have terms of twelve years.
- Maine has a term of seven years.
- New York has a term of fourteen years.

Jury Selection

In selecting a jury, the presiding judge and then the prosecuting and defense lawyers ask potential jurors a series of questions. Discuss the types of questions that lawyers might ask prospective jurors to determine whether they will accept or excuse the potential jurors, and discuss the reasons for those questions. (Questions might be about relationship to or knowledge of the defendant, about membership in organizations that might prejudice the juror for or against the defendant, or about personal convictions that might influence the juror's decisions.)

States use various methods to obtain potential jurors for trials in their state and local judicial jurisdictions. Some states select jurors from the voter-registration lists. Other states choose from all people that have driver's licenses. Recruit a volunteer to research and report to the class on the process that your county or state uses to select jurors.

Visit to a Courtroom

Arrange for the class to visit a local or state courtroom in your area to witness a trial in progress. Before the visit, brainstorm with the students regarding their goals and expectations for the field trip.

If possible, arrange a meeting before or after the trial with the presiding judge. (Meeting before the trial will give the judge a chance to prepare the students for what they will see and for how they should behave in the courtroom. Meeting after the trial will provide the students an opportunity to ask any questions that arose in their minds during the trial.)

State Supreme Courts outside the Capital City

A few states, including the following, have their supreme courts located outside the capital.

- Alaska: in Anchorage, the state's largest city (though the court also hears cases in Fairbanks, Juneau, and other communities as needed)
- California: in San Francisco, with a branch office in Sacramento, the capital, and in Los Angeles, the largest city
- Delaware: in Wilmington
- Louisiana: in New Orleans
- Maine: in Portland, the state's largest city
- Pennsylvania: The court operates co-equal sites in Harrisburg (the capital, located in the central part of the state); in Philadelphia in the east; and in Pittsburgh in the west.
- Tennessee: The court operates coequal sites in Nashville (the capital, located in the central part of the state); in Knoxville in the east; and in Jackson in the west.

six years to a maximum of fourteen years. The number of justices on a court ranges from five to nine, with a majority of the states (twenty-nine) having seven justices.

State Financing

Like the national government, state governments must be financed to pay for natural-resource management; the judicial process; representation in the legislative, executive, and judicial branches; and numerous other services that state governments provide (e.g., police protection and public safety). People often think of taxes as the sole source of state revenue. Although the states' precise funding sources vary, states are financed by a variety of revenue sources.

Taxes paid to the state government actually comprise only about half of the average state's revenue. The next-largest source of income is grants from the national government. Because of the large sums involved, such grants have a significant impact on each state. During times of crisis, state reliance on federal funding increases. For example, when state tax revenues declined in 2009 and 2010 (during a time that the nation's economy was performing poorly), federal grants increased significantly. As noted in the previous chapter, this pattern of increased federal funding and subsequent increased federal involvement in state matters began during the New Deal era.

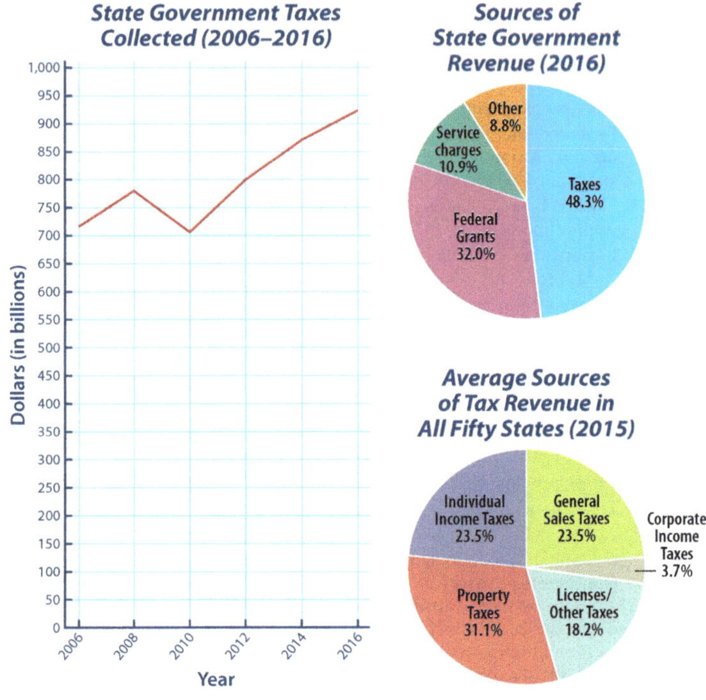

Report on Your State's Supreme Court

Assign a group of students to research and present a report (oral or written) on the members of your state's supreme court. They should include in the report the names and backgrounds of the members of the court, the political composition of the court, the members' views on major issues, and any recent important cases on which the justices ruled.

Analyzing Information

Use the two pie charts and the graph on this page to discuss state revenues. Ask students several questions: What is the difference between what is shown on the two pie charts? Does any information surprise you? What is the primary source of revenue for states? What secondary sources exist? What does the graph indicate about what occurred between 2008 and 2012?

Activity 1: When There Is No Government

This activity provides practice in using resources, writing, analyzing, and evaluating.

Arguments Against Participating in the Lottery

- The odds of winning the largest prizes in the lottery are astronomical (an average of 1 in 12–14 million or more). Playing is poor stewardship of God-given resources (1 Chron. 29:11–14).
- It can lead to addiction—compulsive gambling (1 Cor. 9:27).
- It sometimes increases the temptation toward criminal activities—for example, because people may need to replace the income they have spent on the lottery, they sometimes participate in illegal activities (Prov. 4:14–15).
- It puts states in the position of advertising an act that has been viewed as a vice by many cultures.
- Governments should provide a framework for helping the poor. However, people with the lowest income (those least able to afford it) tend to play the lottery the most. Thus, a lottery disproportionately harms the poor.
- The Bible warns about the dangers of desiring to be rich. It says we should be content with having our basic needs provided (1 Tim. 6:6–10).

Of the various taxes states charge, three are the most common: property tax, general sales tax, and individual income tax. Only seven states do not have an income tax and only five states do not have a statewide sales tax.

A source of state revenue that is not specified in the accompanying pie charts is **lotteries**. Forty-four states have lotteries. The six exceptions are Alabama and Utah, whose heavily religious constituencies have prevented passage of lottery bills; Alaska and Hawaii, neither of which has contiguous neighbors with lotteries to compete for tax revenues; Mississippi and Nevada, which have casinos instead of lotteries; and Wyoming.

Some states place their lottery revenues into the general fund. Typically, however, revenues from state lotteries are designated for specific purposes, such as education, environmental protection, crime control, transportation, or state-park maintenance. Some people complain, however, that when many states designate lottery funds for a certain cause, they also reduce general funding for that cause. State lotteries are the most widespread form of gambling. Perhaps one of the most common arguments offered in favor of using lotteries to increase state revenue is that a lottery is a voluntary tax; only those who play the lottery pay the tax. Proponents also argue that players risk relatively little for a chance to win huge payouts.

States Without Certain Taxes

Seven states do not have a personal income tax and five do not have a statewide sales tax.

No state income tax
1. Alaska
2. Florida
3. Nevada
4. South Dakota
5. Texas
6. Washington
7. Wyoming

No statewide sales tax
1. Alaska
2. Delaware
3. Montana
4. New Hampshire
5. Oregon

Section Review

1. Summarize what the Tenth Amendment says about the power of the states.
2–4. What are the three broad responsibilities of state governments?
5. Which is the only state legislature that is not bicameral?
6. Explain the Missouri Plan for selecting state judges.
7. What is the single largest source of state revenue?
★ What do you think is the best way to choose state judges? Justify your answer.
★ What is the fairest way to finance state government? Support your answer.

Calculating Property Tax

Many variables are involved in determining a property-tax bill, and those variables differ from state to state. The most important variable is the *market value* of the property. (This is supposed to be what a buyer would be willing to pay for the property, but it is actually a number set by a government office and might be inaccurate. Taxpayers who disagree with the stated market value usually have means of appealing the stated value.) The local government sets an *assessment rate*, which might vary from as low as 1 percent of market value to as high as 30 percent or more of market value. The market value is multiplied by the assessment rate. Then any *exemptions* (e.g., deductions for senior citizens or disabled persons) are subtracted from the result, leaving the *taxable value*. The taxable value is then multiplied by the *tax rate*, which is set by the local government; the result is the actual *tax bill*.

Lottery Logistics

If your state has a lottery, invite the students to research how the games operate and the odds of winning games. How are the funds raised by the lottery allocated? What have been the results of the lottery in your state? Debate the idea of having a state lottery and whether the lottery is good for the state and its people.

Section Review Answers

1. The states constitutionally retain all powers not delegated to the national government or prohibited to the states. (p. 141)
2–4. public safety, commercial regulation, and political subdivision oversight (p. 142)
5. Nebraska's legislature (p. 143)
6. The Missouri Plan of selecting judges combines the election and appointment methods. It typically calls for a nonpartisan commission to review a list of potential judges. The members then give the governor the names of those that they consider the most qualified. The governor appoints one of those individuals to fill the judicial vacancy. At the next election, the people vote whether to retain the judge. (p. 145)
7. taxes (p. 146)
★ Some will argue that judges should be directly accountable to the people and thus should be elected. Others say the most qualified candidates might not be the most well-known ones or the best campaigners and that appointment is better. Some will favor the Missouri Plan because it combines election and appointment.
★ Most students will say that taxes and fees are the fairest means of funding state government.

Section II Objectives

1. Identify the various forms of county and municipal government.
2. Explain the role of special districts in local government.

County Names and Numbers

The United States has 3,100 counties. Most of them are named for famous people.

Most common county name
Washington (31)

Second most common
Jefferson (26)

Most common nonpresident county names
Franklin (24), Clay (18), and Montgomery (18)

State that contains the fewest counties
Delaware (3)

State that contains the most counties
Texas (254)

Largest county by population
Los Angeles County, California, has over 10 million residents.

Smallest counties by population
Kalawao County, Hawaii, with approximately 90 residents and Loving County, Texas, with approximately 120 residents.

Largest county by area
San Bernardino County, California (20,105 square miles)

Smallest county by area
Kalawao County, Hawaii (12 square miles)

Guiding Questions

1. What are the various forms of county and municipal government?
2. How do special districts operate in local government?

II. Local Governments

Local government is the level of government with which most people are familiar; the actions of local government affect citizens every day. It is not prescribed in the Constitution, though it is the basic building block of American government.

The Constitution provides for a federal government consisting of national and state governments. Local governments exist within the states, usually as counties, municipalities (cities and towns), and special districts. While there is only one national government and fifty state governments, there are more than 89,000 local governments in the United States.

County Governments

All states have **county** governments to help administer state laws and policies. There are more than three thousand county governments in the United States. In Louisiana, these subdivisions of the state are called **parishes** and in Alaska and New York City, they are called **boroughs**. New York City consists of five boroughs; each constitutes a county.

Each state determines the number and boundaries of the counties within its borders, so the number of counties varies by state. Of course, physical size has much to do with the number of counties a state has. For example, the states with the fewest counties are among the smallest states: Delaware (3), Hawaii (5), Rhode Island (5), and Connecticut (8). The states with the largest number of counties are Texas (254) and Georgia (159). Although Alaska is the largest state geographically, it has only 29 boroughs because its heavily populated areas are generally in the lower half of the state and along the coast.

Voters in each county typically elect, by popular vote, a governing board to administer the county's business. The governing board, which exercises both executive and legislative powers, is usually called either a board of commissioners (county commission) or a board of supervisors. Boards of commissioners are more common and usually consist of three to five members, although larger

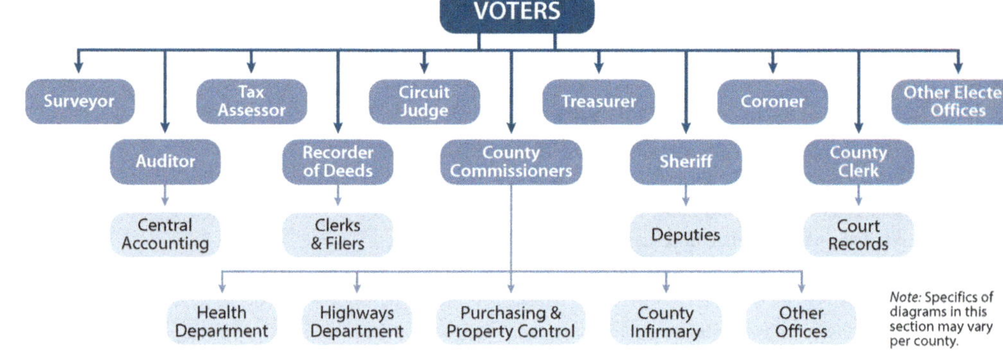

County Organization with Close Voter Control

  ### The Structure of Your County Government

Instruct a group of students to research and present a report (oral or written) regarding your county government's structure. (If the student body of your school represents several different counties, consider assigning a small group for each county.)

Dealing with Local Government

Assign a group of students to write, conduct, and report on a poll to determine which entities of local government the people in your community have the most contact with. The students could list examples of major local-government departments then ask the responders to indicate with which they had dealt in the past year. (If more than one department is marked, the students could ask the responders to rank those departments in order of importance to their needs.)

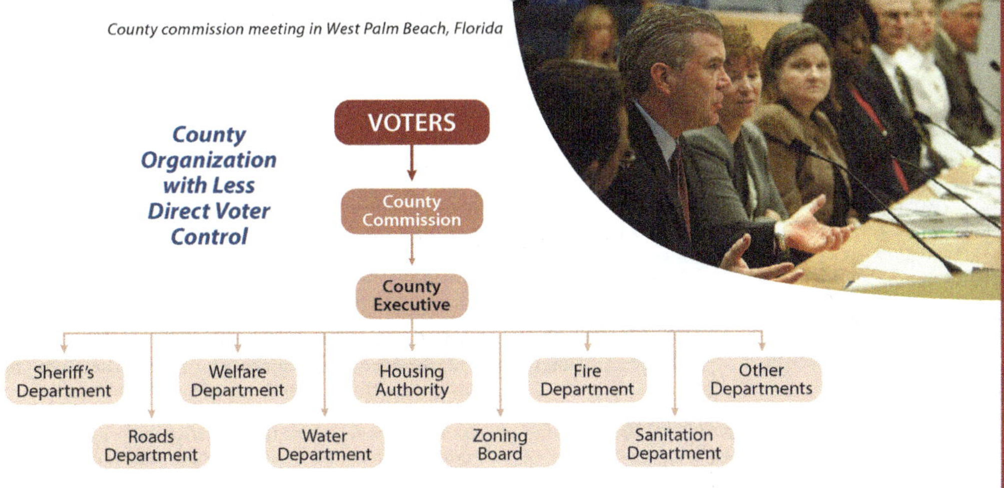

counties might have more; a board of supervisors normally consists of fifteen to eighty members. **Commissioners** or supervisors are elected from different divisions of the county, called districts in some states and townships in others.

In some counties, voters elect a single **county executive**. The title for the person varies—chairman of the county commission, county mayor, or county judge, even though that person does not preside over criminal or civil cases. Having a county executive is more common in larger counties with consolidated, or unified, government (in which a city and its surrounding county are controlled by a single government). The advantage of a **unified government** is that it can avoid duplication of services (police protection, fire protection, a single tax system, etc.). However, opponents of unified government often argue it produces a bigger government with more bureaucracy that is less responsive to the needs of individual citizens.

Although both state and national constitutions restrict county governments' power, counties are still responsible for a wide variety of services. Counties can tax, pass health and zoning ordinances, manage welfare, oversee county roads, operate law-enforcement organizations (commonly called sheriffs' departments), maintain county prison systems, and appoint certain county officers. The county government is also responsible for education. County governments include elected officers with countywide jurisdiction and various boards and commissions to accomplish county responsibilities. The board of commissioners or supervisors oversees the county's daily business. Often, a commissioner or supervisor is assigned to a particular area of service. In other cases, however, commissioners are elected after campaigning for specific service categories (e.g., commissioner of roads, commissioner of waste management, or commissioner of public works).

Examples of Areas with Unified Government

Denver (Denver County), Colorado
Indianapolis (Marion County), Indiana
Jacksonville (Duval County), Florida
Kansas City (Wyandotte County), Kansas
Lexington (Fayette County), Kentucky
Louisville (Jefferson County), Kentucky
Nashville (Davidson County), Tennessee
Philadelphia (Philadelphia County), Pennsylvania

County Offices

Elective or appointed county offices often include the following:

auditor
building-codes inspector
clerk
coroner, or medical examiner
health officer
property controller
purchasing manager
recorder, or register of deeds
sheriff
surveyor
tax assessor
treasurer

The Role of County Governments

Counties were established to be administrative extensions, or agents, of their respective state governments. In this role, they enforced state laws and conducted the business of the state in limited geographic regions. They assessed property values, maintained the peace, and collected taxes. As the roles and responsibilities of state governments expanded, however, so did the work of the county governments. Today, counties are also responsible for conducting elections, trying court cases, maintaining roads, distributing welfare and other forms of relief, and collecting and archiving vital statistics.

National County Government Month

Every April is commemorated as National County Government Month. The purpose of the designation is to highlight the roles played by the thousands of counties across the nation.

The yearly theme varies. For instance, the theme for 2013 was Smart Justice, which focused on the judicial roles of counties. In 2018 the theme was "Serving the Underserved," and the 2019 theme was "Connecting the Unconnected."

Throughout the month, counties may host a variety of activities for constituents. Some counties have recognition ceremonies for both exemplary employees and community volunteers, sponsor essay contests, provide information about various county services, conduct tours of facilities, and present resolutions honoring effective programs and individuals.

Express Your Opinion

Assign the students to write letters to their county executive or mayor (or another local-government official) about an important issue in their local communities. They should state the issue clearly in their letters, recommend action steps, and thank the official for his or her service to local government and the community.

To Unify or Not to Unify

Divide the class into two groups, and debate the pros and cons of unified government for your county or your municipal government. If your county already has a unified government, discuss the positive and negative results that have become apparent since unification occurred.

National County Government Month

Recruit a student to contact your county officials to determine whether your county celebrates National County Government Month. If your county celebrates the month, what activities does it promote in connection with it? If your county does not celebrate the month, try to find out why. The student should report any findings to the class.

City, Town, or Village?

Many students will wonder and might ask about the difference between a city, a town, and a village. In the United States, the definitions are, typically, as follows.

A city is an incorporated, legal entity created and given powers by the state government to perform certain functions for the state and to provide local citizens with certain services. Towns and villages, however, are usually not incorporated, have few (if any) legal powers, and provide few (if any) services. Usually, the services citizens need in those areas are provided by the counties in which the towns and villages are located. Some states, however, sometimes grant powers to towns and villages. Often, the terms *town* and *village* are used interchangeably.

Another distinction between cities, towns, and villages is size or population. Towns have fewer people than cities and might include small urban areas and suburban or rural areas. Villages tend to have even fewer residents than towns and are primarily suburban or rural in nature.

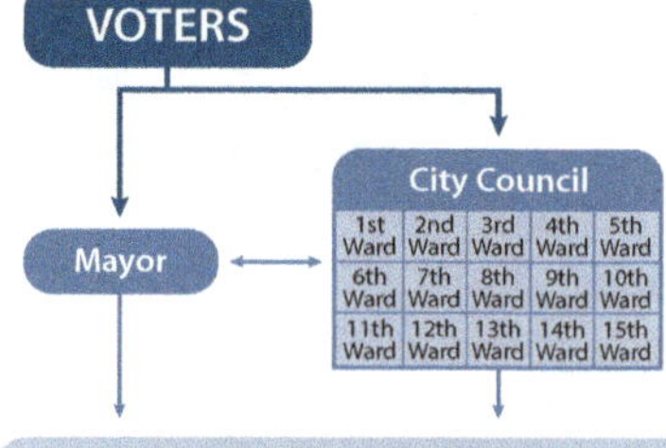

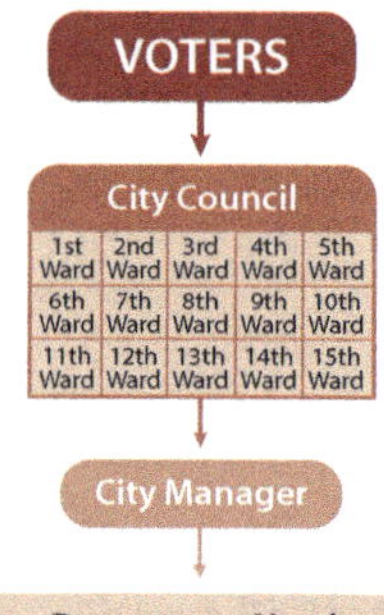

Municipal Governments

Cities are the largest municipalities, which are local systems of government that also include towns and villages. What is true of cities is often true of other municipal entities; only the scale and degree of power vary. There are nearly twenty thousand **municipal governments** in the United States. Cities have historically used three forms of organization: mayor-council, council-manager, and commission government.

Mayor-Council Government

Mayor-council government is one of the oldest forms of municipal government. In this system, government power is divided between the executive authority—a mayor directly elected by the voters—and the legislative authority, a council of individually elected members (usually called councilmen or aldermen) from various voting districts, or wards, within city limits. Sometimes, the mayor is the chairman of the council, but councils often select one of their own members to be the chairman. Either the mayor or the council might be dominant in a particular city, depending on how the city charter was established.

Council-Manager Government

Under **council-manager government**, city council members oversee the general administration of the government, making policy and setting budgets. The council hires a professional manager to oversee the daily administrative functions of the city government as the council has outlined. Ideally, a professional administrator, or manager, can make city government work more efficiently and without the problems of politics. The power wielded by the city manager is determined by the wording of the city charter. Council-manager governments typically also have a mayor; however, he usually promotes and represents the city but has significantly less input with policy and managing city affairs than the city manager.

Commission Government

A less common form of municipal government is the **commission government**. Voters select a body of five to seven people, known as commissioners, who serve as the government. Those commissioners select one of their own number to be their chairman. The other commissioners are assigned to oversee various aspects of the government.

Other Variations for Smaller Entities

Municipalities that are smaller than cities and towns sometimes use other organizational models. For example, a village government might consist of a **board of trustees** elected at-large within village confines.

Mayoral Address

If you live in a small town, invite the mayor to address your class about the operations of that office. If the mayor is unable to come, invite a member of his or her staff to speak about this topic. Students should prepare questions in advance for the speaker.

Council Member

Contact a member of a county council, town council, or city council. Invite the member to come to your classroom to discuss (1) how the council functions, (2) community issues, and (3) possible ways for students to contribute to their communities.

Community-Service Project

Require students to compile an informational brochure about their local government for new residents. They should include such items as contact information for law enforcement and information on garbage collection, codes enforcement, schools, public libraries, post offices, churches, hospitals, banks, political organizations, voter-registration requirements, and driver's license requirements. Publish the end product, and make it available (possibly online or through the students' churches) for newcomers to the community.

Another form of organization is the **town meeting**. Town meetings and modified town meetings are most common in New England and are the best example of direct democracy in the United States. All qualified voters gather on a specified day and elect a board of officers called **selectmen** to make policy decisions. The elected selectmen implement the policies. In some cases, the selectmen appoint a manager to oversee the necessary tasks.

Special Districts

A **special district** is a level of government that is independent of city or county governments and is established to provide specific government functions on a local level within specified boundaries. There are more than thirty-five thousand special districts in the United States.

Perhaps the most common special district is the school district. An elected board determines policies that are administered by a professional who is hired to perform the special district's specific responsibilities. For example, an elected school board could hire a school superintendent to oversee all public schools in a specified area. In most cases, this area involves an entire city's or county's school system (or both if the system is part of a unified government).

Although the school district is the most common special district, many other special districts exist. These include fire departments, soil-conservation districts, mosquito-abatement programs, cemetery commissions, library systems, sanitation districts, and housing authorities. Other special districts supervise public transit and seaports, such as the one served by the Southeastern Pennsylvania Transit Authority (SEPTA).

Services in special districts are financed primarily through direct taxes, user fees (e.g., bus fares), and sales of municipal bonds. Special districts have power to levy taxes for their specific services, charge user fees to those who take advantage of the provided services, and issue municipal bonds to pay for special projects for expansion or maintenance. Funding arrangements for special districts provide districts with a great deal of autonomy from other government entities. In some cases, special districts share boundaries with cities, counties, or other government entities; in other cases, special districts' boundaries might overlap those of other governing bodies.

Ideally, special districts should be more businesslike, more efficient, and less political than formal governmental organizations; however, that does not always occur. Special districts are sometimes inefficient and expensive because they duplicate services performed by similar governmental agencies. Critics argue that the appointed administrators are not always professional and that, since they are not elected, they are not directly accountable to voters or other constituents they serve.

STATE AND LOCAL GOVERNMENT • 151

Special Districts

Special districts are created by county governments or state legislatures to provide specific services that are not already provided by a county or municipality. They are given limited powers to assess and tax users of the services and are usually funded only by those who use or benefit from the services. Members of a special district's governing board are either appointed or elected. The districts sometimes have the authority to sell bonds to raise money for special purposes, such as upgrading equipment or repairing or replacing infrastructure.

Special-District Speaker

Invite a member of a special district in your area (e.g., a fire, roads, or water and sewer district) to speak to the class about the operations of that special entity. Students should prepare questions for the person in advance.

Activity 2: Researching Your State and Local Governments

This activity gives the students experience in using resources and applying and analyzing information about their state and local governments.

Activity 3: Eminent Domain

This activity helps the students understand the growth of government at the local level, especially in the area of eminent domain. It requires them to analyze and evaluate information.

1. Chart and explain typical political party organization on the state and local levels.

2. Explain election and voting processes used in state and local politics.

Section Review

1–2. What are two additional names used for counties?

3–5. What are the three most common forms of municipal government organization?

6–8. Give three examples of special districts.

★ Which form of municipal government do you think is best? Support your answer.

★ In Chapter 1 of this text we listed five obligations of governments. List them and assess whether or not you think your state government fulfills these obligations.

Guiding Questions

1. How are political parties organized at the state and local levels?

2. How do election and voting processes work in state and local politics?

III. State and Local Politics

The term *grass roots* is often used to refer to the lowest level of a group or activity. Political organization for both state and local levels of government begins at the grass roots and emphasizes participation in the electoral process, particularly by voting. The purpose of a political party is to rally support for candidates who agree with that party's views, get them elected to office, and then implement the party's agenda.

Political Party Organization
Party Membership

A **political party** is a group that advances certain common political goals and tries to gain power to implement those goals by selecting candidates in the hope of winning elections. Usually, America has operated under a two-party system, although additional parties frequently arise. Practically speaking, anyone can be a member of a party. If someone tends to vote according to the views of a certain political party, he may refer to himself by that party's label. Many people consider themselves "independents"—that is, they are not allied to either major party. In most elections today, such voters are considered "swing voters," who can turn the outcome in a close race, and they are courted by all serious candidates.

Within political parties there are groups who conflict with one another about one or more key issues. For example, in the 1950s and 1960s, conservative Southern Democrats vied with liberal Northern Democrats. Similarly, in the 1970s and 1980s, conservative Reagan Republicans contended against liberal Establishment Republicans. These groups, called **factions**, are almost always present, but sometimes they can be the determining factor in whether a party wins or loses an election. The strongest party is usually the one that can unite its various factions, at least temporarily, and support a single candidate.

Party Organization: The Precinct

The lowest level of political party organization is the **precinct**. Many municipalities or counties have areas called districts or wards that are used for electing members to the city council, county commission, or some other government body. A ward or district usually contains several precincts.

Interested supporters of a particular party meet within their precinct boundaries, often at the **polling place** (the building in which they vote during elections),

---

Obligations of Governments and the Governed

Use the second critical thinking question on this page (indicated by a star above) to remind students that the five biblical obligations mentioned in Chapter 1 apply to national, state, and local governments.

Also remind students that the obligations of the governed mentioned in Chapter 1 (prayer, participation, submission, and witness) apply at all levels of government.

Section Review Answers

1–2. parish and borough (p. 148)

3–5. mayor-council, council-manager, and commission government (p. 150)

6–8. (any three) school districts, fire departments, soil-conservation districts, mosquito-abatement programs, cemetery commissions, library systems, sanitation districts, housing authorities, public transit systems, and seaports (p. 151)

★ Some students will say the mayor-council form gives voters control over the mayor and the council but gives them little control over department heads. The council-manager form promises greater efficiency and fewer problems with politics but gives voters little direct influence on the manager or department heads.

★ The five obligations of government are to ensure justice, to provide national defense and public safety, to address poverty, to promote moral behavior, and to provide order. Students will provide a variety of answers as they assess whether their state government fulfills these obligations.

to organize the precinct. From among the precinct residents who attend, the voters select officers. Though there are variations depending on the state, these usually include a precinct president, a secretary, a treasurer, and a precinct committeeman. The president conducts the precinct meeting and helps "get out the vote" within the precinct on Election Day. The secretary keeps minutes of the meeting and reports the minutes to the county party office. The treasurer collects any dues or other fees and remits them to the county party office. The precinct committeeman normally represents the precinct at the party's county-wide meetings.

Individual precinct members often present resolutions that are debated at precinct meetings. If approved, they are usually passed along to the county party organization for consideration. (Any resolutions approved at the county level go to the state party and then, if successful there, to the national convention for possible inclusion in the national party platform.)

Party Organization: The County Committee

The precinct committeemen from the county's precincts usually meet regularly (monthly in some areas). They may serve as a **county committee** to oversee the party's business or they elect members to serve on the county committee. That committee elects a chairman, vice chairman, and other officers. These officers attend to the county party's needs and interests by promoting the party, its agenda, and its candidates for the next election, whether local, state, or national. The county chairman also represents the county at the state level.

At county-level meetings, the party introduces various resolutions that affect the party's operations and agenda and promotes—or, in some cases, reprimands—party officials or officeholders. The county officers often invite various party officials, officeholders, or candidates for office to speak to the other party members in attendance. This action is especially important in the months and weeks before an election to energize the party faithful to support party candidates.

The county party holds a county convention, normally every one to two years, to prepare for the next election cycle. Resolutions are presented and debated. As mentioned earlier, those that are approved are passed along to the state organization for consideration. Candidates for office, especially presidential hopefuls and candidates for statewide offices, may be invited to speak.

Party Organization: The State Executive Committee

The chairman of the state party serves as the leader and spokesman for the party. He normally works with a state executive committee to direct the party agenda statewide. One of the chairman's most important roles is to raise funds to wage vigorous campaigns. The goal is to capture as many state offices as possible

Precincts

According to a report from the United States Election Assistance Commission, there were 178,217 precincts at the time of the 2016 elections. The average number of registered voters in each was approximately 900 (though some precincts had substantially fewer and others had a much larger number).

A Political Party at Work

Ask several volunteers to contact leaders of a local political party and attend one of their meetings that is open to the public. Students can report to the class concerning how the party conducted its business. (Try to schedule student representatives to attend some meetings of all major local political parties to ensure that the students view a cross section of the parties.)

Political Party Presentations

Invite some officers of each major local political party to visit your class and participate in a panel discussion on how political parties work in your community. Ask the panel to address the issue of how young people can become active in their respective parties.

Precinct Officers

Invite several precinct officers from the major parties to conduct a panel discussion on how their respective local parties are organized and how they conduct their precinct and county meetings.

Christians and Political Parties

Guide a discussion regarding Christian involvement in political parties. Ask thought-provoking questions such as the following:

- What are some of the benefits of Christian involvement? *(for example, being able to advance Christian concerns, particularly if many Christians become involved in a party)*

- What are some of the dangers? *(Christians may forget that many problems cannot be solved by political means because they are really spiritual issues. Christians may begin to view their parties' positions as biblical positions when there might not be justification for doing so.)*

Bosses of Political Machines: Crump, Bilbo, and Long

As the following three examples show, there are several categories into which political machines fall. Each category involves a different technique that enabled a boss to obtain and keep power.

Edward Hull Crump was a Mississippi-born politician whose political involvement began in Memphis, Tennessee, but whose influence later extended to the halls of Congress. Crump's career began in 1905 when he was named to serve on the Memphis Board of Public Works. In 1907 he became the fire and police commissioner, one of three commissioners who governed the city. The power Crump enjoyed in those roles encouraged him to begin building a political coalition that developed into a machine.

Crump's method was to use two politically weak minority groups to develop a dependable voting bloc. Crump, a Democrat, helped African Americans and Republicans (who were few in West and Middle Tennessee) with problems; in return, both groups helped him on Election Day. Unlike most Democrats of the time, Crump saw blacks as potential voters, so he opposed anything that prevented their exercise of the franchise. Similarly, he courted Republicans, who generally had no electable candidate of their own. Combined, these two groups provided Crump many of the votes needed to win elections for himself and his friends. Crump served as mayor of Memphis for several years. He was also elected to two terms in the US House in the 1930s. By that time, his power had so increased that candidates needed his approval to be elected to almost any position in the state, including the office of governor. Crump's power continued into the 1950s.

In this political cartoon, New York City's Boss Tweed says, "As long as I count the votes, what are you going to do about it?"

Examples of Political Machines and Their Bosses

Bosses of City Machines

Boss Tweed and, later, Richard Croker of Tammany Hall in New York City

Mayor E. H. Crump in Memphis, Tennessee

Mayor Richard Daley in Chicago, Illinois

Bosses of Statewide Machines

Theodore Bilbo in Mississippi

Huey Long in Louisiana

Tom Pendergast in Missouri

Harry Byrd in Virginia

and send victorious party candidates to the state capitol and to Washington, DC, to serve as elected officials. He attends, along with many of the party's major state and national officeholders and other elected delegates, the national party convention. Each political party holds a national convention during the summer of a presidential election year. At that time, the party's candidates for president and vice president are officially selected.

In the past, some states and cities were operated by notorious **political machines**. The machine was an organization by which a strong, authoritarian "boss" or a small group of people commanded the loyalty of supporters and others and rewarded them for providing it. Machines usually operated a highly organized hierarchy and strictly enforced discipline. They were like political "armies" that strong-armed party members to vote for the "right" candidates. Rewards for loyal service included patronage (appointment to a political position), money, and permission to run for office with the help of the machine's resources and influence.

Machines were usually associated with urban government and big-city politics. Historically, many of them focused on new immigrants, not because they truly cared about them and their well-being, but because they saw them as potential votes. Votes, of course, were the key to gaining and keeping political power in an area. For example, bosses might target a newly arrived immigrant; befriend him; help him and his family members get jobs; take groceries to them; or help them in other ways, such as getting them registered to vote and getting them to the polls on Election Day—with instructions on the "right" way to vote. Sometimes bribes were given. At other times, the machine hinted about undesirable consequences that might arise if a person did not support an approved candidate.

Elections

The right to vote is one of the most valuable privileges of a free people. How people vote determines the types of leaders they will have and, consequently, the type of government they will be responsible to obey. State and local governments are responsible for organizing elections.

Defenders of **suffrage** (the right to vote) have fought throughout history to secure that right, to protect it from those who wanted to take it away, and to prevent unscrupulous people from tampering with the voting process. One would think, therefore, that everyone who meets the eligibility requirements would do everything possible to actively exercise the right to vote.

Unfortunately, such is not the case. An alarming number of people do not exercise this precious right and many do not seem alarmed when allegations of election interference or voter intimidation arise.

Director of the Board of Elections

Invite the director of your local board of elections to speak to the students about the privilege of voting, how to register, and how the election process is handled in your local area. Students should prepare questions for the speaker in advance.

Voters' Guide

Instruct students to collect information about an upcoming state or local election. Ask them to find information concerning the offices and issues on the ballot and facts about each candidate's political affiliation, background, qualifications, and views. Then assign students to use the information to create an informative and easy-to-use guide for local voters. Publish the information as a news sheet or brochure, and suggest the students distribute it to potential voters (possibly online or through the students' churches). In future years, you may wish to assign this project as soon as school begins.

According to the Bipartisan Policy Center, during the 1960s, slightly more than 60 percent of eligible voters cast ballots during presidential elections (1960, 1964, and 1968). Over the next few decades, that already low percentage declined further. In the presidential elections of 2004, 2008, and 2016 the percentage slightly exceeded 60 percent again. Turnout for non-presidential elections is usually substantially less. The number of eligible citizens who exercise their right to vote is less in the United States than in most other industrialized nations.

Voter Registration

Voter eligibility and registration requirements vary from state to state. All but one state, North Dakota, require prospective voters to register before voting. All states have various eligibility requirements that are generally the same. The typical state requirements for voting are as follows. (Some states might omit one or more of these requirements or word them differently, but these are the generally accepted requirements of the average state.) To be eligible to vote, a person must

- be a citizen of the United States;
- be a citizen (or resident) of the state (or, sometimes, city or precinct) where voting;
- be eighteen years old by the time of the election, although some states allow seventeen-year-olds to vote in the primary election if they will be eighteen years old by the general election;
- be registered before the deadline (varies from ten days to thirty days before the election, with most states requiring voters to register twenty-nine or thirty days before the election);
- not be registered to vote in any other state, county, or precinct;
- not be deemed mentally incompetent or incapacitated.

Many states prohibit individuals who have been convicted of a felony, a serious crime, from voting. However, many of those states allow convicted felons to regain the right to vote after they have completed their jail sentence. Some other states require the completion of the jail sentence and probation before voting rights are restored.

Forms of Voting

Just as eligibility requirements differ among the states, so do the various methods of voting. Types of ballots and voting machines vary not only among the states but also within states.

All states allow voting in person on Election Day. Many more states permit some form of early voting—in person, by mail, by fax, or by email—before the actual designated day of elections. In addition, a few states now allow voting by internet. Early voting helps reduce time spent waiting in line and increases voter participation. However, a major argument against early voting is that once a vote is cast, it cannot be recalled or changed if the candidate receiving the vote is later determined unworthy of that vote.

State and Local Elections

Elections are basically of two types: **primary elections** and **general elections.** The purpose of primary elections is to determine which of the two or more

Theodore Bilbo of Mississippi was a Democrat who employed the technique of division to win political power. He sought unashamedly to stoke the fires of racial hatred and white supremacy for political gain. This won him a seat in the state senate, the lieutenant governorship, the governor's office, and a seat in the US Senate. With the exception of a few years, he held elected office in the state from 1907 until his death in 1947. Bilbo's power was so great that he weathered charges of bribery; a contempt of court citation; an attempt to expel him from the state senate; and the making of many enemies (including his fellow senator from Mississippi, who refused to talk to him). Bilbo was vitriolic and slanderous in his speeches. He alienated farmers, and he even fired three college presidents and nearly two hundred college professors in the state college system. He also openly admitted active membership in the Ku Klux Klan.

Huey Long of Louisiana was the epitome of political bosses. His political career began on the Louisiana Railroad Commission (later renamed the Louisiana Public Service Commission) in 1918. In 1924 he ran for governor and became one of the first southern politicians to use radio addresses and sound trucks in a campaign. He also began wearing what became his trademark, a white linen suit. Although Long came in third in the gubernatorial race (partly because he opposed the Ku Klux Klan), he was reelected to the commission and gained statewide name recognition that helped him win the governor's post in 1928. He campaigned on the slogan "Every man a king, but no one wears a crown." He openly used class warfare to his advantage, pitting wealthy oil and utility companies against the common man.

As governor, Long was ruthless as he consolidated power. He ousted hundreds

More on Huey Long's Machine

An excellent teacher resource for more information on Huey Long and his machine politics is *Kingfish* by Richard D. White Jr.

Election Results

Assign students to report the results of a recent local election. They should study the lists of individual precinct results and try to arrive at some conclusions about why some areas voted as they did.

Voter Registration Drive

Many of the students are (or will soon be) of voting age. If you have several students who are of voting age but are not registered, conduct an in-class voter-registration drive to register them. If possible, recruit a student who is already registered to secure the materials and lead the drive. Discuss the next election in which the students can exercise their right to vote.

of enemies (and their friends and family members) from state jobs and replaced them with his own friends and supporters. He demanded absolute loyalty. He appeared unannounced on the statehouse floor during debates to ensure that his people voted as he instructed. If they voted against him, he often supported, or even recruited, candidates to oppose them in the next election.

Even when Long won a seat in the US Senate in 1930, he continued to serve as governor until January 1932 (when he was sworn in as US Senator—though his term had officially begun March 4, 1931). In the Senate, he alienated even fellow Democrats by violating the tradition that freshman members must listen quietly; instead, he made fiery speeches that criticized leaders of both parties. He harangued the senators with principles of class warfare and promoted such radical ideas that he sometimes made President Roosevelt's New Deal look conservative. He also delivered blistering speeches against the president and entertained the idea of running against him in the next election.

Called the Kingfish by supporters, Long made frequent trips back to Louisiana to ensure that things were going as he wanted. During one such visit, he was shot in the hallway of the state capitol; he died two days later. Although he was dead, his machine remained in power for decades afterward. His widow replaced him in the Senate. One of his brothers was elected lieutenant governor in 1936 and governor in 1948 and 1956. Another brother became a congressman in 1952. Still another brother was a parish district attorney. His son Russell was a US senator from 1948 to 1987.

candidates within a single party will face the opposing party's candidate in the general election. Unless one party has a powerful incumbent running for reelection who faces no intraparty competition, there are usually two primary contests (one for each major political party). Each primary race normally features at least two candidates.

General election dates for most state and local elections are usually the same as for federal elections. However, in odd-numbered years, a few states hold elections for governor, other executive offices, or state legislators in November. Election dates for city, county, and other local elections vary from state to state.

State elections are administered through each state's election offices. For example, in South Carolina, election offices consist of the State Election Commission, the State Board of Voting Machine Commissioners, and the Board of State Canvassers. Local offices include the County Board of Registration, Commissioners of Election, and the County Board of Canvassers. There are also Election Day officers—poll managers, clerks, and poll watchers (individuals appointed by political parties and candidates to observe the voting on Election Day). Their duties include questioning suspected unqualified voters and watching ballot counting. Each group is to fulfill its responsibilities to ensure a lawful, proper election.

Polling places include schools, churches, fire stations, and other buildings. Opening and closing times for the polls vary by state. After the polls close, supporters may gather at their candidate's headquarters, where they watch the results and hope to celebrate victory. In close races, results are sometimes unknown until the next day. Depending on state laws, in some close races a recount may be demanded by a candidate or required by law if the margin of votes between top candidates is within a certain range. (For example, in some states a recount automatically occurs if the leading candidate wins by 1 percent or less of the vote.)

Primary Elections

Voting in primary elections varies among the states according to whether their primary elections are open, closed, semiclosed, or Top-Two Method. In an **open primary**, any registered voter can vote in either party's primary, but only in one of them. About thirty states use the open primary system. In an open

Open or Closed Primaries?

Discuss the type of primary currently used by your state. Then ask students to debate the pros and cons of open and closed primaries.

primary, there is the likelihood that **crossover voting** will occur. Crossover voting is when a person affiliated with a particular party votes in the primary of an opposing party; thus, a Democrat might vote in the Republican primary or a Republican might vote in a Democratic primary. Sometimes this is done in an attempt to ensure the nomination of the weakest candidate. Such crossover voters hope that their own party's candidate can then win the general election.

In a **closed primary**, on the other hand, only voters registered with a particular party may participate in that party's primary election. Closed primaries allow Democrats and Republicans to participate in their respective primaries, but unaffiliated, or independent, voters are left out of the process. **Semiclosed primaries** allow independents to choose a ballot from one of the two parties. Critics of this primary argue that, like the open primary, semiclosed primaries allow voters who may not share the parties' views to exert undue influence over the choice of candidates. About two dozen states keep their primaries closed or semiclosed.

Who is the winner in the primary? In most states the candidate with the most votes, regardless of the percentage of the total vote, is declared the victor and becomes the party's candidate in the general election. However, almost a dozen states require one candidate to receive a majority of votes in order to proceed to the general election. In those states, if no candidate initially garners a majority, there must be a **runoff election** between the two candidates who received the most votes. The winner of the runoff election, normally held two or three weeks after the primary, earns a spot on the general election ballot.

In addition to open and closed primaries, a few states use a primary system called the **Top-Two method** or a **jungle primary**. All the candidates, regardless of party affiliation, are listed on one ballot. The two that receive the most votes (even if they are members of the same party) advance to the general election. Independent voters prefer this type of primary.

General Elections

Whichever method is used in the primary election, the winners of the respective party primaries face one another in the general election. The winner in that election actually fills the government office.

Typically, voter turnout for general elections is higher than for primaries. When candidates for national office (e.g., for president and senators) are on the ballot, voter participation usually increases even more.

Citizens should remember, however, that state and local elections also have an impact on their lives. Whether voting for mayor, county councilman, road commissioner, governor, or president, every election is important. More information about political parties, election campaigns, and voting is included in Chapters 16 and 17.

Recall, Referendum, and Initiative

Every state has a process whereby the government can place issues on the ballot. Usually, this process requires an action by the state legislature. However, some states give voters, in addition to government officials, ways to make their voices heard above and beyond legislative action. State legislatures do not always

Federal O...

United States President and Vice President

Your vote for the candidates for United States President and Vice President shall be a vote for the electors supporting those candidates.
Vote for one

◯ **Donald J Trump/Mike Pence**
Republican

◯ **Hillary Clinton/Tim Kaine**
Democrat

◯ **Jill Stein/Ajamu Baraka**
Pacific Green, Progressive

◯ **Gary Johnson/Bill Weld**
Libertarian

◯ Write-in

 ### Mock Primary and General Elections

Select two groups of several (i.e., more than two) students to represent different candidates from two parties. Choose some issues on which the candidates in each party differ and conduct a mock primary election to determine a candidate for each party. Then conduct a mock general election to determine which of the two parties' candidates will win.

Recalling a Governor

Scott Walker (R-WI) was elected governor of his state in 2010 by receiving 52 percent of the vote. He took office in January 2011. His top priority was restoring economic stability to the state government. In the 2012–13 fiscal year, Wisconsin faced a potential deficit of $3.6 billion, and state law required that the budget be balanced. Walker advanced a proposal that promised to do that, but opposition began immediately. It was led by labor unions, notably unions for government employees, because the governor's plan called for a reduction in benefits for state employees.

Others opposed Walker because of his conservative position on social issues. His opponents initiated a movement to recall him in November 2011, less than a year after he took office.

According to Wisconsin law, the number of signatures required to trigger a recall of the governor is one-quarter of the number of votes cast in the most recent gubernatorial election. That meant that at least 540,208 voters had to sign petitions calling for a recall.

In late March 2012, Wisconsin officials certified more than 900,000 signatures on petitions. When a new election was held on June 5, 2012, Walker defeated his Democratic opponent by a margin of 53 percent to 46 percent. This incident was only the third time in US history that voters tried to recall a state governor. It was the first time an incumbent governor had won a recall vote.

One reason for Walker's victory was that his economic-recovery plan resulted in a surplus of more than $150 million by May 2012. In 2014 Walker was elected to another term. In 2018 he narrowly lost his bid for a third term.

respond to constituents' demands as people think they should, so voters sometimes have limited power to take matters into their own hands—in an orderly and civilized manner—in one of three ways: by recall, referendum, or initiative.

The procedure known as **recall** allows the people to remove an elected official from office by holding a special election. It differs from impeachment, a legal procedure that normally requires specific charges, presentation of evidence, and a formal trial. Impeachment is used by the legislative branch; however, in a recall voters determine whether an official should lose his position.

Thirty-six states allow recall of certain elected officials at the local or state level. The Constitution does not provide a means of recalling any national officials. Recalls are much more common at the local level than for state offices. There have been only two successful recalls of a governor—North Dakota in 1921 and California in 2003. Gray Davis, the California governor who was removed, was replaced (in a special election) by Arnold Schwarzenegger. A 2012 attempt to recall Wisconsin's governor, Scott Walker, failed.

Scott Walker survived a recall attempt in 2012 and was reelected as Wisconsin's governor in 2014. He lost his bid for another term in 2018.

Referendums allow voters to make changes in their state constitutions and in state or local laws. Two types of referendums are used in state and local governments—legislative and veto. One example of a legislative referendum is when a state legislature, or local governing body, is required to submit a law to the electorate for a direct yes or no vote. This is mandatory in some states for amendments to the state constitution. Another example of a legislative referendum is when a legislative body allows voters to decide an important matter, such as whether to allow a state lottery or the legalization of marijuana. A veto referendum is a very different type of popular participation. This referendum allows the electorate to repeal a piece of legislation or a constitutional amendment. Some form of referendum is used in virtually every state.

Initiative is a means whereby a legally specified number of voters can propose changes to their state constitution or laws. Twenty-four states give their voters this right.

Once such a proposal receives support from the required number of voters, it is placed on the ballot and presented to the voters for their approval or rejection. For example, in 2012 thousands in Wichita, Kansas, signed a petition to add fluoride to the city's drinking water. As a result, the matter was placed on the November 2012 ballot (in that election, the voters rejected the measure).

Section Review

1. What does the term *grass roots* mean?
2. What is a political party?
3. What is the lowest level of political party organization?
4–5. Explain the two types of referendums in state government.
6. What is an initiative?
★ What are the advantages and disadvantages of the ability to recall an elected official?
★ Do you think an initiative is a good idea?

Section Review Answers

1. The term *grass roots* is often used to refer to the lowest level of a group or activity. (p. 152)

2. A political party is a group that advances certain common political goals and tries to gain power to implement those goals by selecting candidates in the hope of winning elections. (p. 152)

3. the local precinct (p. 152)

4–5. The two types of referendums are legislative and veto. Examples of legislative referendums are when a state legislature is required to submit a law to the electorate for a direct yes or no vote or when the legislature allows voters to decide an important matter. A veto referendum allows the electorate to repeal a piece of legislation or a constitutional amendment. (p. 158)

6. An initiative is a means whereby a legally specified number of voters can propose changes to their constitution or laws. (p. 158)

★ An advantage of recall is voters' ability to remove an unqualified or dishonest official from office. A disadvantage may be that a person or group can persuade voters to remove an elected official because that official opposes or supports an issue. Sometimes this is done by distorting the official's views.

★ Some may say the initiative is a great way to place power in the hands of the people. Others may say that it is dangerous because it changes the ways that some laws are enacted.

IV. Interstate and Intergovernmental Relationships

Under the government at the time of the Articles of Confederation, states were continually disputing among themselves, especially over commercial matters and various petty jealousies. One reason for writing the new Constitution was to eliminate, resolve, or otherwise reduce such differences and encourage the states, each with different laws, to interact peacefully with one another. The Constitution addresses this issue in Articles IV and VI by listing responsibilities that the states have to one another and to the national government. Another reason for these stipulations was the founders' strong desire to avoid a powerful, unchecked centralized government. They wanted the states to be a check on the national government.

Interstate Relationships

Although each state retains power to govern itself, no state can exist as a completely independent entity. States are required by Article IV of the Constitution to maintain a certain level of cooperation among themselves.

Full Faith and Credit

Article IV, Section 1, is sometimes called the **full faith and credit clause**. It states:

> Full faith and credit shall be given in each state to the public acts, records, and judicial proceedings of every other state. And the Congress may by general laws prescribe the manner in which such acts, records and proceedings shall be proved, and the effect thereof.

This clause has been interpreted to mean that state drivers' licenses are valid in any state, regardless of the state in which they are issued. Thus, a driver's license issued in Montana will be recognized in Florida. Likewise, a vacationing family from Massachusetts does not need to obtain a driver's license for each state through which they will travel. Furthermore, a contract signed in one state is legally recognized in all states. In addition, a man ordered by a North Dakota court to pay for damages from an accident cannot flee to South Dakota to escape the responsibility of payment. South Dakota must give "full faith and credit" to North Dakota's ruling.

For years, based on this clause, a marriage in one state

Full Faith and Credit

According to Cornell University Law School's Legal Information Institute, "full faith and credit" is "the requirement, derived from Article IV, Section I of the Constitution, that state courts respect the judgments of courts from other states. Thus, a judgment won in one state may be enforced in another, without a relitigation of the underlying issues."

The issues that receive the most attention related to the full faith and credit clause are marriage, domestic violence, protective orders, child custody and support, and interstate adoptions. As noted in the text, the full faith and credit clause was at the center of the disagreement about same-sex marriages prior to *Obergefell v. Hodges* in 2015.

Homosexual Unions

If this topic is discussed in class, the following points will be helpful to the students to understand the biblical position on homosexuality. All students (including those students who struggle with homosexual temptations) should know of confidential counseling resources at your school.

1. The Genesis Creation account reveals that God designed sexual complementarity. He designed humans to be male and female, and He ordained marriage to be the union of one man and one woman for life. Jesus affirmed this in Matthew 19:4–6.

2. The Bible teaches that the Fall disordered humans and creation. This means that humans are often tempted to think and behave in a manner contrary to God's design. It should not surprise Christians that people have strong temptations to do what God forbids.

3. Paul taught that people who practice homosexual behavior can become Christians (1 Cor. 6:9–11). This does not mean that they will stop struggling with temptation, but God transforms those whom He saves so that their old lifestyles no longer characterize them.

4. The key Scripture passages that teach about homosexuality are Leviticus 18:22; 20:13; Romans 1:24–27; 1 Corinthians 6:9–10; and 1 Timothy 1:9–10. Often, people try to dismiss these texts by arguing, for example, that Leviticus's commands cannot still hold since Christians eat shellfish (see Lev. 11:9–12) or by saying that Paul was condemning homosexual prostitution rather than committed homosexual relationships. Others say that Jesus never addressed homosexuality, but Jesus' comments in Matthew 19:4–6 root marriage (and thus the sexual relationship) in the context of one man and one woman for life. The statements elsewhere in Scripture must be interpreted in light of this fundamental reality.

States' Different Laws on Gun Rights

States disagree over the full faith and credit clause, especially on the issue of gun control. Although courts have ruled that the Second Amendment applies to states as well as to the national government, the states still exercise varying degrees of control over guns. The differences are especially evident in their right-to-carry and concealed-carry laws. Such laws are important for people traveling through states other than their own.

Some states (for example, New York, Massachusetts, California, and Connecticut) are stringent in their gun restrictions. Other states (such as Arizona, Alaska, and Wyoming) have much more lenient gun laws. Most states recognize (have reciprocity with) the concealed-carry permits of certain states, but they usually do not recognize all states' permits. It is the gun owner's responsibility to know the states that recognize his state's permit and to carry (or not carry) his gun according to the laws of any state through which he travels.

was recognized in another state. However, in 1993 a dispute arose regarding this matter. In that year, the Supreme Court of Hawaii questioned whether or not it was constitutional for the state to limit marriage to couples of the opposite sex. As Hawaii courts continued to deliberate that issue, a question arose: If same-sex marriage became legal in Hawaii would the full faith and credit clause require other states to acknowledge such unions? If so, one state could then dictate the definition of marriage to the remainder of the nation; thus, religious liberty would be endangered because employers and religious organizations would be forced to accept marriages which violated their religious beliefs. As a result, in 1996 Congress passed and President Bill Clinton signed the Defense of Marriage Act (DOMA), which defined marriage on the federal level as "only a legal union between one man and one woman." It also gave states the right not to recognize same-sex marriages recognized in other states.

Fierce debates soon occurred in individual states regarding whether that state should legalize same-sex marriages. In addition, numerous legal challenges regarding the constitutionality of DOMA were filed. By 2015, more than thirty states allowed homosexual marriage; however, many states still refused to recognize those unions in their states. The issue was settled in June 2015 when the US Supreme Court ruled, in *Obergefell v. Hodges*, that banning same-sex marriages was unconstitutional. As a result, all fifty states are now required to allow the marriage of same-sex couples. Consequently, same-sex unions must be recognized by every state (based on the full faith and credit clause).

Privileges and Immunities

According to Article IV, Section 2, clause 1—the **privileges and immunities clause**—privileges enjoyed by US citizens must be respected in every state.

> The citizens of each state shall be entitled to all privileges and immunities of citizens in the several states.

No state can lawfully restrict a nonresident's legal activities. Nonresidents in a state can work, purchase merchandise, travel, and buy houses with the full privileges and immunities granted to residents of that state. This clause also ensures that nonresidents are guaranteed all legal rights. A state government

Since state taxes help pay for higher education expenses, state colleges may charge nonresidents more than residents.

How Your State Relates to Neighboring States

Assign a group of students to research any historical, recent, or current controversies between your state and neighboring states and report on them. Students should present the background and, if the controversies are settled, the outcome of each controversy. They should also include in the report a description of any positive collaborative efforts that resulted from those controversies between your state and neighboring states.

State Gun Laws

Recruit a student to research and report to the class on your state's gun laws. The report should discuss laws related to transporting or carrying weapons and note the states that have reciprocity with your state.

may not set aside a person's rights because he is a not a resident of that state. This limitation does not, however, restrict the states from making reasonable distinctions between residents and non-residents concerning activities supported by state taxes.

For example, states have the authority to charge out-of-state students more for attending a state university. A student from Georgia will typically pay more to attend Colorado State University than will a Colorado resident. States may also charge nonresidents more for hunting and fishing licenses because state taxes fund the stocking and maintenance of state parks.

Extradition

Article IV, Section 2, clause 2, of the Constitution requires that

> a person charged in any state with treason, felony, or other crime, who shall flee from justice, and be found in another state, shall on demand of the executive authority of the state from which he fled, be delivered up, to be removed to the state having jurisdiction of the crime.

Extradition is the legal process of returning an alleged criminal to the state in which he is charged. The extradition clause was intended to prevent criminals from escaping justice by fleeing to a different state. It has not always been strictly followed. For example, during the period in which slavery was legal, some states protected escaped slaves from recapture once they left slave-state soil. There were other instances in which states did not return individuals who committed crimes. In 1987 the Supreme Court ruled in *Puerto Rico v. Branstad* that the national government had the authority to force a state to extradite a fugitive.

Reciprocity

One means whereby states cooperate with one another to facilitate governing is called **reciprocity**. Reciprocity is a legal arrangement whereby one or more states recognize as valid certain privileges granted or conditions stipulated by one or more other states.

For example, credentials of teachers certified in Georgia are recognized by South Carolina. This occurs because Georgia has an educational reciprocity agreement with that state (as it does with numerous other states). Therefore, teachers certified in Georgia do not have to begin a completely new process to receive a South Carolina teaching license. In turn, Georgia recognizes the certificates of South Carolina teachers. (Each state may have some minor additional requirements the out-of-state individual must meet, but reciprocity means that the person does not have to begin the certification process anew.)

Another example of reciprocity involves the legal carrying of concealed weapons. People who meet the concealed-carry requirements in Kentucky are also able to carry concealed weapons in North Carolina, Tennessee, Ohio, Texas, and numerous other states although those states' laws might be somewhat different from Kentucky's laws. Similarly, people with concealed-carry permits from those states can legally carry concealed weapons in Kentucky.

Extradition Procedure

Alleged criminals often flee to other states to avoid prosecution. A state must follow a procedure, similar to the one below, to obtain an extradition. In this example, New Mexico is the state in which the crime was committed, and Utah is the state to which the accused fled.

1. New Mexico's executive officer, the governor, must ask Utah's executive officer to return the accused.
2. New Mexico's governor must present Utah's governor with a copy of an indictment or an affidavit that was made before a magistrate and charges the accused with a crime.
3. New Mexico's governor or chief magistrate must certify the indictment or affidavit.
4. Utah's governor can then have the accused arrested and secured.
5. After the arrest, Utah's governor must inform New Mexico's governor of the arrest and request an agent from New Mexico to pick up the accused.
6. The fugitive has the right to contest the extradition in court, but he can waive that right.
7. New Mexico has thirty days after the arrest to pick up the fugitive. Otherwise, Utah's authorities can release him.

The Supreme Court and the Tenth Amendment

As noted earlier in the chapter, the Tenth Amendment says that states retain all powers that are not delegated to the national government nor prohibited to the states.

Interest in the Tenth Amendment seemed to revive during the Rehnquist Supreme Court (1986–2005), and it also grew later in response to actions of the Obama administration. Two court cases provide examples of renewed interest in the conflict between the authority of state government and the national government.

In 1993 Congress passed the Brady Handgun Violence Prevention Act, which mandated background checks for anyone purchasing a handgun. Local law-enforcement officials were charged with handling this task. However, two sheriffs claimed that the latter part of the mandate was unconstitutional. Two district courts, one in Montana and the other in Arizona, agreed, but the Ninth Circuit Court of Appeals reversed their rulings.

The issue then was presented to the US Supreme Court in 1997 in *Mack and Printz v. United States*. The majority opinion, written by Justice Antonin Scalia, said that the mandate that state officials must conduct the background checks was unconstitutional because federal requirements for state officials violated the historical understanding of the Constitution. Justice Sandra Day O'Connor concurred, arguing that the Brady Act violated the Tenth Amendment. Justice Clarence Thomas also concurred, declaring the act to be a violation of not only the Tenth Amendment but also the Second Amendment.

Though five justices believed the Brady law was unconstitutional, the other four

Reciprocity Issues

Discuss some issues that involve reciprocity. Examples include professional credentials (for nurses, teachers, lawyers, counselors, etc.), gun rights (transportation, concealed carry, etc.), child-custody issues, and taxation issues involving nonresidents.

Issues in Dispute

Group the students and assign each group to investigate the various disagreements that exist, or have existed, between the states. Disputed issues might include water rights (disputed by North Carolina, South Carolina, and Georgia; Virginia and Maryland; and states that get water from the Colorado River), state boundaries (North Carolina and South Carolina; New Hampshire and Maine), water pollution (Oklahoma and Arkansas), air pollution (Tennessee and North Carolina), taxation of out-of-state workers (Minnesota and Wisconsin), and many other issues.

Tenth Amendment Issues

Instruct students to search current newspapers, news magazines, and internet articles to identify Tenth Amendment issues. They should state how each example is a potential violation of or support for the Tenth Amendment.

justices (Stevens, Souter, Ginsburg, and Breyer) disagreed.

O'Connor's reasoning was in keeping with her earlier argument in *New York v. United States* (1992), challenging the Low-Level Radioactive Waste Policy Amendments Act of 1985. She wrote the majority opinion about the case, arguing that the act violated the Tenth Amendment.

> Where a federal interest is sufficiently strong to cause Congress to legislate, it must do so directly; it may not conscript state governments as its agents.

Some states have become more inclined to oppose the national government's actions, referring to the Tenth Amendment as their defense. The amendment was cited, for example, as the basis for several states' lawsuits against the national government over many mandates in the Patient Protection and Affordable Care Act (often referred to as Obamacare).

President Obama addressing the National Governors' Association in 2016 at the White House

In 1925 the Council of State Governments was established to encourage such cooperation among the states. Other organizations—such as the National Governors' Association and national organizations for state legislators, chief justices, attorneys general, and other state officials—were also founded to promote and continue such cooperation.

Intergovernmental Relationships

The main constitutional provision ensuring the proper, intended distinctions between the national government and the fifty state governments is the Tenth Amendment. This amendment not only protects the states' authority but also reaffirms the federal nature of our government system. In addition, the amendment was designed to prevent the national government from assuming too much power.

The Constitution instituted a governmental system of mixed sovereignty. This is what was originally meant by the term *federal*: each state was to exercise power over its own citizens, and the national government was to exercise power over the whole United States by using its enumerated powers. The relationship between the states and the national government was meant to be one of cooperation, not of superiority versus subservience.

> "The powers not delegated to the United States by the Constitution, nor prohibited by it to the states, are reserved to the states respectively, or to the people."
>
> —Tenth Amendment, US Constitution

Over the years, however, the national government has progressively expanded its authority at the states' expense, often arguing that such action is necessary for fulfilling its enumerated powers. As noted in the previous chapter, New Deal programs, Great Society legislation, the increasing reliance of states on the use of federal grants, and other matters have resulted in an even stronger national government.

Critics charge that Congress has often used the necessary and proper clause and the commerce clause to justify implied powers. Consequently, state authority has declined. During the years that William Rehnquist served as Chief Justice of the Supreme Court (1986–2005), the court issued several decisions (e.g., *New York v. United States*, *Gregory v. Ashcroft*, and *Printz v. United States*) that tended to limit the national government's continued enlargement. But the struggle between the states and the national government remains and, no doubt, will continue.

Section Review

1. Explain the full faith and credit clause.
2. Define *extradition*.
3. What is reciprocity?

4–5. What amendment establishes the proper relationship between state and national governments? What was the amendment designed to prevent?

★ How does the privileges and immunities clause protect American citizens?

Activity 4: Chapter Review

Use this activity to help the students prepare for the chapter test.

Section Review Answers

1. The full faith and credit clause states that public acts, records, and judicial proceedings from one state shall be recognized in all states. (p. 159)

2. Extradition is the legal process of returning an alleged criminal to the state in which he is charged. (p. 161)

3. Reciprocity is a legal arrangement whereby one or more states recognize as valid certain privileges granted or conditions stipulated by one or more other states. (p. 161)

4–5. the Tenth Amendment; to prevent the national government from obtaining too much power (p. 162)

★ It guarantees that a citizen's rights cannot be set aside when he visits a different state and that his legal activities will not be restricted. (pp. 160–61)

Making Connections

1–3. List the three basic responsibilities of every state.

4–6. What are the three most common taxes that states charge?

7–10. Identify at least four of the major leaders, or bosses, of political machines in American history.

Developing Civics Skills

1. Discuss and evaluate Tip O'Neill Jr.'s assertion that "all politics is local."

2. Prepare a brief report explaining whether your state has a strong or weak governorship. Defend your position.

Thinking Critically

1. List the pros and cons of open and closed primaries. What kind of primary do you have in your state?

2. Defend or oppose the use of lotteries as a means of supporting governments.

Living as a Christian Citizen

1. Imagine that you are a member of Congress who voted for the Defense of Marriage Act in 1996. Afterward, you received letters from some of your constituents who wonder why you signed a law that restricts people's freedom. Craft a response to these constituents defending your position.

2. Imagine that your state is considering a bill authorizing gambling to fund educational programs. Write a letter to the editor, providing moral objections to this bill.

People, Places, and Things to Remember

Tenth Amendment
bicameral
unicameral
gubernatorial
governor
lieutenant governor
supreme court
lotteries
county
parishes
boroughs
commissioners
county executive
unified government
municipal governments
mayor-council government
council-manager government
commission government
board of trustees
town meeting
selectmen
special district
grass roots
political party
factions
precinct
polling place
county committee
political machines
suffrage
primary elections
general elections
open primary
crossover voting
closed primary
semiclosed primaries
runoff election
Top-Two method
jungle primary
recall
referendums
initiative
full faith and credit clause
privileges and immunities clause
extradition
reciprocity

CHAPTER REVIEW ANSWERS

Making Connections

1–3. public safety, commercial regulation, and political subdivision oversight (p. 142)

4–6. property tax, general sales tax, and individual income tax (p. 147)

7–10. (any four) Boss Tweed or Richard Croker of Tammany Hall in New York City, E. H. Crump of Memphis, Richard Daley of Chicago, Theodore Bilbo of Mississippi, Huey Long of Louisiana, Tom Pendergast of Missouri, and Harry Byrd of Virginia (p. 154)

Developing Civics Skills

1. American government arises from the grass roots, and officeholders at all levels must be attuned and responsive to the needs and desires of local citizens. The average citizen is most directly involved with state and local governments. (p. 141)

2. Answers will vary. A state's governor is strong if he has line-item veto power over legislative actions. He is also strong if he appoints all cabinet members and if they answer to him. A strong governor has great power over the budget process. A state's governor is weak if he lacks the aforementioned powers. (p. 144)

Thinking Critically

1. A major advantage of an open primary is that it gives independent voters a voice in selecting candidates for the general election. Critics argue it may allow people outside the party to have undue influence over whom the party will select as candidates. A major argument for a closed primary is that it allows party members to decide their candidates without interference by nonmembers who have no stake in the party's integrity or standing. Such nonmembers might try to elect a weak candidate or one who is not committed to the party's platform. The disadvantage of the closed primary is that it does not allow independents to participate. Answers for the second part of the question will depend on the state in which the student lives.

2. Those who defend the use of lotteries may say that lotteries are essentially a voluntary tax. They might argue that people should have the opportunity to participate if they so desire. Those who oppose the lottery may state that gambling often results in the poor being harmed because the people with the lowest income (those least able to afford it) tend to play the lottery the most. Gambling is viewed as a vice in many cultures rather than as good moral conduct and is poor stewardship of God-given resources. It can be addictive. It may harm innocent people in the gambler's family. It sometimes leads to criminal activity as people seek income to participate in the lottery or to replace money lost playing the lottery.

Living as a Christian Citizen

1. You could mention that without DOMA, a judge in a single state might be able to force on the nation a new definition of marriage. Thus, religious liberty would be endangered because employers and religious organizations would be required to accept marriages that violated their religious beliefs. You could state that DOMA therefore protected people's freedom.

2. A student could incorporate some of the answer given for question 2 from the "Thinking Critically" section. A student might also state that though increased funding for education is a good thing, money should be raised in a manner that is less detrimental to society than gambling.

Rotunda of the US Capitol

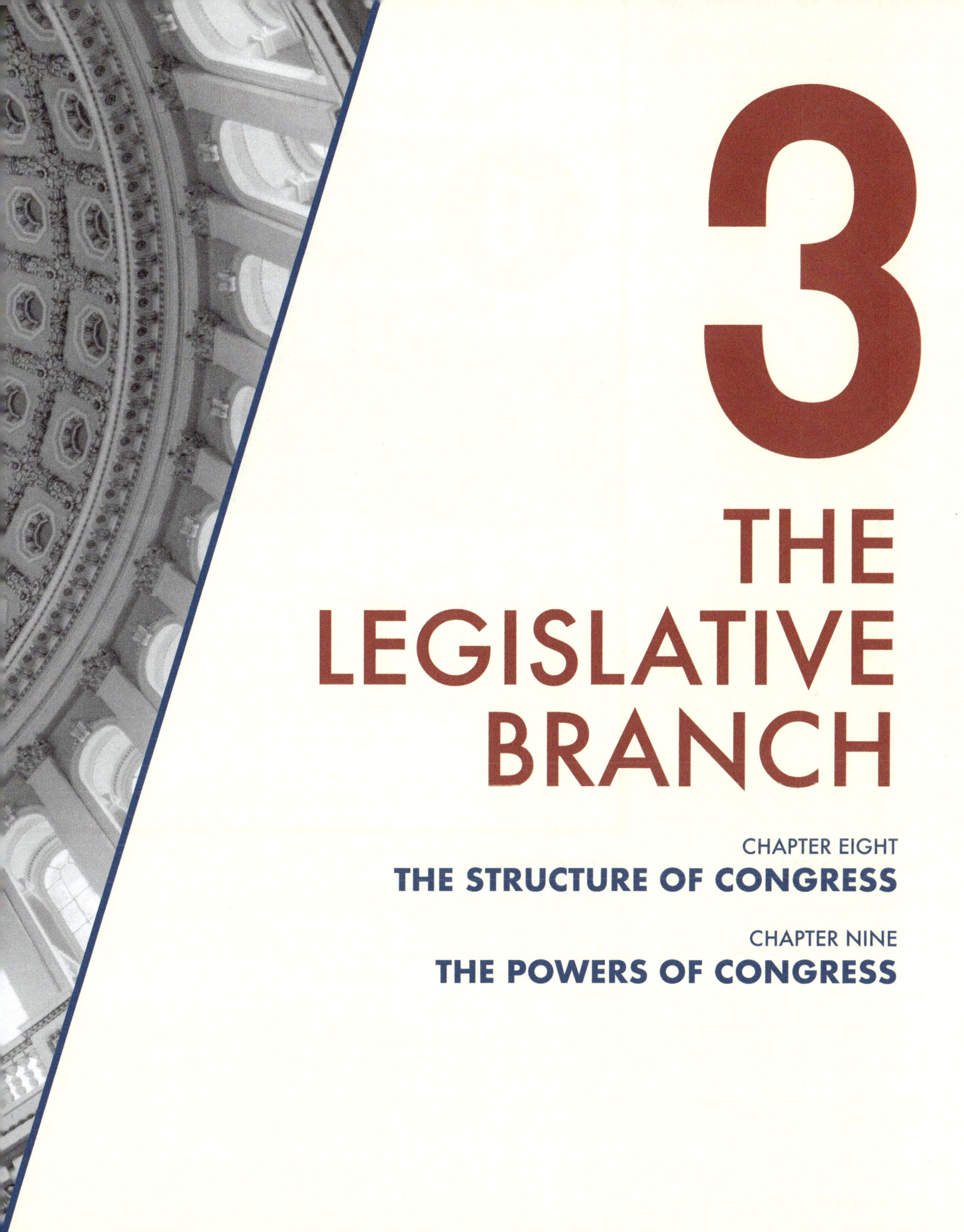

3

THE LEGISLATIVE BRANCH

CHAPTER EIGHT
THE STRUCTURE OF CONGRESS

CHAPTER NINE
THE POWERS OF CONGRESS

1. Analyze the framework of the legislative branch of government.
2. Explain the legislative processes of Congress.

THE STRUCTURE OF CONGRESS

8

If the legislative authority be not restrained, there can be neither liberty nor stability; and it can only be restrained by dividing it within itself, into distinct and independent branches.

—James Wilson
Signer of the Declaration of Independence and US Constitution

Joint session of Congress during a presidential State of the Union address

I. Framework

II. Legislative Workings

BIG IDEAS

1. How is the legislative branch of government organized?
2. What are the legislative processes of Congress?

SUGGESTED MATERIALS

Section I
- A 2020 Census form
- Special speakers (see pp. 171 and 176)
- Activity 1 from Chapter 8 of the *Student Activities*

Section II
- Activities 2–4 from Chapter 8 of the *Student Activities*
- Mock Senate materials (for an optional activity)

Teacher Resources
Visit TeacherToolsOnline.com for resources to enhance the lessons.

Additional Resources

A good resource for this unit is William C. Allen's *History of the United States Capitol: A Chronicle of Design, Construction, and Politics.*

For more information on the history of the US House of Representatives, refer to Robert Remini's *The House.*

The Constitution's framers deliberately made Congress the first branch of government, addressing it in Article I. History reveals why they mentioned the representative assemblies first. The American War for Independence occurred largely because many colonists viewed King George III as a tyrant; consequently, the founders proposed a legislative body to counterbalance executive power and give the people a substantial voice in the national government.

Representative governments date back to the Greeks and Romans. In the late Middle Ages, the English Parliament developed as wealthy noblemen insisted on advising monarchs. When Britain established its colonial empire, American colonists enjoyed a measure of self-government through their colonial assemblies, as illustrated by the House of Burgesses in Virginia. During the War for Independence, the Continental Congress, a representative assembly, guided the American government. Not surprisingly, when the colonists finally gained their independence, the national government under the Articles of Confederation featured a dominant assembly. And in 1789, when the new central government began, Congress was still expected to control America's affairs.

Congressional power peaked in the late nineteenth century. The Reconstruction Congress overrode Andrew Johnson's postwar plans and determined its own procedure for returning the defeated Southern states to the Union. In the era of big business that followed the end of Reconstruction in 1876, Congress cooperated with business and industry leaders. This resulted in a period of unprecedented growth and prosperity. The presidents of that era (from Ulysses S. Grant to William McKinley) are remembered less than presidents from other periods largely because Congress was so dominant.

The twentieth century, however, was a different story. For several reasons, the White House became more dominant in American political life. Theodore Roosevelt expanded the role of the presidency in the national government. He did so through his outgoing personality, the news media, the influence of the office as a "bully pulpit," his initiative in proposing legislation (e.g., the Pure Food and Drug Act), and his aggressive "big-stick" foreign policy. Later, the size of the executive branch bureaucracy increased during both the New Deal of the 1930s and the Great Society of the 1960s. Likewise, during the Cold War, the White House received greater power in foreign policy to stop Communist advances. Despite this increased executive authority, Congress—the main source of legislation—remains a force that presidents cannot ignore (though some modern presidents have tried to bypass Congress by issuing executive orders). This chapter introduces and discusses the structure and workings of the US Congress.

I. Framework

Bicameral Structure

The Great Compromise at the Constitutional Convention led to the creation of a **bicameral**, or two-house, Congress. Big states, such as Virginia, advocated representation based on population; and small states, such as New Jersey, naturally feared the overwhelming power of large states. The Great Compromise resolved the matter. The creation of the House of Representatives, in which representation is based on population, pleased large states; and the creation of the Senate, which is composed of two

One of Andrew Johnson's main political opponents was Radical Republican Thaddeus Stevens, a congressman from Pennsylvania. He told the president, "This is . . . a Government of the people, and . . . Congress *is* the people."

Guiding Questions

1. What is bicameral structure and how does it affect Congress?
2. How do the House and Senate officials lead their respective chambers?
3. What are some of the controversial issues relating to members of Congress?
4. What are some procedures used during a congressional session?

House of Burgesses

One forerunner of the US Congress was the Virginia General Assembly, instituted in 1619, which included the governor, six councilors, and twenty-two burgesses. It eventually became known as the House of Burgesses. (*Burgess* was an English term for a middle-class person or townsman.) Voting was limited to male property owners, who were usually required to own twenty-five to fifty acres or a lot and a house in town. The sheriff conducted elections, and voters announced their choices orally in the presence of the candidates, who typically courted voters with free liquor or invitations to balls and dinners.

Government Comparisons

Direct the students to research and write a report on representative governments in ancient Athens and Rome; their reports should answer the following questions: How were those bodies similar to or different from the American Congress? Did they show favoritism toward the wealthy? Did the common people vote for their representatives? How has the meaning of "representative government" changed over the centuries?

Presidential Advantages

Encourage students to review newspapers, news magazines, and online resources to find examples of how the last two or three American presidents dominated Congress or had an advantage over Congress. The students should examine presidential influence on both domestic and foreign policies.

Sweden's Unicameral Parliament

Since 1971, Sweden's parliament, the Riksdag, has been unicameral. What are the advantages and disadvantages of a unicameral legislative branch?

Power of the Purse

In *Federalist* No. 58, Madison discussed the issue of appropriations (legislation about money).

> [The House], in a word, hold[s] the *purse* that powerful instrument by which we behold, in the history of the British Constitution, an infant and humble representation of the people gradually enlarging the sphere of its activity and importance, and finally reducing, as far as it seems to have wished, all the overgrown prerogatives of the other branches of the government. This *power over the purse* may, in fact, be regarded as the *most complete and effectual weapon* with which any constitution can arm the immediate representatives of the people, for obtaining a redress of every grievance, and for carrying into effect every just and salutary measure. (emphasis added)

Federalist No. 63

This document, written by James Madison or Alexander Hamilton, made the case of including the US Senate in the Constitution. Originally, members of that body were elected by state legislatures. Though the Founding Fathers valued democracy ideologically, they did not believe that more democracy was always better. Thus, they supported the idea of this body not being elected directly by the people.

Madison argued that the Senate would blend stability with liberty. As a smaller body, with only two members from each state, who served six-year terms, the Senate would be less volatile than the House. Madison believed that such stability would cause foreign nations to have greater respect for the new nation.

senators per state, satisfied small states. The British Parliament was a bicameral legislature, as were many of the colonial governments; therefore, the idea of a divided legislature had broad support at the Constitutional Convention. The legislature was the only branch of the national government to be divided.

A two-house legislature, however, has other purposes than just satisfying big states and little states. It also provides for a more cautious pace in passing laws. In enacting laws, the benefits of carefulness outweigh the disadvantage of slowness. Furthermore, the framers of the Constitution believed that the House would better represent the people, particularly the large populations of big states. They designed the Senate, on the other hand, to represent the state governments.

James Madison argues in *The Federalist* No. 58 that "notwithstanding the equal authority which will subsist between the two houses on all legislative subjects, except the originating of money bills [which begin in the House of Representatives], it cannot be doubted that the House, composed of the greater number of members, when supported by the more powerful States, and speaking the known and determined sense of a majority of the people, will have no small advantage in a question."

On the other hand, Madison notes in *The Federalist* Nos. 62 and 63 that the Senate serves as a check on the House, which is the more populous branch. He understood that leaders can violate the trust placed in them. Thus he argued for the "necessity of some institution that will blend stability with liberty." His solution was the Senate, originally chosen by the state legislatures and more distant from the people. While not all the Founding Fathers believed in human sinfulness, they were influenced by the Enlightenment, which taught that government, by bringing people out of an unruly "state of nature," could restrain them. Divided government helps ensure that one branch will not violate the people's freedoms.

House of Representatives

The House of Representatives is the more democratic of the two houses because the number of House members from each state is based on state population. For this reason, California, the most populous state, has more than 50 House members while the seven least populous states (Alaska, Delaware, Montana, North Dakota, South Dakota, Vermont, and Wyoming) have only 1 representative each. Growth and shifts in the nation's population, therefore, are important factors in congressional elections. The Constitution's framers, wisely anticipating this growth and mobility, instituted a **census** (an official count of a country's population) to be taken every ten years beginning in 1790. Such a census, conducted primarily to ensure accurate

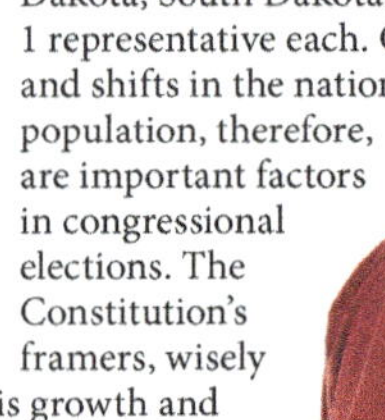

Census

Provide a copy of the 2020 Census form and direct students to examine and discuss it. What is the sole *constitutional* purpose of a census? How does the present form go beyond that constitutional purpose?

A Wealth of Information

A wealth of current and historical information is on the US House and Senate websites. Both have links to information about historical offices of the House and Senate, where the students can find interesting details about past members of the chambers, including facts about who served the longest, who became president, and so forth.

representation, was unique in its time and reflected the founders' commitment to democratic government. Originally, each House member had about 30,000 constituents. Today, with the number of representatives permanently fixed at 435, each member represents approximately 770,000 constitu-

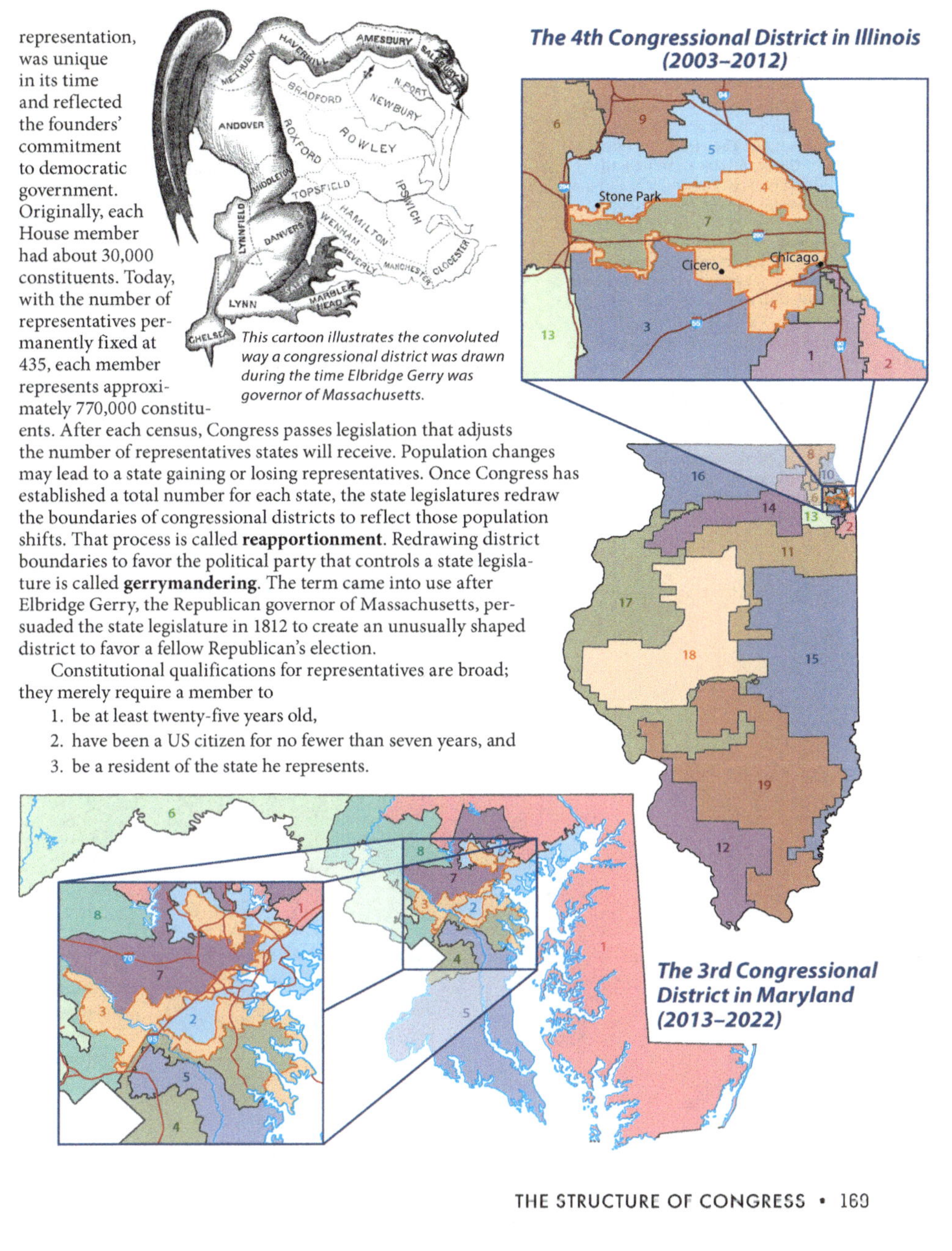

This cartoon illustrates the convoluted way a congressional district was drawn during the time Elbridge Gerry was governor of Massachusetts.

ents. After each census, Congress passes legislation that adjusts the number of representatives states will receive. Population changes may lead to a state gaining or losing representatives. Once Congress has established a total number for each state, the state legislatures redraw the boundaries of congressional districts to reflect those population shifts. That process is called **reapportionment**. Redrawing district boundaries to favor the political party that controls a state legislature is called **gerrymandering**. The term came into use after Elbridge Gerry, the Republican governor of Massachusetts, persuaded the state legislature in 1812 to create an unusually shaped district to favor a fellow Republican's election.

Constitutional qualifications for representatives are broad; they merely require a member to

1. be at least twenty-five years old,

2. have been a US citizen for no fewer than seven years, and

3. be a resident of the state he represents.

Bicameralism

The bicameral structure of the US Congress provides one of the many checks and balances for the American government. Each house of the Congress checks the other and each has some powers that the other body lacks.

These checks and balances reflect the biblical concern that power not be concentrated without ways to hold the powerful accountable.

Gerrymandering

Students should analyze the practice of gerrymandering. What political factors would be considered by the party controlling the state legislature (and therefore in charge of drawing congressional district lines)? How do the places where voters reside relate to how they might vote? Consider characteristics like rural areas, suburbs, or inner cities. Does ethnicity play a role? How can you differentiate between someone who might vote Democratic and someone who might vote Republican?

Discuss the biblical and ethical considerations of gerrymandering. Is justice provided when this tactic is employed? Is the procedure fair to the opposing political party? Does it promote or hinder the idea of having different interests and varying groups fairly represented in Congress?

Single-Member Districts

In addition to making representatives more accountable and accessible to constituents, single-member districts have other advantages. For example, electing one representative from each congressional district has strengthened the two-party system. With this winner-take-all arrangement, a candidate from one of the two major parties will almost certainly win.

In contrast to this system, some other democracies (such as Germany) provide for proportional representation, which means that a party's representation in the lawmaking body is determined by the percentage of the vote it receives regionally or nationally. Supporters of this proportional system argue that it is fairer since it allows minor parties to elect members to the national legislature; however, others argue that it can also allow several small parties to dominate national politics, causing governments to be based on a coalition of parties. They argue that a two-party system with single-member districts generally creates more stable political conditions.

Age, citizenship, and residence requirements, therefore, are the only constitutional restrictions placed on congressmen, and these general restrictions differ little between the two houses. A House member represents a specific **congressional district**. Although the Constitution does not discuss congressional districts, each state draws its congressional boundaries so that each representative is responsible to a roughly equal number of people. This means that each district is a **single-member district**, with one representative elected from a given region. This organization increases House members' accountability and makes them more accessible. Although members are required to live in the state they represent, the Constitution does not mandate that they live within their congressional district. However, few members live outside that area.

The House of Representatives was to be, in the words of Constitutional Convention delegate George Mason, the "grand depository of the democratic principle of the government. . . . It ought to know and sympathize with every part of the community." This principle underlies the limitation of representatives' terms to only two years, with all seats up for election at the same time. The time limit helps make congressmen even more accountable and responsive to those they represent. Answering to

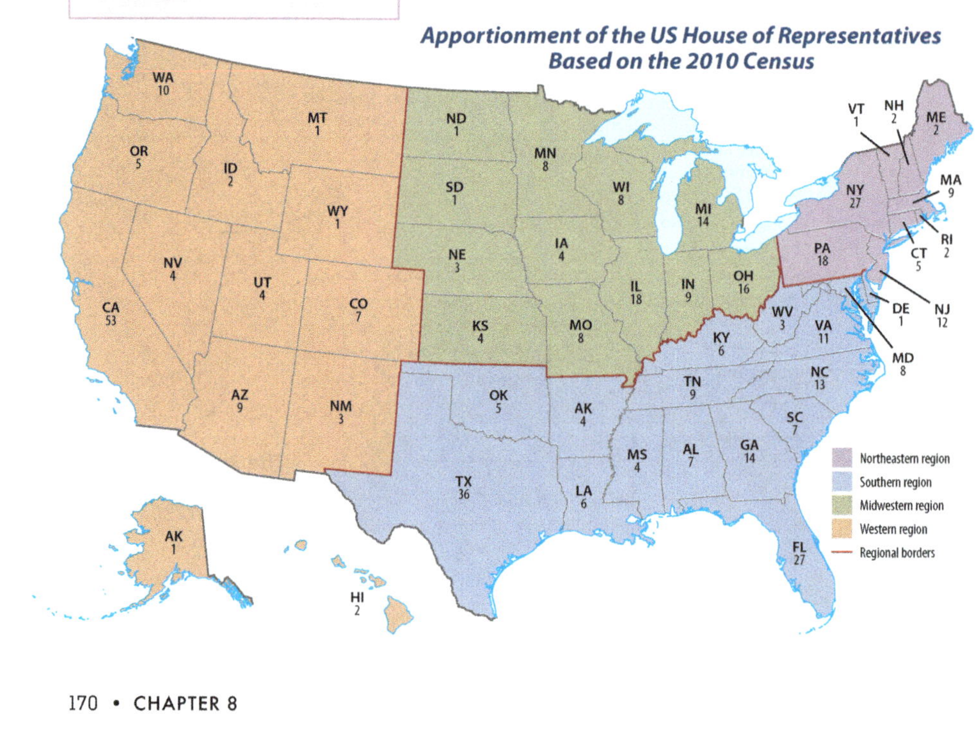

Apportionment of the US House of Representatives Based on the 2010 Census

Operation of the House of Representatives

To help students gain a better understanding of how the House operates, especially on tax and revenue issues, form a mock Ways and Means Committee in the classroom. Ask students to imagine that the government needs more money and that the current president has asked for a tax increase on cigarettes. The committee (the class) must formulate a bill that it will submit to the House for passage.

Appoint a student to chair the committee. He should lead a discussion regarding several questions (e.g., Should we have a tax increase on cigarettes? If so, how much of an increase?). Each question will be decided by a majority vote.

Several controversial questions might arise. For example, should the government promote moral behavior? (Remind the students that one of the obligations of government is to do so.) Is it acceptable to tax harmful products like cigarettes because doing so will discourage people from smoking and reduce secondhand smoke? In other words, is taxing a vice a good way to discourage it? Are there better approaches? Is liberty, even the freedom to harm ourselves, more important than encouraging a moral society? What if the legislation harms tobacco farmers or cigarette manufacturers economically?

As a part of this activity, help students understand that legislation is often complicated.

the residents in one congressional district also tends to make a representative's viewpoint more localized. For example, a congressman would likely oppose a bill to reduce military spending if its passage meant that a business in his district would lose an arms contract (and, potentially, jobs).

Senate

Voters in a congressional district elect House members. But voters elect senators on a statewide, or **at-large**, basis. As a result, senators (except those in the least populated states) have much larger constituencies than their colleagues in the lower house. The Constitution's framers designed the Senate to be less accessible to popular demands and control. In fact, the direct popular election of senators did not occur until 1913 with the passage of the **Seventeenth Amendment**. Before this amendment, members of state legislatures elected senators to represent state governments in the national government. Within the legislative branch, the Senate was to serve as a check and balance to the democratically elected and locally oriented House. Madison himself argued forcefully before his fellow delegates that such a Senate would meet *national* demands "with more coolness, with more system, and with more wisdom, than the popular branch [the House]."

Senate requirements are only slightly more restrictive than those of the House of Representatives. A senator must

1. be at least thirty years old,
2. have been a US citizen for at least nine years, and
3. be a resident of the state he represents.

Differences

There are several differences between the houses even though they are part of one Congress. The differences mainly concern constitutional and operational aspects of the houses.

Political parties also provide an important informal organization to both chambers. Today, with rare exceptions, all members of Congress are either Republicans or Democrats. The majority party determines the leadership, rules, and much of the agenda of Congress; therefore, this party has great influence on the president's success (or failure) in pursuing his policies.

However, one political party's control over both houses does not ensure automatic success for a president of the same party. Jimmy Carter learned this when, on several occasions, enough of his fellow Democrats voted against him to stop some parts of his agenda, including passage of the SALT II arms-control treaty. Similarly, Bill Clinton's healthcare reform failed to pass in Congress although his party, the Democratic Party, controlled both houses. In 2017, Republican Donald Trump failed to obtain a full repeal of the Affordable Care Act, also known as Obamacare, even though his party controlled Congress.

Party members sometimes vote against one another and their president because of regional or ideological differences. When members of different parties unite to support or oppose a bill because of some common interest, they form a **coalition**. In the 1950s, for example, conservative Southern Democrats and conservative Republicans sometimes laid aside their party labels and formed a coalition to oppose liberal legislation. Today, a coalition could be formed if, for example, congressmen of both parties from the South and the Midwest joined to support an agricultural program that would help farmers from their regions. In short, members of Congress sometimes ignore party labels to promote what they believe is best for their constituents.

The Senate and the Power of Treaty Approval

President Woodrow Wilson and the Allies negotiated with Germany after World War I and signed the Treaty of Versailles. The negotiation was a moment of high drama because the Allies had recently defeated the Central Powers. From Wilson's perspective, the treaty, with its provision for the League of Nations, offered the prospect of long-term peace.

Nevertheless, when the treaty was later offered to the US Senate, opposition to the treaty and to the League was strong. The Senate was controlled by the Republicans, and many people in America feared that interest in world problems would divert attention from reforms needed in America. Others, while supporting the treaty in general, wanted to reduce American participation in the League by amending the treaty. Henry Cabot Lodge, the chairman of the Senate Foreign Relations Committee, belonged to the latter group and led the fight against the treaty.

But Woodrow Wilson, a Democrat, refused to modify the treaty, and by 1920 the Senate rejected it. In the same year, Congress passed a joint resolution ending the war, and Wilson vetoed it. In the next year, with a new president, a similar joint resolution passed, and a treaty followed that did not include American membership in the League.

Special Speaker

Invite a guest speaker for the class—someone who can speak authoritatively about Congress. Alternatively, ask the speaker to take part in a video conference with the class. A possible guest includes someone from a congressman's local staff. Members of Congress have offices in their districts, and there might be an office in or near your town. It might be possible to get the member of Congress personally to speak, especially in an election year. A former member of Congress is another possibility. If a congressman or a staffer is not available, perhaps a local college or university professor who teaches political science and specializes in the study of Congress could present to the class.

Professional organizations, such as the American Medical Association or the American Bar Association, also have lobbyists who work on Capitol Hill and who might be willing to talk to the students about lobbyists' work. Instruct the students to prepare questions beforehand for the speaker's presentation.

Role of the Caucus

Very early in the nation's history, the party caucus in Congress played an important role in nominating presidents. Members of a party in Congress would meet formally and choose a nominee. For example, in 1804 the Democratic-Republican Party caucus nominated Thomas Jefferson for president, and he was later elected to that office. Today, the term *caucus* can also mean a meeting of representatives or senators who support a special interest (e.g., the Congressional Black Caucus or the Women's Caucus).

Lyndon Johnson, Majority Leader

Many historians view Lyndon Johnson as the most powerful Senate majority leader. While he was sometimes ineffective as president in the 1960s, Johnson was quite successful in the Senate in the 1950s. Though freshman senators were generally expected to be seen but not heard, Johnson shattered that tradition by becoming the Democratic majority whip in 1951 (only three years after being elected to the Senate). Two years later, he became minority leader; and in 1955, when the Democrats became the majority party, he became majority leader.

How did Johnson rise to power? He had help. Veteran senator Richard Russell of Georgia was his mentor, and the Senate correspondent for the *New York Times* was a fellow Texan who promoted Johnson. Of course, Johnson also worked very hard.

As majority leader, Johnson succeeded through diligence and attention to details. He made sure he knew what was needed to persuade a fellow senator to vote a certain way. He also changed the procedure for determining committee assignments for Democratic senators so that every senator got at least one important committee

Nancy Pelosi served as Speaker of the House from 2007 to 2011. She became Speaker again in 2019.

Mitch McConnell served as minority leader in the US Senate from 2007 until 2015. In 2015, he became majority leader.

Power Structure in Congress	
House of Representatives	**Senate**
Speaker	Majority leader
Majority leader	
Majority whip	Majority whip
Minority leader	Minority leader
Minority whip	Minority whip

Leadership

Selection Process

The power structure within Congress is built largely along party lines. The main purposes of party leadership are to ensure communication between party members and their leaders and to help provide party unity in shaping laws. Each party chooses leaders to coordinate party action on proposals and to strengthen the party's position on a wide range of national issues. The parties select such leadership in a **caucus**. A caucus (or **conference** as Republicans call it), consists of all the members of a party within a house of Congress. The leadership positions that are open to a party depend on its status as the majority or minority party within a branch of Congress. Three key positions are open to the majority party in the House: the Speaker (the House leader), the **majority leader**, and the **majority whip**. The top posts open to the minority party in the House are the **minority leader** and the **minority whip**. In the upper chamber, the Senate majority leadership consists of the majority leader and the majority whip. Similarly, the minority party in the Senate is headed by the minority leader and the minority whip. The vice president of the United States serves as the president of the Senate, but that position is mainly a figurehead role unrelated to the party structure of the upper house. The president of the Senate votes only to break a tie in the Senate.

Leadership Power

The real power inherent in these offices lies in the overall strength of each party and in the skills of individual leaders. In the House, the Speaker generally wields an enormous amount of power. Though he has the right to vote, he does so on rare occasions, such as when there is a tie. The Speaker decides which proposed legislation will be considered, who will be recognized (allowed to speak) from the floor, and who will be assigned to important committees. The majority and minority leaders are floor leaders and spokesmen for their respective parties. They are assisted by party whips, who are primarily responsible for communicating with party members about their views on legislation, encouraging attendance at key voting sessions, and trying to keep all members voting as a bloc. Congressional leaders, however, cannot force party members to vote in a particular way. Rather, these leaders use persuasion, pressure, and political maneuvering to help coordinate their party's response to legislation.

In the Senate, a similar power structure exists. However, there the most powerful position is the majority leader. He controls the flow of legislation in the Senate. His role is similar to that of the Speaker of the House.

The Senate does have a largely honorary position called the **president pro tempore**. It is held by the most senior member of the Senate's majority party. Though this person has little actual power, he is third in the line of presidential succession (behind the Vice President and the Speaker of the House).

Speaker of the House

The **Speaker of the House** is the only House position actually named in the Constitution. The Speaker presides over the House, manages its business, is the official spokesman, and is the body's most powerful officer. The Speaker

The First Congress

Instruct the students to check online resources for information about a documentary history of the first US Congress, which met from 1789 to 1791. The website of the House of Representatives offers a wealth of information through various links. It also includes a section with details regarding the time when New York City was the capital city and another with information about the first Speaker, Frederick Muhlenberg. Encourage students to share interesting facts about the first Congress with the class.

Activity 1: Congress and Its Leaders

This activity enables students to learn more about the current members of Congress and its leaders.

is formally elected by the whole House every two years (unless a vacancy occurs). Because the majority party's choice prevails, the candidate chosen earlier in the majority party's caucus (or conference) will win. Usually, the candidate chosen to be Speaker has served several terms in Congress and in leadership roles during his tenure.

After the vice president, the Speaker is next in the line of presidential succession. He works with the White House on legislation, especially if he and the president are of the same party.

The first Speaker of the House was Frederick A. C. Muhlenberg of Pennsylvania, elected in 1789. The first significant Speaker was Henry Clay of Kentucky. He was elected to that position in 1811 (during his first term in the House). With his own political skills and the powers of the office, he became the first powerful Speaker. He appointed people who shared his views to important committees, and he used parliamentary procedure effectively. Clay served as Speaker for more than ten years (between 1811 and 1825), longer than anyone except Sam Rayburn (who served for more than seventeen years in the twentieth century).

Joseph Cannon of Illinois, who served from 1903 to 1911 (the Fifty-Eighth through the Sixty-First Congresses), is considered by many to be the most powerful Speaker in the history of the House of Representatives. Notoriously profane, Cannon ruled the House with an iron hand. He controlled committee assignments, decided which legislation would come to the floor,

Sam Rayburn

Paul Ryan served as Speaker from 2015 to 2019.

Differences Between the House and the Senate				
Constitutional			**Operational**	
House	**Senate**		**House**	**Senate**
Is the source of all revenue bills	Approves or rejects treaties and major presidential appointments		More centralized leadership	Less centralized leadership
Can impeach	Holds impeachment trials		More efficient procedures	Slower-moving legislation and possible filibusters (or threats of them)
Members have two-year terms. All 435 are up for reelection at the same time.	Senators have six-year terms. One-third face reelection every two years.		Time and rules of debate controlled by Rules Committee and Speaker	Flow of legislation controlled by majority leader (no Rules Committee)
435 members (allocated by population)	100 members (2 per state)		Specialized legislative focus	Broader legislative focus
			High turnover	Moderate turnover
A member must be at least twenty-five, have been a US citizen for seven years, and be a resident of the state he represents.	A senator must be at least thirty, have been a US citizen for nine years, and be a resident of the state he represents.		Focuses on tax and revenue policies	Focuses on foreign policy and judicial appointments, especially Supreme Court nominees
			Limited debate	Less limited and more informal debate

post. But Johnson could also be personally intimidating—grabbing lapels, slapping backs, shaking hands vigorously, and getting directly in someone's face. He was physically imposing, and on the phone he could be blunt, forceful, and sometimes profane. Although Republicans controlled the White House from 1953 to 1961, Lyndon Johnson became a powerful political figure by dominating the Senate.

The Senate President Pro Tempore

The majority party selects the president pro tempore, and he is typically the longest-serving member of that party. The office is usually considered honorary. The president pro tempore serves as long as his party remains in control of the Senate, provided, of course, that he is reelected.

As a general rule, unless there is important business before the Senate, neither the vice president nor the pro tempore (or pro tem) actually presides. Routinely, junior members of the body do so.

But in recent years, the pro tem has been more newsworthy. Whenever Republicans controlled the Senate from 1981 to 2001, Strom Thurmond of South Carolina was the pro tem. He retired after the 2002 election at age 100 as the longest-serving senator in American history, having first been elected to the Senate in 1954. Robert Byrd was then pro tem when the Democrats were in the majority. Byrd later surpassed Thurmond's record and became the longest-serving senator. He died at age ninety-two in 2010 while still in office.

Democrat Daniel Inouye, who served as president pro tempore after Byrd's death, also later surpassed Thurmond's record and thus became the second longest serving senator. In summary, Byrd served over 51 years, Inouye served almost 50 years, and Thurmond served over 47 years.

Speakers of the House

Instruct students to choose one of the Speakers of the House and conduct research on his or her life, paying particular attention to preparation for and becoming the Speaker. What were any major accomplishments? Was the Speaker generally successful or unsuccessful? Why?

State Legislative Officials

Group the students and require each group to review your state government's website and research information on your state's legislature. Direct the students to compare the officers of your state legislature with those of the US House and Senate.

One officer that every state will probably have (other than the clerk) is the parliamentarian. Instruct the students to research the duties of that office. What does a parliamentarian do? You might want to discuss *Robert's Rules of Order* with the students. How can we relate parliamentary procedure to Scripture? (*God ordained government for social order, and we must submit to it. Governments must have rules; otherwise, our society would be chaotic, and the work of the church would suffer.*) In what other areas of life is it necessary to have rules, sometimes just for efficiency's sake?

Groups can present their findings and compare their research.

Sam Rayburn

Democrat Samuel T. Rayburn (1882–1961) was a powerful Speaker of the House. One of the House office buildings in Washington, appropriately, bears his name. He served in leadership positions in the House of Representatives from 1937 to 1961. He served as majority leader from 1937 to 1940 and as minority leader from 1947 to 1949 and 1953 to 1955. He served as Speaker from 1940 to 1947, from 1949 to 1953, and from 1955 to 1961. His years of service covered dramatic periods in American history: the Great Depression, World War II, the Cold War, and the civil-rights movement.

Rayburn's political career began when, at the age of twenty-four, he was elected to the Texas House of Representatives in 1906. In 1912, at the age of thirty, he was elected to Congress. The influence of fellow Texan John Nance Garner helped Rayburn advance in that body. Garner served as minority leader for the Democrats from 1929 to 1931 and as Speaker from 1931 until he became the vice-president in 1933. He served two terms as vice president under President Franklin Roosevelt.

Hard work and close personal ties to key members of the House enabled Rayburn to get important legislation passed and to advance his personal career. He often mediated between southern conservative Democrats, like himself, and more liberal northern Democrats. In 1961 he gained his last major victory as Speaker when he helped push through the expansion of the House Rules Committee; the expansion allowed that committee to become more open to reform legislation.

Women in Congress

Jeannette Rankin was the first female member of Congress. She represented Montana in the House of Representatives from 1917 to 1919 and again from 1941 to 1943. She was a vigorous campaigner and gained support from both parties, although she was a Republican. Her lifework focused on peace and women's rights. She was a strong supporter of women obtaining the right to vote.

Rankin became the only person in Congress to vote against the declarations of war in both world wars. In 1968, when she was in her late eighties, Rankin led about five thousand women in Washington, DC, protesting the Vietnam War.

The first woman to serve as a US senator was Rebecca Felton, a Democrat from Georgia. She was appointed by the governor to fill the position when Senator Tom Watson died in 1922. She actually only served for one day. The first woman *elected* to the Senate was Hattie Caraway, a Democrat from Arkansas, in 1932.

In 1973, there were fifteen women serving in Congress. By 1993, there were fifty-five and for the first time a state (California) had elected two women to the US Senate. By 2003, seventy-five women were serving in Congress:

Jeannette Rankin

one was Senator Hillary Clinton, who represented New York. Clinton became the first former First Lady to hold elective office. By 2019, 127 women were members of Congress. Twenty-five women were serving in the Senate: eight Republicans and seventeen Democrats. One hundred two women were members of the House: eighty-nine Democrats and thirteen Republicans.

Percentage of Women in Congress

1973	15	2.8%
1993	55	10.3%
2003	75	14.0%
2018	107	20.0%
2019	127	23.7%

and thwarted attempts at reform. He was nicknamed Czar Cannon for his heavy-handed rule in the House. However, a rebellion led by progressive members of his own Republican party eventually led to a reduction of the Speaker's power.

In 1994, Newt Gingrich of Georgia became the first Republican Speaker in forty years and during his tenure became a powerful Speaker. Gingrich agreed to limit his time as Speaker to four consecutive terms in exchange for more institutional power for the Speaker, and media attention gave him even greater power. Briefly, some political observers thought he was more powerful than President Clinton, who was weakened by the Republican takeover of Congress (the first since 1954) and the defeat of his healthcare plan. But Gingrich's influence faded quickly. Opponents portrayed him as heartless when he promoted budget cuts, and after a budget skirmish with President Clinton, Gingrich was blamed for the temporary shutdown of the government in late 1995 and early 1996. Dozens of ethics charges were also filed against him, and for the first time in its history, the House voted to reprimand its Speaker. After the Republicans lost congressional seats in the 1998 election, Gingrich resigned both his office and his seat in Congress.

The first female Speaker was Nancy Pelosi of California. Her fellow Democrats elected her to that position in January 2007 and again in 2009 and 2019.

Newt Gingrich

Behind the Scenes

Several officers perform Congress's routine work; without them, that body could not function and laws would never pass. These officials are nonmembers who are hired to do much of the routine work.

Separation of Church and State Blurred

Both the House and the Senate have chaplains. Group the students and assign them to research other examples of how the lines between church and state are sometimes blurred in America. What are the historical reasons for these developments? Are Americans more religious at certain times? Here are some topics for student discussion regarding this issue:

1. The phrase "In God We Trust" being placed on currency
2. The phrase "under God" being added to the Pledge of Allegiance
3. Christian holidays being observed, such as Christmas and Easter
4. Prayer at major public events, such as inaugurations of government officials, patriotic rallies, and even athletic events
5. Prayer during times of national crises

Remind students of the following:

1. *Church* is commonly used in this context to simply refer to religion; however, this is misleading. Churches are institutions; the term is not simply a synonym for religion.
2. It is appropriate for the Christian religion to impact all of life.
3. Christians should beware of the danger of civil religion, in which religious statements and actions are used for political ends rather than for truly Christian ends.

In the Senate, these officials include the following:

- secretary of the Senate: manages various legislative and administrative aspects of the chamber
- sergeant at arms: maintains order in the Senate
- journal clerk: maintains the *Senate Journal*
- legislative clerk: records votes and reports bills, messages, conference reports, and amendments to the Senate
- parliamentarian: advises the presiding officer on official procedures
- official reporters of debates: prepare material for the *Congressional Record*
- chaplain: opens sessions with prayer and also provides counseling to any member of the Senate

In the House, these officials include the following:

- clerk: oversees various administrative duties of the chamber
- sergeant at arms: maintains order in the House
- chief administrative officer: works with the Committee on House Administration to handle the House's finances and operations
- chaplain: opens sessions with prayer and also provides counseling to any member of the House

Controversial Issues

Although members of Congress enjoy positions esteemed by most Americans, they often face criticism regarding a variety of issues. Two such examples are term limits and congressional perquisites (or "perks").

Term Limits

The delegates to the Constitutional Convention rejected a motion to limit House members to one term. But in the late 1980s, Americans became increasingly frustrated with government and politicians. Congress and state legislatures seemed gridlocked, and news of scandals was frequent. For some voters, the solution to such ineffectiveness and ethical problems was **term limits**. These citizens pushed for referendums that would limit the number of terms for state legislators and members of Congress. The movement was also fueled by those who disliked the notion of a "career" politician (one who serves for many years) and preferred a "citizen" legislator (one who serves temporarily and then returns to a nonpolitical career).

Conservative Republicans also pushed for term limits because, before 1994, Democrats had controlled the House for forty years. Because it is often difficult to defeat incumbents in an election, term limits seemed the only viable option to open more seats for Republicans to capture. In 1994, many Republicans running for Congress called for congressional action on term limits. A number of them made a term-limit pledge, promising to serve no more than three terms. But in 1995 the US Supreme Court declared that states could not limit the terms of members of Congress. Therefore, the only way to institute congressional term limits was a difficult one—a constitutional amendment. A subsequent effort to propose such an amendment failed by sixty votes in the House, and the Senate never voted on the measure. However, many Americans continue to support the idea of term limits.

> ### Incumbents
> Rarely are members of Congress who seek reelection defeated. In the past half century, more than eighty percent of Senators and more than ninety percent of House members won their reelection bids.
>
> Why? Name recognition, ability to raise funds, media exposure, voter appreciation for assistance requested from congressional staffers, and ability of members of Congress to obtain federal funds for their states are a few of the reasons incumbents fare well in their reelection campaigns.

1994 Congressional Elections

In the 1994 midterm (nonpresidential) elections, the GOP won a majority in the Senate and took control of the House of Representatives (by winning fifty-two seats in that body). A key reason for the victory was the Contract with America, which nationalized otherwise local congressional races. The Republicans' strategy set a standard for midterm elections by demonstrating that national issues might motivate voters in races for Congress.

What Was the Contract with America?

Republicans presented the Contract with America as a policy statement during the 1994 congressional election campaign. It functioned the way a party platform does during a presidential election. Most Republicans serving in Congress and running for Congress supported the measure. It clarified the differences between Republicans and Democrats and contributed to the Republican victory in Congress in 1994, which resulted in the first Republican House since 1955. The handiwork of Republican leader Newt Gingrich, the Contract with America offered "a detailed agenda for national renewal." It attacked big government and big spending. Its major goals for the first day of the 104th Congress included the following:

- "cut the number of House committees, and cut committee staff by one-third"
- "limit the terms of all committee chairs"
- "require a three-fifths majority vote to pass a tax increase"
- "require all laws that apply to the rest of the country also apply equally to the Congress"
- "select a major, independent auditing firm to conduct a comprehensive audit of Congress for waste, fraud or abuse"

Congressional Terms

Guide a discussion about why the framers instituted two-year terms for House members and six-year terms for senators. Perhaps divide the class into two parts, one for the House and one for the Senate, and ask the following questions:

1. What were the historical reasons for the length of terms? Why would the framers be thinking about such lengths in the late eighteenth century? Would serving two years make House members closer to the people and the public's (sometimes) shifting views? Did the framers want senators to have a more long-term perspective to protect the nation from abrupt changes? Would the Senate then provide more stability?

2. Were the framers of the Constitution careful to prevent America's government from becoming tyrannical, like monarchies in Europe?

3. What are the problems with these term lengths? Are House members constantly campaigning and raising money? Do some senators become too aloof from their constituents?

Term Limits

Discuss arguments for and against term limits. Also discuss the importance of wisdom. For instance, Scripture teaches the importance of placing skilled, wise people in government (see Gen. 41:33; Exod. 18:21; 1 Chron. 26:28–32). Often, wisdom and skill come through experience. Some of the necessary experience for wise legislators comes from fields outside of government, but it is often developed by years of government work. Scripture also warns against corruption in government (Exod. 18:21; Ps. 94:20). Sometimes this corruption manifests itself as legislators seek to acquire more power or to protect their positions.

Women in Politics in Other Countries

In the United States, women could vote in national elections beginning in 1920. This was about the same time that women gained the right to vote in many other countries—though in Switzerland, women could not vote until 1971. Until the 1970s, few women held political office in westernized countries. The women's movement, however, changed that situation in most nations (Japan being the notable exception). Scandinavian countries have had many women serve in representative assemblies and in executive branches. For example, in Norway during the 1980s, 35 percent of the parliament was female, and eight of the eighteen members of the cabinet were women.

For many years, the United States and Great Britain lagged behind many European countries in terms of including women in national politics. However, Margaret Thatcher served as Great Britain's prime minister from 1979 to 1990, and Theresa May held that position from 2016 to 2019.

Among advanced countries, Japan has had the fewest women serve in national government. Japan ranked 165th out of 193 countries in the *Women in Parliament in 2018* report published by the Inter-Parliamentary Union. In that year, 10.2 percent of Japanese House of Representatives lawmakers were female. The report found that the proportion of female members in national parliaments around the globe had increased from 11.3 percent in 1995 to 24.3 percent in January 2019—yet Japan still remains below the 1995 level.

Perquisites

Americans have criticized Congress for its perquisites, commonly called "perks," which are additional benefits that senators and representatives receive by virtue of their office. In 1789, members of the first Congress received $6 a day; the Speaker received $12 a day. In contrast, salaries are now $174,000 a year for House and Senate members; $223,500 for the Speaker; and $193,400 for majority and minority leaders. Critics argue these officials are overpaid; however, considering the high cost of living in Washington, DC, and the high incomes of lobbyists and attorneys, many Americans view congressional pay as reasonable. Members of Congress also have a **franking privilege** (free postage) and allowances for staff, offices, and travel. House members have an average of seventeen full-time staff members; senators have an average of forty-four. Each official's aides and offices (one in Washington and one or more in his home district or state) help the official do his job, which includes casework for constituents. For example, if a constituent has a problem with Social Security, he may solicit help from congressional staff.

Senator Bernie Sanders visiting Afghanistan in 2011

Abuse of the congressional travel allowance often gets unfavorable attention. At times, members of Congress go on trips overseas to gather useful information for debating legislation. Many of these trips can be helpful, but others are unnecessary. Critics dismiss them as **junkets** (seemingly unnecessary trips). Taxpayers are billed for what is sometimes little more than a vacation when leisure activities are the focus more than gathering facts to craft wise legislation.

Members of Congress also enjoy other important benefits. For example, they have a generous pension plan, in addition to their participation in the social security program. But some benefits are intangible. For example, members of Congress gain recognition for federal funds—either grants or contracts—that they bring to their districts; and as government officials, they have regular access to the media, which grants them free publicity. Such publicity may help them gain funds for campaigns. And all members of Congress have power and influence within their own districts and states because of their position in Washington.

Congressional Sessions
Numbering

The first Congress met on March 4, 1789, in New York City. It remained in existence for two years—the length of a House member's term. At the end of that period, the terms of every House member and the term of one-third of the senators expired. The second Congress, elected in 1790, replaced the first Congress and that Congress met for the first time in 1791.

Congresses are numbered each time a new House is elected and the first meeting of the new Congress is always in an odd-numbered year. For example,

Caseworker

Contact the local district office of a member of Congress, and speak to a staff member that deals with constituent services. Such staff illustrate probably the most practical way that a member of Congress can serve the residents in his area. The requests for help are numerous and varied. They range from seeking aid for a grandfather whose Social Security benefits are incorrect, to attempts to secure a flag that flew over the Capitol, to inquiries about a high-school student seeking an appointment to a military academy. Invite one of the staff members to your classroom or to participate in a video conference with the class.

Junkets

Select a student or a group of students to find examples of extravagant junkets and other types of wasteful spending by government officials. Invite the students to present their findings to the class.

Power and Money

Power and money are two forces at work in Washington. Some members of Congress begin with the best intentions of public service yet later succumb to the temptations accompanied by these two forces and, as a result, ruin their lives.

These temptations should not prevent Christians from seeking to become public servants, but Christians should be aware of the potential problems, establish safeguards, and be willing to deny themselves even legitimate power and wealth if they are concerned about the pitfalls each may present. Discuss the kinds of safeguards a Christian public servant should employ to guard himself from these temptations.

the members of the House of Representatives elected in 2016 made up the 115th Congress and those elected in 2018 comprised the 116th Congress. Each Congress lasts for two years and physically convenes (in what is called a session) at least once a year, as the Constitution requires (Article I, Section 4).

Convening

The Congress under the Articles of Confederation provided that the new Congress under the Constitution would meet on March 4, 1789. Thereafter, the Congress elected in November would begin its term a few months later, in March. However, the new Congress was not required to assemble until the first Monday in December—that is, thirteen months after being elected. Travel and communication took a great deal longer in the eighteenth century, and newly elected members needed time to get their affairs in order.

Thus, when the Congress met in December of even numbered years (after a November election), it included members who had been defeated a few weeks earlier and members who had not sought reelection. Such meetings of Congress were called lame-duck sessions. The Twentieth Amendment, ratified in 1933, ended that problem by moving the presidential inauguration from March 4 to January 20 and moving the first session of the newly elected Congress to January 3. When the amendment was ratified, there was great urgency for Congress to convene because of the Great Depression, but the amendment was too late for the 1932–33 period. The revised schedule for a new Congress, to meet in January of odd numbered years, began in 1935. The new inauguration day for the president took effect in January 1937.

Section Review

1. How does the census affect the composition of Congress?
2. What are some major differences between the House of Representatives and the Senate?
3–6. Explain the significance of each of the following Speakers: Frederick Muhlenberg, Henry Clay, Sam Rayburn, and Nancy Pelosi.
★ Why are the majority leader in the Senate, the Speaker in the House of Representatives, and the whips in both houses important to the political process?
★ How has the role of women in Congress changed during America's history?

II. Legislative Workings

Committees

"Congress in committee is Congress at work," said future president Woodrow Wilson when he was a student in graduate school examining this vital part of the national legislative process. Committees are basic to making laws, which is the main power given to Congress by the Constitution. Committees and subcommittees permit Congress to consider a vast number of proposals. Of those, some will be rejected; but many will be debated, refined, and then sent to all the members of Congress for consideration. Those that pass and are signed by the president become law.

Guiding Questions

1. What are the purposes and types of congressional committees?
2. What is the process for passing bills in the United States Congress?

Edmund Burke on Representatives

Burke's remarks given below clearly reflect a biblical worldview regarding government.

> Certainly, gentlemen, it ought to be the happiness and glory of a representative to live in the strictest union, the closest correspondence, and the most unreserved communication with his constituents. Their wishes ought to have great weight with him; their opinion high respect; their business unremitted attention. It is his duty to sacrifice his repose, his pleasures, his satisfactions, to theirs; and above all, ever, and in all cases, to prefer their interest to his own. But, his unbiased opinion, his mature judgment, his enlightened conscience, he ought not to sacrifice to you, to any man, or to any set of men living. These he does not derive from your pleasure; no, nor from the law and the constitution. They are a trust from Providence, for the abuse of which he is deeply answerable. Your representative owes you, not his industry only, but his judgment; and he betrays, instead of serving you, if he sacrifices it to your opinion.
>
> —Edmund Burke, *The Works of Edmund Burke*

Section II Objectives

1. Analyze the purposes and types of congressional committees.
2. Explain the processes for passing bills in the United States Congress.

Section Review Answers

1. It causes reapportionment, in which district lines are redrawn to reflect population changes; the census can change the number of representatives from each state. (pp. 168–69)
2. Answers should be based on the table on page 173 of the student text, called "Differences Between the House and the Senate." (p. 173)
3–6. Muhlenberg was the first Speaker; Clay was the first powerful Speaker; Rayburn was the longest-serving Speaker; and Pelosi was the first female Speaker. (pp. 173–74)
★ The majority leader in the Senate controls the flow of legislation there; the Speaker of the House presides in that chamber and makes decisions about legislation, debate, and service on committees. The whips assist majority and minority leaders by communicating with party members about legislation and encouraging their attendance during key votes. They also try to unite party members behind the party's position on specific bills.
★ The first woman to serve in the House of Representatives began her first term in 1917; thus, for more than a century of our nation's history there were no women in Congress. The first woman to serve in the Senate was appointed in 1922 but only served for a day. The first woman was elected to the Senate in 1932. Eventually more women were elected to Congress, and now there are well over one hundred serving in the House of Representatives and the Senate.

Watergate and Congress

A major catalyst for exposing the wrong-doing of the Nixon administration was the Senate Select Committee on Watergate, which held televised hearings watched by millions of Americans. Senators, like many other Americans, were disturbed about stories linking the White House to crimes that interfered with the 1972 election —a June 1972 break-in at the Democratic Party's Washington headquarters at the Watergate complex, illegal campaign contributions, and other crimes.

Former attorney general John Mitchell acknowledged meeting three times before the break-in with those involved. White House lawyer John Dean, a star witness, then pointed to involvement of key officials in the executive branch. White House aides gave contradictory testimonies as they continued to cover up the scandal.

The most dramatic testimony, however, came in July 1973 when Alexander Butterfield, a White House aide, revealed that conversations in the Oval Office had been taped since early 1971. Those tapes became the center of a legal battle between Nixon, who did not want them used as evidence, and the special prosecutor, who did. In July 1974, the Supreme Court ruled in favor of the special prosecutor. In that same month, the House Judiciary Committee approved three articles of impeachment against the president. Nixon, sensing the inevitable, resigned from the presidency the following month.

The Senate Select Committee on Watergate and the House Judiciary Committee played a key role in ending the presidency of Richard Nixon. Not since Reconstruction had Congress struggled so successfully against a presidency. Separation of powers worked.

Types of Committees

There are four types of committees in Congress: standing, select, joint, and conference. **Standing committees** are permanent committees that are generally more powerful than other types of committees. The most important standing committees are those dealing with finances and legislative procedures. Currently, there are twenty standing committees in the House and sixteen in the Senate. Subcommittees divide a standing committee's work into manageable parts. Members of a subcommittee work on bills; hold hearings; listen to experts testify about proposed bills; and, with the approval of a majority of the subcommittee, report bills to the full committee for further action.

Select committees are created for a specific purpose, generally to investigate a particular problem, and are therefore usually ad hoc (i.e., temporary). (Exceptions include the permanent Senate Select Committee on Indian Affairs and the House Select Committee on Intelligence.) For example, the House of Representatives created the Select Committee on Energy Independence and Global Warming in 2007. It was disbanded in 2011. The House also created a select committee in 2014 to investigate a terrorist attack on the US diplomatic mission in Benghazi, Libya, that resulted in the death of the US ambassador there and three other Americans. The committee ceased functioning in December 2016 after issuing its final report. Probably the most important Senate select committee was the Select Committee on Presidential Campaign Activities (the Watergate Committee) that existed 1973–74. Its investigation into the burglary of the Democratic National

Standing Committees of the 115th Congress (2017–19)			
House committees	**Number of members**	**Senate committees**	**Number of members**
Agriculture	46	Agriculture, Nutrition, and Forestry	21
Appropriations	52	Appropriations	31
Armed Services	62	Armed Services	27
Budget	36	Banking, Housing, and Urban Affairs	25
Education and the Workforce	39	Budget	23
Energy and Commerce	55	Commerce, Science, and Transportation	27
Ethics	10	Energy and Natural Resources	23
Financial Services	60	Environment and Public Works	21
Foreign Affairs	47	Finance	27
Homeland Security	30	Foreign Relations	21
House Administration	9	Health, Education, Labor, and Pensions	23
Judiciary	41	Homeland Security and Governmental Affairs	15
Natural Resources	44	Judiciary	21
Oversight and Government Reform	41	Rules and Administration	19
Rules	13	Small Business and Entrepreneurship	19
Science, Space, and Technology	37	Veterans' Affairs	15
Small Business	23		
Transportation and Infrastructure	61		
Veterans' Affairs	24		
Ways and Means	39		

Who Gets the Bill?

Because students learn much from role playing, instruct them to pretend that they are the Speaker of the House of Representatives. Ask them to imagine that a member of Congress has introduced a bill on a certain subject and that they (the Speaker) must decide which committee will receive the bill. (Since 1995, when Newt Gingrich became Speaker, the Speaker has determined which committee gets each bill.)

Instruct the students to decide which committees will be assigned bills dealing with the following subjects. (See the table on page 178 of the Student Edition that lists standing committees for the 115th Congress.)

1. Constructing new railroad tracks for Amtrak from Richmond, Virginia, to Houston, Texas (*Transportation and Infrastructure*)

2. Granting $50 million for research into additional uses for cottonseed oil (*Agriculture*)

3. Adding staff members to the offices of federal district judges (*Judiciary*)

4. Granting $25 million for research on predicting droughts in the United States (*Science, Space, and Technology*)

5. Exempting companies with twenty-five or fewer employees from inspections by the Environmental Protection Agency (*Small Business or Energy and Commerce*)

6. Restoring diplomatic relations with Iran (*Foreign Affairs*)

7. Abolishing the Internal Revenue Service (*Ways and Means*)

Committee headquarters in June 1972 and related matters was a major factor in the eventual resignation of Republican President Richard Nixon in August 1974.

Joint committees are usually permanent committees composed of members from both the House and the Senate. They generally serve as advisory boards to other congressional committees, particularly on tax matters, but they possess little real power beyond their recommendations.

Conference committees are ad hoc committees drawn from both chambers that meet to devise a compromise regarding different versions of a bill, or proposed law, that emerged from both houses. Although short-lived, these committees are generally successful in getting conference agreements passed by both houses.

Committee Powers

Committees often have life-and-death power over a bill. Because committees (small groups) are designed to represent the Congress at-large, they have great power. For example, if the Republican Party holds 55 percent of the seats in the House, then approximately 55 percent of most House committees must be Republican. Although committees are to reflect the balance of Congress, definite tendencies and interests can make committees anything but representative and unbiased. People usually work better with matters that interest them or promise them a return, and members of Congress are no different. For this reason, many urban representatives seek committee posts concerning housing and government services, and many westerners can be found on committees that deal with water projects and land management.

Advantages of Committees

Although committees cannot provide flawless representation, they do provide certain advantages to Congress. First, they permit Congress to increase its workload and to give more careful attention to proposals and their merits. Committees and subcommittees act as a filter through which bills must pass on their way to becoming law. Each year, thousands of bills, or measures, are introduced, but most do not survive committee scrutiny. In each Congress, which meets for two years, approximately 8,000–10,000 bills are introduced. Typically, only about 5 percent are enacted.

Second, the committee approach encourages expertise in a particular area. Learning much about a subject can make a member of Congress an asset in shaping laws.

Committee Members

In both chambers, each party's selection committee determines who will serve on the committees. Members of Congress typically seek committee assignments that correspond to their expertise or interest (e.g., someone who is in business might want a seat on the Commerce or Small Business Committee) or that allow them to help their constituents in some way. (For example, if a military base is located in a member's district or state, he might want to be on the Armed Services Committee.) Each member is entitled to one committee assignment; however, House members average one to two standing committees, and senators

---

History of Committees in Congress

The framers of the Constitution did not mention congressional committees, but there was considerable historical precedent for their existence. The British Parliament had committees as did both the Confederation Congress and the Continental Congress. John Witherspoon, a minister from New Jersey and a signer of the Declaration of Independence, served on more than 100 committees during his years in the Continental and Confederation Congresses.

Activity 2: Your Representative's and Senators' Committee Assignments

Through this activity, the students learn about their representative in the US House and their two US senators and the committees on which they serve.

Christians and Government

Divide the students into groups that function like committees (e.g., groups on agriculture, appropriations, energy, and natural resources). Provide the groups with a set of possible topics that they can use to each write a bill they will present to the class. Ask them to imagine that they are Christian legislators, and ask them to explain how their Christian worldview affects the bill they propose. For example, for a bill that would allow more oil drilling on federal land, they should explain why Christians would be concerned about conservation, job creation, less expensive energy for the poor, and other topics.

Incumbency

As mentioned in the "Incumbents" margin box on page 175, members of Congress who seek reelection are rarely defeated. How does this affect government? Is this tendency good?

Critics note that incumbency sometimes prevents Congress from adjusting quickly to the people's changing demands. Also, they argue that the longer someone serves in that body, the easier it becomes to be aloof from the people in the district represented. Furthermore, a sense of security might lead to wrongdoing. Sometimes involvement in scandal might be the only reason why an incumbent fails to be reelected.

However, there are positive aspects to the fact that most members of Congress have held their positions for multiple terms. Policy development is complicated; thus, having experienced people in Washington helps to simplify the process. Furthermore, some continuity is important to maintain a stable political system.

A Representative's Interests and Committee Assignments

Congressman John Duncan Jr. represented the Second District of Tennessee from 1988 to 2019. Duncan's early committee assignments in the House of Representatives are a good case study in how needs and interests are often matched in those appointments.

Duncan served on the Committee on Transportation and Infrastructure and on three of its subcommittees. He was chairman of the Subcommittee on Highways and Transit. He was also a member of the Subcommittee on Water Resources and Environment and the Subcommittee on Aviation. He also served on the Committee on Natural Resources and was a member of the Subcommittee on National Parks, Forests, and Public Lands.

Several facts about Duncan's district reveal the reason for his interest in these committees and subcommittees. The Second District encompasses much of East Tennessee, which is served by three major interstate highways (I-81, I-40, and I-75) as well as by I-640 around Knoxville, the largest city in the eastern third of the state.

In addition, McGhee Tyson Airport, in Knoxville, is the air transportation hub of East Tennessee and that city is home to the headquarters of the Tennessee Valley Authority (TVA). One purpose of TVA is to conserve and wisely use water resources in the Southeast. The Second District also includes the Tennessee portion of the Great Smoky Mountains National Park.

Thus, Duncan's committee assignments complemented both his interests and the concerns of his constituents.

Congressman Duncan, seated second member from the left

average three to four standing committees. Members with seniority (i.e., the longest continuous service) generally have priority and tend to receive choice assignments, leaving new members with fewer options.

Chairmen, or **chairs**, of congressional committees have significant powers, though those have been reduced in recent years. For example, committee chairs have a major voice in deciding which bills the committee will consider, the order in which the bills will be discussed, whether a hearing will be held, and whether witnesses should be called to testify about a matter. In addition, the chair manages debate regarding a bill and has much control over the expenditures of the committee. The chair also selects subcommittee chairmen and recommends majority-party members for conference committees.

Traditionally, the chair was the committee member of the majority party who had the greatest seniority. In 1995, however, when Republicans took over the House, important changes were made to committee leadership. Of course, chairmen were still members of the majority party, but no one could serve as a committee chairman for more than three consecutive terms, or six years, and chairmen could not chair their own subcommittees. Seniority continued to be a factor in determining House committee chairs, but it was not the only consideration. Nevertheless, committee chairmen have remained powerful. In the Senate, however, members with the greatest seniority in the majority party still typically serve as chairmen.

The Role of Members of Congress

Discuss the difficulties that a representative or senator faces in trying to represent his constituents properly. Political scientists argue that a member of Congress—or any other representative—acts either as a delegate (votes the way the constituents want) or as a trustee (votes in a way that he thinks is best). The issue at stake is an important one, reaching to the heart of republican (representative) government. Almost every member of Congress acts partly as a trustee but most often as a delegate (doing otherwise would certainly decrease their reelection chances).

Making Laws

Congress's chief constitutional function is to make laws. Those laws affect Americans' daily lives. A member of Congress receives proposals for laws from a variety of sources—the president, committees in Congress, bureaucrats, interest groups, as well as ordinary citizens. Only a House or Senate member, however, can officially submit a **bill**, or proposed law, to Congress. A bill must overcome many hurdles and very few will become law. It is relatively easy to defeat a bill because of the numerous opportunities to do so.

"No legislation for the Union can be safe or wise, which is not founded upon an accurate knowledge of [the] diversities [among the various states], and their practical influence upon public measures. What may be beneficial and politic, with reference to the interests of a single State, may be subversive of those of other States."

—Supreme Court Justice Joseph Story

Basically, three steps are required for a bill to receive congressional approval.

1. A standing committee in both the House and Senate must approve the bill.
2. Both chambers approve it on the floor. (Each chamber might word the bill differently.)
3. If there are differences between the two versions of the bill, a conference committee must resolve them, and its report must be accepted by both houses.

The House and the Senate have similar procedures, and the same bill is usually introduced simultaneously in both places if cosponsors can be found in both chambers.

Introducing a Bill

The first step in a bill's progress to become law begins when a member of Congress introduces the bill; often, several members will cosponsor it to show its broad support. Next, the clerk of the House or Senate gives the bill a number, preceded by "H.R." for the House and "S." for the Senate (e.g., "H.R. 432" means that a bill was the 432nd bill proposed in that session

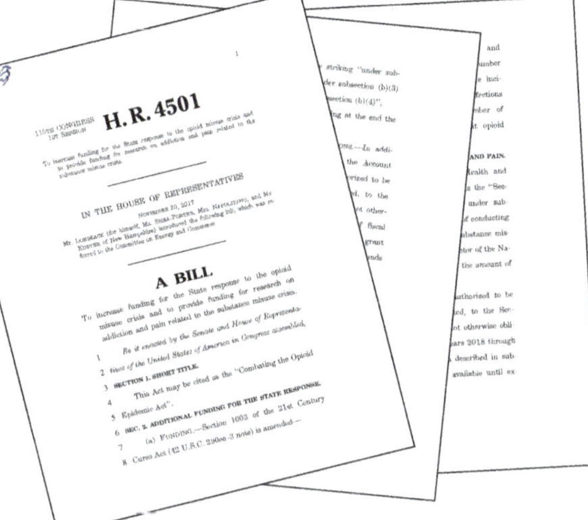

The Hopper or the Clerk?

In the House, a bill is officially introduced when a representative places it in the hopper (a container on the side of the clerk's desk). Of course, the House must be in session; but no permission is needed to present a bill and no statement or speech must be given on the House floor when a bill is presented. The bill then moves to the proper committee.

In the Senate, however, senators introduce bills by giving them to clerks at the presiding officer's desk. This action can be done with or without comments from the Senate floor. If no one objects to a bill, the bill goes to a committee; however, if a senator objects, the bill can be introduced the following day.

Congressman Richard Nixon (left) shown placing a bill in the hopper in 1947

THE STRUCTURE OF CONGRESS • 181

Senate and Confirmation

The Senate controls the fate of nominations made by the president. Responses to those nominations vary. For example, John Tyler failed to obtain approval for four of his five Supreme Court nominees, but Franklin Roosevelt appointed nine men to the Supreme Court without a single rejection by the Senate.

In Chapter 14, we will provide details regarding the Senate's rejection of Ronald Reagan's Supreme Court nominee, Robert Bork, in 1987. Bork, a conservative, was attacked by liberals, who mounted a campaign to prevent his confirmation. (In fact, since then, any presidential nominee who faces strong opposition and questionable attacks is said to be "borked.") Democrats in the Senate were slow to act on George W. Bush's judicial nominees, even on those that were female or Hispanic, because they asserted that some of the nominees were too conservative.

Mock Senate

Refer to page 489 of the Teacher Edition for information on conducting the activity "Mock Senate."

Planned Delay

Thomas Jefferson, in a letter to George Washington, once wrote, "Delay is preferable to error." Discuss that quotation in relation to the legislative process.

Activity 3: A Bill Becomes Law

This activity helps the students understand the process whereby a bill becomes a law.

Celebrities in Congress

Polling data confirms the belief that name recognition is an important factor in getting elected. Some candidates spend millions of dollars in advertising to increase their name recognition. Therefore, it should be no surprise that celebrities, people already famous in nonpolitical fields, are often successful in politics.

Former astronauts John Glenn and Harrison Schmitt were elected to the Senate, and Jack Swigert, another astronaut, was elected to the House but died a week before being sworn in. And show business produced congressmen such as Sonny Bono, who served in the House, and Fred Thompson and Al Franken, who served in the Senate. Thompson is an unusual case: he became famous as a Republican counsel for the Senate Select Committee on Watergate. Then he appeared in several Hollywood films and television programs before serving as a senator from Tennessee from 1994 to 2003.

Athletics also produced several members of Congress including football players Jack Kemp, J. C. Watts, and Steve Largent; football coach Tom Osborne; and basketball players Bill Bradley and Tom McMillen.

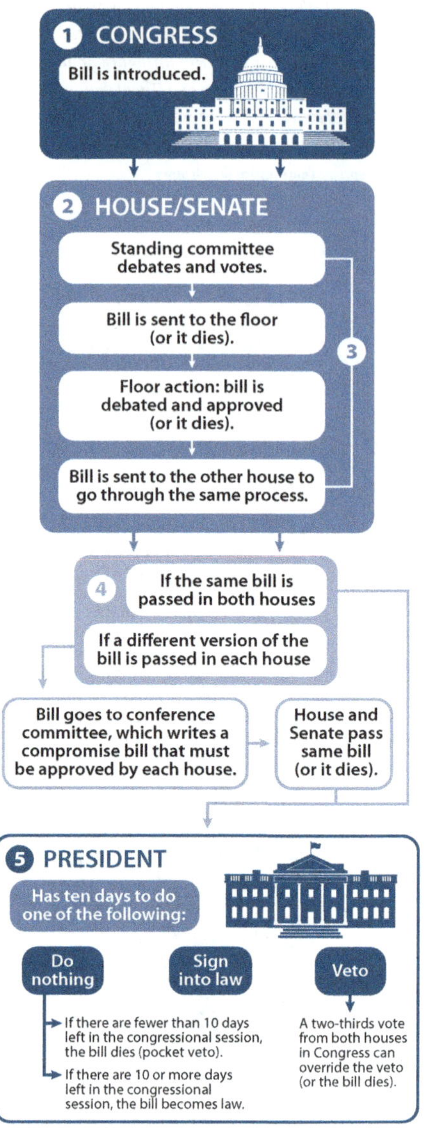

of the House). Congressional staff then print the bill, distribute it, and send it to the appropriate committee(s).

Committee Deliberation

Once in a committee, a bill is typically referred to a subcommittee, which researches it. Sometimes public hearings are held at which witnesses for and against the bill speak. Lobbyists, experts on the topic, and average citizens are among those that may testify. After the hearings, the subcommittee makes changes in the bill, if desired, and then votes on it. If the bill passes, it goes to the full committee, which also votes on it. If the bill is rejected by either the subcommittee or the full committee, the bill is dead. But if it passes both, it advances to the next step.

Full Chamber Vote

Action on the House or Senate floor varies in each chamber. In the House, the Rules Committee must approve the bill, provide the rules for debating it, decide if it may be amended, and schedule a time for considering it on the floor. The only exception is a budget bill, which does not go to the Rules Committee.

The House has four regular ways to vote:
- the voice vote as a group—the Speaker calls for the "ayes" (all members who support the bill answer together) and then the "noes" (all opponents of the bill answer together), and the Speaker announces the result
- the division vote (members in favor stand and are counted; then those opposed stand and are counted)
- the voice vote as individuals, or
- the record vote (electronic).

The record vote is used only if forty-four members want the vote recorded. Each member goes to one of the voting stations, inserts a card that identifies him, and then presses the button that indicates the way he wants to vote. Members' votes appear beside their names on an electronic "scoreboard" above the press gallery. A green light appears if a member votes yea, and a red light if he votes no. The totals of ayes and noes appear on electronic screens on either side of the chamber.

Less frequently used is the teller vote. In this instance, members of the House walk past tellers, or counters, and their votes are recorded.

The Senate uses voice votes or, if eleven senators support the method, roll-call votes, in which

What Makes Good Legislation?

Guide a discussion about characteristics that distinguish good legislation from bad legislation. Discuss not only issues such as moral rightness, constitutionality, and fairness but also qualities such as simplicity, clarity, and brevity.

Mention that bad legislation includes such weaknesses as inclusion of many unrelated issues and often appeals to the emotional rather than the logical. Furthermore, it often embraces bureaucratic red tape, legalese (language intended to confuse), and is excessively lengthy (which causes many, or even most, representatives to not read such a bill before voting on it).

Discuss how Congress can avoid bad legislation and emphasize that good legislation should be based on the biblical purposes of government.

the clerk calls the roll, calling out each of the one hundred senators' names. Each senator responds verbally when his name is called.

Congress has an elaborate system of lights, bells, and buzzers that, in various combinations, communicate important messages to members throughout the Capitol. These messages include quorum calls, which try to gather the minimum number of members needed to conduct official business; calls for voting; indications that a session has adjourned or is in recess; and indications that Congress is in session. Especially important since the terrorist attacks of September 11, 2001, is a new warning system to indicate an emergency.

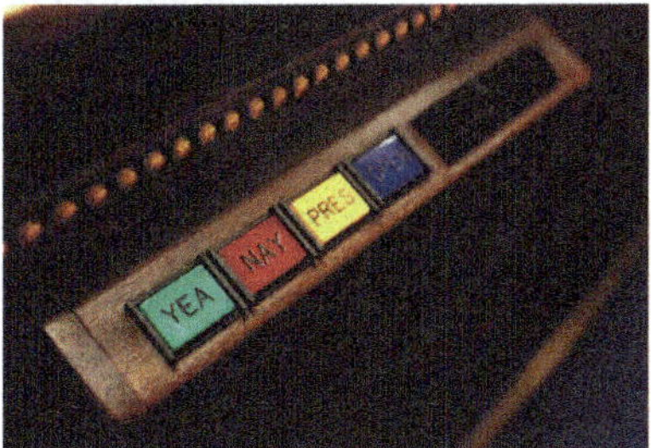
One of the electronic voting devices used by House members

To speed up floor debate on a bill, the House can organize itself into a Committee of the Whole, meaning that it can debate the bill with only one hundred members present. Debate is limited by time, given the size of the House. Members debate the bill on the floor, add amendments (if the Rules Committee allows them), and then vote on the bill. If it passes, it is sent to the Senate (unless it has already been introduced there).

In the Senate, the process moves more slowly. A senator may request an anonymous hold, or a notification, before a certain bill is taken to the Senate floor. This request means that Senate leadership and the bill's sponsor might face opposition from this senator, who might eventually **filibuster** the measure (delay or prevent it through long speeches). The original purpose of a hold was to allow a senator extra time to research the legislation at issue and to consult others when a bill affected his state's interests. Before 1999 such holds were secret, which made them even more powerful. In 2007 the Senate voted to amend its rules to publicize the names of senators placing holds if their holds were not withdrawn within two days; it also voted to limit senators' ability to place anonymous holds. In later Congresses, holds were placed on two-thirds of bills approved in committees. Holds, like filibusters, can be defeated through a successful **cloture** (or limiting debate) motion, which stops debate.

A filibuster is a more formal way of preventing or delaying the passage of a bill. Unlike in the House, where time allowed for debate is limited, debate time in the Senate is unlimited, so opponents of a bill can try to "talk it to death" through long speeches. Filibusters became common in the mid-1800s during Senate debates over slavery. A senator may delay a vote on a bill simply by talking. He may even read from a phone book or other material unrelated to the subject of the bill. Typically, a team of senators will take turns to keep the filibuster going. The longest speech by an individual filibustering senator was that of South Carolina senator Strom Thurmond. In 1957 he spoke for twenty-four hours and eighteen minutes to filibuster a civil-rights bill. In 1964 a group of senators filibustered for eighty-two days. Often, the mere threat of a filibuster will discourage senators from pursuing a particular piece of legislation. Filibusters can be broken only if sixteen senators sign a motion to invoke cloture. Then sixty senators must vote to end debate. If cloture is passed, there can be no more than thirty additional hours of debate on a bill. Thus, a bill needs at least sixty senators to support it for it to progress smoothly through the Senate chamber.

Strom Thurmond

Activity 4: Chapter Review

Use this activity to help the students prepare for the chapter test.

Clinton v. City of New York

Clinton v. City of New York was the court case that led to the Supreme Court's striking down the line-item veto. New York City and healthcare providers, joined by Idaho farmers' cooperatives, filed suit against President Clinton over a tax benefit that he vetoed. The court, by a vote of 6–3, ruled that the line-item veto was unconstitutional. Justice John Stevens declared in the majority opinion that the president has no authority "to enact, to amend, or to repeal statutes."

Conference Committee

Before a bill can be sent to the president, the House and the Senate must produce identical bills. Therefore, after the bill clears both the House and the Senate, it begins the third step toward becoming law—entering the conference committee. In the conference committee, any differences between the two versions of the bill are resolved. The conference committee is composed of a few members from the original committees from both chambers. They devise a compromise on the content of the bill. If the committee members cannot agree, the bill dies. If they do agree, the revised bill is sent back to both houses for approval. At this point, the conference version cannot be amended in either the House or the Senate. If the bill fails to pass in either house, it dies. However, if both chambers pass the bill, it is sent to the president for his approval or veto.

Presidential Signature

The remaining hurdle for a bill to become law is the president's action once the bill is presented to him. He has four options:

1. He can sign the bill, making it law.
2. He can **veto** the bill, killing it. (Congress can override the veto if two-thirds of its members vote for the measure.)
3. He can ignore the bill, but if Congress is in session the bill becomes law within ten days.
4. He can "pocket veto" the bill. If Congress is not in session during the ten days that the president has the bill and if he does not sign it, the bill dies. This is called a **pocket veto**, and it discourages Congress from hastily "stuffing the pocket" of the president with bills at the end of a session. Congress cannot override a pocket veto. The bill may be reintroduced in the next session, but it will have to go through the whole process again.

For a short time, presidents had a fifth option—the line-item veto, which allowed them to veto part of a bill without vetoing it entirely. Congress passed a measure authorizing this option in 1996, and President Bill Clinton exercised the line-item veto eighty-two times before the Supreme Court declared it unconstitutional in 1998. In a 6–3 decision, the Court said that the line-item veto violated the separation of powers because it gave the executive branch some lawmaking power. Only Congress can make laws; a president has to respond to legislation from Congress in its entirety.

President Trump signing the Tax Cuts and Jobs Act in December 2017

Section Review

1–4. Identify the four types of congressional committees and describe the function served by each.

5. What is Congress's chief constitutional function?

6–8. Explain the three basic steps required for a bill to receive congressional approval.

★ Why are committee chairmanships important?

★ Read the quote by Supreme Court Justice Joseph Story on page 181. Explain his statement. Do you agree or disagree?

Legislating from the Bench

Discuss the Supreme Court's decision to eliminate the line-item veto. Could the justification cited by the court also be used to attack judges' practice of "legislating from the bench," which is used by both Supreme Court justices and subordinate judges?

Section Review Answers

1–4. standing committees: permanent and the most powerful; select committees: temporary and created for a specific purpose, usually to investigate a problem; joint committees: usually permanent and composed of members of both houses to advise other committees; conference committees: temporary, drawn from both chambers, and created to devise compromises on bills that have passed both chambers in different forms (pp. 178–79)

5. to make laws (p. 181)

6–8. (a) must receive approval of a standing committee in both the House and Senate; (b) must receive approval of both chambers; (c) and must have any differences between the House and Senate versions of the bill resolved by a conference committee (and the revised bill approved by both chambers) (pp. 181–84)

★ Committee chairs have a major voice in deciding which bills the committee will consider, the order in which the bills will be discussed, whether a hearing will be held, and whether witnesses should testify. In addition, the chair manages debate and has much control over the committee expenditures. He also selects subcommittee chairmen and recommends majority-party members for conference committees.

★ Students may mention that legislation should account for the many differences among states without giving preference to one state. Some will agree that all states should be considered when making laws. Others may prefer to highlight issues in their state of residence or may insist that the more populated states should have more influence.

Making Connections

1–10. Identify the ten leadership positions in the House and the Senate.

11. Who was the first Speaker of the House of Representatives?

12. Which representative served longest as the Speaker of the House?

13. Who was the first female Speaker of the House?

14. What is the function of standing committees in the congressional legislative process?

Developing Civics Skills

1. Do you favor term limits for members of Congress? Defend your answer.

2. Prepare a diagram detailing how a bill becomes a law. Note at what point citizens have the opportunity to respond to a bill.

Thinking Critically

1. Who do you think is more powerful: a representative in the House or a member of the Senate? Defend your answer.

2. Discuss the pros and cons of filibustering in the Senate.

Living as a Christian Citizen

1. In a two-party political system that tends toward gridlock, what biblical principles should a Christian legislator consider to determine how to work with the opposing party?

2. If a legislator opposes legislation that is very popular with the nation as a whole or with the people of his constituency, should he vote with his conscience or should he reflect the will of those whom he represents in Congress?

People, Places, and Things to Remember

bicameral
census
reapportionment
gerrymandering
congressional district
single-member district
at-large
Seventeenth Amendment
coalition
caucus
conference
majority leader
majority whip
minority leader
minority whip
president pro tempore
Speaker of the House
term limits
franking privilege
junkets
standing committees
select committees
joint committees
conference committees
chairs
bill
filibuster
cloture
veto
pocket veto

is taken; (d) sent to a conference committee (if approved by both houses but with differences); and (e) sent to the president to be signed or vetoed (if the final form of the bill is approved by both houses). Citizens can support or oppose a bill from its inception by contacting members of Congress and later the president. If citizens feel that a law is unconstitutional, they can challenge it in the court system (all the way to the Supreme Court).

Thinking Critically

1. A representative typically has fewer people in his district (than a senator), has more direct and regular contact with constituents, and may serve on multiple committees. A senator is one of only 100 rather than one of 435; enjoys a statewide constituency and the accompanying publicity; has greater opportunities for extended, in-depth debate on bills; and may also serve on multiple committees.

2. Filibustering allows senators additional time to research and consider legislation, and it prevents them from making laws rashly. It is a tool that can be used against abuses by those that control a majority of the Senate. However, it slows business and can prevent or delay the Senate from dealing with important issues. It can be used as a partisan, political way of repeatedly blocking the will of the majority.

Living as a Christian Citizen

1. If the opposing party proposes immoral legislation, a Christian legislator should not support it. Scripture clearly teaches that governments should support good and restrain evil (Rom. 13:3–4). A legislator should work with the opposing party if its legislation upholds biblical morality. Christians should serve "not with eyeservice, as menpleasers; but as the servants of Christ" (Eph. 6:6). Christian legislators can show love for their neighbors both in the legislation they support and in their relationships with those of differing political beliefs (Luke 6:35; 10:27).

2. Some will say the legislator should vote with his conscience and be prepared to accept the political consequences (Acts 4–5). Others will argue that he should support the views of his constituents as long as those views do not violate scriptural principles.

CHAPTER REVIEW ANSWERS

Making Connections

1–10. House: Speaker, majority and minority leaders, majority and minority whips. Senate: majority and minority leaders; majority and minority whips; and the vice president. (p. 172)

11. Frederick Muhlenberg (p. 173)

12. Sam Rayburn (p. 173)

13. Nancy Pelosi (p. 174)

14. Committees give a small number of congressmen the opportunity to discuss and debate various issues about legislation and hear testimony for and against proposed legislation. (p. 178)

Developing Civics Skills

1. Some will say the Constitution already allows citizens to remove elected officials by voting them out of office. However, others will argue that the process is largely ineffective because of the advantages of incumbency. Others will oppose term limits because they know of effective officials currently serving who would be prevented from running again if term limits were in place.

2. A bill is (a) introduced in either the House or the Senate; (b) sent to a committee, where testimony is heard and the bill is debated; (c) referred to the full chamber (if approved by the committee), where it is debated and a vote

1. Analyze the uses of Congress's enumerated powers.
2. Describe the implied and nonlegislative powers of Congress.
3. Explain the powers denied to Congress.
4. Evaluate the criticisms of Congress.

THE POWERS OF CONGRESS

9

The people are responsible for the character of their Congress. If that body be ignorant, reckless, and corrupt, it is because the people tolerate ignorance, recklessness and corruption. If it be intelligent, brave, and pure, it is because the people demand those high qualities . . .

—James Garfield

Democratic US Senators Elizabeth Warren from Massachusetts and Chuck Schumer from New York

I. **Enumerated Powers**

II. **Implied and Nonlegislative Powers**

III. **Denied Powers**

IV. **Congressional Criticism**

BIG IDEAS

1. How does Congress use its enumerated powers?
2. What are the implied and nonlegislative powers of Congress?
3. Which powers are denied to Congress?
4. Are the criticisms of Congress valid? Why or why not?

SUGGESTED MATERIALS

Section I
- *United States History* Student Edition, Fifth Edition; BJU Press
- Worksheets about national debt
- Worksheets about *Gibbons v. Ogden*
- Activities 1–2 from Chapter 9 of the *Student Activities*
- Special speakers (see pp. 193 and 196)

Section II
- Video of House or Senate proceedings

Section III
- No materials

Section IV
- Activities 3–5 from Chapter 9 of the *Student Activities*

Teacher Resources
Visit TeacherToolsOnline.com for resources to enhance the lessons.

I. Enumerated Powers

The most important and obvious power of the legislative branch is the power to make laws. The House and the Senate share this power. Specific powers given to Congress in Article I, Section 8, of the Constitution are **enumerated powers**—that is, listed powers. Through the years, Congress has grown more powerful, largely at the expense of the state legislatures.

Financial Powers: Clauses 1, 2, 5, and 6

Article I, Section 8, of the Constitution gives Congress one of the most significant governmental powers: the power to tax. Because the War for Independence was set in motion largely by Parliament's attempts to tax the colonies, the founders ensured that all revenue bills would originate in the House of Representatives, the branch of Congress closest to the people. In practice, the distinction made little difference because the House and the Senate frequently consider tax policy simultaneously and both chambers must approve all bills before they can become law.

The first clause of Article I, Section 8, deals with taxes and explains why they are necessary: "to pay the debts and provide for the common defence and general welfare of the United States." The question of debts was a critical issue

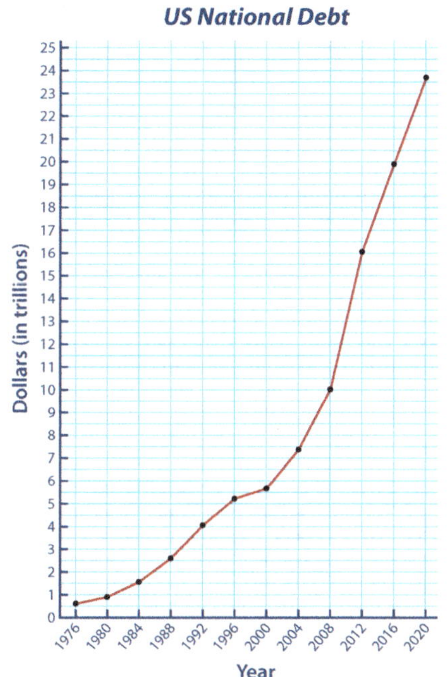

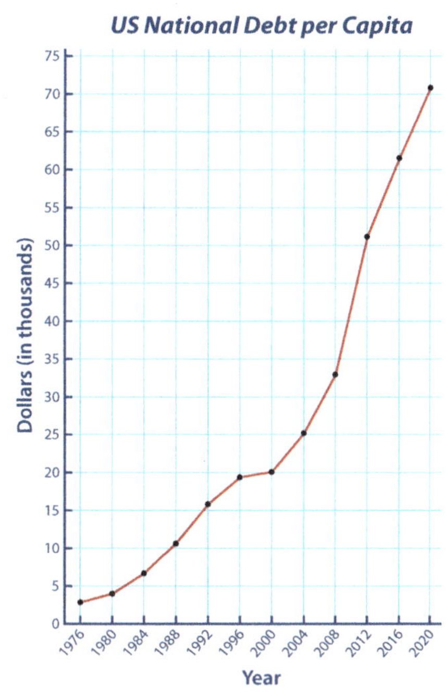

National Debt and the Early Republic

The national debt has been a serious issue from the very beginning of the nation. In 1790, divisions about how to handle it contributed to the development of political parties.

Alexander Hamilton, secretary of the treasury under President Washington, favored funding the federal debt (which was carried over from the Confederation and the Revolutionary War) at face value. In practical terms, this meant that the government paid Americans who owned government bonds. The matter quickly became controversial because many ordinary Americans, needing their money quickly, had already sold their bonds below face value to speculators, who had anticipated that the government would redeem the bonds at face value. The original owners wanted the government to reimburse their losses, but Hamilton noted that tracing all the sales of the bonds would be impossible. Also, failing to pay the current bondholders the full price would be a breach of contract. And Hamilton knew that establishing trust in the nation's financial promises was important to the success of the young nation.

James Madison, however, wanted the original owners, many of them farmers and soldiers, to receive a larger share in the payment program. The fact that most of the debt was owed to northerners also bothered Madison. Nevertheless, Hamilton's plan prevailed.

Taxes and the New Testament

Instruct the students to review the following references to taxes in the New Testament: Matthew 17:24–27; 22:17–22 (see the parallel passages in Mark 12:14–17 and Luke 20:22–26); Luke 23:2; and Romans 13:6–7. Remind the students that context is important in determining what the verses teach. Direct the students to list recurring themes (e.g., pay taxes and submit to government) and any misconceptions concerning taxes. Encourage the students to apply the verses to today's society.

Colonial Taxation

Provide a copy of *United States History* Student Edition, Fifth Edition; BJU Press. Direct a student to turn to the chapter on Independence (Chapter 6), list the various taxes that the British levied against the colonists in the years leading to the War for Independence, and present the taxes to the class. Discuss how responses to these taxes might have influenced the way the Founding Fathers planned the powers of Congress. How does the slogan "No taxation without representation" help people understand Article I, Section 8, of the Constitution?

US National Debt Clock

Find links to current information on the American national debt, as shown by a debt clock. Provide worksheets that contain the following questions and instructions:

1. Look at the website on three different days during a five-day period. By how much did the amount of debt increase or decrease?
2. To whom or to what is most of the national debt owed? (See p. 188 of this text.)
3. What is the difference between the national debt and the budget deficit?
4. After looking at the website's debt clock, describe in a paragraph the growth of the debt over time.

State Debts

Another issue facing the new nation was state debts from the War for Independence. Hamilton proposed that the federal government assume these debts. Generally, southern states had paid much of their debts, but New England states had large unpaid sums and therefore would benefit most from federal payment of their financial liabilities. Again, Madison—being from Virginia, where debts were smaller—fought Hamilton on this issue. In the end, Hamilton compromised. The agreement was that southern states would support Hamilton's debt-assumption program if the new capital would eventually move to the South, on the Potomac River.

Economy in the 1780s

Not all the economic problems in the 1780s were the fault of the Confederation government. Independence from Great Britain meant not only political separation but also disruption of foreign trade. America had to find new markets for its goods, and foreign trade declined temporarily, causing hardship for merchants.

Once the War for Independence was over, trade between the United States and Great Britain improved. And by the late 1780s, Americans discovered new markets in Europe, Africa, and Asia, particularly in China. By 1790 Americans developed important industries, such as shipbuilding, iron making, and textile manufacturing.

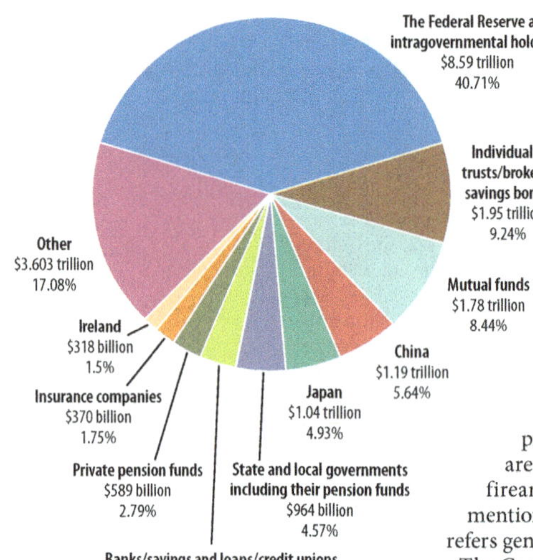

during the first few years of the new national government. During George Washington's first term as president, his secretary of the treasury, Alexander Hamilton, proposed the controversial financial plan that the national government assume federal and state debts. This proposal passed and placed the country on a sound financial footing. In the centuries that followed, however, national debt was an important political issue, especially after the 1980s, when the debt increased dramatically.

Article I, Section 8, also lists some taxes called "duties, imposts and excises." A **duty** is a tax on select imports (goods coming into the country from other nations). **Excises** are taxes on the nation's internal production, sale, or use of items and on certain business practices. Many of these are "hidden taxes" because they are paid by producers who then figure them into the price that a customer is charged. Today, excise taxes are collected on such items as gasoline, tobacco, alcohol, firearms, telephone services, and airline tickets. *Imposts*, mentioned in Article I, Section 8, is related to duty and refers generally to import and export taxes.

The Constitution stipulates how taxes are to be applied. Article I, Section 8, clause 1, says that taxes must be "uniform throughout the United States." All sections of the country have to be taxed the same. Such "direct" taxes, mentioned in Article I, Sections 2 and 9, must be levied or administered based on population and evenly distributed throughout the country, requiring everyone to pay the same amount. However, the **Sixteenth Amendment** instituted the income tax. Ratified in 1913, it allows Congress to tax the income individuals receive. If someone makes more money, he typically pays more taxes.

The power of Congress to impose tariffs (duties) on goods imported to the United States has sometimes been controversial. In the early years of the nation, tariffs not only generated most of the government's revenue but also increased the price of imported goods. Disagreement over tariffs flared and helped spark the Civil War. Nineteenth-century farmers, especially Southern cotton farmers, disliked the fact that the foreign goods they purchased were being taxed to support Northern industry. Since that time, lawmakers have periodically used tariffs to protect domestic industries against foreign competition by raising the price of foreign goods. Such attempts to protect American-made products by raising the price of imports to consumers still generate considerable passion. Thus, many Americans favored the **North American Free Trade Agreement (NAFTA)**, which was first implemented in 1994, because it eliminated many tariffs on Canadian and Mexican goods entering the United States. However, others strongly objected to the legislation. In the 2016 election, candidate Donald Trump called it, "the single worst trade deal ever approved in [the United States]." He claimed the agreement caused the loss of hundreds of thousands of American manufacturing jobs to Mexico and he committed to renegotiating it. In late 2018, President Trump announced that the United States-Mexico-Canada Agreement

Creating the Euro

Just as the United States created a single currency with the dollar, the European Union (EU) introduced the euro in 1999 and began to circulate it in 2002 to facilitate trade among member nations. To create the euro, European countries had to submit their monetary policies to the European Central Bank. Unwilling to surrender such sovereignty, the United Kingdom refused to abandon the pound for the euro. Denmark, one of the original EU members, also did not use the euro. As additional members have joined the EU, some have chosen not to use the euro. Invite students to research the European Union. What countries have adopted the euro? What is the current exchange rate between the US dollar and the euro? What is Brexit? What is the status of Brexit? (Chapter 13 provides some information on the subject, but the students will also need to obtain more current details.)

(USMCA) would replace NAFTA. Trump said the new trade arrangement reached by the three nations was more economically favorable to the United States than NAFTA.

Like clause 1, clauses 2, 5, and 6 deal with the fiscal (financial) powers of Congress. Clause 2 gives Congress the power to borrow money. Given the national debt (it exceeded $23 trillion by 2020), that power has been exercised frequently. The United States borrows from other countries, private banks, and individuals (through sale of bonds).

Clause 5, which gives Congress the power to coin money and regulate its value, has been controversial as well. During the Civil War, millions of "greenbacks" (unsecured paper money) were printed by Congress to help pay for the conflict. Although paper money was once again backed by gold and silver during the late nineteenth century, in 1934 the Supreme Court ruled that Congress had the power to eliminate the gold standard. This initiated an era of fiat money (paper money whose value depends on the trustworthiness of the government that issues it). Clause 6 gives Congress the authority to punish counterfeiters.

Together, clauses 1, 2, 5, 6, and 18 give Congress enormous fiscal powers. Over the years, government officials have interpreted these clauses to mean that the government has power to create a national bank that states cannot tax and to create a Federal Reserve System.

Congress is also authorized (in clause 1) to provide for the "**general welfare** of the United States." James Madison maintained that this phrase simply allowed Congress to spend what was necessary to execute its other constitutional powers. Alexander Hamilton, however, argued that the clause gave Congress additional powers to tax in order to provide additional revenue for the government. Hamilton's view has prevailed.

Though few individuals enjoy paying taxes, doing so is essential. Ensuring justice, providing for national defense and public safety, addressing poverty, promoting moral behavior, and providing order—all obligations of the government to those it governs—require money. Taxes are the primary means for the government to raise the necessary funds.

Commercial Powers: Clause 3

Regulation of commerce (the buying and selling of goods) has been a central issue throughout most of American history. During the colonial period, British control of trade often led to conflict and helped lead to the War for Independence. The

In this 2014 photo, demonstrators oppose NAFTA (on right) and the Trans-Pacific Partnership (TPP) trade deal (on left).

"Legal Tender"

To the left of the portrait of George Washington on a dollar bill is an important statement: "This note is legal tender for all debts, public and private." *Legal tender* means that the government declares the bill to be money and requires that people accept it in payment for debts, whether owed to the government (public) or to individuals or businesses (private).

The statement originally said much more: "This note is legal tender for all debts, public and private, *and is redeemable in lawful money*" (italics added). That last phrase meant that a bank was required to give the bearer of a dollar bill one dollar's worth of gold or silver. Once the United States eliminated the gold standard, it removed that phrase.

Today, a dollar bill is worth intrinsically the value of the ink and paper that compose it. However, because that piece of paper has been declared "legal tender," it is worth whatever the market economy declares it to be— that is, whatever goods or services people will exchange for it. As is true in every country, each bill is backed only by the government's word and people's willingness to accept it.

NAFTA

Today, trade legislation provokes economic and political fights that are similar to those waged over tariffs from the 1790s to the early 1930s. The North American Free Trade Agreement (NAFTA), passed in 1993, is a good example of such legislation. The first Bush administration negotiated a trade agreement with Canada and Mexico to reduce trade barriers and to stimulate trade in North America as the European Union did in Europe. NAFTA was planned to create the world's largest free-trade zone.

Nevertheless, NAFTA revived old debates about the tariff. Bill Clinton, like earlier Democrats, favored low tariffs (and thus NAFTA) which would increase American exports and therefore aid American industry. Many American businessmen also favored the trade agreement, but others opposed it. For instance, some American companies, such as textile manufacturers, worried about competition from cheaper foreign goods. American labor unions also feared that companies seeking cheap labor would relocate to Mexico, taking jobs with them. Even some conservatives, such as Pat Buchanan, opposed NAFTA.

In 1993, the odd coalition of some Democrats and many Republicans made NAFTA law. In the late twentieth century, free trade and regional trade arrangements, like the European Union and that in the Pacific Rim, proved controversial. Tariffs and other trade barriers declined with the rise of globalism.

As noted on pages 189 and 321 of this text, in late 2018 the Trump administration negotiated the United States-Mexico-Canada Agreement (USMCA) to replace NAFTA. Congressional approval is required before the new agreement can be implemented.

The Internet and Clause 3

Examine how the internet has affected congressional and state efforts to regulate commerce. The popularity of e-commerce websites has raised novel issues. To start the discussion, ask a student who is familiar with a commercial website (e.g., eBay or Amazon) to explain how it operates. Discuss some of the following points:

1. Should customers pay sales tax on online purchases? If so, to what government—city, county, state, or national?

2. Should government regulate what is sold online? For example, people have tried to sell kidneys for transplant on eBay.

3. Why have some governments been reluctant to regulate and tax the internet? What is making such taxation more desirable? (*budget deficits and growing national debt*)

4. How does technology affect the issue of taxing and regulating the internet? (*The mechanics of such regulation and taxation can be difficult.*)

5. How successful have e-commerce ventures been? (*After the first frenzied years of e-commerce, the "dot-com bubble" burst; many internet companies declared bankruptcy. Amazon did not become profitable until after fourteen years of existence. As more of these companies become successful, governments have become more interested in taxing them.*)

Industrial Republic?

Beneath the battle for a stronger central government lay the tension between Americans who favored an industrial nation and those who wanted an agrarian one. Alexander Hamilton desired an urban, industrial nation and a strong central government to regulate commerce. Business would thrive, he argued, with a stable economy that had one set of laws and regulations. *Gibbons v. Ogden* (1824) marked a victory for that ideal.

Jefferson, however, held a competing vision for America. He believed that the farm was the source of "the good life" and that local power at the county level, not a strong central government, was most important. He also believed that planters could rule wisely and that some cities were corrupt and had some shiftless people who owned no property and who could be manipulated by politicians. But Jefferson's view declined in America during the latter half of the nineteenth century, when the Industrial Revolution changed America dramatically. By 1920, the census declared America more urban than rural.

From a biblical point of view, Jefferson's ideas that cities were often corrupt and that the farm was the source of the good life disregarded the biblical teaching that depravity resides in the hearts of all people, regardless of environment. Indeed, some of the planters in whom Jefferson placed his trust were entangled in the great national sin of slavery. However, Jefferson's concept of localized, diversified government fits with a biblical recognition of human fallenness and thus emphasizes the need to limit power.

inability of the Articles of Confederation to regulate trade among the states helped lead to the convening of the Constitutional Convention, which developed the new national government. The framers, therefore, intended the Constitution to deal in part with the issue of commerce. Soon, controversy arose over how much power to give Congress. Northerners, representing shipping and merchant interests, wanted the new government to have broad powers. But southerners feared that laws favoring the North would give northerners a competitive advantage over foreigners and that southerners would have more trouble getting their agricultural products to market. Southerners also worried that commerce laws might permit federal interference with slavery. As a result, southerners wanted it to be more difficult for Congress to regulate commerce. They were appeased when the representatives banned export taxes, did not interfere with the practice of slavery, and delayed the end of the slave trade for twenty years.

In the landmark case **Gibbons v. Ogden** in 1824, John Marshall, speaking for a unanimous Supreme Court, gave Congress broad power to regulate **interstate commerce** (commerce between or among the states). In the case, the Court debated whether the state of New York or the US government could regulate trade between New York and New Jersey. Thomas Gibbons had a federal license for trade, and Aaron Ogden's authority came from the New York legislature. Although the Supreme Court left undefined the overlapping powers of the state and federal governments to regulate commerce, it ruled that the federal government has the right to regulate interstate commerce. The Court's decision was popular with many because it ended state trade monopolies and allowed the United States to become a large free-trade zone. However, critics argued it strengthened the federal government at the states' expense.

By the mid-twentieth century, Supreme Court decisions had so expanded Congress's power to regulate interstate commerce that virtually any economic activity, including intrastate commerce (commerce within a state), came under Congress's control. In 1942 the Supreme Court ruled in *Wickard v. Filburn* that even economic activity that is not "commerce" (e.g., a farmer's keeping

Gibbons v. Ogden

Assign the students to research *Gibbons v. Ogden* using the internet and books such as Kelly, Harbison, and Belz's *The American Constitution*; John R. Vile's *Essential Supreme Court Decisions*; and Lawrence M. Friedman's *A History of American Law*. An excellent video is "Gibbons v. Ogden" in the *Equal Justice Under Law* video series (Films for the Humanities & Sciences, 1987; 29 minutes). Distribute worksheets about *Gibbons v. Ogden*, and instruct the students to provide the following information about the case:

1. Historical context: Who were Gibbons and Ogden? What were the facts in the case? What was the legal issue? (*Ogden had a steamboat monopoly granted by New York State; Gibbons challenged it, citing a federal law.*)

2. Verdict (*unanimous in favor of Gibbons*)

3. Author of the opinion (*Chief Justice John Marshall*)

4. Any famous quotations from the decision (*Marshall said that the power of Congress under the commerce clause included "every species of commercial intercourse."*)

5. Significance (*continued Marshall's emphasis on a strong national government*)

his wheat for personal consumption rather than selling it) still affects commerce because its absence in the market affects prices and market conditions.

Defense and Military Powers: Clauses 10–16

Although clause 1 mentions that Congress can tax "to provide for the common defence," Congress's specific military and defense powers are found in clauses 10–16. In ordaining human government, the Lord provided a means for ensuring order and security. When the government of Israel was established, God made provision for the military (Deut. 20). Israel was unique in being commanded to conquer the Promised Land, but it was not unique in having a military (Luke 3:14; Acts 10:1–2).

Clause 10 gives Congress power "to define and punish piracies and felonies committed on the high seas, and offences against the law of nations." This clause authorizes Congress to legislate in the area of international law. Through legislation, Congress may prevent someone from breaking the law of another nation while he is in the United States. For example, Congress has made it illegal to counterfeit foreign currency in the United States. This clause also empowers Congress to establish a military commission for prosecuting war crimes.

Clauses 11–16; clause 18; and Article II, Section 2, clause 1, constitute the **war power** of the national government. This war power is perhaps the single greatest authority given to the national government. Some constitutional scholars argue that the power would exist even if it were unmentioned in the Constitution because each government has a basic right to defend itself.

In clause 11, Congress is given the right to declare war. Nevertheless, because the American president serves as commander in chief, disagreements have arisen over Congress's role in wartime. Most American wars have not been declared by Congress, beginning with an undeclared naval conflict with France (1798–1800). Even the most deadly of all American wars, the Civil War, was not declared, and no wars since World War II have been officially declared by Congress. In the aftermath of the Vietnam War, Congress tried, ineffectively, to restrict presidential war making with the **War Powers Act** (1973). Basically, this measure requires that the president notify Congress within forty-eight hours of committing US troops to military action. He must withdraw such troops after sixty days unless

The President versus Congress

The Cold War changed the way Americans fought wars: presidents often seized the initiative from Congress. The president's ability to act quickly and decisively was used as an argument for moving away from congressional leadership and toward executive leadership in fighting wars. This argument gained credence during the Cold War, when the threat of nuclear war was constant.

After 1945, Soviet forces were taking over Eastern Europe, and President Harry Truman wanted to stop the spread of communism. In 1947, Truman appeared before Congress, not to ask for a declaration of war but to request economic aid for non-Communists in Greece and Turkey. Also, he wanted congressional approval to send Americans to train Greek and Turkish military forces. Congress agreed, and the Truman Doctrine was born. America would aid nations struggling against communism. In this case, containment worked: America's allies in Greece and Turkey won.

A precedent for entering a war by presidential action came a few years later. In 1950, Communist North Korea invaded South Korea, and the United Nations Security Council called for a military response to Communist aggression. Although the UN acted, the Korean War was mostly an American enterprise, and US General Douglas MacArthur was initially in charge. Never before had an American president committed so many troops without a congressional declaration of war.

Current Military Actions

Instruct the students to review newspapers, magazines, and the internet for one example in the news of the United States' current foreign military involvement. Discuss past military involvement in Afghanistan, Iraq, and Korea. America's commitment will probably continue for some time in those places.

Direct the students to answer the following questions about the conflict:

1. How did the trouble start?
2. What are the issues involved?
3. How did America get involved? Did involvement begin because of presidential action?
4. What are America's national interests in the conflict? (*oil, weapons of mass destruction, terrorism, etc.*)
5. Does Congress or the United Nations approve of America's involvement?
6. Do America's allies approve?

Waging War

Guide a discussion about the power to begin a war. As noted in the text, most American wars began with presidential actions rather than by declarations of Congress. Why is this true? Do you think this violates the stipulations in the Constitution? Do you think that lack of direct action by Congress increases or decreases the likelihood of a just war? Why?

Activity 1: War Powers Resolution

In this activity the students answer questions about sections of the War Powers Resolution to enhance their analytical skills.

Louisiana Purchase

Arguments regarding the powers of each branch of government date back to the early years of the nation. For example, the greatest accomplishment of Thomas Jefferson's presidency was the Louisiana Purchase. With this acquisition, the size of the United States more than doubled. Nevertheless, the matter was a problem for Jefferson: the Constitution did not specifically grant the national government power to purchase territory. At first, Jefferson hoped that a constitutional amendment might solve his problem, but he realized that obtaining ratification would take too long (and Napoleon might withdraw his offer).

Eventually, Jefferson agreed with his advisors that the power to make treaties could cover the purchase of territory. In reality, Jefferson's action was expedient: the Louisiana Territory was such a bargain that Jefferson felt differences of constitutional interpretation could not be allowed to impede it.

Wartime Priority—Defense or Civil Rights?

Historically, on America's home front during wartime, the Supreme Court has allowed certain economic and personal freedoms to be curtailed because of the necessities of war. For example, businesses may be heavily regulated, and freedom of speech may be curtailed.

One of the greatest violations of rights in American history occurred during World War II when Japanese Americans were sent to "relocation centers" because of their alleged threat to national security. That action was defended under the war power of the national government and upheld by the Supreme Court—until after the war ended.

In 1988, Congress passed, and President Ronald Reagan signed, legislation paying surviving detainees $20,000 each in redress for their relocations. They were also issued a formal apology. Later amendments provided additional funds for that purpose. In 1991, President George H. W. Bush stated, "The internment of Americans of Japanese ancestry was a great injustice, and it will never be repeated."

More than 120,000 Japanese Americans were placed in internment camps. This one was located in Arkansas.

Congress specifically approves continued use of those forces. The constitutionality of this law remains a matter of dispute.

Of course, Congress can also show its displeasure with undeclared wars by limiting spending and investigating these wars. However, critics note that such actions tend to hurt only the troops, not the president.

Clause 11 also mentions two technical matters related to military action. A **letter of marque** is a license granted by a nation to a private citizen, allowing him to capture merchant ships of another nation. (Letters of marque have not been used in the United States for more than two centuries.) **Reprisal** is a nation's retaliation against another nation when provoked; it might involve seizing property or people. The final portion of clause 11 gives Congress power to deal with prisoners of war. Clauses 12–16 complete the description of Congress's military power.

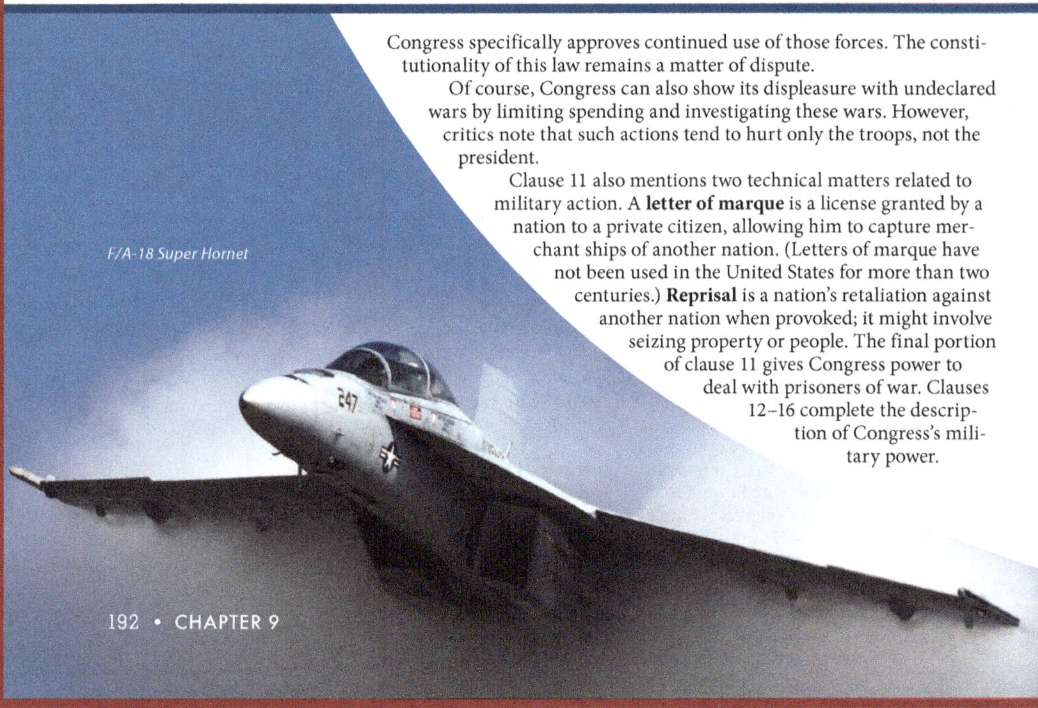

192 • CHAPTER 9

Jubilee

Government decrees, such as those mentioned in this chapter, have been issued for centuries by various nations. Scripture provides an example of a decree that provided release from financial and labor obligations. Have the students read and study Leviticus 25, and discuss the year of jubilee with them. The Lord said that after "seven sabbaths of years" (seven times seven years, or forty-nine years), Israel should observe the jubilee year in the fiftieth year. There were three aspects of this observance.

1. The land and the people were to rest—that meant no sowing or reaping.
2. Land that had been sold because of economic need was to revert without payment to the original owner (some exceptions are mentioned in Leviticus 25).
3. Israelites who had sold themselves into servitude because of economic need were to be freed, along with their children. The implication was that if debtors in bondage were released and their land was returned to them, their debt in general was also forgiven.

Ask the students to suggest practical reasons for the jubilee and discuss spiritual lessons that can be derived from it. Possible answers are as follows:

1. Practical: Rest for the land (conservation) and the people
2. Practical: Opportunity for financial recovery, no matter how desperate a person's situation
3. Practical: Similar to bankruptcy in modern times
4. Spiritual: Reminds us that loving our neighbors as ourselves (Lev. 19:18) has financial components. We should be willing to forgive others' debts under certain circumstances.
5. Spiritual: Reminds us of the greatness of God's love for us. If we find it difficult to forgive debts, we should consider how much God forgave each Christian (cf. Matt. 18:23–35).

Other Powers

Naturalization and Bankruptcies: Clause 4

Clause 4 lists two unrelated provisions—naturalization and bankruptcies; the only element uniting them is the adjective *uniform*, which applies to both. The first sentence of the Fourteenth Amendment clarifies this clause: "All persons born or naturalized in the United States, and subject to the jurisdiction thereof, are citizens of the United States and of the State wherein they reside." The Fourteenth Amendment's main purpose was to handle issues regarding the newly freed African Americans after the Civil War.

Citizenship (belonging to and enjoying all the privileges, rights, and duties as a member of a nation) is granted automatically to those born in the United States. This idea goes back to the feudal law of the Middle Ages and, more specifically, to British common law. The Supreme Court even ruled that children born in the United States to temporary residents are citizens, unless the parents have diplomatic status. Congressional law also grants citizenship to children born outside the United States if one or both parents are US citizens. And in 1924, Congress conferred citizenship on Native Americans who were born in the United States.

Through legislation, Congress has regulated the process whereby foreigners, or aliens, become naturalized citizens. In 1798 the Federalists in Congress, fearing French and Irish immigrants who were tending to vote as Republicans, placed restrictions on immigrants. After heavy immigration from southern and eastern Europe in the late nineteenth and early twentieth centuries, Congress significantly restricted immigration in the 1920s. In 1952 Congress prohibited

Nationalism and Immigration

What is nationalism? It is a political ideology that is based on the premise that an individual's loyalty and devotion should be to his nation or nationality. Is nationalism good or bad? It can be either. Christians should value and seek to preserve all of the good aspects of their nation. This exercises wisdom (Phil. 4:8) and results in gratitude. Furthermore, distinct nations or people groups will last for eternity (Rev. 7:9; 21:24–26). However, Christians should avoid any nationalism that tends to see other ethnic groups as the root of problems within the world or within one's country.

How does one's view of nationalism affect one's attitude toward immigration? Extreme nationalists, with their view of other groups as inferior, would oppose virtually all immigration, but doing so requires one to ignore Jesus' parable of the good Samaritan. In that story, He teaches love for the often despised foreigner. The image of God in all people reminds the Christian that all cultures have positive contributions.

Of course, it is not wrong to set limits on immigration in order to preserve some level of cultural stability. In addition, immigrants are expected to obey the laws established by the nation.

Many argue that a balanced view of devotion to one's nation helps strengthen and unite a country while accepting those in great need and providing them opportunities they would not otherwise enjoy.

A Biblical View of Nations, Nationalism, and Immigration

Nations are part of the order that God established (Acts 17:26) and will continue to exist for all eternity (Rev. 21:23–24, 26; 22:1–2).

The Bible mentions people with varied ethnic backgrounds forming a new group with a cohesive culture (Gen. 24:4; 28:5; 41:50; 46:10; Exod. 12:38; Num. 12:1; Deut. 26:5; Ruth 4:18–22). In fact, the Old Testament model was to permit high levels of immigration (2 Chron. 2:17–18) but to expect high levels of assimilation (Lev. 16:29; 17:15; Num. 19:10; Deut. 14:21).

The Scriptures present the forming of people into nations as a good thing that reflects creational norms. However, it rejects ethnic chauvinism or racism.

Immigration

Discuss current problems regarding immigration. Distinguish between legal and illegal immigration and examine the biblical attitude toward immigrants. Refer to the Lord's instructions to Israel in Exodus 22:21 and Deuteronomy 10:17–19.

Remind the students that racism is wrong and that Christians are all one in Christ (Gal. 3:28). But also note how legal and illegal immigration must be handled if order and security are to be maintained. If you know people whose families immigrated to the United States in recent generations, invite them (or their parents or grandparents) to share their stories about coming to America. Consider asking them to address questions such as the following: Why did they come? How did they travel? Do they still have relatives in their homeland? How often do they return for a visit? Have they acquired or are they in the process of acquiring citizenship? What is involved in becoming a citizen? What was their greatest difficulty in adjusting to life in America?

discrimination based on race, sex, or marital status for those becoming naturalized citizens. During the Cold War, applicants for citizenship could not support or belong to groups that advocated the overthrow of the US government. During the 1960s, however, many restrictions were lifted. By the late twentieth and the early twenty-first century, the majority of the country's immigrants were coming from Asia and Latin America, rather than from Europe.

Congress has also used its power to take away people's citizenship. One can lose American citizenship, for example, by becoming a citizen of another country. In addition, Congress can exclude foreigners from the country or restrict their activities if they live in the country. In 2002 Attorney General John Ashcroft used strong measures to deport people who were believed to be terrorist threats. Of course, any law dealing with immigrants, whether they are legal or illegal, must be weighed in light of the protections and freedoms provided by our laws.

Naturalization and immigration issues have fundamentally affected American government and politics. They have changed the racial and ethnic composition of the country. Because of its heritage of immigration, America is very diverse.

Scripture teaches that nations have the right to regulate immigration and to set expectations for immigrants. But the Mosaic law also set in place protection for immigrants. It stipulated that the "stranger" (a legal immigrant to Israel) must receive equal protection under the law, fair pay, and access to the social benefits that the Israelites enjoyed. The Bible does not address illegal immigration directly, but it does teach that Christians must obey their God-ordained authorities unless those authorities' commands contradict God's stated will. The Bible also warns against treating people unjustly. In relation to immigration, this means that Christians should obey immigration laws. It also means that employers must not take advantage of illegal immigrants by viewing them as cheap laborers to whom they do not owe a fair wage. Most importantly, Christians should remember that all people are made in God's image and are therefore to be treated with love and respect regardless of their legal status.

Clause 4's **bankruptcy** provision was another attempt by the founders to promote uniformity among the states. When a debtor declares bankruptcy (his inability to pay all his debts), it is important that his assets be divided equally and honestly among his creditors. The founders understood that, without federal supervision, states might tend to liberate resident debtors from their out-of-state debts. Despite the constitutional provision that specifically gave Congress the power to make bankruptcy laws, most bankruptcy laws in the nineteenth century were state laws, occasionally modified by state and federal courts to reduce obvious unfairness. Not until 1898 did Congress pass a national bankruptcy law that lasted longer than a few years.

Mail Service: Clause 7

Alexander Hamilton expected the US Post Office to generate revenue for the Treasury. However, even when there was a surplus, Congress wisely used the money to expand the postal service to the frontiers. Although the postal system was called an "odious monopoly" as early as 1843, this government service has never been without some sort of private competition. Through the years, independent delivery companies have forced change on the government system, including a major reduction in postal rates in 1845. In 1896, rural free delivery was inaugurated to provide mail directly to farm families. Undoubtedly the advent of

Activity 2: Design a Stamp

In this activity students will design a stamp that meets the specifications of the Citizens' Stamp Advisory Committee (CSAC).

US Postal Service (USPS)

Stamp Designs

Each year the post office produces stamps with designs ranging from flowers to famous people. How are these chosen?

- Ideas for stamp designs come from the public. Any person may send a suggestion to the Citizens' Stamp Advisory Committee (CSAC) for its consideration.
- The CSAC consists of about a dozen members that are appointed by the postmaster general to help evaluate the merits of proposed design ideas.
- No topics unrelated to America are considered.
- No living person can be honored on a stamp.
- The CSAC recommends about twenty-five or thirty ideas to the postmaster general each year.

Trivia

- operates more than 230,000 vehicles

- employs about 600,000 people (making it the fifth largest employer in the country)
- operates nearly 31,000 post offices
- delivers approximately 150 billion pieces of mail each year
- handles 47% of the world's mail volume
- uses 42,000 zip codes
- receives no tax dollars (relies on the sale of postage, products, and services to fund its operation)

First-Class Postal Rates

1863–1932	2–3¢ (fluctuated)
1958	4¢
1968	6¢
1978	15¢
1988	25¢
1999	33¢
2006	39¢
2007	41¢
2009	44¢
2013	46¢
2014	49¢
2016	47¢
2017	49¢
2018	50¢
2019	55¢

(cents per first ounce for first-class mail)

email and other electronic means of communication will continue to bring more change to the postal system.

Patents and Copyrights: Clause 8

Congress's power to grant patents and copyrights is critical in a democracy. In clause 8, authors and inventors are given "the exclusive right to their . . . writings and discoveries" for "limited times." The time limit prevents Congress from using this provision to create a monopoly. Today, patents and copyrights are known as intellectual property rights. These rights have been expanded to protect photographs and movies as well as computer programs and prescription drugs.

Federal Courts: Clause 9

Clause 9 blurs the doctrine of the separation of powers. By this provision, Congress has the power to create federal courts below the Supreme Court and to provide for other aspects of the national judiciary. This clause must be examined in conjunction with Article III, Section 1, which deals with the courts. Congress has the authority to organize the Supreme Court and determine the number of

THE POWERS OF CONGRESS • 195

Patents and Copyrights

At one time, patents and copyrights applied mainly to authors and inventors, but modern technology has added new elements. Infringement issues about movies, music, software, and prescription drugs (among other things) keep lawyers and government officials busy. Two specific issues with which students will likely be familiar are music piracy and plagiarism. Discuss the widespread nature of these problems and the moral issues involved. You may broaden the discussion to include the following:

1. Should America trade with countries in which widespread piracy of American products occurs?

2. Should Christian consumers support merchants who claim to have name-brand merchandise even though lack of quality and drastically reduced prices indicate that the merchandise is probably fake?

3. How should drug companies' rights be balanced with individuals' rights? In other words, how long should drug companies have exclusive rights to an expensive patented drug when millions of sick people could be helped by a less expensive generic alternative?

Group the students. Assign each group one of the issues discussed in the questions. Instruct each group to research its topic and prepare a report detailing the problem and any proposed solutions. Suggested websites for the activity include the following:

- Office of the US Trade Representative
- Department of Justice
- US Copyright Office
- US Patent and Trademark Office
- US Customs and Border Protection
- Commerce Department and its Commercial Law Development Program
- International Trade Administration
- Department of State and its Bureau of Economic and Business Affairs

Court-Packing Plan

In the 1930s, President Franklin Roosevelt, a liberal Democrat, was frustrated because the Supreme Court had declared seven of nine New Deal laws unconstitutional. Conservative justices in the majority had argued that government's power in dealing with economic matters is limited. Roosevelt believed that the only quick way to get more liberals on the Court was to enlarge it from nine to fifteen justices. Also, he wanted to encourage justices aged seventy or older to retire.

But Roosevelt miscalculated. By implying that older justices were less capable, he offended not only the oldest member of the court—who happened to be the most liberal—but also older members of Congress. Roosevelt attacked an institution that most Americans, regardless of their political views, respected. Others feared what later presidents might try if Roosevelt succeeded with his scheme. Even many Democrats openly opposed the president on the issue.

The court-packing plan failed in Congress, but through a series of events, Roosevelt succeeded in getting the court that he wanted. One justice who had voted with conservatives switched to the liberal side, and the Supreme Court never again ruled against a New Deal program. Several retirements from the court gave the president the opportunity to appoint liberal justices. The court-packing plan damaged Roosevelt politically, but in the long run he achieved his goal of forming a court that was sympathetic to the New Deal.

Court-packing plans emerged again when Democrats suggested enlarging the court in order to appoint more liberal justices after Trump had appointed two conservative ones.

Hearing in a federal courtroom

its justices. The **Judiciary Act of 1789** provided for a chief justice and five associate justices; three circuit courts, where two Supreme Court justices served with one district-court judge; and thirteen federal district courts with one judge each. This legislation also described the judges' jurisdiction (what cases they could take and where they could operate) and operational organization and procedures. Also at this time, state courts were given the right to take some federal cases. During much of the Civil War, there were ten justices on the Supreme Court. In the late 1930s, President Franklin Roosevelt tried, but failed, to expand the number to fifteen. Today, there are nine justices on the Supreme Court, thirteen circuit courts of appeals (which are now a separate entity), and ninety-four district courts. Congress has also created other specialized federal courts, including bankruptcy courts, the Court of International Trade, the US Tax Court, and the Court of Federal Claims.

In addition, Congress has the power to determine the jurisdiction of the federal courts. The only exception is stated in Article III, Section 2, clause 2: "In all cases affecting ambassadors, other public ministers and consuls, and those in which a state shall be party, the Supreme Court shall have original jurisdiction" (serve as the trial court). Congress can also determine the appellate jurisdiction of the Supreme Court, deciding which cases the Supreme Court can hear as appeals from the lower courts.

District of Columbia: Clause 17

Clause 17 gives Congress power to govern a special district, later called the District of Columbia that would become the seat of the national government. This clause also gives Congress the power to make laws governing all other federal properties, such as forts or bases. Today, Congress's authority extends to properties such as post offices, hospitals, hotels in federal parks, and locks and dams. In 1790 Congress established the District of Columbia with land ceded from Maryland and Virginia; however, in 1846, Virginia's portion was returned to the state. Congress took more direct control of the district in 1871 when it abolished the district charter and ruled the district as a territory. The Twenty-Third Amendment, ratified in 1961, gave the district three electoral votes so that its citizens could participate in presidential elections. The next major change occurred in 1967 when Congress instituted a mayor-council form of government, which gave limited self-government to the district. The District of Columbia also has a nonvoting delegate in the House.

Today, disagreements keep the district from obtaining statehood. The District of Columbia is heavily Democratic, and Republicans are not eager to add two more Democratic members to the US Senate and one more Democratic representative to the House. Many scholars also argue that Congress does not have the constitutional authority to grant statehood to the area, since it was specifically established to serve as the seat of the national government and was designated as separate from any state. Other scholars disagree with that assessment.

Christian Attorney

Invite a Christian attorney from your church or community to speak to the students about Christians and law. The purpose of Congress is to make laws, and lawyers help people deal with laws passed by that body and other government entities. The attorney could discuss legal jargon, the importance of written law, fairness and the law, community standards, and the influence of the Bible on American law.

Necessary and Proper Clause: Clause 18

Clause 18, the **necessary and proper clause**, can be read to apply to all the previously enumerated powers in clauses 1–17; it is the basis for the extraordinary powers of Congress and the national government in general. In 1819 Chief Justice Marshall declared in the landmark *McCulloch v. Maryland* case: "Let the end be legitimate, let it be within the scope of the Constitution, and all means which are appropriate, which are plainly adapted to that end, which are not prohibited, but consist with the letter and spirit of the Constitution, are constitutional." Little wonder that this clause has also been referred to as the elastic clause. Historically, this clause has been used to increase the government's power. This clause has been a source of much debate. Early disagreement about its intent can be traced to two of George Washington's cabinet members—Thomas Jefferson and Alexander Hamilton—when they argued about the constitutionality of a national bank. Jefferson did not think the necessary and proper clause permitted the bank. It was not necessary, he argued, because there were other ways that the government could fulfill its responsibilities without creating a bank. Hamilton argued that the clause did authorize the bank. He noted that the Constitution does not say that the laws had to be "absolutely" necessary, just necessary. Therefore, if Congress believed a national bank was needed to fulfill its responsibilities, it had the power to create one.

Because of clause 18, Congress has often exercised greater power over the other branches of government. But congressional power can be limited by the Supreme Court's ability to declare acts of Congress unconstitutional.

Section Review

1. Explain why Article I, Section 8, of the Constitution is so important for Congress.

2. Describe NAFTA and explain why it was controversial.

3. From what sources does the federal government borrow money?

4. Explain why statehood for the District of Columbia is a controversial issue.

★ Using the two graphs on page 187, what are some of the conclusions you can reach concerning the national debt?

★ Why is the necessary and proper clause important?

II. Implied and Nonlegislative Powers

Implied Powers

In addition to its enumerated powers, Congress has inherent, or implied, powers (powers that are needed to exercise enumerated powers). Many of these **implied powers** come from the necessary and proper clause, and some date back to state legislatures, colonial assemblies, or even the British Parliament.

Among the numerous examples of the exercise of implied powers is the creation of the interstate highway system. Enough people questioned the constitutionality of this action that proponents of the highway bill invoked two constitutional provisions to imply that Congress has the constitutional power to build such highways: the provisions for mail delivery and national defense. Another

McCulloch v. Maryland

In 1818, Maryland passed a law taxing bank notes of the Bank of the United States. But James McCulloch, a clerk for the Bank of the United States, did not pay the tax, and the state of Maryland indicted him. McCulloch appealed to the Supreme Court, which ruled in his favor. In a landmark case for the development of national power, the unanimous court said that Congress had the power to create the national bank and that a state could not tax it. The power of the national government was supreme.

The decision echoed rhetoric of the Revolutionary War: the "power to tax involves the power to destroy." A state had deliberately tried to tax and weaken the national government, but the Supreme Court would not allow it.

Section II Objectives

1. Explain the implied powers of Congress.

2. Explain the nonlegislative powers of Congress.

3. Relate the implied and nonlegislative powers of Congress to the biblical purposes of government.

Section Review Answers

1. It clearly lists the powers of Congress. (p. 187)

2. The North American Free Trade Agreement (NAFTA) removed many of the tariffs on goods coming from both Mexico and Canada. Historically, some have welcomed tariffs to protect domestic industry against foreign competition. Others resented the tariffs, especially if it forced them to pay higher prices for US-made goods. (p. 188)

3. other countries, private banks, and individuals (through sale of bonds) (pp. 188–89)

4. The District of Columbia is heavily Democratic, and thus the Republicans are not excited about the possibility of adding more Democratic members to Congress. Many scholars argue that Congress does not have the constitutional authority to grant statehood to DC because it was established to serve as the seat of national government and designed as separate from any state. However, other scholars disagree with this assessment. (p. 196)

★ The national debt is fast increasing. If the national debt were split up among the American population, many would not have the funds on hand to pay for their portion. By 2020, the debt was more than $23 trillion dollars (nearly $70,000 per person).

★ It has been used to expand the government's enumerated powers.

The Extent of Government Involvement

American conservatives are known for preferring limited government to restrictive government and for preferring, in some cases, local government to national government. One reason for these preferences is that many conservatives view human nature as fallen. As a result, conservatives are often suspicious of sweeping plans to fix problems. While the goals of such plans might be good, worthy plans that fail to reckon with human fallenness often multiply problems rather than solve them. Conservatives prefer to make small-scale, and wherever possible, local changes. Experiments implemented on the local level affect fewer people, and successful initiatives on the local level can be adapted and implemented elsewhere.

These conservative ideas align with the biblical doctrine of original sin. They also agree with the scriptural concept that God often preserves societies from being as bad as they could be. The Fall marred, but did not eliminate, the image of God in humans (cf. Gen. 9:6). Conservatives are right, therefore, when they hold to what is good and reform what is evil rather than seeking to raze the whole structure of society. Christians should reject utopian schemes because not only do they know that no paradise will be found until the return of Christ but they also know that in a fallen world removing the constraints of custom and tradition often leads to negative change rather than positive.

Christians should be wary of the libertarian view, though it seems appealing at first glance. Libertarians believe in a limited government but sometimes to an extreme. They believe the best government provides as much liberty as possible. Thus, controlling abortion, recreational drugs,

Facebook CEO Mark Zuckerberg (top) and former FBI Director James Comey (bottom) testifying at US Senate Committee hearings

implied power is Congress's ability to pass resolutions (declarations that lack the authority of law and merely express congressional opinion).

Congress has certain implied judicial powers that are usually associated with courts. Those who violate Congress's mandates can be cited for contempt and punished, possibly with imprisonment. Congress also has power to conduct investigations. To force a person to testify before a committee hearing, Congress can issue a **subpoena** (a legal order to appear as a witness). And to encourage witnesses to give as much information as possible, congressional authorities may grant them immunity, which means that their testimonies cannot be used to charge them with crimes. Famous congressional investigations include the inquiry into the bombing of Pearl Harbor, Senator Joseph McCarthy's notorious pursuit of Communists in the government, the Watergate investigation, the probe into the 2012 attack on the US consulate in Benghazi, Libya, and those dealing with suspected Russian involvement in the 2016 presidential election.

In addition, members of Congress have a right that is usually associated with courts—some immunity from prosecution. Article I, Section 6, clause 1, states in part, "[Members of Congress] shall in all cases, except treason, felony and breach of the peace, be privileged from arrest during their attendance at the session of their respective houses." The framers of the Constitution wanted members of Congress to have as much freedom as possible when legislating.

Since Congress can wage war and the Senate can ratify treaties, the Supreme Court ruled that Congress can acquire territory and govern it. That implied power has obviously been important for America's geographical expansion. And Congress's war power has produced other significant implied powers. During Reconstruction, the Supreme Court ruled that having war power enables Congress to deal with war-induced problems in peacetime. Because any sovereign power has the authority to determine qualifications for citizenship, Congress can also, with its implied powers, produce legislation dealing with immigration and naturalization.

Nonlegislative Powers
Presidential and Vice-Presidential Elections

A seldom-used but significant House responsibility is the power to elect the president if no candidate receives a majority of the electoral votes. Under this arrangement, each state is permitted one vote. This power has been invoked on only two occasions (the 1800 election of Thomas Jefferson and the 1824 election of John Quincy Adams), but it played a role in the strategies of third parties. A third-party candidate might not be able to win, but he might win enough votes to throw the election into the House and thus obtain important concessions from the major parties in exchange for his support.

Like the House, the Senate is charged with electing a major official—the vice president—under the same circumstances. In such a case, each senator gets one vote. Only once has the Senate been required to exercise this power—in the election of 1836.

Congressional Investigation

The purpose of this activity is to show the students Congress's extraordinary powers of investigation. Propose a scandal or other problem that Congress would investigate. (Suggestions include a major company that suspiciously went bankrupt, a homeland-security failure to prevent a serious terrorist attack, a president's violation of campaign spending limits, a space-vehicle disaster, or hundreds of millions of dollars unaccounted for in a Pentagon weapons program.) Write the details so the basic facts will not change. Divide the class into three parts.

The first group will represent the Senate or House committee that investigates the scenario. It could be a select or standing committee. Students should choose a chairperson to oversee the committee and its investigation. The committee can function as a court in some ways by exercising subpoena power, calling witnesses, and citing people for contempt of Congress. The committee cannot, however, convict and sentence; instead, it seeks to discover the facts to see whether Congress can pass a law to correct the problem. This committee, in a sense, is trying to solve a mystery (what happened in the scandal and who is to blame). The committee should prepare a report addressed to Congress summarizing their findings and submitting their recommendations for congressional action.

Another portion of the class will be the accused in the case. They must devise a strategy for defending themselves. The group may select one or two individuals to be specifically accused (e.g., a company CEO or administration department head), and the others in the group can help these individuals "behind the scenes." **Members of each group must keep their group's strategies secret from the other groups.**

The final group will be witnesses, lawyers, or investigators called before the committee. Some members of this group might be senators or representatives not on the committee, while others could be private investigators for the committee. **It is critical that students in this group do not talk to those in the**

Under the **Twenty-Fifth Amendment** ratified in 1967, if there is a vacancy in the vice-presidency, the president nominates and Congress must approve a new vice president by a majority vote. This has been done on two occasions. In 1973 Gerald Ford became vice president after the resignation of Spiro Agnew. In 1974 Nelson Rockefeller became vice president after Richard Nixon's resignation led to Gerald Ford becoming the president. This amendment also provides that Congress will ultimately resolve any disputes over a president's ability to serve.

Ratification and Confirmation

The US Senate has sole responsibility in two important non-legislative areas: treaty **ratification** (formal approval) and confirmation of executive and judicial appointments. Although the president directs foreign policy, his power is checked since all treaties must be approved by a two-thirds vote of the Senate. Perhaps the most graphic example of the Senate's power in ratification was its rejection of the Versailles Treaty after World War I.

During any two-year Congress, the president nominates about four thousand civilians to offices. Most top-level executive and diplomatic positions as well as all federal judicial appointments are subject to Senate **confirmation** proceedings. This group comprises about one-third of the four thousand nominees. Most proceedings are routine, and confirmation is usually a formality, but when nominations involve top policymaking positions, appointees are subject to Senate scrutiny. Confirmation hearings often provide an opportunity for the Senate to present arguments against administration policy, even if a nominee is eventually confirmed. In recent years, growing partisanship has led to more contentious hearings.

Senate confirmation power is also influential in shaping the federal courts, including the Supreme Court, since senators have the last word on who is actually installed. As of early 2019, the Senate has rejected 37 of the president's 163 Supreme Court appointees (this includes sitting Supreme Court justices who were nominated to serve as chief justice), but only 9 of more than 700 cabinet appointees. (At least 15 other appointees withdrew from the process before a confirmation vote occurred.) Since the 1980s, Supreme Court nominations have become increasingly contentious. This was particularly true when the Senate rejected Robert Bork in 1987 by a vote of 42 for and 58 against. In 1991 Clarence Thomas was confirmed as a Supreme Court justice by a slim margin of 52–48, although opponents charged that he was too conservative. Neil Gorsuch, appointed by Donald Trump, was approved by a margin of 54–45 in April 2017. Brett Kavanaugh, another Trump appointee, was approved by a margin of 50–48 in October 2018.

Impeachment

Among the constitutional duties shared by both houses are those involving the power of **impeachment**. Impeachment (formally charging top government

Gerald Ford

Nelson Rockefeller

Neil Gorsuch

and prostitution are not the government's responsibility. However, throughout the Bible (especially in Romans 13) the Scripture is explicit that government's job is to restrain and punish evil. Though Americans who love the concept of freedom, we must understand that complete freedom is not a positive thing for society.

While limited government is a good principle, modern liberals are correct in asserting that sometimes it is best for the national government to act to either preserve the "general welfare" or establish justice. Government's protection of civil rights is an excellent example of the appropriate use of federal power to correct a serious breach in our foundational principle of "freedom and justice for all."

Clarence Thomas

Clarence Thomas's confirmation battle revealed several interesting facets of American politics. Though Thomas is an African American, leading civil-rights groups vigorously opposed his nomination because they perceived him as too conservative. This raised the question of whether ethnicity or ideology was more important to those groups. Many liberals seemed to think that it was necessary for a "real" African American to be liberal.

President George H. W. Bush believed that nominating Thomas was a smart political move. If confirmed, Thomas would replace another black Supreme Court justice, the retiring Thurgood Marshall. Furthermore, it would be difficult for Democrats to vote against Thomas because some black Americans, especially in the South, supported him.

---

other two groups except when testifying. The size of each group can be adjusted to the specific scenario, though the first group will probably be the largest. Every student should have a role.

To help the students with the activity, you might read (or have them read) about the Watergate scandal, one of the biggest scandals in American history. Keith W. Olson's *Watergate* is a good short history of it.

C-SPAN

Record about thirty minutes of House (C-SPAN) or Senate (C-SPAN2) proceedings. Show the video to provide the students at least an idea of what occurs in Congress. If possible, select a time when a major bill is being debated or perhaps a vote being taken; otherwise, the proceedings might be rather uninteresting. Alternatively, encourage students to watch C-SPAN or C-SPAN2 coverage at home. Also, the websites of both the House and Senate provide a link to webcam coverage of their proceedings that also includes previously recorded speeches and debates.

Justices Thomas and Kavanaugh

Instruct students to create two timelines (individually or in groups) showing the progression of events relating to the sexual allegations against Clarence Thomas in his 1991 Supreme Court confirmation hearings and those against Brett Kavanaugh during his 2018 confirmation hearings. Include the timing of the original alleged events as well as the events at the time of the confirmation hearings. Students should compare and contrast the two sets of events as a group or in a brief essay.

officials with "treason, bribery, or other high crimes and misdemeanors" in order to remove them from office [Article II, Section 4]) can be exercised only by the House of Representatives (Article I, Section 2). Only the Senate conducts impeachment trials, and a two-thirds vote is required for conviction (Article I, Section 3). Two presidents have been impeached: Andrew Johnson in 1868 and Bill Clinton in 1998. The Senate acquitted both.

Determining Qualifications

Article I, Section 5, gives Congress the power to determine the "qualifications of its own members"; with that authority, Congress has expelled members. Doing so requires a two-thirds vote of the body in which the individual is a member. The House of Representatives has expelled only five members. Three received that penalty during the Civil War for "support of rebellion." The most recent was in 2002 when Representative Jim Traficant of Ohio was removed for bribery, racketeering, and tax evasion. The Senate has expelled fifteen of its members; fourteen were for supporting the Confederacy during the Civil War. No senator has been expelled since that time. Congress has also **censured**, or condemned, members for conduct that reflected poorly on the institution. Past members have been censured for engaging in sexual misconduct, using offensive language, insulting the Speaker, physically attacking other members, and for financial mismanagement. The last member to be censured was Representative Charles Rangel of New York in 2010 (for improper solicitation of funds, inaccurate financial disclosures, and failure to pay taxes). A lesser punishment, called **reprimand**, is occasionally used in the House of Representatives, though not in the Senate. For example, in 2009 Representative Joe Wilson of South Carolina was reprimanded for shouting, "You lie!" during President Obama's State of the Union address. In 2012 a California representative, Laura Richardson, was reprimanded for having her congressional staff assist her political campaign. Neither censure nor reprimand carries any official punishment; however, sometimes recipients choose not to seek reelection or are defeated when seeking it.

Amendments

Under Article V, Congress has the power to propose amendments to the Constitution. Congress can propose them either by a two-thirds vote of both houses or by calling for a "convention for proposing amendments" when two-thirds of the states ask for it. This latter provision has never been used because many fear that such a convention might seek broader and more dangerous changes to the Constitution. Congress also decides how constitutional amendments are to be ratified: by three-fourths of state legislatures or by three-fourths of state conventions. Only the Twenty-First Amendment (which repealed Prohibition) has been ratified by state conventions.

Section Review

1. Define *resolutions*.
2. How did Congress expand its war powers during Reconstruction?
3–4. In what two ways may Congress propose amendments to the Constitution?
   ★ Distinguish between enumerated, implied, and nonlegislative powers of Congress.
   ★ How can the Senate shape the federal judiciary?

Censure of Joseph McCarthy

During the height of the Cold War and during the Korean War, Senator Joseph McCarthy (R-WI) stirred controversy by making charges that some people in the US government were Communists, were spies for the Communists, or were sympathetic to them. These attacks generated a great deal of attention. The accusation in the late 1940s that Alger Hiss, a State Department employee, had been a Communist spy fueled suspicions. At first the public supported McCarthy's campaign.

Circumstances changed, however, in 1952 with the election of a Republican president, Dwight Eisenhower, who replaced a Democrat, Harry Truman. Now McCarthy's charges put his fellow Republicans on the defensive. Also, in 1953 and 1954, McCarthy's charges about Communists in the government grew more reckless. On December 2, 1954, US senators voted 67 to 22 to condemn McCarthy for conduct that brought shame on the Senate. He died three years later at age forty-eight.

Equal Rights Amendment

"Equality of rights under the law shall not be denied or abridged by the United States or by any State on account of sex."
—The Equal Rights Amendment

One proposed change to the Constitution—the Equal Rights Amendment—proved controversial for about a decade. In 1972, Congress easily approved the proposed amendment, which had first been introduced in 1923. Nevertheless, by 1982 it had failed to gain the necessary approval of three-fourths of the states, although Congress extended the time limit for ratification.

The amendment was brief and vague. No one knew what would or would not be

Section Review Answers

1. declarations that lack the authority of law and merely express congressional opinion (p. 198)
2. Congress believed (and the Supreme Court agreed) that it could deal with peacetime problems that resulted from wars. (p. 198)
3–4. by a two-thirds vote of both houses or by calling for a "convention for proposing amendments" at the request of two-thirds of the states (p. 200)
   ★ Enumerated powers are specifically listed in the Constitution. Implied powers are needed for Congress to exercise its enumerated powers, but are not specifically noted in the document. Enumerated and implied powers may deal with both legislative and nonlegislative functions of Congress. Nonlegislative powers given to Congress would include such matters as impeachment, approval of presidential appointments and treaties, and determining qualification of members of Congress.
   ★ The Senate can exercise its power of confirmation by accepting, rejecting, or influencing executive appointees.

III. Denied Powers

The key to understanding the powers of Congress is an understanding of the **reserved powers**. The Tenth Amendment states that "the powers not delegated to the United States by the Constitution, nor prohibited by it to the states, are reserved to the states respectively, or to the people." These powers kept by the states enable them to legislate for the health and welfare of their citizens.

According to the First Amendment, Congress cannot restrict religious freedom, freedoms of speech and the press, or freedoms to assemble and petition the government. Article I, Section 9, also denies certain powers to Congress. A few of its restrictions state that Congress may not suspend the writ of habeas corpus, pass a bill of attainder, pass an ex post facto law, or tax exports from any state (see p. 101 for a description of these issues).

Section Review

1. Which amendment reserves certain powers to the states?
★ How does the First Amendment restrict Congress's powers?

IV. Congressional Criticism

Americans often level enormous criticism at Congress. Citizens consistently give its members low ratings in opinion polls. In recent years, the approval rating has often been below 20 percent. Congressmen are frequently viewed as self-serving, lazy, indifferent, and corrupt. One reason for this perspective is politics: constituents of one party attack members of Congress from the other party. Of course, citizens also complain about how their representatives vote on certain bills or how they support certain interest groups.

Backdoor Spending

Lawmakers seem to have missed the point of a humorous barb attributed to Everett Dirksen, who represented Illinois in Congress for more than thirty years: "A billion here, a billion there, pretty soon it begins to add up to real money." In spite of the huge national debt, Congress's spending continues to increase, and much of it is "backdoor spending." The following list includes some ways that Congress can spend funds that are basically immune from budget cuts or control, thus pushing the debt to new heights:

1. **Entitlements**: These are government compensation programs that the law requires Congress to protect. Examples of entitlements include Social Security, Medicare, and many Great Society programs. They constitute the majority of the nation's annual budget.

2. Borrowing: Congress has given to many federal agencies the power to borrow billions of dollars.

3. Guaranteed loans: To encourage home ownership, Congress authorized guaranteed loans by underwriting the loans of the Federal Housing Administration and the Veteran's Administration. Consequently, if borrowers fail to pay their debts, the government is obligated to repay their loans.

Critics argue that backdoor spending encourages financial irresponsibility and unaccountable borrowing. Both are threats to America's economic future.

covered in the application of the new law. Conservatives were particularly concerned about how the Supreme Court would later interpret its meaning. Opposition to the amendment by women, especially conservative women, ultimately defeated it. Some feared that the amendment would remove certain legal protections, such as workplace rules that make exceptions for women. Some even argued that changes like unisex toilets would be required. Also, as the feminist movement became more radical in the 1970s, many career women rejected it. Most American women wanted equal treatment but not the radical feminist agenda, which many Americans considered antifamily and antimale. Furthermore, conservatives believed that the Fourteenth Amendment, among other laws, protected women from discrimination, making the Equal Rights Amendment unnecessary.

Section III Objective

Explain the powers the Constitution denies to Congress.

Section IV Objectives

1. Cite various reasons Congress is criticized.
2. Evaluate the criticisms Congress commonly receives.

Section Review Answers

1. the Tenth Amendment (p. 201)
★ Congress cannot restrict religious freedom, freedoms of speech and the press, or freedoms to assemble and petition the government. Congress may not suspend the writ of habeas corpus, pass a bill of attainder or ex post facto law, or tax exports from any state.

Activity 3: The Bible and Poverty

In this activity students will examine passages from the Scriptures regarding poverty and will write a brief essay concerning their findings.

Activity 4: Growing Reliance on Government Support

This activity helps the students understand the dangers of society's increasing dependence on government; it also builds skills in using resources and analyzing material.

Budget "Cuts" the Washington Way

When Washington politicians talk of making spending "cuts," they rarely mean a real reduction in spending. Rather, the politicians usually mean that the rate of spending increase will be less, although total spending will still increase. For example, suppose that a department spent $2 billion for a project in Year 1 and plans to spend $4 billion on that project in Year 2, but Congress mandates a $1 billion cut for that project. Typically, spending will not be reduced to $1 billion. Rather, real spending will increase to $3 billion. The cut affects the amount of increase, so real spending continues to increase. (A proposed $4 billion budget minus a $1 billion cut equals a total of $3 billion, an increase of the department's budget by $1 billion over the previous year.)

Clearly, Congress is an arm of a government that is not distinctively Christian. But because of our republican form of government, it does represent all citizens—including Christians. As citizens, Christians should be careful that their criticisms of Congress are biblically grounded and be cautious about denouncing governmental officials (Acts 23:5; Titus 3:1–2). At the same time, when leaders truly are corrupt, immoral, unjust, or they promote policies contrary to Scripture, the Christian must speak the truth about such matters (Isa. 10:1–2; Dan. 4:27). Christian citizens should hold members of Congress accountable and demand that they follow the highest ethical standards. Furthermore, Christians ought to move beyond mere party labels and personalities and base their evaluations of their leaders on biblical truth.

Pork-Barrel Politics

An ongoing criticism of Congress involves its wasteful spending. The term ***pork barrel*** has become political slang for favors, often very costly ones, obtained for local citizens at the expense of all taxpayers. The term originated in the nineteenth century when pork was salted and kept in barrels. The term conjured images of a politician dipping his hands into the pork barrel, or federal treasury, and pulling out a piece of pork (a federal project for his district).

Pork-barrel politics often includes big spending projects that are designed to help a member of Congress get reelected. Even though unnecessary spending is an abuse of Congress's purse power, it is a considerable part of Congress's legislative program. Pork-barrel spending is often money that is requested by a single member of Congress (that has not been requested by the president nor cleared through a congressional hearing) and used for a local purpose. Pork-barrel spending can fund such things as highway construction, irrigation projects, new post offices, harbor improvements, and military contracts. Congressmen often view this spending as a gift to a hopefully grateful and indebted constituency. However, a pork-barrel project is really not a gift because its cost is paid not only by the taxpayers of the benefiting district but also by the nation at-large.

Two factors contribute to the difficulty of defeating pork-barrel measures. First is the practice of **logrolling**, in which a member of Congress supports a colleague's spending project in exchange for support for his own pork-barrel

The King of Pork? West Virginia Hero? Both?

Robert Byrd (D-WV) served in the US Senate from 1959 until his death in 2010—longer than any other senator in US history. He was well known for garnering an enormous amount of "pork" for his state.

Critics nicknamed him "King of Pork." In fact, he called himself "Big Daddy" in 2006 when he spoke at the dedication of the Robert C. Byrd Biotechnology Science Center, a pork project he obtained for West Virginia. More than forty such pork projects are named for him. And he was unapologetic about his role in the growth of pork-barrel spending. "They call me the 'Pork King,'" he once said. "They don't know how much I enjoy it."

Many in his state saw him as a hero, in large part because of the federal projects he obtained for the state. The legislature approved the placement of a larger-than-life bronze statue of Byrd in the state capitol and named him, "West Virginian of the 20th Century."

Pork-Barrel Politics

Assign students to find examples of what they consider to be wasteful spending by government officials. Display any relevant cartoons and other graphics that the students find while researching. Instruct the students to evaluate their findings. Discuss the possibility that what one person considers to be wasteful may be viewed as an important expenditure by another person. Discuss the graphics and cartoons found. Do you agree or disagree with their portrayal of the issues mentioned?

legislation. Second, pork-barrel projects are often combined with important spending legislation into one omnibus, or all-inclusive, spending bill. Thus, the only way a member can vote against a pork-barrel project is to vote against the entire bill. However, doing so may mean he is helping defeat legislation that he supports. Unfortunately, this approach also protects wasteful spending from a presidential veto since it is shielded by the parts of the bill that the president favors or is hidden in the details of the bill.

Critics of pork-barrel spending cite examples of millions of dollars spent for studies regarding cow flatulence, the use of sheep grazing as a means of weed control, why more Americans do not ride bicycles to work, and growing vegetables in outer space. Of course, not everyone sees pork-barrel spending as extravagant. To some members of Congress, "one person's pork is another person's legitimate spending." Important projects funded by this spending could be viewed as representing constituents and benefiting representatives' districts. After all, advocates argue, if the representatives do not get the money for the people, it will simply go elsewhere.

Seniority System

Generally, members who have served the longest and are in the majority party become chairmen of committees and subcommittees. Critics charge that this system honors political longevity and reelection ability, not wisdom, skill, or ideology. Supporters argue that it rewards experience and ensures that those with expertise, in both policy and procedural matters, are in leadership positions.

Congress's seniority system has weakened in recent years. When the Republicans took control of Congress in the 1990s, they adopted rules to limit committee chairs to serving for six years in that role. They also allowed committee chairs to be elected by secret ballot.

Balance

Criticism of Congress has always been a common pastime in America. Mark Twain, with his typical biting humor, declared, "It could probably be shown by facts and figures that there is no distinctly native American criminal class except Congress." Humorist Will Rogers commented, "The taxpayers are sending congressmen on expensive trips abroad. It might be worth it except they keep coming back." However, it would be unjust to characterize the national legislature only by its most negative aspects. The important and difficult role that the legislative branch plays in national government often goes unappreciated. Congress has two fundamental tasks, neither of which is easy: representation and legislation. As representatives, members of Congress must obey the voice of the people. But which people? How does a member determine whether he is listening to the voice of the majority or to a small but well-organized interest group? A legislator must decide which laws are worth supporting and, in an atmosphere where political compromise determines a bill's future, decide how much he can modify his position.

Another misunderstanding of Congress involves the kind of leadership that it provides. Criticism often declares that Congress is a do-nothing branch—that it is slow to respond to national demands. But Congress, with its bicameral structure and cumbersome legislative process, is designed to act deliberately, not

Logrolling

The term *logrolling* comes from the pioneers' practice of asking a neighbor for help in moving heavy logs when clearing a field. A farmer asked for help with the understanding that he would later return the favor.

Activity 5: Chapter Review

Use this activity to help the students prepare for the chapter test.

Section Review Answers

1. Christians should ensure that their criticisms of Congress are biblically grounded. They should be cautious about denouncing governmental officials (Acts 23:5; Titus 3:1–2). While corruption, immorality, injustice, or policies contrary to Scripture should be condemned, the Christian must speak only the truth about such matters (Isa. 10:1–2; Dan. 4:27; James 1:19–20). Citizens ought to hold members of Congress accountable and demand that they follow the highest ethical standards. (pp. 201–2)

Perks

The following are some congressional perks that some people have noted in their criticisms of Congress:

1. Tax-subsidized life insurance
2. Tax-subsidized comprehensive medical and dental insurance
3. Pensions for members who serve for twenty or more years
4. Free parking in the District of Columbia and at area airports
5. Access to gyms at the Capitol
6. Tax-subsidized services at barbershops and salons

Pass It, Then Read It?

Obamacare bill

In March 2010, Congress was intensely debating the Patient Protection and Affordable Care Act (PPACA), also known as Obamacare. The massive, complex bill exceeded two thousand pages. No Republicans in Congress voted for it and many of them complained that few understood its details. They ridiculed Democratic Speaker of the House Nancy Pelosi for saying, "We have to pass the bill so that you can find out what is in it, away from the fog of the controversy." (Pelosi argued that her comments were taken out of context.) Obamacare narrowly received congressional approval.

In the summer of 2017 Republicans were attempting to pass legislation to repeal Obamacare. The details were again complex. Politicians, this time primarily the Democrats, complained that the proposals were secretive, rushed, confusing, and constantly changing. In the end, the legislation was narrowly defeated.

Unfortunately, members of Congress often vote on extremely complicated bills. The specifics are sometimes difficult to understand and too lengthy to fully comprehend. Many lawmakers admit they regularly support legislation that they have not read. Some defend their actions by saying they depend on their staff members to provide them with summaries of bills on which they must vote.

just decisively. Its approach is characterized by caution and compromise, which in its best sense provides essential balance to presidential leadership. Sometimes the best approach is to do nothing. In the congressional arena, there is as much merit in killing a bad bill as in passing a good one. Many bills are so ill-conceived that if they were passed into law they would be ineffective or dangerous. Thus, the public is served by legislative sifting. Congress is central to America's representative form of government. Its members come from every corner of the nation, and they reflect a diversity of parties, personalities, and opinions. Their work in Washington is immense.

As the first branch of government, Congress provides an important check and balance to the other branches. As the people's branch, it helps unify a diverse country. And as the legislative branch, it passes laws that shape the nation's growth and direction. Despite its failures and the weight of its many responsibilities, Congress continues to have a strong voice in and for the Republic.

Section Review

1. Explain how Christians should be careful about their criticisms of Congress.
2. What are the benefits of a bicameral congress?
3–4. What are two factors that often make it difficult to prevent the defeat of pork-barrel measures?

★ Read the feature box about Senator Robert Byrd on p. 202. Based on the information there, what is your opinion of his fondness for pork? Explain your view.

★ Read the feature box entitled "Pass It, Then Read It?" on this page. What is your opinion on the information presented?

2. A slow, deliberate legislative process protects society from ineffective, dangerous, or ill-conceived laws. It also provides an essential balance to presidential leadership. (pp. 203–4)

3–4. Pork-barrel projects are difficult to prevent because of logrolling and the combining of pork-barrel projects with important spending bills. Logrolling occurs when a congressman supports the proposal of another congressman who supported one of his bills. Without such deals, some congressmen might vote against the pork that many spending bills contain. Attaching pork projects to an important bill forces representatives to either accept the entire bill, including the pork (which may contain measures he supports), or reject the whole bill. (pp. 202–3)

★ Senator Robert Byrd believed strongly that the national government should help his state by supporting government projects there. Consequently, he garnered as many funds for his state as possible. Many in his state appreciated these funds and recognized him as a hero. Some will say that states should focus on funding their own projects rather than looking to the federal government for funds. Some will question if many projects Byrd supported were really worthwhile.

★ Some will say that it is unfortunate that legislators often do not know the full details of a bill on which they are asked to vote. They may say the process should be slowed to give members more time to read bills. Others will say that members must, out of necessity, rely on summaries of bills that their staff members provide. Consequently, it is important to choose staff members wisely.

9 CHAPTER REVIEW

Making Connections

1–2. Describe the two times the House of Representatives invoked its power to elect the president in elections where one candidate failed to win a majority of the electoral votes.

3–4. Which US presidents have been impeached?

5. What was the outcome of each presidential impeachment?

6–7. What are the two ways that Congress can propose an amendment to the Constitution?

8–9. What are the two ways that an amendment can be ratified?

Developing Civics Skills

1. Which house of Congress has the sole responsibility to ratify treaties and confirm executive and judicial nominations? Does this power allow Congress to check executive power? Defend your answer.

2. Contrast the role of each house of Congress in the impeachment process.

Thinking Critically

1. During our nation's history the national government's power has expanded greatly. Is that expansion legitimate? Defend your answer.

2. Explain how the Senate's power to confirm judicial and executive appointments affects the makeup of American government. In your answer, discuss how a senator's beliefs influence his or her views of nominees.

Living as a Christian Citizen

1. Christians must evaluate their political leaders by scriptural standards. Find the most recent party platform of one of the two major parties, and appraise the following provisions: views of marriage, immigration reform, healthcare reform, abortion, and the right of national self-defense. Support your assessment.

2. Imagine that you are a leader for Hispanic outreach for your church. Your pastor has asked you to write a brief statement of your church's position on immigration issues. State a biblical position.

People, Places, and Things to Remember

enumerated powers
duty
excises
Sixteenth Amendment
North American Free Trade Agreement (NAFTA)
general welfare
Gibbons v. Ogden
interstate commerce
war power
War Powers Act
letter of marque
reprisal
citizenship
bankruptcy
Judiciary Act of 1789
implied powers
necessary and proper clause
subpoena
Twenty-Fifth Amendment
ratification
confirmation
impeachment
censured
reprimand
reserved powers
entitlements
pork barrel
logrolling

THE POWERS OF CONGRESS • 205

Thinking Critically

1. Some expanded powers might be reasonable. For example, some students might argue that government control of commerce is efficient. Others, however, might argue that it is better for state and local governments to have more power. And still others might argue that any expansion of government at any level is wrong and unconstitutional.

2. The Senate's power of confirmation often leads the US government to be centrist, or moderate. Many times presidents avoid selecting nominees that might be viewed as too controversial. A senator's beliefs will be reflected in his reactions to nominees and their positions on principles that are important to him.

Living as a Christian Citizen

1. Support of traditional marriage is essential because of scriptural commands (Gen. 2:24) and because studies demonstrate that children benefit from having both a mother and a father. Same-sex "marriage," though now legal in the United States, is unbiblical (Gen. 2:24; 1 Tim. 3:2). Immigration reform and healthcare reform touch on biblical concerns (Deut. 10:18–19; Luke 10:33–34), but Christians may legitimately disagree about the means of reform. Abortion is murder, so support for abortion is clearly unbiblical (Exod. 20:13). While Scripture does give a nation the right to defend itself, it does not necessarily give guidance about when and where to fight and when to make peace.

2. Students should include the following issues. Most important, the church should recognize immigration as a ministry opportunity. When Christians immigrate, the church should recognize the brotherly bond that transcends nationality or ethnicity. When people immigrate to a new country, they are often vulnerable to discrimination; therefore, church members should extend themselves toward immigrants in the congregation to ensure that they are treated justly. Of course, the church must obey the laws of the land, so it should advise illegal immigrants to begin the process of legalization. Christians should also be alert to inconsistencies and injustices that may exist in immigration law and may work politically to see those laws changed.

CHAPTER REVIEW ANSWERS

Making Connections

1–2. The House elected Jefferson in 1800 and John Quincy Adams in 1824. (p. 198)

3–4. Andrew Johnson and Bill Clinton (pp. 199–200)

5. In both instances, the defendants were acquitted by the Senate. (p. 200)

6–7. by a two-thirds vote of both houses or by calling a national convention when two-thirds of the states ask for it (p. 200)

8–9. by three-fourths of state legislatures or by three-fourths of state conventions (p. 200)

Developing Civics Skills

1. The Senate; yes; this power gives the Senate a voice in foreign policy and provides senators a forum for presenting their arguments against administration policy. For example, the Senate has blocked the appointment of some Supreme Court justices and a few cabinet members. That body also refused to ratify the Versailles Treaty after World War I.

2. The House brings charges against the defendant (impeaches), and the Senate conducts the trial. Two-thirds of the Senate must vote to convict in order to remove the official from office.

The City's Planner

The City's Planner

Pierre Charles L'Enfant was born in France in 1754. His father was a painter at the Royal Academy of Painting and Sculpture in Paris who taught his son much in that field. Pierre also became a skilled architect. He came to America during the Revolutionary War and joined the Continental army as an engineer. While serving in the Revolutionary War in 1778, L'Enfant received the rank of captain. In 1779 he was wounded at the siege of Savannah. After this action, he served under George Washington's command and became a major. After Washington became president, he chose L'Enfant in 1791 to be the chief designer of the federal city of Washington. Three years later, after disagreement and personality clashes with the three commissioners overseeing the project, L'Enfant was dismissed.

In 1825, Pierre L'Enfant died penniless and was buried in Prince George's County, Maryland. In 1908, Washington, DC's board of commissioners asked the secretary of war to provide a burial site at Arlington National Cemetery for L'Enfant's remains. A site was approved, and his remains were reinterred at Arlington in April 1909.

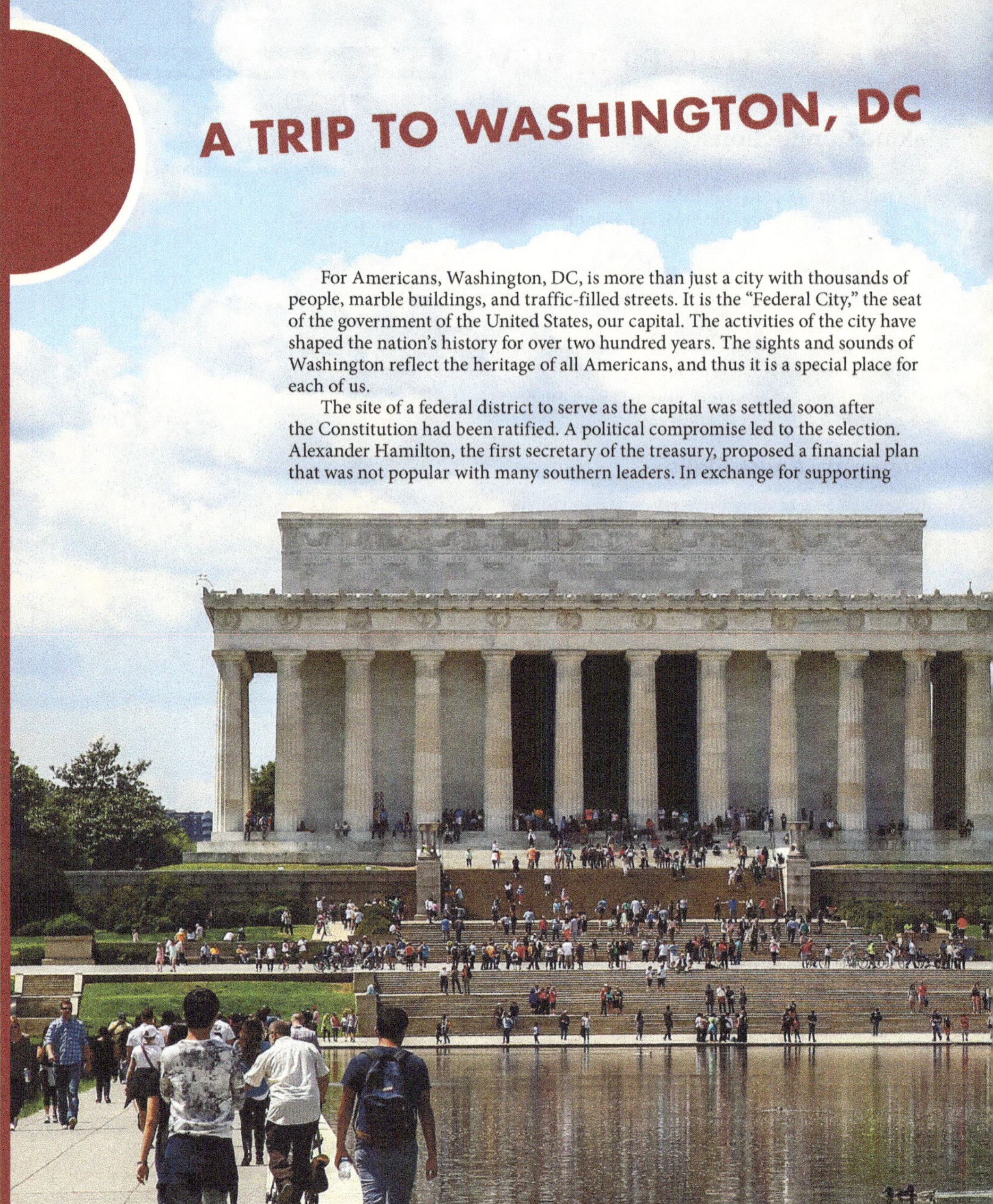

For Americans, Washington, DC, is more than just a city with thousands of people, marble buildings, and traffic-filled streets. It is the "Federal City," the seat of the government of the United States, our capital. The activities of the city have shaped the nation's history for over two hundred years. The sights and sounds of Washington reflect the heritage of all Americans, and thus it is a special place for each of us.

The site of a federal district to serve as the capital was settled soon after the Constitution had been ratified. A political compromise led to the selection. Alexander Hamilton, the first secretary of the treasury, proposed a financial plan that was not popular with many southern leaders. In exchange for supporting

Impressions

Invite students who have visited Washington, DC, to relate their activities and impressions of the city.

his plan, the capital would be located in the South. George Washington himself chose a spot along the Potomac River in 1790. Andrew Ellicott and Benjamin Banneker surveyed the ten-square-mile tract encompassing land from both Maryland and Virginia. (The Virginia land was returned to that state a few decades later.) Then Pierre L'Enfant devised a plan for a city he wanted to call "Washingtonople." L'Enfant claimed that a high point in the tract, then known as Jenkins Hill, was a "pedestal awaiting a monument." Known as Capitol Hill today because it is the site of the Capitol building, this hill became the focal point from which the emerging city grew.

Most of the District of Columbia was still a wilderness of swamps and forests in 1800 when President John Adams, Congress, and the remainder of the government moved into their newly built city. At that time there were only about fifty houses in the central part of the district and one hundred thirty government workers. The fledgling capital grew slowly until the twentieth century, when it swelled into a modern metropolis, with suburbs sprawling far into Virginia and Maryland.

Daniel Chester French's imposing statue of Abraham Lincoln overlooks all who enter the Lincoln Memorial. The classic walls of the memorial, etched with Lincoln's memorable speeches, were completed in 1922. This famous landmark stands between the Potomac River and the giant Reflecting Pool.

Lincoln Memorial

On Lincoln's birthday, February 12, 1915, the first stone of the Lincoln Memorial was laid. When the monument was dedicated on May 30, 1922, the former president's only surviving child, Robert Todd Lincoln, was present. Apart from honoring a president, the memorial has served as a backdrop for various historical events. In 1939 Marian Anderson was not allowed to perform at Constitution Hall because she was African American. Mrs. Roosevelt heard of the incident and was able to have a concert scheduled for her. On Easter Sunday before seventy thousand people and a nationwide radio audience, Marian Anderson gave her concert from the steps of the Lincoln Memorial. In August of 1963, Martin Luther King delivered his "I Have a Dream" speech in front of the memorial.

Korean War Veterans Memorial

Authorized in 1986 and dedicated in 1995, the Korean War Veterans Memorial symbolizes various aspects of the war.

Statues: Some of the nineteen stainless steel statues are shown on the right. They represent the army, marines, navy, and air force. They reflect the sun by day and are illuminated at night. The statues have blowing ponchos to give the column the appearance of movement. Juniper bushes symbolize the rough Korean terrain, and the granite stripes among the statues represent the obstacles overcome in war.

Mural Wall: The black granite wall contains a mural of etchings depicting personnel from all the military branches and their equipment. The reflective quality of the granite creates the image of a total of 38 statues, representing the 38th parallel (the dividing line between North and South Korea when the Korean War began) and the 38 months of war. When viewed from a distance, the wall gives the appearance of the Korean mountain ranges.

Hibiscus Plants: There are beds of the rose of Sharon hibiscus, which is the national flower of South Korea.

Pool of Remembrance: It honors the dead, missing POWs, and wounded from US and UN forces.

Curb: The names of the twenty-two nations who helped to defend freedom and repel communism are engraved on the curb stone along the north entrance.

Honor Roll: Contains all verifiable names of those on active duty who were killed in action, those still listed as missing in action, and those captured as prisoners of war.

"Mount Washington"

George Washington Parke Custis, step-grandson of George Washington, inherited his father's property that overlooked Washington City. Originally the family called the area Mount Washington, but later changed it to Arlington in honor of the family's homestead in eastern Virginia. In 1831, Mary, his only child to survive to adulthood, married Robert E. Lee.

When Custis died in 1857, Mary inherited Arlington. During the Civil War, Mary left Arlington House; and it was soon occupied by federal troops, with General Irvin McDowell making the mansion his headquarters. When land was needed to bury the war dead, soldiers were first buried at Arlington in May of 1864. By 1870 over 15,000 soldiers had been interred, and Arlington would soon become a sacred landmark of the nation.

Museum of the Bible

This museum, which opened in November 2017 just three blocks from the US Capitol, presents the history and impact of the Bible. A large portion of the project, which cost approximately $500 million, was funded by Hobby Lobby and its owners, members of the Green family.

Points of Interest

Instruct each student to research a point of interest from the map of Washington, DC, and write an informational summary. Direct the students to write the assignment as though it were for a brochure, travel magazine, or internet site.

Capitol Designer

Dr. William Thornton was a physician educated in Scotland who rarely practiced his profession. He also was an inventor, painter, and self-taught architect. Thornton submitted his design for the new Capitol, and President Washington approved it. The prize for the chosen design was five hundred dollars and the gift of a city lot.

The Plumbe Story

As a child, John Plumbe emigrated with his parents in 1821 from Wales to the United States. As a young adult, Plumbe learned about photography in Boston; and by 1845 he had his own studio in Washington, DC.

His photography business expanded to include more than two dozen studios in the eastern United States. In 1845 Plumbe was the first photographer to make a portrait of a sitting president, James Polk. His other famous subjects included John Quincy Adams, Dolley Madison, Daniel Webster, Martin Van Buren, and John James Audubon.

Plumbe's 1846 photograph of the White House is thought to be the oldest existing one of the residence. By 1848 with increased competition, Plumbe's studios began to close. He went to California but eventually settled in Iowa in 1854, where he and his brother tried to establish a mill. A financial panic in 1857 ruined Plumbe, and he committed suicide.

A Look Back at the Capitol and the White House

In 1792, commissioners of the newly surveyed federal district authorized contests for architectural designs for both a building to house Congress and a home for the president. A young physician named William Thornton submitted a late entry in January 1793 that outshone the other designs offered for the Capitol. Washington and Jefferson praised Thornton's plan, and the cornerstone for it was laid in September of that year. Construction proceeded slowly. Only the Senate wing was ready for use when Congress occupied it in 1800. The House wing was finished in 1811, but the War of 1812 brought everything to a halt. The Capitol and the president's house were both burned by the British in August 1814.

Charles Bulfinch was responsible for rebuilding the Capitol building after the fire, and the dome visible in the 1846 photograph is of his design. The growing nation with its expanding number of senators and representatives, however, soon outgrew this refurbished building, and additional room was necessary. Thomas U. Walter designed the new Senate and House wings that were added in the 1850s. His new, larger dome was placed atop the rotunda during the Civil War to balance the design. In 1958–62, a major expansion occurred that added additional office space. In 2000, ground was broken for a massive underground visitor center that was completed in 2008.

Irish-born James Hoban submitted the winning design for the president's house. Thomas Jefferson had entered his design anonymously (signed A.Z.), but the Hoban drawings won greater admiration. The house began to take shape on the site L'Enfant had designated for it at one end of the rough path that would be Pennsylvania Avenue. The Capitol building rose at the other end. In 1800 John Adams and his family moved into the still-unfinished house for the last few

The daguerreotypes on these two pages, probably made in 1846 by John Plumbe Jr., are the earliest known photographs of these structures.

The view of the Capitol shows the East Front with the old House wing on the left and the old Senate wing on the right.

210

Plan a Trip!

Assign students to plan a trip to Washington, DC. Using the material in this section, as well as additional resources, the students should determine how long they would like to spend in the city, which sites they would like to visit, and how to maximize their time. Consider giving the students a budget and requiring them to determine transportation, meals, and lodging for the trip. Encourage the students to plan carefully and in such a manner that their work could be used when taking an actual trip to the capital city in the future.

This photograph of the White House depicts the south side of that building as it appeared during James Polk's presidency (1840s).

months of his administration. The main staircase had not been built; walls lacked plaster; and the rooms were damp and cold. Though Abigail Adams stated that she preferred the previous presidential home in Philadelphia, she noted in a letter that "this House is built for the ages to come." Construction continued during the Jefferson administration, and then Dolley Madison was able to add her touch to the mansion before the British arrived.

Eventually, the building became known as the "White House." It was not until the presidency of Theodore Roosevelt, however, that this term was used on official papers. The rebuilt mansion was provided with many new furnishings by James Monroe, and Andrew Jackson finally finished the decoration of the large East Room. As new presidential families moved in during the 1800s and early 1900s, they changed the decor to fit their needs and tastes. Most of the president's administrative offices remained in the original building until the addition of the West Wing in 1902, and the East Wing provided more office space in 1942.

Improvements and repairs to the White House were made constantly, but the ravages of time took their toll on the structure. By the time of the Truman administration, the mansion had become a safety hazard. Rather than demolish this symbol of American government to build a new mansion, a thorough renovation project was begun in 1948. The outside walls were left standing, but the interior was totally dismantled. New foundations were inserted and two levels of basement dug before the house interior was reassembled piece by piece. Since the completion of that project in 1952, the White House has become both a museum of America's presidential past and a comfortable home for the first family.

White House Designer

Born in Ireland, James Hoban emigrated to the United States and established himself as an architect. In 1792 he won the competition for the design of the president's home and oversaw its construction from 1793 to 1800. After the home was burned during the War of 1812, leaving a charred shell, Hoban supervised the restoration work until completion in 1817.

White House Renovation in 1948

During the Great Depression and World War II, needed repairs at the White House were often ignored. Then, early in 1948, in response to the concerns of President Truman and others, engineers confirmed that the White House was in serious need of improvements.

Because of the burning of much of the mansion in 1814; the additions of indoor plumbing, gas lighting, electric wiring, heating ducts; and then major modifications in 1902 and 1927, the White House desperately needed extensive renovation.

Some Capitol Facts

The Capitol building dimensions are 751 feet, 4 inches from north to south; 350 feet at its greatest width; and from the baseline on the east front to the top of the Statue of Freedom (which is above the dome) is 288 feet. That statue faces east, away from the Mall, because the east front is the main entrance. Congress first met in the building on November 17, 1800.

Capitol Rotunda

With a diameter of 96 feet and a height of 180 feet, the Rotunda is the heart of the Capitol and connects the House and Senate sides. An impressive example of architecture, the Rotunda also houses sculpture and paintings. One of the paintings by John Trumbull is *General George Washington Resigning His Commission*. Washington's action, portrayed in the painting, established civilian rule rather than military rule, leading to a democracy rather than a potential dictatorship.

The original dome covering the Rotunda was made of wood and covered with copper. By the 1850s the dome was too small for the enlarged Capitol and was a fire hazard needing constant repair. A new dome made of cast iron included columns, pilasters, brackets, and windows. It was crowned with the Statue of Freedom.

Capitol Star

The Crypt is a large circular area on the first floor of the Capitol with sandstone arches that support the floor of the Rotunda. In the center of the Crypt is a star that marks the point at which the city is divided into four quadrants (and is the basis for how streets in Washington, DC, are numbered and how addresses are designated).

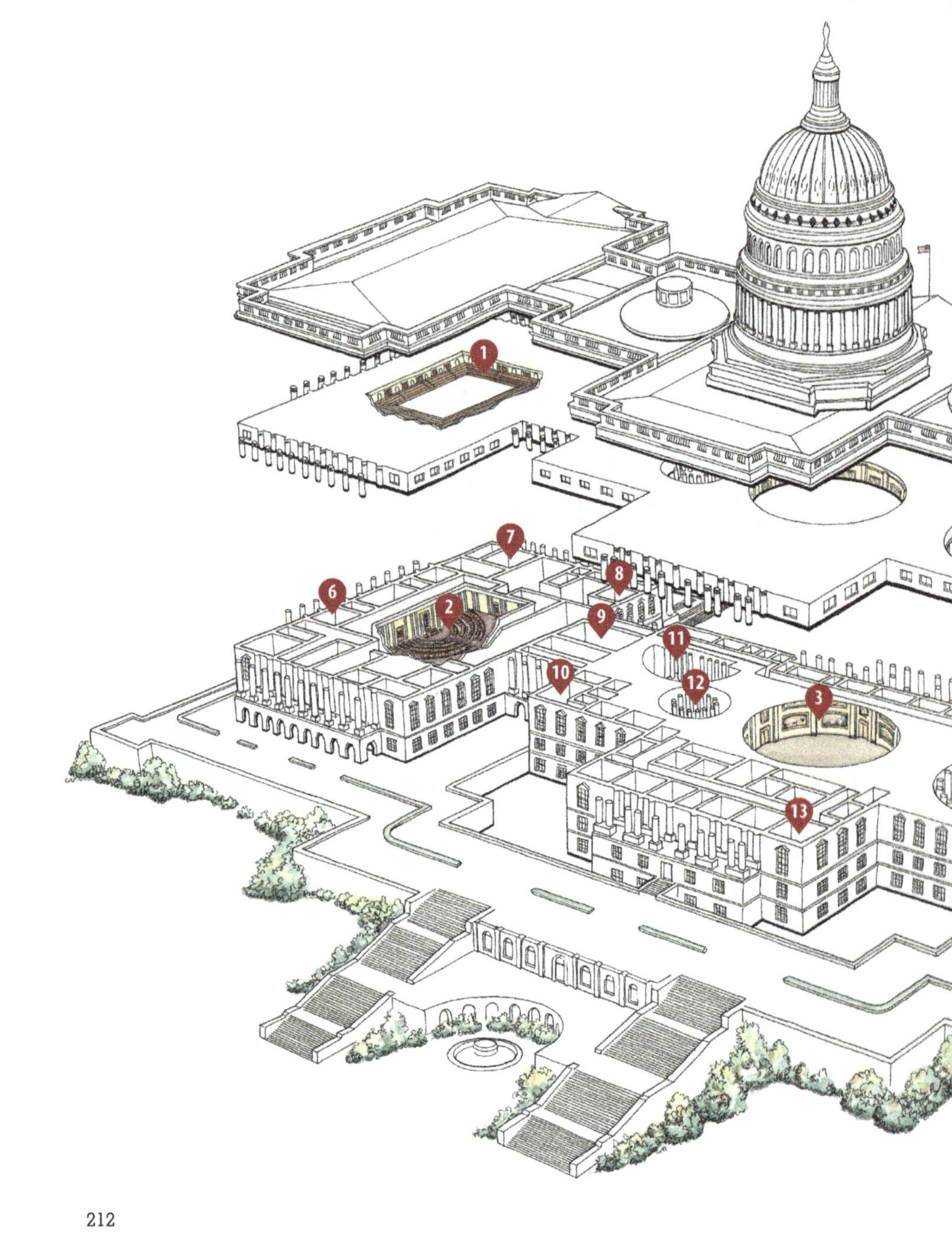

Capitol Tour

Various websites offer a virtual tour of the US Capitol. Ask volunteers to locate one or more of these and share that information with the class.

Quotations and Inscriptions

The Capitol complex displays various quotations and inscriptions. Assign students to research these and share their findings with the class. The following are a few such inscriptions:

> "We defend and we build a way of life, not for America alone, but for all mankind."
> —Franklin Delano Roosevelt (Cox Corridors of the US Capitol)

> "Our government conceived in freedom and purchased with blood can be preserved only by constant vigilance."
> —William Jennings Bryan (Cox Corridors)

"One country, one Constitution, one destiny."
—Daniel Webster (Cox Corridors)

"Preserve me, O God: For in Thee do I put my trust."
—Psalm 16:1 (Prayer Room)

"Annuit coeptis" (God has favored our undertakings)
—over the east doorway, Senate Chamber; also the Prayer Room

The Capitol Building

Artist's Rendering

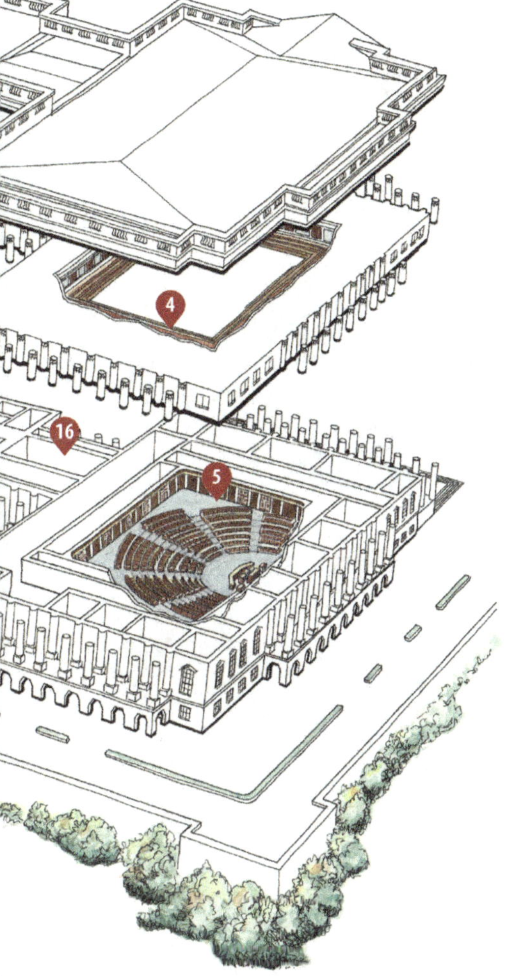

1. Senate Gallery
2. Senate Chamber
3. The Rotunda
4. House Gallery
5. House Chamber
6. President's Room
7. Vice President's Office
8. Senate Majority Leader's Office
9. Senate Conference Room
10. Senate Minority Leader's Office
11. Old Senate Chamber
12. Senate Rotunda
13. House Minority Leader's Office
14. Statuary Hall
15. Speaker's Office
16. House Reception Room

Statuary Hall in the Capitol

This area (#14 on the accompanying diagram) is sometimes referred to as the "Whispering Gallery." The half-dome shape of the hall produces an acoustic effect where in some spots a speaker many yards away may be heard more clearly than one in close proximity. Modern-day echoes occur in different locations from those in the nineteenth century, when the floor and ceiling of the hall were different.

Originally the House Chamber, important historical events occurred in the Hall. In 1824 the Marquis de Lafayette became the first foreign citizen to address Congress. In February 1825 John Quincy Adams was elected president by the House of Representatives when no candidate had secured a majority of electoral votes in the 1824 election. Following his presidency, John Q. Adams served in the House for seventeen years. In 1848, he collapsed at his desk from a stroke and died two days later.

In 1857 the House of Representatives began meeting at its present location. In 1864 Congress invited each state to contribute two statues of prominent citizens to be displayed in the Capitol. Presently, thirty-five of the one hundred are located in the former House Chamber. Statuary Hall today not only houses statues but is used for ceremonial occasions and special events, such as receptions and inaugural luncheons. The room is now officially known as National Statuary Hall.

State Statues

Group the students and assign each group at least two states. Direct the students to locate information concerning the statues those states have displayed in the Capitol. Why were these individuals chosen to represent the state? For what are these individuals most remembered?

Mystery Woman

Chester A. Arthur became president after President Garfield's death in September 1881. The new president caused quite a stir when he placed a photograph of a beautiful woman on a table in Cross Hall, located on the first floor of the White House, and instructed the staff to keep fresh roses on the table. The staff soon learned that she was Nell Arthur, the wife of the president, who had died the previous year.

First and Only

In 1886 President Grover Cleveland became the first and only president to get married in the White House. His daughter, Esther, was the first and only child of a president to be born in the White House.

Christmas at the White House

President Franklin Roosevelt took great delight in watching his children and grandchildren open Christmas gifts. At the White House family Christmas gathering in 1941, the president was so involved with the family and busy with World War II that he did not open his own gifts. Days later, they were found by a housekeeper.

White House Tour

Various websites offer a virtual tour of the White House. Ask volunteers to locate one or more of these and then share that information with the class.

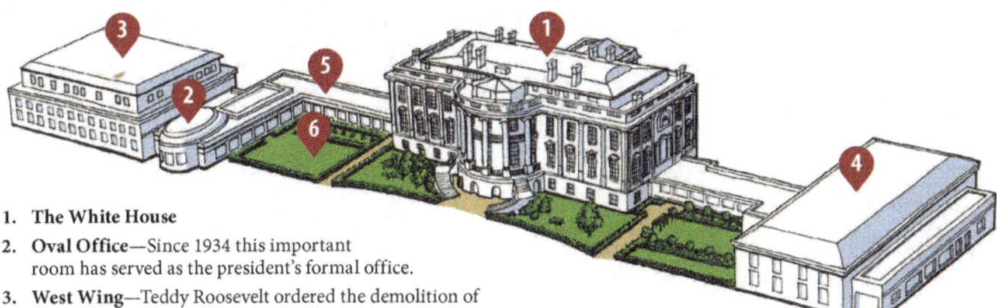

1. **The White House**

2. **Oval Office**—Since 1934 this important room has served as the president's formal office.

3. **West Wing**—Teddy Roosevelt ordered the demolition of a massive greenhouse complex in 1902 for the construction of an executive wing that now contains offices, the Cabinet Room, and press rooms.

4. **East Wing**—Franklin Roosevelt prompted the building of the East Wing in 1941 to provide more office and work space.

5. **James S. Brady Press Briefing Room**—The White House press secretary gives daily press releases to the media concerning the presidential schedule and answers questions concerning the president's policy or position on specific events.

6. **Rose Garden**—This area near the president's offices serves as a beautiful outdoor setting for official receptions. Richard Nixon's daughter Tricia was married in a Rose Garden wedding in 1971.

7. **Diplomatic Reception Room**—The president greets official guests at state functions in this drawing room. Franklin Roosevelt delivered his "Fireside Chats" while sitting before the fireplace in this room.

8. **Map Room**—Franklin Roosevelt used this room as a situation room to follow the course of World War II. Today it serves as a private meeting room for the president or First Lady.

9. **China Room**—Almost every past president is represented in the China Room by either state or family china or glassware. The collection is arranged chronologically.

10. **Vermeil Room**—The White House Vermeil Room, sometimes called the Gold Room, serves as a display room and ladies' sitting room on formal occasions.

11. **Library**—This room served as a laundry area until Theodore Roosevelt's ground floor renovation in 1902 when it became a locker room for male servants. In 1935 the room was remodeled into a library for use by the president, his family, and his staff.

12. **State Dining Room**—This large, formal dining room can hold as many as 140 guests. All presidents have a portrait displayed in different areas of the White House. President Lincoln's is on display here. Carved in the fireplace mantle is an excerpt from a letter written by John Adams in 1800: "I Pray Heaven to Bestow the Best of Blessings on THIS HOUSE and on All that shall hereafter inhabit it. May none but honest and Wise Men ever rule under this Roof."

13. **Red Room**—Furnishings from the Empire period now grace this sitting room where Dolley Madison held receptions.

14. **Blue Room**—This room gained its color during Van Buren's presidency. Several pieces of French Empire furniture in this reception room date from the presidency of James Monroe.

15. **Green Room**—Thomas Jefferson placed a green cloth on the floor of this room, which he used as a dining room. The Monroes made it a sitting room and furnished it in green.

16. **East Room**—The East Room is the White House's largest formal meeting room and the site of many momentous occasions including concerts, weddings, and funerals. At times, White House occupants have found other uses for this room. First Lady Abigail Adams hung laundry to dry in this large and then unfinished room. A century later Teddy Roosevelt's children used it for roller-skating. His portrait is displayed in this room.

17. **Family Quarters**—This section contains bedrooms and other private rooms for the president and his family.

18. **Yellow Oval Room**—The president often uses this parlor for entertaining foreign leaders before state dinners.

19. **Treaty Room**—This room served as the Cabinet Room after the Civil War until the West Wing was built in 1902. The Kennedys redecorated it to resemble the Cabinet Room during the Grant presidency and renamed it because of the treaties that have been and continue to be signed here. Presidents George H.W. Bush, Bill Clinton, and George W. Bush used this room for their private office.

20. **Lincoln's Bedroom**—President Lincoln used this as an office and cabinet meeting room, and it was the site of the signing of the Emancipation Proclamation. It now serves as a guest room furnished with the huge rosewood bed and other furnishings purchased by Mrs. Lincoln.

21. **Queen's Suite**—This bedroom and its neighboring sitting room earned its name in the 1960s after visits from Queen Elizabeth II of Britain, Queen Wilhelmina of the Netherlands, Queen Frederika of Greece, and several other royal ladies.

22. **Third Floor**—The roof of the White House was raised in 1927 to provide additional space for guest rooms, staff quarters, storage, a solarium, and living space for the first family.

Unlimited Access

In 1801, when Thomas Jefferson became president, he transformed the White House's State Dining Room into his private office. Few people were invited to this office, but Jefferson greeted visitors and guests in the adjacent Red Room. Jefferson did allow one creature unlimited access to this area of privacy, his pet mockingbird. Jefferson would place the bird's cage next to a window and often let the bird fly freely around the room.

A Social Taboo

First Lady Eleanor Roosevelt in 1933 began to use the Red Room to host press conferences for women reporters who were excluded from the president's press conferences. In the beginning, Mrs. Roosevelt would knit and discuss cooking and housekeeping topics with the hat-and-gloved women reporters (attired as if attending an afternoon tea). As Mrs. Roosevelt became more involved with social issues and as her traveling increased, the press conference discussions turned to domestic policy topics. Mrs. Roosevelt had lifted a "social taboo" and opened the White House doors to female reporters.

Remembering Vietnam

The Vietnam Veterans Memorial actually includes a Memorial Wall (made of black granite with the names of those men and women who are missing or dead); the Three Soldiers statue (three servicemen looking toward the wall); and the Vietnam Women's Memorial. An American flag flies from a sixty-foot pole. On special occasions a POW/MIA flag is flown under the US flag. These days include Memorial Day, Veteran's Day, and POW/MIA Recognition Day (the third Friday of September).

The Vietnam Veterans Memorial was dedicated in 1982. Standing 150 feet away from this memorial is a statue of three soldiers facing the somber list of war casualties engraved on black granite.

The WWII Memorial was completed in 2004.

Our Honored Fallen

Encourage the students to locate information about a family member who died while serving in the US armed forces. Display each person's name, rank, branch of service, dates of birth and death, the war or conflict in which he or she served (if applicable), and where each is buried. Students may want to attach a photo and brief biography to the sheet. The display area could be decorated with US flags and made a special place of honor.

A statue of George Washington (above) in the Rotunda of the US Capitol. The famous Iwo Jima statue (bottom) stands just outside the Arlington National Cemetery.

Washington Monument

The original plan for this monument consisted of a 600-foot-high decorated obelisk rising from a circular colonnaded building 100 feet high and 250 feet in diameter. The building was to house a large statue of George Washington as well as statues of future presidents and national heroes. The cornerstone was laid on July 4, 1848. Over the next thirty-six years the design changed as completion of the monument was delayed owing to political disagreements, the Civil War, and a shortage of funds.

A Grateful Nation

The Marine Corps War Memorial symbolizes our grateful nation's respect for the honored dead of the US Marine Corps. The monument, shown at left, depicts the raising of the US flag by six marines during the battle of Iwo Jima in World War II. President Eisenhower dedicated the memorial on November 10, 1954, the 179th anniversary of the founding of the US Marine Corps. The monument's base is inscribed with Fleet Admiral Chester W. Nimitz's tribute to the fighting men on Iwo Jima: "Uncommon Valor Was a Common Virtue." The total cost of the monument and site development was funded through donations by US Marines, former Marines, Marine Corps reservists, and friends and members of the naval service. No public funds were used.

Key Dates in Washington, DC's History

1600: Piscataway Native Americans live in the Washington, DC, area.

1791: President Washington chooses site for new permanent capital.

1800: National government moves to Washington, DC.

1802: Congress grants the city of Washington its first municipal charter. Voters, white males who paid taxes and owned property (and had lived in the city for a year), are given the right to elect a twelve-member council. The president appoints a mayor.

1814: The Capitol, the White House, and some other federal buildings (as well as some private homes) are burned by British troops during the War of 1812.

1846: The Smithsonian Institute is established.

1862: Slavery is abolished in DC during the Civil War.

1888: The Washington Monument opens to the public.

1914: Ground is broken for the Lincoln Memorial.

1943: Dedication of the Jefferson Memorial

1961: The Twenty-Third Amendment gives District of Columbia residents voting rights in presidential elections.

1973: Congress approves establishing an elected mayor and thirteen-member council.

1992: The House approves, but the Senate rejects, statehood for Washington, DC.

2001: Terrorist attack destroys part of the Pentagon.

The National Museum of African American History and Culture opened in 2016.

The first Smithsonian Building, often called the "Red Castle on the Mall," houses administrative offices for the Smithsonian.

218

The bronze statue of Thomas Jefferson stands nineteen feet tall above its granite pedestal in the Jefferson Memorial. The memorial's portico faces the large Tidal Basin, which is surrounded by the city's famous cherry trees.

National Air and Space Museum

Main reading room of the Library of Congress

Plaster to Bronze

The Jefferson Memorial was modeled after the Pantheon of Rome. On November 15, 1939, President Franklin D. Roosevelt laid the cornerstone, and he dedicated the memorial in 1943. The memorial's most important change was the replacing of the plaster model statue of Thomas Jefferson with a bronze statue when the World War II restrictions on the use of metals were lifted.

Marine One, the presidential helicopter, lands on the White House lawn.

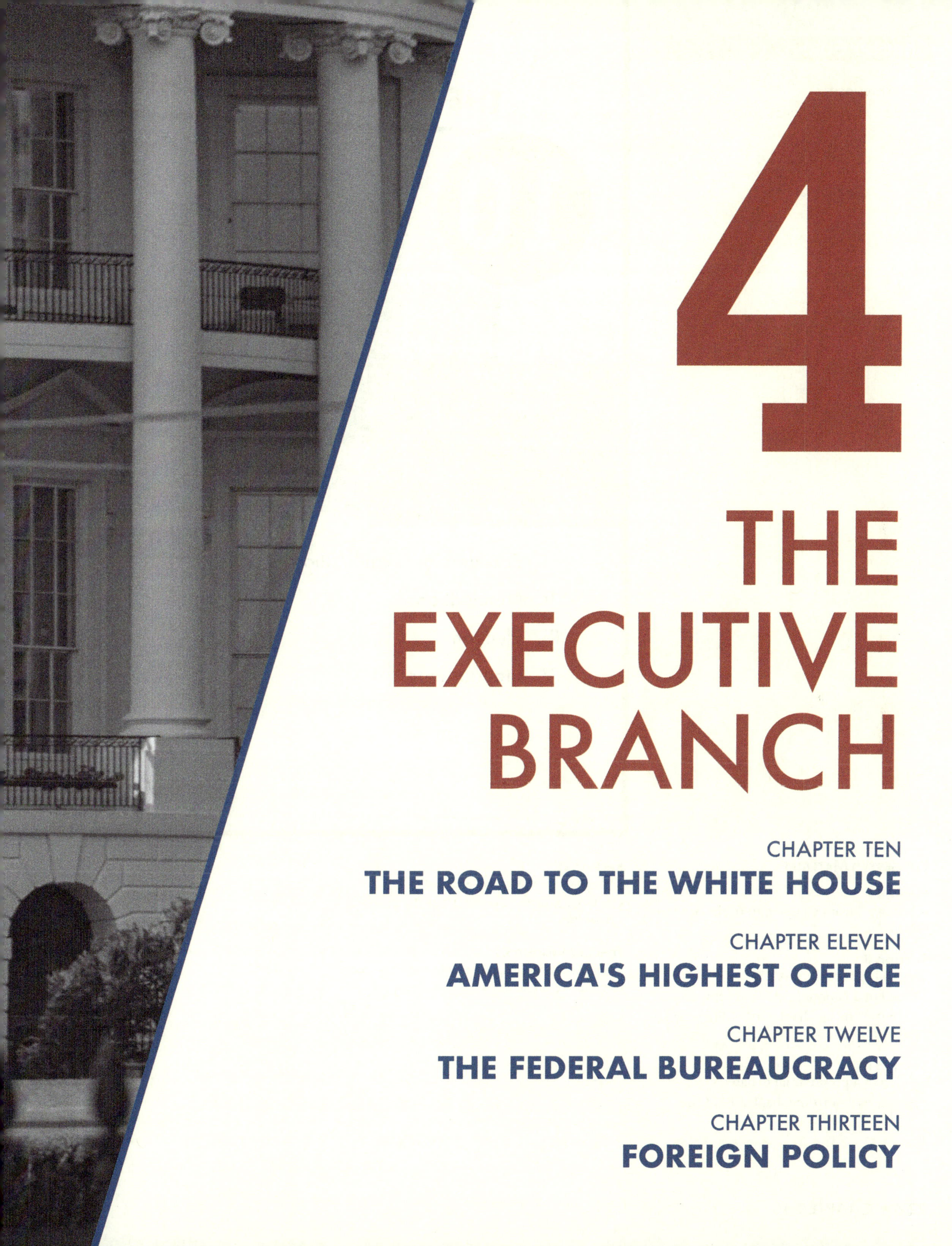

4

THE EXECUTIVE BRANCH

CHAPTER TEN
THE ROAD TO THE WHITE HOUSE

CHAPTER ELEVEN
AMERICA'S HIGHEST OFFICE

CHAPTER TWELVE
THE FEDERAL BUREAUCRACY

CHAPTER THIRTEEN
FOREIGN POLICY

THE ROAD TO THE WHITE HOUSE

10

Three presidents—Barack Obama, Bill Clinton, and George W. Bush—at the White House in 2010

I. **Presidential Qualifications**

II. **Nomination**

III. **Election**

IV. **Inauguration**

BIG IDEAS

1. What qualifications are required to be president?
2. How does the presidential nomination process work?
3. What are the specifics of the election process?
4. What is the significance of the presidential inauguration?

SUGGESTED MATERIALS

Section I
- Activity 1 from Chapter 10 of the *Student Activities*

Section II
- Special speaker (see p. 230)
- Video of a national party convention
- Activity 2 from Chapter 10 of the *Student Activities*

Section III
- Video of a presidential debate
- Activities 3–4 from Chapter 10 of the *Student Activities*

Section IV
- Video of an inaugural address
- Activity 5 from Chapter 10 of the *Student Activities*

Teacher Resources
Visit TeacherToolsOnline.com for resources to enhance the lessons.

The presidency—what political scientist James MacGregor Burns called the "seat of glory, cockpit of raw conflict"—is one of the important power centers of our government. When Patrick Henry first read the Constitution, he grumbled, "It has an awful squinting; it squints towards monarchy. . . . Your president may easily become king." Fortunately, Henry's assessment has proven incorrect. Although the presidency has grown in power and prestige, our nation's chief executive is hardly a king. This chapter examines presidential qualifications, the nomination process, the election process, and the inauguration with its transfer of power.

I. Presidential Qualifications

A study of the presidents of the United States is a study of US history in miniature. The presidents' lives have contributed richly to the American experience, and their names have sometimes characterized periods of the nation's history, such as the Jeffersonian and Jacksonian eras. Some presidents have shaped the nation and its future by the force of their personalities. George Washington, for example, provided leadership and integrity that set a course for the young Republic and established precedents and a pattern for his successors. Theodore Roosevelt embodied a vibrant, burgeoning America waking to its role as a world leader. In contrast, presidents such as Millard Fillmore, Franklin Pierce, and Chester A. Arthur are noted more for their obscurity than for their accomplishments.

In the days of Washington, America was little more than a band of states huddled along the Eastern Seaboard. But by the mid-twentieth century, the United States was a highly industrialized superpower stretching from Maine to California and encompassing Alaska, Hawaii, and even far-flung territories in the South Pacific.

The presidency, like the nation, has experienced change. Yet at least one important feature has remained remarkably unchanged. Despite the growth in government and the demands of a new era, the president is still one person entrusted with the most important office in the land.

The Founding Fathers provided broad, fairly nonrestrictive qualifications for those seeking the presidency. Article II, Section 1, of the Constitution states,

> No person except a natural born citizen, or a citizen of the United States, at the time of the adoption of this Constitution, shall be eligible to the office of president; neither shall any person be eligible to that office who shall not have attained to the age of thirty five years, and been fourteen years a resident within the United States.

These qualifications were intended to ensure that presidents were mature and had lived in the nation long enough to have an understanding of their American heritage. The phrase "natural born citizen" means anyone born in the United States or born outside the United States to US citizens.

Although these qualifications make the office accessible, there have typically been two main avenues to the White House: either a successful military career

"[The presidency] should always be occupied by a man of elevated talents, of ripe virtues, of incorruptible integrity, and of tried patriotism; one, who shall forget his own interests, and remember, that he represents not a party, but the whole nation; one, whose fame may be rested with posterity, not upon the false eulogies of favorites, but upon the solid merit of having preserved the glory, and enhanced the prosperity of the country."

—Supreme Court Justice Joseph Story

Fillmore and Pierce

Although Millard Fillmore and Franklin Pierce are mentioned in the student text as obscure presidents, several notable things (some good, some not) occurred during their administrations. Fillmore became president upon the death of Zachary Taylor. During Fillmore's term in office (1850–53), California was admitted as a free state, New Mexico was granted territorial status, federal officers were obligated to help slaveholders seeking fugitives, and the slave trade was abolished in the District of Columbia.

Despite mounting concerns over slavery, Franklin Pierce (in office from 1853 to 1857) focused his attention on foreign policy. He pressured Great Britain to relinquish its interests in Central America and tried to buy Cuba from Spain. But Pierce was unsuccessful in both foreign-policy attempts.

Additional Unit Resources

Consider consulting the following resources before you teach Chapters 10–13:

DeGregorio, William. *Complete Book of US Presidents.*

Dorr, Robert F. *Air Force One.*

Grace, Catherine O'Neill. *The White House: An Illustrated History.*

Hastedt, Glenn. *Encyclopedia of American Foreign Policy.*

Mieczkowski, Yanek. *The Routledge Historical Atlas of Presidential Elections.*

Polsby, Nelson W., Aaron Wildavsky, Steven E. Schier, and David A. Hopkins. *Presidential Elections: Strategies and Structures of American Politics.*

Siuru, William D., Jr., and Andrea Stewart. *Presidential Cars and Transportation: From Horse and Carriage to* Air Force One, *the Story of How the Presidents of the United States Travel.*

Presidential Qualities

Lead the students in listing ten positive qualities an effective president should possess. Group the students and direct each group to choose two of the ten qualities and discuss why these qualities are important. Remind the students that four key political virtues are prudence, boldness, humility, and respect. Ask them to assess whether the qualities they are discussing relate to these virtues. Invite students to present their conclusions to the class.

Instruct the student to list two to five positive qualities an effective president should possess and explain why these qualities are important. Encourage the student to also examine how these qualities relate to the four virtues mentioned above.

A Natural-Born Citizen

Discuss the possible reasons why the Founding Fathers required the US president to be a natural-born citizen.

Health and Stamina

William Henry Harrison died of pneumonia on April 4, 1841, one month to the day after delivering a one-hour-and-forty-minute inaugural address in the cold on the Capitol's east steps. In contrast, Ronald Reagan served two terms and left office at age seventy-seven and lived until age ninety-three. During his administration, Reagan survived not only a bullet wound from an assassination attempt but also several operations, including one for cancer. He was physically robust, but his survival would have been virtually impossible if medicine were no more advanced in the 1980s than it had been during the 1840s.

In addition to Reagan, three other presidents have lived to age 93 or longer—Gerald Ford, George H. W. Bush, and Jimmy Carter. Carter holds two records. He has had the longest post-presidency of any of the nation's leaders (he left the White House in January 1981), and he has lived longer than any other president.

Dwight D. Eisenhower (top) shown during World War II. Ronald Reagan (bottom) starred in Hellcats of the Navy, *with his future wife, Nancy Davis Reagan, more than two decades before becoming president.*

or holding important government offices. Before entering politics, presidents such as George Washington, Andrew Jackson, Zachary Taylor, Ulysses S. Grant, and Dwight Eisenhower gained leadership experience and fame as high-ranking military officers. Others spent their careers progressing from local to national office. Some presidents have spent time on both paths. Of course, there have been notable exceptions to these approaches to the Oval Office. Herbert Hoover, for example, was an engineer (but he had also held appointive government positions). Ronald Reagan's varied career included stints as an actor, a radio commentator, and a corporate spokesman, and George W. Bush was a businessman and a managing general partner of the Texas Rangers baseball team. But both Reagan and Bush were governors of large states before being elected president. Donald Trump was the first president to hold the office without any prior military or political experience.

Many presidents surmounted great obstacles on their way to the White House. The rough-hewn Andrew Jackson suffered from a variety of physical ailments, including tuberculosis, malarial fever, chronic dysentery, and probably lead poisoning (the result of two bullets lodged in him from duels he survived). His beloved wife died several weeks before his inauguration, in large part due to the stress of the 1828 campaign. Abraham Lincoln was born in poverty, had little formal education, and suffered many political losses before gaining the presidency. Andrew Johnson also grew up in severe poverty. As a teen, he began work as a tailor's apprentice to support his widowed mother, and he did not learn to read or write until his wife taught him. Theodore Roosevelt, on the other hand, was born into a wealthy family; but he was a sickly, asthmatic child. He strove hard and successfully to build a strong body, but the deaths of his wife and his mother (on the same day in the same house) were events from which he never fully recovered. His cousin Franklin fell ill in 1921 and was left paralyzed from the waist down. Bill Clinton was reared by a stepfather who abused Clinton's mother.

Whatever the road taken to the White House, the forces that fashion a president are as varied as the men who have held the office. These presidents, fashioned by wealth, health, and education—or by their lack of these benefits—have played an important role in America's past and will continue to do so in its future.

Section Review

1–3. What are the three qualifications to be a president?

4–5. What two main avenues have traditionally led to the presidency?

★ Read the quote from Supreme Court Justice Joseph Story on page 223. What qualities did he view as necessary for a president? Next, note that one item he listed was "ripe virtues." Read 2 Samuel 23:3; Proverbs 28:2; 29:12; and Titus 3:1–3. What virtues are mentioned in these passages?

★ In addition to the items addressed in the questions above, what additional qualifications do you think are needed for a person to be president?

Presidential Perspective

Instruct the students to describe what they think it would be like to be a candidate for president. Discuss the opportunities and challenges.

Successful Generals

Since the beginning of the US presidency, many have thought military generals would make successful presidents. Guide a discussion about why people think this is true and why a successful general might not make a successful president.

Activity 1: Choosing Qualified Leaders

This activity should help the students understand what the founders expected of the president and of US senators when they were writing the Constitution.

Section Review Answers

1–3. A person must be a natural-born citizen, be at least thirty-five years of age, and have been a US resident for at least fourteen years. (p. 223)

4–5. a successful military career or holding important government offices (p. 223–24)

★ A. Joseph Story's qualities for a president: elevated talents, ripe virtues, incorruptible integrity (Prov. 16:2), tried patriotism, one who forgets his own interests and interests of party and represents the whole nation
B. virtues of a president: just (2 Sam. 23:3); wisdom, understanding or knowledge; honest (Prov. 29:12); respectful (Titus 3:1–3)

★ Answers may include such qualities as ability to communicate, vision, physical stamina, military experience, business experience, government experience, exemplary character, and firm support for traditional values.

II. Nomination

Modern presidential campaigns are not for self-doubters or the faint of heart. The campaign trail is strenuous and exhausting, and each candidate must raise millions of dollars just to stay in the race.

Primary Hurdles

The Constitution offers no guidelines concerning the method of choosing presidential candidates. In the days before party labels existed, the framers of the Constitution hoped that the best men, like cream in milk, would rise to the top: men of talent, intelligence, and experience—men whose only ambition was to serve their country. The candidate who received the most electoral votes (votes cast by electors in the Electoral College) would become president, and the runner-up would become vice president. This ideal system did not survive long in the turbulent world of politics. The nonpartisan selection process changed into a system that was more party oriented and democratic. In many states today, the partisan process of choosing a presidential nominee begins with the presidential primary.

The Rise of Presidential Primaries

The dawn of the twentieth century saw an outcry against the "undemocratic" political party conventions that nominated presidential candidates during much of the nineteenth century. Opponents described these conventions as small groups of men meeting in "smoke-filled rooms" to decide on a candidate. The alternative method proposed giving the people control of party nominations through **direct primaries** (preliminary nominating elections held to select candidates or delegates to party conventions). In 1903 Wisconsin became the first state to allow direct primaries for state offices, and by 1912 fourteen states had adopted **presidential primaries** to select delegates for the national conventions of the political parties. (**Delegates** are party representatives who pledge to support the candidate's nomination at the national party convention.) The 1912 platform of Teddy Roosevelt's Progressive, or Bull Moose, Party called for "nation-wide preferential primaries for candidates for the presidency."

Teddy Roosevelt had a reputation as a vigorous campaigner.

The presidential primary was introduced as an attempt to circumvent party bosses' power to control the national convention and thus the presidential nomination. However, more than half a century passed before the method gained substantial support. The slow adoption of presidential primaries was a result of several factors, including the cost of an extra election to the states and the reluctance of many candidates to campaign for votes in the primaries. In the 1940s, 1950s, and 1960s, some candidates began entering the existing primaries to demonstrate their ability to win votes. For example, John Kennedy's strong showing in the 1960 primaries helped convince Democratic leaders that a Roman Catholic could win support in a nation that was predominately Protestant. In those years, the delegates that a candidate won in the primaries were relatively few and of little consequence, but that situation has changed.

The political and social activism in the 1960s and 1970s helped spur an increase in the number and influence of presidential primaries. The Democrats, who held primaries in fifteen states in 1968, doubled that number in eight years

Section II Objectives

1. Describe the origins, purposes, forms, and course of presidential primaries.
2. Summarize the preparations, participants, and procedures of national party conventions.

Without Campaigning in Primaries

Hubert Humphrey won the Democratic nomination in 1968 without campaigning in any presidential primaries. He was the last major party nominee to do so.

More Campaigning

With the rise of presidential primaries, the overall campaign season became longer and the number of candidates greater. Until the twentieth century, candidates usually did not campaign openly before the convention. Instead, influential friends often worked for those candidates' nomination while the candidates feigned indifference. Today, potential candidates often begin exploratory committees three years or more before the next presidential election.

Positive or Negative

Discuss presidential primaries' positive and negative effects on the average voter. Do the primaries excite a party's voting base? Do average voters ignore what is said in the primaries? How do successful presidential candidates motivate voters and gain their support in the primaries?

The Iowa Caucus

In recent political history the Iowa caucus became one of the first tests for both parties' major presidential candidates. The press and the national leadership in both parties watch to see which candidates generate the strongest support. In the two-year period prior to the 1988 caucuses, thirteen presidential candidates (and almost six hundred staffers) spent approximately 846 days in Iowa. Such efforts have now become typical.

Campaign Rigors

Adlai Stevenson unsuccessfully challenged Dwight Eisenhower for the White House in 1952 and 1956. In the following account, Stevenson gives a candidate's perspective of the tiresome task of campaigning. Though technological advancements and other changes have occurred in the decades since Stevenson was a candidate, his description still provides insight into the grueling campaign process.

"At least for an inexperienced candidate, I suppose we have contrived few more exacting ordeals than a Presidential campaign. You must emerge, bright and bubbling with wisdom and well-being, every morning at 8 o'clock, just in time for a charming and profound breakfast talk, shake hands with hundreds, often literally thousands, of people, make several inspiring, 'newsworthy' speeches during the day, confer with political leaders along the way and with your staff all the time, write at every chance, think if possible, read mail and newspapers, talk on the telephone, talk to everybody, dictate, receive delegations, eat, with decorum—and discretion!—and ride through city after city on the back of an open car, smiling until your mouth is dehydrated by the wind, waving until the blood runs out of your arm, and then bounce gaily, confidently, masterfully into great howling halls, shaved and all made up for television with the right color shirt and tie. . . . Then all you have to do is make a great, imperishable speech, get out through the pressing crowds with a few score autographs, your clothes intact, your hands bruised, and back to the hotel—in time to see a few important people.

"But the real work has just commenced—two or three, sometimes four hours of frenzied writing and editing of the next day's immortal mouthings so you can get something to the stenographers, so they can get something to the mimeograph machines, so they can get something to the reporters, so they can get something to their papers by deadline time. (And I quickly concluded that all deadlines were yesterday!) Finally sleep, sweet sleep, steals you away, unless you worry—which I do.

"The next day is the same."

Stevenson, Adlai E. *Major Campaign Speeches of Adlai E. Stevenson, 1952.* New York: Random House, 1953.

and then had thirty-seven primaries in 1988. By the 2000 election, thirty-nine Democratic primaries were held. Republican primaries increased in similar fashion; that year, they held forty-two primaries. The importance of presidential primaries has continued in the twenty-first century. For example, in the 2016 election, forty-one states held a presidential primary for one or both of the major political parties.

With this significant rise in the number of primaries came a corresponding rise in the number of convention delegates won in the primaries. Thus, serious candidates can no longer avoid participating in the majority of the primaries without risking the loss of too many committed delegates to other candidates.

The states that do not hold presidential primaries generally use a system of district and state conventions generally known as a **caucus**; the Iowa caucuses are the most prominent. At these caucuses, party members participate by the thousands to support certain candidates. But their support does not necessarily correspond to the state delegates' votes for candidates in the national convention in the same way that primary votes usually do. During the course of the various caucus procedures, there is greater room for party leaders to influence the selection of delegates and their support for candidates. Although primaries have gained preeminence, presidential hopefuls cannot afford to ignore the caucus states. Candi-

 **Evaluating Candidates**

To help the students learn how Christians ought to evaluate candidates, ask them to examine the positions of the most recent presidential candidates. Instruct them to determine whether the goals of the various positions are biblical. For those goals that are biblical, instruct the students to discuss whether the means used to achieve them are biblical and effective.

Also, does each candidate exemplify the political virtues of prudence, boldness, humility, and respect? Based on this evaluation, direct the students to decide which candidates a Christian could wisely support.

dates must campaign hard to win support; to influence delegate selection; and, as always, to gain the media spotlight. Therefore, the results of both primaries and caucuses are watched carefully in light of their impact on party nominations.

The Purpose of Presidential Primaries

As we have seen, the party reform effort that resulted in presidential primaries sought to open the nomination process to greater participation and to lessen the party bosses' power to dictate the outcome. Primaries, therefore, have two basic purposes. One purpose is to open the field to more candidates, not just to the ones whom party insiders approve. The primary season is long, expensive, and demanding, but it permits a number of candidates the opportunity to demonstrate their vote-getting ability to the public. Another purpose of the presidential primary is to make national delegate selection more democratic. Because parties are regulated at the state rather than at the national level, the primary process differs from state to state. We will take a general look, however, at primary voting and delegate-selection methods.

In the presidential primary elections, held in the months before the national party conventions, the voters choose the candidate that they want their party to nominate for president. The delegates they send to the party national conventions must then support the candidates according to the dictates of the popular vote in the primaries. Rules for apportioning delegates vary from state to state. Either the winner receives the support of all the state's delegates, or the leading candidates receive delegates according to a system based on the percentage of the vote each candidate received. Thus, after every primary, the candidates can tally the delegate support they have won and compare their total with the number they need to win the nomination at the national convention (a simple majority of the total number of delegates). Because more than two-thirds of the delegates are selected in primary elections, it is typical for the nominee to be determined long before the convention.

Primaries are conducted by the states, and they exist in several forms (see Chapter 7). **Closed primaries** are primaries in which the participants must be registered as members of one party and may vote only for the candidates from the party in which they claim membership.

Steps to Presidential Election	
1	Candidate announces plan to run for the presidency. (He must also file papers required by each state to have his name placed on the ballots of all fifty states.)
2	Candidate campaigns to win delegate (party representatives to the national convention) and voter support.
3	Caucuses and primary elections take place in the states. (These are the methods that the general public uses to help nominate presidential candidates.)
4	The presidential nominee is officially determined at the national party convention, and the general election campaign begins. The candidate attends various events to meet voters, makes speeches, and debates other presidential candidates.
5	Election Day is on the Tuesday after the first Monday of November (many states permit early voting). In reality, voters are selecting a group of electors that will serve as their state's representatives in the Electoral College.
6	The Electoral College votes on the first Monday after the second Wednesday in December. In every state except Maine and Nebraska, all of a state's electoral votes go to the candidate who wins the popular vote in that state. At least 270 electoral votes are required to elect a president.
7	The president is inaugurated on January 20.

Calvin Coolidge used some of the latest available technology, especially radio and amplified sound systems, while campaigning for president.

Iowa Caucus Night

On caucus night, Iowans gather according to party choice in public buildings, designated schools, or private homes. The Republican caucus goers indicate preference for a candidate by paper ballot. The whole caucus then elects delegates and alternates to go to the party's county convention.

Participants in the Democratic caucus divide into groups based on their choice of a candidate. Participants in a group containing fewer than 15 percent of the total number of caucus attendees must either support another candidate or try to get enough undecided attendees to support their candidate so that their group reaches the 15 percent mark. Delegates to the county convention are then elected from the various remaining groups.

After the caucuses end, county parties report their results to state party headquarters in Des Moines. State parties report their results to the media.

Open Primary

In the past in some states that had an open primary, the voter was given two ballots, one for each party. He chose the ballot on which he made his selections and discarded the other. However, today in most states with an open primary, the voter must declare the primary in which he wishes to vote when he enters the polling place.

In **open primaries**, voters do not have to declare their party membership. They simply choose to support candidates from one party or the other; thus, they give voters greater privacy and opportunity in their political participation. This type of primary is popular with independents (voters who are not affiliated with any party) who are the swing voters in any election. However, in an open primary, there is also the likelihood that **crossover voting** will occur when a person affiliated with a particular party votes in the primary of an opposing party (thus, a Democrat might vote in the Republican primary or a Republican might vote in a Democratic primary). One positive of crossover voting is that statistics show that if a party can attract crossover voters in the primary, many of those voters will vote for that party's candidate in the general election.

A more negative side to crossover voting is called **raiding**. Raiding a primary is the aspect of open primaries that political parties fear. When a party has a primary with a strong leading candidate certain of winning the nomination, that party's members could "cross over" to vote for a weak candidate in the opposing party's primary. This tactic, helping nominate a weak candidate from their opposing party, increases the chances that their party's nominee will win in the general election.

Harry Truman campaigned by train, making speeches at numerous whistle stops. His wife, Bess, is on the left.

Although primary elections increased popular participation in the selection of presidential candidates, they also created new problems for the parties. First, primary contests eliminate party leaders' ability to help choose a moderate compromise candidate who will be the most acceptable to the party and most electable with the public. Vocal groups with specific interests can help push a candidate forward in the primaries without regard to his electability in the general election. If a candidate without wide appeal among American voters is nominated, his party will probably suffer a defeat in November. The Republican nomination of Barry Goldwater in 1964 and the Democratic nomination of George McGovern in 1972 are often-cited examples of this risk (though their selections were not entirely due to the presidential primary process).

Second, primaries encourage each faction of a party to enthusiastically and devotedly support its candidate for the primary election. This can create wide divisions within the party that might be difficult to reconcile when the nomination is given to one of the candidates. The result can be the creation of a splinter party or a third party, such as John Anderson's break with the Republicans in 1980. A splinter party risks disunity, and multiple factions drain financial resources that could be used in the general election.

The Course of Presidential Primaries

The early primaries and caucuses have become a key to party nominations. Media attention gained by candidates with good showings in the first few contests helps propel those early leaders toward more primary victories. It also prompts more financial support for candidates who quickly win a reputation for leading the race to gain convention delegates.

The race begins in January and February of the presidential election year. Iowa is the first state to hold caucuses and New Hampshire, shortly thereafter, is the first state to hold a presidential primary. Before these two events, an array of candidates crisscrosses Iowa and New Hampshire for months of campaigning in every possible venue. These initial tests, however, begin a rapid process of elimination. As the numbers are tallied from the **Iowa caucuses** and **New Hampshire primary**, the media quickly label certain candidates as front-runners, others as strong challengers, and still more as losers. Once this starting lineup is assessed, the reporters continue to monitor every step throughout the remaining four months of scheduled primaries and caucuses.

Some people criticize the Iowa caucuses and the New Hampshire primary because Iowa and New Hampshire are not representative of most of the nation. They have relatively small populations and no large cities; in addition, these states are more rural and contain fewer minorities than other states. However, *no* state is *perfectly* representative of the nation; and these states are, in fact, more representative than others, such as Nevada and Alaska. Possibly the biggest problem has been for the Democratic Party, whose activists tend to support more liberal candidates in these early primaries. In fact, the Democratic Party has often found itself with several candidates that are more liberal than its mainstream party members, at least in part because of the early support gained in Iowa and New Hampshire.

It is not a foregone conclusion that early primaries will spell the success or the doom of a particular candidate. For example, Bill Clinton lost the 1992 New Hampshire presidential primary but rebounded in the following primaries to capture the Democratic nomination. Also, John McCain won the 2000 New Hampshire presidential primary only to lose the Republican nomination to George W. Bush.

By 1988 the Democratic parties in the southern states were trying to thwart the impact of Iowa and New Hampshire in the primaries by scheduling many of their primaries on one day. March 8 was termed "Super Tuesday" that year because the party offered primaries in fourteen southern states that held a large number of delegates. The southern states hoped that this prize would help swing a more conservative candidate toward nomination despite any advantage that more liberal candidates had gained in Iowa and New Hampshire. The South's hopes did not materialize, however, largely because of the tremendous African American vote captured by Jesse Jackson. That vote probably diverted strength from moderate candidates and allowed Michael Dukakis to continue as the front-runner. Nevertheless, "Super Tuesday," when the greatest number of US states hold primary elections and caucuses on a single day, continues to have a significant impact on the selection of each party's candidates.

In 2016, Ted Cruz won the Iowa Republican caucuses, and Hillary Clinton lost the Democratic presidential primary in New Hampshire to Bernie Sanders.

229

National Conventions

National party conventions began in the 1830s and continue to be the means of formally nominating presidential candidates and regulating party organization. Until the rise of primaries brought large numbers of committed delegates to the gatherings, conventions were often scenes of political bargaining, deal making, and backslapping as party bosses or campaign leaders sought more support for their candidates. However, for the past half century, a leading candidate has usually entered each convention with enough support from delegates won in primaries to be assured the nomination and remove the need for intense negotiation. Nevertheless, national conventions remain colorful events that elicit a wave of support for party nominees in the general election campaign.

Convention Preparations

Choosing the site of a party convention is an important step. In the past, certain cities were often selected to entice the pivotal states in which they are located to swing their November votes to the party ticket. Now the committee members who make the choice for each party are usually most concerned with locating the convention in a place with an appropriately large convention center and ample hotels, restaurants, and entertainment for the delegates, reporters, campaign workers, and curious onlookers who will flood the city for nearly a week.

Conventions have become expensive productions. Until the 1970s most of the money came from cities and businesses trying to convince each party to locate its meeting in their quarters. The ethical questions raised by this kind of fundraising prompted the federal government to begin allotting a large sum for each of the national party conventions. That funding continued until it was repealed by Congress in 2014.

Conventions for both parties normally meet in either July or August before the November election. Preparations begin well in advance, as does the work of the delegates assigned to each party's Resolutions Committee. The committee formulates the initial party platform to be considered at the convention. A **party platform** is a formal statement of a party's position on current issues; it is drafted at the party's national convention every four years. Interestingly, a nominee might not agree with all planks of his party's platform and is not held to it.

Convention Participants

National conventions have become major events. For example, in 2016, at the Republican convention (held in Cleveland, Ohio), 2,472 delegates were present. In Philadelphia, Pennsylvania, 4,763 delegates attended the Democratic convention. In addition to the official delegate count, each party had thousands of alternates and support staff in attendance. The number of delegates each state is allowed to send varies in accordance with each party's equation for delegate representation. Republican National Convention delegates and alternates are elected by congressional district and state conventions. Democratic National Convention delegates and alternates are chosen by Democratic voters in each congressional district during the state primary election. Additional Democratic delegates include party leaders and elected officials.

The late 1960s and the 1970s saw some dramatic changes in the makeup of the convention delegates in both parties. Before that time, most delegates were party leaders, politicians, businessmen, and other important people who could exert their influence, monetarily or otherwise, on their party. Most of these delegates were white males of middle age or older; consequentially, women, young

Convention Participants

Invite individuals who attended a national convention to relate their experiences to the class. Were they delegates, alternates, or guests? What type of security checks were encountered? Which well-known personalities were present? Do they have photographs or memorabilia to display? What costs were incurred?

In 2016, the Republican National Convention (left) was held in Cleveland, Ohio. The Democratic National Convention (right) was in Philadelphia, Pennsylvania.

people, and minority groups began to protest their exclusion from party conventions. The Democrats were particularly troubled by the protests and antiwar riots that erupted during their 1968 convention in Chicago. In response, the Democratic Party devised guidelines for choosing more women, young people, and minorities to fill delegate slots. These efforts had to be modified, however, when these groups were later overrepresented at the convention. Though the Republican Party did not change its rules to require more diversity at its convention, it has made concerted efforts to increase representation by women, minorities, and younger voters.

The Democratic Party instituted another change in its selection of delegates by including a specified percentage of **superdelegates** (party leaders and office-holders) to serve as uncommitted delegates. The superdelegate position was created because of the need to reform the reforms. The extreme segments of the Democratic Party had begun to send disproportionately large numbers of delegates to the conventions because of their ability to activate support in the primaries. Superdelegates are intended to provide a moderating influence on the outcome of the nomination by supporting the most electable candidate. The Democrats first introduced 568 superdelegates to the 1984 convention, and by the 2000 convention they increased the number to 799. By 2008 the number of super-delegates was 852. In 2016, the number of superdelegates had dropped to 712, but that still accounted for fifteen percent of the total number of delegates. During the 2016 election, superdelegates heavily favored Hillary Clinton rather than her opponent, Senator Bernie Sanders. Sanders argued that superdelegates, who were not chosen during the presidential caucuses and primaries, should not have the same voice as other delegates. Partly as a result of that dispute, in August 2018, the Democratic Party changed its rules. Effective with the 2020 convention, superdelegates will continue to vote on the party rules and the party platform; however, they will not be able to vote on the first presidential ballot unless one of the candidates has secured a majority at the convention with the other delegate votes. In other words, the superdelegates would not be able to cast the determining votes in the nomination process.

At the 2000 Republican National Convention, Republicans began taking steps toward selecting superdelegates. There were 168 superdelegates, fourteen percent of the total delegates, at the 2012 Republican convention in Tampa, Florida. In 2016, there were 173 Republican superdelegates, which was seven percent of the total convention delegates. Though Democratic superdelegates

Site Selection

Selecting a national convention site takes almost a year. To be considered, a city has to have adequate facilities, an adequate infrastructure, and the united support of the city's civic, political, and business leadership. For example, for the site of the 2004 Democratic Convention, Boston, Miami, Detroit, and New York City were considered; Boston was the final choice. The Republicans considered New York City, New Orleans, and Tampa–St. Petersburg and ultimately chose New York City.

As noted with the pictures on this page, the 2016 Democratic convention was held in Philadelphia and the Republicans met in Cleveland. For the 2020 conventions, the Democrats chose Milwaukee and the Republicans chose Charlotte.

Why the Change in Delegate Selection?

Discuss with the class why the conventions' delegate-apportionment system changed in the late 1960s and the 1970s. Two reasons mentioned might be that the new systems

1. encouraged more participation, thus expanding the party base, and
2. encouraged each state to improve voter turnout so each could gain a greater voice in candidate selection.

Discuss some negative aspects of the change. Students might mention that the changes

1. might result in the selection of the most popular, though not necessarily the most capable, candidate and
2. might reduce the ability of the party to prevent a demagogue or other undesirable candidate from being nominated.

Personal Appearance

In 1932, Franklin Roosevelt became the first major party nominee to make a personal appearance at a convention to accept his nomination. Usually, nominees waited at home until official messengers from the convention notified them of the results of the voting.

Today, as a formality, conventions continue to send official representatives to notify a candidate of his nomination; but, of course, the candidate watches his own nomination on television and might be on the way to the convention hall before the party representatives arrive.

are unpledged to any candidate, meaning they can "vote their conscience," Republican Party rules require their superdelegates to vote for whichever candidate won their state in the presidential primary. Therefore, while the function of the Democratic superdelegates is to guard the party against radical candidates, Republican superdelegates were initiated to bring unity to the party by speeding up the nomination process.

Convention Procedures

The obvious purpose of the national convention held by each major political party has always been to nominate that party's candidates for president and vice president. But the convention is also the place for adopting the party platform and launching a unified campaign for the November elections.

The first day of a convention usually consists of routine organizational procedures. National party leaders and temporary officers lead the session by welcoming the delegates, making announcements about activities, and overseeing the election of the convention committees, which consist of delegates attending the convention. The highlight of the first day is usually the **keynote address**

First Lady Michelle Obama speaking at the Democratic National Convention in 2016

(a speech made by a leading party member). This speech overflows with enthusiasm for the party candidates in the coming election while criticizing the opposing party, thus stirring intense passion among the delegates.

Further organizational tasks and the adoption of the party platform generally consume the following day or more of the convention. A committee on rules and order of business recommends the slate of procedural rules and the agenda for the convention. These guidelines are usually slight modifications of those from the previous convention and generally pass without difficulty, but certain changes or points can cause heated arguments on the convention floor before they gain approval. A credentials committee validates all the delegates' claims of eligibility to participate in the convention and prepares the official roll of delegates. Occasionally, the authority of a delegate or even an entire state delegation is challenged, and a determination must be made regarding whether the delegates have been properly selected. Usually, these are minor problems between rival party factions or personalities that can be settled easily with few consequences. However, that is not always the case. Dwight Eisenhower was able to win the Republican nomination in 1952, over his rival Robert Taft, by contesting the credentials of the Taft delegates from several southern states.

A committee on permanent organization recommends a list of permanent officers for the convention. One of these officers is the chairman, who will guide the remaining deliberations and activities. After the officers are approved and installed, the convention really gets down to business by adopting a party platform. The Committee on Platform and Resolutions presents the draft it has prepared, and some debate usually follows. If much of the proposed platform provokes opposition, the proceedings might extend into another day before compromises can be approved. Throughout these days of party work, inspirational speeches are given to help keep enthusiasm alive.

Democratic Superdelegates—Good or Bad?

Selection of Democratic superdelegates has been a subject of much controversy. That disagreement led to a rules change in 2018 that was implemented at the 2020 convention (see p. 231).

Prior to that change, what did opponents of superdelegates assert? *Students might say that their method of selection was less democratic than the method used for other delegates and thus, some voters disliked their involvement in the nomination process. Also, it could cause some to question the legitimacy of a candidate that might be selected because of superdelegates.*

How do you think proponents of the use of superdelegates defended their position? *Supporters argued that superdelegates were elected officials and therefore still represented the people. Their experience in political matters could help prevent the selection of an undesirable candidate, such as a demagogue.*

Next comes the convention's premier event—the nomination of its presidential candidate. Though both parties generally narrow the field to one candidate before coming to the convention, the proceedings remain colorful. Nomination speeches are made for several candidates. In the past, many of these were simply attempts to honor popular party members, such as a state's "favorite son," with speeches rather than serious nominations. Speeches nominating the leading candidates receive the most attention. Each nominating speech is followed by one or more seconding speeches. After hearing the glowing testimonials for these candidates, the convention delegates begin to vote state by state. Reporters tally the votes as they are announced, and interested American viewers watch as the leading candidate reaches the number that puts him over the top. When this happens, the convention floor erupts into celebration with delegates yelling, stomping, whooping, and whistling amid a downpour of balloons and confetti. Often, the demonstration continues for fifteen or twenty minutes until the hall can be quieted enough to allow the voting to conclude.

Although first-ballot nominations are now normal, failure to give one candidate a majority vote on the first roll call, or ballot, remains a possibility. The last time this happened was at the Democratic convention in 1952 when Adlai Stevenson was eventually nominated after three ballots. Primaries now force many delegates to remain committed to certain candidates (at least for specific periods), and this precludes much of the bargaining for delegate votes that took place in the past. Therefore, if large blocks of committed delegates are split among three or more candidates, a convention could again reach an impasse, though not of the magnitude of the 1924 Democratic convention, when John W. Davis had to wait nine days through a total of 103 ballots before he finally won the nomination. Such a convention that requires multiple balloting and an eventual settlement by bargaining and compromise is called a **brokered convention**. Any prolonged and heated situation like this usually impairs a party's unity and strength in the November election.

The final item of business is nominating a vice-presidential candidate. At one time, party leaders made the choice, but now the decision is usually left to the presidential nominee. The choice generally centers on two considerations: geography and ideology. For example, a candidate with liberal ideas from the East might team up with a conservative from the West to **balance the ticket**; in other words, a presidential nominee chooses a running mate who can strengthen his chance of being elected due to specific ideology, geography, ethnicity, gender, or other characteristics. In 1960, John Kennedy, a Roman Catholic from Massachusetts, chose Lyndon Johnson, a Texas Protestant, as his vice-presidential candidate to broaden his support within the party and throughout the country. In 2000, Vice President Al Gore, a Tennessee Protestant, chose Joe Lieberman, a Jewish senator from Connecticut, to balance his ticket.

The 2016 presidential and vice-presidential nominees at their national conventions—Republicans Donald Trump and Mike Pence (top) and Democrats Hillary Clinton and Tim Kaine (bottom)

Dark Horses

Brokered conventions have occasionally resulted in the nomination of a "dark horse," a candidate who received little attention before the impasse but was pushed forward at the convention as a compromise candidate. John W. Davis was an unsuccessful dark horse in 1924. James K. Polk, Franklin Pierce, and Warren Harding were three earlier successful dark horses.

National Conventions

Show the class excerpts from a video of a major party's national convention. Parts of the keynote address, the voting process for the candidate, and the candidate's acceptance speech would be excellent selections for the students to view. Perhaps prepare questions for the students to answer as they watch the video.

Activity 2: A Brokered Convention: The Democratic National Convention, 1924

This activity shows the students that the outcomes of earlier conventions, unlike recent ones, were not always predictable. They often involved numerous votes and political wrangling before delegates selected the presidential candidate for their party.

First to Withdraw

Senator Thomas F. Eagleton was chosen in 1972 to be the Democratic vice-presidential nominee. But after accepting the party's nomination at the national convention, Eagleton became the only person ever to withdraw after accepting the nomination. He did so after it was disclosed that he had received psychiatric treatment.

Section III Objectives

1. Evaluate some influences on campaign strategies.
2. Analyze the role of debates in presidential campaigns.
3. Explain the importance of Election Day.
4. Evaluate the role of the Electoral College.

Although balancing the ticket seems to make political sense in our diverse society, it can damage a candidate's credibility with his main supporters. This is particularly true when a candidate uses ideology to balance a ticket. In 1980 Ronald Reagan surprised his conservative supporters by choosing the more moderate George H. W. Bush as his running mate. In his own campaign, Bush had supported passage of the Equal Rights Amendment and characterized Reagan's economic proposals as "voodoo economics." However, Reagan saw the choice of Bush as his running mate as a way to broaden his support within the Republican Party and to demonstrate his own strength by choosing his closest rival from the primaries. In the end, Reagan won the election.

Where is a party's primary candidate during the convention? The first and second days of the convention often find the candidate on the campaign trail, working his way toward the convention. On the final convention day, the candidate, along with his vice-presidential candidate, gives an acceptance speech that encourages party unity and enthusiasm and then sends the delegates home to work vigorously for the success of the party ticket. With the party's nomination and, hopefully, full support in hand, the candidate begins increasing his campaign efforts as Election Day draws closer.

Section Review

1. What was introduced in the early 1900s as a way of circumventing the control that party bosses held at political party conventions?
2. Identify a second method used by many states to give citizens an opportunity to indicate their preferred presidential candidate.
3. Why is Iowa significant in a presidential election year?
4. Why is New Hampshire important in a presidential election year?
5. In recent years, how has the composition of national convention delegates changed?
6–7. What causes a brokered convention to occur? What happened at the most famous such convention of the twentieth century?
★ Do you think that "balancing the ticket" is a good strategy or a bad one? Explain your view.

Guiding Questions

1. What are some influences on campaign strategies?
2. How do debates affect presidential campaigns?
3. What is the importance of Election Day?
4. What role does the Electoral College play in presidential elections?

III. Election

After campaigning for two years or longer, the candidates who win their party nominations emerge from their conventions to begin the final part of their race—the **general election**. The election, held on the Tuesday after the first Monday in November, determines not only which candidate will occupy the White House for the next four years but also which party will have control of executive appointments and policymaking. At stake are history, leadership, and the most visible job in the world.

Campaign Strategy

A well-laid plan is crucial to a successful campaign. Political strategists must shape the candidate's game plan, and much of that approach hinges on the

Section Review Answers

1. presidential or direct primaries (p. 225)
2. caucuses (p. 226)
3. That state has the first caucuses. (p. 229)
4. That state has the first presidential primary. (p. 229)
5. There are a greater number of women, young people, and minorities, and superdelegates have a large role. (pp. 230–31)
6–7. A brokered convention may occur if large blocks of committed delegates are split among three or more candidates. At the 1924 Democratic convention, John W. Davis had to wait nine days through 103 ballots before he finally won the nomination. (p. 233)

★ Some may say that balancing the ticket makes political sense in our diverse society. Others may mention that it can damage a candidate's credibility with his main supporters.

Campaign Slogans

"Tippecanoe and Tyler Too." Sure, there had been poems and songs in praise of presidential candidates before; but this one-line chant helped sweep William Henry Harrison, the hero of the Battle of Tippecanoe, into the White House in 1840. The slogan linked Harrison's flag-waving nationalism and John Tyler's Virginian southern sectionalism. Since then, campaign slogans have multiplied, adding their promises, accusations, insults, and idealism to the pandemonium of presidential races.

The word *slogan* comes from Gaelic words meaning "army call" or "battle cry," and, indeed, campaigners have learned to use their slogans to rally voters to their cause or sound an attack against their opponents. "Fifty-Four Forty or Fight" (Polk, 1844) and "Let Us Have Peace" (Grant, 1868) both called people to the causes of their time. In 1924 the Democrats claimed that "A vote for Coolidge is a vote for chaos," and after three terms of FDR, Thomas Dewey declared that it was "Time for a Change" in 1944.

Some experts say that the best slogans usually have seven words or fewer, and many memorable campaign lines reflect this. Some are catchy phrases using rhyme or alliteration: "Keep Cool with Coolidge" (1924), "Win with Willkie" (1940), and "All the Way with LBJ" (1964).

A few campaign slogans have been caustic. In 1884 the Republicans labeled the Democrats with "Rum, Romanism, and Rebellion"; and similarly, in 1952 the Democrats were tagged with "Communism, Corruption, and Korea." In 1988 the Republicans poked fun at the Democratic candidate, Michael Dukakis, the son of a Greek immigrant. He was six inches shorter than his opponent, George H. W. Bush. Republicans twisted an old expression "Beware of Greeks Bearing Gifts" (a reference to the story of the Trojan horse) to "Beware of Greeks Wearing Lifts."

One of the most venomous of all popular slogans was one used against Grover Cleveland in 1884. The ditty "Ma! Ma! Where's my pa? Gone to the White House. Ha! Ha! Ha!" accused him of fathering an illegitimate child. The Democrats did not take the jab lying down, however. They responded against Cleveland's opponent with a rousing "Blaine, Blaine, James G. Blaine, the continental liar from the state of Maine!"

Other slogans have concentrated on making promises to the voters. Some pledged prosperity: "A Full Dinner Pail" (McKinley, 1896), "A Chicken in Every Pot" (Hoover, 1928), and "Happy Days Are Here Again" (Roosevelt, 1932). Some promoted freedom: "Return to Normalcy" (Harding, 1920); "Peace and Freedom" (Nixon, 1960). Others emphasized strength: "Let's Make America Great Again" (Reagan, 1980).

Slogans have also been clever: "We Polk'd you in 1844; we shall Pierce you in 1852." Some became ironic: "He kept us out of war" (Wilson, 1916); some were rude: "We don't want Eleanor either" (1940). And some were even comic: "Madly for Adlai" (Stevenson, 1952). Some have backfired, like the Goldwater line in 1964: "In your heart you know he's right." Responses ranged from "Far Right!" to "In your guts you know he's nuts." A few slogans extended the popularity of a candidate. "I Like Ike" worked so well for Eisenhower in 1952 that he used it again with success in 1956.

More recent campaign slogans include "A Kinder, Gentler Nation" (George H. W. Bush, 1988); "Don't Stop Thinking About Tomorrow" (Bill Clinton, 1992); "Ross for Boss" (Perot, 1992); "Prosperity and Progress" (Gore, 2000); "Leave No Child Behind" (George W. Bush, 2000); "Change We Can Believe In" (Obama, 2008); "Stronger Together" (Hillary Clinton, 2016); and "Make America Great Again" (Trump, 2016).

Although it illustrates how little things, even the trivial, may shape voters' thinking, a catchy slogan may actually have an important influence on the outcome of a presidential election. "Old Tippecanoe" surely started something, giving us one of the most colorful and effective weapons in our political arsenal.

Campaign Songs

Campaign songs were popular tools in the nineteenth century. William Henry Harrison's followers sang a tune with the following chorus: "Old Tip [a reference to Harrison's victory at the Battle of Tippecanoe] he wears a homespun coat. / He has no ruffled shirt-wirt-wirt; / But Mat [Martin van Buren] he has the golden plate, / And he's a little squirt-wirt-wirt." Singers punctuated the "wirt-wirts" by spitting tobacco juice through their teeth. In 1932, Franklin Roosevelt's campaign song was "Happy Days Are Here Again," quite a contrast to the dismal state of the Depression economy.

Electoral College's winner-take-all system: if a candidate wins in a state by even a single popular vote, he receives all the electoral votes for that state. (Maine and Nebraska are exceptions.) Therefore, candidates must campaign hardest in the states with the most electoral votes—California, Texas, Florida, and New York, for example. The goal is to capture at least 270 of the 538 electoral votes.

Campaign Focus

Discuss the importance of winning states that have large numbers of electoral votes and the effect this has on campaigns. Note the comparative lack of candidate interest in sparsely populated states.

Titus 3:2

Paul's prohibition of speaking evil of others appears in the context of his instruction that believers are to subject themselves to governmental authorities. The specific word translated "speak evil" is sometimes translated as "to blaspheme." It is a word that refers to slander.

Paul then says that Christians should not be "brawlers." He is not referring to just fist-fights; he's saying that Christians should not be quarrelsome people, always creating controversy. Instead Paul says that Christians should be gentle. That means they should be reasonable, courteous, and easily reconciled with others. Finally, Christians are to show Christlike meekness. They should not retaliate when they are wronged.

Paul's admonition may seem like unrealistic advice for people involved in modern politics; however, if Christians are to avoid being conformed to the world, they must live against the grain of their culture. This does not mean that Christians should avoid denouncing real evils and injustices. But it does mean that they should do so in a simple, forthright way that seeks to persuade others rather than encourage bickering and quarreling.

In 1960 Richard Nixon promised to visit all fifty states during his campaign. He kept his promise, but his strategy wasted valuable time in states that made only meager contributions to his electoral tally. Two basic considerations in any sound campaign strategy are the importance of targeting states with large numbers of electoral votes and of campaigning hard in states where a close race could sweep the electoral votes either way. One factor in this strategy might be the selection of a running mate. As mentioned earlier, a vice-presidential candidate from a key state or other region might help capture votes there.

Addressing issues that concern the public can be a great rallying point for a presidential contender. The candidate who is attuned to popular trends and attitudes and can shape them into campaign issues will generally raise broad support. But a candidate whose ideas are out of touch with those of most voters faces an obvious difficulty. Walter Mondale's suggestion in 1984 that the government raise taxes to help reverse the growing deficit is an example of an idea that lacked popular support—and voters acted accordingly. On the other hand, Ronald Reagan's arguments in 1980 that the economy needed a tax cut and less government regulation struck a chord with the voting public.

In addition to stating their positions on issues, candidates also present voters with reasons not to vote for the other candidate. They may attack an opponent's

previous record. Or they may identify areas in which his positions have changed over time to show that he is inconsistent and unreliable. They may even question another candidate's moral integrity. This is perhaps the most challenging part of a campaign for a Christian candidate or for Christian supporters of a candidate. The apostle Paul prohibits speaking evil of others (Titus 3:1–3). Paul is not prohibiting legitimate criticism, but he is prohibiting angry or abusive speech, insults, slander, and defamation.

Debates

Debates between candidates have long been part of the American political process. The series of debates conducted in 1858 by Abraham Lincoln and Stephen A. Douglas, who were running for a US Senate seat from Illinois, is the most famous. The Lincoln-Douglas debates concerning slavery and national expansion were conducted at a remarkably sophisticated level, considering the limited education of most in the audience.

John Kennedy and Richard Nixon debating in 1960 (top). George W. Bush and Al Gore in one of their debates in 2000 (bottom).

Television provided dramatic change. In 1960, John F. Kennedy and Richard Nixon were the first presidential candidates to broadcast their debates on national television. The television screen showed a well made-up Kennedy versus a haggard, washed-out Nixon, who seemed to be in need of a shave. Many believe the impression each candidate conveyed through this televised debate changed the momentum of the campaign and helped produce a Kennedy victory, though by the smallest of margins.

In 1992 during a debate between George H. W. Bush, Ross Perot, and Bill Clinton, Bush could be seen looking at his watch. Some interpreted this as an indication that he was sorry he could not be somewhere else; this action sent a negative

---

▶ Presidential Debates

Show a video of a presidential debate to your students. Discuss how the candidates interacted with each other, which candidate more effectively communicated positions on major issues, and which candidate looked and acted more presidential. Ask students to explain why they liked or disliked a specific candidate. You may wish to prepare questions for the students to answer as they watch the video.

Activity 3: Presidential Debates

Use this activity to help the students compare and contrast the Lincoln-Douglas debates with the 1960 presidential debates.

message to many viewers. Similarly, in 2000 during the first debate between Al Gore and George W. Bush, Gore's mannerisms of sighing and rolling his eyes were thought to have contributed to his slippage in the polls and ultimate defeat.

Election Day

After all the hands have been shaken, speeches delivered, and television commercials aired, Election Day arrives—the opportunity for the voters to have the last word. The simple civic rite of voting is one of our most important privileges. While many so-called free elections throughout the world are marked by violence and widespread corruption, Americans, by contrast, go to their polling places and, for the most part, vote unhindered and unthreatened. Collectively, some of the most powerful decisions of our day are made not in the Oval Office, the halls of Congress, or even the Supreme Court chamber but in voting machines set up in fire stations, school cafeterias, and church fellowship halls.

Exit Polls

Amid the excitement of voters casting their ballots on Election Day, the news media use exit polls to try to predict the outcome. **Exit polls** are surveys of sample voters as they leave their polling places. By late Tuesday evening, the news media begin to make their projections, tallying the expected number of electoral votes each presidential candidate has secured and keeping an eye on any close congressional races that might affect or change the majority party in either the House or the Senate.

If the race for the White House includes several neck-and-neck contests in key states, it might be nearly dawn before a winner is announced. In the challenged 2000 presidential election between George W. Bush and Al Gore, a month passed before the elected winner was known.

Since the 1980s, early media projections in presidential primaries and elections have brought criticism. With the time-zone differences, East Coast polls close earlier than those on the West Coast. TV news anchors have often called, or projected, a winner in many states before the polls closed on the West Coast. Following the 1980 and 1984 elections, some people thought that West Coast voters were influenced by these media predictions. The media's incorrect call of Florida twice on election night in the 2000 presidential election brought continual criticism of the media and their use of exit polling. Also, the growing number of absentee and early voters increases the possibility that exit-poll results will be distorted.

Exercising a Civil Right

Although voting is one of the most important civil rights, it is also surely one of the most neglected. Frequently, in even the most important elections, less than half of the eligible voters participate. Consider the 2016 presidential election. Hillary Clinton and Donald Trump split the popular vote by 48 percent and 46 percent respectively (other candidates received the remaining percentage). But those numbers represent only the votes cast. About 60 percent of eligible voters participated in that election, which is fairly typical for a presidential election; thus, compared to the total number of eligible voters, Clinton received support from only 29 percent of the electorate while Trump received only 28 percent. In local and state elections, even fewer voters usually cast ballots; as a result, victors are often elected by a smaller percentage of support than presidential candidates.

Author George Jean Nathan observed, "Bad officials are elected by good citizens who do not vote." As citizens, Christians in democratic countries are responsible for helping select rulers. God's requirements for leaders are mentioned

The Commission on Presidential Debates (CPD)

This group was created in 1987. It is a nonpartisan, nonprofit corporation. Its main purpose is to sponsor and produce debates for US presidential and vice-presidential candidates. The CPD staff also prepares educational materials, conducts research to improve the quality of debates, and provides help to countries with developing democracies that are interested in establishing debate traditions in their countries. Some countries helped by the CPD include South Africa, Taiwan, Russia, Ecuador, Japan, and more than two dozen other nations.

Early Voting: Good or Bad?

Schedule a debate in which students evaluate arguments for and against early voting. What are the advantages and disadvantages of allowing people to vote prior to Election Day?

Exercise Your Right

Discuss the importance of voting. Note that only 50.1 percent of the eligible voters turned out in 1988, and only 53.4 percent of those voters actually voted for George H. W. Bush. In other words, just over one-fourth of the electorate determined who the president would be. Assign students the task of locating similar statistics for more recent presidential elections.

Presidential Election 2000

Tuesday, November 7, 2000

7:00 p.m. EST
TV networks begin to project winners of states across the country.

8:00 p.m. EST
Al Gore has been declared winner in Florida, Michigan, and Illinois.

8:47 p.m. EST
Gore declared winner in Pennsylvania.

9:15 p.m. EST
George W. Bush declared winner in Ohio.

10:00 p.m. EST
Gore's Florida win is retracted; networks say too close to call.

11:00 p.m. EST
California, with 54 electoral votes, is called for Gore.

Wednesday, November 8, 2000

12:10 a.m. EST
Gore wins Washington. Bush wins Arkansas.

2:17 a.m. EST
Bush declared winner of Florida.

2:30 a.m. EST
Gore calls Bush to congratulate him on his victory.

3:26 a.m. EST
Bush's lead in Florida drops to fewer than 1000 votes (of almost 6 million votes cast)

3:30 a.m. EST
Gore calls Bush to retract his congratulations.

4:30 a.m. EST
Networks say that Bush may not be the winner (246 electoral votes for Bush and 260 for Gore, with Oregon undeclared and Florida now deemed too close to call).

Friday, November 10, 2000, Through Saturday, January 20, 2001

Nov. 10, 2000: After a statewide machine recount in Florida is completed, Bush leads Gore by about 900 votes. Gore requests a manual recount in 4 of the 67 counties. These are counties that were heavily Democratic. The Gore campaign sought this largely because thousands of ballots were rejected by tabulating machines when voters failed to properly punch the holes in their punch-card ballots. The Gore campaign said a manual inspection of such ballots could reveal the intent of the voters (in case a piece of the ballot was still clinging to the punch hole).

Nov. 12, 2000: Bush campaign seeks a federal injunction to stop hand recounts. They argue that determining the intent of the voter is too subjective. One county might decide to count votes that are not fully punched and another may not. One official might decide that a stray mark indicated an intent to vote for a particular candidate, another might not.

Nov. 13, 2000: US district judge refuses to stop manual recount.

Nov. 15, 2000: Florida's secretary of state asks Florida Supreme Court to stop hand counts. Court denies request.

Nov. 21, 2000: Florida Supreme Court rules that recounts can continue, with November 26 as the deadline for completion.

Nov. 22, 2000: Bush lawyers file appeals with US Supreme Court to stop Florida manual recount.

Nov. 26, 2000: Florida secretary of state certifies count showing Bush ahead by 537 votes and declares Bush the winner. But, a few days later Florida Supreme Court orders the manual recounts to resume.

Dec. 1, 2000: US Supreme Court begins hearing arguments from both sides (first time high court has ever intervened in a presidential election).

Dec. 9, 2000: US Supreme Court, in 5–4 vote, orders a halt to Florida hand counts.

Dec. 12, 2000: US Supreme Court rules that Florida Supreme Court violated constitutional protections in its order for manual recount of thousands of disputed ballots.

Dec. 13, 2000: Al Gore concedes defeat in a televised speech.

Dec. 18, 2000: Electoral College casts votes for the president. George W. Bush, with 271 votes, is officially the winner. Gore received 266 electoral votes. One elector abstained.

Jan. 20, 2001: George W. Bush is inaugurated as 43rd president of the United States.

A Florida election official examining a ballot during a manual recount of the 2000 election

Election Reflections

Instruct each student to interview a parent, grandparent, or older neighbor about the first person for whom he or she remembers voting, the party that candidate represented, and why that candidate received that individual's vote. The students should report the interviewee's responses to the class. Use this activity to generate class discussion about patterns in voting and about how events shape voting.

in several places in the Scriptures, and Christians should consider them carefully when voting. Furthermore, Paul tells Christians to pray for government officials so Christians can live godly lives without persecution or harassment (1 Tim. 2:1–2). Paul's instruction is an extension of God's expectation for believers to participate in civic duties.

Occasionally the candidates for a particular office are so flawed, either morally or in their position on crucial issues, that a Christian has grave difficulty determining how to vote. In such situations most Christians choose to support the individual that most closely aligns with their views even if they disagree with the candidate on significant points. However, some Christians may feel they cannot—in good conscience—vote for any of the contenders. Christians must consistently exercise wisdom. Whatever action is taken, Christians should follow the counsel the prophet Jeremiah gave the Israelites. He instructed them to live in peace with their neighbors and seek prosperity for the community in which they lived (Jer. 29:7). That guidance will serve Christians well as they seek leaders who will govern wisely.

Electoral College

Normally, within a day or two of the election, the outcome is confirmed by the preliminary election counts, but the victorious presidential candidate is not technically elected to office until the Electoral College votes and its ballots are counted by the Senate.

Historically

During the Constitutional Convention of 1787, the founders established a structure for congressional elections under which only the House of Representatives would be elected directly. Senators would be elected by state legislatures (changed to a popular vote by the Seventeenth Amendment in 1913), and the president would be elected by the **Electoral College**. Article II, Section 1, of the Constitution details how the electoral process is to work. The total number of House and Senate members from each state dictates the number of electoral votes that state receives. For example, Kentucky has eight electoral votes (six House members and two senators). California, on the other hand, has fifty-five electoral votes (fifty-three House members and two senators). The popular vote in each state determines which candidate will receive the state's electoral votes.

Why did the Founding Fathers believe that the Electoral College was necessary? Their intention was to give smaller (less populous) states fair representation and to protect the rights of the few against the rights of the many. Without the safeguard of the Electoral College, a few populous states could determine the outcome of a presidential election.

Today

Article II, Section 1, clause 2, of the Constitution states, "Each state shall appoint, in such manner as the legislature thereof may direct, a number of electors." The method of choosing electors varies from state to state. Most are chosen through a political party's state convention during an election year, by the party's executive committee, or in the primary. When a party's candidate wins the popular vote, then that party's electors will participate in the Electoral College vote.

Voting for the Lesser of Two Evils?

Some Christians refuse to vote for either of the two major candidates lest they compromise their principles by voting for the "lesser of two evils." There are situations in which some Christians feel they cannot, in good conscience, vote for any candidate. However, there are several questions that the Christian should ask before reaching this conclusion.

First, what political goals does a Christian wish to see accomplished? Do any of the viable candidates share those goals? Even if they do not, will they promote policies that will advance the Christian's goals? Or do the candidates oppose the Christian's goals?

Second, what means would the candidates adopt to meet those goals? Are they wise? Are they acceptable? Or are they counter-productive?

Third, do the candidates have such glaring moral flaws that a Christian cannot in good conscience place any of the viable candidates in a position of public trust?

In weighing these questions, Christians should recognize that prudence is the wisdom that sees the best means for accomplishing one's intended goal. For example, many Christians would argue that it is prudent, not compromising, to vote for a candidate who opposes abortion but makes some exceptions you would not make. However, they would insist it is compromising to vote for a candidate whose approach would make it more difficult to end abortions.

Christians Voting for Non-Christians

Discuss the issue of Christians voting for non-Christians in elections. Some people have the misconception that the constitutional prohibition against a religious test means that voters should not consider a candidate's religion when deciding whom to vote for. This is not so. For instance, a Christian may choose not to vote for a non-Christian out of a desire to not give that person's religion prominence in the nation. But neither Scripture nor the Constitution mandates that Christians must vote only for other Christians.

Difficult Choices

Often voters state they dislike the choice they face between the candidates of the major political parties who are vying for an office. Is it acceptable to vote for the "lesser of two evils"? Would it be better to boycott the election or to vote for a candidate that has no chance of winning? Use the information in the student text margin box ("For Whom Do We Vote") and the Teacher Edition margin note on this page to initiate a class discussion of this topic.

Why Was the Electoral College Established?

There were numerous reasons the Founding Fathers created the Electoral College. Some of their thoughts are listed below.

- Many of them feared direct election of a president by the people. They worried that a tyrant or demagogue could manipulate public opinion and gain power.

- Many wanted to ensure that smaller states and less populated areas would have a voice in choosing the nation's leader. (Today, direct election would likely mean that candidates would focus their campaigns on the most densely populated areas and ignore many rural areas.)

- Some saw it as a way of sharing power among the governments of the individual states. The Constitution established that each state would receive electoral votes equal to the state's number of representatives in Congress. Each state legislature determines the means by which electors are selected (it was decades before state legislatures began to tie the selection of electors to the popular vote within the state).

Popular Vote or Electoral Vote?

On five occasions the candidate who won the popular vote did not become president. In 1824, Andrew Jackson received the most popular votes, but neither Jackson nor any of the other three major candidates had a majority of the electoral votes. Thus, as stipulated in the Constitution, the election was decided by the House of Representatives. John Quincy Adams was eventually chosen. In the 1876 election, Rutherford B. Hayes lost the popular vote to Samuel Tilden but won the electoral vote. In 1888, the Electoral College chose Benjamin Harrison as president, even though Grover Cleveland had won the popular vote. As noted in this chapter, George W. Bush was chosen by the Electoral College in 2000, but Al Gore narrowly won the popular vote. In the 2016 election, Donald Trump was the electoral vote winner while his opponent, Hillary Clinton, had more popular votes.

Some Americans believe the Electoral College should be abolished and the winner of the popular vote should become president. Others believe the Electoral College serves many useful purposes. For example, they note that it helps prevent the domination of smaller states and rural areas by larger states and urban areas.

In most states, the winner of the popular vote wins all the state's electoral votes. Maine and Nebraska, however, are exceptions. In those two states, the victor in each congressional district receives an electoral vote, and the winner of the statewide vote receives two electoral votes.

No constitutional provision or federal law requires electors to vote according to the results of the popular vote in their states. In twenty-nine states and the District of Columbia, electors are legally bound to support the winner. New Mexico, North Carolina, South Carolina, Oklahoma, and Washington carry this a step further, adding a penalty for not supporting the winner. Even in states that do not legally require it, electors almost always vote for the candidate who won in their state. An elector who does not vote for the presidential or vice-presidential candidate he or she had pledged to support is called a "faithless elector." There have been only sixteen faithless electors in the last hundred years. Seven of those were in the 2016 election (see map on page 241 entitled "The Election of 2016").

The Electoral College has 538 total votes based on congressional representation (435 from the House of Representatives, 100 from the Senate, and 3 from Washington, DC). To win, a candidate must gain 270 of those votes. A national census, taken every ten years, is the only thing that can change a state's number of votes. Changes in a state's population may lead to a change in the number of members the state receives in the House of Representatives and thus in its number of electoral votes.

Congress has ruled that the electors must meet in their respective states to cast their ballots on the Monday after the second Wednesday in December. The ballots are sent to the Senate, where, in joint session with the House, the votes are counted after the new session of Congress convenes in January. The president of the Senate, the US vice president, presides. Vice President George H. W. Bush was able to announce his own election to the presidency in this meeting in 1989, and he was the

Activity 4: The Disputed Election of 1876

Use this activity to help the students understand that disputes over election outcomes are not new. The election of 1876 was the most disputed presidential election before the infamous situation in 2000.

first sitting vice president to do so since Martin Van Buren in 1837. After the 2000 election, Vice President Al Gore presided over his own loss when he announced the election of his opponent, George W. Bush. Likewise, sitting Vice Presidents John C. Breckinridge (1861), Richard Nixon (1961), and Hubert Humphrey (1969) all announced that they had lost their own bid for the presidency when the electoral votes were officially opened and counted.

If no candidate wins a majority in the Electoral College, the House of Representatives chooses the president from among the three leading candidates, with each state casting one vote. Each state's vote is allotted to the candidate preferred by a majority of that state's House members. If there is a tie within a delegation, that state's vote is not counted. Two presidential elections have been decided by the House of Representatives—1800 and 1824. In the first, Thomas Jefferson was chosen over Aaron Burr; in the latter, John Quincy Adams was chosen over Andrew Jackson and William H. Crawford.

If no vice-presidential candidate receives a majority of the electoral votes, the Senate decides between the two candidates who received the most votes in the Electoral College. This has occurred only once, in the election of 1836.

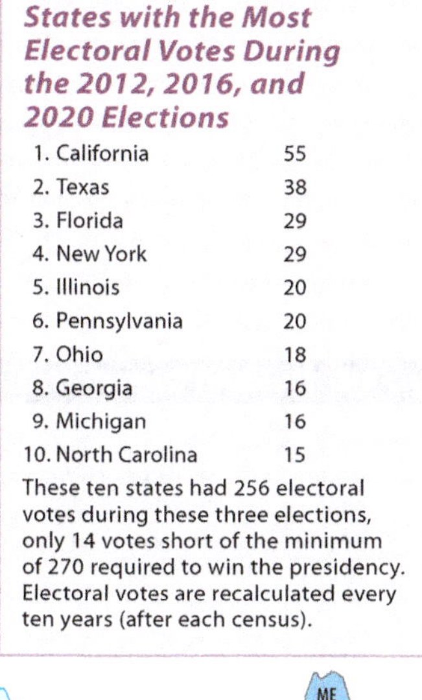

These ten states had 256 electoral votes during these three elections, only 14 votes short of the minimum of 270 required to win the presidency. Electoral votes are recalculated every ten years (after each census).

The Election of 2016

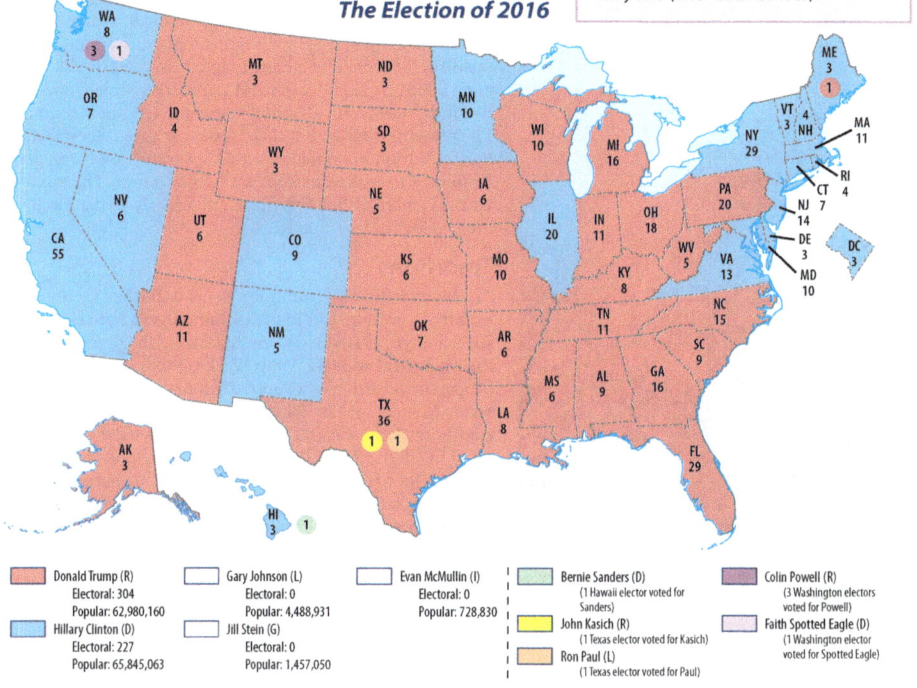

Election of 2016

Ask the students to examine the electoral map above carefully and answer the following questions. What general statements can you make about the various regions of the country and how they voted during this election? Which states had "faithless electors"? Of the ten states with the most electors, how many voted for each political party? If you were a presidential candidate, what campaign strategy would you follow to win election?

Guiding Questions

1. How are the orderly transitions that occur after American elections significant?
2. What are the procedures for a presidential inauguration?

IV. Inauguration

I do solemnly swear (or affirm) that I will faithfully execute the office of president of the United States, and will to the best of my ability, preserve, protect and defend the Constitution of the United States.

Article II, Section 1, clause 7, of the US Constitution

After a US presidential election, it is the ordinary that is so extraordinary. Despite the political rivalry and heated exchanges, despite disagreements with friends or the disappointment of a hard-fought loss, our government endures. Republicans and Democrats, independents and indifferents, are all still Americans after the election. They might be bitter, but there is neither mass bloodshed nor revolution. In Washington, DC, a transition team, not a military coup, oversees the transfer of power. The most visible symbol of this organized and orderly transition is the presidential inauguration.

Traditions

Many inaugural traditions were established by the first inauguration. George Washington gave a special speech after his first swearing-in, setting the precedent for the **inaugural address**. With Washington's second oath of office, the tradition of a Supreme Court justice administering the oath began. Later administrations began more traditions. Jefferson was the first president to be inaugurated in Washington, DC. In 1805 after he took the oath of office for his second term, he mounted his horse and rode back to the White House. A large group of legislators and citizens followed him, and later presidents continued this custom of inaugural parades.

In 1817 the inauguration ceremony was moved outdoors. It had been held in the House of Representatives, but Henry Clay, Speaker of the House, refused to allow senators to bring their cushioned chairs into the "people's" chamber. To Clay's thinking, such plush furnishings

In 1977, Jimmy Carter began the tradition of walking during a portion of the inaugural parade. He was accompanied by his wife, Rosalynn.

The Oval Office

At some point on Inauguration Day, after taking his oath, the new president enters his new office, known as the **Oval Office**, where he will consult with heads of state, his staff, diplomats, and other dignitaries. From this room at times, he will address American citizens or the world by television or radio.

In the last few decades it has become a tradition for the outgoing president to leave a letter for the incoming one. Reading it is one of the first actions the new leader will undertake.

The first Oval Office was constructed in 1909 in the center of the south side of the West Wing. In 1934 it was moved to its present location on the southeast corner, overlooking the Rose Garden (see page 215 for illustration of the West Wing). With each new president, the Oval Office décor changes. Some office features that are not adjusted include the original white marble mantel from the 1909 Oval Office, the two flags behind the president's desk (the US flag and the presidential flag), and the presidential seal in the ceiling.

The Resolute desk is an important piece of White House furniture. In 1854, the HMS *Resolute*, on an Arctic expedition, became trapped in ice and was abandoned. After recovery by an American ship, Congress refitted and returned it to Queen Victoria of England in 1856 as a sign of friendship and goodwill. When the ship was retired from service, the queen authorized a desk be made from its timber and in 1880 had it presented to President Rutherford B. Hayes.

The desk has been slightly altered by a few presidents. President Franklin Roosevelt had the kneehole fitted with a panel carved with the presidential coat of arms. President Ronald Reagan asked that the desk be put on a two-inch base to accommodate his six-foot, one-inch height.

One of the most famous photographs of the Resolute desk shows President Kennedy's son, John Jr., peeking out from behind the kneehole panel. After Kennedy's assassination, the desk traveled as part of an exhibition honoring Kennedy before being displayed at the Smithsonian. It returned to the White House in 1977. Except for Johnson, Nixon, and Ford, every president has used it somewhere in the White House. Since 1961, with the exception of sixteen years, it has been in the Oval Office.

Above, John Kennedy Jr. shown playing beneath the Resolute desk

Nation's Most Famous Office

There is a nationwide network of thirteen presidential libraries operated by the National Archives. One exists for each of the presidents who served from 1929 until 2009 (from Herbert Hoover to George W. Bush). A fourteenth library, for Barack Obama, is in the planning stages. Several of those libraries have replicas of the Oval Office, which have proven to be popular attractions for visitors to those sites.

clashed terribly with the "décor" of republicanism. A compromise was reached so that the new executive would stand before the nation while taking the oath of office.

Road to the Oval Office

Assign a research project in which students trace the campaign of a party's recent presidential nominee. This will serve as a review of the campaign process outlined in this chapter.

Ask students to answer the following questions about the candidate: When did the person announce his or her candidacy? Which personal qualifications were emphasized during the campaign? How successful was the candidate in the Iowa caucuses and in the New Hampshire primary? Which primaries (if any) were won? In what city was the party's national convention held? What were some memorable portions of the acceptance speech at the national convention? Whom did the candidate choose for vice president? What campaign slogans were used? How did he or she perform during the debates? What were the election results (popular vote and electoral vote)?

Inaugural Firsts

- In 1801, Thomas Jefferson was the first to be inaugurated at the Capitol.
- James K. Polk's 1845 inauguration was the first to be reported by telegraph. Samuel Morse sat near Polk on the platform and tapped out the news on a telegraph.
- James Buchanan's 1857 inaugural ceremony was the first to be photographed.
- In 1881, James Garfield's mother was the first mother to attend the inauguration of a son.
- William McKinley's 1897 inauguration was the first to be filmed with a movie camera.
- In 1921, Warren G. Harding was the first to ride to and from his inauguration in an automobile.
- In 1925, Calvin Coolidge became the first president to be heard over radio taking his oath of office.
- Harry Truman's 1949 swearing-in was the first to be televised.
- The first poet to speak at an inauguration was Robert Frost (when John Kennedy became president in 1961).
- Bill Clinton's second inauguration (in 1997) was the first to be broadcast live on the internet.

Transfer of Power

When Washington relinquished the office of the presidency to John Adams in 1797, the first transition of presidential power occurred. Today, that transition begins shortly after the presidential election. After winning at the polls on Election Day, the president-elect has about eleven weeks to develop his new administration. (Because of delays caused by the disputed vote count in 2000, George W. Bush's transition team had only about four weeks to put everything in order.) The transition process has three general parts: final actions by the outgoing president; the allotment of funds to aid the transfer of power to the new president; and the replacement of current personnel with members of the new administration.

Orders and Pardons

Generally, an outgoing president has limited political opportunities. Congress usually sends few major bills for signature, and new legislation will most likely not be considered. But the soon-to-be former president is not without tools or influence.

Executive orders are presidential directives that have the effect and force of law. Usually they involve federal government agencies and officials, rather than citizens or the private sector. The Constitution is not specific regarding executive orders. Article II merely states that "the executive power shall be vested in a president of the United States of America." The president's reason for using these may be personal, practical, or political in nature, and the orders are usually implemented without input or interference from Congress. Often, a president will issue an executive order to achieve a goal that does not have sufficient support to receive Congressional approval. Many presidents will issue a number of executive orders during their closing days in office. Subsequent presidents, however, can issue their own executive orders rescinding their predecessors' orders.

The president may also issue **pardons**. Presidential pardons normally release a convicted person from the remainder of his sentence. Many of these have been controversial. President Washington pardoned the Whiskey Rebellion rebels in 1795, and President Andrew Johnson pardoned most Confederate rebels in 1868. More recent presidential pardons include Gerald Ford's pardon of Richard Nixon in 1974 (although Nixon had not been convicted of any crime, Ford wanted to forestall any potential criminal proceedings and speed the nation's healing) and Jimmy Carter's pardon, in 1977, of those who evaded the draft during the Vietnam War. In the concluding weeks of a president's term, the outgoing leader often exercises his right to pardon, sometimes dozens of individuals. For example, Bill Clinton pardoned 140 people on the last day of his presidency. Such timing is intentional—the criticism received will not affect the president's legislative agenda, since his time in office is ending.

Presidential Transition Fund

Before 1963, presidential transition expenses were funded mainly by the political party organization of the incoming president, and the transition was staffed by volunteers. After realizing the importance of presidential transitions and their effect on government, Congress passed the Presidential Transition Act in 1963. Using some of the funds allocated by this act, the General Services Administration (GSA) coordinates the orientation of the president-elect's cabinet nominees and top executive-branch personnel. Transition funds are available as soon as a presidential winner is declared and continue to be available until shortly after the inauguration.

Executive Orders

Discuss the pros and cons of executive orders. Do you think they are constitutional? If so, when? Always? Sometimes? What are the dangers of executive orders?

Change of Personnel

When a new administration transitions into power, thousands of non-civil-service jobs become vacant in the executive and legislative branches of the federal government. (Civil service jobs are not changed.) These positions include heads of executive-branch agencies; undersecretaries; assistant secretaries; directors of bureaus and services; and members and chairs of various boards, commissions, and committees.

Event
Official Date

The Founding Fathers intended the first presidential inauguration to take place on March 4, 1789, which was the same day the Constitution went into effect. However, it was delayed until April 30 of that year. March 4 continued to be Inauguration Day until 1933 when the crisis of the Great Depression led to a change. Americans wanted quick action from a new president and thus supported the ratification of the Twentieth Amendment, which changed the inauguration date to **January 20**. President Franklin D. Roosevelt was the first president to be inaugurated under the new amendment on January 20, 1937.

Location

Washington's first presidential inauguration took place on the balcony of Federal Hall in New York City, the nation's capital at the time. His second inauguration was in the Senate chamber of Congress Hall in Philadelphia, the second capital of the country. Adams took the presidential oath in the House of Representatives chamber of Congress Hall. Once Washington, DC, became the United States capital, however, most inaugurations took place at different locations in or outside the Capitol Building, the most frequent being on the East Front. Depending on the circumstances, other places have also been necessary. James Monroe, the first president to take his oath of office outside, was inaugurated in front of the Old Brick Capitol, which is now the site of the US Supreme Court Building. When President Abraham Lincoln was assassinated, Andrew Johnson was sworn in at the Kirkwood Hotel in Washington, DC. After Warren Harding's death, Calvin Coolidge took the oath of office at his family home in Vermont; his father, a notary public, administered the oath. After President John Kennedy's assassination, Lyndon Johnson took the oath of office in the conference room aboard *Air Force One* at Love Field in Dallas, Texas. In 1981, President Ronald Reagan moved the ceremony to the terrace of the West Front of the Capitol. That location provides a view of the Mall looking toward the Washington Monument. All presidents since then have used the West Front site.

Inaugural Ceremony

Today, the inaugural ceremony includes more than just the president's taking the oath of office. The ceremony might begin

Outgoing president Harry Truman accompanied incoming president Dwight Eisenhower to the 1953 inauguration (top). President Herbert Hoover accompanied FDR in 1933 (bottom).

"Let [the oath of office] not be deemed a vain or idle form. In all these things, God will bring us into judgement. A President, who shall dare to violate the obligations of his solemn oath . . . may escape human censure, nay, may even receive applause from the giddy multitude. But he will be compelled to learn, that there is a watchful Providence, that cannot be deceived; and a righteous Being, the searcher of all hearts, who will render unto all men according to their deserts."

—Supreme Court Justice Joseph Story

Tense Transition

Though American presidential transitions have always been peaceful, some have been rather strained for the participants. In the following account, Harry Truman describes his conversation with president-elect Dwight Eisenhower on Eisenhower's Inauguration Day in 1953:

> The journey in the parade down Pennsylvania Avenue was quite restrained—as far as the occupants of the Presidential car were concerned. We began our trip in silence. Then the President-elect volunteered to inform me: "I did not attend your Inauguration in [1949] out of consideration for you, because if I had been present I would have drawn attention away from you."
>
> I was quick to reply: "You were not here in [1949] because I did not send for you. But if I *had* sent for you, you would have come."
>
> The rest of the journey continued in silence.

Highs and Lows

George Washington's first inauguration was held on April 30, 1789. Accounts indicate that the temperature reached sixty degrees for that event. Afterward, the inauguration date became March 4, and it remained that day until it was changed to January 20 in 1937.

Ronald Reagan's inaugurals set records. With the exception of Washington's April inauguration, Reagan's was the warmest at fifty-six degrees (in 1981) and the coldest at seven degrees (in 1985).

Read an Inaugural Address

Direct the students to choose presidential inaugural addresses. (You may require each student to choose a different inaugural address.) Ask the students to identify and present the issues that were emphasized in the speech.

▶ Watch an Inaugural Address

Require each student to watch a president's inaugural speech. Ask the students to complete the following questions: What were the major issues included? What were the most memorable quotes? Which remarks drew the most applause from the crowd? What did you like most about the speech? Did you dislike any portions of the speech? If so, why?

Activity 5: Chapter Review

Use this review to help the students prepare for the chapter test and to reinforce the students' knowledge of concepts presented in the chapter.

Famous Passages from Inaugurals

Thomas Jefferson (1801)

"Still one thing more, fellow citizens—a wise and frugal government, which shall restrain men from injuring one another, shall leave them otherwise free to regulate their own pursuits of industry and improvement, and shall not take from the mouth of labor the bread it has earned. This is the sum of good government."

Abraham Lincoln (1865)

"With malice toward none, with charity for all, with firmness in the right as God gives us to see the right, let us strive on to finish the work we are in, to bind up the nation's wounds, to care for him who shall have borne the battle and for his widow and his orphan, to do all which may achieve and cherish a just and lasting peace among ourselves and with all nations."

Franklin D. Roosevelt (1933)

"This great Nation will endure as it has endured, will revive and will prosper. So, first of all, let me assert my firm belief that the only thing we have to fear is fear itself."

John F. Kennedy (1961)

"Let every nation know, whether it wishes us well or ill, that we shall pay any price, bear any burden, meet any hardship, support any friend, oppose any foe, in order to assure the survival and the success of liberty. . . ."

"And so, my fellow Americans: ask not what your country can do for you—ask what you can do for your country."

Ronald Reagan (1981)

"In this present crisis, government is not the solution to our problem; government *is* the problem." (emphasis added)

Inaugural address (top) and parade (bottom) in January 2017

with a musical prelude. The assembly is called to order, and welcoming remarks are given. A prayer and a musical selection might follow. Then the new vice president takes his oath of office. Next, the president-elect takes his oath of office and gives the inaugural address. After a closing prayer or benediction, the national anthem might be played. Some elements of the ceremony vary according to the new president's wishes.

Inaugural Events

Inaugural activities span more than just one day. A few days before the swearing-in ceremony, the celebration of a newly elected president begins, complete with concerts, fireworks, special programs, and other events. On the day of the inauguration, the president-elect usually attends a prayer service. Midmorning, the president-elect and spouse arrive for coffee at the White House with the president and First Lady. Also in attendance are the vice president-elect, the vice president, their spouses, the Congressional Inaugural Committee, and House and Senate members. The president-elect and president share a limousine to the Capitol for the official transfer of power.

Following the ceremony, the new president has a luncheon in the Capitol with family, staff, members of Congress, and others. Meanwhile, the former president's possessions are moved out of the White House and the new First Family is moved in. Mid-afternoon, the inaugural parade begins. The president, the First Lady, and others ride or walk part of the parade route to the reviewing stand, where they watch the rest of the parade. The evening includes multiple inaugural balls around the Washington, DC, area. The president and First Lady visit most balls briefly, as do the vice president and his wife. (The ball gown worn by the First Lady is later exhibited at the Smithsonian.) The following day, the president and First Lady begin a new chapter in America's history.

Section Review

1. What is the most visible symbol of a presidential transition?
2. Why do presidents often issue executive orders?
3. Why was the presidential transition fund established?
4. What day was designated as Inauguration Day from 1789 until 1933?
5. Since 1937 what date has been designated as Inauguration Day?
6–8. Which three cities have served as the capital for the US (list in order)?
★ Do you think it was wise for the Founding Fathers to give the president the right to pardon individuals? What do you think about the manner in which presidents have used this privilege?
★ Read the quote from Supreme Court Justice Joseph Story on page 245. How could you best summarize his statements?

246 • CHAPTER 10

Section Review Answers

1. the presidential inauguration (p. 242)
2. Presidents will often issue an executive order to achieve a goal that does not have sufficient support to receive congressional approval. (p. 244)
3. Congress thought that the presidential transition is so important and has such an effect on government that it should be paid for by the government. (p. 244)
4. March 4 (p. 245)
5. January 20 (p. 245)
6–8. New York City, Philadelphia, Washington, DC (p. 245)
★ Some may say that it is right for presidents to be able to extend mercy through the form of a pardon. Others may say that this power has been abused by granting pardons to undeserving people.
★ The president should take the oath of office seriously and seek to fulfill it. Violating the oath might not bring rebuke from humans; however, God will judge those who violate their oaths.

CHAPTER REVIEW ANSWERS

Making Connections

1–2. One purpose is to open the field to more candidates, not just to the ones whom party insiders approve. Another purpose of the presidential primary is to make national delegate selection more democratic. (p. 227)

3. When a party has a primary with a leading candidate certain of winning the nomination, that party's members could "cross over" to vote for a weak candidate in the opposing party's primary. This tactic helps nominate a weak candidate from the opposing party and increases the chances that the raiding

10 CHAPTER REVIEW

Making Connections

1–2. Explain the two basic purposes of presidential primaries.

3. A negative aspect of crossover voting is known as raiding. Describe this tactic.

4–5. Discuss two disadvantages that presidential primaries pose for the parties.

6–8. Describe two main considerations that often influence a presidential nominee's choice of his vice-presidential candidate. Why are they important?

9. Summarize the role of presidential debates.

10. Explain the statement, "After a US presidential election, it is the ordinary that is so extraordinary."

Developing Civics Skills

1. Trace a likely route that a person's career would take to become president of the United States.

2. If you were elected president of the United States, what would be your inaugural theme, what events would you want to include in your inaugural ceremony, and what topics would you include in your inaugural address?

Thinking Critically

1. A number of critics have charged that election-night news coverage and the use of exit polls should be restricted because of their possible adverse influence on voter turnout. Do you agree with these critics? Why or why not?

2. Should Christians vote for candidates with whom they have significant disagreements? Why or why not?

Living as a Christian Citizen

1. Imagine that you are a legislator who has been asked to state your position on a proposed amendment to abolish the Electoral College in favor of a more democratic system for electing the president. How would your worldview help shape your response to this issue?

2. Select a candidate from a recent presidential primary, and evaluate his or her positions according to a Christian worldview.

People, Places, and Things to Remember

direct primaries
presidential primaries
delegates
caucus
closed primaries
open primaries
crossover voting
raiding
Iowa caucuses
New Hampshire primary
party platform
superdelegates
keynote address
brokered convention
balance the ticket
general election
exit polls
Electoral College
inaugural address
Oval Office
executive orders
pardons
January 20

THE ROAD TO THE WHITE HOUSE • 247

governors have been elected president. (pp. 223–24)

2. Students will provide a variety of answers depending on their personal convictions and opinions.

Thinking Critically

1. Some will agree that the charge is valid, especially because of different time zones. Others will disagree, saying that those who want to vote will vote their convictions regardless of what exit polls or news reports say.

2. Students should address the following kinds of questions in their answers. Will the candidates promote the same values and goals that Christians support? Will the candidates move in the direction that Christians wish, or will they oppose opportunities to achieve goals that Christians desire? The students should note that the prudent voter does not compromise goals and that agreement on every point is not required if a candidate is moving policy in the direction the voter supports.

Living as a Christian Citizen

1. Some students will support such an amendment while others will oppose it. In making a decision, Christians should consider several matters. First, though many proponents of abolishing the Electoral College presume that democracy is the best form of government, the Scriptures do not take a position on that matter. Second, the doctrine of the Fall implies what history demonstrates: majorities can be as tyrannical as monarchs. No system of government is perfect. Majorities and minorities need a check against power. Third, people exist not only as individuals but also as parts of communities. The interests of highly populated communities must be balanced with those of less populated communities. In summary, a Christian should desire that all people be treated fairly and that their concerns be addressed.

2. Students should distinguish between positions that are clearly biblical, those that are unbiblical, and those that are personal preference. Other ideas to consider include issues on which candidates have biblical goals but disagree on how to achieve those goals.

party's nominee will win in the general election. (p. 228)

4–5. They eliminate party leaders' ability to help choose a moderate compromise candidate; they can create wide divisions within a party. (p. 228)

6–8. Geography and ideology; presidential nominees often choose running mates who can strengthen or balance their campaigns. For example, a candidate from the East with liberal ideas might select a conservative from the West to balance the ticket. (p. 233)

9. Debates provide voters an opportunity to compare candidates and their viewpoints. Since debates are televised, physical appearance and even mannerisms can have an effect on voters' perceptions of the candidates. (p. 236–37)

10. The ordinary peaceful transfer of power that America experiences between presidents is extraordinary. There is not mass bloodshed or revolution during the transition period. (p. 242)

Developing Civics Skills

1. Many politicians try to use election to political offices as a springboard to higher offices. Some politicians used their military careers (especially if they became heroes in war) as paths to the presidency. Others became successful in business and used their business connections to pave the way to enter politics. In recent years, several former

AMERICA'S HIGHEST OFFICE

11

I pray heaven to bestow the best of blessings on this house and all that shall hereafter inhabit it. May none but honest and wise men ever rule under this roof.

—President John Adams, in 1800, shortly after moving into what was later called the White House

President Reagan placing a wreath at the Tomb of the Unknown Soldier at Arlington National Cemetery

I. **Presidential Powers**

II. **Executive Organization**

III. **Governing Wisely**

SUGGESTED MATERIALS

Section I
- Activities 1–2 from Chapter 11 of the *Student Activities*
- Video about *Air Force One*
- Video about *Marine One*
- Copies of several presidents' State of the Union addresses
- Video of a State of the Union address

Section II
- Activities 3–4 from Chapter 11 of the *Student Activities*

Section III
- Activities 5–6 from Chapter 11 of the *Student Activities*

Teacher Resources
Visit TeacherToolsOnline.com for resources to enhance the lessons.

The salary of the nation's first chief executive, George Washington, was $25,000 a year. By 1969, the president's salary, which is taxable, was $200,000 per year. Effective January 2001, it was raised to $400,000 annually. In addition, the president receives free housing (the White House), $50,000 annually for expenses, a $19,000 yearly official entertainment allotment, and $100,000 annually for travel costs. Three presidents (Herbert Hoover, John Kennedy, and Donald Trump) have donated all of their salary to charities or other causes.

After leaving office, the president receives a lifetime pension of more than $200,000 a year. Other retirement benefits include lifetime Secret Service protection for them and their spouses. Former presidents also receive paid travel expenses when on official government business, medical treatment in military hospitals, and a state funeral upon death.

Although these benefits certainly provide a comfortable living for the president, the president's compensation is reasonable when compared with the benefits of corporate executives. Though the president of the United States occupies a position of tremendous prestige, power, and responsibility, the job entails hard work, long hours, great obligations, and incredible pressure. Given the demands of the office, most believe the chief executive well earns his salary. To provide a better understanding of America's highest office, this chapter will examine the nature of the office and the forces that have shaped it.

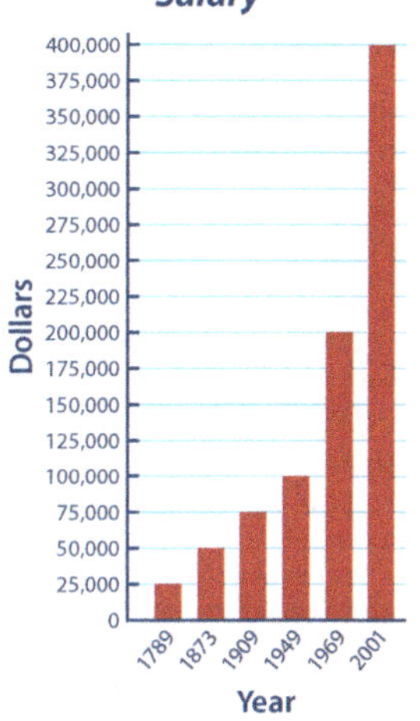

I. Presidential Powers

Chief Executive

"The executive power shall be vested in a president of the United States of America. . . . He shall take care that the laws be faithfully executed." Thus, Article II of the Constitution outlines an important task of the presidency, that of chief executive.

In seeing that laws are "faithfully executed," the president administers and enforces the law through the various departments under his control. For example, Congress might vote to raise, or lower, federal income taxes. If the bill becomes a law, it changes the tax code, but the implementation and enforcement of that change would be carried out through an executive agency—in this case, the Internal Revenue Service (IRS), a part of the Department of Treasury.

As chief executive, the president also administers a vast bureaucracy, which consists of the Executive Office of the President, fifteen cabinet departments, and a wide range of government agencies and corporations. All the cabinet secretaries and undersecretaries and most of the other agencies' top officials (with the exception of the regulatory commissions' officials) are under the direct responsibility of the chief executive. However, with approximately two million employees in the executive branch, sheer size makes it difficult for even the president to control the bureaucracy.

Commander in Chief

One of the most important and most influential roles of the president is his position as commander in chief of the military—a position that underscores the important national principle that civilian power controls military power. This

---

Guiding Questions

1. What are six major areas of presidential responsibility?
2. What constitutional restrictions are placed on the president?
3. What additional powers are given to the president?
4. How have presidents used their powers?

---

1. Analyze six major areas of presidential responsibility.
2. Describe constitutional restrictions placed on the president.
3. Explain additional powers given to the president.

"Mr. President"

The first Congress was faced with a thorny issue when it had to decide how to address the president. Some suggested the title "Your Highness," while "His Majesty, the President" was also considered. Those sounded too much like royalty, but a simple "Sir" was too informal.

Evidently, it was decided that the title "Mr. President" would be used, and it stuck. Ex-presidents are also addressed as "Mr. President" (just as former governors and senators typically continue to be addressed as "Governor" or "Senator").

Presidential Trivia—Part One

The first section of this chapter contains four sets of presidential trivia questions (a total of 33 items). You may use these as an opening activity over a period of several days or as contest questions (perhaps while having the class divided into groups), or for nongraded quizzes. As you discuss the next three chapters, which deal with the executive branch, you may encourage the students to bring other presidential trivia to class.

1. Who was the only president to have a patent issued to him? (*Abraham Lincoln [for a hydraulic device to lift boats over shoals]*)

2. Who was both the eighth president and the eighth vice president? (*Martin Van Buren*)

3. Which president had a foreign capital named for him? (*James Monroe [Liberia was established as a home for freed slaves during the Monroe administration, and its capital is Monrovia.]*)

4. Who was the first president to be born in a hospital? (*Jimmy Carter [born in 1924]*)

5. Which president could barely read or write until his late teens? (*Andrew Johnson [His future wife, Eliza McCardle, who began teaching him when he was about seventeen years of age, helped him master reading, grammar, and math.]*)

Presidential Salary

The chart above indicates that the president's salary doubled in 1969 and then doubled again in 2001. Ask some students to research inflation rates during these periods and make some general statements about how much the president's salary changed in *real* dollars.

Research should indicate (based on reliable inflation calculators) that $100,000 in 1949 would be the equivalent of about $150,000 in 1969, while $200,000 in 1969 would be equal to about $965,000 in 2001. What can we learn from this?

Limits on Presidential Power

The limits of presidential power remain a constant source of controversy. Some people argue that the president is limited to constitutional and statutory powers. Others believe that the president has any power that is not specifically denied to him. Unlike the Constitution's instructions for Congress, its instructions for the president do not include a necessary and proper clause. Therefore, this controversy will no doubt continue.

Many presidents claim executive privilege for certain actions and decisions. During the Watergate scandal, President Nixon claimed that the executive privilege of confidentiality allowed him to refuse a subpoena to turn over recordings of conversations he had had with his advisors. His lawyers said that (1) inherent privileges flow from the president's enumerated powers and that (2) the separation of powers protects the president from judicial prosecution.

In *United States v. Nixon* (1974) Supreme Court Chief Justice Burger wrote, "Nowhere in the Constitution . . . is there any explicit reference to a privilege of confidentiality, yet to the extent this interest relates to the effective discharge of a President's powers, it is constitutionally based." He admitted that matters of national security and diplomacy require secrecy, but he also stated that "the generalized assertion of privilege must yield to the demonstrated, specific need for evidence in a pending criminal trial."

Basically, in *United States v. Nixon* the court concluded that the president does have the right to exercise some executive privilege, but it is limited in scope. How limited? That debate continues.

Presidential Air Travel

The necessity for rapid travel for the president has increased with time. Transportation vehicles have included the Ferdinand Magellan, a custom-built Pullman railroad car; presidential yachts; specially equipped limousines; and planes and helicopters. Today, the president's main means of air travel are *Air Force One* and *Marine One*.

Air Force One

In 1944 President Franklin D. Roosevelt sought the creation of the Presidential Pilot Office (now called the Presidential Airlift Group) to provide air transportation for the president and his staff. For the next two decades, four-engine, propeller-driven aircraft were used. The first jet aircraft, a Boeing 707, was purchased in 1962 to be used as *Air Force One*. Today, the *Air Force One* fleet consists of two specifically outfitted 747-200B aircraft, and its home base is Joint Base Andrews, formerly called Andrews Air Force Base, in Maryland.

Air Force One provides the president and his staff with various services, including secure, encrypted communications systems that are protected against electromagnetic pulse. It is actually a mobile command center, a miniature White House in the sky. It boasts four thousand square feet of area which includes an executive suite, the president's office, two galleys capable of feeding one hundred people, and an operating room with medical equipment. Many items onboard sport the presidential seal, including seat-belt buckles, pillows, blankets, napkins, and cups.

To pilot *Air Force One*, one must have a spotless record, two thousand hours in the cockpit, and worldwide flight experience. The aircraft can fly halfway around the world without refueling and can provide for more than seventy passengers. Reporters are seated in the back of the plane, and VIPs sit in front. The more important the passenger, the closer he sits to the president. The plane is a military aircraft overseen by the air force; every flight is considered a military mission. The plane possesses highly classified defense capabilities, including antimissile devices. The designated *Air Force One* jet is the president's primary source of air travel, but when the president boards any air force aircraft, that aircraft's call sign becomes Air Force One for the duration of the flight. The airplane carrying the vice president is called Air Force Two.

Marine One

Since 1957, the pilots of marine squadron HMX-1 have been responsible for providing all helicopter transportation at home and overseas for the president, the vice president, the president's cabinet members, and foreign dignitaries when directed to do so by the White House Military Office. When the president boards any rotary-wing aircraft, the call sign used is Marine One.

Marine One has a crew of four and can seat up to fifteen passengers. It has a cruising speed of 136 miles per hour, a range of 600 miles, and is capable of reaching an altitude of 14,700 feet.

What Is True Greatness?

Ask the students to list ten people (five living, five dead) that they personally consider to be great leaders. This list may include individuals who have held such diverse occupations as politicians, business executives, and Christian leaders. The students will reference this list later in this chapter (p. 270).

▶ *Air Force One* and *Marine One*

Show a video, or excerpt of one, about *Air Force One* such as the one filmed by *National Geographic*. Likewise, *National Geographic* and other sources provide videos regarding *Marine One*.

fact was illustrated in 1951 during the Korean War when President Truman dismissed Douglas MacArthur, a five-star general in the army, for insubordination. MacArthur had advocated bombing Communist China and expanding the war in an attempt to destroy communism in Asia. The president disagreed, and when the general violated orders not to publicly comment on the dispute, Truman dismissed him. This incident also illustrates the unpopularity that sometimes accompanies the actions of the commander in chief. MacArthur returned home to a hero's welcome. But while many members of Congress lavished praise on the general, some in Congress called for the impeachment of President Truman.

The commander in chief uses his power to respond quickly during an emergency. The earliest example of this was in 1794 when President Washington personally led troops to subdue the Whiskey Rebellion in Pennsylvania. A more modern example occurred after the destruction of the World Trade Center in New York City on September 11, 2001. President George W. Bush responded with the formation of a seventeen-nation coalition whose aim was to defeat the Taliban terrorist network and stop any further terrorist activities. Operation Enduring Freedom began on October 17, 2001, with the bombing of Taliban centers in Afghanistan. President Bush's power to commit US troops stemmed from the 1973 War Powers Resolution, which states under "Purpose and Policy," Section 2(c), that

> the constitutional powers of the President as Commander-in-Chief to introduce United States Armed Forces into hostilities, or into situations where imminent involvement in hostilities is clearly indicated by the circumstances, are exercised only pursuant to (1) a declaration of war, (2) specific statutory authorization, or (3) a national emergency created by attack upon the United States, its territories or possessions, or its armed forces.

The president also has a vast national security and intelligence apparatus at his disposal with which he carries out **covert operations** (activities unknown to the public and sometimes even to Congress). Congress votes to apportion money to agencies that guard the country's security—of which the **Central Intelligence Agency (CIA)** is

President Johnson visiting US troops in South Vietnam in 1966

Lobby of CIA headquarters

Declaring War

Congress, not the president, has the power to declare war. When the president needs a formal declaration of war, he must gain the support of Congress. To gain this support, the president usually gives a speech to Congress or sends a message to that body.

In his request on April 2, 1917, for a formal declaration of war against Germany, President Wilson stated that the United States would be "glad" to fight for "the ultimate peace of the world" and for "the liberation of its peoples, the German peoples included." Wilson changed the way the Executive Office uses military power when he said, "The world must be made safe for democracy."

The President as Commander in Chief

In 1969, President Nixon included the following words in a letter to the parents of a young man killed in the Vietnam War: "Of all the hardships of war, the cruelest are the losses of men such as your son." Similarly, President Reagan stated that his most difficult task as president was having to talk with the families of US Marines who were killed in the bombing of the US Marines' barracks in Beirut, Lebanon, in 1983.

Activity 1: President vs. King

In this activity the students study Alexander Hamilton's comparison, in *Federalist* No. 69, of presidents and kings. This activity enhances the students' skills in using original sources and improves their analytical skills.

Lesser-Known Presidents

Instruct students to write reports about some of the lesser-known presidents of the United States, such as John Tyler, Zachary Taylor, Millard Fillmore, Franklin Pierce, Chester Arthur, and Calvin Coolidge. Each student might also present an oral summary of the report to the class.

Covert Operation: A Presidential Secret

In 1893, Grover Cleveland had been president for only a few weeks of his second term when he ordered one of the most secret presidential covert operations in history. Earlier, he had noticed a "rough spot" on the roof of his mouth. Over the next few weeks, it grew noticeably. Cleveland finally had doctors examine it, and they determined that it was cancerous and should be excised.

But the summer of 1893 was a politically perilous time. The country was entering what became known as the Panic of 1893, which Cleveland believed was precipitated by the inflation-producing Sherman Silver Purchase Act of 1890. He was pushing Congress to repeal the act. It would not have been good timing for the public to know that the president was ill. They might have become hysterical. Cleveland's opponents might have used the moment to prevent repeal. Cleveland decided that if the surgery must be done, it would be done secretly.

On July 1, 1893, President Cleveland boarded the *Oneida*, the private yacht of his friend Commodore Elias Benedict, in New York, ostensibly heading out for a four-day fishing trip. (Another story the White House planted was that Cleveland was having a bad tooth extracted.)

Among others onboard were Dr. Joseph Bryant, his assistant Dr. W. W. Keen, and a dentist, Dr. Ferdinand Hasbrouck. A room on the yacht was converted to an operating room. As the yacht traveled at half speed up the East River, the doctors administered ether as an anesthetic. They removed the tumor and, when they discovered that the tumor had spread to the molars of the jaw, about half the president's palate. Dr. Kasson Gibson, a

the best known—but provides only limited oversight of them. The Kennedy administration's support of an invasion at the Bay of Pigs; the Reagan administration's support of anti-Communist forces in Nicaragua, Afghanistan, and Angola; George H. W. Bush's administration's involvement in Panama and the Persian Gulf; and the war on terrorism under Clinton and George W. Bush depended heavily on the CIA to implement directives from the president.

Diplomatic Leader

The constitutional basis for the president's role as diplomatic leader is found in Article II, Section 2, clause 2, where we read that the president "shall have power, by and with the advice and consent of the Senate, to make treaties, provided two-thirds of the senators present concur; and he shall nominate, and by and with the advice and consent of the Senate, shall appoint ambassadors, other public ministers and consuls." As with his other constitutional roles, the president's role as diplomatic leader is balanced with the foreign policy responsibilities of Congress. However, his authority in this sphere remains formidable.

President Trump and Russian President Vladimir Putin held a summit in Helsinki, Finland, in July 2018.

In initiating and implementing treaties or other foreign-policy activities, the president has access to important information and management resources—the State Department, the National Security Council (NSC), and the CIA. Given these resources, along with a measure of political cooperation with the Senate, the president generally gains approval for treaties. There have been, however, notable exceptions to this rule. Woodrow Wilson, for example, failed to gain Senate ratification for the Treaty of Versailles in 1919, and President Carter was unable to persuade the Senate to approve SALT II in 1979.

In addition to treaty-making powers, the president also has the power of **executive agreement**, whereby he can have a written "understanding" with another head of state to take a particular action. Congress has little or no control over executive agreements as long as an agreement does not violate the law. Executive agreements underscore the independence that the president has in implementing foreign policy. For example, Lyndon Johnson used executive agreements to escalate the war in Vietnam, and Richard Nixon ended American involvement in that country through an executive agreement with the North Vietnamese.

Presidents use executive agreements far more frequently than treaties as they do not require Senate approval. However, an executive agreement only lasts as long as future presidents wish to keep it. Because treaties require a two-thirds majority vote of the Senate, it is often difficult for them to receive approval; however, they are more enduring. On the other hand, executive agreements are easy to implement but are also easy for the current or a future president to change.

Executive Agreements

Discuss the pros and cons of executive agreements. Are they mentioned in the Constitution? Why might a president rely on them rather than on legislation or formal treaties? Are they good or bad for American freedom? Are there dangers inherent in their use?

Camp David

During World War II, President Franklin D. Roosevelt sought an area near Washington, DC, to be used as a presidential retreat. Officials from the National Park Service sought a place located close to the capital with an elevation that would provide relief for FDR's health issues. Ensuring security for the president was another major concern.

One of the possibilities presented to the president was located in the Catoctin Mountains of Maryland. It contained a camp that had been built for federal government agents and their families. FDR submitted his ideas for construction of a retreat and in May 1942 work began. Roosevelt named the hideaway Shangri-La, in reference to the fictional Himalayan paradise in James Hilton's book *Lost Horizon*. But President Eisenhower later renamed the facility **Camp David** (in honor of his grandson) because he thought the name Shangri-La was too unusual.

Over the years, many presidents have taken advantage of Camp David to advance diplomacy. There, FDR discussed war strategy with British prime minister Churchill, President Eisenhower hosted Soviet leader Nikita Khrushchev, and President Nixon met with Soviet premier Leonid Brezhnev. President Carter held meetings that led to the signing

President Kennedy at Camp David with his daughter (on horseback) and son (by his side) in 1963

of the Camp David Accords. In addition, President Clinton hosted a Middle East summit; and after September 11, 2001, President George W. Bush met with his national security advisors.

Many presidents have enjoyed recreational activities there with family and friends. FDR worked on his stamp collection. Truman walked, watched films, and drove the camp jeep. Eisenhower shot skeet and golfed. The Kennedys rode horses and enjoyed family outings. The Johnsons bowled at the camp's bowling lanes. Nixon wrote speeches and enjoyed the swimming pool. In winter, Ford rode around the camp on a snowmobile. The Carters bicycled. The Reagans rode horses and spent more time there than any other First Family—more than 500 days. George H. W. Bush pitched horseshoes, had large family gatherings, and celebrated the only wedding to be held at Camp David.

The Clintons partook of Thanksgiving dinners. George W. Bush continued the Bush family tradition of family gatherings on holidays. He made 149 visits during his two terms to the camp. Barack Obama liked the area less than the Bushes but still visited 39 times during his eight years in office. President Trump preferred spending time at one of the Trump resorts, but occasionally visited Camp David.

The retreat has changed over the years as different administrations improved the facility. While FDR used it only during the summers, Truman had heat installed to allow year-round use. Eisenhower added air conditioning, an area for practicing golf, a skeet range, and a bowling alley.

Kennedy added the stables. Nixon enlarged the facility, adding more buildings and a swimming pool. The Reagans redecorated and beautified the area with flowers. George H. W. Bush added horseshoe pits and a chapel built with private donations.

Camp David provides a place away from the rest of the world for the president's family and friends to gather as well as a place to entertain heads of state or to discuss many of the nation's most pressing matters. Of course, visits to Camp David are by invitation only. Navy personnel operate the site and troops from the marine barracks in Washington, DC, provide permanent security.

Israeli Prime Minister Menachem Begin, President Carter, and Egyptian President Anwar Sadat (left to right) at Camp David in 1978

prosthodontist, fashioned a vulcanized rubber palate so that the president could speak.

On August 7, Cleveland addressed a special session of Congress, urging the members of Congress to repeal the Sherman Silver Purchase Act. Congress, still unaware of the president's operation, complied by repealing the act. Not until nine years later did the public learn that the country had been without a conscious president for one and a half hours.

Diplomatic Leadership

Dealing with foreign affairs is one of the president's many difficult tasks. Comments from presidents give us a glimpse of the challenges they faced.

After the European phase of World War II ended in 1945, President Truman attended the Potsdam Conference in Germany. While meeting with other Allied leaders, he wrote the following to his wife: "I like Stalin. He is straightforward. Knows what he wants and will compromise when he can't get it. His foreign minister isn't so forthright."

President Kennedy, responding to letters sent to him in 1962 by Soviet premier Nikita Khrushchev, wrote, "The continuation of this threat, or a prolonging of this discussion concerning Cuba by linking these problems to the broader questions of European and world security, would surely lead to an intensification of the Cuban crisis and a grave risk to the peace of the world."

Presidential Trivia—Part Two

6. Which two sons of presidents became presidents? (*John Quincy Adams and George W. Bush*)

7. Who were the two oldest presidents to take office? (*Donald Trump was 70 years, 220 days old and Ronald Reagan was 69 years and 349 days old when each began his presidency.]*)

8. Which president weighed the most? (*William Howard Taft [He is reported to have weighed between 335 and 350 pounds while president; a new, larger bathtub was installed in the White House to accommodate him.]*)

9. Who was the only preacher to become president? (*James Garfield was a Disciples of Christ lay preacher.*)

10. Who was the first president to be the target of an assassination attempt? (*Andrew Jackson [An insane house painter named Richard Lawrence fired two pistols at Jackson as the president was leaving a funeral held at the Capitol on January 30, 1835. Both weapons misfired, and Jackson was unharmed.]*)

11. Which president had the most children? (*John Tyler [fifteen by two wives]*)

12. Which presidents had ancestral ties to passengers on the *Mayflower*? (*John Adams, John Quincy Adams, Zachary Taylor, Ulysses S. Grant, James Garfield, Calvin Coolidge, Franklin Roosevelt, George H. W. Bush, and George W. Bush*)

13. Which president had to borrow money to attend his inauguration? (*George Washington; though he was a wealthy planter with a large estate, he had limited cash when he needed to leave for New York, so he had to borrow money to finance his trip.*)

Legislative Leader

During the twentieth century, the president's influence in relation to Congress grew. The Great Depression, the two world wars, the Cold War, and increased technological changes all made the president the chief beneficiary of increasing federal power.

As late as 1885, political scientist (and future president) Woodrow Wilson complained that the president exerted virtually no legislative influence. Presidents could suggest legislation in their annual message, but domestic policy belonged to Congress. Yet only a decade later the presidency began its rise to dominance in the constitutional system. Both William McKinley and Theodore Roosevelt skillfully advanced their own bills through Congress. Woodrow Wilson, who had earlier criticized congressional leadership, presented his reform program in person with all the force he could muster, even going over the heads of stubborn congressmen to make his case to the people. During the crisis of the Great Depression, Franklin Roosevelt, with large Democratic majorities supporting him, made many laws himself. Congress set aside its traditional procedures to pass his "emergency" bills quickly and even reduced its own powers, surrendering them to the executive branch and the federal bureaucracy.

President Trump meeting with congressional leaders and other officials in the Oval Office

Along with his ability to set a legislative agenda, the president can exercise **veto** power over Congress. If the president opposes a bill passed by Congress, he may veto it, or refuse to sign it into law. Although vetoes may be overridden by a two-thirds vote in both houses of Congress, historically this has been difficult to accomplish. An additional veto power of the president, which cannot be overridden, is the **pocket veto**. If the president leaves a bill unsigned for ten days during a congressional adjournment (in a sense, putting it in his pocket and forgetting about it), that bill is automatically vetoed. If the president ignores a bill while Congress is in session, then the bill becomes law without the president's signature. Presidential veto is a powerful weapon—less than five percent of them have been overridden.

In the 1990s many conservatives wanted to give the president the **line-item veto**, which allows the president to veto part of a bill without vetoing the entire bill, so that he could more easily cut "pork" from legislative bills. This measure would give him more legislative power. In 1996, Congress approved the practice; but the Supreme Court struck it down as unconstitutional in 1998, stating that Congress does not have the authority to give the president legislative power. The Court further stated that if Congress wanted to give the president that power, it would have to pass a constitutional amendment. Such an amendment has never gained sufficient support for passage.

Presidential Vetoes	
2,575 vetoes as of March 2019	
Regular vetoes	1,509
Pocket vetoes	1,066
Vetoes overridden	111 (4.3%)
Most vetoes	
Franklin Roosevelt	635
Grover Cleveland	584
Harry Truman	250
Dwight Eisenhower	181
Ulysses S. Grant	93
Theodore Roosevelt	82
Ronald Reagan	78

Presidential Legislation

Assign a student or a group of students to gather information about legislation that the current president is trying to get passed in Congress. Alternatively, ask students to determine whether the president might be considering vetoing any legislation. Identify the issues that these items of legislation address. Should a Christian support or reject this legislation? Why?

Since the advent of television, preparation for this yearly speech has become even more intense. Before President George W. Bush's 2004 State of the Union address, the White House website gave Americans a behind-the-scenes look at the preparations for the speech. It included video clips of cabinet secretaries talking about the speech as well as photographs of the president and others involved with the preparations. Similar descriptions and other coverage have documented the efforts of the president and his staff in advance of this occasion.

State of the Union Address

Article II, Section 3, of the Constitution states that the president "shall from time to time give to the Congress information of the state of the Union, and recommend to their consideration such measures as he shall judge necessary and expedient." The president uses his annual **State of the Union (SOTU) address** to establish a legislative agenda, rally his party members, reach out to opponents, and influence public opinion. The address is given before a joint session of the House and Senate in the House chamber in the Capitol.

The first State of the Union address, called the Annual Message at the time, was delivered by George Washington to both the House and Senate in the Senate chamber. Thomas Jefferson, however, disliked delivering the message in person and instead sent a written message to be presented to Congress. The practice of submitting a written address continued until 1913, when Woodrow Wilson began delivering the address in person again.

The title Annual Message was changed to the title State of the Union in 1947. With the advent of television, President Johnson changed the time of the address in 1965 to the evening (rather than midday) to reach a greater audience. In 1986, the address was postponed for the first time because of the explosion of the space shuttle *Challenger* on the day of the scheduled speech. In 1999, President Clinton was the first president to give a State of the Union address to Congress when it was considering his removal from office after his impeachment.

First Lady Laura Bush with guests at the 2005 SOTU address

Shortest SOTU Address
In word count: George Washington, 1790 (1,089 words)

Longest SOTU Address
In minutes: Bill Clinton, 2000 (1 hr., 28 min., 49 sec.)

First SOTU Address on Radio
Calvin Coolidge, 1923

First SOTU Address on TV
Harry Truman, 1947

First Evening SOTU Address
Lyndon Johnson, 1965

First Live Webcast SOTU Address
George W. Bush, 2002

Chief of State

The president of the United States is both the national leader and a national symbol. As chief of state, the president represents America at home and abroad by hosting or visiting foreign dignitaries and by leading important ceremonial events. When laying the wreath at the Tomb of the Unknown Soldier, lighting the White House Christmas tree, attending the funeral of a world leader, or throwing the first pitch of baseball season, the President is acting in his role as chief of state. Although the glitter of ceremony might seem far removed from the president's business of politics and governing, the president's presence on such occasions is an important part of our national experience.

On the opening day of baseball season, presidents (such as Hoover above) often toss the first pitch.

A Presidential Address

Secure copies of a president's State of the Union address. Ask students to read the address and discuss the issues that the president highlighted. What were the problematic issues mentioned? What solutions did the president propose? Can a Christian agree with the proposed solutions? Why or why not?

State of the Union Address

Record or locate a video of one of the current president's State of the Union addresses. Play the video, or selected portions, for the class. Discuss Congress's responses to the address. How well does the president communicate his ideas both to Congress and to the electorate?

Comparing Philosophies in State of the Union Addresses

Obtain copies of several presidents' State of the Union addresses. Divide the class into three or four groups, and distribute to each group the speeches of two presidents who have starkly different political philosophies (e.g., Jefferson and Adams, John Quincy Adams and Jackson, Coolidge and Franklin Roosevelt, or Reagan and Obama). Instruct students to note the political differences between the proposals mentioned in the respective addresses.

Differences

What are some of the differences between a US president and a prime minister? Presidents are chosen by the Electoral College, whereas prime ministers are normally chosen by national legislatures. Presidents appoint individuals to cabinet positions from the public and private sectors while prime ministers appoint people from the legislature. A president is not required to have a majority in Congress in order to hold the office. Prime ministers must have a majority in the legislature because the majority party chooses the prime minister (if no party controls the legislature, then a coalition government must be formed). If people lose confidence in prime ministers' leadership, the prime ministers might lose power even though their parties hold the majority.

State Dinners

A **state dinner** is a special dinner hosted by the president and the First Lady to honor a visiting foreign leader, such as a monarch, president, or prime minister. It provides an opportunity to renew ties and strengthen the relationship between the United States and the country of the visiting head of state.

Representatives of the two nations begin preparations for the dinner months ahead of time. The guest list includes specific officials from the country being honored, elected US officials, cabinet members, business and community leaders, educators, and entertainers. Once the list is complete, the White House calligraphers prepare the invitations.

The dinner often occurs in the White House State Dining Room. (State dinners have also taken place in the East Room and the Rose Garden.) After the menu is approved, it is prepared by the White House chef, pastry chef, and kitchen staff. The White House florist creates the floral arrangements. Other decisions involve table settings, entertainment, and seating arrangements. Tradition-

President and Mrs. Bush (shown on right) with President and Mrs. Fox of Mexico at a 2001 state dinner

ally, couples are not seated side by side, and guests receive envelopes containing seating assignments when they arrive at the White House.

State dinners are carefully orchestrated and are designed to both impress and entertain guests. Typical of such occasions was the one hosted by President George W. Bush for Mexican president Vicente Fox. The events of the evening began with the president and First Lady greeting their guests of honor at the White House North Entrance, which is reserved for formal occasions. In the Yellow Oval Room, President Bush, the First Lady, President Fox, and Mrs. Fox had a private meeting before descending to the East Room. There the other guests had gathered for a reception, with the Marine Band presenting the music. The guests then moved to the State Dining Room for the president's official welcome, President Fox's response, and dinner. During dessert, brass and stringed instruments provided music. After dinner, everyone returned to the East Room for special musical entertainment. And the evening officially ended with a fireworks display, viewed by the guests from the balcony off the Blue Room.

Americans' identification with their president has been most evident during times of national tragedy. Millions mourned the death of Franklin Roosevelt, who had led the country through the Great Depression and a global war. Few Americans old enough to remember 1963 can forget the assassination of President Kennedy and the resulting national grief. Similarly, the wounding of President Reagan during a 1981 assassination attempt brought a nationwide outpouring of concern and prayers for his recovery.

In the United States, the roles of chief of state and the head of the government are both assigned to the president. In Britain, and in a number of other nations, those jobs are divided between two people—the monarch and the prime minister. Our system produces a strange relationship for a president; Americans usually react positively to him when he acts as head of state but negatively when he supports legislation they dislike. Britain on the other hand, can love the monarch and hate the prime minister without this confusion of roles.

Presidential Trivia—Part Three

14. Who was the youngest president elected to office? (*John Kennedy [He was 43 years and 236 days old at the time of his inauguration.] However, Theodore Roosevelt took office at a younger age [42 years and 322 days] when he succeeded to the presidency upon the death of William McKinley.*)

15. Who was the first president to visit a foreign nation while in office? (*Theodore Roosevelt; he traveled to Panama in 1906.*)

16. What man's father and son became presidents? (*John Scott Harrison [His father was William Henry Harrison, and his son was Benjamin Harrison.]*)

17. Who was the only president to earn a PhD? (*Woodrow Wilson; he received the degree in political science from Johns Hopkins University in 1886.*)

18. Who was the tallest president? (*Abraham Lincoln [six feet four inches tall]*)

19. Which two former presidents died on the same day? (*John Adams and Thomas Jefferson [They both died on July 4, 1826, which was the fiftieth anniversary of the signing of the Declaration of Independence.]*)

20. Which president had the shortest life? (*John Kennedy [46 years and 177 days]*)

21. Who served as president and vice president but was not elected to either office during a presidential election? (*Gerald Ford [He was appointed vice president following the resignation of Spiro Agnew, and he succeeded to the presidency upon the resignation of Richard Nixon.]*)

22. Which president was the last surviving signer of the Constitution? (*James Madison [died on June 28, 1836]*)

23. Which presidents were assassinated? (*Abraham Lincoln, James Garfield, William McKinley, and John Kennedy*)

Party Leader

The Founding Fathers did not envision the president as leader of his political party because political parties did not exist at the time. Nevertheless, the president's role as political leader is an important aspect of his authority.

Generally, a presidential candidate controls his party through personnel and by his position. The presidential nominee works closely with the chairman of his political party to exercise control over the personnel appointed to policymaking positions within the party. If elected as president, the nominee continues to be the spokesman for his party through the high visibility of that office.

As party leader, the president returns to the campaign trail to help elect congressional or gubernatorial candidates of his party. Although the president must be the leader of all Americans, his partisan leadership and loyalty are expected and understandable, given the importance of the two-party system in this country and every president's dependence on his political party to get elected.

Restrictions

Our Founding Fathers endured six years of bloodshed to gain independence from, what they perceived to be, a hostile monarchy. With this in mind at the

Presidential Protection

The **Secret Service**, the major source of presidential protection today, was established in 1865 to stop the counterfeiting of money. It was part of the Treasury Department until 2003 when it became a division within the Department of Homeland Security. After the 1901 assassination of President William McKinley, Congress asked that the Service protect the nation's leader. The following year, the Secret Service acquired full responsibility for doing so while also continuing its other responsibilities.

At the request of President Warren Harding, the White House Police Force was organized in 1922 to protect the White House and to assist with providing security for the president. In 1930, that group was placed under the control of the Secret Service. After an assassination attempt on President Harry Truman in 1950, Congress passed legislation to extend Secret Service protection to the president's immediate family, the president-elect, and the vice president (if he desired it).

Congress further extended protection, in 1962, to the vice president-elect and, in 1965, to former presidents and spouses throughout the former president's lifetime. In 1968, Congress authorized guarding the widow of a former president until the widow died or remarried. Minor children of former presidents became entitled to protection until the age of sixteen. In 1971, Secret Service coverage was expanded to visiting heads of a foreign nation.

As a cost-saving measure, in 1994 Congress passed legislation to limit protection of former presidents to ten years after they left office. The law was to apply to presidents who were first inaugurated after January 1997. However, in 2013, that law was repealed. With the increase of terrorism, Congress wanted to ensure the safety of former presidents for life.

President Reagan was wounded in a 1981 assassination attempt along with a Secret Service agent, a police officer, and a White House official.

Presidential Influence

Former and sitting presidents exert influence on their parties. Two men that had tremendous such impact were Ronald Reagan (Republican) and Bill Clinton (Democrat). Invite students to research the influence of these men on their parties while they were in and after they left office.

Political Parties

George Washington and some of the other Founding Fathers were skeptical of political parties. They were concerned that such associations would draw people away from doing what was best for the nation and cause them to focus on what was best for their parties. This was a legitimate concern. However, ideally, parties should allow people of like conviction to work together to achieve what they believe is best for the nation.

Constitutional Convention, they set about to forge an executive branch in which presidential power was limited by the Constitution, checked by the legislative and judicial branches, and yet broad enough to lead the nation effectively.

Tenure

Article II of the Constitution deals with the restrictions and responsibilities of the executive branch. Although some of these are clearly outlined, many are vague and have therefore been defined by interpretation or precedent. For example, the Constitution plainly states (in Article II, Section 1, clause 1) that a president's **tenure**, or term of office, will be four years. However, presidents since Washington have interpreted this restriction as simply applying to the length of a single term but not restricting the number of terms. In light of this, Washington served two terms, establishing an important precedent for his successors—one that survived for nearly a century and a half until Franklin Roosevelt's unprecedented third- and fourth-term elections in 1940 and 1944.

Franklin D. Roosevelt

With the passage of the **Twenty-Second Amendment** in 1951, the president was restricted to two terms. A vice president who succeeds to the presidency to finish an uncompleted term may not exceed a total of ten years in the highest office (up to two years of his predecessor's term plus two full terms of his own). If a successor serves more than two years of a predecessor's term, he can be elected for only one more term. When President Kennedy was assassinated, Vice President Lyndon Johnson became president and finished Kennedy's remaining term of fourteen months. Johnson then ran for reelection and won. And he could have run again because another four-year term would not have exceeded the ten-year limit. This was not the case for President Ford. He was only eligible for one additional term because he finished President Nixon's remaining term of two years and five months. (However, Ford lost his bid to gain that additional term when he was defeated in the 1976 election by Jimmy Carter.)

The Twenty-Second Amendment provides an additional limitation on presidential power because the two-term restriction can result in a lame-duck period for the president. A president is considered a **lame duck** when he has lost an election or is ineligible for reelection and yet must serve the remainder of his term. This position tends to decrease his effectiveness with Congress because members of Congress no longer have to be concerned about his ability to muster widespread support at the polls. In effect, the president sometimes becomes a figure that is easier to attack or ignore.

Chief executives have usually had a more difficult time during a second term, but much depends on the president's popularity and the political composition of Congress. For example, Ronald Reagan won a landslide reelection in 1984 and maintained a slim Republican majority in the Senate, thus continuing his successful legislative record. However, in 1986 the Republicans lost their Senate majority. Because Reagan was ineligible to seek another term, and thereby unable to take his cause to the electorate in a national election, his legislative ability was hampered.

Impeachment

Another constitutional restriction on the presidency is impeachment. Article II, Section 4, states,

> The president, vice president and all civil officers of the United States, shall be removed from office on impeachment for, and conviction of, treason, bribery, or other high crimes and misdemeanors.

"If I Were . . ."

Ask the students to write a paragraph on one of these topics: "If I Were President for a Day . . ." or "If I Were Elected President, the First Two Things I Would Do . . ." Then read selected essays to the class. Discuss the constitutionality of the desires that are expressed. Also discuss how the proposed actions would please or antagonize individuals or groups.

The Twenty-Second Amendment

Discuss the advantages and disadvantages of the Twenty-Second Amendment. Does the two-term limit properly restrain excessive presidential power, or does it thwart the will of the people by not allowing them to decide how long a president should hold office?

This restriction is the ultimate check on the power of the office. It underscores a fundamental principle of democratic government—that no one, including the president, is above the law. **Impeachment** (bringing charges against the president or other major federal officials) requires a majority vote in the House of Representatives. Conviction on those same charges requires a two-thirds majority vote in the Senate. A vote of conviction in the Senate can result only in the official's removal from office. If laws have been broken, it is the courts' responsibility to prosecute after the dismissal.

Richard Nixon resigned in August 1974 because of the threat (and likelihood) of impeachment. By that time it was clear the president had repeatedly lied to the American public regarding his involvement in the Watergate scandal. Andrew Johnson and Bill Clinton hold the distinction of being the only presidents to be impeached. Neither impeachment trial, however, resulted in removal from office. Johnson's case provides a good example of the vagueness of the impeachment clause and its use for political ends.

Andrew Johnson sought a speedy and lenient reconstruction process for the South following the Civil War. His program was

Andrew Johnson

Impeachment Procedures

The Constitution does not give a specific plan for the impeachment process, but the House and Senate have historically followed a basic pattern.

House of Representatives' Role

The House of Representatives is granted "sole power of impeachment" in Article I, Section 2, clause 5, of the Constitution.

1. House custom is to begin with a resolution giving the Judiciary Committee the authority to investigate the charges.

2. Investigations and hearings of the charges are held by the House Judiciary Committee.

3. If the charges are supported by the Judiciary Committee's findings, an impeachment resolution, which includes articles of impeachment, is issued to the full House. If the committee's findings prove that impeachment is not justified, a resolution to that effect is issued to the full House.

4. The House considers the resolution. If any one of the articles of impeachment is adopted by the House, the official is considered impeached, and the matter goes to the Senate for trial.

Senate's Role

In Article I, Section 3, clause 6, the Constitution says that "the Senate shall have the sole power to try all impeachments."

1. A certain number of House members (traditionally five to eleven) function as "managers" (prosecutors) at the Senate trial. They are chosen by the House Speaker or by ballot.

2. Lawyers representing the impeached official present the defense. The impeached official can cross-examine witnesses and has the right to testify, as in any criminal trial.

3. The jury is the full Senate.

4. The Constitution states that the chief justice of the Supreme Court will preside over the trial if the president of the United States is being tried.

5. At the trial's end, the Senate meets in closed session to discuss the verdict. Each senator is allowed fifteen minutes of debate.

6. Senators vote on each article of impeachment in open session. A two-thirds vote, of those present, is required for conviction. The Constitution says that federal officials will be removed from office when impeached and convicted. If no article is approved by a two-thirds vote, the official is cleared of the accusations.

7. A vote to disqualify the convicted official from holding future federal office could be held by the Senate and would be decided by a majority.

Presidential Trivia—Part Four

24. Which president served for the shortest length of time? (*William Henry Harrison [one month]*)

25. Which president was elected unanimously by the Electoral College? (*George Washington [with 69 votes in 1789 and with 132 votes in 1792]*)

26. Who was the only president to serve two nonconsecutive terms? (*Grover Cleveland [1885–89 and 1893–97]*)

27. Who was the shortest president? (*James Madison [five feet four inches tall]*)

28. What state was birthplace to the most presidents? (*Virginia; eight presidents were born there.*)

29. Who was the first president to receive a Nobel Peace Prize? (*Theodore Roosevelt [He received it in 1906 for mediating the treaty to end the Russo-Japanese War.]*)

30. How many presidents have received the Nobel Peace Prize? (*Four; Theodore Roosevelt, Woodrow Wilson, Jimmy Carter, and Barack Obama*)

31. Which president was born on a national holiday? (*Calvin Coolidge [July 4, 1872]*)

32. More presidents attended which college than any other college? (*Eight presidents attended Harvard [John Adams, John Quincy Adams, Rutherford B. Hayes, Theodore Roosevelt, Franklin Roosevelt, John Kennedy, George W. Bush, and Barack Obama]*)

33. What former president was elected to the Confederate Congress during the Civil War? (*John Tyler [He died, however, before he could take his seat.]*)

One Vote Short

Edmund G. Ross was a journalist and printer by trade, a Civil War soldier, and a participant in politics. In 1865, when Senator James Lane of Kansas died, the governor appointed Ross to fill the vacancy, and in 1867 Ross was elected to the office for the term expiring in 1871. During this term, Andrew Johnson's impeachment occurred. When the trial occurred in the Senate, Ross said he could find no grounds for Johnson's removal as president and voted against it. As a result, many viewed Ross as a traitor to the Republican Party. He lost his bid for reelection to the US Senate in 1871.

Later, he moved his family to the New Mexico Territory, and when Grover Cleveland became president, Ross was appointed governor of the territory. He held that position from 1885 to 1889.

John F. Kennedy wrote about Ross in his book *Profiles in Courage* and portrayed him as a hero. Others have disagreed with that assessment. Some have argued that Ross accepted a bribe to vote against Johnson's removal. Others have noted that his "no" vote was motivated by his dislike of Benjamin Wade, the Senate's president pro tempore. According to the law at the time, Wade would have become president if Andrew Johnson had been removed from office.

Bill Clinton

Presidential Executive Orders Issued Since 1923

Coolidge (1923–29)	1,203
Hoover (1929–33)	968
F. Roosevelt (1933–45)	3,721
Truman (1945–53)	907
Eisenhower (1953–61)	484
Kennedy (1961–63)	214
L. Johnson (1963–69)	325
Nixon (1969–74)	346
Ford (1974–77)	169
Carter (1977–81)	320
Reagan (1981–89)	381
G. H. W. Bush (1989–93)	166
Clinton (1993–2001)	364
G. W. Bush (2001–9)	291
Obama (2009–17)	276
Trump (2017–March 2019)	102

in keeping with Abraham Lincoln's desire "to bind up the nation's wounds." Because of his sympathetic dealings with the former Confederate states and his stubbornness in his interactions with those who disagreed with him, Johnson faced strong opposition from the Radical Republicans in Congress. That group controlled both houses of Congress and sought to institute harsher measures on the southern states than Johnson would support. In March 1867, Congress passed the Tenure of Office Act over Johnson's veto. The law made it illegal for the president to remove any appointee who had been approved by the Senate unless the Senate also approved the dismissal. Johnson believed the legislation was unconstitutional and violated it. In 1868, the Radical Republicans impeached Johnson. Though the charges against the president largely stemmed from his violation of the 1867 law, the impeachment was primarily an act of political revenge. The case then went to the Senate for a trial, and Johnson was acquitted by just one vote. The Senate's action not only demonstrated the legislature's check over the executive branch but also helped remove impeachment as a tool of partisan politics.

In 1998 **Bill Clinton** was impeached by the House for the criminal acts of perjury and obstruction of justice. The prosecution argued that President Clinton, in an attempt to conceal his adulterous affair with White House intern Monica Lewinsky, committed perjury when he lied under oath to a grand jury and that he obstructed justice by tampering with evidence and witnesses. The prosecution concluded that the president should be removed from office. But the defense emphasized that President Clinton's actions stemmed merely from his attempt to hide his extramarital affair. They claimed that any wrongdoing of which he might be guilty did not constitute "high crimes and misdemeanors." Thus, they said, the circumstances did not justify the president's removal from office. The Senate, after hearing the prosecution and defense arguments, acquitted Clinton on both charges—with forty-five voting to convict him on the perjury charge and fifty voting that he was guilty of obstruction of justice.

Reaction by Americans to the Clinton impeachment and trial varied. Many accused the president, age forty-nine, of using his position to forge a sexual relationship with a twenty-two-year-old subordinate. Many believed that no one, not even the president of the United States, was above the law and that his actions merited his removal from office. Others argued that the issue was a private matter.

Additional Powers
Executive Orders

The Constitution and certain acts of Congress give the president the legal authority to issue **executive orders** (presidential directives having the force of law). In 1947 President Truman issued an executive order creating the National Security Council (NSC). In 1965 President Johnson, concerned about a

The Importance of Character

Guide a discussion about the importance of character for political leaders. Ask the students whether they would vote for a person who had been convicted of a crime or a person who had committed adultery if he also had many skills as a political leader. Help the students understand that although political skill is an important qualification for holding government positions, having a moral sense is vital. Justice is based on morality. A person should have moral discernment to serve in the government.

Comparing Two Impeachments

Guide a discussion regarding the impeachments of Andrew Johnson and Bill Clinton. How were they similar? How were they different? Were the impeachments justified? Do you think the Senate should have convicted the presidents? What lessons can Americans, including future presidents, learn from these two events?

famine in India, issued an order to the secretary of agriculture about the Indian food situation. With an executive order in 1983, President Reagan initiated a study to determine whether the National Aeronautics and Space Administration (NASA) should develop a manned, permanently based space station. In 2016, President Obama signed an executive order that established the Commission on Enhancing National Cybersecurity. These are examples of just a few of the approximately fourteen thousand executive orders that have been issued since the mid-1800s.

Some executive orders have been controversial, thus earning both praise and condemnation. For example, President Franklin Roosevelt issued an order in February 1942, just two months after the bombing of Pearl Harbor, that authorized the removal of Japanese Americans from the West Coast and their placement in internment camps. In July 1948, President Truman ordered an end to segregation in the armed forces. A September 1957 executive order from President Eisenhower empowered the Arkansas National Guard to protect African American students who were attempting to integrate Central High School in Little Rock, Arkansas.

Some argue that the president's ordinance power has allowed him greater opportunity to intervene in national and world affairs. However, critics contend that such authority has been abused by many presidents and used as a means of implementing controversial policies that might not pass as congressional legislation. Like executive agreements, executive orders may be changed by a later president.

Headline regarding one of President Truman's executive orders

Appointment Power

Good leaders surround themselves with good people and delegate authority to them. The Founding Fathers understood the principle of delegating responsibility and granted the power of appointment to the president through Article II, Section 2, clause 2, which states,

> He shall have power, by and with the advice and consent of the Senate, to make treaties, provided two-thirds of the senators present concur; and he shall nominate, and by and with the advice and consent of the Senate, shall appoint ambassadors, other public ministers and consuls, judges of the Supreme Court, and all other officers of the United States, whose appointments are not herein otherwise provided for, and which shall be established by law: but the Congress may by law vest the appointment of such inferior officers, as they think proper, in the president alone, in the courts of law, or in the heads of departments.

Ben Carson was appointed by President Trump to serve as Secretary of Housing and Urban Development (HUD) in 2017.

AMERICA'S HIGHEST OFFICE • 261

Activity 2: The Proper Attitude Toward the Powers of the Presidency

Use this essay by Mike Pence to help the students improve their reading comprehension and analytical skills by using resources.

With this constitutional provision, the president may appoint cabinet members and their top aides, ambassadors and other diplomats, heads of independent agencies, all federal judges, US marshals and attorneys, and the commissioned officers of the armed forces.

Use of Powers

The Constitution both restricts and outlines presidential power; however, the exercise of that power has varied considerably, depending on the occupants of the White House. Some presidents, such as Calvin Coolidge and William Howard Taft, had a rather passive view of presidential power. For instance, Taft said,

> The President can exercise no power which cannot be fairly and reasonably traced to some specific grant of power. . . . Such specific grants must be either in the Federal Constitution or in an act of Congress passed in pursuance thereof. There is no undefined residuum of power which a President can exercise because it seems to him to be in the public interest.

Taft's predecessor could not have been more different. Theodore Roosevelt found the presidency to be, in his words, a "bully pulpit"; from that "pulpit" Roosevelt took a broad view of his power.

> My belief was that it was not only [the president's] right but his duty to do anything that the needs of the Nation demanded unless such action was forbidden by the Constitution or by the laws. Under this interpretation of executive power I did and caused to be done many things not previously done by the President and the heads of the departments. I did not usurp power, but I did greatly broaden the use of executive power.

Regardless of a president's personal definition of power, certain general responsibilities are clearly outlined in the Constitution: chief executive, commander in chief, diplomatic leader, legislative leader, chief of state, and party boss. The president wears many "hats," and the complexity of his job description often requires that he act in more than one role at a time—as when he travels overseas to negotiate as a diplomatic leader while also representing the United States as the chief of state.

Section Review

1. Explain the president's responsibility to "faithfully execute" the nation's laws.

2–3. Distinguish between the president's treaty-making powers and executive agreements.

4–5. What is the difference between a regular veto and a pocket veto?

6. Why was the Secret Service originally established?

7. Explain the limits on how long a president can serve that were enacted in the Twenty-Second Amendment.

8–10. Who were the only two presidents ever to be impeached? For what constitutional reason were they not removed from office?

★ How did the various State of the Union addresses mentioned in this chapter differ? Why do you think they differed?

★ When is the president considered a lame duck? What does this mean?

Section Review Answers

1. The president enforces and administers the law through the various departments under his control and also administers a vast bureaucracy. (p. 249)

2–3. Treaties must be ratified by a two-thirds vote of the Senate, but executive agreements do not require congressional approval. Executive agreements give the president more flexibility but are less permanent. (p. 252)

4–5. A regular veto occurs when a president refuses to sign a bill into law; it can be overridden by a two-thirds vote in both houses of Congress. A pocket veto occurs when the president leaves a bill unsigned for ten days during a congressional adjournment; it cannot be overridden. (p. 254)

6. to stop the counterfeiting of money (p. 257)

7. The Twenty-Second Amendment restricted the president to two terms. A vice president who succeeds to the presidency to finish an uncompleted term may not exceed a total of ten years as president (up to two years of his predecessor's term plus two full terms of his own). (p. 258)

8–10. Andrew Johnson and Bill Clinton; two-thirds of the Senate did not vote to convict either president (pp. 259–60)

★ Washington's address was the shortest. Jefferson sent a written message to Congress, and that tradition continued until 1913 when Woodrow Wilson reinstated delivering the address in person. Clinton's address was the longest. The various addresses reflect the presidents' personalities and the circumstances at the time of their speeches.

★ A president is considered a lame duck when he has lost an election or is ineligible for reelection and yet must serve the remainder of his term. The term lame duck describes the president's decreased effectiveness with Congress because he cannot gather widespread support for a future election.

First Ladies

The title "**First Lady**" normally refers to the wife of the president. In cases where the wife is deceased or disabled (or the president is single, as was true of James Buchanan), the title refers to the person who serves as White House hostess.

Though their names do not appear on the ballot, though their "position" is not subject to Senate confirmation, though they receive no pay, and though they have no duties prescribed by law, the wives of presidents have great responsibility and often great power.

The First Lady's primary responsibility, since the time of Martha Washington, has been to receive and entertain the president's guests. This job includes greeting and socializing with visitors—foreign rulers, dignitaries, and Americans from all walks of life. In addition she also supervises the staff who will serve during the visits, approves menus, and oversees details such as seating arrangements, tableware, and entertainment.

As a hostess, probably none have surpassed Dolley Madison. She not only served during her husband's administration but earlier had sometimes worked as hostess for Thomas Jefferson, a widower. She aided later administrations as well. Her reputation for graciousness, warmth, and wit made her as famous as her husband. When the British burned the White House during the War of 1812, Dolley Madison's winsome personality helped both her husband and the people of Washington get through those difficult years.

Beyond the traditional role as hostess, the duties of the president's wife have increased through the years. She accompanies the president on many trips at home and abroad where she must act as a representative for her husband or the nation, and most modern First Ladies also make some of these trips on their own. She usually lends her support to certain charities or political causes, and she often undertakes special projects for the White House or other public concerns. In addition to these taxing responsibilities, a First Lady must answer the tons of mail she receives from the public and, of course, offer the continual support that her husband needs during his presidency. This position of personal confidante has allowed many First Ladies to exert important influence on their husbands' careers and decisions. Edith Wilson, for example, carried on the routine administrative chores at the White House while her husband was recovering from a stroke. Although the president's enemies referred to her as "Mrs. President," her skill in helping her husband was such that the nation was not aware of the severity of Woodrow Wilson's condition. Harry Truman depended on his wife, Bess, for her political insight and her advice, and with a good-natured humor often referred to Bess as "Boss."

With the tremendous responsibilities and the scrutinizing spotlight placed on the president's wife today, it is little wonder that First Lady Betty Ford observed that the task is "much more of a 24-hour job than anyone would guess."

Dolley Madison

Dolley Madison enlivened the capital with her flair for entertaining, and she remained a prominent social influence until her death in 1849. In an attempt to promote bipartisan cooperation, during her time in the White House she invited members of both political parties to the same social functions (rather than holding separate ones for each political party).

One of the events for which she is best remembered occurred during the War of 1812. In August 1814, as the British army was attacking Washington, DC, she refused to leave the White House until servants rescued the Gilbert Stuart portrait of George Washington that was located in the state dining room.

"First Lady"

It is unclear when this term was first used to refer to the wife of the president. Though it may have been used earlier, the title gained nationwide recognition in 1877 when Mary C. Ames, a newspaper writer, used it to refer to President Rutherford B. Hayes's wife. She called Lucy Hayes "the First Lady of the Land." A 1911 comedy about Dolley Madison, titled *The First Lady in the Land*, popularized the title further. By the 1930s, it was widely used.

"I Am Still Determined . . ."

With a focus on her husband's comfort and happiness, Martha Washington followed her husband to Revolutionary War battlegrounds and eventually to the presidency. In a letter to a friend, Mrs. Washington wrote, "I cannot blame him for having acted according to his ideas of duty in obeying the voice of his country." As for herself, "I am still determined to be cheerful and to be happy, in whatever situation I may be; for I have also learnt from experience that the greater part of our happiness or misery depends upon our disposition, and not upon our circumstances."

Foreign Born

Only two first ladies were born outside the United States. The first was John Quincy Adams's wife, Louisa Catherine Adams, and the second was Melania Trump.

Adams was born in London to an English mother and an American father. Her husband's political enemies called her "English" and drew attention to her heritage. Many viewed this in a negative light since her husband's term in office began about ten years after the War of 1812 and many Americans had not forgotten the British attack upon the United States during that conflict.

"A Heart as True as Steel"

When Rutherford B. Hayes began courting his future wife, Lucy Webb, he wrote about her in his diary: "Her low sweet voice is very winning . . . a heart as true as steel. . . . Intellect she has too. . . . By George! I am in love with her!"

"Crete"

James A. Garfield courted Lucretia "Crete" Rudolph for five years. Their courtship officially began when James sent her the first of what would become 1,200 letters the two shared. A few months after his inauguration as president, she fell gravely ill, apparently from malaria and nervous exhaustion. Garfield was profoundly distressed. In a letter to her, he wrote, "When you are sick, I am like the inhabitants of countries visited by earthquakes. They lose all faith in the eternal order of things." Though she recovered, her husband died later that year.

Angelica Van Buren

When Angelica Singleton visited Washington in the 1830s to call on her relative Dolley Madison, Dolley took her to the White House to meet Martin Van Buren and his sons. The eldest son, Abraham, was charmed by the young lady, and they soon married. Thereafter, Angelica served as the White House hostess for her widower father-in-law.

Angelica Van Buren

Mary Lincoln

Mary Lincoln

Undeniably temperamental, excitable, and extravagant, Mary Lincoln received excessive criticism and little sympathy during her husband's war-torn administration.

Frances Cleveland

At twenty-one, Frances Cleveland was the youngest First Lady and the only one married in the White House. Though her husband was twenty-eight years older, they were happy together, and Frances found popularity as a young wife and mother. Two of their five children were born while Cleveland was president, one actually at the White House.

Frances Cleveland

Grace Coolidge

As both a teacher and trustee for the Clarke School for the Deaf, Grace Coolidge was a lifelong supporter of deaf education. Mrs. Coolidge posed for her official portrait with her collie, Rob Roy, one of the Coolidges' favorite pets.

Grace Coolidge

Eleanor Roosevelt

Mrs. Roosevelt served as eyes, ears, and legs for her handicapped

Eleanor Roosevelt

Activity 3: Comparing First Ladies

Use this activity to help the students think about the background of some First Ladies and their contributions while holding that position.

husband. She traveled, spoke, and wrote on behalf of her own public concerns as well as for the president. She became a notable influence in American politics.

Bess Truman

The 150-year-old White House was renovated during the Truman administration, and Bess Truman spent part of her years as First Lady living across the street in Blair House.

Bess Truman

Jacqueline Kennedy

Jacqueline Kennedy

The care of two small children and an extensive project of restoring the historic furnishings of the White House occupied much of Jackie Kennedy's time as First Lady. In 1961, she established the White House Historical Association. Its mission is to protect and preserve the history of the president's residence.

Nancy Reagan

Nancy Davis left a successful acting career of her own to marry the then-actor Ronald Reagan. She adapted to political life as he became governor of California and later president. As First Lady she lent her support to several public service programs, including an anti-drug campaign.

Nancy Reagan

Barbara Bush

As First Lady, Mrs. Bush continued to support causes that she had promoted during her many years in public life: literacy, cancer research, and helping the homeless. She did more than simply speak out on these issues; she also set an example by volunteering with homeless children and assisting in a Washington soup kitchen.

Barbara Bush

Hillary Rodham Clinton

Mrs. Clinton, a former attorney, took a very active political role in her husband's administration. She headed a task force on health care reform, but the plan it endorsed failed to receive congressional approval.

Hillary Rodham Clinton

Treasure

William Howard Taft called his wife Helen a "treasure." Taft said she was "self-contained, independent, and of unusual application." When Taft was president, it was Helen who requested that Japanese cherry trees be planted around the Tidal Basin.

A Symbol

Lou Hoover was First Lady when the Great Depression began. Using personal funds, she paid for the reproduction of furniture owned by Monroe for a period sitting room in the White House and for the restoration of Lincoln's study (for her husband's use).

The Hoovers entertained elegantly but used their own private funds for such social events while the country suffered worsening economic depression. Herbert Hoover only learned the full extent of his wife's many charitable gifts after her death in 1944. She had helped the education, he stated, "of a multitude of boys and girls." He said she was ideal for the position she had held: "a symbol of everything wholesome in American life."

Hillary Rodham Clinton

Hillary Rodham attended Wellesley College where she became a prominent student leader. Her peers selected her to become the first-ever student speaker at the school's commencement ceremony. After college, she enrolled in Yale Law School, where she was one of just twenty-seven women in her graduating class of more than two hundred students. While there, Hillary began dating one of her classmates, Bill Clinton. They were married in 1975, and their only child, a daughter named Chelsea, was born in 1980.

First Ladies

Instruct the students to write a report about one of the First Ladies. Direct the students to focus on the time in which she occupied the White House. For what is she most remembered from that period? Is she known for a particular initiative or for supporting a specific cause? Choose students to present a summary of their reports to the class.

Teacher and Librarian

After graduating from college in 1968, Laura Welch began teaching second grade in Dallas, Texas. She later taught elementary school in Houston before becoming a librarian. She married George W. Bush in 1977 and gave birth to twin daughters, Barbara and Jenna, in 1981. She is the only First Lady to have given birth to twins. With her background as an educator, after becoming First Lady she championed the cause of accessible, quality education.

Michelle Robinson Obama

Michelle Robinson graduated from Princeton University in 1985 and from Harvard University Law School in 1988. While working at a prestigious Chicago law firm, she was assigned to mentor her future husband when he worked there as a summer associate. They were married in 1992. Malia, their first daughter, was born in 1998, and a second daughter, Sasha, was born in 2001. Though she was a native of Chicago, the Obamas remained in Washington, DC, after her husband's second presidential term ended in 2017 while their younger daughter was completing high school. The Obamas retained their Chicago home and, in 2019, also purchased an estate in Massachusetts on the island of Martha's Vineyard.

Melania Trump

Melania Trump was born in Slovenia in April 1970 (part of Yugoslavia at the time). She moved to New York in 1996 and became a naturalized US citizen a decade later. She married Donald Trump in 2005. She is the only non-native English speaking First Lady. Mrs. Trump speaks several languages, including French, German, and Italian.

At the conclusion of her husband's second term, she became the first First Lady to be elected to the United States Senate. From January 2001 until January 2009, she represented New York in that body. For the next four years she served as President Obama's secretary of state. She ran as the 2016 Democratic presidential candidate.

Laura Bush

A former teacher and librarian, Laura Bush initially drew attention to education and her national initiative called Ready to Read, Ready to Learn. After the September 11 attacks on the United States, Mrs. Bush channeled her energy toward helping the nation, especially children, through the difficult recovery process. Mrs. Bush became the first First Lady to record a full presidential radio address.

Laura Bush

Michelle Obama

Mrs. Obama, a Harvard Law School graduate, worked in the Chicago law firm in which her future husband then joined as an intern. She was associate dean of student services at the University of Chicago and served on the boards of several organizations.

As First Lady, she installed beehives and planted a family garden at the White House. She volunteered at homeless shelters and soup kitchens. She was an advocate for health, wellness, and nutrition causes.

Michelle Obama

Melania Trump

Mrs. Trump, a former model, is the wife of the 45th president of the United States. Born in Slovenia, she later moved to the United States. She is only the second First Lady born outside America (Louisa Adams, daughter of an American merchant and later the wife of John Quincy Adams, was born in England). She speaks several languages.

Mrs. Trump has used her position to embrace a number of causes. She has raised awareness of opioid abuse and has addressed numerous issues related to improving the social, emotional, and physical well-being of children.

Melania Trump

II. Executive Organization

The vice president is part of the executive branch. The first person to hold that office, John Adams, commented, "I am Vice President. In this I am nothing, but I may be everything." Indeed, the most important part of the vice president's responsibilities is to be ready to assume the presidency if something happens to the nation's leader.

The president's immense task of governing is administered through three major levels of the executive bureaucracy: the Executive Office of the President, the cabinet departments, and additional administrative agencies. The civilian employees of the vast executive bureaucracy number about two million. Although large and complex, it has become indispensable to modern American government.

Vice President
Constitutional Direction

The Constitution lists two vice-presidential responsibilities. According to Article I, Section 3, clause 4, "the vice president of the United States shall be president of the Senate, but shall have no vote, unless they be equally divided." Thus, the vice president votes only to break a tie. The second vice-presidential duty given is considered the office's main purpose for existence. Article II, Section 1, clause 6, states the following:

> In case of the removal of the president from office, or of his death, resignation, or inability to discharge the powers and duties of the said office, the same shall devolve on the vice president, and the Congress may by law provide for the case of removal, death, resignation or inability, both of the president and vice president, declaring what officer shall then act as president, and such officer shall act accordingly, until the disability be removed, or a president shall be elected.

Thus the president's powers and duties "devolve," or pass to, the vice president if the president is unable to fulfill his duties. Many men have found the second spot a dull, dead-end job. Having political ambitions while being overshadowed by a powerful chief executive can be a frustrating experience. Eight vice presidents have become president because of the death of the chief executive. One became the nation's leader when a president resigned. Five additional vice presidents were elected to the presidency.

Expanding Role

As noted in Chapter 10, the vice-presidential candidate is often chosen during the presidential campaign for the political "balance" that he can bring to the ticket. In the past, this was often the most important contribution that the vice president made to his chief's administration. In recent years, however, the vice president has assumed greater responsibility and more visible leadership roles, such as serving on the National Security Council, leading presidential commissions, and representing the president at official state ceremonies (such as the funerals for heads of state). He also makes speeches in support of the president's policies and helps members of the president's party get elected to office.

> *"The opportunities afforded by the vice-presidency, particularly the presidency of the Senate, do not come—they are there to be seized. . . . The Vice President's influence on legislation depends on his personality and his ability, and especially the respect which he commands from the senators. Here is one instance in which it is the man who makes the office, not the office the man."*
>
> —Harry Truman

Section II Objectives

1. Outline the responsibilities of the vice president.
2. Explain the origin and role of the Executive Office of the President (EOP).
3. Describe the cabinet departments and other administrative agencies.

Vice-Presidential Song

"Hail, Columbia" is the official vice-presidential anthem. It is used as the ceremonial entrance march for the nation's second-highest official. "Hail to the Chief" is the anthem for the president.

Vice-Presidential Salary

In 1789, the salary for the first vice president was set at $5,000. By 2001, it was $171,500. It was later increased to $230,700 and was raised in 2019 to $235,100.

Vice-Presidential Watch

Invite a student or group of students to collect recent news information concerning the current vice president. Discuss the types of activities, events, or issues on which the news focuses. Discuss a recent speech delivered by the vice president. Also note how often the vice president has been present in the Senate. Has he had to break any ties? If so, with what did that legislation deal?

More on the Vice-Presidency

An excellent source for more information about changing attitudes toward the vice-presidency is "We're Number 2!" by Tony Horwitz in *Smithsonian* (July–August 2012).

A Regular Attendee

Vice President Calvin Coolidge was the first vice president to become a regular attendee of cabinet meetings.

Vice-Presidential Residence

Before 1974, vice presidents and their families lived in their own homes. However, the cost to secure their private homes greatly increased over the years. Congress, after years of debate, agreed to renovate the house at the Naval Observatory as the vice-presidential home. Vice President Walter Mondale, who held the office from 1977 to 1981, was the first vice president to move into the residence.

Twenty-Fifth Amendment

As noted earlier, the most important role of the vice president is to succeed the president upon his death or disability. This constitutional function was first tested in 1841, when William Henry Harrison caught a cold while delivering his nearly two-hour-long inaugural speech in a cold drizzle. He died of pneumonia a month later. Vice President John Tyler then succeeded Harrison, leaving a vacancy in the vice-presidency; the Constitution had no provision for dealing with this issue. For a combined total of more than thirty-seven years in our nation's history, presidents have served without vice presidents. Before 1967 the Constitution did not provide a way to choose a vice president if the vice-presidency became vacant. President Lyndon Johnson was the last president to lack a vice president for a substantial part of his presidency (from November 1963 to January 1965).

This situation was remedied in 1967 with the **Twenty-Fifth Amendment**, whereby any vice-presidential vacancy is to be filled through a nomination by the president and confirmation by a majority vote in both houses of Congress. As noted in Chapter 9, the passage of this amendment was timely, considering that the provision was used in 1973 after the resignation of Vice President Spiro Agnew when President Nixon appointed Gerald Ford to fill the vacancy. The following year Ford succeeded to the presidency upon Nixon's resignation. Ford

Role of the Vice President

The office of vice president has historically had little respect, and it has been the brunt of countless jokes, even among vice presidents. John Adams referred to it as "the most insignificant office that ever the invention of man contrived." John Nance Garner referred to himself as FDR's "spare tire." Woodrow Wilson's vice president, Thomas Marshall, joked that there were two brothers, and one ran away to sea, while the other one became vice president—and nothing was ever heard of either of them again. Teddy Roosevelt said that the vice-presidency "is not a steppingstone to anything except oblivion," but in his case and for a few others, it was a steppingstone into the presidency.

Thanks to Harry Truman the vice-presidency took on much greater responsibilities and even a little respect. Truman, whom FDR did not prepare for taking over the presidency, determined that his vice president would be prepared; he made Vice President Alben Barkley part of the National Security Council and regular cabinet meetings. Since that time, vice presidents have generally played fairly significant roles in the various administrations.

Perhaps the most influential vice president in recent history was Dick Cheney, George W. Bush's vice president. Barack Obama also enjoyed a good relationship with his vice president, Joe Biden, and often sought his input regarding important issues.

Joe Biden (right) was vice president from 2009 to 2017. Mike Pence (left) became vice president in 2017.

Tie-Breaking Senate Votes

Who Cast the Most?

John C. Calhoun	31
John Adams	29
George Dallas	19
Schuyler Colfax	18
George Clinton	14
Richard Johnson	14

Who Cast None?

John Tyler
William King
Andrew Johnson
Thomas Hendricks
Theodore Roosevelt
Charles Fairbanks
Calvin Coolidge
Lyndon Johnson
Gerald Ford
Nelson Rockefeller
Dan Quayle
Joe Biden

Activity 4: John Nance Garner on the Vice Presidency

Use this activity to show the students one vice president's perspective on the vice-presidency and to develop the students' comprehension and analytical skills as they use resources.

then nominated Nelson Rockefeller, and Congress confirmed him, creating an unprecedented situation in which both the presidency and the vice-presidency were filled by men who were not elected by the voters.

The Constitution stated that when there was a vacancy in the office of president, the powers and duties of that office would be assumed by the vice president. As mentioned in Chapter 5, when William Henry Harrison died in 1841, some argued that John Tyler should merely be viewed as an acting president. Tyler did not accept that interpretation and insisted on being called president. All other vice presidents who assumed the office upon a president's death followed Tyler's example. The Twenty-Fifth Amendment clarified the accepted practice by stating clearly that when the presidency was vacant, the vice president would be president.

Presidential Disability

If a president knows that he will be incapacitated for a brief period of time, he may decide to transfer his duties to the vice president for that time period. The president does this by giving a written declaration to the president pro tempore of the Senate and to the Speaker of the House of Representatives.

In 1985 when President Reagan had surgery, Vice President George H. W. Bush became acting president for a few hours. In 2002, with the nation at war with terrorists, President George W. Bush was sedated while undergoing a medical procedure. Vice President Dick Cheney served as president for more than two hours. In 2007, Cheney was again president for about two hours when Bush underwent another medical procedure.

The Executive Office of the President

As America grew, so did its problems and the demands on the president. Franklin Roosevelt decided to confront the complexities of these national demands that were gradually paralyzing presidential power by their sheer weight. In 1936 he appointed a committee to study the problem. That committee's report opened with a sentence that stated the problem in capsule form: "The President needs help." The eventual result of this report was the 1939 formation of the Executive Office of the President (EOP). The EOP consists of White House offices and agencies that help develop and implement the president's programs and policies.

The EOP probably exerts more influence on the president's policies and legislative program than any other segment of the executive branch. Top aides serving in the **White House Office** (part of the EOP) include the president's press secretary; counsel, or legal advisor; and physician. The First Lady's chief of staff and press secretary are also assistants to the president. Approximately four hundred members comprise the White House Office. The president's top aides often have daily access to him and even travel with him on weekends and vacations. It is not unusual for presidents to place longtime friends in positions as aides and confidants. President Carter gave Hamilton Jordan and Jody Powell, friends from his early days in Georgia politics, top

John Tyler

Line of Presidential Succession

The line of presidential succession is as follows, from the vice president to the latest cabinet office. During the State of the Union address, one person in the line of succession is absent from the speech in case of an attack on the Capitol Building. This practice of appointing a "designated survivor" has been especially important since the 9/11 terrorist attacks.

Vice President

Speaker of the House

President Pro Tempore of the Senate

Secretary of State

Secretary of the Treasury

Secretary of Defense

Attorney General

Secretary of the Interior

Secretary of Agriculture

Secretary of Commerce

Secretary of Labor

Secretary of Health and Human Services

Secretary of Housing and Urban Development

Secretary of Transportation

Secretary of Energy

Secretary of Education

Secretary of Veterans Affairs

Secretary of Homeland Security

The EOP

Franklin Roosevelt's decision to form the Executive Office of the President (EOP) is a major example of the power of precedent and the lasting impact of seemingly insignificant decisions. The EOP has become an indispensable part of the executive branch.

advisory posts. A similar relationship existed between President Reagan and his longtime California supporters Edwin Meese and Caspar Weinberger.

A variety of agencies within the Executive Office serve the president in management, intelligence, and economics. Primary among these are the **National Security Council (NSC)** and the **Office of Management and Budget (OMB)**. With its close ties to the Central Intelligence Agency (CIA) and the Defense and State Departments, the NSC plays an important role in intelligence gathering, policy formulation, and crisis management. The OMB prepares the nation's annual budget for Congress and coordinates policy among departments. The OMB director exercises such control over the budget and how it reflects the president's policies that his selection by the president is subject to Senate approval. Chapter 12 gives greater insight into the EOP and its agencies.

The Cabinet

The **cabinet** offices of the executive branch were developed to assist the president in his constitutional duties and to meet the demands of America's growth. The term *cabinet* comes from the French word for a closed or private room where a king would meet with his advisors.

George Washington with his cabinet (above) and George H. W. Bush with his cabinet (below)

In Britain, where cabinet government first developed, cabinet members are generally drawn from the majority party in Parliament and serve both an executive and a legislative function. In the United States, by contrast, cabinet members, usually called secretaries, are not members of Congress. **Cabinet secretaries** are individuals responsible to the president for the departments that they head.

The Constitution makes no mention of a cabinet; however it does state, in Article II, Section 2, that the president "may require the opinion, in writing, of the principal officer in each of the executive departments." In 1789 President Washington's cabinet consisted of four departments. Over the years, new departments were added and some were consolidated. Today there are fifteen cabinet offices: State, Treasury, Defense, Justice, Interior, Agriculture, Commerce, Labor, Health and Human Services, Housing and Urban Development, Transportation, Energy, Education, Veterans Affairs, and Homeland Security. Each of the fifteen cabinet departments has substantial office space in various buildings in the capital city.

Additional participants at cabinet meetings include cabinet-rank officials, though they are not actually cabinet members. These typically include the president's chief of staff, the administrator of the Environmental Protection Agency (EPA), the US trade representative, the director of the Office of Management and Budget, the ambassador to the United Nations, and the director of national intelligence (DNI). The vice president also attends these meetings. Chapter 12 discusses the president's cabinet in greater depth.

Administrative Agencies

Beneath the cabinet departments are a variety of administrative agencies. This executive level consists of more than fifty agencies and service commissions that manage a wide array of concerns, ranging from environmental protection to postal service to space exploration. The directors of these administrative agencies are nominated by the president and confirmed by the Senate. (We examine the operation and importance of these bureaucratic agencies more closely in the next chapter.)

True Greatness

What character qualities should great leaders demonstrate? Lead a class discussion regarding this question and make a list of those items mentioned by students. Contrast the world's view of greatness with the biblical view by reminding students that the Scriptures mention many important aspects of good leadership. Among them, leaders should be prudent (Proverbs 8:12–16), bold (Eph. 6:20), humble (Daniel 4:17), and respectful (Titus 3:1–3).

Next, instruct the students to refer to the list of ten people they compiled at the beginning of the chapter. Ask students to evaluate those individuals. Were they, or are they, truly great? Assess them using the charac-

ter qualities noted in the Bible. If students have written a report about a lesser-known president (see assignment at the bottom of page 251) or one about a First Lady (see assignment at the bottom of page 265), ask the students to evaluate those individuals. Were they truly great?

Mention the fleeting nature of fame, and note that many heroes never make headlines (for example, missionaries laboring for years in difficult fields who build a lasting work for Christ). Emphasize the importance of choosing proper role models.

Checkup Time

As you discuss the topic of the next section ("Governing Wisely"), refer to some of the lessons learned in the previous note. Also, use this as an opportunity to remind students that all Christians should demonstrate, by their daily lives, obedience to the Scriptures. Even those not in leadership positions benefit by exercising good leadership qualities. Are we prudent? Bold? Humble? Respectful? If not, what steps should we take to change our lives?

1–3. What are the two responsibilities that the Constitution places on the vice president? Identify duties that have been added to those responsibilities over the years.

4–5. What is the EOP? What is its function?

6–7. What are the two primary agencies of the EOP?

★ Do you think the Twenty-Fifth Amendment was needed? Why or why not?

★ How do cabinet offices assist the president in the performance of his duties?

III. Governing Wisely

Avoiding Pitfalls

Because of his exceptional authority and responsibility, a president might be tempted to use his extraordinary powers illegally and immorally. The attention he attracts by occupying this powerful human office might be enough to divert him from the just use of his authority. Presidents ensnared by arrogance have damaged their country, their reputations, and their political influence—as Richard Nixon and Bill Clinton demonstrated.

Christians should obey the command of 1 Timothy 2:1–2 to pray and give thanks for all who are in authority so that they might have quiet and peaceable lives. They should also submit to the authority of the president as long as that submission does not violate Scripture. Any president who wants to rule well must, like King Solomon, acknowledge his need of a wisdom beyond himself, a wisdom that can come only from God.

Assessing Presidents

All presidents are discussed extensively in history books and other writings. However, it is difficult to determine which were great and which were not. Former presidents have moved up and down in the lists of comparative greatness depending on who was passing judgment and when the presidents were being judged. Still, we can be certain that Pierce, Buchanan, and Harding will never surpass Washington, Lincoln, and Jefferson on any rational scale of greatness.

Great presidents have been clear about their goals and have retained a self-confidence about their objectives that was unshaken by popular opinion. More importantly, great presidents have successfully met the challenge of national crises (e.g., the establishment of the new constitutional system under Washington and the maintenance of the Union under Lincoln). Refusing to face a crisis is almost

> **Guiding Questions**
>
> 1. What are common pitfalls of the presidency?
> 2. What factors influence assessments of presidents?

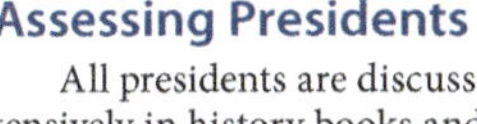

Presidents (left to right) George H. W. Bush, Barack Obama, George W. Bush, Bill Clinton, and Jimmy Carter in 2009

---

1. Identify pitfalls of the presidency.
2. Appraise the factors that influence assessment of presidents.

Presidential Retirement

Many presidents are relieved to retire from the presidency and its constant demands. Upon his inauguration, John Adams wrote to his wife, Abigail, and gave her the following account concerning George Washington:

> A solemn scene it was indeed and it was made more affecting to me, by the presence of the General, whose countenance was as serene and unclouded as the day. . . . Methought I heard him think, "Ay! I am fairly out and you fairly in! See which of us will be happiest."

Similarly, James Buchanan told Lincoln on Inauguration Day 1861, "If you are as happy, my dear sir, on entering this house as I am in leaving it and returning home, you are the happiest man in this country!"

However, not all presidents have retired from politics. John Quincy Adams left the presidency in 1829 and was then elected to the House of Representatives in 1830. He was elected to nine terms in that chamber and served as a voice of the rising abolitionist movement until his death in 1848. Andrew Johnson was elected to the US Senate in 1875, six years after leaving the White House; however, he died before he was able to take office.

Section Review Answers

1–3. He is to succeed the president if the president dies, resigns, or becomes incapacitated. He presides over the Senate, where he can vote only to break a tie. Added extraconstitutional responsibilities include representing the president at various state functions, such as funerals for heads of state; making speeches in support of administration-favored policies; and helping members of the president's party get elected to office. He also serves on the National Security Council and leads presidential commissions. (p. 267)

4–5. The Executive Office of the President consists of White House offices and agencies that help develop and implement presidential programs and policies. (pp. 269–70)

6–7. Its two primary agencies are the National Security Council (NSC) and the Office of Management and Budget (OMB). (p. 270)

★ Some will say the amendment was needed to provide a process for a new vice president when that position was vacated. Others may say that it is fine to have a vacant position rather than to fill it with someone who was not elected.

★ The cabinet members advise the president and head the various departments of the executive branch.

Activity 5: Comparing Presidents

Use this activity to help the students consider the background of some presidents and some of the challenges they faced while in office.

Presidential Success

Ask the students how they would decide whether a president was successful. Use the comments to underscore the broad expectations Americans have for their presidents.

Ranking the Presidents

Arthur M. Schlesinger Jr., a sometimes-controversial historian, polled fifty-five historians in 1948, seventy-five in 1962, and thirty-two in 1996. In all three surveys, Lincoln was given first place, Washington was second, and FDR was third. In the first two surveys, Wilson was ranked fourth and Jefferson was fifth; however, in the last survey, fourth place went to Thomas Jefferson and fifth place to Andrew Jackson.

The Difference between Effectiveness and Greatness

Historian George Bancroft writes that President James K. Polk set and achieved four goals for his administration. Another historian, Daniel Walker Howe, concluded that Polk was the most successful president because he accomplished those goals within a single term.

However, Pastor James W. Alexander, who lived during Polk's presidency, examined Polk's achievements in light of Polk's role in the Mexican War. Calling the war a "war of pretexts," Alexander saw Polk's term of office as a dark period in American history.

Some critics of Polk would argue that he was not great, though he may have been effective, because they believe his policies violated the teaching of God's Word.

Humility and Greatness

We tend to think that kingdoms are won by fighting; however, Jesus said the poor in spirit, those who are humble because they recognize there is no goodness in themselves, inherit the kingdom (Matt. 5:3). Jesus also said that the meek will inherit the earth (Matt. 5:5). The story of Saul's demise and the rise of David (1 and 2 Samuel) clearly shows that God favors the humble and rejects the proud.

Ranking the Presidents

Determining the best and the worst of the US presidents is no easy task. Opinions vary widely, even among scholars.

A typical list of the best presidents usually includes the following (though the order is debated):

Abraham Lincoln
George Washington
Franklin Roosevelt
Thomas Jefferson
Theodore Roosevelt
Harry Truman
Woodrow Wilson
Dwight Eisenhower
Ronald Reagan

A typical list of the worst presidents is shown below (though again the order is a matter of dispute):

Warren G. Harding
James Buchanan
Andrew Johnson
Franklin Pierce
John Tyler

Many writers argue that Richard Nixon and Ulysses S. Grant should also be included on the list of the worst presidents. Others disagree with that assessment.

---

a sure ticket to the bottom rungs of presidential greatness. Likewise, choosing especially incompetent or corrupt advisors—as Grant, Harding, and Nixon did—often results in lower rankings. On the other hand, some presidents whose terms were blessed with relative peace and prosperity might have been judged more highly had they been tested in the crucible of a national emergency.

Another factor in determining the rankings is the political philosophy of those doing the ranking. Those who have a broad constructionist view of the Constitution tend to give higher rankings to presidents who increased the power, size, and functions of the government. Those who hold a strict constructionist view will rank such presidents lower.

Although even great presidents have had significant moral flaws, most presidents have had a strong desire to serve their country and its people. As noted author Russell Kirk wrote, "Nearly all presidents of the United States, whatever their antecedents, have been gentlemen."

Christ defined the quality for a true greatness unaltered by time, circumstances, or polls: service. He explained to His disciples that if anyone wants to be great, he should minister, or serve (Matt. 20:26–27). Often, the world's definition of greatness is not greatness at all; it is mere popularity. There is an important difference between popularity and greatness. Popularity means having the favor of many people, but this favor does not survive well over time. In contrast, greatness transcends the glitter and noise of popular acclaim and focuses on immortal things. Greatness comes through giving, serving, and following Christ's example.

Section Review

1. Describe pitfalls each president faces.

2–3. What is the difference between popularity and greatness?

☆ Who do you think are the five greatest presidents? Explain your choices.

☆ Who do you think was the worst president? Why?

Presidential Ranking

Poll the students on how they would rank the most recent half-dozen presidents, and present your findings to the class. Ask the students to defend their rankings.

Why Are There Differences?

Conduct a class discussion comparing the various surveys of presidential greatness. Focus on the top five or ten presidents. Why are there differences between the surveys? Discuss how political preferences and worldviews may influence the results.

Activity 6: Chapter Review

Use this chapter review to help the students prepare for the chapter test and to reinforce the students' knowledge of chapter concepts.

Section Review Answers

1. the tendency to use powers illegally and immorally or to allow attention he receives to divert him from using his authority justly (p. 271)

2–3. Popularity means having many people's favor, and it does not usually last very long. In contrast, greatness transcends popular acclaim and focuses on immortal things. True greatness comes through giving, serving, and following Christ's example. (pp. 271–72)

☆ Answers will vary.

☆ Answers will vary.

CHAPTER REVIEW

Making Connections

1. What important national principle is underscored by the president serving as commander in chief?

2. Explain the powers the president exercises as the nation's diplomatic leader.

3–6. List four tasks the president performs in the role as chief of state.

7. Why did the Founding Fathers not envision the president as leader of his political party?

8. Describe the appointment powers of the president.

9–14. List six officials that normally meet with the cabinet though they are not official members of that body.

Developing Civics Skills

1. Assess the use of executive orders by presidents. Has this power been used appropriately? What are advantages and disadvantages of their use?

2. Within the context of a recent presidential campaign or policy debate, find an argument that concerns a moral issue, such as abortion, marriage, or religious liberty. Expose the root assumptions of the argument, and evaluate them.

Thinking Critically

1. Do modern presidents tend to spend too much of their first term campaigning for a second term? Why or why not? What do you think would be best for the country?

2. Evaluate the wisdom of allowing the president to serve as a party leader.

Living as a Christian Citizen

1. In your opinion, which president is a good example of leading as a servant? Support your answer.

2. Imagine that you have been elected president. Devise a document that states your top five legislative priorities. Explain why you chose these priorities and why you prioritized them as you did. Take the present political situation into account.

Developing Civics Skills

1. Some argue that the president's ordinance power has allowed him greater opportunity to intervene in national and world affairs. However, critics contend that such authority has been abused by many presidents and used as a means of implementing controversial policies that might not pass as congressional legislation. Executive orders may be changed by the next president.

2. A student evaluating a pro-abortion position could highlight the assumption that a fetus is not a human or that it lacks human rights until birth. A student evaluating arguments about homosexuals' rights could highlight the assumption that homosexual desires ought to be embraced and acted upon (rather than resisted along with other kinds of sinful desires). A student evaluating opposition to religious liberty could highlight the assumption that religion is just a way of disguising bigotry rather than the core of a person's identity.

Thinking Critically

1. Those who say yes might point to possible motivations such as the desire to stay in power or to continue carrying out an agenda. Some will say that this practice is good for the country, while others will insist that it is selfish and harmful for the country.

2. Some might note that the president's status allows him to move party agenda forward. Since a president is elected on a party platform, his supporters expect him to advance party policies. Others will argue that making the president a party leader may increase resistance from the opposing party for otherwise noncontroversial legislation. It may therefore result in polarization that is not in the country's best interest.

Living as a Christian Citizen

1. Students should demonstrate that their chosen presidents acted with the desire not to make a mark on history but to serve the nation.

2. Students should demonstrate an awareness of policy issues with which a president should be concerned and provide a realistic assessment of what may be possible to achieve.

CHAPTER REVIEW ANSWERS

Making Connections

1. that civilian power controls military power (p. 249)

2. The president can make treaties and appoint ambassadors, other public ministers, and consuls. He has access to important information and management resources—the State Department, the National Security Council (NSC), and the CIA. Using the power of executive agreement, he can have a written "understanding" with another head of state to take a particular action. (p. 252)

3–6. laying the wreath at the Tomb of the Unknown Soldier, lighting the White House Christmas tree, attending a world leader's funeral, or throwing the first pitch of baseball season (p. 255)

7. political parties did not exist (p. 257)

8. The president may appoint cabinet members and their top aides, ambassadors and other diplomats, heads of independent agencies, all federal judges, US marshals and attorneys, and commissioned officers of the armed forces. (pp. 261–62)

9–14. the president's chief of staff, the administrator of the Environmental Protection Agency (EPA), the US trade representative, the director of the Office of Management and Budget, the ambassador to the United Nations, and the director of national intelligence (DNI) (p. 270)

Chapter Goals

1. Evaluate the development of the US bureaucracy.
2. Analyze the bureaucratic structure of the executive branch.
3. Evaluate the practices of the federal bureaucracy.

THE FEDERAL BUREAUCRACY

12

The true test of a good government is its aptitude and tendency to produce a good administration.

—*Alexander Hamilton*

The Douglas Dam in east Tennessee, one of the dozens of dams operated by the Tennessee Valley Authority (TVA), a US government corporation

I. **Bureaucratic Development**

II. **Bureaucratic Structure**

III. **Bureaucratic Practices**

BIG IDEAS

1. How did the US bureaucracy develop?
2. How does the bureaucratic structure of the executive branch work?
3. Are the practices of the federal bureaucracy effective?

SUGGESTED MATERIALS

Section I
- Activity 1 from Chapter 12 of the *Student Activities*
- Video about the New Deal

Section II
- Copies of a transcript of a White House gaggle or briefing
- Video about the White House
- Video about the cabinet
- Color photograph of the Great Seal
- Video about the Bureau of Engraving and Printing
- Video about the Pentagon
- Activities 2–3 from Chapter 12 of the *Student Activities*

Section III
- Activities 4–5 from Chapter 12 of the *Student Activities*

Teacher Resources
Visit TeacherToolsOnline.com for resources to enhance the lessons.

In almost every US election, office seekers make promises about harnessing our government's bureaucracy, a giant organization of officials and civil servants. These political hopefuls usually receive a hearty round of applause from their constituents when they campaign to halt the growth of the bureaucracy and even reduce its size.

The bureaucracy is an easy target. In the minds of many, the term conjures images of waste, inefficiency, red tape, and mountains of paperwork. Though that description is sometimes accurate, it overlooks the positive aspects of an essential part of our government. Effective governing requires efficiency, structure, rules, and procedures. Bureaucracy should serve as the vehicle for providing those ingredients necessary for properly managing government. Sometimes it functions well, while other times it falls far short of its goals.

I. Bureaucratic Development

Overview

Bureaucracy Defined

The term *bureaucracy* refers to an administrative system in which agencies staffed largely by nonelected officials perform specific tasks in accordance with standard procedures. Much of the federal bureaucracy's work involves the implementation and administration of laws or programs. For this reason, most of the federal bureaucracy is within the executive branch. The executive branch contains many **bureaucrats** (civil servants dedicated to the details of administrative procedure). The popular image of a bureaucrat is a white-collar individual laboring through stacks of paperwork. But employees in the federal bureaucracy actually perform a variety of tasks. Besides fulfilling administrative and clerical duties, members of the bureaucracy might deliver mail, work as computer technicians or plumbers, or serve as nurses.

When defining *bureaucracy*, one must remember the principle of **delegation**: committing, or entrusting, a task or power to another. Modern society involves a complex interaction of social, economic, and technological forces combined with an attitude that often favors government intervention in a broad range of issues. Responding to people's problems and managing government resources is a tremendous responsibility—a responsibility much too great for the president and his advisors alone.

The need for a bureaucracy becomes clear when one looks at the biblical purposes of government. One such purpose is to defend the nation. Though the president is the commander in chief, he cannot defend the nation alone. He needs a military and he needs people to manage, equip, and train it. Another purpose of the government is to ensure justice. Again, the president cannot personally enforce justice throughout the nation—a department of justice is needed. There is a hint of the need for a bureaucracy in Exodus 18. In that passage Moses is advised to delegate some of his responsibility for ensuring justice for Israel to other men because the task is too great for him to handle alone.

The Internal Revenue Service (IRS) is the government agency responsible for collecting federal income taxes. Above, the most commonly used tax form.

Federal Hall

New York City provided the facilities for the Congress that operated under the Articles of Confederation from 1785 to 1789. When the new federal government began in 1789, New York City was the nation's temporary capital. Local businesses hoped to convince the new Congress to make New York City the permanent seat of government, but Congress moved to Philadelphia for a decade (1790–1800). In late 1800, Congress moved again; this time to Washington, DC.

After Congress left New York City, Federal Hall served as the local city hall until it was demolished in 1812. In 1842, another Federal Hall was built on the original site, and the building is now designated as a national memorial. On September 2, 2002, more than three hundred members of Congress convened a special ceremonial session at Federal Hall to honor the victims and heroes of the September 11, 2001, terrorist attacks. It had been 212 years since Congress had met in New York City.

Congressional Attempt to Control Cabinet Appointments

Despite Congress's 1789 decision that the president could remove cabinet officials without Congress's approval, Radical Republicans tried to wrest that privilege from President Andrew Johnson in 1867 by passing the Tenure of Office bill. When Johnson vetoed the bill, Congress overrode the veto and then impeached Johnson when he fired Secretary of War Edwin Stanton. The Tenure of Office Act was amended in 1869 and repealed in 1887. In 1926, the US Supreme Court evaluated a similar law in *Myers v. United States*. In that decision, the Court noted that the Tenure of Office Act had been unconstitutional.

Bureaucratic Features

America's bureaucracy has three key features:

1. Hierarchical authority: The organization is constructed like a pyramid, with the chain of command going from top to bottom.
2. Job specialization: A specific division of labor exists within the organization; each worker has specified responsibilities.
3. Formalized rules: Rules enable the bureaucracy to work according to established regulations, methods, and procedures.

Bureaucratic Benefits

America's bureaucratic features produce benefits that allow people to work together on large and complex tasks more efficiently:

1. Hierarchical authority can increase agency speed by limiting conflicts concerning who has the authority to make decisions.
2. Efficiency and productivity are promoted by job specialization because workers can focus on a specific task using their specialized skills and knowledge.
3. Work can continue when workers leave the organization and new workers replace them because decisions are based on defined standards, not on someone's preferences.

Federal Hall in New York City

"[The president] shall nominate, and by and with the advice and consent of the Senate, shall appoint ambassadors, other public ministers and consuls, judges of the Supreme Court, and all other officers of the United States, whose appointments are not herein otherwise provided for, and which shall be established by law: but the Congress may by law vest the appointment of such inferior officers, as they think proper, in the president alone, in the courts of law, or in the heads of departments."

—*Article II, Section 2, Clause 2*

History and Growth
The First Congress

In 1789 the first Congress, meeting at New York City's Federal Hall, considered a bill that would create the State Department. Both houses discussed whether appointed officials could be removed by the president alone. Some wanted officials to be removed only with the Senate's consent. James Madison, speaking for the Washington administration, argued that if the president were restricted in his ability to remove subordinates, he would be unable to control them. Furthermore, he argued that the president would be unable to perform his constitutional obligation to "take care that the laws be faithfully executed." Madison's view won by a narrow margin. The result was that the Department of State and all other created cabinet departments would be administered by people whom the president could remove. Congress kept the right to appropriate money, investigate the administration, and shape the laws that would be implemented by the administration.

Advantages and Disadvantages

Discuss the advantages and disadvantages of bureaucratic organization. Advantages might include a chain of command, development of expertise, and standardized procedures for orderly and impartial decision making. Disadvantages might include a lack of accountability, overlapping authority, and failure to meet certain needs because of a rigid, impersonal approach.

Bureaucratic Benefits

Encourage students to list ways in which the bureaucracy benefits their lives during a single day. Ask students to assess whether the items they have named align with the five biblical obligations of government (ensuring justice, providing for national defense and public safety, addressing poverty, promoting moral behavior, and providing order).

Civil Service

Since the Constitution has little to say concerning civilian employees, Washington and Thomas Jefferson, the first secretary of state, set the early standards for the **civil service** (the civilian employees who perform the administrative tasks of government). Washington recognized that the new government's success would depend on whom he appointed to office. He wanted the most qualified individuals and made selections accordingly. The next president, John Adams, continued Washington's method of choice. The third president, Thomas Jefferson, agreed with Washington's standard of fitness for office but combined it with political acceptability, replacing Federalists with members of his own Democratic-Republican Party.

Spoils System

Upon entering the White House in 1829, Andrew Jackson initiated the spoils system when he gave government posts as a reward for campaign support. He reasoned that since public-office duties were simple, any intelligent person could fill the office. Jackson also thought that many should have the privilege of serving in government and that holding office too long would lead to tyranny and inefficiency. He felt that people were entitled to have the party they placed in power also placed in control of government offices from the top to the bottom. The spoils system grew as many saw it as a method of building and holding on to power.

Civil War Effects

A major turning point in bureaucratic development was the Civil War, which led to the hiring of many new officials. The war illuminated the federal government's administrative weaknesses. Reformers demanded a better civil service, arguing that state governments could not deal with the rapid postwar industrialization and emerging national economy alone.

Post–Civil War

The political motivation behind the job assignments did not always put the most qualified people into office. President Grant acknowledged the inadequacy of the spoils system when he said, "There is no duty which so much embarrasses the Executive and heads of departments as that of appointments. . . . The present system does not secure the best men and often not even fit men for public place." Since the president could hire or fire these employees at will, however, the bureaucracy was highly responsive to the president's wishes.

Job and favor seekers pull at President Grant from all sides.

Spoils versus Merit

Discuss the advantages of the spoils system over the merit system and vice versa. Direct the students to include the following considerations in their discussion.

Offering someone a job in exchange for political support is akin to a bribe. God warns against placing those willing to accept bribes in positions of civil leadership (Exod. 18:21; 23:8; Prov. 17:23; 29:4). God also commends those who are able to act skillfully (Prov. 22:29). These considerations tilt a biblical evaluation toward the merit system and away from the spoils system.

However, another consideration is more ambiguous. A president is usually elected based on a platform of his ideas. As he works to implement his platform, it would be wise to appoint subordinates who will forward his goals rather than oppose them.

Analyzing Political Cartoons

Guide a discussion about the political cartoon on this page. What is the thesis? Is it an accurate portrayal of events? What are some factors to consider when analyzing political cartoons?

As the system increased in size, many positions were filled with ill-equipped people. Inefficiency and corruption occurred, and many people began calling for reform. But not until President James Garfield was shot and killed by a disappointed office seeker did a horrified nation and President Arthur, former vice president under Garfield, demand reform. That reform came sixteen months after Garfield's death through the **Pendleton Act** of 1883 establishing quality, or **merit**, of one's work as the new standard for hiring and promoting civil employees. It also established the Civil Service Commission (the predecessor of the Office of Personnel Management) and abolished the old patronage, or spoils, system.

Between 1861 and 1901, the number of federal employees increased by more than two hundred thousand with the creation of new agencies to handle the growing economy. These agencies were created to serve (research, gather statistics, distribute benefits, etc.), not to regulate. Not until the 1887 establishment of the Interstate Commerce Commission, the first regulatory agency, did the federal government begin to regulate the economy.

Wars and the New Deal

Government regulation of the economy greatly expanded as a result of US involvement in World War I. During wartime, restrictions on administrative actions are set aside to meet the increased needs and demands brought about by war; thus the number of government employees increases. Once wars end, however, many of those new employees remain in their positions, causing a net growth in government.

The origins of much of our current bureaucracy can be traced to the New Deal and World War II. The New Deal established government agencies to help Americans who lost homes, jobs, and savings during the Great Depression. The Federal Emergency Relief Administration (FERA) provided funds directly to the needy. The Civilian Conservation Corps (CCC) and the Tennessee Valley Authority (TVA) and other agencies put millions of people to work on public projects. The Social Security Act established a pension program and a state and federal system to provide unemployment insurance. The New Deal led many Americans, from both political parties, to expect the federal government to solve the country's economic and social problems.

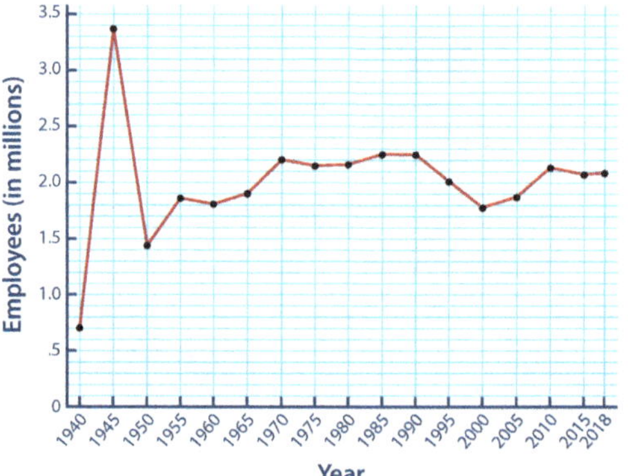

Executive-Branch Civilian Employment
(does not include the US Postal Service)

World War II brought further bureaucratic changes: some government agencies (such as the CCC) shut down, and their employees were transferred to military service or defense jobs. The war also expanded the number of business personnel involved in administering industrial production and other aspects of the economy.

The US Supreme Court began upholding laws that permitted Congress to authorize agencies to make whatever decisions seemed necessary for solving problems or serving the public interest. During World War II, the government began relying heavily on income taxes from individuals and corporations (as well as on deficit spending) to pay for its activities. The government also used the additional funds

Fireside Chats

During the Great Depression and World War II, President Franklin D. Roosevelt shared his plans for the nation through his fireside chats via radio. Ask your students to find and listen to one of the chats or a portion of one. Discuss FDR's ideas and how well he communicated them to the nation. Discuss the fears that arose during the Great Depression and World War II and how FDR comforted the nation through the chats. Also discuss how attempts to solve the nation's problems during this time period led to the expansion of the bureaucracy.

Activity 1: The Case for Bureaucracy

Use this enrichment activity to help the students develop skills in analysis and evaluation.

New Deal

Try to obtain a video relating to the New Deal. If possible, use one that notes how government bureaucracy increased as legislation from that period was implemented.

to increase many programs and support more administrators.

Pay and Benefits

Congress sets the pay and other job conditions for federal workers. Civil service pay at the lower and middle levels compares fairly with salaries in the private sector. However, pay for upper-level positions often cannot compete with private-sector salaries. Holiday, vacation, sick-leave, disability, and life-insurance benefits are frequently better in the private sector. Notwithstanding, civil service employees typically have better benefits in the areas of retirement, health insurance, and retiree health insurance.

Political Activities

Federal employees were first limited in their political activities by the Hatch Act of 1939. The law allowed federal workers to vote in elections, but they could not participate in partisan political activities. Critics of the Hatch Act said that unnecessary, unjustifiable limits had been placed on federal workers' political and civil rights, but the Supreme Court rejected several First Amendment challenges to the law. In 1993 federal employees were given greater political opportunities, and additional changes were made later. Today, federal employees may help register new voters, contribute money to candidates and parties, participate in campaigns and rallies, and hold office in a political party. However, they cannot be a candidate in partisan elections, participate in party work on government property or while on the job, solicit political contributions, or use a government position to influence an election.

Today

Today most of the rank and file of the federal bureaucracy are hired through the merit system, and generally they may hold lifelong tenure if they so choose. They are paid and promoted on the basis of written evaluations by their superiors and are protected from disciplinary actions or dismissal for partisan reasons. However, the president still maintains appointive power over approximately four thousand positions. Many of these are top policymaking posts, such as secretaries (cabinet offices), undersecretaries, directors, and commissioners. Thus, the president has a measure of control over the bureaucratic pyramid, and his appointments act as important tools in seeing that his policies are implemented.

Protesters denouncing any changes to the social security system, which was established as part of the New Deal

Section Review

1. Define *bureaucracy*.
2–4. Identify three benefits of bureaucracy.
5–6. Contrast the spoils system and the merit system.
   ★ How does war expand bureaucracy?
   ★ Do you think the limitations on the political activities of federal employees are justified? Why or why not?

The Hatch Act

The impetus for the Hatch Act was allegations of partisan politicking and vote buying by some New Deal agencies, notably the Works Progress Administration. It appears that jobs and government projects were promised in return for political support, especially at the state and county levels of government. Historian Burton Folsom has criticized FDR by writing, "If we probe deeply into [Franklin] Roosevelt's popularity, we almost always discover the presence of patronage—the creating and the manipulating of federal jobs to strengthen his political support" (*New Deal or Raw Deal?*, 169). Many FDR supporters discount Folsom's assessment.

The outcry against such practices during the New Deal era prompted New Mexico senator Carl Hatch to introduce a bill called "An Act to Prevent Pernicious Political Activities"; it passed in 1939 as the Hatch Act. In 1947 and 1973, the act was challenged in the Supreme Court but was upheld both times.

Congress amended the act in 1993 and 2012. As a result, most federal employees can engage in many, though certainly not all, campaign activities. For example, employees still cannot be a candidate for office in a partisan election, solicit political contributions, or engage in political activities while at work or while on federal property. Additional regulations also apply.

Section Review Answers

1. an administrative system in which agencies staffed largely by nonelected officials perform specific tasks in accordance with standard procedures (p. 275)

2–4. It has a hierarchical authority structure that can increase agency speed by limiting conflicts over who has decision-making authority; it promotes efficiency and productivity through job specialization; and it allows work continuity as decisions are based on defined standards rather than personal preferences. (p. 276)

5–6. Under the spoils system, the president used government positions to reward campaign supporters. Since the president could hire or fire at will, the bureaucracy was highly responsive to his wishes. But the spoils system did not necessarily put the most qualified people in office. The merit system, established by the Pendleton Act, based employment on quality (merit). (pp. 277–78)

★ During wartime, restrictions on administrative action are often set aside to meet the increased needs and demands brought about by war; thus, the number of government employees increases. After the war, many remain in their positions, causing a net growth in government.

★ Some will say that the limitations are not justified and cite the First Amendment (though the Supreme Court has rejected several such arguments). Others will say that the limits are justified in order to prevent the use of their position to influence an election.

1. Describe the major departments within the executive branch.
2. Outline how the federal bureaucracy functions.

Taft's Changes

In 1909, President Taft changed the shape of the president's office to an oval and located the office in the center of an expanded West Wing. This arrangement enabled the president to work more closely with his staff and enabled future presidents to be more involved in the operations of government.

II. Bureaucratic Structure

As noted earlier, the vast bureaucratic machine of the executive branch is organized like a pyramid—one with a very broad base. At the pinnacle is the chief executive, the president. Beneath him stretches an array of agencies that are both stunning in their number and bewildering in their organization. The federal bureaucracy is so vast that one of President Jimmy Carter's aides, who was responsible for reorganizing the bureaucracy, could not even determine how many agencies existed.

Executive Office of the President

The first level of the bureaucracy beneath the president is the **Executive Office of the President (EOP)**. This powerful segment of the executive branch is largely a policymaking and management level that has the greatest access to the president and is the most responsive to his ideas. The Executive Office was formed during the administration of Franklin Roosevelt to help the president manage the burdens of modern government. (Refer to the previous chapter.) The size and responsibilities of the Executive Office have greatly expanded since its inception. The principal agencies within the Executive Office include the White House Office, the Office of Management and Budget, and the National Security Council.

The White House Office

The people closest to the president on a daily basis are the members of the White House Office, often merely called the **White House staff**. Its members serve him by communicating his policies to both the appropriate agencies and the American public. Top aides within the White House exercise an enormous amount of influence as they operate behind the scenes. Typically, presidents appoint close friends or longtime supporters to these top posts because of the trust and confidentiality required. Such closeness between a president and his aides is understandable, but it can be dangerous. Advisors who try to shield the president from damaging information or who simply tell him what he wants to hear can do great, even irreparable, harm to a president's credibility and to the country.

The integrity of an advisor obviously has a great effect on the integrity of his advice. For example, the dishonesty of President Nixon's advisors, H. R. Haldeman and John Ehrlichman, and their involvement in the Watergate affair led to coverups, criminality, and eventually the downfall of the president.

The White House Office includes the chief of staff, staff secretary, Office of Management and Administration, presidential personnel director, counsel to the president, Press Office, and Office of Communications. The president's **chief of staff** advises him on issues of politics, policy, and management; selects key people for the White House staff; and controls and manages staff members,

John Kelly served as President Trump's chief of staff from July 2017 until January 2019.

Chief of Staff

Choose a student to write a brief biography about the current chief of staff. What were his accomplishments prior to receiving this appointment? Why was he chosen? How is he viewed by the media (the student should read some news stories relating to his performance). What have been some of his successes and failures during his tenure? Invite the student to present the information to the class.

their work, and the information and paperwork that reach the Oval Office. The chief of staff is often a guest on television news programs.

The staff secretary also helps control the paper flow to the president and follows up on the paper flow out of the Oval Office. In addition, he or she oversees the Office of the Executive Clerk, Office of Records Management, and Office of Correspondence.

The Office of Management and Administration is the backbone of the White House staff. This office administers staff salaries; allots passes, staff positions, meal privileges, and parking places; manages the budgets for the White House and the Executive Office; liaisons and works in association with the Secret Service; and manages the White House computer systems.

The presidential personnel director plays an essential role in filling critical government positions. Of the president's four thousand appointees, approximately twelve hundred must be confirmed by the Senate.

The counsel for the president, described as the "presidency's lawyer," monitors ethics matters, coordinates the president's message and agenda within the executive branch, negotiates with Congress on the president's behalf, recommends actions to the president, and interprets the law throughout the executive branch. The counsel for the president is the legal protector of the office.

The Press Office serves the president, the White House staff, and reporters. This office channels information, represents constituents, and aids in administration and communication planning. The White House press secretary is the official spokesman for the administration and meets daily with the White House press corps.

The White House communications director is said to be the presidential "fire-walker" ("takes the heat" from the press), reflecting the strength and style of the president. The director works with the president, chief of staff, press secretary, and others in the White House, and is tasked with coordinating all messages coming from the White House and making sure they accurately reflect the President's position.

For many years the president's office was located on the second floor of the White House. As the nation and the presidential staff grew, additional space was needed. In 1902, under President Theodore Roosevelt, the president's offices were moved from the Executive Residence to the addition named the West Wing.

The **West Wing** is the center of activity for the White House staff. The president's

Sarah Huckabee Sanders became White House press secretary in July 2017.

Kellyanne Conway, one of President Trump's chief advisors, speaks outside the West Wing.

President Nixon had the White House indoor swimming pool covered and converted the area into press offices and a briefing room. The White House press corps assembles in the area for gaggles and briefings. The room contains forty-nine assigned theater seats (added by President Reagan).

In 2000 the room was renamed the James S. Brady Press Briefing Room in honor of James Brady, the White House press secretary who was shot and seriously injured during an assassination attempt on President Reagan in 1981. The room was renovated in 2007 at a cost of nearly $8.5 million. (See illustration on p. 215.)

The Blue Goose

The Brady Press Briefing Room contains the standard podium used by all who address the press except the president. The special podium used only by the president and called the Blue Goose is armored and weighs several hundred pounds. It is often transported around the world for the president to use in his foreign travels.

Gaggles

Gaggles are informal briefings by the press secretary that are usually about fifteen minutes long. Sometimes they include the president's schedule for the day and comments on important news issues.

Briefings

Formal press briefings are usually thirty-five to forty minutes long. The press secretary makes a few opening remarks and then answers questions from the press corps. The briefings do not end until the senior correspondent present says, "Thank you."

Press Secretary

Choose a student to write a brief biography about the current White House press secretary. What were his or her accomplishments prior to receiving this appointment? Why was the person chosen? Evaluate the relationship between this person and the media. Is it an amiable one? A combative one? Ask the student to develop a class presentation.

Gaggle or Briefing

Locate a transcript of a White House gaggle or briefing (some are normally available on the White House website). Instruct the students to read copies of the transcript. Direct them to identify the major topics of discussion.

The White House

Show a video, or excerpt of one, about the White House. One such video is *Inside the White House* filmed by *National Geographic*.

The Roosevelt Room

Across the hall from the Oval Office is the original location of President Theodore Roosevelt's office. This room was named the Roosevelt Room by President Nixon in 1969. President Nixon did this to honor both Theodore Roosevelt, who had the West Wing built, and Franklin Roosevelt, who had implemented another expansion of it.

On the Roosevelt Room's mantle is the Nobel Peace Prize given to Theodore Roosevelt in 1906 for his mediation between Russia and Japan. He was the first American and the first sitting president to receive this award. Today, the Roosevelt Room is used as a conference room and as the place in which large groups are assembled before they are admitted to the Oval Office. It also contains a multimedia center for presentations.

Oval Office, the offices of the executive staff (including the vice president), the Cabinet Room, the Roosevelt Room, and the Brady Press Briefing Room are in this section of the White House.

The **East Wing** of the White House was later added. Office space for the First Lady and her staff is located there.

The Office of Management and Budget

The Office of Management and Budget (OMB) wields great influence for an administration. In addition to preparing the president's annual budget for Congress, the OMB serves as a clearing-house by coordinating programs among various agencies and by evaluating budgetary requests from executive departments. The OMB also exercises important control over the president's legislative program. A proposal that originates from a bureaucratic agency must generally get OMB approval before it ever reaches the president.

The National Security Council

The National Security Council (NSC) is the president's policymaking group concerning security and intelligence matters. The NSC was formed in 1947, early in the Cold War, to advise the president on military policy and covert operations and to manage crises. Later, presidents appointed a National Security Advisor to coordinate the work of this group.

During the Truman and Eisenhower years, the NSC was largely an information-gathering agency. However, amid the Vietnam War, the NSC took an increasing role in formulating and implementing foreign policy and advising on military activity. For example, Henry Kissinger, the National Security Advisor for President Nixon, personally negotiated an end to American involvement in Vietnam and prepared the way for summits with both China and the Soviet Union.

Presidents normally receive national security briefings daily and periodically convene meetings of the NSC. The president chairs such meetings and regular attendees include the vice president; the national security advisor; the secretaries of state, defense, energy, and the treasury; the chairman of the Joint Chiefs of Staff (the nation's highest ranking military official); and the director of national intelligence. The chief of staff to the president, counsel for the president, and assistant to the president for economic policy often also attend meetings. The attorney general and the director of the Office of Management and Budget are invited to attend sessions pertaining to their responsibilities. When appropriate, the heads of other executive departments and agencies are also in attendance.

Other EOP Agencies

The Executive Office of the President includes other agencies that advise and assist the chief executive. In 1988, the Office of National Drug Control Policy was established, headed by a director that the media labeled the nation's "drug czar." This agency acts as an advisory and planning agency.

The Office of the United States Trade Representative advises the president on all matters of foreign trade. Its representative, who is appointed by the president and confirmed by the Senate, carries the rank of ambassador and represents the president in foreign-trade negotiations.

The Office of the Vice President aids the vice president in performing his duties. The Office of Faith-Based and Community Initiatives was created by President George W. Bush in January 2001. (President Obama later renamed this agency the Office of Faith-Based and Neighborhood Partnerships.) Its purpose is

National Security Advisor

Choose a student to write a brief biography about the current national security advisor. What were his accomplishments prior to receiving this appointment? Why was he chosen? Has his work received much attention in the media? If so, how is he generally perceived? Ask the student to develop a presentation.

The Eisenhower Executive Office Building (EEOB)

On May 7, 2002, President George W. Bush dedicated the Old Executive Office Building to former president Dwight David Eisenhower. The building is located next to the West Wing on the White House premises.

Many national figures have participated in historic events that took place in this building. Winston Churchill walked its corridors, and on the day Pearl Harbor was bombed, Secretary of State Cordell Hull met there with two Japanese representatives.

Presidents and secretaries of state, war, and the navy have had offices in the building. President Hoover used the secretary of the navy's office for a few months after a fire damaged the Oval Office on Christmas Eve 1929. Richard Nixon had a private office in the building during his presidency.

Since the 1960s, all vice presidents, beginning with Lyndon B. Johnson, have had offices in this building (though the vice president also has an office in the West Wing). Today, the former office of the secretary of the navy is used by the vice president for meetings and press interviews. It has been considered a ceremonial office since its restoration.

to seek ways to involve religious and other private groups more directly in many of the government's social-welfare programs.

The Office of Global Communications was established in 2003 and became a part of the EOP. The agency's purpose is to coordinate important communications with people throughout the world, incorporating the president's ideas into new and existing programs. Other EOP offices include the Council of Economic Advisers, the Office of Policy Development, the Council on Environmental Quality, the Office of Science and Technology Policy, and the Office of Administration.

Cabinet

History and Purpose

The cabinet constitutes the second level of the bureaucracy. The **cabinet** (offices of the executive branch developed to assist the president in his constitutional duties and to meet the demands of America's growth) is not specifically mentioned in the Constitution or established by Congress but is a result of custom and habit. The Constitution's only possible reference to a cabinet is under Article II, Section 2, clause 1, in which the president is given the power to "require the opinion, in writing, of the principal officer in each of the executive departments, upon any subject relating to the duties of their respective offices." Not until 1907 in an act of Congress was the cabinet officially mentioned.

THE FEDERAL BUREAUCRACY • 283

Christmas Eve Fire

On Christmas Eve 1929, staff detected a fire in the West Wing attic. President Hoover and the First Lady were hosting a children's Christmas party at the White House when news of the fire reached them. The president left with his aides to secure important documents, but the First Lady stayed with the children, allowing the party to continue and avoiding panic. Though firefighters battled intense heat and freezing temperatures, the fire ruined much of the West Wing. Unfortunately, the White House was uninsured; Congress had to pass a special appropriation for construction.

Hoover welcomed reporters back in April, "You will be more comfortable and so will I." The West Wing had a new feature—air conditioning.

Office of Global Communications

After the attacks of September 11, 2001, the president decided to create an office that would focus on spreading a positive image of the United States around the world. In early 2003, President George W. Bush issued an executive order officially creating the Office of Global Communications for the purpose of accomplishing that task.

Later, the president delivered a radio address in which he stated some of the nation's priorities.

> This is America's agenda in the world. From the defeat of terror, to the alleviation of disease and hunger, to the spread of human liberty, we welcome and we need the help, advice, and wisdom of friends and allies.

The Office of Global Communications was shuttered by executive order in 2005.

Cabinet Sites

Assign one of the cabinet departments to a student, or assign all fifteen to fifteen different students. Ask participating students to access their department's website, write down that department's mission statement and goals, and list additional interesting information found. Guide a discussion about the information they find most interesting. You may assign this task in conjunction with Activity 2 (p. 288) for this chapter.

Cabinet Meetings

James Madison's cabinet met in the White House's East Room, where it discussed the issues that led to the War of 1812.

On November 6, 1902, Theodore Roosevelt's cabinet became the first to meet in the West Wing.

The Great Seal of the United States

After many important government documents (such as treaties and other international agreements, appointments of important officials, and communications from the president to foreign leaders) are signed, a seal is affixed to each in order to prove authenticity or to certify accuracy. Documents that have been signed by the president and countersigned by the secretary of state have the seal affixed by an officer of the Department of State.

As the nation's first secretary of state, Thomas Jefferson became the first in a long line of secretaries to have custody of the Great Seal. It is used approximately two to three thousand times each year.

President Kennedy meeting with cabinet members and other advisors during the Cuban Missile Crisis in October 1962

Cabinet members advise the president and serve as administrative heads of the executive departments. The expansion and the responsibilities of the cabinet departments reflect the growth of the country, advances in technology, and increased government involvement in areas of life beyond what the Founders ever envisioned.

Presidents have had varied opinions regarding the effectiveness of the cabinet. William Howard Taft said, "[The Constitution] contains no suggestion of a meeting of all the department heads, in consultation over general governmental matters. The Cabinet is a mere creation of the President's will. . . . It exists only by custom. If the President desired to dispense with it, he could do so." A number of presidents have relied more on unofficial advisory groups than on their cabinets. Andrew Jackson's group was called the Kitchen Cabinet, while Franklin Roosevelt's was called his brain trust. Likewise, Harry Truman and John Kennedy depended heavily on the advice of trusted friends. Nonetheless, thousands of bureaucrats work together within the cabinet departments to fulfill the responsibilities of their departments.

Today, fifteen cabinet divisions serve the president: the Departments of State, the Treasury, Defense, Justice, the Interior, Agriculture, Commerce, Labor, Health and Human Services, Housing and Urban Development, Transportation, Energy, Education, Veterans Affairs, and Homeland Security. Most of these departments are headed by a **secretary**, an undersecretary, and various assistant secretaries. These positions are filled by presidential appointment with a vote of approval by a majority of the Senate. Each department enables the president to make more informed decisions when carrying out the executive branch's administrative duties, and each has its own building complex in Washington, DC, or nearby in Virginia. The following summary lists the cabinet departments in the order they were created and reflects the order of presidential succession.

Department of State

One of the four original cabinet departments, the State Department is responsible for issuing passports, visas, and travel warnings to US citizens and providing information when emergencies occur outside the United States. The secretary advises the president on foreign policy and represents the United States in foreign-policy negotiations. State Department agencies include the Foreign Service and the Bureau of Consular Affairs.

Department of the Treasury

The Treasury Department, also an original cabinet department, is responsible for collecting taxes, borrowing money for the government, minting coins, and

The Cabinet

Show a video, or excerpt of one, about the cabinet and its role in the executive branch.

printing bills. Its agencies include the US Mint and the Internal Revenue Service (IRS).

Originally the Bureau of Alcohol, Tobacco, Firearms and Explosives (ATF), the Customs Service, and the Secret Service all resided in the Treasury Department. However, today, the ATF is overseen by the Justice Department, and Customs and the Secret Service have been moved to the Department of Homeland Security.

Department of Defense

Another original cabinet department, first called the Department of War, is now known as the Department of Defense. Its primary function is ensuring national security. Thousands of department personnel work in the Pentagon. Defense Department agencies include the Joint Chiefs of Staff, the Army, the Navy, the Marine Corps, the Air Force, and the Office of the Inspector General. The inspector general is the principal advisor to the secretary of defense concerning fraud, abuses, and deficiencies, and he helps avoid duplication among the military departments while ensuring effective coordination.

US Treasury's Bureau of Engraving and Printing in Washington, DC

"To be prepared for war is one of the most effectual means of preserving peace."
—George Washington

Pentagon, headquarters of the US Department of Defense

Great Seal Features

The features on the seal's obverse (front) have important meanings:

- The American bald eagle stands for the United States of America.
- The shield on the eagle's breast contains thirteen alternating red and white stripes with a blue field across the top. (Red stands for hardness and valor; white stands for purity and innocence; and blue stands for vigilance, perseverance, and justice.) The thirteen stripes stand for the thirteen original colonies. The shield represents Congress uniting the states.
- The olive branch stands for peace. (Note that the eagle is looking toward peace.)
- The thirteen arrows stand for war.
- The ribbon in the eagle's beak contains the phrase *e pluribus unum*, which is Latin for "out of many, one" (many states were born into one nation).
- The constellation over the eagle's head denotes a new state taking its place among other sovereign powers.

The features on the seal's reverse (back) are also significant:

- The thirteen-step unfinished pyramid stands for the thirteen original states.
- The roman numerals at the pyramid's base add up to 1776, the year of the nation's founding.
- The eye surrounded by rays of light is the Eye of Providence (God) surrounded by glory.
- The phrase *annuit coeptis* is Latin for "He (God) has favored our undertakings."
- The phrase *novus ordo seclorum* is Latin for "a new order of the ages," which proclaims the beginning of the new American era in 1776.

The Great Seal

Display a color photo of the Great Seal, or ask each student to bring a one-dollar bill to class. Instruct the class to make a list of each feature on the seal's obverse (front, with the eagle) and reverse (back, with the pyramid). Using the side-margin information on pages 284–85, identify and discuss the symbolism of each feature as a class. More information concerning the history of the seal may be obtained from the Department of State's website.

Bureau of Engraving and Printing

Show a video, or excerpt of one, about this agency.

The Pentagon

Show a video, or excerpt of one, about the Pentagon. One such video is *Inside the Pentagon* filmed by *National Geographic*.

Department of Justice

The last of the four original cabinet departments, the Justice Department was titled the Attorney General's Office until 1870. The head of the Department of Justice is addressed as "attorney general" rather than as "secretary." The department enforces federal laws, gives legal advice to the president, represents the US court system, and oversees federal prisons. Agencies in this department include the Federal Bureau of Investigation (FBI), US Drug Enforcement Administration (DEA), Civil Rights Division, and Criminal Division.

Department of the Interior

In 1849, the Department of the Interior became part of the cabinet. The department manages public lands, national parks, wildlife refuges, hydroelectric power plants, Native American affairs, mining, and the nation's water, energy, and mineral resources. Some of the agencies included in the Department of the Interior are the National Park Service, the US Fish and Wildlife Service, the Bureau of Indian Affairs, and the US Geological Survey.

Department of Agriculture

Raised to cabinet status in 1889, the Department of Agriculture (USDA) is the United States' largest conservation agency. Some of the USDA's functions are inspecting food, managing school-lunch and food-stamp programs, helping farmers and ranchers, managing national forests, and helping promote US agricultural products overseas. Some agencies within the USDA are the Food and Nutrition Service and the Food Safety and Inspection Service.

USDA inspectors (above). National Park Service ranger talks with visitors at Olympic National Park in Washington state (below).

Department of Commerce

In 1903 the Department of Commerce and Labor was added to the cabinet. The Department of Labor became a separate entity in 1913. Today, the Commerce Department's functions include promoting international trade, encouraging economic growth, conducting the census, issuing patents and trademarks, and protecting ocean and coastal resources and developing them economically. Some agencies within the department are the National Oceanic and Atmospheric Administration (NOAA), the Bureau of the Census, and the Patent and Trademark Office.

Department of Labor

The Department of Labor enforces work laws, such as those instituting the minimum wage and requiring safe working conditions; promotes job-training programs; and addresses childcare issues. The Bureau of Labor Statistics and the Occupational Safety and Health Administration (OSHA) are two of the Labor Department's agencies.

NOAA vessel in Alaska at Glacier Bay

Department of Health and Human Services

The roots of the Health and Human Services Department (HHS) go back to 1789 with the establishment of a marine hospital to care for seafarers. In 1953, the Department of Health, Education, and Welfare was created. The Education Department became a separate department in 1979, and in 1980 the Health and Welfare Department became the Department of Health and Human Services. This department's functions include promoting healthcare programs, preventing and controlling diseases, administrating Medicare and Medicaid, and enforcing food and drug laws. It has the largest budget among the cabinet departments. Two of the agencies within the Health and Human Services Department are the Centers for Disease Control and Prevention (CDC) and the Food and Drug Administration (FDA).

Department of Housing and Urban Development

The origins of the Department of Housing and Urban Development (HUD) began with the US Housing Act of 1937. The act's purpose was to provide low-income families with safe, sanitary shelter and economic opportunity. In 1965 the Department of Housing and Urban Development obtained cabinet status. HUD oversees public housing, home financing, and fair housing, and it helps the homeless. The Office of Fair Housing and Equal Opportunity is a HUD agency.

Department of Transportation

In 1966 the Department of Transportation was established. It oversees highways, mass transit, air travel, railroads, pipelines, and maritime laws. Agencies under Transportation Department administration include the Federal Aviation Administration (FAA) and the Federal Highway Administration. (The US Coast

Commerce Building Inscriptions

The following quotations are among the inscriptions on the Herbert C. Hoover Building, headquarters of the Department of Commerce:

"Commerce among nations should be fair and equitable."
Benjamin Franklin

"The patent system added the fuel of interest to the fire of genius."
Abraham Lincoln

"Let Us Raise a Standard to Which the Wise and Honest Can Repair."
George Washington

Transportation Prehistory

Before there was a Department of Transportation, President Washington signed a bill in 1790 authorizing the construction of ten fifty-foot, two-masted boats to aid in guarding the coast against smugglers.

In 1806 President Jefferson authorized the first federal highway, the National Road, which would connect Ohio with the Eastern Seaboard. It was also called the Cumberland Road.

Commerce Building Inscriptions

Display one of the inscriptions from the Department of Commerce building (see the side margin). Discuss the meaning of the quotation as well as the possible biblical principles represented in the quotation.

Teen Labor Laws

Invite a student or small group of students to access the Department of Labor's website. Instruct the participating students to obtain a list of jobs that teens of various ages can and cannot legally do. Also select a different student or group of students to access your state's teen labor restrictions. Ask each student or group to relate any findings to the class. Compare and contrast federal and state rules.

Guard and the Transportation Security Administration were previously included in this department. After the September 11, 2001, terrorist attacks, however, President George W. Bush requested that those agencies be transferred to the Department of Homeland Security.)

Department of Energy

The oil crisis in 1973 brought greater attention to problems regarding energy. That crisis and other concerns led to the establishment of the Department of Energy in 1977. This department oversees energy technology and nuclear-weapons research, including the operations of the research plants in Oak Ridge, Tennessee (the Oak Ridge National Laboratory and the Y-12 National Security Complex). It also manages through contractors the Hanford Site in Washington State, the Sandia National Laboratory and the Los Alamos National Laboratory in New Mexico, the Lawrence Livermore National Laboratory in California, and others.

Today the Energy Department's focus includes ensuring our energy security, maintaining the safety and reliability of our nuclear stockpiles, conducting nuclear experiments, cleaning up environmental Cold War–era nuclear wastes, and transferring nuclear technology to civilian uses. The Energy Department also administrates the Office of Nuclear Energy.

Department of Education

President Andrew Johnson created the first Department of Education in 1867. Its purpose was to collect information and statistics about the nation's schools. However, many people thought that the department would have too much control over local schools, so it was demoted to the Office of Education in 1868. From 1953 to 1979, the agency was part of the Health, Education, and Welfare Department. But education programs expanded in the 1970s, and the Department of Education gained cabinet status in 1979. The Education Department gives federal aid to public schools and oversees educational research. Agencies within the department include the Office of Elementary and Secondary Education and the Office of Postsecondary Education.

Department of Veterans Affairs

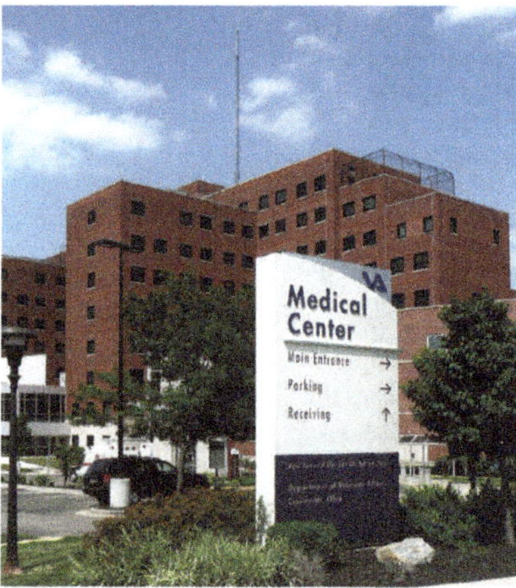

Veterans Medical Center in Cincinnati, Ohio

In 1636 the Pilgrims passed a law stating that the Plymouth colony would support soldiers disabled by wounds suffered during the Pequot War. In 1776, the Continental Congress encouraged enlistments during the War for Independence by promising pensions for disabled soldiers. Thus, there is a long history of concern for veterans in our nation.

In 1989 a cabinet-level position called the Department of Veterans Affairs was created. At that time, President George H. W. Bush said, "There is only one place for the Veterans of America, in the Cabinet Room, at the table with the President of the United States of America."

The department oversees benefits, pensions, and medical programs for veterans and maintains military cemeteries. It operates over twelve hundred healthcare facilities, including medical centers and clinics, across the nation. Agencies within the department include the Veterans Health Administration and the National Cemetery Administration.

Activity 2: The Cabinet

This enrichment activity enhances skills in using resources while familiarizing the students with the current cabinet secretaries.

Department of Homeland Security

The Department of Homeland Security (DHS) was created after the September 11, 2001, terrorist attacks on the World Trade Center and the Pentagon. The department's mission is to prevent terrorist attacks within the United States, reduce America's vulnerability to terrorism, and minimize damage from and speed recovery following attacks. It also assists after natural disasters.

The Department of Homeland Security was originally a part of the Executive Office of the President, but it was elevated to cabinet status in 2002. A few of the preexisting agencies and organizations that became part of the DHS include the US Customs Service, the Federal Law Enforcement Training Center, and the Secret Service (all were formerly under the Treasury Department). The Immigration and Naturalization Service also came under the authority of DHS, as did the Nuclear Incident Response Team (formerly under the Energy Department) and the Coast Guard (formerly under the Defense Department).

The most visible newly established agency under DHS is the **Transportation Security Administration (TSA)**, which screens all passengers and baggage at airports. The TSA has been the subject of much criticism since its inception following the 9/11 terrorist attacks. Although most airline passengers recognize the need for screening to ensure safety, some have argued that the physical pat-downs and electronic screening used are violations of passenger privacy and of the Fourth Amendment guarantee against "unreasonable searches and seizures."

TSA agents screen passengers (above). NASA launched the space shuttle Discovery *in 1998 (below).*

Independent Agencies

The third and final level of the bureaucratic pyramid consists of independent agencies. These agencies are independent because they do not fit within the fifteen cabinet departments. Because of their particular, sensitive functions, some agencies, especially regulatory commissions, need protection from partisan political pressures. Agencies are divided into three groups: independent executive agencies, government corporations, and independent regulatory commissions. All of these agencies are part of the executive branch and are accountable to the president.

Independent Executive Agencies

Most independent agencies fit into the category of independent executive agencies. Some of these agencies have multimillion-dollar budgets, employ thousands of people, and are organized like cabinet departments, but they do not have cabinet status. An example is the National Aeronautics and Space Administration (NASA). Most independent executive agencies, however, have relatively few employees and small budgets and draw very little attention. An example is the American Battle Monuments Commission which has a few hundred employees.

"Independent" Agencies

Discuss the irony of the phrase "independent agencies." Is it really possible for independent agencies to be independent if the directors of those organizations are nominated by and answerable to the president? How does their dependence on congressional appropriations or subsidies affect their ability to be independent?

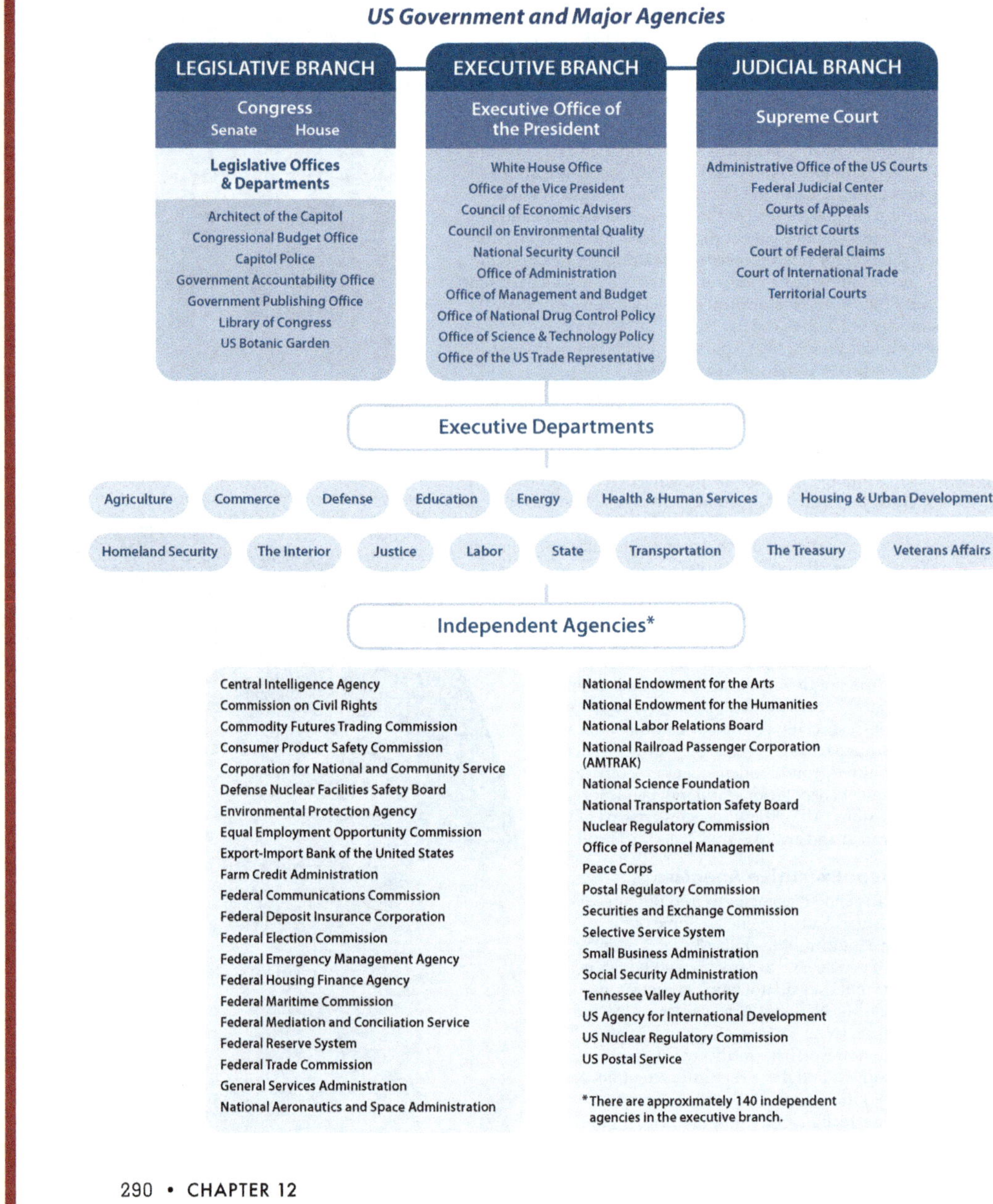

Unchecked Bureaucracy

Discuss the ways that an unchecked bureaucracy would undermine democratic processes, particularly because the bureaucracy can write specific regulations. Discuss where the blame would lie for an unchecked bureaucracy: with the president, Congress, or citizens themselves?

Government Corporations

Congress established government corporations to administer certain businesslike activities. The government assumes these responsibilities because they may not be profitable enough for a private company to perform them.

The first government corporation was the Bank of the United States, established in 1791. However, not until World War I and the Great Depression of the 1930s did Congress establish many corporations to oversee emergency programs. Today there are more than fifty government corporations. Examples include the US Postal Service and the Tennessee Valley Authority (TVA). (TVA operates dams and locks to control flooding and to facilitate river transportation in the Southeast. It also generates electricity with coal, nuclear, and hydroelectric plants to sell and distribute.)

Independent Regulatory Commissions

Although the president has appointive power over the commissioners and directors of regulatory commissions, these officials are not accountable to him for how they run their agencies. Regulatory agencies affect everything from highways and airways to food and water.

The scope and power of regulatory commissions have generated a chorus of complaints from industry and individuals alike. Although bureaucratic overreach can result from the strictness and independence with which some regulatory commissions operate, regulation is still necessary. Humans, being sinners, cannot always be trusted to do what is right. Since they are tempted to do whatever is right in their own eyes (Judg. 21:25), humans need accountability. As noted in Chapter 1, maintaining justice is the primary biblical purpose for government, but many bureaucratic regulations reflect one or more of the purposes of government. For example, if employers show a tendency to save thousands of dollars rather than create safe workplaces for their employees, the government may rightly pass laws that outline and enforce safety measures. Such workplace safety regulations can

Food and Drug Administration (FDA) laboratory

<table>
<tr><td colspan="4" align="center">**Major Federal Regulators**</td></tr>
<tr><td></td><td>**Agency**</td><td>**Year created**</td><td>**Major functions**</td></tr>
<tr><td rowspan="3">Trade</td><td>Food and Drug Administration (FDA)</td><td>1906</td><td>Ensures the safety and effectiveness of drugs and medical devices and the safety and purity of food. Regulates labeling and oversees more than $2 trillion worth of products used by consumers.</td></tr>
<tr><td>Federal Trade Commission (FTC)</td><td>1914</td><td>Has broad discretion to curb unfair trade practices, protect consumers, and maintain competition.</td></tr>
<tr><td>Antitrust Division</td><td>1933</td><td>Attempts to promote and protect the competitive process and the American economy through the enforcement of antitrust laws.</td></tr>
</table>

The FTC

The Federal Trade Commission (FTC) is responsible for such items as product warranties, stickers that show the energy costs of home appliances, and the care labels that are attached in clothes.

The FDIC

The Federal Deposit Insurance Corporation (FDIC) insures savings, checking, and other deposit accounts in commercial banks and savings institutions. Accounts are insured for $250,000 per depositor. Securities, mutual funds, or similar types of investments offered by banks and other institutions are not protected by FDIC insurance.

Major Federal Regulators			
	Agency	Year created	Major functions
Finance and competition	Federal Deposit Insurance Corporation (FDIC)	1933	Promotes safe, sound banking practices and, along with the states, exercises regulatory power over state-chartered banks not in the Federal Reserve System. Insures deposits in member banks up to $250,000.
	Federal Communications Commission (FCC)	1934	Regulates interstate and international communications by radio, television, wire, satellite, and cable. Has jurisdiction over the fifty states, the District of Columbia, and US possessions.
	Securities and Exchange Commission (SEC)	1934	Protects investors, maintains the integrity of the securities market, and enforces public-disclosure and securities-fraud laws.
Consumer protection	Federal Aviation Administration (FAA)	1958	Regulates civil aviation to promote safety and fulfill national-defense requirements, operates the air-traffic control system for civil and military aircraft. Regulates US commercial space transportation.
	National Highway Traffic Safety Administration (NHTSA)	1970	Sets and enforces safety standards for motor vehicles and equipment; investigates safety defects; promotes the use of safety devices (seat belts, child-safety seats, air bags, etc.); and conducts research on driver behavior and traffic safety.
	Environmental Protection Agency (EPA)	1970	Develops and enforces standards for clean air and water, controls pollution from pesticides and toxic substances, approves state pollution reduction plans, and rules on environmental-impact statements.
	Occupational Safety and Health Administration (OSHA)	1971	Works in partnership with federal and state governments to save lives, prevent workplace injuries, and protect the health of American workers.
	Consumer Product Safety Commission (CPSC)	1972	Tries to reduce product-related injuries to consumers by mandating better design, labeling, and instruction sheets.

EPA scientists at work

promote justice, public safety, and order. Not surprisingly, precedent for these kinds of measures is found in the law God gave to Israel (e.g., the laws in Exod. 21:28–32).

Some bureaucratic edicts may be burdensome, insensitive, or dictatorial. Because bureaucrats are themselves both fallible and sinful, a good governmental system should provide a check on the bureaucracy as well. Oftentimes, however, if an employer or business is concerned for others, then some of the reasonable regulations may not seem so burdensome. As the apostle Paul observes in Romans 13:3, "Rulers are not a terror to good works, but to the evil."

Operation of the Bureaucracy

The federal bureaucracy has become a quasi-legislative, quasi-executive, and quasi-judicial system. Its broad powers that have accumulated over time give it an influential role in the connection between government and the people.

The bureaucracy serves a legislative role by recommending bills to Congress and the president, generally through the Office of Management and Budget. Of course, the Constitution empowers Congress to pass bills that become **statutory law** (law that has been passed by the legislature and signed by the president). However, such laws are often written in vague terms owing to a lack of information, fear of offending constituents, or a desire to allow enforcement officials to interpret the laws as they see fit. The bureaucracy has the responsibility to devise specific regulations, rules, and procedures that implement congressional statutes. These regulations have the force of law and are known as **administrative law**. Examples of administrative laws include the regulations of the Social Security Administration; the rules of the Environmental Protection Agency (EPA); and the workplace requirements of the Occupational Safety and Health Administration (OSHA). The creation of laws by nonelected officials is a formidable power. Critics argue that this growth has occurred because of congressional inaction and because bureaucrats have sought to extend their control.

In its judicial role, the bureaucracy provides due process for individuals or groups involved in disputes with an agency. (Due process provides all parties involved the right to a fair hearing and the right to appeal bureaucratic decisions.)

In addition to implementing administrative law, each bureaucratic unit exercises its responsibility in specific areas. At times, there might be some overlapping of responsibilities; in law enforcement, for example, both the FBI and the Drug Enforcement Administration (DEA) might investigate a case involving the importation of illegal narcotics. However, most agencies serve a specific need of a particular group. The members of such groups are known as **clients**. An individual might be the client of more than one agency at a time; for example, a retired veteran might seek help from both the Social Security Administration and Veterans Affairs. Clients are not always provided a service in the form of benefits, though. Certain agencies function as regulators and controllers. For example, the Environmental Protection Agency (EPA) regulates the development and use of pesticides, and the Internal Revenue Service regulates all taxpayers.

FBI agents removing documents after executing a search warrant

Bureaucracies operate according to clearly defined procedures. These methods, known as **standard operating procedures** (SOPs), have both a positive side and a negative one. Positively, they help ensure that everyone is treated alike and that decisions are less subjective. Negatively, SOPs are rigid, making it difficult for individuals with exceptional situations to receive prompt help. SOPs might seem to make the relationship between agency and client impersonal; however, when adhered to, these rules usually help control bureaucratic authority by limiting the discretionary power of bureaucrats. For example, when housing assistance is provided to low-income families, clearly defined procedures and conditions help prevent bureaucrats from exercising their own judgment to exclude a client who might otherwise qualify for help.

Activity 3: Is Administrative Law Constitutional?

This activity presents arguments against the constitutionality of administrative law. Students will read and then analyze and evaluate information dealing with this topic.

1. Summarize why the federal bureaucracy has been called the fourth branch of government.

2. Describe ways the bureaucracy is held accountable for its actions.

3. Delineate the problems created by a powerful bureaucracy.

4. Describe some distinctives and achievements of American bureaucracy.

Section Review

1. What is the first level of bureaucracy beneath the president?

2–3. State the purpose of the National Security Council. Describe its origin.

4. Define *cabinet*.

5. Discuss the Constitution's possible reference to the cabinet.

6. How do cabinet members obtain their positions?

7. What was the first government corporation in the United States?

8–9. Contrast statutory and administrative law.

10. Which agency regulates the development and use of pesticides?

★ Why is the Executive Office of the President such a powerful segment of the executive branch?

★ Why is regulation by the government necessary?

Guiding Questions

1. Why has the federal bureaucracy been called the fourth branch of government?

2. How is the bureaucracy held accountable for its actions?

3. What problems exist within the federal bureaucracy?

4. What are some distinctives and achievements of American bureaucracy?

III. Bureaucratic Practices

The Fourth Branch

Congress, the president, and the courts all exercise constitutionally derived power as three separate but interdependent branches of the national government. Given its power and pervasiveness, the federal bureaucracy is sometimes referred to as the **fourth branch** of government. There are four major causes for this description: size, skills, separation of powers, and desire for security.

Size

The growth in the number and size of federal agencies has made the bureaucracy the largest segment of the national government; the bureaucracy has about two million civilian employees in the executive branch alone. Size creates problems of supervision. The president cannot micromanage all the federal departments. In fact, the Executive Office of the President, originally created to help the president supervise the bureaucracy, has become so large that it too now requires supervision.

Skills

The skills that many agency officials provide also strengthen the independence of the bureaucracy. Having expertise in a variety of technical fields—such as pollution control, aircraft design, laser weaponry, and census statistics—means their advice is often sought on legislative matters. These agency officials often control the information Congress receives and thereby influence legislation and shape policy.

Separation of Powers

Another factor supporting the idea that the bureaucracy acts as a fourth branch of government is the bureaucracy's tendency to increase its independence by taking advantage of the separation of powers between the three major branches of government. For example, an agency having strong ties with a congressional committee might seek its help on a proposal that has met with executive resistance. This might result in legislation that could force the president

Section Review Answers

1. Executive Office of the President (EOP) (p. 280)

2–3. To serve as the president's policymaking group concerning security and intelligence matters; it was formed in 1947, during the Cold War, to advise the president on military policy and covert operations and to serve as a crisis management team. (p. 282)

4. offices of the executive branch developed to assist the president in his constitutional duties and to meet the demands of America's growth (pp. 283–84)

5. Article II, Section 2, clause 1, gives the president the power to "require the opinion, in writing, of the principal officer in each of the executive departments, upon any subject relating to the duties of their respective offices." (p. 283)

6. by presidential appointment with Senate approval (p. 284)

7. the Bank of the United States (p. 291)

8–9. Statutory law is passed by the legislature and signed by the president. Administrative law is the collection of regulations developed by the federal bureaucracy to implement congressional statutes. (p. 293)

10. Environmental Protection Agency (EPA) (p. 292)

★ It has the greatest access to the president and is the most responsive to his ideas.

★ Students may say that humans are sinners and will not always do right. Many regulations fulfill the government's obligations to its citizens in promoting the general welfare.

to consider the program. For example, the FBI maintained considerable independence from both the president and the attorney general for decades because of its strong congressional ties. This dynamic has changed in recent years.

Desire for Security

The independence of the federal bureaucracy is further illustrated by agencies' intense struggles to control their internal affairs. For example, in the past, bureaucrats who disclosed evidence of waste and mismanagement did so at the risk of their own jobs. These whistleblowers, those who make public disclosures of wrongdoing, have been fired, demoted, retired, or relocated for making public complaints about costly bureaucratic bungling. Fortunately, recent laws have been passed attempting to prevent such retaliation.

The so-called fourth branch is powerful and pervasive. Its capacity for independence is certainly great given its size, its role in implementing law, and its complex responsibilities. The president and Congress, however, both have powerful checks that can be used to help curb the power of the giant bureaucratic machine.

Accountability

Bureaucrats operate under congressional **oversight** (the process of examining a department's compliance with the law and scrutinizing its budget requests). Congress has power over how agencies function. With the exception of a few presidential offices and commissions, no federal agency may exist without congressional approval. Before the 1960s, Congress passed statutes giving broad discretion to regulatory agencies, such as the Federal Communications Commission. Since the 1960s, however, Congress has tended to restrict agency discretion. Also, agencies may not spend **appropriations** (money budgeted by Congress to fund programs) unless the money is first authorized and set aside by Congress. There has been a trend toward requiring annual authorizations to strengthen congressional control over certain executive agencies. These agencies include NASA and those that administer foreign aid or procure military equipment for the Defense Department.

The bureaucracy poses a threat to democratic government when it fails to respond to the voice of the people and their elected representatives or when it attempts to rule instead of serve. Congress, the president, and the public, however, can restrict bureaucratic power through various means. Congress can exercise checks over the bureaucracy by authorizing the **Government Accountability Office (GAO)** to audit an agency's finances and monitor its activities. Since

> *"In framing a government which is to be administered by men over men, the great difficulty lies in this: you must first enable the government to control the governed; and in the next place oblige it to control itself."*
>
> **The Federalist No. 51**

Like all military equipment, the US Army Abrams tank is financed through congressional appropriations.

Secrets

Bureaucrats often prefer to keep their procedures and decisions secret, and bureaucracies may patronize and intimidate citizens by claiming to have technical expertise that citizens supposedly have no right to question or understand. For example, the Internal Revenue Service (IRS) sends out thousands of letters each year to clarify its position on special cases; but until the FOIA was passed, the IRS kept most of these special cases secret. Critics said the secrecy was to protect the agency against its own inconsistencies.

Even after passage of the FOIA, agencies retained nine exemptions (including those related to national security, personal privacy, and law enforcement) and a host of effective tactics to delay release of information. Inquirers often have to go to court or wait months for an official response to their inquiries. Information may be filed in such a way that it is difficult to locate, and agencies may also block the release of unrestricted information if releasing it would require releasing protected information at the same time.

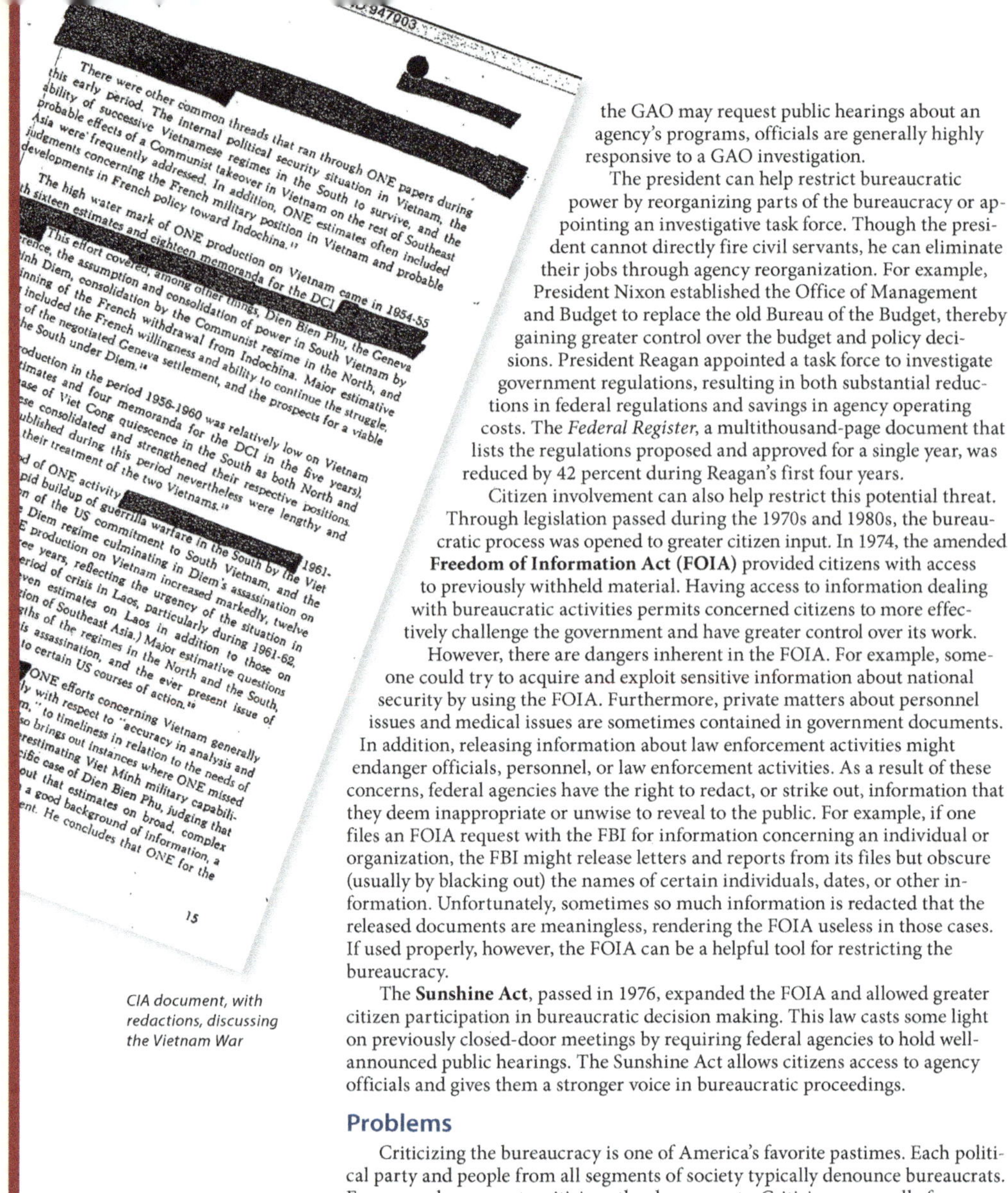

CIA document, with redactions, discussing the Vietnam War

the GAO may request public hearings about an agency's programs, officials are generally highly responsive to a GAO investigation.

The president can help restrict bureaucratic power by reorganizing parts of the bureaucracy or appointing an investigative task force. Though the president cannot directly fire civil servants, he can eliminate their jobs through agency reorganization. For example, President Nixon established the Office of Management and Budget to replace the old Bureau of the Budget, thereby gaining greater control over the budget and policy decisions. President Reagan appointed a task force to investigate government regulations, resulting in both substantial reductions in federal regulations and savings in agency operating costs. The *Federal Register*, a multithousand-page document that lists the regulations proposed and approved for a single year, was reduced by 42 percent during Reagan's first four years.

Citizen involvement can also help restrict this potential threat. Through legislation passed during the 1970s and 1980s, the bureaucratic process was opened to greater citizen input. In 1974, the amended **Freedom of Information Act (FOIA)** provided citizens with access to previously withheld material. Having access to information dealing with bureaucratic activities permits concerned citizens to more effectively challenge the government and have greater control over its work. However, there are dangers inherent in the FOIA. For example, someone could try to acquire and exploit sensitive information about national security by using the FOIA. Furthermore, private matters about personnel issues and medical issues are sometimes contained in government documents. In addition, releasing information about law enforcement activities might endanger officials, personnel, or law enforcement activities. As a result of these concerns, federal agencies have the right to redact, or strike out, information that they deem inappropriate or unwise to reveal to the public. For example, if one files an FOIA request with the FBI for information concerning an individual or organization, the FBI might release letters and reports from its files but obscure (usually by blacking out) the names of certain individuals, dates, or other information. Unfortunately, sometimes so much information is redacted that the released documents are meaningless, rendering the FOIA useless in those cases. If used properly, however, the FOIA can be a helpful tool for restricting the bureaucracy.

The **Sunshine Act**, passed in 1976, expanded the FOIA and allowed greater citizen participation in bureaucratic decision making. This law casts some light on previously closed-door meetings by requiring federal agencies to hold well-announced public hearings. The Sunshine Act allows citizens access to agency officials and gives them a stronger voice in bureaucratic proceedings.

Problems

Criticizing the bureaucracy is one of America's favorite pastimes. Each political party and people from all segments of society typically denounce bureaucrats. Even some bureaucrats criticize other bureaucrats. Criticisms generally focus on seven categories of bureaucratic problems—waste, conflict, duplication, red tape, vague goals, obscure bureaucratic language, and resistance to change.

Activity 4: Bureaucracy Cartoon

In this activity students will draw and explain a political cartoon dealing with the government bureaucracy.

Ensuring justice, providing for national defense and public safety, addressing poverty, promoting moral behavior, and providing order are all obligations of the government to those it governs. Meeting these obligations in a society that has more than three hundred million is no small task. A sizable government is required. Nevertheless, the role of government should not operate within or take over the functions of the many other institutions, such as the home and the church. Tasks that can be competently performed by the proper institution should not be assumed by the government. Unfortunately, there sometimes exists a tendency with the nation's bureaucratic structure to do so.

Waste

Possibly the most frequent criticism leveled at the federal bureaucracy regards **waste** (the mismanagement of money, time, and personnel). The extent of government waste is staggering. President Reagan tried to tackle the problem by appointing the Grace Commission to investigate federal agencies. The commission report, released in 1984, revealed that the federal bureaucracy had numerous deficiencies. It noted that unlike businesses, which are concerned about maximizing profits, government agencies have few incentives to keep costs down. In a business, if an employee cuts costs, the firm can add the savings to its profits and the employee might even receive a raise or a bonus. But if a government employee cuts costs, he receives no reward and his agency cannot keep the savings because the money goes back to the Treasury.

One problem that increases bureaucratic waste is the budgeting process within most agencies. Typically, when preparing the annual budget, agency departments ask for more funds than they actually need. Then, if a department's request is reduced by Congress, the agency will still have the amount of money it really desires. In addition, if a department has not spent all its previously appropriated funds as the end of the budget year approaches, it will often try to quickly spend those funds for fear that its new request will be cut. These practices result in the waste of much taxpayer money.

Conflict

Some agencies, misunderstanding one another's purposes, seem to work against each other; this results in conflict. Agencies often engage in power struggles for bigger budgets, larger staffs, and greater jurisdiction. Departments are often at odds with one another over basic goals. For example, the State Department might want to reduce the number of weapons being produced with the intent of fostering better relations with other countries. However, the Defense

Wasteful Spending

Citizens Against Government Waste (CAGW) was established in 1984. It produces publications that are critical of pork-barrel projects.

For example, in 2003 this group identified specific examples of the government's wasteful expenditures:

- $250,000 to implement the National Preschool Anger Management Project
- $9.5 million for various wood-research projects
- $4 million for the International Fertilizer Development Center
- $800,000 for the Grammy Foundation and $90,000 for the American Film Institute
- $750,000 for the Baseball Hall of Fame, $350,000 for the Rock and Roll Hall of Fame, and $90,000 for the National Cowgirl Museum and Hall of Fame

CAGW's annual report, *The Congressional Pig Book Summary* (Pig Book), listed these projects in 2019 as examples of irresponsible government spending:

- $1.8 billion for sixteen additional F-35 aircraft (CAGW states that the airplane has performed poorly and has been troubled with cost overruns and delays.)
- $960 million for the Littoral Combat Ship (CAGW says it has been ridden with excessive costs and a poorly defined mission.)
- $13 million for Save America's Treasures grants, which has previously funded the restoration and operation of local museums, opera houses, and theaters
- $9 million for a fruit fly quarantine program
- $863,000 to help eliminate the brown tree snake

Analyzing Political Cartoons

Guide a discussion about the political cartoon on this page. What is the cartoon implying? What is the basis of the cartoon (how does it connect to the material in the text)? Refer to the feature box on page 439 of this text for more information about political cartoons.

Doublespeak

The defense sector provides some of the best examples of the twisted language of gobbledygook. For example, tents are "frame-supported tension structures," being caught in an ambush is "engaging the enemy on all sides," and a neutron bomb is referred to as a "radiation-enhancement device."

The private sector is just as skilled at this doublespeak. Greeting cards are now "social expression products," and public restrooms have been referred to as "guest relations facilities." The manufacturers of Rolls-Royce, unwilling to say that their cars might break down, did admit that a Rolls could "fail to proceed."

Department might think the production necessary for long-term national security. Departments also compete with one another for limited appropriations.

Duplication

In April 2014, *USA Today* discussed GAO reports which identified problems with more than two hundred federal programs. One of the most common issues cited was multiple government agencies performing the same or similar tasks. Such duplication results in enormous inefficiency. The GAO found that eleven government agencies were involved in autism research; eight were searching for soldiers missing in action; and ten different offices within the Department of Health and Human Services worked with minority communities regarding AIDS. Unfortunately, numerous additional examples of duplicated efforts, resulting in the waste of taxpayer money, have been documented.

Red Tape

Bureaucratic paperwork, or **red tape**, can be one of the most frustrating problems that individuals and businesses confront when dealing with government agencies. Businesses are particularly hard-hit by government red tape as they attempt to comply with confusing and, at times, conflicting demands from a variety of agencies covering everything from pollution control to employment practices to health and safety standards.

One example of red tape is the enormous amount of paperwork often required to accomplish a seemingly simple task. Multiple forms must sometimes be completed, many of which ask for the same information. Perhaps even more disheartening are the instances in which individuals calling an agency with a question receive conflicting or even contradictory answers. The Internal Revenue Service and the Social Security Administration are frequently cited as examples of agencies that misinform and confuse citizens this way.

Vague Goals

When Congress does not establish clear goals for an agency, the agency will sometimes exercise broad powers. Often interest groups will take advantage of imprecise wording or ambiguous statements to demand that an agency support that group's agenda. Leaders of a federal agency often devise and implement regulations based on their own interpretation of ill-defined objectives.

Obscure Bureaucratic Language

Another problem with the bureaucratic system is the use of **bureaucratese** (vague, jargon-filled, and unnecessarily complicated language) to describe something clear and simple. Critics argue that doublespeak, language used to conceal or confuse or even misrepresent the truth, frequently appears in bureaucratic regulations and documents.

Bureaucratic language is not simply an alternative writing style. In many cases it is an effort to obscure the truth. The Bible, in contrast, emphasizes the importance of clearly speaking truth. Government officials should heed the example set by King Solomon, a wise and learned ruler whose writings in the book of Proverbs are direct and clear. His words, even centuries later, ring with simplicity and truth.

Bureaucratic Red Tape

Group the students and assign each a government agency. You may designate such federal agencies as the Internal Revenue Service or the Social Security Administration and local agencies such as a building and permits department or a zoning agency. Encourage students to research how much paperwork and time go into some typical inquiries or applications involving these entities. Students can present their findings to the class.

Resistance to Change

The federal bureaucracy is large, powerful, and expensive. Politicians annually promise to curb bureaucratic power, but, ironically, many of the offices that were established to control federal agencies and implement presidential policies eventually became part of the bureaucratic machine. In short, the bureaucracy resists change and tends to be self-perpetuating. President Carter learned this, much to his disappointment, when his attempts to reorganize and trim the bureaucracy met with stubborn resistance. More than two decades earlier, President Truman underscored the problem of the bureaucracy's resistance to change in his remarks about his successor, Dwight D. "Ike" Eisenhower. Eisenhower was a former general who was accustomed to giving orders to soldiers and having those orders implemented immediately and efficiently. Truman lamented, "He'll sit here, and he'll say, 'Do this! Do that!' *And nothing will happen.* Poor Ike—it won't be a bit like the Army. He'll find it very frustrating."

Presidents have long bemoaned the unresponsiveness of the federal bureaucracy. The distance between presidential policy and bureaucratic implementation can be great indeed. Foot-dragging, quiet opposition, or just the long paper trail down the bureaucratic pyramid can produce significant delays in enacting a White House request.

Part of the difficulty between presidents and their bureaucratic subordinates involves the basic issue of time. Presidents serve for a few years, but many bureaucrats can expect to keep their jobs until retirement. (Cabinet officials and most of the EOP change with each administration.) If a department particularly resents a White House policy, bureaucrats can slow action or even stop it.

Nonetheless, many presidents have attempted to tame the bureaucracy. For example, President Nixon sought to correct its unresponsiveness by placing some of his appointees in lower-level positions to increase the likelihood of action on his policies. In the 1990s the Clinton administration tried to streamline government through its National Performance Review, more popularly called "reinventing government." This program's focus was different from previous efforts that sought to strengthen presidential power or incorporate independent agencies into a few big departments. It attempted to "cut red tape," "empower employees," and "put customers first." The ultimate goal of the program was "to create a government that works better and costs less." Some positive changes did occur. The Office of Personnel Management simplified the way that bureaucrats are hired and fired, and many agencies created customer service standards.

Distinctiveness

All modern societies, whether democratic or undemocratic, have bureaucracies. However, four aspects of the United States' constitutional system and political traditions give its bureaucracy a distinctive character. First, the president and Congress share political authority over the bureaucracy. High-ranking appointed officials have at least two masters: congressional committees and the executive branch. Divided authority often enables bureaucrats to play one branch of government against another.

How [Economically] Free Is the Land of the Free?

Each year the Heritage Foundation ranks the world's national economies according to how much freedom from government regulation they enjoy. In 2013, the United States was ranked tenth but had slipped to eighteenth place by 2018. The following list shows the twenty most economically free nations from the foundation's *2019 Index of Economic Freedom* (one means "most free").

1. Hong Kong	11. Iceland
2. Singapore	12. United States
3. New Zealand	13. Netherlands
4. Switzerland	14. Denmark
5. Australia	15. Estonia
6. Ireland	16. Georgia
7. United Kingdom	17. Luxembourg
8. Canada	18. Chile
9. United Arab Emirates	19. Sweden
10. Taiwan	20. Finland

Sphere Sovereignty

As the Creation Mandate is implemented, clearly not everyone can do everything. Consequently, different institutions have developed. Scripture specifically says some are ordained by God: family, government, and church. Others, though not specifically instituted by God, serve good purposes in carrying forward the Creation Mandate: schools, hospitals, restaurants, construction companies, etc. Each institution has duties to fulfill in its own way. A family should not operate like a military unit, a school should not function like a family, and a construction company should not conduct business like a church.

In the nineteenth century some Protestant theologians considered how institutions should relate to each other. They concluded that institutions are sovereign within their own spheres. For instance, though a church should train parents regarding raising children, it does not actually rear them. Similarly, though churches should speak about moral issues of government policy and regulation, they cannot pass laws or execute civil punishments.

People live in a variety of spheres. For instance, if an employer attends an evening class that is taught by someone he supervises during the day, he is clearly under his employee's authority when that employee is his teacher. During the day job, however, the employer is the employee's authority.

Sometimes, however, spheres overlap. For instance, if a father physically harms his family, the government should intercede to protect them, and the church should discipline him. Because the government has the role of ensuring justice, it often has the authority to correct injustices within other institutions. However, it should not seize control of other institutions; that would violate their sovereignty.

Sovereignty

Outline the concepts of sphere sovereignty and subsidiarity and guide students in a discussion of the concepts' strengths and weaknesses.

Why do even conservatives who are not Protestants or Catholics tend to like these theories? *They aim to keep government overreach in check.*

Which of these systems would likely be more effective in helping limit government power? *Sphere sovereignty, because it assumes numerous parallel sovereign spheres, whereas the subsidiarity principle teaches that all entities, other than the church, lie under government authority.*

What are some weaknesses of sphere sovereignty? *It is sometimes difficult to determine the different spheres and to resolve when they do and do not overlap.*

Activity 5: Chapter Review

Use this activity to help the students prepare for the chapter test.

Subsidiarity

Nineteenth-century Roman Catholics developed a similar, though hierarchical, view to sphere sovereignty. God, church, and state were at the top; "intermediary institutions," such as families, businesses, and schools were next; and individuals were on the third level. Within this structure the Roman Catholics enunciated the principle of subsidiarity that says it is wrong for entities higher in the hierarchy to do for lower entities what the lower entities can do for themselves. So the government should not do what individuals, community groups, or businesses can do for themselves.

A number of non-Catholic conservatives have embraced the terms "intermediary institutions" and the subsidiarity principle while not accepting all Catholic teaching regarding the hierarchy of society.

Second, most federal agencies share their functions with related agencies in state and local governments. Some federal agencies, such as the Postal Service, deal directly with the people, but others, such as those associated with education or housing, work primarily with state agencies.

Third, Americans exhibit an interest in preserving and even demanding their rights—an interest fueled by the political and social movements of the 1960s. Lawsuits and various political actions have made personal rights a central focus. American government agencies receive greater public scrutiny, with more potential court challenges, than agencies in almost any other nation.

Fourth, the American bureaucracy has a different range and style from other bureaucracies. Most governments in western Europe are socialistic to a degree and own, operate, or strictly regulate large parts of their countries' economies. Though not a socialist society, the US government does extensively regulate privately owned enterprises.

Achievements

Technological advances such as developing the atomic bomb, which brought a swift end to World War II, and landing Americans on the moon were the work of federal agencies and their bureaucracies. In addition, groups within the bureaucracy provide numerous consumer services. Each year, the US Postal Service handles millions of letters and packages efficiently. Though Americans complain when their mail gets delivered to the wrong address or when the sorting machines mutilate their magazines, America still has one of the most efficient postal systems in the world.

The interstate highway system, a bureaucratic effort, is the largest road system in the world. The bureaucracy also operates the Social Security Administration, which distributes retirement benefits to millions of Americans. And federal agencies are involved in consumer protection through agencies such as the Consumer Product Safety Commission and the National Highway Traffic Safety Administration.

In 1971, the Apollo 15 mission landed Americans on the moon for the fourth time.

We often overlook the fact that every day millions of bureaucrats work hard and faithfully in their responsibilities. Clearly, the bureaucracy is a necessary part of modern American government.

Section Review

1–4. Summarize four reasons why the bureaucracy is sometimes called the fourth branch of government.

5. Describe how Congress uses the Government Accountability Office to check the federal bureaucracy.

6–7. Name two ways in which the president can restrict bureaucratic power.

★ What are the advantages and disadvantages of the Freedom of Information Act (FOIA)?

★ List seven categories of bureaucratic problems. Which do you think is the worst? Explain your answer.

Section Review Answers

1–4. Size: The bureaucracy is the largest segment of the national government. Skills: bureaucrats, partly because of their expertise, have much influence within the government. Separation of powers: Bureaucracy tends to increase its independence by taking advantage of the separation of powers between the major branches of government. Desire for security: The bureaucracy seeks to control

its internal affairs and sometimes hides details regarding bunglings. (pp. 294–95)

5. It can authorize the GAO to audit an agency's finances and monitor its activities. It can also request public hearings about the agency's programs. (pp. 295–96)

6–7. by reorganizing parts of the bureaucracy which might eliminate jobs; by appointing an investigative task force (p. 299)

★ Having access to information dealing with bureaucratic activities permits concerned citizens to more effectively challenge the government and have greater control over its work. It can be a helpful tool in restricting bureaucracy. However, there are dangers as well. Someone could try to acquire and exploit sensitive information about national security by using the FOIA. Information about medical records and law enforcement activities may be shared that could cause harm to individuals or investigations. Consequently, some information can be redacted (blacked out). This can make some documents meaningless.

★ Bureaucratic problems fall under the categories of waste, conflict, duplication, red tape, vague goals, obscure bureaucratic language, and resistance to change. Students will provide varying answers for the second part of the question.

Making Connections

1. Explain the relationship between delegation and the federal bureaucracy.

2. What is the connection between Exodus 18 and the idea of bureaucracy?

3–5. The bureaucracy in the executive branch is organized like a pyramid. At the top is the president. What are the other three levels of that pyramid?

6–9. Originally, there were four cabinet departments. List them.

10–12. Many presidents have attempted to improve or reform the federal bureaucracy. Summarize the efforts of Presidents Nixon, Reagan, and Clinton that are noted in this chapter.

Developing Civics Skills

1. What legitimate complaints would you make about the federal bureaucracy, and what would you do to correct the problems you see?

2. Based on your experience at the Department of Motor Vehicles (or a similarly named agency that handles driver's licenses and/or purchase of vehicle tags), suggest five improvements that could be implemented to make this state-level bureaucracy more efficient.

Thinking Critically

1. Does the existence of a bureaucracy threaten the separation of powers in the federal government? Support your answer.

2. Read the quote from *The Federalist* No. 51 shown in the margin on page 295. Explain the idea the author is expressing.

Living as a Christian Citizen

1. Defend the concept that both laws grounded in God's revelation and bureaucrats who are upright, moral people are necessary for just government.

2. Some unnecessary bureaucratic growth arises from selfishness on the part of government officials. List some examples where this is true.

People, Places, and Things to Remember

bureaucracy
bureaucrats
delegation
civil service
Pendleton Act
merit
Executive Office of the President (EOP)
White House staff
chief of staff
press secretary
West Wing
East Wing
cabinet
secretary
Transportation Security Administration (TSA)
statutory law
administrative law
clients
standard operating procedures
fourth branch
oversight
appropriations
Government Accountability Office (GAO)
Freedom of Information Act (FOIA)
Sunshine Act
waste
red tape
bureaucratese

THE FEDERAL BUREAUCRACY • 301

---

government through his National Performance Review. (pp. 295–99)

Developing Civics Skills

1. Complaints might involve abuse of power, confusing regulations and jargon, red tape, inefficiency, rudeness, delays, and waste. Answers to the second part may mention that citizens can elect officials who want to improve bureaucratic procedures, expect bureaucratic due process for any wrongdoing, access information through the FOIA, and participate in meetings held by bureaucrats. (pp. 295–98)

2. Answers may include improvements such as tracking the number of people who visit the Department of Motor Vehicles (or similar agencies) at certain times to determine how many staff members are needed to process matters quickly. Allowing customers to rate the friendliness and efficiency of the clerks would create an incentive for better service.

Thinking Critically

1. The federal bureaucracy assumes the characteristics and powers of all three branches and can undermine checks and balances. In addition, bureaucratic powers are frequently derived from a broad interpretation of the Constitution.

2. Madison argues that although government must have the power to control those it governs, the government itself must be controlled.

Living as a Christian Citizen

1. Law, to be just, must be based on basic moral realities. Christians recognize that God's revelation is the only true moral norm. But just laws alone do not make a just government. Those who enforce the law must also be moral and trustworthy themselves. Exodus 18:13–26 mentions many of these principles.

2. Unnecessary bureaucratic growth can happen when competing departments, in seeking to protect their domains, duplicate one another's work. Also, growth occurs in unnecessary spending to avoid unwanted budget cuts. In these situations the issue is selfishness—failure to heed the second-greatest commandment (Matt. 22:37–39).

Chapter Review Answers

Making Connections

1. Delegation involves committing a task or power to another. Managing the executive branch is too much for the president to handle alone, so much is delegated to the bureaucracy. (p. 275)

2. In Exodus 18, Moses is advised to delegate some of his responsibility for ensuring justice in Israel to others because he cannot handle the task alone. Acting on this advice, Moses creates a small bureaucracy. (p. 275)

3–5. Executive Office of the President (EOP); the cabinet; independent agencies (pp. 280–89)

6–9. Departments of State, Treasury, Defense (War), and Justice (pp. 283–86)

10–12. President Nixon replaced the old Bureau of the Budget with the Office of Management and Budget to gain greater control over the budget and policy decisions. Nixon also placed appointees in lower-level bureaucratic positions to increase the likelihood of action on his policies. President Reagan used a task force to investigate government regulations, thereby substantially reducing the regulations and the operating costs of agencies. Reagan also appointed the Grace Commission to investigate federal agencies. President Clinton sought to streamline

FOREIGN POLICY

13

My policy has been, and will continue to be, . . . to be upon friendly terms with, but independent of, all the nations of the earth.

—George Washington

US Secretary of State Mike Pompeo with the vice foreign minister of Vietnam in July 2018

I. Foreign Policy Goals

II. Foreign Policy Development

III. Policymakers

IV. Policy Methods

V. Challenges Abroad

BIG IDEAS

1. What are America's foreign policy goals?
2. What changes in American foreign policy have occurred throughout history?
3. How similar and different are the roles of various individuals and groups involved in the implementation of foreign policy?
4. How effective are the different methods for administering foreign policy?
5. What challenges face US security?

Red carpet, crisp uniforms, and a brass band provide an impressive backdrop as the president of the United States welcomes a visiting head of state to the White House. In Riyadh, Saudi Arabia, an Arab businessman checks the Pepsi dispenser at his Kentucky Fried Chicken (KFC) franchise. Over a dry California lakebed, an air force test pilot soars upward as he pulls back on the stick of an experimental aircraft. From his office near Washington, DC, a federal agent works feverishly to track an internet virus originating somewhere in the Far East. In another government office, a clerk prepares to issue a passport to an American citizen who is going to a foreign mission field and to issue another to an American businessman going to his company's headquarters in Europe. All these events reflect some aspect of American foreign policy.

I. Foreign Policy Goals

Despite changes in political leadership, advances in military technology, and turmoil in places around the globe, certain basic goals remain central to American **foreign policy**: national security, alliance security, international stability, and economic development.

Although the goals remain largely the same, the means of achieving them change. For example, during the Cold War (1945–91), the United States countered attempts by the Soviet Union to spread communism throughout the world; but after the collapse of the Soviet Empire and the rise of global terrorism, the United States sought to make Russia, the Soviet Union's largest successor state, an ally. Likewise, before the Great Depression, the United States believed that its economic interests were best served by maintaining high tariffs; but later in the century, the United States helped form the General Agreement on Tariffs and Trade (GATT) and its successor, the World Trade Organization (WTO). Both groups promoted reduction, or elimination, of tariffs. In each case, the US government pursued a foreign policy that its leaders perceived to be in the nation's best interest at that time.

National Security

A primary goal of foreign policy is **national security** (protecting the nation and its citizens and property abroad). This aligns with one of the biblical purposes of government—to provide national defense and public safety for a nation's citizens.

American security was rarely threatened in the nineteenth century. After winning its independence, the United States experienced a foreign invasion only during the War of 1812. Sheltered by two oceans, flanked by weak neighbors, and guided by a policy of isolation from turbulent Europe, America faced few challenges to its safety.

But beginning with World War II, threats increasingly arose against American security. Because of increased technology in air and naval warfare, the two oceans on each side of the country no longer provided essential insulation from foreign threat. After the Japanese attack on Pearl Harbor in December 1941, the United States shifted decisively from isolationism to internationalism. And concern about national security only deepened during the Cold War. In response to the Soviet nuclear threat, the United States maintained a large peacetime military

The Yom Kippur War

In 1973, Egypt and Syria (helped by other Arab nations) launched surprise attacks against Israel on that nation's holiest day, Yom Kippur. During the conflict, Russia supplied the Arab nations—and the United States supplied Israel—with munitions and intelligence. In response to the United States' action, the Organization of Petroleum Exporting Countries (OPEC) instituted an oil embargo against the United States and raised prices by 70 percent for America's allies in Western Europe. The economic impact was immediate and resulted in several legislative measures in the United States, including approval for the construction of the trans-Alaskan oil pipeline. The Yom Kippur War demonstrates the impact that foreign instability can have on the United States.

Seeking Peace in the Middle East

As noted in the text, every president since Harry Truman has been forced to deal with conflict and uncertainties in the Middle East. Optimists hoped that the Camp David Accords would hasten an end to the problems between Israel, its Arab neighbors, and other Muslim nations in the Persian Gulf region. But conflicts continued. President Reagan's attempt to restore peace in Beirut in 1983 led to the bombing of the US Marines' barracks there. George H. W. Bush engaged in a war with Iraq. Bill Clinton had trouble with the Libyan leader, Muammar al-Qaddafi, and was forced to deal with various terrorist incidents in the region. George W. Bush responded to terrorist attacks by invading Afghanistan and fighting Iraq again. The Obama and Trump administrations also faced significant challenges in the region.

force, sought to ease tensions diplomatically, and fought "limited wars" against communism in Korea, Vietnam, and Central America. Even after the fall of the Soviet Union in 1991, maintaining national security in America continued to be a costly necessity because of the growth of international terrorism.

Alliance Security

One way for the US government to protect America is to support its allies abroad. Such support might involve diplomatic cooperation, economic assistance, or military intervention. For instance, twice in the twentieth century the United States fought beside its friends in Europe.

Leaders of NATO countries meeting in Belgium

Sometimes support for allied nations is solidified by a formal **alliance** (a treaty that unites its participants in a common cause). Military alliances often include a collective security, or mutual defense, pact, promising that an attack on one member will be treated as an attack on all. Following World War II, the United States helped form the North Atlantic Treaty Organization (NATO) to present a united front against the Soviet Union and its satellite states. Even today, NATO remains a significant part of US foreign policy.

International Stability

Another method of protecting American security is to encourage international stability. The United States has often taken the lead in trying to end war or threats of war by diplomacy. Given the modern interdependence of nations, cooling global hot spots to prevent violence from spreading to other areas has become a foreign policy objective. The United States promotes international stability through direct diplomacy by acting as a diplomatic intermediary between hostile nations and by working through international organizations, such as the United Nations (UN).

President Clinton (center) meeting with the prime minister of Israel and an Arab leader in 1993

For instance, the United States has long tried to promote stability in the oil-rich Middle East, where the United States has important economic interests. The United States has close ties with Israel, a nation surrounded by Arab countries, some of which are openly hostile to their neighbor. But the United States has also tried to maintain good relations with those Arab nations. During the 1973 Yom Kippur War, Arab nations halted oil shipments to the United States and other nations that supported Israel in its war with Egypt, Syria, and other Arab states. Through skillful diplomacy, Secretary of State Henry Kissinger forged a shaky peace between Israel, Egypt, and Syria that resulted in the lifting of the oil embargo. In 1978 President Carter brought the leaders of Israel and Egypt together to build a "framework for peace" in the Middle East. The result was the Camp David Accords, by which the Israelis made territorial concessions while the Egyptians recognized Israel as a nation.

Securing Security

Discuss the connection between alliance security and national security. You might emphasize, for example, that many of our allies are absolutely dependent on imported oil (e.g., Western Europe imports over 85 percent, and Japan imports almost all its oil). Because a complete elimination of oil to our allies would literally shut down those countries, it was in the interest of the United States to keep the sea-lanes open with its large fleet during the "tanker war" between Iraq and Iran (1980–88). (The conflict was called a tanker war because Iraq and Iran attacked oil tankers headed to and from each other's ports.)

Nevertheless, all attempts at making peace in the Middle East have been limited at best. Every president since Harry Truman (who recognized the statehood of Israel) has faced his own Middle East crisis, and each has had to nurture—or try to resuscitate—the peace process.

The search for lasting peace is often elusive. Greed, hatred, and selfishness provoke conflicts and bar the way to their resolution. Nevertheless, the Christian diplomat should remember Jesus' words: "Blessed are the peacemakers." Though such a diplomat's work can only anticipate the peace that Christ's return to earth will bring, his efforts can provide relief for many people and, in some cases, allow new openings for the gospel.

Economic Development

Economic development is another important part of American foreign policy. US goals are to stimulate economic expansion in developing nations (sometimes called Third World countries) and thereby help them establish the markets necessary for capitalist economies and, consequently, increased political freedom. Although private trade and investment abroad have stimulated most foreign economic development, the US government has also given direct assistance to countries stricken by war, famine, and natural disasters. Relief (usually given in the form of American goods) has been provided to millions abroad. For instance, after World War II, the United States responded to European devastation with the **Marshall Plan**. From 1948 to 1951, that program supplied billions of dollars to western Europe to rebuild shattered economies and bolster democracy.

The Marshall Plan shipped goods and provided money to western Europe.

The Marshall Plan well illustrated an important goal of American economic aid—building self-sustaining economies rather than encouraging dependence on American dollars. After helping rebuild Europe and Japan, America sent assistance to underdeveloped nations in Asia, Africa, and Latin America, though usually with fewer positive results.

Section Review

1–4. What are the four basic goals of American foreign policy?

5. Why did concern for national security increase during the Cold War?

6. After the collapse of the Soviet Union, why was national security still an important concern?

7. How has the growing interdependence of nations affected foreign policy?

★ What is the relationship between foreign policy and the biblical purposes of government?

★ What are the potential positive effects of economic development for both the receiving nation and the donor country? In your opinion, which country benefits more?

Describe the changes in America's foreign policy from 1790 to the present.

Washington's Isolationism

President Washington emphasized independence. He believed that America should welcome strong trade ties with Europe but avoid Old World politics. As he said, "The great rule of conduct for us in regard to foreign nations is in extending our commercial relations, to have with them as little *political* connection as possible." (emphasis added)

To the Shores of Tripoli

For years the kingdoms of the Barbary Coast (Morocco, Algiers, Tripoli, and Tunisia) demanded tribute for the safe passage of ships. If demands were not met, the kingdoms would capture ships, holding crews for ransom or selling them into slavery. The United States paid the tribute for a decade, but when Algiers demanded higher tributes, Congress sent the navy to the Mediterranean to protect American shipping. The US Navy was successful in this venture, securing free passage for US shipping and gaining international respect for the young country. Marines also played a significant role, which is celebrated in the second line of their hymn— "to the shores of Tripoli."

Guiding Question

How has American foreign policy changed from 1790 to the present?

II. Foreign Policy Development

Isolation: 1790–1890

The dominant theme of foreign policy during America's first century was **isolationism**, a plan first formulated during the Washington administration. Alexander Hamilton, the first secretary of the treasury, urged strong ties with Great Britain, whereas Thomas Jefferson, the first secretary of state, advocated a pro-French policy. George Washington, however, believed that America's fortunes should not be tied to Europe; he insisted that America should be tied to *no* other nation.

Although *isolationism* is the term generally used to characterize nineteenth-century American foreign policy, the expression is somewhat misleading. The United States did not eliminate foreign contacts. The fledgling nation fought one undeclared naval war with France over freedom of the seas and another against Muslim pirates in the Mediterranean. It declared war on Britain, in what became known as the War of 1812, partly because the British were forcing American sailors to serve in their navy and partly because Britain did not allow free use of the seas. In addition, it established and maintained a brisk foreign trade. Throughout the nineteenth century, the United States established strong commercial ties in Europe, Africa, and Asia. In 1853 Commodore Matthew Perry negotiated the first treaty between Japan and a Western nation. On the heels of these developments, American missionaries took the gospel to China, and Adoniram Judson became the first to preach the gospel in Burma.

America's nineteenth-century policy of isolation can be best described as America's effort to preserve its independence while it busied itself with continental expansion. One of the clearest assertions of this policy was the **Monroe Doctrine**; this statement was issued in 1823 in response to the fear that Euro-

Presidential Thoughts About Isolation

"Europe has a set of primary interests which to us have none; or a very remote relation. Hence she must be engaged in frequent controversies, the causes of which are essentially foreign to our concerns. . . . Our detached and distant situation invites and enables us to pursue a different course. . . . It is our true policy to steer clear of permanent alliances, with any portion of the foreign world. . . . [But] we may safely trust to temporary alliances for extraordinary emergencies."
—*George Washington, Farewell Address (September 1796)*

George Washington

Thomas Jefferson

James Monroe

"[The United States should pursue] peace, commerce, and honest friendship with all nations, entangling alliances with none."
—*Thomas Jefferson, First Inaugural Address (March 1801)*

"We owe it, therefore, to candor and to the amicable relations existing between the United States and . . . [European countries] to declare that we should consider any attempt on their part to extend their system to any portion of this hemisphere as dangerous to our peace and safety."
—*James Monroe, Monroe Doctrine (December 1823)*

Loving Neighboring Nations

In addition to the portion of George Washington's Farewell Address quoted in the student text above, Washington offered the following advice:

Observe good faith and justice towards all nations; cultivate peace and harmony with all. Religion and morality enjoin this conduct; and can it be, that good policy does not equally enjoin it? It will be worthy of a free, enlightened, and at no distant period, a great nation, to give to mankind the magnanimous and too novel example of a people *always guided by an exalted justice and benevolence.* (emphasis added)

Discuss how a government can exemplify a "people always guided by an exalted justice and benevolence." What would this involve (e.g., no exploitation or arm twisting), and how could it magnify God in the eyes of the world? Ask the students about the role of the golden rule and the second-greatest commandment ("thou shalt love thy neighbour as thyself"). How should these two laws affect our relationships with other nations?

Isolationist for a Reason

Discuss the historical and geographic context of isolationist policies during the Washington and Jefferson administrations. For example, the United States had a weak military and was preoccupied with westward expansion, while Europe was embroiled in a series of wars between France and shifting coalitions led by Great Britain.

peans might threaten the United States by reasserting control over weak Latin American states that had recently declared independence from Spain.

The Monroe Doctrine restated a long-standing policy of opposition to any further European presence in the Western Hemisphere, although at the time the doctrine was mostly brash talk from a nation whose capital had been burned by British troops only nine years earlier. Fortunately, the British themselves had a trading interest in a free Latin America and effectively defended the Monroe Doctrine with their own navy.

As the United States grew stronger, so did the Monroe Doctrine. Several presidents threatened European countries with military force because of their violations of the doctrine. For example, Kennedy invoked the Monroe Doctrine in 1962 when he opposed a Soviet attempt to install missiles in Cuba. The policy was also used in the 1980s to justify arming an anti-Communist army fighting Nicaragua's Soviet- and Cuban-backed regime.

Expansion: 1890–1910

By the last decade of the nineteenth century, the United States was an emerging force in the world community and had an important manufacturing sector. With the continental frontier now nearly tamed, the United States abandoned isolationism for both an increased participation in international commerce and a craving for colonies. One excuse for the latter was that America's new steam-powered navy needed stations in the Pacific and the Caribbean where ships could refuel (with coal). In 1898 the United States annexed the Hawaiian Islands and took some of Spain's

Having expanded with new territories, Uncle Sam declines a dose of antiexpansionist policy "cure" while President McKinley (right) fits him for larger clothes.

Pacific and Caribbean holdings—the Philippines, Guam, and Puerto Rico. The following year, the United States acquired some of the Samoan Islands as well as Wake Island. It also announced the Open Door Policy (that is, that all nations should have equal access to Chinese ports) in an attempt to preserve its markets in China. As the nineteenth century closed, the United States had emerged as a major world power.

Vacillation and Uncertainty: 1910–40

The late nineteenth and early twentieth centuries had been the height of **imperialism** (the extension of power by one country over another people or country). America's involvement in empire-building was intense but short-lived. Expansionism declined as domestic concerns reasserted themselves. Yet because it was now a world power, the United States had embarked on a course of global involvement from which it could not turn back. Although Woodrow Wilson won reelection in 1916 using the slogan "He kept us out of war," America entered World War I the following year.

Missionaries and Foreign Policy

Adoniram Judson was America's first missionary to Burma (present-day Myanmar). Before his arrival, others (including Felix Carey, the oldest son of missionary William Carey) took the gospel to the Burmese.

Judson's missionary work was intertwined with foreign affairs. In his early years as a missionary, Judson spent a great deal of time seeking an edict of religious toleration from Burma. Later, when Burma and Great Britain went to war, the Burmese put him in prison. He tried to communicate that he was American, not British, but to little avail. After the war, Judson was tasked to serve as a translator between the British and the Burmese since he knew both languages. The British retained some Burmese territory and permitted Judson to establish his mission work in that area.

Today, missionaries are still affected by the foreign policy of their nations and of the nations to which they minister. For example, American missionaries have very little access to nations such as Iran or North Korea, but they have much more access to South Korea. Also, Americans' reputation abroad can affect how the gospel is received when it is presented by American missionaries.

Growth of Missionary Activity

Discuss the rapid growth of missionary activity during the early years of the nineteenth century. In Britain it sprang from the Wesleyan revival and in America, from the Second Great Awakening.

Discuss also the influence of missionaries today. How do they affect our relationships with other countries? What impact do missionaries have on the attitudes, beliefs, and perceptions of ordinary citizens in foreign countries?

Historical Perspective

Direct the students to read Woodrow Wilson's second inaugural address. Instruct them to examine Wilson's statements concerning the war in Europe, noting his desire to avoid taking part in the war.

Wilson the isolationist became Wilson the internationalist and the architect of the League of Nations, an organization that he believed would inaugurate an era of world peace. Yet, for all Wilson's dreams and dedicated efforts to see the United States join the organization, isolationist feeling remained strong enough for the US Senate to reject American membership in the League.

While Adolf Hitler was rebuilding the German war machine during the 1930s, the United States was passing neutrality legislation in a naïve attempt to avoid another European conflict. By 1940, Hitler had conquered most of Europe,

Japanese attack on Pearl Harbor

and Britain stood alone against him. During the presidential campaign of that year, both the incumbent Franklin Roosevelt and the challenger Wendell Willkie opposed involvement in the war. In October, Roosevelt declared, "I have said this before, but I shall say it again and again and again: Your boys are not going to be sent into any foreign wars." However, within fourteen months America found it had no choice but to enter World War II.

Obligation: 1941–91

The Japanese attack on Pearl Harbor, on December 7, 1941, helped propel the United States to become a superpower. The United States poured men and materiel (the equipment and supplies of a military force) into the effort to liberate the Pacific from the Japanese; at the same time, it subsidized battered Allies—Britain, France, and the Soviet Union—in an effort to destroy the German war machine in Europe.

Unfortunately, along with German defeat came Soviet conquest of Eastern Europe. By 1949 the Chinese mainland and the northern part of Korea had also fallen to Communist tyranny. Against the threat of expanding communism, isolation was not only dangerous but also impossible.

Hostilities between the two superpowers—the United States and the Soviet Union—and their allies became known as the **Cold War**. Three strategies shaped American foreign policy during this period. The first was **nuclear deterrence**, discouraging Soviet aggression by building a nuclear arsenal so large that the Soviets faced massive retaliation if they attacked the United States or its allies. As the Russians responded with their own nuclear buildup, this strategy gave way to a second one—**mutual assured destruction** (known by its appropriate acronym **MAD**). This policy was based on the idea that the superpowers would refrain from attacking each other because of the certainty that each would be destroyed.

A third US foreign policy strategy was **containment**, confronting the Communists with counterforce whenever they tried to expand their empire. At times, the policy of containment turned the Cold War into hot wars, as occurred in Korea and Vietnam.

A nuclear missile test launched from a US submarine during the Cold War

League of Nations

Ask students to read the Covenant of the League of Nations, noting the purpose for that body, its organization, and its obligations. The organization's purposes were to "promote international cooperation and to achieve international peace and security" by abolishing war, promoting open relations between nations, establishing international law, and maintaining "justice and a scrupulous respect for all treaty obligations."

Guide a discussion about Italy's invasion of Ethiopia in 1935. Both nations were members of the League of Nations, but the organization took little real action against Italy for its conquest of Ethiopia. Discuss what this revealed about the League of Nations' tendencies.

But America's loss in Vietnam dealt a blow to the idea of containment. North Vietnam, supported by the Soviets and Communist Chinese, forced the American military into a long and costly struggle in which fifty-eight thousand Americans died in an effort to protect the region from Communist domination. The last American troops withdrew in 1973, and South Vietnam fell to the Communists two years later. The "domino theory" was proved partly true when Laos and Cambodia also fell to Communists soon afterward. (The domino theory stated that if one Southeast Asian country were to fall to communism, other neighboring countries, too, would soon fall.)

Ronald Reagan's election to the presidency in 1980 was a significant event in the US struggle against the Russians and their allies. Reagan openly dubbed the Soviet Union an "evil empire" and rebuilt the American military to a level that the Soviet economy could not match. Furthermore, Reagan promised to roll back communism by supporting anti-Communist insurgents abroad. Weakened by its pathetic economy and by its own "Vietnam" in Afghanistan, the Soviet Empire collapsed soon after the fall of the Berlin Wall in 1989. In 1991 the Soviet Union disintegrated into fifteen separate nations.

Transition: 1991 to the Present

The relative peace of the 1990s strengthened economic growth around the world. The former Communist nations and developing nations sought to integrate into a world economy.

The United States now stood alone as the world's only superpower. Instead of facing a single threat from the Russians, it encountered smaller, more unpredictable dangers from nearly every part of the globe. The United States moved cautiously in assessing its new role, struggling to maintain the peace while also trying to avoid becoming the world's policeman. But it found itself involved in more and more police actions.

After Iraqi dictator Saddam Hussein invaded Kuwait and threatened to manipulate a sizable percentage of the world's known oil reserves, a multinational coalition of forces led by the United States defeated the Iraqis in the 1991 Persian Gulf War. Nevertheless, because the United States feared offending its allies and suffering more casualties, Saddam Hussein was allowed to remain in power. In that decade, American forces were also engaged in peacekeeping operations in the conflicts of the Balkans, Somalia, and Haiti.

US helicopters during the Vietnam War

Cold War

Cold war refers to conflict that consists of threats, propaganda, subversion, enormous military expenditures, and political posturing. Occasionally, for example in Korea and Vietnam, it expands into actual military conflict.

Many people attribute the term *cold war* to Bernard Baruch, an American millionaire and statesman of the early 1900s. He is said to have coined the term in a congressional debate in 1947. But the *Oxford English Dictionary* credits British author George Orwell (who wrote *Animal Farm* and *1984*) as the first author to pen *cold war* in English. Orwell used the term in an article entitled "You and the Atomic Bomb," published in the *Tribune* on October 19, 1945. In that article, he argued that the atomic bomb would take power away from the public and further consolidate the power of governments, which would become "at once unconquerable and in a permanent state of 'cold war.'" In America, writer Walter Lippman popularized the term in his series of articles entitled The Cold War.

Activity 2: Foreign Policy Development

In this activity the students use recognition and application skills as they list specific events that developed foreign policy during certain periods in US history and identify the goals of each policy.

The Patriot Act

In late October 2001, within weeks of the attacks on the World Trade Center and the Pentagon, Congress passed and President George W. Bush signed the Patriot Act. Major provisions of the legislation included the following:

1. It made information sharing among law-enforcement agencies easier.

2. It made knowingly harboring a terrorist illegal.

3. It authorized "roving wiretaps" to allow easier surveillance of terrorists' cell-phone communications.

4. It allowed the government to detain foreign nationals suspected of terrorism for up to seven days without charging them.

5. It gave the government greater subpoena power over the email records of suspected terrorists.

6. It tripled the number of border guards on the US-Canada border.

7. It eliminated the statute of limitations for most egregious terrorist acts.

Critics of the law say that some provisions are too broadly written. They claim the power given to government agencies can be used to curtail civil liberties of American citizens.

US Marines topple a statue of Saddam Hussein in Iraq (April 2003).

Osama bin Laden, leader of al-Qaeda until he was killed by US troops in May 2011

On September 11, 2001, however, American optimism about national security in the post–Cold War world evaporated when Muslim terrorists seized four planes and killed more than three thousand people in attacks on the World Trade Center and the Pentagon. The following month, President George W. Bush sent troops to Afghanistan to eliminate the leaders of **al-Qaeda**, the terrorist group responsible for the attacks, and to remove the Taliban (the Muslim extremist regime that controlled the nation's government) from power. In March 2003, American troops, aided by military forces from Britain and several other nations, attacked Iraq. This was deemed part of the continued war on terrorism. Within weeks, Saddam Hussein was overthrown.

As the second decade of the twenty-first century began, protecting the United States from foreign threats remained as complicated as ever. US forces pulled out of Iraq in December 2011, and the United States began a troop reduction in Afghanistan in 2012. Attempts to counter terrorism on a grand scale prompted questions about the balance between national security and individual liberty at home and the limits to which the United States should, or could, exercise its superpower status abroad.

In July 2015, the Obama administration reached a controversial agreement with Iran that was supported by several other major nations. As part of the deal, Iran promised to not develop nuclear weapons. In May 2018, President Trump withdrew the United States from the accord after citing concerns that Iran was not being monitored effectively and the agreement could not ensure a nuclear-free Iran.

Tensions between America and North Korea worsened as their dictator, Kim Jong-un, continued his development of nuclear weapons. At meetings in June 2018 and February 2019, President Trump and the North Korean leader discussed peaceful resolutions to the problems between the two nations.

Section Review

1. Explain how the Monroe Doctrine demonstrated isolationism.

2–7. List six areas the United States acquired during the 1890s.

8. Explain why the period from 1910 to 1940 is referred to as a time of vacillation in American foreign policy.

9–11. Explain the three strategies that shaped US foreign policy during the Cold War.

12. What was the greatest blow to the idea of containment?

★ How did the terrorist attacks of September 11, 2001, affect American foreign policy? Evaluate the success of the actions taken after the 9/11 attacks.

Osama bin Laden

The apprehension of bin Laden took ten years. Discuss why that was not accomplished earlier. Also, discuss the ethical decisions involved in killing him.

Section Review Answers

1. The Monroe Doctrine sought to preserve American independence (isolationism) by ensuring that other countries were not involved in the affairs of the Western Hemisphere. (pp. 306–7)

2–7. the Hawaiian Islands, the Philippines, Guam, Puerto Rico, some of the Samoan Islands, and Wake Island (p. 307)

8. During this period, America moved between a policy of isolation (which it followed before and after World War I) and a policy of global involvement (which it followed during the world wars). (pp. 307–8)

9–11. The three strategies that shaped US foreign policy during the Cold War were nuclear deterrence (discouraging Soviet aggression by building a nuclear arsenal so large that the Soviets faced massive retaliation if they attacked the United States or its allies), mutual assured destruction (also called MAD, this policy was based on the idea that the superpowers would refrain from attacking each other because of the certainty that each would be destroyed), and containment (confronting the Communists with counterforce whenever they tried to expand their empire). (p. 308)

12. the fall of South Vietnam to communism (p. 309)

★ The attacks precipitated two foreign wars (in Afghanistan and Iraq). Those wars had mixed results. The Taliban was driven out of Afghanistan temporarily, but it has retaken control of some areas. The war in Iraq removed Saddam Hussein from power, but infighting between Muslim factions continues, and US prestige in the region has suffered.

III. Policymakers

The President

The president occupies center stage in the making of American foreign policy because of the powers granted to him by the Constitution and those he has acquired by tradition. In his role as commander in chief, the president heads the military forces of the United States. In his roles as chief diplomat and chief executive, he represents the country abroad and initiates treaties and agreements with foreign leaders. He also appoints the secretaries of state and defense (the heads of the departments that deal most directly with foreign policy) as well as the diplomatic corps.

Given the extent of the president's power, it is hardly surprising that presidents' personalities and interests have shaped foreign policy. For instance, Theodore Roosevelt enjoyed the power of the presidency as few other chief executives have, and his foreign policy reflected his exciting and aggressive nature. He ordered American troops to the Dominican Republic to collect that country's debts to European investors. Earlier, after the Colombian government tried to hike the price of a right of way for an isthmian canal, Roosevelt provided military assistance for a revolution that led to the creation of the nation of Panama. The new government then reached an agreement with the United States by which a canal could be built. When Roosevelt sent the American navy—the Great White Fleet—around the world, a group of congressmen threatened to cut its funding. "Very well," replied Roosevelt. "The existing appropriation will carry the Navy halfway around the world, and if Congress chooses to leave it on the other side, all right."

Roosevelt's initiatives stimulated national pride and deterred potential enemies of the United States, at least temporarily. But Roosevelt's foreign policy resulted in some unintended consequences. Among those was the growing resentment among Latin American nations of American power.

The Foreign Policy Bureaucracy

Advisors within the executive branch help the president shape and implement foreign policy. Five agencies and departments are heavily involved in this process.

National Security Council

The **National Security Council (NSC)** supplies information and guidance for the president regarding national security. It has a staff that works at the direction of the **national security advisor**, who is appointed by the president. As noted in the last chapter, when the president meets with this group, regular attendees include the vice president; the national security advisor; the secretaries

President Theodore Roosevelt used US military force to help obtain permission to build a canal through Panama.

Section III Objectives

1. Explain how the president helps shape foreign policy.
2. Describe the work of agencies and departments within the executive branch that are involved in foreign policy.
3. Explain how Congress impacts policy-making for foreign affairs.
4. Analyze media influence on foreign policy.

American Involvement in the Dominican Republic

Theodore Roosevelt sent marines to the Dominican Republic to prevent European interference in the Western Hemisphere. (Some people argue that this action was only a pretense for American involvement in the country.) When asked whether he wanted to annex the country, Roosevelt replied that his desire to annex the Dominican Republic was like the desire a "gorged boa constrictor might have to swallow a porcupine wrong-end-[up]." Nevertheless, marines remained in the Dominican Republic for eight years.

The Great White Fleet

See Chapter 18 in *UNITED STATES HISTORY*, Fifth Edition (BJU Press) for more information about the Great White Fleet.

Making Enemies

While some of the antipathy that other nations have for the United States is due to jealousy or fear, others have such a view because they dislike how America has sometimes dealt with their own or other nations.

Ask the students to consider times the United States wronged other nations in seeking its own interests (e.g., by protecting dictators because they were the enemies of America's enemies). Remind students about the role of the golden rule and the second-greatest commandment. Discuss the government's duty to ensure justice in executing foreign policy. Also mention to students that politics is often a matter of prudence. Sometimes the United States may support an imperfect ruler because the alternative would be worse for Americans and for other nations.

Secretary of State Henry Kissinger

German-born Henry Kissinger received three degrees at Harvard (BA, MA, and PhD), where his 388-page senior thesis precipitated a rule limiting the length of senior theses. Later, he served as national security advisor to Presidents Nixon and Ford from 1969 to 1975 and as secretary of state for those presidents from 1973 to 1977.

Kissinger became a dominant force in American foreign policy during the 1970s. He dealt with China and other foreign dictatorships to secure US interests. In 1973 he was awarded the Nobel Peace Prize for his work in bringing the Vietnam War to an end.

Secretary of State in Line for the Presidency?

Kissinger was born in Germany in 1923 and was not a natural-born citizen of the United States. However, as secretary of state he was fourth in the line of presidential succession (after the vice president, the Speaker of the House, and the president pro tempore of the Senate). But since he did not meet the constitutional requirements of the presidency, he could not have succeeded to that office.

A similar situation occurred when Madeleine Albright served as President Clinton's secretary of state from 1997 to 2001. She, too, was not a natural-born US citizen (she was born in Czechoslovakia in 1937); as a result, she could never have assumed the office of president.

President Trump meeting with some of his national security advisors

Passports

A **passport** is an official document that identifies a traveler and confirms his citizenship. Before the terrorist attacks of September 11, 2001, Canada, Mexico, and many Caribbean countries did not require Americans to carry passports while on short visits. Since that time, they and all other countries require travelers to show passports. In addition, many countries require each traveler to have a **visa**, especially if a visitor plans an extended stay. A visa is an official endorsement of a passport by the government of the country being visited. Visas are usually obtained from foreign consulates in the United States.

The State Department issues passports to US citizens. A prospective traveler applies by completing a form, submitting proof of citizenship and identity, and supplying two identical passport photographs. The length of time a passport is valid depends on how old its owner is when it was issued. If the person is sixteen or older, the passport is valid for ten years; if the person is fifteen or younger, it is good for five years.

of state, defense, energy, and the treasury; the chairman of the Joint Chiefs of Staff (the nation's highest ranking military official); and the director of national intelligence. The chief of staff to the president, counsel for the president, and assistant to the president for economic policy often also attend these meetings. The attorney general and the director of the Office of Management and Budget are invited to attend sessions pertaining to their responsibilities. Heads of other executive departments and agencies attend when needed.

The president normally receives national security briefings daily. During periods of international tension, such as the aftermath of the September 11 attack, the national security advisor and other close advisors, such as the chief of staff, form a crisis management team.

State Department

The Department of State is the oldest and most prestigious cabinet office. Many distinguished individuals have headed the department, including Thomas Jefferson (and five other future presidents), John Marshall, Daniel Webster, and Henry Clay.

The **secretary of state** oversees more than seventy thousand employees, many of whom serve abroad as part of the Foreign Service, maintaining diplomatic relations in more than 180 countries. On the frontline of State Department foreign policy are embassies and consular offices. **Embassies** are government offices or residences that are typically located in foreign capitals. Each is headed by an **ambassador**, who acts as the president's personal representative. The ambassador, a presidential appointee, requires Senate approval. The majority have Foreign Service experience, although a number of posts are awarded as political favors. An ambassador's responsibilities are to keep the US administration informed about affairs in the country to which he is assigned and to protect Americans and American interests within his area of responsibility.

While the United States has just one ambassador and one embassy in each foreign nation, there may be several consular offices, or **consulates**, in larger nations. These are typically located in the main cities of states or provinces, and each is led by a consul.

Consulates and embassies offer legal assistance to traveling Americans and provide immigration advice. In addition, they provide passport

Obtaining a Passport

Many students will not know how to obtain a passport. Use the following steps to help the students learn how to procure their own passports.

1. Applicants must complete an application for a passport. (An application can be obtained from the State Department via the internet.) Make copies so that the students can read the application.
2. Applicants must have proof of US citizenship.
3. Applicants must have proof of their identity.
4. Applicants must have two recent, identical color photographs of themselves (these must be clear two-by-two inch facial shots). These photographs can be made at most photo shops.
5. Applicants must pay appropriate fees.

Passport

Invite students who have a passport to bring it to class. Allow other students to examine the passport and discuss any questions that may arise.

Ambassadors and Embassies

Show a video, or excerpt of one, regarding the work of ambassadors. One such video is *Ambassador: Inside the Embassy* filmed by *National Geographic*.

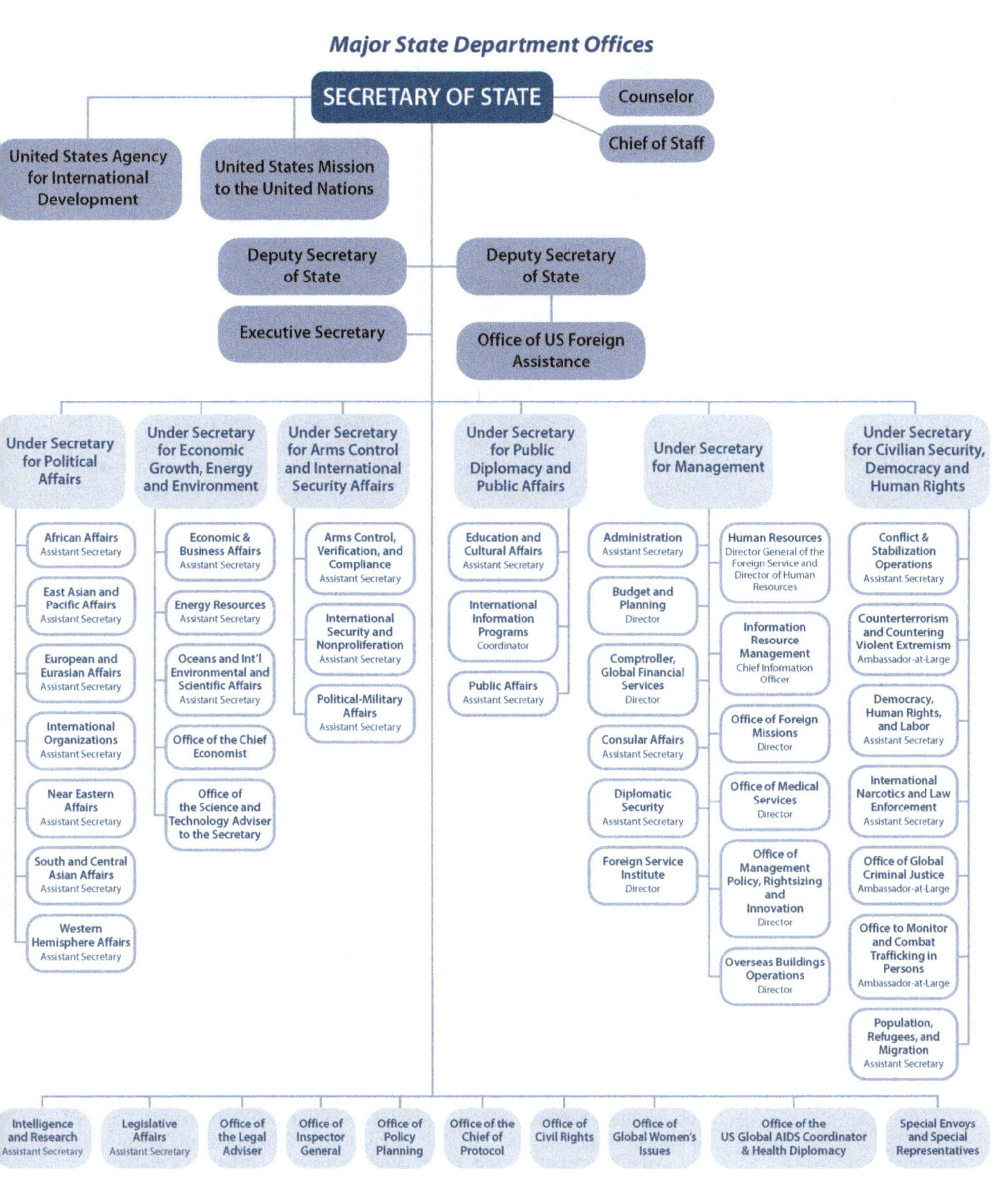

FOREIGN POLICY • 313

Secretaries of State Who Became Presidents

Thomas Jefferson was not only the first secretary of state but also the first secretary of state to become president. Other former secretaries of state who became presidents were James Madison, James Monroe, John Quincy Adams, Martin Van Buren, and James Buchanan. During the first half century or so of our history, the office of secretary of state was viewed almost as a steppingstone to the presidency. More recently, however, holding a state governorship or serving as a US senator has been a better credential for presidential hopefuls.

Secretary of State Condoleezza Rice

Condoleezza Rice was born in Alabama in 1954. She was the only child of a Presbyterian preacher and a teacher. She overcame the racism of the 1950s and 1960s to earn her bachelor's, master's, and doctoral degrees before becoming a professor of political science at Stanford University. She then became the first African American and the first woman to be provost of Stanford. In 2001, Rice became the first woman to be the national security advisor; and in 2005, she became the first black woman to be the secretary of state.

After leaving the State Department in 2009, Rice rejected calls to run for president and instead returned to private life. In 2012, Rice and South Carolina businesswoman Darla Moore became the first female members of the Augusta National Golf Club (home to the Masters Tournament).

State Department Hierarchy

Direct the students to analyze the chart shown above. What general statements can you make from an examination of the chart? What questions does it bring to mind? What do the offices and positions indicate about the priorities of the State Department?

Spying

Embassies often serve as more than a diplomatic arm of government. This was especially true during the Cold War when nations used them to covertly gather information about the country in which the embassy was located.

The Pentagon

Most citizens are somewhat familiar with the Pentagon, but here are a few facts that many probably do not know. The Pentagon, with 6.5 million square feet of space, contains more than two times the floor space of the Empire State Building. More than 25,000 employees work there.

Just one of its five sides would hold the Capitol. It has approximately 100,000 miles of telephone lines, on which 200,000 calls are made a day. The building is just over 77 feet high, and each of the five outside walls is 921 feet long. It contains over 7,700 windows, more than 16,000 light fixtures, nearly 300 restrooms, and almost 700 drinking fountains. The Pentagon site covers nearly 600 acres (29 of which are the building itself and 67 are used for parking).

According to *Infoplease,* the corridors are a total of 17.5 miles long, and there are 131 stairways, 19 escalators, and 13 elevators. A shopping area, numerous snack bars, cafeterias, dining rooms, banks, a subway station, and a bus platform make the Pentagon a "city within a city."

On September 11, 2001, the crashing of American Airlines flight 77 into the complex killed 189 people, including the 64 aboard the aircraft. The crash damaged or destroyed more than 200,000 square feet of the building.

US embassy in Berlin, Germany

assistance to Americans who are residents or visiting the region. They also encourage commercial contacts as well as the exchange of educational and scientific ideas.

Department of Defense

The Defense Department, headed by the **secretary of defense**, is the national government's largest agency. Formed in 1947 when the Department of War and the Department of the Navy were combined, the Department of Defense comprises about 1.3 million men and women in uniform (excluding more than 800,000 National Guard and Reserve forces) and over 700,000 civilian employees. These personnel provide the force necessary to maintain American security.

There are three major levels in the Defense Department's organization. The secretary of defense heads the department. The congressional act that created the department ordered that the secretary be a civilian who has not served in active military duty for at least ten years (in 2008, it was changed to seven years). This provision is intended to reflect the constitutional principle that military power should be subordinate to civilian power. On two occasions, Congress has waived the requirement when approving the president's choice for defense secretary. The first occurred when President Truman named General George C. Marshall to that position in 1950 and the second in 2017 when President Trump appointed retired general James Mattis.

The Founding Fathers were well aware of military tyranny in both history and their contemporary world, and they were determined not to allow the military to play a dominant role in the US government. Some even advocated the extreme position of limiting the entire army to three thousand soldiers. Nevertheless, liberty had to be defended from aggressors without as well as from enemies within. As James Madison wrote in *Federalist* No. 41, the realities of greed and aggression make security against foreign danger a necessity. Therefore, the demands of both a free society and national security were balanced by establishing a military force that could be checked at several points by civilian authority.

The principle of civilian control extends to the second level of the defense organization as well. Assisting the secretary of defense are civilian officials who work at the **Pentagon**, the huge Defense Department headquarters located just outside Washington, DC, in Arlington, Virginia. These civilian officials, including the secretaries of the army, navy, and air force, are joined by top military officers—the **Joint Chiefs of Staff (JCS)**—in helping the secretary of defense shape defense policy. The Joint Chiefs are the highest-ranking officers of the army, navy, air force, marines, and national guard. Membership in this elite group is not based on seniority; rather, the Joint Chiefs are presidential appointees subject to Senate confirmation. At one time, JCS members had command authority over their military branches, but today they serve only as military advisors. The civilian and military officials at this level comprise the Armed Forces Policy Council, the major policymaking and coordinating group of the defense establishment.

Two Arms of Foreign Policy

The **State Department** and the **Defense Department** administer the two arms of American foreign policy—international relations and national security. The department secretaries are usually influential members of the president's cabinet.

Federalist No. 41

In *Federalist* No. 41, James Madison argues in favor of the powers given to the national government in the Constitution. Instruct the students to read the essay and answer the following questions to understand Madison's argument:

1. What issue does *Federalist* No. 41 address? (*the powers given to the national government in the Constitution*)

2. In what two ways does Madison think that the Constitution may be considered? (*[1] in relation to the "sum or quantity of power which it vests in the government, including the restraints imposed on the States" and [2] in relation to the "structure of the government and the distribution of . . . power among its several branches"*)

3. According to Madison, what two important questions must be asked about the powers granted to the national government? (*[1] "whether any part of the powers transferred to the general government be unnecessary or improper" and [2] "whether the entire mass of them be dangerous to the portion of jurisdiction left in the several States"*)

4. According to Madison, what two issues must be considered when power is given to the government? (*[1] "whether such a power [is] necessary to the public good" and [2] how "to guard as effectually as possible against a perversion of the power to the public detriment"*)

5. List the six classes of power delegated to the government. (*[1] "security against foreign danger," [2] "regulation of the intercourse with foreign nations," [3] "maintenance of harmony and proper intercourse among the States," [4] "certain miscellaneous objects of general utility," [5] "restraint of the States from certain injurious acts," and [6] "provisions for giving due efficacy to all these powers"*)

6. According to Madison, under what conditions would it be safe to forgo a standing army? (*"If a federal Constitution could chain the ambition or set bounds to the exertions of all other nations, then indeed might it prudently chain the discretion of its own govern-*

A third level of the Department of Defense comprises the military branches themselves: the army, navy, and air force. The army is the largest branch, operating primarily on land with infantry, artillery, tank, engineering, and chemical-warfare units. The navy, with its fleet of approximately three hundred ships, maintains sea-lanes and, when necessary, delivers troops and firepower to hostile areas. The Marine Corps is part of the navy but functions as a separate military branch. A primary mission of the marines is to secure landing beaches for sea, air, and land operations when invasions take place. The air force, originally part of the army, was reorganized as a separate branch in 1947. The air force maintains both tactical (short-range) and strategic (long-range) aircraft as well as advanced missile systems. Each branch also maintains its own special-operations units (small groups of elite, specially trained people who perform precision missions, often in secret and behind enemy lines). For example, the army has the Rangers, the Green Berets, and Delta Force, while the navy has the SEALs. The air force and marines have special operations groups as well.

Department of Homeland Security

Following the terrorist attacks of September 11, 2001, President George W. Bush responded with the largest reorganization of government since 1947. The new **Department of Homeland Security** addresses a relatively new aspect of foreign relations—terrorist attacks on American soil. The department's responsibilities fall into five major categories: Border and Transportation Security; Emergency Preparedness and Response; Chemical, Biological, Radiological, and Nuclear Countermeasures; Information Analysis; and Infrastructure Protection. Several older government agencies were reassigned to this massive new department, including the Secret Service, the Coast Guard, the Federal Emergency Management Agency (FEMA), and most parts of the Immigration and Naturalization Service (INS).

Central Intelligence Agency

The **Central Intelligence Agency (CIA)** is another important element in the making and implementation of American foreign policy. The CIA is the chief gatherer of intelligence, or information activities, in foreign countries. Intelligence gathering is as old as ancient warfare. For example, according to Numbers 13, Moses sent twelve spies on a fact-finding mission to Canaan. Later, Joshua, himself a former spy, sent two spies to Jericho in preparation for its conquest. In American history, George Washington made effective use of espionage during the War for Independence.

Nevertheless, intelligence gathering is not all cloak-and-dagger operations. The CIA gathers information from such obvious sources as foreign newspapers, radio broadcasts, and websites as well as from covert operations and satellite reconnaissance.

Color guard representing the branches of the US military

FEMA personnel assisting after Hurricane Katrina devastated much of New Orleans, Louisiana in 2005

Intelligence

The American intelligence community is larger and more complex than is popularly believed. In addition to the CIA and the NSC, there is the State Department's Bureau of Intelligence and Research (INR), and each branch of the military has an intelligence branch. Furthermore, the Defense Department includes the Defense Intelligence Agency (DIA), which is answerable to the Joint Chiefs, and the National Security Agency (NSA), the nation's high-technology cryptologic organization. Each of these agencies, along with several others, are part of the United States Intelligence Community (IC). That agency is headed by the Director of National Intelligence.

---

ment, and set bounds to the exertions for its own safety.")

7. Explain how Madison uses King Charles VII of France as an argument for the necessity of having a standing army. (*Charles VII established an army during peacetime. Europe followed his example, and this prevented a "universal monarch" from ruling Europe. As Madison says, "Security against foreign danger is one of the primitive objects of civil society."*)

8. Explain how Madison refutes the charge that the constitutional power to "lay and collect taxes, duties, imposts, and excises, to pay the debts, and provide for the common defense and gen-

eral welfare of the United States" is so broad that it allows unlimited abuse of power. (*The Anti-Federalists took a point out of context to justify their position. As Madison points out, the Constitution does limit the government's powers.*)

9. Do the six classes of power delegated to the government, a standing army, and the power to levy taxes reflect biblical purposes of government? *Yes. "Security against foreign danger" (the first class mentioned) and a standing army relate to providing for national defense; "regulation of the intercourse with foreign nations" and "maintenance of harmony and proper intercourse among the States" (classes two and three) relate to provid-*

ing order; "restraint of the States from certain injurious acts" (class five) relates to ensuring justice; "provisions for giving due efficacy to all these powers" (class six) and the power to levy taxes are necessary for the government to implement its biblical purposes. "Certain miscellaneous objects of general utility" (class four) is rather vague but appears to refer to the government carrying out its responsibilities.

Congress

The president's superior position in making foreign policy is unquestioned; however, his power is at least nominally shared with Congress. As noted in Chapter 9, the Senate is constitutionally empowered to approve treaties by a two-thirds vote. Senators may also attach reservations and conditions to a treaty that were not part of the original agreement.

Ratified treaties generally require wide, bipartisan support since the two-thirds requirement means that one-third plus one may kill a treaty. Treaties have sometimes faced significant difficulties receiving approval in the Senate (e.g., the Treaty of Versailles during the Wilson administration and the SALT II agreement during the Carter administration). Thus, most presidents have relied on executive agreements, which do not require Senate approval, in foreign policy matters.

The Senate's power to approve nominees for State and Defense Department positions provides it with a forum for discussing foreign policy. Similarly, having the power to control appropriations gives Congress influence in such areas as defense spending and foreign aid.

Congress also has the constitutional power to declare war, but presidents have frequently authorized military action without congressional approval. Congress, on the other hand, has never declared war without presidential approval.

The Treaty of Versailles was rejected by the US Senate after World War I.

The Media

No discussion of foreign policy would be complete without considering the media—particularly television. Today, satellites can beam live images from distant corners of the world to American living rooms. The media's ability to provide world news, commentary, and analysis nearly instantaneously is a powerful force in shaping public opinion and thus in influencing foreign policy.

This ability to influence public opinion can make government more responsible by making citizens aware of events. Conversely, the media has enormous power in deciding what to report—or not to report. Unfortunately, there have been instances when some media outlets have presented distorted analyses of foreign events.

The debate about news coverage during the Vietnam War is just one example of the controversy concerning media influence.

US soldiers being interviewed during the Vietnam War

Bias in the Media

Instruct the students to record instances of conservative or liberal bias that they find in newspapers, magazines, news broadcasts, or internet news sites. Invite them to report the results and to suggest how the news reports might read if they were less biased.

During that war, sometimes called the first "television war," Americans were supplied daily with graphic images and a tally of casualties. As polls indicated a growing disenchantment with the war, many blamed the change in the public's perspective on the television coverage. Those critics argued that events such as the Tet Offensive, launched by the Vietnamese Communists in 1968, were unfairly presented. They noted that although American and South Vietnamese troops ultimately repelled that attack, the media concentrated on the early successes the Communists had on the battlefield, emphasizing that Communists had stunned their enemy with the display of strength. Furthermore, critics note that because the press had access to the South Vietnamese army, reporters could film South Vietnamese mistreatment of prisoners of war, but North Vietnamese atrocities remained largely invisible and unreported because they were out of American camera range.

Much disagreement continues to surround the topic of media coverage. Yet, all agree that the media can have much impact on American foreign policy.

Section Review

1–3. Identify three of the president's constitutional roles that give him primary control over foreign policy.

4. What is the purpose of the National Security Council?

5. What is the difference between an embassy and a consulate?

6–7. How has Congress sought to ensure that military power in the United States is subordinate to civilian power at both the first and second levels of the Department of Defense?

★ Of the five areas for which the Department of Homeland Security is responsible, which two do you think are most important? Why?

★ Does media coverage help or hinder American foreign policy? Explain your answer.

IV. Policy Methods

Foreign policy is shaped through methods as subtle as a diplomat's smile and as forceful as a missile striking foreign soil. Throughout its history, the United States has used a variety of methods to achieve its foreign policy goals.

Diplomacy

The United States' first diplomatic mission began during its fight for independence when Benjamin Franklin sailed to France in 1779. Today, the United States has diplomatic relations with more than 180 countries of the world.

Preserving good relations with America's allies is not the only use of diplomacy. The United States maintains diplomatic relations with a number of hostile nations as well and usually engages in diplomatic discussions before resorting to force. Of course, the threat of force, even if unused, can powerfully influence diplomacy. President Theodore Roosevelt popularized the phrase "Speak softly and

Section Review Answers

1–3. commander in chief, chief diplomat, and chief executive (p. 311)

4. to supply information and guidance for the president concerning matters of national security (p. 311)

5. Embassies are government offices or residences, typically located in foreign capitals, that are headed by ambassadors, who act as personal representatives for the president. The United States has just one ambassador and one embassy in a foreign nation. However, the United States may have several consular offices, or consulates, in large nations; they are usually located in main cities of states or provinces. (p. 312)

6–7. The secretary of defense must be a civilian who has not served in an active duty position for at least seven years. Many civilian officials, including the secretaries of the army, navy, and air force, also work to shape defense policy. (p. 314)

★ Students will provide a variety of answers.

★ Some will say that the media's ability to influence public opinion can make government more responsible by making citizens aware of events. Others will argue that the media can be selective in reporting or present distorted analyses of foreign events.

In this 1905 cartoon, President Theodore Roosevelt is shown carrying his "big stick."

carry a big stick," which means that just *having* a powerful military sends a message.

Indirect diplomacy can also be used to encourage negotiations between foreign nations that are hostile to one another. For instance, the United States has long sought to act as a peace mediator between Israel and its Arab neighbors, including the Palestinians.

Although a host of Foreign Service workers carry out diplomacy in daily operations, today the secretary of state and president also perform high-level diplomatic missions. Condoleezza Rice, who served as secretary of state from 2005 to 2009, traveled more than a million miles during her tenure. Hillary Clinton, the next person to hold that position (2009–13), visited 112 countries and traveled more than 956,733 miles. John Kerry, secretary of state from 2013 to 2017, traveled to some 90 countries and logged more than 1.3 million miles.

Treaties and Multinational Organizations

Two additional tools used in achieving foreign policy goals are treaties and multinational organizations. **Treaties** are formal agreements made between nations or groups of nations. Treaties are popularly associated with the ending of wars, but they can also settle boundary disputes, establish commercial relations, and decide legal issues.

Treaties can be called by various names, including *agreement*, *convention*, *charter*, *accord*, and *protocol*. As noted earlier in the chapter, formal treaties require ratification by two-thirds of the Senate, as described in Article II, Section 2, of the Constitution, but presidents have the ability to sign **executive agreements** with foreign heads of state. Executive agreements do not require Senate ratification. Although they have the same effect in international law as treaties, they are not valid in the United States to the extent that they conflict with federal statutes. An important difference

Secretary of State John Kerry (right) meeting with the foreign minister of Qatar in 2014

between the two is that while treaties endure until Congress changes them, executive agreements may be retained, altered, or discarded by the next president.

Often the outgrowth of treaties, **multinational organizations** are bodies established to allow nations to work collectively on certain issues. **Globalization** (the increasing integration of world markets, politics, and culture) has made an isolationist foreign policy practically impossible. Nevertheless, the United States must determine whether it has a sufficient common interest with other nations or multinational organizations before committing itself to a treaty relationship.

Today, the United States is party to many treaties and multinational organizations. Perhaps the most prominent of the latter is the United Nations.

United Nations

The **United Nations (UN)** was created in 1945, at the end of World War II, with the stated purpose of maintaining world peace and upholding human rights. It offered hope as an instrument for peace by providing a forum for nations to negotiate their differences rather than go to war. It has a mixed record as a peacemaker, with more failures than successes. The organization has grown to include 193 countries. Virtually every nation (exceptions include Taiwan, which is claimed by the People's Republic of China, and Kosovo) is now a member.

The following six major divisions of the United Nations act as decision-making and policy-implementing bodies.

The **Secretariat** is the main administrative body of the UN. The **secretary-general**, who serves as the chief administrative officer of the UN, heads this part of the UN.

The **General Assembly** is the primary representative body of the UN and consists of one voting delegate, often called an ambassador, from each member nation. The **Security Council** deals with peace and security issues. It has five permanent members (China, France, Russia, the United Kingdom, and the United States) and ten other member nations serving two-year terms.

UN General Assembly

The **Economic and Social Council** promotes fundamental human rights as defined by the UN. It is composed of representatives from fifty-four member nations (each serving three-year terms) within five broad geographic regions.

The Trusteeship Council oversaw the independence of several small territories. It suspended operation in 1994 when its last trust territory obtained independence.

The **International Court of Justice**, sometimes called the World Court, is located at The Hague in the Netherlands. It is the main judicial body of the UN. It deals with legal disputes between member nations and handles other matters relating to international law. It consists of fifteen judges of different nationalities who are elected for nine-year terms by the General Assembly and the Security Council.

The goals of the UN are to bring peace, security, and development to the world. It promises to defend human rights and to promote justice around the world. But justice and rights are moral issues that must be determined by a moral standard. A pluralistic organization like the United Nations has no ultimate standard on which to ground its moral aspirations. As a result, it promotes abortion as a human right. Critics of the organization argue that its moral rootlessness was

Funding the United Nations

In order to fund the UN's regular budget, the General Assembly assesses each of its 193 member nations a contribution amount. That amount is based on each country's "capacity to pay" as determined by examining that nation's economic data. The minimum amount assessed to any country is .001 percent of the agency's annual regular budget, while the maximum is 22 percent.

For decades, the United States has been the largest contributor to the UN's regular budget. Currently the United States funds 22 percent of the budget, while China (the next highest contributor in 2019), pays about 12 percent. The twelve countries assigned the highest assessments actually contribute nearly 75 percent of the total budget. In addition, the US pays approximately 28 percent of the UN's peacekeeping expenses.

In addition to the regular budget and the peacekeeping budget, the UN provides money for numerous humanitarian projects through the budgets of their other agencies.

Disagreements between the UN and the US government regarding expenditures and policies have led to the United States withholding payments on a number of occasions. Doing so is intended to "encourage" changes in UN management.

Pluralism in the United States

The religiously pluralistic United States faces the same kinds of problems in determining right and wrong as the pluralistic UN. Without using the Bible as the standard, Americans cannot agree on the basic values that should guide the nation's morality.

UN Paper

Ask the students to research the history, structure, and activities of the United Nations and submit reports on their findings.

NATO Expansion

When the Cold War ended in 1991, there were sixteen members of NATO. Since that time, thirteen additional countries have joined. All thirteen had been communist controlled during the Cold War.

Hungary, the Czech Republic, and Poland joined NATO in 1999. In 2004, Bulgaria, Estonia, Latvia, Lithuania, Romania, Slovakia, and Slovenia became members. Two additional countries—Albania and Croatia—were added in 2009, and Montenegro became the twenty-ninth member in 2017.

President Trump speaking to the UN General Assembly

on full display in 2001 when a secret vote resulted in the United States being removed from the Commission on Human Rights although Sudan and Libya—both major violators of human rights—were retained as members. Although this commission was replaced in 2006 with the UN Human Rights Council, the new council also failed to address the problem of how morality is determined. In June 2018, the United States announced its withdrawal from the council, citing concerns about human rights violations by a number of nations that were a part of that group.

The United States provides substantial financial support for the United Nations. It pays about 22 percent of the UN's overall budget and contributes approximately 28 percent of the monies allotted for peacekeeping missions. This has long been a controversy among Americans.

Military Relations

To meet the threat of an expansionist Soviet Union after World War II, the United States and its allies formed several regional military alliances. The first and most important of these was the **North Atlantic Treaty Organization (NATO)**, established in 1949 by the United States, Canada, and ten nations in western Europe. Each of the twelve nations promised to provide military support for any member that was attacked. By the end of the Cold War, membership had increased to sixteen.

Since that time, NATO has focused on peacekeeping missions, such as those in the Balkans during the 1990s. During the same period, NATO accepted many former Communist-bloc countries as members to promote cooperation between these nations and the West. NATO has also addressed the issues of weapons of mass destruction, human-rights violations, and global terrorism. Following the September 11, 2001, terrorist attacks on the United States, NATO members joined the anti-terrorism campaigns in Afghanistan, Iraq, and other places. In 2011, NATO used military force to support Libyan rebels who were fighting to topple the dictator in their country, Muammar al-Qaddafi. NATO has continued to grow, and in 2017, it welcomed Montenegro as its 29th member.

Another military agreement involving the United States is the Inter-American Treaty of Reciprocal Assistance, usually known as the Rio Pact. The United States and a number of Latin American countries signed this treaty in 1947 in Rio de Janeiro. Like NATO's constitution, the Rio Treaty states that an attack on one treaty member is to be regarded as an attack on all. Today, seventeen countries are members of this group.

In addition to NATO and the Rio Pact, the United States has a number of **bilateral treaties** (agreements that involve only two nations) in which it promises to assist the other nation in case of attack. Such treaties exist with Japan, the Philippines, and South Korea.

Economic Relations

Although there has been a general trend toward open markets worldwide, close economic ties between nations have largely been the product of regional agreements such as the one formed by the twenty-eight European nations in the

Activity 3: Two Views of American Involvement in Foreign Affairs

This activity provides students with two views regarding American involvement with other nations.

European Union (EU). While this confederation does have political implications, it is foremost an economic alliance (member nations have eliminated trade barriers, including tariffs, on products produced within the EU). In 2002 the EU introduced the euro, a common currency that most EU nations adopted.

Although the United States has shied away from a union as binding as the EU, it has engaged in its own regional economic agreement. In 1994, the **North American Free Trade Agreement (NAFTA)** took effect. This agreement between the United States, Canada, and Mexico called for the gradual elimination of almost all tariffs and other trade restrictions between the three nations. NAFTA has opened new markets for American products, but critics contend that it has also allowed the importation of low-priced goods with which some American companies cannot compete. As noted in Chapter 9, the agreement became a campaign issue in the 2016 presidential election. In late 2018, the Trump administration negotiated the United States-Mexico-Canada Agreement (USMCA) to eventually replace NAFTA. The president praised the new trade arrangement as more economically advantageous for the United States than NAFTA.

The United States also engages in broader attempts to lower world trade barriers. Once a part of the UN, the General Agreement on Tariffs and Trade (GATT) acted as an international body for breaking down such barriers between nations until the **World Trade Organization (WTO)** replaced it in 1995. The WTO has been opposed by many labor organizations as well as some consumer advocates and environmentalists. Some meetings of the WTO have been marked by violent protests.

Almost 190 nations, including the United States, compose the **International Monetary Fund (IMF)**. This organization works to maintain world economic stability by providing funds to nations that are in financial crisis or that are rebuilding their economies. Member nations also receive technical assistance with monetary transactions.

Foreign Aid

America has shared its prosperity with the world. Since the end of World War II in 1945, it has provided hundreds of billions of dollars in foreign aid to other nations. The belief that such aid, if properly directed, can promote economic and political stability in the world is an important, and controversial, part of US foreign policy.

The **US Agency for International Development (USAID)** is chiefly responsible for delivering that foreign aid. Organized during the Kennedy administration, this agency provides both food and health and education services to needy countries while promoting free government and free-market economies in recipient nations. One goal of foreign aid is to help nations achieve economic prosperity. Notable successes include Taiwan and South Korea, but there have also

European Union flag

What is Brexit?

In June 2016 approximately 52 percent of British voters supported a referendum calling for the United Kingdom to withdraw from the European Union. Brexit (British exit) was a controversial and complicated matter. In March 2017, the nation began the multiyear process of withdrawing from the EU.

The World Trade Organization's Principles of Trade

More than 160 nations are members of the WTO. They agree to conduct trade among themselves based on the following principles. (The source for the information below is *Development, Trade, and the WTO*, edited by Bernard Hoekman et al.)

Nondiscrimination: Members must apply the same trade policies to all members equally.

Reciprocity: Policies that apply to one member must apply to all members.

Binding and enforceable commitments: Any country can change its trade policies, but it can do so only through negotiations, and other countries can challenge such changes through proper WTO procedures. Agreements thus arrived at are binding and enforceable by the WTO.

Transparency: Members' trade policies must be published, must be reviewable upon request, and may be challenged. Any proposed changes must be announced.

Safety valves: Member nations can have trade restrictions "to attain noneconomic objectives," ensure "fair competition," and fulfill other approved purposes. Exceptions can also be made for developing nations and regional free-trade zones.

End *All* Foreign Aid?

Sometimes congressmen propose ending all foreign aid, especially when they see recipients of such aid opposing US policies and interests. Such proposals become even more attractive when one considers the United States' financial woes. Is it viable to end all foreign aid? Why? If not, how can the United States deal with nations that receive aid yet often do not support American interests?

The International Monetary Fund (IMF)

The IMF began when 29 countries signed the Articles of Agreement in 1945. The purpose of the organization is to maintain a stable international economy. The IMF accomplishes this goal by encouraging international cooperation, overseeing national and global exchange rates, lending to needy countries, and providing training for developing nations.

Lending is perhaps the IMF's most well-known function. Member countries contribute to the IMF according to the size of their economies—larger economies pay more money. Thus, the United States is the largest contributor. Other major contributors, though paying significantly less than the United States, are Japan, China, Germany, France, and the United Kingdom.

been many failures. Critics of foreign aid argue that funds are often wasted and that the people who most need the assistance receive only a small portion due to corruption and mismanagement in the nation receiving the funds. They note that recipient governments have sometimes discouraged land reform and private enterprise, and in those cases USAID has not met its goals.

Sanctions

In some ways, **sanctions** are the reverse of foreign aid. In international affairs, the term *sanctions* refers to measures taken against a nation to influence

Protesters denouncing US sanctions imposed on Venezuela (May 2011)

its actions. Sanctions are usually economic in nature. For example, a nation imposing a sanction may restrict the flow of certain goods to or from the sanctioned country as well as stop loans, military assistance, and economic aid.

Both the president and Congress have power to impose sanctions. The president's power is detailed in the International Emergency Economic Powers Act (IEEPA) of 1977. He can establish sanctions if a nation poses an "unusual and extraordinary threat . . . to the national security, foreign policy, or economy of the United States."

In the past, the United States has imposed sanctions on Iraq, North Korea, Libya, Sudan, Cuba, and other nations. The EU, the United States, and other countries imposed sanctions on Russia in 2014. That move was in response to the Russian annexation of Crimea (part of a neighboring nation, Ukraine) and Russian support for rebel forces inside Ukraine.

Military Action and Espionage
Military Action

Attack on World Trade Center, September 11, 2001

As was noted earlier in the chapter, military action is usually used only when diplomacy has failed, although in some instances (such as the Mexican-American War of 1846–48) the United States did little to discourage war. In other cases, military action was taken in response to a threat to American security. For instance, the United States took military action after the devastating terrorist attacks of September 11, 2001, by invading Afghanistan. The government there, controlled by Muslim extremists known as the Taliban, was providing safe haven to al-Qaeda, the terrorist group responsible for the attacks. And in some cases, an attack might be preemptive (in other words, an attack launched to prevent something from occurring), as was the US invasion of Iraq when US intelligence sources thought that the country might use chemical and biological weapons (weapons of mass destruction).

God's Word does not forbid war. However, wars ought to be just, in other words, fought for a just cause—self-defense (cf. Ex. 22:2–3) or in defense of those suffering injustice. The goal of war should not be conquest, economic gain, or revenge. In addition, wars should be a last resort. Because of the value of human life

No Fear

Discuss how a Christian should respond to the threat of terrorism. Guide the students as they conclude that Christians have a responsibility to love their enemies and do good to those who try to harm them. Christians should trust Christ rather than be fearful or hateful. However, remind students that the government has the God-given responsibility to protect the nation against terrorist attacks and bring the perpetrators of attacks to justice.

Intelligence and International Relations

Discuss the importance of intelligence operations to international relations. Note that in the past, when communication and transportation were slower, rapid intelligence gathering was more difficult. The growth of the intelligence community following World War II paralleled America's increased role in world affairs. Should the United States spy on other countries? On allies? On enemies? Why?

(Gen. 9:6) and the preference for peace (Deut. 20:10; Prov. 3:29–31; Rom. 12:18), all reasonable steps to avoid war should be taken. Considering the value of human life, greater harm or death than is necessary to achieve victory must be avoided.

Espionage

To maintain national security, the US government must sometimes gather information and take action without revealing those activities to either the American public or other nations. The FBI carries out such operations within the United States; the CIA and the **National Security Agency (NSA)** do so in foreign countries. A primary purpose of the NSA is to collect and process information and data relating to national security.

The history of US intelligence includes such notable successes as cracking the Japanese code during World War II. With the ability to read Japanese military communications, the United States discovered enemy plans to invade Midway Island. The result was a decisive US victory, which is widely regarded as the turning point of the Pacific war. Today, American intelligence organizations have the important responsibility of investigating terrorist activities both at home and abroad.

Section Review

1–2. What is the difference between a treaty and an executive agreement?

3–8. Identify the six major divisions of the United Nations.

9–11. Name three countries with which the United States has bilateral treaties to assist if they are attacked.

12. Why do critics of foreign aid say that it is often unsuccessful?

★ Interpret the phrase "Speak softly and carry a big stick" in relation to diplomacy.

★ Assess the financial support the United States provides the United Nations. Discuss the amount and whether it is a wise or unwise use of American funds.

V. Challenges Abroad

As we have seen, national security is a primary goal of American foreign policy. Nevertheless, the United States' position as the world's only superpower poses additional challenges in maintaining that security.

Wars and Weapons

World War I was once called "the war to end all wars," but the world continues to be consumed by conflict. Even well-intentioned efforts to conclude wars have been thwarted by humans' sinful nature. The cause of wars has not changed: they are the result of human lusts (James 4:1). But modern methods of warfare certainly differ from those of even the recent past.

Terrorism

Terrorism is an attempt to achieve goals by using fear to intimidate people and governments and thereby coerce them to do what the terrorists want. Often it involves the practice of psychological warfare against civilians. Small groups who

Just War Principles

The position of justified war is distinct from two opposing positions: pacifism, which rejects war, and realpolitik, which rejects moral considerations in matters such as war ("All's fair in love and war"). Realpolitik is not an acceptable option for Christians since there is no area of life where biblical morality does not apply.

Christians recognize that peace is God's intention for the world. When nations or groups break the peace, God has authorized governments to restore it—even though it may necessitate a war to do so. Thus the first criteria for a just war is that it is waged by a lawful government. God has not given the sword to the church (holy wars are not just wars) or to individuals, but to the government (Rom. 13:4).

Unjust wars bring the unjust deaths of those who bear God's image (Gen. 9:6). Those who seek to restore peace ought to be motivated by love for their neighbor (Matt. 22:39). Just wars are never wars of aggression but are always in self-defense or in defense of allies.

Because of the concern for human life, just wars are also fought as a last resort and should be fought in moral ways. Since war is fought out of love to protect the innocent, it should avoid targeting those who are not fighting. Furthermore, soldiers ought not to massacre those who are surrendering. These principles provide moral guidelines for those who are considering war or actively fighting in one.

Section V Objectives

1. Identify challenges that face US national security.

2. Determine a Christian response to national security challenges.

Section Review Answers

1–2. A treaty is a formal agreement made between nations or groups of nations that requires Senate approval. An executive agreement is an agreement between heads of state that does not require Senate approval. (pp. 318–19)

3–8. the Secretariat, General Assembly, Security Council, Economic and Social Council, Trusteeship Council, and International Court of Justice (p. 319)

9–11. Japan, Philippines, and South Korea (p. 320)

12. They say funds are often wasted and that people who need assistance the most receive only a small portion due to corruption and mismanagement in the nation receiving the funds. They say that some recipient countries discourage land reform and private enterprise. (p. 322)

★ The mere existence of force, even when unused, can powerfully influence diplomacy by serving as a deterrent to undesirable conduct.

★ Some may say that the United States is justified in supporting the United Nations at such a high percentage due to the United States' large role in global peacekeeping. Others may say that the United States should not bear so much of the financial burden of the United Nations. Reasons students might cite for not providing so much support to the UN include that funds are not always managed well and that the US support is very large considering it is just one of the 193 members.

Joseph John Rochefort

Intelligence played a large part in the US Navy's victory at the Battle of Midway in June 1942. That intelligence was gathered by Joseph John Rochefort and his associates at Station Hypo in Pearl Harbor.

Rochefort knew that the Japanese intended to launch a massive attack against a target identified as AF on June 4. He confirmed his suspicion about the target's identity by persuading Admiral Chester Nimitz to order a false message be sent from the base at Midway. When the base at Midway falsely reported that it had a problem with its fresh water supply, the Japanese intercepted the message and reported to their superiors that AF was having water problems. This confirmed Rochefort's identification of AF. This information allowed Nimitz to arrange an ambush that resulted in a major victory, which many consider a turning point of the war in the Pacific. The US Navy lost 150 planes, 1 carrier, 1 destroyer, and 307 men. The Japanese, however, lost approximately 250 planes, 4 carriers, a heavy cruiser, and more than 3,000 men. This defeat ended Japan's advance in the Pacific.

Admiral Nimitz recommended Rochefort for the Distinguished Service Medal for his part in the victory at Midway, but the medal was denied. In fact, he never received recognition during his lifetime for the work he did regarding Midway. But President Reagan did award Rochefort the medal posthumously in 1986. That same year Rochefort was also awarded the Presidential Medal of Freedom and in 2000 was inducted into the National Security Agency's Hall of Fame.

Members of ISIS

stand no chance of winning a conventional war frequently resort to terrorism. Decades ago, the Palestine Liberation Organization (PLO) and the Irish Republican Army (IRA) were among the best known of groups who used terrorist activities to advance political goals. Others, such as the Japanese doomsday cult Aum Shinrikyo, have practiced terrorism for broad religious purposes. Currently, the best known Muslim extremist groups include al-Qaeda, Hamas, Hezbollah, and the **Islamic State in Iraq and Syria (ISIS)**. These four groups, and numerous clones, use terrorism in an attempt to—politically, religiously, and culturally—bring about a world with a Muslim worldview.

Terrorism is not new; an assassination by terrorists in the city of Sarajevo was the spark that ignited World War I. But terrorism has become more effective for several reasons. First, because of improved communications, terrorists can recruit and network with others, and they can maximize the psychological impact of an attack. For instance, most Americans saw pictures of planes hitting the World Trade Center twin towers and the subsequent collapse of the buildings on the day it happened. Second, terrorism can be implemented relatively inexpensively. One person with one bomb or one vial of toxins can attack hundreds, even thousands. Anthrax attacks in 2001 struck fear throughout the nation although only four tainted letters were found. Third, because of technological advances, the threat that terrorists can now build weapons of mass destruction far more easily and cheaply is greater than ever before.

Simply securing America's borders is a difficult responsibility. The United States has more than seven thousand miles of land border and more than twelve thousand miles of coastline. Furthermore, terrorists can now enter the United States electronically. The potential for cyberterrorism threatens the disruption of government and commerce as well as aspects of personal life.

Rogue Nations

Although there is no clear definition of *rogue nation*, the term usually refers to nations that seek to develop weapons of mass destruction; that supply, support, or provide safe havens for terrorist organizations; that disregard international law and violate human rights; and that threaten regional or world security.

Many nations fall under this broad definition, but only the most serious international threats are labeled rogue nations or "pariah (outcast) states." In his 2002 State of the Union address, President George W. Bush called three such nations—Iraq, Iran, and North Korea—an "Axis of Evil." During the early years of his administration, President Trump identified Iran, Venezuela, Syria, and North Korea (prior to his summits with the North Korean dictator) as rogue countries.

Regional Conflicts

Several chronic conflicts threaten regional and world security, and the United States has often become involved in attempts to settle them peacefully. India and Pakistan have intermittently wrestled for control of Kashmir, a mountainous region separating the two countries, for decades. The conflict has since taken an even more perilous turn because both nations have developed nuclear weapons.

US Borders

Land:	7,479 miles
US-Canada border:	5,525 miles
Atlantic to Pacific:	3,987 miles
Alaska:	1,538 miles
US-Mexico border:	1,954 miles
Coastline:	12,383 miles
Atlantic:	2,069 miles
Gulf:	1,631 miles
Pacific:	7,623 miles
Arctic:	1,060 miles

Axis of Evil

Obtain a copy of President Bush's 2002 State of the Union address. Read the portion of the speech that deals with the Axis of Evil. Instruct the students to answer the following questions:

1. What characteristics of North Korea, Iran, and Iraq prompted President Bush to label them the Axis of Evil?
2. What dangers did President Bush predict in his speech?
3. What solutions did President Bush propose in his speech?

Discuss the need to listen to speeches critically to follow their intended message.

Fourth-Generation Warfare

The style of combat by the Taliban in Afghanistan and the Muslim extremists in Iraq reflects a trend in warfare, first given the name **fourth-generation warfare** in 1989. That term refers to a decentralized form of fighting. Many times it includes low-intensity guerilla warfare (rather than big, decisive battles) and is usually waged by religious, political, or ideological groups, such as al-Qaeda, rather than by countries. The rise of fourth-generation warfare is partly due to the inability of governments to control such groups within their own borders.

Incapable of funding large armies, terrorist groups fight superior powers by harassing them with ambushes, attacking civilians and symbolic structures, and using the media to instill fear. Meanwhile, they also cultivate support among ideological sympathizers throughout the world. These groups are often funded through a global network of supporters and sustained by fanatically loyal members who are willing to die—even commit suicide—for their cause.

Preventing attacks from such groups is more difficult than thwarting conventional enemies, partly because large population centers that are most susceptible to terrorist attacks are hard to protect. Retaliating against terrorists is also challenging because they are not necessarily associated with a single nation. Democratic nations find it difficult to maintain morale in a protracted war or to resist responding in kind to the atrocities of their enemies. Often, the most effective deterrents to terrorist acts threaten the civil rights and liberties of innocents.

In response to the 2001 terrorist attacks on the World Trade Center and the Pentagon, the United States initiated several changes in its foreign policy. It established coalitions with nations who were not normally allies in order to pursue al-Qaeda and other terrorist groups throughout the world. Further, the president convinced Congress to create a new cabinet-level department to handle homeland-security issues, and he declared that he was willing to use preemptive strikes against potential aggressors. In addition, new legislation enhanced federal and state law-enforcement powers to pursue and arrest individuals suspected of terrorist activities.

To the east, another equally long-standing conflict is that between China and Taiwan. Because Communist China considers Taiwan part of its empire, China regularly threatens to conquer the small island and has carried out military exercises nearby. From an economic standpoint, the United States is interested in peace between these nations because both are major, and equally valuable, trading partners. Economic ties between China and Taiwan have grown in the twenty-first century and might help smooth relations and aid peace.

Russia has long been involved in a regional conflict with Muslim Chechnya, a republic near the Caucasus Mountains that has unsuccessfully fought for its independence. The combination of Russia's heavy-handed military tactics and the Chechens' terrorist attacks has fully sustained a bitter conflict that originated several centuries ago.

Likewise, the decades-old dispute between Israelis and Palestinians (and between Israel and Muslim nations generally) seems incurable. A number of US presidents have tried to broker a peace agreement, seeing it as a crucial first step toward Middle East peace; however, distrust, bitterness, and extreme religious and ethnic hatred have made Middle East peace agreements difficult, if not impossible.

Weapons of Mass Destruction

Despite the fall of the Soviet Union in 1991, the threat of nuclear war continues. At least eight nations (United States, Russia, United Kingdom, France, China, India, Pakistan, and North Korea) have nuclear weapons, weapons capable of killing millions of people. Almost certainly, Israel also possesses such weapons. There is much concern among world leaders that other countries,

The Evil of War

Not all wars are evil, but all wars reveal the evil nature of fallen humanity. This distinction, however, is not always easy to make. The awful nature of war makes it difficult to imagine any war as just, but some wars are necessary if justice is to prevail. In the Old Testament, God ordered Israel to engage in war against other nations. These wars were just because they served the purpose of punishing evil.

There would be no warfare on the earth today if sin had not entered the world. Instead of questioning God's existence or His goodness (as some people often do) when war arises, people should realize that the reality of war incriminates humanity. Why, if humans are inherently good, is there continual conflict on the earth? The answer does not lie merely in outside influences, such as injustice or oppression, but also in the human heart, which is dead in sin.

Handling Foreign Policy

Group the students and assign each a current foreign-policy matter that is receiving much publicity. Ask each group to evaluate the causes for the challenge and the potential effects of various US responses. Remind them to consider how a Christian worldview may affect preferred responses to the matter.

WMDs

Weapons of mass destruction (WMDs) became a major issue during the 2004 presidential election. After invading and defeating Iraq, the Bush administration was embarrassed because of the lack of evidence of WMDs there (the alleged presence of these weapons was a primary reason for invading Iraq). Secretary of State Colin Powell was forced to admit that information he presented to the UN, in a bid for support for the invasion, might have been based on flawed intelligence.

as well as some terrorist organizations, will acquire such weapons. A cheaper, though still deadly, alternative is a radiological weapon, or "dirty bomb." These weapons are conventional explosives surrounded by radioactive material. The explosions and the number of casualties that these weapons cause might not be greater than those caused by a conventional bomb, but public panic about radioactivity and the cost of cleanup measures—especially in large cities—could paralyze a local economy for years.

Another threat is that of chemical and biological weapons. Chemical weapons use substances such as mustard gas, sarin, and VX (a neurotoxin, or nerve agent) to poison the enemy. Chlorine gas and other chemical weapons have recently been used against civilians in the Syrian civil war. **Biological weapons** use fatal diseases or organic toxins as weapons. Examples include ricin, smallpox, and botulinum toxin. Anthrax, mentioned earlier, a particularly deadly disease, was mailed to members of Congress and members of the media in 2001. No government officials were infected, but five other people died. Although biological and chemical weapons are easier to create than to use, the fear of such potent agents of death makes them powerful psychological weapons.

Postal workers (in white) in Liverpool, England, after they had contact with a suspicious substance that was feared to be anthrax.

The use of both biological and chemical weapons has been banned by international treaty, and the United States has been active in talks to reduce nuclear arms. Nevertheless, it is important for the United States to develop defenses against these **weapons of mass destruction (WMDs)**. Since the Reagan administration, the United States has been interested in creating a national missile-defense system. And although the United States does not use chemical and biological weapons, its scientists are actively seeking to develop antidotes for such weapons.

Globalization

Globalization, mentioned earlier in the chapter, is a term often used by politicians and economists. From an economic standpoint, it is the integration of world markets through increased communications, foreign investment, and free trade. It allows businesses and (to a lesser extent) other institutions to operate as though national borders did not exist. Globalization also results in some integration of politics, society, and culture.

Globalization is a natural outgrowth of the communications revolution, which has helped connect our world. The fall of the Soviet Union also aided its development: the Soviet Union's failed socialist experiment prompted many other governments to turn their economic policies toward open-market capitalism.

The United States faces several foreign policy challenges in a "globalized" world. First, not just businesses have more influence on government in a global environment, but terrorists can use global integration to their advantage as well. For instance, terrorist groups have used mobile phones, satellite connections, and global markets to plan and fund their attacks.

Second, globalization has heightened the debate between free trade and protectionism. Free trade stimulates most businesses and raises the standard of living. But industries endangered by this expanded free trade may lobby the government for legislation to protect special-interest groups.

 ### Terrorism Facing Other Countries

Group the students and assign each group a country that has faced major terrorist threats (e.g., the United Kingdom, France, Israel, Iraq, Afghanistan, Egypt, and Turkey). After researching terrorist attacks committed within their assigned nation, ask each group to present their findings to the class. Then lead a discussion about some of the similarities and differences regarding terrorism in these nations.

Third, globalization has rapidly disseminated many different ideas and cultures. There are obvious benefits to globalization's spread of ideas. For instance, oppressive regimes have found it increasingly difficult to keep democratic notions from their people.

Finally, foreign countries are concerned that globalization will increase American political and economic power. Therefore, globalization has intensified another foreign policy challenge to the United States—anti-Americanism.

As barriers between nations fall, Christians must recognize the opportunities now available. First, better communication between continents allows for closer ties between believers and easier transmission of the gospel. Second, globalization helps ease the differences between cultures. This helps reduce the amount of resistance some nations offer to missionary efforts. Third, globalization makes missionary work more feasible. Though a country may close its doors to traditional missionaries, Christians may find opportunities through nonreligious vocations in closed countries to share the gospel.

Anti-Americanism

Some people contend that the United States is often guilty of "cultural imperialism" (promoting its culture at the expense of others). American culture *is* perhaps the largest export of the United States. Through television, movies, popular music, and the internet, the world has been flooded with American culture. American soft drinks, hamburgers, and clothing can be purchased even in Third World countries. There, American culture is both embraced and resented as it challenges local cultures.

Fear of American political power has also encouraged anti-Americanism. The simple existence of its strong military has troubled many non-Americans. As a result, in 2003 when the United States attacked Iraq, a country controlled by a notorious dictator, many nations opposed American use of force. There have also been attempts to form coalitions of power to balance that of the United States. Although the European Union is largely an economic alliance, many EU leaders would like it to become a political coalition in the future. And an alliance between Russia and China might someday counter the political strength of the United States.

Conclusion

During its decades as a superpower, the United States has protected itself as well as its allies. US naval power helps keep the sea-lanes open, making it easier for nations to trade. Efforts to foster trade around the world have increased the standard of living for millions of people. Furthermore, America's military and economic powers allow it to place pressure on other nations to not engage in human rights abuses.

US foreign policy often assists in the implementation of the biblical purposes of government: advancement of justice, provision of defense, reduction of poverty, promotion of morality, and maintenance of order. At other times, American policies have hindered accomplishing those goals. For example, some presidents

Bangalore, India (top), and Ho Chi Minh City, Vietnam (above)

"The only thing the world hates more than unilateral American leadership is no American leadership."

—Condoleezza Rice,
Former national security advisor and secretary of state

Globalization and Christianity

Christianity is a global religion. People of every tribe, language, people group, and nation will be included among the redeemed (Rev. 5:9). The church is not confined to a single nation, culture, or people group but spans the globe. Because all people bear the image of God, Christians are concerned for the well-being of everyone. Globalization thus may help the spread of the gospel and may give Christians the opportunity to minister around the world.

Nations are part of God's good created order. They will persist into the new creation (Rev. 21:24–25). Christians also recognize that responsibility increases with proximity. A father has a greater responsibility to care for his own children than he does for the neighbor's and than he does for a child across the world. This does not mean that Christians do not show concern for those distant from them (especially as globalization brings remote people closer), but it does mean that a Christian should avoid the trap of "loving humanity" while not loving the real humans interacted with day by day.

In the debates about globalization and nationalism, perhaps Christians should not take either side. Instead, in applying a biblical worldview, Christians ought to recognize the proper concerns and the sinful tendencies of each.

Activity 4: Chapter Review
Use this activity to help the students prepare for the chapter test.

Cultural Relativity

In the nineteenth and early twentieth centuries, European colonial powers often wronged conquered peoples, partly because they thought their European culture superior to cultures found elsewhere in the world. The United States is often accused of "cultural imperialism" because its culture—and often its sinful aspects—has spread around the world. Many people have argued for "cultural relativity," meaning that no culture should be judged as superior to any other culture; rather, each culture should be judged by its own set of values.

This is an unrealistic proposition. Why? Because a logical conclusion of cultural relativism is that no one should criticize or attempt to change cultures that oppress women, enslave children, threaten others' peace, or deny certain classes of people the right to participate in government if doing these things are consistent with those cultures' values.

Although many people recognize that cultural relativism is ethically unsatisfying, they differ as to what standard should be used to judge the morality of a culture. Some resort to the UN's Universal Declaration of Human Rights as the standard, but adopting this pronouncement merely shifts the source of the standard from an individual culture to a consensus of human cultures. In other words, humans remain the standard by which humanity is judged.

A Christian understands that the Bible is the only unchangeable, absolute standard for judging culture because Scripture is the revelation of an unchanging God. When God promised in Malachi 3:5 to judge Israel for its sorcery, lying, adultery, oppression, and maltreatment of immigrants, He clarified the nature of an immoral culture. Also, God's judgment on Sodom and Gomorrah revealed that a perverse culture is unacceptable in His sight.

Conversely, the Ten Commandments reveal that cultures that forbid murder, theft, covetousness, disrespect for parents, and the worship of false gods please the Creator. Micah 6:8 declares that cultures that promote justice, protect life, help the poor and weak, and keep God's commandments are good cultures.

Because humans in all cultures are sinners, the Christian expects every culture, including Western culture, to be critiqued by God's Word. Because all cultures are developed by people who bear God's image, the Christian should expect to find something of value in every culture. But Christians must strongly reject the idea that all cultures are morally equal. While all cultures are flawed, some are more flawed than others and in greater need of gospel transformation. Saying this is not imperialistic but rather a necessary truth in ministering God's grace to the nations.

have given foreign aid to organizations that promote abortion or LGBT rights, while other administrations have endorsed wars that some Christians would consider unjust.

Foreign policy is closely connected with issues important to Christians—issues that are sometimes complicated. Some are issues for which the Bible provides no direct guidance; others are matters on which Christians may disagree about the application of biblical principles. When should military power be used? What military alliances should be formed? What economic policies should be followed? What trade agreements are beneficial for Americans? Christians must develop wisdom to know how to best apply Scripture to such complex circumstances.

Section Review

1. Define *terrorism*.

2–4. Name three reasons terrorism has become so effective.

5–8. Identify four regional conflicts that continue to influence foreign policy.

★ What challenges face US foreign policy as a result of globalization? If you were president, how would you address these challenges?

328 • CHAPTER 13

Making Connections

1–4. Summarize the four basic goals that are central to US foreign policy.

5–6. Identify the cabinet departments that administer the two arms of American foreign policy and summarize their respective responsibilities.

7. What aspect of foreign relations does the Department of Homeland Security handle?

8–11. What is the only absolute standard by which cultures can be judged? Provide three examples from this standard based on the box "Cultural Relativity" on page 328.

12. Explain why American culture is perhaps the largest export of the United States.

Developing Civics Skills

1. Analyze why the Constitution gives the executive branch the greatest control over foreign policy.

2. What conditions in the world make an isolationist policy difficult to uphold today?

Thinking Critically

1. What is the proper Christian attitude toward the threats of this age?

2. Why have efforts to bring about world peace failed? Support your answer with Scripture.

Living as a Christian Citizen

1. Select a war or military action in the last 150 years of US history and analyze whether the United States' entrance and conduct during that conflict followed the principles of a just war.

2. Identify a foreign policy challenge that the United States has faced in the last 20 years and formulate a response to that challenge from a biblical worldview.

People, Places, and Things to Remember

foreign policy
national security
alliance
Marshall Plan
isolationism
Monroe Doctrine
imperialism
Cold War
nuclear deterrence
mutual assured destruction (MAD)
containment
al-Qaeda
National Security Council (NSC)
national security advisor
passport
visa
secretary of state
embassies
ambassador
consulates
secretary of defense
State Department
Defense Department
Pentagon
Joint Chiefs of Staff (JCS)
Department of Homeland Security
Central Intelligence Agency (CIA)
treaties
executive agreements
multinational organizations
globalization
United Nations (UN)
Secretariat
secretary-general
General Assembly
Security Council
Economic and Social Council
International Court of Justice
North Atlantic Treaty Organization (NATO)
bilateral treaties
European Union (EU)
North American Free Trade Agreement (NAFTA)
World Trade Organization (WTO)
International Monetary Fund (IMF)
US Agency for International Development (USAID)
sanctions
National Security Agency (NSA)
terrorism
Islamic State in Iraq and Syria (ISIS)
rogue nation
fourth-generation warfare
chemical weapons
biological weapons
weapons of mass destruction (WMDs)
cultural imperialism

FOREIGN POLICY • 329

Developing Civics Skills

1. Answers may include the goals of engendering international respect and allowing for a quick response to an emergency.

2. Answers may include the rise of nuclear weapons, modern means of transportation, America's position as the only superpower, and dependence on world trade.

Thinking Critically

1. Students will provide varying answers. God told the Israelites to "seek the peace of the city" where He sent them in exile, even if He sent them to a city that was part of a pagan empire (Jer. 29:7). Even though ultimate peace will not come until the return of the Prince of Peace (Isa. 9:6), Christians should seek the welfare of non-Christians in the world (Deut. 10:17–18; Isa. 1:17; Luke 10:27–37). For example, Christians do a good work when they justly broker a peace between warring parties that stops the fighting and provides relief from the widespread suffering that war typically brings.

2. In the New Testament, James says that wars and fighting occur because people desire pleasures that others have. They desire what others have, and they kill to get it (James 4:1–2). (James uses war as a metaphor for interpersonal conflicts, but the principle still applies.) Though God's people may long for peace, the wicked often make war necessary (Ps. 120:7; Eccles. 3:8). Lasting peace will not be found until Christ purges the earth of evil.

Living as a Christian Citizen

1. Students should apply the just war principles they have learned to a specific war or military action.

2. Students should reference the biblical purposes for government outlined in their text and identify specific biblical passages or teaching in their response.

CHAPTER REVIEW ANSWERS

Making Connections

1–4. National security focuses on protecting the nation and its citizens and property abroad; alliance security involves supporting allies abroad; international stability involves seeking to end wars or threats of war by diplomacy; and economic development involves stimulating economic expansion in developing nations. (pp. 303–5)

5–6. The State Department oversees foreign embassies and maintains foreign diplomatic relations; the Department of Defense is in charge of defending the country from foreign aggression. (pp. 312, 314–15)

7. The Department of Homeland Security focuses on protecting the nation from terrorist activities on American soil. (p. 315)

8–11. Scripture; examples of biblical standards include Malachi 3:5, the Ten Commandments, and Micah 6:8. (p. 328)

12. Through television, movies, popular music, and the internet, the world has been flooded with American culture. Its reach has expanded so that American soft drinks, hamburgers, and clothing can be purchased even in the Third World. (p. 327)

Exterior of US Supreme Court Building in Washington, DC

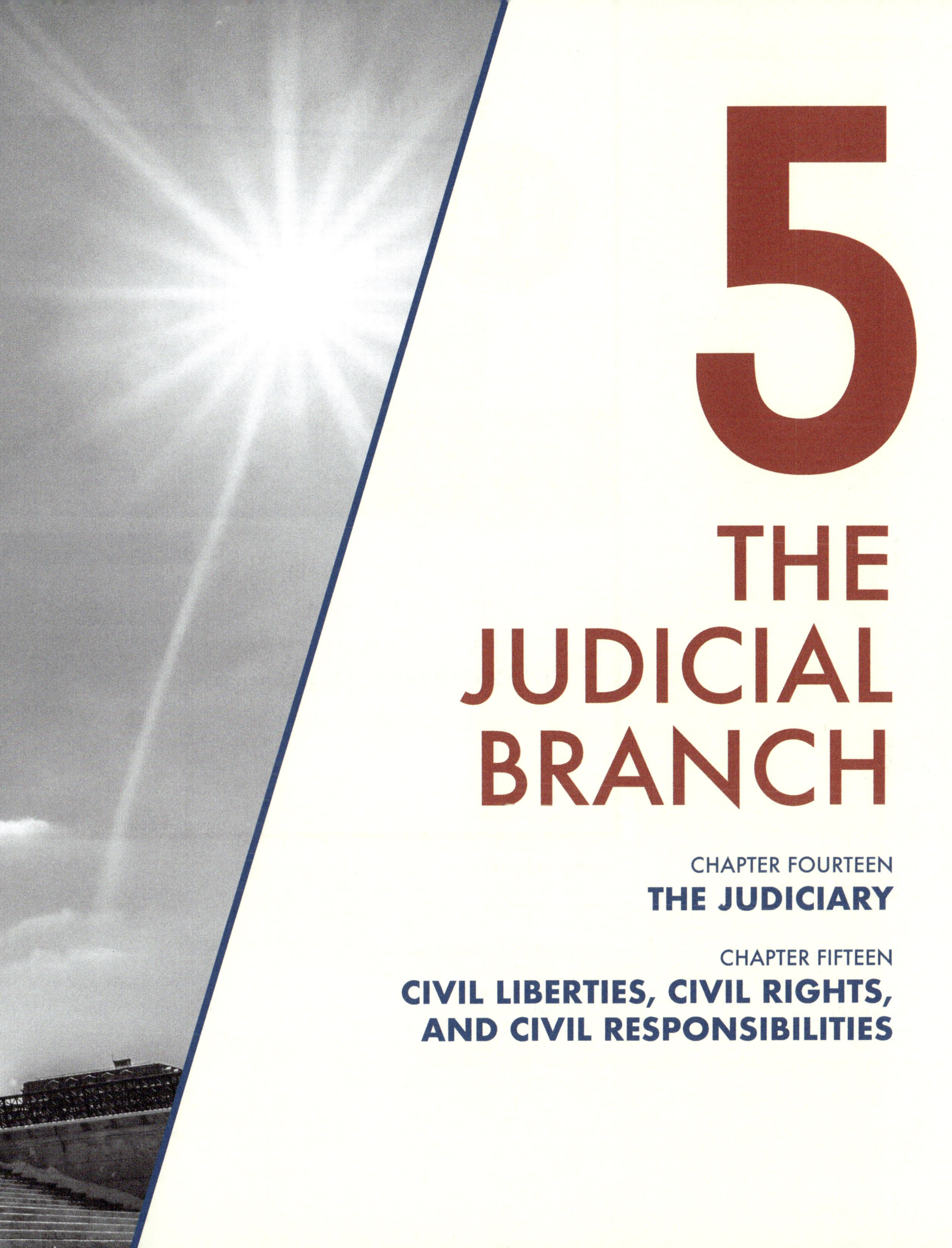

5

THE JUDICIAL BRANCH

CHAPTER FOURTEEN
THE JUDICIARY

CHAPTER FIFTEEN
CIVIL LIBERTIES, CIVIL RIGHTS, AND CIVIL RESPONSIBILITIES

1. Analyze the sources of American law.
2. Explain the structure of the United States judicial system.
3. Outline the process for the selection of judges.
4. Evaluate the judiciary branch's role in legal change.

THE JUDICIARY

14

The most sacred of the duties of a government [is] to do equal and impartial justice to all its citizens.

—Thomas Jefferson

In the courtroom of the US Supreme Court, some of the great lawgivers of history are displayed along with allegorical figures relating to justice. Above on the left are Hammurabi and Moses with Solomon on the right. The winged figure holding a Roman fasces next to him symbolizes Authority.

I. Sources of American Law

II. Structure of the Courts

III. Selection of Judges

IV. Constitutional and Legal Change

BIG IDEAS

1. What are the sources of American law?
2. What is the structure of the judicial system?
3. How are judges selected?
4. What is the judiciary's role in constitutional and legal change?

SUGGESTED MATERIALS

Section I
- Activity 1 from Chapter 14 of the *Student Activities*
- Materials for a mock trial (for an optional activity)

Section II
- No materials

Section III
- Activity 2 from Chapter 14 of the *Student Activities*
- Special speaker (see p. 346)

Section IV
- Activities 3–5 from Chapter 14 of the *Student Activities*

Teacher Resources
Visit TeacherToolsOnline.com for resources to enhance the lessons.

Additional Unit Resources
For this unit (Chapters 14–15), consider reading the following books as background for teaching the material:
- Robert H. Bork's *Coercing Virtue: The Worldwide Rule of Judges*
- William H. Rehnquist's *The Supreme Court*
- Clarence Thomas's *My Grandfather's Son*

In *The Roots of American Order* (1974), Russell Kirk tells the story of a Menshevik (a moderate socialist) who escaped to the Black Sea city of Odessa during the Russian Revolution. The Menshevik discovered the city in anarchy.

> Bands of young men commandeered street-cars and clattered wildly through the heart of Odessa, firing with rifles at any pedestrian, as though they were hunting pigeons. At any moment, one's apartment might be invaded by a casual criminal or fanatic, murdering for the sake of a loaf of bread. In this anarchy, justice and freedom were only words. "Then I learned that before we can know justice and freedom, we must have order," my friend said. "Much though I hated the Communists, I saw then that even the grim order of Communism is better than no order at all. Many might survive under Communism; no one could survive in general disorder."

Indeed, most would probably prefer oppressive laws that produce order to unrestrained freedom, which is anarchy. But such laws are not just. Law in its truest sense originates from God and stands above all human government. Judges, the human interpreters of law, can impose order even when they reject the law of God, but society needs scriptural morality to restrain human wickedness. Only then can any legal system truly be "a government of laws and not of men."

I. Sources of American Law

Scriptural Foundation

Ensuring justice is one of the fundamental obligations that people have toward one another. God makes it His glory to execute justice (Deut. 10:17–18; Ps. 99:4). Justice was a fundamental requirement for Israel to remain in the land of promise (Deut. 16:20). God calls on people to act justly, especially on behalf of those who are unable to defend themselves (Deut. 27:19). Micah 6:8 teaches that doing justice, loving mercy, and walking humbly with God sum up a believer's obligation before Him. The Lord reveals in Amos 5 that He actually prefers justice over formal worship. In the New Testament, Jesus blesses those who hunger and thirst for righteousness (Matt. 5:6). And the Bible closes with God exercising ultimate justice for all people (Rev. 20:11–15).

But what is justice? To be just is to respect the rights of another human being. Some of these rights are natural and God-given. Because a person is made in the image of God, he has the right to be treated as a bearer of God's image. The image of God is the foundation for all natural human rights. But natural rights are not the only rights that humans possess. A legislature can confer specific rights. For instance, the Bill of Rights says that Americans have the right to deny soldiers lodging in their homes. This is not necessarily a natural right, but it is a right held by Americans.

Remember, however, that laws can be unjust. Laws are unjust when they infringe on people's God-given rights. The most obvious unjust American laws permitted the enslavement of humans. Justice respects people's God-given and conferred rights (insofar as those conferred rights are consistent with biblical principles).

Contemporary theorists who discuss justice often deny the concepts of God-given rights and the image of God in man. Because modern nations are pluralistic,

✝ Divine Law

Discuss Christ's definition of divine law. Mention that while most people think of law as negative (as a list of "don'ts"), God's law is fundamentally positive. For example, Christ said that the two greatest commandments are to love God and love others (Matt. 22:37–40). The law plays an important role for the Christian. Jesus, in the Sermon on the Mount, taught that Christians' good works are like lighted cities set on hills—visible to all for God's glory (Matt. 5:14–16).

But how can Christians know what works are good and which are not? Discernment comes through God's law. This is why Jesus did not come to abolish the law (Matt. 5:17–20). Indeed, obedience to the law attracts people to see how great and wise God is (Deut. 4:1–8).

It is true that Christians are now under the New Covenant rather than the Mosaic Covenant, so certain Old Testament laws are not directly applicable to the Christian (1 Cor. 9:20–21). But one of the most important aspects of being under the New Covenant is that the Holy Spirit indwells believers and empowers them to be faithful to the law of God (2 Cor. 3:3, 5–6; Ezek. 36:26–27).

God's Law

Sometimes people ask why Christians believe that Old Testament laws prohibiting murder, homosexuality, and idolatry remain valid while laws about not wearing mixed fabrics and offering sacrifices no longer need to be followed. The answer is that Christians live under the New Covenant rather than the Mosaic Covenant. The apostle Paul taught that Christians are released from the old written law but now serve in the new (covenant) way of the Spirit (Rom. 7:6).

Sacrifices are no longer offered because Jesus established the New Covenant with the once-for-all sacrifice of Himself on the cross (Heb. 10:11–18). Laws like not wearing mixed fabrics are not part of the New Covenant because they were illustrations or teaching tools. Their purpose has been fulfilled (Gal. 3:24–26).

However, laws about worshiping other gods, sexual relations and marriage, or murder are always valid. They don't change from covenant to covenant. They reflect God's eternal character and the order or structure that He built into creation.

US Law and Old Testament Law

God's laws in the Pentateuch are different from modern law codes. Modern codes specifically enumerate legal requirements. The Old Testament laws God provided Israel were general laws (such as the Ten Commandments) that set broad guidelines plus very specific laws that acted almost like case studies. Old Testament law was not exhaustive. If a person committed an injustice that was not explicitly covered by the law, a wise judge would determine from general principles and similar past cases what the judgment should be for that particular crime.

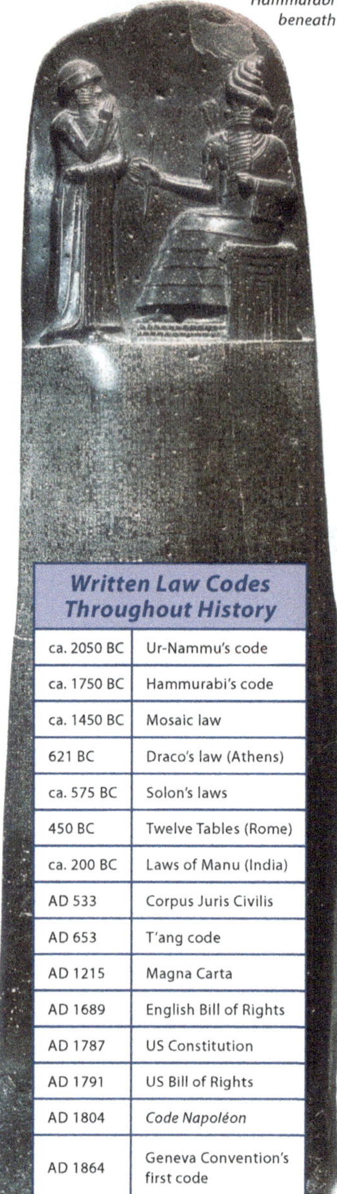

Hammurabi (standing) with his code of laws inscribed beneath him on a seven-foot stone pillar

Written Law Codes Throughout History	
ca. 2050 BC	Ur-Nammu's code
ca. 1750 BC	Hammurabi's code
ca. 1450 BC	Mosaic law
621 BC	Draco's law (Athens)
ca. 575 BC	Solon's laws
450 BC	Twelve Tables (Rome)
ca. 200 BC	Laws of Manu (India)
AD 533	Corpus Juris Civilis
AD 653	T'ang code
AD 1215	Magna Carta
AD 1689	English Bill of Rights
AD 1787	US Constitution
AD 1791	US Bill of Rights
AD 1804	Code Napoléon
AD 1864	Geneva Convention's first code

having citizens of many religions and worldviews, they seek to develop theories of justice that do not require decisions about right and wrong. Some theorists argue that justice is served when the most people get the greatest good. But what about the rights of the minority? And what is the greatest good? This question requires a moral judgment. Others argue that justice is secured when people have freedom to make choices according to their own ideas about what constitutes a good life. But what happens when people's conceptions of "the good life" clash? Clearly, the moral dimension of justice is inescapable.

God's standard of justice is His own character (Deut. 32:4); therefore, **justice** is conformity to God's character. God has revealed His divine character in the Bible, and to the extent that any human law does not conform to His character, that law is unjust.

Historical Foundation

Although the first-known law code was produced by Ur-Nammu of Ur in about 2050 BC (roughly the time of Abraham), undoubtedly the most famous ancient law materials are those of Hammurabi, a Babylonian king (ca. eighteenth century BC). The **Code of Hammurabi**, consisting of 282 laws, was developed by compiling, organizing, and simplifying existing laws.

In ancient Greece, the best minds gave themselves to philosophy; but in Rome, men of leisure and intelligence more often considered law. At the beginning of the Roman Republic, laws were unwritten and patricians (members of the upper class) used them to maintain their power. Later, they were placed in writing, publicly displayed, and called the Law of the Twelve Tables (fifth century BC).

As the Romans expanded their laws, they found commonsense solutions to everyday legal problems. To generalize about how future cases should be decided, a respected class of private experts combined the reasoning of legal decisions made over centuries. Even during the grimmest periods of imperial autocracy, Romans never abandoned the beliefs that law remained above the desires of any particular ruler and that it could not be altered arbitrarily. Eventually, in AD 533, the Roman emperor Justinian collected many Roman legal materials from previous centuries and published an organized compilation called the **Corpus Juris Civilis** (Body of Civil Law). It is also called the Code of Justinian.

After the fall of the Roman Empire, knowledge of Roman law never entirely disappeared in the West, but a sophisticated legal system was not common during much of the Middle Ages. By the tenth or eleventh century, though, interest in Justinian's code revived as legal problems once solved by the Romans reappeared in the courts of European cities. After centuries of examination, scholars managed to blend the best elements of the *Corpus Juris Civilis* into local legal materials and write their own law codes. Perhaps the most famous of these is the *Code Napoléon* (1804).

During the Middle Ages and the Renaissance, England did not accept the *Corpus Juris Civilis* and instead developed its own

Courthouse Visit

Visit a local courthouse and attend part of a trial. Discuss the necessity of upholding and enforcing laws.

system: the **common law**—common because it was not local feudal law but was common to the whole realm of England. Unlike legal systems of continental Europe that were based on the codified Roman law, the common law was grounded in case law, a body of opinions written by royal judges who, at least in theory, followed the **precedents** (prior authoritative rulings) of those who came before them. (This practice of rendering judicial decisions on the basis of precedents is called *stare decisis* [STAR-ee dih-SEYE-sis]. The phrase means "to stand by that which is decided," or "let the decision stand.") Therefore, even though common law was not codified, in a sense it closely resembled the legal system of Rome, in which legal experts generalized about commonsense solutions to practical problems on the basis of past experience.

Before the thirteenth century, English courts used three common methods to determine guilt or innocence—trial by ordeal, trial by battle, and compurgation (wager of law). It was believed that through these methods God would reveal the truth regarding the accused.

Trial by ordeal included carrying a hot iron nine feet or plucking a stone out of a pot of boiling water. The resulting burned hand would then be bound. If after three days the hand were not infected, the accused would be considered innocent. But if "unhealthy matter" were found, he would "be deemed guilty and unclean." The ordeal of cold water was usually reserved for the lowest classes. After the hands of the accused were tied together behind his bent knees and a rope was bound around his waist, he was gently lowered into a pool of water "so as not to make a splash. If he [sank] down to the knot [around his waist] he [would] be drawn up saved; otherwise [he would] be adjudged a guilty man by the spectators." In addition to trial by ordeal, accusations could be settled by having two disputing parties fight each other. The victor in combat judged

Depiction of a suspect required to plunge his hand into a pot of boiling water

Common Legal Terms

Affirm—To approve the decision of a lower court

Appeal—To petition a higher court to review a lower-court decision

Appellate jurisdiction—A court's power to decide appeals

Brief—A legal document that presents arguments supporting a client's position in a case

Civil law—1. The division of law dealing with private citizens' legal rights in disputes with other citizens 2. A system of law based on codified Roman law and distinguished from common law

Common law—A system of law developed in England and based on tradition and the courts' decisions rather than on legal codes; distinguished from civil law

Constitutional law—The division of law dealing with the constitutional interpretation of laws and government actions

Criminal law—The division of law that treats crimes prosecuted by the government

Original jurisdiction—A court's power to hear a case before it is considered by any other court

Precedent—A court decision that serves to guide subsequent decisions in related cases

Reverse—To rule against a lower-court decision by virtue of a higher court's authority

Stare decisis—Literally, "let the decision stand"; a principle of law that bases decisions on judicial precedent

Writ of certiorari—An order from a superior court (especially the US Supreme Court) to a lower court to send the entire record of a case for review; *certiorari* is Latin for "to be made more certain."

Pagans Who Fear God

When Abraham sojourned among the Philistines, he was concerned that there was no fear of God among them. But the Philistines' reaction to Abraham's sin demonstrated that they knew right from wrong (Gen. 20). When Abraham sinned against the Philistine king and the Egyptian pharaoh, they challenged him for doing what he should not have done (Gen. 12:18; 20:9–10; cf. 26:10–11; 1 Cor. 5:1). How was it that these pagan kings could rebuke the man of God for his sin? Where did they get their sense of right and wrong?

Romans 2:14–15 teaches that God wrote His law on the human heart so that people's consciences accuse or excuse their actions. The conscience is fallible. It may be weak, defiled, seared, or evil (1 Cor. 8:7; 1 Tim. 4:2; Heb. 10:22). Nonetheless, it often provides people with knowledge of right and wrong, even when they do not have access to Scripture. The law written on the heart explains how pagan nations could develop law codes that in many instances truly distinguished between right and wrong.

Mock Trial

Conduct a mock criminal trial. (See page 498 for details.) This role-playing activity teaches judicial procedures and illustrates the rights of the accused.

If your school or a neighboring one has a mock trial team, suggest that students observe one of their proceedings. Perhaps review videos of mock trials on the internet to show to the class.

The Influence of Roman Law

Roman law survived the fall of Rome for several reasons.

1. The codification of Roman law in 533 by Emperor Justinian (ca. 483–565) provided later scholars with a comprehensive account of a highly developed legal system that they could modify for their own use.

2. Parts of Roman law were preserved by the medieval church in its canon law.

3. The "reception" of Justinian's code—that is, its reintroduction—began in about the eleventh century, at a time when European culture was once again becoming sophisticated enough to have a use for it. The code was written in a book; this was an advantage during a period in which the written word had nearly magical authority. In addition, the code was written in Latin, which made it readable to all educated people. And it was a challenging puzzle to people with intelligence and curiosity.

Code Napoléon

Unlike English law, French law was a confusing mixture of Roman law derived from Justinian's code and a Germanic customary law; French law also differed depending on location. Customary law dominated in the north of France, and Roman law dominated in the south. Three hundred or more towns and villages had their own local legal systems. In a famous quip that was hardly an exaggeration, French philosopher Voltaire said that a French traveler changed laws as often as he changed horses. The law was so confusing that even judges were suspected of not understanding it.

There were attempts to organize French law as early as the fifteenth century, but the French Revolution (1789–99) made codification easier because it abolished feudal privileges and local customary law. The revolutionaries were interested in producing a law code because it would help unify France and because constructing a logically organized legal code reflected the contemporary faith in reason.

Shortly after Napoleon Bonaparte's coup d'état of 1799, he appointed a four-man commission of distinguished jurists to draft a uniform civil code for France. The commission sensibly decided that its business was to conserve and organize what had existed in the past rather than try to create new laws. The commission sounded decidedly unrevolutionary (and almost English) when it declared that "codes of people develop in time; properly speaking, one does not make them."

Eventually, Napoleon's Council of State debated a draft of the code. Although Napoleon was only thirty-two years old and unlearned in the law, he made important contributions to the final document; his force of character also ensured that the project stayed on track. At first the French legislature hindered passage of the code, but after Napoleon further consolidated his power in 1802, he made that body more to his liking.

The completed *Code Napoléon* (or *Code Civil*, as it is known today) was declared the law of France in 1804. It is about 120,000 words long (about the length of a substantial book) and is written in clear, precise French. French novelist Stendhal (Marie-Henri Beyle) said that the code was, for him, a model of literary clarity and simplicity.

The importance of *Code Napoléon* was magnified when French armies exported it to northern Italy, parts of Germany, and even Poland. After Napoleon made his brother Louis king of Holland, he told him to adopt the French civil code. "The Romans gave their laws to their allies," said Napoleon. "Why should not France have hers adopted in Holland?" In 1808 the code was modified to become the law of Louisiana, and even after Napoleon's fall, his code became the basis for legal systems in Quebec, Egypt, Greece, and many Latin American countries.

English Common Law

According to page 337 of the student text, "England took its legal system to its colonies, so the common law is usually dominant wherever English is the primary language." In what other countries besides the United States would you expect to find common-law systems? Guide a discussion about this question, and then read aloud the following information:

Canada (except Quebec); Australia; New Zealand; Caribbean islands, such as Jamaica and Trinidad and Tobago; and other countries use common-law systems.

Ireland's legal system is based on English common law but has been substantially modified by native legal traditions.

English (along with ten other official languages) is spoken in South Africa, which was an English colony; but the Dutch were the first Europeans to settle the country, so the South African system is based on both Roman-Dutch law and English common law.

victor in the dispute. A third method for settling legal matters was by compurgation, which was essentially a character test. The accused had the right to swear his innocence and then present a number of people to swear that his oath was trustworthy.

Eventually, English common law encouraged the development of jury trials, which were much more rational than the older methods; and, because juries made their decisions secretly, jury trials were also mysterious enough to be regarded as revealing the mind of God.

Like other western European countries, England took its legal system to its colonies, so the common law is usually dominant wherever English is the primary language. In England, the common law had been developed by and for the royal courts; however, it was not codified. Over the centuries, it had developed into an unusual quilt of complicated legal fictions with no explanatory guide.

Ten years before the American War for Independence, William Blackstone (1723–80), Oxford's first professor of English law, produced a key to the system in his **Commentaries on the Laws of England** (1765–69). The *Commentaries* was a bestseller in America and strongly influenced the American founders.

Although Blackstone was a Tory who opposed the American struggle for liberty, his book probably restrained whatever urge American lawyers had to abandon common law and devise their own legal code. Furthermore, Blackstone, like most people of his generation, believed that the common law was derived from God's law. Blackstone thought that God expressed His law through both creation, as a **natural law** given to all men (what the apostle Paul refers to in Romans 2:14–15), and the **revealed law** contained in the Bible. "Upon these two foundations," said Blackstone, "the law of nature and the law of revelation, depend all human laws; that is to say, no human laws should be suffered [allowed] to contradict these."

The adoption of the common law was advantageous for the new Republic for several reasons. First, the common law was a product of human experience, not the pronouncement of a ruler or committee of experts. Second, the common law was not created by the ruler but was, rather, the source of his power. Finally, the common law, with its emphasis on a law that existed from time immemorial, reflected Christian truth.

William Blackstone

"The historic phrase 'a government of laws, and not of men,' epitomizes the distinguishing character of our political society."

—Justice Felix Frankfurter, concurring in *United States v. United Mine Workers*, 330 U.S. 258 (1947)

Section Review

1. What is one of the fundamental obligations that people have toward one another?

2. Explain God's standard for justice.

3–4. Who compiled the *Corpus Juris Civilis*? What is it?

5–6. What was English common law? How was it different from the legal systems used in most of Europe?

7. Explain how William Blackstone's *Commentaries on the Laws of England* affected the American colonies.

★ Why was adopting English common law advantageous for the colonies?

What Is Equity?

Until at least the middle of the seventeenth century, common law was a law for aristocrats; it hardly touched average people. Strange to our way of thinking, other systems of law existed alongside English common law, which was common to all of England but not to all Englishmen. These other legal systems included feudal law, ecclesiastical law, traders' law (laws for merchants), and the law of the high seas (admiralty).

An unusual rival to common law was equity, a legal system administered by the king's chancellor in a totally separate system of courts. Common law had power over things but not people: it could declare who owned a piece of property but could not force an illegitimate possessor to hand the land over to its owner. Equity, however, had power over people but not things. Equity courts (which did not allow juries) could not decide ownership of land, but they could issue injunctions to force illegitimate possessors of land to return the lands to their rightful owners. If anyone refused to return land, an equity court could hold him in contempt of court.

Although law and equity gradually merged during the nineteenth (and, in some jurisdictions, well into the twentieth) century, law and equity were still separate systems when the Constitution was written. That is why Article III, Section 2, clause 1, reads (in part), "The judicial power shall extend to all cases, in law and equity, arising under this Constitution." Even today, only judges—not juries—can issue injunctions and hold people in contempt of court.

Activity 1: The Principles of Blackstone's *Commentaries*

This enrichment activity helps the students understand William Blackstone's thinking and how his views helped form the foundation of America's legal system.

Section Review Answers

1. ensuring justice (p. 333)

2. God's standard of justice is His own character (p. 334)

3–4. Justinian (a Roman emperor); an organized compilation of Roman legal materials from previous centuries (p. 334)

5–6. Common law was common throughout the whole realm of England. It was grounded in case law, a body of opinions written by royal judges who, at least in theory, followed precedents. The legal systems of continental Europe were based on codified Roman law. (pp. 334–35)

7. It probably restrained any urge Americans had to abandon common law for a new legal code; it also taught that God expressed law through His Word as well as through nature. (p. 337)

★ The common law was a product of human experience; it was the source of the ruler's power; it emphasized a law that existed before civilization, thereby reflecting Christian truth.

II. Structure of the Courts

Judicial Federalism

Each of the thirteen original American states already had common-law courts in place when the Constitution was written. The relationship that these preexisting state courts would have with the new national courts created by the Constitution was a delicate issue that the founders chose not to answer during the summer of 1787 as they wrote that document.

The founders almost certainly understood that national courts would have to exercise judicial review over state courts, but they could not have imagined the modern Supreme Court's power to make public policy. In *Federalist* No. 78, Alexander Hamilton called the proposed federal judiciary the "least dangerous" branch of the new government.

Article III, Section 1, of the Constitution was written as concisely and vaguely as possible. It vested the nation's judicial power "in one Supreme Court, and in such inferior courts as the Congress may from time to time ordain and establish."

According to Article III of the Constitution, federal courts are empowered to hear the following cases:

- constitutional violations
- congressional violations
- treaty violations
- lawsuits between foreign countries and the United States or an American citizen
- cases involving US ambassadors or consuls
- cases involving crimes committed at sea aboard American vessels
- cases involving crimes committed on federal lands or federal property
- lawsuits between states or citizens of different states

Although the Constitution establishes the general bounds of federal jurisdiction (i.e., the areas in which the federal government has the power to make legal decisions and judgments), Congress establishes the jurisdiction of a particular court within these constitutional boundaries.

Congress quickly established a more elaborate federal judicial system, and the United States soon had a unique system of coexisting federal and state courts—**judicial federalism**—an organizational scheme that had never been tried before.

Despite a vast expansion of federal power, state courts are still important today. More than 95 percent of the nation's legal actions—tens of millions of cases—are heard in state courts each year. Once a case is decided in the highest court of a state, it will not be admitted into the federal system unless there is a federal question involved.

Nevertheless, some cases can be heard in either state or federal courts, as, for example, in a civil suit where the amount at issue is more than $75,000 and the parties reside in different states. Likewise, the kidnapping of a

US Court Systems

STATE COURT SYSTEM
- State Supreme Court
- State Appeals Courts (not all states)
- State Trial Courts

FEDERAL COURT SYSTEM
- US Supreme Court
- US Courts of Appeals
- US District Courts

Judiciary Levels

Ask each student to draw a chart of the three levels of the national judiciary and relate it to your region by listing, on the chart, the nearest federal district court, the nearest federal circuit court of appeals, and the US Supreme Court.

federal marshal might be prosecuted in either a state or federal court. Furthermore, criminal suspects can sometimes be tried for the same activity in both state and federal courts. For instance, a suspect charged with a racially motivated beating might be tried in state court for the beating itself and then be tried in federal court for violating the victim's civil rights. The Supreme Court has ruled that such prosecutions do not violate the Fifth Amendment's prohibition against double jeopardy (being tried twice for the same offense).

District Courts

By passing the **Judiciary Act of 1789**, the first Congress created a system of inferior courts and launched the United States Supreme Court as well. The act created thirteen **district courts**, the trial courts of the federal judicial system. Today the United States has ninety-four district courts in the fifty states, the District of Columbia, Puerto Rico, and three territories (Guam, the US Virgin Islands, and the Northern Mariana Islands). There are more than 670 judges that serve these courts. Each state has from one to four districts, depending on its population. District courts exercise **original jurisdiction**, meaning that they are the first to hear a case before any other court considers it. Like most state courts, district courts use a **grand jury** (a panel of citizens who considers the prosecution's case against the accused and determines whether there is enough evidence against the accused to warrant a jury trial to determine guilt or innocence). A

The US Marshals Service

The US Marshals Service is the oldest federal law-enforcement agency, having been created by the Judiciary Act of 1789. It is the enforcement arm of the US court system.

The marshals gained fame because of their law-enforcement activities in the West during the nineteenth century. But they also recovered fugitive slaves, helped break the Pullman Strike (a famous railroad strike in 1894), en-

US Deputy Marshals in 1892

forced Prohibition, and protected abortion clinics.

The following are some of the most famous US Marshals:

- Phoebe Couzins was the first female marshal (1887).
- Frederick Douglass, former slave, became the marshal for the District of Columbia in 1877.
- Brothers Morgan, Virgil, and Wyatt Earp served as marshals in Tombstone, Arizona Territory (1879–81).
- Wild Bill Hickok was a deputy US Marshal in Kansas (1865).
- Bat Masterson was famous for his law-enforcement deeds in the West, but President Theodore Roosevelt appointed him deputy marshal for the Southern District of New York (1905–7).
- Bass Reeves, one of the first African American marshals,

Heavily armed members of the US Marshals Special Operations Group outside a federal courthouse in Buffalo, New York (October, 2002)

arrested more than three thousand criminals (1875–1907).
- John Marshall was the first black American to serve as director of the US Marshals Service (1999–2001).

Governing Fallen Humanity

Shortly after the War for Independence, some American thinkers had grand ideas about dispensing with common law and developing law codes that would turn a judge, in Jefferson's words, into "a mere machine." But by the end of the 1780s, it was clear that this vision had gone awry. Instead of having clear and simple law codes, the state legislatures were influenced by special interests and developed complicated law codes to benefit some people over others. In addition, the laws covered some aspects of life but not others. As a result, some suggested that the states should devise general principles of justice and ensure that wise and honest judges applied these principles. But how could people ensure that the judges would be wise and honest if the legislators were not?

Ensuring justice in a world of fallen people is difficult. No system can perfectly counteract people's fallen tendencies, but some systems do work better than others. This is why the American founders endeavored to establish checks and balances between the branches of government.

US Marshals

Select a student to collect information regarding the history of US Marshals and to find the name of the US Marshal in your district. Ask the student to present the findings to the class.

Why Are Grand Juries "Grand"?

Grand juries are grand only because they are larger than petit, or trial, juries. (*Grand* is French for "large"; *petit* is French for "small.") Federal grand juries have twenty-three members and can be impaneled for months at a time, although they are usually impaneled for only a few days per week at most. (State grand juries are usually smaller, sometimes smaller than trial juries.)

The role of the grand jury is to indict, or charge, a suspect with a crime. Grand juries meet in secret, and people ordered to testify before them do not have to be told the nature of the crime being investigated. Suspects are not entitled to cross-examine witnesses, nor (in most jurisdictions) are they allowed to bring their lawyers into court. Grand juries do not hold trials, nor do they determine guilt or innocence. Their job is simply to decide whether there is enough evidence to charge a suspect with a crime.

The theoretical purpose of grand juries is to insulate suspects from government officials, especially police and other criminal-justice professionals, should there be insufficient evidence to warrant prosecution. But prosecutors have considerable influence over grand juries. No judge is involved with a grand jury, and most suspects are indicted.

petit jury, or a **trial jury**, then hears a case and decides its outcome. Each year, more than three hundred fifty thousand cases, about 85 percent of the federal judicial workload, are heard in federal district courts.

The president, with the consent of the Senate, appoints a US attorney and a US Marshal for each district. The attorney and his assistants prosecute criminal cases and represent the federal government in all civil cases. The marshal and the deputy marshals typically serve subpoenas, summonses, and arrest warrants. They also protect federal witnesses and juries, transport criminals, and manage assets seized in federal law-enforcement activities. In addition, the men and women of the US Marshal Service pursue and arrest federal fugitives (they are responsible for the apprehension of more than half of all federal fugitives that are captured).

Circuit Courts of Appeals

The circuit courts of appeals are the second tier, or level, of the federal judicial system. The Judiciary Act of 1789 established three circuits. Today there are thirteen circuit courts of appeals—eleven circuits plus one each for the District of Columbia and the Federal Circuit. The oddly named US Court of Appeals for the Federal Circuit has a national jurisdiction but reviews only specialized appeals, such as tax, patent, and trademark cases and claims against the federal government. Until 1982 it was two different courts: the Court of Customs and Patent Appeals and the Court of Claims.

Originally, two Supreme Court judges and a district judge were assigned to each circuit. That meant that justices of the Supreme Court regularly "rode circuit," often thousands of miles annually. Although some people argued that

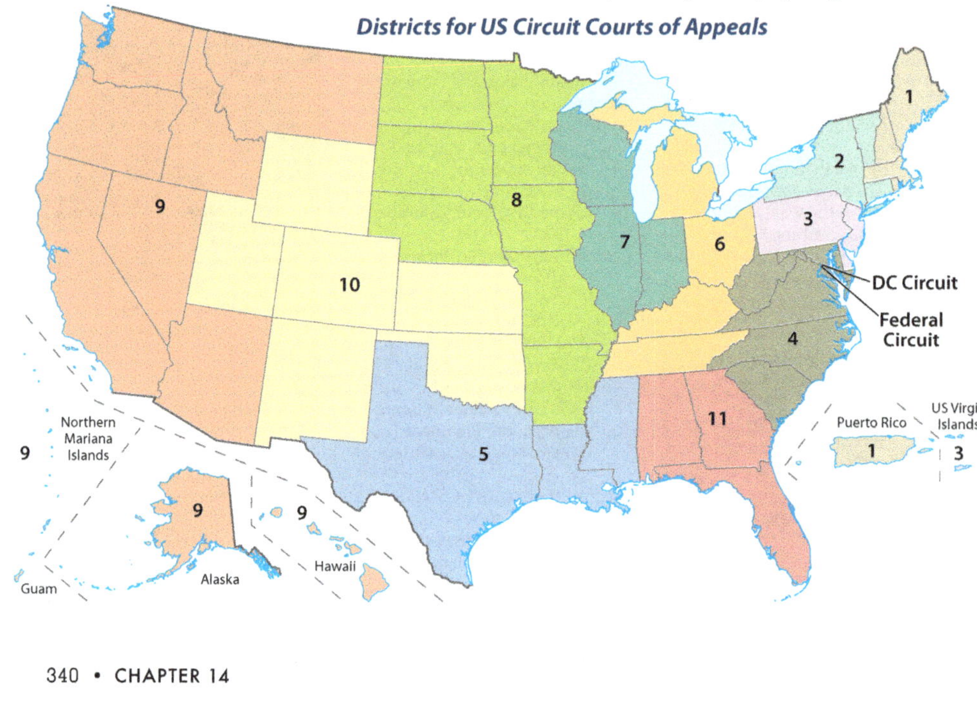

Districts for US Circuit Courts of Appeals

US Circuit Courts of Appeals

Guide a visual analysis of the map above. What general conclusions can be drawn? Invite the students to speculate regarding why the districts are of varying geographical proportions. How are adjustments made for circuits that have larger populations (refer students to the text for the answer)?

Ask a student to research the Ninth Circuit Court. What makes this court distinctive? Encourage the student to prepare a presentation for the class.

this practice brought national justice closer to the people, it also required judges to have a good deal of physical stamina. Further, as Gouverneur Morris wryly noted, "riding rapidly from one end of [the] country to the other" was not the best method of becoming learned in the law.

As their name implies, circuit courts of appeals have **appellate jurisdiction** only; that is, they do not hold trials but only hear appeals from the district courts in their circuits, examining the actions and rulings of district judges for possible errors in procedure or legal interpretation. Circuit-court judges usually sit in rotating panels of three and decide most cases on the basis of written briefs, although occasionally they may sit *en banc* (as a group). Only a very small percentage of decisions from the circuit courts are successfully appealed to the Supreme Court.

Today, there are 179 circuit-court judges and the number of judges assigned to each circuit is roughly determined by that circuit's population. Some circuit courts have so many members that they operate like small legislatures. The Ninth Circuit Court, based in San Francisco, is by far the largest, serving more than 65 million people with 29 judges.

The Supreme Court

The United States Supreme Court is the third and highest tier of the federal judicial system and perhaps the most powerful court in the world. But at the beginning of the Republic, it was so feeble that the government had difficulty attracting able men to serve on it. Alexander Hamilton preferred to practice private law rather than join the Court. John Jay, the first chief justice, had so little responsibility that he was sent to England, to negotiate a treaty, while still holding office. When he returned, he resigned to become governor of New York. Later, when asked to rejoin the Court, Jay refused on the grounds that the US Supreme Court lacked not only "energy, weight, and dignity" but also "public confidence and respect."

The period of Supreme Court weakness gradually ended after John Marshall became chief justice in 1801. Marshall had a brilliant mind and an amiable, unassuming personality that easily won others to his views. Marshall's leadership attracted able associates, and the early nineteenth-century Court was also blessed with a number of long tenures, an unblemished record of honesty, and high legal craftsmanship. By 1900 the Supreme Court had certainly become equal in not only power but also prestige to Congress and the president.

Justices and Their Jurisdiction

Supreme Court judges are known as **justices**. The Constitution does not stipulate a specific number of justices, and the first Congress appointed six. From 1801 to 1807, there were five members and between 1807 and 1869 the number ranged from seven to ten. Since 1869 nine justices—one **chief justice** (the highest ranking judge) and eight **associate justices**—have composed the Supreme Court. There have been nine justices for so long that another number would be considered revolutionary, even though naming more or fewer would be constitutional, provided it is done according to the constitutionally stipulated procedure. In fact, Franklin Roosevelt tried to do just that in the late 1930s when he tired of the justices' declaring his New Deal measures unconstitutional and proposed a plan for increasing the number on the court. The resulting public outcry was so great, however, that he backed down from any further attempt to "pack" the Court with New Deal sympathizers.

Chief Justices

The chief justice is only the first among equals, but he can use his traditional privileges to influence the Court. In conference, the chief justice always states his opinion first, but he votes last. If he votes with the majority, he decides who will write the opinion, and he can therefore choose a justice who closely approximates his own views.

Supreme Court Justices

Direct attention to page 348 of this text. Ask the students whether any justices have retired, resigned, or died since this book was published. If so, who replaced those individuals? How old are the present members of the Court? Which members have served the longest?

The Supreme Court is empowered to exercise both original and appellate jurisdiction. Nevertheless, original-jurisdiction cases (which are usually cases about one state suing another or cases involving US ambassadors and consuls) compose only a tiny fraction of the Court's caseload. The vast majority of cases come to the Supreme Court on **writ of certiorari** (suhr-shee-uh-RAR-ee) (Latin for "to be made more certain") from the federal circuit courts and state supreme courts.

Caseload

During the first half of the nineteenth century, the caseload of the Supreme Court was so light that arguments often rambled on for days. In the famous case of *Dartmouth College v. Woodward* (1819), Daniel Webster spoke for more than four consecutive hours.

With the rapid growth of American industry and the expansion of federal power following the Civil War, the Court's caseload escalated. Congress appointed full-time circuit-court judges in 1869 and gave them their modern powers in 1891. Even with these reforms, the Supreme Court was still hearing hundreds of cases a year. Many of these cases were mundane, having arrived at the Supreme Court only because they involved citizens of different states or because they originated in the territories.

In 1925, Congress reduced the Court's caseload dramatically by granting the Court nearly unlimited discretion to choose which cases and what issues it wanted to decide. Although litigation continues to swamp state and lower federal dockets, the Supreme Court has been virtually untouched by the flood below. Beginning with the 1990s, the number of cases argued before the court has actually declined. Now the Court hears fewer than a hundred cases per year. This is less than two percent of the thousands for which it receives appeals each year. After the Court decides which cases it will hear, all remaining ones are denied review; this allows the lower-court rulings to stand.

Petitions for writ of certiorari, or "cert," are delegated to the justices' law clerks—some of the best and brightest of the nation's recent law-school graduates. The clerks write short memos about the cases, and the justices vote in conference about which of the cases to hear. Review of a case will be granted if four justices agree to hear it. As a rule, the Court takes only cases that lower courts have disagreed on or those that involve significant matters of public policy.

Decision Making

Supreme Court sessions begin on the first Monday in October and continue through the following June. The nine-month term has alternating two-week sessions, with court days running Monday through Wednesday. Justices meet on Wednesday afternoons and Fridays to discuss that week's cases and to vote on the outcomes.

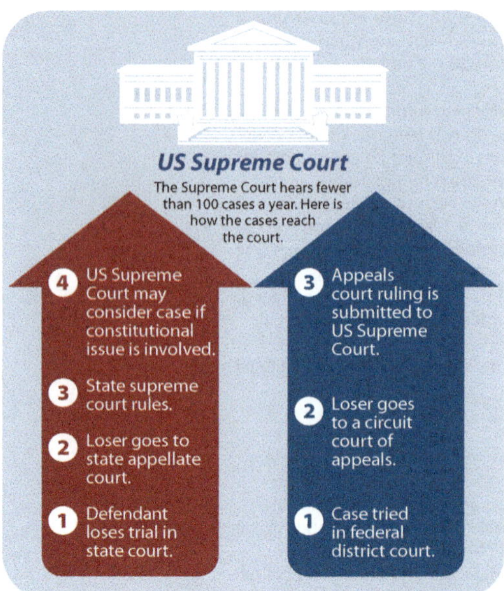

Roads to the US Supreme Court

Instruct the students to analyze the diagrams above. How do the two ways in which cases reach the Supreme Court fundamentally differ?

When the Supreme Court accepts a case, lawyers for each side present written briefs detailing their positions. (*Brief* is a figure of speech: in major cases the combined briefs can be as long as a book.) The case is then argued for exactly one hour, thirty minutes per side. But justices may interrupt with questions—and otherwise take the lawyers' time—whenever they choose. Following each two-week session, there is a two-week recess in which the justices and their clerks write draft opinions and study those written by other justices.

A case is won by a simple majority vote of the justices. However, which side "won" is sometimes less important than the legal principles established in the written opinions of the justices. Supreme Court opinions present the arguments and points of law the justices used in deciding the case. These opinions can establish new precedent which can only be changed by Congress or sometimes only by changing the Constitution; thus, they are very important.

If the chief justice votes with the majority, he—or someone he assigns—writes the **majority opinion**. It details the reasons the decision was made. If the chief justice is in the minority, the senior justice on the winning side assigns the writing of the opinion. Justices on the losing side frequently issue **dissenting opinions** to explain why they oppose the majority opinion. Justices who agree with the majority for different reasons than those presented in the decision may issue **concurring opinions**.

Justices' written opinions have tended to grow longer and more legalistic, and dissents and concurrences have become more numerous. Each associate justice now has four law clerks (the chief justice is permitted five, but often hires fewer)

Presenting the Case

When lawyers present oral arguments before the Supreme Court, the justices will sometimes talk among themselves, read briefs, look at their watches, or act very disinterested. Justices may also interrupt the presentations at will. Occasionally they attempt to help a lawyer, but more often they question lawyers' arguments. When two justices disagree, they may argue back and forth, using a hapless lawyer as their middleman. Some justices have a reputation for regularly interrupting presentations; others rarely say a word in court.

Homes of the US Supreme Court

Although it is the highest court of the United States, the Supreme Court did not have its own building for the first 145 years of its existence. During those years, the Court met in many different buildings in three different cities, even meeting in a private home after the British burned Washington, DC, during the War of 1812.

The Court spent its first two sessions, February 1–10 and August 2–3, 1790, at the Royal Exchange in New York City. When the United States capital moved to Philadelphia, the Supreme Court met in Independence Hall for two days in 1791. The session was short because the Court had no cases to hear. For the next decade, the Court met in the east wing of Philadelphia's Old City Hall, and Congress met in the west wing of the building.

When the government moved to Washington, DC, the Supreme Court convened in a number of different rooms in the unfinished Capitol until it was given a specially designed courtroom, now restored as the Old Supreme Court Chamber. The Court occupied this space from 1819 to 1860.

After the Senate left for larger quarters, the Supreme Court met in the Old Senate Chamber from 1860 to 1935.

Finally, Chief Justice William Howard Taft persuaded Congress to appropriate funds for a permanent Supreme Court building in 1929. Built in the style of a Greco-Roman temple, the current home of the Supreme Court is 304 feet wide by 385 feet long. Construction cost $9,395,566—almost $350,000 under budget! Neither Taft nor the architect, Cass Gilbert, lived to see the building completed in 1935.

Philadelphia's Old City Hall

Recent Decisions

Discuss recent Supreme Court decisions and assess whether they align with scriptural principles.

to "draft" (write) his decisions, so it has become easier for each justice to put his individual stamp on each decided case. Unfortunately, the Court is sometimes so splintered by concurring decisions that a majority decision is more of a plurality decision. Deciphering what the Court actually decided becomes an exercise in logic splitting. Although under unusual circumstances (such as the disputed 2000 presidential election) the decision-making process may be hurried along, the Court generally does not announce its decision for several months after oral arguments (though decisions are announced before the Court's summer recess begins in June).

Section Review

1. Define *judicial federalism*.
2–4. Identify the three tiers of federal courts.
5–6. Distinguish between the work of a grand jury and a petit jury.
7–9. Describe the three kinds of opinions that a Supreme Court justice may write about a decided case.
★ Why do few cases reach the Supreme Court?
★ Do you think the Supreme Court should listen to more cases each year? Explain your answer.

III. Selection of Judges

State Judges

State judges are chosen in three basic ways (with a number of complex variations): by popular election (the vote of the people), appointment by the governor, or appointment by the state legislature. The election may be partisan (meaning that a candidate runs as a member of a political party) or nonpartisan (meaning that he runs without a party label). Only two states, South Carolina and Virginia, allow the legislature to choose state judges; legislative selection has been criticized for resulting in the election of judges who have a great deal of political clout—especially judges who are past and present members of the legislature.

States that allow the governor to choose state judges often restrict his power by requiring that he pick from a committee-approved list or by requiring that his choice be approved by the state senate. A more formal attempt to reduce the influence of partisan politics is the **Missouri Plan**, which more than half of the states use for the selection of some judges. In this plan, the governor appoints a judicial candidate from a short list nominated by a judicial commission. The new judge assumes office but then must be approved by voters in a later election, usually a year or more later. No opposition candidate is allowed; the voters can only approve or disapprove of the new judge. Proponents of this method of judicial selection argue that it produces better-qualified judges who are not dependent on their political connections. Opponents assert that because voters rarely vote against a judge who has no opponent, reliance on the judicial commission places too much power in the hands of a small group of lawyers.

Unlike federal judges who serve for life (technically, "during good behaviour"), in the states' systems the vast majority of judges serve for stated terms, typically

Section Review Answers

1. a system of coexisting state and federal courts (p. 338)
2–4. district courts, circuit courts of appeals, and the Supreme Court (pp. 339–41)
5–6. A grand jury is a panel of citizens who considers the prosecution's case against the accused and determines whether there is enough evidence against the accused to warrant a jury trial to determine guilt or innocence. A petit jury, or trial jury, is used to hear a case and decide its outcome. (pp. 339–40)
7–9. A majority opinion is written to justify and explain the decision. A dissenting opinion is written by a judge who wants to explain why he rejects the majority position. A concurring opinion is written by a judge who agrees with the majority opinion but for reasons different from those presented in the majority opinion. (p. 343)
★ Congress gave the Supreme Court the authority to choose which cases and what issues it wants to decide.
★ Some may agree that the Supreme Court should be able to decide the number of cases it takes to keep its workload manageable and thus should limit the number of cases they consider. Others may say the Supreme Court should be willing to hear additional cases because there are many that involve issues of national importance that are never considered.

ranging from four to twelve years. Also unlike the federal system, most of the states have mandatory retirement ages for judges, usually ranging from seventy to seventy-five years old.

Federal Judges

According to Article II, Section 2, of the Constitution, the president appoints all federal judges with the approval of the Senate. Presidents almost always select judges from their own political party. A prospective federal judge for a district court is subject to the long-standing, though unwritten, tradition of **senatorial courtesy**. This practice gives a senator from the nominee's home state the power to block the appointment if he does not approve of the individual. Sometimes a senator and the president engage in political horse-trading: the senator agrees to vote for a piece of legislation that the president wants, and the president agrees to nominate a judicial candidate whom the senator prefers.

The president usually has more control over circuit-court nominations than he does over district-court nominations because the circuits cover several states. Nevertheless, his choices are still limited by the political need to balance the courts by gender, ethnicity, and geographic region.

Federal judges hold office until death or retirement unless impeached by the House of Representatives and removed by the Senate. Only eight federal judges have been impeached and removed. The first occurred in 1803–4. The most recent incident was in 2010 when federal judge G. Thomas Porteous of Louisiana was found guilty of accepting bribes and committing perjury (making false statements while under oath).

Life terms tend to protect judges from political pressure; this insulation might encourage a thoughtful approach to the judicial process. Likewise, elderly judges can use their years of experience to better unravel complex legal questions. Sometimes, however, such judges are tempted to continue in office even after they have clearly become mentally or physically unfit to serve.

Supreme Court Justices

Supreme Court nominations are so important and so rare that it is difficult to formulate any general rule about whom the president might nominate when the opportunity arises. Although he obviously prefers to choose someone with similar ideological views, he will try not to nominate a candidate that the Senate will reject. As with lower-court nominations, the president will consider gender and ethnicity in selecting a nominee. For example, when Thurgood Marshall, the first African American justice, retired in 1991, President George H. W. Bush nominated another black American, Clarence Thomas, to succeed Marshall. In 1981 President Ronald Reagan appointed the first female justice and in 2009 President Barack Obama selected Sonia Sotomayor to be the first Hispanic justice.

Chief Justice Warren Berger (left) swearing in Sandra Day O'Connor (right). She was the first female Supreme Court justice.

Judicial Confirmation

Until recent decades, it was uncommon for judicial nominees to district and circuit courts to meet more than token resistance in the Senate. But today the increased politicization of the confirmation process and the importance (or near

Impeached and Removed

The following federal judges were impeached and removed from office:

- John Pickering in 1804, on charges of mental instability and intoxication on the bench
- West H. Humphreys in 1862, on charges of refusing to hold court and waging war against the US government
- Robert W. Archbald in 1913, on charges of improper business relationships with litigants
- Halsted L. Ritter in 1936, on charges of favoritism in the appointment of bankruptcy receivers and practicing law while sitting as a judge
- Harry E. Claiborne in 1986, on charges of income-tax evasion and remaining on the bench following criminal conviction
- Alcee L. Hastings in 1989, on charges of perjury and conspiring to solicit a bribe
- Walter L. Nixon in 1989, on charges of perjury before a federal grand jury
- G. Thomas Porteous in 2010, on charges of accepting cash and other favors from lawyers who had dealings with his court; making false statements under the penalty of perjury

Judge Selection

Instruct the students to research the method your state uses to select state judges and relate the information to the class.

Senate Rejection

During a nineteen-month period from late 1968 to 1970, four Supreme Court nominees failed to receive Senate approval. Two had been submitted by a Democratic president and two by a Republican president.

During the last months of the Johnson administration, Chief Justice Earl Warren announced his intention to retire. Johnson nominated Abe Fortas, a Supreme Court associate justice and personal friend, to replace Warren. Johnson then nominated another close friend, Homer Thornberry, to take Fortas's seat. However, both names were withdrawn in October 1968 after supporters were unable to break a filibuster led by Republicans and conservative Democrats.

After Republican Richard Nixon became president in 1969, he nominated Warren Burger to replace Earl Warren, who had delayed his retirement. Burger was confirmed by the Senate. Nevertheless, after Abe Fortas resigned his seat in the summer of 1969, Nixon's next two nominees, Clement Haynsworth and G. Harrold Carswell, were rejected by the Senate.

finality) of decisions made at the circuit-court level have led to Senate challenges, filibusters, and foot-dragging on presidential nominations to all federal courts.

Supreme Court nominees are, appropriately, subjected to the most scrutiny. Each nominee's professional qualifications are examined, and the American Bar Association rates suitability for office. Unfortunately, sometimes such scrutiny becomes an attempt to discover information that will allow political opponents to embarrass the prospective justice (and the president) and torpedo the nomination.

Likewise, at the hearings themselves, some hostile senators ask questions intended to induce a political blunder from the nominee. The prospective justice

The Bork Nomination

Political opposition to Supreme Court nominees intensified after the turn of the twentieth century when it became clear that Supreme Court decisions could impact public policy in ways that were virtually irreversible. Nevertheless, President Ronald Reagan's unsuccessful nomination of Robert Bork, a well-known law professor and judge, to the US Supreme Court in 1987 proved something of a milestone in the evolution of the confirmation process. Political liberals were candid in their determination to not allow a staunch conservative like Bork a seat on the Supreme Court.

Democrats had regained control of the Senate in 1986, and Bork had frequently and comprehensively expressed his views on a variety of constitutional subjects. As a result, the Bork nomination was denounced by such liberal stalwarts as the American Civil Liberties Union (ACLU), the People for the American Way, and the nation's largest labor organization—the American Federation of Labor and Congress of Industrial Organizations (AFL-CIO). Millions of dollars were spent on the media campaign that denounced the nomination.

Bork had outstanding credentials. He was a professor at Yale Law School for fifteen years, had served as solicitor general in the Nixon and Ford administrations, and in 1982 received unanimous confirmation as a federal circuit court of appeals judge. Former president Gerald Ford and retired chief justice Warren Burger both testified on Bork's behalf at the confirmation hearings when he was nominated to the Supreme Court.

The Senate hearings dragged on for eighty-seven hours over a twelve day period. No previous nominee had ever faced such a lengthy process. Bork himself testified for more than thirty hours, and he outlined his legal philosophy in greater detail than any previous nominee. Ironically, Bork's candid discussion of his judicial beliefs probably derailed his chances of winning confirmation. His outspokenness and distinct conservative views regarding constitutional law led to the Senate rejecting his nomination by a vote of 42–58.

Since the Bork ordeal, presidents have sometimes nominated "stealth nominees" for federal court positions (one of whom, David Souter, was confirmed as a Supreme Court justice in 1990). Such nominees have a meager paper trail, and their views about controversial issues are, at least officially, shrouded in mystery.

Furthermore, most Supreme Court nominees now say as little as possible about their political ideologies regarding controversial issues, such as abortion, immigration, and affirmative action.

The rejection of the Bork nomination was an important event with lasting political implications. The *Oxford English Dictionary* defines *bork* as US political slang, with this definition: "To defame or vilify (a person) systematically, especially in the mass media, usually with the aim of preventing his or her appointment to public office; to obstruct or thwart (a person) in this way."

Invite a Judge

Invite a judge to speak to the class. Ask the judge to describe a typical workday, responsibilities, and judicial career path. In advance, encourage students to write questions they would like to ask. If time permits, allow students to ask additional questions as well.

Longest-Serving Supreme Court Justices

More than 110 individuals have served on the US Supreme Court. William O. Douglas, who served for thirty-six years (1939–75), holds the record for the longest tenure. Serving for thirty-four years were Stephen Field, John Paul Stevens, John Marshall, and Hugo Black. John Harlan, William J. Brennan, William Rehnquist, and Joseph Story served for thirty-three years. In all, fifteen justices have served thirty or more years.

Quotes from one of those longtime justices, Joseph Story, are featured in several chapters of this book. Story played a critical role in the formation of US jurisprudence. Born during the War for Independence to a Patriot family (his father attended the Boston Tea Party), he distinguished himself academically, eventually attending and excelling at Harvard University. After graduation, he established a successful law practice and served in the Massachusetts House of Representatives as well as the US Congress. Story was only thirty-two when President James Madison nominated him to the Supreme Court, the youngest justice ever appointed.

Story actively participated in rulings by writing opinions; few other justices matched his output. In addition to sitting on the Supreme Court, he taught law at Harvard and was a popular legal writer and speaker. Law schools have used several of his works as textbooks. His *Commentaries on the Constitution of the United States* remains important to understanding what led to the writing of the US Constitution and how it should be interpreted. *Commentaries'* authority has influenced hundreds of court decisions regarding constitutional issues.

Joseph Story

President Clinton (left) appointed Ruth Bader Ginsburg (center) to the Supreme Court in 1993.

Brett Kavanaugh (right) was appointed by President Trump in 2018 to serve on the Supreme Court.

attempts to create distance from earlier decisions or writings that might be seen as politically incorrect and usually insists on not giving opinions about issues that might someday arise before the Supreme Court.

In the cases of Robert Bork (in 1987) and Clarence Thomas (in 1991), confirmation hearings were especially bitter because different parties controlled the presidency and the Senate. In 2018 fiery hearings ensued when Republicans held only a narrow majority in the Senate at the time Republican President Trump nominated Brett Kavanaugh (his nomination was eventually approved by a vote

Change of Mind

Supreme Court justices occasionally change their minds before the Court's decision is published. Though quite rare, sometimes when opinions are drafted and circulated among members of the Court, the refined opinions may gather support from justices who did not originally vote for that side.

Two examples of this, both occurring in 1992, involved Justice Anthony Kennedy. In *Planned Parenthood v. Casey*, his original vote would have overturned *Roe v. Wade*, but he reversed himself, turning a 5–4 decision to overturn into a 5–4 decision to uphold. In *Lee v. Weisman*, a case involving prayer at public school graduations, he initially supported the right to such prayer but, after drafting his opinion on the matter, changed his mind. This produced a 5–4 ruling against school-sponsored public prayer.

Static or Ever-Changing Document?

Discuss whether the Constitution is a static document that should be interpreted to mean exactly what it says or whether it is a living, ever-changing document.

Judicial Training

As noted earlier in the chapter, in the legal systems of Western Europe a prospective magistrate or judge usually follows a different system of training and a separate career path from those who wish to become lawyers. In addition, European judges often sit as panels, and some members of those panels are remarkably young by American standards.

Supreme Court Appointments

The current Court consists of appointees spanning several presidential administrations. As of 2019, four of the justices were near or over age seventy. The oldest member of the Court is Ruth Bader Ginsburg (b. 1933). Stephen Breyer was born in 1938, Clarence Thomas in 1948, and Samuel Alito in 1950. The aging court increases the likelihood of new justices being appointed in the near future. The chart at right lists the current Court members, the presidents who appointed them, and the day each justice took the judicial oath.

Clarence Thomas	George H. W. Bush	October 23, 1991
Ruth Bader Ginsburg	Bill Clinton	August 10, 1993
Stephen G. Breyer	Bill Clinton	August 3, 1994
John Roberts	George W. Bush	September 29, 2005
Samuel Alito	George W. Bush	January 31, 2006
Sonia Sotomayor	Barack Obama	August 8, 2009
Elena Kagan	Barack Obama	August 7, 2010
Neil Gorsuch	Donald Trump	April 10, 2017
Brett Kavanaugh	Donald Trump	October 6, 2018

Members of the US Supreme Court in November 2018: (standing from left) Justices Neil Gorsuch, Sonia Sotomayor, Elena Kagan, Brett Kavanaugh, (seated from left) Stephen G. Breyer, Clarence Thomas, Chief Justice John Roberts, Justices Ruth Bader Ginsburg, and Samuel Alito

of 50–48). As noted in an earlier chapter, during President Obama's last year in office, Republicans refused to schedule a hearing on his Supreme Court nominee, Merrick Garland.

Even after the Senate confirms a presidential nominee, there is no guarantee that the new justice will help move the Court in the direction the president would like to see it go, especially over the twenty or thirty years of the justice's tenure. As the late constitutional scholar Alexander Bickel once reflected, "You shoot an arrow into the far-distant future when you appoint a justice, and not the man himself can tell you what he will think about some of the problems that he will face."

Activity 2: Criteria for Supreme Court Justices

This enrichment activity enables the students to become more familiar with the criteria whereby US Supreme Court justices are chosen.

Presidential disappointment in Supreme Court nominees has been a recurring lament in American history. Jeffersonian Republicans nominated a series of justices who they thought would challenge John Marshall; but once seated on the Court, most consistently voted with the chief justice. Similarly, when Dwight Eisenhower was asked whether he made any mistakes during his term of office, he replied, "Yes, two, and they are both sitting on the Supreme Court."

Section Review

1–3. Identify three ways that state judges are chosen.

4–5. Distinguish between partisan and nonpartisan elections.

6. Explain the Missouri Plan.

7. How has the judicial confirmation process changed in recent decades?

★ Do you think federal judges should serve for life? Explain your answer.

★ How did Robert Bork's nomination become a milestone in the confirmation process?

IV. Constitutional and Legal Change

From the perspective of the twenty-first century, it is difficult to imagine the frailty of the Supreme Court two hundred years ago. As mentioned earlier, Chief Justice John Marshall crafted the Court's rise in prestige and power.

A fundamental question that had to be resolved was whether Congress or the individual states, rather than the Supreme Court, would determine when the Constitution had been violated. In *Marbury v. Madison* (1803), Marshall cautiously declared the doctrine of **judicial review** (the Court's right to declare government actions unconstitutional). In Marshall's view, it was "emphatically the province and duty of the judicial department to say what the law is."

Likewise, as a strong nationalist, Marshall took seriously the Constitution's **supremacy clause**, contained in Article VI, that declared the Constitution and the laws of the United States "the supreme law of the land; . . . any thing in the constitution or laws of any state to the contrary notwithstanding." In the case of *McCulloch v. Maryland* (1819), the Marshall Court ruled that state taxation of the second Bank of the United States was unconstitutional, although chartering banks was not a power specifically granted to Congress in the Constitution. But the chartering power could be implied from the necessary and proper clause, said Marshall, and the Maryland law must therefore be unconstitutional because "the power to tax involves the power to destroy."

The Marshall Court also increased the power of the federal government in other ways: for instance, it made federal commerce laws supreme over state laws and guaranteed the sanctity of contracts that would have otherwise been violated by state action. Jefferson called the judiciary a "corps of sappers and miners" chipping away at state power, but there is no doubt that private property and economic prosperity benefited from the Court's decisions.

Guiding Questions

1. What is judicial review?
2. How do Supreme Court decisions impact the legal system?

John Marshall

---

1. Define *judicial review*.

2. Evaluate the impact of Supreme Court decisions on the legal system.

John Marshall

John Marshall grew up on the Virginia frontier, but his father was a member of the Virginia gentry, and Marshall was related, through his mother's family, to the Randolphs and the Lees. He was a cousin to Thomas Jefferson. Marshall had only about a year of formal schooling and a second year of tutoring by a clergyman. But he had the advantage of observing his father serve as a surveyor, justice of the peace, vestryman, and sheriff; this was the practical school of the Virginia gentry. Apparently, Marshall also pored over some of the copies of Blackstone's *Commentaries* that arrived from London.

During the War for Independence, Marshall fought at Brandywine, Germantown, and Monmouth, and he wintered at Valley Forge. He said that his nationalist views were forged during the war when he, in his own words, "associated with brave men from different states, who were risking life and everything valuable in a common cause" and "was confirmed in the habit of considering America as [his] country and Congress as [his] government."

Curbing Court Power

Ineffective attempts to curb the power of the Supreme Court date back to the first decade of the nineteenth century. In 1805, John Randolph of Virginia proposed a constitutional amendment that would have permitted the president to remove a justice with the approval of both houses of Congress. The amendment did not pass.

Section Review Answers

1–3. State judges are chosen by popular election (the vote of the people), appointment by the governor, or appointment by the legislature. (p. 345)

4–5. In a partisan election, a candidate runs as a member of a political party. In a nonpartisan election, a candidate runs without a party label. (p. 344)

6. In the Missouri Plan, the governor appoints a judicial candidate from a short list nominated by a judicial commission. The new judge assumes office but then must be approved by voters in a later election, usually a year or more later. No opposition candidate is allowed; the voters can only approve or disapprove of the new judge. (p. 346)

7. Until recent decades, nominees to district and circuit court positions normally met only token resistance in the Senate. But today the increased politicization of the confirmation process and the importance (or near finality) of decisions made at the circuit-court level have led to Senate challenges, filibusters, and foot-dragging on presidential nominees to federal courts. Supreme Court nominees are subjected to the most scrutiny. (p. 349)

★ Some will favor judges serving for life, citing reasons such as protection from political pressure and the benefit of judges having long years of experience. Some will oppose, citing that judges might be tempted to continue in office even after they have clearly become mentally or physically unfit to serve.

★ In the Bork confirmation hearings, liberal senators were candid in their determination to not allow a seat on the Supreme Court to go to a staunch conservative like Bork. Bork was the last Supreme Court nominee to fully discuss his legal views during a Senate hearing; other nominees have had meager paper trails and tend to shroud their true beliefs in mystery or have avoided questions during the hearings about political ideology.

Federal Judges and Judicial Milestones

The oldest federal judge, Joseph W. Woodrough, was 104 when he died in 1977 while serving as a senior judge for the Eighth Circuit Court of Appeals.

As of 2020, the oldest serving Supreme Court justice, Oliver Wendell Holmes Jr., was 90 years and 10 months old when he retired in 1932.

The youngest federal judge was 25-year-old Thomas Jefferson Boynton, appointed by Abraham Lincoln in 1863.

The youngest Supreme Court justice was 32-year-old Joseph Story, who received his commission in 1811.

The longest-serving Supreme Court justice was William O. Douglas, who served from 1939 to 1975.

The first African American federal judge was William Henry Hastie, appointed in 1950.

The first female federal judge was Florence Allen, appointed in 1934.

The first Hispanic federal judge was Reynaldo G. Garza, appointed in 1961.

The first Asian American federal judge was Herbert Choy, appointed in 1971.

Marbury v. Madison (1803)

William Marbury

James Madison

After John Adams lost the 1800 presidential election to Thomas Jefferson, Adams attempted to pack the judiciary with Federalists before Jefferson could be inaugurated in March 1801. As Adams's secretary of state, John Marshall was in charge of certifying and delivering the new judicial commissions (which had been approved by the US Senate). Marshall managed to deliver most of them before he left office.

The Republicans were furious at the appointment of these "midnight judges" (a reference to the allegation that Adams was still signing these appointments at midnight on his last day in office). Jefferson ordered the new secretary of state, James Madison, to withhold the undelivered commissions. Four Federalists who had been promised positions, including William Marbury, sued Madison for their commissions and asked the Supreme Court to issue a writ of mandamus (Latin for "we command") ordering Madison to hand them over.

John Marshall, by then the chief justice of the Supreme Court, faced a dilemma. If the Court ruled for Madison, it would admit its inability to enforce the law.

If, on the other hand, the Court ruled for Marbury, Madison might refuse to deliver the commissions anyway, and the refusal would likewise reveal the Court's inability to enforce the law. Worse, the Jeffersonians might impeach Marshall. (A modern judge would likely recuse, or disqualify, himself from deciding such a case. After all, Marshall himself was responsible for not delivering the four commissions.)

Marshall found an ingenious solution to the problem. The Supreme Court ruled that Marbury had a legitimate grievance and that the government should grant him his commission. Nevertheless, Marshall also ruled that the Court had no power to issue a writ of mandamus because the provision in the Judiciary Act of 1789 that gave the Court that power was unconstitutional. Marshall cleverly managed to lecture Jefferson on the injustice of withholding the commissions while avoiding a showdown with the Republicans.

Marbury v. Madison marks the Supreme Court's first use of judicial review to strike down a law Congress passed. But the Supreme Court did not do so again for fifty-four years—until the disastrous Dred Scott decision. Over the course of the nation's history, the Supreme Court has declared congressional acts unconstitutional more than 175 times. With far greater frequency, it has declared state laws invalid because they violated the Constitution.

Ironically, federal power over the states was also indirectly enhanced by one of the most misguided Supreme Court decisions in its history—the Dred Scott case (1857), in which Chief Justice Roger Taney tried to settle the question of slavery by judicial ruling. Taney's declaration that African Americans could not be citizens of the United States unleashed a storm of Northern protest that helped lead to the Civil War.

Later, the Supreme Court sought to further define the responsibilities of the states to their citizens by expanding the interpretation of the Fourteenth Amendment (which had been ratified in 1868, three years after end of the Civil War). While intending to undo the Dred Scott decision and prevent civil discrimination against blacks, the Court also interpreted the amendment's due process clause to include corporations seeking relief from state regulatory legislation.

Activity 3: *Marbury v. Madison* (1803)

Use this activity to help the students better understand the US Supreme Court's role in judicial review.

While the Court heard many cases involving business and the Fourteenth Amendment, the Court virtually ignored Southern blacks, the intended beneficiaries of the amendment.

The Great Depression, which began in 1929, brought great challenges to the Supreme Court. As noted earlier in the chapter, when the court ruled much of Franklin Roosevelt's New Deal legislation unconstitutional, Roosevelt struck back with a plan to "pack" the Court with justices of his own choosing. For each justice over age seventy who did not retire, he wanted the right to appoint an additional justice up to a maximum of six. Many Americans were shocked by the president's attack on the institution of the Supreme Court and as a result, his plan was rejected. However, deaths and retirements of justices (along with a change in viewpoint of one of the justices) soon gave the president the opportunity to appoint replacements that took a more favorable view of New Deal measures.

Many justices named by Roosevelt were still sitting on the Court when Dwight Eisenhower selected Earl Warren to be chief justice in 1953. The Warren Court became the second most influential in American history after that of John Marshall. It wrote the unanimous decision in

This cartoon depicts Franklin Roosevelt's (right) proposed new justices as his puppets.

Activism Versus Restraint

There are several major philosophies of constitutional interpretation. A textualist interprets the Constitution (and all legislation) according to what the words of the text meant at the time of their writing. Purposivism takes into consideration the purpose of the legislation or the supposed intent of the legislators. A judge who follows this philosophy will rule in a way that he thinks upholds the purpose of the law, even if his ruling departs from the actual wording of the law. A consequentialist considers what he thinks the best, most just outcome would be and shapes his ruling to reach this outcome.

Overall, these philosophies can be divided into two major tendencies. **Judicial restraint** respects the laws as they are written, respects previous court decisions, and strikes down laws as unconstitutional only when they clearly are. **Judicial activism** seeks to correct injustices and shape policy even if that means departing from the clear meaning of the law.

Textualists support judicial restraint and argue that judges should apply only the clear statements of the Constitution to make their decisions. Proponents of judicial activism view the Court's role as that of policymaker, interpreting the Constitution to meet present needs.

Today, judicial restraint is usually equated with conservatism, and judicial activism with liberalism. Of course, the line between the two positions is often less clear than is frequently believed. The Constitution's statement that the "vice president of the United States shall be president of the Senate" is obvious on its face, but it is more difficult to unambiguously understand phrases such as "due process," "unreasonable searches and seizures," or "make no law respecting an establishment of religion."

Judicial Decisions

Strict and broad constructionism are two categories for describing how appellate judges rationalize their decisions.

Specific methods of how judges view the Constitution to reach decisions include the following:

Originalism: The Founding Fathers' purposes are explored to reveal constitutional truths that are applicable to contemporary situations.

Literalism: The actual words of the Constitution are interpreted literally—taken to mean what they say.

Historical meaning: The words of the Constitution are literally interpreted, but they are also examined for their historical meaning.

Stare decisis: Interpretation is based on precedents set by earlier cases involving similar issues.

Methods of judicial decision making that depend less on the Constitution include the following:

Logical reasoning: The terms and the major and minor premises of arguments are identified before a judge comes to a logical conclusion.

Balancing: The interests of an individual and the government are balanced against one another. Decisions favor the overruling interest in each case.

Role based: Decisions follow a judge's interpretation of the proper role of the court: judicial activism or judicial restraint.

Ideology: Decisions rely less on constitutional interpretation than on personal ideology (conservatism, liberalism, etc.).

Politics: Decisions are influenced by public opinion, partisan politics, or interest groups.

Activity 4: The Originalist Perspective

This activity explains how an originalist perceives the law and implies that a judge should interpret the law responsibly.

The Warren Court

During the Warren Court era of the 1950s and 1960s, some congressmen and state appellate judges attacked the Supreme Court's extension of its power. David Lawrence, editor of *US News & World Report,* urged taking the nomination of justices out of the president's hand and making Court seats elective for short terms. A campaign was even launched to impeach Chief Justice Warren; billboards and bumper stickers shouted, "Impeach Earl Warren." Some conservative organizations found the effort a valuable fundraising tool, but the Supreme Court continued to make what many called activist rulings. Warren was not impeached.

Alexis de Tocqueville

In *Democracy in America* (1835) Alexis de Tocqueville wrote,

> If I were asked where I place the American aristocracy, I should reply, without hesitation, that it is not composed of the rich, who are united together by no common tie, but that it occupies the judicial bench and the bar. . . .

> . . . Scarcely any question arises in the United States which does not become, sooner or later, a subject of judicial debate.

An African American parent explains, on the steps of the Supreme Court, the significance of Brown v. Board of Education *(1954).*

Jim Obergefell speaks to reporters shortly after the case bearing his name was decided (2015).

Brown v. Board of Education of Topeka, Kansas (1954), which called for an end to segregation in schools. The Warren Court also ruled that police cannot use evidence seized without a warrant; that suspected criminals must be informed of their rights, according to *Miranda v. Arizona* (1966); that states must redraw their congressional districts on the basis of "one man, one vote"; and that prayer and Bible reading in public schools are unconstitutional. Conservatives complained that the Warren Court was too liberal.

Despite complaints from liberals that post–Warren Courts have been too conservative, succeeding decades have witnessed increased attacks against biblical morality by Supreme Court decisions. The late twentieth-century Court created a "right of privacy," that was not mentioned in the Constitution. That new right was the basis for *Roe v. Wade* (1973), the infamous decision that legalized abortion, and *Lawrence v. Texas* (2003), a decision that invalidated state laws against sodomy (thus making same-sex sexual activity legal). In *Obergefell v. Hodges* (2015), the court required all US states to recognize same-sex marriages. Thus, there has been a slow but steady decay in reliance on biblical principles from US judges and justices.

In 1868, Joel Bishop, a respected attorney and legal scholar, said,

> When . . . there is a concurrence of all the circumstances essential to a sound administration of justice, . . . "Almighty God" appears in the midst of the tribunal where it sits, and reveals the right way to the understandings of the judges, as surely as he appears in the tempest.

Such language has largely been absent from our nation's legal writings for many years.

Section Review

1. Why was the *Marbury v. Madison* decision so significant?
2. Summarize Chief Justice John Marshall's ruling in *McCulloch v. Maryland.*
3–4. Contrast the philosophies of judicial restraint and judicial activism.
★ Why was the *Obergefell v. Hodges* ruling significant?

Activity 5: Chapter Review

Use this activity to help the students prepare for the chapter test.

Section Review Answers

1. *Marbury v. Madison* established the concept of judicial review, whereby the Supreme Court determines whether government actions are constitutional. (p. 349)
2. State taxation of the second Bank of the United States was unconstitutional. Though chartering banks was not a power specifically granted to Congress in the Constitution, the chartering power could be implied from the necessary and proper clause. The Maryland law must therefore be unconstitutional because "the power to tax involves the power to destroy." (p. 349)
3–4. Advocates of judicial restraint argue that judges should apply only the clear statements of the Constitution to make their decisions. Judicial activists seek to correct injustices and shape policy even if it means departing from the clear meaning of the law. (p. 351)
★ Answers may include that the ruling showed the continued steady decay in reliance on biblical principles from US judges and justices.

CHAPTER REVIEW

Making Connections

1. What contribution did William Blackstone make to American law?

2–3. What percentage of the nation's legal actions do state courts hear? What does this indicate about the importance of state judiciaries in American jurisprudence?

4–6. What are the major differences between jurisdictions of the district courts, the circuit courts, and the Supreme Court?

Developing Civics Skills

1. Analyze the significance of *Miranda v. Arizona*.

2. Evaluate the impact of *Roe v. Wade* since 1973.

Thinking Critically

1. How do society's prevalent ideas about justice contrast with the Bible's standard of justice?

2. Respond to this statement: "The Supreme Court, which hears fewer than one hundred cases a year, is nevertheless more powerful than the district courts, which hear more than three hundred fifty thousand cases a year."

Living as a Christian Citizen

1. Imagine that you are given the responsibility of drafting the judicial section of a constitution. Outline the provisions that you would incorporate in your draft, and explain why you selected them. Be sure to specify whether the judges in your system are tasked with bringing about just outcomes or upholding specific laws.

2. Choose a justice-related topic that is controversial in the present culture, and defend a biblical position on it. (You may want to build on an answer to the first question in the Thinking Critically section.)

People, Places, and Things to Remember

justice
Code of Hammurabi
Corpus Juris Civilis
common law
precedents
stare decisis
Commentaries on the Laws of England
natural law
revealed law
judicial federalism
Judiciary Act of 1789
district courts
original jurisdiction
grand jury
petit jury (trial jury)
appellate jurisdiction
en banc
justices
chief justice
associate justices
writ of certiorari
majority opinion
dissenting opinions
concurring opinions
Missouri Plan
senatorial courtesy
Marbury v. Madison
judicial review
supremacy clause
McCulloch v. Maryland
judicial restraint
judicial activism
Brown v. Board of Education of Topeka, Kansas
Roe v. Wade
Obergefell v. Hodges

CHAPTER REVIEW ANSWERS

Making Connections

1. Blackstone's *Commentaries on the Laws of England* influenced American founders to not abandon common law and devise their own legal code. This helped ensure that Americans had a legal system that acknowledged God as the source of law. (p. 337)

2–3. More than 95 percent; this indicates that state judiciaries are a vital aspect of American jurisprudence. (pp. 338–39)

4–6. The district courts have original jurisdiction. The circuit courts of appeals have appellate jurisdiction over all district courts in their circuits (but the US Court of Appeals for the Federal Circuit has nationwide jurisdiction). The Supreme Court has both appellate and (in a few special cases) original jurisdiction over the entire country. (pp. 339–42)

Developing Civics Skills

1. Some will say that the ruling has had an enormous impact on the legal system. Every time an arrest is made, the decision has an effect (suspected criminals must be informed of their rights).

2. In this case, the Supreme Court applied a "right to privacy" in the Constitution (from a previous decision) to legalize abortion. Since then, more than sixty million abortions have occurred in the United States.

Thinking Critically

1. Students should note the prevalence of two wrong ideas about justice: that justice means respecting everyone's individual freedom and that justice means providing the greatest good for the greatest number of people. These views are the basis of arguments favoring homosexual marriage, abortion, pornography, etc. The Bible's standard for justice is God's character. An act will be unjust if it does not conform to His character. In creating humans in His image, God passes to them the foundation for all natural rights; for example, they may not be killed unjustly (Gen. 9:6) or selfishly used for personal pleasure (Rom. 13:10).

2. This statement is true because although the Supreme Court hears significantly fewer cases than inferior courts, it makes the final decision on the meaning of the law and the Constitution; it also decides whether legislation and actions conform to the Constitution's principles. In addition, there is no appeal beyond the Supreme Court, so the Court is automatically more powerful than inferior courts.

Living as a Christian Citizen

1. Answers will vary. In an ideal society, judges would try to bring about justice. However, this ideal can be achieved only when a society shares a cohesive worldview about what is right and wrong, just and unjust. This was the system in place in Old Testament Israel. In a pluralistic society, it is better for legislatures to craft laws and rule according to the law, even if a particular outcome is unjust. This system gives each faction in a society a chance to make a public case (through its elected representatives) for what it believes is just. This system also protects citizens from arbitrary judgments.

2. Answers will vary. See the answer to the first question in the Thinking Critically section for a list of some controversial issues and the ways that students may respond to them.

CIVIL LIBERTIES, CIVIL RIGHTS, AND CIVIL RESPONSIBILITIES

15

High school students pledging allegiance to the American flag

I. Civil Liberties Guaranteed in the First Amendment

II. Other Constitutional Civil Liberties

III. Civil Rights

IV. Civil Responsibilities

BIG IDEAS

1. Which civil liberties are guaranteed in the First Amendment?
2. What additional civil liberties are mentioned in the Constitution?
3. What civil rights are provided to all Americans?
4. What are the civil responsibilities of citizens?

SUGGESTED MATERIALS

Section I
- Activities 1–2 from Chapter 15 of the *Student Activities*
- Special speaker (see p. 360)

Section II
- Activity 3 from Chapter 15 of the *Student Activities*

Section III
- No materials

Section IV
- Activities 4–5 from Chapter 15 of the *Student Activities*

Teacher Resources

Visit TeacherToolsOnline.com for resources to enhance the lessons.

Since all people are created in God's image, everyone has basic natural rights given by God. The Declaration of Independence recognizes this when it says that "all men . . . are endowed by their Creator with certain unalienable Rights." Governments can recognize these natural rights and may supplement them with stated civil liberties and rights. Today, US citizens enjoy greater civil liberties and civil rights than most of the people of the world. But a nation that values liberty must also value the divine limits placed on those liberties. Without limits liberties degenerate and become harmful to society. This chapter examines American liberties and rights and concludes with a brief discussion of the responsibilities that our privileged citizenship requires.

As we reflect on these matters, the words of Joseph Story, Supreme Court justice, should challenge us. He said,

> Let the American youth never forget that they possess a noble inheritance, bought by the toils, and sufferings, and blood of their ancestors. . . . It may, nevertheless, perish in an hour, by the folly, or corruption, or negligence of its only keepers, THE PEOPLE. Republics are created by the virtue, public spirit, and intelligence of the citizens. They fall, when the wise are banished from the public councils, because they dare to be honest. . . . "

I. Civil Liberties Guaranteed in the First Amendment

The terms *civil liberties* and *civil rights* are often used interchangeably, but there is an important distinction between them. **Civil liberties** are individual freedoms that must be protected *from* government. For instance, Americans are promised that their freedoms of worship and speech will not be arbitrarily limited by government intrusion.

Civil rights, on the other hand, concern the right to be free from unequal treatment and refers to the government's role in protecting liberties for all people. For instance, the Civil Rights Act of 1964 prohibited discrimination due to race, sex, religion, or national origin.

Nevertheless, the distinction between civil liberties and civil rights has been aptly described as murky and blurred. Even legal scholars often disagree on the differences between the two terms and, unfortunately, use them synonymously.

Freedom of Religion

Many of our most cherished civil liberties are outlined in the First Amendment to the Constitution, and the Supreme Court continues to define these rights. The first declaration of the Bill of Rights defends freedom of religious conscience: "Congress shall make no law respecting an establishment of religion, or prohibiting the free exercise thereof." The two parts of this provision—the **establishment clause** and the **free-exercise clause**—create a natural division by which to examine the first portion of the First Amendment.

1. Distinguish between civil liberties and civil rights.
2. Appraise civil liberties that are protected by the First Amendment.

Freedom of Political Conscience

Almost immediately after the Reformation of the sixteenth century, divisions, or denominations, arose within Protestantism. Besides the Roman Catholic Church, other churches (such as Lutheran, Reformed, Anglican, Anabaptist) emerged in Europe. In most parts of the continent, each ruler would choose the religion for the area he ruled. Those of other religious persuasions often faced the choice of persecution or emigration. Later, religious toleration was embraced to reduce conflict between different religions.

At the founding of the United States, multiple denominations already existed in the country. The founders recognized this and prohibited the national government from establishing any one religion as the nation's religion.

However, each state was permitted to establish a particular denomination as its official religion or to require religious tests for government officials. These tests existed in a number of states in the early years of our nation. For instance, New Jersey required government officials to be Protestant. North Carolina required officeholders to acknowledge the authority of Scripture. And Tennessee allowed neither atheists nor those who denied heaven or hell to hold governmental office. As the nineteenth century progressed, the state governments dropped these and similar requirements.

Religious Tolerance

Lead a discussion that evaluates different approaches to religious toleration. Help students see that although not all religions are equally valid, the Bible does not permit any kind of coercion in religion. To force someone to join a false religion is to disobey the two greatest commandments. To require someone to adhere to the Christian faith is to misunderstand the nature of Christianity, which requires spiritual regeneration.

The Bible does not grant the government prerogatives such as appointing ministers or paying their salaries. Many theologians believe that when a government establishes a state church, it oversteps its God-given prerogatives (see Isaac Backus's *An Appeal to the Public for Religious Liberty Against the Oppressions of the Present Day*).

There is nothing unbiblical in making religious requirements for public office in a largely Christian nation as long as the Christians do not act coercively toward others. But in a pluralistic nation, in which there are many religions represented among the populace, Christians are wise to support broad religious liberty because it gives true religion the freedom to flourish.

Wall of Separation

After Jefferson was elected president, the Danbury Baptist Association wrote to him, congratulating him for his victory and praising him as a defender of religious liberty (refer to activity three in Chapter 3 of the *Student Activities* that accompanies this text for more details). President Jefferson responded with a letter containing the phrase "wall of separation between church and state." This phrase led to the principle known today as separation of church and state.

However, the meaning of the phrase has been debated. Daniel Dreisbach, a scholar on this issue, argues that Jefferson wanted to prevent the national government from interfering with either the church or the states' religious dealings. But in 1947 the Supreme Court decided in *Everson v. Board of Education of the Township of Ewing* that Jefferson's phrase calls for complete separation of the church (often understood as religion) and the state, from local levels to the national government.

Establishment Clause

A chaplain talking with a soldier at a US base in Afghanistan

"Congress shall make no law respecting an establishment of religion, or prohibiting the free exercise thereof; or abridging the freedom of speech, or of the press; or the right of the people peaceably to assemble, and to petition the government for a redress of grievances."

—First Amendment, US Constitution

It is not accidental that the First Amendment was worded in such a way to prevent Congress, but not the states, from establishing a religion. When the First Amendment was adopted, the Congregational Church was still the official church in Connecticut and Massachusetts. In addition, several states required public officers to be Protestants and to affirm the authority of Scripture. The establishment clause of the First Amendment was therefore intended to protect the religious diversity of the states from the power of the national government, not to make the government an enemy of religion.

The founders understood that the success of republican government depends on the morality of its citizens. To support that morality, Congress appointed chaplains to the armed forces (and to Congress itself) and granted tax exemptions to religious organizations. There was no suggestion that Congress was thereby establishing a religion or violating the First Amendment.

By the end of the nineteenth century, state religious establishments had been dismantled. Yet the Supreme Court continued to allow Bible reading in schools, released-time programs for religious instruction, and state funding for transportation to private religious schools. In 1952 William O. Douglas, one of the most liberal New Deal Supreme Court justices, wrote, "The First Amendment, however, does not say that in every and all respects there shall be a separation of Church and State. . . . We are a religious people whose institutions presuppose a Supreme Being. . . ."

Nevertheless, in the 1960s the Supreme Court began to imply that there *was* a complete "wall of separation" between church and state. Although that phrase does not occur in the Constitution (it is derived from a letter written by Thomas Jefferson), the Supreme Court began to require a separation between religion and all levels of government. In **Engel v. Vitale** (1962), the Supreme Court forbade government-authorized prayers in public schools, even if such prayers were nonsectarian (i.e., not associated with a specific religious denomination) and noncompulsory. A year later, the Court struck down a Pennsylvania statute that required a daily reading of ten Bible verses in Pennsylvania public schools.

In **Lemon v. Kurtzman** (1971), the Supreme Court ruled that state statutes affecting religion must meet three requirements (known now as the "*Lemon* test") to be acceptable: (1) the state law must have a "secular legislative purpose"; (2) it can neither advance nor inhibit, or restrict, religion; and (3) it cannot foster an "excessive government entanglement" with religion. If any of the three requirements is not met, then the government's action is unconstitutional.

Arguments regarding the *Lemon* test have fostered such debates as whether adding a Santa

Should nativity scenes be permitted on public property? The issue has been a matter of controversy.

Public School Prayer

Discuss the advantages and disadvantages of requiring prayer in public schools. For example, a Christian's public prayer might encourage Christian students and teachers and be a testimony to the lost. But the rule might also cause people to pray rote prayers simply to meet the legal requirement. (For example, before the Supreme Court outlawed teacher-led prayer in public schools in *Engel v. Vitale* [1962], the Lord's Prayer was often recited in a completely mechanical way.) Ask students whether it would be spiritually preferable to require prayer or Bible reading.

You might note that there is little value in a generic prayer offered before lessons that are taught from a non-Christian worldview.

Nativity Scenes

Discuss the question, "Should nativity scenes be permitted on public property?" Some of the following questions can provide focus.

Do nativity scenes violate the establishment clause? *Most who favor an originalist interpretation of the Constitution would say that is doubtful. However, several court decisions in the late twentieth century held that religious displays on public property must not endorse a particular religion and that elements like a nativity scene can only be permitted if it is part of a larger secular display representing the Christmas season.*

Why have nativity scenes become a point of debate in some communities? *If a largely religious local community has historically* had nativity scenes on public property, forced removal of the scene is often viewed as a war on religion. But, as communities become more secular and religiously pluralistic, having specifically Christian symbols on public property can be offensive to a greater number of people. Of course, Christians want the right to observe a Christian holiday.*

What should Christians think of the solution of making nativity scenes part of a larger secular display? *Some would say that this reflects a secular concept of religion that is contrary to the Christian belief that Christ was born as the true ruler of all the earth. Others would say that at least the nation's Christian heritage is represented in the display.*

Madison's *Memorial and Remonstrance* of 1785

In 1784 the Virginia Assembly proposed to tax property owners to support a Christian denomination of each taxpayer's choice. The proposition pitted James Madison and Thomas Jefferson against Patrick Henry and George Mason before either the US Constitution (1789) or the Bill of Rights (1791) had been written.

Henry and Mason supported the tax as a means of upholding morality while Jefferson and Madison opposed it as an intrusion on religious freedom. Because Jefferson was serving as the US minister to France, Madison led the opposition with his *Memorial and Remonstrance*. Madison's basic points were (1) that one's duty to God can be "directed only by reason and conviction, not by force or violence"; (2) that a government that has the power to

tax on behalf of religion *generally* might eventually force citizens to conform to a specific religious establishment; and (3) that past attempts, throughout many centuries, to support religion by taxation had caused much harm.

As a result, petitions and memorials signed by more than eleven thousand Virginians deluged the Virginia state legislature, and nine out of ten signers condemned the tax. They believed that government did not have the right to oversee the workings of the church.

The legislature allowed the bill to die and voted instead to adopt Jefferson's Virginia Statute for Religious Freedom, which asserted that "no man shall be compelled to frequent or support any religious worship, place, or ministry whatsoever."

Statue of Madison in the Library of Congress

Claus and some elves to a manger scene makes it secular enough to be displayed in a public space. In writing their court decisions, various Supreme Court justices have applied the test in different ways that appear to be contradictory. For example, while the Court has frequently upheld nativity scenes displayed in public spaces as a display of our religious heritage, cases surrounding the public display of the Ten Commandments are usually ruled a violation of the *Lemon* test.

Free-Exercise Clause

More recently, questions have arisen in connection with the free-exercise clause of the First Amendment. This clause protects religious practices, ensuring the freedom of people not only to believe what they choose but also to act on those beliefs.

In recent years some have noted a troubling tendency on the part of some in government to speak of "freedom of worship" rather than of the more expansive "free exercise of religion." Worship is what occurs in a church, synagogue, mosque, or temple. But a person's religious practices affect all of life.

Two recent cases exemplify this current debate. The evangelical owners of Hobby Lobby and the

A Jewish man working on a prayer shawl

Prayer

When Congress approved the First Amendment on September 24, 1789, it did not intend to prohibit government-sponsored prayer. On the very next day, the House of Representatives passed a resolution calling for a day of national prayer and thanksgiving. George Washington responded, "It is the duty of all nations to acknowledge the providence of Almighty God, to obey His will, to be grateful for His benefits, and humbly to implore His protection and favor." According to the logic of some, both Congress and George Washington violated the First Amendment.

Both houses of Congress open each session with a prayer. This tradition dates back to the Continental Congress in the 1770s. Some have objected to this practice. But, in *Barker v. Convoy* (2017), a federal district court judge noted that the Supreme Court has ruled that opening prayers do not violate the establishment clause. Paul Ryan, Speaker of the House at the time, applauded the ruling and said, "Since the first session of the Continental Congress, our nation's legislature has opened with a prayer to God. Today, that tradition was upheld and the freedom to exercise religion was vindicated."

Was Madison Right?

Guide a discussion using the feature box on this page regarding Madison's *Memorial and Remonstrance*. Ask students whether they agree or disagree with Madison's three basic points. Help students realize that although part of Madison's discourse has an Enlightenment or rationalist tone to it, the basic points have much merit. Refer to "Religious Tolerance" at the bottom of page 355.

Congressional Chaplains

Select a student or a group of students to locate information about the current Senate or House chaplain. The students should report information to the class regarding his background and his responsibilities. This information may be obtained from the websites of the House and Senate.

Public Accommodations

Public accommodations laws were created as part of the effort to secure civil rights for black Americans. Prior to such laws, there were parts of the country where they could not find a place to stay, eat, use the restroom, or purchase gas while traveling because of discrimination. Such laws state that public and most private facilities cannot discriminate on the basis of "race, color, religion, or national origin."

LGBTQ+ activists want to use public accommodations laws to require certain Christian business owners (e.g., cake makers, florists, photographers) to participate in events or to create works of art that violate their conscience. Since there are usually numerous other businesses that would be willing to bake a cake celebrating a "gender transition" or to photograph a same-sex wedding, the issue seems not to be one of access to services but rather an effort to target, harass, or even close businesses operated by Christians and others with conscience objections to LGBTQ+ beliefs and practices.

Schenck v. United States (1919)

In 1917, Charles Schenck, a member of the American Socialist Party, was convicted of violating the Espionage Act by distributing fifteen thousand leaflets to young men of draft age. The leaflets encouraged readers to "assert [their] rights" and refuse to "submit to intimidation." Schenck was convicted but appealed to the US Supreme Court. The Court upheld his conviction. In doing so, Justice Oliver Wendell Holmes Jr. stated, "The question . . . is whether the words used are used in such circumstances and are of such a nature as to create a clear and present danger that they will bring about the substantive evils that Congress has a right to prevent."

Mennonite owners of a furniture company both argued that a regulation that required their health care plans to provide coverage for items that could induce abortions violated their religious beliefs. In **Burwell v. Hobby Lobby Stores** (2014) the Supreme Court, while not directly ruling in connection with the free exercise clause, held that the government should have found ways to achieve its health care goals without violating the religious beliefs held by the owners of these companies. In **Masterpiece Cakeshop v. Colorado Civil Rights Commission** (2018) the Court ruled in favor of a Christian baker who argued that while he would sell his goods to any customer, he could not create custom cakes for same-sex weddings without violating his religious beliefs. The Supreme Court ruled that the Colorado Civil Rights Commission showed hostility to the religious beliefs of the baker. Since these cases were limited in their scope, similar cases are likely to come before the Supreme Court.

The government must also protect public safety and morality, so free exercise of religion cannot be absolute. For example, the Court, in *Reynolds v. United States* (1879), upheld laws forbidding the Mormon practice of polygamy although late nineteenth-century Mormons claimed that polygamy was a matter of religious duty for them. Chief Justice Morrison Waite noted that the government would certainly have to prohibit human sacrifice even if it were a sincerely held religious belief.

Jack Phillips, owner of Masterpiece Cakeshop in Lakewood, Colorado

Freedoms of Speech and Press

Freedom of expression through speech and print is fundamental to personal liberty and to the success of a free society. Freedom of conscience is of little value without freedom of communication, and a democratic government requires an informed public that arises from the free exchange of ideas. Freedom of expression restrains arbitrary government and allows unpopular views to be heard and even prevail if they have merit. For this reason, totalitarian governments suppress free speech.

Defending the principle of free expression can involve defending someone's right to say obnoxious things. Even so, reasonable people acknowledge that there are limits to what a person may lawfully say or write. Justice Oliver Wendell Holmes Jr. stated, "The most stringent protection of free speech would not protect a man in falsely shouting fire in a theatre and causing a panic."

Limitations on Speech

The government may legitimately restrict speech. Such limitations include speech that threatens public safety, speech that attempts to overthrow the government or endanger national security (**sedition**), speech that damages an individual's reputation (defamation), and speech that is obscene.

The government may restrict *disruptive speech* (speech that threatens public safety and public order), but it may not restrict speech that is simply disagreeable. In the landmark case *Schenck v. United States* (1919), the Supreme Court established the **clear-and-present-danger test**, which declares that punishable speech involves genuine danger and actually incites violence, rather than simply endorsing it. The courts have also upheld local laws prohibiting speech that disturbs the peace as, for instance, by the use of amplifiers.

Although treason, sabotage, and spying are all actions that have fairly clear legal definitions, sedition has been more difficult for the

Religious Rights

Lead a discussion regarding religious rights. Ask students to describe the rights at issue in the cases of *Burwell v. Hobby Lobby Stores* and *Masterpiece Cakeshop v. Colorado Civil Rights Commission*. How do these cases relate to the free-exercise clause?

Note that from a biblical worldview, it is clearly unjust to deprive someone of their business because of their refusal to participate in something that Scripture teaches is sinful. What is the best way of balancing public accommodations and religious liberty?

Activity 1: Freedom of the Press

Use this activity to provide the students experience in reading and analyzing original sources.

courts to define. The government certainly has a right to defend itself against **subversion** (attempts to undermine its authority and existence). In 1940, Congress passed the **Smith Act**, making it illegal to advocate the violent overthrow of the government, to teach others to take such actions, or to be a member of an organization that conspires to overthrow the government. In 1948, Eugene Dennis, general secretary of the American Communist Party, and eleven other party members were prosecuted under the Smith Act for teaching and promoting the overthrow of the United States government. The Supreme Court upheld the Smith Act in *Dennis v. United States* (1951). However, the Supreme Court later began to interpret the Smith Act in a way that made it virtually unenforceable and made sedition a crime nearly impossible to prove in court.

Generally, the government may not suppress a story before its publication. In 1969, Daniel Ellsberg, a former Defense Department analyst, stole classified documents that outlined the progress of American involvement in the Vietnam War. In 1971, Ellsberg made the documents available to the *New York Times* and other newspapers. When Richard Nixon's Justice Department sought to ban publication of the papers, citing a threat to national security, the *New York Times* defended itself in court in ***New York Times Co. v. United States*** (1971)—the Pentagon Papers case. The Supreme Court ruled for the *New York Times* on the grounds that the government was attempting to exert **prior restraint** on the publisher. But the Court did not exclude the possibility that the *New York Times* could be prosecuted *after* the Pentagon Papers were published.

Defamation denotes malicious words, whether spoken (**slander**) or written (**libel**), that damage a person's reputation. Private individuals can, and do, sue for defamation. But in *New York Times Co. v. Sullivan* (1964), the Supreme Court ruled that attacks on public officials, even if inaccurate, are constitutionally protected unless made in "reckless disregard" of the truth. Eventually, public figures lost much of their ability to sue for defamation, and this inability lowered the barrier to gossiping about the famous.

The courts have long agreed that obscenity does not have the protection of the First Amendment, but they no longer agree on what constitutes obscenity. Attempts at definitions have degenerated with the culture. In *Miller v. California* (1973), the Supreme Court gave communities greater ability to set their own obscenity standards, stating that sexually explicit material is supposed to have some "serious literary, artistic, political, or scientific value" to avoid being judged obscene. Censorship of movies was largely abandoned in 1967 and replaced with a voluntary rating system. Today, pornographic films are almost never banned, just rated.

Free Speech and Business

Commercial speech has never enjoyed the same protection as other forms of speech. For instance, local laws may limit the distribution of commercial advertising and the posting of "for sale" signs on private property, and the Federal

---

The Zenger Trial and Its Precedent

In 1733, John Peter Zenger, publisher of the *New York Weekly Journal*, printed an article that criticized colonial governor William Cosby. Angered by the attack, Cosby eventually had Zenger arrested and tried for libel.

Zenger, defended by Philadelphia lawyer Andrew Hamilton, built his case around his insistence that what he had printed was true. In 1735, the jury deliberated for only ten minutes and acquitted Zenger. The case established the precedent that truth is a defense against accusations of libel and slander, even if the person criticized is a public official. It was also an important step toward establishing freedom of the press.

Christians and Obeying Laws

The Bible teaches that Christians must disobey earthly laws if those laws require them to disobey God's laws (Acts 5:29). This principle is illustrated in the Bible by the midwives' refusal to kill Hebrew babies (Exod. 1), the Hebrew youths' refusal to bow to an idol (Dan. 3), Daniel's refusal to stop praying (Dan. 6), and Peter's refusal to stop preaching the gospel (Acts 5). Christians must obey their rulers because rulers are God's servants (Rom. 13:1–7). But when it becomes necessary for Christians to disobey a government command, they should accept the consequences.

Terminiello v. City of Chicago (1949)

In *Terminiello v. City of Chicago*, the Supreme Court privileged free speech above a local community's right to protect law and order. In 1946, Arthur Terminiello, a defrocked Catholic priest, delivered a scurrilous, anti-Semitic speech in a prominently Jewish area of Chicago. As he vigorously condemned a large protesting crowd that had gathered outside the auditorium—he called the protesters "slimy scum," "bedbugs," and other names—the crowd responded by throwing rocks and stink bombs through the windows and tried to break down the doors. Police assigned to maintain order then arrested Terminiello under a local ordinance that forbade speech that "stirs the public to anger."

One problem for the courts to consider was that the Chicago disturbance was not precipitated by Terminiello or his supporters but by members of the audience who disagreed with his views.

Writing for a 5–4 majority, Justice William O. Douglas argued that the Chicago ordinance was overly broad in its restriction of speech. Douglas maintained that the "vitality of civil and political institutions in our society depends on free discussion" and that speech should be restricted only if it is "likely to produce a clear and present danger of a serious substantive evil that rises far above public inconvenience, annoyance, or unrest."

Dissenters on the Court attacked the majority opinion as an assault on the states' right to maintain law and order. Justice Robert Jackson wrote that the "local court that tried Terminiello was not indulging in theory. It was dealing with a riot and with a speech that provoked a hostile mob and incited a friendly one, and threatened

---

Terminiello v. City of Chicago

After reading the material in the side margin about *Terminiello v. City of Chicago*, discuss the case with your students, first asking whether they would have voted with the majority or the minority. If they choose the majority, remind them that mob violence is dangerous, even deadly, and at best restricts the freedom of others.

If they choose the minority, remind them that a pastor preaching against abortion or LBGTQ+ "rights" in his own church could conceivably be arrested for disturbing the peace if a crowd opposing him gathered outside and threw stink bombs and tried to break down the doors of the church.

Help the students understand that Western law often attempts to achieve justice without rendering moral judgments. Almost all speech is protected because it is difficult in a religiously pluralistic society to agree about what speech is acceptable. But cases such as the *Terminiello* case demonstrate that ensuring justice requires making moral judgments.

Warning labels on cigarette packages

Trade Commission can prohibit advertising that is obviously false or makes claims that cannot be proven.

Perhaps the best-known example of restriction of business speech is government regulation of tobacco advertising. In 1965, Congress required tobacco manufacturers to put the Surgeon General's warning on cigarette packages. Later restrictions forbade tobacco companies to advertise on television and radio. Since 1998, tobacco companies have been unable to use cartoons to advertise tobacco products and have been unable to advertise on billboards or buses. Nevertheless, in 2001 the Supreme Court ruled that a Massachusetts law further restricting tobacco advertisements was an unconstitutional breach of commercial free speech.

Symbolic Speech

The Supreme Court has also protected **symbolic speech** (the expression of ideas through actions instead of words). For example, the Court protected such "expressive activity" as wearing the American flag on the seat of one's pants or superimposing a peace symbol on the American flag.

In 1984, Gregory Lee Johnson burned an American flag outside the Republican National Convention. He was arrested and convicted under a Texas law prohibiting desecration of the flag. In *Texas v. Johnson* (1989), the Supreme Court reversed the conviction in a 5–4 decision, ruling that flag burning is a form of symbolic speech and is thereby protected by the Constitution. The ruling precipitated a nationwide uproar. Congress immediately passed the Flag Protection Act, which the Supreme Court struck down the following year. There was talk of

Flag Etiquette

Because the American flag symbolizes the nation and its freedoms, the flag should be treated with respect. The following guidelines are taken from the US Flag Code:

1. When reciting the Pledge of Allegiance to the flag, a person should stand at attention facing the flag with his right hand over his heart. When not in uniform, men should remove head coverings.

2. Flags should be flown "only from sunrise to sunset" unless "properly illuminated."

3. Flags should not be flown in bad weather unless they are all-weather flags.

4. "No other flag or pennant should be placed above or, if on the same level, to the right of" the American flag.

5. The flag "should not be dipped to any person or thing."

6. The flag "should never be displayed with the union [the blue section] down, except" to signal an emergency.

7. The flag "should never touch anything beneath it, such as the ground, the floor, water, or merchandise."

8. The flag "should never be used as wearing apparel, bedding, or drapery."

9. The flag should not have words or pictures placed on it.

10. The flag "should never be used for advertising purposes."

11. "No part of the flag should ever be used as a costume or athletic uniform." But it may be attached to military or civilian uniforms.

12. When no longer fit for display, the flag "should be destroyed in a dignified way, preferably [and ironically] by burning."

Folding of the flag at a ceremony honoring veterans

Flag Etiquette

Use the flag etiquette information on this page to guide a discussion. Mention that the First Amendment's free speech protections prevent the direct enforcement of the US Flag Code.

Ask questions such as the following: Are there some guidelines that surprise you? Are there parts that you regularly see ignored? Do you think some of the etiquette should be changed?

Respecting the Flag

Invite an individual to discuss flag etiquette with the class. Many former or present members of the military might have sufficient knowledge in this area to do so. Prior to the speaker's arrival, encourage students to write questions they would like to ask. If time permits, allow students to ask additional questions as well.

Flag Burning

Discuss whether burning the flag should be illegal. In preparation, assign some students to research *Texas v. Johnson* (1989) and present their findings.

Ask students why a constitutional amendment would be necessary to ban flag burning. Is such an amendment a good idea? Are there positives and negatives to such an amendment? How likely is passage of such an amendment?

a constitutional amendment to reverse the decision, but both public interest and flag burning waned simultaneously.

Freedoms of Assembly and Petition

The freedom to stage peaceful demonstrations, to circulate petitions, or to write letters supporting (or opposing) a particular cause is a natural extension of the free-speech clause. Likewise, the freedom to organize into groups to influence public opinion, public officials, and legislation is also basic to our political system.

Nevertheless, the freedoms of assembly and petition protect only peaceful activity, not riots, property destruction, or the obstruction of streets and businesses. Courts have consistently

Protesters burning the US flag in Washington, DC

upheld local governments' right to enforce **time-place-manner laws** that may, for instance, restrict demonstrations to particular streets, sidewalks, or public parks during specified periods of time. Local governments may also require that demonstrators acquire permits in advance.

Furthermore, assembly and petition rights do not supersede property rights. Citizens outraged over a city council ruling may legitimately demonstrate in front of city hall, but they may not trample the mayor's lawn. Using a shopping mall for public petitioning and demonstrations is a much thornier issue. Most courts have considered shopping malls private property; others have ruled that malls are diversified enough to be considered "public forums" for First Amendment purposes.

Freedom of association is not mentioned in the Constitution, but the Supreme Court has inferred it from the rights of free speech and petition. When the state of Alabama ordered the National Association for the Advancement of Colored People (NAACP) to surrender its membership lists, the Supreme Court ruled in 1957 that members of the organization should be able to "pursue their

lawful private interests privately and . . . associate freely with others in doing so." Likewise, in *Boy Scouts of America v. Dale* (2000), the Supreme Court ruled that the Boy Scouts could revoke the membership of an assistant scout leader who was an avowed homosexual, despite a New Jersey antidiscrimination law. Otherwise, said the Court, the government would be forcing a private organization to admit a member it did not want. (In 2015,

Participants in the large pro-life rally held each January in Washington, DC

Speech and Press Limits Under Oppression

The freedoms of speech and press are often severely limited by dictatorial regimes. After the execution of Soviet KGB chief Lavrenti Beria in 1953, librarians throughout the USSR were sent a paste-in addition to the *Great Soviet Encyclopedia*. The addition, which lengthened an entry on the Bering Strait, conveniently covered the biographical sketch of Beria, who had been rendered a nonperson.

Activity 2: First Amendment Freedoms

This activity provides students with the opportunity to apply what they have learned regarding the freedoms mentioned in the First Amendment.

Exercising Civil Liberties

To underscore the practical nature of civil liberties, instruct students to list the various ways in which they exercised their First Amendment freedoms during the past week. Discuss these instances in class.

the Boy Scouts removed its ban on homosexual leaders, but that decision was not made because of court rulings.)

Section Review

1–2. Contrast civil liberties and civil rights.

3–6. Identify and describe the three-part test that courts use to determine the constitutionality of state laws regarding religion.

7–8. Explain the difference between slander and libel.

9. What precedent did the Zenger trial establish regarding slander and libel?

10. Define *symbolic speech*.

★ Do you think a constitutional amendment should be adopted that bans the burning of the US flag? Explain your answer.

★ What are the limitations on Americans' freedoms of assembly and petition?

Guiding Questions

1. What security rights are guaranteed by the Constitution?
2. What does the Constitution guarantee regarding fair judicial procedures?
3. Is there a constitutional right to privacy?

II. Other Constitutional Civil Liberties

The first ten amendments to the Constitution, the Bill of Rights, were originally written to apply to the national government. Though many state constitutions had their own bill of rights, or other provisions, that protected many civil liberties for citizens, there was inconsistency and incompleteness in those protections. After the ratification of the Fourteenth Amendment in 1868, the Supreme Court began to apply the protections of the Bill of Rights to state laws using that amendment's due process clause. This extension of the Bill of Rights to all levels of government is called **incorporation**. The Fourteenth Amendment reads in part that

no state shall make or enforce any law which shall abridge the privileges or immunities of citizens of the United States; nor shall any state deprive any person of life, liberty, or property, without due process of law; nor deny to any person within its jurisdiction the equal protection of the laws.

In *Gitlow v. New York* (1925), the Court first applied the Fourteenth Amendment to a state law restricting free speech. During the New Deal era, the nationalization of the Bill of Rights increased. Incorporation was greatly accelerated by the Warren Court (the name for the Supreme Court from 1953–69, the period in which Earl Warren served as chief justice). Today most of the Bill of Rights has been brought under the umbrella of the Fourteenth Amendment. This expansion of the Bill of Rights means that most state laws must conform to requirements established by the Supreme Court.

The incorporation of the Bill of Rights into the Fourteenth Amendment has enhanced the power of the judiciary, altered the nature of federation, and enlarged the scope of constitutional rights. Two categories of these expanded rights will be examined here: security rights and rights of the accused.

Security Rights

The security of an individual and his property is protected by the Second, Third, and Fourth Amendments.

Section Review Answers

1–2. Civil liberties are individual freedoms that must be protected from government. Civil rights concern the right to be free from unequal treatment and the government's role in ensuring liberties for everyone. (p. 355)

3–6. The three-part test is the "Lemon test." According to it, statutes affecting religion must have a "secular legislative purpose," can neither advance nor inhibit religion, and cannot foster an "excessive government entanglement" with religion. (p. 356)

7–8. Slander is spoken malicious words; libel is written malicious words. The only defense against accusations of libel or slander is to prove that what was printed or spoken is true. (p. 359)

9. It set the precedent that if the truth is being stated it is neither slander nor libel (even if the person criticized is a public official). (p. 359)

10. Symbolic speech is the expression of ideas through actions rather than words. (p. 360)

★ Students may argue that an amendment outlawing flag burning might be seen as a slippery slope of limiting civil liberties. Others may say that an amendment would specifically disallow flag burning while still protecting other civil liberties.

★ Assemblies must be peaceful, and they must not destroy private property. In addition, local governments have the right to enforce time-place-manner laws.

The Second Amendment: The Right to Bear Arms

The Second Amendment reflects an underlying right of self-defense. State legislatures may, to a degree, regulate the sale and possession of firearms and designate how they may be carried (whether openly or concealed). The Supreme Court has also upheld a federal law that bans the interstate transport of unregistered sawed-off shotguns and silencers, since such items are hardly "necessary to the security of a free state." Other court cases have affirmed individuals' gun rights. For example, in *McDonald v. Chicago* (2010), the Court ruled that the states are subject to the Second Amendment; and in *District of Columbia v. Heller* (2008), the Court ruled that states cannot arbitrarily deny individuals the right to possess firearms for such lawful purposes as self-defense in their homes.

The Third Amendment: No Forced Quartering of Troops

The Third Amendment prohibits the forced quartering of troops in private homes during peacetime. Forced quartering of British troops was such a major irritant before the War for Independence that Jefferson included it as a complaint against King George III in the Declaration of Independence. The issue remained a bitter memory thereafter. The Third Amendment was violated during the War of 1812 and the Civil War, but these violations were never challenged in the courts.

The Fourth Amendment: No Unreasonable Searches or Seizures

The Fourth Amendment protects citizens from "unreasonable searches and seizures." A legal search takes place when there exists **probable cause** that a crime has been committed or is about to be committed. Generally, a legal search also requires a search warrant. The Supreme Court has determined that a search necessitates a warrant if the person searched has an expectation of privacy that society regards as reasonable.

Nevertheless, when a proper arrest is made, it is unnecessary to obtain a warrant to search a person or the area under his immediate control (such as a car he is driving at the time). Search warrants are also unneeded for searches of vehicles when there is probable cause to suspect contraband (such as drugs or stolen property), when police are in "hot pursuit," or when evidence is in danger of being destroyed. In addition, search warrants are unnecessary when the owner of a building gives his consent to a search (although the police are not supposed to obtain the consent by force or intimidation). Abandoned property (such as trash left on curbs or thrown in dumpsters) may also be searched without a warrant.

Mandatory drug testing has been contested as an illegitimate search, but the courts have upheld the constitutionality of such tests for athletes and prospective employees. The Supreme Court has also ruled that "reasonable" administrative searches in schools or

Gun Laws

Gun laws are often hotly debated. Many of your students—and, even more likely, their parents—will have strong views on the matter, especially if they are hunters or know someone who has been injured by a gun. The issue provides excellent material for an organized class debate.

Divide the class into two groups. One should be assigned to argue that present guns laws are sufficient and do not need modification. The other could be assigned to argue for stricter control laws. Require the groups to research the legal and practical issues involved in the matter. A moderator should pose questions to both sides based on the groups' research. Rebuttal time should be permitted.

Activity 3: The Second Amendment

In this activity students are assigned to read the Second Amendment and to answer questions about it. Reference to outside sources may be necessary.

Miranda Rights

In 1976, Miranda rights were read in both English and Spanish to a man who had just killed someone in a barroom brawl. The dead man was Ernesto Miranda, whose earlier Supreme Court case led to the requirement that defendants must be read their rights.

workplaces (e.g., searches of lockers or backpacks) do not require search warrants.

Advances in technology have added a different dimension to rules about search and seizure. The Supreme Court ruled, for example, that electronic eavesdropping violates privacy and is therefore illegal without a warrant, but the Court allows wiretaps and "bugs" in investigations related to national security.

The Warren Court created the **exclusionary rule** in *Mapp v. Ohio* (1961). The rule holds that evidence obtained illegally (e.g., evidence obtained without a proper search warrant) is inadmissible in court. The purpose of the exclusionary rule was to restrain the police from making illegal searches and seizures, but the new rule also allowed some criminals to escape punishment, especially before the police could adjust to the new requirements. The Supreme Court gradually relaxed the exclusionary rule. For instance, the Court ruled in 1984 that evidence obtained by an officer acting reasonably and in good faith cannot be excluded from testimony simply because a warrant was defective.

Fair Judicial Procedures

The Fifth, Sixth, Seventh, and Eighth Amendments guarantee fair judicial procedures. The rights of those accused of crimes are listed and a fundamental assumption of our court system is supported: a person is innocent until proven guilty.

The Fifth Amendment

The Fifth Amendment provides important protections for the accused. A citizen accused of criminal activity cannot be forced to answer for a major federal crime unless indicted by a grand jury. (The requirement of a grand jury has not been incorporated into the due process clause of the Fourteenth Amendment and so is not obligatory for state court systems.) More importantly, the amendment protects citizens from **double jeopardy** (being tried twice for the same crime) unless a crime violates both a federal law and a state law. In addition, the Fifth Amendment protects citizens from **self-incrimination**. No one is required to admit in a criminal case anything that could be used against him in court. The burden of proof rests on the prosecution.

To protect citizens from self-incrimination while they are being held in police custody, the Supreme Court ruled in *Miranda v. Arizona* (1966) that it would throw out any conviction in which a suspect was not informed of his constitutional rights against self-incrimination. The case established the **Miranda warning** (a list that the police must recite to the accused before questioning):

All arrested individuals must be given the Miranda warning.

1. The accused has the right to remain silent to avoid self-incrimination.
2. If he chooses to speak, what he says can be used against him in court.
3. He has the right to an attorney. If he cannot afford counsel, an attorney will be provided by the state.
4. He has the right to end police questioning whenever he chooses.

The Miranda warning is one of the most familiar features of the American criminal-justice system because it is so often repeated on television shows and in movies. Although there have been complaints that the Miranda rule hinders

The Exclusionary Rule

Assign two groups of students to research the exclusionary rule and debate its advantages and disadvantages. Comments about the rule are often sharp and contradictory. Consider, for instance, the following opinions:

1. "When agents of the executive branch (the police) disregard the terms of search warrants, or attempt to bypass the warrant-issuing process altogether, the judicial branch can and should respond by 'checking' such misbehavior. The most opportune time to check such unconstitutional behavior is when prosecutors attempt to introduce illegally seized evidence in court. Because the exclusionary rule is the only effective tool the judiciary has for preserving the integrity of its warrant-issuing authority, any legislative attempt to abrogate the rule should be declared null and void by the Supreme Court."
   —Timothy Lynch, Cato Institute

2. "What the rule really does is endanger innocent victims, while letting criminals escape. . . . The social costs of this policy are immense."
   —Edwin Meese, US attorney general under Ronald Reagan

3. "For the first century after American independence, the remedy for an unreasonable search was simple: sue the offending officer for compensatory or punitive damages under trespass or tort law. . . . No court, in England or America, excluded evidence in criminal trials until the Supreme Court invented the exclusionary rule in the 1886 *Boyd* case. Even friends of the rule agree the Court's reasoning was mystifying. . . . But the Court has never explained why, if the exclusionary rule is not required by the Constitution, the justices had any business imposing it on the states in the first place."
   —Jeffrey Rosen, *New Republic*

criminal justice, the evidence is inconclusive—at least since the police have adjusted to the new rule.

The Fifth Amendment also ensures that no citizen may "be deprived of life, liberty, or property, without due process of law"—that is, only after a fair and proper trial. However, courts have upheld the government's right to declare that land is needed for a public use, such as for the construction of a new road, but it must pay the owner "just compensation" for the property. The power the government possesses to take private property for public use is called **eminent domain**.

The Sixth Amendment: Rights in Criminal Courts

Additional procedural rights protecting the accused include the Sixth Amendment right to a "speedy and public trial" in criminal cases. The Sixth Amendment also ensures the right of a trial by an impartial jury. This right can be waived by the accused, and the Supreme Court has ruled that the right does not apply if the penalty for the charge is less than six months in prison. Generally in a criminal case, a unanimous jury must be convinced beyond reasonable doubt that the accused is guilty.

Furthermore, the Sixth Amendment ensures that the accused will be "informed of the nature and cause of the accusation," that he will be able to face his accusers, that he will have the opportunity to gather witnesses to show his innocence, and that he will have an adequate defense. Courts appoint a lawyer called a public defender to defend those who cannot afford to hire their own lawyer.

The Seventh Amendment: Rights in Civil Trials

The Seventh Amendment guarantees the right to jury trials for civil cases involving disputes between citizens if the disputed amount exceeds twenty dollars. Civil trials decide issues between individuals or groups of people, and they encompass such things as disputes over land ownership, breaches of contract, and negligence in automobile accidents. In criminal trials, the state prosecutes the accused violator of criminal law whereas in civil trials private citizens confront each other.

The Eighth Amendment: No Cruel, Unusual, or Unjust Punishments

The Eighth Amendment protects the accused from being assigned bail higher than necessary to ensure that he will appear in court and submit to punishment if convicted. The Eighth Amendment also protects those convicted of crimes from being subjected to "cruel and unusual punishments."

Most cases that have been presented to the Court regarding this provision involve **capital punishment** (the death penalty). Opponents of capital punishment contend that the death penalty is cruel and unusual regardless of the reason or the manner that it is administered. In *Furman v. Georgia* (1972), the Supreme Court discarded all state death-penalty statutes on the grounds that they were too vague and too inconsistently applied. In the words of the majority, the randomness of executions was "cruel and unusual in the same way that being struck by lightning is cruel and unusual." Although two justices believed that the death penalty was unconstitutional in all circumstances, the majority could agree only that the *existing* death-penalty statutes were unacceptable. Perhaps the Court thought that its decision might end capital punishment anyway.

Typical Criminal-Justice Process for Federal Crimes
1. Arrest
2. Booking: The suspect is photographed and fingerprinted, and his personal information is recorded.
3. Initial appearance: The accused meets with a magistrate within hours of arrest to hear the charges, be reminded of his rights, and be considered for bail.
4. Preliminary hearing: A judge determines whether there is enough evidence to continue the judicial process.
5. Grand-jury review: A grand jury hears evidence and decides whether to issue an indictment (this is applicable in federal courts and in twenty states).
6. Arraignment: The accused appears in trial court; the judge reads the indictment; and the accused enters a plea ("guilty," "not guilty," or "no contest").
7. Trial
8. Sentencing (if the defendant is found guilty): The judge decides what punishment the convicted person will receive.

Gideon v. Wainwright (1963)

In 1961, Clarence Gideon, a Florida drifter, was accused of stealing; at his trial, he requested a court-appointed lawyer. The judge denied his request because, under Florida law, state courts could appoint defense lawyers only for those charged with capital offenses. This forced Gideon to act as his own lawyer, and the trial ended in his conviction. From prison, Gideon wrote an appeal to the Supreme Court, which then appointed prominent Washington attorney (and future member of the Supreme Court) Abe Fortas to present his case to the Court.

In *Gideon v. Wainwright* the Supreme Court unanimously ruled, based on the Sixth and Fourteenth Amendments, that states are required to provide an attorney to defendants in criminal cases who cannot afford to hire one. The *Gideon* ruling marked an important step for the incorporation of the rights of the accused.

Later, an attorney was provided for Clarence Gideon and his case was retried. The jury acquitted him.

Who Was Miranda?

Invite students to research the origin of the Miranda warning by reading about *Miranda v. Arizona* (1966) and Ernesto Miranda.

Discussion: Eminent Domain

Discuss the following topic: "Eminent Domain: Should There Be a Limit on Government's Taking of Private Property?"

More on Eminent Domain

For more detailed information regarding eminent domain, refer to *Abuse of Power: How the Government Misuses Eminent Domain* by Steven Greenhut.

What Does the Bible Say About Capital Punishment?

Since all humans are made in God's image, every human has the right to life (Gen. 9:6). This means that murder is one of the worst crimes that can be committed. Accordingly, God decreed that death should be the penalty for inflicting death (Gen. 9:6). The Scriptures indicate that government is to oversee the enactment of the death penalty.

Some people object to the death penalty because the sixth of the Ten Commandments reads, "Thou shalt not kill." However, it is important to note that the Hebrew word translated "kill" refers specifically to murder and manslaughter. Thus, the command does not prohibit all killing— just murder and manslaughter. Second, the Mosaic law itself commanded death for murder, manslaughter (with alternatives for involuntary manslaughter), and fifteen other crimes.

The death penalty for murder is rooted in the concept of the image of God in humans. For those who deliberately take life, the death penalty is a just reward.

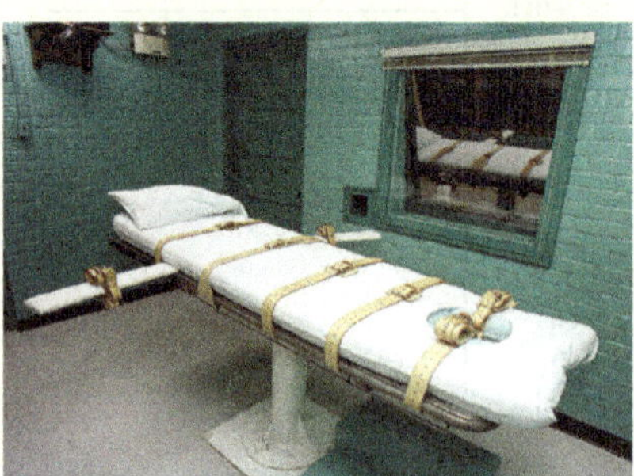

Room used to administer lethal injections in a Texas prison

Instead, many states passed *mandatory* death-penalty statutes, which would almost certainly have increased the number of American executions. However, the Court struck those laws down. Other states passed laws that made capital punishment possible under "special circumstances" (e.g., torturing a victim, killing a police officer, or killing more than one person). These laws have generally survived Supreme Court scrutiny. In any case, few murderers are executed, and those who are to be executed usually spend many years on death row appealing their sentences.

Constitutional Protection

In Article I, Section 9, the Constitution offers additional protection from oppressive and unfair laws. First, if the authorities do not bring charges against and try an arrested person, the defendant may apply for a **writ of habeas corpus** (literally, "you should have the body"). This forces officials to release the individual from custody.

In addition, **bills of attainder** (which permit punishment without a trial) and **ex post facto laws** (which criminalize activities that were not crimes when they were committed or require harsher punishments than were mandated at the time of the act) are prohibited.

Right to Privacy?

The Constitution does not explicitly state that Americans have the right to privacy (that is, the right to be left alone). However, the Supreme Court has inferred that right in some of its rulings. In *Griswold v. Connecticut* (1965), the Court ruled unconstitutional a law that forbade even married couples the use of contraceptives. Justice William O. Douglas, who wrote the decision, asserted that although a right of privacy is not mentioned in the Constitution, the Bill of Rights has "penumbras, formed by emanations from [the document's] guarantees."

Capital Punishment

Divide the class into two groups. Assign one group to support capital punishment and the other to oppose it. Ask the students to present their arguments in class.

(This phrase means that the Bill of Rights has a gray area formed by the implications of its guarantees.) Eight years later, the Court ruled that the right to privacy extended to a woman's decision to have an abortion in **Roe v. Wade** (1973). This legalization of abortion throughout the country has had enormous consequences.

Strict constructionists, or originalists, have denounced the Court's creation of a constitutional right to privacy. Of course, a Christian cannot support any human-declared "right" for something that God has declared immoral, such as abortion. Since 1973, both Congress and the states have attempted to restrict abortions in various ways. Sometimes the Court accepts the restrictions; sometimes it rejects them.

Pro-lifers in Minnesota protesting against Roe v. Wade

Section Review

1–3. List three amendments that guarantee security rights and briefly summarize those rights.

4–10. Identify circumstances when authorities may search without a warrant.

11–14. What four protections for citizens are mentioned in the Fifth Amendment?

15–20. What rights are guaranteed to accused persons by the Sixth Amendment?

21–22. In addition to the Fifth and Sixth Amendments, list and briefly summarize two other amendments that deal with rights of the accused.

★ On what fundamental assumption is the US court system based? Why is this important?

III. Civil Rights

Civil liberties are the individual freedoms that are promised to Americans. Many of these have been explained in this chapter. *Civil rights* deal with the right to be free from unequal treatment based on certain characteristics such as race, sex, religion, and national origin. A civil rights violation occurs in certain situations when an individual faces discrimination on the basis of a protected characteristic, such as the ones noted above. From the late nineteenth century through the present, minorities' and women's struggles for full political rights have resulted in constitutional guarantees being interpreted, expanded, and sometimes created by the US Supreme Court.

The concept of due process is a key component in protecting the rights and liberties of citizens. It legally requires that the government must respect the liberties and rights owed to a person and that the government must act fairly and reasonably to defend those rights. **Substantive due process** means that the content of laws must protect a person's basic freedoms. **Procedural due process** means the laws must be justly administered and enforced.

> **Guiding Questions**
>
> 1. What are substantive and procedural due process?
> 2. What struggles did African Americans face in their effort to obtain civil rights?
> 3. What are the voting rights and voting requirements for citizens?

1. Define *substantive due process* and *procedural due process*.
2. Describe the struggles African Americans faced in their effort to obtain civil rights.
3. Describe voting rights and requirements.

Section Review Answers

1–3. The Second Amendment protects the right to "keep and bear arms"; the Third prohibits forced quartering of troops; and the Fourth prohibits "unreasonable searches and seizures." (pp. 362–63)

4–10. when searching a properly arrested person or an area under his immediate control (e.g., the car he was driving); when searching vehicles if there is probable cause to suspect contraband; when the police are in "hot pursuit"; if evidence is in danger of being destroyed; when the owner of a building gives consent; when searching abandoned property; and when conducting administrative searches in schools or workplaces (pp. 363–64)

11–14. indictment by grand jury required for major federal crimes; no double jeopardy, which is being tried for the same crime twice; no self-incrimination, being made to act as a witness against one's self; due process of law is required in order to deprive a person of life, liberty, or property (pp. 364–65)

15–20. the right to "speedy and public trial[s]," right to a trial by an impartial jury, right to be "informed of the nature and cause of the accusation[s]," right to face accusers, right to obtain witnesses to show innocence, and right to have a lawyer for defense (p. 365)

21–22. The Seventh guarantees the right to jury trials in certain civil cases; the Eighth prohibits excessive bail and cruel or unusual punishments. (p. 365)

★ the belief that a person is innocent until proven guilty; under this principle, the accuser (not the accused) has the burden of proof

Separate but Equal

Chief Justice Earl Warren, writing the unanimous opinion for the *Brown* case, stated, "We conclude that, in the field of public education, the doctrine of 'separate but equal' has no place."

From a biblical point of view, the "separate but equal" doctrine is problematic because the separate accommodations for black people were unequal and because the separation was based on premises that violated the biblical teaching that all people are image bearers of God.

Poll tax receipt issued in Fannin County, Texas, in 1907

Rights for African Americans

The **Fifteenth Amendment**, ratified in 1870, gave adult black men the right to vote. However, despite that constitutional guarantee, black citizens were effectively denied that right in many southern states after Reconstruction ended in 1877. During the nineteenth century, jurisdictions throughout the country required prospective voters to pass a **literacy test** on the grounds that responsible voting requires at least a basic understanding of political issues. But literacy tests in the South were not applied evenhandedly and, in fact, were specifically designed to deprive blacks of the right to vote. For example, voting officials were notoriously lenient about certifying illiterate whites while often providing much more rigorous tests for black Americans. In addition, poor blacks were often barred from voting because they could not afford to pay the **poll tax**, a fee required before one could vote. Many states also passed a **grandfather clause**. It exempted an individual from the poll tax and the literacy test if his grandfather was eligible to vote before 1867. No black citizens met this requirement. (The **Twenty-Fourth Amendment**, ratified in 1964, ended poll taxes in national elections.)

In the 1940s and 1950s, more and more Americans realized that racism continued to be a national issue. The United States had just defeated the archracist Adolf Hitler and hoped to minimize Communist propaganda about ethnic inequality in the United States. While northern blacks could exercise considerable economic and political clout, southern blacks still had few political opportunities in states where they were largely denied the vote. The federal courts became somewhat reluctant champions of civil rights for blacks during the 1940s and 1950s.

In 1948 the Supreme Court prevented states from enforcing housing covenants (neighborhood contracts) that were ethnically discriminatory. More importantly, in a series of cases, the Court struck down segregation in education; this culminated in *Brown v. Board of Education of Topeka, Kansas* (1954), which declared segregated school facilities to be in violation of the Fourteenth Amendment. This reversed *Plessy v. Ferguson* (1896) which had established the "separate but equal" doctrine (which permitted separate schools for black and white children provided the facilities were equivalent).

By the mid-1950s, the American civil rights movement had passed from courtroom arguments to mass protests. Civil rights activists, such as Martin Luther King Jr., Rosa Parks, and Ralph David Abernathy challenged discrimination against African Americans in the South with boycotts and demonstrations. Even after King's house in Montgomery, Alabama, was bombed in 1956, King continued to advocate nonviolent disobedience of southern laws that sustained ethnic segregation and unequal treatment.

Rosa Parks (in dark coat and hat) in Montgomery, Alabama, after African Americans won the right to sit anywhere on city buses

Is Gay Rights a Civil Rights Issue?

Supporters of gay rights say that just as some Christians wrongly used the Bible to support slavery and oppose integration, Christians are now wrongly using the Bible to oppose LGBTQ+ rights. Various arguments are used to explain away the Bible's clear teaching that same-sex desires and actions are sinful (Matt. 19:4–5; Rom. 1:26–27). Guide students through a discussion by noting the following facts:

1. A premise is that LGBTQ+ rights are comparable to civil rights for African Americans. This premise does not hold since sexual behavior is by nature subject to moral evaluation, whereas skin color is not.

2. Christians who supported slavery with the Bible had to employ a selective reading of Scripture to do so. They neglected the implications of the Bible's opposition to manstealing and the slave trade (Exod. 21:16; Deut. 24:7; 1 Tim. 1:9–10). They contradicted biblical prohibitions against racism (Gen. 1:26–27; Mark 12:31; Luke 10:30–37) by supporting race-based slavery. And they did not follow the Mosaic law's teachings that slaves were to be freed every seven years (Deut. 15:12–15) and that perpetual slaves had to voluntarily agree to serve for life (Deut. 15:16–17). Christians who supported slavery adopted distorted readings because of the cultural pressure to support slavery.

The same is true of many professing Christians who employ a selective reading of Scripture to support LGBTQ+ rights. The culture pressures Christians to find a way to shift their position, and some adopt strained readings of Scripture to accommodate that pressure.

3. Many evangelical Christians were at the forefront of seeking an end to slavery in both the United States and in Great Britain. The teaching of Scripture motivated them in the fight for slaves' freedom.

This strategy proved shrewd and highly effective, especially when southern law-enforcement officers were filmed brutalizing nonviolent demonstrators. After King's assassination in 1968, he was widely viewed as both a martyr and a national hero.

In 1964, Congress, spurred by President Lyndon Johnson, passed the landmark **Civil Rights Act of 1964**. Afterward, virtually no business—hotel, cafeteria, gas station, or theater—could discriminate on the basis of ethnicity. Under its provisions, the Justice Department was authorized to enforce voting rights and to promote racial integration in public schools, in keeping with the *Brown* decision. The act also created the Equal Employment Opportunity Commission (EEOC) to oversee the elimination of discriminatory hiring practices.

President Johnson (left) shakes hands with Martin Luther King Jr. (right) after the signing of the Voting Rights Act in August 1965.

Voting Rights

The right to vote (also called the franchise) is one of the most cherished freedoms in the United States. It has been expanded over the course of our nation's history and has been a crucial part of the struggle for civil rights for all Americans. At first, the franchise was limited to adult white male property owners. In the early nineteenth century, property requirements were gradually abolished. In theory, adult black men were allowed to vote as a result of the Fifteenth Amendment in 1870. As noted earlier, many were continued to be denied this right. In 1920, all adult women received the vote with the ratification of the **Nineteenth Amendment**. Finally, all those between eighteen and twenty-one years of age were allowed to vote by the **Twenty-Sixth Amendment**, ratified in 1971.

An equally important change was the **Voting Rights Act of 1965**. It helped sweep aside state poll taxes, literacy tests, and other devices that prevented blacks from voting. It also authorized the attorney general and the Justice Department to supervise local elections in areas where voter discrimination was suspected and gave the Justice Department power to review any changes in state election laws in those areas. Southern politics faced dramatic changes as white officeholders were suddenly made responsible to black voters as well as to white ones. Amendments to the Voting Rights Act were adopted in 1970, 1975, 1982, and 2006.

"Let each citizen remember, at the moment he is offering his vote, that . . . he is executing one of the most solemn trusts in human society, for which he is accountable to God and his country."

—Samuel Adams

Voting Requirements

Voters must be citizens of the United States and at least eighteen years old. In addition, citizens must satisfy the **residency requirements** of their states. Those requirements are used to ensure that voters have some knowledge of the issues and the candidates in their locality—and that they have not suddenly appeared in a district simply to manipulate an election. Although residency requirements vary from state to state, the maximum requirement is thirty days' residence in a particular **precinct**, or voting district.

Registration is another requirement for voting. Every state except North Dakota requires that voters be properly enrolled with local election officials. Typically, on election day a registered voter goes to the polling place in his precinct,

The Nisei and Civil Rights

In 1942, the possibility that thousands of people of Japanese descent might serve as spies or saboteurs on the West Coast of the United States seemed a very real threat. As a result, the US government forced about 150,000 people of Japanese descent, including children and the elderly, to leave their homes in California and parts of Washington, Oregon, and Arizona. Most did not have time to store or sell their household goods at a fair price. Some were able to move to states farther east, but most were held in internment camps. Allowed to take only a few belongings with them, many families lost virtually everything they owned, except what they could carry.

Many internees spent years in the camps. Entire families lived in cramped, hastily constructed one-room quarters. Nevertheless, 30,000 Nisei (Japanese American) men from relocation camps volunteered for American military service and fought with distinction in Europe or served in military intelligence units in the Pacific.

In 1988, President Ronald Reagan signed the Civil Liberties Act of 1988, which gave a presidential apology and a symbolic payment of $20,000 to each living Japanese American internee and evacuee who lost liberty or property because of the federal government's discriminatory action during World War II. The act also created the Civil Liberties Public Education Fund to teach children and the rest of the public about the internment period.

The 1980 congressional commission that investigated Japanese relocation during World War II blamed this episode in American history on "race prejudice, war hysteria, and a failure of political leadership."

Helpful Resources Regarding LGBTQ+ Issues

When discussing these issues it is important both to uphold the Scripture's teaching and to oppose hateful and derogatory speech regarding those with same-sex temptations. Students should understand that while a Christian cannot embrace a sin as an identity, a Christian can struggle with same-sex temptations. All Christians face temptations, and this matter is a struggle for some Christians.

Helpful resources for teachers in thinking through these issues include the following:

• Rosaria Champagne Butterfield, *Secret Thoughts of an Unlikely Convert: An English Professor's Journey into Christian Faith*

• Kevin DeYoung, *What Does the Bible Really Teach about Homosexuality?*

Voting

Explain the voter-registration process, and give the location of the nearest local election office where eligible citizens may register. (Prospective voters can often register at other locations, such as shopping malls, schools, motor vehicle registration offices, and even by mail or online.) Instruct the students to find the location of their polling place and the name of their precinct and bring that information to class. Some of the students might be old enough to register to vote. If so, encourage them to do so and become involved in the electoral process.

where an official checks for that voter's name on the list of registered voters. If everything is in order, the voter may cast his ballot.

Registration is a simple process but usually must be completed at least a few weeks before an election. (That amount of time varies from state to state.) Online registration is available in most states and makes the registration process even easier. Unless a voter changes residence or fails to vote for several years, he remains registered on his precinct rolls. (If a voter fails to vote in a specified number of years or elections, his name may be purged from the voter lists.) Registration not only identifies qualified voters but also prevents voter fraud. Without registration requirements, dishonest voters could vote for their candidates in more than one precinct. Registration helps prevent people from taking literally the old joke about voting "early and often."

In addition to the citizenship, age, residency, and registration requirements, thirty-four states now request or require some form of identification for a person to vote. In about half of those states, a photo is requested or required. In several states, the ID must be government issued (the 2006 election was the first in which any state made this a requirement). Proponents see requirements for identification as a common sense way of protecting against voter fraud. They insist it helps prevent voter impersonation, increases public confidence in the election process, and helps ensure election integrity. Opponents argue that electoral fraud is extremely rare in the United States and that the requirements are merely a way to create barriers to voter participation. They assert that they place an undue burden on minority groups, the elderly, and others who are less likely to possess identification, particularly photo IDs. They also maintain that such requirements impose unnecessary costs and administrative burdens on elections administrators.

Lawsuits have been filed against many of the voter ID requirements on the basis that they are discriminatory with an intent to reduce voting by those who traditionally support the Democratic party. Such challenges state that the requirements violate the civil rights of some voters. Parts of voter ID laws in several states have been overturned by courts.

A voter enters a polling place in Arlington, Virginia

Section Review

1–2. List and explain the two types of due process.

3. What did the Fifteenth Amendment do?

4. What is a poll tax?

5. Which amendment ended the poll tax in national elections?

6. Why were the protests led by Martin Luther King Jr. so effective?

7–11. What are five typical requirements that a person must meet in order to vote in the United States?

★ Why do you think the privilege of voting was limited to property owners in our nation's early history? What would be some positives and negatives of this requirement?

★ Should voters be required to present identification before being allowed to cast a ballot? Explain your answer.

Section Review Answers

1–2. Substantive due process means the substance of laws must protect a person's basic freedoms. Procedural due process means laws must be justly administered and enforced. (p. 367)

3. gave adult black men the right to vote (p. 368)

4. A poll tax is a fee required before a person can vote. (p. 368)

5. the Twenty-Fourth Amendment (p. 368)

6. His protests were nonviolent. Also the public was surprised when law enforcement officials in the South often responded with brutality. (pp. 368–69)

7–11. A person must be a citizen of the United States, be age eighteen or older, satisfy the residency requirements of their state, register in advance (except in North Dakota), and in many states provide identification at the polling place. (pp. 369–70)

★ Students may say that such a requirement ensured that stable individuals elected officials (those who owned property were less likely to move from place to place). Also, because legislation often affected property owners the most, many wanted to limit voting rights to those individuals. The negative is the restriction did disfranchise many Americans who were affected by government actions.

★ Some might say yes, it is not an undue burden since individuals commonly must present an ID in numerous situations. Presenting an ID at the time of vote helps prevent voter fraud because there is the potential of someone claiming to be another person (even claiming to be someone deceased). Others would oppose the requirement because it unduly affects the elderly and minorities.

IV. Civil Responsibilities

Americans often speak of our liberties and our rights. We speak less frequently of our responsibilities. Yet, all three are crucial parts of our heritage and all three are essential to maintaining a free society.

Understanding Liberties and Rights

Where do liberties and rights originate? Some are given by law. For instance, voting rights are protected by the Constitution (especially the Fifteenth, Nineteenth, and Twenty-Sixth Amendments). However, some rights clearly come from God. Genesis 9:6 reveals that certain rights are based on the way that God made humans and on the way that God made His world to work. For example, every human has a right to life. Because all humans bear God's image, no human ought to be murdered (Gen. 9:6). The government may take human life only when it is a just punishment (Gen. 9:6; Rom. 13:4). Since human trafficking involves stealing the victim's life, it is also a violation of the right to life. For this reason, human trafficking was punishable by death in the Mosaic law (Exod. 21:16; Deut. 24:7). God created a world in which people create value by their work. Therefore, individuals have a right to be paid for their work (Lev. 19:13; Jer. 22:13–17) and a right to own property (Exod. 20:15, 17). Because all people bear the image of God, the vulnerable of society have a right to be treated fairly by those who are more fortunate (Exod. 22:21–27; 23:6–9).

However, an overemphasis on liberties and rights produces two major problems. The first is the multiplication of rights. The second is the neglect of responsibilities.

An example of the first can be found in Article 24 of the United Nations Universal Declaration of Human Rights: "Everyone has the right to rest and leisure, including reasonable limitation of working hours and periodic holidays with pay." Part of this statement reflects an important biblical truth—God created the world in six days and rested one day. Thus, a society in which certain people are given no rest from work is an unjust society (Exod. 20:10). However, it is difficult to believe that everyone has a right to "periodic holidays with pay." Throughout human history many people have worked for themselves as farmers or artisans. No such "right" applied to them.

One reason for the multiplication of rights is the effort of some groups to achieve the impossible goal of equality

1. Explain the origins of liberties and rights.
2. Describe the dangers of an overemphasis on liberties and rights.
3. Explain the responsibilities citizens have to their government and present a biblical view of civil rights.

Guiding Questions

1. What are the origins of liberties and rights?
2. What are the dangers of an overemphasis on liberties and rights?
3. What responsibilities do citizens have toward government?

Activity 4: The Duties of Citizenship

Use this speech by President Calvin Coolidge to help the students better understand American citizens' duty to vote.

Bill of Responsibilities

Ask the class to devise a bill of responsibilities to emphasize the proper relationship between rights and responsibilities.

Activity 5: Chapter Review

By answering the questions in this activity, the students will review chapter information.

of condition. The Bible teaches that all humans are equally image bearers of God (Gen. 1:26). It is right, therefore, for all people to be equal before the law (Exod. 23:3, 6). Likewise, equality of opportunity should exist in a society. However, equality of condition is a different matter. Achieving equality of condition would require an impossible amount of government supervision and would intrude in private lives and institutions to such an extent that it would ultimately destroy freedom. It will not even exist in eternity (Luke 19:17, 19).

Even more problematic, the multiplication of rights has led to some claiming as rights things that are contrary to God's law and the order of His creation. For instance, some claim that mothers have the right to take the life of their unborn children. Others say that people have a right to change their sex. Some insist that any couple who wishes to marry has a right to do so, even if they are of the same sex. Some say that people have the right to use harmful drugs. And others say that everyone should have the right to choose when to end their life. Each of these instances involves calling evil good and good evil (Isa. 5:20). No government ought to create a right that violates God's law.

Fulfilling Responsibilities

The second problem with the overemphasis on rights is that it can lead to a neglect of responsibilities. Imagine a society in which everyone insists on their own rights but in which they refuse to take the responsibility for upholding the rights of others. Such a society would not function well. Nor would a society in

which people refuse to submit to their government or participate in it. Rights necessarily involve responsibilities. Since all people have God-given rights, all people have God-given responsibilities.

When governments grant people civil liberties and civil rights, they are also placing responsibilities on people. These include a duty to submit to government by obeying laws, serving on juries, paying taxes, and engaging in numerous other ways. Citizens should also participate in a government that is "of the people, by the people, [and] for the people." Voting, voicing opinions, and supporting political candidates are just a few means of doing so.

Volunteers working at the campaign office of a 2014 US Senate candidate in Georgia

Christians must not forfeit their opportunities to work for the best possible society in which to live out their faith and to spread the gospel. Maintaining liberties, protecting rights, and fulfilling responsibilities are vital aspects of supporting and preserving our nation.

Section Review

1–2. What two major problems occur when liberties and rights are overemphasized?

3. What is one reason for the multiplication of rights?

4–8. List five rights individuals sometimes claim that are contrary to God's law and God's order.

★ Choose three civil responsibilities that each Christian should fulfill. Explain why these are important.

Section Review Answers

1–2. the multiplication of rights and the neglect of responsibilities (p. 371)

3. Some groups try to achieve the impossible goal of equality of condition. (pp. 371–72)

4–8. They claim the right of mothers to take the lives of their children; the right to change one's sex; the right to marry someone of the same sex; the right to use harmful drugs; and the right to end one's life. (p. 372)

★ Students may mention obeying laws that do not oppose God's law, paying taxes, serving on juries, voting, voicing opinions, and supporting political candidates. In Romans, Paul says that God ordained the authorities and citizens are to submit to them, each side meeting its responsibilities to the others. In addition, in order for a democratic nation to remain free, its citizens must fulfill their responsibilities by participating in government.

CHAPTER REVIEW ANSWERS

Making Connections

1. The free exercise clause says that Congress cannot make a law which restricts a person from believing and practicing his or her religious ideas. (pp. 357–58)

2–3. He said, "The most stringent protection of free speech would not protect a man in falsely shouting fire in a theatre and causing a panic." Holmes was saying that free speech does have limits. For example, no one has the right to endanger others by shouting something that falsely causes panic. (p. 358)

4. With incorporation, the Supreme Court began using the Fourteenth Amendment's due process clause to extend

15 CHAPTER REVIEW

Making Connections

1. Summarize the free-exercise clause in the First Amendment.
2–3. Write and explain the famous statement Justice Oliver Wendell Holmes made about the freedom of speech.
4. Explain the significance of the process known as incorporation (as it relates to the Bill of Rights).
5. Summarize the Voting Rights Act of 1965.

Developing Civics Skills

1. What change in the interpretation of the Constitution, beginning in the 1960s, led the Supreme Court to ban government-authorized prayers and required Bible reading in public schools?
2. Are the terms *gay rights* and *abortion rights* based on a true or a false understanding of civil rights? Support your answer. Identify consequences that have resulted from the interpretation that gay rights and abortion rights are civil rights.

Thinking Critically

1. Does the government have a right to enforce time-place-manner laws on the public preaching of the gospel? Support your answer.
2. Does the Constitution support a right to privacy?

Living as a Christian Citizen

1. In this chapter we see that free speech entails defending others' right to sometimes say obnoxious things. Write a brief statement that could serve as guidance for a legislator in framing limitations on free speech.
2. Explain the purpose of the establishment clause of the First Amendment. Describe and defend changes that you would make to the amendment's position on religion if you were a legislator in the first Congress.

as street preaching that uses a loud public address system or blocks pedestrian or vehicular traffic.

2. The Constitution does not explicitly state that Americans have the right to privacy. Some students may argue that for many of the first ten amendments to be practiced there is an assumed right to privacy; for example, the Fourth Amendment protecting a citizen from unlawful search and seizure would imply privacy. Other students may argue that if the framers wanted to guarantee a right to privacy they would have written it specifically into the Constitution.

Living as a Christian Citizen

1. Students should note that in a democratic society, free political speech is necessary for the political process to function. A student might argue from Scripture for the restriction of some religious speech; for instance, a student could advocate limiting false religions' proselytization. However, this would not be prudent in a pluralistic society because Christians' religious speech might also be prohibited. Christians should advocate restrictions on obscene, violent, and sensual expression. These kinds of speech degrade a society, and governments have a right to censor them.

2. The purpose of the establishment clause was to keep the national government from establishing a national religion but to allow the states to establish a state religion if they chose. Students may present differing views regarding possible changes to the clause, but students might argue that in the 1780s Congress should have required government officials to confess a basic creed that all Christians could accept. (Many states initially required this.) Such a creed would not infringe on other religious groups' right to worship, but it would mark the United States as a nation committed to Christianity. Other students would oppose this, arguing that it would be preferable to maintain Article VI, clause 3 of the Constitution.

the protections of the Bill of Rights to citizens in relation to state laws. This enhanced the power of the judiciary, altered the nature of federation, and enlarged the scope of constitutional rights. (p. 362)

5. The Voting Rights Act of 1965 helped eliminate state poll taxes, literacy tests, and other devices that prevented blacks from voting. It also authorized the attorney general and the Justice Department to supervise local elections and review state election law changes in areas where voter discrimination was suspected. (p. 369)

Developing Civics Skills

1. In the 1960s, the Supreme Court began to imply that there is a complete "wall of separation" between church and state.
2. A false understanding; groups advocating these "rights" are asking the government to sanction immoral behavior. By granting sinful behavior the status of a civil right, the government violates the religious liberties of Christians (and others) who reject the purported rights.

Thinking Critically

1. Some may say that in order to maintain law and order, the government could regulate certain public activities, such

Opening of the 1904 Republican National Convention in Chicago

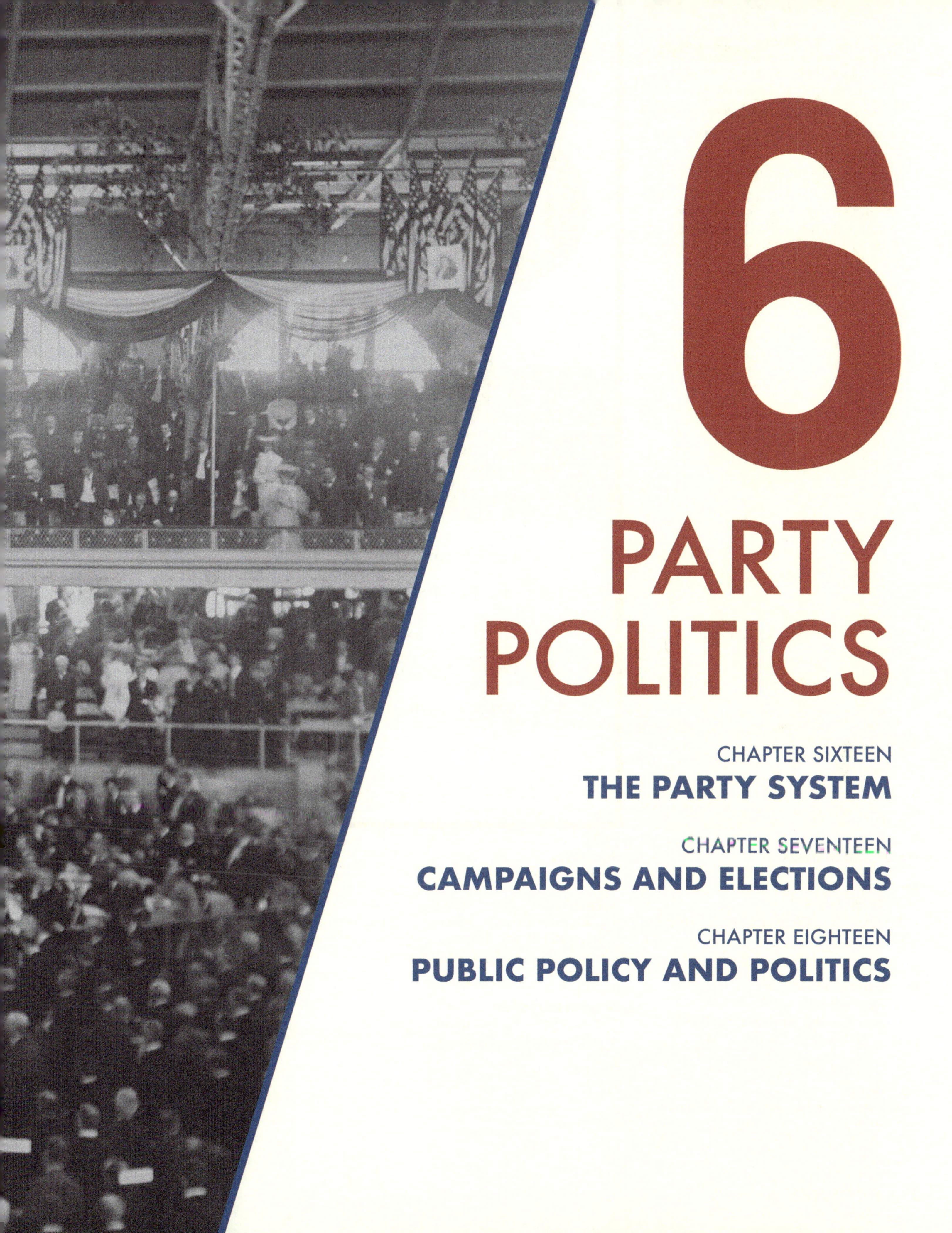

6

PARTY POLITICS

CHAPTER SIXTEEN
THE PARTY SYSTEM

CHAPTER SEVENTEEN
CAMPAIGNS AND ELECTIONS

CHAPTER EIGHTEEN
PUBLIC POLICY AND POLITICS

Chapter Goals

1. Describe political parties and their functions.
2. Analyze the two-party system.
3. Identify the different types of third parties.
4. Delineate the organization of political parties.
5. Analyze the reasons for the decline of political parties in the United States.

THE PARTY SYSTEM

16

If a political party does not have its foundation in the determination to advance a cause that is right and that is moral, then it is not a political party; it is merely a conspiracy to seize power.

—*Dwight D. Eisenhower*

2004 Democratic National Convention in Boston, Massachusetts

I. Parties and Their Functions

II. The Two-Party System

III. Third Parties

IV. Party Organization

V. Party Decline

BIG IDEAS

1. What are political parties and what are their functions?
2. How does the two-party system operate?
3. What are the different types of third parties?
4. How are political parties organized?
5. Why have political parties in the United States declined?

SUGGESTED MATERIALS

Section I
- Campaign materials
- Activity 1 from Chapter 16 of the *Student Activities*

Section II
- Activities 2–3 from Chapter 16 of the *Student Activities*
- A copy of Washington's Farewell Address
- Lyrics and music from 1860s campaign songs

Section III
- Activity 4 from Chapter 16 of the *Student Activities*

Section IV
- Special speakers (see pp. 392–93)

Section V
- Video of a recent presidential debate or the Nixon-Kennedy debate
- Activity 5 from Chapter 16 of the *Student Activities*

Teacher Resources
Visit TeacherToolsOnline.com for resources to enhance the lessons.

Politics describes the exercise of public power, the art and energy of governance. In this text, we first examined the foundations and constitutional provisions that comprise the American governmental system. Then our study showed how the three branches of government work on a national level. Often we can clearly see the exercise of public power through the functioning of government. Our attention now turns to how citizens group themselves to engage in politics.

What is the character of America's political parties? What should be the Christian's role in the American political system? With a basic understanding of America's party system, a Christian can determine the degree of individual involvement for this avenue of service.

I. Parties and Their Functions

Mugwump and Anti-Masonic, Greenback and Gold Bug, Federalist and Free-Soil, Green and Grassroots, Democrat and Dixiecrat are just some of the parties and factions within factions that have entered America's colorful political glossary. A few of these groups survive today; others are only historical curiosities. Despite their diversity, all political parties share a common definition—associations that represent certain political philosophies and promote certain political goals. This definition applies to all parties, both major and minor.

Party Defined

The simple definition of *political party* above could be applied to a multitude of organizations that are not really parties, such as labor unions and pro-life groups. The key point that distinguishes political parties from groups that are simply politically oriented is that **political parties** are organized to gain power by winning elections. This distinction is especially true for the country's major parties.

The two **major parties** that have been the dominant political competitors for well over a century and a half are the Democratic and Republican Parties. **Minor parties**, or **third parties**, are smaller and are usually organized around a particular issue. The positions that minor parties promote might later be adopted by the major parties if public support builds for those particular causes.

The Constitution never mentions political parties, probably because many of its framers distrusted factions; yet many of these men would soon become the leaders of a very partisan struggle, the ratification process. The Constitution's chief architect, James Madison, observed in *Federalist* No. 10 that the causes of political division, or faction, are "sown in the nature of man," and he referred to humans' "fallible . . . . reason and . . . self-love" as significant motivations that result in factions. Madison also noted that

> we see [these causes of faction] everywhere. . . . A zeal for different opinions concerning religion, concerning government, and many other points, [and] . . . an attachment to different leaders ambitiously contending for pre-eminence and power.

The Republican Party's elephant and the Democrat Party's donkey have been political symbols since the nineteenth century.

Campaign Materials

Because of the frequency of American elections, it is probable that one or more political campaigns will be underway at some level as you teach this chapter. Call or visit a party's or a candidate's headquarters, and request signs, bumper stickers, and other materials that you can use for display (perhaps along with drawings of a donkey and an elephant) to show the candidates' contrasting views. A collage might be appropriate for the forthcoming election.

Multiparty Struggles

In multiparty systems, opinions and interests about a variety of issues result in limited-issue political parties. These parties often result in unstable coalition governments, and power struggles frequently take place in the government itself. In a two-party system, however, ideological struggles usually take place within the parties; this tends to make the government itself more stable.

Tocqueville on Parties

"The political parties which I style great are those which cling to principles more than to their consequences; to general, and not to especial cases; to ideas, and not to men. These parties are usually distinguished by a nobler character, by more generous passions, more genuine convictions, and a more bold and open conduct than the others."

Washington on Parties

George Washington saw clear dangers in "factions," or political parties, and he warned against them in his 1796 Farewell Address.

Madison was, of course, referring to the variety of divisions, the opinions and shades of opinion, that exist throughout any society on various subjects. As President Washington neared the end of his eight years in office, he warned against the formation of political parties in his Farewell Address.

Yet, in a society that permits free speech and association, political parties are natural; and in a government that represents diversity, political parties are inevitable.

Party Functions

Political parties provide a bridge between the governed and their government. They are channels for expressing political opinion and for electing the men and women who will represent those positions.

Nominating Candidates

A political party's major purpose is to **nominate**, or name, candidates for public office. A party's candidates are usually chosen through a party caucus, a party convention, or a party primary. The nominated candidates are then announced to all voters. Afterward, parties work for their candidates, helping them win their elections by providing access to funds, endorsements, volunteers, and professional staff members. These nominating methods have proven effective both as a democratic means of choosing a party's candidates and as a means of securing votes for them.

Governing

After candidates are nominated and elections have been won (or lost), parties continue to play an important role through the process of governing. Party ties provide a basis for both legislative cooperation and obstruction. Congress is actually structured along party lines, with the majority party in the House and the Senate empowered to control top committee posts and set the legislative agenda. The president can also use party ties to help push legislation through Congress, uphold vetoes, and determine executive and judicial appointments. Much of the business conducted by Congress and state legislatures is based on **partisanship** (strong devotion to a political party).

Watchdogs

Parties act as watchdogs over one another. This is especially true of the party out of power (i.e., the party that does not control the presidency). The behavior and policies of the party in power are watched carefully and often criticized; this can help make the controlling party more accountable to the people. However, the party out of power must be concerned about how it is perceived by the public. Is it merely opposing the party in power, or is it exhibiting a greater loyalty to the nation?

Moderating Influence

Generally, political parties provide an important moderating influence over competing and even conflicting political forces. In the US governing system, the major parties have tended to lessen extremism at both ends of the spectrum and bring diverse interests together in a consensus over broad principles (though some have argued this has been less true in recent years).

For Good or for Evil?

Exodus 23:2 warns against following the crowd in doing evil. Like all other groups united to achieve a specific purpose, political parties can be forces for either good or evil, depending on their objectives. Exodus 23:2 reminds us how easy it is for people to assent to wrongdoing when many other people are committed to a bad course of action. Ask students to discuss how this verse applies to American politics today.

Instruct your student to write a paragraph that shows how Exodus 23:2 applies to American politics today.

Activity 1: Party Functions

In this activity each student will choose a major political party and use media sources to illustrate each party function.

Parties' moderating influence entails both benefits and dangers. Its chief benefit is reducing the disruptive influence of political extremists while seeking to find common ground for opposing demands. This characteristic explains much about our government system's tendency to move to the middle through political compromise. The drawbacks of parties' moderating influence include the potential for suppressing unpopular dissent, resisting needed policy changes, compromising moral principle, and making centrist parties too much alike.

Section Review

1–2. Explain the differences between major and minor political parties.

3. Summarize James Madison's conclusion about the causes of political division.

4. What is the major purpose of a political party?

5. What role does a political party play in governing the nation?

★ How do political parties serve as a moderating influence?

II. The Two-Party System

Today, whenever political parties are mentioned, most Americans automatically think of Republicans and Democrats. This fact reflects a dominant feature of American politics—the **two-party system**. Other parties have existed and currently exist in the country, but most of the electorate identifies with one of the two major parties.

Reasons for Formation
Tradition

The history of the American two-party system dates to our earliest struggles as a nation. Partisan struggles and personality conflicts surrounding the ratification of the Constitution produced two political camps—the Federalists and the Anti-Federalists. These camps were the basis of the two-party system. This system also reflects a British influence, seen in the conflicts between Whigs and Tories in Parliament.

Competition

Although our two-party system has been well entrenched for more than two centuries, it has not always been a contest between equals. At times, one of the major parties has dominated the other, either regionally or in one or more branches of the national government. The House of Representatives, for example, was controlled by the Democratic Party from 1955 to 1995. At the presidential level, the Democrats held the White House continuously from 1933 to 1953, but the Republicans won seven of the ten presidential elections between 1952 and 1988.

Competition between the two parties is also unequal in certain areas of the country. In fact, certain states could best be described as having a one-party system because of the total dominance of the Democratic or Republican Party. For instance, after the Civil War ended in 1865, the Democratic Party dominated the politics of the South. The then-new Republican Party was the party of Lincoln and Radical Reconstruction—meaning that it was not the party of many successful Southern politicians. The South, for all practical purposes, had a one-party system (and was thus called the "**Solid South**") until the 1960s, when

---

Section II Objectives

1. Explain why a two-party system developed in America.

2. Analyze the characteristics of a two-party system.

3. Summarize the historical development of parties.

4. Identify party systems in other nations.

The British Whig Party

Whig is a shorter form of *whiggamore*. It was first used for seventeenth-century Scottish Presbyterians, who opposed the succession of the Roman Catholic Duke of York (James II). In British parliamentary circles, the term *Whig* was used to refer to those who opposed royal influence in government and wanted to increase parliamentary control and influence.

The British Tory Party

Tory was originally the name given to Irish outlaws. The name was later applied to supporters of the Duke of York. Tories believed in the divine right of kings (the hereditary right to the throne), had strong ties with the Anglican Church, and supported the exclusive power of the king.

John Locke

The Whig Party of England was inspired by John Locke. He promoted the idea that a nation's sovereignty rests in the will of the people, not in the king's so-called divine right to rule.

Section Review Answers

1–2. Major parties emphasize gaining power by winning elections; minor (third) parties are smaller, are usually organized around a particular issue, and often influence the major parties. (p. 377)

3. Madison believed that political divisions originate in the nature of humanity, which is motivated significantly by "fallible. . . . reason and . . . self-love." (pp. 377–78)

4. The primary purpose of political parties is to nominate, or name, candidates for public office. (p. 378)

5. Party ties provide a basis for legislative cooperation and obstruction; the majority party in the House and in the Senate controls top committee posts and sets the legislative agenda; and the president can use party ties to push legislation through Congress, uphold vetoes, and make executive and judicial appointments. (p. 378)

★ The major parties tend to reduce extremism and bring diverse interests together in a consensus over broad principles. (pp. 378–79)

The 2000 and 2016 Elections

In the 2000 election, 675 counties across the nation supported Gore; 2,463 counties supported Bush. In 2016, Hillary Clinton won the popular vote in 487 counties, while Trump won in 2,626 counties.

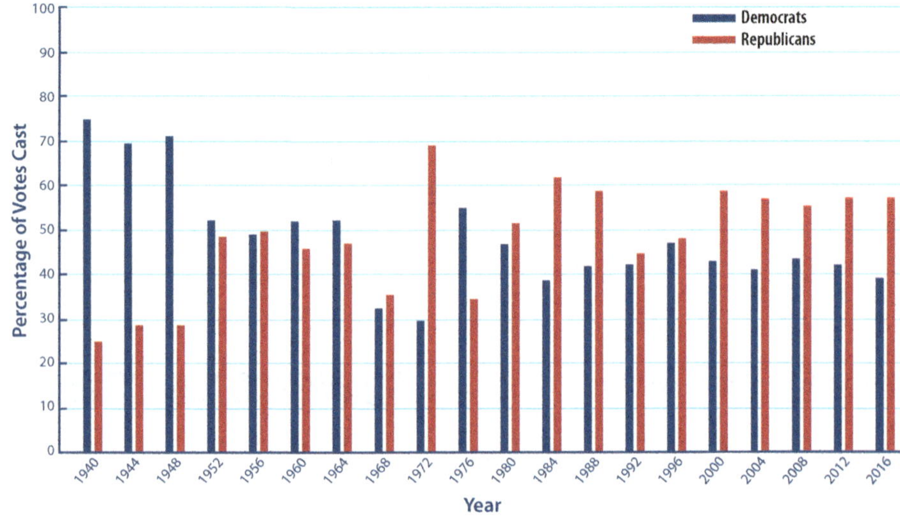

the Republicans, with their more conservative appeal, began gaining acceptance in the region. Since that time, Republican presidential candidates have generally found the states of the old Confederacy to be an important power base. A notable exception occurred in 1976 when Jimmy Carter, former Democratic governor of Georgia won the presidency.

This political shift in the South shows the growing competitiveness between the major parties. Party strength might vary on the local level—Democrats usually control major cities and Republicans normally dominate rural areas—however, the two-party rivalry on the whole remains strong.

The best indication of national competitiveness is the voting tally for the only office that all eligible Americans, from Maine to Maui, can cast ballots—the presidency. In 1960, for example, John Kennedy defeated Richard Nixon for the presidency by fewer than 120,000 votes out of more than 68 million cast. Nixon came back in 1968 to edge out Democrat Hubert Humphrey by a close 43.4 percent to 42.7 percent margin. The 1976 election was a close contest between Democrat Jimmy Carter's 50.1 percent of the electorate and Republican Gerald Ford's 48 percent. In the 2000 election, Democrat Al Gore won the popular vote with about 540,000 more votes than Republican George W. Bush out of approximately 105 million votes cast (though Bush won the presidency with a majority of electoral votes). In 2016, Democrat Hillary Clinton outpolled Republican Donald Trump by approximately three million votes (more than 136 million people voted in the election). However, Trump was victorious in the Electoral College.

Electoral System

The American electoral system encourages a two-party system through single-member districts and election law. Most elections held in the United States, from the national level to the local level, are single-member district elections.

Party Support in the South

Instruct the students to review the chart above. Ask the following questions based on the chart: In which three elections did the Democratic candidate receive approximately 70 percent or more of the vote in the South? In which election was this true for the Republican candidate? What is significant about the 1952 election? The 1972 election? The 1976 election? What other information can you learn from reviewing this chart?

Urban versus Rural

In recent presidential elections, the Democratic Party proved to be strong in urban areas while Republicans dominated rural areas. Divide the class into groups, and instruct them to discuss the possible reasons for urban Democratic dominance and rural Republican dominance. What influences could alter this trend?

Encourage the student to list reasons for urban Democratic strength and rural Republican strength.

Single-member districts are legislative districts that have only one representative. Single-member district elections are used in a winner-take-all system based on a candidate's receiving the largest number of votes cast for an office. On the national level, in all states (except Maine and Nebraska) the presidential candidate who receives the largest number of votes receives all of that state's electoral votes. Minor parties are discouraged because people usually perceive that there are only two electable candidates. Voters often do not want to "waste" votes on a minor-party candidate.

In the United States, most election law is state rather than federal law. Most of the people who make these election laws are Republicans or Democrats. The two major parties work together in a **bipartisan** manner (a spirit of two-party cooperation) to shape laws that make it difficult for a third-party candidate to get on the ballot. As a result, third-party candidates for president find it especially difficult to be listed on the ballot in every state.

Characteristics
Diverse Support Through Broad Appeal

America's diversity is mirrored in its two major parties. People of different ethnicities, religions, incomes, and professions come together to support their particular parties. The reasons for this diverse support, however, often differ.

How People Voted in the 2016 Presidential Election

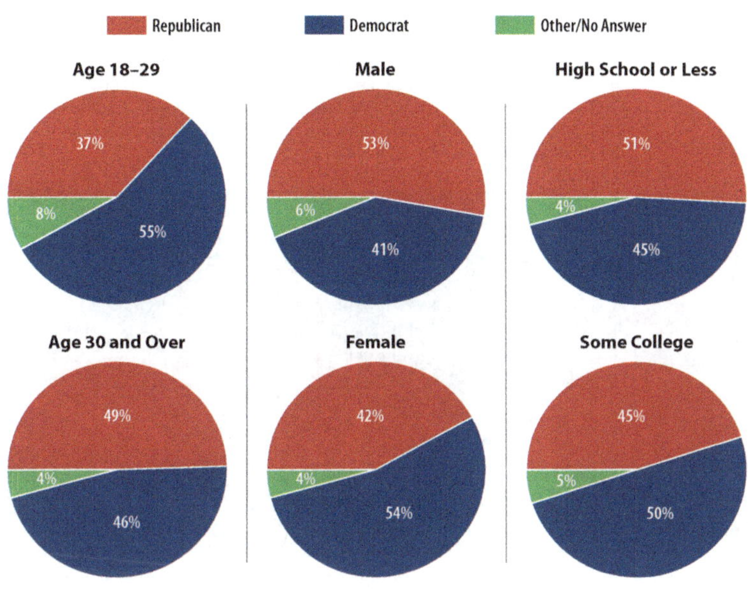

Maine and Nebraska

Electors in Maine and Nebraska are apportioned using a district method. Two electors are chosen at large (the presidential electors of the party whose candidates for president and vice president received the most votes statewide), and the remainder are chosen according to the popular vote in each congressional district. Maine changed to the district system for the 1972 election, and Nebraska changed its election law in 1991.

Dirty Politics?

Discuss the popular notion that politics is "dirty." Why is this attitude common in the United States? Is politics necessarily dirty? In what ways do political parties simply reflect their political environment?

Suggested points to include in the discussion are as follows:

1. Politics, by its nature, involves compromise; and compromise might be perceived as immoral, especially when ethical principles seem to be at stake.

2. Politicians often exaggerate the virtues of their positions and denigrate those of their opponents. Sometimes they state outright falsehoods.

3. Political scandal seems common because it is frequently reported in the media. (Remind the students that in our country, the media often investigates government. The media might not cover similar incidents in the private sector because, obviously, they are private. Less information about private malfeasance is available to the media, and the public is less interested in it—except when it involves the public.)

4. The dirtiness of politics is largely determined by individual candidates and officeholders and by the political environment in which they operate. For instance, during the Tweed era in New York City politics (ca. 1855–75), corruption was normal political behavior. The same could be said of some other cities and towns at various periods of history (e.g., Chicago during Prohibition).

5. For many, politics and political campaigns become so all-consuming that the only thing that matters is that your party or candidate wins. This has led many politicians and campaigns to engage in unethical behavior. Discuss with the class whether it is right to pursue unethical political practices or support an immoral candidate so that a good piece of legislation might pass or to prevent an opposing party's candidate from being elected.

Platform Pitfalls

A platform can cause problems for a candidate if it is too specific or seems to make too many concessions to special-interest groups. In 1988, the Democrats produced a brief, vague platform to avoid the problems they created for themselves in 1984 with a detailed platform that seemed to promise something to almost everybody.

For example, Christians concerned about abortion might support the Republican Party because of its pro-life platform. Some businessmen might support the Republican ticket because it advocates for lower taxes and the free market. Similarly, the Democratic Party draws support from a broad cross section of society because many groups like the party's emphasis on urban programs and public health.

Because diverse groups identify with each major party for varying reasons, a party must have broad appeal. As mentioned earlier, the main purpose of political parties is to win elections. Therefore, both parties try to reach a majority of voters with a broad, moderate message. This is why opposing candidates might sound quite similar on a number of issues: they are trying to reach the same voters—those in the middle. Candidates that many voters perceive as extreme do not usually win elections. This was true of Republican Barry Goldwater in 1964 when many thought he was too conservative and of Democrat George McGovern in 1972 when many thought he was too liberal. Historically, the parties' closeness on some issues and the middle-of-the-road appeal that both parties make actually enhance the stability of our political system. When the two parties grow further and further apart on issues, elections become more bitter, leaving the country deeply divided.

Different Viewpoints

The similarities between the parties apply to some issues but not all of them. Similarity is not sameness. The two parties have clear differences on a number of issues. A **party platform** (a formal statement of a party's position on current issues) is written at a party's national convention every four years and provides evidence of these distinctions. For example, the 2016 Democratic platform had this to say about abortion:

> We believe unequivocally, like the majority of Americans, that every woman should have access to quality reproductive health care services, including safe and legal abortion. . . . We believe that reproductive health is core to women's, men's, and young people's health and wellbeing. We will continue to stand up to Republican efforts to defund Planned Parenthood health centers.

Controversy surrounds the money that the government gives Planned Parenthood, the largest abortion provider in the country.

The Prophet Daniel

Encourage students to reflect on the life of Daniel. Were the five issues mentioned in the "Dirty Politics?" note (page 381) present in his day?

How was Daniel able to serve effectively in high office in a pagan empire? What does his willingness to suffer indicate? Emphasize to students that Daniel was willing to lose his life in order to maintain his principles.

Interpreting Charts

Ask students to review the pie charts on the previous page. Lead a discussion regarding what can be learned from this information. In 2016 where was support for the Republican Party the strongest? For the Democratic Party? In which categories are the differences between the support received by each party significant? In which are they not? What other information can be determined from the charts?

In contrast, the 2016 Republican platform declared:

> We assert the sanctity of human life and affirm that the unborn child has a fundamental right to life which cannot be infringed. . . . We oppose the use of public funds to perform or promote abortion or to fund organizations, like Planned Parenthood, so long as they provide or refer for elective abortions. . . . We support the appointment of judges who respect traditional family values and the sanctity of innocent human life.

Most political candidates from a party adhere to the party's platform. However, not all candidates do so, and the party leadership lacks the ability to force such agreement. These internal disputes can cause confusion among voters.

Broader differences exist between the two parties. For example, a 1980 survey of the Democratic National Committee revealed that 36 percent of its members described themselves as **liberal**. (A liberal is one whose political view seeks to change the political, economic, and social status quo—often by government intervention.) On the other hand, only 1 percent of the Republican National Committee members described themselves as liberal; and 63 percent of the committee's members described themselves as **conservative**, compared to a slim 4 percent of conservatives on the Democratic side. (A conservative is one whose political view defends against major changes in the political, economic, and social institutions of society while seeking to improve conditions with reform as needed.) Since 1980, the philosophical rift has only deepened between the political camps. Nevertheless, the Republican Party is not conservative enough for many conservatives, nor is the Democratic Party liberal enough for many liberals. This simply reflects the middle-of-the-road focus that the major parties often embrace.

Party Membership

Another important characteristic of the two major parties is the nature of party membership. A person can be a Democrat or a Republican simply by declaring himself one or the other; party membership is a matter of personal identification, not requiring formal admittance.

Many factors determine why a person may identify with one party over another. Of course, agreement on issues and ideology attracts many voters to a particular camp. Economic conditions can also affect allegiances. In some areas, it is nearly impossible for members of one political party to get elected using its party label, so some of that party's candidates will run on their opponents' ticket. The term RINO, "Republicans in Name Only," is sometimes used to describe Democrats who run as Republicans (though the term is also used by conservative Republicans to refer to moderate or liberal Republicans who do not adhere to the party's limited-government, free-market, pro-family stances).

Yet the single most influential factor in most people's choice of a party or political philosophy is their family background. Candidates and campaigns come and go, but a political philosophy often bridges generations. Although commitment among party members might be quite strong, the loose, nonbinding nature of party identification results in shifts of allegiance.

"In effect, anyone who considers himself a Democrat is a Democrat; anyone who considers himself a Republican is a Republican. . . . No obligations intrude on the party member. He can be a member without applying for admission, a beneficiary without paying dues or contributing to campaigns, a critic without attending meetings, an interpreter without knowing party vocabulary. . . . To the citizen who takes politics casually, it may be the best of all worlds. The typical American['s]. . . . principal participation in party life is through the act of voting— sometimes for his party and sometimes not."

—William Keefe, political scientist
Parties, Politics, and Public Policy in America

Conservatives and Liberals

The differences between liberalism and conservatism are addressed again in Chapter 18. Refer to the chart and explanation on page 422 and the accompanying notes in the Teacher Edition of that chapter.

Differing Views

Divide the class into three groups to study and discuss conservative, libertarian, and liberal views on a range of issues, such as divorce laws, marriage laws, obscenity laws, gun-control laws, and business regulation. Instruct students to evaluate these positions in light of a Christian worldview.

Using the same three groups, assign each the task of reviewing the most recent party platform of the Republican, Democratic, or Libertarian Parties. Ask students to evaluate the party positions in light of a Christian worldview.

Liberal, Moderate, or Conservative?

Invite the students to identify the top five political figures in your state and the political party each represents. Are these political figures conservative, liberal, or moderate? Instruct students to justify their conclusions through the political figures' statements and voting records.

The Federalist Party

The Federalist Party included merchants, bankers, manufacturers, most professionals, and some wealthy farmers. In foreign policy, Federalists were typically pro-British.

The Democratic-Republican Party

This party, also referred to as the Jeffersonian Party, was strongly supported by small farmers, small shopkeepers, frontier settlers, and craftsmen. In foreign policy, Jeffersonians were usually pro-French.

Thirty-Six Ballots

The election of 1800 marked the first peaceful transfer of power between political parties and the first of two occurrences in which a president was elected by the House of Representatives. Prior to the Twelfth Amendment, each Electoral College member voted for two people. The person with the most votes became president, and the person with the second-most votes became vice president. In the election of 1800, Thomas Jefferson and Aaron Burr tied, and the House of Representatives had to break the tie. Alexander Hamilton, who liked Burr even less than he liked Jefferson, argued that House members should vote for Jefferson. After thirty-six ballots, Jefferson became president and Burr became vice president.

Stability

The two-party system provides more stability than a **multiparty system**. In multiparty politics, common among many European democracies, several parties compete for majority support. With so many factions dividing the electorate, it is very difficult for one party to win a majority. Some of these parties come together, forming a **coalition** (a temporary alliance of several groups) to gain a majority and thereby gain control of the government. But these party coalitions do not always hold together; their separation may force frequent elections, hence sometimes leading to instability in the government.

Flexibility

The two-party system is more flexible than a one-party system. Having two parties provides an open forum for competing ideas, a requirement for the ability to meet the demands of democratic government. Thus, American politics is very stable. A one-party system, such as those in Cuba and the People's Republic of China, simply rubber-stamps the decisions of a dictator. Individual dissent is rarely tolerated, and organized dissent seldom exists within the official political party. Voting in a one-party election is a peculiar sort of charade.

Development and Direction
Jefferson and Jackson

As already mentioned, the struggle concerning ratification after the Constitutional Convention was waged between two political camps that could be called parties: the Federalists, who favored the Constitution, and the Anti-Federalists, who opposed it in part or in whole. After ratification of the Constitution, political differences persisted both in Congress and in President Washington's cabinet. The growing political rift was fueled by arguments between Alexander Hamilton and Thomas Jefferson concerning tariffs, foreign policy, a national bank, and constitutional interpretation. Hamilton headed the Federalist Party; Jefferson led the opposing group, known as the Democratic-Republican Party (the party was sometimes called Republicans, but it should not be confused with the modern Republican Party, which was founded in 1854).

The Jeffersonian victory in 1800 swept the Federalists out of power and began a period of one-party domination. The Federalist Party slid steadily toward extinction when it opposed the War of 1812 and ceased to compete for national office after its presidential candidate carried only three states in the 1816 election. For the quarter century that followed 1800, the Virginia dynasty of Jefferson, Madison, and Monroe ruled the presidency while their followers controlled both houses of Congress. With the lack of effective party competition, the Jeffersonian era gradually became less partisan. The problems with the nonpartisan system became quite apparent after the 1824 election, and the results of that election transformed American politics.

In 1824, William Crawford, General Andrew Jackson, John Quincy Adams, and Henry Clay (all members of the Democratic-Republican Party) competed in a four-man nonpartisan race for the presidency. When no one gained a majority in the Electoral College, the election had to be settled by the House of Representatives. In these situations, according to the Twelfth Amendment, the House must elect the president from the top three contenders—Jackson, Adams, and Crawford in this case. Since

Alexander Hamilton

Thomas Jefferson

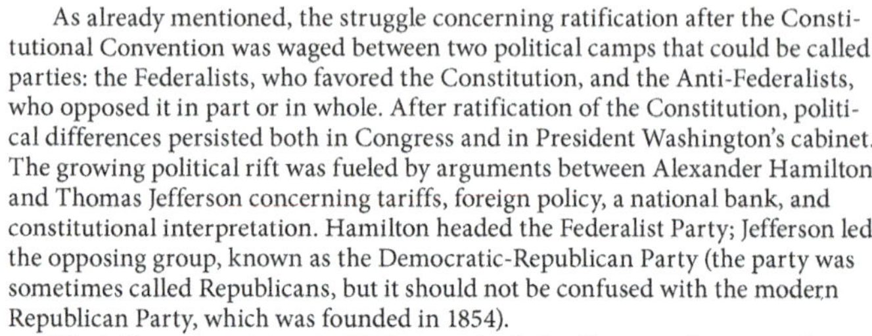

Two-Party Competition

The American party system has undergone three major periods of competition.

- Federalists vs. Democratic-Republican period (1790s–1820s)
- Democratic vs. Whig period (1820s–1850s)
- Republican vs. Democratic period (1850s to the present)

Coalition Government

Create a coalition government by dividing the class into at least five different "parties." Assign key platform positions to each party. The "Hawk Party," for example, could advocate a strong defense buildup and increased veterans' benefits. The "Dove Party" could favor nuclear disarmament and defense cuts. Other parties might include a "Green Party" that represents environmental concerns and a "Populist Party" that has an amalgamated platform drawn from each of the other parties.

Distribute descriptions of each party's platform. Each party should study its positions, make a compromise-and-alliance strategy, and develop a compromise platform with two or more other parties to achieve a majority. The first coalition to gather a numerical majority of the class controls the government. After a coalition becomes dominant, introduce a "national emergency" that threatens the coalition's fragile party alliances. The coalition-building process should then start again.

Jackson won the popular and most electoral votes, he was expected to be the House choice. Clay, however, who had received the lowest number of electoral votes, became the "kingmaker." As Speaker of the House, Clay threw his support to Adams. When he became president, Adams appointed Clay to be his secretary of state. Jackson and his supporters cried foul, accusing Adams and Clay of making a "corrupt bargain." Although no proof of a prior deal exists, Jackson's supporters soon began organizing to win the White House in 1828. Their efforts opened a new chapter in party development.

Martin Van Buren, a senator from New York and later Jackson's successor in the presidency, organized Jackson's campaign. In a break with old attitudes, Van Buren believed that the decline of two-party competition had hurt the democratic process by encouraging regional candidates to seek the White House. Those regional candidacies could leave the country divided and (as in the previous contest) force elections to be decided by a few House members.

In the 1828 campaign, the Democratic-Republican Party split. President John Quincy Adams sought reelection as a National Republican while Jackson's group was called the Democrats. Jackson's triumph that year and the subsequent era that he dominated produced several notable results for political parties. First, organized competition broadened voter participation. Voter turnout in 1828 was substantially higher than in previous elections (partly due to interest in that election; partly due to the elimination of the requirement, in many states, that adult men own property in order to vote; and partly due to the excitement of being able to vote for the first time).

Second, the nomination process expanded through the use of the **convention**. The convention, first used by the Anti-Masonic Party in 1831 and then by the Democratic Party in 1832, is an assembly of party representatives, or **delegates**, selected from each state to nominate candidates for president and vice president. Before the advent of the convention, a party's nominees were chosen by a **caucus** (a small meeting of a party's top leaders and legislators in Congress). As democratic participation expanded, the closed-door nature of the caucus was attacked, and the nominating convention eventually became an established practice.

Third, Andrew Jackson implemented **patronage**. Also called the **spoils system**, it is the practice of giving jobs to friends and other supporters. Beginning in 1828, patronage was possibly the single most influential factor in building party organization for half a century. With the arrival of a new administration, many firings and hirings occurred as party supporters were rewarded with government positions at all levels. Naturally with this arrangement, a person seeking a government position had greater incentive to boost voter turnout for his party's candidate.

Finally, the party system gave birth to the **political campaign** (an organized effort by a political party or candidate to attract voter support in an election). Jackson's strong personality and party organization led his opponents to form a new party, the Whigs. The Whigs quickly excelled in the new art of campaigning. They especially noted Jackson's common-man appeal. By 1840, they had outgeneraled the general's party, running a war hero of their own, William Henry Harrison, as candidate against the incumbent Democrat, Martin Van Buren. Harrison, the hero of the Battle of Tippecanoe nearly thirty years earlier,

John Quincy Adams

Andrew Jackson

Lowest and Highest Voter Turnouts for Presidential Elections

The following three presidential elections had the *highest* voter turnout (that is, percentage of eligible voters who participated in the election):

- 1876 (81.8 percent)
- 1860 (81.2 percent)
- 1840 (80.2 percent)

The following three presidential elections had the *lowest* voter turnout:

- 1924 (48.9 percent)
- 1996 (49.0 percent)
- 1920 (49.2 percent)

The First National Convention

The Anti-Masonic Party held the first national convention in 1831 in Baltimore. The Democrats quickly followed the example of this minor party by nominating Andrew Jackson at a convention in 1832.

The Whig Party in America

For most of its existence in US politics, the Whig Party focused on internal improvements, such as building roads, canals, and railroads and deepening rivers. This concentration on internal improvements was of great interest to westerners, who were isolated and needed markets. When the Whig Party disintegrated, most Whigs became Republicans (e.g., Abraham Lincoln was originally a Whig), but a few became Democrats or joined fringe parties.

Getting Out the Vote

By 1840 a party's ability to get out the vote was a clear indication of its strength. From that year through 1900, the percentage of eligible voters who cast ballots in presidential elections was 70 percent or higher. Afterward, turnout dropped. In the twenty-five presidential elections of the twentieth century, turnout was below 60 percent in fifteen. Since 1900, turnout has never reached 70 percent.

Activity 2: Voter Turnout in Presidential Elections

Use this enrichment activity to enhance the students' analytical skills and their skills in using charts.

Why Is Voter Turnout So Low?

Discuss various factors that might explain why voter turnout is not higher. (Reasons might include disillusionment with party politics, a weak choice of candidates, little distinction among parties, a lack of viable third parties, and the various preoccupations of life.)

Washington's Farewell Address

Obtain a copy of George Washington's Farewell Address. Read and discuss Washington's advice on political parties. Ask the students the following questions: What issue do you think was on Washington's mind when he gave this advice? Has his warning come true?

Activity 3: Washington's Farewell Address

This activity offers excerpts from Washington's Farewell Address and questions about it to aid the development of the students' analytical skills and use of original sources.

Whigs and Democrats

Party competition between the Whigs and Democrats remained strong after Jackson left office. During the next four elections, control of the White House changed hands with each election. In 1844, Democrats ran a dark horse, James K. Polk of Tennessee, while the powerful Henry Clay and his running mate Theodore Frelinghuysen represented the Whigs. The Whig campaign song proclaimed,

> Rah! Rah! The country's risin'
>
> For Henry Clay and Frelinghuysen!

But it was wrong. Third-party candidate James Birney diverted enough votes from Clay to give the election to Polk.

Conscience Whigs versus Cotton Whigs

The 1850s brought division within the Whig Party over the slavery issue. The northern Conscience Whigs favored abolishing slavery and stopping its spread into new territories. The southern Cotton Whigs opposed this viewpoint. By the 1860s, most southern Whigs had become part of the Democratic Party, and most northern Whigs had joined the newly formed Republican Party.

William Henry Harrison's 1840 presidential campaign successfully developed many features still used in modern political campaigns.

had John Tyler as his running mate. "Tippecanoe and Tyler too!" and "Van, Van is a used-up man" were popular Whig Party rallying cries.

The loud and rowdy campaign of 1840 featured slogans, campaign buttons, placards, large rallies, a campaign newspaper, and large quantities of hard cider. The Whig Party was the first party to create a popular image greater than the candidate himself and "sell" it to the public. They wrongly portrayed the well-to-do Harrison, son of one of the signers of the Declaration of Independence who later served as Virginia's governor, as a common man of the frontier who was born in a log cabin. They portrayed his opponent as "Matty," a lightweight dandy (a man who focuses on clothes and manners and gives little thought to important issues).

Harrison rode to the White House on his log-cabin theme, and the Whigs introduced the country to one of its most colorful sideshows—the presidential campaign. The success of their venture was underscored by the fact that about 80 percent of all eligible voters—the third-highest total in the nation's history—voted in the election.

Civil War and Afterward

Unity in the Democratic Party diminished considerably by 1860, when Republican Abraham Lincoln won the presidency in a four-way race. Union victory in the Civil War ensured Republican success until well into the twentieth century. During the period from 1860 to 1932, only two Democrats won the White House: Grover Cleveland (twice in nonconsecutive terms) and Woodrow Wilson (twice).

However, this situation changed abruptly in 1932 during the Great Depression. The election of Democrat Franklin Roosevelt broke the Republican hold on the presidency and its dominance in Congress. Roosevelt's unprecedented and unrepeatable (because of the Twenty-Second Amendment) string of four victories, along with Harry Truman's win in 1948, gave the Democrats control of the White House for twenty years. Still, since Eisenhower's 1952 election, Republicans have controlled the highest office more often than Democrats.

The Powerful Few

Although party conventions allowed more individuals to participate in the nomination process, convention delegates were often chosen by party cau-

Grover Cleveland

Woodrow Wilson

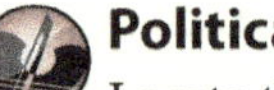

Political Songs

Locate the lyrics and music of some of the campaign songs in previous presidential elections. Direct the students to read the lyrics and discuss what is being said about the candidates. If the music is available, encourage a group of students to perform the songs for the class. Discuss reasons why political songs are not very popular today.

cuses committed to a particular candidate or political boss. This meant that the outcome of a nomination remained in the hands of a few power brokers. And the candidates themselves were often those who survived deals made in "smoke-filled rooms." Early in the twentieth century, demands for reform of the entire nominating process brought another important change in party development—the **primary**, sometimes called a nominating primary. This is a state or local election in which voters select the candidates who will run on each party's ticket in the general election. For example, if two Democrats want to be elected to the US House of Representatives for a particular congressional district, they must compete for their party's support in a primary election. The winner will be the Democratic nominee and will face the Republican nominee in the general election.

Primaries have been examined in earlier chapters and will be discussed again in the next chapter, but one point is clear: primaries have significantly changed political parties by shifting the power focus from the party organization to the campaign organization. The candidates now play a much greater role in choosing the issues, raising money, and mobilizing the voters than in the past. There have been both positives and negatives to this change.

Other Party Systems

Multiparty System

In this system, common in most European democracies, several major and many minor parties compete for public offices. Each party often emphasizes a

Comparison: Political Parties in the United States and Mexico

A strong two-party system has dominated American political history. Third parties routinely fail and disappear. Americans have become so accustomed to two-party politics that it is hard to imagine any other kind of political life. For much of the twentieth century, however, Mexico had quite a different tradition—one-party rule. From 1929 to 2000, Mexico's Institutional Revolutionary Party (in Spanish, *Partido Revolucionario Institucional* or PRI) dominated the presidency. Having ruled for more than seventy years, the PRI was the longest-ruling party in the world at the time of its loss in 2000.

While dozens of countries were fighting in World War I, Mexico suffered a bloody civil war (1910–1920) over political succes-

sion that cost more than a million lives. From that horrible experience came a new constitution and the National Revolutionary Party, the forerunner of today's PRI. Mexico's leaders, revolutionary rivals,

PRI candidate José Antonio Meade lost the 2018 Mexican presidential election.

decided that all questions about political succession would be resolved within one political party instead of by devastating civil wars. As a result, one party, the PRI, dominated for over seventy years. Leaders within the party chose candidates and everyone agreed to support them. Nomination by the party ensured election to office. The PRI controlled not only the presidency but also the governors, Congress, and the state assemblies.

However, the PRI's power ended, at least temporarily, in 2000 with the election of Vicente Fox. He was the leader of the National Action Party. Years of corruption, economic woes, and political turmoil eventually led to the defeat of the once-invincible PRI.

A Classic Example of a Multiparty System

In some multiparty systems, the small parties are extremely competitive and represent specific points of view. France's Fourth Republic (1946–58) provides a classic example. In many elections, no party came close to securing a majority in the National Assembly. Therefore, the government was composed of coalitions of many parties that lasted only as long as they avoided contentious and important issues. These coalitions were torn apart when divisive issues surfaced and the government could not respond to the problems affecting society.

This situation changed under Charles de Gaulle in 1958. The French ratified the Fifth Republic, which combined the presidential and parliamentary systems and gave the president greater powers and a specific term in office.

Influencing Factors

Ask the students to discuss the ways their homes or churches might influence their political attitudes. These attitudes might relate to political ideology as well as party preference.

specific interest (such as religious belief, political ideology, or economic class) or section of the country. Those who support the multiparty system maintain that the system allows broader, more diverse representation of the populace. However, this diversity proves to be the most significant weakness of the system because one party is often unable to win a majority of the votes. As mentioned earlier, this makes it necessary for two or more parties to combine their strength by forming a coalition to gain a majority of votes in the legislative body (and thus control the government). These coalitions can produce odd alliances that do not always hold together very well or very long. Italy is one of the most striking examples of this problem. Between 1946 and 2016, control of the government there changed 65 times. In Britain, which has fewer parties, control changed 25 times during the same period.

One-Party System

Most of today's dictatorships have a **one-party system** of government in which only one political party is allowed. An elite few who control the party rule the country using a centralized bureaucracy and an effective police force. As noted earlier in the chapter, this is true in Cuba and the People's Republic of China.

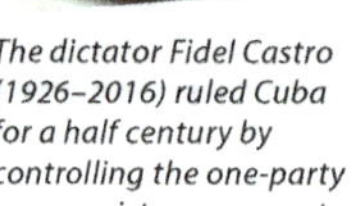

The dictator Fidel Castro (1926–2016) ruled Cuba for a half century by controlling the one-party communist government.

Section Review

1–2. What are two ways in which the American electoral system encourages a two-party system?

3–7. Identify five characteristics of the two-party system.

8–11. Identify four significant political results of Andrew Jackson's election to the presidency in 1828.

12–13. What was possibly the single most influential factor in building party organization after 1828? Why was it so influential?

14. What is a nominating primary?

★ Why does a two-party system provide more stability than a multiparty system?

★ How have primaries changed political parties?

Guiding Questions

1. What are the different types of third parties?
2. Why are third parties important?

III. Third Parties

A number of minor parties also compete in the political arena, although they rarely see their candidates elected. These third parties have faced numerous obstacles within a system dominated by two parties. With many state election laws making it difficult for third parties to even get their candidates placed on the ballot, most voters do not take these parties seriously enough to desert one of the established parties. Despite these barriers, third parties, even short-lived ones, have had an important impact on American politics, often by taking votes away from one candidate and thereby giving the election to his major opposing candidate.

Section Review Answers

1–2. single-member districts and election law (pp. 380–81)

3–7. diverse support through broad appeal, different viewpoints, party membership by personal identification, stability, and flexibility (pp. 381–84)

8–11. Organized competition broadened voter participation, the nomination process expanded through the use of the convention, the spoils system was introduced, and modern political campaigning came into existence. (p. 385)

12–13. Patronage, or the spoils system; the spoils system gave a person greater incentive to get involved in a party and to encourage voter turnout for his candidate. (p. 385)

14. Nominating primaries are state or local elections to select the party nominees for the general election. (p. 387)

★ In multiparty systems, many factions divide the electorate, making it difficult for one party to win a majority. Coalitions between these parties do not always hold together.

★ Primaries shift the power focus from the party organization to the campaign organization. Now candidates play a greater role in choosing the issues, raising money and mobilizing the voters than in the past.

Types of Third Parties

Single-Issue Parties

Single-issue parties are third parties that form because of one burning issue—often one that is so controversial that major parties avoid taking a strong position on it or prefer to ignore it. For instance, the antebellum Free-Soil Party opposed the expansion of slavery into the West. In more recent times, the Right-to-Life Party has opposed the legalization of abortion. Such single-issue parties gain a small but fiercely loyal political following. When an issue is resolved or public sentiment moves the major parties to adopt the cause, the corresponding third party declines and soon becomes a historical footnote.

Ideological Parties

Parties that rise from political and social ideas are called ideological parties. Some of these are the result of Marxist influence. For example, the Socialist Labor Party had a presidential candidate in every election from 1892 until 1976; however, the highest number of votes received was approximately 54,000. Between 1924 and 1984, the Communist Party had a nominee in almost every presidential contest; likewise, its most successful contender received only a small number of the millions of votes cast (approximately 103,000 in 1932). The Socialist Party USA was more successful when its candidate, Eugene V. Debs, received over 900,000 votes in 1912 and again in 1920.

The Libertarian Party, which tends to be conservative on economic matters and liberal on social issues, has fared better than many other ideological parties. Its most successful presidential nominee, Gary Johnson, received one percent of the vote in 2012 (approximately 1.3 million votes) and over three percent in 2016 (more than 4.4 million votes). The Green Party, which emphasizes environmental matters, had its greatest electoral success in the 2000 presidential election when its candidate received almost three percent of the national total (approximately 2.9 million votes). Its 2016 candidate received approximately 1.5 million votes, just over one percent of all ballots cast.

Depression Parties

Difficult economic times often produce political unrest and have led to the formation of minor parties. The saying "misery loves company" characterizes these depression parties, which usually gather strength in rural pockets of the South and Midwest. These grassroots parties of discontent, such as the Populist Party of the 1890s, gradually lose strength as the economy improves. However, depression parties have left their stamp on American politics and government. For example, the federal income tax (Amendment XVI), the direct election of senators (Amendment XVII), and federal regulation of banks and railroads all originated in depression-party platforms.

Splinter Parties

As their name implies, **splinter parties** are minor parties that split from major parties, generally over policy but sometimes over personality conflicts. Whereas depression parties have affected legislation, splinter parties' greatest impact has been on elections. No splinter party has won a national election, but a splinter party often determines who will win by splitting the parent party's strength and throwing the election to the opposition.

George Wallace (in 1968) and Ross Perot (in 1992 and 1996) were among the more successful third-party presidential candidates.

The Popular Vote

Eugene V. Debs ran for president on the Socialist Party ticket in every election except one between 1900 and 1920. In 1900 he received substantially less than 1 percent of the popular vote. He received 3 percent in 1904, 2.8 percent in 1908, 6 percent in 1912, and 3.4 percent in 1920. He never received a single electoral vote.

Ideology and Idolatry

Political ideologies become idolatrous when they claim that something good is actually evil. People think that society will be rescued by adhering to a particular pattern of belief according to their ideology. For example, in socialism, individual ownership and class hierarchy are seen as evil, and common ownership is seen as the ultimate good. In libertarianism, the expansion of government is seen as evil, and the autonomous individual is seen as the ultimate good.

Ideologies often err on three points: they identify something good in God's creation as the fundamental evil; they identify something other than God as the ultimate good; and they look to something other than Christ to bring about the ultimate "solution" (redemption).

Ideology and Idolatry Chart

Draw a table with three columns and as many rows as ideologies you choose to discuss. On each row, write the particular ideology being discussed. Label the columns "Evil," "Ultimate Good," and "Proposed Solution." Choose one or more controversial ideologies and instruct students to answer the following questions for each: What do people claim is evil based on this ideology? What do they find to be the ultimate good instead of looking to God? What is the means of redemption (provided solution) in this idolatrous ideology? Mention that choosing something besides God in the ultimate good column is basically idolatry, whatever form it takes.

Teacher Resources

A good resource on ideologies and idolatry is David T. Koyzis's *Political Visions and Illusions: A Survey and Christian Critique of Contemporary Ideologies*. For a similar approach, refer to Russell Kirk's *The Politics of Prudence*.

The Bull Moose Platform

In 1912 the platform of the Progressive, or Bull Moose, Party included women's suffrage; direct election of senators; initiative, recall, and referendum at the federal level; tariff reform; and legislation about child labor and the minimum wage.

Ralph Nader

Ralph Nader (1934–) is best known as a consumer advocate and third-party presidential candidate. He gained public attention in 1965 when he published *Unsafe at Any Speed*, a critique of American automobile safety (later criticized by the National Highway Traffic Safety Administration), which helped lead to the 1966 National Traffic and Motor Vehicle Safety Act.

With fellow activists (called Nader's Raiders), Nader became involved in nuclear, environmental, and international trade issues. In 1992, he ran as a presidential candidate in both the Democratic and Republican New Hampshire primaries and in the Massachusetts Democratic primary. He was a candidate for the Green Party in the 1996 and 2000 presidential races. In the extremely close election of 2000, he was accused of siphoning Democratic votes, which contributed to the Republican victory. In 2004, he was the presidential nominee of the Reform Party, and in 2008 he represented the Peace and Freedom Party.

Green Party presidential candidates have included Ralph Nader (in 1996 and 2000) and Jill Stein (in 2012 and 2016).

This was precisely what happened in the 1912 election. Theodore Roosevelt's Progressive ("Bull Moose") Party, which splintered from the Republican Party, divided that party's votes. The consequence of that action was that Democrat Woodrow Wilson won a landslide victory in the Electoral College. If the popular votes for the Republicans and Progressives had been combined, Wilson would have been defeated.

Most splinter parties are identified with a person and an election year. For example, in addition to Theodore Roosevelt's Bull Moose Party in 1912, there were Robert La Follette's Progressive Party in 1924; Strom Thurmond's States' Rights Democratic ("Dixiecrats") Party and Henry Wallace's Progressive Party in 1948; and George Wallace's American Independent Party in 1968. When an election is over and a prodigal candidate returns to his old party, his splinter party, having lost both its candidate and its cause, either disappears or takes a lower profile.

The Most Successful Third-Party Campaigns

Year	Candidate	Party	Popular votes	Electoral votes
1892	James B. Weaver	People's (Populist)	1,027,329	22
1912	Theodore Roosevelt	Progressive	4,119,207	88
1924	Robert M. La Follette	Progressive	4,822,856	13
1948	Strom Thurmond	States' Rights Democratic	1,169,021	39
1960	Harry Byrd	Democratic	116,248	15
1968	George Wallace	American Independent	9,906,473	46
1992	Ross Perot	Independent	19,743,821	0
1996	Ross Perot	Reform	8,085,294	0

Importance

As noted, although most Americans have not supported third-party candidates, third parties have influenced the American political system. Even a relatively small one can play an important role in a close contest. In 2000, Green Party candidate Ralph Nader received almost 3 percent of the popular vote and

Some Third Party Candidates in the 2016 Election

Party	Candidates (president and vice president)
Constitution Party	Darrell Castle and Scott Bradley
Green Party	Jill Stein and Ajamu Baraka
Libertarian Party	Gary Johnson and William Weld
Prohibition Party	James Hedges and Bill Bayes
Reform Party	Rocky De La Fuente and Michael Steinberg
Socialist Party USA	Emidio Soltysik and Angela Walker
Socialist Workers Party	Alyson Kennedy and Osborne Hart

Is a Vote for a Third Party Wasted?

Debate whether a vote cast for a third-party candidate is a wasted vote. Does voting for a third-party candidate merely give the advantage to a major party candidate? Would it be better to vote for the lesser of two evils rather than "waste" a vote on a third-party candidate who cannot win? Should voters support third-party candidates in order to send a message to the major political parties (that those parties should nominate better candidates or should change positions on certain issues)?

Guide the students to answer these questions by distinguishing between compromise and prudence. A prudent voter will not vote for a candidate who will hinder the voter's political goals from being realized. Many might vote for a candidate who will further certain goals even if that candidate does not support all the beliefs of each voter. Prudent voters also weigh the issues that they value. They consider which issues are grounded in biblical mandates, which are tied to political philosophy, and which are largely based on preference.

You may wish to revisit the three margin notes on page 239 ("Christians Voting for Non-Christians," "Difficult Choices," and "Voting for the Lesser of Two Evils") as well as the box in the Student Edition entitled, "For Whom Do We Vote?" These will help you prepare for the assigned debate.

Third-Party Positions

Ask volunteers to research the third parties listed on this page and report to the class on their positions.

The Perfect Party

Divide the class into two to four groups (depending on class size). Ask each group to determine the "perfect" political party position on such issues as immigration, management of natural resources, trade, abortion, euthanasia, and LGBTQ+ matters. Instruct each group to choose a party name, symbol, and chairman. Ask each party chairman to introduce the party and its position on issues.

probably took enough votes away from Democrat Al Gore to allow a victory by Republican George W. Bush.

In addition, third parties call attention to issues that are important to many voters or to the hardships faced by Americans. They often represent citizens who feel that they are ignored by the major parties.

Third parties continue to be a visible, important part of the American political scene. Notable third parties today include the Constitution Party, Green Party, Libertarian Party, Prohibition Party, Reform Party, Socialist Party USA, and Socialist Workers Party.

Gary Johnson was the Libertarian Party's presidential candidate in 2012 and 2016.

Section Review

1–4. Identify four types of third parties.

5–6. What are two reasons third parties that develop around a single issue decline or disappear?

★ How important are third parties? Evaluate their influence on the American political system.

IV. Party Organization

Party organization more closely resembles a scattered army than a streamlined corporation. Sometimes, party organization is diagrammed as a pyramid of national control over state levels with power flowing to a base of county and precinct organizations. That diagram does not portray reality. The US party system is actually highly decentralized. Some have suggested a diagram should show power flowing from the grassroots levels upward to the national party.

In fact, the amounts of organizational, financial, and political strength among a party's many components widely differ. There is also a remarkable degree of independence in the relationship between party levels. Each division of party organization, from the national level to the precinct, corresponds to an electoral division—a fact that underscores the purpose of each division.

> **Guiding Questions**
>
> 1. Why are US political parties fragmented?
>
> 2. How are the two major national parties organized?
>
> 3. How are the political parties organized at state and local levels?

Reasons for Political Parties' Fragmented Nature
Membership Strength

A party's effectiveness at any level often depends on the strength and motivation of its membership. A party can set a date for precinct members to meet, but no law requires attendance at such a meeting. Although every citizen in this country lives in a precinct, only a small fraction of people ever attend precinct meetings. A party's success at even the most basic organizational level depends largely on individual initiative; this should challenge and encourage Christians to

Should a Christian Be a Libertarian?

The principles of libertarianism often conflict with a biblical worldview. Many libertarians object to "legislating morality"; they say that laws cannot force people to be good. Yet the Bible teaches that government has a duty to punish the evil and praise the good. Laws cannot punish every evil; even the Mosaic law made concessions for the hardness of people's hearts. But the law can have a powerful influence. For example, when the law prohibits discrimination based on race, it plays a positive role by signaling to society that racism is unacceptable. And if the law permits indecency in films or allows people to use recreational drugs, society becomes more tolerant of indecency and drug use.

Libertarians seek to reduce government's role in restraining individuals. Libertarians also tend to have a much more positive view of human nature than do many Christians or conservatives. They fail to recognize that public virtue is a necessary condition for limited government. People are not just individuals but are a part of communities. Finally, libertarians have a skeptical view of government's role. Christians can agree with libertarians' desire to limit the reach and power of government while keeping in mind that government is a God-given institution established for the good of nations.

Section IV Objectives

1. Explain the fragmented nature of political parties.

2. Outline the components of the two major parties at the national level.

3. Describe the organization of political parties at the state and local levels.

Activity 4: Third Parties in American Politics

Use this activity to familiarize the students with some of the major third parties in American history.

Section Review Answers

1–4. Some parties form around a single issue of great importance to their members. Others are based on commitment to a particular political or social idea. Still others form as a result of depressed economic conditions. Some split from major parties. (p. 389)

5–6. because the issue is resolved or because the major political parties adopt the issue as a result of public sentiment (p. 389)

★ Although most Americans have not supported third-party candidates, third parties influence the American political system. Even a relatively small one can play an important role in a close contest. For example, in 2000, Green Party candidate Ralph Nader received almost 3 percent of the popular vote and probably took enough votes away from Democrat Al Gore to allow a victory by Republican George W. Bush. In addition, third parties call attention to issues important to many voters or to the hardships faced by Americans. They often represent citizens who feel that they are ignored by the major parties.

European Parties

Political parties in Europe select candidates in a different manner than US political parties. European party leaders select their parties' candidates, and each party typically runs its candidate's campaign. Once elected, each official is expected to vote for his or her party's position on the issues. The voters make their choices based on party label.

Longest Convention

At the 1924 Democratic National Convention, it took 103 ballots to select John W. Davis as the party's candidate.

Memorable Convention

At the 1932 Democratic National Convention, Franklin D. Roosevelt flew to Chicago to personally deliver an acceptance speech. This action was unprecedented but has since become a tradition at the political conventions of both parties.

A precinct meeting in Seattle, Washington

get involved. Although humans' fundamental need of redemption demands a divine rather than a political solution, believers can be "salt" in society in many ways, including through involvement in community politics.

Any registered voter can attend precinct meetings, at which precinct officers are elected. And a percentage of each precinct's members can attend a party's county convention. At the convention, the county party chairman and committeemen are elected, as well as delegates and alternates to the state convention. At the state party convention, a party's state chairman and vice-chairmen are elected. During presidential election years, committeemen to the national party committee and delegates to the national convention are also elected at the state convention. Thus, precinct participation directly affects the election of national committees.

Federalism

The basic goal of the two major parties is to gain control of government by winning elective office. In the United States, a half-million elected positions exist at local, state, and national levels. This dispersal of power encourages fragmentation by making parties operate at many different levels at the same time.

Nominating Process

Since candidates are nominated within a party, the selection process lends itself to potential infighting. Although all party members hold allegiance to the same national party, they often become divided over a nomination. These intraparty conflicts usually result from two major factors. The first factor is the power of the position. A candidate who wins a nomination wins leadership in the party and gains access to its resources. The second factor is internal party variety. America's two-party system brings a variety of factions and interests, along with their leaders and potential candidates, together under a single party label. Sometimes unity is difficult to achieve.

These two factors can result in stimulating competition, but at other times they can lead to bitter rivalry. Party nominees must often act quickly to heal party wounds and forge a united front for the general campaign. Candidates who fail to reach out to their in-party rivals might regret it on Election Day.

National Organization

A national party has four components. The national chairman and the national committee serve largely in an administrative capacity, whereas the national convention and the congressional campaign committees serve an electoral function.

National Convention

The national convention may be the most familiar aspect of party organization for most Americans. Conventions, which meet in the summer of every presidential election year, usually attract heavy media coverage. The primary purposes of the convention are to nominate a party's candidates for president and vice president and to approve a party's platform position on various issues. The

Precinct Officer

Invite a precinct officer to tell the class about the activities that occur at a precinct meeting.

Meeting Summary

If it is a year when precinct reorganization is taking place, recruit some students to attend a precinct meeting and write a brief summary of the experience.

County or State Delegate or Alternate

Invite someone who has been a delegate or alternate to a county or state party convention to share that experience with the class.

hundreds of delegates who attend a national convention represent the state level. (Chapter 10 presents a closer look at national conventions and national delegates.) In recent years, presidential primaries have tended to determine a party's nominee well before the convention, leaving only the question of whom the nominee will select as the vice-presidential running mate.

National Committee and National Chairman

The national committee of each major party is responsible for the party's administration between national conventions. More importantly, it helps raise money and supply technical assistance in congressional races and important state races. The national committees of the two parties differ in both composition and approach. Both committees are composed of a committeeman and a committeewoman elected by state conventions from each state and a number of territories. In addition, the **Republican National Committee (RNC)** includes state party chairmen. However, the **Democratic National Committee (DNC)** has a much larger membership. It includes all state chairmen and vice-chairmen as well as over two hundred members elected by Democrats in all fifty states and the territories. The RNC generally concentrates on strengthening national ties to state organizations and thereby building a more unified party. The DNC traditionally places more emphasis on presidential politics and has been less intent at building strong state organizations.

A meeting of DNC officials in Washington, DC

In theory a national chairman is the head of his party, a leader elected by members of the national committee. In reality the party's presidential nominee handpicks a chairman after the national convention, and the national committee rubber-stamps his choice. Traditionally, the national chairman has more prestige than power. The chairman of the party in power answers to the incumbent president; whereas, the chairman of the party out of power has the rather thankless task of presiding over an array of factions and candidates jockeying for power and the next nomination.

Congressional Campaign Committees

Another component of party organization at the national level is the congressional campaign committees. The Democrats and the Republicans have committees for both the House and the Senate. These organizations operate independently of their party's national committee, providing money and expertise to help reelect incumbents to Congress and to assist promising challengers in their bids for national office.

State and Local Levels

State

State party organization centers on a state committee headed by a state chairman in an arrangement similar to that at the national level. The chairman and central committee work to further their party's interests in the state by building

---

Party Official

Hold a classroom forum by inviting a party official (such as a city or county chairman) to discuss the importance of campaign volunteers and grassroots organizing.

Campaign Volunteers

Discuss the importance of volunteers to political campaigns. High-school students can make significant contributions to a campaign in many ways (e.g., by placing campaign signs in strategic locations, distributing campaign literature, stuffing envelopes, and polling voters). Emphasize that the nature of our party system, particularly on the local and state levels, provides opportunities for Christians who are motivated, organized, and qualified to assume leadership and be "salt" in our political system.

1. Analyze the changes that have contributed to the decline of American political parties.
2. Describe the role of independent voters in the political process.
3. Explain the impact of media on political campaigns.
4. Assess the impact of party decline on American politics.

Party Cohesion

Parties provide cohesion by serving as vehicles for cooperation both within Congress and between Congress and the president. This certainly does not mean that parties always ensure that matters run smoothly, nor would such efficiency necessarily be good for the country. Simply following the party line can smother genuine debate. However, parties do provide a peaceful framework that encourages factions and regions to cooperate rather than divide further.

an effective organization, fostering party unity, recruiting candidates, and soliciting campaign funds. State committee members are generally elected from the county level in a convention or a primary. The influence of these state committees varies considerably since it is tied to the political competitiveness within a state. For example, if the Democratic Party controlled virtually every state office from the governor to the local sheriffs, this unbalanced situation would probably be reflected in the two major parties' state machinery. In this case, the Republican state organization would probably not be well organized or well funded, nor would it command as much media attention as the Democratic organization.

Local

As discussed in Chapter 7, local party divisions across the country vary considerably in structure and strength. The structure usually follows an electoral map of a state. States are divided into congressional districts. Many municipalities or counties also have areas known as **wards**, or districts, for the purpose of city council and county commission elections. These wards are then subdivided into precincts. Precincts are the smallest units of election districts and party administration. These grass-roots organizations provide the widest opportunity for political involvement because they administer essential party efforts, such as voter registration, candidate recruitment, campaign support, and poll management.

Section Review

1–2. Identify the two major purposes of a party's national convention.

3–4. What group manages national-party activities during the time between national conventions? Who is the party leader, at least in theory, during that time?

★ What are three major factors that contribute to the fragmented nature of political parties?

Guiding Questions

1. What changes have contributed to the decline of American political parties?
2. What is the role of independent voters in the political process?
3. How has the media impacted political campaigns?
4. How has party decline affected American politics?

V. Party Decline

Like a mirror, political parties in America reflect the changes that have occurred in American society over the past two centuries. A number of trends have created shifts in the purpose and effectiveness of party organizations. Recent trends have weakened the traditional party, making it more a vehicle for nominating than a means of governing.

In the past, strong parties served as a cohesive force in government. For example, they provided control over factions, coordination in policymaking, and cooperation between the legislative and executive branches. They helped build consensus among members and around important ideas and policies. They helped identify and promote qualified candidates. Some argue that weaker parties have increased the number of celebrity candidates and have led to greater polarization of the public.

Critics of strong political parties hail the recent weakening of parties as an improvement in the political process. They cite the tight control that past party bosses often held and note their negative impact on democratic government. They argue that strong parties often ignored issues important to the average voter.

Executive Committee Meeting

Select a student or a group of students to attend a political party's executive committee meeting. (A precinct committeeman or president has information concerning when and where these meetings are held.) Instruct the student(s) to take notes on what happens at the meeting and summarize the information for the class.

Section Review Answers

1–2. to nominate the party's candidates for president and vice president and to approve the party platform (p. 392)

3–4. the national committee; the national chairman (p. 393)

★ membership strength, federalism, and the nominating process

Changes

Primary Laws

In the early twentieth century, reformers introduced the primary to open the nominating process to broader participation. By placing the state parties under some degree of state regulation, primary laws reduced the power of party regulars and insiders to control delegates and nominations. It is important to remember that there are two types of primaries—the nominating primary (in which voters select the candidates who will run on each party's ticket in the general election) and the **presidential primary** (in which voters elect the state party's delegates, who will go to their political party's national convention to select the party's presidential candidate).

Presidential primaries were slow to gain momentum. Most delegates to the parties' national conventions continued to be chosen in party-run caucuses, meaning that party bosses continued to dominate nominee selections. But this undemocratic vestige came under severe attack in 1968, particularly in the Democratic party, and was swept away, with mixed results.

Social Upheaval

The forces of social upheaval that characterized the 1960s seemed to converge on the streets of Chicago outside the 1968 Democratic National Convention. Members of the radical Students for a Democratic Society (SDS) and the Youth International Party ("Yippies"), along with thousands of other antiwar demonstrators and rights activists, clashed with police and National Guardsmen before a nationwide television audience.

Against this backdrop, the Democrats nominated Vice President Hubert Humphrey. Humphrey had entered the presidential race late and thus had not been involved in any presidential primaries; however, he was the choice of party leaders, such as President Lyndon Johnson and Chicago mayor Richard Daley. The violence and charges of corruption surrounding Humphrey's nomination helped lead to widespread campaign reform.

National guardsmen and antiwar protesters outside the 1968 Democratic National Convention in Chicago

Primary and Delegate Increase

Two important party changes in the post-1968 era were an increased number of presidential primaries and an increased number of national delegates determined in those primaries. Today more than 70 percent of the national delegates are chosen through the primary system. These democratizing changes have brought significant results by opening the nominating process to greater participation. Also, the reform movement has resulted in greater party involvement by **interest groups** (groups formed around a particular issue or agenda). The system is more accessible for such groups attempting to influence a nomination, and candidates for the nomination can solicit various special interests to piece

US Senator Rand Paul (R-KY) addressing one of the nation's most influential interest groups, the National Rifle Association (NRA)

Is More Representation Better?

In *Federalist* No. 58, James Madison discussed representation and noted a disadvantage of party democratization.

> The people can never err more than in supposing that by multiplying their representatives beyond a certain limit, they strengthen the barrier against the government of a few. Experience will forever admonish them that, on the contrary, *after securing a sufficient number for the purposes of safety, of local information, and of diffusive sympathy with the whole society,* they will counteract their own views by every addition to their representatives.

Daniel Moynihan, who served as a Democratic US senator from New York from 1977–2001, noted, "Only the innocent assume that the more persons who are involved in a process, the more democratic it is. Power gravitates to the special and organized, as against the general interest."

Theologian D. A. Carson has argued that democracy is not a guarantee of freedom, truth, or morality. He states,

> Democracy remains the best way of making government more or less accountable. Nevertheless, even when a democratically elected government *is* acting accountably in line with the desires of the majority of voters, it does not follow that those desires will be for good or wise things. . . .

> . . . Doubtless democracy, especially classic liberal democracy, is the best form of government for establishing at least minimal standards of accountability to the governed . . . but it does not follow that it is always the best regime—and it has the potential for becoming as tyrannous as any other regime.

together an acceptable coalition of support. Of course, these groups expect to receive political dividends for their support if their candidate wins the office.

Campaign Expense

Another result of the changes in the nomination process is that campaigns are now much longer and much more expensive than those in the past. Because of the transcontinental proportions and an often crowded field of contenders, many candidates start today's presidential primary marathon by organizing and actively campaigning two years or more before an election.

The race officially begins in January and February of the presidential election year. As mentioned in Chapter 10, Iowa is the first state to hold caucuses and New Hampshire, shortly thereafter, is the first state to hold a presidential primary. Candidates must also amass considerable funds if they hope to sustain a strong campaign, and the money comes mostly from private, not party, sources. For the 2016 presidential election, the candidates spent approximately $2.5 billion. That year, congressional candidates spent an additional $4.3 billion, and billions more were spent on state and local races. That amount will likely continue to quickly rise; for example, in 2018 congressional candidates spent more than $5 billion campaigning for office.

Party Democratization

In general, party democratization resulting from primary and delegate-selection reforms has broken the parties down into component special interests and competing campaign organizations; this contributes to a political process that is, ironically, less democratic. In the last half of the nineteenth century, approximately 75–80 percent of eligible voters participated in presidential elections. No presidential election in the twentieth or twenty-first century has seen that level of participation.

Independent Voters
Yellow-Dog Demise

"I'd rather vote for a yellow dog than a Republican," declared die-hard partisans of the Democrats' Solid South in the 1940s and 1950s. "Yellow-dog voting" refers to the practice of casting a vote solely based on party label. It frees the voter from thinking about issues or candidates' qualifications or character. Such voting contributes to incumbents' reelection and influence, regardless of the quality of their service.

Yellow Dog Democrats, as such voters came to be known, and their counterparts in the Republican Party have declined in number; in fact, the percentage of voters who say that a candidate's party is the first consideration in how they vote has significantly decreased over the past century. This reflects the dramatic rise in the number of **independent voters** (voters who have no declared party affiliation). In a Gallup poll, one-third of the voters in the 1988 presidential election identified themselves as independents. That percentage has generally been trending upward. Other Gallup polls indicate that independents comprised 43 percent of voters in 2014 and 42 percent in late 2017.

Party Switching

The rise in the number of independent voters has not only weakened party control but also destabilized election trends and their aftermath. For one, the number of independent voters has contributed to an increase in landslide victories (that is, where the winner receives at least 55 percent of the vote) in presiden-

More Democracy?

Discuss the idea that government is improved by having more representatives involved in governing. Present the quotes, given in the margin note above, from James Madison and Daniel Moynihan. What warnings do these men cite? Are they justified in their concerns?

Then discuss the quote, also in the margin note, by theologian D. A. Carson. What biblical worldview ideas would support the matters he raises?

Independent Voters

Do independent voters make a difference in presidential elections? Select a group of students to research information about the real impact of independent voters in those elections and discuss the findings with the class.

tial contests. Between 1828 and 1900 three landslide victories occurred; however, party-switching independents contributed to eleven such lopsided victories during the twentieth century.

A number of Republicans supported Lyndon Johnson in 1964, and this significantly increased his electoral tally over Barry Goldwater. In 1980 and 1984, a quarter of Democrats, the so-called Reagan Democrats, defected from their party to support the top of the Republican ticket. In 1988 George H. W. Bush drew heavily from this same group to defeat Democrat Michael Dukakis. While there was no landslide in the 2000 presidential contest, the same block of independent voters created uncertainty. Republican George W. Bush and Democrat Al Gore were extremely close in their vote totals. As Election Day neared, America was kept guessing as to how the independents would vote.

In addition, **ticket splitting** (voting for candidates of different parties for different offices), has become increasingly prevalent with the rise of independents. On many occasions voters have shown a strong ticket-splitting tendency by sending a Republican to the White House and Democrats to Congress. Ticket splitting is even more predominant in state and local elections; this sometimes hampers governing because of the awkward, highly charged, partisan atmosphere that arises when the governor and lieutenant governor, for example, are from opposite parties.

Media Impact

Television

Television has had a powerful influence on the effectiveness of our party system. Candidates with enough money can largely bypass the party apparatus and reach voters directly via media. It is no longer necessary for a candidate to devote years of loyal service to a party to win its nomination. Because television reaches millions of homes instantaneously, the pursuit of office has become more of a personal matter than a party one. News organizations also affect campaign issues by choosing the issues that will be addressed during their public broadcasts and by deciding how much coverage they will give to each candidate's campaign. Columnist George Will observed:

> Campaigning today is one of the purest forms of individual entrepreneurship available in an age of bureaucratized enterprises. A candidate enlists a small staff, raises capital, invests it in marketing his product (himself) and the market decides.

Internet and Social Media

The internet has brought great change to campaigning methods. Especially with various social media (e.g., Twitter, Facebook, Instagram), it offers quick ways for candidates and voters to send and receive information. The internet also allows people to conveniently volunteer their time and energy and even donate money. In 2003, Howard Dean, who was seeking the 2004 Democratic nomination for the presidency, used the internet to raise $11 million in just six months. In 2007 Republican Ron Paul raised $2 million online in a single day for his 2008 presidential bid. Yet, the internet as a fundraising tool was perfected by the Obama campaign—raising $500 million in 2008 and $690 million in 2012, mostly from small donors.

The next chapter discusses other changes in political campaigning caused by past and present technology. Today, a caravan of photographers, aides, and journalists with microphones, smart phones, and other electronic devices constantly

Media Image

Ray Price, a former speechwriter and media advisor for President Nixon, provided his view of politics in the age of television.

> We have to be very clear on this point: that the response is to the image, not to the man, since 99 percent of the voters have no contact with the man. It's not what's there that counts, it's what's projected—and, carrying it one step further, it's not what he projects but rather what the voter receives. It's not the man we have to change, but rather the received impression. And this impression often depends more on the medium and its use than it does on the candidate himself.

Television's Impact

Locate a video of a recent presidential debate or one of the Nixon-Kennedy debates, and play it for the class. After watching all or part of the debate together, discuss the students' impressions of the candidates and the candidates' ability to communicate their positions on key issues.

Fake News?

In recent years the term *fake news* has been used a great deal. Guide a discussion of this phrase. What does it mean? Do you think it is accurately or inaccurately used? How do you think its use has affected American opinion of the press? What are ways in which the news media could improve how it is perceived by the public?

Activity 5: Chapter Review

Use this activity to help the students prepare for the chapter test.

follows candidates on the campaign trail. The sophistication of a campaign staff might be better judged by whether it includes a makeup artist.

Despite the forces that have weakened the party system, political parties show no signs of becoming extinct. The majority of the electorate continue to identify with one of the major parties, and even many independents lean toward one. Parties, as vehicles of self-government, will probably continue to adapt to social and technological changes and continue to offer opportunities for political participation and leadership.

Section Review

1–2. Which two important party changes occurred, in part, because of the 1968 election?

3. What is yellow-dog voting?

4–6. Many refer to yellow-dog voting as intellectually lazy because voters do not have to think about three things. Identify those.

★ Do you think the weakening of political parties in America has been a positive or negative development? Explain your answer.

★ How have television, the internet, and social media influenced election campaigns?

Section Review Answers

1–2. an increase in the number of presidential primaries and an increased number of national delegates drawn from those primaries (p. 395)

3. the practice of casting a vote solely based on party label (p. 396)

4–6. issues, candidates' qualifications, or their character (p. 396)

★ Some might describe the weakening as good, noting that President Washington warned of the dangers of political parties. They might cite the tight control past party bosses often held, negatively impacting democratic government, or might argue that strong parties often ignored issues important to the average voter. Other students may disagree and note that in the past strong parties served as a cohesive force by controlling factions, coordinating policymaking, and promoting cooperation between the legislative and executive branches, as well as helping to identify and promote qualified candidates. Some may argue that weaker parties have increased the number of celebrity candidates and have led to greater polarization of the public.

★ Answers will vary. Television, the internet, and social media have negatively influenced election campaigning by magnifying candidates' physical looks and personality qualities, often at the sacrifice of debates about issues and ideological views. Used properly, however, these media can make news almost instantaneously available to the public, enable rapid responses to candidates' accusations or promises, and inform voters about the differences between candidates. These media also make it easy to volunteer for or donate to a campaign.

CHAPTER REVIEW ANSWERS

Making Connections

1. Parties try to gain power by winning elections. Other groups promote certain issues, or causes, and hope to influence the major parties. (p. 377)

Making Connections

1. Describe what sets political parties apart from other groups that are organized to promote political causes.

2. How does the existence of political parties affect the workings of Congress?

3–4. What is a party platform? Why is it significant?

5. Discuss the importance of the 1840 presidential election.

6–7. Distinguish between a nominating primary and a presidential primary.

8. How have the internet and social media impacted campaign fundraising?

Developing Civics Skills

1. How loyal should a Christian be to a political party? Describe a circumstance when a person might vote a split ticket.

2. Compare the most recent Republican and Democratic party platforms. Identify issues that align with a Christian worldview, issues that do not align with a Christian worldview, and issues with goals that Christians may agree with but may disagree on how to achieve.

Thinking Critically

1. President Washington opposed the development of political parties. In your opinion, was this justified? If so, what actions might have prevented partisanship? If not, why not?

2. Should Christians be active in politics? Defend your answer.

Living as a Christian Citizen

1. Write a brief statement of personal political philosophy. Include biblical justification for your position.

2. If you were given the opportunity to sit on a party's platform committee, what issues would you consider important to address? How does the Christian faith relate to the issues you chose?

People, Places, and Things to Remember

political parties
major parties
minor parties
third parties
nominate
partisanship
two-party system
Solid South
single-member districts
bipartisan
party platform
liberal
conservative
multiparty system
coalition
convention
delegates
caucus
patronage
spoils system
political campaign
primary
one-party system
splinter parties
Republican National Committee (RNC)
Democratic National Committee (DNC)
wards
precincts
presidential primary
interest groups
independent voters
ticket splitting

THE PARTY SYSTEM • 399

2. Congress is structured along party lines; the majority party controls committees and agendas. The president can use party ties to help push legislation through Congress. (p. 378)

3–4. A formal statement of a party's position on current issues, written at each party's national convention every four years. The platform is significant because it tells voters what the party believes about major issues. (p. 382)

5. In this election, the Whigs ran a masterful campaign. Using slogans, campaign buttons, placards, large rallies, a campaign newspaper, and other tactics, they promoted their candidate on an unprecedented scale. (p. 385–86)

6–7. In a nominating primary, voters select a candidate to represent their party in the general election. In a presidential primary, voters elect delegates to the national convention that will vote for a particular candidate to represent the party in the general election. (p. 395)

8. They have made raising large amounts of money quickly, from many individuals, significantly easier. (p. 397)

Developing Civics Skills

1. Party loyalty is important but not as important as loyalty to Christ. Candidates and issues change, but a believer's commitment to the Word of God must be absolute. For example, one might vote a split ticket if some of the party's candidates take immoral stands.

2. Students should particularly note views on issues that the Bible speaks to directly, such as marriage, abortion, religious liberty, and religious groups' participation in the public square. Regarding issues with agreement on goals but disagreement on how to achieve them, Christians must use scripturally guided wisdom to determine the most effective course of action.

Thinking Critically

1. The only way to prevent the development of political parties is to outlaw organized opposition to government leaders and policies. This prohibition would strike a blow against freedoms of speech, assembly, petition, and association, destroying the democratic nature of the government.

2. Christians have as much stake in retaining freedoms as other citizens do, so they should work to preserve them. Christians must pray that their leaders will allow them to live their Christian faith (1 Tim. 2:1–2). But it is wrong for people to pray for God to do something and then refuse to do their part (e.g., to pray for a good grade but fail to study). Thus, it is wrong for Christians to pray for godly leaders and then ignore God-given opportunities to select their leaders. God calls Christians to be involved in political matters to varying degrees.

Living as a Christian Citizen

1. Example: Because the Fall affected every society, Christians see many societal issues that need reform. All Christians should be salt and light in their communities (Matt. 5), and some may find political opportunities in bringing about necessary reform. Knowing the impossibility of human-organized utopias, reform efforts would avoid revolutions, which usually substitute one broken system for another—damaging much in the process. Instead, Christians should work to preserve what God calls good in society and to repair what can be mended. Accurate knowledge of human nature avoids both total cynicism and pure optimism in political philosophy. The Bible offers true guidance on how people, though all are fallen, can live together peacefully.

2. Students should make valid connections between Scripture and issues they would include in the party platform.

CAMPAIGNS AND ELECTIONS

17

Let each citizen remember, at the moment he is offering his vote, that … he is executing one of the most solemn trusts in human society, for which he is accountable to God and his country.

—Samuel Adams

Senator Bernie Sanders of Vermont addressing supporters at one of his presidential campaign rallies

I.   Candidate Nomination

II. The Campaign Trail

III. Elections and Voting

IV. Campaign Finance

BIG IDEAS

1. How are candidates nominated?
2. How does the campaigning process work?
3. What happens during the election process and on Election Day?
4. How are campaigns financed?

SUGGESTED MATERIALS

Section I
• Activity 1 from Chapter 17 of the *Student Activities*

Section II
• Activity 2 from Chapter 17 of the *Student Activities*

Section III
• Activities 3–4 from Chapter 17 of the *Student Activities*

Section IV
• Activity 5 from Chapter 17 of the *Student Activities*

Teacher Resources
Visit TeacherToolsOnline.com for resources to enhance the lessons.

Politics in a free society involves a rich array of competing ideas, choices, personalities, and power. Add to this mix color, comedy, cameras, hand-shaking, speechmaking, baby-kissing, and excessive quantities of barbecue, and you have the American political campaign. John Quincy Adams said, "A stranger would think that the people of the United States have no other occupation than electioneering."

This chapter examines this important American spectacle primarily from congressional, state, and local perspectives. It will review and provide additional details about some items discussed in Chapters 7, 10 (which discusses presidential campaigns and elections), and 16.

I. Candidate Nomination

Preliminaries

A major function of US political parties is candidate **nomination** (selecting a candidate to represent the party for public office), a key step in the election process. However, before securing the nomination, each candidate faces such preliminary tasks as meeting requirements for holding public office, assembling a staff, establishing a campaign strategy, and campaigning for the party's nomination.

Office Requirements

Each public office has specific requirements that a person must fulfill to become a viable candidate. The US House and Senate office requirements are established in Article I, Sections 2 and 3, of the Constitution. Senate candidates must be at least thirty years old and have been US citizens for nine years. House candidates must be at least twenty-five years of age and have been US citizens for seven years. Both senators and representatives must live in the state in which they are elected.

Requirements for state-level elected positions vary. In Idaho, for example, governor and lieutenant-governor candidates must be at least thirty years of age, be US citizens, and have been residents of Idaho for two years before the election. Pennsylvania has the same age requirements as Idaho for governor and lieutenant-governor candidates, but candidates must be state residents for seven years before the election. Vermont has no age requirement for governor. In 2018, a fourteen-year-old received almost five thousand votes (approximately seven percent of the votes cast in the Democratic primary) when he sought the state's highest office.

Local office requirements also vary within each state, depending on the county. Requirements usually include completing and submitting appropriate forms, paying filing fees, and establishing a campaign contribution account and headquarters. It is important for potential candidates to understand the requirements and commitments before announcing their candidacies.

Senator Kamala Harris (D-CA) announced in January 2019 that she was seeking the Democratic nomination for president in 2020.

Core Campaign Staff

In small campaigns, core personnel might have multiple responsibilities, but the following roles must be filled:

Campaign manager: Manages the campaign operation, develops a campaign plan, and oversees staff and volunteers. Has a knowledge of the community and a solid relationship with key community political leaders.

Finance coordinator: Manages campaign finances, develops a fundraising strategy, oversees fundraising events, and knows campaign-finance rules and regulations.

Treasurer: Oversees campaign expenses and files financial reports.

Press secretary: Develops a press plan, is the point of contact for reporters, and communicates the campaign message through free media.

Field coordinator: Coordinates voter-contact efforts, including meetings and door-to-door and phone contact.

Volunteer coordinator: Motivates the volunteers and keeps them busy and properly directed.

Staff, Strategy, and Primary Campaigning

Recruiting campaign and staff workers is a temporary but important first step toward being elected to office. The **incumbent** (the current officeholder) often enlists some staff from his previous campaign(s), while challengers recruit their own workers.

Campaign workers are typically divided into three groups. One group consists of unpaid, trusted senior advisors. These individuals usually have no personal political ambition but provide counsel for a candidate regarding important questions. A second group consists of citizen volunteers who perform the routine jobs of the campaign. These volunteers might be seeking excitement, hoping for a future government appointment, supporting certain issues, or merely exercising civic responsibility. Consultants compose the third group of campaign workers. They are paid professionals who help a candidate become more informed about subjects that are important to interest groups and constituents. They also advise candidates about issues on which the media focus. Christians who participate in any of these groups can exert a godly influence by helping candidates to support biblical solutions to America's problems.

With core staff and advisors, a candidate develops a strategy for the campaign. Strategic choices must be made and the primary must be won. These choices include developing a campaign theme, deciding whether to focus on a positive or negative approach in advertising, securing a finance chairman who will raise funds and properly use them, and gaining the support of local party members. Once the primary is won, the campaign expands, campaign strategy is refined, and more intense campaigning begins. Incumbent candidates and candidates who are not challenged for their party's nomination generally have more campaign funds available; this gives them an advantage over candidates from opposing parties who faced a primary challenger. Candidates who face competitors for their party's nomination usually must raise more money to mount an effective campaign.

Mitt Romney (far left) on his campaign bus when he was the Republican presidential nominee in 2012. Though he lost that bid, he was elected to represent Utah in the US Senate in 2018.

Political Participation

Remind the students that political participation can build relationships that provide opportunities for sharing the gospel. It may also open the door to greater political involvement in the future, in which a student could influence a party's policy positions.

Activity 1: Becoming a Candidate

This activity provides students valuable insight into tasks that must be completed and issues that should be considered before launching a political campaign.

Methods of Nomination

Today, the United States has four commonly used methods of nomination: petition, caucus, convention, and direct primary.

Petition

The petition method is widely used at the local level for municipal offices in small communities and nonpartisan (i.e., separate from any party label) positions, such as school boards. A **petition** is a formal document signed by a required number of qualified voters on behalf of a candidate in the election district. State law usually requires a petition to nominate independent and minor-party candidates. Specifics of this process vary by city and state.

Caucus

Originally, caucuses were composed of a few like-minded, influential individuals who selected the candidates they would support in the upcoming elections. As political parties developed, the caucus was officially implemented, and membership expanded. But with westward expansion and the spread of democracy, Americans increasingly disliked the closed, unrepresentative nature of the caucus. This dislike escalated with the four-candidate 1824 presidential race noted in the last chapter. That election became a race of competing personalities and regions of the country, with no candidate receiving a majority of the popular or electoral votes. The contest was then thrown into the House of Representatives because of the Twelfth Amendment. This event helped lead to the death of the caucus method of choosing presidential party candidates. Today in presidential election years, one or both of the major parties in some states continue to use the caucus method to select delegates to the party's national convention. The caucus is also used, mainly in New England, for selection of candidates for local positions.

Convention

The convention, a more representative method, replaced the caucus during the Jacksonian era. At the local level, party members met to select candidates for local offices and delegates to represent each precinct at the county convention. There, county-office candidates and delegates to the state convention were selected. At the state convention, delegates chose party nominees for governor and other statewide offices. In presidential election years, they chose national convention delegates who then participated in the selection of the presidential and vice-presidential nominees for each party. Unfortunately, party bosses began to control many state and national conventions until the 1870s, when many people sought to change the corrupted system. Today, many third parties use state conventions to nominate their candidates.

Direct Primary

The **direct primary**, mentioned in earlier chapters, is a preliminary election to select the party's candidate for the general election, to elect delegates to a political party's convention, or both. It originated in Wisconsin

State convention of the Libertarian Party in Montana

Primary Differences

Discuss the differences between caucuses and primaries. A caucus involves a small percentage of voter participation and is often more easily managed by party bosses. A primary involves a larger percentage of voter participation and is less controlled by party bosses.

In 1845 Congress passed legislation establishing the first Tuesday after the first Monday in November as Election Day during a presidential election year.

November was the most convenient month for farmers and other rural workers to travel to the polls. Planting occurred in the spring, and summer was the time for working the fields and tending the crops, so those seasons would not do. By November, fall harvest was complete, and the weather was still mild enough for travel.

in 1903 and soon afterward replaced the convention as the main nominating method in the American political process. Most states mandate that primaries be the method by which parties choose candidates for the US Senate and House, for governors and legislatures, and for most local offices. Some states select their candidates by a combination of the convention and primary systems. To assist with primaries, states set the dates for primary elections; furnish election officials, polling places, ballots, and registration lists; and oversee the primary (as they do other elections).

Because laws regarding state primaries are complex and confusing, a review of the various types of primaries is appropriate. In a **closed primary**, participants must be registered as members of one party and may vote only for candidates from the party to which they belong. On primary-election day, registered voters go to their precinct polling places, where their names are on a list of party members. Each voter is given his or her party's ballot and votes. Because only party members can vote, independents (unaffiliated voters) do not participate in closed primaries, although they may vote in the general election. **Semiclosed primaries** allow independents to choose a ballot from one of the two parties. About two dozen states keep their primaries closed or semiclosed.

The **open primary** (a primary in which voters do not have to declare their party membership) is also found in about two dozen states. On primary-election day, any qualified voter may tell a precinct official which party's primary ballot he desires; or, in some states, the voter may take both major party ballots but vote on only one.

No longer in use is the **blanket primary**, or "wide-open" primary. Three states—Alaska, California, and Washington—formerly used this kind of primary. All voters received identical ballots that included the names of all the candidates. Voters could then choose to vote in the Republican primary for one office and in the Democratic primary for another. In 2000, however, the Supreme Court ruled this type of primary election unconstitutional.

A few states (such as Washington, Nebraska, and California) use a primary system called the **Top-Two method**. All the candidates, regardless of party affiliation, are listed on one ballot. The two that receive the most votes (even if they are members of the same party) advance to the general election. This method is also called a **jungle primary**.

Whichever method used in the primary election, the winners of the respective primaries face one another in the **general election**. The winner in that

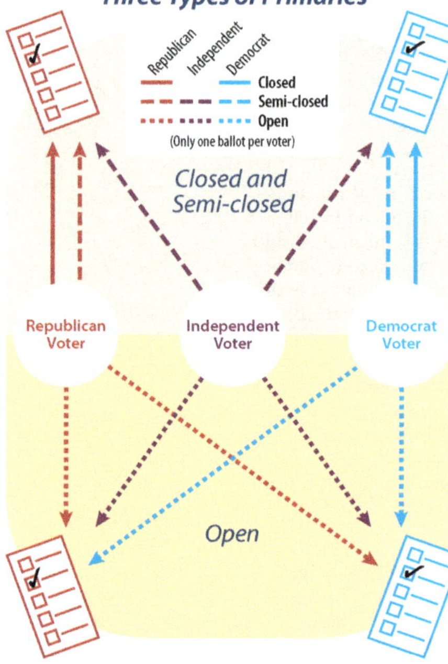

Voters enter a polling place in Kernersville, North Carolina

Which Primary Is Best?

Discuss the pros and cons of open and closed primaries. Identify the type of primary used in your state. If your state uses the Top-Two method, discuss the advantages and disadvantages of that method.

election, which is held on the Tuesday after the first Monday in November, actually fills the government office.

Section Review

1–4. Identify four preliminary tasks that a candidate faces when running for public office.

5. Define *incumbent*.

6–9. Identify four methods used to nominate candidates.

10. Define *direct primary*.

★ What is the difference between the blanket primary and the open primary?

★ Which type of direct primary do you think is best? Justify your answer.

II. The Campaign Trail

The intensity of a long campaign is an important test of a candidate's physical and mental strength. Weeks of travel, speechmaking, and scrutiny from the media enable voters to see how well a candidate withstands pressure and might reveal a candidate's true nature. Rutherford B. Hayes said that "nothing brings out the lower traits of human nature like office-seeking. Men of good character and impulses are betrayed by it into all sorts of meanness."

Marco Rubio (R-FL) was first elected to the US Senate in 2010.

CAMPAIGNS AND ELECTIONS • 405

Section II Objectives

1. Explain the advantages of incumbency in campaigns.

2. Describe how the coattail effect impacts elections.

3. Analyze the media's influence on political campaigns.

Section Review Answers

1–4. meeting the office requirements, assembling a staff, establishing a campaign strategy, and campaigning for the party's nomination (p. 401)

5. the current officeholder (p. 402)

6–9. petition, caucus, convention, and direct primary (p. 403)

10. a preliminary election to select a party's candidate for the general election, to elect delegates to a political party's convention, or both (p. 403)

★ In a blanket primary, all candidates from all parties are on one ballot, and the voter chooses one candidate for each elected office. In an open primary, the voters do not have to declare party membership and can choose which party ballot they desire.

★ Some students may say a closed primary is best because those voting have an honest interest in electing the best candidate for their party. Some may say the Top-Two method is better because it de-emphasizes political parties. Some may provide reasons for favoring the open primary, such as that it allows independent voters to participate.

Campaigns, Incumbents, and Coattails

The Congressional Campaign

Congressional campaigns are less competitive than presidential campaigns. Most incumbents who seek reelection win it. Incumbents often distance themselves from the problems in Washington, DC, and hold the president or others responsible; furthermore, they try to take credit for improvements since they help make the laws. Congressional elections place importance on specific voter groups, such as pro-life voters or the growing Hispanic community.

Daniel Inouye

Incumbents

Candidates who challenge incumbents or vie for an open seat usually begin campaigning at least a year, and often longer, before the general election. Incumbents are generally spared all the preliminary rigors because they have many advantages—name recognition, financial backing, the powers of their office, and goodwill they have created by assisting their **constituents** (residents of a district who are represented by an elected official) with problems. As noted, because of well-entrenched incumbents, most congressional races are not very competitive. From 1960 to 2018, over 90 percent of US House incumbents seeking reelection retained their seats, and over 80 percent of US Senate incumbents retained theirs.

Longest-Serving Senators as of 2019

Senator	Party/State	Total Tenure in Office	Years Served	Reason for Leaving
Robert Byrd	Democrat, West Virginia	51 years, 176 days	January 3, 1959–June 28, 2010	Died
Daniel Inouye	Democrat, Hawaii	49 years, 349 days	January 3, 1963–December 17, 2012	Died
Strom Thurmond	Democrat then Republican, South Carolina	47 years, 159 days	December, 14, 1954–April 4, 1956 and November 7, 1956–January 3, 2003	Retired
Ted Kennedy	Democrat, Massachusetts	46 years, 292 days	November 7, 1962–August 25, 2009	Died
Patrick Leahy	Democrat, Vermont	44 years+	January 3, 1975–	

Longest-Serving US Representatives as of 2019

Representative	Party/State	Total Tenure in Office	Years Served	Reason for Leaving
John Dingell	Democrat, Michigan	59 years, 21 days	December 13, 1955–January 3, 2015	Retired
Jamie Whitten	Democrat, Mississippi	53 years, 60 days	November 4, 1941–January 3, 1995	Retired
John Conyers	Democrat, Michigan	52 years, 336 days	January 3, 1965–December 5, 2017	Resigned
Carl Vinson	Democrat, Georgia	50 years, 61 days	November 3, 1914–January 3, 1965	Retired
Emanuel Celler	Democrat, New York	49 years, 305 days	March 4, 1923–January 3, 1973	Lost renomination

Coattail Effect

The **coattail effect** is the ability of a strong candidate at the top of a ticket (usually a candidate for president or, in a year with no presidential election, a governor or US senator) to attract votes for other members of his party who are running for lesser offices. For instance, in 1980, Republicans gained twelve Senate seats when their candidate, Ronald Reagan, was elected president. Those seats provided a Republican majority in that body for the first time since the 1952 election (when many Republican members of Congress had ridden the

Incumbents or Challengers

Assign students to research the most recent statewide elections. Was there a greater percentage of incumbents or challengers elected? If challengers were elected, discuss possible reasons for their success.

Coattail Effect

Discuss the coattail effect and its uncertainties. Note that the coattail effect is not necessarily limited to presidential elections. A strong candidate for the Senate, a governorship, or another high office can sometimes help those of his party who are seeking lower offices.

coattails of their presidential nominee, Dwight Eisenhower). But since voters do not always vote a **straight ticket** (vote for all the candidates of one party), the coattails of the winning presidential candidate are not always long enough to help party members running for other offices. In 1976 for example, Jimmy Carter's victory brought an increase of only one Democratic senator and one representative. The same was true in 1988, when Republicans lost two seats in the House although they easily won the White House. Generally speaking, the greater the popularity of a party's presidential candidate, the greater the opportunity for the coattail effect to operate. Therefore, congressional, state, and local candidates tie their fortunes to the top of the ticket if a presidential candidate (or governor or US senator in a non-presidential election year) is popular and a likely winner in the state or district.

Campaigning and the Media
Newspapers and Magazines

In the 1896 presidential election, Democrat William Jennings Bryan traveled thousands of miles and gave hundreds of speeches, and many newspaper reporters joined him on the campaign trail. William McKinley, his opponent, conducted a "front porch" campaign from his residence in Canton, Ohio. Instead of traveling to the voters, more than 500,000 people were brought by train to his home. There McKinley addressed the crowds. His staff then issued his remarks to newsmen who sent them to newspapers throughout the country by telegraph. Republican National Committee chairman Mark Hanna raised large sums of money and distributed millions of pamphlets. Hanna also mounted a negative campaign, implying that if Bryan were elected, many people would lose their jobs. With this election, the media began to be widely used in political campaigns.

William McKinley (at right on porch in dark suit) speaking to a crowd at his home during the 1896 presidential election

Competing Campaign Styles

The year 1896 was a watershed in campaign styles. The Republican presidential candidate, William McKinley, used a front-porch campaign. It epitomized the nineteenth-century approach, in which it was considered undignified to campaign personally for oneself.

In contrast, Democratic candidate William Jennings Bryan's vigorous speechmaking tours set the stage for the campaign style of the twentieth century. McKinley's campaign manager and financier, Mark Hanna, feared that Bryan's energetic campaign might work. He encouraged McKinley to follow Bryan on the stump, but McKinley good-naturedly declined, saying that he might "as well put up a trapeze on [his] front lawn and compete with some professional athlete as go out speaking against Bryan."

Since McKinley refused to go to the people, Hanna decided to bring the people to McKinley. He arranged for delegations of people from around the nation to travel by tens and hundreds to Canton, Ohio, to see the distinguished-looking McKinley, hear brief campaign speeches, and carry home enthusiasm for the Republican ticket. Railroads provided special trains with excursion rates for these pilgrimages. McKinley's front lawn was trampled to dust during the campaign, and his neat picket fence was gradually appropriated by souvenir hunters. Despite his low-key approach, McKinley won the election.

Campaign Memorabilia

Invite students to bring campaign buttons, bumper stickers, literature, and other campaign memorabilia to show and discuss. Note the slogans and other attention-getting devices that are used on the memorabilia.

Campaign Circumstances

Identify the current US senators serving your state and the representative serving your district. Discuss any interesting circumstances involved in their campaigns and elections.

The Treason of the Senate

In 1906, William Randolph Hearst increased the influence of his publishing empire by supporting the demand for direct election of senators. Hearst hired David Graham Phillips, a veteran reporter, to write critical pieces depicting senators as individuals who were controlled by financiers and industrialists. The articles became a series called The Treason of the Senate. The public was so motivated by the articles that they kept pushing for reform, which came about in 1913 with the passage of the Seventeenth Amendment.

During the early twentieth century, newspapers and magazines were the major information sources for voters.

Radio

In October 1920, KDKA in Pittsburgh became the first commercially licensed radio station in the country. Shortly afterward, it broadcast the election returns in Warren Harding's win over James Cox. Radio could quickly inform the nation of campaign events and election results; it was first used by campaign teams during the 1924 presidential race, especially by Calvin Coolidge's staff. Even after radio was largely superseded by television, the medium remained an important channel for political speech, as, for instance, in the talk shows (most of which were conservative) that became popular during the 1990s. Many such programs continue to be influential.

Television

In the nineteenth century, apart from drawings and photographs, most Americans never saw their president during his administration, much less the various candidates vying for office during an election year. The 1952 presidential campaign witnessed the first significant use of television; suddenly, candidates had a medium that was both a blessing and a curse. A candidate could reach millions of homes with his message, outline his plans for the nation, and even target advertising to appeal to various groups. But television could become a "one-eyed monster" for a candidate when embarrassing incidents or ill-chosen words gained nationwide exposure. Little things can sidetrack a campaign, such as a candidate's attempts to recover from a gaffe. Senator Bob Dole's quest for the 1988 Republican presidential nomination was impaired by a fit of frustration. In a live interview, an angry Dole told George H. W. Bush, "Stop lying about my record"; the negative image haunted Dole during the race.

Since television is primarily a visual medium, superficial factors become more noticeable. The fact that a candidate simply "looks good" on television can become a deciding factor in many voters' minds. Some analysts believe that the

physical contrast between John Kennedy and Richard Nixon, particularly apparent during the first of their four debates in the 1960 presidential election, had an impact on that race (mentioned in Chapter 10). Kennedy appeared handsome, cheerful, and rested whereas Nixon, who had recently been released from the hospital, was sweaty, pale, and seemed to need a shave (unlike Kennedy, he declined to have makeup applied for the event).

Television also influences congressional campaigns. During one of the televised debates between candidates for the US Senate in New York, Republican candidate Rick Lazio challenged Democratic candidate Hillary Clinton to pledge she would limit the use of outside funds in the race. He walked over to Clinton, thrust out a written pledge, and asked her to sign it. Lazio wanted his opponent to make a commitment on television, but viewers thought he "invaded" Clinton's personal space. The negative image of Lazio was burned into voters' minds and contributed to his loss in that 2000 election.

Republican Rick Lazio (left) and Democrat Hillary Clinton (right) were opponents in the 2000 US Senate race in New York.

Yellow Journalism's Influence

Yellow journalism has significantly influenced US history. Discuss with the students how the Treason of the Senate articles (see the side-margin information above) encouraged the public to keep pressure on Congress and helped change the Constitution. If the articles had not been written, would the direct election of senators have occurred? Or was the adoption of the Seventeenth Amendment inevitable?

In the 1984 presidential campaign, the incumbent, Ronald Reagan, made a weak showing in his first debate with the Democratic challenger, Walter Mondale. Although Reagan had enjoyed immense popularity, his seemingly confused responses during a single televised hour raised questions about his age and competence. As Reagan prepared for the second debate, his closest friends, thinking that he had been bombarded with too many facts and figures, begged his advisors to "let Reagan be Reagan." During the next debate, Mondale pounced on the age issue against the seventy-three-year-old president. In a surprising twist, Reagan shot back, "I am not going to exploit for political purposes my opponent's youth and inexperience." The quip was funny, and the audience and both candidates laughed. With that one-liner, Reagan steadied the shaky image he presented in the first debate. Such incidents involve no party platform and address no key campaign issues; yet, magnified by television, they can become crucial factors in winning voters.

Presidential-campaign debates often succeed or fail based on one memorable quip or gaffe. For instance, Reagan used a clever line when debating Mondale (right) in 1984.

State and local candidates usually employ the television medium by running **spots** (paid advertisements) or using "**free media**" (coverage of campaign activities on programs, including news programs). Free media does not cost a campaign any money and aids in name recognition for an unknown candidate.

Internet

The internet has provided the latest tools to aid the candidate's campaign. As part of their campaign strategy, candidates establish an internet presence including websites that enable voters to become more informed and to volunteer their support, both time and finances. Websites also keep voters informed of campaign appearances and of a candidate's responses to opponents' attacks. Furthermore, voters can interact by sending and receiving information and can subscribe to receive email updates. Voters may become concerned about the condition of a campaign if online information and websites are no longer updated.

Social media, such as Facebook and Instagram, has extended the reach of campaign communications. During Barack Obama's campaigns, his staff analyzed Facebook data to increase voter engagement. In 2016 Donald Trump was the first candidate to extensively use Twitter during a presidential campaign. Such use highlighted some of the advantages of social media. It can bypass the traditional media and take the candidate's message directly to the American public. It also reaches younger voters that candidates desperately want to energize politically. Media campaigns are a necessity today in American politics, but purchasing time on radio or television is very expensive; social media is free media, which, if used correctly, can bolster any campaign. However, social media has also had a negative impact on elections. Untrue or distorted information can be

As president, Trump's tweets repeatedly criticized news outlets that alleged he had conspired with Russians to win the 2016 election. An investigation by Special Counsel Robert Mueller (2017–19) found no evidence of such collusion.

Positive or Negative

During an election year, encourage the students to bring newspaper or internet articles to class or summarize television presentations about a major party candidate at the state or local level. Instruct the students to identify whether the information portrays the candidate positively or negatively. Designate an area in the classroom for the positive items and another area for the negative items.

Discuss the potential impact these items might have on the candidate's campaign. Also, review the margin note at the bottom of page 397 and consider discussing fake news.

Political Virtues

Use the articles or summaries suggested under "Positive or Negative" (at left) or assign students to read, watch, or listen to additional media coverage of political campaigns.

Ask students the following questions about the news stories to focus on political virtues: Do they indicate that candidates and voters are being prudent? Do some focus on candidates boldly standing for what is right and for the common good? Are there instances given where a politician is shown to be humble? Are examples given of candidates and citizens, with differing positions, showing respect for each other?

Activity 2: The Role of New Media in Political Campaigning

This activity exposes the students to information about how political workers use new media as powerful tools in election campaigns.

effortlessly posted and fool undiscerning readers. Furthermore, although foreign governments have meddled in past elections, social media has made it easier to do so. After the 2016 election, Russians were shown to have interfered in a variety of ways, particularly by posting false information on social media, yet there was no proof they had successfully influenced the election results.

Section Review

1–4. Name four advantages of incumbents when they seek reelection.

5–6. Define *coattail effect*, and describe how it works.

7–8. During the early twentieth century, which two forms of media provided the most information for voters?

9–11. List three advantages of a candidate using social media.

★ What are some advantages and disadvantages of a candidate using television?

★ What impact do televised debates have on voters?

Guiding Questions

1. What happens on Election Day?
2. How have voting requirements changed?
3. What role do social, religious, economic, and other factors play in American elections?
4. What are the different methods of voting?

III. Elections and Voting

Federal Elections

Election laws in the United States are mainly state laws because most elected offices are state and local offices. Only the specifics regarding the election of the president, the vice president, and both houses of Congress were established by the Constitution. Article I, Section 2, clause 1, states that House of Representative members will be elected by the people every two years, and clause 4 says that vacancies will be filled by special elections called by state governors. Article I, Section 3, clause 1, directs each state legislature to choose senators for terms of six years. In 1913, however, the Seventeenth Amendment was ratified, allowing senators to be elected directly by the people. Senate vacancies may be filled by special election or, in some states, appointment by the governor.

Election Day

Candidates prepare for Election Day by drafting two brief speeches—a victory speech and a concession speech. The candidates' staffs continue working that day to get supporters out to vote at their **polling places** (the location in a specific precinct where residents go to vote). Polling places include schools, churches, and fire stations. In the evening, after the polls close, supporters gather at their candidate's headquarters, where they watch the results and hope to celebrate victory. In close races the results are sometimes unknown until the next day or later.

> *"The electors [voters] see their representative not only as a legislator for the state but also as the natural protector of local interests in the legislature; indeed, they almost seem to think that he has a power . . . to represent each constituent . . ."*
>
> —Alexis de Tocqueville

The Voter

The opportunity to vote in America is a responsibility, a privilege, and a constitutional guarantee. The Fifteenth Amendment gave voting rights to all adult male citizens regardless of ethnicity, and the Nineteenth Amendment gave adult women the right to vote. The Twenty-Third

Section Review Answers

1–4. name recognition, financial backing, the powers of their office, and the goodwill they have created by assisting their constituents (p. 406)

5–6. The coattail effect is the ability of a strong candidate at the top of the ticket to attract votes for other members of his party who are running for lesser offices. For example, a less popular candidate for the US House of Representatives might still be elected because of the popularity of the same party's presidential candidate. (pp. 406–7)

7–8. newspapers and magazines (p. 408)

9–11. It can bypass the traditional media and take the candidate's message directly to the American public. It also reaches younger voters that candidates desperately want to energize politically. It is a free media. (p. 409)

★ The advantages of television are that the candidate can reach millions of homes with his message, outline his plans for the nation, and target advertising to appeal to various groups. Disadvantages of television are the effects of little mistakes like embarrassing moments or ill-chosen words that gain nationwide exposure. As a visual medium, superficial factors are more noticeable. Purchasing advertising time is expensive.

★ Debates often place an emphasis on the outward image or performance ability of the candidate. One such example was the physical contrast between Kennedy and Nixon in the 1960 presidential debates. An example of poor performance was in the US Senate race in New York (in 2000) when Rick Lazio appeared to be invading Hillary Clinton's personal space. The use of witty statements, such as that of Ronald Reagan in his 1984 debates with Walter Mondale, sometimes attracts more attention than detailed substance during a debate.

Amendment extended the right to vote in presidential elections to citizens of Washington, DC. The Twenty-Fourth Amendment eliminated poll taxes, and the Twenty-Sixth Amendment extended voting rights to eighteen-year-olds. Unfortunately, in presidential elections since World War II, only slightly more than half the eligible voters have exercised their constitutional right. An even smaller number normally vote in other elections.

Many people have expressed their thoughts about voting, including former presidents. John Quincy Adams said, "Always vote for principle, though you may vote alone, and you may cherish the sweetest reflection that your vote is never lost." John F. Kennedy said, "The ignorance of one voter in a democracy impairs the security of all."

Registration

In the forty-nine states that require voters to **register** (to officially enroll for the purpose of voting), the minimum requirements are the same. A person must be a US citizen, at least eighteen years old, and a resident (one who lives in a particular place for a specific period of time) of the state in which he or she will vote. Each state may impose additional requirements, and most do. For example, most states mandate that voter registration be closed a specified number of days before an election. In many states, an individual convicted of a felony, imprisoned, or judged mentally incompetent cannot vote.

Election night crowd of Hillary Clinton supporters in New York City (November 2016)

CAMPAIGNS AND ELECTIONS • 411

Poll Watchers

Typically political parties, candidates, and groups concerned about a particular item on the ballot can appoint poll watchers. They observe at a polling place but may not interfere with either voters or election officials. However, their mere presence may help ensure that laws and procedures are properly followed. Rules and requirements regarding these individuals vary from state to state.

The Exception

As mentioned in other chapters, North Dakota is the only state that does not require voters to register prior to voting in an election.

Voter Requirements

Group students and assign the following tasks. One group should locate the state's voter requirements. Another should investigate the various ways individuals can register to vote. Other groups may research the voting requirements for neighboring states and chart the similarities and differences between the states' requirements. Each group should report its findings to the class.

Poll-Watcher Requirements

Assign a student to locate your state's requirements regarding poll watchers and relate the information to the class. (This information can usually be found on the secretary of state's website.)

Activity 3: State Election Laws

This activity enables the students to further develop the skill of using outside resources while gaining knowledge about state election laws.

Should Christians Consider a Candidate's Religion?

When Al Smith and John F. Kennedy ran for the presidency, their Roman Catholicism bothered some voters. In response, Kennedy pledged his support for the separation of church and state and promised that the pope would not sway his policy decisions. Similarly, Mitt Romney's Mormon faith was a campaign issue in the primaries for the 2008 and 2012 elections.

The Constitution declares that the state cannot impose religious tests on candidates, but voters may take a candidate's religion into account when they are assessing candidates. For example, a Christian may choose not to vote for a candidate because he does not want that candidate's religion to gain public prominence, or may vote against a professing Christian because that candidate's morals or policies are inconsistent with his profession.

Voter registration office in Miami, Florida

Alfred E. Smith (left) and John Kennedy (right)

A person can register by mail or in person at city hall or the county courthouse. Since the passage of the National Voter Registration Act, or "Motor Voter Law," in 1993, a person can also register when applying for or renewing a driver's license or at various state agencies, such as an employment or welfare office. In addition to stipulations of that law, many states allow individuals to register to vote online, at libraries, at churches, or at fire stations.

Profile

The profile of the American electorate has changed dramatically since our Constitution was written. At that time, the voters were adult white males who were property owners. Voting rights were eventually extended to freed slaves, women, and eighteen-year-olds. Today, candidates must take into account such diverse factors as geographical location, gender, age, religious background, ethnicity, education, income, and occupation of the people in a voting area.

Geography has a significant impact on elections. For the past few decades, Democrats have done better in the heavily populated areas in and around cities, while Republicans perform better in rural areas, small towns, and many suburbs.

Gender and age are also important to the major political parties. Women and voters under age forty-five tend to vote for Democratic candidates. There have been exceptions to this; for example, Ronald Reagan in 1984 and George H. W. Bush in 1988 were able to win more younger voters. In 2000 George W. Bush and Al Gore received an equal percentage of votes from these groups.

Religious backgrounds can influence elections. Voters in the early years of American politics were mainly Protestants, but increased immigration brought Catholics, Jews, and voters of other religions to the polls. In 1928 Alfred E. Smith, a Catholic, ran for president. His campaign failed in part from the reluctance of many Protestants to vote for him. Similarly, some Protestants opposed another Catholic candidate, John Kennedy, in 1960; however, Kennedy's winning the White House made him the first, and so far only, Catholic president. In 2012 Mitt Romney became the first Mormon to win the nomination of a major party for president. Though he lost the election, his religious background seemed to have little impact on the race. However, religion does influence voters' positions on many issues. Religious conservatives, for example, tend to support candidates who are pro-life and take conservative stands on other important issues.

Activity 4: Summarizing Recent Elections

This activity asks the students to review and analyze the results of the most recent election.

"The Ignorance of One Voter . . ."

John F. Kennedy said, "The ignorance of one voter in a democracy impairs the security of all." Guide a discussion about what Kennedy meant by his statement.

Political parties also focus on voters' ethnic backgrounds. Beginning in the late nineteenth century, Democrats heavily courted immigrants who were settling in the cities. During the Depression in the 1930s many African Americans shifted their support from Republicans to Democrats, and by the mid-1960s an even larger percentage voted Democratic (today, the overwhelming majority of black Americans support Democratic candidates). In 2000 the Hispanic vote was divided, with more Cuban Americans voting with Republicans and a large percentage of Mexican and Puerto Rican Americans voting with Democrats. Today, approximately two-thirds of Hispanics support the Democratic party.

Methods of Voting
Historical

America's early historical voting method was by voice. The voter expressed aloud his voting preference; this was considered a "man's" way of voting. However, as the number of voters increased, corruption took place. Candidates tried to buy votes and sometimes resorted to intimidation. In the 1800s voters began writing their choices on pieces of paper and putting these handmade ballots in the ballot box. Political parties and candidates started making their own ballots, but this created its own set of problems. Today, individual state election commissions, state boards of elections, or secretaries of state choose and certify the methods and equipment used for voting.

Paper Ballots

The system of secret ballots, or Australian ballots, first saw use in 1856 in the Australian state of Victoria. The official paper ballots listed all candidates and issues and allowed voters to privately mark their choices. Voters then placed their ballots in a secured ballot box. By 1890 almost the entire United States had switched to this method of voting. In many rural and small communities, paper ballots continue to be used.

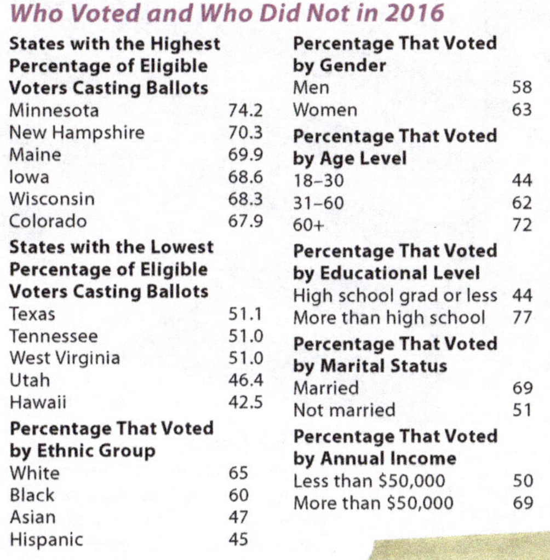

Who Voted and Who Did Not in 2016

States with the Highest Percentage of Eligible Voters Casting Ballots		Percentage That Voted by Gender	
Minnesota	74.2	Men	58
New Hampshire	70.3	Women	63
Maine	69.9	**Percentage That Voted by Age Level**	
Iowa	68.6	18–30	44
Wisconsin	68.3	31–60	62
Colorado	67.9	60+	72
States with the Lowest Percentage of Eligible Voters Casting Ballots		**Percentage That Voted by Educational Level**	
Texas	51.1	High school grad or less	44
Tennessee	51.0	More than high school	77
West Virginia	51.0	**Percentage That Voted by Marital Status**	
Utah	46.4	Married	69
Hawaii	42.5	Not married	51
Percentage That Voted by Ethnic Group		**Percentage That Voted by Annual Income**	
White	65	Less than $50,000	50
Black	60	More than $50,000	69
Asian	47		
Hispanic	45		

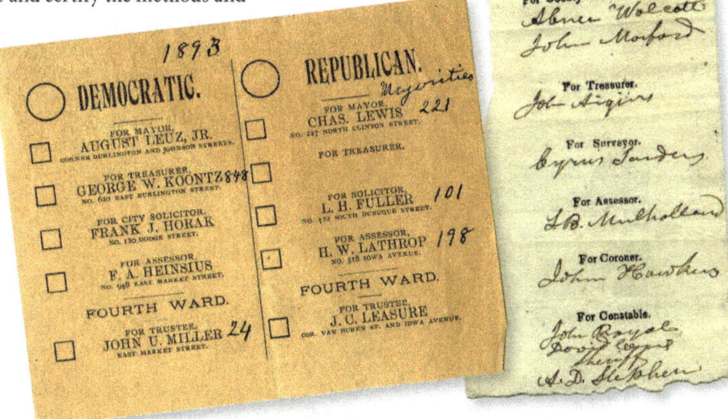

An Australian, or secret, ballot (left) used in Iowa City, Iowa, in 1893. A paper ballot (right) used in Iowa Territory in 1839.

Australian Ballot

In 1856 the use of a secret ballot was implemented in various parts of Australia. The practice was intended to help protect voters from intimidation and pressure. When the secret ballot was later adopted in the United States, it was called the Australian ballot.

Hispanic Support

Discuss possible reasons that Cuban Americans tend to support the Republican Party, whereas Mexican and Puerto Rican Americans tend to support the Democratic Party.

Election 2016 Data

Instruct students to analyze the voting data on page 413 of the Student Edition for the 2016 presidential election. Discuss their ideas regarding reasons for the results in each category.

History of Absentee Voting

Absentee ballots were first used in colonial times. During the Civil War, absentee voting increased as soldiers in the field were allowed the opportunity. In 1896, some states allowed absentee voting for civilians who would be away from home on Election Day.

During World War II, the "soldier ballot" was adopted by the federal government, and certain officers were given election duties. After the war, the states extended absentee voting to service personnel, their families, and civilians who traveled with the armed forces.

Today, virtually anyone who is unable to go to his precinct on Election Day may vote by absentee ballot. In some states a person must give a legitimate reason to vote by absentee ballot, but many do not have such a requirement. Oregon, Washington, and Colorado mail ballots to all voters. Also, thirty-nine states and the District of Columbia allow early voting.

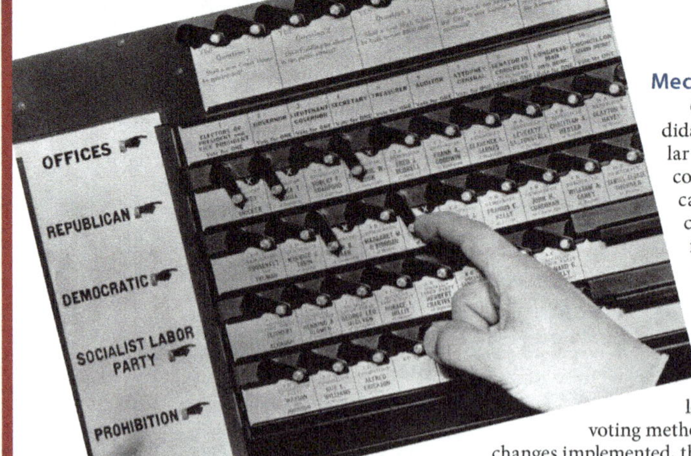

Mechanical-lever voting machine

Mechanical-Lever Machines

On a lever voting machine, each candidate or ballot issue is given a particular lever, and a voter pulls down levers corresponding to the votes he wishes to cast. The first official lever voting machine was demonstrated in New York in 1892. By 1930 most major US cities had adopted this method, and by the 1960s more than half of all US voters were using it. After the controversial 2000 presidential election, Congress passed the Help America Vote Act of 2002 (HAVA). This legislation was designed to upgrade voting methods and procedures. As a result of the changes implemented, these machines were retired by 2010.

Punch Cards

By 1996 more than a third of the nation used the punch-card system for voting. This method required a voter to punch holes in a card beside the printed names of the preferred candidates or issues. The voter then placed the card into a ballot box. After the polls closed, the ballots were placed into a tabulating device at the precinct, where the punched holes were counted for each candidate or issue. The last use of this voting method was in 2014.

Optical Scan

On an optical-scan ballot card, a voter fills in an empty oval, a circle, or a rectangle next to the candidate favored. The cards are counted by machines that scan the darkened areas. This system is similar to the answer sheets used by students for classroom and standardized tests.

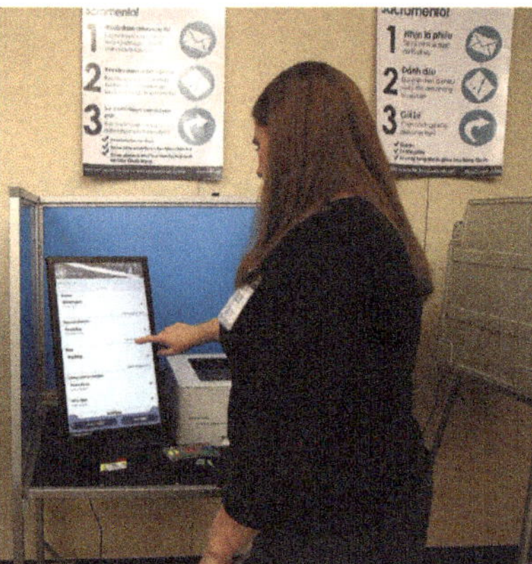

Touch-screen voting machine

Touch Screens

Rather than marking a paper ballot, voters in many precincts utilize a touch screen device that displays the options for candidates and issues. After completing all selections, a box marked "vote" must be pressed to record the choices.

Voting by Mail

Voting by mail is used mostly by **absentee voters**—individuals unable to vote in person during the regular voting times. This category includes those at college or on business trips, the ill or disabled, and those serving in our military forces. These voters apply for absentee ballots during a specific time period before an election. They mark their ballots, seal them, and return them to appropriate election officials before the election. To encourage greater voter participation, some states now allow practically anyone to cast an absentee ballot before an election. Three states—Oregon, Colorado, and Washington—conduct all elections by mail.

 **Mock Primary and General Elections**

Refer to the suggested activity at the bottom of page 157 of the Teacher Edition. If you did not have an opportunity to enact it during the discussion of Chapter 7, consider doing so now.

Internet Voting

Internet voting has drawn mixed reactions. Many people point to potential problems such as viruses, voter fraud, voter secrecy violations, inaccurate voter counts, blocked access, and interference by hackers. Others view internet voting as a way of increasing voter participation, eliminating waiting in lines, and reducing election costs.

Section Review

1. Define *polling place*.
2–4. Which amendment extended voting rights to eighteen-year-olds? To women? To all ethnic groups?
5–7. What are the three minimum requirements to register to vote?
8. Explain how the 1993 "Motor Voter Law" changed voter registration.
★ Why is the secret ballot so important in ensuring the integrity and reliability of elections?

IV. Campaign Finance

Running for public office at federal and state levels has become a multimillion-dollar pursuit. As money became a campaign necessity, some candidates tried to purchase their way into office, and many interest groups tried to gain political favors with their campaign contributions. As a result, in the early 1900s campaign financing drew attention for reform. But it was not until the 1970s that stricter laws were passed to govern campaign finance and that the **Federal Election Commission (FEC)** was established to enforce the legislation. However, due to misuse and perceived misuse of campaign financing, the reform movement continued, at least sporadically, throughout the 1990s and into the twenty-first century.

> **Guiding Questions**
>
> 1. What do the laws state regarding campaign funding?
> 2. What campaign finance reforms have been instituted?
> 3. What is the impact of campaign funding reform?

Laws

Federal Legislation

In 1907 federal law made corporate campaign contributions to specific candidates illegal, and contributions by interest groups to specific candidates were made illegal in 1943. But because political campaigns still received much of their funding through individuals, many people thought that additional change was needed. Eventually, four major pieces of legislation were passed that impacted campaign finance on the federal level—the Federal Election Campaign Act (FECA) of 1971, the FECA amendments of 1974 and 1976, and the Bipartisan Campaign Reform Act (BCRA) of 2002.

Campaign money raised for a specific candidate in federal elections that must be spent according to federal laws and restrictions is called **hard money**. Because labor-union contributions to federal candidates were made illegal in 1943, soft money came into being. **Soft money** includes campaign money raised apart from federal regulations and given to local, state, and national party organizations to be used

"Politics has become so expensive that it takes a lot of money even to be defeated."
—Will Rogers, humorist

Section IV Objectives

1. Describe the laws that govern campaign funding.
2. Analyze the campaign finance reforms that have been instituted.
3. Assess the impact of campaign funding reform.

Theodore Roosevelt

In President Theodore Roosevelt's 1905 message to Congress, he said that all political contributions by corporations should be forbidden by law. Roosevelt did not, however, oppose campaign contributions by individuals who owned and operated corporations. He also proposed that the public should finance federal candidates' campaigns through political parties.

Early Reform Laws

1867: The first federal campaign-finance legislation was the 1867 Naval Appropriations Bill. This law stopped federal officers from asking for campaign contributions from navy-yard workers.

1883: The Pendleton Civil Service Reform Act of 1883 expanded the 1867 Naval Appropriations Bill to include all federal civil-service workers. Before this act, government workers were expected to make campaign contributions or possibly lose their jobs.

Internet Voting

Ask students to research any current uses of the internet in governmental elections on the local, state, or national level. Instruct them to state the current status, successes, and failures of internet voting in a one-page report. Discuss their findings.

Section Review Answers

1. the location in a specific precinct where residents go to vote (p. 410)
2–4. the Twenty-Sixth Amendment, the Nineteenth Amendment, and the Fifteenth Amendment (p. 410–11)
5–7. A voter must be a US citizen, at least eighteen years old, and a resident of the state in which he will vote. (p. 411)
8. It allowed people to register to vote when applying for or renewing a driver's license or at various state agencies such as employment or welfare offices. (p. 412)
★ The secret ballot allows voters to privately mark their choices and vote in a secure way; it thus prevents intimidation and retribution if someone does not vote the "right" way, and it ensures that votes reliably reflect the will of the people.

Presidential-Campaign Expenditures in 2016					
Candidate	Party	Amount raised ($)	Amount spent ($)	Popular votes	Cost per vote ($)
Clinton	Democratic	$1.4 billion	$1.425 billion	65,845,063	$21.64
Trump	Republican	$957.6 million	$957.5 million	62,980,160	$15.20
Johnson	Libertarian	$12 million	$12 million	4,488,931	$2.67
Stein	Green	$3.7 million	$3.6 million	1,457,050	$2.47
McMullin	Independent	$1.6 million	$1.6 million	728,830	$2.20
Castle	Constitution	$68,036	$68,036	203,010	$0.34

for "party-building" activities, such as voter-registration efforts and get-out-the-vote drives. It also includes money raised by **political action committees**, or **PACs**, that are established by interest groups. That money is used to make contributions to individuals' campaigns, to a political party, or to support specific causes. Only PACs registered with the FEC can contribute to candidates seeking federal offices.

To better understand how soft money and PACs work, imagine that you are employed by General Motors and a member of the United Auto Workers (UAW), whose PAC is the UAW Voluntary Community Action Program (UAW V-CAP). You, along with other autoworkers, might be concerned over competition from foreign-owned automakers. You could contribute money to the UAW, which would in turn give those funds to UAW V-CAP. In an election year, the PAC would contribute the funds to the political party of candidates who call for protection of American manufacturing, to specific candidates, or to groups that support that cause.

Presidential candidates can receive some financial support through the Presidential Election Campaign Fund. Established in 1971, this fund uses tax money that individuals designate (by checking a box on their federal tax return) for this account. The donated amount is three dollars per person. Candidates who prove that they have widespread support can get money from this fund. Candidates demonstrate such support by collecting at least $100,000 from individual donations of $250 or less from twenty or more states, with each state contributing at least $5,000 toward the goal. During presidential primaries, most candidates can qualify for federal money (from this fund) equal to the amount they receive in contributions from individuals. During the general election they can acquire a specific lump sum. However, to receive this money candidates must agree not to exceed specified spending limits. From 1976 until 2008, presidential candidates regularly accepted these campaign funds. However, since 2008, many candidates have rejected this money because they do not want the constraints imposed by spending limits.

The *Buckley v. Valeo* Case

In 1974 legislation was passed limiting the amount of money that could be given to federal candidates by individuals and PACs. It also limited candidate spending from personal and family resources, total campaign expenses, and **independent expenditures** (funds spent by a person or group trying to help elect or defeat a candidate without the candidate's knowledge or support). Soon afterward, a suit was filed in federal court claiming that these provisions were unconstitutional. The plaintiffs said that important political communications cost money and that limiting such spending actually restricted speech; thus, the legislation violated the First Amendment. In 1976, the US Supreme Court ruled, in **Buckley v. Valeo**, that the restrictions did indeed violate the First Amendment by limiting a candidate's ability to spend his own money, restricting a campaign's total expense, and limiting independent expenditures. But the court upheld the

Election Expenses

Instruct the students to list and discuss probable expenses incurred by presidential, state, and local candidates.

Funding

Guide a discussion about the fundraising methods used by the major political parties.

constitutionality of limiting individuals' and committees' donations. The Court also ruled that if a candidate voluntarily accepts public financing, he is subject to campaign spending limits.

State Laws

Local and state campaign-finance laws largely govern the activity of state and local candidates and the activity of PACs at those levels. These laws vary depending on the location.

However, federal laws do stipulate that no candidates (national, state, or local) can accept contributions from foreign nationals (foreign governments, political parties, corporations, associations, and partnerships). In addition, federal regulations prohibit national banks and corporations organized by the authority of congressional act (for example, federal savings banks) from making contributions or expenditures in connection with any federal, state, or local election.

Additional Reform

After the efforts of the 1970s, it was not until the 1990s that reform once again received much attention. During that decade, Congress discussed measures that called for reducing political ads on television and voluntary state-by-state spending limits; they debated whether labor unions could spend union dues on political activities; they argued whether to limit, or even prohibit, PAC contributions; and they considered whether to raise the amount that individuals can donate for political purposes. The pressure for reform continued into the early twenty-first century, and specific proposals were given serious consideration.

McCain-Feingold Act

In 1995 Senators John McCain (R-AZ) and Russell Feingold (D-WI) began their joint work on campaign finance reform. Though the bill they authored failed to pass Congress, their efforts continued. Two members of the House of Representatives, Chris Shays (R-CT) and Marty Meehan (D-MA), joined the two senators to support reform in 2001. Eventually, reform legislation passed and was signed by President George W. Bush in March 2002. Although the law was modified from the original proposal advanced by the two senators, it is still often called the **McCain-Feingold Act**. The official name is the Bipartisan Campaign Reform Act (BCRA) of 2002.

John McCain (left) with Russell Feingold (right)

A stipulation included in the bill prohibited, with limited exceptions, national political parties, federal candidates, and officeholders from soliciting or receiving soft money contributions in federal elections. It also barred corporations—including non-profit corporations such as the American Civil Liberties Union (ACLU), the National Right to Life Committee, and Planned Parenthood—and unions from using their treasury funds to finance advertisements (issue ads) that referred to federal candidates within 60 days of a general election or 30 days of a primary election or caucus. The act strengthened laws that supervised the disclosure of how much is contributed to political campaigns and who contributed.

Campaign Reform

Discuss why Democrats typically support campaign finance reform and why Republicans (John McCain was the most notable exception) generally oppose such reform.

Bans

Discuss the reasoning behind banning foreign national campaign contributions. Discuss whether members of Congress should continue to have the franking privilege (some assert that it is just a means of incumbents obtaining publicity for themselves).

Protesters outside the US Supreme Court denouncing the Citizens United v. Federal Election Commission *decision*

At the signing of this reform law, President Bush stated that the act had flaws; but he asserted that despite its shortcomings, it would improve the political system. Soon afterward, Senator Mitch McConnell (R-KY) filed a lawsuit to block the new law. He stated that it violated Americans' First Amendment right to take part in the political process. Over the next few years, the Supreme Court issued decisions involving the legislation. In December 2003, in *McConnell v. Federal Election Commission*, the Court upheld most of the regulations. However, other rulings by the Court struck down specific portions. The most significant decision was rendered by the Court in **Citizens United v. Federal Election Commission** in January 2010. In that decision, the Court ruled as unconstitutional the parts of the act that kept corporations and unions from spending money to support or denounce individuals in elections. The Court stated that corporations and unions are to be treated as any individual would be treated in regard to political expression, which is protected by the First Amendment. Supporters of free speech hailed the ruling as a victory. Others feared that the decision would lead to even more lavish spending in campaigns and to greater corruption.

Challenges

Campaign-finance debates continue. In spite of reforms, the amount of money spent on political races continues to skyrocket. Many argue that money has become the dominating force in the political arena. Others note that the grass-roots effort of one-on-one campaigning by candidates and their supporters can make the biggest difference in the minds of voters.

Many Christians might avoid involvement in campaigns and elections or might want to participate only by voting and praying. After all, 1 Timothy 2:1–2 urges believers to pray for all people, especially for those who are in authority, so that Christians can live quiet, peaceable lives.

When the apostle Paul wrote this to Timothy and the other Christians with him, the people at that point in history could not choose their own civil authorities. Today, however, God has provided Americans the opportunity to help select their leadership. This is indeed a special gift. Praying for one's country and voting for candidates who uphold Christian principles are important responsibilities. Still, the Lord might want a Christian to do more, especially in one-on-one grass-roots efforts. Christians should seek what the Lord desires of them and combine action with their prayers.

Section Review

1–2. Explain the difference between hard and soft money.

3. What are *independent expenditures*?

4. What is the official name of the McCain-Feingold Act?

5. What did the Supreme Court rule in *Citizens United v. Federal Election Commission*?

★ What roles can Christians legitimately play in the electoral process?

Activity 5: Chapter Review

This is a review of all major terms and other information in the chapter.

Section Review Answers

1–2. Hard money is raised for a specific candidate in federal elections that must be spent according to federal laws and restrictions. Soft money is raised apart from federal regulations and given to local, state, and national party organizations for "party-building" activities. (pp. 415–16)

3. funds spent by a person or group trying to help elect or defeat a candidate without the candidate's knowledge or support (p. 416)

4. Bipartisan Campaign Reform Act (BCRA) of 2002 (p. 417)

5. The court ruled unconstitutional the parts of the McCain-Feingold Act that kept corporations and unions from spending money to support or denounce individuals in elections. (p. 418)

★ Christians should pray for their leaders and may vote. They may also actively campaign for candidates and run for office.

CHAPTER REVIEW ANSWERS

Making Connections

1–2. Senate: A candidate must be at least thirty years old, be a resident of the state in which he is elected, and have been a US citizen for nine years; House: A candidate must be at least twenty-five years old, be a resident of the state in which he is elected, and have been a US citizen for seven years. (p. 401)

3–5. unpaid senior advisors, citizen volunteers, and consultants (p. 402)

6–11. set the dates for primary elections; furnish election officials, polling places,

Making Connections

1–2. What are the office requirements for US Senate and House of Representatives candidates?

3–5. What are three categories of workers that candidates use to mount an effective campaign?

6–11. Name six things that states do to assist with primary elections.

12. Explain the relationship between the coattail effect and straight ticket voting.

13. Explain how the American electorate has changed since the Constitution was written.

14–15. List two reasons many people called for campaign financing reforms in the early 1900s.

Developing Civics Skills

1. How has television influenced presidential election campaigns, and how has it changed campaigning?

2. What is the significance of *Buckley v. Valeo*?

Thinking Critically

1. What are the potential uses and misuses of the internet and social media in campaigns? Should Congress pass legislation to prevent misuse? Support your answer to the second question.

2. Identify the voting method that, in your opinion, is the most accurate, timely, and secure. Explain why you chose that method.

Living as a Christian Citizen

1. How should a Christian determine his or her level of involvement in political campaigns?

2. Culture influences the political possibilities that are available to legislators. At the same time, legislation shapes culture. Choose a currently debated issue, and explain how the interdependent relationship between politics and culture has affected that issue. What conclusion should Christians draw from your observations?

People, Places, and Things to Remember

nomination
incumbent
petition
direct primary
closed primary
semiclosed primaries
open primary
blanket primary
Top-Two method
jungle primary
general election
constituents
coattail effect
straight ticket
spots
free media
polling places
register
absentee voters
Federal Election Commission (FEC)
hard money
soft money
political action committees (PACs)
independent expenditures
Buckley v. Valeo
McCain-Feingold Act
Citizens United v. Federal Election Commission

---

2. The Supreme Court ruled that the legislation violated candidates' First Amendment rights by limiting their ability to spend their own money, restricting campaigns' total expenses, and limiting independent expenditures. But the Court upheld the constitutionality of limiting individuals' and committees' donations and stated that if a candidate accepts public financing, he is subject to campaign spending limits.

Thinking Critically

1. Students may answer that candidates can use these media to easily and quickly reach voters. Candidates misuse these media when posting untrue or distorted information. Social media has made foreign interference easier in the US election process. For the second question, some might say that the government must ensure truth in campaigning, but others might say that truth is a defense against lies and that this issue should be decided by public opinion. Others might say that candidates who think they have been libeled or slandered can seek legal action (e.g., by suing their attackers).

2. Answers will vary. Students may choose from the following methods: hand-marked paper ballots, optical-scan ballots, touch screens, voting by mail, or internet voting.

Living as a Christian Citizen

1. Students should note that individuals have different callings. In deciding what to do, a Christian should consider vocation, obligations, opportunities, and what is at stake in each election. Some may decide to participate in a campaign, and others may decide to run for office or participate in other ways.

2. Issues will vary. Students should note how the media influences what culture tolerates in legislation and how legislation shapes culture by signaling what is culturally acceptable. For instance, divorce became more culturally acceptable (and more common) after no-fault divorce laws were passed. Christians should learn from this that passing laws legislating morality is proper. But one cannot create a moral society by law alone. Christians should promote morality in other spheres of culture as well and be examples to the world.

---

ballots, and registration lists; and oversee elections (p. 404)

12. The coattail effect is the ability of a strong candidate at the top of a ticket (usually a candidate for president or, if not a presidential election, a governor or US senator) to attract votes for other members of the party who are running for lesser offices. By having a strong candidate at the top of the ticket, the coattail effect could cause someone who otherwise would not vote a straight party ticket to do so. (pp. 406–7)

13. When the Constitution was first written, only adult white males who owned property could vote. Voting rights were eventually extended to all ethnicities, women, eighteen-year-olds, and citizens of Washington, DC, leading to greater diversity in the electorate. (pp. 410–11)

14–15. Because some candidates tried to purchase their way into office, and many interest groups tried to gain political favors with their campaign contributions. (p. 415)

Developing Civics Skills

1. Answers will vary. Television promotes appearance as a major factor for choosing a candidate and encourages sound bites over substance and detail. Television ads make campaigning very expensive.

1. Explain important terms relating to the interaction between the government and the public.
2. Define *public policy*.
3. Analyze the role of public opinion in governing.
4. Describe the purposes and types of interest groups and their impact on government.
5. Evaluate the media's influence on politicians and the public.

PUBLIC POLICY AND POLITICS

18

The foundation of our national policy will be laid in the pure and immutable principles of private morality.

—*George Washington*

Martin Luther King Jr. (center) with other participants at the August 1963 March on Washington

I. Government and the Public

II. Public Policy

III. Public Opinion

IV. Interest Groups

V. Mass Media

BIG IDEAS

1. What are some important terms related to the interaction between the government and the public?
2. What is public policy?
3. How does public opinion play a role in governing?
4. What are the purposes and types of interest groups, and how do they impact government?
5. How does media influence politicians and the public?

SUGGESTED MATERIALS

Section I
• No materials

Section II
• Activity 1 from Chapter 18 of the *Student Activities*

Section III
• Activity 2 from Chapter 18 of the *Student Activities*

Section IV
• Activity 3 from Chapter 18 of the *Student Activities*

Section V
• Political cartoons

• Activities 4–5 from Chapter 18 of the *Student Activities*
• Instructions for obtaining information under the Freedom of Information Act
• Political and product advertisements

Teacher Resources

Visit TeacherToolsOnline.com for resources to enhance the lessons.

The governor of Florida declares a state of emergency after a hurricane devastates several counties within the state. Congress passes an education bill requiring greater accountability for student achievement in the nation's schools. The municipal government of Gypsum, Colorado, approves the installation of speed bumps near a high school to curtail speeding.

In each of these cases, government is acting at the state, federal, or local level. But why does government respond to these particular issues and not to others? This chapter discusses the nature of public policy and the nongovernmental forces that help shape it.

I. Government and the Public

Every government—including the most autocratic and repressive—interacts with the public at some level, even if only to suppress its civil liberties. But in a democratic government, elected representatives compose a government that is "of the people, by the people, [and] for the people." Consequently, government action in a republic should be both a reaction to and a reflection of public attitudes.

Definitions

Public policy consists of the plans adopted by the government to handle problems and accomplish goals. Such policy is heavily influenced by how the public views matters. Most Americans have opinions about political issues that they ponder silently or reveal only to close friends. But pollsters can collect personal views on issues ranging from increases in local property taxes to reductions in national defense and from gun control to national health care. Collectively, ideas about political issues compose a public opinion.

Political scientist V. O. Key defined **public opinion** as "those opinions held by private persons which governments find it prudent to heed." There are two noteworthy characteristics of public opinion. First, government does not gauge public opinion simply by determining the opinions of the average American. There are many "publics" with opinions. Members of a manufacturing association would likely favor trade restrictions, whereas dockworkers and import merchants would probably favor free trade. The elderly have strong opinions about Social Security benefits. Most farmers support agricultural subsidies. Government considers the opinions of these and many more segments of society, and then it responds to those issues it deems significant in the political arena.

Second, interest in issues varies. Some issues, such as abortion, education reform, and capital punishment retain public interest for decades. Others, however, are as short-lived as fads or only important to a limited number of people (for instance, the citizens of a small town where a major factory is to be closed).

PUBLIC POLICY AND POLITICS • 421

1. Explain *public opinion* and *public policy*.
2. Distinguish between liberalism and conservatism.

Liberalism

The core belief of liberalism is the freedom of the individual. In the nineteenth century, liberals wanted government to protect the freedom of the individual. They believed that the state's primary role is to protect private property. Later, liberals added "freedom from want" to the freedoms that individuals should have and gave the government the role of protecting it.

Modern liberalism is usually a mix of the following three parts: (1) Reform liberalism, which recognizes the need to protect individuals from injustices. (2) Equality liberalism, which focuses on the state of the poor, sometimes going far beyond the biblical example. In fulfilling this role, the government often crowds out those who are better able to help the poor. (3) Freedom-from-morality liberalism, which directly opposes the government's biblical purpose to reward good and punish evil. This liberalism permits and protects evil and seeks to mitigate its consequences. Big-government liberalism is typically a combination of the three types of liberalism.

Today, it is necessary to distinguish "big-government liberals" from "classical liberals," who are now considered economic conservatives.

Current Events Display

Encourage students to bring articles from newspapers and magazines to post on a current events display. Discuss the issues of public concern mentioned in the articles and the public policies that result from that concern.

Types of Liberalism

Divide the students into groups to contrast possible biblical views in modern liberalism and classical liberalism.

The students should consult Exodus 20–23 to see what God permits a government to rule over.

Should a Christian Be a Conservative?

Certain types of conservatism and Christianity are similar. The Christian believes that in a fallen world no perfect system can be developed to alleviate the world's problems. He is therefore, like traditional conservatives, suspicious of utopian schemes. The Christian also believes that God graciously restrains sinfulness. There is much good and even wisdom in existing social structures. Thus, like the traditional conservative, the Christian desires to learn from traditions and opposes sweeping away existing culture to make way for proposed utopias. The Christian, however, should avoid idealizing the past; sin is a problem affecting every era. Both Christians and traditional conservatives believe in enduring moral norms, although the basis for those norms may be explained differently.

However, some forms of conservatism do not align with Christianity. Conservatives may seek to conserve traditions that are opposed to a biblical worldview. When *conservative* is used as a political label, it can describe a wide variety of policies and positions, many of which may not be Christian (or even traditionally conservative).

Neoconservatives

According to Republican journalist Irving Kristol, neoconservatism is not so much a movement as it is a persuasion. It began with the 1965 publication of *The Public Interest* by disenchanted liberals whom Kristol defined as "liberal[s] who [were] mugged by reality." Neoconservatism tends to accept the New Deal (but reject the Great Society), the idea of good and evil, and the need for a strong military capable of preemptive attacks.

President Franklin Roosevelt (center) signing legislation in 1934

Conservative or Liberal?

The terms *conservative* and *liberal* describe political ideologies. The following characterize these opposing viewpoints.

Conservatives tend to support

- lower taxes
- less government regulation of business
- reductions (or less rapid growth) in welfare programs
- increased spending for defense programs
- harsher penalties for crime

Liberals tend to support

- higher taxes
- more government regulation of business
- increased spending for welfare and other social programs
- more regulations regarding the environment
- greater protection for "diversity," including homosexuality

Liberalism and Conservatism

Frequently, public opinion—and the public policy that it helps create—can be categorized as either liberal or conservative. During the early twentieth century, the terms *liberalism* and *conservatism* acquired their modern political meanings. President Franklin Roosevelt added to individual freedom, a concept championed by nineteenth-century liberalism (also called classical liberalism), the vague promise of freedom from want. Since that time, liberals have also emphasized personal moral "freedoms," resulting in support for abortion rights, easy divorce, and redefinition of marriage. These "freedoms" have negative social consequences. Liberals often respond to issues by demanding extensive government intervention to deal with them. As a result, **liberalism** has come to refer to policies that favor government action and government expansion.

American conservatives remained influenced by classical liberalism's emphasis on individual freedom and the limits this emphasis places on government. As a result, **conservatism** often refers to a reluctance to expand government authority, especially if such expansion de-emphasizes individual responsibility.

Foundational to the conservative worldview are the twin ideas that human nature is always a mixture of good and evil and that societies must embrace moral standards. Consequently, conservatives tend to believe that government must exercise authority to restrain human wickedness; however, the government should itself be limited so that it does not trample individual freedoms.

Conservatives also value cultural traditions, including religious traditions. Because of their skepticism about the goodness of humans, conservatives tend to be suspicious of schemes to fix the world and respectful of the wisdom found in traditional ways of behaving and believing. But conservatives recognize that these traditions were formed by fallible people and thus are sometimes in need of reform.

Some politicians and other citizens prefer to call themselves **moderates** rather than liberals or conservatives. To some degree, the term *moderate* means whatever its bearer wants it to mean. Generally, moderates favor a middle ground between conservative and liberal positions.

Section Review

1–2. Define *public policy* and *public opinion*.

3–4. Identify two noteworthy characteristics of public opinion.

5–6. Explain the basic modern implications of the words *liberalism* and *conservatism*.

★ Define the term *moderate*. Evaluate the wisdom of holding moderate views in politics.

Liberals and Conservatives

Discuss the meanings of *liberalism* and *conservatism*, and note the basic attitudes of liberals and conservatives on several matters of current political interest.

Section Review Answers

1–2. Public policy consists of the plans adopted by the government to handle problems and accomplish goals. Public opinion consists of "those opinions held by private persons which governments find it prudent to heed." (p. 421)

3–4. Government does not gauge public opinion simply by determining the opinions of the average American, and some issues retain lasting interest, while others are short-lived. (p. 421)

5–6. Liberalism now refers to policies that favor government action and expansion. Conservatism generally refers to a reluctance to expand government authority, especially at the expense of individual responsibility. (p. 422)

★ To some degree, the term *moderate* means whatever its bearer wants it to mean. Generally, moderates favor a middle ground between conservative and liberal positions. For the second part of the question, some will criticize taking the "middle of the road" on issues and say moderates lack the fortitude to take firm stands. Other students may endorse taking a moderate position, noting that sometimes the liberal and conservative positions are both wrong.

II. Public Policy

Divisions

The Preamble of the Constitution outlines several goals of government—establishing justice, ensuring domestic tranquility, providing for the common defense, promoting the general welfare, and securing the blessings of liberty. These goals generally define the arena of public policy.

A more basic way of examining public policy is to divide it between domestic and foreign policy. **Domestic policy** frequently involves economics, law, education, health, energy, environment, and civil liberties within the nation's borders. **Foreign policy** includes diplomacy, trade relations, war, and other matters involving our relationship with other countries.

Development

The development of public policy is like a highway. Issues, like cars, can enter or exit the process at various stages, travel at different speeds, and stay for different lengths of time. Traffic constantly changes and the road is often difficult to navigate.

Issue Identification

Before public policy can be developed, government must identify which issues to deal with. Obviously, not every issue demands a response from government. You might have burned your toast this morning, but you would hardly ask the government to do something about it. On the other hand, if there were a sudden rash of burglaries in which household merchandise was being stolen, you might seek the assistance of local government by requesting more police patrols, stricter enforcement of laws, and stiffer penalties for convicted burglars.

Measured against the governments of Europe and Canada, the United States government is *comparatively* uninvolved in the private lives of its citizens. Nevertheless, since the Great Depression, the national government has become involved in many issues that were once handled by state or local governments, private organizations, or individuals. A growing number of Americans are looking to the national government to solve problems for them.

Christians acknowledge that God established government for particular functions. But government is not the only institution that God has ordained. When the state tries to do the work of the family, the church, or the local business, it hinders these other

1. How are domestic policy and foreign policy defined?
2. How is public policy developed and implemented?

When Should an Issue Become Public Policy?

An issue usually does not become public policy unless it meets the following criteria:

1. It affects a sizable portion of the public (i.e., it is *pervasive*).
2. It has a significant impact on the public (i.e., it is *extensive*).
3. It is perceived by the public as a problem that government has a constitutional responsibility to solve (i.e., it is *relative*).

1. Define *domestic policy* and *foreign policy*.
2. Describe how public policy is developed and implemented.

Social Policy

Public policy is made up of monetary and fiscal policy (both studied in economics) and social policy. Generally, the issues relating to social policy concern protection against risk and insecurity, promotion of equal opportunity, and assistance to the poor.

Social Security and Medicare for the elderly consume a huge portion of the budget. Educational policy issues are frequently discussed as a way to increase equal opportunities and to reduce assistance to the poor in the long term.

Overlapping Public Policy

Some matters related to domestic policy also affect foreign policy. Among these are international economics and the environment.

Activity 1: Today's Issues

This activity requires the students to identify major issues of domestic and foreign policy, distinguish between the conservative and liberal positions on these issues, and formulate biblical positions regarding them.

The President's Management Agenda

The president's management agenda details matters of current national interest regarding technology and work. As of 2020, these include modernization of the government's IT systems, data accountability, and the federal workforce.

institutions from functioning as they should. The government has the unique role of preventing injustice in the other institutions. It should also pass laws that help these institutions flourish. This means that the government will be involved in addressing societal problems. But ideally this involvement will be indirect and the various other institutions of society will be empowered to directly address the problems within their spheres of influence.

Agenda Setting

The issues that government decides to address are said to be on its **agenda**. The agenda reflects the relative importance of issues: some are at the top, and others are at the bottom. Often, the president outlines the government's agenda in his inaugural address and his annual State of the Union addresses, although other government branches also help establish the agenda. Depending on what issues the government targets, the agenda can be described as conservative or liberal.

President George W. Bush delivering a State of the Union address. Vice President Dick Cheney and Speaker of the House Nancy Pelosi are behind him.

Policy Formation

In the next phase, policy formation, government forms a response to a problem. In some cases, this response might be to do nothing at all, depending on the ideology of the party in power. Historically, the legislative branch of government has been most influential in policy formation. Much of the work is done in committees within Congress, such as the Committee on Agriculture, the Committee on Oversight and Government Reform, the Committee on Small Business, the Committee on Veterans' Affairs, and the Select Committee on Homeland Security. These and other committees help craft laws that become some of the most visible forms of public policy.

During the last century, both the executive and judicial branches of government have become more involved in creating public policy. Executive orders, treaties, and diplomatic agreements are instruments of the executive branch; likewise, court decisions shape public policy. For example, during the 1950s and 1960s, the Warren Court followed a course of judicial activism that has since been continued in many court decisions. Unlike the legislative and executive branches of government, the national judiciary does not answer directly to the people through elections. As a result, the courts can, to a considerable extent, ignore public opinion when they make public policy.

Implementation

After it is formed, public policy must be implemented by the executive branch and its bureaucracy—or, in the case of foreign policy, by the diplomatic corps or the military. Ideally, the policies implemented will help solve the problems facing the public. Many factors, however, can limit the success of a public-policy decision. For example, a decision might be sound in theory but unworkable in practice, or a court might declare a possible solution unconstitutional. Or, despite the soundness of a public-policy decision, the decision might involve an issue the government cannot resolve effectively.

 ### Agenda Setting and Policy Formation

Encourage the students to work individually or in groups to create a policy agenda for the school. Items should be listed in order of priority, from the most important to the least. Students should draft "bills" which could be passed into "law" (if the administration agrees). Instruct them to think through potential issues and problems which may arise and to devise solutions.

Optional: If the school adopts any of these agenda items, students should revisit the matter at a later time, comparing results that aligned and differed from the original plan.

Section Review

1–2. Identify the two broad categories of public policy.

3–5. What are three stages of public-policy development?

★ Contrast the involvement of the executive and judicial branches in public-policy development.

III. Public Opinion

Like the government's agenda, public opinion is linked to ideology. What people believe affects what they say and how they act. How their opinions form is as varied as their life stories.

Origins of and Influences on Opinion

Family

One of the most important influences on public opinion is the family. What people learn from their parents and home environments often helps establish who they are as adults. God designed the family to teach truth and shape coming generations (Prov. 1:8–9; 4:1–9). Sadly, the family has come under pressure from many directions. This can be seen in government policy and in the family's portrayal by entertainment media. Unfortunately, an enduring family of a father, mother, and children is becoming less common and less cherished.

Peers

Another factor in determining opinion is the influence of peers. Peers can be extremely influential on the views and conduct of young people, especially during the teen years. Scripture affirms the importance of choosing friends wisely to ensure positive peer influence (Prov. 13:20).

Events

Circumstances also contribute to how people think about public issues. An important national or international event can galvanize public opinion. For example, after the terrorist attacks of September 11, 2001, Americans were more willing to have their civil liberties curbed to ensure their safety.

Media

The types of information and entertainment provided by newspapers, magazines, radio, television, movies, the internet, and various social media and the amount of time devoted to those media greatly influence how one thinks about the world and public-policy issues. Popular entertainment often carries social or political messages, influencing public opinion. For example, television shows may promote the idea that casual sex is acceptable or that opposition to same-sex marriage is bigoted.

Hundreds of March for Our Lives rallies occurred on March 24, 2018. Participants (including those above in Washington, DC) called for stronger gun control laws.

Other Influences on Public Opinion

Schools and churches are not the only institutions that influence public opinion. Government can also have an influence. Many politicians, especially the president, receive a considerable amount of media coverage and work hard to put some kind of "spin" on stories and issues. Sometimes this is effective, and other times it is not.

The economic states of the country and of individuals create constantly shifting opinions as people's financial well-being shifts.

Interest groups with more money than others are able to advertise more, usually resulting in greater attention for their message.

What Does the Government Do with Public Opinion?

How does the government respond when elections and polls have taken place and the results have been determined? It may add items to its agenda or adjust policy. Sometimes the government does not do much with public opinion except to use it to shape those things that influence public perception.

Rejection of Early Influences

Already Gone by Ken Ham, Britt Beemer, and Todd Hillard showcases foundational reasons behind the movement of the younger generation of Americans who grow up in church and leave the faith.

Ben Shapiro (top) is a conservative political commentator. Protesters (above) at the University of California, Berkeley, denounced his September 2017 speech there. Both speeches and demonstrations contribute to shaping public opinion.

Institutions

School and church can occupy large portions of a young Christian's time. Because the vast majority of American youth attend public schools, those schools have a huge impact on children's opinions. Furthermore, surveys relating to political views and opinions of college professors repeatedly indicate that liberal bias is common at many American colleges.

The influence of religious groups in the United States is in flux. Mainline Protestant churches were once at the center of American civic life, but when many of these churches abandoned the gospel, their membership and influence began declining. Evangelical churches grew in political influence from the late 1970s to the first decade of the twenty-first century, but some observers are concerned that a lack of doctrinal and worldview instruction has led the next generation to hold only loosely to Christian doctrinal and ethical teachings. Many young people who grew up with a generally Christian background have abandoned distinctively Christian doctrine. In addition, the United States has grown diverse with religions such as Islam, Buddhism, and others. Greater numbers of Americans now identify themselves as nonreligious, preferring to ignore spiritual questions.

Scripture

When a person becomes a Christian, he becomes a new creature (2 Cor. 5:17). The Holy Spirit works in the believer's mind to increasingly conform his thinking to align with the mind of Christ. Through the Spirit's use of Scripture, Christian minds are renewed and transformed so they are increasingly not conformed to the thinking of the present age (Rom. 12:2). This transformation includes how Christians think about politics. This does not mean that Christians will agree about every political question. The Bible does not directly address every political issue, and wisdom is needed to apply the Bible's teaching to various matters. But the Bible does contain specifics about many ethical and moral issues. Furthermore, it provides guidance about the government's role and the manner in which Christians should engage in the political realm.

Public opinion is a reflection of people's values. As such, public opinion provides insight into the worldview of people on many issues.

Measuring Public Opinion

Elections

Because the people are the ultimate source of power in a democratic government, it is natural for government leaders to seek reliable measures of public opinion. For more than two hundred years, the primary expression of public opinion on political issues has been the ballot box. A winning candidate considers his victory an endorsement of his public record or his stand on issues. Although election results indicate the public's general attitude, they are limited as a tool for measuring public opinion.

Polls and Voting

Using one of the policy items created in the group activity on page 424, take a poll of student opinions on the matter. Write the issue, worded as a question, on Google Forms and include a place to choose "yes" or "no." Collect the results. Direct the students to assemble the data into a spreadsheet and create a graph of student choices. This class is one "public." Compare with other classes ("publics") if there is more than one section. If there is not another section, take the same poll among teachers and graph the results. Notice that different publics may have various opinions. If the school leadership is willing, take a vote of all students on the issue.

Perceptions

In the early twentieth century, political candidates and officeholders had to rely mainly on their own perceptions of public opinion. As they mingled with voters, they elicited opinions about matters of public interest. Officeholders also received letters and telegrams supporting or opposing certain government actions. And they read editorials and letters to editors in influential newspapers. Based on these opinions, candidates would develop campaign strategies and, if they were elected, make decisions about public policy. However, the development of reliable opinion polls during the middle to late decades of the twentieth century gave politicians a new and valuable, though imperfect, tool for measuring public opinion.

Opinion Polls and Surveys

Opinion polls (surveys of what the public thinks about particular subjects) were not unknown before the 1930s. Occasional polls were taken even in the 1800s, but they were usually unreliable. Among the first practitioners of scientific polling was George Gallup, who introduced a more rigorous sampling technique during his mother-in-law's 1932 campaign to become secretary of state of Iowa. The success of Gallup's methods in predicting the outcome of the Iowa election was followed by a similar success in the 1936 presidential election.

Today, the public is bombarded with statistics from political polls, particularly during election years. Besides independent pollsters, political candidates conduct their own surveys; presidential candidates now spend millions of dollars on polling alone. Why do candidates desire to know voters' major concerns, the percentage of blue-collar workers and minorities supporting them, or the public's perception of their honesty and leadership skills? Among other things, select polling information can be used as political propaganda, and polling data also alerts candidates to their own vulnerabilities and indicates how they can improve their campaigns.

In 1936, *Literary Digest* conducted a poll and used its findings to predict a victory for the Republican challenger, Alfred Landon, over Franklin Roosevelt in that year's presidential election. The magazine calculated that Landon would take thirty-two states with 370 electoral votes while FDR would win only sixteen states and 161 electoral votes. The actual outcome was a landslide victory for FDR. Landon lost his home state of Kansas and won only the electoral votes of Vermont and Maine.

Why was the *Literary Digest* poll so inaccurate? *Literary Digest* mailed ten million post cards to people, asking that they indicate their presidential preference; 2.4 million people responded. The *Digest*'s mistake was preparing its mailing list from telephone listings, automobile registrations, and its own list of subscribers. In 1936 the United States was in the depths of the Depression. Large numbers of Americans did not have telephones or cars—and FDR received greater support from people who did not own either. In the same election, George Gallup predicted the correct result by surveying a much smaller group—50,000 people. However, his survey group was a representative sample of the voters who participated in the election.

Modern pollsters often take their samples from lists of registered voters. Others further narrow their surveys to include those who are both registered and likely to vote. Scientific polls obtain a **representative sample** by polling voters from all regions, economic groups, political parties, and other major divisions

*George Gallup, pollster (top);
Alfred Landon (bottom)*

George Gallup

George Gallup (1901–84) earned a PhD in journalism; taught at Drake University, Northwestern University, and Columbia University; and worked for the advertising company Young & Rubicam of New York. While in New York, Gallup established the American Institute of Public Opinion (AIPO), which in 1935 successfully predicted the winner of the 1936 presidential election. Since its inception, the Gallup organization has rarely been incorrect in predicting a presidential election (1948 and 2012). To remain neutral and trustworthy, Gallup refused to vote once he began taking polls. He reasoned that his vote might persuade others to vote a certain way and that he could not expect others to tell him whom they voted for if he would not tell them whom he voted for.

Major Opinion Polls and Polling Organizations

Of the more than two hundred polls and polling organizations, the following are some of the major ones:

- Gallup, Inc.
- Pew Research Center for the People and the Press
- Rasmussen Poll
- Roper Center for Public Opinion Research

Activity 2: Opinions About Public Opinion

In this activity the students analyze the opinions of two presidents and relate these opinions to modern public opinion.

How Poll Accuracy Has Changed

The final Gallup Poll conducted before the 1948 presidential election showed Thomas Dewey defeating incumbent Harry Truman, 49.5 percent to 44.5 percent. But the actual voting result showed almost the reverse: Truman had 49.6 percent, and Dewey had 45.1 percent. Since that time, accuracy has tended to improve, especially when polls are taken close to elections.

The night before the 2016 election, poll averages showed Clinton with a lead over Trump of 46.8 percent to 43.6 percent, respectively. In the actual election, Clinton received 48.1 percent and Trump 46.1 percent of the popular vote. Because Trump won the electoral college, he won the presidency.

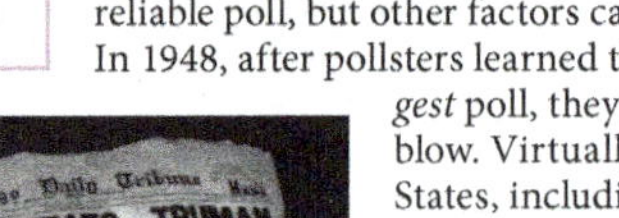

A sample public-opinion survey

Why People Vote as They Do

A person might vote for a candidate for several reasons, including the following:

1. Approving of the party platform
2. Disliking the opposing party's platform
3. Liking the candidate's personality
4. Family has always voted for that candidate's party

Harry Truman celebrates his upset victory over Thomas Dewey by displaying the *Chicago Daily Tribune's erroneous headline.*

in appropriate proportions so that surveys will represent the portion of the population expected to vote. Of course, no matter how carefully a survey sample is chosen, there will still be a margin of error.

Despite the *Literary Digest* fiasco, Americans often hear the results of unrepresentative polls. Informal polls, often called **straw polls**, do not attempt to use valid sampling techniques but are conducted for a variety of purposes, especially to liven up boring news stories. For instance, a television reporter may poll a few passersby on a street corner regarding their favorite sports teams, but if they are outside a stadium on game day, the result will be skewed. This shows that the types of businesses or churches nearby may cause more than a representative number of people from certain economic, ethnic, religious, or age groups to be polled, thus distorting the results of a survey.

Another kind of straw poll requires participants to call and register their opinions in response to a question posed on a television program or in a newspaper. In some cases, a viewer or reader must pay a fee for the call, and thus only those willing to pay are surveyed. Many internet news and opinion sites include straw polls. But these polls are limited to people who use the internet, and results reflect the type of people who visit that site. A conservative site tends to have conservative results, while a liberal site tends to have liberal results. Clearly, straw polls cannot be regarded as accurate reflections of public opinion.

Roadblocks to Measuring Public Opinion

Choosing a representative sample is necessary to ensure a reliable poll, but other factors can also reduce a poll's accuracy. In 1948, after pollsters learned the lessons of the *Literary Digest* poll, they suffered another humiliating blow. Virtually every major poll in the United States, including the Gallup Poll, predicted a victory for Thomas Dewey over Harry Truman in the presidential election. But to the pollsters' dismay, the voters disagreed. Several factors contributed to the polls' errors. One problem was many pollsters stopped surveying voters well before Election Day. The few polls taken during the weeks immediately before the November election indicated growing support for Truman. Later reports indicated that many voters did not make their decision until a few days before the election, and Truman apparently captured most of their votes. Pollsters learned that polls can be considered accurate only at the time the data is gathered.

Recent Opinions

Discuss opinion-poll indications and outcomes in recent elections. The election of 2016 between Trump and Clinton (or 2000 between Bush and Gore) lends itself particularly well to this, since the popular vote and the electoral college vote did not match.

In 2000, Gallup Polls showed voter opinions flip-flopping at least five times between the first week of August and the November presidential election. Results ranged from 39 percent for Al Gore and 55 percent for George W. Bush (Aug. 11–12) to 51 percent for Gore and 40 percent for Bush (Oct. 2–4). Shortly before the 2016 election, the vast majority of polls predicted a victory for Hillary Clinton. Instead, Donald Trump was elected president.

George W. Bush (left) *and Al Gore* (right) *were presidential candidates in 2000.*

The wording of questions and the conditions under which a poll is taken can affect a poll's reliability. A question that leads a participant to choose a particular answer is an inappropriate method for discovering public opinion. For instance, if a pollster asked, "Do you want to clean up the nation's polluted waters?" nearly everyone's response would be yes. However, the overwhelmingly positive reply to that question could not be used to imply that most Americans would support a particular piece of environmental legislation; nor would the reply indicate that they consider clean water a major public issue. Also, connotations of the words used in pollsters' questions can affect the outcome of a poll. For instance, in one survey 24 percent of those polled said that the nation was spending too little on "welfare," but 68 percent said that the nation was spending too little on "assistance to the poor."

Polling conditions can also affect poll results. Is the poll taken in person, by telephone, or in a written questionnaire? Often people are inclined to be more candid and truthful when they do not have to give their answers face to face. In addition, the manner or appearance of a pollster can affect participants' replies. For this reason, major polling operations use professional pollsters.

Although more than two hundred major polling organizations operate in the United States, polls are not a final authority on any public-policy issue. Polls merely reflect some features of the complex mosaic that is public opinion.

The Danger of Public Opinion

Government leaders have many reasons to consider public opinion and allow it to guide their policymaking decisions. Foremost is the fact that the public voted them into office and can vote them out again. Even so, government leaders understand that public opinion is far from infallible. In fact, it can be very fickle and, at times, completely misguided. A single misleading piece of evidence may lead the public to rush to judgment, or a demagogue may be able to stir popular emotions with charismatic appeals, as Adolf Hitler did in Germany.

Evidence of public opinion's instability is abundant. For example, airplane and factory accidents have resulted in public demands for greater security and improved safety standards; yet when government's attempts to meet these demands result in delays, increased costs, and bureaucratic inconveniences, public responses can shift from support to complaints. The public might praise a candidate's promises to increase aid for the poor, the elderly, and the disabled; but if the candidate is elected and keeps those promises, he might be criticized for raising the necessary taxes to support such programs. Obviously, politicians must follow public opinion cautiously. Making a wise but politically unpopular

What Makes a Good Survey?

Some surveys are better than others. The following are helpful tips to remember when writing poll questions:

- Ask very few open-ended questions, if any.
- Do not ask "leading" questions. Remain neutral.
- Balance the answer choices.
- Ask only one question at a time.
- Create a variety of questions.
- Make most questions optional so that people are not forced to answer questions they do not know or understand.
- Test the survey before using it.

Student Survey

Invite the students to develop poll questions concerning opinions on current political issues. Analyze the wording of the questions, and discuss the basic requirements for obtaining significant survey results with these questions (see the side margin note on this page).

Encourage the students to use the poll questions to survey opinion on current political issues. For example, students may interview people in different age brackets, equal numbers of men and women, or only those people who are registered voters.

1. Identify the purposes of interest groups.

2. Distinguish between the various types of interest groups.

3. Describe the activities of interest groups.

Interest Group Formation

Interest groups form when there is action that could and potentially should be taken to solve some type of problem, but an individual cannot take the action alone. For example, a homeowner could build a driveway but not a highway. Purpose-driven groups, such as those formed during the civil rights movement, exist for the intended result of solving societal problems.

Pontius Pilate (left)

decision is better than making a bad decision dictated by a volatile public. A good example of the danger of following public opinion is Pontius Pilate who, despite his own better judgment, allowed the roar of the crowds to sway him to crucify Jesus Christ.

Unfortunately, politicians are not the only ones who allow ill-informed opinions to influence their actions. Christians must constantly be wary of violating scriptural convictions to please others. (See John 12:42–43.)

America's representative government was designed to allow government leaders to make decisions contrary to public opinion if doing so in the interest of the public good. Thus, while elected officials should respond to public opinion, they also ought to weigh the merits of their decisions beforehand. Ideally, this foresight will prompt them to act in the public interest regardless of pressure by current public opinion.

Section Review

1–6. What are six areas of life that influence our opinions?

7. According to Romans 12:2, how should a Christian's opinions be formed?

8. What importance does a representative sample have for an opinion poll?

9. Why is the wording of an opinion-poll question significant?

★ Why should politicians be wary of public opinion?

Guiding Questions

1. What are the purposes of interest groups?

2. What major types of interest groups exist?

3. In what activities do interest groups participate?

IV. Interest Groups

Sharing their views with pollsters is not the only way that Americans can express their opinions to government leaders. Citizens who hold similar opinions can also form **interest groups** (also called pressure groups) to influence government officials and the public about a political issue or group of issues.

Purposes

Interest groups have long been a pervasive force in American society. Farmers' organizations, merchants' groups, consumer-protection lobbies, and other such groups have sprung up, often as grass-roots movements, to eventually wield considerable political power.

Nevertheless, interest groups are not political parties because their scope of activity is narrower. Their concerns often focus on one major area—such as business or trade laws, gun control (or gun rights), agricultural policies, or benefits for the aged—whereas political parties must be concerned with *all* aspects of public policy. (No single-issue political party has ever been successful in electing national officeholders.) In general, interest groups are more concerned with influencing governmental policies than with electing particular candidates.

During the twentieth century, interest groups increased in both power and number. This change was partially a result of political parties' decline, as well as several other factors. With the growth of governmental power, more groups organized to influence governmental policies. Improved communication and transportation also allowed people to associate more easily and to reach the public, media, and politicians with their message. Increased education and affluence

---

Fickle Public

Discuss the dangers of developing public policy based on public opinion. Remind the students that the Founding Fathers avoided making the United States a pure democracy because of this concern. Discuss whether their concern was biblical. Note the biblical teaching that rulers need wisdom (Prov. 8:15–17) and that the majority of people do not seek it (Matt. 7:13).

Section Review Answers

1–6. family, peers, events, media, institutions, and Scripture (pp. 425–26)

7. The Holy Spirit's renewing of a Christian's mind will transform that person's ideas about politics, aligning them in accordance with scriptural principles. (p. 426)

8. A representative sample will survey appropriate proportions of citizens in order to yield reliable information about the target group. (pp. 427–28)

9. Different wordings might lead people to particular responses, especially if the question is vague or uses terms that have strong connotations. (p. 429)

★ Politicians must be careful because public opinion can change quickly or be based on incorrect information. Furthermore, just because the majority of people favor something does not mean that it is the correct action to take.

have provided the time and resources that citizens need to address their political concerns.

Interest groups both help and hinder our political system. Many provide valuable expertise and information (such as studies and data) to government officials regarding the products or positions they support. However, sometimes the information provided is inaccurate or misleading; for example, over many years groups that represented the tobacco industry and tobacco farmers tried to convince Congress that smoking was not a substantive health risk.

Christians may rightfully participate in interest groups that have proper goals and methods. Political participation is a freedom to be exercised. Even James Madison, who saw the danger of factions (which would include political parties and interest groups), supported their existence. To abolish them completely, he recognized, would be to undermine liberty as expressed in the First Amendment: "the right of the people peaceably to assemble, and to petition the government for a redress of grievances."

Kinds of Interest Groups

The nation's interest groups are countless, ranging from small community parent-teacher organizations interested in improving local schools to nationwide organizations with millions of members, such as the American Association of Retired Persons (AARP). The variety of these groups makes classifying them difficult. However, many interest groups can be organized under the following major headings.

Economic Groups

Since the late nineteenth century, business associations have dominated the interest-group landscape. Many arose in response to the growing power of labor unions and the increase of government regulation. Today, approximately 70 percent of interest groups represented in Washington are business associations or trade organizations. Among the most powerful are the National Association of Realtors, the United States Chamber of Commerce, and the National Federation of Independent Business. With the resources available to them, business interest groups can exert pressure that might seem overwhelming. Nevertheless, conflicts among these groups tend to reduce their influence.

Labor unions are also economic interest groups. Workers in various fields have created associations that seek economic benefits and better working conditions for their members. Democrats have traditionally enjoyed the support of labor unions and often rely on that support. The **AFL-CIO**, the largest labor organization, has over twelve million members in its affiliated unions; and despite declining membership since the mid-twentieth century, unions remain powerful voices in American politics.

Such professionals as doctors, lawyers, accountants, and teachers have formed organizations. The American

Labor union march on the Brooklyn Bridge in New York City

The AFL-CIO

Samuel Gompers established the American Federation of Labor (AFL) in 1886 to protect skilled laborers. In 1935, John L. Lewis created the Committee for Industrial Organization (CIO) to organize labor, whether skilled or unskilled. The CIO originally consisted of a few AFL union leaders. Because of disagreements, however, relations between the two organizations deteriorated, and these ties dissolved when the AFL expelled the CIO unions in 1936. In 1938, the CIO became the Congress of Industrial Organizations. During World War II, the AFL and the CIO began to work together for the good of all workers and finally merged in 1955 to form the AFL-CIO.

Christian Involvement

Note that a Christian must be careful not to join a group whose positions or methods are contrary to scriptural principles (2 Cor. 6:14–18).

Interest Groups

Direct the students to investigate local interest groups or interest groups that friends or relatives belong to. Instruct them to record the purpose, positions, goals, and activities of these groups.

NRA

The National Rifle Association (NRA) was founded in 1871 in New York by two veterans who were disappointed at the lack of shooting skills their troops exhibited during the Civil War. The association's first president was Union General Ambrose Burnside.

Opposition to the NRA from the very beginning forced the group to move to New Jersey the next year. Rapid expansion then pushed them to Ohio.

Before World War II, the NRA formed the Legislative Affairs Division to deal with situations it perceived as attacks on the Second Amendment. In 1940, the NRA helped to rearm Great Britain against the threat of Nazi invasion, since the British had passed a series of gun-control laws between the world wars that had taken away most guns in the country. In 1949, the NRA began offering hunter-education courses.

Today, the NRA's many certified instructors train many gun owners each year. It conducts the Eddie Eagle GunSafe® Program for children in preschool through fourth grade, using the slogan "STOP. DON'T TOUCH. RUN AWAY. TELL A GROWNUP." The NRA also publishes several magazines, including *American Hunter* and *American Rifleman*.

A National Institutes of Health official speaks at an AMA conference.

Medical Association (AMA) is one of the most powerful of these interest groups. The Motion Picture Association of America, the Independent Insurance Agents & Brokers of America, the National Education Association, and the American Bar Association are other professional organizations. People involved in agriculture also have organizations that speak to the government on their behalf. Among them are the American Farm Bureau Federation, the US Cattlemen's Association, and the National Cotton Council of America.

Social Groups

Other interest groups focus on social issues. Most of these organizations perform a variety of functions, including providing benefits for their members, but they also attempt to influence government. One of the largest of these groups, mentioned earlier, is AARP. Among its chief concerns are health and welfare topics, such as low-cost medication and defending the Social Security system. Interest groups such as the Council for Exceptional Children represent children and youth with disabilities as well as those that are gifted. The Sierra Club and Greenpeace concern themselves with environmental policy. People for the Ethical Treatment of Animals (PETA) supports an animal-rights agenda that many consider to be radical.

Several civil-rights interest groups were formed during the 1960s and 1970s. Highly visible is the National Organization for Women (NOW). Civil-rights interest groups often try to increase their influence by taking an inclusive title. For instance, NOW tries to portray itself as representative of all women. However, its membership (according to the group's estimate) is about 500,000 members—of the more than 170 million females in the United States. Concerned Women for America (CWA) has about the same number of members as NOW; however, CWA embraces traditional, conservative values while NOW is known for its support of liberal causes.

Sierra Club rally

Single-Issue Interest Groups

Although many interest groups have a wide range of concerns, many others are **single-issue interest groups** concerned with a particular issue, such as abortion or gun control. For example, the National Right to Life Committee is well known for its support of pro-life legislation. The **National Rifle Association (NRA)**, one of the best known and most influential interest groups in the country, supports gun rights, promotes gun safety, and

Interest Group Debate

Divide the students into groups based on whether they think interest groups are good or bad for America. Allow a few minutes for students from each viewpoint to state the reasons behind their choices. Try to involve as many participants as possible so that a variety of reasons are presented. Encourage students to change sides at any time if they are persuaded.

Students who think interest groups are good for America might state that if there are enough of these groups they would compete, ending up with thoughtful compromise in legislation. Since elections are spread out over time, there is also more potential political participation when citizens are involved in interest groups.

Those who are against interest groups may state that some groups are too powerful for others to have much influence. Groups with more money might crowd out those with less.

opposes almost all gun control legislation. NARAL Pro-Choice America, formerly know as the National Abortion Rights Action League (NARAL), opposes restrictions on abortion.

Religious and Ideological Groups

As American culture increasingly fragments, organizations arise to support various religious and ideological beliefs. In the 1980s the Moral Majority, composed largely of religious conservatives, helped Ronald Reagan win the White House twice. Another conservative group, the Christian Coalition, helped Republicans gain control of the House and the Senate during the 1990s. Not all Christians or conservatives would identify with these groups, and not all religious groups reflect Christian or conservative values. For instance, the Council for Secular Humanism and other anti-Christian organizations have staged marches in Washington, DC.

Other ideological groups include Americans for Democratic Action (ADA). That group has worked consistently for abortion rights, lesbian and gay rights, and the removal of Christian influence in public life. People for the American Way also supports both an anti-Christian and an anti-conservative agenda. The Heritage Foundation is a well-known think tank that embraces conservative causes.

Civic Groups

Other interest groups operate to further some civic cause or responsibility. For instance, the League of Women Voters promotes greater public participation in elections. Common Cause supports a variety of causes, including government reform. The Family Research Council (FRC) and the American Family Association (AFA) promote topics of vital interest to traditional families.

Interest Groups' Activities

Interest groups use a variety of techniques to influence public policy. Those that support issues with widespread public acceptance might use highly visible tactics, while those that support issues less favored by the public might be more discreet while working to change public opinion.

Lobbying

One important tactic is **lobbying** (the attempt to influence public officials to support a special interest). Large interest groups often maintain a staff in Washington, DC, to compile information and chart strategies designed to win the support of members of Congress. The lobbyists who present the information to the lawmakers, either in personal conversations or in meetings with congressional committees, are usually experienced lawyers or former officeholders who can gain the attention of policymakers.

Many supporters and opponents of gun control legislation are active members of interest groups.

Senator James Inhofe (R-OK) addressing the Values Voter Summit, an annual meeting sponsored by the Family Research Council (FRC).

K Street in Washington, DC, has been home to numerous national lobbying firms.

Think Tank

A think tank is a body of experts providing advice on specific political or economic problems. These groups gather information on and evidence about these issues and create proposed solutions.

Iron Triangle

The term *iron triangle* is sometimes used when interest groups work together with Congress and the bureaucracy. Congress and bureaucrats rely on the information given by these groups. Large interest groups generally have more money to spend on this kind of research than a government agency would. Congress may then pass laws that bureaucracies enforce. In this way, interest groups influence the passing of legislation in their interest and even at times write bills that become laws.

Outsider Lobbying

Certain interest groups focus on influencing the public rather than influencing government. This is often called "grassroots lobbying." These groups tend to advertise, organize protests, and push members to contact officials.

Influences on Ideologies

Guide a discussion about how students' own family, gender, educational background, and political experience may cause them to tend toward certain interest groups. Are their parents involved with any interest groups? What types of interest groups are the students interested in?

Harry and Louise

When President Clinton tried to push through his healthcare reform plan, the Health Insurance Association of America ran expensive ads for about a year featuring a couple named Harry and Louise. These ads are credited with helping to prevent Clinton's plan from passing into law.

Protecting Trees

Julia "Butterfly" Hill spent 738 days (more than two years) from 1997 to 1999 in a giant redwood, which she called Luna, to prevent it from being cut down. She came down after an agreement was reached to protect the tree and donate money to forestry research. Not all tree activists have fared well. In 2002, twenty-two-year-old Beth O'Brien died after falling from a tree in which she was protesting.

For many years, lobbyists invited members of Congress to expensive restaurants for meals or asked them to speak at meetings of the lobbyist's organization in return for generous compensation. Large monetary gifts, goods, and payments for expensive trips and entertainment were common. Some critics declared these practices were little better than bribery, although members of Congress regularly insisted that they remained unswayed by such actions. Recent national legislation has curtailed such perks. Today, members of the House and Senate are limited to accepting gifts, including meals, less than $50 in value. However, many states still allow state and local lawmakers to receive gifts and money in much larger amounts than the federal limit.

Public Persuasion

In addition to lobbying public officials, interest groups may try to attract public support for their causes and then use that support to influence officials. Groups might use media appearances and advertisements to sway public opinion, or they might send newsletters or direct-mail advertising to citizens. Most interest groups now have websites and make extensive use of the internet, especially social media; some groups even produce "report cards" that grade the voting records of individual politicians on issues that are important to those groups. Interest groups also encourage citizens to contact their representatives personally and support or oppose a particular piece of legislation.

Protests and Rallies

Organizing picket lines, sit-ins, marches, and other forms of protest might form an advantageous strategy for some interest groups. For example, environmentalists have engaged in sit-ins high up in trees to prevent loggers from cutting

down those trees. In 1999 a conglomeration of interest groups, some with violent agendas, staged numerous protests, both in the United States and abroad, against the World Trade Organization. The most famous of those protests occurred in Seattle, Washington.

The August 1963 March on Washington, DC, by more than two hundred thousand people seeking improved civil rights for blacks, was organized as a peaceful protest by groups that included the National Association for the Advancement of Colored People (NAACP), the Congress of Racial Equality (CORE), and the Southern Christian Leadership Conference (SCLC). Martin Luther King's "I Have a Dream" speech, delivered at that event, became one of the most famous in American history. The March helped bring the passage of the Civil Rights Act the following year.

Martin Luther King Jr. delivered his most famous speech at the March on Washington in August 1963.

Involvement in Political Action Committees

Another political activity of interest groups is involvement in political campaigns. The groups usually establish **political action committees (PACs)** to work on behalf of candidates whom the groups deem favorable to their goals. PACs not only enlist campaign workers but also make monetary contributions to the

---

Harry and Louise

Show a clip of a Harry and Louise ad that was run during the Clinton administration. What was the intent of the ad? Discuss the possible effects on the public. Divide students into small groups and instruct them to jot down ideas about a matter of current public interest and to film a thirty-second video influencing the public to believe a certain point of view about the issue. Allow time to present and evaluate the videos.

Activity 3: Contacting Public Officials

In this activity students learn how to contact lawmakers.

"I Have a Dream" Speech

Direct the students to locate and watch King's "I Have a Dream" speech. Instruct them to evaluate the last five minutes in particular. Ask what they notice about King's powers of persuasion. How was this method of protest eventually successful?

PAC Money

Discuss the effect of PAC money on campaigns, and point out that good candidates might be reluctant to enter a race in which an incumbent has considerable PAC support.

campaigns themselves. Most PAC money goes to incumbents for two reasons: interest groups have greater access to politicians already in office, and the money might help win support on issues that arise before, as well as after, an election. Even incumbents who have only token or no opponents in a reelection campaign might receive thousands of dollars in PAC money for their campaigns. Large PAC contributions to incumbents discourage possible challengers. Obviously, interest groups intend these contributions to promote the reelection of an incumbent and hold him sympathetic to their political opinions.

At one time, members of Congress were allowed to keep unspent campaign funds for personal purposes. Beginning in 1980, Congress passed laws to phase out and eventually ban this practice. Today, excess funds must be transferred to the campaigns of other candidates, given to a political party, or donated to charities. However, regulations vary widely in each state regarding excess campaign funds raised in state and local races. In some cases, personal use is still allowed.

Court Action

Some interest groups focus their efforts on the judiciary by advocating positions in court cases important to their causes. Most visible of these groups is the **American Civil Liberties Union (ACLU)**, which has chapters in every state. In the name of civil liberty, the organization champions diverse causes such as free speech, abortion rights, legalization of marijuana, abolition of the death penalty, and antidiscrimination. Though the ACLU usually supports causes embraced by liberalism, in some cases it has aligned with conservative issues. It attempts to ban prayer in schools or at school functions, the public display of religious symbols, and Christian Christmas displays on public property. The American Center for Law and Justice (ACLJ), the Alliance Defending Freedom (ADF), and Liberty Counsel are three of the conservative legal groups that have argued cases to protect the First Amendment rights of religious conservatives and have opposed most of the positions supported by the ACLU.

In some court cases, an interest group might act as an **amicus curiae**, or "friend of the court" (amici curiae, the plural). Although not a party in a case, an amicus curiae may testify or file briefs in an attempt to influence a court's decision. Obviously, some court cases have implications far beyond the matters at hand and might set legal precedents affecting an interest group's position.

Although interest groups wield considerable power, there are counteracting factors. First, voters can replace elected leaders when those officials blatantly ignore the interests of their constituents. Second, for every interest group, there is probably another group working just as hard to gain support for the opposite position. Thus, elected officials often allow all sides to present their views before making a decision on a public issue.

A "friend of the court" brief filed by the ACLU

Section Review

1–2. What is an interest group? What is another name for an interest group?

3–7. Identify five major kinds of interest groups, and give an example of each.

8. Define *amicus curiae*.

★ Interest groups use a variety of activities to influence public policy. Explain one of these.

Section Review Answers

1–2. a group sharing a similar opinion about a political issue or group of issues and uniting to further their views; pressure group (p. 430)

3–7. Examples may include the following: (a) economic—US Chamber of Commerce, (b) social—AARP, (c) single-issue interest—NRA, (d) religious and ideological—Moral Majority, and (e) civic—League of Women Voters. (pp. 431–33)

8. an individual or group that testifies or files legal briefs as a "friend of the court" to influence a court's decision (p. 435)

★ Interest groups can influence public policy through lobbying; the media; direct mailings; protests and rallies; campaign involvement, especially through political action committees (PACs); and court action. Explanations will vary.

1. Evaluate the major types of media that shape public opinion.
2. Summarize the powers and the limitations of media.
3. Evaluate how politicians use media.
4. Describe the impact of media propaganda.

Colonial American Newspapers

In 1690, Benjamin Harris published one issue of a newspaper in Boston, but he was forced to stop because he did not obtain the proper license from the governor and because he criticized British treatment of French prisoners in the French and Indian War. In 1704, Boston postmaster John Campbell published the first continuous newspaper, the *Boston News-Letter*, which had governor approval and ran until the War for Independence began. Two weekly newspapers began in 1719: the *Boston Gazette* and Philadelphia's *American Weekly Mercury*. James Franklin established the *New England Courant* in 1721, and his brother Benjamin Franklin (after running away from his apprenticeship under James) published the *Pennsylvania Gazette* beginning in 1729.

Who Uses Newspapers Today?

Most television and internet sources rely heavily on newspapers to give them pertinent stories. About 7 percent of Americans claim to read newspapers as their main source of news. Educational elites tend to use newspapers as their method of obtaining news coverage rather than using other available broadcast or online sources.

Guiding Questions

1. What are the major types of media that shape public opinion?
2. What are the powers and limitations of the media?
3. How effectively do politicians use media?
4. What is the impact of media propaganda?

V. Mass Media

In Chapter 16 we discussed the impact of media on the decline of political parties. In Chapter 17 we discussed its impact on campaigning. In this section, we will focus on mass media's influence on public policy and politics.

Politicians and interest groups use **mass media** to their advantage as they seek to gain public support. Their messages can reach thousands—even millions—of potential voters through radio, television, newspapers, magazines, the internet, and social media. But the media, by exercising its influence, helps create public policy.

America's first newspaper, the Boston News-Letter

Major Types of Media
Newspapers

America's oldest form of mass media is the newspaper. John Campbell launched what could be called the first American newspaper in 1704 with his *Boston News-Letter*, but colonial papers had small circulations and narrow business interests. In the years before the War for Independence, newspapers began to cover issues related to American dissatisfaction with the British government, but circulations remained low.

During the early national period, newspapers were usually mouthpieces of major parties. For instance, the *Gazette of the United States* promoted the Federalist position, and the *National Gazette* espoused Democratic-Republican views. The era of the partisan paper reached its heyday during the Jackson presidency (1829–37). Several newspaper editors actually became part of Jackson's administration. By the 1830s, newspapers began pursuing a mass audience. Copies of the *New York Sun* sold for a penny, giving rise to the name *penny press*. Penny-press papers emphasized emotional and dramatic stories that might appeal to the less educated reader. In 1841 the *New-York Tribune* became the first national paper when it started distribution in the Midwest and West. During the Civil War, readers eager for war news boosted circulation of the *New York Herald* to one hundred thousand.

Through the late nineteenth and early twentieth centuries, newspapers covered social issues, often with considerable sensationalism. At the same time, they also tried to increase circulation by giving the impression of objectivity (i.e., that they had no connection with any party or interest group). By and large, major media have attempted to maintain this impression to the present, although charges of media bias are common and often justified.

During the twentieth century, many printing improvements were made, including the ability to print photographs in color. Satellite technology permitted large daily newspapers to distribute issues more quickly by printing them at regional distribution centers rather than at a central location. Today, some of the US newspapers with the largest circulation, or number of readers, are *USA Today*, the *New York Times*, the *Wall Street Journal*, and the *Washington Post*.

In the News

Encourage the students to analyze the news presented in telecasts, newspapers, and news magazines, preferably all from the same period of time but by different news outlets. Instruct the students to list the subjects and lengths of the major stories or articles and any obvious slant to the news. They should also observe reporters' body language (e.g., a raised eyebrow, nod or shake of the head, sneer, or frown). Instruct the students to compare the findings from each of the sources.

The influence of newspapers eroded as new forms of media technology emerged. This was partly due to newspapers being unable to match the speed of radio, television, or the internet in breaking news. Neither can newspapers compete with the visual appeal of television or the internet. As a result, the number of newspaper readers has declined over the past few decades. Many newspapers dramatically reduced staff or have ceased publication.

Radio

Within ten years of Guglielmo Marconi's 1895 invention of the radio, amateur radio operators had moved beyond transmitting Morse-code signals to sending words and music. Commercial radio originated in 1920 when KDKA Pittsburgh began broadcasting. The radio's usefulness in politics soon became apparent when that station relayed the results of the 1920 presidential election, in which Warren G. Harding and Calvin Coolidge triumphed over James Cox and Franklin Roosevelt.

By 1933 two-thirds of American homes had radios, and radio broadcasts had become part of American life. People increasingly relied on the radio for news as well as entertainment. Throughout the Depression and World War II, President Franklin Roosevelt reassured the nation with radio broadcasts known as fireside chats. Presidents have continued to use radio since that time.

Today, there are thousands of radio stations operating in the United States. National Public Radio (NPR), which was formed in 1970, acts as a major source of news and arts programming. NPR provides its programs for more than one thousand public radio stations across the country. Although the quality of its news coverage is good, some critics argue that its viewpoint leans toward the left on the political spectrum.

In the late 1980s conservatives launched commercial talk-radio programs. The number of such programs grew quickly over the decades that followed. Among the most popular hosts were Rush Limbaugh, Sean Hannity, and Laura Ingraham.

Radio offers advantages over other forms of media. First, radio programs are easily accessible, and people can listen while driving or engaged in another activity. Second, radio programs are much cheaper to broadcast than television programs. Third, radio often offers listeners a degree of interaction. For example, many programs allow listeners to call program hosts and express their views while remaining relatively anonymous.

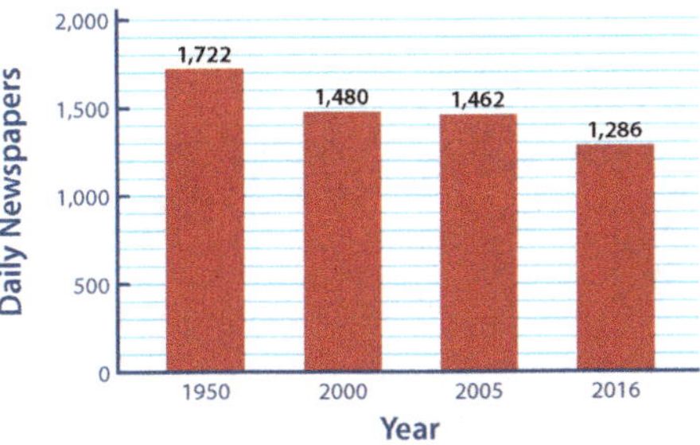

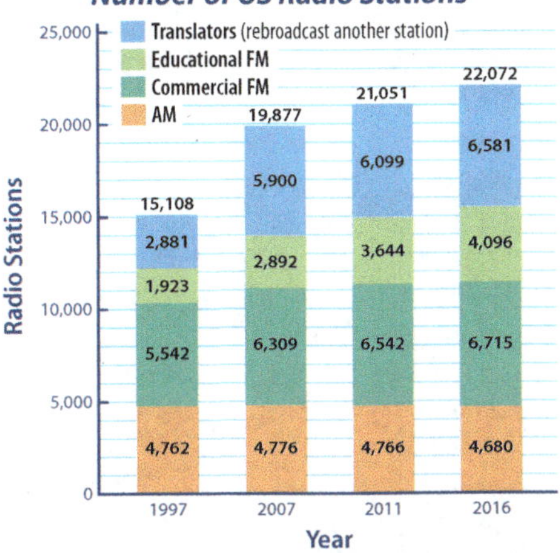

Rush Limbaugh

Christians and Talk Radio

Because many talk-radio hosts are sympathetic to Judeo-Christian values, they have attracted a large Christian audience. However, many of these hosts are not born again, and their worldviews may be inconsistent with a biblical worldview. Therefore, Christians need to use caution when listening to radio programs. Christians also need to be cautious about the spirit of some talk radio. Peter reminded believers to respond to others with meekness and respect (1 Pet. 3:14–15). And Paul reminded Titus to teach believers to be gentle, not quarrelsome (Titus 3:1–2). Talk radio that does not foster this kind of spirit can be harmful to growing in Christlikeness.

Who Uses Radio Today?

While radio has been largely displaced by television, it is still quite useful in the field of politics. Certain stations, especially those carrying conservative talk shows, cater to certain niche groups. About 14 percent of Americans use radio as their main source of news information.

Reading Graphs

Request students to analyze the graph of the number of radio stations on this page in the Student Edition and ask the following questions: Which category of stations remains basically the same? Which category has expanded the most? Why do you think this growth has occurred?

Educational Radio

Listen as a class to brief examples of educational radio.

Who Uses Television Today?

While the percentage of Americans viewing news online is increasing, as of December 2018, television still led all media at 44 percent as the preferred method of obtaining news.

Who Uses the Internet and Social Media Today?

Approximately 34 percent of Americans gather news primarily from the internet and social media. Of course, there is much overlap in where people get news, such as when an individual reads a newspaper article on that newspaper's website or watches an online video of a news broadcast.

Advantages and Disadvantages of Online News Sources

There are certain advantages to using the internet and social media for news. The internet can keep pace with constantly changing stories. It can be updated almost immediately. Internet (as well as radio and some television) information is generally free as opposed to newspapers.

However, social media sources may often be blatantly biased toward one viewpoint or another. The ability of the internet to update quickly may push news outlets to create more stories, leading to the possibility that stories may be less informative and more sensational because of the need to stay ahead of competitors and keep audience attention. News may be advanced or withheld based on the likely audience and the desired response of those who see it.

Television

Although the television was introduced at New York City's World's Fair in 1939, not until after World War II did improvements in technology and a rise in household income make it commercially viable. In just a few years three major networks dominated the airwaves—CBS, NBC, and ABC. Besides entertainment, the networks eventually brought the nightly news into homes. The nation witnessed on television such events as the Cuban missile crisis, the Vietnam War, civil-rights demonstrations, race riots in major cities, and men walking on the moon. With so many Americans relying on only a few sources of information, the major television networks quickly gained enormous power to influence opinions.

That power continues today, though somewhat diluted by the rise of cable television and the internet. Alternative networks, such as Cable News Network (CNN) and Fox News, now compete for ratings with the network giants. Another alternative to major networks' coverage of politics is **C-SPAN**, a public-service network created by the American cable-television industry. One of the network's goals is to provide the public with coverage of House and Senate proceedings "without editing, commentary or analysis and with a balanced presentation of points of view."

Television's primary advantage over other forms of media is its ability to break into regular programming and deliver news quickly with images and action. Critics of television news argue that its images sometimes appeal to emotions more than to intellect. They also note that television tends to reduce news to sound bites (brief snippets of information). While doing so allows more news to be presented between commercials, the coverage sometimes provides misinformation or oversimplifies complex issues.

The CNN headquarters is in Atlanta, Georgia (top). C-SPAN busses (above), with their mobile studios, have toured the country since 1993.

The Internet and Social Media

In the 1990s internet usage grew rapidly, and websites of every conceivable nature appeared alongside advancements in communication technology. Newspaper, radio, and television news outlets later created online versions of their publications and programs to tap this market. Government at all levels soon used the internet to reach the public. For instance, the White House, the House of Representatives, and the Senate all developed websites, as did such governmental agencies as the Library of Congress, the National Archives, and the National Park Service.

In addition, the internet and social media can be used to target specific groups of potential voters. Political campaigns use both to spread political statements. They allow for rapid responses to opposing campaigns' messaging and

Overlapping News Sources

Choose a current news story and direct the students to find the same story on as many sites as possible. Can it be found in newspapers? on the radio? on television? on the internet? on social media? Are there differences or are the stories the same? Take a straw poll of which form of media the students would most likely use if looking up the news story outside of class.

free a candidate from the restriction of press releases or formal statements that may be filtered by the press. Both also hold politicians accountable because they provide instant access to scores of previous speeches and statements. However, as is true of other forms of mass media, they can disperse inaccurate information.

Powers and Limits
Legal Rights

The First Amendment guarantees freedom of the press and thereby gives the media power to print or broadcast information without fear of government reprisal. This guarantee helps protect the media from government control or censorship that could allow officials to suppress information that they do not want made public. For instance, the *Washington Post* first uncovered the Watergate scandal, which eventually led to the resignation of President Nixon. Without freedom of the press, Nixon's wrongdoing might never have been revealed.

Thus, American media enjoys freedoms that are almost unparalleled elsewhere in the world, including the freedom from **prior restraint**. This freedom means that the government cannot review and censor information before

This political cartoon shows President Nixon, during the Watergate scandal, tangled in a spider's web of recording tapes.

Political Cartoons

Probably the most concise language in the world is that of political cartooning. The best political cartoons combine art, humor, satire, and a pointed political message.

Political cartoons have been drawn in America for more than two centuries. However, political cartoons did not become a regular part of the daily newspaper until the late nineteenth century, when print technology made cartoon reproduction fast and inexpensive. Today, political cartoons are a standard feature of the nation's newspapers. Some newspaper subscribers look at the editorial cartoon before reading the paper.

With the expansion of media, political cartoons have become common on the internet and in social media.

Interpreting political cartoons requires an understanding of a few of their basic characteristics. Caricature (exaggerating certain features of a subject) often distinguishes figures in a drawing and sometimes makes a statement about a person. Symbols, too, are an important part of political cartooning. Some of the more common ones include a star-spangled "Uncle Sam," who represents the United States, and a donkey and an elephant, which symbolize the Democratic and Republican Parties, respectively. What an artist cannot convey through caricature or symbolism, he conveys through labels and captions.

Although political cartoons can be a powerful political force, cartoons, by nature, are limited. Even the best cartoons can usually express only one idea forcefully, and none can examine a complex issue in detail. And, of course, political cartoons reflect the political prejudices of their creators.

The decline of newspaper numbers and the quickness by some readers to take offense have contributed to the publication of fewer political cartoons.

Deep Throat

The Watergate scandal produced one of America's best-kept journalistic secrets—the identity of Bob Woodward's anonymous source, Deep Throat. Woodward and his partner, Carl Bernstein, reporters for the *Washington Post*, wrote a series of articles about the Watergate scandal in which they cited an anonymous source who had an important government position. Woodward kept his promise not to reveal his source's identity unless Deep Throat gave him permission to reveal his identity or died. Many theories arose in this silence—informants at the FBI, the CIA, or the White House among the most popular—identifying anyone from Alexander Haig to Henry Kissinger as Deep Throat. Despite the books and articles that claimed to identify Deep Throat, no one could be sure until Woodward revealed his source. In 2005, an ailing W. Mark Felt, former deputy director of the FBI, claimed to be Deep Throat. Within hours of his confession, the *Washington Post* confirmed his claim. He died in 2008.

Some Famous Editorial Cartoonists

Some famous editorial cartoonists are Thomas Nast, famous for exposing the corruption of Boss Tweed and Tammany Hall; Bill Mauldin with his World War II GI characters Willy and Joe; and Theodor Geisel, better known today as Dr. Seuss. More recent political cartoonists include Herbert Block, better known by his signature—Herblock; Jeff MacNelly, who wrote the *Shoe* comic strip; and conservative cartoonist Michael Ramirez.

Political Cartoons

Provide several political cartoons from recent newspapers, magazines, or websites, and analyze them with the students while referring to the "Political Cartoons" feature box on this page.

Activity 4: Mass Media Cartoon

This activity asks the students questions about political cartoons to encourage development of analytical and evaluation skills.

Reporting on Wars

Journalists who choose to cover wars in person expose themselves to potential injury, capture, or death. More than two hundred journalists have died in crossfire since 2001. Countries in the Middle East such as Syria, Afghanistan, and Iraq see more war-zone deaths of journalists than most other countries.

The Freedom of Information Act

The Freedom of Information Act, often abbreviated FOIA, was passed in 1966 and has been amended several times since. Under the FOIA, citizens may apply for access to documents held by agencies in the executive branch. Elected officials, the judicial branch, private institutions, and state and local governments are exempt. Agencies are required to respond within twenty days, but response time is usually longer. Making a request does not ensure that the requested information will be received; agencies are allowed to refuse to release information if that information falls under one of the nine exemptions listed in the FOIA. The FOIA helps ensure that the populace has access to public information. As James Madison said, "A popular Government, without popular information, or the means of acquiring it, is but a prologue to a farce or a tragedy; or, perhaps both."

it is presented to the public. The only exception to this media freedom occurs in wartime. During World War I, for example, President Wilson created the Committee on Public Information (CPI), an agency authorized to keep unpatriotic and antiwar information from the newspapers.

Nothing like the CPI exists in the United States today, but wartime restrictions on freedom of the press remain controversial. Throughout the Vietnam War, reporters were allowed to accompany troops in action. Critics of the press argued that images they broadcast or reports they wrote were often biased and were partially responsible for making the war unpopular at home. When the United States fought the Gulf War of 1991, only a few reporters were allowed to accompany the troops. Military officers also denied reporters access to certain areas of the war zone. These restrictions were very unpopular with the press and led to changes during the 2003 war in Iraq. In that conflict, reporters were given greater access to troops and combat areas than a decade earlier. Many journalists were "embedded" or stationed with various military units.

Except when under limited wartime restrictions, the US media enjoys additional freedom to scrutinize government actions. For instance, the **Freedom of Information Act (FOIA)**—discussed in Chapter 12—gives the media (as well as private individuals) broad powers to investigate the federal bureaucracy's files. The government may, however, exclude from disclosure information that is vital to national security and redact (strike out) details that might jeopardize certain government actions or endanger certain people.

Although not a legal freedom at the federal level, freedom of confidentiality is held by the media in some states. To gather sensitive information, reporters might rely on secret sources. Of course, such sources do not usually want their identities revealed to the public or in court. In more than forty states and the District of Columbia, the media enjoys some legal protection of confidentiality through **shield laws**. In states with no shield laws or in states that have qualifications attached to their shield laws, reporters who refuse to divulge a source may be jailed for contempt of court. For instance, William Farr, a reporter for the *Los Angeles Herald Examiner*, spent forty-six days in prison for protecting a source related to the 1971 trial of murderer Charles Manson. In another occurrence, *New York Times* reporter Judith Miller spent three months in jail in 2005 for refusing to disclose a source who had revealed the name of a CIA agent to her.

Powers of Presentation

In addition to many legal protections, the media also possesses much freedom in how it presents the news. A newspaper story can be given a front-page headline, buried on a back page, or cut completely. A long lead story on television immediately conveys the idea that the subject is important. Not all publishers and broadcasters present their material with the conscious intention to influence public policy, but by selecting which items of news will be discussed in the time or space available, they do exert such influence. On the other hand, some newscasters, writers, editors, and producers readily admit that one of the most enjoyable aspects of their work is influencing public opinion. Their critics argue that such individuals often present only their version of news to the public.

Indeed, the words and pictures used in media can have tremendous impact. A political candidate can be portrayed with a smile or a frown or can be labeled as "reactionary" or "moderate." Also, the body language of a newscaster can communicate a bias for or against a subject. Furthermore, media can influence

A reporter during the Gulf War of 1991

FOIA Letter

Request information under the Freedom of Information Act. (Instructions can be obtained from the United States Department of Justice.) Choose an issue that the class or student would like more information about. Write a letter or email (or complete the online form) requesting this information. Grades should be based on how well the students follow the instructions provided by the government and on how clearly they present the requests. Note that information requested is not free of charge and that responses to FOIA requests may take a significant amount of time.

public perception by what they do *not* say—reporting only part of a story.

The media sometimes predicts voting outcomes, and these predictions can in themselves affect a political campaign. For instance, a reporter might say, "Candidate A needs to win 40 percent of the vote in this primary to establish himself as a major candidate." If candidates fail to meet the media's expectations, their viability might be damaged. On the other hand, candidates who exceed the media's expectations might receive extra coverage, which often leads to further gains in public recognition. Of course, most candidates realize the pitfall

of high expectations and usually try to lower the public's expectations so that if a modest prediction is exceeded, the public will view that gain as a victory.

Many Americans believe that the media often shows bias in its coverage of events; furthermore, that assumption appears to be growing. For example, in a survey completed in October 2017 by the Gallup/Knight Foundation, only 32 percent of Americans said that the media was careful to separate fact from opinion (compared with 58 percent of Americans who felt that way in a 1984 survey conducted by MORI Research for the American Society of Newspaper Editors). In that same 2017 Gallup/Knight Foundation survey, 45 percent of Americans indicated there was a great deal of political bias in news coverage (compared with only 25 percent of Americans who felt that way in a 1989 survey by the Pew Research Center).

In recent presidential campaigns, voters have repeatedly said they thought journalists favored the Democratic candidate over the Republican. For example, just a few weeks before the 2008 election, a Pew Research Center report stated the following:

> Voters overwhelmingly believe that the media wants Barack Obama to win the [2008] presidential election. By a margin of 70% [to] 9%, Americans say most journalists want to see Obama, not John McCain, win on Nov. 4. Another 8% say journalists don't favor either candidate, and 13% say they don't know which candidate most reporters support. . . .

> . . .At this stage of the 2004 campaign, 50% of voters said most journalists wanted to see John Kerry win the election, while 22% said most journalists favored George Bush. In October 2000, 47% of voters said journalists wanted to see Al Gore win and 23% said most journalists wanted Bush to win. In 1996, 59% said journalists were pulling for Bill Clinton.

Other surveys indicate that in the 2012 and 2016 presidential campaigns most Americans continued to believe that media coverage favored the Democratic

Regulating Television

The Communications Act of 1934 established the Federal Communications Commission (FCC) as an independent agency within the executive branch. The FCC regulates the programming of television and radio on American soil. The five commissioners who lead the FCC are presidential appointees, subject to Senate confirmation, and serve five-year terms.

The FCC requires that broadcast media stations exist for the "public good." The Fairness Doctrine, which said that equal time must be given to both sides of an issue, was loosely enforced until Reagan's presidency. Today, radio and television outlets must allow candidates to purchase the same amount of ad space and must allow a candidate to give a rebuttal if attacked on the open air. Obscenity, indecency, and profanity are censored on network television (but not on cable television).

In 1996, the Telecommunications Act attempted to restrain pornography on the internet, but it was partly struck down as a violation of free speech. In 1998, the Child Online Protection Act was passed but similarly failed to survive challenge in the federal court system.

nominee (Obama and Hillary Clinton, respectively). During the 2016 contest, Donald Trump popularized the term "fake news" to describe most of the negative press coverage he received. He continued using that term extensively throughout his presidency.

In 2012 the Center for Responsive Politics, a nonpartisan research group, noted that major media companies made significantly higher contributions to the Obama campaign than to that of his opponent, Mitt Romney. In 2016 the Center for Public Integrity, another nonpartisan group, surveyed 430 individuals employed in journalism who contributed money to the presidential nominees that year. It found that almost 90 percent of them donated to Hillary Clinton rather than to her opponent, Donald Trump.

Legal Limits

Two limits to the media's freedom under the First Amendment are laws against **libel** and **slander**. Libel is *published* false statements that injure one's reputation, whereas slander is *oral* communication that does the same. Politicians and other public figures are less protected from libel and slander than private citizens. As noted in Chapter 15, in *New York Times Co. v. Sullivan* (1964), the Supreme Court ruled that published attacks on public officials, even if inaccurate, are constitutionally protected unless made in "reckless disregard" of the truth. Thus, public officials have no grounds for a libel lawsuit unless they can demonstrate "actual malice"—that is, that the source of the libel acted in reckless disregard of the truth by knowingly printing a falsehood.

The chairman of the FCC speaking at a meeting

The First Amendment additionally limits the media by not protecting socially offensive communication, known as **obscenity** (determining what constitutes obscenity is often a matter of controversy). Government regulation is another legal limitation. The **Federal Communications Commission (FCC)** licenses and regulates American radio and television stations. Although the FCC does not decide broadcast content, it can impose fines on stations for broadcasting obscene language or false advertising. The FCC does not currently regulate the internet. Congress passed the Communications Decency Act (1996) to control pornography on the internet, but a year later the Supreme Court struck down the law as unconstitutional.

Marketplace Limits

With relatively few legal limits, mass media exercises great influence over the American public. However, one factor that limits media power is the vast information marketplace in the United States. Politicians are held accountable to the public on Election Day, but the media is held accountable every time people "vote" by changing channels, stations, or newspapers. If a media source alienates its audience, people can find something more to their liking. Cable and satellite television, internet news sites, and radio talk shows now provide a smorgasbord of political views from which to choose. Some see the media turning politics into a form of entertainment or spectacle as networks work to retain their audiences. The decentralization of political information seems to be a trend that will continue to shape American interaction with media.

Factitious

Factitious is a game that requires students to discern fake news from real news. It includes middle school and high school levels (as well as college). Students must decide whether the brief articles provided are true or fake. Playing this game should demonstrate that although something may appear to be factual, it may not be.

Using the Media for Politics

Because politicians recognize the tremendous power wielded by the media, they make every effort to use its influence to their best advantage. From the president down, politicians employ press secretaries and advisors who portray their activities in the most flattering light or help them prepare for press interviews.

Candidates try to keep their poise, their smiles, and their appeal before the public by standing in front of the cameras and talking with reporters as much as possible. If polls reveal a particular voter-perceived weakness, candidates will often try to modify public opinion during their next appearance on camera with a new line in a speech or a new setting for photographs. A stylish haircut and appropriate attire for the occasion are important for the candidate.

The political parties' national nominating conventions have become largely media events. Democrats and Republicans try to use the extensive coverage they receive to present a positive view of their platforms and their candidates. In fact, the media coverage of presidential campaigns now practically demands that parties choose candidates who are both politically and telegenically qualified. Unfortunately, so much attention focuses on a candidate's image that an otherwise superb choice for president can be effectively disqualified by drab physical appearance or lackluster speaking ability. Conversely, a candidate who has no substantial knowledge or experience but has an attractive face and is well-spoken can be elected by a wide margin. This fact should encourage Christians to look beyond outward appearance when determining for whom they will vote.

Using the Media for Propaganda

Most people think of propaganda as false information distributed by dictators, like Nazis or Communists. However, the actual definition of the word is neither so narrow nor so sinister. **Propaganda** means simply the use of various techniques to select and manipulate information to persuade or influence people effectively. Virtually everyone uses propaganda. A teenager

News media critics say reporters spend too much time creating negative images. President Ford (shown here after falling) was one recipient of such publicity.

Basic Propaganda Techniques in Politics

Name calling
Calling an opponent by a name that has a negative connotation, such as *ultraconservative*, *left wing*, *radical*, *extremist*, or *far right*, without explanation

Plain folks
Creating the image of a common person (instead of an aloof politician) by using slogans such as "Friend of the common man" and "One of us" and by having a candidate appear with factory workers, farmers, and other "average Americans"

Bandwagon
Attempting to persuade people to follow a crowd by insisting that "everyone else" is voting for a candidate, implying that there is something wrong with those who do not "jump on the bandwagon"

Testimonial
Using celebrity endorsements to create the impression that important people will vote for a certain candidate

Card stacking
Using select data from polls, government reports, and other sources to support one side of an issue while disregarding contrary information

Glittering generalities
Making broad statements that sound good but lack substance, such as "My party stands for peace and prosperity" or "We will fight poverty"

Transfer
Identifying with a symbol, such as the Statue of Liberty or the American flag, in an attempt to transfer the widespread admiration for that symbol to a candidate

Washed-Out

Nixon's washed-out appearance in the 1960 presidential debate is often mentioned, but it is not often noted that he had just spent two weeks in the hospital, recovering from a knee injury. Nixon was twenty pounds underweight and pale, and his choice to forgo makeup only intensified his pale appearance and five o'clock shadow. These factors combined to give television viewers the impression that Kennedy won the debate. Nixon learned from his mistake and fared better in later debates.

Telegenic Qualities

Discuss the telegenic "qualifications" for presidential candidates and their effect on the political system. Some past presidents might have found it more difficult to gain nomination in the age of television, such as the 325-pound William Howard Taft, and Franklin Roosevelt, who was confined to a wheelchair and braces as a result of polio. Point out the superficiality of basing political decisions on appearance. The Bible says that people look at outward appearances, but God looks at a person's heart (1 Sam. 16:7). God recognizes that people prefer attractive rulers, but He warns that such rulers may not be the wisest or the best (1 Sam. 8; 10:17–24).

Political and Product Ads

Provide political and product ads for the students to analyze the use of propaganda techniques.

Activity 5: Chapter Review

This activity reviews information from the entire chapter.

who tells his parents that he wants something because all his friends have it is using a type of propaganda. Advertisers constantly use propaganda techniques as they bombard the public with reasons to buy their products (e.g., "Most doctors recommend Brand X").

Propaganda's persuasive qualities have not gone unnoticed by politicians and interest groups, and both use propaganda constantly in their campaigns. Not only is media used to disseminate this propaganda, but also the media can add propaganda of its own.

Propaganda can be true and influence people for good ends. However, it tends to break down a listener's resistance, making contrary information easy to disregard. In other words, propaganda circumvents the rational by emphasizing the emotional. Therefore, propaganda has great potential for abuse by those with evil purposes. Americans (particularly Christian Americans) must be aware of the pervasive use of propaganda devices so that they can justly weigh information about public policy rather than blindly follow a mass appeal. American democracy is endangered if the public allows itself to be manipulated through the clever use of propaganda into making unwise political decisions.

Conclusion

Christians should strive to anchor their convictions in Scripture rather than in the opinions of politicians, political parties, interest groups, and the media. Christians will continue to differ with one another over nonessential issues (matters on which compromise is legitimate), but they must always remember that biblical truth should never be subject to the whims of popular opinion.

Lady with a Lamp (1946 Version)

According to a recent Nationwide survey:

MORE DOCTORS SMOKE CAMELS THAN ANY OTHER CIGARETTE

TRY CAMELS ON YOUR "T-ZONE"

CAMELS Costlier Tobaccos

This 1946 cigarette advertisement is an example of propaganda.

Section Review

1–5. Identify five major forms of media.

6–7. Identify what FOIA stands for and identify the rights that the FOIA provides.

8. What material can be excluded from the information released by a FOIA request?

9. Define *propaganda*.

★ How can the media manipulate the information it relays to the public?

★ List seven basic propaganda techniques. Which two do you think are most effective? Explain your answer.

Section Review Answers

1–5. newspapers, radio, television, the internet, and social media (pp. 436–38)

6–7. FOIA stands for the Freedom of Information Act, which was passed to give the public, especially the media, access to the federal government's bureaucratic information. (p. 440)

8. information that is vital to national security or that might jeopardize certain government actions or endanger certain people (p. 440)

9. the use of various techniques to select and manipulate information to persuade or influence people effectively (p. 443)

★ Students may answer that the media can manipulate public perception by giving certain information more extensive or prominent coverage, omitting information, choosing connotative words and pictures in their coverage, and setting arbitrary expectations.

★ Name calling, plain folks, bandwagon, testimonial, card stacking, glittering generalities, and transfer. Answers will vary for the second part of the question.

CHAPTER REVIEW ANSWERS

Making Connections

1–3. Liberalism has come to refer to policies that favor government action and government expansion. Conservatism refers to a reluctance to expand government authority, especially if such expansion de-emphasizes individual responsibility. Generally, moderates favor a middle ground between conservative and liberal positions. (p. 422)

4. In the development of public policy, issues can enter or exit the process at various stages, travel at different speeds, and stay for different lengths of time, just as cars travel on a highway. (p. 423)

18 CHAPTER REVIEW

Making Connections

1–3. Briefly distinguish between liberalism, conservatism, and the views of moderates.

4. Compare the development of public policy to a highway.

5–8. Identify four conditions that can make opinion polls unreliable.

9. Define *lobbying*.

10. Explain how lobbying Congress has changed in recent years.

Developing Civics Skills

1. Identify three current public-policy issues, and note a possible liberal response and a possible conservative response to each one.

2. How has the emergence of PACs affected congressional elections?

Thinking Critically

1. Should government leaders presume that public opinion is reliable? Why?

2. What are some dangers of propaganda?

Living as a Christian Citizen

1. Would you agree or disagree with a politically active Christian friend who told you that he viewed conservatism as the political ideology that best matches a Christian worldview? Why?

2. If you worked for an interest group, how would your faith shape the policy proposals that you would make?

People, Places, and Things to Remember

public policy
public opinion
liberalism
conservatism
moderates
domestic policy
foreign policy
agenda
opinion polls
representative sample
straw polls
interest groups
AFL-CIO
single-issue interest groups
National Rifle Association (NRA)
lobbying
political action committees (PACs)
American Civil Liberties Union (ACLU)
amicus curiae
mass media
C-SPAN
prior restraint
Freedom of Information Act (FOIA)
shield laws
libel
slander
obscenity
Federal Communications Commission (FCC)
propaganda

5–8. failure to survey a representative sample, failure to keep polls current, poorly worded questions, and poor polling conditions (pp. 428–29)

9. Lobbying is the attempt to influence public officials to support a special interest. (p. 433)

10. Students should mention the elimination of most expensive gifts and services. The maximum value of gifts to members of Congress is limited to $50. (p. 434)

Developing Civics Skills

1. Examples include (a) an increase in gun violence: liberal—pass new gun-control laws / conservative—strictly enforce existing laws while assisting institutions that can address root problems; (b) an oil shortage: liberal—tax oil companies in order to invest in research of alternative fuels / conservative—drill for more oil; and (c) a budget deficit: liberal—increase taxes / conservative—cut spending.

2. PACs give money and campaign support to congressional candidates, and their large contributions to incumbents' campaigns discourage challengers limited by smaller budgets.

Thinking Critically

1. Government leaders should take public opinion seriously since citizens are intended to have a significant voice in our system, but generally, because public opinion can be fickle or misguided, leaders should not presume that it is always right.

2. Propaganda tends to break down a listener's resistance, making contrary information easy to disregard. It can circumvent the rational by emphasizing the emotional and has great potential for abuse by evil purposes. American democracy is endangered if the public allows itself to be manipulated through the clever use of propaganda into making unwise political decisions.

Living as a Christian Citizen

1. Students may say that conservatives' emphasis on the existence of evil in human nature fits with the doctrine of human depravity. Christians also agree with conservatives that society must embrace moral standards. Conservatives respect cultural tradition, so they tend to respect Christianity because of its contributions to Western civilization. But conservatives recognize that traditions are formed by fallible people and thus acknowledge the need for reform. Yet Christians cannot be uncritical conservatives. The tradition lauded by secular conservatives includes philosophies incompatible with Christianity; the Christian should proclaim that only Christ can provide the foundation that society needs. A secular conservative might believe in moral norms, but the only reliable place to find them is in Scripture. Without a clear moral vision, a conservative will not know what to conserve and what to reform.

2. Answers will vary. Christians who work in public-policy organizations should recognize God-ordained institutions in society (such as family, church, and government) and propose policies that further those institutions' efforts to fulfill their God-given roles. Christians should evaluate the status quo by Scripture and look for ways to align it with scriptural values.

A. PARTY CONTROL OF CONGRESS

Congressional Session		House Parties*			Senate Parties			President	Party in Power
		Majority	Minority	Others	Majority	Minority	Others		
1st	1789–91	Ad—37	Op—28		Ad—18	Op—8		Washington	Ad
2nd	1791–93	Ad—39	Op—30		Ad—16	Op—13		Washington	F
3rd	1793–95	Op—54	Ad—51		Ad—16	Op—14		Washington	F
4th	1795–97	DR—59	F—47		F—21	DR—11		Washington	F
5th	1797–99	F—57	DR—49		F—22	DR—10		J. Adams	F
6th	1799–1801	F—60	DR—46		F—22	DR—10		J. Adams	F
7th	1801–3	DR—68	F—38		DR—17	F—15		Jefferson	DR
8th	1803–5	DR—103	F—39		DR—25	F—9		Jefferson	DR
9th	1805–7	DR—114	F—28		DR—27	F—7		Jefferson	DR
10th	1807–9	DR—116	F—26		DR—28	F—6		Jefferson	DR
11th	1809–11	DR—92	F—50		DR—27	F—7		Madison	DR
12th	1811–13	DR—107	F—36		DR—30	F—6		Madison	DR
13th	1813–15	DR—114	F—68		DR—28	F—8		Madison	DR
14th	1815–17	DR—119	F—64		DR—26	F—12		Madison	DR
15th	1817–19	DR—146	F—39		DR—30	F—12		Monroe	DR
16th	1819–21	DR—160	F—26		DR—37	F—9		Monroe	DR
17th	1821–23	DR—155	F—32		DR—44	F—4		Monroe	DR
18th	1823–25	DR—189	F—24		DR—43	F—5		Monroe	DR
19th	1825–27	Ad—109	J—104		J—26	Ad—22		J. Q. Adams	DR
20th	1827–29	J—113	Ad—100		J—27	Ad—21		J. Q. Adams	DR
21st	1829–31	D—136	NR—72	5	D—25	NR—23		Jackson	D
22nd	1831–33	D—126	NR—66	21	D—24	NR—22	2	Jackson	D
23rd	1833–35	D—143	NR—63	34	NR—26	D—20	2	Jackson	D
24th	1835–37	D—143	NR—75	24	D—26	W—24	2	Jackson	D
25th	1837–39	D—128	W—100	14	D—35	W—17		Van Buren	D
26th	1839–41	D—125	W—109	8	D—30	W—22		Van Buren	D
27th	1841–43	W—142	D—98	2	W—29	D—22	1	W. Harrison; Tyler	W
28th	1843–45	D—147	W—72	4	W—29	D—23		Tyler	W
29th	1845–47	D—142	W—79	6	D—34	W—22		Polk	D
30th	1847–49	W—116	D—110	4	D—38	W—21	1	Polk	D
31st	1849–51	D—113	W—108	11	D—35	W—25	2	Taylor; Fillmore	W
32nd	1851–53	D—127	W—85	21	D—36	W—23	3	Fillmore	W

Congressional Session		House Parties			Senate Parties			President	Party in Power
		Majority	Minority	Others	Majority	Minority	Others		
33rd	1853–55	D—157	W—71	6	D—38	W—22	2	Pierce	D
34th	1855–57	Op—100	D—83	51	D—39	Op—21	2	Pierce	D
35th	1857–59	D—132	R—90	15	D—41	R—20	5	Buchanan	D
36th	1859–61	R—116	D—83	39	D—38	R—26	2	Buchanan	D
37th	1861–63	R—108	D—44	31	R—31	D—15	3	Lincoln	R
38th	1863–65	R—85	D—72	27	R—33	D—10	9	Lincoln	R
39th	1865–67	R—136	D—38	19	R—39	D—11	4	Lincoln; A. Johnson	R D/NU
40th	1867–69	R—173	D—49	4	R—57	D—9		A. Johnson	D/NU
41st	1869–71	R—171	D—67	5	R—62	D—12		Grant	R
42nd	1871–73	R—136	D—104	3	R—56	D—17	1	Grant	R
43rd	1873–75	R—199	D—88	5	R—47	D—19	7	Grant	R
44th	1875–77	D—182	R—103	8	R—46	D—28	1	Grant	R
45th	1877–79	D—155	R—136	2	R—40	D—35	1	Hayes	R
46th	1879–81	D—141	R—132	20	D—42	R—33	1	Hayes	R
47th	1881–83	R—151	D—128	14	R—37	D—37	2	Garfield; Arthur	R
48th	1883–85	D—196	R—117	12	R—38	D—36	2	Arthur	R
49th	1885–87	D—182	R—141	2	R—42	D—34		Cleveland	D
50th	1887–89	D—167	R—152	6	R—39	D—37		Cleveland	D
51st	1889–91	R—179	D—152	1	R—51	D—37		B. Harrison	R
52nd	1891–93	D—238	R—86	8	R—47	D—39	2	B. Harrison	R
53rd	1893–95	D—218	R—124	14	D—44	R—40	4	Cleveland	D
54th	1895–97	R—254	D—93	10	R—44	D—40	6	Cleveland	D
55th	1897–99	R—206	D—124	27	R—44	D—34	12	McKinley	R
56th	1899–1901	R—187	D—161	9	R—53	D—26	10	McKinley	R
57th	1901–3	R—200	D—151	6	R—56	D—32	2	McKinley; T. Roosevelt	R
58th	1903–5	R—207	D—176	3	R—57	D—33		T. Roosevelt	R
59th	1905–7	R—251	D—135		R—58	D—32		T. Roosevelt	R
60th	1907–9	R—223	D—167	1	R—61	D—31		T. Roosevelt	R
61st	1909–11	R—219	D—172		R—60	D—32		Taft	R
62nd	1911–13	D—230	R—162	2	R—52	D—44		Taft	R
63rd	1913–15	D—291	R—134	10	D—51	R—44	1	Wilson	D

Congressional Session		House Parties			Senate Parties			President	Party in Power
		Majority	Minority	Others	Majority	Minority	Others		
64th	1915–17	D—230	R—196	9	D—56	R—40		Wilson	D
65th	1917–19	R—215	D—214	6	D—54	R—42		Wilson	D
66th	1919–21	R—240	D—192	2	R—49	D—47		Wilson	D
67th	1921–23	R—302	D—131	2	R—59	D—37		Harding	R
68th	1923–25	R—225	D—207	3	R—53	D—42	1	Harding; Coolidge	R
69th	1925–27	R—247	D—183	5	R—54	D—41	1	Coolidge	R
70th	1927–29	R—238	D—194	3	R—48	D—46	1	Coolidge	R
71st	1929–31	R—270	D—164	1	R—56	D—39	1	Hoover	R
72nd	1931–33	R—218	D—216	1	R—48	D—47	1	Hoover	R
73rd	1933–35	D—313	R—117	5	D—59	R—36	1	F. Roosevelt	D
74th	1935–37	D—322	R—103	10	D—69	R—25	2	F. Roosevelt	D
75th	1937–39	D—334	R—88	13	D—76	R—16	4	F. Roosevelt	D
76th	1939–41	D—262	R—169	4	D—69	R—23	4	F. Roosevelt	D
77th	1941–43	D—267	R—162	6	D—66	R—28	2	F. Roosevelt	D
78th	1943–45	D—222	R—209	4	D—57	R—38	1	F. Roosevelt	D
79th	1945–47	D—244	R—189	2	D—57	R—38	1	F. Roosevelt; Truman	D
80th	1947–49	R—246	D—188	1	R—51	D—45		Truman	D
81st	1949–51	D—263	R—171	1	D—54	R—42		Truman	D
82nd	1951–53	D—235	R—199	1	D—49	R—47		Truman	D
83rd	1953–55	R—221	D—213	1	R—48	D—47	1	Eisenhower	R
84th	1955–57	D—232	R—203		D—48	R—47	1	Eisenhower	R
85th	1957–59	D—232	R—203		D—49	R—47		Eisenhower	R
86th	1959–61	D—282	R—153	1	D—65	R—35		Eisenhower	R
87th	1961–63	D—264	R—173		D—64	R—36		Kennedy	D
88th	1963–65	D—258	R—176		D—66	R—34		Kennedy; L. Johnson	D
89th	1965–67	D—295	R—140		D—68	R—32		L. Johnson	D
90th	1967–69	D—248	R—187		D—64	R—36		L. Johnson	D
91st	1969–71	D—243	R—192		D—57	R—43		Nixon	R
92nd	1971–73	D—255	R—180		D—54	R—44	2	Nixon	R
93rd	1973–75	D—243	R—192		D—56	R—42	2	Nixon; Ford	R
94th	1975–77	D—291	R—144		D—61	R—37	2	Ford	R
95th	1977–79	D—292	R—143		D—61	R—38	1	Carter	D
96th	1979–81	D—278	R—157		D—58	R—41		Carter	D

Congressional Session		House Parties			Senate Parties			President	Party in Power
		Majority	Minority	Others	Majority	Minority	Others		
97th	1981–83	D—243	R—192		R—53	D—46	1	Reagan	R
98th	1983–85	D—269	R—166		R—55	D—45		Reagan	R
99th	1985–87	D—254	R—181		R—53	D—47		Reagan	R
100th	1987–89	D—258	R—177		D—55	R—45		Reagan	R
101st	1989–91	D—260	R—175		D—55	R—45		G. H. W. Bush	R
102nd	1991–93	D—267	R—167	1	D—56	R—44		G. H. W. Bush	R
103rd	1993–95	D—258	R—176	1	D—57	R—43		Clinton	D
104th	1995–97	R—230	D—204	1	R—52	D—48		Clinton	D
105th	1997–99	R—226	D—207	2	R—55	D—45		Clinton	D
106th	1999–2001	R—223	D—211	1	R—55	D—45		Clinton	D
107th†	2001–3	R—220	D—213	2	D—50 R—50 D—50 R—50	R—50 D—50 R—49 D—48	 1 2	G. W. Bush	R
108th	2003–5	R—229	D—205	1	R—51	D—48	1	G. W. Bush	R
109th	2005–7	R—233	D—201	1	R—55	D—44	1	G. W. Bush	R
110th	2007–9	D—233	R—202		D—49	R—49	2	G. W. Bush	R
111th	2009–11	D—257	R—178		D—57	R—41	2	Obama	D
112th	2011–13	R—242	D—193		D—51	R—47	2	Obama	D
113th	2013–15	R—234	D—201		D—53	R—45	2	Obama	D
114th	2015–17	R—247	D—188		R—54	D—44	2	Obama	D
115th	2017–19	R—241	D—194		R—51	D—47	2	Trump	R
116th	2019–21	D—235	R—199		R—53	D—45	2	Trump	R

Note: Interpretation of the information in this table is based on data from the US Senate and US House websites. This information may differ from that in other sources.

**Note:* Ad = Administration; D = Democratic; DR = Democratic-Republican; F = Federalist; J = Jacksonian; NR = National Republican; NU = National Union; Op = Opposition; R = Republican; W = Whig.

†The Democrats held the majority from January 3 to January 20, 2001, due to the deciding vote of outgoing Democratic vice president Al Gore. Senator Tom Daschle was majority leader at that time. Beginning on January 20, 2001, Republican vice president Dick Cheney held the deciding vote, giving the majority to the Republicans. Senator Trent Lott resumed his position as majority leader on that date. On May 24, 2001, Senator Jim Jeffords of Vermont announced his switch from Republican to Independent status, effective June 6, 2001. Jeffords also announced that he would caucus with the Democrats; this changed control of the Senate from the Republicans back to the Democrats. Senator Tom Daschle became majority leader again on June 6, 2001. On October 25, 2002, Senator Paul Wellstone (D-MN) died, and Independent Dean Barkley was appointed to fill the vacancy. The election on November 5, 2002, brought Senator James Talent (R-MO) to office; he replaced Senator Jean Carnahan (D-MO). This shifted the balance once again to the Republicans, but no reorganization was completed at that time since the Senate was out of session.

B. PRESIDENTIAL ELECTIONS

Year	Number of States in Union	Major Candidates*	Parties**	Popular Votes	Approx. Popular Vote (%)	Electoral Votes
1789	11	**George Washington** John Adams Other candidates				69 34 35
1792	15	**George Washington** John Adams George Clinton Other candidates				132 77 50 5
1796	16	**John Adams** Thomas Jefferson Thomas Pinckney Aaron Burr Other candidates	F DR F DR			71 68 59 30 48
1800	16	**Thomas Jefferson** Aaron Burr John Adams Charles C. Pinckney John Jay	DR DR F F F			73 73 65 64 1
1804	17	**Thomas Jefferson** Charles C. Pinckney	DR F			162 14
1808	17	**James Madison** Charles C. Pinckney George Clinton	DR F DR			122 47 6
1812	18	**James Madison** DeWitt Clinton	DR F			128 89
1816	19	**James Monroe** Rufus King	DR F			183 34
1820	24	**James Monroe** John Quincy Adams	DR I			231 1
1824	24	**John Quincy Adams** Andrew Jackson Henry Clay William H. Crawford	DR DR DR DR	108,740 153,544 47,531 40,856	31.0 43.8 13.6 11.6	84 99 37 41
1828	24	**Andrew Jackson** John Quincy Adams	D NR	647,286 508,064	56.0 44.0	178 83
1832	24	**Andrew Jackson** Henry Clay William Wirt John Floyd	D NR AM D	687,502 530,189 101,051	54.5 37.5 8.0	219 49 7 11
1836	26	**Martin Van Buren** William H. Harrison Hugh L. White Daniel Webster W. P. Mangum	D W W W W	764,176 550,816 146,107 41,201	50.8 36.7 9.7 2.7	170 73 26 14 11
1840	26	**William H. Harrison** Martin Van Buren	W D	1,275,016 1,129,102	53.1 46.9	234 60

Year	Number of States in Union	Major Candidates	Parties	Popular Votes	Approx. Popular Vote (%)	Electoral Votes
1844	26	**James K. Polk** Henry Clay James G. Birney	D W L	1,337,243 1,299,062 62,300	49.6 48.1 2.3	170 105
1848	30	**Zachary Taylor** Lewis Cass Martin Van Buren	W D FS	1,360,099 1,220,544 291,501	47.4 42.5 10.1	163 127
1852	31	**Franklin Pierce** Winfield Scott John P. Hale	D W FS	1,601,274 1,386,580 155,210	50.9 44.1 5.0	254 42
1856	31	**James Buchanan** John C. Frémont Millard Fillmore	D R Amer	1,838,169 1,341,264 873,000	45.3 33.1 21.6	174 114 8
1860	33	**Abraham Lincoln** Stephen A. Douglas John C. Breckinridge John Bell	R D D CU	1,866,452 1,382,713 847,953 592,906	39.8 29.5 18.1 12.6	180 12 72 39
1864	36	**Abraham Lincoln** George B. McClellan	R D	2,213,665 1,805,237	55.0 45.0	212 21
1868	37	**Ulysses S. Grant** Horatio Seymour	R D	3,012,833 2,703,249	52.7 47.3	214 80
1872	37	**Ulysses S. Grant** Horace Greeley	R D	3,597,132 2,834,125	55.6 43.9	286 —[a]
1876	38	**Rutherford B. Hayes** Samuel J. Tilden	R D	4,036,298 4,300,590	48.0 51.0	185 184
1880	38	**James A. Garfield** Winfield S. Hancock James B. Weaver	R D GL	4,454,416 4,444,952 308,578	48.5 48.1 3.4	214 155
1884	38	**Grover Cleveland** James G. Blaine Benjamin F. Butler John P. St. John	D R GL Proh	4,874,986 4,851,981 175,370 150,369	48.5 48.2 1.8 1.5	219 182
1888	38	**Benjamin Harrison** Grover Cleveland Clinton B. Fisk Anson J. Streeter	R D Proh UL	5,439,853 5,540,309 249,506 146,935	47.8 48.7 2.2 1.3	233 168
1892	44	**Grover Cleveland** Benjamin Harrison James B. Weaver John Bidwell	D R P Proh	5,556,918 5,176,108 1,027,329 264,133	46.1 43.0 8.5 2.2	277 145 22
1896	45	**William McKinley** William J. Bryan	R D/P	7,104,779 6,502,925	51.1 47.7	271 176
1900	45	**William McKinley** William J. Bryan John G. Woolley	R D Proh	7,207,923 6,358,133 208,914	51.7 45.5 1.5	292 155

Year	Number of States in Union	Major Candidates	Parties	Popular Votes	Approx. Popular Vote (%)	Electoral Votes
1904	45	**Theodore Roosevelt** Alton B. Parker Eugene V. Debs Silas C. Swallow	R D S Proh	7,623,486 5,077,911 402,895 258,536	57.4 37.6 3.0 1.9	336 140
1908	46	**William H. Taft** William J. Bryan Eugene V. Debs Eugene W. Chafin	R D S Proh	7,678,908 6,409,104 420,793 253,840	51.6 43.1 2.8 1.7	321 162
1912	48	**Woodrow Wilson** Theodore Roosevelt William H. Taft Eugene V. Debs Eugene W. Chafin	D Prog R S Proh	6,293,454 4,119,207 3,483,922 901,551 206,275	41.9 27.4 23.2 6.0 1.4	435 88 8
1916	48	**Woodrow Wilson** Charles E. Hughes A. L. Benson J. Frank Hanly	D R S Proh	9,129,606 8,538,221 585,113 220,506	49.4 46.2 3.2 1.2	277 254
1920	48	**Warren G. Harding** James M. Cox Eugene V. Debs P. P. Christensen	R D S FL	16,152,200 9,147,353 919,799 265,411	60.4 34.2 3.4 1.0	404 127
1924	48	**Calvin Coolidge** John W. Davis Robert M. La Follette	R D Prog	15,725,016 8,386,503 4,822,856	54.0 28.8 16.6	382 136 13
1928	48	**Herbert Hoover** Alfred E. Smith	R D	21,391,381 15,016,443	58.2 40.9	444 87
1932	48	**Franklin D. Roosevelt** Herbert Hoover Norman Thomas	D R S	22,821,857 15,761,841 884,781	57.4 39.7 2.2	472 59
1936	48	**Franklin D. Roosevelt** Alfred M. Landon William Lemke	D R U	27,751,597 16,679,583 882,479	60.8 36.5 1.9	523 8
1940	48	**Franklin D. Roosevelt** Wendell Willkie	D R	27,244,160 22,305,198	54.8 44.8	449 82
1944	48	**Franklin D. Roosevelt** Thomas Dewey	D R	25,602,504 22,006,285	53.5 46.0	432 99
1948	48	**Harry S. Truman** Thomas Dewey Strom Thurmond Henry Wallace	D R SR Prog	24,105,695 21,969,170 1,169,021 1,157,328	49.8 45.4 2.4 2.4	303 189 39
1952	48	**Dwight D. Eisenhower** Adlai E. Stevenson II	R D	33,778,963 27,314,992	55.1 44.4	442 89
1956	48	**Dwight D. Eisenhower** Adlai E. Stevenson II	R D	35,581,003 25,738,765	57.6 42.1	457 73

Year	Number of States in Union	Major Candidates	Parties	Popular Votes	Approx. Popular Vote (%)	Electoral Votes
1960	50	**John F. Kennedy** Richard Nixon Henry F. Byrd	D R D	34,227,096 34,107,646 116,248	49.7 49.6 0.2	303 219 15
1964	50	**Lyndon Johnson** Barry Goldwater	D R	42,825,463 27,146,969	61.1 38.5	486 52
1968	50	**Richard Nixon** Hubert Humphrey George Wallace	R D AI	31,710,470 30,898,055 9,906,473	43.4 42.7 13.5	301 191 46
1972	50	**Richard Nixon** George McGovern	R D	46,740,323 28,901,598	60.7 37.5	520 17
1976	50	**Jimmy Carter** Gerald Ford	D R	40,825,839 39,147,770	50.1 48.0	297 240
1980	50	**Ronald Reagan** Jimmy Carter John Anderson	R D I	43,901,812 35,483,820 5,719,437	50.7 41.0 6.6	489 49
1984	50	**Ronald Reagan** Walter Mondale	R D	54,455,472 37,577,352	58.8 40.6	525 13
1988	50	**George H. W. Bush** Michael Dukakis	R D	48,886,597 41,809,476	53.4 45.6	426 111
1992	50	**Bill Clinton** George H. W. Bush Ross Perot	D R I	44,908,254 39,102,343 19,743,821	43.0 37.4 18.9	370 168
1996	50	**Bill Clinton** Bob Dole Ross Perot	D R Ref	47,401,185 39,197,469 8,085,295	49.2 40.7 8.4	379 159
2000	50	**George W. Bush** Al Gore Ralph Nader	R D G	50,456,062 50,996,582 2,882,955	48.3 48.9 2.8	271 266
2004	50	**George W. Bush** John Kerry	R D	62,039,073 59,027,478	50.7 48.3	286 251
2008	50	**Barack Obama** John McCain	D R	69,456,897 59,934,814	52.9 45.7	364 174
2012	50	**Barack Obama** Mitt Romney Gary Johnson	D R Lib	65,446,037 60,589,084 1,275,971	51.4 47.6 1.0	332 206
2016	50	**Donald Trump** Hillary Clinton Gary Johnson Jill Stein	R D Lib G	62,980,160 65,845,063 4,488,931 1,457,050	46.7 48.8 3.3 1.1	304 227

Note: Winners are in bold-faced type. Most candidates receiving less than 1 percent of the popular vote have been omitted; thus the percentage of popular votes given for any election year might not total 100 percent. Before 1824, most presidential electors were chosen by state legislatures, not by popular vote.

**Note:* AI = American Independent; AM = Anti-Masonic; Amer = American; CU = Constitutional Union; D = Democratic; D/P = Democrats and Populists; DR = Democratic-Republican;

F = Federalist; FL = Farmer-Labor; FS = Free-Soil; G = Green; GL = Greenback-Labor; I = Independent; L = Liberty; Lib = Libertarian; NR = National Republican; P = People's; Prog = Progressive; Proh = Prohibition; R = Republican; Ref = Reform; S = Socialist; SR = States' Rights; U = Union; UL = Union Labor; W = Whig.

[a]Greeley died shortly after the election; the electors supporting him then divided their votes among minor candidates.

C. PRESIDENTS OF THE UNITED STATES

President	Term(s)	Political Party	Home State	Vice President
George Washington	1789–97	None	Virginia	John Adams
John Adams	1797–1801	Federalist	Massachusetts	Thomas Jefferson
Thomas Jefferson	1801–9	Democratic-Republican	Virginia	Aaron Burr George Clinton
James Madison	1809–17	Democratic-Republican	Virginia	George Clinton Elbridge Gerry
James Monroe	1817–25	Democratic-Republican	Virginia	Daniel D. Tompkins
John Quincy Adams	1825–29	Democratic-Republican	Massachusetts	John C. Calhoun
Andrew Jackson	1829–37	Democrat	Tennessee	John C. Calhoun Martin Van Buren
Martin Van Buren	1837–41	Democrat	New York	Richard M. Johnson
William H. Harrison	1841	Whig	Ohio	John Tyler
John Tyler	1841–45	Whig	Virginia	
James K. Polk	1845–49	Democrat	Tennessee	George M. Dallas
Zachary Taylor	1849–50	Whig	Louisiana	Millard Fillmore
Millard Fillmore	1850–53	Whig	New York	
Franklin Pierce	1853–57	Democrat	New Hampshire	William R. King
James Buchanan	1857–61	Democrat	Pennsylvania	John C. Breckinridge
Abraham Lincoln	1861–65	Republican	Illinois	Hannibal Hamlin Andrew Johnson
Andrew Johnson	1865–69	Democrat/National Union	Tennessee	
Ulysses S. Grant	1869–77	Republican	Illinois	Schuyler Colfax Henry Wilson
Rutherford B. Hayes	1877–81	Republican	Ohio	William A. Wheeler
James A. Garfield	1881	Republican	Ohio	Chester A. Arthur
Chester A. Arthur	1881–85	Republican	New York	
Grover Cleveland	1885–89	Democrat	New York	Thomas A. Hendricks
Benjamin Harrison	1889–93	Republican	Indiana	Levi P. Morton
Grover Cleveland	1893–97	Democrat	New York	Adlai E. Stevenson
William McKinley	1897–1901	Republican	Ohio	Garret A. Hobart Theodore Roosevelt

President	Term(s)	Political Party	Home State	Vice President
Theodore Roosevelt	1901–9	Republican	New York	Charles W. Fairbanks
William H. Taft	1909–13	Republican	Ohio	James S. Sherman
Woodrow Wilson	1913–21	Democrat	New Jersey	Thomas R. Marshall
Warren G. Harding	1921–23	Republican	Ohio	Calvin Coolidge
Calvin Coolidge	1923–29	Republican	Massachusetts	Charles G. Dawes
Herbert Hoover	1929–33	Republican	California	Charles Curtis
Franklin D. Roosevelt	1933–45	Democrat	New York	John Nance Garner Henry A. Wallace Harry S. Truman
Harry S. Truman	1945–53	Democrat	Missouri	Alben W. Barkley
Dwight D. Eisenhower	1953–61	Republican	Pennsylvania	Richard M. Nixon
John F. Kennedy	1961–63	Democrat	Massachusetts	Lyndon B. Johnson
Lyndon B. Johnson	1963–69	Democrat	Texas	Hubert H. Humphrey
Richard M. Nixon	1969–74	Republican	California	Spiro T. Agnew Gerald R. Ford
Gerald R. Ford	1974–77	Republican	Michigan	Nelson A. Rockefeller
Jimmy Carter	1977–81	Democrat	Georgia	Walter F. Mondale
Ronald Reagan	1981–89	Republican	California	George H. W. Bush
George H. W. Bush	1989–93	Republican	Texas	Dan Quayle
Bill Clinton	1993–2001	Democrat	Arkansas	Al Gore
George W. Bush	2001–9	Republican	Texas	Richard Cheney
Barack Obama	2009–17	Democrat	Illinois	Joe Biden
Donald Trump	2017–	Republican	New York	Mike Pence

D. JUSTICES OF THE US SUPREME COURT

Justice*	Tenure	Years of Service	Life Span
John Jay	1789–95	5	1745–1829
John Rutledge**	1790–91	1	1739–1800
William Cushing	1790–1810	20	1732–1810
James Wilson	1789–98	8	1742–98
John Blair	1790–95	5	1732–1800
James Iredell	1790–99	9	1751–99
Thomas Johnson	1792–93		1732–1819
William Paterson	1793–1806	13	1745–1806
John Rutledge	1795		1739–1800
Samuel Chase	1796–1811	15	1741–1811
Oliver Ellsworth	1796–1800	4	1745–1807
Bushrod Washington	1798–1829	31	1762–1829
Alfred Moore	1800–04	3	1755–1810
John Marshall	1801–35	34	1755–1835
William Johnson	1804–34	30	1771–1834
H. Brockholst Livingston	1807–23	16	1757–1823
Thomas Todd	1807–26	18	1765–1826
Gabriel Duvall	1811–35	23	1752–1844
Joseph Story	1812–45	33	1779–1845
Smith Thompson	1823–43	20	1768–1843
Robert Trimble	1826–28	2	1777–1828
John McLean	1830–61	31	1785–1861
Henry Baldwin	1830–44	14	1780–1844
James M. Wayne	1835–67	32	1790–1867
Roger B. Taney	1836–64	28	1777–1864
Philip P. Barbour	1836–41	4	1783–1841
John Catron	1837–65	28	1786–1865
John McKinley	1838–52	14	1780–1852
Peter V. Daniel	1842–60	18	1784–1860
Samuel Nelson	1845–72	27	1792–1873

Justice	Tenure	Years of Service	Life Span
Levi Woodbury	1845–51	6	1789–1851
Robert C. Grier	1846–70	23	1794–1870
Benjamin R. Curtis	1851–57	6	1809–74
John A. Campbell	1853–61	8	1811–89
Nathan Clifford	1858–81	23	1803–81
Noah H. Swayne	1862–81	19	1804–84
Samuel F. Miller	1862–90	28	1816–90
David Davis	1862–77	14	1815–86
Stephen J. Field	1863–97	34	1816–99
Salmon P. Chase	1864–73	8	1808–73
William Strong	1870–80	10	1808–95
Joseph P. Bradley	1870–92	21	1813–92
Ward Hunt	1873–82	9	1810–86
Morrison R. Waite	1874–88	14	1816–88
John M. Harlan	1877–1911	33	1833–1911
William B. Woods	1881–87	6	1824–87
Stanley Matthews	1881–89	7	1824–89
Horace Gray	1882–1902	20	1828–1902
Samuel Blatchford	1882–93	11	1820–93
Lucius Q. C. Lamar II	1888–93	5	1825–93
Melville W. Fuller	1888–1910	21	1833–1910
David J. Brewer	1890–1910	20	1837–1910
Henry B. Brown	1891–1906	15	1836–1913
George Shiras Jr.	1892–1903	10	1832–1924
Howell E. Jackson	1893–95	2	1832–95
Edward D. White**	1894–1910	16	1845–1921
Rufus W. Peckham	1896–1909	13	1838–1909
Joseph McKenna	1898–1925	27	1843–1926
Oliver W. Holmes Jr.	1902–32	29	1841–1935
William R. Day	1903–22	19	1849–1923
William H. Moody	1906–10	3	1853–1917

Justice	Tenure	Years of Service	Life Span
Horace H. Lurton	1910–14	4	1844–1914
Charles E. Hughes**	1910–16	5	1862–1948
Edward D. White**	1910–21	10	1845–1921
Willis Van Devanter	1911–37	26	1859–1941
Joseph R. Lamar	1911–16	5	1857–1916
Mahlon Pitney	1912–22	10	1858–1924
James C. McReynolds	1914–41	26	1862–1946
Louis D. Brandeis	1916–39	22	1856–1941
John H. Clarke	1916–22	6	1857–1945
William H. Taft	1921–30	8	1857–1930
George Sutherland	1922–38	15	1862–1942
Pierce Butler	1923–39	16	1866–1939
Edward T. Sanford	1923–30	7	1865–1930
Harlan F. Stone**	1925–41	16	1872–1946
Charles E. Hughes**	1930–41	11	1862–1948
Owen J. Roberts	1930–45	15	1875–1955
Benjamin N. Cardozo	1932–38	6	1870–1938
Hugo L. Black	1937–71	34	1886–1971
Stanley F. Reed	1938–57	19	1884–1980
Felix Frankfurter	1939–62	23	1882–1965
William O. Douglas	1939–75	36	1898–1980
Frank Murphy	1940–49	9	1890–1949
Harlan F. Stone**	1941–46	4	1872–1946
James F. Byrnes	1941–42	1	1882–1972
Robert H. Jackson	1941–54	13	1892–1954
Wiley B. Rutledge	1943–49	6	1894–1949
Harold H. Burton	1945–58	13	1888–1964
Fred M. Vinson	1946–53	7	1890–1953
Tom C. Clark	1949–67	17	1899–1977
Sherman Minton	1949–56	7	1890–1965
Earl Warren	1953–69	15	1891–1974
John Marshall Harlan II	1955–71	16	1899–1971
William J. Brennan Jr.	1956–90	33	1906–97
Charles E. Whittaker	1957–62	5	1901–73
Potter Stewart	1958–81	22	1915–85
Byron R. White	1962–93	31	1917–2002
Arthur J. Goldberg	1962–65	2	1908–90
Abe Fortas	1965–69	3	1910–82
Thurgood Marshall	1967–91	24	1908–93
Warren E. Burger	1969–86	17	1907–95
Harry A. Blackmun	1970–94	24	1908–99
Lewis F. Powell Jr.	1972–87	15	1907–98
William H. Rehnquist**	1972–86	14	1924–2005
John Paul Stevens	1975–2010	34	1920–
Sandra Day O'Connor	1981–2006	24	1930–
William H. Rehnquist**	1986–2005	19	1924–2005
Antonin Scalia	1986–2016	29	1936–2016
Anthony Kennedy	1988–2018	30	1936–
David H. Souter	1990–2009	18	1939–
Clarence Thomas	1991–		1948–
Ruth Bader Ginsburg	1993–		1933–
Stephen G. Breyer	1994–		1938–
John Roberts	2005		1955–
Samuel Alito	2006–		1950–
Sonia Sotomayor	2009–		1954–
Elena Kagan	2010–		1960–
Neil Gorsuch	2017–		1967–
Brett Kavanaugh	2018–		1965–

Note: Chief justices are in bold-faced type.
**Listed twice because he served as both an associate justice and as chief justice.

E. HOW TO WRITE TO PUBLIC OFFICIALS

I. Tips for Writing to Your Member of Congress

The following hints regarding how to write to a member of Congress were suggested by congressional sources and the League of Women Voters:

- Write to your own senators or representative, not to those of other states.
- Write when the Senate or House is discussing a bill, either when it is in committee or on the floor.
- Use your own words, not those of a form letter.
- Do not write too often. Choose issues carefully.
- Refer to all bills by their numbers, if possible.
- Consider including a copy of an editorial from a local paper if it is pertinent to the issue.
- Do not just criticize or identify a problem; offer a solution or a better approach.
- If you are an expert in a particular area, share your expertise with the member, but do not pretend to have political influence.
- Write to thank the member when he does something right, not just when you disagree with him.
- Write to ask a question or to resolve a problem dealing with the government bureaucracy.
- Be brief. Keep your letter or email to four hundred words or fewer (about one page). Use the appropriate form of address.

II. Correct Form for Emails and Letters

Email subject line: Identify the bill number or topic related to your message (e.g., H.R. __________ [House bill] or S. __________ [Senate bill]).

Format for the body of the message:

>Your name
>Address
>City, State ZIP
>
>Dear Mr. President:
>   or
>Dear Mr. Vice President:
>   or
>Dear Senator __________ (last name):
>   or
>Dear Representative __________ (last name):

When writing to the chairman of a committee, the Speaker of the House, or a cabinet secretary, address him or her in these ways:

>Dear Mr. Chairman:
>Dear Madam Chairwoman:
>Dear Mr. (or Madam) Speaker:
>Dear Mr. (or Madam) Secretary:

Closing your message:

>(To the president)   Very respectfully yours,
>(To other officials)   Sincerely yours,

III. Letter Addresses

President
The President
The White House
1600 Pennsylvania Avenue NW
Washington, DC 20500

Vice President
The Vice President
1600 Pennsylvania Avenue NW
Washington, DC 20501

Senator or Chairman of a Senate Committee
Honorable __________ (last name)
United States Senate
Washington, DC 20510

Representative, Chairman of a House Committee, or Speaker of the House
Honorable __________ (last name)
House of Representatives
Washington, DC 20515

Member of the Cabinet
Honorable __________ (last name)
The Secretary of __________ (department name)
(Each cabinet department has an individual street address that you will need to locate.)

IV. Email Addresses

You can obtain these by checking the official website of the House of Representatives, the Senate, the White House, the vice president, or appropriate cabinet agency.

The American's Creed

William Tyler Page

Many people are surprised to learn that the United States has an official national creed. William Tyler Page—a descendant both of Carter Braxton, a signer of the Declaration of Independence, and of John Tyler, tenth president of the United States—wrote it in 1917 and submitted it in a national contest. His entry won over more than three thousand other entries. On April 3, 1918, the US House of Representatives adopted Page's entry as the official creed of the nation. It captures and summarizes the basic philosophy of American patriotism and is sometimes used in the naturalization ceremony for new Americans.

As you study American government this year, look for reasons Page might have included each phrase of his statement of Americanism. How has America followed (or failed to follow) this statement of ideals? How can you fulfill your responsibilities as an American?

I believe in the United States of America as a government of the people, by the people, for the people, whose just powers are derived from the consent of the governed; a democracy in a Republic; a sovereign Nation of many sovereign States; a perfect Union, one and inseparable; established upon those principles of freedom, equality, justice, and humanity, for which American patriots sacrificed their lives and fortunes.

I therefore believe it is my duty to my country to love it; to support its Constitution; to obey its laws; to respect its flag, and to defend it against all enemies.

Blessed is the nation whose God is the Lord.

— Psalm 33:12

GLOSSARY

A

absentee voters—Individuals unable to vote in person during the regular voting times

absolute monarchs—Monarchs who hold unlimited power

administrative law—Regulations that have the force of law and are drawn up by government bureaucracy to implement congressional statutes

agenda—Those issues that the government decides to address

Age of Enlightenment—Philosophical and intellectual movement in eighteenth-century England that emphasized reason and thought; its principles are reflected in the Declaration of Independence

Air Force One—Name of the custom-built plane dedicated to transporting the US president; Air Force One—call sign used to identify any plane transporting the president

alliance—Treaty uniting its participant nations in a common cause; usually military in nature

al–Qaeda—Terrorist group responsible for the September 11, 2001, attacks on the World Trade Center and the Pentagon

ambassador—The president's personal representative to a host country and head of the embassy

amendment proposal—First phase of the amendment process that formally recommends an amendment to the Constitution

American Civil Liberties Union (ACLU)—Special interest group, often supports causes embraced by liberalism

American Federation of Labor and Congress of Industrial Organizations (AFL-CIO)—Largest American labor union

amicus curiae—"Friend of the court," an interest group not involved in a court case but testifying or filing a brief in an attempt to influence the court's decision because of the potential legal precedent that could be set

anarchy—Absence of government

Annapolis Convention—Convention of five states in 1786 at which Alexander Hamilton proposed to reconvene the following year in Philadelphia, where the representatives drew up the Constitution

Anti-Federalists—Members of state ratification conventions who rejected the proposed Constitution

appeal—To petition a higher court to review a lower-court decision

appellate jurisdiction—A court's power to decide appeals; a case must first have been tried in a lower court before it can be appealed in a higher court

appropriation—Money budgeted by Congress to fund programs

Articles of Confederation—Ratified by the Second Continental Congress in 1781; created a weak central government based on the consent of the newly formed state governments

associate justices—Supreme Court judges that serve alongside the chief justice

at-large—Representing an entire region like a state or city rather than a particular district or precinct

autocracy—Form of government in which one person rules with supreme authority, a dictatorship

B

bail—Money paid to guarantee a court appearance, allowing the accused to be free while awaiting trial

balance the ticket—Practice in which a presidential nominee chooses a running mate for specific ideology, geography, ethnicity, gender, or other characteristics in order to strengthen the chance of being elected

bankruptcy—Constitutional provision allowing a debtor who is unable to pay all his debts to divide his assets equally among his creditors; allows a judge to supervise the debtor's finances

bicameral—Legislative branch of a national or state government that is divided into two separate houses, an upper chamber and a lower chamber

bilateral treaties—Agreements that involve only two nations

bill—A legislative proposal that becomes law if passed by both the House and Senate and receives the president's approval

bill of attainder—Legislative act permitting punishment without a trial

Bill of Rights—First ten amendments to the Constitution that protect citizens' democratic rights by limiting the power of the government over its citizens

biological weapons—Fatal diseases or organic toxins used as weapons

bipartisan—Cooperation between two major parties to support a common goal

blanket primary—Primary in which ballots list all candidates and voters can vote in one party's primary for one office and another party's primary for a different office, also called a "wide-open" primary

block grants—Federal grants-in-aid that combine several categorical grants under a general umbrella to simplify the use of the funds in local governments but involve fewer federal regulations and less red tape

board of trustees—Group of people elected at-large in a municipality (small village or town) to serve as the government

boroughs—Administrative units in Alaska and New York City; see **county**

boycott—An act of protest in which business is withheld or refused

brief—A legal document that presents arguments supporting a client's position in a case

broad constructionists—Those who take a broad and more flexible approach to constitutional interpretation

brokered convention—A convention that requires lengthy balloting and an eventual settlement by bargaining and compromise

Brown v. Board of Education of Topeka, Kansas—The Supreme Court decision declaring segregated school facilities to be in violation of the Fourteenth Amendment

Buckley v. Valeo—Supreme Court ruling that 1974 legislation restricting candidate spending during elections violated the First Amendment; upheld the constitutionality of (a) limiting individuals' and committees' donations and (b) applying campaign spending limits on candidates who voluntarily accept public financing

bureaucracy—An administrative system staffed largely by nonelected officials who perform specific tasks in accordance with standard procedures; much of its work involves the implementation and administration of laws and programs

bureaucrats—Civil servants dedicated to the details of administrative procedure

bureaucratese—Vague, sprawling language and wordy jargon used in bureaucratic regulations and documents

Burwell v. Hobby Lobby Stores—The Supreme Court case which held that the government should find ways to achieve its health care goals without violating the religious beliefs of company owners

C

cabinet—Offices of the executive branch developed to assist the president in his constitutional duties and to meet the demands of America's growth; currently consists of fifteen departments

cabinet secretaries—Individuals responsible to the president for the departments that they head

Camp David—Secure presidential retreat in the Catoctin Mountains of Maryland which provides a place for the president to spend time with family and friends, entertain heads of state, and hold meetings to discuss pressing national matters

capital punishment—The death penalty

categorical grants—Federal programs requiring federal oversight; grant monies for specific purposes within state and local governments

caucus—**1.** A small meeting of a political party's top leaders and legislators in Congress **2.** A form of district and state conventions used to nominate candidates in areas that do not hold primaries **3.** A meeting of all members of a party in the House or Senate, also called a **conference** by Republicans

censured—Condemnation by Congress of members whose conduct reflected poorly on the institution

census—Official government counting of the population taken every ten years that determines how many representatives each state may elect

Central Intelligence Agency (CIA)—The chief agency for gathering intelligence or information activities in foreign countries

chair—Head of a congressional committee

checks and balances—Principle of keeping each branch of government in check through the powers of the other branches and limiting the concentration of power in any one branch

chemical weapons—Substances such as mustard gas, sarin, and VX (a nerve agent) used to poison the enemy

chief justice—The highest ranking US judge

chief of staff—Member of the president's staff who advises on issues of politics, policy, and management; selects key people for the White House staff; controls and manages staff members, their work, and the information and paperwork that reach the Oval Office; appears regularly on media to represent the president

citizenship—Belonging to and enjoying all the privileges, rights, and duties as a member of a nation

Citizens United v. Federal Election Commission—The Supreme Court decision that ruled as unconstitutional parts of the McCain-Feingold Act that kept corporations and unions from spending money to support or oppose individuals in elections

civic thinking—Having an understanding of the political ideas and institutions that shape America's government, an appreciation for America's heritage, and an ability to evaluate current issues and national direction

civil liberties—Individual freedoms that must be protected from government

civil rights—Concerns the right to be free from unequal treatment and refers to government's rule in protecting liberties for all people

Civil Rights Act of 1964—Congressional act that prohibited discrimination on the basis of ethnicity

civil service—The civilian employees who perform the administrative tasks of government

clear-and-present-danger test—Test established by the Supreme Court in *Schenck v. United States* that punishable speech involves genuine danger and actually incites violence, rather than simply endorsing it

clients—Members of groups whose needs are served by government agencies

closed primary—Primary election in which only registered members of political parties may participate; voters may vote only for candidates from the party they belong to

cloture—A motion by sixteen or more senators to limit debate on a bill; passes with support of sixty or more senators; if invoked, bill has no more than thirty additional hours of debate; often used to end a filibuster

coalition—Temporary alliance formed by members of different parties who unite to support or oppose a bill because of some common interest

coattail effect—The ability of a strong candidate at the top of a ticket (such as a candidate for governor or president) to attract votes for other members of his party who are running for lesser offices

Code of Hammurabi—The most famous code of ancient law compiled by the Babylonian king Hammurabi in the eighteenth century BC

Cold War—Period between the end of World War II and the fall of the Soviet Union, during which the United States and the Communist bloc coexisted and competed without actually waging war against one another

collective security—Agreement stating that an attack on one ally is an attack on all; results in a unified response; also called mutual defense

Commentaries on the Laws of England—Written by William Blackstone as a key to understanding the English system of law; a bestseller in America and strongly influenced the American founders

commissioners—Elected supervisors from county divisions who serve on the county's governing board

commission government—Form of municipal government overseen by an elected body of five to seven people

common law—Law that applies to the whole country, not just a portion of it

concurring opinions—Opinions written by Supreme Court justices who agree with the majority vote but for different reasons than those presented in the decision

confederate government—System in which regional governments retain supremacy while delegating a few tasks to the national government

conference—Meeting of all Republicans within a house of Congress

conference committees—Ad hoc (temporary) committees drawn from both chambers of Congress that meet to work out a compromise regarding different versions of a bill, or proposed law, that emerged from both houses

confirmation—Senate proceedings that some government appointees have to go through to be approved for their positions

Congress—Legislative branch of US federal government; composed of a lower house called the House of Representatives and an upper house called the Senate

congressional district—Geographic area represented by a House member

Congressional Record—The journal, or record, of Congress's daily proceedings

Connecticut (Great) Compromise—Proposal by Roger Sherman for the composition and structure of the new Congress as a compromise between the Virginia and New Jersey Plans; proposed that representation in the lower house be based on state population and in the Senate be equal for all states regardless of size

conservatism—Political philosophy that shows a reluctance to expand government authority, especially at the cost of individual responsibility

conservative—One whose political view defends against major changes in the political, economic, and social institutions of society while seeking to improve conditions with reform as needed

constituents—Residents of a district who are represented by an elected official

Constitution—Document signed in 1787 and ratified by all thirteen original colonies; replaced the Articles of Confederation and outlined the US government

Constitutional Convention (1787)—Convention held in Philadelphia in 1787 at which the delegates discarded the Articles of Confederation and drew up the Constitution; originally called the Philadelphia Convention

constitutional law—Division of law dealing with the constitutional interpretation of laws and government actions

constitutional monarchy—Form of monarchy in which a democratically elected parliament operates the government and the monarch is a ceremonial head of state

consulate—State Department office established in a major foreign city to offer assistance to traveling and resident Americans, encourage commercial contacts, and exchange educational and scientific ideas; led by a consul

containment—Cold War policy whereby the United States confronted the Soviet Union with counterforce whenever it tried to expand Communist control

convention—National, state, or county-level assembly of political party representatives, or delegates, elected from each state for the purpose of establishing a platform, electing party leadership, and nominating candidates

Corpus Juris Civilis—Collection of many Roman laws and other legal materials from previous centuries compiled by Justinian in AD 533

council-manager government—Form of municipal government in which city council members control the general administration (making policy and setting budgets) while a manager oversees daily administrative functions

county—Administrative unit into which states are divided to help with the administration of state laws and policies

county committee—Group elected by county precinct committeemen to oversee a party's business or elect committee members and attend to the county's needs and interests

county executive—County official elected to oversee a county commission's work; sometimes called the county mayor

covert operations—National security and intelligence activities authorized by the president but unknown to the public and, to a large extent, even to Congress

Creation Mandate—God's command for humans to exercise good and wise dominion over His world

criminal law—Division of law concerning criminal actions and punishments

crossover voting—In an open primary, when members of one party vote in an opposing party's primary, often these voters will also vote for that party's candidate in the general election

C-SPAN—Public-service television network created by the American cable-television industry to provide the public with coverage of House and Senate proceedings "without editing, commentary or analysis and with a balanced presentation of points of view"

cultural imperialism—Promoting one nation's culture at the expense of other cultures

culture wars—Conflict between groups with different ideals, beliefs, and philosophies

D

Declaration of Independence (1776)—The formal declaration of independence from England that justified the American colonies' break with England and established the principles of government for the new nation

Defense, Department of—Cabinet department responsible for the defense of the nation; formerly known as the Department of War

deism—Religious philosophy that taught reason, rather than Scripture, was the way people came to know God

delegated powers—Powers specifically assigned to the national government by the Constitution; powers which define the limits of the government's authority

delegates—**1.** Historically, the representatives at the Constitutional Convention **2.** Political party representatives who pledge to nominate candidates for president and vice president at the party convention **3.** Nonvoting members of the House of Representatives who represent various US territories and the District of Columbia

delegation—The act of committing or entrusting a task or power to another

democracy—Form of government in which the people participate and have a voice in how they should be ruled

Democratic National Committee (DNC)—Elected by state conventions to run the national Democratic administration between national elections, raise money, and supply technical assistance in important races

Department of Homeland Security—Cabinet-level department created after the September 11, 2001, terrorist attacks; tasked with preventing further terrorism against the United States, reducing vulnerability to terrorism, and minimizing damage from and speeding recovery following attacks that occur

dictatorship—Form of authoritative government which the acts without the people's consent or input

direct democracy—Form of government in which the people directly affect a government's policies and actions through voting; also called pure democracy

direct primary—Preliminary election held to select candidates or delegates (or both) to party conventions

dissenting opinion—The written opinion of Supreme Court justices voting in the minority; gives reasons for opposition to the majority decision

district courts—The ninety-four federal judiciary trial courts in the fifty states

District of Columbia v. Heller—Supreme Court ruling that states cannot arbitrarily deny individuals the right to possess firearms for such lawful purposes as self-defense in their homes

domestic policy—Government policy dealing with economic, law, education, health, energy, environment, and civil liberties issues within the nation's borders

double jeopardy—Trying a person twice for the same crime

dual federalism—System in which national and state governments are sovereign within their own spheres

due process—Certain rules that the government must follow by which a person cannot be imprisoned, have his property taken away, or be sentenced to death without a fair and proper trial

duty—A tax on select imports (goods coming into the country from other nations); also called a tariff

dynasty—A monarchy with hereditary succession

E

East Wing—The section of the White House accommodating the First Lady and her staff

Economic and Social Council—A body of the United Nations that promotes fundamental human rights

elastic clause—The clause in the Constitution granting Congress the power to carry out its listed powers; another name for the **necessary and proper clause**

Electoral College—System used to indirectly elect the US president; each state has a number of electors equal to that state's representation in Congress

electoral votes—Votes cast by electors in the Electoral College

embassy—Primary State Department office or residence in a foreign capital for diplomacy, immigration services, and assistance for Americans overseas, headed by an ambassador

eminent domain—The right of government to take private property for public purposes while compensating the property owner

en banc—As a group; describes occasional instances when all judges of a circuit court hear a case

Engel v. Vitale—Supreme Court decision forbidding government authorized prayers in public schools, even if they were nonsectarian and noncompulsory

English Bill of Rights—Document signed by William and Mary in 1689; marked the beginning of democratic government in England by limiting the monarchy's power and asserting the people's rights; the most important development in constitutional government since the Magna Carta

entitlements—Government compensation programs that the law requires Congress to protect

enumerated powers—Powers specifically granted to the national government by the Constitution; sometimes called expressed powers

equality—A democratic principle (political or legal) characterized by equal justice and an equal right to vote

establishment clause—Stipulation in the First Amendment that prevents the government from establishing any religion as the official national religion; in subsequent court cases, it was interpreted as justification for a wall of separation between church and state

European Union—A primarily economic alliance of twenty-eight European nations

excises—Taxes on the production, sale, or use of items and on certain business practices

exclusionary rule—Supreme Court ruling stating that illegally obtained evidence is inadmissible in court

executive agreement—A nonbinding presidential agreement made with another head of state in which both sides agree to carry out a particular action; used by the president in implementing foreign policy

executive branch—enforces the nation's laws, headed by the president

Executive Office of the President (EOP)—First level of the bureaucracy beneath the president; largely a policy-making and managing level that consists of White House offices and agencies that help develop and implement the president's programs and policies

executive orders—Presidential directives or actions that have the effect and force of law

exit poll—Surveys of sample voters as they leave their polling places

ex post facto law—Criminalizes activities that were not crimes when they were committed or requires harsher punishments than were mandated at the time of the act; forbidden by the Constitution

extradition—Legal process of returning a criminal (who fled to another state) to the state where the crime was committed in order to stand trial

F

factions—Groups within a political party who compete with one another over key issues, sometimes determining the win or loss of an election

Federal Communications Commission (FCC)—Federal agency that licenses and regulates radio and television stations

Federal Election Commission (FEC)—Federal agency that governs campaign finance

federalism—Division of governmental power into two or more levels, usually national and state governments, which simultaneously exert authority over the people

Federalist Papers—Collection of essays explaining and defending constitutional provisions of power and predicting dire consequences if the Constitution were rejected

Federalists—Advocates of the proposed Constitution

Fifteenth Amendment—Constitutional amendment that guaranteed voting rights regardless of ethnicity

filibuster—Tactic used in the Senate to prevent or delay a bill's passage with long speeches

First Continental Congress (1774)—Assembly in Philadelphia at which colonial representatives issued a list of grievances and defined the colonists' political rights

First Lady—Title of the wife of the president or the person serving as White House hostess

foreign policy—Government policy dealing with diplomacy, trade relations, war, and other matters involving the nation's relationship with other countries

formula grants—Categorical grants that are governed by demographic formulas, such as unemployment figures, in a given area

fourth branch of government—Term often used to describe the federal bureaucracy because of its power and pervasiveness

fourth-generation warfare—Decentralized form of fighting which includes low-intensity guerilla warfare and is usually waged by religious, political, or ideological groups rather than by countries

franchise—The right to vote; also called **suffrage**

franking privilege—The right of members of Congress to send official mail free of charge

freedom of association—Freedom inferred from the freedoms of speech and petition that gives individuals the right to "pursue lawful private interests privately…and associate freely with others in doing so"

Freedom of Information Act (FOIA)—Gives media and individual citizens access to previously withheld material in federal bureaucracy files; information may be redacted to protect national security

free-exercise clause—Stipulation in the First Amendment that protects religious practices from government restriction within broad, reasonable boundaries

free media—Coverage of campaign activities, including news programs, that does not cost the campaign money

full faith and credit clause—Constitutional clause requiring states to acknowledge one another's public acts, records, and judicial rulings

G

General Assembly—**1.** Name given to many states' legislative branches **2.** Primary representative body of the United Nations with delegates from each member nation

general election—Election to fill an elective office; allows candidates who win their party nominations to run against each other; at the national level, it is held on the first Tuesday after the first Monday in November

general welfare—Fiscal power granted by the Constitution for Congress to spend what is necessary to execute its other consitutional powers

gerrymandering—**1.** Redrawing district lines so black voters had less influence **2.** Redrawing district lines to favor the political party that controls a state legislature

Gibbons v. Ogden—Supreme Court decision granting Congress broad power to regulate interstate commerce

globalization—The increasing integration of world markets, politics, and culture

government—Any system of public rule or authority

Government Accountability Office (GAO)—Congressional office authorized to audit an agency, monitor its activities, and hold public hearings about its programs

governor—Chief officer of a state's executive branch, elected directly by the people of the state

grandfather clauses—Provisions for voters to avoid literacy tests or poll taxes if their grandfathers were eligible to vote before 1867; designed to prevent black voters from voting

grand jury—Jury that considers the prosecution's case against the accused and determines whether there is enough evidence against the accused to warrant a jury trial for guilt or innocence

grants-in-aid—Transfer of monies from federal to state and local governments; used to implementing national policies on the local level

grass roots—Lowest level of a group or activity; support for a political party on the local level

Great Society—Federal programs aimed at eliminating poverty, supervising voting rights, and promoting greater national involvement in education and health care

gridlock—Political stalemate or deadlock resulting from checks and balances; occurs, in part, when different political parties control different branches of government

gubernatorial—Of or relating to a governor

H

hard money—Campaign money raised for a specific candidate in federal elections and spent according to federal laws and restrictions

House of Burgesses (1619)—First representative assembly in the New World

House of Representatives—Lower house in Congress; representation based on state population

human depravity—Result of the marring of God's image in humans though sin which affects every part of each human's being (mind, will, and emotions)

I

image of God—Qualities of humans that reflect God's character (reason, moral capacity, spirituality, sociability, and emotion), enabling humans to exercise wise and responsible dominion over God's world as He commanded

impeachment—To formally charge the president, federal judges, or other government officials with "treason, bribery, or other high crimes and misdemeanors"

imperialism—Extension of power by one country over another people or country

implied powers—Powers not stated in the Constitution but are needed to exercise enumerated powers

inaugural address—Speech given by the president after taking the oath of office

incorporation—**1.** Process establishing a city as a legal government body by granting it a charter authorized by the state **2.** Protections of the Bill of Rights applied across all levels of government through the due process clause of the Fourteenth Amendment

incumbent—Current officeholder

independent expenditures—Funds spent by a person or group to help elect or defeat a candidate without the candidate's knowledge or support

independent voters—Voters who have no declared party affiliation

indirect democracy—Form of government in which the people elect individuals to operate the government on their behalf; also called representative democracy

initiative—Method whereby a legally specified number of voters can propose changes to their state constitutions or laws

interest groups—Groups formed around a particular issue or agenda by individuals that share similar opinions in order to influence government officials and further certain views; also called pressure groups

International Court of Justice—Main judicial body of the United Nations; sometimes called the World Court

International Monetary Fund (IMF)—UN agency that seeks to maintain world economic stability by providing funds to nations that are in financial crisis or that are rebuilding their economies

interstate commerce—Commerce between or among the states

Iowa caucuses—First and most prominent state caucus held during a presidential election year

Islamic State in Iraq and Syria (ISIS)—Muslim extremist group that uses terrorism in an attempt to bring about a world with a Muslim worldview

isolationism—Foreign policy that avoids strong ties to other nations; basic US foreign policy from 1790 to 1890

J

January 20—Date for the presidential inauguration established by the ratification of the Twentieth Amendment

Joint Chiefs of Staff (JCS)—Highest-ranking officers from each branch of the US military who act as military advisors to the president and the secretary of defense

joint committees—Permanent committees of both House and Senate members; act as advisory boards to other congressional committees, particularly on tax matters

judicial activism—Philosophy of legal interpretation that seeks to correct injustices and shape policy even if that means departing from the clear meaning of the law

judicial branch—Interprets the law and oversees criminal cases; determines whether laws are constitutional

judicial federalism—Judicial system of coexisting federal and state courts

judicial restraint—Philosophy of legal interpretation that respects the laws as they are written and previous court decisions, striking down laws only when they are clearly unconsitutional

judicial review—Judicial branch's power to review the constitutionality of laws passed by the legislative branch or of actions taken by the executive branch

Judiciary Act of 1789—Congressional act establishing the Supreme Court and a system of inferior federal courts, described the judges' jurisdiction (what cases they could take and where they could operate) and their operational organization and procedures

jungle primary—Primary election in which all candidates are list on the ballot regardless of party affiliation; the two candidates who get the most votes (even if they are from the same party) advance to the general election; also called **Top-Two method**

junkets—Seemingly unnecessary trips made by members of Congress at the taxpayers' expense

justice—Conformity to God's character; the principle of moral rightness and respect of other's rights

justices—Supreme Court judges

K

keynote address—Speech made at a national convention by a leading party member

L

lame duck—Official still in office but has not been reelected; often refers to a president who lost an election or cannot stand for reelection and must serve out the rest of his term

legislative branch—Primary function is to make laws

legislative referendum—Allows electorate to decide important matters or legislation by a direct yes or no vote

legislature—Lawmaking body

Lemon v. Kurtzman—Supreme Court ruling that state statutes affecting religion must meet three requirements to be acceptable: (1) the state law must have a "secular legislative purpose"; (2) it can neither "advance nor inhibit…religion"; and (3) it cannot foster an "excessive government entanglement" with religion

letter of marque—License granted by a nation to a private citizen, allowing the capture of merchant ships of another nation

libel—Published (written) false statements defaming a person to injure his reputation

liberal—One whose political view seeks to change the political, economic, and social status quo often by government intervention

liberalism—Political philosophy that favors policies requiring government action and government expansion

lieutenant governor—Second to governor, similar to a vice president; duties vary by state but generally a relatively weak, sometimes merely symbolic office, succeeds to the governorship if anything prevents the governor from performing his duties

limited government—Principle that government does not have absolute power, only what the people have given it; government limited by law under which the rights people possess cannot be taken from them

line-item veto—Presidential power that allowed the president to veto part of a bill without vetoing the entire bill

literacy tests—Tests that required voters to be literate to vote

litigation—Legal proceedings, such as lawsuits

lobbying—The attempt to influence public officials to support a special interest

local government—Organized government that provides order and leadership in local communities, such as counties and towns

logrolling—The practice in which a member of Congress supports a colleague's spending project in return for support for his own pork-barrel legislation

lotteries—Form of gambling that some states use as a source of state revenue, typically designated for specific purposes, such as education or transportation

Loyalists—Colonists who remained loyal to Britain during the War for Independence for political, religious, and economic reasons; often called Tories

M

Magna Carta—List of demands King John of England was forced to sign in 1215; restored the feudal rights of English barons, its detailed principles established it as a foundational document of constitutional government

majority leader—Leader chosen by the party with the most members in the House or Senate; in the House, is next to the Speaker in authority, but in the Senate, is the most powerful member

majority opinion—Document justifying and clarifying a Supreme Court decision; written by one of the justices voting with the majority

majority rule—Principle of government asserting that a numerical majority of the electorate can make decisions that bind the entire electorate

majority whip—Chosen by the party with the most members in the House or Senate to assist the majority leader; responsibilities include overseeing communication, tracking votes, and summarizing bills

major parties—The Republican and Democratic parties, the dominant political competitors in American politics

Marbury v. Madison—Supreme Court ruling that established the principle of judicial review of acts of Congress

Marine One—Name of the designated helicopter for the president; Marine One—call sign identifying any rotary-wing aircraft the president boards

Marshall Plan—The US response to European devastation after World War II; supplied billions of dollars to western Europe to rebuild shattered economies and bolster democracy

mass media—Major forms of public communciation (radio, television, newspapers, magazines, internet, and social media) and their associated organizations

Masterpiece Cakeshop v. Colorado Civil Rights Commission—Supreme Court ruled in favor of a Christian baker who argued that while he would sell goods to any customer, he could not create custom cakes for same-sex weddings without violating his religious beliefs

Mayflower Compact—Agreement of temporary government established by the Pilgrims before they settled in the New World, based on the idea of a covenant

mayor-council government—Form of municipal government that divides power between executive (a mayor directly elected by the voters) and legislative (a council of individually elected members from various voting districts, or wards, within city limits)

McCain-Feingold Act—Legislation that reformed campaign financing; prohibited soft money contributions in federal elections and strengthened campaign contribution disclosure laws

McCulloch v. Maryland—Supreme Court ruling that state taxation of the Bank of the United States was unconstitutional

merit—**1.** The quality of one's work **2.** In the civil service, the standard for employment

minority leader—Leader chosen by the party with the second-most members in the House or the Senate

minority whip—Chosen by the party with the second-most seats in the House or Senate to assist minority leader; responsibilities include overseeing communication, tracking votes, and summarizing bills

minor parties—Small political parties, usually organized around a particular issue; also called third parties

Miranda v. Arizona—Supreme Court ruled that it would throw out any conviction in which a suspect was not informed of his constitutional rights, particularly against self-incrimination

Miranda warning—List of rights and warnings that the police must inform the accused of before questioning

Missouri plan—Nonpartisan method of selecting state judges; the governor appoints a judicial candidate from a short list nominated by a commission, the candidate must be approved by voters in a later election

moderates—Adherents of a middle-of-the-road, pragmatic ("whatever works") political philosophy that has no firm ideology

monarch—Leader of a monarchy who usually inherits the position and rules for life

monarchy—Form of government in which supreme (but not sole) authority is invested in a single person, such as a king or queen; that authority is sometimes checked by other governmental bodies

Monroe Doctrine—Foreign-policy declaration by James Monroe in 1823 that the United States would not tolerate interference in the Western Hemisphere by European powers

Mount Vernon—Home of George Washington

multinational organization—A body established to allow nations to work collectively on certain issues

multiparty system—Political system in which several parties compete for (but rarely gain) majority support

municipal governments—Local systems of government varying in size from small towns to large cities

mutual assured destruction (MAD)—Cold War policy based on the idea that superpowers would refrain from attacking each other because of the certainty that each would be destroyed by nuclear weapons

N

National Guard—Modern state-run militia under the dual control of state and federal governments

National Rifle Association (NRA)—Interest group that supports gun rights, promotes gun safety, and opposes almost all gun control legislation

national security—Protecting the nation and its citizens and property abroad

national security advisor—Director of the National Security Council; appointed by the president to advise on matters of national security

National Security Agency (NSA)—National-level agency that collects and processes information and data relating to national security

National Security Council (NSC)—Agency within the Executive Office that serves the president by gathering intelligence, formulating policy, and conducting crisis management in areas affecting national security and foreign policy

naturalization—The process by which a foreign-born person gains citizenship

natural law—Principle stating that all people have a conscience and can recognize the moral truths that exist in nature

necessary and proper clause—Authorizes Congress to make any laws necessary for executing its designated constitutional powers; also called the elastic clause

New Deal—Series of social and economic programs instituted in the 1930s by Franklin D. Roosevelt providing federal funds to address the poverty and unemployment of the Depression

New Hampshire primary—First primary held in a presidential election year

New Jersey Plan—Proposal by William Paterson for the composition and structure of the new Congress in response to the Virginia Plan; it called for a unicameral congress, preserving the one-state, one-vote principle of the Confederation

New York Times Co. v. United States—Supreme Court reaffirmed that the government may not exercise prior restraint on a publisher to prevent publication of certain information

Nineteenth Amendment—Constitutional amendment that granted women the right to vote

nominate—Naming a candidate for public office; a political party's major purpose

nomination—Selecting a candidate to represent the party for public office

North American Free Trade Agreement (NAFTA)—Agreement between Canada, Mexico, and the United States eliminating many tariffs and other trade restrictions on goods

North Atlantic Treaty Organization (NATO)—Military alliance established in 1949 to provide military support for any member that was attacked; membership has expanded to include many former European satellites of the former Soviet Union

nuclear deterrence—Initial Cold War policy that sought to discourage Soviet aggression by building a nuclear arsenal so large that the Soviets faced massive retaliation if they attacked the United States or its allies

O

Obergefell v. Hodges—Supreme Court decision that required all US states to recognize same-sex marriages

obscenity—Socially offensive communication that is not protected by the First Amendment

Office of Management and Budget (OMB)—Executive agency that prepares the nation's annual budget for Congress and coordinates policy among departments

oligarchy—Form of dictatorial government ruled by an elite group that is sometimes self-appointed and divides the governmental departments among its members

one-party system—Political system that allows only one political party, an elite few from that party rule the country using a centralized bureaucracy and police force

open primary—Primary in which voters do not have to declare party membership; a voter can choose which party's primary to vote in but only one

opinion polls—Surveys of what the public thinks about particular subjects

original jurisdiction—A court's power to hear a case before it is considered by any other court

Oval Office—The US president's office in the West Wing where he consults with heads of state, his staff, diplomats, and other dignitaries

oversight—Process by which Congress examines a government department's compliance with the law and scrutinizes its budget requests

P

pardon—President's power to completely forgive a crime and its punishment

parishes—Administrative units in Louisiana; see **county**

parliamentary system—Government with inseparably linked legislative and executive branches; candidate whose party wins the most votes in a district becomes that district's representative in Parliament, the majority party in Parliament then appoints the chief executive, the prime minister

partisanship—Strong devotion to a political party

party platform—Formal statement of a party's position on current issues; drafted at a party's national convention every four years

passport—Official document that identifies a traveler and confirms citizenship; in the United States, it is issued by the State Department

patriotism—Love and devotion to one's country, concern for its social, political, and spiritual welfare

patronage—Practice of giving government jobs to friends and other supporters; also called the spoils system

Pendleton Act—Established the Civil Service Commission; set quality of work as the new standard for hiring and promotion of civil employees and abolished the old patronage (spoils) system

Pentagon—Headquarters of the Department of Defense, located in Arlington, Virginia, outside Washington, DC

petition—Form of nomination with a formal document signed by a specific number of qualified voters on behalf of a candidate in the election district

petit jury—Jury that hears the case against an indicted person and decides its outcome; also called **trial jury**

Plessy v. Ferguson—Supreme Court decision establishing the "separate but equal" doctrine (that permitted separate schools for black and white children provided the facilities were equivalent); reversed by **Brown v. Board of Education of Topeka, Kansas**

pluralism—The coexistence of a diversity of ethnic, social, religious, and political backgrounds; various groups, with different views of right and wrong, all living in the the same society

pluralistic society—Society of diverse religious, ethnic, and political groups with differing opinions and coexisting ideas

pocket veto—Automatic veto of a bill if the president leaves the bill unsigned after ten days while Congress is not in session; it cannot be overridden

political action committees (PACs)—Formed by interest groups on behalf of candidates whom they deem favorable to their goals; they enlist campaign workers and raise monitary contributions

political campaign—Organized effort by a political party or candidate to attract voter support in an election

political ideology—Set of related beliefs based on an underlying worldview that focuses on solving societal problems with the application of political power

political machines—Organizations by which a strong, authoritarian "boss" or small group commands the loyalty of supporters and others and rewards them for their loyal and reliable support

political party—Group organized to gain power by running candidates to win elections, thereby advancing and implementing certain common political goals

polling place—Location in a specific precinct where residents go to vote

poll tax—Tax required before one could vote; used in some states to prevent poor African Americans from voting; abolished by the **Twenty-Fourth Amendment**

popular government—System of government in which power resides with the people, rather than with a monarchy or an elite group

popular majority—The majority of all citizens or at least the majority of all voters who participate in their government through free elections

popular sovereignty—Philosophy of government that asserts the people as the ultimate source of their government's authority

pork barrel—Political slang for favors obtained for local citizens at the expense of all taxpayers; often consist of big spending projects designed to help a member of Congress be reelected

Preamble—Constitution's introduction, explaining its nature and purpose

precedent—Court decision that guides subsequent decisions in related cases; a prior authoritative ruling

precinct—Lowest level of election districts and party administration

president—Chief executive officer and head of the executive branch of the United States, responsible for enforcing laws passed by the legislative branch

presidential primary—Primary election in which voters indicate their preference for their party's presidential candidate and elect state party delegates to represent their choice at the national convention

presidential system—Government that holds the executive and legislative branches both separate and equal; the people elect the head of the executive branch independently of the legislative branch

president pro tempore—Senate position held by the most senior member of the majority party; limited authority but third in line of presidential succession following the vice president and the Speaker of the House

press secretary—Official spokesman for the White House administration who meets daily with the White House press corps

primary—State or local election that determines which of the two or more candidates within a single party will face the opposing candidates in the general election

prior restraint—A government's ability to review and censor or suppress a story before its publication; American media enjoys freedom from this restriction

privileges and immunities clause—Constitutional guarantee that privileges enjoyed by US citizens must be respected in every state

probable cause—Reasonable evidence that a crime has been committed or is about to be committed

procedural due process—Principle that laws must be justly administered and enforced

Prohibition—The nationwide ban on the manufacture, sale, and transportation of liquor from 1920 to 1933

project grants—Categorical grants that allow the national government great discretion in deciding how much aid will be given to a project

propaganda—Techniques used to select and manipulate information to persuade or influence people effectively

public opinion—Reflections of individuals' values taken collectively that inform government plans

public policy—Plans adopted by the government to handle problems and accomplish goals

Q

quorum—Minimum number of members needed to transact business in the House or the Senate

R

raiding—To abuse crossover voting in an open primary by attempting to get a weak candidate of the opposing party nominated thus improving the chances of one's own candidate winning in the general election

ratification—Formal approval of a constitution, constitutional amendment, or treaty

reapportionment—Process of redrawing the boundaries of congressional districts to reflect population shifts

recall—Procedure that allows the removal of an elected official from office by holding a special election

reciprocity—Legal arrangement whereby states cooperate with one another to facilitate governing

red tape—Bureaucratic paperwork

referendum—Permits voters to make changes in their state constitutions and in state or local laws

register—To officially enroll for the purpose of voting

registration—A voting requirement for voters to be properly enrolled with local election officials

representative democracy—See **indirect democracy**

representative majority—Majority of elected officials, such as members of Congress

representative sample—An accurate representation of the population surveyed in an opinion poll

reprieves—Temporary postponement of punishment

reprimand—Rebuke of a House representative for misconduct; lesser punishment than censure

reprisal—A nation's retaliation against another nation when provoked

republic—State in which the supreme power rests in the people or their representatives

Republican National Committee (RNC)—Committee elected by state Republican parties to run the national party between national elections, raise money, and supply technical assistance in important races

reserved powers—Constitutional powers not delegated to the national government or denied to states and their citizens

residency requirements—Requirements to ensure that voters have some knowledge of the issues and candidates in their locality and to prevent voters from suddenly appearing in a district to manipulate an election

revealed law—Revelation of God's law through Scripture

revenue sharing—Federal aid program that allocated portions of the national government's tax revenues to the states

righteousness—Conformity to a standard (conformity to the character of God)

Roe v. Wade—Supreme Court decision legalizing abortion

rogue nation—Nation that seeks to develop weapons of mass destruction; supplies, supports, or provides a safe haven for terrorist organizations; disregards international law and violates human rights; and threatens regional or world security

runoff election—Second election between the two candidates who received the most votes if no candidate receives a majority of votes in the initial election

S

sanctions—Measures taken against a nation to influence its actions; the reverse of foreign aid

Second Continental Congress—Colonial assembly that convened in 1775; tasked with handling the military emergency around Boston and discussing a formal declaration of independence

Secretariat—Main administrative body of the United Nations

secretary—Title of the heads of the cabinet departments; appointed by the president, confirmed by the Senate

secretary-general—Chief administrative officer of the United nations and head of the Secretariat

secretary of defense—Head of the Department of Defense

secretary of state—Head of the Department of State

Secret Service—Federal law enforcement agency in Washington, DC mandated by Congress to protect the president, also investigates counterfeiting of money

Security Council—Division of the United Nations that deals with peace and security issues; composed of five permanent members and ten other member nations serving two-year terms

sedition—Speech that attempts to overthrow the government or endanger national security

select committees—Temporary congressional committees created for a specific purpose, generally to investigate particular problems

selectmen—Those elected at a town meeting to make policy decisions for a local government

self-incrimination—Giving testimony that could implicate oneself in a criminal case

semiclosed primaries—Primary elections that allow independents to choose a primary ballot from one of the two major parties

Senate—Upper house in Congress; equal representation for each state (two senators)

senatorial courtesy—Tradition of giving a senator from a nominated federal judge's home state the power to block the appointment if he does not approve of the nominee

separation of powers—Principle of dividing national power into separate branches of government (legislative, executive, judicial) to prevent any group or individual from gaining too much control

September 17, 1787—Date on which the delegates signed the offical engrossed copy of the Constitution

sergeant at arms—Official in each house of Congress responsible for finding absent members needed to make up a quorum

Seventeenth Amendment—Constitutional amendment that provided for the direct popular election of senators

Shays's Rebellion—Uprising of debtor farmers led by Daniel Shays over farm foreclosures and prison sentences for indebtedness; quickly suppressed but generated fear throughout state legislatures, making them open to the Philadelphia (Constitutional) Convention

shield laws—Laws protecting journalists' right to refuse divulging the identity of a secret source

single-issue interest groups—Pressure groups that are concerned with one particular issue

single-member district—Legislative district that have only one representative

Sixteenth Amendment—Constitutional amendment that approved the national income tax, based on individual income

slander—Defaming a person verbally

Smith Act—Law making it illegal to advocate the violent overthrow of the government, to teach of others to take such actions, or to be a member of an organization that conspires to overthrow the government

social contract theory—Principle that people agree to submit to a government in exchange for the protection of their rights

soft money—Campaign money raised apart from federal regulations and given to local, state, and national party organizations or PACs to be used for "party-building" activities, such as voter-registration efforts and get-out-the-vote drives

Solid South—Term identifying the practically one-party system that dominated the south until the 1960s

Speaker of the House—Most powerful officer of the House of Representatives, elected by House members; presides over the House, manages its business, and is its official spokesman

special district—Level of government independent of city or county governments, established to provide specific government functions on a local level within specified boundaries

splinter parties—Minor parties that split from major parties, generally over policy but sometimes over personality conflicts

spoils system—Practice of giving government jobs to friends and other supporters; also called patronage

spots—Paid advertisements

standard operating procedures (SOPs)—Clearly defined procedures that bureaucracies operate within

standing committees—Permanent congressional committees, generally quite powerful

stare decisis—Literally, "let the decision stand"; rendering judicial decisions on the basis of precedents

State, Department of—Cabinet department responsible for advising the president on foreign policy; representing the United States in foreign-policy negotiations; issuing passports, visas, and travel warnings to US citizens; and giving information when emergencies occur outside the United States

state dinner—Special dinner hosted by the president and First Lady to honor a visiting foreign leader, such as a monarch, president, or prime minister

State of the Union (SOTU) address—President's annual report to Congress establishing the president's legislative agenda; may be delivered either in writing or orally to a joint session of Congress

statutory law—Law passed by the legislature and signed by the president

straight ticket—Vote for all the candidates of one party

straw polls—Informal, unscientific polls

strict constructionists—Philosophy of constitutional interpretation emphasizing the importance of the Constitution's text and holding that any interpretation should be kept to a minimum

subpoena—Legal order requiring a person to appear in court as a witness

substantive due process—Principle that the content of laws must protect a person's basic freedoms

subversion—Attempts to undermine government authority and existence

suffrage—The right to vote; also called **franchise**

Sunshine Act—Law expanding the Freedom of Information Act to allow greater citizen participation in bureaucratic decision making by granting citizen access to federal agencies and officials through public hearings

superdelegates—Party leaders and officeholders who serve as uncommitted delegates at party conventions

supremacy clause—Constitutional clause that sets the US Constitution, the laws of the national government, and treaties as the "supreme [highest] law of the land"

Supreme Court—**1.** Highest court of the United States, responsible for interpreting the law (including determining whether a law is constitutional) **2.** Highest state court, responsible for interpreting the law and overseeing criminal cases

symbolic speech—Expression of ideas through actions instead of words

T

Tenth Amendment—Declares that the people or the states constitutionally retain all powers not specifically delegated to the national government or prohibited to them; designed to prevent the national government from assuming too much power

tenure—Term of office

term limits—Limits on the number of terms for state legislators and members of Congress

terrorism—An attempt to achieve goals by using fear to intimidate people and governments and thereby coerce them into doing what the terrorists want

third parties—Small political parties, usually organized around a particular issue; also called **minor parties**

Three-Fifths Compromise—Settlement at the Constitutional Convention permitting three-fifths of a state's slaves to count toward its representation in the House, but a slave state would also have to pay taxes on the slaves at the same rate

ticket splitting—Voting for candidates of different parties for different offices

time-place-manner laws—Local government ordinances restricting public demonstrations to particular locations during specified periods of time; may require demonstrators to obtain permits in advance

Top-Two method—Primary election in which all candidates are list on the ballot regardless of party affiliation; the two candidates who get the most votes (even if they are from the same party) advance to the general election; also called a **jungle primary**

totalitarianism—Government ruled by an elite class (such as the military, the wealthy, or a powerful family) that wields absolute power, often seeking to control every aspect of the people's lives

town meeting—Local government event open to all qualified voters who gather on a specified day to elect a board of officers, or selectmen, to make policy decisions

Transportation Security Administration (TSA)—Agency under the Department of Homeland Security that screens all passengers and baggage at airports

treason—Crime which consists of a US citizen going to war against the United States or giving aid and comfort to the enemies of the country

treaty—Formal agreement between nations or groups of nations

trial jury—Jury that hears the case against an indicted person and decides its outcome; also called a **petit jury**

Twenty-Fifth Amendment—Constitutional amendment prescribing that any vice-presidential vacancy be filled through a nomination by the president and confirmation by a majority vote in both houses of Congress

Twenty-Fourth Amendment—Constitutional amendment ending poll taxes in national elections

Twenty-Second Amendment—Constitutional amendment limiting the president to two terms, plus up to two years of a predecessor's term if left unfilled

Twenty-Sixth Amendment—Constitutional amendment allowing all those between eighteen and twenty-one years of age the right to vote

two-party system—Political system dominated by two major parties whom most of the electorate identity with

U

unicameral—Legislature made up of only one house

unified government—A city and its surrounding county both controlled by a single government; also called consolidated government

unitary system—Authority given by the people to one centralized level of government that then creates other levels of government to help administer the law

United Nations (UN)—International organization founded in 1945 to maintain world peace and uphold human rights

United States Agency for International Development (USAID)—The US agency chiefly responsible for delivering foreign aid and providing both food and health and education services to needy countries while promoting free government and free-market economies in recipient nations

V

veto—President's power to stop a bill passed by Congress by refusing to sign that bill into law; may be overridden with a two-thirds vote in both houses

veto referendum—Allows the electorate to repeal a piece of legislation or a constitutional amendment

Virginia Plan—Proposal for the composition and structure of the new congress by James Madison; called for a bicameral legislature, with the number of representatives based on state population or on the amount of revenue a state provided for the national government

visa—Official endorsement of a passport by the government of the country being visited

Voting Rights Act of 1965—Legislation that swept aside state poll taxes, literacy tests, and other devices that prevented black voting

W

ward—Division of a municipality or county for the purpose of city council and county commission elections; also known as a district

war power—Congress's constitutional authority to declare war; implicitly grants the government the basic right to defend itself

War Powers Act—Law intended to rein in the presidential power to commit US troops in undeclared wars and foreign conflicts; requires the president to notify Congress within forty-eight hours of committing US troops into military action and to withdraw such troops after sixty days unless Congress specifically approves continued use of those forces.

waste—Bureaucratic mismanagement of money, time, and personnel

weapons of mass destruction (WMDs)—Nuclear, radiological, chemical, and biological weapons designed to affect large numbers of the population in a single attack

West Wing—Section of the White House accommodating the Oval Office, the offices of the executive staff (including the vice president), the Cabinet Room, the Roosevelt Room, and the Brady Press Briefing Room

White House Office—President's top aides, including press secretary, physician, and counsel (legal advisor), who interact with the president on a daily basis and are responsible for communicating presidential policies to both the appropriate agencies and the American public; part of the Executive Office of the President; also called White House staff

white primaries—Restricted party primaries and candidate selection to whites only

World Trade Organization (WTO)—International body promoting free trade, the reduction or elimination of tariffs, and the breaking down of trade barriers between nations; replaced the General Agreement on Tariffs and Trade (GATT)

writ of certiorari—Literally, "to be made more certain"; an order ("writ") from a superior court (especially the Supreme Court) to a lower court to send the entire record of a case for review

writ of habeas corpus—Literally, "you should have the body"; a court order that forces authorities who arrest a person to quickly bring him before a judge and charge him with a crime or else to release him

INDEX

A

abortion, 33, 38, 44, 45, 47–48, 50, 51, 84, 205, 341, 347, 353, 381, 382, 388, 421–22, 432–33, 435. See also *Roe v. Wade*

Abrahamic Covenant, 15–16

absentee voting, 237, 414

ACLU (American Civil Liberties Union), 417, 435

Adams, John, 28, 56–58, 69, 76, 168, 244, 248, 267, 268, 277, 350, 384–85, 401, 408

administrative agencies, 267, 270

administrative law, 293

agenda setting, 424. *See also* public policy

Age of Enlightenment. *See* Enlightenment

Agnew, Spiro, 268

air force. *See under* armed forces

Air Force One, 245, 250

Alito, Samuel, 348

alliance, 102, 303, 304, 321, 327, 384

Alliance Defending Freedom (ADF), 435

al-Qaeda, 310, 322, 324–25

al-Qaddafi, Muammar, 320

ambassador(s), 178, 270, 282, 312

amendment process. *See* Constitution: amendment process of

amendments, constitutional, 27, 76, 82, 141, 170, 175, 183, 192, 200, 245, 247, 362

First, 42, 85, 112, 118, 201, 355–57, 359, 361, 416, 418, 431, 435, 439, 442

Second, 84, 113, 362–63

Third, 113, 362–63

Fourth, 82, 113, 362–63

Fifth, 113, 341, 364–65

Sixth, 114, 364–65

Seventh, 87, 114, 364–65

Eighth, 114, 364–66

Ninth, 114

Tenth, 92, 115, 127, 141, 162, 201

Eleventh, 107, 115

Twelfth, 115, 120, 402

Thirteenth, 109, 116

Fourteenth, 86, 116–17, 193, 352, 362, 364

Fifteenth, 116, 141, 368, 369, 408

Sixteenth, 86, 101, 117, 130, 171, 188, 389

Seventeenth, 92, 95, 117, 126, 171, 389, 407

Eighteenth, 119, 120

Nineteenth, 118, 369

Twentieth, 96, 119, 177, 245

Twenty-First, 85, 119, 120, 194

Twenty-Second, 20, 84, 103, 120, 258, 386

Twenty-Third, 103, 120, 170, 196, 408

Twenty-Fourth, 121, 368, 408

Twenty-Fifth, 84, 104, 121, 199, 268

Twenty-Sixth, 122, 141, 369, 408

Twenty-Seventh, 87, 112, 122

American Association of Retired Persons (AARP), 431–32

American Center for Law and Justice (ACLJ), 435

American Civil Liberties Union, 347, 414

American Family Association (AFA), 433

American Federation of Labor and Congress of Industrial Organizations, (AFL-CIO), 431

Americans for Democratic Action (ADA), 433

American government, 11, 14, 21–22, 25, 74, 92, 112, 141, 148, 167, 194, 211, 267, 300, 303–5, 312, 320,

amicus curiae, 435

amnesty, 105

anarchy, 5, 17, 64

Andrews Air Force Base, 250

Annapolis Convention, 65

Anti-Americanism, 327

Anti-Federalists, 73–77, 379, 384

appellate jurisdiction, 107, 196, 335, 341, 342

appropriations, 100, 101, 295, 316

Aquinas, Thomas, 58–59

Aristotle, 88

armed forces, 12, 86, 99, 100, 251, 261–62, 356

air force, 250, 285, 303, 312

army, 26, 63, 86, 100, 105, 134, 251, 285, 295, 299, 312, 314

marines, 310, 314–15

navy, 63, 86, 100, 105, 224, 253, 283, 285, 306-07, 310, 311–12

Armed Forces Policy Council, 312

army. *See under* armed forces

Arthur, Chester, 223

Articles of Confederation, 19, 31, 62–65, 67, 69, 71, 76, 94, 110, 136, 159, 167, 177, 190

Ashcroft, John, 162, 194

assistant to the president for economic policy, 282, 312

associate justices, 196, 341

Athens, 18, 22, 27

attorney general, 81, 104, 105, 194, 269, 282, 286, 295, 369

autocracy, 16

"Axis of Evil," 321

B

Bacon, Henry, 23

backdoor spending, 201

bail, 26, 114, 123

balancing the ticket, 234

bankruptcy, 99, 194, 196

Benghazi, Libya, 178, 198

bicameral legislature, 94, 143, 167–72

Biden, Joe, 268

bilateral treaties, 320

bill becoming law. *See* legislation, process of

bill of attainder, 101–2, 201

Bill of Rights, 6, 23, 25, 27, 29, 59, 72, 76, 86, 112, 114, 116, 122, 127, 335–36, 342, 355, 356, 362, 367. *See also* amendments, constitutional

biological weapons, 322

Bipartisan Campaign Reform Act (BCRA), 415, 417

Bishop, Joel, 352

Blackstone, William, 338–39

Commentaries on the Laws of England, 338

blanket primary. *See* primary
block grants, 132
board of trustees, 150
Boniface VIII, 46
Bork, Robert, 89, 199, 346–47
boroughs, 148
Boston Massacre, 57
boycott(s), 57
Boy Scouts of America v. Dale, 361
Brady Press Briefing Room, 215, 282
Breyer, Stephen, 348
brief, 335, 343, 435
broad constructionists, 82
brokered convention, 233–4
*Brown v. Board of Education of
    Topeka, Kansas*, 353, 368–69
Bryan, William Jennings, 407
Buchanan, James, 263, 271, 272
Buckley v. Valeo, 416
Bull Moose Party. *See*
    Progressive Party
bureaucracy, 82, 130, 149, 167,
    221, 249, 254, 267, 275,
    277–80, 283, 292–294,
    295–297, 299–300, 424
bureaucrat(s), 275, 284, 292,
    293, 295, 296, 299
bureaucratese, 298
Bush, Barbara, 265
Bush, George H. W., 192, 215,
    234, 235, 236, 253, 269,
    270, 271, 288, 345, 348,
    397, 408, 412
Bush, George W., 31, 222, 224,
    251, 252, 253, 255, 156,
    269, 271, 282, 283, 288,
    310, 315, 324, 348, 380,
    391, 397, 411, 412, 417, 424, 429
Bush, Laura, 266
Byrd, Robert, 202

C

cabinet, 21, 104, 105, 119, 144,
    197, 199, 244, 249, 250,
    256, 262, 267, 268, 269,
    270, 276, 279, 282, 283,
    284, 286, 287, 288, 289,
    299, 312, 384. *See also*
    names of cabinet departments
Cabinet Room, 215, 282
cabinet secretaries, 249, 270
Cameron, David, 20

campaign(s), 33, 47, 178, 200,
    222, 224, 225–27, 230,
    232, 234–36, 238, 242,
    279, 401–2, 404–7, 409, 411–14
Campaign Reform Act of
    2002, 415, 417
campaign slogan(s), 235
Camp, David, 253
Camp David Accords, 253, 304
Cannon, Joseph, 173
capital punishment, 365, 421
Carter, Jimmy, 171, 242, 258,
    271, 304, 316, 380
Carson, Ben, 261
categorical grants, 132–33
caucus, 172, 173, 226, 378, 385,
    386, 394, 395, 402–3, 414
censure, 200, 245
census, 70, 95, 101, 117, 137,
    168, 287, 294
Central Intelligence Agency (CIA),
    251–52, 270, 315, 323, 440
chair, 180
Challenger, 255
checks and balances, 16, 82, 88,
    89–90, 98, 105
chemical weapons, 326
Cheney, Dick, 268, 269, 424
chief executive, 15, 19, 20, 21,
    68, 144, 223, 249, 310. *See
    also* president
chief justice(s), 81, 90, 93, 96,
    129, 162, 196, 259, 343,
    345, 347, 349, 350, 353, 362
chief of staff, 269, 270, 282
chief of state, 255, 256, 262. *See
    also* president
China, People's Republic of, 18, 282
Christian Coalition, 433
church and state relations, 44–46,
    50, 356
Churchill, Winston, 283
circuit courts of appeals, 107,
    196, 340–41
citizenship, 86, 95, 99, 116, 141,
    170, 193, 312, 355, 370
*Citizens United v. Federal
    Election Commission*, 414
civic thinking, 36
civil law, 100, 334, 335
civil liberties, 76, 355, 362, 367,
    372, 414, 421, 423, 425, 435
civil rights. *See* rights: civil
Civil Rights Act of 1964, 355, 369

civil service, 36, 105, 244, 277–79
Civil Service Commission, 278
Civil War, 43, 116, 117, 121,
    125, 129, 130, 188, 189,
    191, 193, 196, 200, 210,
    277, 343, 352, 363, 379,
    386, 387, 436
Clay, Henry, 54, 173, 242, 312, 384
clear-and-present-danger test,
    358–59
Cleveland, Frances, 264
Cleveland, Grover, 235, 240,
    254, 264, 381, 386
client(s), 293
Clinton, Bill, 31, 90, 106, 160,
    171, 184, 200, 225, 231,
    252, 253, 255, 259, 260,
    271, 348, 441
Clinton, George, 73, 268
Clinton, Hillary Rodham, 31, 174,
    229, 231, 233, 235, 237, 240,
    241, 265, 314, 315, 380, 381,
    395, 406, 429, 442
closed primaries. *See* primaries
cloture, 183
coalition, 16, 171, 384, 388, 396
coattail effect, 406–7
Code Napoléon, 336, 337
Code of Hammurabi, 334
Coercive Acts, 57
Cold War, 167, 194, 254, 282,
    288, 303, 308, 310, 320
commander in chief, 99, 105, 116,
    144, 191, 249, 251, 262, 275,
    311. *See also* president
*Commentaries on the
    Constitution of the United
    States*, 349
*Commentaries on the Laws of
    England* (Blackstone), 338
Commerce Clause, 67, 162, 190
commissioners, 26, 148, 149,
    150, 210, 279, 291
commission government, 150
Commission on Human Rights, 320
common law, 114, 193, 335, 337–38
Communications Decency Act
    (1996), 442
communism, 47, 235, 251,
    303–4, 308–9, 333
Communist Party, 16, 359, 389

compromise(s), 33, 38, 55, 66,
    67–72, 91, 179, 182, 184,
    203, 204, 206, 228, 233,
    239, 243, 379
Concordant of Worms (1122), 45
concurring opinion, 343
confederate government, 18–19
conference, 172, 173, 175, 178,
    179, 184, 245, 250, 342
conference committees, 179, 180
confirmation, 105, 121, 199, 263, 268
Congress, 21, 27, 29, 30, 42,
    43, 57, 58, 61, 62, 63, 67,
    68, 70, 72, 84–91, 93–102,
    126, 129, 133–35, 141, 143,
    159, 160, 162, 167, 169,
    249, 251, 252, 254, 255,
    257, 258, 260, 261, 262,
    268, 269, 270, 276, 278,
    279, 281–83, 288, 290,
    293, 294, 295, 297, 298,
    310, 312, 313, 315, 318,
    319, 322, 340, 341, 343,
    344, 347, 350–51, 355,
    356, 359, 360, 361, 367,
    369, 378, 384, 385, 386,
    387, 393, 396, 405, 407,
    410, 413–14, 421, 424, 431,
    433–35, 438, 442
  congressional committees in, 179,
      180, 184, 299
  controversial issues, 175–76
  criticism of, 175, 201–4, 289, 297
  leadership in, 172–75
  legislative workings, 177–84
  powers of, 96, 125–26, 187–201
  sessions of, 176–77
  structure of, 167–84
  See also House of Representa-
      tives; Senate
congressional campaigns, 392,
    393, 406
congressional committees. See
    Congress: congressional
    committees in
congressional district, 169–70,
    230, 240, 352, 394
congressional elections, 96, 168, 239
Congressional Record, 97, 175
Congress of Racial Equality
    (CORE), 434
Connecticut Compromise, 69, 70
conservatism, 422

conservative(s), 233, 254, 346, 352,
    383, 412, 422, 433, 435, 437
Constantine, 41
constituents, 30, 151, 158, 169, 170,
    171, 176, 179, 180, 201, 203,
    275, 281, 293, 402, 404
Constitution, 28, 31, 32, 42,
    54, 59, 125–28, 249, 255,
    258, 259, 260, 262, 267,
    268, 269, 270, 272, 277,
    283, 284, 293, 310, 315,
    336, 339, 340, 343, 344,
    346, 347, 349, 350, 351–53,
    355–57, 361–71, 367, 377,
    379, 384, 387, 401, 410,
    412, 416, 423
  amendment process of, 85–87,
      93, 110
  articles
      I, 21, 84, 88, 94, 125–7, 141,
        167, 177, 187, 188, 198, 200,
        201, 259, 267, 366, 401, 407
      II, 27, 63, 82, 88, 103, 115, 116,
        121, 125, 191, 200, 223, 239,
        242, 244, 249, 252, 255, 258,
        261, 267, 270, 346
      III, 88, 94, 107, 195, 196, 340
      IV, 18, 28, 108, 133, 159–61
      VI, 351
  characteristics of, 81–87
  foundational principles, 87–93
  influences on, 55–72
  interpretation of, 82–84
  Preamble, 76, 92, 94, 423
  principles of, 26–27
  ratification of, 73–78
  text, 107–11
  See also amendments,
      constitutional
Constitutional Convention, 27,
    55, 66–72, 75, 76, 111, 123,
    138, 167, 168, 170, 175,
    190, 239, 258, 384
constitutional law, 71
constitutional monarchies, 15
constitutional rights. See
    rights: constitutional
Constitution Party, 390
consulates, 312
containment, 308–9
Continental Congress, 62, 71,
    100, 167, 288. See also First
    Continental Congress;
    Second Continental Congress

convention(s), 225, 226, 227,
    230, 231, 233–38, 378,
    385–86, 402, 403
  county, 391, 403
  national, 85, 153–54, 391 225–27,
      230, 233, 381, 392–93, 394,
      402–03
  party, 225, 230, 231, 403
  state, 230, 239, 391, 393, 403
Coolidge, Calvin, 227, 245, 255,
    260, 262, 268, 405, 437
Coolidge, Grace, 264
copyrights, 99, 195
Corpus Juris Civilis, 334
Council for Secular Humanism, 433
council-manager form of gov-
    ernment, 150
Council of Economic Advisors, 283
Council of Environmental
    Quality, 283
counterfeiting, 99, 257
counties, 22, 128, 142, 148–49,
    238, 393
county commission, 148
county committee, 153
county executive, 149
covert operations, 251, 252, 282, 315
Creation Mandate, 4
criminal-justice process, 365
criminal law, 335, 365
crossover voting, 157, 228
C-SPAN, 438
cultural imperialism, 327–28
cultural relativity, 328
culture wars, 49

D

Dartmouth College v. Woodward, 343
Davis, Gray, 158
Dean, Howard, 397
debates. See presidential debates
Declaration of Independence,
    6, 9, 25, 32, 58, 59, 62, 66,
    69, 75, 166, 355, 363, 386
defamation, 236, 358–59. See
    also libel; slander
Defense of Marriage Act, 160
delegated powers, 21, 125
delegation, 63, 126, 232, 241, 275
Delta Force, 312
democracy, 17–18, 21–29, 31–34,
    35–38, 151, 195, 305, 403, 411,
    444

Democratic National
Committee (DNC), 383, 393
Democratic Party, 171, 229,
231, 254, 259, 266, 370, 409
Democratic primary. *See* primary
Democratic-Republican Party,
277, 384–85
Dennis v. United States, 359
Department of Agriculture, 270, 286
Department of Commerce, 99,
270, 287
Department of Defense, 270,
285, 311, 312, 313
Department of Education, 37,
270, 288
Department of Energy, 270, 288
Department of Health and
Human Services, 270, 287, 298
Department of Homeland
Security (DHS), 257, 270,
285, 288, 289, 312
Department of Housing and
Urban Development, 270, 287
Department of Justice, 118,
270, 275, 286, 369
Department of Labor, 270, 287
Department of State, 270, 276,
284, 311
Department of the Interior, 270, 286
Department of the Navy, 311
Department of the Treasury,
249, 270, 275, 284
Department of Transportation,
270, 287
Department of Veterans
Affairs, 270, 288
Department of War, 311
dictatorship, 16
diplomacy, 106, 253, 304, 314–
15, 304, 317–18, 322, 423
direct democracy, 18, 25–28, 151
director of national intelli-
gence, 270, 282, 312
direct primaries. *See* primaries
disruptive speech, 358
dissenting opinion, 345
district. *See* ward
district courts, 99, 107, 196, 338–41
District of Columbia, 70, 100,
103, 120, 170, 196, 207,
240, 292, 339–42
District of Columbia v. Heller, 363
divine law. *See* revealed law
divorce, 7, 44, 48, 49, 142, 145

Dole, Bob, 408
domestic policy, 254, 423
double jeopardy, 364
Douglass, Frederick, 339
Douglas, Stephen A., 236
Douglas, William O., 347, 356, 366
Dred Scott case, 350, 352
dual federalism, 129
due process, 24, 113, 116, 128,
293, 350
Dukakis, Michael, 229, 235, 397
Duncan, John, Jr., 180
duty, 8, 9, 11, 12, 60, 63, 90, 98,
100–02, 188-89, 262, 267,
277, 314, 349, 358, 372
Dwight, Timothy, 43
dynasty, 15

E

Earp, Wyatt, 339
Economic and Social Council, 316
Edict of Milan, 41
EEOC (Equal Employment
Opportunity Commission), 369
Eisenhower, Dwight D., 132,
134, 224, 226, 232, 235,
245, 253, 254, 260, 261,
272, 349, 376, 407
Eisenhower Executive Office
Building, 283
elastic clause. *See* necessary and
proper clause
elections, 18, 24, 29, 36, 77,
95–97, 103, 117, 120–22,
143, 152, 154–57, 168,
170, 196, 198, 222, 225,
227–29, 232, 237, 239, 241,
279, 370, 402–4, 407–9,
411–12, 414, 424, 433. *See
also* congressional elec-
tions; general elections;
presidential elections;
runoff elections
Electoral College, 27, 31, 72, 77,
86, 91, 225, 227, 235, 238,
239, 243–246, 380, 381,
384, 389, 409
Ellsberg, Daniel, 359
Emancipation Proclamation, 116
embassies, 311
eminent domain, 113, 365
en banc, 342,
Engel v. Vitale, 357
English Bill of Rights, 23, 25–26

English government, 23–25
Enlightenment, 27, 58–59, 92, 168
entitlements, 201
enumerated powers, 98–102,
125, 162, 187-97
Environmental Protection
Agency (EPA), 270, 292, 293
equality, 6, 17, 18, 25, 27–29, 32,
33, 38, 68, 86, 371–72
Equal Rights Amendment, 86, 234
espionage, 108
establishment clause, 43, 355, 356
European Union (EU), 19, 317, 324
excise taxes, 98, 188
exclusionary rule, 364
executive agreement, 252
executive branch, 10, 19, 21, 68,
85, 88, 90, 103–06, 144,
167, 184, 244, 245, 249,
254, 275, 278, 280, 281,
283, 289, 290, 294, 299,
424. *See also* president
Executive Office of the
President (EOP), 21, 249,
269, 270, 280, 282, 283,
289, 290, 294
executive orders, 167, 244, 260,
261, 424
Executive Residence, 281
exit polls, 237,
ex post facto law, 101, 102, 201, 366
extradition, 108, 129, 161

F

factions, 17, 31, 33, 152, 228, 232,
377, 384, 392, 393, 394, 431
Fall, 4–5
Family Research Council (FRC), 433
Federal Bureau of Investigation
(FBI), 286, 293, 295, 296, 323
Federal Communications
Commission (FCC), 290,
292, 295, 442
Federal Election Campaign
Act (FECA), 415
Federal Election Commission
(FEC), 290, 411–12, 415
federal election(s), 121, 156, 415, 417
Federal Emergency
Management Agency
(FEMA), 290, 315

federal government, 19, 21, 65, 70, 76, 101, 109, 112, 115, 117, 125, 126, 130, 131, 132, 135, 148, 190, 230, 244, 245, 253, 278, 338, 340, 349
Federal Housing Administration, 201
federalism, 19, 27, 91–92, 125, 129–30
    defined, 19, 125, 141, 338, 392
Federalist Papers, 23, 73–74
    No. 1: 73–74
    No. 6: 23
    No. 9: 23
    No. 10: 76, 377
    No. 14: 76
    No. 18: 23
    No. 38: 23
    No. 41: 312
    No. 46: 138
    No. 48: 88
    No. 51: 81–82
    No. 58: 168
    No. 62: 168
    No. 63: 23, 168
    No. 70: 23
    No. 74: 74
    No. 78: 90, 340
Federalists, 73–77, 193, 350, 377, 379, 384
Federal Reserve System, 189, 290, 292
Federal Rights, 179
Felton, Rebecca, 174
filibuster, 183
Fillmore, Millard, 85, 223
First Continental Congress, 57, 69
First Lady, 174, 215, 232, 246, 255, 256, 263–66, 282
flag etiquette, 360
Flag Protection Act, 361
Ford, Gerald, 80, 199, 268, 347, 380
foreign policy, 167, 173, 199, 252, 303, 304, 305–6, 308, 310, 311, 313–14, 315, 318, 319, 320, 323, 324, 325, 423–24
Foreign Service, 284, 312, 318
formula grants, 132, 137
fourth branch, 294, 295
fourth-generation warfare, 319
franchise, 32, 118, 369. *See also* rights: voting
franking privilege, 97, 176

Franklin, Benjamin, 58, 62, 69, 78, 111, 317
free speech, *See* rights: free speech
freedom, 12, 17, 18, 21, 24, 26, 37, 38, 43, 47, 59, 63, 81, 198, 235, 296, 298, 299, 333–34, 357, 361, 372, 431, 439
    economic, 299
    individual, 44, 47, 76, 88, 355, 367, 422
    of assembly, 112, 113, 201, 356, 361
    of association, 32, 93, 361, 378
    of expression, 32, 33, 112, 358
    of media, 439–42
    of petition, 112, 201, 356, 361
    of religion, 32, 41, 93, 112, 128, 201, 355, 357
    of speech, 43, 93, 97, 112, 192, 201, 356, 358–61, 362, 378, 435
    of person, 32
    of the press, 32, 93, 112, 201, 356, 358–61, 439
    political, 32, 305
Freedom of Information Act (FOIA), 296, 440
free-exercise clause, 355, 357–58
free media, 406–7
French, Daniel Chester, 23
full faith and credit clause, 159–60
Furman v. Georgia, 365–66

G

Gallup, George, 427
Garfield, James, 37, 121, 186, 278
Garland, Merrick, 89, 348
General Agreement on Tariffs and Trade (GATT), 303, 317
General Assembly, 143, 319
general elections, 155–56, 157, 403–4, 412, 414
general welfare, 92, 94, 98, 187, 189, 423
George III, 56
Germany, 12, 16, 19, 37, 106, 126
gerrymandering, 117, 169
Gibbons v. Ogden, 190
Gingrich, Newt, 174
Ginsburg, Ruth Bader, 347, 348
Gitlow v. New York, 362
Gladstone, William, 78
globalization, 315, 323–24
Goldwater, Barry, 228, 382, 397

Gore, Al, 31, 233, 236, 237, 238, 240, 241, 380, 381, 391, 397, 411, 412, 429, 441
Gorsuch, Neil, 90, 199, 348
government
    American, 21, 22, 25, 74, 92, 112, 141, 148, 167, 194, 211, 267, 300
    biblical worldview of, 3–6, 38, 44–50
    branches, 19, 21–22, 68, 74, 85, 88–91, 99, 125, 142–43, 146, 197, 204, 245, 258, 294, 377, 424
    Christian responsibility toward, 7–10, 36–38, 41–50
    church and state, 45–47
    confederate, 18–19
    defined, 3
    federal, 18-19, 125–37, 148, 190, 230, 244, 245, 253, 278, 338, 340, 349
    history of, 41–43
    levels, 18
    national, 17, 19, 21, 62, 63, 67, 68, 69, 76, 82, 87, 88, 89, 90, 91, 93, 95, 100, 102, 110, 125, 127–35, 137, 141–42, 146, 148, 159, 161, 162, 167, 168, 171, 188, 190–91, 196, 197, 203, 294, 356, 379, 423
    necessity of, 3–4
    obligations of, 9–11
    shut down, 90
    state, 22, 125–26, 141–47, 152–58, 160
    types of, 15–17
    unified, 149–51
    unitary, 18
    See also specific types of government
Government Accountability Office (GAO), 290, 295–96
governor, 73, 75, 77, 84, 108, 109, 117, 125, 126, 143–145, 156–158, 161, 169, 174, 265, 342, 345–46, 401, 403, 407, 410.
    See also gubernatorial appointments
Grace Commission, 297
grass roots, 152, 394, 418, 430
grandfather clause, 368
grand jury, 55, 113, 260, 339, 364, 365

Grant, Ulysses S., 167, 224, 254, 272
grants
    block, 132–33
    categorical, 132
    formula, 132
    grants-in-aid, 131
    project, 132
grants-in-aid, 131
grass roots, 152, 418
Great Compromise. *See* Con-
    necticut Compromise
Great Depression, 137, 254,
    278, 291, 303, 386, 423
Green Berets, 312
Green Party, 389, 390
gridlock, 33, 90
Griswold v. Connecticut, 82–84, 366
gubernatorial appointments, 143–44
gun control, 421, 425, 430, 432–33
gun rights. *See* rights

H

habeas corpus, writ of, 101, 201
Haley, Nikki, 144
Hamilton, Alexander, 65,
    73–74, 90, 111, 188, 189,
    194, 197, 206, 274, 306,
    338, 341, 384
Hammurabi, 334
Harding, Warren, 257, 405, 437
hard money, 415
Harrison, William Henry, 85, 235,
    268, 269, 385–86
Hayes, Rutherford B., 405
health care, 130, 275
Help America Vote Act (HAVA), 410
Henry, Patrick, 57, 62, 75, 223, 357
Heritage Foundation, 299, 433
Hickok, Wild Bill, 339
Hitler, Adolf, 16, 37, 308, 368, 429
Hobbes, Thomas, 17
Hoover, Herbert, 224, 245, 249, 283
hopper, 181
House of Burgesses, 55, 167
House of Representatives, 21,
    27, 68, 70, 86, 89, 92, 94,
    95, 98, 103, 104, 106, 115,
    119, 121, 122, 143, 167–74,
    177, 178, 180, 187, 200,
    239–42, 245, 259, 269,
    346, 348, 378, 379, 384,
    385, 387, 393, 402, 407,
    414, 433–34, 438

Housing and Urban
    Development (HUD), 261, 287
Hughes, Charles Evans, 84
human depravity, 3–5, 16. *See
    also* Fall
human rights, *See* rights: human
Humphrey, Hubert, 380, 395
Hussein, Saddam, 16, 309–10

I

image of God, 4–5, 8, 33–34, 44
immigration, 179, 193, 198,
    312, 346, 412
Immigration and Naturalization
    Service (INS), 289, 315
impeachment, 74, 89, 95–96,
    105–6, 108, 158, 173, 199,
    200, 251, 255, 258–60
imperialism, 307, 327, 328, 328
implied powers, 125–27, 162, 197–98
inaugural address, 32, 242,
    245–46, 306, 424
inauguration, 31, 78, 115, 119,
    177, 223, 224, 242–46
incorporation, 362
incumbent, 156, 308, 385, 393,
    401–2, 409, 435
independent expenditures, 416
independent voters, 396–97
India, 36, 261
indirect democracy, 18
individual rights. *See* rights
initiative, 157, 158, 167, 266, 391
Innocent III, 22, 46
Inter-American Treaty of
    Reciprocal Assistance
    (Rio Pact), 317
interest groups, 87, 135, 181,
    201, 298, 395, 430–36,
    444. *See also* pressure groups
International Court of Justice, 319
International Emergency
    Economic Powers Act
    (IEEPA), 322
International Monetary Fund.
    (IMF), 321
internet, 28, 155, 406, 411, 425,
    428, 434, 436–39, 442
internet voting, 415
interstate commerce, 65, 70, 190–91
Interstate Commerce
    Commission, 190, 278
interstate highway system, 99,
    132, 197, 300

Intolerable Acts, 57
Iran, 16, 310, 324
Iraq, 16, 310, 320, 322, 324, 325,
    327, 440
Irish Republican Army (IRA), 324
Internal Revenue Service (IRS),
    118, 249, 275, 285, 293, 298
Islamic State in Iraq and Syria
    (ISIS), 321
isolationism, 303, 306–7
Israel, 3, 7, 15–16, 18, 35, 46,
    191, 194, 275, 292, 304–5,
    318, 325, 328, 333

J

Jackson, Andrew, 211, 224, 240,
    241, 277, 381, 384, 385, 436
Jay, John, 64, 73, 341
Jefferson, Thomas, 28, 32, 37,
    55, 58, 59, 62, 69, 75, 76,
    90, 114, 129, 197, 198, 210,
    241, 255, 263, 272, 277,
    306, 312, 332, 350
Jesus Christ, 16, 86, 430
John (King of England), 24
Johnson, Andrew, 106, 200,
    224, 244, 245, 259, 268,
    272, 288
Johnson, Gary, 389, 390, 416
Johnson, Lyndon B., 130, 233,
    245, 252, 255, 258, 268,
    283, 369, 395, 397
Joint Chiefs of Staff (JCS), 282,
    285, 312, 314
joint committees, 179
judges, 46, 60, 83, 84, 89, 97,
    100, 105, 107, 110, 112,
    128, 144–45, 261, 262,
    276, 319, 333, 335–36,
    339–42, 344–345, 349–52, 383
judicial activism, 351, 424
judicial branch, 21–22, 68, 88,
    107, 144, 290, 333–352
judicial federalism, 338
judicial restraint, 351
judicial review, 83, 90, 107, 338,
    349, 350
Judiciary Act of 1789, 196, 339,
    340, 350
jungle primary. *See* primary.
junkets, 176

justice, 5, 6, 24, 29, 32, 37, 60,
    61, 74, 90, 92, 94, 96, 108,
    161, 189, 275, 291–92, 297,
    335–36, 353, 355, 357, 362, 366
justices of the US Supreme
    Court, 89, 145, 162, 196,
    199, 223, 224, 242, 245,
    251, 252, 342–49, 352–53
Justinian, 336, 337

K

Kagan, Elena, 348
Kant, Immanuel, 17
Kavanaugh, Brett, 347–48
Kennedy, Jacqueline, 265
Kennedy, John F., 121, 233,
    236, 243, 249, 253, 256,
    258, 260, 284, 307, 380,
    406, 408, 409, 411, 412
Kerry, John, 318, 441
keynote address, 232
King, Martin Luther, Jr., 368,
    369, 434
Kissinger, Henry, 282, 304
Kitchen Cabinet, 284
Kuwait, 16, 308

L

lame duck, 119, 258
Lawrence v. Texas, 353
lay investiture controversy, 45
League of Nations, 307
Lee, Robert E., 129
legal tender, 189
legislation, process of, 180–84
legislative branch, 21, 85–102,
    187, 290
legislative government, 55
legislature, 19, 20, 21, 30, 60,
    61, 63, 64, 68, 74, 94–96,
    100, 103, 109, 116–18, 126,
    129, 133, 134, 143, 144,
    145, 147, 157, 158, 168–69,
    190, 202, 203, 239, 293,
    333, 336, 344, 357, 410
Lemon test, 356–57
Lemon v. Kurtzman, 357
letter of marque, 192
libel, 112–13, 359, 442. *See also*
    defamation
liberalism, 351, 421–22, 435
Libertarian Party, 389–91, 403

liberty, 17, 25, 27, 28, 29, 32, 33,
    34, 36, 37, 38, 43, 58, 59,
    60, 72, 76, 77, 78, 81, 87,
    88, 89, 90, 92, 93, 94, 113,
    116, 160, 168, 354–55, 358,
    362, 365, 423, 431, 435, 443
Liberty Council, 357, 435
Library of Congress, 99, 219,
    290, 438
lieutenant governor, 144, 397, 401
limited government, 23–25,
    55–56, 88, 112, 125, 383
Lincoln, Abraham, 207, 224,
    236, 245, 271, 272, 379, 386
Lincoln, Mary, 264
Lincoln Memorial, 23, 207
line-item veto. *See* veto: line-item
literacy tests, 117, 368, 369
lobbying, 433–34
local government, 22, 28, 55,
    128, 135, 140, 148–58, 423
Locke, John, 25, 42, 59
logrolling, 202–3
lotteries, 147

M

MacArthur, Douglas, 251
Madison, Dolly, 263
Madison, James, 8, 21, 28, 29,
    37, 55, 64, 67, 71, 73, 75,
    81, 88, 110, 111,112, 122,
    129, 138, 168, 189, 276,
    314, 347, 350, 357, 377, 431
Magna Carta, 23-25
majority leader, 172, 173
majority opinion, 38, 343
majority-plurality representation, 30
majority rule, 29–32
majority whip, 172
Mapp v. Ohio, 364
Marbury v. Madison, 90, 107, 350
Marine One, 220, 250
marines. *See under* armed forces
Marshall, John, 81, 90, 129,
    190, 341, 342, 347–48, 349, 353
Marshall Plan, 305
Marshall, Thomas, 268
Marshall, Thurgood, 345
Mason, George, 72, 75, 170, 357
mass media, 346, 436, 439, 442, 445
Masterson, Bat, 339
Mattis, General James, 314
May, Theresa, 20
Mayflower Compact, 42

mayor-council form of govern-
    ment, 196
McCain, John, 229, 417
McCain-Feingold Act, 414
McConnell, Mitch, 418
*McConnell v. Federal Election
    Commission*, 414
McCulloch v. Maryland, 127, 197, 351
McDonald v. Chicago, 363
McGovern, George, 228, 382
McKinley, William, 167, 254,
    257, 307, 407
mechanical-lever voting ma-
    chine, 414
Memorial and Remonstrance
    (Madison), 356
merit, 105, 204, 223, 278–79, 358
Miller v. California, 359
minority leader, 172
minority rights. *See* rights: minority
minority whip, 172
Miranda rights, 31
Miranda v. Arizona, 353, 364
Miranda warning, 364
Missouri Plan, 145, 346
moderates, 422
monarch, 15
monarchy, constitutional, 15
Mondale, Walter, 409
Monroe, James, 14, 211, 215,
    245, 306, 384
Monroe Doctrine, 306-7
Montesquieu, 18, 88
    Spirit of Laws, The, 18
Moral Majority, 433
moral responsibility, 38
Morris, Gouverneur, 67, 71, 92,
    111, 342
Mount Vernon, 64
Muhlenberg, Frederick A. C., 173
multinational organizations, 315
multiparty system, 384, 387–88
municipal governments, 150
municipalities, 22, 148, 150, 152, 394
mutual assured destruction
    (MAD), 308

N

Nader, Ralph, 390
National Abortion Rights
        Action League (NARAL), 433
National Aeronautics and Space
        Administration (NASA), 261,
        289, 295
National Assessment of
        Educational Progress
        (NAEP), 37
National Association for the
        Advancement of Colored
        People (NAACP), 361, 434
National Cemetery
        Administration, 288
national debt, 135, 187–89, 201
national defense, 5, 8, 189, 197,
        297, 303, 421
National Guard, 100, 261, 314
National Performance Review, 299
National Public Radio (NPR), 437
National Rifle Association
        (NRA), 395, 432
National Right to Life
        Committee, 417, 432
national security, 192, 251, 253,
        303–5, 310, 314, 322–323,
        358–59, 364, 440
national security advisor, 282,
        311–12, 327
National Security Agency (NSA), 323
National Security Council
        (NSC), 252, 260, 267, 268,
        270, 280, 282, 329
National Voter Registration
        Act ("Motor Voter Law"), 412
naturalization, 60, 99, 193–94,
        289, 315
natural law, 42, 58, 337
navy. *See under* armed forces
necessary and proper clause,
        84, 100, 126, 128, 162, 197
New Deal, 130, 131, 137, 146,
        162, 167, 278, 343, 352–53,
        357, 362
New Jersey Plan, 67–70
New York Times Co. v. Sullivan,
        359, 442
*New York Times Co. v. United
        States*, 359

Nixon, Richard, 74, 125, 130,
        133, 179, 181, 199, 236,
        241, 244, 252, 259, 271,
        272, 282, 283, 296, 299,
        346, 380, 385, 408, 439
nominating primaries. *See* primaries
nomination, 385–87, 392,
        401–3, 408, 412
nomination process, 222, 223,
        227, 231, 232, 385–86, 396
nominating methods, 378
Norris, George W., 143
North American Free Trade
        Agreement (NAFTA),
        188–89, 317
North Atlantic Treaty
        Organization (NATO),
        304, 316–17, 320
nuclear deterrence, 308
nuclear weapons, 288, 309, 321, 322

O

Oak Ridge National Laboratory, 288
Obama, Barack, 6, 83, 84, 89,
        90, 162, 190, 200, 222,
        235, 253, 260, 261, 268,
        271, 282, 310, 345, 348,
        397, 441–42
Obama, Michelle, 232, 266,
Obamacare, 171, 190, 204
obscenity, 358-59, 442
Occupational Safety and Health
        Administration (OSHA), 293
Office of Administration, 283, 290
Office of Global
        Communications, 283
Office of Management and
        Budget (OMB), 270, 280,
        282, 290, 293, 296, 310
Office of Nuclear Energy, 288
Office of Personnel
        Management, 299
Office of Policy Development, 283
Office of Post Secondary
        Education, 288
Office of Science and
        Technology Policy, 283
Office of Strategic Services
        (OSS), 252
Obergefell v. Hodges, 353
oligarchy, 16
O'Neill, Thomas P. "Tip," Jr., 141
one-party system, 379–80, 384, 388
open primaries. *See* primaries

Operation Enduring Freedom, 251
opinion polls, 427
optical scan ballot, 414
original jurisdiction, 107, 196,
        335, 339, 341, 342
Oval Office, 31, 84, 215, 224,
        237, 243, 281–83
oversight, 142, 178, 179, 252,
        278, 295, 424

P

Palestine Liberation
        Organization (PLO), 321
pardons, 74, 105, 144, 244
parishes, 148
Parks, Rosa, 368
Parliament, 20, 55–56, 88, 126,
        167, 168, 197, 270, 379
parliamentary system, 20, 88, 126
partisanship, 199, 378
party platform, 153, 205, 230–
        32, 381, 382, 389, 409, 428
passport, 303, 311
patents, 99, 195
patriotism, 12, 223
patronage, 105, 154, 278, 385.
        See also spoils system
Paul, Rand, 395
Paul, Ron, 397
Pearl Harbor, 59, 198, 261, 283,
        303, 308
Pelosi, Nancy, 172, 174, 204, 424
Pence, Mike, 233, 268
Pendleton Act, 278
Pentagon, 285, 289, 310, 314, 325, 359
Pentagon Papers, 359
People for the American Way, 433
Perot, Ross, 235, 236, 389, 390
Perry, Matthew, 306
petition, 26, 31, 43, 112, 158,
        201, 335, 361, 403, 431
petit jury, 341
Philadelphia Convention. *See*
        Constitutional Convention
Pierce, Franklin, 223, 272
Pilgrims, 42
Planned Parenthood, 382–83, 417
Plessy v. Ferguson, 368
PLO (Palestine Liberation
        Organization), 321
pluralism, 41, 43, 44, 49, 50. *See
        also* pluralistic society
pluralistic society, 31, 40
plurality, 30

pocket veto. *See* veto: pocket
political action committee
      (PACs), 416, 434, 445
political campaign, 200, 385,
      401. *See also* campaigns
political cartoons, 439
political ideologies, 47
political machine, 154
political parties, 49, 74, 90, 103,
      113, 134, 152–54, 156, 157,
      170, 171, 225, 226, 228,
      278, 377, 378, 383, 384,
      385, 387, 388, 394, 401–2,
      409, 413–14, 427, 430–31,
      436, 443, 444
politics, 13, 19, 42, 45, 47, 56,
      62, 141, 150, 154, 194,
      201, 202, 224, 225, 257,
      263, 280, 319, 326, 344,
      369, 377, 379, 384, 387–89,
      392–93, 401, 409, 412,
      426, 431, 436, 437, 438, 442
polls, 31, 154, 156, 201, 237, 244,
      258, 272, 317, 396, 408–10,
      412, 414, 428–29, 443
   exit, 237
polling place, 152–53, 369–70, 404
poll tax, 121, 368, 369
popular government, 17–18
popular majority, 29–30
popular sovereignty, 92–93, 114
Populist Party, 389
pork-barrel politics, 202–3
poverty, 5, 8, 33, 43, 49, 130,
      189, 224, 297
Powell, Colin, 241, 269
Preamble, 92, 94
precedents, 84, 129, 223, 337
precincts, 152–53, 369–70, 391,
      393, 403, 408, 410
president, 17, 19, 21, 23, 27, 31,
      62, 66, 67, 70–72, 74, 77,
      78, 82, 84–86, 88–91, 93,
      96–99, 103–7, 111, 115–22,
      126, 130, 132, 134, 137,
      144, 154, 157, 160, 162,
      171–74, 177, 179, 181, 182,
      184, 188, 191, 192, 196,
      198–200, 202, 203, 207,
      210, 215, 223–27, 232,
      238–47, 249–71, 275–84,
      286, 289, 291, 293, 378,
      381, 384, 385, 390, 392,
      393, 404–7, 409, 424, 429, 443

presidential campaigns, 225–
      34, 406–7, 413, 441, 443
presidential debates, 160, 75,
      182–83, 227, 234, 236,
      356, 408–10
presidential elections, 120, 155,
      170, 196, 379, 391, 392,
      393, 395, 396, 401–18, 426
   in 1800: 103, 241, 384
   in 1816: 384
   in 1824: 241, 384, 396, 402
   in 1828: 385
   in 1832: 385
   in 1836: 103, 198, 241
   in 1840: 385
   in 1860: 385, 386
   in 1876: 240, 385
   in 1892: 389, 410
   in 1896: 235, 405
   in 1912: 389
   in 1920: 235, 385, 389, 437
   in 1924: 385, 389, 405
   in 1928: 385
   in 1932: 386
   in 1936: 427
   in 1940: 235, 258
   in 1944: 235, 258
   in 1948: 386, 390, 428
   in 1952: 379, 386, 405
   in 1960: 155, 225, 233, 235, 236
      404, 406, 409
   in 1964: 155, 381, 396
   in 1968: 155, 380, 390
   in 1972: 381
   in 1976: 258, 380, 389, 407, 415–16
   in 1980: 237, 396, 405
   in 1984: 239, 258, 389, 396, 406,
      409
   in 1988: 238, 396, 405, 406, 409
   in 1992: 240
   in 1996: 385
   in 2000: 226, 237, 238, 240, 241,
      380, 381, 387, 389, 390, 396,
      406, 409–10, 429, 437, 441
   in 2004: 441
   in 2008: 397, 416, 441
   in 2012: 389, 397, 409, 441-42
   in 2016: 31, 188–89, 198, 232–34,
      266, 380, 381, 382, 389, 407,
      409, 413, 429, 441–42
presidential inauguration, 223–246
presidential primaries. *See* primaries
presidential succession, 87, 96,
      106, 119, 121, 172, 173, 269

presidential system, 19–20
Presidential Transition Act, 244
president pro tempore, 96, 97,
      104, 119, 121, 172
press secretary, 215, 269, 281
pressure groups, 430
primaries, 117, 155–57, 378,
      386–87, 392, 393–95, 404, 416
   blanket, 403
   closed, 157, 227, 403
   Democratic, 226, 401, 403
   direct, 225, 403
   jungle, 157, 404.
         also called Top-Two method
   nominating, 387, 395
   open, 156–57, 228, 403
   presidential, 225–232, 416
   Republican, 226, 403
   semiclosed, 157, 403
   Top-Two method, 156, 403
   white, 117
   winner-take-all, 235
primary elections, 227–29, 404
prior restraint, 359, 439
privileges and immunities
      clause, 160–61
probable cause, 113, 363–64
procedural due process, 367
Progressive Party, 389–90
Prohibition, 85, 200, 339
Prohibition Party, 390–91
project grants, 132
propaganda, 368, 427, 443–44
property rights, *See* rights:
      property rights
proportional representation,
      30, 67, 69
proposal, 31, 65, 67, 68, 70,
      85–87, 90, 158, 188, 282,
      294, 417
public opinion, 38, 92, 421–22,
      424–30, 433–34, 440, 443
public policy, 48, 112, 421–25,
      427, 429–30, 433, 436, 440, 444
punch-card ballots, 238
pure democracy, 18, 28

Q

quorum, 64, 97, 104, 115, 116, 183

R

radiological weapon, 326
Randolph, Edmund, 68, 75
Rangers, 312

Rankin, Jeannette, 174
ratification, 62–63, 72–76,
    85–87, 92, 93, 110, 118–20,
    122, 199, 245, 252, 318,
    362, 369, 377, 379, 384
Ravitch, Diane, 37–38
Reagan, Nancy, 265
Reagan, Ronald, 125, 128, 130,
    192, 224, 234, 243, 245,
    296, 297, 309, 326, 345,
    405–6, 409, 433
reapportionment, 95, 137, 143,
    145, 169
recall, 74, 158
reciprocity, 161
Reconstruction, 116–17, 368, 379
red tape, 133, 275, 296, 298
Reeves, Bass, 339
referendum, 126, 157–58, 321
Reform Party, 390–91
Reformation, 41, 59
registration, voter, 145, 155,
    394, 411, 416
"reinventing government"
    (REGO), 299
Rehnquist, William, 162
relations between church and
    state, 44–46, 50
religion, free exercise. *See*
    rights: religious rights
religious toleration, 42
representative democracy, 18, 28
representative majority, 29–30
representative sample, 427–28
reprieves, 74, 105, 144
reprimand, 174, 200
reprisal, 90, 99, 102, 192
republic, 17, 18, 23, 25, 27, 28,
    32, 38, 55, 59, 65, 70, 73,
    129, 204, 223, 325, 421
Republican National
    Committee (RNC), 383,
    393, 407
Republican Party, 174, 179,
    231–32, 234, 277, 349–50,
    379–81, 383–84, 386, 389,
    394, 396
Republican primaries. *See* primaries
"Republicans in Name Only"
    (RINO), 383
reserved powers, 127, 129, 201
residency requirements, 369
revealed law, 337
revenue sharing, 132, 133

Revolutionary War. *See* War
    for Independence
Reynolds v. United States, 358
Rice, Condoleezza, 315
Right-to-Life Party, 389, 417, 432
righteousness, 6–7, 50, 333
rights, 9, 32–33
    abortion and homosexual, 84,
        422, 433, 435
    civil, 6–8, 112, 183, 192, 339, 355,
        367–70, 372, 432, 438
    constitutional, 6, 58, 60, 128, 362,
        364
    free speech, 44, 358, 360–62, 378,
        418, 435
    gun, 363, 430, 432
    human, 319, 320, 324
    individual's, 17, 23, 25, 72, 108,
        114–15, 141, 160–61, 193
    minority, 31
    property, 195, 361
    religious, 112, 357–58
    states', 62, 75–76, 102, 115, 125–
        28, 133
    unalienable rights, 6, 25, 58, 60,
        355
    voting, 32, 86, 117, 119, 120, 122,
        130, 141, 154–55, 369, 408,
        410–12
    women's, 174
Roberts, John, 348
Rockefeller, Nelson, 199, 268
Roe v. Wade, 47, 353, 367. *See*
    also abortion
rogue nations, 321
Roman government, 22–23, 41,
    336–37, 339
Roman Republic, 22–23, 336
Romney, Mitt, 402, 412, 442
Roosevelt, Eleanor, 264–265
Roosevelt, Franklin, 130,
    137–38, 154, 226, 249–50,
    280–82, 307, 386, 422, 427, 437
Roosevelt Room, 282
Roosevelt, Theodore, 167,
    223–24, 254, 262, 281, 311,
    317, 318, 339, 390

S

Sadat, Anwar, 253
sanctions, 322
Scalia, Antonin, 89
Schenck v. United States, 358–59
Schwarzenegger, Arnold, 158

SEALs, 315
Second Continental Congress, 58
Secretariat, 316
secretary-general, 319
secretary of defense, 104, 285, 314
secretary of energy, 269
secretary of state, 104, 238,
    266, 277, 306, 312, 318,
    350, 385, 427
secretary of the treasury, 101,
    104, 188, 206, 306
secret ballot, 203, 413
Secret Service, 249, 281, 285, 289, 315
secularism, 44–45, 48
sedition, 358–59
select committees, 178
selectmen, 151
self-incrimination, 364
semiclosed primaries, *See* primaries
Senate, 21, 68, 70–72, 74, 86,
    89, 91, 94–98, 103–7, 110,
    115–19, 121–22, 126, 143,
    167–68, 171–76, 178–84,
    187, 196, 198–200, 202,
    210, 213, 236–237, 239–41,
    245–46, 276, 281–82, 284,
    290, 307, 311–13, 315, 341,
    344, 346–47, 349–51, 378,
    393, 401, 403–7, 433–34, 438
senatorial courtesy, 345
separation of church and state,
    44–45
separation of powers, 21–22,
    63, 88, 89, 141–42, 184, 195, 294
September 11 attacks, 183, 251,
    253, 266, 288, 289, 310,
    312, 315, 320, 322, 425
sergeant at arms, 97, 175
Shays's Rebellion, 65
Sherman, Roger, 58, 62, 67, 69, 111
shield laws, 440
single-issue interest group, 432
single-member district, 170, 380–81
slander, 112, 236, 359, 442. *See*
    also defamation
slavery, 67, 70, 76, 86, 95, 101,
    108–10, 116–17, 130, 161,
    183, 190, 236, 350, 389
slogans, 238–39
Smith Act, 359
social contract, 42, 59
Socialist Labor Party, 389
Socialist Party, 389–90
Socialist Worker's Party, 390

Social Security Administration, 290, 293, 298, 300
soft money, 415–17
Solid South, 379–80, 396
Somalia, 17, 309
Sotomayor, Sonia, 345, 348
Souter, David, 346
South Africa, 91
Southern Christian Leadership Conference (SCLC), 434
Soviet Union, 18, 282, 303–4, 307–8, 316, 322–23
Speaker of the House, 95–97, 104, 119, 121, 122, 141, 172–73, 242, 269, 385, 424
Spirit of Laws, The (Montesquieu), 21
splinter parties, 389
spoils system, 105, 277, 385. *See also* patronage system
spots, 409
Stamp Act, 56–57
standard operating procedures (SOPs), 293
standing committees, 178–80
stare decisis, 335
state courts, 107, 145, 196, 338–39
State Department. *See* Department of State
state dinners, 215, 256
state executive committee, 153–54
state government. *See* government: state
state legislature, 63, 94, 109, 117, 157–58, 169, 344, 357, 410
State of the Union address (SOTU), 105, 166, 200, 255, 269, 324, 424
states' rights. *See* rights: states'
statutory law, 293
Stevens, Thaddeus, 167
Stevenson, Adlai, 226–27, 236–37
Story, Joseph, 83, 181, 223, 245, 251, 347, 355
straight ticket, 407
straw polls, 428. *See also* informal polls
strict constructionists, 82, 87, 367. *See also* judicial restraint
subpoena, 114, 198
substantive due process, 367–68
subversion, 359
suffrage, 68, 110, 118, 154, 155
Sunshine Act, 296
superdelegates, 231–32

supremacy clause, 110, 195, 349
Supreme Court, 21, 69, 81–84, 88–90, 96, 99–100, 105, 107, 112, 114, 121, 127–29, 144–45, 160–62, 173, 175, 181, 184, 189–93, 195–96, 198–99, 223, 237–38, 242, 245, 251–52, 254, 259, 261, 276, 278–79, 290, 339–45, 347–50, 352, 355–68, 403, 413–14, 442
symbolic speech, 360–61

T

Taft, William Howard, 187–88, 262, 284, 343
Taney, Roger, 350
taxes, 98–99, 101–17, 146–47, 249, 275, 278, 284, 381
Taylor, Zachary, 85, 224
tenure, 60, 173, 174, 258, 260
Tenure of Office Act, 260
term limits, 74, 75, 175
terrorism, 99, 179, 252, 257, 289, 303–4, 309, 317, 320–21
Texas v. Johnson, 361
third parties, 30, 198, 377, 381, 387–90
Thomas, Clarence, 199, 347–50
Three-Fifths Compromise, 70, 95
Thurmond, Strom, 183, 389, 390, 406
ticket splitting, 396
time-place-manner laws, 361
Tocqueville, Alexis de, 38, 129
Tomb of the Unknown Soldier, 255
Top-Two method, 156, 403. *See also* primary: jungle
Tories, 379
totalitarianism, 16
touch-screen voting, 414
town meeting, 151
townships, 22, 128, 149
Transportation Security Administration (TSA), 289
treason, 26, 74, 97, 106, 108, 161, 198, 200, 258
treaties, 72, 88–89, 102, 105, 107, 110, 125, 127–28, 173, 198–99, 215, 252, 261, 315, 317
trial jury. *See* petit jury
Truman, Bess, 265
Truman, Harry, 120, 228, 245, 254–55, 257, 263, 267–68, 272, 282, 284, 299, 305, 314, 428

Trump, Donald, J., 31, 90, 171, 188, 199, 224, 233, 237, 240–41, 249, 310, 312, 314, 320–21, 324, 347–48, 380, 409, 416, 429, 442
Trump, Melania, 266
Trusteeship Council, 319
two-party system, 152, 257, 379–80, 383–84, 387, 392,
Tyler, John, 85, 268–69, 272, 386

U

unalienable rights. *See* rights: unalienable
UN Human Rights Council, 316
unicameral legislature, 143
unified government, 149, 151
unitary government, 18
United Auto Workers (UAW), 416
United Nations (UN), 270, 304, 315–16
United Nations Universal Declaration of Human Rights, 371
United States Agency for International Development (USAID), 321–22
United States-Mexico-Canada-Agreement (USMCA), 188–89, 317
Ur-Nammu, 334
US government. *See* American government
US Marshals Service, 341
US Postal Service, 99, 194–95, 278, 290–91, 300

V

Van Buren, Angelica, 264
Van Buren, Martin, 241, 264, 385
Vererans Health Administration, 288
veto, 68, 89–90, 98, 127, 129, 144, 158, 182, 184, 203
    line-item, 90, 184, 254, 260
    pocket, 98, 183
vice president, 21, 84, 96, 103–4, 105–6, 115–17, 119–22, 144, 154, 172–73, 198–99, 225, 232–33, 240, 246, 250, 257–58, 267–70, 278, 282–83, 290, 385, 390, 392, 407
Vietnam War, 122, 174, 191, 244, 282, 296

Virginia Plan, 67–71
visa, 311
voter registration, 145, 155
voter turnout, 157
voting, 10, 12, 18, 30–32, 37, 67,
       76, 85–86, 98, 109, 115–17,
       120–22, 130, 137, 141,
       145, 150, 152, 154–157,
       172, 182–83, 227–28, 233,
       236–37, 239, 260
    registration for, 145, 155
voting rights. *See* rights: voting
Voting Rights Act of 1965, 369
Voting Rights Act of 1970, 369

W

Waite, Chief Justice Morrison, 358
Walker, Scott, 158
Wallace, George, 389–90
"wall of separation," 356
ward, 150, 152–53, 393
War for Independence, 56–58,
       62, 100, 167, 187, 189, 338,
       348, 363, 436
War of 1812, 43, 59, 210, 303,
       306, 363, 384
war power, 191–92, 198
War Powers Act, 99, 191
Warren, Earl, 353, 362
Washington, DC, 27, 30, 52, 59,
       86, 88, 95, 120, 125, 132,
       134, 137, 154, 170, 174,
       176, 204, 206–7, 209, 223,
       240, 242, 245–46, 253,
       263, 284–85, 303, 312,
       344, 404, 408, 425, 433–34
Washington, George, 55,
       57–58, 64, 66, 70, 75, 77,
       104, 111, 120, 189, 207,
       217, 223–24, 242, 249, 255,
       263, 270, 272, 285, 302,
       305–6, 315, 420
waste, 149, 297, 381
Watergate scandal, 259, 280, 439
weapons of mass destruction
       (WMDs), 320, 322, 324–26
Webster, Daniel, 312, 342
welfare programs, 35, 283, 422
West Wing, 211, 215, 243, 281,
       283, 385
Whig Party, 384, 386

White House, 85, 88, 162, 167,
       173, 210, 220, 222–24,
       226, 234–35, 237, 242–43,
       246, 248–50, 255–56, 257,
       260, 262–66, 379, 384–86,
       396, 405, 409, 433, 438
White House Military Office, 250
White House Office, 269, 280, 290
white primaries. *See* primaries: white
Willkie, Wendell, 235, 308
Wilson, Joe, 200
Wilson, Woodrow, 83, 177,
       252, 254–55, 272, 307, 386, 390
winner-take-all. *See* primaries:
       winner-take-all
women's rights. *See* rights: women's
World Trade Center, 251, 289,
       310, 322, 324–25
World Trade Organization
       (WTO), 303, 321, 434
worldview. *See* government:
       biblical worldview of
World War I, 118, 130, 199,
       278, 291, 307, 316, 321
World War II, 12, 34, 37, 81,
       105, 120, 126, 191–92, 215,
       224, 252–53, 278, 300,
       303–5, 307, 315–16, 318,
       320, 408, 411, 437–38
writ of certiorari, 335, 342
writ of habeas corpus, 101, 201, 366
writ of mandamus, 350

Y

Y–12 National Security
       Complex, 288
Yale College, 43
Yellow Dog Democrats, 396

Z

Zenger trial, 359

PHOTO CREDITS

Key: (t) top; (c) center;
(b) bottom; (l) left; (r) right
(bg) background

Cover

front eurobanks/Shutterstock.com; **back** Craig Oesterling/BJU Press/Campaign buttons courtesy of Joseph Jarrell

Front Matter

i, ii, iii Craig Oesterling/BJU Press/Campaign buttons courtesy of Joseph Jarrell; **iv t** Ivan Batinic / Alamy Stock Photo; **iv b** NiKreative / Alamy Stock Photo; **v t** "George Washington (Lansdowne portrait)" by Gilbert Stuart/National Portrait Gallery/Wikimedia Commons/Public Domain; **v ct** Inspired By Maps/Shutterstock.com; **v cb** "Jeannette Rankin cph.3b13863"/Library of Congress/Wikipedia/Public Domain; **v b** MPI/Archive Photos/Getty Images; **vi** © iStock.com/f11photo

Unit Openers

viii–1 © iStock.com/AndreyKrav; **52–53** Michael Ventura / Alamy Stock Photo; **164–65** © iStock.com/drnadig; **220–21** Ivan Batinic / Alamy Stock Photo; **330–31** stock_photo_world/Shutterstock.com; **374–75** Library of Congress, LC-DIG-ds-11910

Chapter 1

2 Brendan Hoffman/Getty Images News/Getty Images; **3** © iStock.com/rehtse_c; **4** © iStock.com/RyanJLane; **6l** Chip Somodevilla/Getty Images News/Getty Images; **6r–7t** Getty Images/iStockphoto/Thinkstock; **7b** UpperCut Images/Getty Images; **8** © iStock.com/Prathaan; **9** AP Photo/Amarillo Globe-News, Henry Bargas; **10t** Blend Images/HILL STREET STUDIOS/Media Bakery; **10b** © iStock.com/Image Source; **11** Spencer Platt/Getty Images News/Getty Images; **12** peresanz/Shutterstock.com

Chapter 2

14 © iStock.com/OlegAlbinsky; **15** AP Photo; **16** Hulton Deutsch/Corbis Historical/Getty Images; **17** AFP/Getty Images; **19** Unusual Films; **20l** Ondrej Deml/Shutterstock.com; **20r** Bloomberg/Getty Images; **21** Lanmas / Alamy Stock Photo; **23l** Brent Wong/Shutterstock.com; **23c** Chepe Nicoli/Shutterstock.com; **23r** © iStock.com/traveler1116; **24** SuperStock / Alamy Stock Photo; **25** "Declaration of Independence" by John Trumbull/Wikimedia Commons/Public Domain; **26l** A. Burkatovski / Fine Art Images / SuperStock; **26r** "Portrait of Queen Mary II of England (1662–1694)" by Godfrey Kneller/Wikimedia Commons/Public Domain; **27** © iStock.com/CastaldoStudio; **28** © iStock.com/baona; **29** Xinhua / Alamy Stock Photo; **31** Win McNamee/Getty Images News/Getty Images; **33** © iStock.com/dibrova; **34** © iStock.com/littleny; **35t** Richard Levine / Alamy Stock Photo; **35b** © iStock.com/RiverNorthPhotography; **37** © iStock.com/monkeybusinessimages

Chapter 3

40, 42b 3LH / SuperStock; **42t** Science History Images / Alamy Stock Photo; **43t** "Timothy Dwight (1752–1817)" by John Trumbull/Wikimedia Commons/Public Domain; **43b** Wasin Pummarin/123RF; **44** Stan Rohrer / Alamy Stock Photo; **46t** DEA/G. NIMATALLAH/De Agostini/Getty Images; **46b** alysta/Shutterstock.com; **47l** B Christopher / Alamy Stock Photo; **47r** Win McNamee/Getty Images News/Getty Images; **48** © iStock.com/steph; **49l** Jim West / Alamy Stock Photo; **49r** Bloomberg/Getty Images

Chapter 4

54 "Scene at the Signing of the Constitution of the United States" by Howard Chandler Christy/The Indian Reporter/Wikimedia Commons/Public Domain; **55** Matt Purciel / Alamy Stock Photo; **56t** Public Domain; **56bl, br, 57t, 65** North Wind Picture Archives / Alamy Stock Photo; **57b** ClassicStock / Alamy Stock Photo; **58** "Writing the Declaration of Independence, 1776" by Jean Leon Gerome Ferris/Library of Congress/Wikimedia Commons/Public Domain; **59** © lawcain - Fotolia.com; **61** Division of Political History, National Museum of American History, Smithsonian Institution.; **64** Carolyn M Carpenter/Shutterstock.com; **66t** "George Washington (Lansdowne portrait)" by Gilbert Stuart/National Portrait Gallery/Wikimedia Commons/Public Domain; **66b** Inspired By Maps/Shutterstock.com; **69** Architect of the Capitol; **71t, 75t, 75b** Stock Montage/Archive Photos/Getty Images; **71c** "James Madison by Gilbert Stuart 1804"/Wikimedia Commons/Public Domain; **71b** Library of Congress, Manuscript Division, James Madison Papers; **73t** Courtesy National Gallery of Art, Washington; **73c** "James Madison" by John Vanderlyn/Wikimedia Commons/Public Domain; **73b** John Jay Homestead State Historic Site, Katonah, NY, Office of Parks, Recreation and Historic Preservation (JJ.1958.306) (cropped); **74** "Federalist Papers"/Wikipedia/Public Domain; **75ct** Library of Virginia; **75cb** Granger, NYC; **77** 3LH / SuperStock; **78** Joseph Sohm/Corbis Documentary/Getty Images

Chapter 5

80 NiKreative / Alamy Stock Photo; **82** French School/Getty Images; **83** Bloomberg/Getty Images; **84** 506 collection / Alamy Stock Photo; **93** © iStock.com/CastaldoStudio; **94** © iStock.com/Jonathan P. Larsen; **99** JIM WATSON/AFP/Getty Images; **103** © iStock.com/Pgiam; **106** AP Photo/Peter Lennihan; **107** Tinnaporn Sathapornnanont/Shutterstock.com; **114** BRENDAN SMIALOWSKI/AFP/Getty Images; **118l** Pictorial Press Ltd / Alamy Stock Photo; **118r** Library of Congress / S.Dupuis / Alamy Stock Photo

Chapter 6

124 Roschetzky Photography/Shutterstock.com; **125** Bloomberg/Getty Images; **126** © iStock.com/querbeet; **127** Rob Thompson/SCDOT; **129** "John Marshall" by Henry Inman/Wikimedia Commons/Public Domain; **130t, b** BJU Photo Services; **131** Granger, NYC; **133** Darryl Heikes/UPI Photo/Newscom; **134** Everett Collection Historical / Alamy Stock Photo; **137** © iStock.com/f11photo

Chapter 7

140 © iStock.com/gregobagel; **141** AP Photo/Scott Stewart; **142, 143t, 149** ZUMA Press, Inc. / Alamy Stock Photo; **143b** © iStock.com/traveler1116; **144** "Governor Nikki Haley's official photo for her second term" by Sam Holland/Flickr/Public Domain; **151** Tupungato/Shutterstock.com; **154** Granger, NYC; **157** Leon Werdinger / Alamy Stock Photo; **158** Scott Olson/Getty Images News/Getty Images; **160** Norma Jean Gargasz / Alamy Stock Photo; **162** White House Photo / Alamy Stock Photo

Chapter 8

166 Rob Crandall / Alamy Stock Photo; **167** North Wind Picture Archives / Alamy Stock Photo; **168** Age Fotostock / Spencer Grant / Media Bakery; **169** "The Gerry-Mander" by Elkanah Tisdale/Wikimedia Commons/Public Domain; **172t, 183t** Scott J. Ferrell / Congressional Quarterly / Alamy Stock Photo; **172b** "Mitch McConnell official portrait 112th Congress"/United States Senate/

Wikimedia Commons/Public Domain; **173t** Collection of the U.S. House of Representatives; **173b** Aaron P. Bernstein/Getty Images News/Getty Images; **174t** "Jeannette Rankin cph.3b13863"/Library of Congress/Wikipedia/Public Domain; **174b** MPI/Archive Photos/Getty Images; **176** U.S. Navy/Getty Images News/Getty Images; **180** Scott J. Ferrell/CQ-Roll Call Group/Getty Images; **181l** Government Publishing Office/Public Domain; **181r, 183b** Bettmann/Getty Images; **184** BRENDAN SMIALOWSKI/AFP/Getty Images

Chapter 9

186 AP Photo/J. Scott Applewhite; **189** Sipa via AP Images; **190** Carolyn Franks/Shutterstock.com; **192t** Pictorial Press Ltd / Alamy Stock Photo; **192b–93b** BlueBarronPhoto/Shutterstock.com; **193t** Erik S. Lesser/Getty Images News/Getty Images; **195l** neftali/Shutterstock.com; **195r** © iStock.com/rappensuncle; **196** AP Photo/The Billings Gazette, James Woodcock; **198t** Xinhua / Alamy Stock Photo; **198b** SAUL LOEB/AFP/Getty Images; **199t** "Official portrait of President Gerald R. Ford (February 25, 1976)" by David Hume Kennerly/Gerald R. Ford Presidential Library and Museum/Public Domain; **199c** Wally McNamee/Corbis Historical/Getty Images; **199b** AP Photo/Evan Vucci, File; **202** Chris Maddaloni/CQ-Roll Call Group/Getty Images; **204** Bloomberg/Getty Images; **206–7bg** Michael Rosebrock/Shutterstock.com; **207** Oksana Tysovska/Shutterstock.com; **208–9bg** Hey Darlin/DigitalVision Vectors/Getty Images; **208t** Orhan Cam/Shutterstock.com; **208cl, 218b** travelview/Shutterstock.com; **208cr** © iStock.com/OlegAlbinsky; **208b** Simfalex/Shutterstock.com; **209t** © iStock.com/AlexandreFagundes; **209b** © iStock.com/zodebala; **210–11bg** Donald Walker/Shutterstock.com; **210** "Capitol1846" by John Plumbe/Wikipedia/Public Domain; **211** "White House 1846" by John Plumbe/Library of Congress/Wikimedia Commons/Public Domain; **216–17bg** Alessio Catelli/Shutterstock.com; **216t** Anton_Ivanov/Shutterstock.com; **216c** © iStock.com/TalbotImages; **216b** © iStock.com/Lingbeek; **217t** AP Photo/J. Scott Applewhite; **217b** M DOGAN/Shutterstock.com; **218–19bg** Cvandyke/Shutterstock.com; **218t** Efrain Padro / Alamy Stock Photo; **219l** Jennifer Wright / Alamy Stock Photo; **219r** ymgerman/Shutterstock.com

Chapter 10

222 Mark Wilson/Getty Images News/Getty Images; **224t** Trinity Mirror / Mirrorpix / Alamy Stock Photo; **224b** Historical/Corbis Historical/Getty Images; **225, 243b, 245b** Bettmann/Getty Images; **226** Tony Evans/Timelapse Library Ltd./Hulton Archive/Getty Images; **227** "Pres. Coolidge & radio equipped auto LOC npcc.11988"/Library of Congress/Wikimedia Commons/Public Domain; **228, 236t, 245t** AP Photo; **229t** AP Photo/Chris Carlson; **229b, 243t** JEWEL SAMAD/AFP/Getty Images; **231l, 233b, 242** ZUMA Press, Inc. / Alamy Stock Photo; **231r** SAUL LOEB/AFP/Getty Images; **232** Paul Morigi/WireImage/Getty Images; **233t** Chip Somodevilla/Getty Images News/Getty Images; **235t** Independent Picture Service / Alamy Stock Photo; **235b** Courtesy of Busy Beaver Button Museum; **236b** AP Photo/Ed Reinke, File; **238** Robert King/Hulton Archive/Getty Images; **240** Nigel Bowles / Alamy Stock Photo; **246t** charlie archambault / Alamy Stock Photo; **246b** AB Forces News Collection / Alamy Stock Photo

Chapter 11

248 National Archives/Public Domain; **250l** "Air Force One on the ground" by SSGT Alex Lloyd, USAF/Wikimedia Commons/Public Domain; **250r** "Naeapaxr VH071 whitehouse"/Wikimedia Commons/Public Domain; **251t** "President Lyndon B. Johnson in Vietnam: With General William Westmoreland decorating a soldier" by Yoichi Okamoto/Wikimedia Commons/Public Domain; **251b** Danita Delimont/Gallo Images/Getty Images; **252** ITAR-TASS News Agency / Alamy Stock Photo; **253t** "Weekend at Camp David. President Kennedy, John F. Kennedy, Jr., Caroline Kennedy (riding "Tex"). Camp David, MD." by Robert L. Knudsen/Wikimedia Commons/Public Domain; **253b, 261b** ZUMA Press, Inc. / Alamy Stock Photo; **254** MediaPunch Inc / Alamy Stock Photo; **255t** PAUL J. RICHARDS/AFP/Getty Images; **255b** Library of Congress, LC-DIG-npcc-18568; **256** MIKE THEILER/AFP/Getty Images; **257** "Photograph of chaos outside the Washington Hilton Hotel after the assassination attempt on President Reagan"/Wikimedia Commons/Public Domain; **258** "CT 09-109(1)"/FDR Presidential Library & Museum/Flickr/CC By 2.0; **259** North Wind Picture Archives / Alamy Stock Photo; **260, 265rb** Richard Ellis / Alamy Stock Photo; **261t** Steve Skjold / Alamy Stock Photo; **263** "Dolley Madison" by Gilbert Stuart/Wikimedia Commons/Public Domain; **264lt** "Angelica Singleton Van Buren (Mrs. Abraham Van Buren)" by Henry Inman/Wikimedia Commons/Public Domain; **264lb, 272r** Everett Historical/Shutterstock.com; **264c** Library of Congress; **264rt** Archive PL / Alamy Stock Photo; **264rb** Stock Montage/Archive Photos/Getty Images; **265lt** Lisa Larsen/The LIFE Images Collection/Getty Images; **265lb** AP Photo; **265c** The White House; **265rt** Allstar Picture Library / Alamy Stock Photo; **266l** White House Photo Office; **266c** Alex Wong/Getty Images News/Getty Images; **266r** ANDRZEJ HULIMKA/AFP/Getty Images; **268** SAUL LOEB/AFP/Getty Images; **269** "Official White House portrait of John Tyler" by George Peter Alexander Healy/Wikimedia Commons/Public Domain; **270t** Bettmann/Getty Images; **270b** "President Bush participates in a full cabinet meeting in the cabinet room" by Susan Biddle/National Archives/Wikimedia Commons/Public Domain; **271** AP Photo/J. Scott Applewhite; **272l** "George Washington" by Rembrandt Peale/Wikimedia Commons/Public Domain; **272c** "Abraham Lincoln poses in Gardner's new gallery. Imperial albumen print." by Alexander Gardner/Wikimedia Commons/Public Domain

Chapter 12

274 "Douglas Dam" by Tennessee Valley Authority/Flickr/CC By 2.0; **275t, b** Department of the Treasury/Internal Revenue Service/Public Domain; **276** photo.ua/Shutterstock.com; **277** Library of Congress; **279** Danita Delimont / Alamy Stock Photo; **280** MediaPunch Inc / Alamy Stock Photo; **281t** ZUMA Press, Inc. / Alamy Stock Photo; **281b** Mark Wilson/Getty Images News/Getty Images; **283** © Leonid Andronov/Fotolia; **284** Bettmann/Getty Images; **285t** EVA HAMBACH/AFP/Getty Images; **285b** DoD photo by Master Sgt. Ken Hammond, U.S. Air Force; **286t** Stock Connection Blue / Alamy Stock Photo; **286b** © iStock.com/fdastudillo; **287** "ship5058"/NOAA Photo Library/Flickr/CC By 2.0; **288** "Cincinnati VA Medical Center"/Veterans Health/Flickr/Public Domain; **289t** Kevork Djansezian/Getty Images News/Getty Images; **289b** "KSC-JohnGlenn-0015 (31144905310)"/NASA/Public Domain; **291** "Testing for Arsenic in Rice (6783)"/The U.S. Food and Drug Administration/Flickr/Public Domain; **292l** "EPA scientists surveying aquatic life. 2009, OR."/USEPA/Flickr/Public Domain; **292r** Patti McConville / Alamy Stock Photo; **293** MARK RALSTON/AFP/Getty Images; **295** "140821-A-SF231-268" by Sgt. Leon Cook, U.S. Army/Flickr/Public Domain; **296** National Archives/Public Domain; **300** "Apollo 15 flag, rover, LM, Irwin" by Astronaut David R. Scott/NASA/Wikimedia Commons/Public Domain

Chapter 13

302 "Secretary Pompeo Visits Vietnamese Ministry of Foreign Affairs" by U.S. Department of State/Flickr/Public Domain; **304t** Alexandros Michailidis/Shutterstock.com; **304b** Georges MERILLON/Gamma-Rapho/Getty Images; **305** National Archives/Public Domain; **306l** "George Washington" by Gilbert Stuart/Clark Art Institute/Wikipedia/Public Domain; **306c** John Parrot/Stocktrek Images/Getty Images; **306r** Everett - Art/Shutterstock

.com; **307**t, **318**t Everett Historical/Shutterstock.com; **307**c, b Robert Wajda - https://www.presidentialelection.com; **308**t "USS West Virginia;014824"/U.S. Navy/Wikimedia Commons/Public Domain; **308**b "Poseidon C-3 SLBM"/Wikimedia Commons/ Public Domain; **309** Wally McNamee/Corbis Historical/Getty Images; **310**t Wesley Bocxe/Science Source/Getty Images; **310**b Getty Images News/Getty Images; **311** Bettmann/Getty Images; **312**t White House Photo / Alamy Stock Photo; **312**bl topseller/ Shutterstock.com; **312**br "Pasaporte-eua"/Mkt3000/Wikimedia Commons/Public Domain; **314** © iStock.com/ewg3D; **315**t RP Images / Alamy Stock Photo; **315**b "FEMA - 17298 - Photograph by Jocelyn Augustino taken on 08-30-2005 in Louisiana"/Wikimedia Commons/Public Domain; **316**t Library of Congress; **316**b tim page/Corbis Historical/Getty Images; **318**b US State Department / Alamy Stock Photo; **319** Drop of Light/Shutterstock.com; **320** Geisler-Fotopress GmbH / Alamy Stock Photo; **321**t baona/iStock/ Getty Images Plus/Getty Images; **321**b Dinendra Haria / Alamy Stock Photo; **322**t AFP/Getty Images; **322**b Spencer Platt/Getty Images News/Getty Images; **324**t Handout / Alamy Stock Photo; **324**b Jim Schwabel/Shutterstock.com; **326** PA Images / Alamy Stock Photo; **327**t Nils Versemann/Shutterstock.com; **327**b © iStock.com/VasukiRao

Chapter 14

332 MCT/Tribune News Service/Getty Images; **334** Print Collector/Hulton Archive/Getty Images; **335** Chronicle / Alamy Stock Photo; **337** "Sir William Blackstone from NPG"/Wikimedia Commons/Public Domain; **339**l LegendsOfAmerica.com; **339**r J.P. MOCZULSKI/AFP/Getty Images; **343** Nikreates / Alamy Stock Photo; **345** Official White House Photograph; **346, 352**t Bettmann/Getty Images; **347**t Everett Historical/Shutterstock .com; **347**bl Mark Reinstein/Corbis Historical/Getty Images; **347**br SOPA Images/LightRocket/Getty Images; **348** Chip Somodevilla/ Getty Images News/Getty Images; **349** "John Marshall" by Henry Inman/Wikimedia Commons/Public Domain; **350**l Attributed to Rembrandt Peale, Collection of the Supreme Court of the United States; **350**r "James Madison by Gilbert Stuart 1804"/Wikimedia Commons/Public Domain; **351** Fotosearch/Archive Photos/Getty Images; **352**b Alex Wong/Getty Images News/Getty Images

Chapter 15

354 Image Source/Getty Images; **355** Chip Somodevilla/Getty Images News/Getty Images; **356**t John Moore/Getty Images News/ Getty Images; **356**b Karl Gehring/The Denver Post/Getty Images; **357**t Stephen St. John/National Geographic Image Collection/ Getty Images; **357**b Ira Berger / Alamy Stock Photo; **358** Hyoung Chang/The Denver Post/Getty Images; **360**t James Leynse/Corbis Historical/Getty Images; **360**b The Old Major/Shutterstock.com; **361**t, **364** Chris Hondros/Getty Images News/Getty Images; **361**b Alex Wong/Getty Images News/Getty Images; **363**t Robert Nyholm/Shutterstock.com; **363**b Bill Pugliano/Getty Images News/Getty Images; **366** PAUL BUCK/AFP/Getty Images; **367** AP Photo; **368**t H.S. Photos / Alamy Stock Photo; **368**b Don Cravens/ The LIFE Images Collection/Getty Images; **369** Alpha Historica / Alamy Stock Photo; **370** Rob Crandall/Shutterstock.com; **372** Jessica McGowan/Getty Images News/Getty Images

Chapter 16

376 Digital Focus / Alamy Stock Photo; **377** stevezmina1/ DigitalVision Vectors/Getty Images; **378**t Frank Cezus/ Photographer's Choice/Getty Images; **378**b michelmond/ Shutterstock.com; **382**l NurPhoto/Getty Images; **382**r Olivier Douliery/Getty Images News/Getty Images; **384**t Courtesy National Gallery of Art, Washington; **384**b John Parrot/Stocktrek Images/Getty Images; **385**t "John Quincy Adams" by George Peter Alexander Healy/Wikipedia/Public Domain; **385**b "Andrew

jackson head" by Ralph Eleaser Whiteside Earl/Wikipedia/Public Domain; **386**tl, tr, **395**t Bettmann/Getty Images; **386**c Everett Historical/Shutterstock.com; **386**b Stock Montage/Archive Photos/ Getty Images; **387** AP Photo/Rebecca Blackwell; **388** Mondadori Portfolio/Mondadori Portfolio Premium/Getty Images; **389**t LunaseeStudios/Shutterstock.com; **389**b Courtesy of Busy Beaver Button Museum; **390**t The Front Collection/Corbis Historical/ Getty Images; **390**b REUTERS / Jonathan Ernst - stock.adobe.com; **391** Scott Olson/Getty Images News/Getty Images; **392** Stephen Brashear/Getty Images News/Getty Images; **393** Mark Wilson/ Getty Images News/Getty Images; **395**b Bloomberg/Getty Images; **396** ronwadebuttons.com

Chapter 17

400 Kenneth Gabrielsen/Getty Images Entertainment/Getty Images; **401** AP Photo/Rich Pedroncelli; **402** The Washington Post/Getty Images; **403** AP Photo/Bobby Caina Calvan; **404** Brian Blanco/Getty Images News/Getty Images; **405** Orlando Sentinel/ Tribune News Service/Getty Images; **407** Used by Permission from McKinley Presidential Library & Museum, Canton, Ohio.; **408** RICHARD DREW/AFP/Getty Images; **409**t Historical/Corbis Historical/Getty Images; **409**b AP Photo; **411** Anadolu Agency/ Getty Images; **412**t Joe Raedle/Getty Images News/Getty Images; **412**bl George Rinhart/Corbis Historical/Getty Images; **412**br Bettmann/Getty Images; **413**l, r State Historical Society of Iowa, Iowa City; **414**t SuperStock/Getty Images; **414**b Justin Sullivan/ Getty Images News/Getty Images; **417** New York Daily News Archive/New York Daily News/Getty Images; **418** Bill Clark/CQ-Roll Call Group/Getty Images

Chapter 18

420 Robert W. Kelley/The LIFE Picture Collection/Getty Images; **421** Joe Raedle/Getty Images News/Getty Images; **422, 427**b, **428**b Bettmann/Getty Images; **424** ImageCatcher News Service/ Corbis Historical/Getty Images; **425** Pacific Press/LightRocket/ Getty Images; **426**t SOPA Images/LightRocket/Getty Images; **426**b AP Photo/Josh Edelson; **427**t Hulton Archive/Archive Photos/Getty Images; **427**c ClassicStock / Alamy Stock Photo; **428**t "Voter poll" by RadioFan/Wikimedia Commons/CC By-SA 3.0; **429** New York Daily News Archive/New York Daily News/ Getty Images; **430** Freedom Studio/Shutterstock.com; **431** Drew Angerer/Getty Images News/Getty Images; **432**tl AP Photo/J. Scott Applewhite; **432**tr Jer123/Shutterstock.com; **432**c Chris Pancewicz / Alamy Stock Photo; **432**b Barry Lewis / Alamy Stock Photo; **433**t RichLegg/E+/Getty Images; **433**c Bill Clark/CQ-Roll Call Group/Getty Images; **433**b bakdc/Shutterstock.com; **434** Francis Miller/The LIFE Picture Collection/Getty Images; **435** National Archives/Public Domain; **436** The Picture Art Collection / Alamy Stock Photo; **437** John Medina/WireImage/Getty Images; **438**t John Greim/LightRocket/Getty Images; **438**b B Christopher / Alamy Stock Photo; **439**t Artmim/Shutterstock.com; **439**b Library of Congress/Corbis Historical/Getty Images; **440** Chip HIRES/ Gamma-Rapho/Getty Images; **442** Bloomberg/Getty Images; **443** Wally McNamee/Corbis Historical/Getty Images; **444** Apic/Hulton Archive/Getty Images

Back Matter

446–59bg AXL/Shutterstock.com; **459** Library of Congress, LC-DIG-npcc-15199

All maps from Map Resources

Mock Senate

Adapted by Gail L. Nicholas, Bob Jones Academy

This activity and necessary forms may be found at TeacherToolsOnline .com. Forms include information sheets as well as forms needed for Senate activities.

Basic Outline

   I. Basic Planning
  II. Instructional Information
 III. Student Responsibilities and Instructions for Participation
 IV. Instructions for the Senate

A simulation of the activities of Congress in the government classroom can be a profitable educational experience for your students. The project requires individual research, group cooperation, and creative and higher level thinking. It also reinforces and enhances students' knowledge of how our government works and how government leaders deal with current political issues.

Although this activity is highly recommended, in order for the simulation to be effective, the teacher must be familiar with the workings of Congress and must have resources available to help the students understand their roles and the procedures of Congress. Prior planning by the teacher is essential, but if that groundwork is well laid, the actual simulation should progress with minimal teacher assistance and coordination. The first attempt at this project may reveal some unforeseen difficulties that require additional information, organization, or adjustments, but the experience will help you develop the mock Senate into an activity that will enhance your government classes for years to come. Students often comment afterward that the activity is a memorable experience and that it helped them understand governmental processes and evaluate current political events.

I. Basic Planning

The instructions and forms provided for this project are intended to help reflect actual congressional activities as accurately as is practical. However, the size and make-up of your class, the materials available, and the time constraints you must deal with may make it advisable to omit or modify some of the project's steps at your discretion. Instructions and forms are given for Senate procedures. Because of its smaller size and less complicated procedures, this project will focus on the Senate chamber for the purpose of role-playing.

You should reserve a block of fifteen class days for the actual simulation. In addition, some time will be needed in advance of the project for role assignments and the researching of the members of the Senate who will be portrayed by the students. It is important that the chapters on Congress (Chapters 8 and 9) have been taught and that the students understand how a bill becomes a law.

During the week before the simulation begins, you should introduce your students to the requirements and procedures for the project and make some preparatory assignments. When the simulation is complete, you should reserve one class day for grading. On that day, the students will collect all their materials and hand them in.

II. Instructional Information

The following information provides insights into the preparation and proceedings of the project. This section is followed by the student instructions (which give additional procedural information).

A. Description of the Activity

The students are assigned to role-play actual members of the United States Senate. These roles include the president pro tempore, the secretary, and various Democratic and Republican senators (their number should be based on the current ratio).

The students will participate in the legislative process of writing bills, meeting in committees, debating bills, voting, and sending bills for further approval.

Each student's grade is based on the amount of congressional work accomplished. This work includes making speeches, writing bills and resolutions, and participating in daily activities.

B. Objectives of the Activity

1. Biblical Objectives
   - God wants us to know about those in authority over us (1 Thess. 5:12).
   - God expects us to submit to all authority (Rom. 13:1–7; Titus 3:1–2; Heb. 13:17).
   - God considers our speech important (Ps. 37:30; 39:1; 119:13, 27, 46, 54; 141:3; Prov. 10:11; 12:6; 15:1; Col. 4:6; 1 Pet. 3:15).
   - God wants us to pray for our rulers (1 Tim. 2:1–2).
   - God wants us to be orderly (1 Cor. 14:40).
2. Classroom Objectives
   - Procedures for how a bill becomes a law
   - Basic parliamentary procedures
   - Research skills
   - Current-events analysis
   - How to apply current events to the Constitution
   - Skills needed to work in a group
   - Speaking and writing skills
   - Political party viewpoints and issues
   - Objective thinking on controversial issues
   - Organization
   - Creative thinking
   - Decision making
   - Congressional vocabulary
   - Procedures for writing to a senator

C. Sources

To a large extent, the success of this simulation depends on the students' ability to faithfully portray the attitudes and actions of the senators whose roles they are playing; and this ability, in turn, depends on the availability of information about the senators, including information about their political views and their voting records. The best resource for each student is the Senate website (senate.gov). This website contains valuable links to all Senate members and is invaluable to students in role-playing.

CQ Press (a division of Sage Publications) publishes a number of extremely useful books for this project. You might want to ask for a catalog of its publications and to be placed on its mailing list so that you will be aware of new and updated materials as they become available. Below is a list of some of its most helpful books which are currently available (and updated on a regular basis):

Politics in America 2014: The 113th Congress (most current print version); updated online every two years. This book contains extensive biographical information about each senator and representative, an analysis of his work in Congress, his voting record, information about the committees he serves on, and a description of the states and districts he represents.

Congressional Roll Call (most recent edition currently 2013). This book describes the bills and resolutions that were brought up for a vote before the House or Senate in a session of Congress, and it records every congressman's vote on these matters.

Congressional Procedures and the Policy Process, 11th edition, by Walter J. Oleszek, 2019. This publication provides a detailed description of procedures that will give essential information to the teacher and helpful insights to the students as they play their roles.

In addition to these reference books, the students should constantly consult newspapers and news magazines for information on current congressional issues and activities. Online state newspapers would be a good way to follow events in the states being represented. Recent copies of the *Congressional Record* will also be helpful. To clarify parliamentary procedures, have a copy of *Robert's Rules of Order* available. This standard work by Henry M. Robert is available in economical paperback editions.

D. Requirements

The following list is a guide of requirements for grading the project. Note that not only the quantity but also the quality of the work should be considered.

1. Participation: subjective grade based on the teacher's observations of active participation and interaction

2. Introduction of bills and resolutions (one must be a constitutional amendment): at least three introductions for an A, two for a B, and one for a C

3. Short speeches on any subject for the *Congressional Record*: at least six for an A, five for a B, three for a C, and two for a D

4. Debate speech on a bill or resolution before the floor: at least three for an A, two for a B, and one for a C

5. Time spent outside the classroom: each student is expected to spend at least five hours of outside time in research and preparation for the Senate.

6. Record of daily activities (daily log): each student is expected to keep a daily record of his activities during the class hour. Each day the daily logs from the previous day should be placed on the secretary's desk.

Check the daily logs on a daily basis and continuously observe the activities of the students. The students will collect all their speech forms, bills, and other materials (from the various committee files, speech files, secretary's records, etc.) on the last day of the project. These will then be turned in for grading. The students should also keep a continuous record of all the speeches that they have given and bills that they have introduced. Forms are provided for this record. If, when materials are collected, a speech or bill is lost, the record will help you find verification for the speech or bill in the journal.

E. Materials

The following materials will be needed for the mock Senate:

1. Posterboard to make calendars, committee charts, etc.
2. Folders for committees, blank forms, speech reports, etc.
3. Gavel
4. Date stamp and pad for use by clerk and secretary (optional but helpful)
5. Paper clips and stapler
6. File drawers or boxes to keep student files, committee files, forms, and other materials
7. Notebooks with dividers for use as journals
8. Adequate copies of the necessary forms
9. Bell
10. Podium

F. Procedures

About six weeks before the simulation is to begin, determine the number of Democratic and Republican senators that will be needed to achieve the proper ratio in your classroom. You may wish to assign capable students to the leadership roles: president pro tempore, secretary, and the majority leader and minority leader and whips for each class you teach. Assign other students to roles as other senators in accordance with the current Democrat to Republican ratio. Note that the students should portray senators that have served long enough in Congress to have established voting records and discernible political views. Try to develop an appropriate mixture of liberals and conservatives, northerners and southerners, some with many years of experience and some with fewer, etc. You may also want to include some minority representation among the "legislators." Note that the student who will act as secretary of the Senate will not be an actual member of Congress but will, however, have extensive record-keeping responsibilities during the simulation. The teacher could play this role instead of a student.

Instruct each student to obtain information from the assigned senator's website. A profile sheet, which is included with the forms, should be completed by each student on the assigned senator and on the state represented. Then, in the intervening time before the simulation, be sure to have your students take note of the current events related to Congress and any mention in newspapers and magazines of their senator in particular. Encourage students to follow their senators on social network sites.

During the week prior to the beginning of the simulation, there are several preparatory steps that should be completed. Introduce the students to the available reference materials. The information for both of these assignments can be found in *Politics in America* and on individual senator websites. Distribute copies of the pages from the Teacher Edition that detail student responsibilities as well as specific instructions for the Senate. Discuss the general guidelines for the activity as listed in the instructions. Show the forms that will be used for the assignments, and explain their use.

Explain the parliamentary procedures that will be used, noting the guide for these procedures in the student instructions. A mock debate is useful at this time to help acquaint the class with parliamentary language and procedures. Also, allow the students to meet in party caucuses at this time. The majority leader and minority leader will act as chairmen for these caucuses, and, using parliamentary procedures, the party members of each party should choose one senator to act as a whip for their party (if not assigned by the teacher), sign up for committees, elect committee chairmen, etc.

Make nameplates for each "senator," noting political party affiliation and the state represented. Also, have each student bring a file folder (with pockets) to class. The student should keep the materials he works with in this file and carry it with him during the activity. He will be responsible for gathering the forms for his speeches, bills, resolutions, and other activities from their locations on the last day of the project. All materials will be placed in the folder and given to the teacher on that day.

The secretary has duties and requirements that differ from those of the actual senators. During the week before the mock Congress begins, the secretary should be preparing the journals and devotional schedules while familiarizing himself with his duties.

Also, determine the committee assignments. The committees, listed on page 178 of the student text, may be combined at your discretion. You probably will not want more than four separate committees per class with each senator having membership on two. Two different committees will meet each day from Monday through Friday, and each student will serve on two committees. (Not all student senators will be able to serve on the same actual committees as the senator they portray.) Adjust the committee assignments as necessary according to the proper Democrat to Republican ratio. One of the majority party members of each committee should be chosen in the party caucus as chairman.

In final preparation for the actual simulation, assign the writing of one short speech on any subject for the *Congressional Record* and the writing of at least one bill to be completed before the simulation begins. The students will then be ready to use these beginning on the first day of the simulation. In the classroom, have copies of the necessary forms for these and the other procedures.

The actual procedures for conducting the Senate and the responsibilities of the leaders are explained in the student handouts. For further clarification of the processes involved, see *Congressional Procedures and the Policy Process*.

Whenever the congressional and committee activities for the day are completed before the class hour ends, have the students use the time to complete their logs or records, do further research, and prepare materials for the next day.

G. Suggestions

1. Allow the students to use the words of actual speeches, letters, and legislation presented by their senators, as found online, in newsletters, the *Congressional Record*, and other sources. This will help the students play their roles more accurately and eliminate some of the need for invention.

2. Make a chart showing the detailed steps of how a bill becomes a law, and post it in the classroom. You will be able to refer to it while giving instructions for the activity, and the students will be able to refer to it to help them chart the course of their activities.

3. Spend some time before the simulation discussing the political attitudes and policies generally favored and opposed by Democrats and Republicans as well as by liberals and conservatives. Help your students use this information to analyze the positions of the senators they are representing so that they may portray them more realistically.

4. Collect the pictures of the senators, and use them to make a bulletin board titled with the current number of the Congress in session (e.g., "The 116th Congress").

5. If possible, watch C-SPAN coverage of congressional activities, and show segments of the floor debates and other actions to your students in advance of their simulation.

6. Stress current events involving congressional actions and particular senators throughout the government course to familiarize your students with the roles they will be playing.

7. Encourage the students to have their bills, amendments, and speeches prepared early to keep the activities moving and to avoid having many presentations during the last few days of the project. This may require setting a mandatory schedule or even assigning all bills to be written before the simulation begins. It is generally wise to require that all bills and resolutions be submitted at least one week before the end of the simulation.

III. Student Responsibilities and Instructions for Participation

A. Written Requirements for the Senate

(*Note:* All the following speeches may be made extemporaneously, but credit will be given only if the speeches are written and handed in. All speeches may be read. No memorization is required.)

1. *Congressional Record* Speeches
   a) Speeches must be written on the form provided.
   b) These speeches may cover any current subject. They are not debate speeches but rather speeches that express the opinion of your senator. Be sure to role-play in these speeches. Watch for your senator or state being in the news and write speeches on this.
   c) Some suggested subjects are national issues (inflation, unemployment, taxes, foreign policies, and domestic policies), international issues (European and US relationship, Latin American problems, or the death of a foreign leader), congratulations (recognizing people from your state who reach their hundredth birthday, receive a scholarship, or win a national championship or national title), agreement or disagreement with the president, and agreement or disagreement with another senator.
   d) Only one *Congressional Record* speech may be given per day per senator.

2. Debate Speeches
   a) These speeches must be written on the form provided. Make sure that each bill's or resolution's title and number are indicated.
   b) Debate speeches should include the following:
      (1) Statement of support or opposition
      (2) Reason for support or opposition
      (3) Benefits or problems that will arise if the bill or resolution is passed
      (4) If necessary, an indication that the bill or resolution is written poorly or is incomplete. Offer an amendment if you desire. (Amendments to bills and resolutions should be made and presented to the presiding officer when they are brought before the floor.)
      (5) End by reminding the Senate of how you plan to vote. The final sentence should be "I yield the floor."

3. Daily Logs: A log is to be handed in for each day in the Senate. The logs for the previous day should be placed on the desk of the secretary at the beginning of the class hour (the secretary should give them to the teacher). The teacher will use the daily logs to help determine your participation grade, so these must be completed on a daily basis. Your log should be a description of what you did during the hour (speeches, committee work, voting, logrolling, etc.). Be specific. Be sure you record outside time on each log daily.

4. Legislation (*Note:* Bills and joint resolutions apply to the entire nation, whereas concurrent and simple resolutions apply only to the congressional chambers. All legislation should be written in the subjunctive mood. No mention of yourself [I, we, etc.] should be in the legislation. Resolutions may have "Whereas" statements preceding the actual legislation. Bills will not have such statements.)
   a) Bills
      (1) Bill forms are used for most legislation. Bills become laws that must be followed by the entire nation. Those laws are permanent until another bill overrides them or the courts overrule them.
      (2) Each bill should have five to six sections: Section 1—definitions (if needed), Section 2—specifications of what is to be done, Section 3—controlling agency (who will carry out the specifications), Section 4—penalties if the law is disobeyed, Section 5—funding (if needed), and Section 6—enactment date
      (3) Article I, Section 8, of the Constitution lists the areas in which Congress may make laws.
      (4) Bills originating in the Senate will be designated "S." (The numbers will be assigned by the secretary.)

Senators will hand their bills to the secretary for numbering after they are introduced.

    (5) Each bill should be typed or written neatly with all lines numbered. If you run out of room on the front of the bill form, continue on the back, and number each line you write there.

b) Joint Resolutions

    (1) Joint resolutions in the Senate should be designated "S. J. Res."

    (2) The following legislation should be written on a joint resolution form: constitutional amendments, opinions or suggestions for the president, requests for commemorative holidays or stamps, temporary actions taken by the government, and amendments to bills that were passed by previous Congresses.

c) Concurrent Resolutions

    (1) Concurrent resolutions in the Senate should be designated "S. Con. Res."

    (2) Concurrent resolutions deal with matters concerning both chambers of Congress, not with the nation as a whole.

    (3) Concurrent resolutions deal with the following: expression of congressional opinions, expression of congressional purposes, and permissions needed for both chambers to act, such as permission for a recess of three days or longer. A concurrent resolution setting the end date and time for your mock Senate should be passed.

d) Simple Resolutions

    (1) Simple resolutions in the Senate should be designated "S. Res."

    (2) Simple resolutions deal with matters of one chamber. They are considered only by the body in which they were introduced. They are not sent to the other chamber, and they do not apply to the entire nation.

    (3) Simple resolutions deal with matters such as chamber rules of order or needs. For example, the House once passed a simple resolution to have water pitchers at the representatives' desks.

B. Procedural Instructions for the Senate

1. Methods for Voting

a) Unanimous consent: this method is used in the Senate on trivial matters, such as dispensing with the reading of the *Journal* ("If there are no objections, . . .").

b) Voice vote: the chair says, "All in favor, say Aye. All opposed, say No." The decision as to which side wins is made by the chair; if there is a dispute concerning his decision, a roll-call vote should be demanded from the floor.

c) Standing vote: all those for the measure are asked to stand or raise their hands and then all those opposed do the same.

d) Roll-call vote: this gives an accurate record of how each member voted. When a motion is made for a roll-call vote, one-fifth of the members must approve the motion. The name of each senator is called from the roll (in the *Journal*), and in response each senator states his vote. Each senator's vote is recorded by the clerk or secretary and placed in the *Journal*. In the House, this is done electronically. In the Senate, this is done as a Teller Vote in which each senator walks to the presiding desk and tells his vote to a teller who in turn repeats the vote for the entire Senate to hear.

2. Parliamentary Procedures to Be Followed in the Senate

Parliamentary procedures are used as a tool for conducting the business of the Senate. The better you learn to use this tool, the more adept you will be in fulfilling your roll in the mock Senate. The following basic principles govern the procedures, and the accompanying table describes the various motions that will be used:

a) The chair must recognize a member before the member can speak.

b) The chair (whether it be the president pro tempore or a committee chairman) must always be addressed before a speaker continues ("Mr. President, I . . .").

c) Motion is a noun. Move is a verb. When making a parliamentary motion, you say, "I move. . . ." ("Mr. President, I move that we adjourn until tomorrow, April 21, 2014, at 8:00 a.m.")

d) The chair should respond with a complete restatement of the motion ("The motion has been made to adjourn until tomorrow. . . ."). The motion must be seconded ("Do I hear a second?"). Then a vote must be taken.

e) See *Robert's Rules of Order* for further clarifications.

IV. Instructions for the Senate

A. Daily Order of Business for the Senate

(The president pro tempore should follow this agenda.)

1. First Hour Business

a) Declare a quorum; tell the secretary the names of those who are absent.

b) Call on a senator for devotions and prayer (according to the devotional schedule). Remind the person who will do the devotional the following day that he is scheduled. (*Note*: The devotionals should not be made according to the religious beliefs of the senators whose roles are being played. Set aside role-playing for this devotional time.)

c) Call for the reading of the *Journal* from the previous day, unless by unanimous consent it is disposed of. (Say, "Unless there is an objection, the *Journal* from the previous day stands approved.")

d) Call for *Congressional Record* speeches. (Say, "Senators may now make remarks for the *Congressional Record*.")

e) From this point on, it is in order (appropriate) to make a motion to move a bill or resolution from the calendar for consideration.

    (1) The motion must be approved unanimously.

    (2) A motion to set a time limit on debate is also in order. (It must be unanimous.) See debate rules for more information.

f) Announce the day's committee meetings.

g) Ask for messages from the House about legislation (Say, "Are there any messages from the House?"). The teacher may act as the messenger. The messenger should say, "Mr. President, the House has passed House bill/resolution and requests the concurrence of the Senate." The legislation may be considered right away if there is unanimous consent. If legislation is not considered immediately, send the House legislation to a committee.

h) Call for reports from standing committees. ("Are there any reports from standing committees?")

i) Call for introduction of legislation by making the following announcements:

    (1) "Senators may now introduce bills." (After each senator reads his bill, he should give the bill to the secretary.)

(2) "Senators may now introduce joint resolutions."

(3) "Senators may now introduce concurrent resolutions."

(4) "Senators may now introduce simple resolutions."

   j) Call for a motion to adjourn First Hour business. (If there is no Second Hour business, send the senators to their committees.)

   k) First Hour business should end by a time halfway through your class hour unless by unanimous consent a motion is made to extend the time. The time of the ending of First Hour should be set by a simple resolution introduced by one of the senators.

2. Second Hour Business

   a) As soon as First Hour is adjourned, the president pro tempore should call Second Hour to order. This is the time in which bills are debated straight down the calendar order. (See debate rules for more information.)

   b) The president pro tempore calls for consideration of bills and resolutions. These are read by number and title as they appear on the calendar. If requested, entire bills or resolutions should be read. Then debate begins.

   c) When the debate time is over, call for a motion to adjourn or recess. Give the date and time that the session will be reconvened.

3. Unfinished Business

   a) Whenever a motion to adjourn interrupts a debate, the bill or resolution being considered is placed on an unfinished-business list.

   b) Unfinished business is considered on a day when there is extra time. The legislation should be taken in the order that it was added to the list.

B. Senate Debate Rules

1. The Senate may not introduce money-raising bills, but it may debate such bills sent over from the House.

2. Debate may not be limited in the Senate except by unanimous consent or by cloture. (With unanimous consent, the objection of one person prevents the debate from being limited.)

3. No senator may rise to speak more than twice on an issue. If a senator speaks twice on a bill or resolution, he may also speak twice on each amendment to that bill or resolution.

4. Once recognized by the chair, a senator may speak as long as he wishes on any subject. He may yield temporarily for questions or for the consideration of other business. If a senator wants to ask the person with the floor a question, he should rise and say, "Mr. President, will the speaker yield for a question?" The president pro tempore will then ask the speaker to yield. The speaker will answer as follows: "Mr. President, the speaker will yield" or "Mr. President, the speaker will not yield until the end of my speech."

5. After a bill or resolution has been debated and there is no objection to ending the debate (by approving the motion "I move the previous question on the [name and number of the legislation]"), the following motion should be made: "Mr. President, I move that S. XX entitled be engrossed." (Engrossment means to print the bill in its final form.) This motion should be seconded and then voted on. (*Note*: Debate cannot end unless everyone agrees to it.) When the engrossed bill is returned to the Senate, a formal vote is taken (roll call) during first hour business to pass the bill or resolution. This is the vote that counts. If the bill or resolution passes, it is sent to the House. A bill that passes is now called an act.

6. If time (the class period) runs out during a debate, the Senate has two options:

   a) A motion is made to adjourn. The bill or resolution is then placed on the unfinished-business list. This is a way to temporarily kill or stall the bill's passage.

   b) A motion is made to recess. The bill or resolution is then debated at the beginning of the hour on the following day. In other words, a recess means that the day has been suspended and will be continued the following day. Daily logs should have the previous day's date on them if a recess is called, and the debate continues the following day. The debate picks up wherever it left off when the motion for a recess was made.

C. Filibuster Rules and Cloture Rules

1. The purpose of a filibuster is to kill a bill, delay the vote on a bill, or gain concessions on a bill.

2. Ways to filibuster are as follows:

   a) You may introduce an endless number of amendments. They can be germane or non-germane. They must be written out and handed to the president pro tempore at the time you introduce them.

   b) You may talk to excess on the bill or any subject you choose. You could even read from a book. Others should use this time to logroll.

3. During a filibuster, it is in order for other senators to leave the floor of the Senate and work on other Senate business. Talking must be kept at a minimum so that the debate on the Senate floor can be heard over everything else.

4. Cloture (a method used to end the filibuster) can be done in the following way:

   a) Present to the president pro tempore a petition signed by the Senate.

   b) One class hour later (two days in the real Senate), a vote is taken on the petition. Three-fifths of the Senate must agree. If this motion for cloture passes, then each senator has one minute of debate before a vote is taken on the bill or resolution.

D. Duties of the President Pro Tempore of the Senate

1. Chair the Senate using correct parliamentary procedure.

2. Prepare an agenda each day on the proper form. Refer to the "Daily Order of Business" section.

3. Assign all introduced bills and resolutions to their correct standing committees.

4. When you wish to speak on an issue, assign the chair to another member of the Senate (preferably the majority leader). In order to yield, say, "I yield the chair to the senator from [state]." When you want the chair back, the person to whom you yielded should say, "I yield the chair back to the president pro tempore." You will also give the required number of speeches, etc.

5. Be prepared to debate important issues and lead (along with the majority leader) your party members.

6. Set the debate calendar with the majority and minority leaders.

7. You must always be prepared because the success of this activity depends on you. If you are absent, be sure the majority leader knows so that he can take the chair.

8. Hand in your agenda at the end of the class hour on a daily basis. (The agenda is required of you in place of a daily log.)

9. During the debates, keep track of how many times each senator speaks. Keep track of each speech's length if there is a time limit.

E. Duties of the Secretary of the Senate

1. Prepare and keep the *Journal*, which will include the following:
    a) A place to record bills and resolutions that are introduced. These record pages should have seven columns labeled as follows: Date, Number, Introduced By, Title, Committee Assignment, Date Reported, and Outcome.
    b) An alphabetical list of all senators to use for roll-call votes
    c) A day-by-day account of Senate business. This must be signed by the president pro tempore at the end of each day.
    d) A list of the committees and who is on each one
    e) A pocket in which to keep bills that are to be engrossed. (Write the final forms of the engrossed bills on act forms, and recopy resolutions on resolution forms.)
2. As senators introduce bills and resolutions, they will hand them to you. You should do the following:
    a) Number the bills and resolutions. Pieces of legislation in each category (bills, joint resolutions, concurrent resolutions, and simple resolutions) are numbered consecutively beginning with 1. (This means that there will be bills numbered 1, 2, 3, etc.; joint resolutions numbered 1, 2, 3, etc.)
    b) Enter them in the *Journal*.
    c) Have the president pro tempore assign them to committees.
    d) Receive them from the president pro tempore, and record the committee assignment for each one.
    e) Place them in the proper committee folders.
3. When bills and resolutions are reported back to the Senate floor, do the following:
    a) Record them in the *Journal* as reported.
    b) Give each report document a number; begin with 1, and number consecutively.
    c) Give the bills calendar numbers, and place them on the Senate calendar. Make the calendar on posterboard, and divide it into four columns: Date, Calendar Number, Bill or Resolution, and Outcome.
4. Prepare a devotional schedule for the duration of the mock Senate.
5. With the stamp, date all speeches that have been delivered in the Senate. (They should be handed to you immediately after they are given.) Place them in a folder marked for speeches. Keep them sorted according to student names so that they may be handed back to the students more easily on the last day of the Congress.
6. See that all bills and resolutions passed by the Senate are first signed by you and the president pro tempore and then sent to the House (given to the teacher). You should keep the original bill and resolution forms as well as the report forms in file folders for later distribution.
7. You will not be role-playing a senator but will do only the duties of the secretary.

F. Duties of the Chairmen of Committees

1. At the first meeting of your committee, do the following:
    a) Choose a chairman pro tempore to preside when you are absent. He should be from the majority party. This could also be done in a caucus meeting.
    b) Choose a secretary to keep minutes. These minutes should be placed in the committee folder at the end of the meeting.
    c) Choose a ranking minority party member to represent the minority party within the committee. The above offices should be chosen by taking nominations and then electing each officer with a majority vote from those in the committee. These offices could be decided in the caucus meetings of each party: the majority party would choose chairmen and vice chairmen of the committees, and the minority party would choose ranking members.
2. You must report to the Senate what the committee has done. Good secretary minutes will aid in this report; the report must be written out and will replace one of your speeches.
3. See that the following rules are followed in your committee: Senators should address you as Mr. Chairman (or Madam Chairman).
    a) A quorum must be present. A quorum is half of the members with at least one minority party member present.
    b) An agenda must be presented to each committee member at least one day in advance of the committee meeting. Use the following format for your agenda:
        Agenda for the Committee on ________
        Date of Meeting ________
        • List bills (by number and title) that will be discussed.
        • List reports to be considered. (You will not have these until Congress has been in session for a while.)
    c) Leave a copy of each committee's agenda in the committee folder.
    d) Bills reported to the Senate must be approved by a majority of the committee members, one of whom must be of the minority party.
4. You are responsible to see that someone on the committee completes a report form for each bill or resolution approved by your committee. (The person who writes the report for a bill should put his name on the report form, not the name of the person who wrote the bill.) The bill (or resolution) should be stapled to the report form.
5. After bills have been reported to the Senate, you must see the majority leader if you wish your bills to have priority under the unanimous consent rule.
6. Appoint floor managers for bills that have been reported from your committee.
    a) The floor manager lines up support for a bill.
    b) The ranking minority party member often takes the job of floor manager against the bill. He organizes a filibuster if one is desired.
7. If your committee seems to be getting very few bills, assign members to write legislation on a topic that is related to your committee.

G. Committee Action on Bills and Resolutions/Mark Up Sessions

1. Bills and resolutions will be placed in the committee folders. These bills and resolutions are not to be taken out of the classroom. Once a committee has discussed a piece of legislation, place the paper back into that committee's folder, or report the legislation (using the report form) during First Hour business on the following day. As soon as the report is made to the entire Senate floor, the report form and the legislation reported should be given to the president pro tempore.
2. When a committee discusses legislation, it can act on the legislation in any of the following ways:
    a) Consider it and vote to report it favorably.
    b) Amend it by writing any changes and clipping them to the legislation. The amendment should be clear about which part of the legislation is receiving changes and about what these changes are. The committee must have a majority vote in order to amend anything.

c) Rewrite the legislation entirely and introduce the new bill or
   resolution.
   d) Reject the legislation. Mark it "killed" or "pigeonholed" and
   place it in the back of the folder.
   e) Report it unfavorably. (This is rarely done.)
3. All committee members must remember that the committee
   chairman is completely in charge of the committee meeting.

H. Duties of the Majority Leader

1. Since most legislation is debated by the Senate during the morning
   hour by means of unanimous consent, the majority leader needs
   to have a plan for seeing that legislation that aligns with what his
   party and the President of the United States believe is brought
   before the Senate on a priority basis. Work with the president pro
   tempore as well as the minority leader.
2. With the president pro tempore and the minority leader, make a
   calendar for bills and resolutions that will be brought to the Senate
   floor for debate two days in advance.
3. Check with each member of your party on a regular basis to make
   sure that he is with you on the issues.
4. Line up people to speak on bills and resolutions in order to win
   over the opposition.
5. Take the chair if the president pro tempore is absent or when he
   wishes to speak from the floor.

I. Duties of the Minority Leader

1. With the president pro tempore and the majority leader, make a
   calendar for bills and resolutions that will be brought to the Senate
   floor for debate two days in advance.
2. Check with each member of your party on a regular basis to make
   sure that he is with you on the issues.
3. Line up people to speak on bills and resolutions in order to win
   over the opposition.

J. Duties of the Whips

1. Work with the leader of your party to keep party members in-
   formed of legislation soon to be considered.
2. Take polls in the chamber to see how members plan to vote.

Kind of motion	Motion	Purpose	Is a second required?	Is it debatable?	Can it be amended?	What vote is required for passage?	May it be used to interrupt a speaker?
Main	To make a main motion	To introduce business	Yes	Yes	Yes	Majority	No
Subsidiary	To postpone indefinitely	To suppress action	Yes	Yes	No	Majority	No
	To postpone to a certain time	To defer action	Yes	Yes	Yes	Majority	Yes
	To lay on the table	To defer action	Yes	No	No	Majority	No
	To take from the table	To consider a tabled motion	Yes	No	No	Majority	No
	To reconsider	To consider a defeated motion again	Yes	Yes	No	Majority	No
	To rescind	To repeal a previous action	Yes	Yes	Yes	Two-thirds	No
	To amend	To modify a motion	Yes—one-third must second.	Yes	Yes	Majority	No
	To amend an amendment	To modify an amendment to a motion	Yes—one-third must second.	Yes	No	Majority	No
	To refer to a committee (Be specific.)	To allow further study	Yes	Yes	Yes	Majority	Yes
	To move the previous question	To end debate and force an immediate vote	Yes	No	No	Two-thirds	No
	To limit or extend debate (House only)		Yes	Yes	The time may be amended.	Two-thirds	No

Kind of motion	Motion	Purpose	Is a second required?	Is it debatable?	Can it be amended?	What vote is required for passage?	May it be used to interrupt a speaker?
Incidental	To suspend the rules (House only)	To take action contrary to standing rules	Yes	No	No	Two-thirds	No
	To modify or withdraw a motion	To modify or withdraw a motion	No	No	No	Majority	No
	To divide a motion	To consider parts of a motion separately	Yes	No	Yes	Majority	No
	To object to the consideration of a question	To suppress action	No	No	No	Two-thirds	Yes
	To call for a roll-call vote	To verify a voice vote	Yes	No	No	One-fifth	No
	To appeal a decision of the chair	To reverse a decision of the chair	Yes	No	No	Majority	Yes
	To rise to a point of order or parliamentary procedure	To correct a parliamentary error or ask a question	No	No	No	Decision of the chair	Yes
Privileged	To call for the orders of the day	To force consideration of a postponed motion	No	No	No	Decision of the chair	Yes
	To rise to a question of privilege	To make a personal request during debate	No	No	No	Decision of the chair	Yes
	To recess	To dismiss the meeting for a stated period of time	Yes	Yes	The time may be amended.	Majority	No
	To adjourn	To dismiss the meeting	Yes	No	The time may be amended.	Majority	No
	To fix a time for reassembly	To arrange the time of the next meeting	Yes	The time is debatable.	The time may be amended.	Majority	Yes

Mock Trial

Conducting a mock trial may provide an interesting activity to help the students understand judicial procedures. The major requirement for this project is to have detailed information about the proceedings of a court case. This information may be compiled from newspaper reports of a recent trial, books documenting court cases, or an educational unit prepared for this purpose. Websites such as Social Studies School Service and Teachers Pay Teachers offer several mock trial exercises.

Note that real-life trials often involve some unsavory characters as well as descriptions of activities that are unbecoming to a Christian. Therefore, the students should be advised to play their roles with propriety.

Assign your most capable students to the roles of judge, prosecuting attorney, and defense attorney. Other roles will be those of defendant, witnesses, jurors, bailiff, and clerk. The following trial script and instructions may help the trial start smoothly. A local attorney may be able to give you or your class further insights into courtroom procedures.

Mock Trial Script

BAILIFF: Oyez! Oyez! Oyez! All rise for the Honorable Judge ____________ for ______*(judicial district)*______ .

JUDGE: Be seated.

BAILIFF: God save the United States and this honorable court.

JUDGE: What case is this?

CLERK: Your Honor, the court hears Case ____________, *The State vs.* ____________.

JUDGE: Are the attorneys for the prosecution present and prepared to proceed?

PROSECUTING ATTORNEY: We are.

JUDGE: Are the attorneys for the defense present and prepared to proceed?

DEFENSE ATTORNEY: We are.

JUDGE: Let the record show that all parties in this case are present and prepared. Mr. Prosecutor, would you please read the indictment?

PROSECUTING ATTORNEY: Mr./Mrs./Miss ____________ is charged with ____________________.

JUDGE: (*Give instructions to the jury.*)

CLERK: (*Swear in the jury.*)

JUDGE: (*Continue giving instructions to the jury. For example, "During the course of the trial, we may have to recess. You may not discuss the case with anyone. Report anyone who contacts you about the case."*)

Do you have any questions before we begin?

(*to the prosecutor*) Mr. Prosecutor, you may present your opening statements.

PROSECUTING ATTORNEY: (*Read statements. Begin with "Ladies and gentlemen of the jury, . . ."*)

JUDGE: Mr. Defense Attorney, you may present your opening statements.

DEFENSE ATTORNEY: (*Read statements. Begin with "Ladies and gentlemen of the jury, . . ."*)

JUDGE: Mr. Prosecutor, you may call your first witness.

PROSECUTING ATTORNEY: The prosecutor calls Mr./Mrs./Miss _______________ to the witness stand.

WITNESS: (*Step onto the witness stand, and raise your right hand to take the oath.*)

CLERK: Do you swear to tell the truth, the whole truth, and nothing but the truth in this case, under penalty of perjury, so help you God?

WITNESS: I do.

CLERK: State your full name and occupation, and be seated on the witness stand.

(The prosecuting attorney proceeds to question his witness, and then the defense attorney is allowed to cross-examine the witness. Other witnesses for the prosecution are called in like manner and then witnesses for the defense. The attorneys make final statements, and the judge gives the jury final instructions and sends it out to deliberate. When the jurors return, the judge asks whether they have reached a verdict, and one juror replies.)

Map of the United States
Olympia
Mt. Rainier
Mt. St. Helens
Washington
Columbia R.
Salem
Montana
North Dakota
Badlands
Bismarck
Helena
Oregon
Boise
Idaho
South Dakota
Black Hills
Pierre
Wyoming
Rocky Mountains
Great Salt Lake
Nevada
Cheyenne
Platte R.
Nebraska
Salt Lake City
Carson City
Sacramento
Sierra Nevada
Utah
Denver
Colorado
Pikes Peak
Lincoln
Kansas
California
Colorado R.
Arkansas R.
Grand Canyon
Arizona
Santa Fe
Oklahoma
Oklahoma City
Phoenix
New Mexico
PACIFIC OCEAN
Texas
Alaska
Yukon R.
Austin
Juneau
Rio Grande
Honolulu
Hawaii
0   200 Miles
0   100 Miles

Minnesota
Lake Superior
Lake Michigan
Lake Huron
Lake Ontario
Lake Erie
Wisconsin
Saint Paul
Michigan
Madison
Lansing
Iowa
Des Moines
Illinois
Springfield
Indiana
Indianapolis
Columbus
Ohio
Missouri
Missouri R.
Topeka
Jefferson City
Frankfort
Kentucky
Ohio R.
West Virginia
Charleston
Washington, DC
Richmond
Virginia
Harrisburg
Pennsylvania
Trenton
New Jersey
Dover
Annapolis
Delaware
Maryland
New York
Albany
Boston
Massachusetts
Providence
Hartford
Rhode Island
Connecticut
Vermont
Montpelier
Green Mountains
Maine
Augusta
Concord
New Hampshire
Raleigh
North Carolina
Columbia
South Carolina
Atlantic Ocean
Arkansas
Mississippi R.
Nashville
Tennessee
Little Rock
Alabama
Atlanta
Mississippi
Georgia
Louisiana
Jackson
Montgomery
Baton Rouge
Tallahassee
Florida
Appalachian Mountains
Gulf of Mexico
N
W   E
S
Key
Above 12,000 ft.
9,000–12,000 ft.
6,000–9,000 ft.
3,000–6,000 ft.
0–3,000 ft.
0   250   500 Miles

Explaining the Gospel

One of the greatest desires of Christian teachers is to see their students repent and believe in Christ. Relying on the Holy Spirit, you should take advantage of the opportunities that arise for presenting the gospel. You may find the following outline helpful, especially when dealing individually with a young person.

1. The Lord God is King over all His creation (Rev. 4:11).
- God created everything that is (Gen. 1–2).
- God created the world with laws about how His world is to work and the way people are to live.

2. All have sinned—including me (Rom. 3:23).
- Since Adam first sinned, all people are born rebels against the rule of God (Rom. 5:12).
- God has made me in His own image so that I might declare His glory by being like Him (Gen. 1:26–27).
- But I am a sinner. I disobey God's Word. The Bible teaches that I am to love God more than anything or anyone (Mark 12:30). It also teaches that I should love other people at all times (Mark 12:31). But I don't enjoy doing what God wants me to do, I don't delight in obeying my parents, and I don't like being kind to other people.
- God will punish me for my rebellion and sin (Rom. 6:23). God hates sin, and there is nothing I can do to get rid of my sin. I can try to change my behavior, but I can never change my heart.

3. Jesus died and rose again for me (Rom. 5:8).
- God loves me even though I am a sinner.
- He sent His Son, Jesus Christ, to live a perfect life and to die on the cross, suffering the punishment for my sin.
- Three days later, God raised Jesus from the dead and made Him the ruler of His eternal kingdom. Jesus is alive today. This is the gospel of Jesus Christ: He died on the cross and was raised up to be God's appointed King (1 Cor. 15:1–4).
- God desires to restore me to bear His image fully by making me like His Son, the perfect image bearer of God (Rom. 8:29).
- God gives a new heart—new loves and desires—to every one of His children (Ezek. 36:26–27).

4. I need to put my trust in Jesus (Rom. 10:9–10).
- I must repent (turn away) from my sin and let Jesus control my life. I must also believe what God has done through Jesus (Mark 1:15).
- If I repent and believe in what Jesus has done, I am putting my trust in Jesus.
- Everyone who is trusting in Jesus is forgiven of sin.
- Everyone who is trusting in Jesus submits to having Him as his King.
- Everyone who has been saved by God will continue trusting and obeying Jesus for the rest of his life (Heb. 3:14).

When talking individually with a young person, ask questions to discern sincerity or any misunderstanding. What is sin? Are you a sinner? What is the gospel? What does it mean to repent? Read the verses from your Bible. If a student shows genuine sorrow for sin and a sufficiently accurate understanding of the basics of the gospel, encourage him to call on the Lord as you listen. Perhaps he will pray something like the following:

> God, I know that You hate sin. But I also know that You love me. I believe that Jesus died for me and rose from the dead for me. I now turn away from my sin, and I am trusting in Jesus to forgive me and to be my King forever. I want to follow Him wherever He leads me.

Show the student the Bible's command that believers unite together in regular fellowship (Heb. 10:24–25), and encourage him to get involved right away in a gospel-preaching church. Tell him that whenever he sins, he will be forgiven as he confesses his sins to God (1 John 1:9).